SECOND
CANADIAN EDITION

PSYCHOLOGY
EVALUATING CONNECTIONS

Gregory J. Feist
San Jose State University

Erika L. Rosenberg
University of California, Davis

Jennifer A. Stamp
Dalhousie University

Jennifer A. Poole
Langara College

McGraw Hill Education

PSYCHOLOGY: EVALUATING CONNECTIONS SECOND CANADIAN EDITION

ISBN-13: 978-1-25-902460-3
ISBN-10: 1-25-902460-1

1 2 3 4 5 6 7 8 9 0 TCP 1 9 8 7 6

Printed and bound in Canada.

Director of Product Management: *Rhondda McNabb*
Product Manager: *Scott Hardie*
Senior Marketing Manager: *Margaret Greenfield*
Product Developer: *Brianna McIlwain*
Senior Product Team Associate: *Marina Seguin*
Supervising Editors: *Cathy Biribauer, Shannon Martin*
Photo/Permissions Editor: *Derek Capitaine*
Copy Editor: *Valerie Adams*
Plant Production Coordinator: *Sarah Strynatka*
Manufacturing Production Coordinator: *Sheryl MacAdam*
Cover Design: *Dianne Reynolds*
Cover Image: *Mike Harrington/Getty Images Royalty Free*
Interior Design: *Katherine Strain*
Page Layout: *SPi Global*
Printer: *Transcontinental Printing Group*

www.mhhe.com

To our daughters,
Yasemin and Zehra
Alexandra and Shannon

— J.S. and J.P.

To our most precious collaborative work,
Jerry and Evan

— G.F. and E.R.

About the Authors

Gregory J. Feist

Gregory J. Feist is Associate Professor of Psychology in Personality and Adult Development at San José State University. He has also taught at the College of William & Mary and the University of California, Davis. He received his PhD from the University of California, Berkeley, and his undergraduate degree from the University of Massachusetts–Amherst.

Dr. Feist is widely published in the psychology of creativity, the psychology of science, and the development of scientific talent. One of his major goals is establishing the psychology of science as a healthy and independent study of science, along the lines of the history, philosophy, and sociology of science.

Toward this end, Dr. Feist has published a book entitled *Psychology of Science and the Origins of the Scientific Mind* (2006, Yale University Press), which was awarded the 2007 William James Book Prize by the Division of General Psychology, American Psychological Association (APA). In addition, he is the founding president of the International Society for the Psychology of Science and Technology. His work on creativity had been recognized with awards from the *Journal of Research in Personality* as well as the Division for Psychology of Aesthetics, Creativity and the Arts (Division 10) of the American Psychological Association. His teaching efforts have been recognized with outstanding teaching awards at both UC Berkeley and UC Davis. Dr. Feist is also co-author with his father, Jess Feist, of the undergraduate text *Theories of Personality.*

In his spare time, Dr. Feist enjoys cycling and skiing. Married to Erika Rosenberg, Dr. Feist is the father of Jerry and Evan.

Erika L. Rosenberg

Erika L. Rosenberg is an emotions researcher, health psychologist, and teacher of meditation. Her research on emotion has examined how feelings are revealed in facial expressions, how social factors influence emotional signals, and how anger affects cardiovascular health. Dr. Rosenberg received her PhD in psychology from the University of California, San Francisco, where she studied with Paul Ekman. Dr. Rosenberg served on the faculties at the University of Delaware and the College of William & Mary, and currently is at the Center for Mind and Brain at the University of California, Davis, where she is a senior investigator on the Samantha Project, a multidisciplinary study of how intensive meditation affects cognition, emotion, and neuropsychology. She is a co-author of studies from this project, which are published in *Psychological Science, Emotion, and Psychoneuroendocrinology.*

Dr. Rosenberg is a world-renowned expert in facial expression measurement using the Facial Action Coding System (FACS). She consults with scientists, artists, and the entertainment industry on the use of FACS in a variety of contexts, including her role as scientific consultant on the Fox TV show *Lie to Me.* She teaches FACS workshops worldwide.

A long-time practitioner of meditation, Erika Rosenberg serves on the faculty of Nyingma Institute of Tibetan Studies in Berkeley, where she teaches meditation courses and workshops for working with emotions in daily life. Recently, she helped develop a secular compassion-training program with Geshe Thupton Jinpa, PhD, at the Center for Compassion and Altruism Research and Education at Stanford University, where she is a senior teacher. Dr. Rosenberg has presented this program to His Holiness the Dalai Lama and has taught the program at Google and throughout the Bay Area, and she now co-directs the Compassion Cultivation Teacher Training Program. Dr. Rosenberg is also a Senior Fellow at the Mind and Life Institute.

Dr. Rosenberg and her husband, Gregory Feist, have two sons, Jerry and Evan. They live in the San Francisco Bay Area.

Jennifer A. Stamp

Jennifer A. Stamp received her BSc in neuroscience from Dalhousie University in 1994 and her PhD in anatomy from Cambridge University in 2000, where she investigated the impact of hormones on responses to psychological stress in rats. Upon completing her PhD, she returned to Dalhousie for postdoctoral research in the departments of Pharmacology and Anatomy and has published on a number of topics in neuroscience, including chronic stress, sleep deprivation, sex differences, and addiction.

Dr. Stamp currently holds a position as a university teaching fellow in the Department of Psychology and Neuroscience at Dalhousie, where she has been since 2003. She has played an active role in undergraduate teaching and research, concentrating in the areas of introductory psychology, neuroanatomy, pharmacology, addiction, and social psychology. She has a keen interest in innovative teaching approaches, which grew from her experience teaching psychology and neuroscience for the Dalhousie Integrated Science Program. She has been involved in several initiatives using technology in teaching and has developed several online courses. She has received many teaching awards and grants and is regularly involved in a number of outreach programs, particularly with high school students. Dr. Stamp also participates in public outreach activities and graduate teaching as a member of CARD (the Centre for Addiction Research at Dalhousie).

Dr. Stamp developed a love of cycling as a graduate student in Cambridge. She continues to ride as her primary means of commuting, as much as the Canadian weather will allow. She also works regularly on her finger calluses on the guitar and banjo and occasionally manages to play a recognizable tune. She has two daughters, Yasemin and Zehra.

Jennifer A. Poole

Jennifer A. Poole received her BA (Honours) from the University of Waterloo and her MA and PhD in psychology from Simon Fraser University. For her doctoral research, she examined the influence of attachment representations on emotion encoding and memory in young adults. She has also studied the impact of empathy on prosocial behaviour in children. She has been an instructor of psychology at Langara College in Vancouver, British Columbia, since 1995, including tenure as Department Chair.

Dr. Poole has taught numerous courses in psychology, including introductory psychology, developmental psychology, social psychology, research methods, and statistics. She is passionate about teaching and has an interest in using technology to enhance student learning. For many years, she has combined the best aspects of face-to-face and online teaching formats to create hybrid (or mixed mode) courses. She is an advocate for the Scholarship of Teaching and Learning (SoTL). In her recent research, she examines factors that enhance student engagement and performance, as well as student perceptions of learning in mixed mode courses. She is a member of the Society for the Teaching of Psychology (Division 2) of the American Psychological Association, as well as the Association for Psychological Science (APS), and frequently attends the National Institute on the Teaching of Psychology (NITOP).

Dr. Poole currently resides in Vancouver. She has two daughters, Alexandra and Shannon. She loves to sing and has been known to perform in musical theatre productions. She is a passionate supporter of the arts, having served on various executives and organized numerous fundraisers. Her favourite pastimes include "hanging out" with her family and taking her dog on long walks.

Brief Contents

Contents

5 Consciousness 164

6 Memory 202

13 Personality: The Uniqueness of the Individual 482

15 Psychological Disorders 566

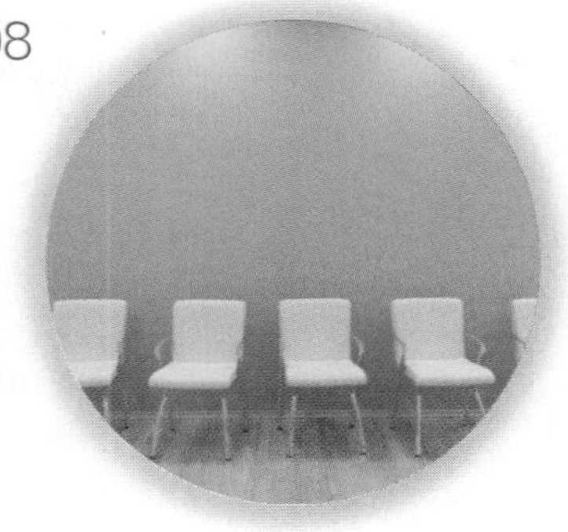

Foreword by Paul Ekman

Perhaps it was because I had never taken Introductory Psychology that I became a psychologist—or so I used to quip at the start of undergraduate lectures. Fifty years ago the textbooks for introductory courses were a turn-off. Most were dry and segmented. The only reason to read them was to pass introductory psychology in order to get to the higher-level courses you really wanted to take. It was an obstacle you had to jump over. Things have changed!

This textbook is—I hesitate to use the word—fun to read, enlightening, useful, and provocative. I recommend it to anyone—not just undergraduates—who wants a contemporary overview of psychology. In fact, people with no intentions of studying psychology will find this book engaging and interesting, and useful to their life. Wow.

Make no mistake—this is not a how-to book. It is not going to tell you how to get rid of whatever bothers you or find a mate or choose a career or become the most charming person in the world. But it will fascinate you; in each chapter you will learn about the cutting edge of knowledge, how science is done, what it means, and why it is important to understand that most complex of all subjects—why we do what we do and when and how we do it.

My own specialty for 40 years has been the study of facial expressions, and in the last decade or so I have reached out to develop a theory about emotion itself and how to lead a better emotional life. So I was surprised to find that when I read Chapter 11, "Motivation and Emotion," I learned something new. This is a comprehensive book; the coverage, even from a specialist's view, is amazing. And in each chapter the reader learns about both the breakthrough discoveries that have fundamentally altered the field of psychology and those scientists responsible for them.

I still find it a bit amazing that I should be ending a foreword to a textbook with the phrase "have fun."

About the Text

Many people think they already "know" psychology. Our daily lives are filled with thoughts, memories, emotions, and interactions with others, so why do we need a scientific discipline devoted to these topics? After all, aren't we all experts? Research in psychology suggests otherwise. Personal events in our lives are viewed from a very biased perspective, so we often let our preconceptions get in the way of evaluating evidence. Virtually all of our students enter Introductory Psychology with a full set of preconceived notions—many of them incorrect. *Psychology: Evaluating Connections*, second Canadian edition, is designed to move students beyond what may seem obvious, to have them re-evaluate the thoughts and beliefs they bring to the course.

Social psychologist Stanley Milgram once said, "Understanding grows because we examine situations in which the end is unknown" (Milgram, 1964). We encourage our students to question preconceived notions, putting their ideas—and the ideas of others—to the test. Throughout this text we demonstrate the importance of challenging assumptions and experiences—whether as a student or as a researcher—to understand that no one perspective tells the whole story. It is through asking open-ended questions, those that might not yield certain, convenient, or comfortable answers, that we can truly uncover new knowledge.

CHALLENGING ASSUMPTIONS

Psychology: Evaluating Connections, second Canadian edition, guides students along their path to discovery by challenging their assumptions. With this in mind, each chapter begins with several Challenge Your Assumptions questions, such as "Eyewitness memories are usually accurate," or "More money leads to greater happiness." Students are prompted to question their own perspective by thinking critically and evaluating evidence. Responses to the assumption questions can be found in call-outs throughout the chapter.

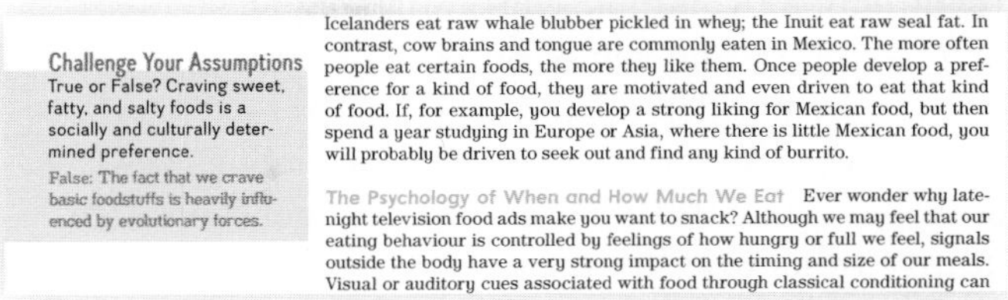

Challenge Your Assumptions
True or False? Craving sweet, fatty, and salty foods is a socially and culturally determined preference.

False: The fact that we crave basic foodstuffs is heavily influenced by evolutionary forces.

Icelanders eat raw whale blubber pickled in whey; the Inuit eat raw seal fat. In contrast, cow brains and tongue are commonly eaten in Mexico. The more often people eat certain foods, the more they like them. Once people develop a preference for a kind of food, they are motivated and even driven to eat that kind of food. If, for example, you develop a strong liking for Mexican food, but then spend a year studying in Europe or Asia, where there is little Mexican food, you will probably be driven to seek out and find any kind of burrito.

The Psychology of When and How Much We Eat Ever wonder why late-night television food ads make you want to snack? Although we may feel that our eating behaviour is controlled by feelings of how hungry or full we feel, signals outside the body have a very strong impact on the timing and size of our meals. Visual or auditory cues associated with food through classical conditioning can

CHANNELLING CURIOSITY

Curiosity is the cornerstone of scientific inquiry and psychology is an excellent introduction to scientific thinking because the topics are inherently interesting. A typical introductory psychology class is a jigsaw puzzle of diverse students with different reasons for taking the course, but all share an interest in discovering why humans (and other animals) do the things we do. Throughout each chapter we've included numerous critical thinking questions to encourage students to think beyond the textbook and relate to the material at a deeper level. This curiosity-driven approach aims to pull students, rather than push them, into learning.

Psychology provides insight into why people behave and think the way they do.

What questions might researchers in different subdisciplines of psychology seek to answer in studying riot behaviour, for example?

EVALUATING CONNECTIONS

A major overarching theme of this text is *evaluating connections*. Topics in psychology lend themselves to connectivity and integration. For instance, understanding most psychological disorders requires consideration of environments from prenatal to social, and biological factors from genes to molecules, neurons, and brain systems. *Psychology: Evaluating Connections,* second Canadian edition, pays careful attention to multiple causality, moving students beyond "black-and-white" or "either/or" thinking to include diverse perspectives.

Our presentation of psychology emphasizes several connective themes that provide a cohesive, integrative framework for the course, and inspire students to make active connections themselves.

Connections between Psychologists and Their Scientific Discoveries Connecting scientists with their discoveries brings psychology to life. This is the purpose of the "Groundbreaking Research" feature in each chapter. This feature highlights breakthrough discoveries that have fundamentally altered the field of psychology and tells the story of the scientists responsible for them.

Groundbreaking Research

The Universality of Facial Expressions of Emotion

If you were to visit an exotic place, such as the Amazon rain forest, could you expect your smile to be greeted with a smile from the local inhabitants? Or might they do something else? More generally, can we expect facial expressions of emotion to mean the same thing to people from different cultures? In the late 1960s, Paul Ekman went to a remote culture to find out whether facial expressions of emotion were universal or culturally specific. His research broke new ground, not just in our understanding of expression, but in helping launch the field of emotion research in psychology as well.

EMOTION EXPRESSION: CULTURALLY DETERMINED OR UNIVERSAL?

In the 1960s, most social scientists believed that behaviour was strongly determined by a person's environment. Anthropologists, for instance, proposed that facial expressions of emotion were **culturally relative;** that is, expressions varied across cultures and could be understood only in their cultural context. After all, anthropologists in the field had observed cultures in which people acted playfully at funerals and those in which people showed expressions of fierce anger at joyous festivals (Ekman, 1973).

cultural relativism
the idea that behaviour varies across cultures and can be understood only within the context of the culture in which they occur.

Trained as a behaviourist who emphasized the effects of environment on behaviour, a young psychologist named Paul Ekman thought the anthropologists were right. By the mid-1960s, however, he was beginning to question that view. Ekman's mentor, Silvan Tomkins,

Connections between Topics across Psychology Not surprisingly, textbook chapters too often come across as isolated topics. In *Psychology: Evaluating Connections,* second Canadian edition, we include a "Connections" feature to link topics that are discussed in more than one chapter of the book to reinforce the interrelatedness of subfields in psychology.

Connection
The autonomic nervous system both activates and relaxes physiological systems.
See Chapter 3, LO4

Behavioural-Expressive Changes. Emotions create expressive changes in the face and voice, as well as behavioural tendencies toward particular types of action (Frijda, 1986). People show their emotions—knowingly or not—through both verbal and non-verbal means, such as changes in facial behaviour and vocal intonation. Although researchers have studied both facial and vocal expressions of emotion, the most extensive body of research has focused on facial expressions.

Connections among Topics within each Chapter Not only do we connect ideas and topics *between* chapters, we also connect them *within* each chapter. Every chapter ends with an integrative section called "Evaluating Connections" that integrates and reviews the important material covered in the chapter.

Evaluating Connections in Motivation and Emotion

Living a Happy Life

The idea that emotion and motivation are intertwined seems obvious when we're faced with hunger, thirst, sexual attraction, or social isolation. As Beck Weathers's story at the beginning of the chapter clearly illustrates, when our very survival is threatened, these two powerful psychological forces join together. Certainly we all have a strong will to survive. But what do we really want in our day-to-day lives? Not surprisingly, most people would answer that they simply want to be happy. But what does it mean to be happy and how do we achieve happiness in our lives? In this section we discuss the pursuit of happiness in the context of motivation and emotion.

Life Satisfaction around the World

Throughout this chapter, the word *happiness* was used to describe a brief, emotional state, but it can also be used to mean a long-term sense of satisfaction with life. In order to capture this broader meaning, researchers usually measure **life satisfaction,** the overall evaluation we have of our lives (Diener et al., 1999). Psychologists consider life satisfaction to be a subset of **subjective well-being,** which also includes satisfaction in different domains, such as career, family, finances, and social networks.

life satisfaction
the overall evaluation we make of our lives and an aspect of subjective well-being.

subjective well-being
state that consists of life satisfaction, domain satisfactions, and positive and negative affect.

Most countries measure their wealth in terms of a statistic called the *gross national product* (GNP), the value in goods, services, and income produced by a country in one year. Often evaluated on a per-person basis, a high GNP is considered a sign of a country's economic success. So why, in 1972, did the King of Bhutan decide to measure the wealth of his nation differently? In response to criticism that his country was poor, King Jigme Singye Wangchuk argued

Connections between Psychology and Students' Experience In *Psychology: Evaluating Connections,* second Canadian edition, we link psychological concepts to tangible, real-world experiences. We use "Psychology in the Real World" to show how psychological research can directly affect people's lives.

Psychology in the Real World

Social and Emotional Learning in Schools

If you ask most people what you are supposed to learn in elementary school, they might say, "Reading, writing, math, science, history. . . ." How many people would say, "I learned how to regulate my anger"? Yet today many schools are teaching just that. Psychologists and educators argue that the development of skills for recognizing and regulating emotions is just as important to success in life as is academic achievement. And new research backs up this assertion. The past decade or so has seen the development and implementation of programs designed to teach young children skills for managing their emotions and promoting social adjustment. These social-emotional learning (SEL) programs constitute an important application of the psychology of emotion to the real world.

Mark Greenberg, director of the Prevention Research Center for the Promotion of Human Development at Penn State University, initiated much of the research on SEL. Through applied psychological research, he and his colleagues have evaluated the effectiveness of the prevention programs developed by the centre. One of those programs is PATHS (Providing Alternative THinking Strategies), a groundbreaking program developed by Greenberg and Carol Kusché (Greenberg & Kusché, 1998; Kusché & Greenberg, 1994). The PATHS program gives teachers a detailed curriculum for improving children's emotional awareness and regulation skills and enhancing their social competence.

An example of an exercise in the PATHS program is the turtle story and lesson, which is aimed at developing self-control. Children are told about a turtle that gets into trouble with other turtles in various situations because he does not stop to think. He gets some help from "wise old turtle," who tells him that when he just can't handle his anger and feels aggressive, he should go into his shell and consider what the best way to respond might be.

The PATHS program uses a modified version of the turtle story to teach children the technique of pulling back and mulling over options when they are upset in order to gain self-control and reduce aggressive behaviours. Kids learn to time themselves out when they get upset by "playing turtle" and thinking about what to do next. Other exercises are designed to help children identify their feelings, develop empathic understanding, and recognize that it's okay to have all feelings but that not all behaviours are okay.

Research using controlled intervention trials in which classrooms were randomly assigned to receive the PATHS curriculum or not (thereby continuing as usual) has shown that PATHS leads to improvements in social and emotional skills in high-risk children, reduction of aggressive behaviours in both normal and special-needs children, fewer depressive symptoms in special-needs kids, and improvements in classroom functioning (Conduct Problems Prevention Research Group, 1999a, 1999b; Kam, Greenberg, & Kusche, 2004). Other prevention programs, such as Head Start, have also applied the theory and methods of emotion research to decrease behaviour problems in schools, and initial results are promising (Izard et al., 2004).

Now, more than a decade after the implementation of major SEL programs, it is possible to see how the development of socio-emotional learning might be linked to academic success. A large-scale meta-analysis of more than 500 studies shows that SEL programs significantly improve children's academic performance (Durlak et al., 2007). Specifically, children who participate in these programs have better attendance and less disruptive classroom behaviour; they like school more and have higher GPAs.

ADDITIONAL FEATURES

RESEARCH PROCESS FIGURES

In most chapters, Research Process figures promote a deeper understanding of the science of psychology by focusing on a single study from the text. Each figure emphasizes the four key steps involved in all research: asking a question clearly, designing a clean study that addresses the question, collecting data and interpreting the results, and drawing conclusions about what these results mean to people in general and to other scientists in particular.

Research Process

1 Research Question

Are there differences between men and women in their interest in casual sex? The researchers hypothesized that men are more eager for casual sex than are women.

2 Method

Clark and Hatfield (1989) developed a brief survey to address the research question. Research assistants who were college students approached students of the opposite sex. After a brief introduction, the research assistant would ask each student one of these questions: "Would you go out with me tonight?" "Would you come over to my apartment tonight?" or "Would you go to bed with me tonight?"

Said "Yes"
Men
Women
Question
"Would you go out with me tonight?" 56% 50%
"Would you come over to my apartment tonight?" 69% 6%
"Would you go to bed with me tonight?" 75% 0%

3 Results

This table gives responses to the various questions, by gender.

4 Conclusion

Men and women were equally likely to agree to go on a date with someone they didn't really know. As the proposal became increasingly intimate, however, women backed off. Consistent with the hypothesis, men were much more likely than women to agree to have sex.

QUICK QUIZ QUESTIONS

By applying research in relevant areas of psychology, especially memory, we can make it easier for students to master key concepts. For this reason, we have broken up the content in each chapter into short chunks and included a few multiple-choice "Quick Quiz" questions at the end of each major section. These questions prompt students to think about what they have read and put it to use.

Quick Quiz 11.1: Motivation

1. Which model of motivation can be compared to the thermostat in your house?
   a. evolutionary
   b. drive reduction
   c. optimal arousal
   d. hierarchical
2. Which of the following hormones does *not* stimulate hunger?
   a. orexin
   b. ghrelin
   c. neuropeptide Y
   d. cholecystokinin
3. Most research on weight loss has reported that
   a. losing weight is very difficult for most people.
   b. losing weight is relatively easy, but keeping it off is very difficult.
   c. keeping weight off is relatively easy for most people.
   d. losing weight is relatively easy and so too is keeping it off.
4. Brain imaging research has found that during orgasm
   a. some parts of the brain "shut down" and become deactivated.
   b. most of the brain becomes very active.
   c. only the brain stem is active.
   d. the insula becomes very active.

Answers can be found at the end of the chapter.

Psychology: Evaluating Connections, Second Canadian Edition

The chapters in *Psychology: Evaluating Connections*, second Canadian edition, follow a fairly typical sequence. One distinction is the placement of "Memory" (Chapter 6) before "Learning" (Chapter 7). Learning and memory are intimately linked, which is one reason many universities offer courses on the combined topics of learning and memory. To some extent, it might not matter which chapter comes first. Learning, however, depends on memory processes—as evidenced by the fact that learning is disrupted in people with memory deficits. For this reason, we believe that setting up a basic foundation of memory processes facilitates the understanding of learning.

CHAPTER-BY-CHAPTER CHANGES

Psychology: Evaluating Connections, second Canadian edition, includes over 650 new research citations. But research is only part of the story. Each chapter also contains substantial changes, beginning with "Challenge Your Assumptions" questions and critical thinking questions throughout the chapter to keep students thinking actively about the material. Coverage of psychological disorders, such as categories and definitions, has been updated to reflect the publication of the fifth edition of the *Diagnostic and Statistical Manual of Mental Disorders (DSM-5)*.

Chapter 1: Introduction to Psychology

- New chapter-opening vignette on the effects of technology on human behaviour.
- New material on applying the field of psychology to real life, including a brief discussion on careers that are useful for an undergraduate degree in psychology.
- Updated material on industrial/organizational psychology.
- A more critical approach in discussing psychological perspectives.
- New section "No One Perspective Tells the Whole Story."
- Updated material on studying electronic social interactions.

Chapter 2: Conducting Research in Psychology

- New material emphasizing scientific thinking, including discussion of Andrew Wakefield and his fraudulent research on vaccines and autism spectrum disorder.
- New discussion on types of questions science can answer.
- Expanded discussion on evaluating research approaches, including updated figures on descriptive methods and independent versus dependent variables.
- New descriptions of physical trace and archival research, and delivering online surveys.

- New section on measurement scales and their properties.
- Expanded coverage of descriptive and inferential statistics.
- Updated Evaluating Connections section with recent research on the impact of poverty on the brain

Chapter 3: The Biology of Behaviour

- Expanded coverage of glial cells and epigenetics.
- New Psychology in the Real World feature on mirror therapy for phantom limb pain, with an emphasis on neuroplasticity.

Chapter 4: Sensing and Perceiving Our World

- Expanded coverage of synesthesia.
- An updated map of taste receptors on the tongue.

Chapter 5: Consciousness

- Deeper coverage of some of ethical issues surrounding the study of consciousness.
- Reorganization of the Sleep section so that the discussion on dreaming follows the discussion on the rhythmic nature of sleep.
- New Research Process figure on using brain imaging to communicate with comatose patients.

Chapter 6: Memory

- New section on process models of memory.
- More emphasis on false memory and less on Schacter's "Seven Deadly Sins."
- New Groundbreaking Research section on the 2014 Nobel Prize work by O'Keefe, Moser, and Moser on spatial maps and spatial memory.
- Updated Psychology in the Real World feature on manipulating memory with drugs.

Chapter 7: Learning

- Reorganization of content to reduce the number of sections and improve flow of material.

Chapter 8: Language and Thought

- New opening vignette focusing on growing up in a multilingual house.
- Expanded discussion on the definition of language, including pragmatics.
- New coverage of the long-term effects of family environment on language development.
- Updated research on the cognitive benefits of bilingualism.
- New contemporary examples of biases in thinking.

Chapter 9: Intelligence, Problem Solving, and Creativity

- New chapter opener on child prodigies with current Canadian examples.
- A new section on the frontal lobes and creativity.
- An updated Evaluating Connections section on genius, intelligence, and creativity.

Chapter 10: Human Development

- Expanded discussion on theory of mind research with Canadian examples.
- New Research Process figure on the development of object permanence.
- New sections on gender identity development, and ethnic, career, and sexual identity development in emerging adulthood.
- Expanded coverage of young adulthood.
- Addition of critical evaluation of Erikson's theory.
- Updated coverage of digital technology's impact across every stage of development.

Chapter 11: Motivation and Emotion

- New chapter opener on Beck Weathers's survival on the fatal Mount Everest expedition.
- Updated coverage of Maslow's hierarchy of needs.
- Updated Evaluating Connections section on happiness.

Chapter 12: Stress and Health

- New chapter opener that highlights individual responses to stress.
- New Evaluating Connections section on social support, caregiver burnout, and the power of belief.

Chapter 13: Personality: The Uniqueness of the Individual

- Simplified coverage of quantitative trait loci approach.
- New research findings on measurement of personality from social media sources.

Chapter 14: Social Behaviour

- Reorganization of the chapter material.
- New discussion of applied research on cognitive dissonance.
- Addition of belief in a just world theory, the elaboration likelihood model on persuasion, benefits of kindness, and cooperation and the prisoner's dilemma.
- Updated coverage on social exclusion, and media violence and aggression.
- New Psychology in the Real World feature on the impact of social networking sites.
- New Canadian examples.

Chapter 15: Psychological Disorders

- Extensive revision and chapter reorganization incorporating all the new diagnoses of psychological disorders according to the *DSM-5*.
- New discussions surrounding the changes in categories, the impact on diagnoses and treatments, and the role of biology.
- Additional discussion on the role of culture in psychological disorders, critical evaluation of categorization using the *DSM-5*, and stigma surrounding mental illness in Canada.
- Expanded and updated coverage in Psychology in the Real World on Internet Gaming Disorder.
- New Groundbreaking Research feature on the discovery of dopamine.
- New Research Process figure on gene–environment interaction in depression.

Chapter 16: Treatment of Psychological Disorders

- A more critical approach in discussing psychological therapies.
- New sections on challenges in evaluating treatment effectiveness, new directions in therapy, and preventing disorders.
- Updated coverage on the effectiveness of antidepressants, psychological therapies, and combined approaches.
- New Psychology in the Real World feature on how to choose a therapist in Canada.

MARKET–LEADING TECHNOLOGY

McGraw Hill Education connect®

Learn without Limits

McGraw-Hill Connect® is an award-winning digital teaching and learning platform that gives students the means to better connect with their coursework, with their instructors, and with the important concepts that they will need to know for success now and in the future. With Connect, instructors can take advantage of McGraw-Hill's trusted content to seamlessly deliver assignments, quizzes and tests online. McGraw-Hill Connect is a learning platform that continually adapts to each student, delivering precisely what they need, when they need it, so class time is more engaging and effective. Connect makes teaching and learning personal, easy, and proven.

Connect Key Features:

SmartBook®
As the first and only adaptive reading experience, SmartBook is changing the way students read and learn. SmartBook creates a personalized reading experience by highlighting the most important concepts a student needs to learn at that moment in time. As a student engages with SmartBook, the reading experience continuously adapts by highlighting content based on what each student knows and doesn't know. This ensures that he or she is focused on the content needed to close specific knowledge gaps, while it simultaneously promotes long-term learning.

Connect Insight®
Connect Insight is Connect's new one-of-a-kind visual analytics dashboard—now available for instructors—that provides at-a-glance information regarding student performance, which is immediately actionable. By presenting assignment, assessment, and topical performance results together with a time metric that is easily visible for aggregate or individual results, Connect Insight gives instructors the ability to take a just-in-time approach to teaching and learning, which was never before available. Connect Insight presents data that helps instructors improve class performance in a way that is efficient and effective.

Simple Assignment Management

With Connect, creating assignments is easier than ever, so instructors can spend more time teaching and less time managing.

- Assign SmartBook learning modules.
- Instructors can edit existing questions and create their own questions.
- Draw from a variety of text specific questions, resources, and test bank material to assign online.
- Streamline lesson planning, student progress reporting, and assignment grading to make classroom management more efficient than ever.

Smart Grading

When it comes to studying, time is precious. Connect helps students learn more efficiently by providing feedback and practice material when they need it, where they need it.

- Automatically score assignments, giving students immediate feedback on their work and comparisons with correct answers.
- Access and review each response; manually change grades or leave comments for students to review.
- Track individual student performance—by question, assignment or in relation to the class overall—with detailed grade reports.
- Reinforce classroom concepts with practice tests and instant quizzes.
- Integrate grade reports easily with Learning Management Systems including Blackboard, D2L, and Moodle.

Instructor Library

The Connect Instructor Library is a repository for additional resources to improve student engagement in and out of the class. It provides all the critical resources instructors need to build their course.

- Access Instructor resources.
- View assignments and resources created for past sections.
- Post your own resources for students to use.

Instructor Resources

- **Instructor's Manual:** This manual includes chapter outlines, key terms, and Innovative Instruction suggestions. Each Connection annotation is reinforced and expanded on to facilitate teaching psychology as an extensively connected discipline.
- **Test Banks:** Our text-specific Test Bank comprises more than 2400 multiple-choice questions. Our conceptual Test Bank provides instructors with an additional bank of multiple-choice questions which will challenge students to think more conceptually. All test questions are categorized according to learning objective and Bloom's taxonomy. Both test banks are available through EZ Test Online—a flexible and easy-to-use electronic testing program—that accommodates a wide range of question types and allows instructors to add their own questions. Test items are also available in Word (Rich text) format.
- **Microsoft® PowerPoint® Lecture Slides:** Prepared by the text authors, these slides cover the key points of each chapter and include figures and visuals from the text.

Superior Learning Solutions and Support

The McGraw-Hill Education team is ready to help instructors assess and integrate any of our products, technology, and services into your course for optimal teaching and learning performance. Whether it's helping your students improve their grades, or putting your entire course online, the McGraw-Hill Education team is here to help you do it. Contact your Learning Solutions Consultant today to learn how to maximize all of McGraw-Hill Education's resources.

For more information, please visit us online: http://www.mheducation.ca/he/solutions

Acknowledgments

Psychology: Evaluating Connections, second Canadian edition, would not have been possible without the support of our colleagues. In sharing our enthusiasm for teaching introductory psychology, they gave invaluable advice about recent research findings, topic coverage, and writing. On countless occasions, when we ran out of coherent sentences after hours of staring at the computer screen, awkwardly worded paragraphs were repaired with swift and constructive comments. Particular thanks go out to Leanne Stevens, Leslie Phillmore, Rahia Mashoodh, Tracy Taylor-Helmick, Tara Perrot, Heather Schellinck, and Christopher Hoyt.

We would also like to thank our students for their valuable insights and inspiration they provide us with every day. This book would not have been possible without you!

We are also appreciative to our colleagues who recommended changes for the second Canadian edition of *Psychology: Evaluating Connections*. Their expert knowledge and valuable suggestions helped to direct and improve this book:

Derek Fisher, *Mount Saint Vincent University*
Peter Graf, *University of British Columbia*
Mark Holder, *University of British Columbia*
Jacqueline Kampman, *Thompson Rivers University*
Heather Poole, *University of Ottawa*
Will Shead, *Mount Saint Vincent University*
Lisa Sinclair, *University of Winnipeg*
Greg Tyndall, *College of New Caledonia*

—Jennifer Stamp and Jennifer Poole

Introduction to Psychology

CHAPTER

1

CHAPTER OUTLINE

Challenge Your Assumptions

True or False?

- ☐ Psychology is all about curing mental illness.
- ☐ Psychology is made up of many different subfields.
- ☐ Genetic influence on our thoughts and actions is set at birth and can't be changed.
- ☐ Psychologists agree that most of human thought and behaviour cannot be explained by one perspective.

LEARNING OBJECTIVES

LO1 Define psychology, including its scope, goals, and methods.

LO2 Name and describe the different subdisciplines of psychology.

LO3 Describe the evolution of clinical psychology from prehistoric to modern times.

LO4 Discuss the roots and early scientific foundations of psychology.

LO5 Summarize the nature–nurture debate.

LO6 Define and describe mind–body dualism.

LO7 Summarize the evolution of human behaviour, including the roles of natural selection and adaptation.

In the spring of 2011, revolution spread throughout Egypt. After decades of violent oppression and despotic rule, everyday Egyptians wanted change. Revolutions have existed as long as rulers and governments have, but something new accelerated the spread of these uprisings: social networking sites. Organized protests were planned and carried out over Twitter, Facebook, and YouTube. Eighteen days after the revolution started, it successfully and relatively bloodlessly deposed the government.

In another instance of online social interaction, Tonya was skeptical of online dating. She had already been married, had a 12-year-old daughter, and was not finding anyone to date (Schipani, 2014). Her parents offered to buy her a subscription to an online dating service and at first she resisted. Within a few weeks she was matched with Frank, who had had no luck after a year of online dating. After exchanging emails for some time, Tonya and Frank finally went on their first date and immediately hit it off: Their date lasted nine hours, and they talked about everything from children to religion. Tonya now says, "There really is someone out there who is so good for me—so smart, funny. He's never let me down. We're just so stinkin' happy" (Schipani, 2014). They soon got married and now are expecting their first child.

These two events give just a small hint of the wide-ranging ways that online technologies have changed social interaction and human behaviour. Here are some others:

- Millions of people have free or very inexpensive access to online learning through massive open online courses (MOOCs), such as Coursera or Udacity.
- We can immediately be in contact with friends and family via texting and email, and with wider circles of people via social networking sites such as Twitter, Facebook, Instagram, and Snapchat, to name a few.
- Online psychotherapies have helped many individuals and couples dealing with mental illness and broken relationships.
- Sexting photos have had traumatic effects on people's lives and even ruined politicians' careers.
- A baby died of malnutrition and neglect because a couple in South Korea were spending 14–16 hours a day raising a virtual baby on the website Prius Online (Elder, 2014).
- Distracted driving (much of which involves mobile device use) is a factor in about 4 million motor vehicle crashes in North America each year (Canadian Automobile Association, 2014).

In many ways, people behave online much the way they do in everyday life, but with the capacity to affect more people, both known and unknown, and potentially with more widespread impact. What happens to social interactions when they become primarily electronic? Do the depths of our friendships increase or decrease through social media? Does technology make our attention scattered, or does it improve our ability to do more than one thing at a time? These are important questions; our interactions and social connections, or networks, can influence everything from opinion to eating patterns to one's likelihood of quitting smoking (Christakis & Fowler, 2007, 2008). Do Facebook and other social networks operate in ways that resemble real-world networks? What are the consequences of electronic interaction for our social lives? Each of these questions centres on understanding the effects of technology on thought, feeling, and behaviour.

You might assume that social networks only enhance social life. The surprise from psychological science is that social networking both improves and impairs our relationships (Garrett & Danziger, 2008). People use "friending" on social networks to widen their social circles, which can translate into real-life social benefits (Lange, 2008). These media help us reach people we might not otherwise communicate with at all (such as long-lost cousins). Yet social networking can also reduce interactions with close friends to short electronic statements and lessen the amount of face-to-face time. In addition, technology in general increases our likelihood to multi-task, which makes it harder for us to engage in any one task deeply (Bowman, Levine, Waite, & Gendron, 2010; Foerde, Knowlton, & Poldrack, 2006).

As psychology begins to identify the pros and cons of this overlap between real and virtual worlds, the ways to navigate this realm in a healthy manner become clearer.

You may be wondering just how the study of people's use of technology in all its many forms relates to the study of psychology. The answer is that it involves people thinking, behaving, and interacting, which is what psychology is all about. At the end of this chapter, we will return to the topic of electronic social interactions, connecting specific research questions to the various fields of study within psychology.

WHAT IS PSYCHOLOGY?

Wherever there are people, even online, there is psychology. In one sense, you have been a psychologist for most of your life. Every time you try to explain what someone else is doing—and why—you are thinking psychologically. You do it when you say your friend dominates conversations, because he is self-absorbed. Or when you conclude that your big sister is bossy, because she is older and always gets what she wants. We think and live psychology every day.

LO1 Psychology Defined

Many fields of study aim to understand people's thoughts and actions. Literature helps us understand people through its methods of storytelling, character exploration, setting, and imagery. History helps us understand people through description and analysis of past events and artifacts. Anthropology is the study of human culture and origins. Sociology seeks to understand people in terms of large-scale social forces and group membership rather than individuals. Psychology is unique in that it is the *science* of understanding individuals—animals as well as people. Formally defined, **psychology** is the scientific study of thought and behaviour. The root word *psyche* comes from the Greek for "mind," but modern psychology is as likely to study the brain and behaviour as it is the "mind."

psychology
the scientific study of thought and behaviour.

One important aspect of this definition is the emphasis on psychology as a science. Psychologists rely on objective, verifiable evidence to draw conclusions about the way individuals think and behave. Rather than merely relying on the opinions of experts or authorities, they are trained to systematically observe and measure behaviours. For example, some psychologists, referred to as *experimental psychologists,* conduct laboratory research on basic processes, such as emotion, motivation, learning, cognition, or sensation and perception. Many of these psychologists conduct their studies at colleges or universities, where they also teach.

But wait, you might be thinking, don't psychologists treat people with mental illness or try to help us figure out how our parents messed us up? Yes, some psychologists do these things too. These professional psychologists practise or *apply* psychology to diagnose and treat problems of thought and behaviour. But these psychologists are also trained in research and many of them conduct experiments. The point is that psychology is *both* a clinical practice and a science. The clinical practice side encompasses the services provided in therapists' offices, schools, hospitals, and business. The science side covers the empirical research that is used to understand how and why people and animals do the things they do. And these two traditions often overlap—research informs clinical practice and vice versa.

As researchers and/or clinical practitioners, psychologists have four main goals. The first is to *describe* the way we think and behave. For example, a psychologist might be interested in identifying the techniques used by introductory psychology students to study for their exams. Do students read the text more than once? Do they make notes on what they've read? Do they make up practice questions? Do they review their notes? Do they test themselves? Description is often the first step in understanding an aspect of human or animal nature. A second goal of psychology is to *explain* behaviour, which involves identifying the

Challenge Your Assumptions

True or False? Psychology is all about curing mental illness.

False: Psychologists not only diagnose and treat mental illness but also test hypotheses using the scientific method. Psychology is both a practice and a science.

underlying causes of behaviour. For example, a psychologist may try to answer this question: Why do certain study techniques produce more successful outcomes on exams than others? Once researchers understand the underlying causes of behaviours, they may be interested in *predicting* when future behaviours or mental processes are likely to occur. For example, knowing that a good night's sleep leads to improved exam performance (Covington & Omelich, 1987; Hill & Wigfield, 1984; Kelly, Kelly, & Clanton, 2001), we can predict that students who pull all-nighters before exams will not perform as well as those who get a good eight hours' sleep. The fourth goal of psychology involves *changing* thoughts and behaviour. Many psychologists apply research results to bring about desired behaviours. For example, university counsellors may hold workshops for students on study techniques in order to enhance academic performance.

In contrast to scientific and clinical psychology, popular psychology is what we find in homes, radio talk shows, many Internet news sites, and TV news reports. What sets scientific psychology apart from popular psychology—often referred to as *pseudo* or *pop psychology*—are the methods used in each. As you will see in Chapter 2, "Conducting Psychological Research," and throughout this book, the methods of psychologists are quite different from those of laypeople, who sometimes rely on an unreliable body of knowledge known as *common sense.*

Perhaps because of the ubiquity of popular psychology, most people you talk to on the street don't think of psychology as a science; rather they probably only think of it as a clinical practice. The editors of *Scientific American,* for instance, commented that "whenever we run articles on social topics, some readers protest that we should stick to 'real science'" ("The Peculiar Institution," 2002, p. 8).

As we will see throughout this book, not only is psychology a science, but it is also considered a core science, along with medicine, earth science, chemistry, physics, and math (Boyack, Klavans, & Börner, 2005). Core sciences are those that have many other disciplines organized around them.

Why Should You Study Psychology?

Reasons for studying psychology vary from person to person. Maybe your advisor suggested it would be a good course to take or maybe you're taking the course because it satisfies a general education requirement. Psychology is considered a part of a good general education because its content is useful to many fields. It is also relevant to your life.

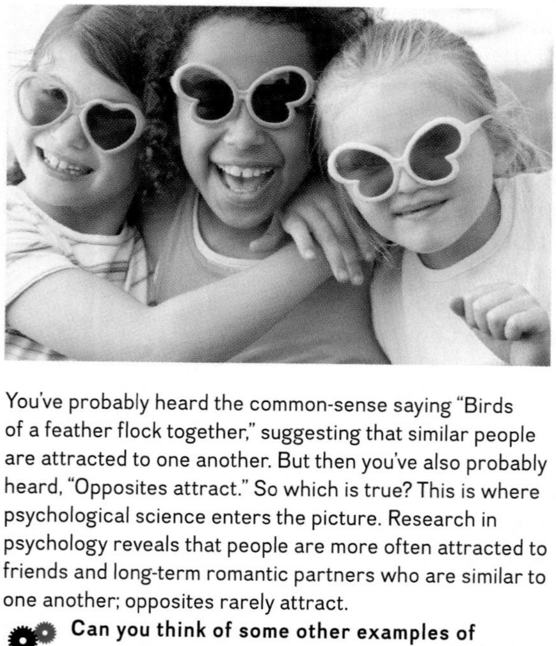

You've probably heard the common-sense saying "Birds of a feather flock together," suggesting that similar people are attracted to one another. But then you've also probably heard, "Opposites attract." So which is true? This is where psychological science enters the picture. Research in psychology reveals that people are more often attracted to friends and long-term romantic partners who are similar to one another; opposites rarely attract.

Can you think of some other examples of common-sense ideas about behaviour? How can we determine if these beliefs are accurate?

Adopting a scientific perspective on human behaviour helps you develop a curiosity for how behaviour works. It also fosters an appreciation for how much of human thought and behaviour cannot be explained from one perspective. As you move through this text, you will find that many of the concepts you learn, such as memory, have several definitions depending on how you look at them. *Memory,* for instance, can refer either to a specific recalled event (such as your memory of last summer's vacation) or to the process by which we recall such information.

Studying psychology not only makes you more aware of how people work but also makes you more aware of how *you* work—very practical knowledge to have in many settings. Understanding others' thoughts, feelings, and motives—as well as your own—may help you be a more effective doctor, lawyer, businessperson, or friend. Understanding how children learn, think, reason, and play will help you if you become a parent or a teacher. To learn how one recent university graduate has applied her knowledge of psychology in her life, read the "Psychology in the Real World" box.

Psychology in the Real World

Why Psychology Is Important to My Life by Amanda Yzabo (Student at the University of British Columbia)

For me, studying psychology has meant so much more than learning concepts for an exam. Every day I see how it applies to my life. Material from class and the textbook come alive in my daily encounters. For instance, I now understand what affects my own productivity and what increases my motivation. I know that stress sometimes serves as a major stimulant for me and activates me to work, but it also wears down my immune system. Also, too much stress impairs the quality of my work. From Intro Psych, I learned that these experiences are consistent with what research on motivation, stress, and health tells us.

As a curious student, I always enjoy understanding something new. One thing I appreciated with this class is how all of the fields of psychology overlap and interconnect. For example, different people see and perceive events differently. In other words, social and personality psychology are closely connected to memory, sensation, and perception. What we perceive and remember overlaps with our social environment and our personality. Perceiving and remembering is almost like a camera lens, but the lens has filters—your personality and previous experiences filter what you take in, what sense you make of it, and what you recall.

Additionally, for me, connections between the subfields are clearer when I look at an area that interests me—diagnoses and treatments for depression. In order to understand both the causes of and treatments for depression, you need to appreciate how the biological origins of depression, such as hormones and neurotransmitters, are affected by life experiences, such as stress and trauma. If we don't integrate the biological and social approaches to understanding disorders, then we won't be very successful at diagnosing and treating them.

My knowledge of psychology provides constant explanations for the kinds of relationships I see all around me. For example, as I learned in my psychology courses, research shows that children who were bullied at home will be more likely to befriend someone meek so they can achieve dominance. Sure enough, a close friend of mine recently admitted she was a bully in grade school because it was the one place she was tougher than those around her. At home she was picked on, and so she wanted to dominate when she could at school. Psychology allowed me to better understand this not-so-desirable behaviour in my friend. Similarly, I learned that people who do not receive much human contact and were not held as children will likely have difficulty forming bonds and close attachments as adults. I have seen this play out among numerous friends and acquaintances. Both of these cases show the importance of caregiving behaviour in the formation of social relationships.

By turning what I learn in my classes outward, I can better understand the actions of others. I am more effective at motivating others and myself because I better understand individual differences and different types of motivation that stem from internal and environmental sources. I am more conscious about what motivates me. Sometimes I am more motivated by an internal source, such as when I participate in a sport, because I enjoy the game. Other times, I am more motivated by external sources, such as when I work to earn a high grade in a class.

Most importantly, the things I learned in Introductory Psychology have laid a foundation for all my future studies in psychology and even other courses. As I have studied more about the clinical applications of psychology, I have become more conscious of the role of a listener and speaker and have greatly improved my listening skills. Psychology has taught me techniques for learning, like scheduling study time over several days, getting a good night's sleep, rehearsing material, and making information personal and relevant. Intro Psych can help you not only to understand other people but also to do well in university.

Psychology has helped me so much in my everyday life that I want to continue to take as many psychology classes as I can and then pursue a doctoral degree in psychology. My motivation to learn more than what is required originated from the sampling of fields covered in introductory psychology. It is only in Intro Psychology where you learn about everything in psychology—from the brain and genetics to learning, memory, and perception; from development and aging to social groups and disorders of the mind. Intro Psych has been a wonderful foundation for understanding my own and other people's thought and behaviour—and after all, isn't that what psychology is all about?

The study of psychology is as old as the human species. Before people wondered about the stars, rocks, and planets, no doubt they tried to figure out themselves and others. They did, after all, form relationships, have children, and protect their families. Human babies could not survive without others to care for them. Perhaps that is why people fascinate us. From our very first days, we humans are inherently interested in other humans—for survival. Newborns

What can I do with an undergraduate degree in psychology? Although you can't work as a psychologist (you need a graduate degree—a master's and/or PhD—to do that), there are many careers that an undergraduate degree in psychology is useful for. Some career options include sales representative, technical writer, research assistant, correctional officer, marketing researcher, psychiatric assistant, and so forth. An undergraduate degree in psychology also provides useful preparation for many professional programs, including law, medicine, management, social work, speech pathology, audiology, counselling, and education. For more information on careers in psychology, check out the website of the Canadian Psychological Association: http://www.cpa.ca/students/career/careersinpsychology.

prefer faces to almost any other object. Our very existence is social, and as you will learn, our brains have evolved mechanisms and structures that allow us to understand others in a remarkably complex way (Dunbar, 1996; Frith & Frith, 2010).

As you begin your study of this field, you will learn just how broad the field of psychology is. You may even find a subfield that dovetails with another interest you have already developed.

Quick Quiz 1.1: What Is Psychology?

1. Psychology is best defined as the scientific study of
   a. mental illness.
   b. behaviour.
   c. neuroses.
   d. thought and behaviour.
2. As a field, psychology is
   a. the practice of diagnosing and treating mental illness.
   b. a social science.
   c. a biological science.
   d. all of the above.
3. How does psychology differ from the related field of sociology?
   a. Psychology studies systems; sociology studies cultures.
   b. Psychology studies cultures; sociology studies people.
   c. Psychology studies individuals; sociology studies groups.
   d. Psychology studies groups and cultures; sociology studies human behaviour.
4. A researcher is interested in differences in aggression between boys and girls. She observes ten-year-old boys and girls on the playground during recess over the course of a week and records how they behave. The primary goal of this research is to ________ boys' and girls' aggressive behaviour.
   a. describe
   b. explain
   c. predict
   d. change

Answers can be found at the end of the chapter.

LO2 SUBDISCIPLINES OF PSYCHOLOGY

As a science and a practice, psychology is divided into various areas of investigation. Just as this book consists of chapters on different topics in psychology, the field of psychology is divided into more than 25 distinct, but increasingly interrelated, subdisciplines. Figure 1.1 gives a breakdown of the percentages of doctorates awarded in Canada and the United States in 2008 in each of the major subdisciplines we discuss.

cognitive psychology
the study of how people perceive, remember, think, speak, and solve problems.

developmental psychology
the study of how thought and behaviour change and remain stable across the life span.

Cognitive psychology is the study of how we perceive information, how we learn and remember, how we acquire and use language, and how we solve problems. For example, a researcher who is concerned with how people visualize objects in their minds is studying cognitive psychology.

Developmental psychology explores how thought and behaviour change and show stability across the life span. This perspective allows us to appreciate that organisms—human or otherwise—change and grow; thus, psychological functions likely change as well. Developmental psychologists ask such questions as these: How do our reasoning skills or emotional skills change as we age? How does parent–infant bonding affect adult relationships? Does old age bring wisdom?

Behavioural neuroscience studies the links among brain, mind, and behaviour. Neuroscience is a field that cuts across various disciplines and subdisciplines of psychology. One can study brain functions involved in learning, emotion, social behaviour, and mental illness, to name just a few areas. The more general subdiscipline of **biological psychology** includes research on all areas of connection between bodily systems and chemicals and their relationship to behaviour and thought. An example of research in biological psychology appears in Chapter 12, "Stress and Health," where we discuss the effects of stress on hormones and behaviour. Neuroscience and biological psychology overlap substantially. The latter is an older term that is being replaced by *behavioural neuroscience* in contemporary psychology. Using non-invasive advanced imaging techniques and electrical recordings, behavioural neuroscientists study the structure and functions of the living brain.

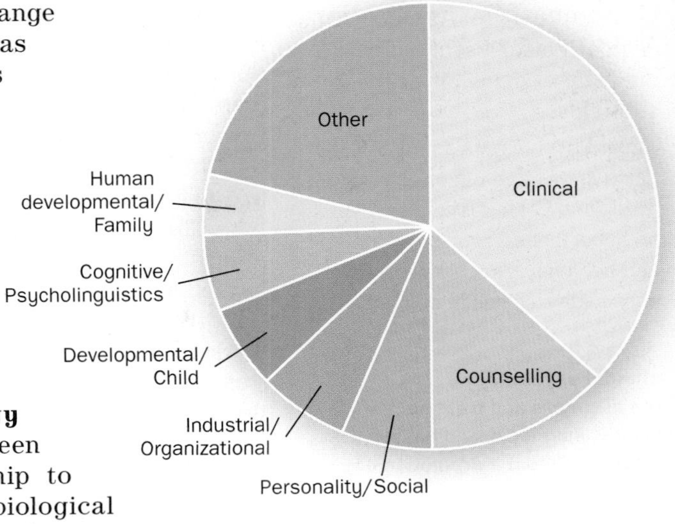

FIGURE 1.1
PERCENTAGE OF PHDS AWARDED IN THE SUBFIELDS OF PSYCHOLOGY IN 2008. (Adapted from Mulvey & Grus, 2010.)

Personality psychology considers what makes people unique as well as the consistencies in people's behaviour across time and situations. Personality research addresses questions such as whether our personal traits and dispositions change or stay the same from infancy to childhood to adulthood. A question from this area, for example, might be whether the consistent tendency to be friendly, anxious, or hostile affects one's health, career choice, or interpersonal relationships or whether a friendly or anxious child will necessarily have the same characteristics as an adult.

Social psychology considers how the real or imagined presence of others influences thought, feeling, and behaviour. Research on prejudice and racism, for example, looks at how a person of one group perceives and treats people in other groups. Social psychologists ask questions like: How does the presence of other people change an individual's thoughts, feelings, or perceptions? Why is someone less likely to help a person in need when there are many people around than when there is no one else around? Why do otherwise non-aggressive people sometimes behave quite aggressively in certain situations? Why are we attracted to particular kinds of people?

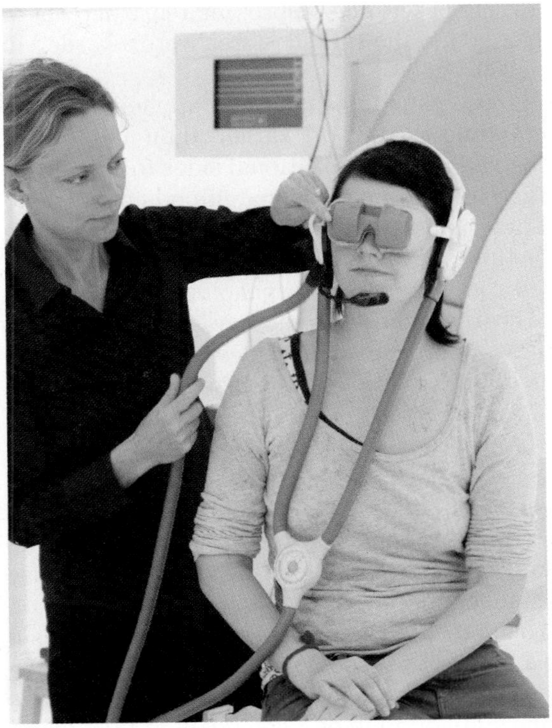

The woman wearing the goggles and headgear is being prepared for a neuroimaging exam in a neuroscience lab.

behavioural neuroscience
the study of the links among brain, mind, and behaviour.

biological psychology
the study of the relationship between bodily systems and chemicals and how they influence behaviour and thought.

personality psychology
the study of what makes people unique and the consistencies in people's behaviour across time and situations.

social psychology
the study of how living among others influences thought, feeling, and behaviour.

Challenge Your Assumptions

True or False? Psychology is made up of many different subfields.

True: Psychology has many subfields and is not just one overall discipline. Each subfield examines an important component of thought and behaviour, such as cognition, personality, or social influence.

clinical psychology
the diagnosis and treatment of mental, emotional, and behavioural disorders and the promotion of psychological health.

health psychology
the study of the role that psychological factors play in regard to physical health and illness.

educational psychology
the study of how students learn, the effectiveness of particular teaching techniques, the social psychology of schools, and the psychology of teaching.

industrial/organizational (I/O) psychology
the application of psychological concepts and questions to work settings.

sports psychology
the study of psychological factors in sports and exercise.

forensic psychology
the field that blends psychology, law, and criminal justice.

Connection

Are police, parole officers, and judges more skilled at detecting liars than others? No—although research suggests they are more confident in their judgments.

See Chapter 11, "Detecting Deception."

Clinical psychology focuses on the diagnosis and treatment of mental, emotional, and behavioural disorders and ways to promote psychological health. Some clinical psychologists also conduct research and teach. Clinical psychologists work in universities, medical settings, or private practice. As you can see from Figure 1.1, clinical psychology is the single largest subdiscipline in psychology. In Canada and the United States, since the late 1940s, the main approach to training in psychology has been the scientist-practitioner model, in which people with PhDs in clinical psychology should be both therapists and researchers—or at least be trained to be both (Benjamin, 2007). Indeed, psychology is a practice as well as a science.

A related field is *counselling psychology.* Counselling psychologists tend to work with less severe psychological disorders than clinical psychologists. They treat and assess relatively healthy people and assist them with career and vocational interests. Training for counselling psychologists is more likely to occur in schools of education than in psychology departments (Norcross et al., 1998).

Other professionals who provide therapy include social workers, couple and family therapists (who generally have master's degrees), and psychiatrists. Psychiatrists have training in medicine and an MD degree; in addition to offering therapy, they can prescribe drugs.

Health psychology examines the role of psychological factors in physical health and illness. Topics in health psychology range from studies of how stress affects people's lives and is linked to illness and immune function to research on the role of social factors in how people interact with health care professionals. Some health psychologists work in disease prevention, treatment, and rehabilitation; thus, this area involves clinical practice as well as research.

Educational psychology draws on several other areas of psychology to study how students learn, the effectiveness of particular teaching techniques, the dynamics of school populations, and the psychology of teaching. This field also attempts to understand special populations of students such as the academically gifted and those with special needs. Educational psychologists are usually academics, theorists, or researchers. *School psychology* is a related field that is generally practised by counsellors in school settings. Approximately 9 percent of the doctorates in psychology in Canada and the United States were awarded in educational or school psychology in 2005–2006.

Industrial/organizational (I/O) psychology is an applied science, meaning that it involves understanding real-world rather than laboratory behaviour (Aamodt, 2010). The industrial and organizational sides focus on two distinct sets of problems. The *industrial* side involves matching employees to their jobs and uses psychological principles and methods to select employees and evaluate job performance. For this reason, the industrial side of I/O psychology is also sometimes referred to as personnel psychology. The *organizational* side of I/O aims to make workers more productive and satisfied by considering how work environments and management styles influence worker motivation, satisfaction, and productivity. I/O is one of the fastest-growing subdisciplines in psychology, with a nearly 50 percent increase in the number of PhD programs in this area in North America between 1986 and 2004 (Rogelberg & Gil, 2006).

Two of the smaller and newer disciplines in psychology are sports psychology and forensic psychology. **Sports psychology** examines the psychological factors that affect performance and participation in sports and exercise (Weinberg & Gould, 2007). For instance, sports psychologists might focus on improving athletic performance through techniques such as relaxation and visualization. **Forensic psychology** is a blend of psychology, law, and criminal justice (Adler, 2004). Forensic psychologists make legal evaluations of a person's mental competency to stand trial, the state of mind of a defendant at the time of a crime, the fitness of a parent to have custody of children, or allegations of child abuse. Occasionally, they develop criminal profiles of the type of person who might have committed a particular crime.

Clearly, psychology is a diverse field of study. How many psychologists are there working in the world today? It is estimated that 500 000 people have been trained as psychologists worldwide (Tikkanen, 2001). The American Psychological Association (APA), an organization that includes psychologists from all over the world, has more than 150 000 members (APA, 2009). In Canada, many psychologists join the Canadian Psychological Association (CPA), which has a membership of over 6700 (CPA, 2010).

As you study the chapters of this text, you may find that one area of psychology especially excites you. Keep in mind, however, that psychology is about how humans think and behave. Thus, all of the topics are useful, many of them are closely intertwined, and there are many reasons for studying psychology, even if you don't become a psychologist. The field of psychology is the outcome of millions of years of humans' interest in their fellow human beings (Feist, 2006). As we will see next, however, the formal history of the field is not quite so old.

Psychology provides insight into why people behave and think the way they do.

What questions might researchers in different subdisciplines of psychology seek to answer in studying riot behaviour, for example?

Quick Quiz 1.2: Subdisciplines of Psychology

1. What subdiscipline of psychology examines how thoughts, feelings, and behaviours change over the life span?
   a. developmental psychology
   b. cognitive psychology
   c. personality psychology
   d. educational psychology
2. A psychologist has conducted a series of studies on what part of the brain is most active during a memory task. She is probably
   a. a developmental psychologist.
   b. a behavioural neuroscientist.
   c. a cognitive psychologist.
   d. an industrial/organizational psychologist.
3. The main difference between a clinical and counselling psychologist is that counselling psychologists treat
   a. people with more severe psychological disorders.
   b. children more than adults.
   c. people with less severe psychological disorders.
   d. people with learning disabilities only.

Answers can be found at the end of the chapter.

THE ORIGINS OF PSYCHOLOGY

In this section, we look briefly at the origins of the two main forms of psychology: clinical practice and science. The practice of psychology has deeper roots in human history than does the science of psychology. Prehistoric evidence tells us of efforts to heal people's suffering from disturbances of the mind, sometimes in ways we now find alarming. The foundations for psychology as a science date back to the ancient Greeks, and the modern science of psychology originated in the 1870s (Robinson, 1995). First, we consider the practice of psychology.

LO3 A Brief History of the Practice of Clinical Psychology

Disorders of thought and behaviour are no doubt as old as humans—indeed, there is evidence that primates (monkeys and apes) are afflicted with psychological disorders such as depression, anxiety, repetitive and functionless behaviours, and self-injuries (Maestripieri et al., 2006; Novak, 2003; Troisi, 2003). Like any trait shared between species, these behaviours must go back to the ancestors of both species, in this case approximately 6 million years.

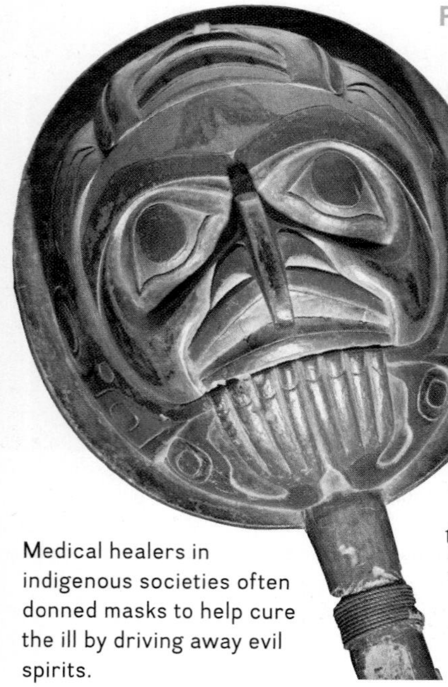

Medical healers in indigenous societies often donned masks to help cure the ill by driving away evil spirits.

Prehistoric Views As far back as the Stone Age (7000 years ago and maybe even as long as 50 000 years ago), humans tried to cure one another of various mental problems. Most prehistoric cultures, including many North American indigenous peoples, had medicine men or women, known as **shamans,** who would treat the possessed by driving out the demons with elaborate rituals, such as exorcisms, incantations, and prayers. For example, the False Face society was an Iroquois healing group that utilized grotesque wooden masks to frighten the evil spirits believed to cause illness (Snow, 1996).

Occasionally, some of these shamans appeared to practise the oldest of all known surgical procedures, trephination. *Trephination* involves drilling a small hole in a person's skull, usually less than two centimetres in diameter (Alt et al., 1997; Weber & Wahl, 2006). Some of these surgeries may have been for medical reasons, such as an attempt to heal a brain injury. Some may also have been performed for psychological reasons—notably, to release the spirits and demons they believed possessed the afflicted person. Anthropological evidence suggests that a surprisingly large percentage of people survived such surgeries—which today's scientists can confirm by identifying bone growth after the procedure—and the surgeons must have had moderately sophisticated knowledge and understanding of the brain (Alt et al., 1997; Weber & Wahl, 2006).

shamans
medicine men or women who treat people with mental problems by driving out their demons with elaborate rituals, such as exorcisms, incantations, and prayers.

Ancient Views Around 2600 BCE (Before the Common Era), the ancient Chinese moved away from supernatural explanations of psychological disorders toward natural and physiological explanations (Tseng, 1973). Specifically, they made connections between a person's bodily organs and their emotions. The heart housed the mind; the liver, the spiritual soul; the lung, the animal soul; the spleen, ideas and intelligence; and the kidneys, will and vitality. The ancient Egyptian and Greek physicians also sought natural explanations for psychological disorders, fighting against commonly held beliefs that mental disorders came from the gods (Harris, 2013). In the second century BCE, the ancient Egyptians apparently used narcotics to treat pain (Finger, 1994). The Greek physician Hippocrates (460–377 BCE) was the first to write about a man suffering from a phobia of heights—what we now call acrophobia.

Although native North American medicine relied on spiritual healing, a great deal of its practice also depended on the use of herbs or botanicals to treat both mental and physical illness (Toledo & Toledo-Pereyra, 2003). Herbs were prepared according to their traditions, using boiling water and other cooking techniques. For example, many First Nations tribes used the inner bark of the willow tree ground into powder and mixed with water to relieve headaches, toothaches, and joint pain (Moerman, 1998). Why did this treatment work? We now know that willow bark contains salicin, an anti-inflammatory agent—also the active ingredient of one of today's most commonly used medicines, aspirin (Mahdi, Mahdi, & Bowen, 2006)!

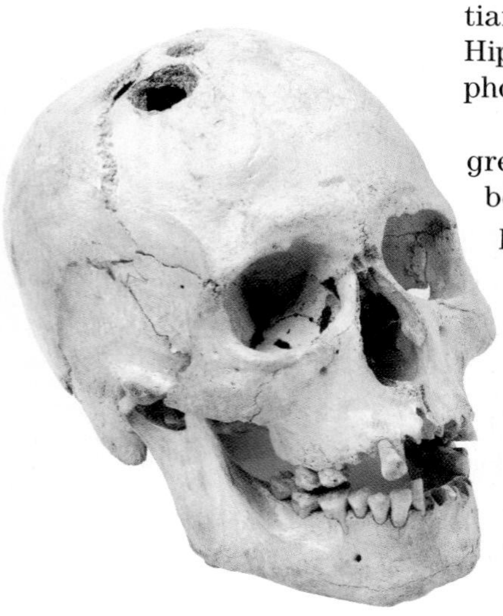

The hole in this skull may have been created by trephination, a prehistoric practice believed to release spirits or demons responsible for psychological disturbances.

What do you think actually happens to those who undergo such a procedure?

Medieval to Early Modern Views In medieval Europe from approximately 400 to 1400 CE (Common Era), psychological disorders were again attributed to supernatural causes. In the worldview that dominated this era and the Renaissance (from about 1400 to the early 1600s), people were thought to be possessed by demons, spirits, and the devil—not by physical disorders. These views were taken to an extreme during the Inquisition, when the Catholic Church investigated witchcraft and heresy as part of a broad campaign to eliminate dissent from established Church dogma. Some witchcraft practices were viewed as harmless and even beneficial, but others were branded as the work of the devil. In order to distinguish good witchcraft from bad, Church officials held inquisitions and trials (Robinson, 1995), using several techniques to determine whether

In the Middle Ages, people who were judged to be witches could be burned at the stake. Some of them may have had psychological disorders that caused them to behave strangely.

Although we see these as very outdated reactions to those who may be mentally ill, can you think of modern-day reactions that one day may also seem as outdated?

a person was a witch. Sometimes the accused was prodded with a metal pole and spears; if she felt no pain, she was protected by the devil and therefore was a witch. In another common method, the *float test*, the woman's hands and feet were tied, and she was thrown into a lake or river. If she floated, she had to be guilty because only the devil could make someone float; if she sank, she was innocent—but had drowned (Robinson, 1995). The most common punishment for the infrequent survivor of the float test—deemed to be a witch—was being burned at the stake. To be fair, there were numerous writers during the 14th to 16th centuries who argued that witchery was caused not by spirits and supernatural elements but rather by natural ones, such as hallucinations or "melancholia"—what we would now call depression (Robinson, 1995; Veith, 1965).

During the witch hunts of the 16th and 17th centuries, the first facilities for the mentally ill—called **asylums**—were built throughout Europe. The most famous, or infamous, of these was located at St. Mary of Bethlehem in London, England. Although it had served as a hospital for the mentally ill and others since the 1300s, Henry VIII designated it as a hospital for the insane in 1547. It was really no more than a storage house for the mentally ill and other social castaways. For the most part, early efforts to "treat" mental illness focused on removing afflicted people from society rather than helping them adjust to society. The conditions were deplorable and chaotic—patients were put in windowless and filthy rooms and were chained and shackled to the walls. The local population, including William Shakespeare, called the place *Bedlam*, a shortened version of "Bethlehem," and that is how the term came to be associated with chaotic and noisy conditions.

asylums
facilities for treating the mentally ill in Europe during the Middle Ages and into the 19th century.

In response to these inhumane conditions, reform movements in support of **moral treatment** emerged in Europe and North America. The main idea was to provide a relaxing place where these patients would be treated with dignity and care. The first major proponent of humane therapies was the French physician Philippe Pinel, in 1783. In North America, the first practitioner of moral treatment

moral treatment
the 19th-century approach to treating the mentally ill with dignity in a caring environment.

was Dorothea Dix. After visiting a prison in 1841 and witnessing the abhorrent and inhumane treatment of the inmates, some of them suffering from psychological disorders, Dix vowed to change these conditions. Over the next 40 years, she personally helped open 30 homes throughout North America (Nolen-Hoeksema, 2007). Moral therapies were among the first forms of treatment that regularly helped people get better.

Late 19th to Early 20th Century Views The last decades of the 1800s also saw the emergence of the first truly modern view of psychological disorders—the idea that they are simply one form of illness and should be treated as all medical conditions are, with appropriate diagnosis and therapy. This view is now known as the "medical model" perspective in clinical psychology. In the 1880s and 1890s, the German psychiatrist Emil Kraepelin collected data on the various kinds of psychological disorders and began systematically classifying and diagnosing them (Shepard, 1995). He popularized the term *dementia praecox* (premature dementia), which he later changed to *schizophrenia,* to refer to the major thought disorder known previously as "split mind." He was also the first to distinguish thought disorders (schizophrenia) from the mood disorders of melancholia (depression) and manic depression (bipolar disorder) (Jablensky & Woodbury, 1995). In short, his views were a major influence on diagnostic categories formulated during the 20th century.

psychoanalysis
a clinically based approach to understanding and treating psychological disorders; it assumes that the unconscious mind is the most powerful force behind thought and behaviour.

Around the turn of the 20th century in Austria, Sigmund Freud developed a form of therapy called psychoanalysis. A clinical approach to understanding and treating psychological disorders, **psychoanalysis** assumes that the unconscious mind is the most powerful force behind thought and behaviour and that dreams have meaning and are the most direct route to the unconscious mind (Freud, 1900/1953). It also assumes that our experiences during childhood are a powerful force in the development of our adult personality. Psychoanalysis assumes that people use psychological defences to protect themselves against threatening impulses, thoughts, feelings, and fantasies. Lastly, it assumes that the unconscious blocking, or repression, of disturbing thoughts and impulses—especially sexual and aggressive impulses—is at the heart of all maladaptive adult behaviour.

Sigmund Freud

Psychoanalysis gained immense popularity in the first half of the 20th century, spawning many new therapies, collectively referred to as the *psychodynamic approach* (Berzoff, Flanagan, & Hertz, 2011). While these therapies continued to emphasize the role of unconscious influences on maladaptive behaviour, many downplayed Freud's emphasis on sexual urges. Today, modern psychodynamic therapies have evolved to focus on how early relationships with family members unconsciously influence later relationships in life, for example (Kernberg, 2000).

As we will see in later chapters, Freud is a controversial figure in psychology. On the one hand, his theories contributed to broadening the field of psychology to include the study and treatment of psychological disorders (Fisher & Greenberg, 1996; Westen, 1998). For many contemporary psychological scientists, however, it is hard to reconcile his largely untestable theories with the rigorous methods of science (Crews, 1996). Although recent psychological research has revealed that many aspects of our mental processing occur outside conscious awareness, it's not clear that these processes resemble Freud's view of the unconscious mind (Bargh, 2014; Ramus, 2014).

Connection
Recent research suggests that some of our mental processing, such as encoding new memories, occurs automatically—that is, outside our conscious awareness.
See Chapter 6, LO5.

Modern Views By the mid-20th century, three of the major modern developments in clinical psychology had emerged: psychotherapy, drug therapy, and modern criteria for diagnosing mental disorders. For example, one common form of modern therapy—cognitive-behavioural therapy—focuses on changing a person's maladaptive thought and behaviour patterns by discussing and rewarding more appropriate ways of thinking and behaving. Although we will consider the modern diagnostic criteria in detail in Chapter 15 ("Psychological Disorders") and *psychotherapy* (psychological assessment and treatment by a trained therapist) and drug therapy in detail in Chapter 16 ("Treatment of Psychological Disorders"), it is appropriate to conclude our discussion of the history of psychology as a clinical practice with a brief introduction to the classification system that guides the diagnosis of psychological disorders today.

While it cannot be denied that Freud has had a profound influence on the philosophy, art, film, and literature of the 20th century (Burnham, 2012), psychologists often disagree on his importance to the field of psychology.

Why do you think Freud stirs up so much controversy?

There are currently two widely established systems for classifying mental disorders: the *International Classification of Diseases* produced by the World Health Organization (WHO, 1992) and the *Diagnostic and Statistical Manual* published by the American Psychiatric Association. When diagnosing psychological disorders, North American psychologists tend to use the *Diagnostic and Statistical Manual* (Evans et al., 2013). Currently in its fifth edition, this standardized reference is referred to as the *Diagnostic and Statistical Manual-5*, or *DSM-5* (American Psychiatric Association, 2013). Originally published in 1952, the *DSM* includes diagnoses for more than 250 psychological disorders. The various editions of the *DSM* have incorporated new findings and added new disorders, objectively describing the behaviours and symptoms of each disorder so that psychologists from all perspectives can agree on a single diagnosis for an individual with a given set of symptoms. You might find it surprising to know, however, that this goal of universal agreement often is not achieved, so different clinicians hold different views about what constitutes a mental disorder. Occasionally, the *DSM* authors have even removed behaviour patterns (such as homosexuality, which was deleted from the list of disorders recognized by the American Psychiatric Association in 1973) that do not meet updated diagnostic criteria. Further, practitioners from the various subfields do not always agree with each other about the definitions of a given disorder. Cognitive-behavioural practitioners view depression, for example, as the patient's distorted thinking ("I am worthless"), whereas psychodynamic practitioners might consider the same person's depression (and expressed thoughts) to be the result of unconscious disturbing family relationship patterns that need to be made conscious. Clearly, perspective matters when it comes to psychological treatment, and we must continually question what we know from the perspective we are adopting.

empiricism
the view that all knowledge and thoughts come from experience.

LO4 A Brief History of Scientific Psychology

As with all sciences, scientific psychology can claim philosophy as one of its parent disciplines. By the middle of the 1800s, however, psychology had grown away from philosophy to become a science. Let's look briefly at this history.

The Philosophy of Empiricism Perhaps the most important philosophical question for psychology is the nature of knowledge and how human beings create knowledge. Does knowledge come from reflection and thinking or from experience? In the 4th century BCE, the Greek philosopher Plato argued for the former and his student Aristotle for the latter. In the 17th century Europe, however, the English philosopher John Locke established the view that knowledge and thoughts come from experience, a point of view known as **empiricism.** Specifically, Locke argued that the

Psychotherapy techniques, including psychoanalysis, focus on the client's mental state. Through talking with their therapist, clients learn about their moods, feelings, thoughts, and behaviours and how to better respond to life's challenges.

mind begins as a *tabula rasa,* or blank slate, onto which experience writes the contents of the mind (Locke, 1690/1959).

This view that the mind simply receives what our sensory organs—eyes, ears, nose, skin, and tongue—take in from the outside world is very important in philosophy and psychology. In contrast to scientists, however, philosophers do not collect data to test their ideas. Psychology gained its independence from philosophy when researchers started to examine and test human sensations and perception using scientific methods. Psychology as a modern empirical science tests predictions about behaviour with systematic observations and gathered data. In the mid- to late 1800s, many German universities were starting scientific laboratories in physics, chemistry, and medicine. In the 1870s, they opened the first laboratories in psychology.

psychophysics
the study of how people psychologically perceive physical stimuli, such as light, sound waves, and touch.

The Psychophysics of Human Perception The starting point for empiricism is that we know and experience the world through our five senses of seeing, hearing, tasting, smelling, and touching. Because of the profound influence of the empiricists, the first researchers in psychological science developed the field of **psychophysics** to examine the subjective experience of physical sensations. If the mind consists only of what we sense, then understanding the senses will lead to a direct understanding of the mind. German psychophysics researchers in the 1860s focused on the sensations of touch, vision, hearing, and smell. Whereas physicists study the physical properties of light and sound, psychophysicists study human perception of light and sound.

Connection

Helmholtz's work laid the foundation for several areas of psychology, including sensation and perception. For example, he proposed that three types of receptors in the retina were responsible for our ability to perceive the world in colour. This theory, known as the "trichromatic (three colour) theory of colour vision," continues to explain and guide research on how we see colours.

See Chapter 4, LO7.

One important principle of psychophysics is that the perception of physical properties is not the same as the physical properties themselves. To demonstrate, let's consider the classic question, What weighs more, a pound of feathers or a pound of bricks? You might be thinking, "How dumb do they think I am? I've heard that so many times. They weigh the same! A pound is a pound." Maybe . . . for that answer is true only for the objective, physical property of weight. The *perceived* weight of the two—a psychological property—would be very different. Researchers found that when people's estimates of the weights of both items are empirically tested, contrary to common sense, people think a pound of bricks weighs two to three times more than a pound of feathers (Benjamin, 2014). If you don't believe us, try it for yourself. Psychophysics is all about this relationship between the physical and psychological worlds.

In essence, the scientists who first developed psychophysics—Ernst Weber, Gustav Fechner, and Hermann von Helmholtz—were the first experimental psychologists. Ernst Weber (1795–1878) did some of the first research in perception. For instance, he investigated the smallest change in weight or length that people could discern—what became known as *Weber's Law,* which we will discuss in Chapter 4 ("Sensing and Perceiving Our World"). Gustav Fechner (1801–1889) went on to refine some of Weber's principles of perception (Fancher, 1996). In 1860, he published *Element der psychophysik,* a text of the "exact science" of the relationship between body and mind (Hearnshaw, 1987). This publication is often regarded as the beginning of experimental psychology. Another German, Hermann von Helmholtz (1821–1894), a physician and physicist, made important contributions to the study of memory, physiology, and colour vision (Benjamin, 2014). In addition, he was the first to calculate the speed of a nerve impulse at about 27 metres per second. Specifically, he measured *reaction times* or how long it took people to respond after he stimulated various parts of their legs. Helmholtz found that people took longer to react when their toe was stimulated than when their thigh was stimulated—an important discovery for the time when the prevailing belief was that all mental processes occurred instantaneously!

Wilhelm Wundt

Psychology blossomed into a full-fledged science with the help of Wilhelm Wundt (1832–1920), one of Helmholtz's students. In 1879, Wundt set up a psychology laboratory in Leipzig, Germany, now considered the birthplace of experimental psychology. Although others went before Wundt, he is credited with giving psychology its independence from philosophy and physiology (Benjamin, 2014; Fancher, 1996). He did so by applying the scientific methods of physiology to questions of philosophy (Benjamin, 2014). Before Wundt, people evaluated the question of how the mind worked only by way of argument, not by scientific investigation. By establishing a laboratory, Wundt created a place where the best young minds could learn the science of psychology. And come to learn they did. Wundt single-handedly trained more than 180 students in his laboratory. Of these, more than 100 came from countries other than Germany and then returned to their native countries, taking their knowledge of experimental psychology with them. One of Wundt's American students, James Mark Baldwin, founded the first Canadian laboratory of experimental psychology at the University of Toronto in 1891 (Hoff, 1992).

William James

Another American, G. Stanley Hall (1844–1924), also went to Germany to learn from Wundt. Additionally, Hall studied with William James at Harvard; James is considered the founder of psychology in North America. Hall holds the distinction of earning the first PhD (1878) in psychology as James's student. Hall opened the first psychology laboratory in the United States at Johns Hopkins University in Baltimore, Maryland. He also founded the American Psychological Association (APA) and became its first president in 1892; the Canadian Psychological Association (CPA) was founded decades later, in 1939. Hall started the first scientific journal in American psychology, the *American Journal of Psychology*. Finally, he was able to persuade both Sigmund Freud and his famous protégé Carl Jung to make their only journey to the United States and give lectures at Clark University in Massachusetts in 1909. G. Stanley Hall was also the teacher and mentor of Francis Cecil Sumner (1895–1954), the first African American to earn a PhD in psychology (1920). From 1928 until his death in 1954, Sumner chaired the psychology department at Howard University, in Washington, DC, where he conducted research on equality and justice.

Mary Whiton Calkins

Another of William James's students, Mary Whiton Calkins (1863–1930), became the first female president of the APA in 1905. Harvard was an all-male university until 1920, and the male students did not want to have a woman in class, so she and James conducted their coursework in James's home. Calkins went on to complete the requirements for a PhD, although Harvard would not grant her the degree simply because she was a woman (Benjamin, 2014). Nevertheless, Calkins had an accomplished academic career. She taught at Wellesley College and conducted much research on dreaming, attention, and self-image (Furomoto, 1981). James acknowledged her to be among the best students he had ever encountered (Benjamin, 2014).

Margaret Floy Washburn (1871–1939) was another woman who substantially contributed to the development of psychology as a science in the early part of the 20th century. She was the first woman to be awarded a PhD in psychology in 1894. Her thesis on the influence of visual imagery on judgments of tactual distance and direction was the first foreign study Wundt published in his journal, *Philosophische Studien* (1895) (Johnson, 1997). She went on to have a distinguished career, publishing her influential book, *The Animal Mind*, a review of perception, learning, and memory in various animal species. In 1921, she became the second female president of the APA; the next female president of the APA would not appear for another 50 years (Benjamin, 2014). The first female president of the CPA, Mary Wright, was elected in 1968 (Austin, Rutherford, & Pyke, 2006). Today, almost 50 percent of the faculty employed in psychology departments across

Margaret Floy Washburn

Canada and the United States are women (American Psychological Association, 2009).

Structuralism and Functionalism What is the best way to understand the human mind—by examining its parts or its function? In the last decades of the 1800s, psychology weathered its first major scientific debate with two different perspectives on how to study thought and behaviour. The field was divided over whether it was more important to study the *elements* or the *functions* behind human thought and behaviour. Focus on the elements of mind led to the school of thought known as *structuralism*, whereas focus on the functions of the mind led to the school of thought known as *functionalism*. Edward Titchener (1867–1927), a British-American psychologist trained by Wilhelm Wundt, coined both terms.

structuralism
a 19th-century school of psychology that argued that breaking down experience into its elemental parts offered the best way to understand thought and behaviour.

introspection
the main method of investigation for structuralists; it involves looking into one's own mind for information about the nature of conscious experience.

According to **structuralism,** breaking down experience into its elemental parts offers the best way to understand thought and behaviour. Structuralists believed that a detailed analysis of experience as it happened provides the most accurate glimpse into the workings of the human mind. Their method was **introspection,** looking into one's own mind for information about the nature of conscious experience. Structuralists divided each experience into its smallest elements. Wundt and Titchener, the chief proponents of structuralism, wanted to describe human experience in terms of the elements that combined to produce it (Benjamin, 2014). For example, structuralists, like chemists describing elements, would not describe a peach as "a good peach," but rather would describe their experience with the peach as sweet, round, slightly orange, fuzzy, wet, and juicy. Structuralists were primarily interested in studying the conscious experience of sensations, emotions, and images (Goodwin, 2012).

functionalism
a 19th-century school of psychology that argued it was better to look at why the mind works the way it does than to describe its parts.

Influenced by Charles Darwin's theory of natural selection, psychologists who supported **functionalism** thought it was better to look at why the mind worked the way it did, rather than to describe its parts. The functionalists asked, "Why do people think, feel, or perceive, and how did these abilities come to be?" Functionalists used introspection as well. William James, the most famous functionalist, relied on introspection as a primary method of understanding how the mind worked. However, other functionalists moved beyond introspection to incorporate more objective measures of observation, applying psychology to the study of everyday problems, such as how children learn (Goodwin, 2012).

James's and Wundt's methods of introspection were impressive attempts to describe the conscious mind. Eventually, however, introspection failed as a method of science because of difficulties in reaching a consensus as to what the experiences were. As a result, because of overreliance on introspection in the laboratory as its primary research method, structuralism eventually died out. Although functionalism also faded away as a "school of thought," the functionalists are credited with pioneering work in many contemporary areas of psychology, such as developmental psychology, clinical psychology, and industrial/organizational psychology (Benjamin, 2014). Together, structuralism and functionalism contributed to the rise of psychology as the science of *observable* behaviour.

behaviourism
a school of psychology that proposed that psychology could be a true science only if it examines observable behaviour, not ideas, thoughts, feelings, or motives.

Behaviourism In 1913, a little-known 34-year-old psychologist, John Watson, directly challenged the use of introspection. He founded **behaviourism,** which asserts that psychology can be a true science only if it examines observable behaviour, not ideas, thoughts, feelings, or motives. In Watson's view, mental experiences are hypothetical concepts, for they cannot be directly measured.

As long as psychology focused on such internal states, it would forever be a false science. Behaviourism is an extreme form of environmentalism, the view that all behaviour comes from experience interacting with the world. It is the school of psychology that most clearly expresses John Locke's ideas about our minds being a blank slate at birth.

Borrowing from his predecessors, Watson's early research investigated stimulus-response relationships in animals. He used white rats to study how changes in the nerve fibres of the rat's brain (stimulus) affected maze learning (response). However, as we shall see in Chapter 7 ("Learning"), he is probably most known for his dramatic demonstration of instilling a fear of white rats in an 11-month-old boy known as Little Albert. We don't want to give away the plotline here, but suffice it to say his work with Little Albert revealed how complex human behaviours, particularly emotional responses, could be influenced by environmental events, and provided an approach to the study of the growth and development of children (Fuchs & Evans, 2013).

This dolphin is being trained by means of shaping, a behaviourist technique that rewards animals for small changes in behaviour as they learn a desired behaviour pattern, such as leaping out of the water on cue.

Can you think of undesirable human behaviours that could be shaped with rewards to lessen them or to make them go away?

A decade or so after behaviourism emerged, it became the dominant force in experimental psychology in North America. Its most famous figure, B.F. Skinner (1904–1990), was largely responsible for making behaviourism the major approach in experimental psychology, a position it held for nearly 50 years. Like Watson, Skinner believed that psychology should have two goals—the prediction and control of behaviour. He called his approach the *experimental analysis of behaviour* (Skinner, 1938). He modified Watson's ideas and argued that consequences shape behaviour. Specifically, he studied learning in animals, mostly rats and pigeons, under controlled laboratory conditions. As discussed in Chapter 7, his work focused on changing behaviour by strengthening it through the use of reinforcers and suppressing it through punishment. For example, if you feed your dog Fido from the table, Fido is likely to keep begging for more food. Since you have rewarded, or reinforced, his begging behaviour by feeding him from the table, he is likely to continue begging. Skinner was also interested in applying what he learned about animal behaviour to people's well-being. In 1971, he published his most famous and controversial book, *Beyond Freedom and Dignity,* which ended up on the *New York Times* bestsellers list. In the book, he argued that freedom was largely an illusion; environmental forces controlled people's lives. As you might imagine, such a view of human nature was not well received by everyone.

Connections

Watson, Skinner, and behaviourism have had a tremendous impact on the treatment of problem behaviours in children and psychological disorders, such as fear and anxiety.

See Chapter 7, LO2, LO4; Chapter 16, LO3.

Although many psychologists considered Skinner's approach extreme, he was highly esteemed for his scientific contributions and did much to advance psychology as a scientific discipline (Benjamin, 2014). He was ranked as the field's most important contributor in a survey completed by 93 psychology department chairpersons in 1990, the year of his death (Estes, Coston, & Fournet, 1990). His work and that of other behaviourists on the basic laws of learning continues to have important implications for education and the treatment of psychological disorders. By the 1970s, however, researchers' interest in studying mental processes expanded, and as a result, behaviourism's popularity declined (Robins, Gosling, & Craik, 1999).

Connections

Humanistic personality psychologists developed theories of personality based on humans at their best and striving to be better. They also developed therapies to treat psychological disorders.

See Chapter 13, LO5; Chapter 16, LO2.

Humanistic and Positive Psychology During the first half of the 20th century, the two major schools of thought in psychology were split along the divide between practice and science. On the therapeutic side were psychoanalysis and Freud, and on the scientific side were behaviourism and Skinner. In the 1940s and 1950s, Abraham Maslow and Carl Rogers presented an alternative to both of these perspectives. They offered a rather straightforward criticism of psychology: Both psychoanalysis and behaviourism ignored people at their best, and neither approach considered what it meant to be psychologically healthy. Specifically, humanists thought psychoanalysis' emphasis on aggressive and sexual urges was too pessimistic, overlooking people's capacity for joy. And behaviourism's focus on observable events made it too "mindless," ignoring people's "inner world" and their capacity to hope and aspire. Maslow and Rogers proposed an alternative called **humanistic psychology,** which promoted personal growth and meaning as a way of reaching one's highest potential.

humanistic psychology
a theory of psychology that focuses on personal growth and meaning as a way of reaching one's highest potential.

Humanistic psychology holds a more optimistic view of human nature. Humanists believe that people are inherently good and possess the capacity for free will; that is, people can shape their own lives. As such, humanists believe that people can do more for themselves than either behaviourism or psychoanalysis would predict (Association for Humanistic Psychology, 2001). Today, most applications of humanistic psychology are found in education or clinical psychology.

The humanistic movement waned by the late 1970s, mostly because it had moved away from its research and scientific base. Like introspection in the late 19th century, humanistic psychology came under criticism for using research methods that were too subjective (Shiraev, 2015). Humanistic psychology surfaced again in the late 1990s, however, when Martin Seligman and Mihály Csíkszentmihályi started the positive psychology movement (Seligman & Csíkszentmihályi, 2000). **Positive psychology** shares with humanism a belief that psychology should focus on studying, understanding, and promoting healthy and positive psychological functioning. It does so with a better appreciation than humanistic psychology for the importance of studying well-being from a scientific perspective. As you will see in this text, much of contemporary psychology embraces the positive psychological view.

positive psychology
a scientific approach to studying, understanding, and promoting healthy and positive psychological functioning.

Cognitivism After Watson banished thoughts, feelings, and motives as the focal point of the modern science of psychology in the 1910s, research into these topics nearly disappeared from the field for almost 50 years. Two events kept them in the minds of psychologists, however. First, in the 1920s and 1930s, a movement in Germany called Gestalt psychology attracted worldwide attention. Led by Max Wertheimer (1880–1943), **Gestalt psychology**—after the German word for "whole form"—proposed that perception occurs in unified wholes, where the whole is more than the sum of its parts. As the Gestaltists suspected, our brains actively shape sensory information into perceptions. For an example of this phenomenon, look at Figure 1.2. You see a triangle within three circles, but no triangle actually exists. The brain, however, organizes your perception of the markings on the page into the shape of a triangle.

Gestalt psychology
a theory of psychology that maintains that we perceive things as wholes rather than as a compilation of parts.

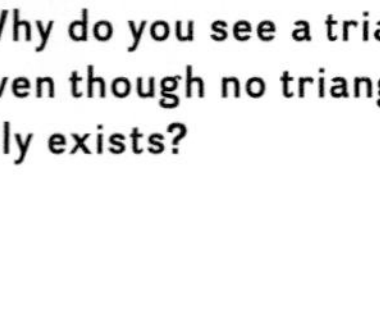

FIGURE **1.2**
A DEMONSTRATION OF GESTALT PSYCHOLOGY.
Why do you see a triangle even though no triangle actually exists?

Second, mental processes returned to psychology full force in the 1950s and 1960s—just when the influence of behaviourism was at its peak. The new emphasis was really a forgotten focus on the processes that fascinated Fechner, Wundt, and Helmholtz in the 19th century: sensation, perception, and mental processes. The term *mental,* however, had lost its appeal. Instead, a new word for thought and mental processes appeared: *cognition* (Benjamin, 2007; Gardner, 1987).

By the 1960s the field of cognitive science had been born, with a focus on the scientific study of thought (Gardner, 1987). The excitement of this new field was captured in a seminal book, *Cognitive Psychology,* written by Ulric Neisser (1967). In addition to freeing itself from the label *mental,* cognitive science made use of a new modern metaphor for the human mind—the computer. A fairly recent innovation at the time, the computer seemed to have a lot in common with the human mind. Computers store, retrieve, and process information, just as the brain stores, retrieves, and processes sensations, memories, and ideas. Sensation was the input; perception was the interpretation and processing of the input; and behaviour and thoughts were the output. By the 1980s, cognitive science combined many disciplines in addition to psychology—namely, linguistics, philosophy, anthropology, artificial intelligence, and neuroscience (Gardner, 1987).

Connection

Jean Piaget, a Swiss psychologist, studied the cognitive errors children make and provided key insights into the mental world of children.

See Chapter 10, LO4.

The British psychologist Frederick Bartlett (1886–1969) wrote a book that promoted a cognitive psychological view in the 1930s. Bartlett stated that memory is not an objective and accurate representation of events but rather a highly personal reconstruction based on one's own beliefs, ideas, and point of view. For example, racial–ethnic stereotypes are frameworks that can alter memory (Graham & Lowery, 2004). If a witness to a crime holds a bias about how likely a crime is to be perpetuated by a person of a certain racial–ethnic background, the witness may misremember the appearance of the accused. This example illustrates that, as Bartlett argued, when people remember, they reconstruct experience in terms of what is most relevant to them rather than providing an unbiased account of events. Bartlett showed that our cognitive frameworks organize how we experience the world. This view is now well accepted in psychology, though Bartlett's insights were unappreciated in North America for decades (Benjamin, 2007).

Behavioural Neuroscience By the 1980s, more and more psychologists had become receptive to the ideas that who we are and what we do and think are very much a result of brain activity. Many related fields with older origins, such as biology, chemistry, and physics, came together with newer fields of psychology, behavioural genetics, and computer science to form the interdisciplinary subject of **neuroscience** (Society for Neuroscience, 2010). Neuroscientists study the structure and function of human and animal brains. As described earlier, *behavioural neuroscientists* attempt to link psychological processes, such as sensation, learning, and emotion, to activities in the brain. For example, a behavioural neuroscientist might record the electrical or chemical activities in rats' brains as they run through a maze to obtain food rewards. Another way to examine the brain–behaviour link might be to remove specific parts of rats' brains to see how performance on the maze is affected.

neuroscience
the interdisciplinary study of the structure and function of human and animal brains.

Much of the early work in this field may be traced to McGill University in Montreal. It was there that Canadian neurosurgeon Wilder Penfield (1891–1976) researched the effects of brain injury and surgery on behaviour. He pioneered the *Montreal procedure,* a successful treatment for patients with epilepsy, which involved destroying nerve cells where the seizures originated (Todman, 2008). Another important figure in this area was Donald O. Hebb (1904–1985), a McGill psychologist who also worked with Penfield. In 1949, he published his seminal work, a book titled *The Organization of Behavior: A Neuropsychological Theory.* In his book, Hebb proposed a theory of cell assembly, which also became known as Hebbian learning or Hebb's law. Simply put, he suggested that repeated stimulation of brain cells leads to physical changes in the cells—"what fires together, wires together." Recently described (along with Darwin's *Origin of Species*) as one of the two most important books in biology (Adams, 1998), his innovative

Donald O. Hebb

Connection

Another pioneer, Brenda Milner, a student of Hebb, was the first to study the effects of brain damage on memory. She studied one of psychology's most famous patients, H.M.

See Chapter 6, LO1.

ideas set the stage for contemporary developments in neuroscience (Posner & Rothbart, 2004). We will return to a discussion of Hebb's work in Chapter 6, "Memory," and Chapter 7, "Learning."

As was suggested earlier in this chapter, research in neuroscience has exploded in the last few years, largely as a function of powerful new brain-imaging techniques (e.g., PET scans, fMRIs, etc.). These techniques will be discussed in detail in Chapter 3, "The Biology of Behaviour." The last decade has seen research in behavioural neuroscience expand to many subdisciplines of psychology, including developmental, social, clinical, and personality psychology. To take just one recent example, Goldapple and colleagues (2004) have observed that cognitive therapy for depression brings about reductions in the activity level of front regions of the brain involved in depressive or negative thinking. In contrast, antidepressant medication appears to exert its effect mostly upon the more "primitive" centres of the brain that regulate mood. Such a finding has important implications for how clinicians treat depression. Some argue that the multidisciplinary nature of neuroscience will serve to integrate the practical and scientific sides of psychology, leading to a more coherent and cohesive scientific discipline (Rand & Ilardi, 2005).

socio-cultural perspective
an approach to psychological research that emphasizes cross-cultural differences in thinking and behaviour.

individualist culture
a culture in which people tend to view themselves as autonomous individuals and to emphasize the needs of individuals.

collectivist culture
a culture in which people tend to view themselves in connection to others; the needs of the group are more important than the needs of individuals.

Socio-culturalism In reviewing the important figures in the history of psychology, it may have become obvious to you that they share similar demographic characteristics. Most notably, early pioneers were Caucasian men of Western European origins who also happened to conduct research on mostly middle- and upper-class male participants (Hall, 1997). Beginning in the 1980s and 1990s, some psychologists began to question the universality of many Western psychological theories and the research generated by them (Norenzayan & Heine, 2006). Many of these researchers adopted a **socio-cultural perspective** to study mental processes and behaviour. Psychologists who take a socio-cultural approach examine *cross-cultural differences* in the causes and consequences of behaviour with the goal of determining whether psychological theories and research apply to all humans, or only to specific populations.

Let's consider a specific example of how a socio-cultural perspective might be relevant to the study of psychology. Suppose you have grown up in a culture that emphasizes individual autonomy, achievement, and success—an **individualist culture** (Triandis, 2003). In this culture, it is important to have a strong sense of identity and feel good about oneself; these are characteristics that people idealize and strive to attain. In such a culture, you might expect people to evaluate themselves in an extremely positive light, perhaps seeing themselves as better than others, because a positive sense of self is valued by the culture. But what if you've grown up in **collectivist culture**—where group needs are more important than individual needs? In this culture, interconnectedness is the ideal way of being. The ideal person in this culture is someone who understands his or her connections to others and works hard to promote positive group interactions (Triandis, 2003). Would such individuals be as likely to view themselves in an enhanced positive light? Wouldn't such an evaluation (e.g., "I'm better than you") undermine harmonious group functioning? Indeed, research shows that people from individualist

Growing up in an individualistic or collectivist culture can shape our views about ourselves.

Can you think of situations in which cultural differences in thinking might lead to misunderstandings?

(Western) cultures, like Canada and the United States, are more likely to engage in strategies of self-enhancement than are people from collectivist (Eastern) cultures, like Japan (Ross, Heine, Wilson, & Sugimori, 2005). Such findings have led researchers to conclude that individualism/collectivism affects the frequency, form, and function of self-enhancement—it clearly depends on the culture you grow up in!

The socio-cultural perspective has become increasingly important as societies, like Canada and the United States, become more culturally diverse. Although the example just given suggests that countries differ in their individualistic versus collectivist orientations, it is important to note that you may find differences in these perspectives within countries, as well. For example, many Aboriginal peoples in Canada have the values of collectivism in their traditional cultures, as often seen when dealing with issues such as land management, community decision making, and educating and raising children. An understanding of the unique experiences of such culturally diverse individuals promotes tolerance and reduces the potential for misunderstandings and conflicts in intercultural interactions. Throughout this text, you will see many examples of how culture impacts the way we think and behave.

Evolutionary Psychology The early 1990s saw the beginning of a new biological perspective on psychology—**evolutionary psychology.** John Tooby and Leda Cosmides (1992) are credited with jump-starting the field with the publication of the chapter "The Evolutionary Foundations of Culture" in a seminal book on evolutionary psychology. Like neuroscience, evolutionary psychology is a hybrid discipline that draws insights from other fields, such as biology, cognitive science, anthropology, economics, and computer science. Like the early functionalists, evolutionary psychologists apply evolutionary principles, such as *natural selection* (1859) and *adaptation* (Williams, 1966), to explain the development of mental characteristics and behaviour. We will return to a more detailed discussion of some specific principles of evolution in the next section of this chapter.

evolutionary psychology
the psychological approach that applies evolutionary principles to explain the development of mental characteristics and behaviours.

Evolutionary psychologists study a wide range of topics across many *content areas* of psychology, such as developmental psychology, social psychology, clinical psychology, perception, linguistics, and so on. For example, an evolutionary psychologist might use an evolutionary perspective to study the emotional attachments infants form with their parents, why jealousy is a common characteristic of romantic relationships, how attractiveness influences mate selection, or why fear of snakes is so common. While evolutionary psychology seeks to explain universal mental characteristics and behaviours such as these, it also sees cultural diversity as one of the most important aspects of human nature that needs explanation (Tooby & Cosmides, 1992). For some, evolutionary psychology has the potential to unify the disparate field of psychology within a single, logically integrated theoretical framework (Tooby & Cosmides, 2005). We will see many examples of the application of evolutionary theory to the study of psychology throughout this text.

Our review of the history of psychological science, summarized in Figure 1.3, has only scratched the surface of how psychologists think about human thought and behaviour, about mind, body, and experience. Debates and theories about how and why we think and act the way we do go back thousands of years. Some of the key debates remain unresolved to this day, primarily because in many cases no one perspective explains the whole story of how things work. These systems of thought have profoundly influenced the development of psychology. Let's now consider the major ways of thinking about mind, body, and experience that have shaped modern psychological science.

5000 BCE
Trephination is used to release the spirits and demons from the mind

460–377 BCE
Hippocrates describes a patient suffering from mental disorder

1690
John Locke proposes that the mind is a blank slate to be written on by experience

1860
Gustav Fechner publishes *Elemente der Psychophysik,* establishing the discipline of psychophysics

1879
Wilhelm Wundt opens first psychology laboratory in Leipzig, Germany

1890
William James publishes *Principles of Psychology,* a text in 2 volumes

1891
James Mark Baldwin founds the first psychology laboratory in Canada at the University of Toronto

1892
G. Stanley Hall, a founding father of the American Psychological Association (APA), becomes its first president

1900
Sigmund Freud introduces his psychoanalytic theory of behaviour with the publication of *Interpretation of Dreams*

1905
Mary Whiton Calkins becomes first female president of the APA

1912
Max Wertheimer develops the principles of Gestalt psychology

1913
John B. Watson establishes behaviourism to study observable behaviour

1920
Francis Cecil Sumner becomes first African American to earn PhD in psychology

1932
Frederick Bartlett lays the foundation for cognitive science with his book *Remembering*

1938
B.F. Skinner publishes *The Behavior of Organisms,* outlining his version of behaviourism

1949
Donald O. Hebb publishes *The Organization of Behavior: A Neuropsychological Theory*

1950
Karen Horney publishes *Neurosis and Human Growth* outlining her psychoanalytic social theory as an alternative to Freud's psychosexual theory

1951
Carl Rogers publishes *Client-Centered Therapy,* advocating a new humanistic approach emphasizing personal growth

1953
Abraham Maslow's *Motivation and Personality* outlines the stages of growth leading to personal fulfillment

1955
Brenda Milner meets and begins to study H.M., a landmark case contributing to memory understanding

1965
Jean Piaget publishes *The Child's Conception of Number*

1974
Eleanor Maccoby and Carol Jacklin publish a seminal book on gender, *The Psychology of Sex Differences*

1992
John Tooby and Leda Cosmides publish a landmark chapter "The Evolutionary Foundations of Culture" that jump-starts evolutionary psychology

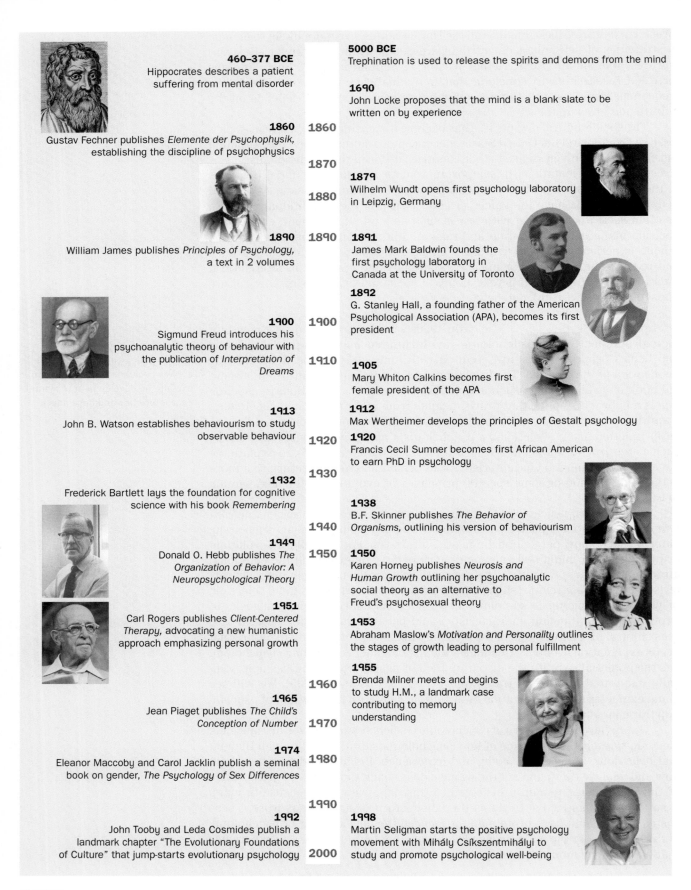

1998
Martin Seligman starts the positive psychology movement with Mihály Csíkszentmihályi to study and promote psychological well-being

1860 1870 1880 1890 1900 1910 1920 1930 1940 1950 1960 1970 1980 1990 2000

FIGURE 1.3
KEY FIGURES AND EVENTS IN THE HISTORY OF PSYCHOLOGY.

Quick Quiz 1.3: The Origins of Psychology

1. What perspective in psychology assumes the unconscious is the most powerful force behind most behaviour?
   a. trephination
   b. cognitive psychology
   c. structuralism
   d. psychoanalysis
2. __________ argued that thoughts, feelings, and motives are unimportant in understanding human behaviour.
   a. Behaviourists
   b. Psychoanalysts
   c. Functionalists
   d. Gestalt psychologists
3. Positive psychology is a modern form of which school of thought?
   a. structuralism
   b. humanism
   c. functionalism
   d. introspectionism

Answers can be found at the end of the chapter.

WAYS OF THINKING ABOUT MIND, BODY, AND EXPERIENCE

The topics covered by psychology sit in the middle of age-old debates and theories about the origins of human thought and behaviour. Three major ways of thinking about human experience continue to influence the field today: the nature–nurture debate, the mind–body problem, and evolutionary theory.

LO5 The Nature–Nurture Debate

For millennia, thinkers have argued over what determines our personality and behaviour: innate biology or life experience (Pinker, 2004). This conflict is known as the *nature–nurture debate*. The nature-only view is that who we are comes from inborn tendencies and genetically based traits.

Consider this scenario. You are at a restaurant and you see a young family trying to eat a meal. A two-year-old girl is running in circles around a table and won't sit down, despite her parents' best efforts. You mention to the parents that she is quite active. The exhausted mom answers meekly, "Yes, she was born that way!" Other patrons of the restaurant might quietly disapprove of the parents' inability to control the child. Chances are, though, the mom is right. The girl was probably always active, and there may be little they can do to get her to sit down. In fact, a great deal of evidence indicates that our personalities are influenced by genetic factors and remain consistent across the life span (Plomin & Caspi, 1999).

The nurture-only side states that we are all essentially the same at birth, and we are the product of our experiences. As we have already considered, John Locke (1690/1959) popularized the idea that the newborn human mind is a blank slate on which the experiences of life are written. This accumulation of experiences makes us who we are. This view means that anything is possible. You can be anything you want to be. This notion is a very Western, very North American idea. It stands as the cornerstone of democracy, free will, and equality (Pinker, 2002).

Pitting nature against nurture, however, gets us nowhere. It creates a false split, or false dichotomy, that hinders our understanding of the mind and behaviour. Almost nothing in psychology can be categorized as either nature or nurture—not learning, not memory, not cognition, not emotion, not even social behaviour! These forces work together almost all the time; they are interdependent.

Throughout this book, we will point out many cases in which environmental and genetic forces work together to shape who we are (Rutter, 2002). For

example, in the processes of learning and remembering, certain genes in the brain are turned on or off by what happens to us (Kandel, 2006). New connections between brain cells result from these changes in the genes. Consequently, the brains of people and animals reared in richly stimulating environments differ from the brains of people reared in understimulating, neglectful, or abusive environments.

Given how much biological and environmental forces interact and influence each other, we introduce the term *softwire* to reflect this new way of thinking about nature and nurture. **Softwiring,** in contrast to hardwiring, means that biological systems involved in thought and behaviour—genes, brain structures, brains cells, and so on—are inherited yet are still open to modification from the environment (Herbert & Rich, 1999; Ottersen, 2010). Much of who we are is more softwired than hardwired.

Here's an example of softwiring: Research reveals that people whose mothers developed an infection during pregnancy are more likely to develop schizophrenia than people whose mothers were healthy during pregnancy (Brown, 2006). Risks of this disorder in offspring increase sevenfold in mothers infected with the flu virus and 10- to 12-fold in mothers infected with rubella, the virus that causes German measles (Brown, 2006; Brown et al., 2004). Evidence suggests that the crucial event here may be the fact that the mothers are mounting an immune response against an infectious agent during key stages of neural development in pregnancy (Fruntes & Limosin, 2008). A baby of the same genetic makeup who was not exposed to the virus and immune response would be less likely to develop the disorder.

How has nature interacted with nurture to influence who you are today?

softwiring
the view that in contrast to hardwiring, biological systems—genes, brain structures, and brain cells—are inherited but open to modification from the environment.

nature through nurture
the position that the environment constantly interacts with biology to shape who we are and what we do.

These examples illustrate how what we are born with and what we are exposed to interact to create thought and behaviour. For decades many psychologists have shied away from the idea of an interrelationship, clinging to the nature–nurture debate. Old habits do indeed die hard. But to fully appreciate human behaviour, we must take a broader view. All creatures are born with genetic instructions, but from the beginning, even before birth, environmental factors alter the ways in which genes are expressed. Throughout life, genetic factors, such as a familial predisposition toward anxiety, assert themselves. Rather than pitting nature against nurture, we use the phrase **nature through nurture** (sometimes also referred to as the *interactionist perspective*), whereby the environment—be it the womb or the world outside—interacts continuously with biology to shape who we are and what we do (Begley, 2007; Pinker, 2004; Ridley, 2003).

Connection

Our genetic code is not set in stone at birth. Genes are turned on or off by experiences we have, foods we eat, and even foods our mothers ate while pregnant with us.

See Chapter 3, LO2.

LO6 Mind–Body Dualism

How is the mind related to the body and brain? Are they one and the same or two distinct entities? Since its inception, psychology has been burdened by another big idea of Western thinking—*mind–body dualism*. In the 17th century René Descartes, a French philosopher and mathematician, offered proofs of many important concepts in mathematics (Crump, 2001). He proposed one idea that crippled the social sciences for years, stating that the mind and the body are separate entities, an idea often referred to as *mind–body dualism*. From this perspective, the mind controls the body. The body can occasionally control the mind too, but mainly when we abandon good judgment, such as in the throes of passion. Mostly, in Descartes's view, mind and body are separate.

Challenge Your Assumptions

True or False? Genetic influence on our thoughts and actions is set at birth and can't be changed.

False: Experience can and does change how and when genes get expressed.

Dualism, the separation of mind and body, allows for many ideas central to Western thinking: For example, a soul survives bodily death, the mind is separate from the brain, and humans are superior to animals. Like nature versus nurture, mind–body dualism represents a false dichotomy—in the sense of being either–or. Mind and body are both useful concepts, but they are exquisitely intertwined. That which we call *mind*, our thoughts, feelings, and ideas—our entire mental world—results from the functioning of our *brain*, which is indeed part of the body.

Both the nature–nurture and mind–body dichotomies have influenced Western thought and the development of psychology as a field. Notice that we have been talking about *Western* thinking. Indeed, modern psychological science grew from the marriage of Western philosophy and physiology, with Wundt's laboratory in Leipzig as the first child. In contrast, systems of thought from elsewhere in the world—especially Eastern philosophy—have long emphasized the interdependence of body and mind (Begley, 2007; Tulku, 1984). In Eastern thought, body and mind are very much seen as part of one whole. Native North Americans also viewed mind and body as interconnected, together with spirit. Their traditional healing practices were holistic, designed to restore balance (or wellness) between all three parts (Portman & Garrett, 2006). Psychological science is, at last, beginning to arrive at this same conclusion—mind and body are connected—but it has taken over a century to get there.

LO7 The Evolution of Behaviour

One principle that plays an important role in understanding human behaviour is evolution. The basics of this theory are more complex than most of us realize. Here we briefly explain the fundamental processes of evolution.

Evolution means "change." With respect to biological species, **evolution** is the change over time in the frequency with which specific genes occur within a breeding species (Buss, 1999). What does the frequency of gene transmission have to do with behaviour? Our genes contain instructions for making all the proteins in our bodies. Proteins, in turn, make up a lot of what we are: cell membranes, hormones, enzymes, and muscle tissue, for instance. These constituents carry out our intentions, in our brains, and in our bodies. Thus, behaviours have genetic bases that are affected by many environmental factors. Human interaction with the world influences which genes are passed on to future generations, and these in turn shape human behaviour. These changes take place by *natural selection*.

evolution
the change over time in the frequency with which specific genes occur within a breeding species.

First described by the 19th-century English naturalist Charles Darwin (1809–1882), **natural selection** is formally defined as a feedback process whereby nature favours one design over another, depending on whether it has an impact on reproduction. This process takes a long time to work, but it ultimately shapes who we are and how species evolve. Charles Darwin's genius and great contribution was not the theory of evolution itself but rather his explanation of *how evolution works*, that is, by natural selection.

natural selection
a feedback process whereby nature favours one design over another because it has an impact on reproduction.

Natural selection occurs by chance. Every once in a while, genes change for no apparent reason. Spontaneous changes in genes, called *chance mutations*, can alter the design of a structure or a set of behaviours. Let's suppose, for example, that a chance mutation in a population of green beetles results in a brown beetle. If the brown beetle is less visible to predators, it might have more success in surviving and reproducing. When it reproduces, the brown beetle passes on its "brown" genes to its offspring. The brown offspring have a better survival rate, which means they are more likely to reproduce. Eventually, this physiological trait becomes common among members of the species. The complete change takes many generations, but eventually the entire beetle species will be brown (Tooby & Cosmides, 1992). The key in natural selection is that the behaviours have to increase reproductive success, because reproduction and gene transmission drive the whole process.

Charles Darwin

The accumulation of chance mutations underlies evolutionary change. Each generation is a product of beneficial modifications from its evolutionary

In Industrial England in the 1800s, the peppered moth, which was originally mostly white, blended into the white lichen on trees. Pollution killed the white lichen on trees and put the original white moth in danger of being easy prey. Some started to become darker to blend in with the lichenless trees. Can you see both moths in each image? The white one on the right is so well camouflaged that a red circle had to be drawn to show its location.

How does this exemplify Darwin's idea of natural selection?

adaptations
inherited solutions to ancestral problems that have been selected for because they contribute in some way to reproductive success.

past. Natural selection creates structures and behaviours that solve adaptive problems. Among the adaptive problems that our early human ancestors faced were avoiding predators, choosing nutritious foods, finding a mate, and communicating effectively with others. **Adaptations** are inherited solutions to ancestral problems that have been naturally selected because they directly contribute in some way to reproductive success (Tooby & Cosmides, 1992). Adaptations evolved to solve problems in past generations—not current ones. In other words, we are living with traits and tendencies that benefited our ancestors. Even though these tendencies might not seem to enhance our fitness in today's world, eons spent in harsher environments have left us predisposed to perform certain social behaviours when a situation calls forth ancient patterns. Consider, for example, our preference for fatty foods. In our evolutionary past, eating fat was a good strategy. Early humans, as hunter-gatherers, did not know when they would find food. If they found fat, they ate it, because fat could be stored on the body and used later when food might be scarce. For this reason, humans evolved to like fat. Modern society, however, offers easy access to food. Now eating fat is not the best strategy, because we don't need to store it for future use. More food will be available when we need it. So we eat fat, store it up, and carry it around as extra weight. Human cravings have not changed much, even though our environments have.

Nothing illustrates more vividly than evolution how nature and nurture work together. Depending on how they enable organisms to respond to their environment, certain characteristics of animals predominate or not—like the brown colour of the beetle and peoples' preference for eating fat. Nature and nurture work together to create our bodies (including our brains) and behaviour. They are interdependent—that is, they depend on and interact with each other.

Early hunters, like the ones portrayed in this ancient rock painting from the Tadrart Acacus Mountains of Libya, ate fat when it was available and their bodies stored the excess in order to survive when food was scarce. This adaptation has persisted for thousands of years, even though for most people access to food is not a problem.

Quick Quiz 1.4: Ways of Thinking about Mind, Body, and Experience

1. Which phrase most accurately reflects a modern perspective in psychology?
   a. nature over nurture
   b. nature versus nurture
   c. nurture over nature
   d. nature through nurture
2. In evolutionary theory, inherited solutions to ancestral problems are termed
   a. natural selection.
   b. adaptations.
   c. psychoanalysis.
   d. traits.
3. Mind–body dualism proposes that
   a. the mind influences the body and the body influences the mind.
   b. the mind and body are one.
   c. the mind and body are separate.
   d. the mind and body are both adaptations.

Answers can be found at the end of the chapter.

NO ONE PERSPECTIVE TELLS THE WHOLE STORY

As we have seen in this chapter, in order to fully appreciate the complexity of human thought and behaviour, one must consider a wide variety of perspectives—no one perspective tells the whole story. As summarized in Figure 1.4, psychology's perspectives provide different ways of viewing human nature. One or more perspectives frame research questions posed by researchers in each of the subdisciplines of psychology. Throughout this text we highlight diverse explanations of human thought and behaviour.

Consider the psychological disorder of schizophrenia, for example. For years people attributed the development of this disorder mostly to upbringing, arguing for a pure "nurture" explanation. Then biological explanations, such as an imbalance of particular neurotransmitters, became fashionable. The most recent research suggests that schizophrenia emerges from an interaction of biological and environmental influences—in a very real sense, elements of both explanations are correct (Moffitt, Caspi, & Rutter, 2005). The more open we are to diverse perspectives, the better able we will be to explain the whole and often surprising picture of human behaviour.

We believe strongly that modern psychological science tells us that we must combine multiple perspectives in order to come to a complete understanding of

Challenge Your Assumptions

True or False? Psychologists agree that most of human thought and behaviour cannot be explained by one perspective.

True: Human thought and behaviour are so complex and determined by so many different factors that no one perspective can fully capture the richness of human psychology.

Perspective	Psychoanalytic	Behavioural	Humanistic	Cognitive	Neuroscience	Socio-cultural	Evolutionary
Focus	How the unconscious mind and childhood experiences influence maladaptive behaviour	How the environment shapes our behaviour through stimuli and consequences	How free will and striving for personal growth and meaning shapes our thinking and behaviour	How we think, using processes, such as retrieval and storage in memory, perception, and attention	How brain structure and function is linked to thought and behaviour	How culture shapes the way we think and act	How our behaviours are shaped through natural selection and adaptation
Examples of subdisciplines using this perspective	Personality, clinical, counselling	Clinical, industrial-organizational, educational, forensic	Personality, clinical, counselling	Cognitive, developmental, social, sports, industrial-organizational	Biological, developmental, cognitive, social, clinical	Developmental, social, clinical	Biological, developmental, social

FIGURE **1.4**

A SUMMARY OF PSYCHOLOGY'S PERSPECTIVES.

Suppose a researcher is interested in studying bullying. Can you think of some examples of questions generated by each perspective to shed light on this issue?

human thought and behaviour. As we have seen, one of the overarching themes of multiple perspectives is the proverbial nature–nurture question. Psychological science shows that almost every fundamental aspect of human behaviour—whether it is brain development, learning, intelligence, perception, personality, social behaviour, or psychological disorders—develops from a complex interplay of biological and environmental forces, of nature and nurture.

Evaluating Connections in Psychology

Studying Electronic Social Interactions

There are nearly a dozen ways a person can interact with others electronically—via email, blogs, cell phones, chat rooms, texting, instant messaging, audio or video chats, gaming (either solo or multiplayer), videos, photos, bulletin boards, and social networking sites (SNSs). Humans have taken to electronic forms of interaction like fish to water. As a form of behaviour that is evolving at a rapid pace, electronic social interaction holds great interest for psychologists in all of the subfields you read about in this chapter. Let's consider how psychologists from some of these different areas might study electronic communication and its effects on human behaviour and thought.

Cognitive Psychology

Cognitive scientists typically are interested in how we learn, remember, think, or reason. They are also interested in attention. The widespread use of mobile devices has sparked a number of research questions. The most obvious one concerns how drivers can pay attention to driving while talking on a mobile device. Researchers who have examined the effect of talking on a hands-free mobile device while driving report that a person's ability to operate a car while doing so is significantly impaired and is even similar to the ability to drive while drunk (Caird, Willness, Steel, & Scialfa, 2008; Strayer, Drews, & Couch, 2006). In addition, attitudes and beliefs about how dangerous and how common mobile phone use is while driving predict using phones while driving (Hafetz et al., 2010; Zhou, We, Rau, & Zhang, 2009): Those who think most about receiving phone calls and think about their phones while they are off are most likely to have accidents while driving (O'Connor et al., 2013).

Developmental Psychology

Developmental psychologists study how we change over the life span. They might ask questions like these: At what age is a person too young to form electronic social networks? At what age does participation in Internet social networks peak? Will they always be for the younger generation, or will people 60 and older use them? Does gender affect interest and participation in SNSs? How have cell phones and other electronic methods of communicating changed the way teenagers interact with others?

Researchers have already given us answers to some of these questions. Some suggest that older teenage girls and young women are more likely to participate in social networking sites than are boys and young men (Boyd, 2007; Hargittai, 2008). Among university students, men are more likely to use SNSs to begin new relationships, whereas women are more likely to use them to maintain existing relationships (Muscanell & Guadagno, 2012). Electronic interactions are popular with adolescents because of psychological factors: identity, autonomy, intimacy, and sexuality (Subrahmanyam & Greenfield, 2008; Walsh, White, & Young, 2009). One reason the popularity of electronic interactions declines with age may be that these issues decline in importance as one moves from early adulthood to middle and late adulthood (Erikson, 1982; Harris Interactive, 2008).

Social Psychology

More than just about any other area of psychology, social psychology lends itself to a rich set of research questions regarding electronic interactions. Texting in particular and mobile device use in general are the primary tools for staying connected to friends and peers (Harris Interactive, 2008; Walsh et al., 2009). One of the first Internet applications for social purposes was online dating services. Such forms of electronic interaction may be a preferred method of contact for people with high social anxiety (Stevens & Morris, 2007). Although most people who use online dating services tend to be over 30, university-age teens and young adults are increasingly using them as well (Stevens & Morris, 2007; Valkenburg & Peter, 2007). Contrary to what some people originally thought, however, electronic interactions cannot easily be used to hide one's "real personality" and to avoid ever having real face-to-face contact with others. Research on this phenomenon suggests that people use the Internet not simply to interact with others from afar but also to arrange real face-to-face meetings (Couch & Liamputtong, 2008).

Electronic interactions have led to new behaviours and language as the boundaries between public and private have broken down. For instance, being *privately public* means connecting with many other people, while being relatively non-public about revealing who you are. Being *publicly private* means you disclose a lot of details of your private life and may or may not limit access to your site (Lange, 2008).

Another electronic behaviour is the concept of "friending," which raises ancient issues of being "popular," socially excluded, rejected, or accepted. In one tragic case of online rejection, a 13-year-old girl was so distraught over being rejected by a boy online that she committed suicide. The even greater tragedy, however, was that the boy did not exist: A neighbour's mother allegedly made him up to get back at the girl for making disparaging remarks about her daughter.

How does technology change how we learn, think, feel, and behave with others?

Personality Psychology

A personality psychologist could ask many questions about electronic interaction and presentations. For example, are people who interact extensively with other people via Facebook more or less outgoing than those who do not? Moreover, how much of people's personality is reflected in their Facebook profiles? Research consistently finds that people who are extraverted are more likely than introverts to use Facebook and have a wider network of social relationships (Amichai-Hamburger & Vinitzky, 2010; Nadkarni & Hofmann, 2012). Yet introverts are more likely than extraverts to spend more time on Facebook and have a more favourable attitude toward it (Orr et al., 2009).

Health Psychology

A recent innovation is using mobile devices to deliver health information and provide support for patients in managing their medical treatment of chronic diseases, such as asthma, high blood pressure, and diabetes. One study had children and adolescents with diabetes use a text messaging system, called *Sweet Talk,* to ask questions about aspects of their self-care, including monitoring their blood glucose levels; care providers answered queries and provided treatment updates (Franklin, Waller, Paglieri, & Greene, 2008). Compared to those receiving conventional insulin therapy, children and adolescents who used Sweet Talk reported greater beliefs in their ability to self-manage their diabetes and they were more likely to adhere to their insulin treatment schedules. Mobile devices have also been used successfully in interventions aimed at changing unhealthy behaviours. For example, text messaging has helped people quit smoking, lose weight, and increase physical activity levels (Riley et al., 2011).

Clinical Psychology

Clinical psychologists can diagnose disorders of technology use but also use the same technologies to help treat people with various kinds of disorders. When do SNSs and other electronic interactions become a problem? Can one become "addicted" to such behaviour, and can such interactions become dangerous to those involved? One of the main criteria for a mental illness is that it interferes with everyday life and functioning. If one is online for 10–12 hours a day, is that healthy? What about the danger involved in meeting someone in person whom you know only from online interaction? Sexual predators use these connections to meet victims. They contact potential victims through chat rooms, instant messages, and email. According to one study, one in seven teens and preteens (ages 10–17 years) have been sexually solicited online (Ybarra & Mitchell, 2008).

Connection

Can a person actually become addicted to online activities? What does it mean to be addicted to electronic interaction?

See Chapter 15, LO1.

There is also the psychologically interesting phenomenon of creating an alternative personality, or avatar, in the gaming world. People sometimes take on personalities that are very different from their own in an online world that allows them to say things they would not in direct, face-to-face contact. This ability to be people we are not has allowed psychotherapists to use avatar personality games, such as Second Life®, to help people overcome their social anxieties in real life (Gottschalk, 2010; Lisetti et al., 2009). Similarly, video services such as Skype and Google Chat are increasingly used to connect psychotherapist and patient.

We hope this chapter has helped you to appreciate the richness and excitement of psychology as a clinical practice and science. More than that, we hope it encourages you to become an active and critical student of human behaviour: Don't believe everything you think, and question how conclusions are drawn—even conclusions in this text. We hope that at this point, as a first step toward active learning and investigating, you are asking, How do psychologists know all of this? How do they do research? In the next chapter, we discuss the techniques by which psychological scientists study mental processes and behaviour. Welcome to the fascinating world of psychology.

Quick Quiz 1.5: Evaluating Connections in Psychology

1. What area of psychology would be concerned with studying changes in the patterns of cell phone use as people age?
   a. clinical psychology
   b. cognitive psychology
   c. developmental psychology
   d. social psychology
2. Researchers have found that
   a. operating a car while using a mobile device is as dangerous as driving while drunk.
   b. adolescent boys are more likely to use SNSs than teen females.
   c. personalities can be completely disguised during online interactions.
   d. extroverts are likely to spend more time on Facebook than introverts.

Answers can be found at the end of the chapter.

Chapter Review

WHAT IS PSYCHOLOGY?

- Psychology is the scientific study of thought and behaviour. We can see psychology all around us—in our own thoughts and feelings, in the behaviour of our friends and relatives, and in how we interpret others' behaviours. As a field, it prepares us well not only for life in general, but also for a wide variety of professions in which relating with other people plays a key role.
- As a discipline, psychology is both a practice and a science. Clinical psychologists and counsellors treat mental, emotional, and behavioural disorders and promote psychological health. Clinical psychologists also conduct research on psychological disorders and health. They practise psychology. As a science, psychology is the field of study in which researchers examine how the mind works and the rules that govern behaviour within and between individuals. Psychology has four main goals: to describe, explain, predict, and change behaviour.

SUBDISCIPLINES OF PSYCHOLOGY

- As a broad field, psychology comprises several subdisciplines, or areas of focused study, including cognitive, developmental, social, personality, health, educational, and industrial/organizational psychology. Neuroscience explores the links among brain, mind, and behaviour and thus cuts across other subdisciplines.

THE ORIGINS OF PSYCHOLOGY

- The practice of psychology goes back to prehistoric times. Thousands of years ago humans drilled holes in the skull to treat brain injury and perhaps mental anguish as well. In the Middle Ages, the mentally ill were often treated as if possessed by demons. A few hundred years later, asylums served as storage houses for the severely mentally disabled.
- The late 1800s and early 1900s witnessed the beginning of more humane and more sophisticated treatment of people with psychological disorders. Around the turn of the 20th century, Sigmund Freud developed psychoanalysis to treat people suffering from disorders. By the middle of the 20th century, modern diagnostic criteria for mental disorders, psychotherapy, and drug therapy had emerged.
- The history of psychology as a science is not nearly as old as that of clinical practice, although its origins in philosophy go back to the ancient Greeks. Psychological science emerged from a tradition of empiricism and observations of the world. John Locke's 17th-century view of the mind as a blank slate on which experience writes the contents influences psychology to this day.
- The first psychological scientists did experimental work in perception and laid the groundwork for psychophysics. Only when laboratories started to empirically examine and test human sensations and perception did psychology gain its independence from philosophy and become a science.
- Wilhelm Wundt opened the first laboratory in experimental psychology in Leipzig, Germany, in 1879. Key figures in the birth of scientific psychology in North America include William James and G. Stanley Hall.
- The biggest development in psychological research in North America was the birth of behaviourism in the early 20th century. According to behaviourism, all behaviour comes from experience. Founded by John Watson, behaviourism reached its pinnacle with B.F. Skinner.
- Behaviourism proved a very useful model for developing methods of studying learning in humans and animals, but it left the unobservable world of the mind unexplained. This all changed with the cognitive revolution of the 1950s and 1960s. Initially, cognitive science used the computer as a model for the way the human mind processes and stores sensations, memories, and ideas.
- By the 1980s, many psychologists were interested in studying how thoughts and behaviours are linked to underlying brain activity. Research in the interdisciplinary field of neuroscience expanded rapidly, largely due to innovative new brain-imaging techniques. A number of early pioneers in the field were researchers at McGill University, including Wilder Penfield, Donald Hebb, and Brenda Milner.
- The socio-cultural approach to psychology grew in the 1980s and 1990s as psychologists realized the importance of studying cross-cultural variations in thought and behaviour. Research has revealed differences between cultures who value autonomy (individualist cultures) and cultures where group connection is important (collectivist cultures).
- In the 1990s, a new biological approach to studying psychology emerged. Using evolutionary theory, evolutionary psychologists attempt to explain how and why specific human and animal characteristics and behaviours have developed over time.

WAYS OF THINKING ABOUT MIND, BODY, AND EXPERIENCE

- Psychological science in the 21st century has reintegrated biological and environmental explanations of human thought and behaviour. The fully modern view squares explanations of behaviour with the principles of evolution. It also surpasses old absolutes like the nature–nurture debate and mind–body dualism.

NO ONE PERSPECTIVE TELLS THE WHOLE STORY

- Multiple perspectives are often needed to fully explain the complexity of human thought and behaviour.

EVALUATING CONNECTIONS IN PSYCHOLOGY

- The world of electronic interaction provides a context for research in many subdisciplines of psychology. For example, personality psychologists have examined which types of people are more likely to use social networking sites (SNSs); social psychologists have studied whether SNSs operate like real-life social networks; and developmental psychologists have begun to explore how the use of email, SNSs, and texting varies by age and gender.

Quick Quiz Answers

Quick Quiz 1.1: 1. d 2. d 3. c 4. a **Quick Quiz 1.2:** 1. a 2. b 3. c **Quick Quiz 1.3:** 1. d 2. a 3. b
Quick Quiz 1.4: 1. d 2. b 3. c **Quick Quiz 1.5:** 1. c 2. a

CHAPTER 2

Conducting Research in Psychology

CHAPTER OUTLINE

Challenge Your Assumptions

True or False?

- ☐ Psychology is not a science.
- ☐ Spending money on ourselves makes us happier than spending money on others.
- ☐ Knowing what you're looking for in an experiment has no effect on the outcome.
- ☐ Eating sugar makes children hyperactive.

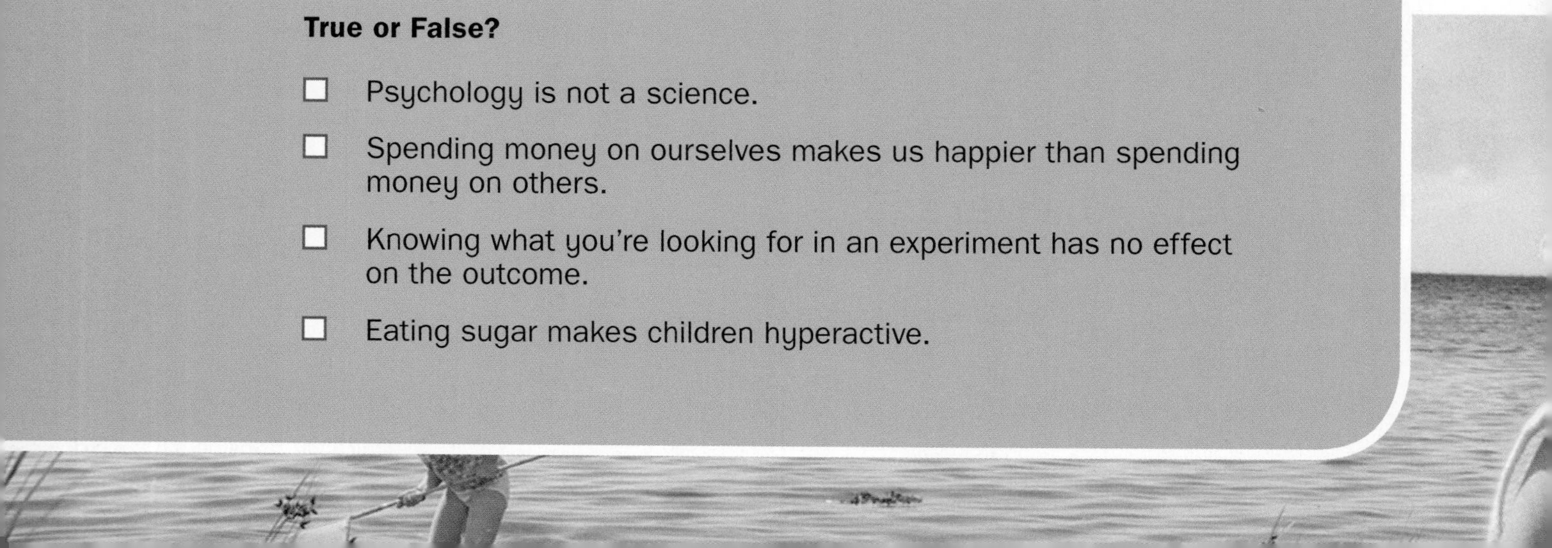

LEARNING OBJECTIVES

- **LO1** Describe some of the limits of everyday thinking and observation.
- **LO2** Explain what makes psychology a science.
- **LO3** Compare and contrast the different kinds of descriptive studies and explain the importance of random sampling.
- **LO4** Describe the strengths and weaknesses of correlational studies and define positive and negative correlations.
- **LO5** Describe the main characteristics of an experimental study that allow researchers to isolate cause and effect.
- **LO6** Differentiate among the various types of measurement scales used to operationally define variables.
- **LO7** Compare and contrast commonly used measures of psychological research.
- **LO8** Explain how to use descriptive and inferential statistics to analyze and interpret data.
- **LO9** Discuss some research challenges that involve the ethics of studying humans and animals.

You are at your apartment near campus one summer day when the police knock at your door. After they confirm your identity, they say that you are being arrested on suspicion of armed robbery. The police handcuff your hands behind your back, put you in the squad car, and take you down to the station. There you are booked, fingerprinted, and placed in a detention cell. You are then blindfolded and driven to a nearby prison, where you are stripped, sprayed with a delousing agent, and made to stand nude and alone in the cell yard. Finally, you are given a uniform, photographed, and assigned to a prison cell. But you have done nothing, and the people who arrested you knew this.

This scenario may seem far-fetched, but it actually happened to ten male college students in the summer of 1971 in Palo Alto, California. They had previously agreed to participate in a "psychological study on 'prison life' in return for payment of $15 a day" (Haney, Banks, & Zimbardo, 1973, p. 73). Yet the police officers who arrested them said nothing about a connection between their arrest and their agreement to participate in such a study. Philip Zimbardo conducted this study—now known as the Stanford Prison Experiment—to examine whether normal people might behave in extreme ways when thrust into situations that place extreme demands on them. In this case, they readily took on roles that made them powerful or powerless (Haney et al., 1973). Zimbardo chose 21 carefully screened male student volunteers and randomly assigned them to be either "guards" or "prisoners" in a simulated prison environment for two weeks. All were briefed beforehand about what conditions would be like in the mock prison. All the students signed a form, consenting to participate. Six days into the simulation, however, the experiment had taken such an unexpected turn that Zimbardo had to end the study—the students were playing their roles too well. Prisoners went back and forth between plotting riots and having emotional breakdowns—getting sick and crying, for instance. Guards became extremely authoritarian, restricting the prisoners' personal freedom almost completely. They dehumanized the prisoners by referring to each one only by his assigned number—never by name. They put anyone suspected of "disobeying" and being "a bad prisoner" in solitary confinement. The line between fiction and reality, between assigned role and true identity, blurred. In fact, half of the "prisoners" had to be released ahead of schedule because they were experiencing extreme emotional distress as a result of their "incarceration."

The Stanford Prison Experiment was widely criticized for being unethical and unscientific (Savin, 1973). Many felt that the information learned about human behaviour did not justify the emotional turmoil experienced by the student participants, and that the study should never have been conducted in the first place. Others challenged the study's design, suggesting that it lacked experimental control and that the conclusions drawn by the experimenters were largely subjective (Banuazizi & Movahedi, 1975).

Regardless of these criticisms, Zimbardo's study has served not only as a springboard for additional research on group behaviour, but also as a strong incentive for prison reform. Interest in this study continues today, and it takes on new significance in light of more recent cases of prisoner abuse, such as the mistreatment of Iraqi prisoners by American soldiers following the 2003 U.S. invasion of Iraq (Zimbardo, 2007). In addition, the Stanford Prison Experiment has contributed to our current standards in the ethical treatment of research participants, one of the many topics of research methods in psychology that we will cover in this chapter. We begin this chapter by looking at psychology as a science and the methods of scientific inquiry applied in psychological research. We will then turn to the subject of how psychologists collect, analyze, and interpret data—processes that become the building blocks of knowledge in the field.

THE NATURE OF SCIENCE

Science is about testing intuitive assumptions regarding how the world works, observing the world, and being open-minded to unexpected findings. Some of science's most important discoveries happened only because the scientists were open to surprising and unexpected results. Fundamentally, science entails collecting observations, or *data*, from the real world and evaluating whether the data support our ideas or not. The Stanford Prison Experiment fulfilled these criteria, and we will refer to this example several times in our discussion of research methods, measures, and ethics.

LO1 Common Sense and Logic

Science is more than common sense, logic, and pure observation. Although reason and sharp powers of observation can lead to knowledge, they have limitations. Take common sense—the intuitive ability to understand the world. Often common sense is quite useful. Don't go too close to that cliff. Don't arouse that sleeping bear. Don't eat that rotten food. Sometimes, though, common sense leads us astray. In psychology, our intuitive ideas about people's behaviour are often contradictory or flat-out wrong. For example, it is intuitive to most of us that who we are is influenced by our parents, family, friends, and society. But it is equally obvious, especially to parents, that children come into the world as unique people, with their own temperaments, and people who grow up in essentially the same environments do not have identical personalities. To what extent are we the products of our environment, and how much do we owe to heredity? Common sense cannot answer that question, but science can.

Connection

How do psychologists tease apart the question of how much of a personality trait is influenced by genetics and how much by environment? A common approach is to study twins (both identical and fraternal) who are reared apart or reared together.

See Chapter 3, LO2.

Another problem with common sense is that we often use the benefit of hindsight to confirm what we believe, sometimes referred to as the **hindsight bias** or "I-knew-it-all-along-phenomenon." Imagine that you receive a letter from a publisher stating that the publisher is going to print your short story. You tell your friend that you knew that it would be published all along. However, your friend reminds you that before you received the letter, you had told him that you were very uncertain about whether the publisher would accept your short story. Clearly, you are engaging in hindsight bias. Publication of your short story seemed more predictable in retrospect (i.e., after you knew it had been accepted). Research shows that you are not alone in your 20/20 hindsight—hindsight bias is widespread (Blank, Musch, & Pohl, 2007). Hindsight bias is problematic because it can make common sense unreliable. We need the methods of science to help us separate fact from illusion.

hindsight bias
the tendency to overestimate our ability to predict an event, *after* the event outcome is known.

Logic is also a powerful tool in the scientist's arsenal. But it can tell us only how the world *should* work, not how the world actually works. Sometimes the world is not logical. A classic example of the shortcoming of logic is seen in the work of the ancient Greek philosopher Aristotle. He argued that heavier objects should fall to the ground at a faster rate than lighter objects. Sounds reasonable, right? Unfortunately, it's wrong. For 2000 years, however, the argument was accepted simply because the great philosopher Aristotle wrote it and it made intuitive sense. It took the genius of Galileo to say, "Wait a minute. Is that really true? Is that the way the world works? Let me do some tests to see whether it is true." He did and discovered that Aristotle was wrong (Crump, 2002). The weight of an object does not affect its rate of speed when falling. Science, therefore, must combine logic with research and experimentation.

Connection

What other biases may hinder our ability to think scientifically? The confirmation bias can lead people to pay attention to information that is consistent with their beliefs while ignoring evidence that contradicts their beliefs.

See Chapter 8, LO9.

The Limits of Observation

Science also relies on observation, but even observation can lead us astray. Our knowledge of the world comes through our five senses, but our senses can be fairly easily fooled, as any good magician or artist can demonstrate. Even when

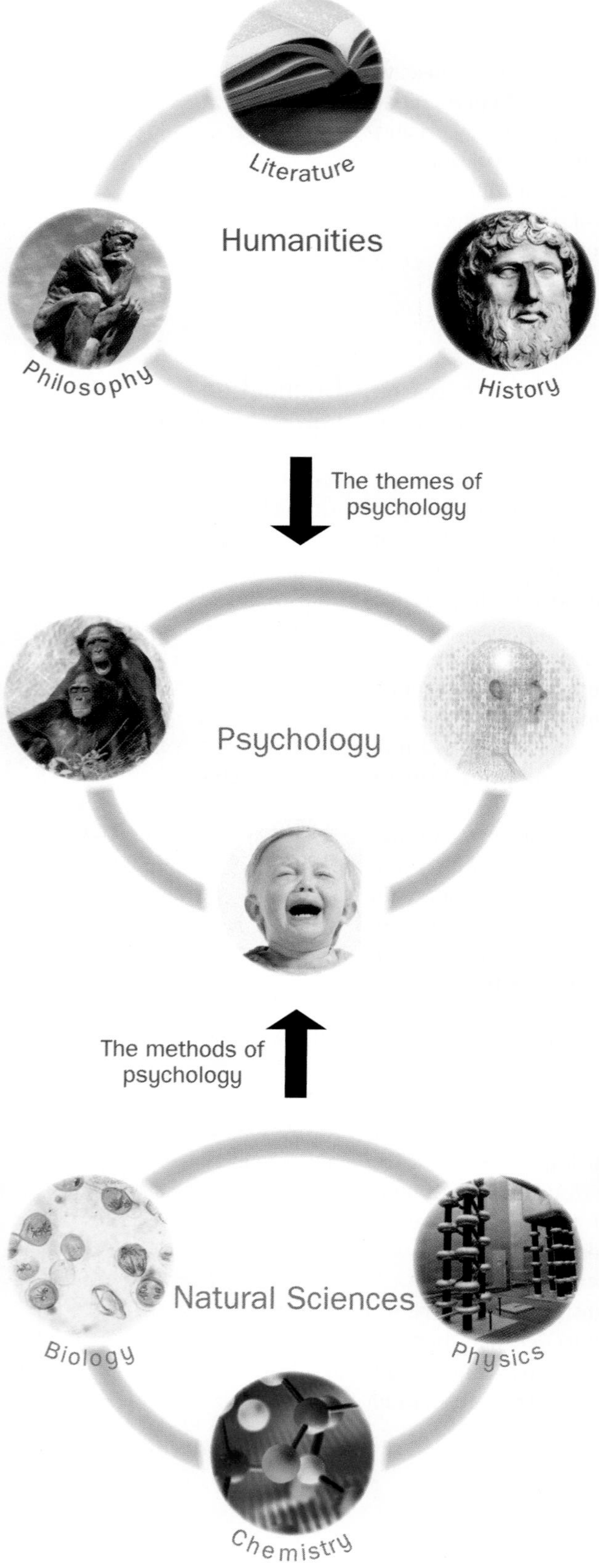

FIGURE 2.1
PSYCHOLOGY: ITS THEMES AND METHODS

Reality can be different from what we think. Our perceptions are not the same as what is really out there. Camouflaged animals are just one example.
Can you think of other common examples of observations that don't reflect reality?

we are not being intentionally fooled, the way in which the brain organizes and interprets sensory experiences may vary from person to person.

Another problem with observation is that people tend to generalize from their observations and assume that what they witnessed in one situation applies to all similar situations. Imagine you are visiting another country for the first time. Let's say the first person you have any extended interaction with is rude, and a second briefer interaction goes along the same lines. Granted, you have lots of language difficulties; nevertheless, you might conclude that all people from that country are rude. After all, that has been your experience. Those, however, were only two interactions, and after a couple of days, you might meet other people who are quite nice. The point is that one or two cases do not a generalization make. Scientists must collect numerous observations and conduct several studies on a topic before generalizing their conclusions.

LO2 Scientific Principles in Psychology

Is physics a science? As we saw in Chapter 1, few would argue that it is not. In contrast, many people do not view psychology as a science. Why not? Perhaps it has something to do with the topics psychologists study. Free will and determinism, love and loss, relationships and emotion are examples of some of the themes that have characterized intellectual inquiry in the humanities over the years. Psychologists have studied some of these same ideas. So what is special about psychology, as opposed to the study of philosophy, history, or literature? The critical difference is that psychology relies on systematic, empirical methods of observation. It is these methods that we share with the natural sciences, such as biology, physics, and chemistry (see Figure 2.1). It is these methods that make psychology a science.

Many philosophers and scientists have tackled the question of what science is, but behavioural psychologist B.F. Skinner's answer may be one of the best. He concluded that science is (1) cumulative, (2) a process more than a product, and (3) an attitude (Skinner, 1953). Let's take a closer look at each of these characteristics and how they apply to psychology.

Science Is Cumulative Are works of contemporary literature more advanced than those of Shakespeare, Tolstoy, or Virginia Woolf? Many literate people would argue that they are not—that these are products of different styles or periods, but that none is superior to the others. Do we know more today about the physical and biological realms than Galileo, Newton, or Darwin did? The answer in this case has to be yes. Scientific knowledge is unique in comparison to knowledge in the humanities, music, art, literature, and philosophy. Science progresses and advances cumulatively. In science, the knowledge base builds on itself and advances in ways that the kind of knowledge the humanities focus on does not.

Science Is a Process More than a Product Many students tend to think of science as a set of facts, such as the parts of the body or the structure of a cell. But science is also an active enterprise. It is a way of exploring how the world operates, understanding the causes of events, and predicting what might happen under similar conditions in the future more than it is a set of answers. It is a process of gaining knowledge that is ever changing, relatively reliable, but always imperfect. Even the best science is open to modification. Appreciating the way science advances means asking questions, wondering how to test your own ideas, and trying to improve on what is already known.

Science Is an Attitude At the core of science is a way of thinking. **Scientific thinking** involves the cognitive skills required to generate, test, and revise theories (Koslowski, 1996; Kuhn, Amsel, & O'Loughlin, 1988; Zimmerman, 2007). What we believe or theorize about the world and what the world is actually like, in the form of evidence, are two different things. Scientific thinking keeps these two things separate. In other words, scientists remember that belief is not the same as reality.

Science begins with questioning and rejecting authority—including scientific authority. The first attitude of science, therefore, is to *question authority*. Be skeptical. Don't just take the word of an expert; test ideas yourself. The expert might be right, or not. That advice extends to textbooks—including this one. Wonder. Question. Ask for the evidence. Also be skeptical of your *own* ideas. Our natural inclination is to really like our own ideas, especially if they occur to us in a flash of insight. And remember, hindsight bias shows us that we can hold beliefs that are not accurate reflections of reality. Believing something does not make it true.

As expressed by cosmologist and astrophysicist Carl Sagan (1987), the second attitude of science is *open skepticism*. Doubt and skepticism are hallmarks of critical and scientific reasoning. The French philosopher Voltaire put scientific skepticism most bluntly: "Doubt is uncomfortable, certainty is ridiculous"; however, skepticism for skepticism's sake is also not scientific, but stubborn. Scientists are ultimately open to accepting whatever the evidence reveals, however bizarre it may be and however much they may not like it or want it to be the case. For example, could placing an electrical stimulator deep in the brain turn off depression like a switch? That sounds like a far-fetched treatment, worthy of skepticism, but it does work for some people (Mayberg et al., 2005). Be skeptical, but let the evidence speak for itself.

The third scientific attitude is *intellectual honesty*. When the central tenet of knowing is not what people think and believe, but rather how nature behaves,

Challenge Your Assumptions

True or False? Psychology is not a science.

False: Psychologists often use the scientific method to test hypotheses; therefore, psychology is a science.

Science is an attitude that requires we keep open eyes and questioning minds. Scientists can become quite passionate when they feel scientific principles are being undermined. In October 2014, more than 800 scientists from outside Canada representing 32 countries signed an open letter asking Prime Minister Stephen Harper to remove communication restrictions on Canadian government scientists.

scientific thinking
the process of using the cognitive skills required to generate, test, and revise theories.

Connection

As a neuroscientist working on Parkinson's disease, Helen Mayberg found something unexpected about brain circuitry. Initially, she was skeptical. But because she was also curious and open to the evidence, she decided to pursue it further. Her curiosity and openness led to her discovery that placing an electrical stimulator deep inside the brain could turn off depression.

See Chapter 16, LO9.

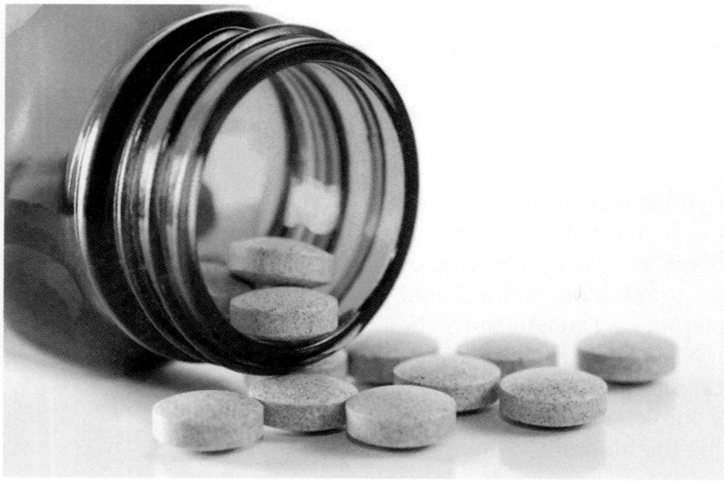

Are antidepressants effective at alleviating depression? The pharmaceutical companies would certainly like us to believe so. However, recent research suggests that these medications may be no more effective for some people than taking sugar pills (Kirsch et al., 2008, Kirsch, 2014). Science, itself, is open to skepticism.

Can you think of some ideas you've had that you no longer believe?

then we must accept the data and follow them wherever they take us. If a researcher falsifies results or interprets them in a biased way, then other scientists will not arrive at the same results if they repeat the study. Every so often we hear of a scientist who faked data in order to gain fame or funding. For the most part, however, the fact that scientists must submit their work to the scrutiny of other scientists helps ensure the honest and accurate presentation of results.

All science—whether physics, chemistry, biology, or psychology—shares these general properties of open inquiry that we have discussed. Let's now turn to the specific methods used by scientists in the process of acquiring new and accurate knowledge of the world.

The Scientific Method

Science depends on the use of sound methods to produce trustworthy results that can be confirmed independently by other researchers. The **scientific method** by which scientists conduct research consists of five basic processes: **O**bserve, **P**redict, **T**est, **I**nterpret, and **C**ommunicate (O-P-T-I-C) (see Figure 2.2). In the *observation* phase of a study, researchers examine previous research findings, and/or make personal observations of some phenomenon in the world. Then, during the *prediction* stages of a study, they develop expectations about the observed phenomenon. They express their expectations as a **theory,** defined as a set of related assumptions from which testable predictions can be made. Theories organize and explain what we have observed and guide what we will observe (Popper, 1965). To put it simply, theories are not facts—they explain facts. Our observations of the world are always either unconsciously or consciously theory-driven, if you understand that theory in this broader sense means little more than "having an expectation." In science, however, a theory is more than a guess. Scientific theories must be tied to real evidence, they must organize observations, and they must generate expectations that can be tested systematically.

Connection

How does critical thinking relate to scientific thinking? Like scientific thinking, critical thinking is a process that involves analyzing, evaluating, and drawing conclusions based on facts and evidence.

See Chapter 8, LO10.

scientific method
the procedures by which scientists conduct research, consisting of five basic processes: observation, prediction, testing, interpretation, and communication.

theory
a set of related assumptions from which scientists can make testable predictions.

hypothesis
a specific, informed, and testable prediction of the outcome of a particular set of conditions in a research design.

A **hypothesis** is a specific, informed, and testable prediction of what kind of outcome should occur under a particular condition. For example, a study recently appeared that suggests that caffeine increases sex drive in female rats (Guarraci & Benson, 2005). The hypothesis may have stated, "Female rats who consume caffeine will seek more couplings with male rats than female rats who do not consume caffeine." This hypothesis specifies a particular form of behaviour (coupling with male rats) in a specific group (female rats) under particular conditions (under the influence of caffeine). The more specific a hypothesis is, the more easily each component can be changed to determine what effect it has on the outcome.

To *test* their hypotheses (the third stage of the scientific method), scientists select one of a number of established research methods, along with the appropriate measurement techniques. The methods, which we will discuss in detail, involve choosing a plan for the design of the study, the tools that will create the conditions of the study, and the tools for measuring responses, such as how often each female rat allows a male to mount her. We will examine each of these elements in the section "Research Methods in Psychology."

Research Process

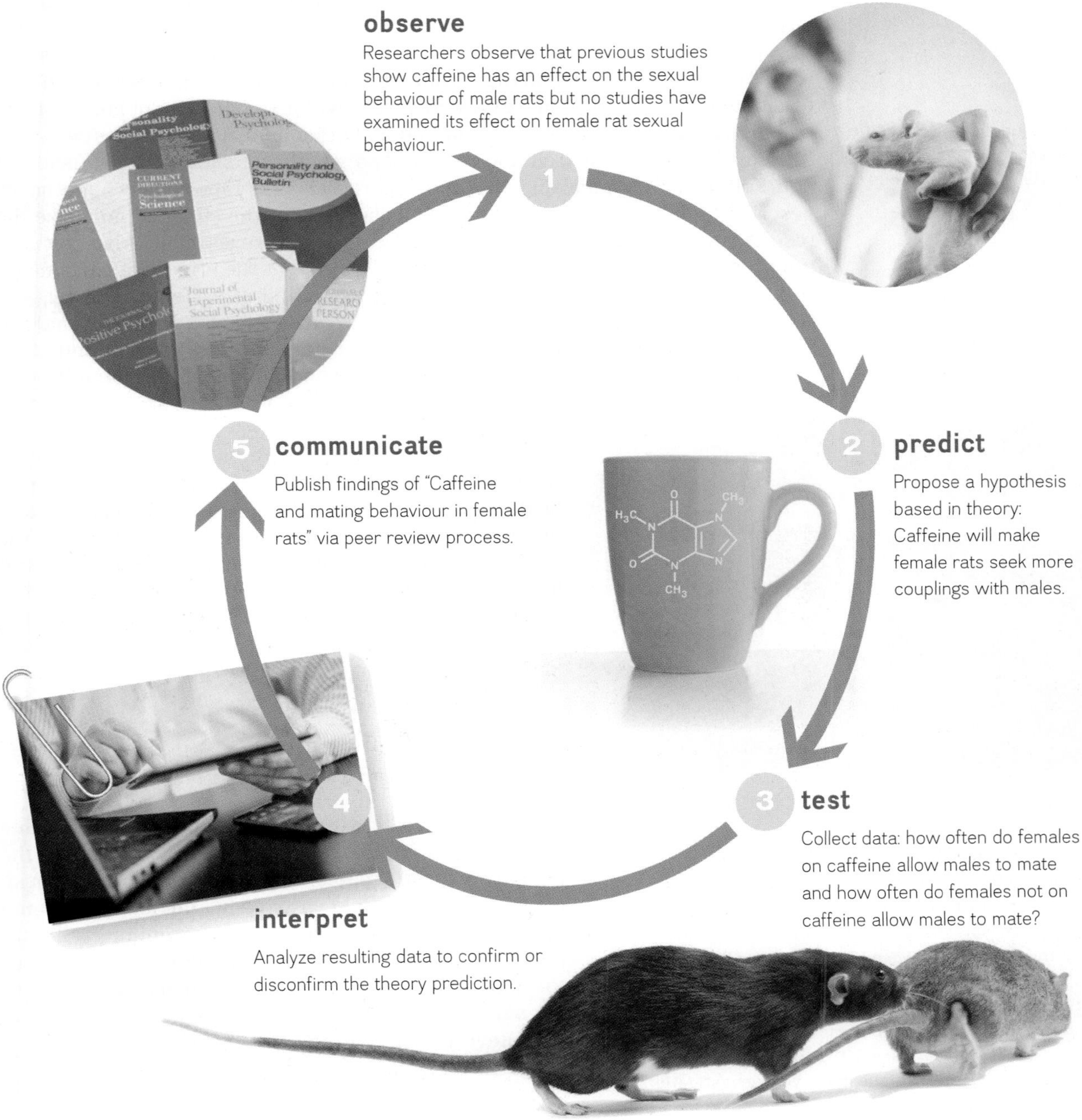

1
observe
Researchers observe that previous studies show caffeine has an effect on the sexual behaviour of male rats but no studies have examined its effect on female rat sexual behaviour.
2
predict
Propose a hypothesis based in theory: Caffeine will make female rats seek more couplings with males.
3
test
Collect data: how often do females on caffeine allow males to mate and how often do females not on caffeine allow males to mate?
4
interpret
Analyze resulting data to confirm or disconfirm the theory prediction.
5
communicate
Publish findings of "Caffeine and mating behaviour in female rats" via peer review process.

FIGURE **2.2**

THE SCIENTIFIC METHOD. The scientific method consists of an ongoing cycle of observation, prediction, testing, interpretation, and communication (OPTIC). Research begins with observation, but it doesn't end with communication. Publishing results of a study allows other researchers to repeat the procedure and confirm the results.

In the fourth step of the scientific method, scientists use mathematical techniques to *describe* and *interpret* the results and determine whether they are significant (not just a matter of chance) and closely fit the prediction or not. Do psychologists' ideas of how people behave hold up, or must they be revised? Let's say that more of the caffeine-consuming female rats coupled with males than did non-consuming females. Might this enhanced sexual interest hold for all rats or just those few we studied? Statistics, a branch of mathematics that we will discuss shortly, helps answer that question.

The fifth stage of the scientific method is to *communicate* the results. Generally, scientists publish their findings in an established, peer-reviewed professional journal. The **peer-review** process involves scientists submitting their research reports to scientific journals so that other qualified scientists can carefully evaluate the research and recommend whether it should be published or not. Following a standardized format, the researchers report their hypothesis, describe their research design and the conditions of the study, summarize the results, and share their conclusions. In their reports, researchers also consider the broader implications of their results. What might the effects of caffeine on sexuality in female rats mean for our understanding of caffeine, arousal, and sex in female humans? Publication also serves an important role in making research findings part of the public domain. Such exposure not only indicates that colleagues who reviewed the study found it to be credible, but it also allows other researchers to repeat and/or build on the research.

peer-review
the practice of judging the scientific merit of research through review by other scientists with expertise.

replication
the repetition of a study to confirm the results; essential to the scientific process.

Replication is the repetition of a study to confirm the results. The advancement of science hinges on replication of results. No matter how interesting and exciting results are, if they cannot be reliably duplicated, the findings must have been accidental. Whether a result holds or not, new predictions can be generated from the data, leading in turn to new studies. This is how the process of scientific discovery is cumulative. Previous knowledge builds on older knowledge.

In 1998, Dr. Andrew Wakefield published a scientific paper claiming that autism spectrum disorder was often caused by vaccines for measles, mumps, and rubella. There were many problems with the paper from the outset, not the least of which was its small, unrepresentative sample size (12 children). Many scientists and medical panels could not confirm the results and were highly skeptical of Dr. Wakefield's findings. Unfortunately, the paper created quite a bit of publicity, and many parents ignored standard vaccination schedules, leading to numerous deaths from preventable diseases. In January 2011, the original 1998 paper was deemed fraudulent in a seven-year investigation by the *British Medical Journal.* The investigation concluded that Dr. Wakefield had altered the results of his study to make vaccines appear to be the cause of autism spectrum disorder. Although the peer-review process seems to have failed in this instance, other researchers' inability to replicate Dr. Wakefield's findings led to the eventual retraction of the paper.

What Science Is Not: Pseudoscience

Do you believe that the planets and stars determine our destiny, that aliens have visited Earth, or that the human mind is capable of moving or altering physical objects? Certainly, astrology, unidentified flying objects (UFOs), and extrasensory perception (ESP) are fascinating topics to ponder. As thinking beings, we try to understand things that science may not explain to our satisfaction. In fact, many of us seem quite willing to believe things that science and skeptics easily dismiss. For example, in a survey of 1765 Canadian adults, Ornstein (2002) reported that

- Fifty-five percent believe some people possess psychic powers or extrasensory perception (ESP).
- Forty-two percent have had personal experience with precognition (i.e., experiencing an event before it happened).

- Thirty percent believe in astrology charts.
- Eighteen percent claim to be in communication with the dead.

People often claim there is "scientific evidence" for certain unusual phenomena, but that does not mean the evidence is truly scientific. There is also false science, or *pseudo*science. **Pseudoscience** refers to practices that appear to be and claim to be science, but in fact do not use the scientific method to come to their conclusions. What makes something pseudoscientific comes more from the way it is studied than from the content area. Pseudoscience practitioners (1) make no real advances in knowledge, (2) disregard well-known and established facts that contradict their claims, (3) do not challenge or question their own assumptions, (4) tend to offer vague or incomplete explanations of how they came to their conclusions, and (5) tend to use unsound logic in making their arguments (Derry, 1999; see Figure 2.3).

Philosophy, art, music, and religion, for instance, would not be labelled pseudoscience because they do not claim to be science. They often seek to answer questions that science can't address. Science is limited by its methods. We can only use it to answer questions about the world for which we can make direct observations, using the scientific method (Gould, 1997; Popper, 1965). Some questions, such as those dealing with the morality of assisted suicide or the existence of God, for example, are untestable and therefore, beyond the scope of science. That doesn't make them less significant or interesting; it just makes them non-scientific.

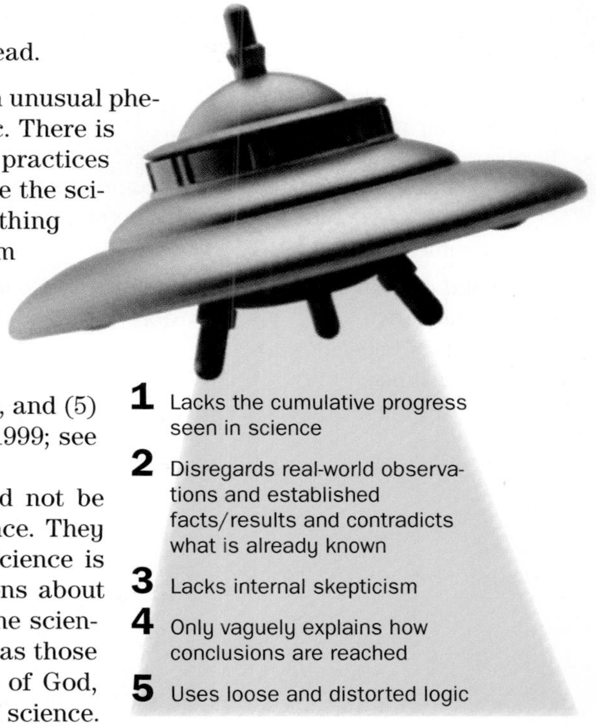

1 Lacks the cumulative progress seen in science
2 Disregards real-world observations and established facts/results and contradicts what is already known
3 Lacks internal skepticism
4 Only vaguely explains how conclusions are reached
5 Uses loose and distorted logic

FIGURE **2.3**
THE CHARACTERISTICS OF PSEUDOSCIENCE. Pseudoscience is marked by the absence of validated scientific methods. Skepticism is the best approach to claims that aren't supported by hard scientific evidence.

pseudoscience
claims presented as scientific that are not supported by evidence obtained with the scientific method.

In contrast, pseudoscience often makes claims that *are* testable, but fails to provide the adequate evidence, using valid scientific methods. Pseudoscientific claims have been made for alchemy, creation science, intelligent design, attempts to create perpetual motion machines, astrology, alien abduction and extraterrestrial explanations of UFOs, psychokinesis, and some forms of mental telepathy.

Perhaps the most pervasive pseudoscience is astrology, which uses positions of the sun, moon, and planets to explain an individual's personality traits and make predictions about the future. There simply is no credible scientific evidence that the position of the moon, planets, and stars and one's time and place of birth have any influence on personality and its development or one's life course (Shermer, 1997). And yet 30 percent of respondents to the Project Canada survey (Ornstein, 2002) said they believed in horoscopes. Why do many of us persist in these beliefs? As the late Barry Beyerstein, psychology professor at Simon Fraser University and founder of the British Columbia Skeptics Society, argued, "Pseudosciences invite us to buy into the desirable but unobtainable dream of abundance, health, and happiness for all" (Beyerstein, 1996, p. 32). We are more likely to believe in something, especially if it makes us feel good, and it requires minimal effort or sacrifice to believe.

Remember, open skepticism is the hallmark of science. If there is scientifically sound evidence for something—even if it is difficult to explain—and it has been replicated, then we can accept it. The key is to know how to distinguish sound from unsound evidence.

Tarot card readers claim that they can use their cards to predict future events in your life.

What makes Tarot reading a pseudoscience?

Quick Quiz 2.1: The Nature of Science

1. The scientific method consists of
   a. observing, predicting, and testing.
   b. observing, predicting, and trying.
   c. observing, predicting, testing, and communicating.
   d. observing, predicting, testing, interpreting, and communicating.
2. Which of the following is NOT a characteristic of science?
   a. It is cumulative.
   b. It is a set of beliefs.
   c. It is an attitude.
   d. It requires intellectual honesty.
3. Scientific theories are
   a. a set of related assumptions that guide and explain observations and allow testable predictions to be made.
   b. educated guesses.
   c. hunches.
   d. hypotheses.
4. What distinguishes science from pseudoscience?
   a. use of statistics
   b. content area studied
   c. open skepticism
   d. the search for truth

Answers can be found at the end of the chapter.

RESEARCH METHODS IN PSYCHOLOGY

Given that science involves testing ideas about how the world works, how do we design studies that test our ideas? This question confronts anyone wanting to answer a psychological question scientifically. Let's turn to the methods and tools psychologists use.

Principles of Research Design

research designs
plans of action for how to conduct a scientific study.

Like other sciences, psychology makes use of several types of **research designs**—plans for how to conduct a study. The design chosen for a given study depends on the question being asked. Some questions can best be answered by randomly placing people in different groups in a laboratory to see whether a treatment causes a change in behaviour. Other questions have to be studied by questionnaires or surveys. Still other questions can best be answered simply by making initial observations and seeing what people do in the real world. And sometimes researchers analyze the results of many studies on the same topic to look for trends.

Connection
What are the four main goals of psychological research?
See Chapter 1, LO1.

In this section we examine variations in research designs, along with their advantages and disadvantages. We begin by defining a few key terms common to all research designs in psychology.

A general goal of psychological research is to measure change in behaviour, thought, or brain activity. A **variable** is anything that changes or "varies" within or between subjects. People differ or vary from one another on age, gender, weight, intelligence, anxiety, and extraversion. These are all examples of variables. Psychologists do research by predicting how and when variables influence each other. For instance, a psychologist who is interested in whether girls develop verbal skills at a different rate than boys focuses on two variables: gender and vocabulary.

variable
a characteristic that changes or "varies," such as age, gender, weight, intelligence, anxiety, and extraversion.

population
the entire group a researcher is interested in; for example, all humans, all rats, all Rhesus monkeys, all adolescents, all boys, all girls, all university students.

All researchers must pay careful attention to how they obtain participants for a study. The first step in obtaining a sample is for the researchers to decide the makeup of the entire group, or **population,** in which they are interested. In psychology, populations can be composed of, for example, all rats, all Bonobos, all humans, all adolescents, all boys, all girls, all university students, or all students at a particular school.

Can you think of a problem that would occur if a researcher tried to collect data directly on an entire population? There are many, but the most obvious are time and money. Most populations are too large to survey or interview directly. So researchers draw on small subsets from each population. These subsets of the population are known as **samples.** A sample of the population of university students, for instance, might consist of students enrolled in one or more universities in a particular geographic area. Research is almost always conducted on samples, not populations. If researchers want to draw valid conclusions or make accurate predictions about the population, it is important that they have samples that accurately represent the population in terms of age, gender, ethnicity, or any other variables that might be of interest. When polls are wrong in predicting who will win an election, it is often because the polled sample did not accurately represent the population.

In the British Columbia provincial election of 2013, the incumbent Liberals were returned to power, despite advance poll predictions of an easy NDP victory. Why did the polls get it so wrong? Was the sample of people polled not representative of those who actually voted? Did a large portion of people change their minds on election day? Did those who said they'd vote for the NDP not bother voting on election day? Pollsters are perplexed!

samples
subsets of the population studied in a research project.

LO3 Descriptive Studies

Many creative ideas for studies start with researchers identifying a gap in the research literature. Others come from specific experiences, or events. Suppose you watch a report on the evening news about a young woman not being helped as she is stabbed and repeatedly attacked, eventually dying. What is more, the attack occurs in an apartment complex in which 38 other people later confess that they either heard or saw the attack. Only one of the 38 did as much as call the police. This case is a real-life story that happened in Queens, New York, in 1964 to a woman named Kitty Genovese. Her case was so shocking that it drove two psychologists—Bibb Latané and John Darley—to begin conducting research on this phenomenon. The area of research known as the "bystander effect" was born.

The point is that single events and single cases can sometimes lead to new ideas and new lines of research. When researchers are interested in a particular question or topic that is relatively new to the field, often the wisest first move is

Connection

The "bystander effect" explains why individuals in crowds may not help others in need. When in a group, individual responsibility is diffused and people tend to think that helping is someone else's responsibility.

See Chapter 14, LO11.

Researchers often work with a small sample of the population they're interested in.

Can a small sample represent the larger population? If so, how is that done?

descriptive designs
study designs in which the researcher defines a problem and variable of interest but often makes no prediction and does not control or manipulate anything.

to use a descriptive design. In **descriptive designs,** researchers don't necessarily make any predictions and do not control or manipulate any variables. They simply define a problem of interest and describe as carefully as possible the variable(s) of interest. The basic question in a descriptive design is: What is the nature of the phenomenon? For example, what is love? What sorts of behaviours do couples display to demonstrate their love for one another? What does aggression look like on the playground? What makes girls' aggression different from boys' aggression? The psychologist makes careful observations, often in the real world outside the research lab. Descriptive studies usually occur during the exploratory phase of research in which the researcher is looking for meaningful patterns that might lead to some predictions later on; they do not involve testing hypotheses. Possible relationships or patterns are noted and then used in other designs as the basis for testable predictions (see Figure 2.4). Three of the most common kinds of descriptive methods in psychology are case studies, naturalistic observations, and interviews/surveys.

descriptive studies

What type of questions might be researched?	What is the most suitable method for answering the question?	What is the best use for this kind of study?	What is the main limitation of this kind of study?
Single variable, such as: **How do people flirt?**	Case study	To study rare or unusual phenomena in detail To generate hypotheses for future research	Lack of generalizability to other people Cannot look at cause and effect
	Naturalistic observation	To describe naturally occurring behaviour in the real world To generate hypotheses for future research	Lack of control over variables Cannot look at cause and effect
	Surveys and interviews	To describe thoughts or behaviours of large numbers of people	If sample is non-random, results will not be generalizable Biased responses

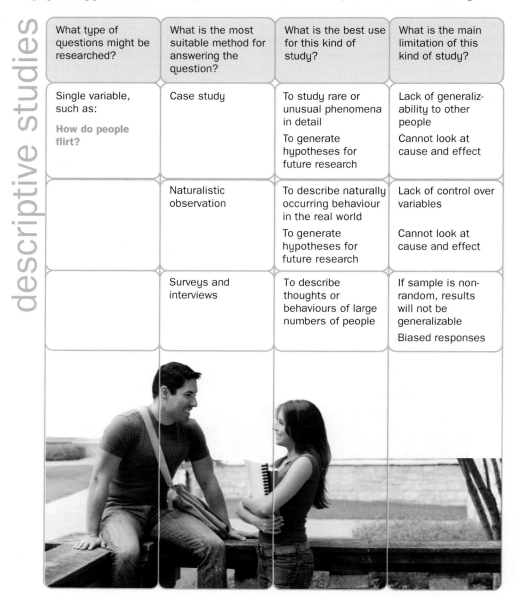

FIGURE **2.4**
CHARACTERISTICS OF DESCRIPTIVE STUDIES. In descriptive studies, researchers look for patterns that might help them create testable hypotheses.

Case Study A **case study** involves observation of one person, often over a long period of time. Case studies are most often used to provide detailed descriptions of remarkable and rare events. Consider the case of D.S., a young Brazilian man who suffered a head injury in a traffic accident. Although he recovered his cognitive abilities, he kept insisting that his parents had been replaced by identical-looking doubles, or imposters—a symptom of a rare neurological condition, known as Capgras syndrome (Hirstein & Ramachandran, 1997). What was interesting about D.S.'s case was that he never treated either parent as an imposter when speaking to them over the telephone—the difficulty arose only when he saw them. The study of D.S. and others with this rare condition has shed light on the brain structure and functioning involved in identifying other people. Sometimes studying the lives of extraordinary individuals, such as Vincent van Gogh, Abraham Lincoln, Marie Curie, Albert Einstein, or even Adolf Hitler, can tell us much about creativity, greatness, genius, or evil. An area of psychology called *psychobiography* examines in detail the lives of historically important people and provides an example of the richness and value of case studies and studying individual lives over time (Elms, 1993; Runyan, 1982; Schultz, 2005). Like other descriptive research, case studies do not test hypotheses but can be a rich source for hypotheses. Because case studies are based on one-on-one relationships, often lasting years, they offer deep insights that other descriptive methods often miss. They also allow researchers to study phenomena that are unethical or impractical to examine in any other way. One has to be careful with case studies, however, because not all cases are generalizable to other people. That is why we don't stop with case studies, but use them to develop testable and more general predictions.

case study
a study design in which a psychologist observes one person over a long period of time.

Naturalistic Observation A second kind of descriptive method is **naturalistic observation,** in which the researcher observes and records behaviour in the real world. The researcher tries to be as unobtrusive as possible so as not to influence or bias the behaviour of interest. Naturalistic observation is more often the design of choice in comparative psychology by researchers who study nonhuman behaviour (especially primates) to determine what is and is not unique about our species.

naturalistic observation
a study in which the researcher unobtrusively observes and records behaviour in the real world.

archival research
research involving the use of already existing records of information.

Developmental psychologists occasionally also conduct naturalistic observations. For example, the developmental psychologists Debra Pepler of York University and Wendy Craig of Queen's University have made detailed naturalistic observations of bullying on school playgrounds (Pepler & Craig, 1995). Children wear wireless microphones, and a hidden, remote video camera records their interactions as they roam the playground during recess. Although most children report that bullying is unpleasant to watch and that they wouldn't join in, the naturalistic observations have suggested otherwise! Peers are present during 85 percent of bullying episodes, and many are active participants in the bullying. Only 19 percent attempt to intervene to stop the bullying (Hawkins, Pepler & Craig, 2001). Pepler and Craig are now examining intervention strategies to reduce bullying problems (Craig & Pepler, 2007).

Primatologist Jane Goodall is famous for her observational studies of chimpanzees in the wild.

Some forms of naturalistic observation are less intrusive than others. Sometimes behaviours can be observed indirectly through public records or other environmental evidence. Researchers who conduct **archival research,** examine previously compiled information, such as governmental documents (e.g., health records), newspaper clippings, and personal papers, to gain insights into people's behaviour. For example, Moulden, Firestone, Kingston, and Wexler (2010) described the characteristics of teachers who had committed sexual offences against youth by accessing a Royal Canadian Mounted Police database. Other researchers observe **physical traces** of behaviour in an environment. That is, they examine a particular setting for remnants or reflections of the activities or characteristics of the people who recently used it. In one study, for instance, researchers systematically collected and analyzed people's garbage to measure what people actually consume (e.g., cigarette boxes or empty alcohol bottles) as opposed to what they *say* they consume (Rathje & Murphy, 2001). In another study, Gosling, Ko, Mannarelli, and Morris (2002) examined people's university dorm rooms and work spaces to gain insights into their personality.

physical traces
physical evidence of people's activities in a particular setting.

The advantage of naturalistic observation is that it gives researchers a look at real behaviour in the real world, rather than in a controlled setting where people might not behave naturally. As with case studies, naturalistic observations are useful for generating hypotheses for future studies. Relatively few psychologists use naturalistic observation, however, because conditions cannot be controlled—researchers have to wait for the behaviours to unfold before their eyes. As a result of this lack of control, cause-and-effect relationships between variables cannot be demonstrated.

Interview and Survey Two related and widely used techniques for gaining information about peoples' thoughts and behaviours are interviews and surveys. They both involve asking people directly or indirectly what they think, feel, or have done. They also both involve specific questions, usually asked precisely the same way to each respondent. Answers can be completely open-ended, allowing the person to answer however she or he wants. More often than not, however, the possible answers are restricted to some kind of rating scale, such as 1 for "completely disagree," 3 for "neither disagree nor agree," and 5 for "completely agree." Historically, interviews were conducted mostly face-to-face, but now both interviews and surveys are more often carried out over the phone or the Internet. Researchers may thus survey thousands of individuals on almost any topic, such as abortion, sex, legalization of marijuana, voting, or gay marriage—a distinct advantage over the other descriptive research methods we have described previously.

Americans and Canadians were shocked by Alfred Kinsey's initial reports on male and female sexual behaviour. Kinsey was the first researcher to survey people about their sexual behaviour. For better or worse, his publications changed our attitudes about sex.

The well-known Kinsey surveys of male and female sexual behaviour provide one famous example of survey research (Kinsey, Pomeroy, & Martin, 1948; Kinsey et al., 1953). Data was gathered primarily by means of subjective interviews with over 18 000 participants (Bullough, 1998). Make no mistake—just publishing such research was shocking to many people, and it led to an uproar both in the scientific community and in the general public at the time. Alfred Kinsey reported, for instance, that up to 50 percent of the men and only about half as many (26 percent) of the women interviewed had had extramarital affairs. Another widely cited finding was that approximately 10 percent of the population could be considered homosexual. The impact of Kinsey's research has been profound. By itself it began the science of studying human sexuality and permanently changed people's views. For example, Kinsey was the first to consider sexual orientation on a continuum from 0 (completely heterosexual) to 6 (completely homosexual) rather than as an either–or state with only two options. This approach remains a lasting contribution of his studies.

FIGURE 2.5

SAMPLING. For practical reasons, research is typically conducted with small samples of the population of interest. If a psychologist wanted to study a population of 2200 people (each face in the figure represents 100 people), he or she would aim for a sample that represents the makeup of the whole group. Thus, if 27 percent of the population were blue, the researcher would want 27 percent of the selected sample to be blue, as shown in the pie chart on the left. Contrary to what many students think, *representative* does *not* mean that all groups have the same numbers.

However, Kinsey's research also highlights some of the numerous pitfalls in collecting data via large-scale interviews and surveys, one being the inclusion of people who are not representative of the group at large. Think about your own response when you are contacted via phone or email about participating in a scientific survey. Many of us don't want to participate and ignore the request. So how does a researcher know that people who participate are not different from people who don't participate? Maybe those who participate are older or younger, have more education or have less education. In other words, we need to know that the information we collect comes from people who represent the group in which we are interested, which is known as a **representative sample** (see Figure 2.5). To obtain such a representative sample, survey researchers often rely on the method of *random sampling.* A **random sample** is a type of sample in which every member of the population has an equal likelihood of being selected for the survey. Kinsey's research was criticized because he did not use representative sampling (Bullough, 1998; Ericksen, 1998). He oversampled people in Indiana (his home state) and prisons, for example, raising questions about how generalizable his results were to the American public.

A second challenge in conducting survey research involves biased responses. If the topics being surveyed are controversial, sensitive, or personal, such as sexual behaviour, people are likely to respond in ways that may not honestly reflect their true beliefs. In other words, people might tell researchers what they want to hear rather than what they really believe. This tendency toward favourable self-presentation is known as the **social desirability bias.** Kinsey interviewed people face-to-face about the most personal and private details of their sexual behaviour, raising the possibility that some may not have been perfectly honest in their responses (Ericksen, 1998).

Is it possible that new technology (notably, the ability to deliver surveys online) could help to overcome some of these problems with survey research? There is some evidence to suggest that samples from Internet studies are more diverse in terms of gender, socioeconomic status, geographic region, and age (Gosling, Vazire, Srivastava, & John, 2004), and thus, more representative of populations under study than traditional samples (Gosling, Sandy, John, & Potter, 2010). However, it is not clear that the anonymity afforded by the Internet reduces biased

For the first time, in 2003, Statistics Canada included a question on sexual orientation as part of its Canadian Community Health Survey (Statistics Canada, 2004). Among the 135 000 respondents aged 18 to 59, 1.0 percent said that they were gay or lesbian, and 0.7 percent considered themselves bisexual.

How do you explain the lower percentage of Canadians identifying themselves as homosexual compared to Kinsey's results?

representative sample
a research sample that accurately reflects the population of people one is studying.

random sample
a type of sample in which every member of the population had an equal likelihood of being selected to participate in a survey.

social desirability bias
the tendency toward favourable self-presentation that could lead to inaccurate self-reports.

Is there a connection between sugar consumption and children's activity level? How might you measure each of these variables?

responses by participants. Recent evidence suggests that people's tendency to answer questions in a socially desirable manner is practically the same in online versus traditional surveys (DoDou & de Winter, 2014). Let us now turn to a discussion of the research designs used for determining relationships between variables.

LO4 Correlational Studies

Once an area of study has developed far enough that predictions can be made from descriptive studies, then a researcher might choose to test hypotheses by measuring variables and determining the extent to which one relates to the other. **Correlational designs** measure two or more variables and their relationship to one another. In correlational designs, the basic question is: "Is *X* related to *Y?*" For instance, "Is sugar consumption related to increased activity levels in children?" If so, how strong is the relationship, and is increased sugar consumption associated (correlated) with increased activity levels, as we would predict, or does activity decrease as sugar consumption increases? Or is there no clear relationship?

correlational designs
studies that measure two or more variables and their relationship to one another; not designed to show causation.

Connection

What type of research design can a researcher use if he or she is interested in how certain thoughts or behaviours change with age? Developmental psychologists often use cross-sectional or longitudinal designs.

See Chapter 10, LO1.

Correlational studies are useful when the variables cannot be manipulated. For instance, it would be unethical to raise one group of children one way and another group another way in order to study parenting behaviour. But we could use a good questionnaire to find out whether parents' scores are consistently associated with particular behavioural outcomes in children. In fact, many questions in developmental psychology, personality psychology, and even clinical psychology are examined with correlational techniques.

The major limitation of the correlational approach is that it does not establish whether one variable actually causes the other or vice versa. Parental neglect (variable *X*) might be associated with antisocial behaviour in adolescence (variable *Y*), but that does not necessarily mean that neglect causes antisocial behaviour. It might, but it might not. It could be that antisocial behaviour causes or elicits parental neglect—antisocial adolescents are not very nice to be around! Or the two variables may not be causally related to one another at all. They may only appear to be related because some other third variable (e.g., poverty) is causing differences in both adolescent antisocial behaviour and parental neglect. For example, poverty may cause adolescents to feel bad about themselves and act out. Poverty may also cause parents to be neglectful because they have to work many jobs. Figure 2.6 depicts these three different plausible causal explanations for a correlational finding. We must always be mindful that correlation is necessary for causation but not sufficient by itself to establish causation (see Figure 2.7).

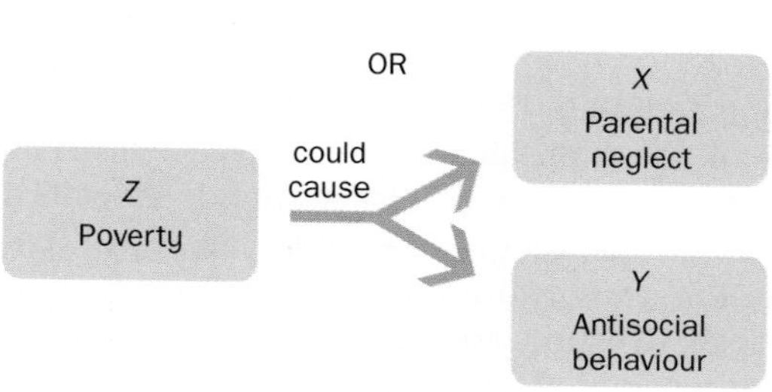

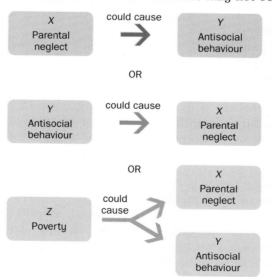

FIGURE **2.6**
POSSIBLE CAUSES OF CORRELATION. If *X* (parental neglect) and *Y* (antisocial behaviour) are correlated, then there are at least three possible causal explanations: *X* causes *Y*, *Y* causes *X*, or *Z* (some other variable, such as poverty) causes both *X* and *Y*.

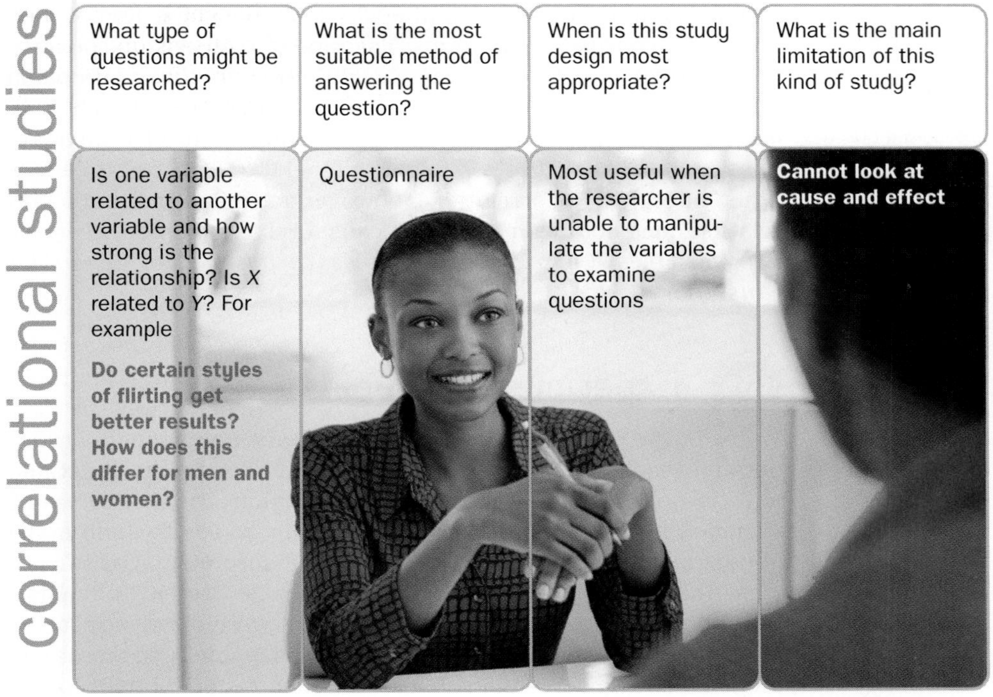

correlational studies
What type of questions might be researched?
What is the most suitable method of answering the question?
When is this study design most appropriate?
What is the main limitation of this kind of study?
Is one variable related to another variable and how strong is the relationship? Is X related to Y? For example
Do certain styles of flirting get better results? How does this differ for men and women?
Questionnaire
Most useful when the researcher is unable to manipulate the variables to examine questions
Cannot look at cause and effect

FIGURE **2.7**

CHARACTERISTICS OF CORRELATIONAL STUDIES. These studies measure two or more variables and their relationship to one another.

Psychologists often use a statistic called the correlation coefficient to draw conclusions from their correlational study. **Correlation coefficients** tell us whether two variables relate to each other and the direction of the relationship. Correlations range between −1.00 and +1.00, with coefficients near 0.00 telling us there is no relationship between the two variables. This means that knowing about one variable tells you nothing about the other. A classic example of a correlation exists between height and weight. Generally, the taller people are, the more they will weigh. As a correlation approaches ± 1.00, the strength of the relationship increases.

correlation coefficient
a statistic that ranges from −1.0 to +1.0 and assesses the strength and direction of association between two variables.

Correlation coefficients can be positive or negative. If the relationship is positive, then as a group's score on *X* goes up, its score on *Y* also goes up. If the relationship is negative, then as a group's score on *X* goes up, its score on *Y* goes down. For instance, let's consider the correlation between students' scores on the final exam in an introductory psychology course and the number of lectures that they attended. By calculating a correlation, we know whether students who attend many lectures are likely to do well on the final. Figure 2.8a shows a **scatterplot** of the positive correlation between student final exam scores and lecture attendance for a hypothetical sample of 20 students. Each dot represents one student's score on the final exam and the number of lectures they attended per month. Now let's suppose that we were to calculate the correlation between the number of alcoholic beverages consumed over the semester and final exam scores. Figure 2.8b shows the negative correlation that we might expect between these two variables. In this graph, each dot represents one student's score on the final exam and their alcohol consumption per week. As students increase their consumption of alcohol, their final exam scores decrease. Figure 2.8c shows the zero correlation we might expect between students' shoe size and their final exam performance. Not surprisingly, these two variables are unrelated in this sample.

scatterplot
a graph depicting a correlation between two variables.

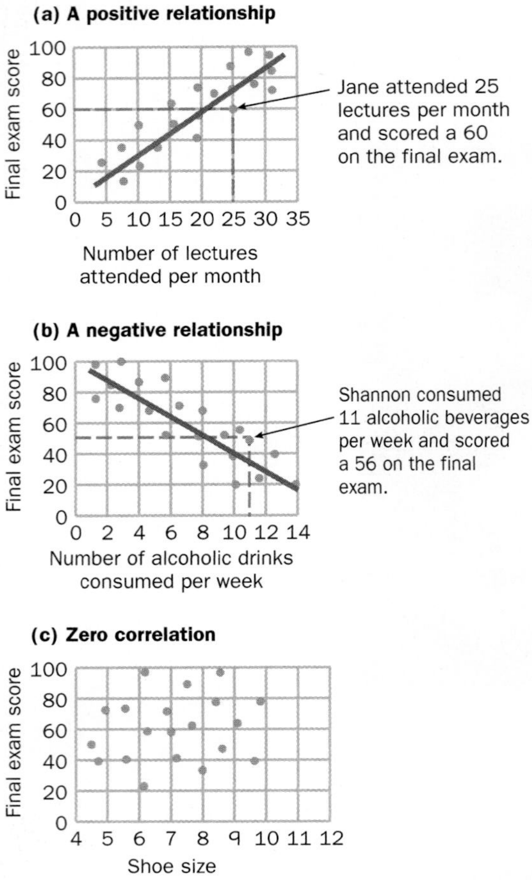

FIGURE **2.8**

THREE TYPES OF CORRELATION. The scatterplots illustrate the three main types of correlations for hypothetical data from 20 students. Graph (a) shows a positive relationship between lecture attendance per month and final exam scores. Graph (b) shows a negative relationship between number of drinks consumed per week and final exam scores. Graph (c) shows a zero correlation between shoe size and final exam scores.

It is important to note that positive relationships are not "better" than negative relationships. The type of relationship (positive or negative) merely indicates the direction of the relationship between the variables. Thus, a negative correlation of −.78 indicates a stronger relationship between variable X and Y than a correlation of +.44 because −.78 is closer to −1.00 than +.44 is to +1.00. When interpreting correlations, however, keep in mind that a correlation does not mean there is a causal relationship between the two variables. *Correlation is necessary but not sufficient for causation.*

LO5 Experimental Studies

Which of the following scenarios would make you happier—going out and buying something new for yourself or buying something new for your friend? The answer seems obvious, right? Or does it? Common sense might suggest that treating yourself would make you happier than treating your friend. But surprisingly, that's not what the research shows. The University of British Columbia's Elizabeth Dunn and her colleagues (2008) were interested in the relationship between spending choice and happiness. In one study, they had people complete online questionnaires about their happiness and types of spending they engaged in. The researchers found that personal spending (i.e., buying gifts for oneself) was unrelated to happiness but spending money on others was positively correlated with happiness. Of course, as we learned in the last section, the correlational nature of this study makes it impossible to draw the conclusion that prosocial spending *causes* increased happiness. A plausible alternative explanation for the finding is that an unmeasured third variable, such as materialism (i.e., valuing financial success and material possessions) causes people to be happier and spend more on others. So in order to test the hypothesis that spending money on others causes increases in happiness, Dunn and her colleagues (2008) conducted a second study—an *experiment.*

Often people use the word *experiment* loosely to refer to any research study, but in science an experiment is something quite specific. An experiment is often viewed as the "golden standard" of research design because it allows the researcher the most control over the experimental situation. A true **experiment** has two crucial characteristics:

1. Experimental manipulation of a predicted cause—the independent variable—and measurement of the response, or dependent variable.
2. Random assignment of participants to control and experimental groups or conditions—meaning that each participant has an equal chance of being placed in each group.

The **independent variable** in an experiment is a factor (or attribute) that is manipulated by the experimenter under controlled conditions. The independent variable is the condition that the researcher predicts will cause a particular outcome. The **dependent variable** is the outcome, or response to the experimental manipulation. You can think of the independent variable as the "cause" and the dependent variable as the "effect," although reality is not always so simple. If there is a causal connection between the two, then the responses *depend* on the treatment; hence the name *dependent variable.*

experiment
a research design that includes independent and dependent variables and random assignment of participants to control and experimental groups or conditions.

independent variable
a factor that is manipulated by the experimenter under controlled conditions to determine whether it causes the predicted outcome of an experiment.

dependent variable
in an experiment, the outcome or response to the experimental manipulation.

So how did Dunn and her colleagues design an experiment to examine the relationship between spending and happiness? In her second study, she manipulated spending choice (independent variable) and measured happiness (dependent variable). Specifically, she gave participants $20 to spend by the end of the day but half of them were told to spend the money "on a bill, an expense, or a gift for themselves" (Dunn et al., 2008, p. 1688) (personal spending condition), whereas the other half were instructed to spend the money "on a gift for someone else or a charitable donation" (Dunn et al., 2008, p. 1688) (prosocial spending condition). The participants then rated their happiness at the end of the day after they had spent the money. The researchers found that participants who spent money on others were happier than those who spent money on themselves, providing support for the conclusion that spending money on others causes us to be happier than spending money on ourselves.

Challenge Your Assumptions

True or False? Spending money on ourselves makes us happier than spending money on others.

False: People who have spent money on others report being happier than those who have spent money on themselves.

Let's look at a few more examples of independent and dependent variables. Earlier we mentioned the hypothesis that sugar consumption makes kids overly active. If we redesign this sugar-activity example of a correlational study as an experiment, sugar levels would now become the independent variable and activity level the dependent variable. Recall the study of the effect of caffeine on sex drive in rats. Is caffeine the independent or dependent variable? What about sex drive? One of the main shortcomings of the Zimbardo Stanford Prison Experiment was its failure to include obvious dependent variables. That is, the researchers had few ways of measuring how the prisoners and guards behaved as a result of their being assigned to those conditions. They simply observed what happened—and what happened was a lot of conflict and emotional turmoil. In this sense, the prison study was more descriptive than experimental. Figure 2.9 features other examples of independent and dependent variables.

Random assignment is the method used to assign participants to different research conditions to guarantee that each person has the same chance of being in one group as another. Elizabeth Dunn randomly assigned participants to either the personal or prosocial spending condition. Recall that Zimbardo randomly assigned students to be either "prisoners" or "guards" in the Stanford Prison Experiment. Random assignment is achieved either with a random numbers

random assignment
the method used to assign participants to different research conditions so that all participants have the same chance of being in any specific group.

FIGURE **2.9**
INDEPENDENT AND DEPENDENT VARIABLES. Remember: The response, or dependent variable (DV), depends on the treatment. It is the treatment, or independent variable (IV), that the researcher manipulates.

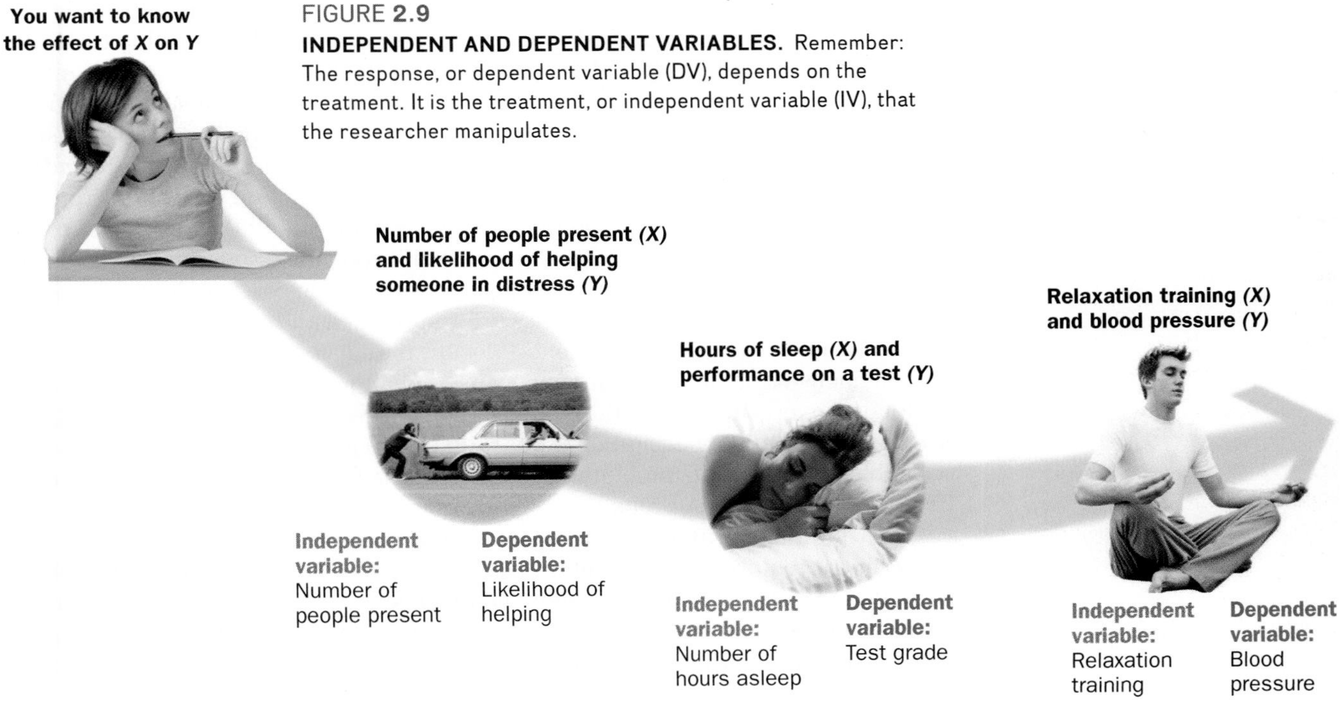
You want to know the effect of X on Y
Number of people present (X) and likelihood of helping someone in distress (Y)
Independent variable: Number of people present
Dependent variable: Likelihood of helping
Hours of sleep (X) and performance on a test (Y)
Independent variable: Number of hours asleep
Dependent variable: Test grade
Relaxation training (X) and blood pressure (Y)
Independent variable: Relaxation training
Dependent variable: Blood pressure

generator or some other unbiased technique, such as tossing a coin. Random assignment is critical because it assures that *on average* the groups will be similar with respect to all possible variables, such as gender, intelligence, motivation, and memory when the experiment begins. If the groups are the same on these qualities at the beginning of the study, then any differences between the groups at the end of the experiment are likely to be the result of the independent variable.

experimental group
a group consisting of those participants who will receive the treatment or whatever is predicted to change behaviour.

control group
a group of research participants who are treated in exactly the same manner as the experimental group, except that they do not receive the independent variable or treatment.

placebo
a substance or treatment that appears identical to the actual treatment but lacks the active substance.

Experimenters randomly assign participants to either an experimental group or a control group. The **experimental group** consists of those participants who will receive the treatment or whatever is thought to change behaviour. In the sugar consumption and activity study, for example, the experimental group would receive a designated amount of sugar. The **control group** consists of participants who are treated in exactly the same manner as the experimental group, but with the crucial difference that they do not receive the treatment. Instead, they often receive no special treatment or, in some cases, they get a **placebo,** a substance or treatment that appears identical to the actual treatment but lacks the active substance. In a study on sugar consumption and activity level, an appropriate placebo might be an artificial sweetener. So the experimental group would receive the actual treatment (sugar), and the control group would be treated exactly the same way but would not receive the actual treatment (instead the control group might receive an artificial sweetener). Can you identify the experimental and control groups in Dunn's study on prosocial spending and happiness?

Why is it so important for experimental and control groups to be equivalent at the outset of an experimental study? We must minimize the possibility that other characteristics could explain any difference we find after we administer the treatment. If two groups of children are similar at the start and if one group differs from the other on activity level after receiving different amounts of sugar, then we can conclude that the treatment caused the observed effect. That is, different levels of sugar consumption caused the differences in activity level.

In our hypothetical study on sugar and activity, for instance, we would want to include equal numbers of boys and girls in the experimental and control groups and match them with respect to age, ethnicity, and other characteristics, so that we could attribute differences in activity level following treatment to differences in sugar consumption. Suppose we didn't do a good job of randomly assigning participants to our two conditions, and the experimental group ended up with 90 percent boys and the control group had 90 percent girls. If, after administering the sugar to the experimental group and the placebo (sugar substitute) to the control group, we found a difference in activity, then we would have two possible explanations: gender and sugar. Either being male or female caused the difference or consuming large amounts of sugar did. In this case, gender would be a **confounding variable**—an additional variable whose influence cannot be separated from the independent variable being examined (sugar consumption). Because most of the people in the experimental group were male and consumed sugar, we do not know whether male gender or sugar consumption was responsible for the difference in active behaviour. These two variables are confounded and cannot be teased apart.

confounding variable
a variable whose influence on the dependent variable cannot be separated from the independent variable being examined.

The power of the experimental design is that it allows us to say that the independent variable (or treatment) caused changes in the dependent variable, as long as everything other than the independent variable was held constant (see Figure 2.10). Random assignment guarantees group equivalence on a number of variables and prevents ambiguity over whether effects might be due to other differences between the groups.

In addition to random assignment to control and experimental groups, a true experiment requires experimental control of the independent variable. Researchers must treat the two groups alike and make sure that all environmental conditions (such as noise level and room size) are equivalent. Again, the goal is to make sure that nothing affects the dependent variable besides the independent variable.

In the experiment on sugar consumption and activity level, for example, the researcher first must randomly assign participants to either the experimental group (in which participants receive some amount of sugar) or the control group (in which participants receive some sugar substitute). The outcome of interest is activity level, and so each group might be videotaped for a short period of time, 30 minutes after eating the sugar or saccharin (the sugar substitute). Figure 2.11 illustrates this experimental design. But what if it turns out that the room in which the experimental group was given the sugar was several degrees warmer than the room where the control group received the sugar substitute, and our results showed that the participants in the warmer room were more active? Could we conclude that sugar led to increased

experimental studies

What type of questions might be researched?	What is the most suitable method of answering the question?	What is the best use for this kind of study?	What is the main limitation of this kind of study?
Does the independent variable cause the dependent variable? Does *X* cause *Y*? **Do smiles with raised eyebrows versus those without lead to more offers of dates?**	Random assignment of participants, controlled experimental conditions in a lab setting	Most useful for the researcher to infer cause	**Results cannot always be applied to the real world**

FIGURE **2.10**
CHARACTERISTICS OF EXPERIMENTAL STUDIES. Only in true experimental designs, in which researchers manipulate the independent variable and measure its effects on the dependent variable, can cause-and-effect relationships be determined.

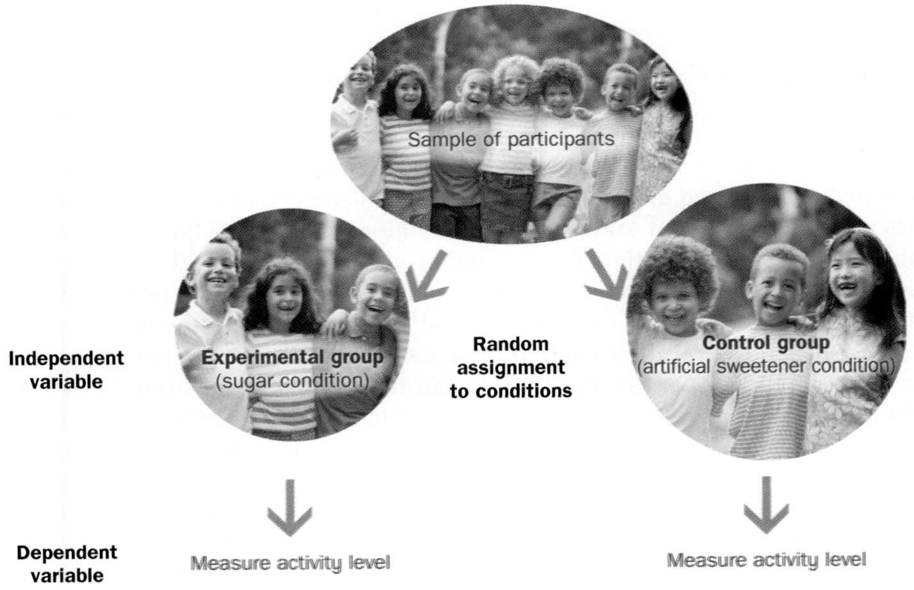

FIGURE **2.11**
DOES SUGAR IMPACT CHILDREN'S ACTIVITY LEVEL? Researchers randomly assign participants to an experimental or control group and then measure both groups on the dependent variable.

activity level? No, because the heat in that room may have caused the increase in activity level. In this case, room temperature would be the confounding variable. Experimenters must carefully consider all variables that might influence the dependent variable and control them (e.g., making sure room temperatures are equal).

How much participants and experimenters know about the experimental conditions to which participants have been assigned can also affect outcome. In **single-blind studies,** participants do not know the experimental condition to which they have been assigned. This is a necessary precaution in all studies to avoid the possibility that participants will behave in a biased way. For example, if participants know they have been assigned to a group that receives a new training technique on memory, then they might try harder to perform well, a result known as participant expectancy effects. **Participant expectancy effects** occur when participants' knowledge about the experimental condition affects their behaviours or responses. This would confound the results. One criticism of the Stanford Prison Experiment was that participants knew the roles they were expected to take on, as "prisoner" or "guard," and so they acted out these stereotypic roles (Banuazizi & Movahedi, 1975). Thus, the oppressive and tormenting behaviour of the "guards" and the passive, depressive behaviours of the "prisoners" were a product of this particular role-playing situation, and not necessarily a reflection of "real" prison environments.

single-blind studies
studies in which participants do not know the experimental condition (group) to which they have been assigned.

participant expectancy effects
results that occur when the behaviour of the participants is influenced by their knowledge of the experimental condition.

Another possible problem can come from the experimenter knowing who is in which group and unintentionally treating the two groups somewhat differently. This could result in the predicted outcome simply because the experimenter biased the results. In the Stanford Prison Experiment, Phillip Zimbardo acted in the dual roles as principal researcher and as the prison superintendent. In his role of prison superintendent, he could have influenced the behaviours of "guards" and "prisoners," unwittingly eliciting particular responses from them. He, himself, admits to getting so caught up in the study that he did not end it soon enough (Zimbardo, Maslach, & Haney, 2000). In **double-blind studies,** neither the participants nor the researchers (at least the ones administering the treatment) know who has been assigned to which condition. Ideally, then, neither participants nor those collecting the data should know which group is the experimental group and which is the control group. The advantage of double-blind studies is that they prevent experimenter expectancy effects. **Experimenter expectancy effects** occur when the behaviour of the participants is influenced by the experimenter's knowledge of who is in which condition (Rosenthal, 1976, 1994). See the Groundbreaking Research section in this chapter for the story of how experimenter expectancy effects were discovered.

double-blind studies
studies in which neither the participants nor the researchers administering the treatment know who has been assigned to the experimental or control group.

experimenter expectancy effects
results that occur when the behaviour of the participants is influenced by the experimenter's knowledge of who is in the control group and who is in the experimental group.

Meta-Analysis

As important as results from an individual study may be, the real power of science comes from the cumulative overall findings from all studies on a given topic. If a topic or question has been sufficiently studied, researchers may choose to stand back and analyze all the results of these numerous studies. For example, a researcher interested in the effects of media violence on children's aggressive behaviour might want to know what all of the research—not just one or two studies—suggests. The method for examining so many research studies is known as **meta-analysis,** and it involves combining the results of all the published and even unpublished results on one question and drawing a conclusion based on the entire set of studies on the topic. To do a meta-analysis, the researcher has to convert the findings of each study to a standardized statistic known as effect size. **Effect size** is a measure of the strength of the relationship between two variables or the magnitude of an experimental effect. The average effect size across all studies tells us what the literature as a whole says on a topic or question. In short, meta-analysis tells us whether all of the research on a topic has or has not led to consistent findings and what the size of the effect is.

meta-analysis
a research and statistical technique for combining all research results on one question and drawing a conclusion.

effect size
a measure of the strength of the relationship between two variables or the magnitude of an experimental effect.

Quick Quiz 2.2: Research Methods in Psychology

1. Dr. Lovejoy wanted to do research on real-world conditions that lead to aggression in ten-year-old children. She defined aggression as "intent to harm another person" and went to a local elementary school and videotaped a ten-minute recess period. She then observed the behaviour of every child and counted the number of times each child acted aggressively. This is an example of what kind of research design?
   a. descriptive
   b. correlational
   c. case study
   d. experimental
2. If Dr. Lovejoy wanted to examine whether certain personality traits make aggression more likely, she would most likely use what kind of research design?
   a. descriptive
   b. correlational
   c. interview
   d. experimental
3. Researchers have consistently found that married men live longer than single men. From this finding, we can conclude that
   a. if a man gets married he adds years to his life.
   b. marriage causes men to live longer.
   c. being single causes men to die earlier.
   d. marriage may or may not cause men to live longer.
4. In research on whether sugar causes hyperactivity, researchers randomly assign children to receive no sugar, small amounts of sugar, or large amounts of sugar. They then observe and measure activity levels. In this case, the sugar level is the
   a. outcome variable.
   b. dependent variable.
   c. independent variable.
   d. control condition.
5. In contrast to other kinds of research designs, a true experimental design must have two things:
   a. random assignment of participants to conditions and statistical analysis.
   b. random assignment of participants to conditions and manipulation of an independent variable.
   c. manipulation of an independent variable and dependent variable.
   d. hypothesis testing and observation.

Answers can be found at the end of the chapter.

Groundbreaking Research

Experimenter Expectancy Effects

You don't have to be a scientist to understand that it would be wrong and unethical for an experimenter to tell participants how to behave and what to do. Even for the participants to know what group they are in or what the hypotheses of the study are is bad science and biases behaviour. Can what the experimenter knows change the behaviour of the participants?

HOW ROSENTHAL DISCOVERED EXPERIMENTER EFFECTS

In the mid-1950s, Robert Rosenthal was conducting an experiment to complete his PhD thesis. Rosenthal hypothesized that people who believed they were successful would be more likely to see success in others. To test this idea, he conducted an experiment in which he told one group of participants that they had done well on an intelligence test and another group they had done poorly on an intelligence test. Rosenthal randomly assigned participants to be in one of these conditions (there was also a neutral control condition where participants were not given any feedback after the intelligence test). Then he asked both groups to look at photographs of people doing various tasks and rate how successful they thought the people in the photos were. He reasoned that people told they did well on an intelligence test should see more success in photographs of people doing various tasks than people who were told they did not do well on the test.

Robert Rosenthal

As a good scientist, Rosenthal compared the average test scores of the participants assigned to different conditions *before* giving them any feedback on their performance—that is, before the experimental treatment. The reason is simple: If the treatment causes a difference in behaviour for the different groups, the researcher needs to make sure the groups started out behaving the same way before treatment. Otherwise, the researcher does not know if the difference is due to the treatment or to some pre-existing condition. To Rosenthal's dismay, the groups did differ before receiving treatment. They were also different in exactly the way that favoured his hypothesis!

Given random assignment, the only difference in the groups at the outset was Rosenthal's knowledge of who was in which group. Somehow by knowing who was in which group he unintentionally created behaviours that favoured his hypothesis. He was forced to conclude that even when trying to be "scientific" and "objective," researchers can subtly and unconsciously bias results in their favour.

And so began Rosenthal's research into what he termed *experimenter expectancy effects.* His research revealed that characteristics of the experimenter, such as age, ethnicity, personality, and gender, influence participants' behaviour whenever an experimenter interacts directly with the participants in a study (Rosenthal, 1976). He also stumbled upon a more general phenomenon known as self-fulfilling prophecy. A **self-fulfilling prophecy** is a statement that changes events to cause a belief or prediction to become true. If you say, "I am going to fail this exam" and do not study, then that belief has become self-fulfilling when you do fail the exam.

self-fulfilling prophecy
a statement that affects events to cause the prediction to become true.

Challenge Your Assumptions

True or False? Knowing what you're looking for in an experiment has no effect on the outcome.

False: Even when being careful, if the researcher is aware of the hypothesis, he or she may unconsciously act differently and unintentionally affect the behaviour of the participants.

WHAT QUESTIONS REMAIN?

Within ten years, more than 300 other studies confirmed Rosenthal's results (Rosenthal & Rubin, 1978). Studies showed that experimenter expectancies affect animal participants as well as humans (Rosenthal & Fode, 1963). Rosenthal's demonstration of experimenter expectancy effects and self-fulfilling prophecies led to the development of double-blind procedures in science that we discussed earlier in the chapter.

What role might the self-fulfilling prophecy have played in your education?

Expectancy effects have also been studied in classrooms. If a teacher believes that a particular student is "smart" and "special," that teacher may unwittingly treat the student differently, give more detailed feedback, and give the student more challenging material. In turn, these actions could create a higher-performing, "smarter" student. Teacher expectations might become a self-fulfilling prophecy.

That is precisely what Rosenthal and Jacobson (1968, 1992) found in classrooms where 20 percent of the children were assigned randomly to be "late bloomers"; their teachers were told they would start to show real intellectual gains in the coming year. Sure enough, these late bloomers showed more improvement over the year than any other group of students. Follow-up research one and two years later found that these "late blooming" students had also shown slightly more improvement on intelligence tests than control students. In more than four decades since the original study, dozens of similar studies have confirmed this self-fulfilling prophecy effect in the classroom—although the effect is often not as strong as Rosenthal and Jacobson had reported (Jussim & Harber, 2005).

What other questions does this research raise? Is every researcher and teacher, every research participant and student equally susceptible to expectancy effects? In the workplace, might employer expectations affect employee behaviour? What about the relationship between medical doctors and their patients?

Quick Quiz 2.3: Groundbreaking Research—Experimenter Expectancy Effects

1. One explanation for the experimenter expectancy effect is
   a. double-blind studies.
   b. self-fulfilling prophecy.
   c. confounding variables.
   d. experimental manipulation.

2. The best way to lessen the effects of experimenter expectancy is to design a study that uses
   a. single-blind methods.
   b. double-blind methods.
   c. random assignment.
   d. quasi-experimental methods.

Answers can be found at the end of the chapter.

LO6 MEASURING VARIABLES

When psychologists conduct research, they not only use a variety of research designs to conduct their studies, but they also use a vast array of tools to measure variables relevant to their research questions. The tools and techniques used to assess thought or behaviour are called **measures.** Researchers' descriptions of the way that they measure or manipulate their variables are called **operational definitions.** For example, suppose a researcher is interested in studying the variable of self-esteem. One of the ways the researcher might assess this variable is by asking participants to rate how they feel about themselves on a seven-point scale, where 1 indicates that they feel "extremely bad" about themselves and 7 indicates that they feel "extremely good." This specific description of the measurement of self-esteem is an operational definition of the variable.

measures
the tools or techniques used to assess thought or behaviour.

operational definitions
researchers' specific descriptions of the way that variables are measured or manipulated.

When researchers operationally define their variables, they assign categories or numbers to represent different levels of each variable. Taken together, the categories or numbers assigned to each level of a particular variable form a **measurement scale.** There are four different types of measurement scales: nominal (or categorical), ordinal, interval, and ratio (see Figure 2.12).

measurement scale
the categories or numbers assigned to each level of a variable.

If the levels of a variable are simply labels or categories without any numeric meaning, then the scale is a **nominal scale.** Examples of variables defined by nominal scales include sex, whose levels are male and female, or dog breed, whose levels in a study might be pug, boxer, and poodle. The independent variable in an experiment is often a nominal or categorical variable. For example, type of role assigned ("prisoner" or guard") in the Stanford Prison Experiment is a nominal variable because the two levels reflect different categories.

nominal scale
a scale of measurement in which the levels of a variable are represented by categories.

An **ordinal scale** of measurement applies when numbers are used to rank order levels of a variable. Birth order (first, second, third) is an example of a

ordinal scale
a scale of measurement in which the numbers on the scale represent an ordered series (or rank order) along a continuum.

	Scale values have unique meanings	Scale values can be rank ordered	Equal intervals between scale values	Scale has an absolute zero point	Examples	
					Variable	Scale values (operationally defined by researcher)
Nominal	✔				citizenship student status	Canadian/American/ Chinese full-time/part-time
Ordinal	✔	✔			university letter grades socioeconomic status	A/B/C/D low/medium/high
Interval	✔	✔	✔		temperature intelligence	in degrees celsius in IQ points
Ratio	✔	✔	✔	✔	weight reaction time	in kilograms in seconds

FIGURE **2.12**
MEASUREMENT SCALES AND THEIR PROPERTIES. Depending on how researchers operationally define their variables, variables will be represented by one of four measurement scales: nominal, ordinal, interval, or ratio.

variable using an ordinal scale. In ordinal scales, it's the order of the values that's important; differences between the numbers on the scale are not really meaningful. For example, is the difference between being "first born" and "second born" the same as the difference between being "second born" and "third born?" We can't really say.

interval scale
a scale of measurement in which the intervals between numbers on the scale are all the same size.

In a variable with an **interval scale,** the numbers representing the different levels of the variable *are* assumed to represent equal intervals. For example, in the measure of self-esteem just described, it is often assumed that the difference between someone scoring 1 and someone scoring 2 represents the same quantitative difference in self-esteem as between a person scoring 6 and another person scoring 7. Most researchers in psychology assume that rating scales, like the self-esteem one, are interval scales, although there is some disagreement on this issue (Sheskin, 2007).

ratio scale
a scale of measurement in which there are equal intervals and an absolute zero point.

The final type of measurement scale, a **ratio scale,** applies to a variable represented by a numeric scale that has equal intervals and an absolute zero point (i.e., there are no values on the scale below zero). An example of a variable defined using a ratio scale is annual income. Having an absolute zero means that we can make statements like "a person who earns $40 000 annually earns *twice as much* as someone who earns $20 000." It also means that if someone reports an annual income of zero, he or she literally has "no income." As we will see in a later section, "Making Sense of Data with Statistics," a variable's measurement scale affects the type of statistical technique we can use to analyze our data.

reliability
consistency of measurement over repeated occasions.

One of the goals of psychological measurement is to develop measures that are both reliable and valid. **Reliability** refers to consistency of results. If a measure is reliable, it should yield similar results across occasions. For example, if you use the measure of self-esteem just discussed, you would expect that people who score high today should also score high tomorrow or any other day that you conduct your research (assuming that self-esteem doesn't fluctuate very much on a day-to-day basis). If a person's score on the measure changes depending on the day you conduct your research, then it's not clear how the results of your study should be interpreted. In contrast, **validity** refers to how accurately your measure assesses the psychological quality it is trying to measure. So while the self-rating of how people feel about themselves seems to be a valid way of assessing self-esteem, asking people to rate the extent to which they like Frosted Flakes does not. We will return to a more detailed discussion of reliability and validity in Chapter 9.

validity
the degree to which a test accurately measures what it purports to measure, such as self-esteem, and not something else.

Measures in psychological science tend to fall into three categories: self-report, behavioural, and physiological. To study complex behaviours, researchers may employ multiple measures (see Figure 2.13) or multiple operational definitions.

LO7 Self-Report Measures

self-reports
written or oral accounts of a person's thoughts, feelings, or actions.

Self-reports are people's written or oral accounts of their thoughts, feelings, or actions. Two kinds of self-report measures are commonly used in psychology: interviews and questionnaires. In an interview, a researcher asks a set of questions, and the respondent usually answers in any way he or she feels is appropriate. The answers are often open-ended and not constrained by the researcher. (See the section "Descriptive Studies" for additional discussion on interviews.)

In a questionnaire, responses are limited to the choices given in the questionnaire. In the Stanford Prison Experiment, the researchers used several questionnaires to keep track of the psychological states of the prisoners and guards. For example, they had participants complete mood questionnaires many times during the study so that they could track any emotional changes they experienced. Participants also completed forms that assessed personality

	Description	Use	Limitations
self-reports	Participants' written or oral accounts of thoughts, actions, and feelings.	Interviews and questionnaires	Social desirability bias Lack of clear insight into one's own behaviour
behavioural measures	Objective observation of actions in either natural or lab settings.	Small-scale studies on behaviour	Time required to train coders and conduct coding Participants may modify their behaviour
physiological measures	Data collection of bodily responses under certain conditions.	Studies to determine the magnitude of physiological change	Specialized training on expensive equipment, on how to collect measurements, and on data interpretation
multiple measures	Several measures combined to acquire data on one aspect of behaviour.	Offset limitation of any single measurement Complex behaviours to study	Expensive and time consuming

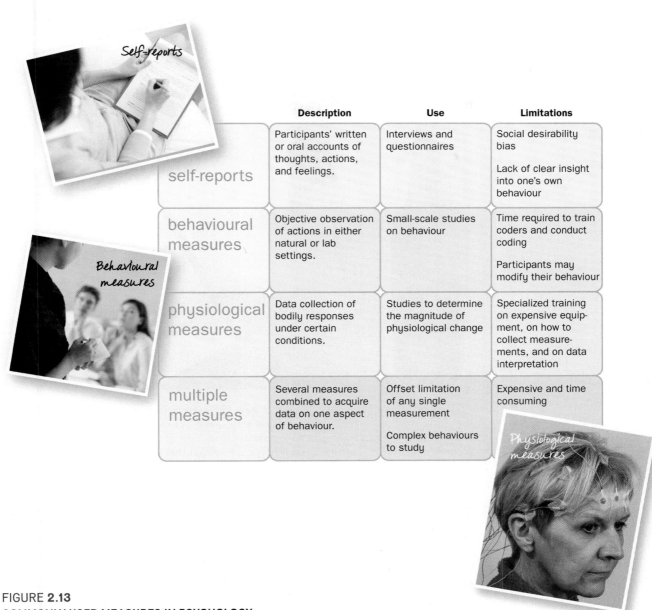

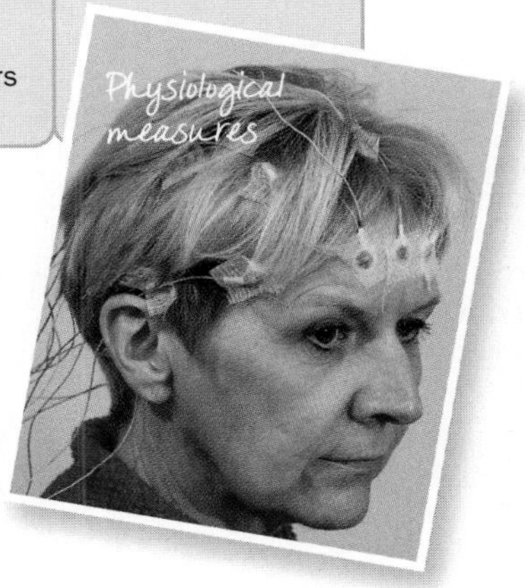

FIGURE **2.13**

COMMONLY USED MEASURES IN PSYCHOLOGY.

Why does the best research strategy involve using as many techniques as possible to study the same question?

characteristics, such as trustworthiness and orderliness, which might be related to how they acted in a prison environment (Haney et al., 1973).

Self-report questionnaires are easy to use, especially in the context of collecting data from a large number of people at once or in a short period of time. They are also relatively inexpensive. If designed carefully, they can also provide important information on key psychological variables. A major problem with self-reports, however, is that people are not always the best sources of information about themselves. Why? Sometimes people do not want to reveal what they are thinking or feeling to others for fear of looking bad, the tendency to social desirability that we discussed earlier. Presented with questions about social prejudice, for example, respondents might try to avoid giving answers that would suggest they were prejudiced against a particular group. Another problem with conclusions about human thought and behaviour based on self-reports is that we have to

Connection

How can we measure prejudice occurring outside of conscious awareness? Researchers use the Implicit Associations Test, which measures people's reaction times to word pairings presented on a computer screen.

See Chapter 14, LO8.

New technologies offer even more efficient ways for researchers to collect self-reports. Conroy et al. (2014) had people record their physical activity and alcohol use in smartphones at the end of the day, for 21 days at a time, at three different times throughout one year. They found that on days when people are more active (Thursdays to Sundays), they tend to drink more than on days they are less active (Mondays to Wednesdays).

assume that people are accurate witnesses to their own experiences. Of course, there is no way to know exactly what a person is thinking without asking that person. It is also true, however, that people do not always have clear insight into how they might behave (Nisbett & Wilson, 1977). A growing body of evidence suggests that much of what we think and feel occurs outside of our conscious awareness, and as such, is unavailable for accurate introspection (Wilson & Dunn, 2002).

Behavioural Measures

behavioural measures measures based on systematic observation of people's actions or animals' activities either in their normal environment or in a laboratory setting.

Behavioural measures are based on the systematic observation of people's actions or animals' activities either in their normal environment (that is, naturalistic observation) or in a laboratory setting. For example, a psychologist interested in aggression might bring people into a laboratory, place them in a situation that elicits aggressive behaviour, and videotape the responses. Afterward, research assistants would observe the videotapes and, using a prescribed method, score the level of aggressive behaviour exhibited by each person. It is important for researchers to train research assistants to evaluate the video and make sure that the data are being scored in a *reliable* manner—that is, that any two observers make consistent observations.

Behavioural measures are less susceptible to social desirability bias than are self-report measures. They also provide more objective, direct measurements, because they come from a trained outside observer, rather than from the participants themselves. This is a concern for researchers on topics for which people do not always provide accurate information in self-report instruments. In the study of emotion, for example, measuring people's facial expressions from videotape can reveal things about how people are feeling that participants might not want to reveal on questionnaires (Rosenberg & Ekman, 2000). Typically, researchers employ behavioural measures because they are interested in natural human or animal behaviour.

One drawback of behavioural measures is that people may modify their behaviour if they know they are being observed, watched, and/or measured. One way to reduce the likelihood of this reactive behaviour is by measuring behaviours that people cannot control. For example, a researcher might videotape a person's eye movements to assess their mental effort when performing a task—most people don't know that their blink rate slows when they are concentrating (Oh & Jeong, 2012; Jiang, Tien, Huang, Zheng, & Atkins, 2013)! Another drawback of some types of behavioural measurement is that it is often time-intensive, in terms of the time required to train coders in using the coding schemes, to collect behavioural data, and to prepare the coded data for analysis. As a case in point, one of the most widely used methods for coding facial expressions of emotion requires intensive training, on the order of 100 hours, for people to be able to use it correctly (Ekman, Friesen, & Hager, 2002)! However, for other types of behavioural measurement, just the opposite is true—automated recording by a computer leads to very precise, less time-intensive data collection. For example, some researchers might rely on computers to record the time it takes participants to perform various tasks, such as solving a problem or reading a series of words. Thus, the challenges and strengths of various behavioural measures really depend on what the researcher is trying to study.

Researcher Matthias Mehl designed this Electronically Activated Recorder, or EAR, a digital voice recorder, to record the conversations of young women and men over several days. Contrary to the popular belief that women are more talkative than men, he found no sex differences in daily word use. He found that both men and women use on average 16 000 words per day (Mehl, Vazire, Ramirez-Esparza, Slatcher, & Pennebaker, 2007).

What are some advantages and disadvantages to collecting data via observation?

Physiological Measures

Physiological measures provide data on bodily responses. For years, researchers relied on physiological information to index possible changes in psychological states—for example, to determine the magnitude of a stress reaction. Research on stress and anxiety often measures electrical changes in involuntary bodily responses, such as heart rate, sweating, and respiration, as well as hormonal changes in the blood that are sensitive to changes in psychological states. Some researchers measure brain activity while people perform certain tasks to determine the rate and location of cognitive processes in the brain.

physiological measures measures of bodily responses, such as blood pressure or heart rate, used to determine changes in psychological state.

We will look at specific brain-imaging technologies in Chapter 3. Here we note simply that they have enhanced our understanding of the brain's structure and function tremendously. However, these technologies, and even more simple ones, like heart rate, often require specialized training in the use of equipment, collection of measurements, and interpretation of data. Further, some of the equipment is expensive to buy and to maintain. Outside the health care delivery system, only major research universities with medical schools tend to have them. In addition, researchers need years of training and experience in order to use these machines and interpret the data they generate.

Multiple Measurement

Every measure has both strengths and weaknesses. The best way to compensate for the limitations or disadvantages of any particular kind of measurement tool is to use more than one type of measure. **Multiple measurement,** the use of several measures to acquire data on a single aspect of behaviour, avoids some of the limitations of individual measures. For example, the researcher who was studying prejudice and wants to avoid social desirability bias might want to include in the study a self-report measure and a behavioural measure, such as observations of how likely an individual is to help a member of a different group. Using the two measures together provides a more accurate portrait of someone's prejudice by building on the strengths of both and offsetting their weaknesses. Multiple measures yielding the same result can be used to demonstrate the *validity,* or accuracy, of any single measure.

multiple measurement the use of several measures to acquire data on one aspect of behaviour.

Some studies call for multiple measures, not just because the researchers are trying to offset the limitations of measurement tools, but also because the phenomena under study are complex. One area that requires multiple measures is research on emotions. By their nature, emotions are multifaceted; they create changes in thought, action, bodily systems, and conscious experience. When angry, for example, one individual might contemplate the situation that brought forth the anger, have thoughts of retribution, feel impelled to lunge or attack (but not necessarily act on this impulse), show a facial expression of anger, and experience any number of physiological changes, such as warm skin and a racing heart. Which one of these elements of the emotional response is a definitive measure of anger? We discuss this issue in more detail in Chapter 11, where we examine emotions, but at this point, it is enough to say that emotion is all of these things and no single one of these things. Complex, multifaceted phenomena, such as emotions, can be understood best by measuring the different systems involved.

Quick Quiz 2.4: Measuring Variables

1. A researcher is interested in studying aggression among NHL hockey teams. She decides to operationally define aggression by recording the total number of minutes each team spends in the penalty box. What type of measurement scale has she used to define aggression?
   a. nominal
   b. ordinal
   c. interval
   d. ratio
2. An advantage of self-report questionnaires is that they are easy to administer to large numbers of participants. A disadvantage of questionnaires is that
   a. they cost too much.
   b. people do not always accurately report their true thoughts or feelings.
   c. scoring responses is subjective.
   d. they have low reliability.
3. One advantage of behavioural measures compared to self-reported measures is that they
   a. are less prone to social desirability bias.
   b. are less time-intensive.
   c. are always more valid.
   d. cost less.
4. A psychologist who is interested in how brain activity relates to behaviour will most likely use which kind of measure?
   a. interview
   b. questionnaire
   c. behavioural measure
   d. physiological measure
5. Multiple measurement is used to
   a. avoid limitations on any one kind of measurement.
   b. capitalize on the strengths of each kind of measurement.
   c. understand complex and multifaceted behaviours.
   d. all of the above.

Answers can be found at the end of the chapter.

LO8 MAKING SENSE OF DATA WITH STATISTICS

statistics
the collection, analysis, interpretation, and presentation of numerical data.

Once researchers collect data, they must make sense of them. Raw data are difficult to interpret. They are, after all, just a bunch of numbers. It helps to have some way to organize the information and give it meaning. To make sense of information, scientists use **statistics,** mathematical procedures for collecting, analyzing, interpreting, and presenting numerical data. Researchers use statistics to describe and simplify what their data look like and to understand how variables relate to one another. There are two classes of statistics: descriptive and inferential.

Descriptive Statistics

descriptive statistics
measures used to describe and summarize research data.

frequency distribution
a graph of the scores on a variable, arranged by the number of times each score was obtained.

The first step in understanding research results, involves summarizing and organizing data using **descriptive statistics.** One common way of describing data is to plot the scores in tables or graphs. Graphs provide a visual way of determining what scores occur most frequently. For example, suppose your psychology class has just completed a pop quiz and your instructor wants to summarize the class performance. She could plot a **frequency distribution**—a graph of the number of students who received each particular mark on the quiz (see Figure 2.14). Frequency distributions can be plotted for variables that are operationally defined using all types of measurement scales—nominal, ordinal, interval, or ratio. Another way to describe data is by calculating *measures of central tendency*—single numbers that summarize a set of scores. There are three different ways to calculate central tendency, namely, the mean, median, and mode. The **mean** is the arithmetic average of a series of numbers. It is calculated by adding all the numbers together and dividing by the number of scores in the series. An example of a mean is your GPA, which averages the numeric grade points for all of the courses you have taken. The **median** is the score that separates the lower half of scores from the upper half. The **mode** is simply the most frequently occurring score. Figure 2.14 shows how each of these descriptive statistics is calculated for our sample of pop quiz scores.

mean
the arithmetic average of a series of numbers.

median
the score that separates the lower half of scores from the upper half.

mode
a statistic that represents the most commonly occurring score or value.

The mean is the most commonly used measure of central tendency. It has the advantage that it takes into account every person's score on a variable in its calculation. However, one problem with the mean is that it is susceptible to extreme scores. For example, suppose we want to know the average annual income in a small sample of seven families. Let's say that the family incomes, arranged in order from lowest to highest, are: $20 000, $25 000, $30 000, $35 000, $40 000, $45 000, and $2 000 000. Notice that six of the incomes are modest and the seventh is very high. The mean of these incomes is $313 571. Does that number seem very representative of the "average" family in this sample? No—the mean has been affected by that one really high income. In this instance, the median, or $35 000, provides a better description of the "average" family's income.

Whether you calculate a mean, median, or mode also depends on how you have operationally defined your variable, and the underlying properties of the

Quiz scores for class of 14 students

Student	Quiz Score (out of 7)
Lee	5
Smith	4
Sandhu	7
Reed	4
Poole	2
Aenderson	3
Chan	6
Alexander	3
Yee	5
Roja	4
Bergeron	3
Roi	4
Iljac	4
Romanov	4

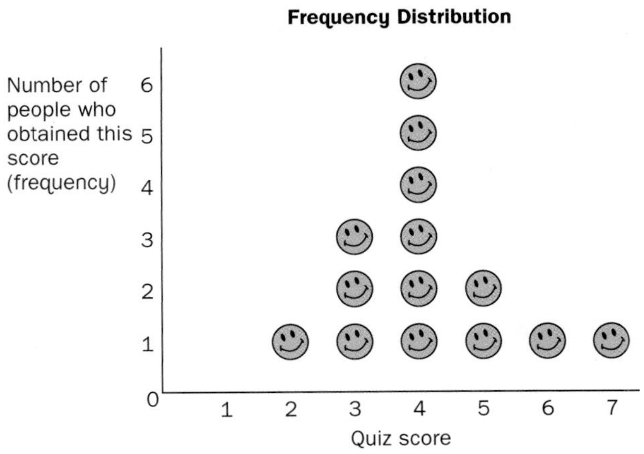

$$\textbf{Mean} = \frac{5+4+7+4+2+3+6+3+5+4+3+4+4+4}{14} = \frac{58}{14} = 4.14$$

Median = 4 (because ten scores are ≥ 4 and ten scores are ≤ 4)

Mode = 4 (because six people scored 4, only three scored 3, only one scored 2, only two scored 5, only one scored 6, and only one scored 7)

Range = highest score − lowest score = 7−2 = 5

FIGURE **2.14**

A SUMMARY OF CLASS QUIZ PERFORMANCE. This table shows how each student performed on the pop psychology quiz, marked out of 7 points. The class data has been organized and summarized in the frequency distribution—each happy face represents one student quiz score.

measurement scale used (see our previous discussion on measurement scales in the section, "Measuring Variables"). Not all measures of central tendency can be meaningfully calculated for all measurement scales. For example, imagine that you are interested in studying people's religious affiliation. You give people a questionnaire asking them to identify whether they are "Hindu," "Muslim," "Buddhist," "Christian," "Jewish," "Atheist," and so forth. The only measure of central tendency that can be calculated with this nominal scale is the mode—you can count up the number of people who fall into each religious category and report the religious affiliation with the highest frequency. Most commonly, variables are measured using interval or ratio scales, making it appropriate to calculate all measures of central tendency, as in our class quiz performance example in Figure 2.14.

Sometimes scores vary widely among participants, but the mean, median, and mode do not reveal anything about how spread out—or how varied—scores are. For example, one person's 3.0 GPA could come from getting B's in all of his or her courses, while another person's 3.0 could result from getting A's in half of his or her classes and C's in the other half. The second student had much more variable grades than the first. *Measures of variability* are numbers that are calculated to summarize the extent to which a sample of scores differs from one another. These measures can only be meaningfully calculated on interval and ratio data. The most easily calculated measure of variability is the **range**—the numerical difference between the highest and lowest score in a data set (see Figure 2.14). The weakness of the range, however, is that it only looks at the highest and lowest scores; it fails to take into account all the other scores in the distribution. Thus, the most common way to represent variability in data is to calculate the **standard deviation,** a statistical measure of how much scores in a sample vary around the mean. A higher standard deviation indicates more variability (or more spread); a lower one indicates less variability or less spread. So in the example just given, the student with all B's would have a lower standard deviation than the student with A's and C's (see Figure 2.15).

range
the difference between the highest and lowest score in a sample.

standard deviation
a statistical measure of how much scores in a sample vary around the mean.

inferential statistics
statistical tests calculated on sample data to make conclusions about populations.

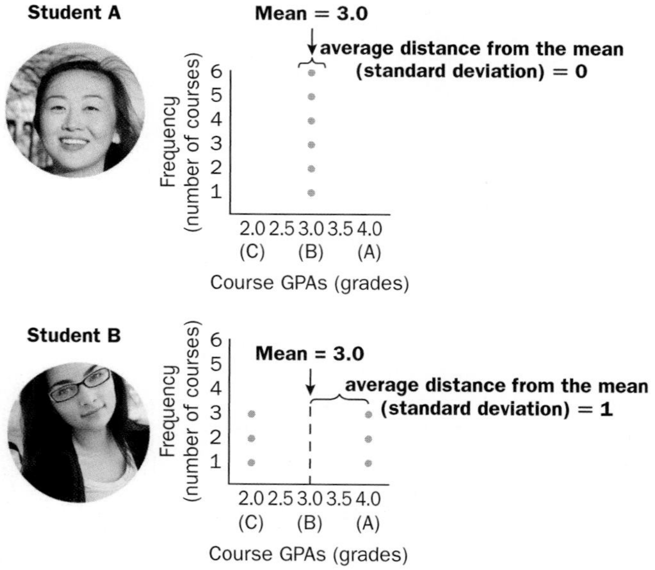

FIGURE **2.15**

SAME MEAN, DIFFERENT VARIABILITY. Each graph shows one student's course grades for each of six courses taken during one semester—each circle represents a GPA in one course. In both distributions, the mean GPA is the same: 3.0. However, the variability of each student's scores differs. Student A's scores are all centred at the mean. The average difference of these scores from the mean (or the standard deviation) is 0. In contrast, student B's scores are spread out from the mean. The average difference of these scores from the mean (the standard deviation) is 1.0.

Inferential Statistics

Whereas descriptive statistics are used to summarize patterns in our data, **inferential statistics** are used to draw conclusions. Inferential statistics are calculated using mathematical formulas that allow researchers to determine how much confidence they should have in the results of a study. They allow a researcher to draw inferences or make conclusions about populations based on evidence from samples.

Let's look at an example, by returning to a question we considered earlier: Does sugar cause hyperactive behaviour in children? We will make the common-sense prediction that sugar does cause hyperactive behaviour. We randomly assign 100 children to consume sugar (experimental group); another 100 children consume an artificial sweetener (control group). We then wait 30 minutes—to let the sugar effect kick in—and observe their behaviour for an additional 30 minutes. We video record each child's behaviour and code it on number of "high-activity acts." If sugar causes activity levels to increase, then the sugar group's number of high-activity acts should be higher than those of the control group. We calculate the mean number of high-activity acts for each group. We find that the experimental (sugar) group exhibited an average of 9.23 high-activity behaviours in the 30 minutes after eating the sugar; the control (artificial sweetener) group exhibited an average of 7.61 such behaviours. On the face of it, our hypothesis seems to be supported. After all, 9.23 is higher than 7.61. But is this difference in high activity behaviours big enough to be considered a "real" difference or is it a product of chance? Perhaps our sugar group had more children with high activity levels to begin with in comparison to our control group, despite our attempts to equalize the groups through the use of good experimental design techniques, such as random assignment. To answer this question, we must rely on inferential statistics.

There are many different techniques, or statistical tests, we can use to make inferences about the population from which our sample is drawn. Each statistical test is calculated with a different mathematical formula using information from our data. The type of statistical test calculated for a particular data set depends on the design of the study and whether the variables are measured using nominal, ordinal, interval, or ratio scales. In our sugar-activity level study, we are interested in whether the observed difference between the two means ($9.23 - 7.61 = 1.62$) in our sample is a chance occurrence or not. Thus, we would calculate a **t-test**—a type of inferential statistic that tests for differences between means. The mathematical formula for a t-test uses information from our study about the group means, variability (i.e., differences in high activity behaviours among children in our study), and sample size (i.e., the number of children in our study).

t-test
a particular type of inferential statistic designed to test differences between two means.

When the result of a statistical test tells us that our finding is real and not just random, we say that the result has **statistical significance.** Thus, in order to confirm our hypothesis that sugar affects activity level, we need to calculate a t-test on our observed difference in mean activity behaviours and demonstrate that this result is statistically significant. In general, the larger our difference between group means, the smaller the variation in activity levels among children within each group, and the larger the number of children sampled, the more likely we are to obtain a statistically significant result for our t-test. A statistically significant result tells us nothing about the size of the observed difference between means—that is, whether 1.62 is a big or small difference. It just tells us that this 1.62 difference in activity is unlikely to have occurred by chance. As we saw earlier, the magnitude of an experimental effect can only be determined by calculating an estimate of *effect size.* Today, many researchers advocate that it is not enough to report inferential statistics—the importance of the findings, or the effect sizes, need to be stated too (APA, 2010).

statistical significance
a statistical statement about the likelihood that an obtained result occurred by chance.

Even if we obtain a result that is statistically significant, it doesn't mean that we can be 100 percent certain that the result is not random. For any result, there is always some likelihood that chance is operating—we can never completely eliminate it. The amount of evidence required to accept that a finding is unlikely to have arisen by chance is known as the **significance level.** Typically, in psychology, we accept a result as statistically significant if we expect it to have occurred by chance less than 5 percent of the time; that is, we would expect chance to be responsible for the outcome 5 or fewer times in 100 repetitions of the study. We report this significance level as $p < .05$, where p stands for probability (or likelihood).

significance level
the standard used to decide statistical significance.

Suppose we calculate the t-test for our sugar-activity level study and find that the difference between means is *not* statistically significant (i.e., the likelihood of our result occurring due to chance is greater than 5 percent, $p > .05$). In this instance, we must conclude that children who eat sugar are no more active than those who do not. Our hypothesis is not supported, and we are forced to conclude that we have no evidence that sugar increases activity level. In fact, such a result is consistent with previous research on the topic of sugar and activity level (Kanarek, 1994; Krummel, Seligson, & Guthrie, 1996; Wolraich, Wilson, & White, 1995), despite what most of us want to believe!

Challenge Your Assumptions

True or False? Eating sugar makes children hyperactive.

False: There is no evidence supporting the belief that sugar intake directly affects hyperactivity.

As useful and helpful as statistics are to make sense of data and make inferences about populations, be aware that they also can be and are used to mislead people. To see how, read "Psychology in the Real World: Beware of Statistics in Advertising."

Psychology in the Real World

Beware of Statistics in Advertising

Learning about research methods plays a crucial role in understanding psychological science, but it offers huge practical advantages as well. You can learn how to look at claims in the news and advertisements with a critical eye. Much of what you learn in this class may be forgotten not long after you leave university. But you are bombarded with advertisements dozens of times each day, something that will continue throughout your life. So let's look briefly at three scenarios that will help you to be a more critical and intelligent consumer of information.

Scenario 1

A billboard advertising a popular hybrid vehicle: *"The car more people would buy again."*

That sounds great! Not only is the car good for the environment (which is one reason to get it), but it also gets great mileage (which will save you money), *and* people like it (they must if they say they would buy it again). Are you sold yet?

Wait a minute. What did the ad actually say? The car more people would buy again. *More* than what? The meaning of this claim depends entirely on what this vehicle is being compared to. The implication is that more people would buy this car again than would buy any other car. But what did they actually compare it to?

- Other hybrids?
- All other cars?
- A horse and buggy?

These are things you need to know. Otherwise it is impossible to judge what the statement means, but advertisers regularly leave such information out and hope you will fill in the blank with what helps them most. In this case, they hope and assume you fill in the blank with "all other cars."

Scenario 2

In an ad in the morning paper, Company B reports on a recent lab study showing that just a half ounce of its new drug—let's call it "No-Cold"—killed 37 202 germs in a test tube in less than 15 seconds (adapted from Huff, 1954).

The implication is that "No-Cold" is a great cold medicine—perhaps better than others—on the basis of these hard scientific data. After all, it killed more than 37 000 germs! Let's take this claim apart. Can you see what is wrong with this statement? Here are a few things to consider:

1. The fact that a substance works well in a test tube does not mean it will work in the human throat or respiratory tract. The test tube is a controlled environment, whereas a host of factors interact in the human body. Temperature, moisture, other bacteria, the human immune system, and phlegm are just a few examples of such factors.
2. The ad doesn't say what kind of germs "No-Cold" killed. Were they the ones that cause colds? (The common cold is caused by a variety of viruses.) Medical researchers still have little idea of the specific viruses (germs) that cause colds, though some of them have been isolated. Were these germs even relevant to colds? Were they even viruses? Can you identify any other problems with the ad?

Scenario 3

Graphic displays of data can be misleading.

Consider Figures 2.16a and 2.16b, both of which depict the billions of dollars spent on education over a one-year period. Figure 2.16b seems to show a much bigger increase in spending on education than Figure 2.16a. If you look closely, however, both depict a $2 billion increase in spending over a one-year period. The information contained in each picture is exactly the same, but the slopes of the lines differ dramatically. This difference stems from how the illustrations' vertical axes are segmented. If you want to imply that the spending increases in education are insufficient, then you might graph them as shown in Figure 2.16a, which has $2 billion increments, so it shows a gradual increase across the year. Figure 2.16b, on the other hand, uses $0.2 billion increments. Businesses, journalists, and politicians can mislead people by graphically distorting data.

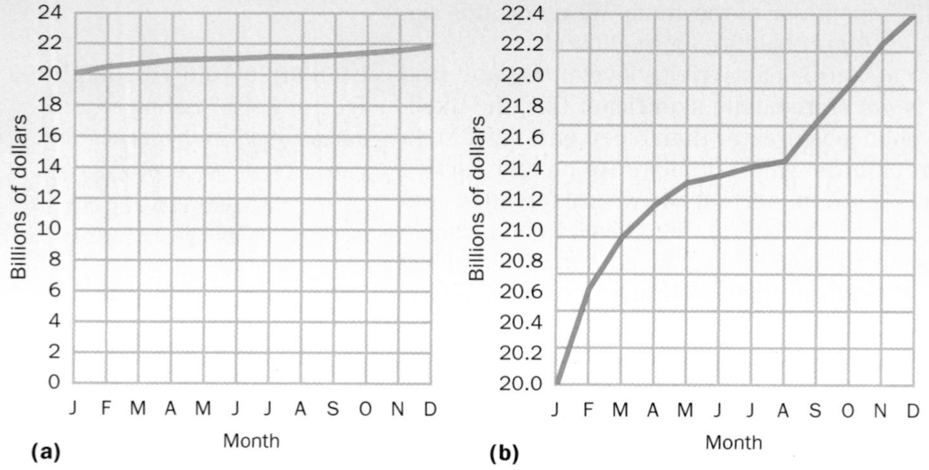

FIGURE 2.16
BILLIONS OF DOLLARS SPENT ON EDUCATION.

If you wanted to persuade someone that education spending is out of control, which graph would you use to make your case?

Quick Quiz 2.5: Making Sense of Data with Statistics

1. If two sets of scores have the same mean, then
   a. they must have the same variability.
   b. they must have similar variabilities.
   c. they must have different variabilities.
   d. their variabilities could be the same or they could be different.
2. For the following set of data, 3, 5, 5, 1, 1, 4, 1,
   a. the mean is 4.
   b. the mode is 1.
   c. the median is 1.
   d. the range is 2.
3. Scores that are widely spread apart have a
   a. high standard deviation.
   b. low standard deviation.
   c. high mean.
   d. low reliability.

Answers can be found at the end of the chapter.

LO9

RESEARCH ETHICS

Due to current ethical guidelines, some of the most important and classic studies in psychology could not be performed today. One of them is the Stanford Prison Experiment, which you read about at the beginning of this chapter. This experiment subjected participants to conditions that so altered their behaviour that the researchers had to intervene and end the study early. In 1971, there were few ethical limitations on psychological research. Since then, and partly as a consequence of studies like the Stanford Prison Experiment, professional organizations and universities have put in place strict ethical guidelines to protect research participants from physical and psychological harm.

Ethics are the rules governing the conduct of a person or group in general or in a specific situation; stated more simply, ethics are standards of right and wrong. What are the ethical boundaries of the treatment of humans and animals in psychological research? In psychology today, nearly every study conducted with humans and animals must pass through a rigorous review of its methods by a panel of experts. If the proposed study does not meet the standards, it cannot be approved.

ethics
the rules governing the conduct of a person or group in general or in a specific situation—or more simply, standards of right and wrong.

Another notable example of research that would violate current ethics guidelines was a classic series of studies by Stanley Milgram in the early 1960s. Milgram's landmark research on obedience is discussed in more detail in Chapter 14, but we mention it here for its pivotal role in the development of ethical guidelines for human psychological research. Like many social psychologists of the mid-20th century, Milgram was both fascinated and horrified by the atrocities of the Holocaust and wondered to what extent psychological factors influenced people's willingness to carry out the orders of the Nazi regime. Milgram predicted that most people are not inherently evil and argued that there might be powerful aspects of social situations that make people obey orders from authority figures. He designed an experiment to test systematically the question of whether decent people could be made to inflict harm on other people.

Connection

Social psychologists have demonstrated both in the lab and in the real world that otherwise normal folks can be pressured to do cruel things, such as give people electric shocks to the point of knocking them unconscious (or so they believe).

See Chapter 14, LO6.

Briefly, Milgram's studies of obedience involved a simulation in which participants were misled about the true nature of the experiment. Thinking that they were part of an experiment on learning, they administered what they thought were electrical shocks to punish the "learner," who was in another room, for making errors. In spite of protest from the "learner" when increasingly intense shocks occurred, the experimenter pressured the "teachers" to continue administering shocks. Many participants were clearly upset and concerned about what was happening to the "learner." Some people withdrew from the study, but most of the participants continued to shock the learner. After the study, Milgram fully explained to his participants that, in fact, the "learner" was never shocked or in pain at all (Milgram, 1974).

Milgram's study provided important data on how easily decent people could be persuaded by the sheer force of a situation to do cruel things. What is more, Milgram conducted many replications and variations of his findings, which helped build knowledge about human social behaviour. But was it worth the distress it exerted on the participants? One could ask the same of the Stanford Prison Experiment. Although the prison experiment also contributed to our knowledge about the impact of situational factors on individual behaviours and led to some reform in prisons, it is hard to know whether the deception of the participants and the emotional breakdowns some of them experienced was worth it. Do you think it was worthwhile?

Ethical Research with Humans

The Milgram study is one of the most widely discussed studies in the history of psychology. A number of psychologists were quite upset over the study and protested it on ethical grounds (Baumrind, 1964). The uproar led to the creation of explicit guidelines for the ethical treatment of human subjects. In Canada, researchers are expected to adhere to the ethical policy statement published by a consortium of three federal funding agencies, the Tri-Council (Canadian Institutes, 2010), and the code of ethics, published by the Canadian Psychological Association (CPA, 2000). Some of the ethical principles all psychological and medical researchers must follow include:

1. *Informed consent.* Tell participants in general terms what the study is about, what they will do and how long it will take, what the known risks and benefits are, that they have the right to withdraw at any time without penalty, and whom to contact with questions. This information is provided in written form and the participant signs it, signifying consent. If a participant is under the age of 18, informed consent must be granted by a legal guardian.
2. *Respect for persons.* Safeguard the dignity and autonomy of the individual and take extra precautions when dealing with study participants who are less likely to understand that their participation is voluntary, such as children.
3. *Beneficence.* Inform participants of the costs and benefits of participation; minimize costs for participants and maximize benefits. For example, many have argued that the Milgram study was worth the distress (cost) it may have caused participants, for the benefit of the knowledge we have gained about how readily decent people can be led astray by powerful social situations. In fact, many of the participants said that they were grateful for this opportunity to gain knowledge about themselves that they would have not predicted (Milgram, 1974).
4. *Privacy and confidentiality.* Protect the privacy of the participant, generally by keeping all responses confidential. Confidentiality ensures that participants' identities are never directly connected with the data they provide in a study.
5. *Justice.* Benefits and costs must be distributed equally among participants. Participants from a wide range of social groups should be recruited. Groups should only be excluded when scientifically justifiable.

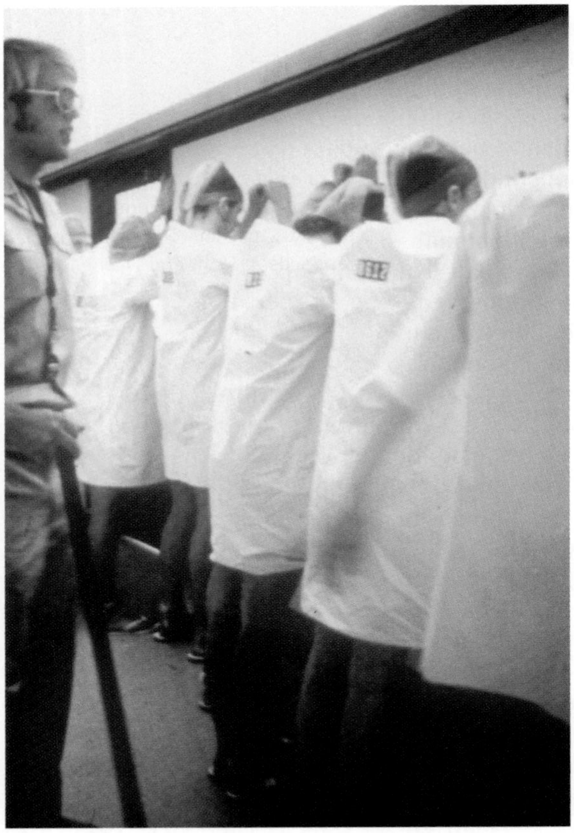

In the Stanford Prison Experiment, college students assigned to the role of either a prison guard or a prisoner acted their parts so well that the distinction between reality and the world created for this study disappeared. The extreme distress experienced by some of the prisoners forced the researchers to end the simulation earlier than planned.

Do you think the experimenter pushed the participants too far?

In Milgram's study, participants were led to believe they were taking part in a learning study, when in fact they were taking part in a study on obedience to authority. Is this kind of deception ever justified? The answer (according to the Tri-Council and

CPA) is that deception is to be avoided whenever possible but it is permissible if these conditions are met: it can be fully justified by its significant potential scientific, educational, or applied value; it is part of the research design; there is no alternative to deception; and full debriefing occurs afterward. **Debriefing** is the process of informing participants of the exact purposes of the study—including the hypotheses—revealing any and all deceptive practices and explaining why they were necessary to conduct the study and ultimately what the results of the study were.

debriefing
the explanation of the purposes of a study following data collection.

Debriefing is required to minimize any negative effects (e.g., distress) experienced as a result of the deception. Deception comes in different shades and degrees. In the Stanford Prison Experiment, all participants were fully informed about the fact that they would be assigned the roles of a prisoner or a guard. In that sense there was no deception. But they were not informed of the details and the extent to which being in this study would be like being in a real prison. They were not told upfront that if they were assigned to the "prisoner" role, they would be strip-searched. When they were taken from their homes, the "prisoners" were not told this was part of the study. Not informing participants of the research hypotheses may be deceptive but necessary to prevent biased and invalid responses. Not telling participants that they might experience physical pain or psychological distress is a much more severe form of deception and is not ethically permissible.

Today, to ensure adherence to ethical guidelines, **research ethics boards (REBs)** evaluate proposed research before it is conducted to make sure research involving humans does not cause undue harm or distress. Should Milgram's study have been permitted? Were his procedures ethical by today's standards? To this day, there are people who make strong cases both for and against the Milgram study on ethical grounds, as we have discussed.

research ethics boards (REBs)
organizations that evaluate research proposals to make sure research involving humans does not cause undue harm or distress.

Ethical Research with Animals

Human participants are generally protected by the ethical guidelines we itemized in the previous section. What about animals? They cannot consent, so how do we ethically treat animals in research?

The use of non-human species in psychological research is even more controversial than research with humans. There is a long history in psychology of conducting research on animals. Typically, such studies concern topics that are harder to explore in humans. We cannot, for instance, isolate human children from their parents to see what effect an impoverished environment has on brain development. Researchers have done so with animals. The subfields of biological psychology and learning most often use animals for research. For instance, to determine what exactly a particular brain structure does, one needs to compare individuals who have healthy structures to those who do not. With humans this might be done by studying the behaviour of individuals with accidental brain injury or disease and comparing it to the behaviour of normal humans. Injury and disease, however, never strike two people in precisely the same way, and so it is not possible to reach definite conclusions about the way the brain works by just looking at accidents and illness. Surgically removing the brain structure is another way to determine function, but this approach is obviously unethical with humans. In contrast, non-human animals, usually laboratory rats, offer the possibility of more highly controlled studies of selective brain damage. For example, damage could be inflicted on part of a brain structure in one group of rats while another group is left alone. Then the rats' behaviours and abilities could be observed to see if there were any differences between the groups.

To keep up to date with Canadian regulations on research ethics, many employers (such as universities) require their researchers to complete an online tutorial, such as the *TCPS 2 Course on Research Ethics* available at http://tcps2core.ca.

Animals cannot consent to research, and if they could, it is unlikely they would agree to any of this. Indeed, it is an ongoing debate

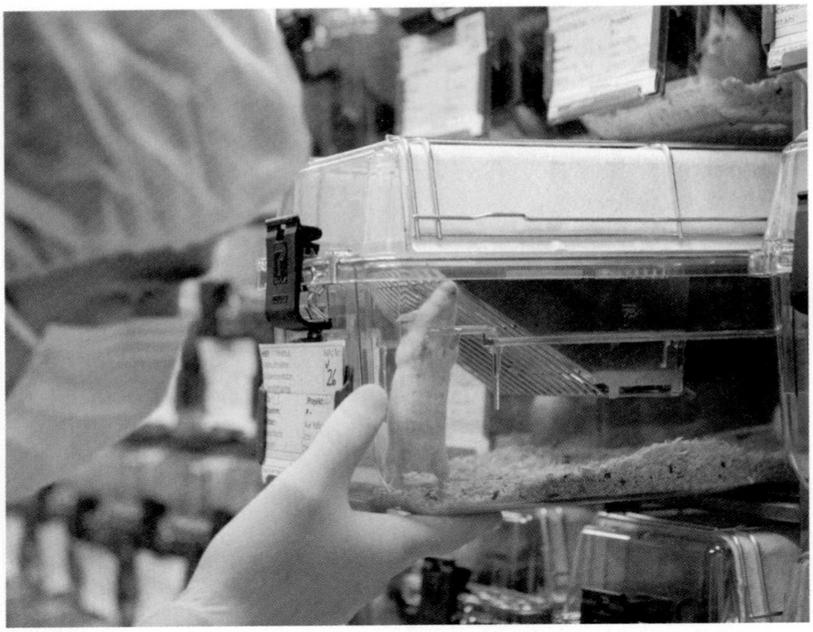

In 2013, the Canadian Council on Animal Care commissioned a survey asking Canadians what they think about the use of animals in research (CCAC, 2013). Fifty-four percent reported that "the welfare of the animal is important in determining what is an acceptable or unacceptable use of animals" (CCAC, 2013, p. 3); 30 percent felt that "the benefits of using animals to advance science and medicine outweigh the welfare of animals" (CCAC, 2013, p. 3).

What do you think? What are the pros and cons of using animals for scientific research?

as to how much animal research should be permissible at all. Because animal research has led to many treatments for disease (e.g., cancer, heart disease), as well as advances in understanding basic neuroscientific processes (such as the effects of environment on brain cell growth), it is widely considered to be acceptable. Animal research is acceptable, that is, as long as the general conditions and treatment of the animals is humane. Approximately 3 million animals are used every year in Canada for teaching and research purposes (Canadian Council on Animal Care, 2011). Most of these are fish, mice, or rats.

If informed consent is the key to ethical treatment of human research participants, then humane treatment is the key to the ethical use of animal subjects. In Canada, all research involving the use of animals must adhere to the guidelines outlined by the Canadian Council on Animal Care (CCAC, 1993). Federal and provincial laws generally require housing the animals in clean, sanitary, and adequately sized structures—failure to do so can result in criminal prosecution. In addition, there are separate REBs to evaluate proposals for animal research. They require researchers to ensure the animals' comfort, health, and humane treatment, which also means keeping discomfort, infection, illness and pain to an absolute minimum at all times. If a study requires euthanizing the animal, it must be done as painlessly as possible.

As is true of all ethical issues, complex and legitimate opposing needs must be balanced in research. The need to know, understand, and treat illness must be balanced against the needs of participants and animals to have their well-being and rights protected at all times. Consequently, the debate and discussion about ethical treatment of humans and animals must be ongoing and evolving.

Quick Quiz 2.6: Research Ethics

1. Which of the following scenarios best exemplifies *informed consent?*
   a. A researcher informs participants about the study's research hypotheses after they have participated.
   b. A researcher recruits a diverse sample of participants.
   c. A researcher explains the known risks and benefits of a study to participants before they participate.
   d. A researcher ensures that all participant responses are treated as anonymous and confidential.
2. Current guidelines on research ethics state that when studying humans, deception
   a. must be avoided whenever possible.
   b. can be used only if it's part of the research design.
   c. must be followed by debriefing.
   d. must be fully justified.
   e. all of the above.
3. Ethical guidelines for research with non-human animals state that
   a. informed consent is always required.
   b. ethical and humane conditions must exist throughout the research process.
   c. computer modelling must always be tried before research with animals.
   d. deception can be used if fully justified.

Answers can be found at the end of the chapter.

Can Experience Change the Brain?

Can enriching experiences actually improve brain function and/or make the brain grow faster? Can impoverished experiences negatively impact brain growth? By looking at different research approaches to this topic and at some of the ethical issues involved, we can see why certain methods are chosen over others and get a sense of the cumulative nature of science.

In the early 1960s a group at the University of California, Berkeley, decided to study the effects of different environments on the brains of rats (Bennett et al., 1964; M. Rosenzweig et al., 1962). In numerous experimental studies, the researchers randomly assigned genetically similar rats to either enriched or impoverished environments for up to 30 days. The enriched environments included many opportunities and apparatus for play and activity, such as running wheels and climbing tubes, as well as food and water. The impoverished environments provided only food and water. As you might have guessed, the independent variable in these experiments was how enriched the environment was; the dependent variables were change in brain size and/or changes in the growth of brain cells. The researchers found that rats raised in enriched environments showed evidence of growth in brain tissue compared to the animals reared in the impoverished environments. Using an experimental design with random assignment (the groups of rats were equivalent at the beginning of each experiment), the researchers replicated their basic finding many times. By doing so, they established that rats raised in the enriched conditions did indeed develop more brain tissue and thicker cortexes.

These experiments all involved true experimental designs, in which the animals were randomly assigned to different environmental conditions, all aspects of the study were tightly controlled, and the animals were euthanized afterward to allow for detailed study of brain structure. One of the main reasons we study these phenomena in animals is to learn how these processes work in humans, but ethical limitations prevent human research. Thus, the animals serve as models for how human brain organization and function might be modified by experience.

Do rats serve as good models for how things happen in humans? Although rat and human brains have many similarities, they also have a multitude of anatomical differences. This suggests that not everything about brain growth is identical between humans and rats and therefore rat brain organization is not a perfect model for understanding human brain organization.

Research on humans is necessary to know whether environmental enrichment or deprivation causes changes in the human brain, but the ways in which we can study such processes in humans are limited. Clearly it would be unethical to randomly assign babies to live in either enriched or impoverished environments for several years so that we could assess differences in their behaviour or brain activity. Which research designs might be appropriate to address these questions with humans?

Probably the most rigorous design that one could apply in this context is a **quasi-experimental design**, which is much like an experimental design except that it makes use of naturally occurring groups rather than randomly assigned ones. For example, some humans grow up in more enriched, cognitively stimulating environments than others, benefiting perhaps from access to books, computers, and many interactions with parents. Instead of assigning people to these conditions (cognitively stimulating versus not), quasi-experimental designs take advantage of the fact that people are already in these different groups in the real world. In order to lessen confounds, however, it is important to make sure these naturally occurring groups are very similar on other traits, except for the ones being studied.

quasi-experimental design
a research method similar to an experimental design except that it makes use of naturally occurring groups rather than randomly assigning subjects to groups.

Quality of early home environments is associated with changes in the structure and function of the brain.

How does the quality of early home environments actually change the brain?

Several recent quasi-experimental studies have focused on differences in brain structure and function among children from families of differing socioeconomic status, or SES (Hackman, Farah, & Meaney, 2010). Researchers use measures of parental income and education to create SES groups (low, medium, and high) and then compare children in these different groups on brain structure and function. According to studies of brain images, preschoolers who have grown up in low-SES environments have less dense front regions of the brain (responsible for planning and control) than preschoolers from higher-SES environments, despite starting out with similar brain size and density at birth (Hanson et al., 2013). This finding suggests that children exposed to poorer-quality environments have brains that are not as good at regulating impulsive behaviours as children from higher-quality environments. Consistent with this idea, Hanson et al. (2013) also found that these preschoolers with less dense brains exhibited more problem behaviours. Further, studies comparing brain activity levels for children from low- versus high-SES backgrounds reveal less active front regions of the brain when working on tasks requiring attention (Kishiyami, Boyce, Jiminez, Perry, & Knight, 2009). Other studies, using cognitive tests assumed to measure underlying brain systems, reveal that children from low-SES environments perform more poorly on tests of language and executive function (i.e., planning and organizing) compared to children from higher-SES environments (Farah et al., 2006; Noble, Norman, & Farah, 2005).

Taken together, these findings suggest that environments can change the brain, but because the researchers relied on naturally occurring groups based on SES, the results are correlational, *not* causal. That is, we cannot conclude that impoverished environments cause changes in the brain. Only true experiments, with random assignment, allow us to draw conclusions about cause and effect, so any group differences observed in a quasi-experimental design cannot be attributed to a specific cause. Remember that correlation is not causation, but causation does require correlation.

Quick Quiz 2.7: Evaluating Connections in Psychological Research

1. What is an enriched environment in animal research?
   a. a living situation that provides ample opportunity for play and activity
   b. a living environment that provides optimal nutritional enrichments as well as adequate sleeping space
   c. a living space with room and plenty of water
   d. a living situation with all of the latest toys and games
2. What is the most rigorous study design that can be used to study the effects of enrichment on brain development in humans?
   a. experimental design
   b. case study
   c. correlational design
   d. quasi-experimental design

Answers can be found at the end of the chapter.

Chapter Review

THE NATURE OF SCIENCE

- Science is about empirically testing our ideas and learning whether our understanding of the world is correct.
- The key attitudes of science are skepticism, openness to new ideas based on evidence, and intellectual honesty.
- The scientific method by which research is conducted can be summed up by OPTIC: Observing, Predicting, Testing, Interpreting, and Communicating. Scientists start with observations of the world, make predictions once they see a pattern, devise a study to test predictions, interpret results with the aid of statistics and decide whether the prediction was correct or not, and publish their work to clearly describe findings to others. These new findings lead to new predictions, and the whole process begins anew.
- Pseudoscience lacks cumulative progress, disregards empirical facts, lacks skepticism of its own assumptions, and vaguely describes how it came to its conclusions, which often stem from loose and distorted logic.

RESEARCH METHODS IN PSYCHOLOGY

- Psychologists use three types of research designs to test their ideas: descriptive designs, correlational designs, and experimental designs.
- In descriptive designs, researchers simply observe and describe what they see. They address the question: "What is the nature of the phenomenon?" They don't manipulate anything.
- In correlational designs researchers measure two or more things carefully to see whether or not they are related. They address the question: "Is *X* related to *Y*?" These designs use correlational statistics to interpret the results and to make and test hypotheses, but do not allow researchers to draw any conclusions about causality.
- Researchers use correlation coefficients to assess the strength and direction of association between two variables.
- In experimental designs, researchers randomly assign participants to conditions and carefully manipulate the predicted cause (independent variable), then look for differences in outcome (dependent variables). True experiments address the question: "Does *X* cause *Y*?"

MEASURING VARIABLES

- When researchers operationally define their variables, they assign categories or numbers to represent different levels of each variable. There are four types of measurement scales: nominal, ordinal, interval, and ratio.
- Psychological researchers draw on several types of tools to measure variables relevant to their research questions. These measures fall into three major categories: self-report, behavioural, and physiological.
- Self-reports are people's written or oral accounts of their thoughts, feelings, or actions.
- Behavioural measurements involve systematic observation of people's actions in either their normal life situations (naturalistic observation) or laboratory situations.
- Physiological measures include various types of measures of bodily responses. Each measure has strengths and weaknesses. By employing multiple measures, researchers offset the limitations of any given measure.

MAKING SENSE OF DATA WITH STATISTICS

- Descriptive statistics organize data for interpretation and help researchers evaluate their hypotheses. The mean is the arithmetic average of a set of data. The median is the score that separates the lower half of scores from the upper half. The mode is the most frequently occurring score.
- Variability is the spread between the lowest and highest values in a set of data. The range is the difference between the highest and lowest score. The standard deviation indicates variability around the mean.
- Inferential statistics allow researchers to make conclusions about populations based on sample evidence. Researchers use statistical significance to determine the likelihood that a finding occurred by chance.

RESEARCH ETHICS

- Ethics are standards of right and wrong that guide people's behaviour.
- Professional ethics have been developed to protect the rights of humans and animals who participate in psychological research. Researchers must obtain informed consent from human participants before a study begins. Animals cannot provide informed consent, but strict ethical guidelines exist to ensure humane living conditions and treatment.

EVALUATING CONNECTIONS IN PSYCHOLOGICAL RESEARCH

- Research on environmental enrichment and brain growth using experimental designs with animal models and correlational studies with humans illustrates how numerous methodological issues unfold in a given research area.

Quick Quiz Answers

Quick Quiz 2.1: 1. d 2. b 3. a 4. c **Quick Quiz 2.2:** 1. a 2. b 3. d 4. c 5. b
Quick Quiz 2.3: 1. b 2. b **Quick Quiz 2.4:** 1. d 2. b 3. a 4. d 5. d
Quick Quiz 2.5: 1. d 2. b 3. a **Quick Quiz 2.6:** 1. c 2. e 3. b **Quick Quiz 2.7:** 1. a 2. d

The Biology of Behaviour

CHAPTER

3

CHAPTER OUTLINE

Challenge Your Assumptions

True or False?

- ☐ Genes can be influenced by our experiences and behaviours.
- ☐ Learning increases the number of neurons in your brain.
- ☐ People can be classified as left brained or right brained, depending on whether they are analytical or artistic.
- ☐ In people who are blind, vision areas of the brain do not function.
- ☐ Nerve cells cannot regenerate like other cells in the body.

LEARNING OBJECTIVES

- LO1 Describe three principles of behavioural genetics.
- LO2 Identify the five research strategies that are used to determine the role genes play in behaviour.
- LO3 Draw a flow chart to demonstrate the components of the nervous system, including divisions of the CNS and PNS.
- LO4 Compare and contrast the organization and function of the sympathetic and parasympathetic nervous systems.
- LO5 Label the parts of a neuron and identify the role each plays in neuronal transmission.
- LO6 Compare and contrast sensory neurons, motor neurons, and interneurons.
- LO7 Describe how messages are sent between neurons.
- LO8 Describe how an action potential carries a message along a neuron.
- LO9 Describe the processes of neurotransmitter degradation and reuptake.
- LO10 Identify the locations and main functions of the hindbrain, midbrain, and forebrain.
- LO11 Identify the anatomical and functional divisions of the cortex.
- LO12 Explain the concept of cerebral asymmetry and give examples of asymmetrical brain functions.
- LO13 Describe examples of neuroplasticity in the brain.
- LO14 Describe how psychologists measure brain activity.

Take a look at the painting in Figure 3.1. It is pleasing, colourful, and nicely done. It features realistic colour, perspective, and shadowing. It seems, perhaps, not extraordinary—except by virtue of its maker. He cannot see at all.

Born blind to an impoverished family in Turkey, Esref Armagan started drawing at a young age; later he began painting with oils and acrylics. Armagan has been actively painting for over 30 years. His work strikes us not only for its beauty but also for how it depicts objects in a way that a sighted person would see them. How can someone who has never seen anything in his life create beautiful paintings that depict realistic images? It seems as if his brain is doing something that his eyes cannot.

FIGURE **3.1**

PAINTING BY ESREF ARMAGAN, A BLIND PAINTER. Besides being beautiful to look at, Armagan's vivid, realistic paintings and drawings challenge conventional thinking about the brain and its ability to adapt and overcome limitations imposed on it. **Can you think of how Armagan is able to paint with colour, shadow, and perspective, even though he has never seen any of these?**

The skills of Esref Armagan both suggest that our experience of the world is not a direct representation of what is out there. The brain can change our experiences—give us visual memories for tactile experiences. The brain is both fixed and flexible in how it acts.

While most of us use the rear portion of our brains to process visual information, Esref Armagan uses that area when he paints by the feel of his hands.

In this chapter and the one that follows, we will explore what is known about how the brain works, how it supports behaviour, and how it is transformed by experience. Our main task in this chapter is to introduce the biological systems that are most relevant to a basic understanding of psychology. In so doing, we will look at the role of heredity and evolution in shaping the brain and behaviour, and explore the workings of the nervous system.

LO1 GENES AND BEHAVIOUR

We seldom have trouble accepting the idea that heredity is responsible for outward family resemblances, such as the shape of the nose and face, height, and the colour of our hair and skin. But when it comes to behaviour, many of us are uncomfortable with the idea that heredity might determine what we think and do. Yet heredity very much influences behaviour and experience, although it does not operate on thought and behaviour in a simple, deterministic way.

chromosome
a coiled-up thread of DNA.

DNA (deoxyribonucleic acid)
molecule that contains genes.

genes
small segments of DNA that contain information for producing proteins.

Before we can explore how heredity and behaviour interact, we must know something about the structures and mechanisms involved in heredity. A **chromosome** is a cellular structure that holds our genetic information in threadlike strands of DNA. Humans have 23 pairs of chromosomes in the nucleus of each cell of the body, except red blood cells, which do not have nuclei. **DNA (deoxyribonucleic acid),** the genetic material that makes up chromosomes, is a large coiled molecule that contains genes. **Genes** are small segments of DNA that contain information for producing proteins. These proteins in turn make up most chemicals and structures in the body (see Figure 3.2). Genes influence specific characteristics, such as height or hair colour, by directing the synthesis of proteins. So although our DNA contains the "recipe" for who we are, it is our proteins that make it all happen. All of the genetic information contained in our DNA makes up our **genome.**

For some traits, such as height, eye colour, and personality, individuals in a population differ dramatically from one another. This diversity is strongly influenced by the fact that the genes responsible for these characteristics often take different forms. These different forms are known as **alleles** (Clark & Grunstein, 2000; Starr & Taggart, 2004). Individuals inherit one allele from each parent; sometimes both alleles have the same form, but not always. Each gene in an allele pair can produce different characteristics, so the combination of alleles inherited from our parents directly determine some traits. **Dominant genes** show their effect even if there is only one copy of that gene in the pair, while **recessive genes** show effects only when both alleles are the same. The specific collection of genes that we carry as part of our genetic make-up is called our **genotype,** while our observable characteristics are referred to as our **phenotype.**

The genetic underpinnings of behaviour are more complex that those for physical traits. To understand how heredity affects behaviour, psychologists turn to the science of **behavioural genetics.** Three principles of behavioural genetics are especially relevant in psychology:

1. The relationship between specific genes and behaviour is complex; behaviours derive from dozens or hundreds of genes—not one or two.
2. By studying human twins and adoptees, or by manipulating genes in animals, behavioural geneticists may disentangle the contributions of heredity and environment to behaviour.
3. The environment influences how and when genes affect behaviour.

Let's consider each of these principles in turn.

genome
all the genetic information in DNA.

alleles
different forms of a gene.

dominant genes
genes that show their effect even if there is only one allele for that trait in the pair.

recessive genes
genes that show their effects only when both alleles are the same.

genotype
the genetic make-up of an individual.

phenotype
an individual's observable characteristics.

behavioural genetics
the scientific study of the role of heredity in behaviour.

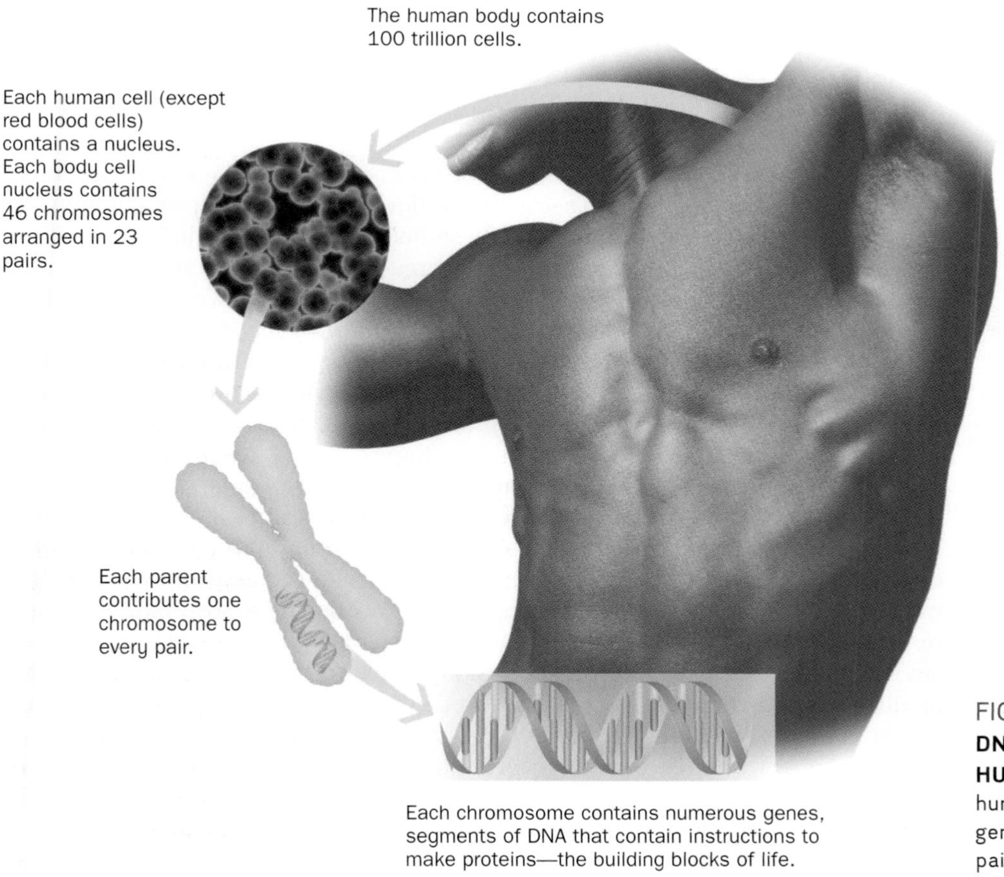

The human body contains
100 trillion cells.
Each human cell (except red blood cells) contains a nucleus. Each body cell nucleus contains 46 chromosomes arranged in 23 pairs.
Each parent contributes one chromosome to every pair.
Each chromosome contains numerous genes, segments of DNA that contain instructions to make proteins—the building blocks of life.

FIGURE **3.2**
DNA, CHROMOSOMES, AND THE HUMAN CELL. Every cell in the human body contains the same genetic material distributed in 23 pairs of chromosomes.

The Complex Connection between Genes and Behaviour

The connection between genes and behaviour is complex. To understand how genes influence behaviour, we must abandon the notion of simple causation (Rutter, 2006). Many of our inherited physical characteristics, such as body temperature, need to be maintained within a narrow range. Behaviour, on the other hand, needs to be flexible to cope with the demands of an ever-changing environment. Therefore, genes seldom make behaviours a certainty. For example, no single gene causes anxiety. Anxiety is influenced by both genetic and environmental factors that make it more likely to trouble some people than others.

Connection

Genetics influence about 50 percent of the differences in performance on intelligence tests, leaving about the same amount to be explained by non-genetic influences.

See Chapter 9, LO4.

In a few cases, having a specific gene guarantees an outcome—such as the incurable neuromuscular disease called Huntington's disease, which is carried by dominant allele for a specific brain protein. Because the abnormal allele is dominant, inheriting only one parental copy means that offspring will develop the disorder. More typically however, a specific gene plays only a small part in creating a given behaviour, and genetic influence itself is only part of the story. Environmental events such as smoking during pregnancy, early childhood experiences, stress or trauma, and enriched environments all interact with genes to make specific behaviours more or less likely.

monogenic transmission
the hereditary passing on of traits determined by a single gene.

polygenic transmission
the process by which many genes interact to create a single characteristic.

The hereditary passing on of traits determined by a single gene, such as Huntington's disease, is known as **monogenic transmission.** However, the number of potential outcomes for most traits and behaviours is not small. There is wide variation in intelligence, for example, and numerous genes are thought to contribute. When many genes interact to create a single characteristic, the process is known as **polygenic transmission.** Other examples of polygenic traits include skin colour, personality traits (such as whether a person is likely to be adventurous), height, and weight (Clark & Grunstein, 2000; Ebstein, 2006).

LO2

Genes and the Environment

heritability
the extent to which a differences in a characteristic are influenced by genetics.

Traits clearly vary across individuals. For instance, if you take a look around at your lecture classroom you will see a huge range height and body weight amongst your classmates. To what extent are these height and weight differences influenced by genetics and environment? The degree to which variation within a group can be statistically accounted for by genetic differences is known as **heritability,** and is usually expressed numerically as the *heritability coefficient.* This number ranges between 0, (trait differences are due entirely to environment) to 1 (trait differences are due entirely to genes). Research shows that the heritability coefficient for height is about 0.8 (Weedon & Frayling, 2008), while that for weight is lower, approximately 0.6 (Silventoinen & Kapiro, 2008). Environmental factors such as diet and exercise affect weight much more than height.

But how do researchers conduct studies to determine heritability coefficients? In order to tease apart the role of genes and environment on behaviour experimentally, researchers would have to hold one of these factors constant while varying the other one. That is hard to do because, for obvious ethical reasons, researchers cannot assign people to grow up in the same or different environments. Nor can researchers assign people to be either genetically alike or different. Fortunately, nature does both of these things for us. In humans, researchers use twin studies, adoption studies, twin-adoption studies, and gene-by-environment studies to study heritability. Researchers take advantage of genetically similar and different people by studying twins, siblings, and unrelated individuals reared together or apart. Researchers using non-human animals have a greater degree of control over environmental conditions and can therefore ask more direct questions about the influence of environment on behaviour. Recent advances in genetic engineering techniques have also allowed the manipulation of the genome in animal models.

Twin Studies Most of us know or have known at least one set of twins. Maybe it is hard to tell them apart because they look identical, or maybe they're different genders and would never be mistaken for each other. **Fraternal twins** develop from two different eggs fertilized by two different sperm, as are any two siblings born at separate times. Because they develop from two fertilized eggs, or *zygotes,* they are also referred to as *dizygotic* twins. Thus, genetically speaking, fraternal twins are no more alike or different than are non-twin brothers and sisters. They may be of the same sex or of different sexes. **Identical twins** develop from a single fertilized egg that splits into two independent cells, and therefore are also referred to *monozygotic* twins. As a result, identical twins develop from embryos with identical genetic information, and they must be of the same sex.

fraternal twins
twins that develop from two different eggs fertilized by two different sperm.

identical twins
twins that develop from a single fertilized egg that splits into two independent cells.

Fraternal and identical twins provide a natural population for research to determine how much of a trait is due to genetics and how much is due to environment. The logic of **twin studies,** studies comparing pairs of fraternal and identical twins, is straightforward. Fraternal twins share half as many genes on average as identical twins (50 percent compared to 100 percent). If a trait is genetically influenced, identical twins should be more similar in that trait than fraternal twins will be. If genetics play no role, identical twins will be no more alike than fraternal twins in that specific trait.

twin studies
research into hereditary influence comparing pairs of fraternal and identical twins.

Adoption Studies Researchers have also studied adopted individuals and compared them to their biological and adoptive parents. Such studies are known as **adoption studies.** Adopted children share none of their genes but most of their environment with their adopted families. Offspring share 50 percent of their genes with each biological parent and none with their adoptive parents. Yet they share most of their environment with their adoptive parents and none (or little) with their biological parents. If environment is most influential, people will be more similar on a trait to their adoptive parents than to their biological parents. But if genetics is more influential, people will be more similar to their biological parents than to their adoptive parents. If both genetics and environment matter, people will display traits from their biological and adoptive parents. For example, an adoption study on intelligence would support the power of the environment over genetics if adopted children were more like their adoptive parents than their biological parents in intelligence. In contrast, if adopted children are more similar to their biological parents than adoptive parents in intelligence, we might conclude that genetics are more powerful.

adoption studies
research into hereditary influence in which adopted people are compared to their biological and adoptive parents.

twin-adoption studies
research into hereditary influence on twins, both identical and fraternal, who were raised apart (adopted) and who were raised together.

Twin-Adoption Studies A problem inherent in twin studies is that because identical twins look and act more alike than do fraternal twins, they may also be treated more similarly than regular siblings. Thus, it can be difficult to untangle genetic from environmental effects on any given outcome. In addition, a problem with adoption studies is that they only include people who are 50 percent genetically similar (biological parents and offspring) and those who are 0 percent similar (adoptive parents and adoptees)—not those who are genetically identical. The best solution to both of these problems is to study twins, both identical and fraternal, who were raised apart (adopted) and those who were raised together. This is exactly what **twin-adoption studies** do.

Twins form a natural population for teasing apart the influences of genetics and environment on development.

The logic of the twin-adoption approach is simple yet powerful. Identical twins are 100 percent alike genetically, whereas fraternal twins, like all siblings, share only 50 percent of their genes. Adopted children and their adoptive parents and siblings share no genes. If genes play a strong role in a trait, then the greater the genetic similarity, the greater the similarity on the trait should be. That is, similarity should be strongest in identical twins reared together and next in identical twins reared apart. It should be modest in siblings and biological parent–offspring reared together. Similarity should be weakest in adopted siblings and adoptive parent–offspring. As we will see in later chapters, this pattern holds for intelligence, mental disorders, and even personality, suggesting a moderately strong genetic component to these outcomes.

gene-by-environment interaction research
a method of studying heritability by comparing genetic markers, allowing researchers to assess how genetic differences interact with environment to produce certain behaviours in some people but not in others.

Connection
How do stress and abuse interact with genes to increase vulnerability to depression?
See Chapter 15, LO4.

Gene-by-Environment Studies A fourth technique in the study of heritability, **gene-by-environment interaction research,** allows researchers to assess how genetic differences interact with environment to produce certain behaviour in some people but not in others (Moffitt, Caspi, & Rutter, 2005). Instead of using twins, family members, and adoptees to vary genetic similarity, gene-by-environment studies directly measure genetic variation in parts of the genome itself and examine how such variation interacts with different kinds of environments to produce different behaviours. Individuals do not differ in whether or not they have a gene, but rather in the form that gene takes. For example, the same gene in different people might vary in the number of particular DNA sequences it has. Some DNA sequences are long in some people and short in others. Differences in the length of DNA sequences represent a *genetic marker*. Researchers first have to locate these genetic markers from blood or saliva samples. Then they assess crucial environmental experiences such as trauma and stress in people with and without the genetic marker. Finally, they determine whether individuals with the genetic marker who were raised in a particular environment are more or less likely to develop some trait, such as extraversion, violence, high intelligence, or schizophrenia. For example, genetic markers interact with a stressful environment to make depression more likely in some people than in others. Researchers report that people who have a short form of a specific DNA sequence linked to depression are more likely to become depressed when under great stress than are individuals who have the long form of the same DNA sequence (Caspi et al., 2003; Kendler et al., 2005).

Gene Manipulation in Non-human Animals Genetic engineering has enabled researchers to manipulate the genes in experimental animals in ways that are not possible in human studies. Researchers have a much higher degree of control of environmental conditions in animal research and recent techniques in molecular biology have allowed specific genes to be targeted, something that is not feasible (or ethical) in humans. There are a number of techniques used to investigate the role of genetics in specific behaviours, but usually involve one of two strategies: conditional manipulation of gene expression or permanent alteration of the genome.

antisense
a synthetic DNA sequence used to block the expression of a gene.

viral-mediated gene transfer
technique whereby a gene is packaged into a virus and injected into a brain region.

Gene manipulation usually involves inactivation or overexpression of the gene of interest. Inactivation can be done by manipulating the gene through the use of genetic sequences. One strategy is to inject a genetic sequence, called **antisense,** to block the gene from being translated into protein. If a specific gene plays a crucial role in a particular behaviour, then inactivation of this gene should lead to observable changes. For instance, *brain-derived neurotrophic factor,* or BDNF, is a brain protein thought to support memory processes, and inactivation of this gene with antisense methods produces memory impairment in rats (Seoane et al., 2010). Novel genes can be introduced by packaging the sequence of interest into a virus and introducing it into the brain, where the virus makes many copies of the gene. This **viral-mediated gene transfer** has been used to introduce genes implicated in human disorders into animal models. For instance, injection of the abnormal form of the human Huntington's gene into the rat brain produces neurodegeneration similar to that observed in the human disorder (de Almeida et al., 2002).

The second genetic engineering strategy, manipulation of the genome itself, is most often carried out in mice. Similar to the genetic manipulation techniques just described, changes to the genome usually involve inactivation of an existing gene or introduction of a new gene. The main difference is that genome manipulations in mice involve altering DNA sequences before conception, whereas antisense and viral-mediated techniques are usually carried out in adult animals. Therefore genome alterations are present not only in adulthood, but also throughout prenatal and postnatal development. Inactivation of a gene in this manner is called a **knockout,** while introduction of a novel gene (often of human origin) produces a **transgenic.** These mouse models have contributed a great deal our understanding of the influence of genes on behaviour. For instance, knockout mice that lack the appetite-suppressing hormone leptin are obese compared to control mice, largely due to overeating (Ahima et al., 1996). A rare form of this genetic deficiency is also found in humans, which also results in obesity and overeating (Dardeno et al., 2010). Introducing abnormal genes implicated in neurodegenerative disorders has led to the development of a number of transgenic mouse models of human disease, such as Huntington's disease and Alzheimer's disease, and has vastly increased our understanding of gene–environment interactions (Manelled & Chesselet, 2002; Elder et al., 2010).

knockout
an animal, usually a mouse, that has had a specific gene removed from its genome.

transgenic
an animal, usually a mouse, that has a foreign gene inserted into its genome.

Challenge Your Assumptions

True or False? Genes can be influenced by our experiences and behaviours.

True: Genes continue to get turned on or off throughout our lives by what we eat, drink, and are exposed to.

Epigenetics: How the Environment Changes Gene Expression

A third—and in many ways, the most important—principle of behavioural genetics is a relatively new one: Environmental events influence how and when genes are activated or deactivated. Genes can be changed by an individual's behaviours and experiences, and behaviours can be modified by genetic differences. This principle is seen most clearly in **epigenetics** (Rutter, 2006). Epigenetics concerns changes in the way genes get expressed—that is, are activated or deactivated—without changing the sequence of DNA. The food we eat, the drugs we take, and our exposure to certain chemicals in the environment are a few things that can have epigenetic consequences.

epigenetics
concerns changes in the way genes are turned on or off without a change in the sequence of DNA.

Currently, the most well-understood mechanism of epigenetic change involves the methylation process of DNA. Remarkably, when we eat or drink certain things, exercise, or are exposed to particular chemicals in the environment, molecular tags known as methyl groups can get attached to specific nucleotides in the DNA, often targeting cytosines (see Figure 3.3). These tags turn off particular genes, regardless of the actual genetic sequence around them.

Because of the need for detailed genetic analysis, epigenetic research tends to be conducted mostly with non-humans, such as rats and mice. Genetically obese rats pass their genes on to their offspring, who also tend to be obese. However, if obese rats are fed a specific diet (e.g., onions, beets, and garlic), they remain obese, but tend to have offspring that are normal weight. It turns out that particular diets can actually affect gene expression by turning on switches that attach to DNA and turn on or off the gene. This result offers a compelling illustration of epigenetics.

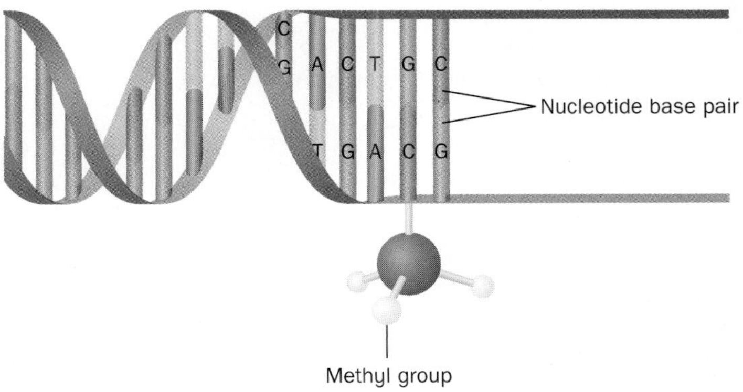

FIGURE **3.3**

DNA METHYLATION. Methyl groups tag DNA at particular sites. These tags act as off switches and silence genes. Incredibly, these methyl group tags come about purely by what happens to us—our diet, drugs, or exposure to certain chemicals. Genes, therefore, are not destiny but simply a starting point for biological structures.

The field of study known as epigenetics examines how experience can turn genes on or off.

What implications does this have for what we eat, drink, and are exposed to early in life?

An equally compelling example of epigenetics is the effect of parental nurturing on gene expression. Nurturing behaviour in rats can produce calmer, less-stressed offspring because of changes in the way that particular stress genes get expressed (Weaver, Cervoini, & Champagne, 2004). Rats that lick their offspring (a nurturing behaviour) set in motion changes that produce less-stressed pups. Licking turns on biochemical pathways that allow for enhanced expression of receptors that terminate the stress response in the growing brains of rat pups. Increasing the numbers of these stress receptors makes these pups calmer and less likely to become startled (Watters, 2006). Although it is not feasible to experimentally manipulate parental care in humans (it would not be ethical to randomly assign children to receive low parental care), these findings in rats have been also observed in correlational studies in humans. Researchers at Carleton University in Ottawa have found that shy children were more likely to suffer from stressful reactions (anxiety and loneliness) during their first year of school if their mothers had *fretful* parenting styles compared to shy children whose mothers were more *warm* and *supportive* (Coplan et al., 2008). More extreme cases of low parental care have revealed that early life experiences can have effects on how genes are expressed, much the same as observed in rats. Studies by Michael Meaney's group at McGill University have found that the brains of suicide victims who experience childhood abuse contained fewer of the stress-termination receptors than those who did not experience abuse as children (McGowan et al., 2009). These findings suggest that early life experiences can have long-lasting effects on gene expression.

Quick Quiz 3.1: Genes and Behaviour

1. Genes occur in pairs, or alternate forms of each other, called
   a. chromosomes.
   b. alleles.
   c. base-pairs.
   d. ribosomes.
2. Which people share 0 percent genetic similarity?
   a. pairs of monozygotic twins
   b. pairs of dizygotic twins
   c. adoptive parents and their adoptive children
   d. siblings
3. Nurturing behaviour in rats can produce calmer, less-stressed offspring because of changes in genes that are involved in stress reactions. This is an example of
   a. epigenetics.
   b. genetic engineering.
   c. recessive genes.
   d. dominant genes.

Answers can be found at the end of the chapter.

THE NERVOUS SYSTEM

The human genome contains an estimated 25 000 to 35 000 genes, about *half* of which code for proteins expressed in the brain (Rutter, 2006). The functions of most of these genes are not yet known, but researchers have begun to discover that some of these genes are critical to normal brain development and function. Recall that the neurodegenerative disorder Huntington's disease is caused by a mutation to a single gene. Abnormalities in other brain genes can lead to even more profound impairments, such as an overall reduction in brain size, called *microcephaly,* caused by a mutation in the oddly named gene *sonic hedgehog* (Gilbert et al., 2005). Ultimately, the integrity of the nervous system is critical to everything we experience and do. All voluntary actions and automatic processes of the body result from the activity of nerve cells, which are organized in a net of circuits far more complex than any electrical system you could imagine. Let's look at the organization and basic elements of the nervous system and at how the nervous system transmits information.

LO3 LO4

Organization of the Nervous System

The human nervous system has two main parts and several components, as depicted in Figure 3.4. It is divided into the **central nervous system (CNS),** which includes the brain and spinal cord, and the **peripheral nervous system (PNS),** which consists of all the other nerve cells in the body. The peripheral nervous system includes the somatic nervous system and the autonomic nervous system. The **somatic nervous system** is made up of nerves that innervate skeletal muscle, which control voluntary movement, as well as those involved in the reception sensory information from the external environment, such as vision and hearing. The **autonomic nervous system (ANS)** serves the involuntary systems of the body, such as the internal organs and glands.

Autonomic means "self-governing," and to a large extent the structures served by the autonomic nervous system control bodily processes over which we have little conscious control, such as changes in heart rate and blood pressure. The ANS has two main branches: the **sympathetic nervous system** and the **parasympathetic nervous system.** The nerves of these systems control muscles in organs such as the stomach, small intestine, and bladder and in glands such as the sweat glands. The sympathetic branch of the ANS is responsible for what the physiologist Walter Cannon (1939) labelled the *flight-or-fight response;* that is, it activates bodily systems in times of emergency. The main function of the sympathetic nervous system is activating the body, for example, by increasing the

central nervous system (CNS) the part of the nervous system that comprises the brain and spinal cord.

peripheral nervous system (PNS) the part of the nervous system that comprises all the nerve cells in the body outside the central nervous system.

somatic nervous system peripheral motor nerves involved in control of voluntary movement as well as sensory nerves involved in the reception of stimuli from the external environment.

autonomic nervous system (ANS) all the nerves of the peripheral nervous system that serve involuntary systems of the body, such as the internal organs and glands.

sympathetic nervous system the branch of the autonomic nervous system that activates bodily systems in times of emergency.

parasympathetic nervous system the branch of the autonomic nervous system that usually relaxes or returns the body to a less active, restful state.

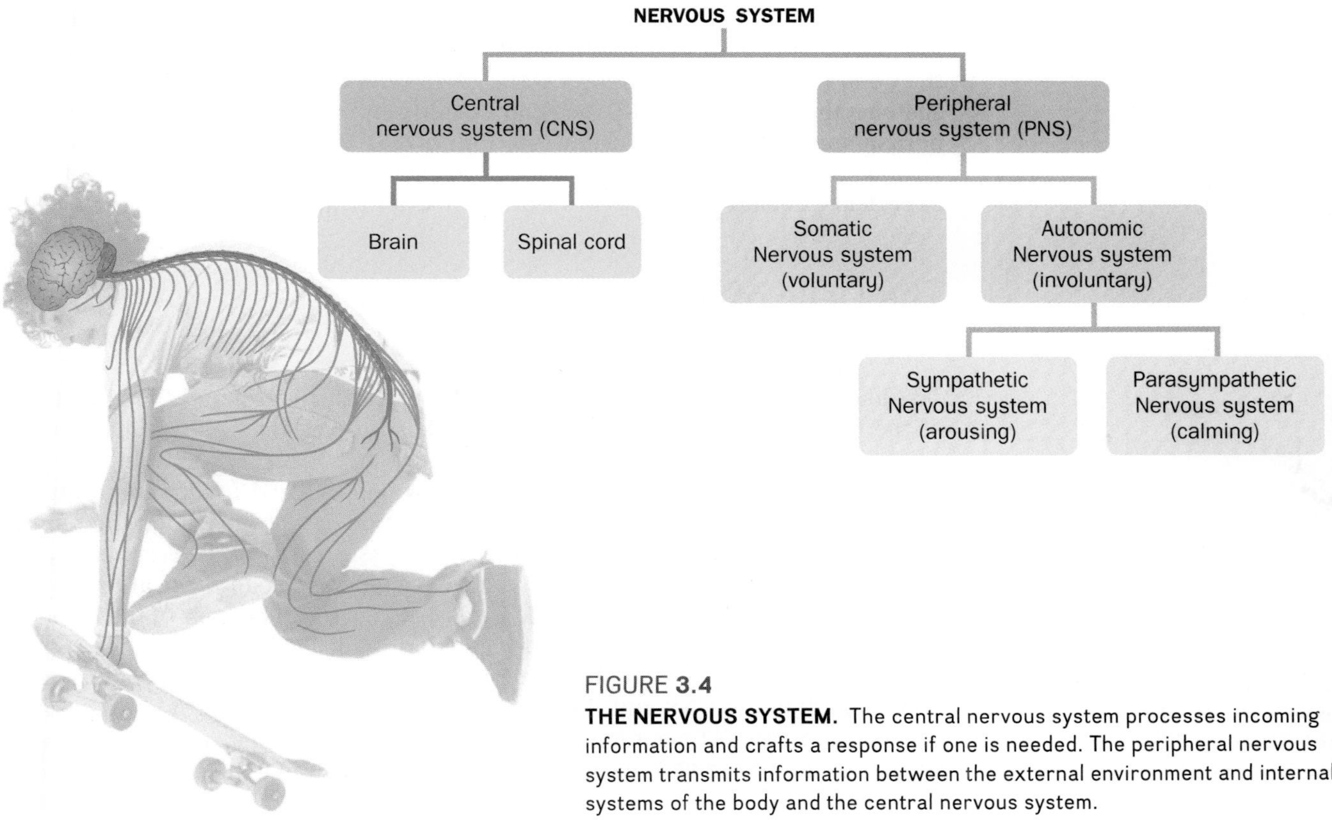

FIGURE **3.4**

THE NERVOUS SYSTEM. The central nervous system processes incoming information and crafts a response if one is needed. The peripheral nervous system transmits information between the external environment and internal systems of the body and the central nervous system.

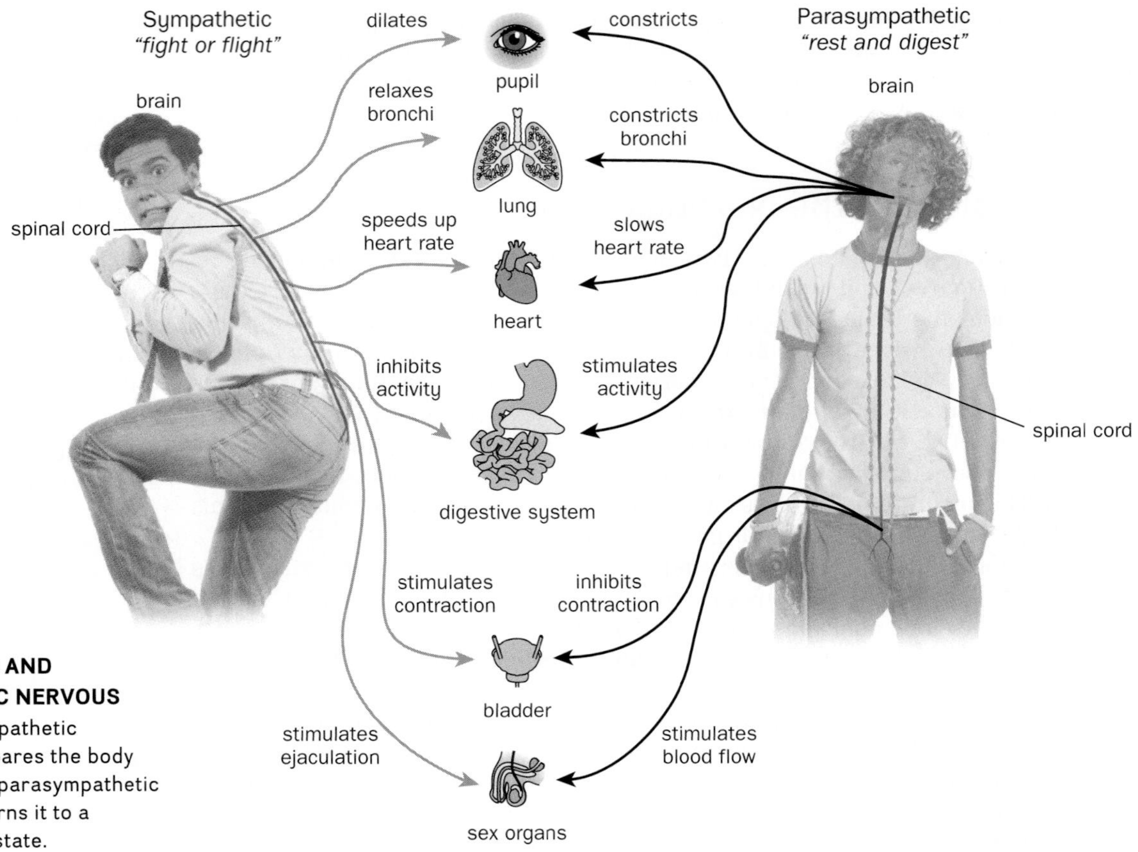

FIGURE **3.5**
THE SYMPATHETIC AND PARASYMPATHETIC NERVOUS SYSTEMS. The sympathetic nervous system prepares the body for action, while the parasympathetic nervous system returns it to a relaxed and resting state.

heart rate, dilating the pupils of the eyes, or inhibiting digestion. The function of the parasympathetic branch of the ANS is largely one of relaxation, or returning the body to a less active, restful state, often referred to as *rest and digest.* The systems that are aroused by the sympathetic nervous system are relaxed by the parasympathetic nervous system (see Figure 3.5). Because of its effects on these various bodily systems, the ANS produces many of the physical sensations we experience during emotional arousal, such as a racing heart or sweaty palms.

The Cells of the Nervous System: Glial Cells and Neurons

Just like any other body tissue or organ, the basic structural and functional unit of the nervous system is the cell. What makes the nervous system unique is its remarkable diversity of cell types (Emery & Barres, 2008). The liver has only five different types of cells, each with its own specialized function and unique shape. In comparison, there are hundreds of different cell types identified in the brain, spinal cord, and PNS (Masland, 2004). Classification of different cell types in the nervous system is often based upon shape, and some of these are shown in Figure 3.6. Despite the seemingly infinite assortment of types, cells of the CNS and PNS can be broadly classified into two categories: glial cells and neurons.

glial cells
central nervous system cells that provide structural support, promote efficient communication between neurons, and serve as scavengers, removing cellular debris.

Glia is the Greek word for glue. Indeed, **glial cells** serve the primary function of holding the CNS and PNS together. Specifically, they provide structural support, promote efficient communication between neurons, and remove cellular debris (Kandel, 2000). We now know that they also play an important role in communication between neurons as well (Allen & Barres, 2005; Pfrieger, 2002).

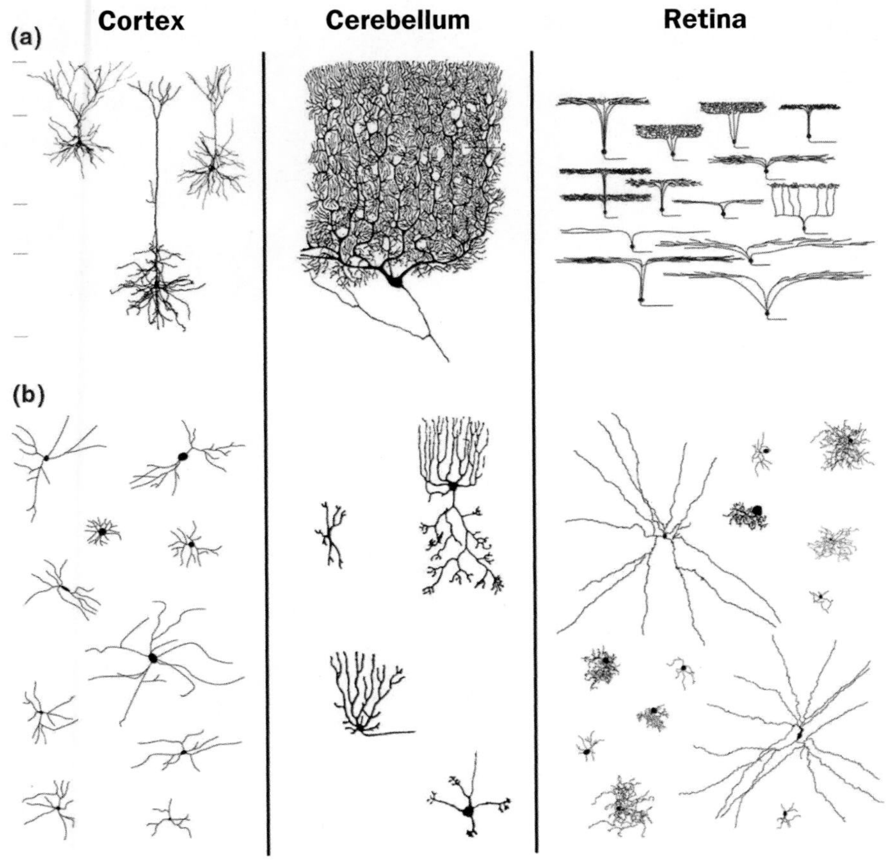

FIGURE 3.6
DIVERSITY OF CELLS IN THE NERVOUS SYSTEM. Neuron types for three regions of the nervous system: the cortex and cerebellum (CNS), and the retina (PNS). Neurons that communicate with other distant regions (a) are usually larger than those that communicate locally (b). (From Masland, R.H. (2004). Neuronal cell types. *Current Biology, 14;* R496–500.)

Different types of glial cells carry out specialized functions, and like neurons, are often classified based upon their shape. The importance of glial cells in nervous system functioning is highlighted by their sheer abundance; in fact, about 90 percent of the cells in the brain are glial (Ndubaku & de Bellard, 2008).

Neurons are the cells that process and transmit information throughout the nervous system. Within the brain, neurons receive, integrate, and generate messages. By most estimates, there are more than 10 billion neurons in the human brain. Each neuron has approximately 10 000 connections to other neurons, making for literally trillions and trillions of neural connections in the human brain (Nauta & Feirtag, 1979; Hyman, 2005). Thus, it is understandable that some scientists consider the human brain to be the one of the most complex structures in the known universe. In order to learn how neurons communicate with each other, it is critical to understand the structure of an individual neuron and how each of its parts contributes to the reception and transmission of information in the nervous system.

neurons
the cells that process and transmit information in the nervous system.

LO5 LO6

The Structure and Types of Neurons Whereas most cells in the body have a round shape, neurons are spidery, with long branches and projections (see Figure 3.6). Neurons are so small they cannot be seen with the naked eye, and only a strong microscope can magnify them enough to be viewed and described. In the late 1800s, the Spanish anatomist Santiago Ramón y Cajal deciphered the precise nature and structure of nerve cells, which he named neurons. Cajal was an artist who, while studying anatomy for his drawing, became fascinated by the structure of the body. He then went on to study medicine. His ability to see, imagine, and draw came together in his observations of the neuron. It was Cajal who identified the three major parts of the neuron: cell body, dendrites, and axon. Indeed, Cajal's original sketch of these structures was an amazingly accurate representation.

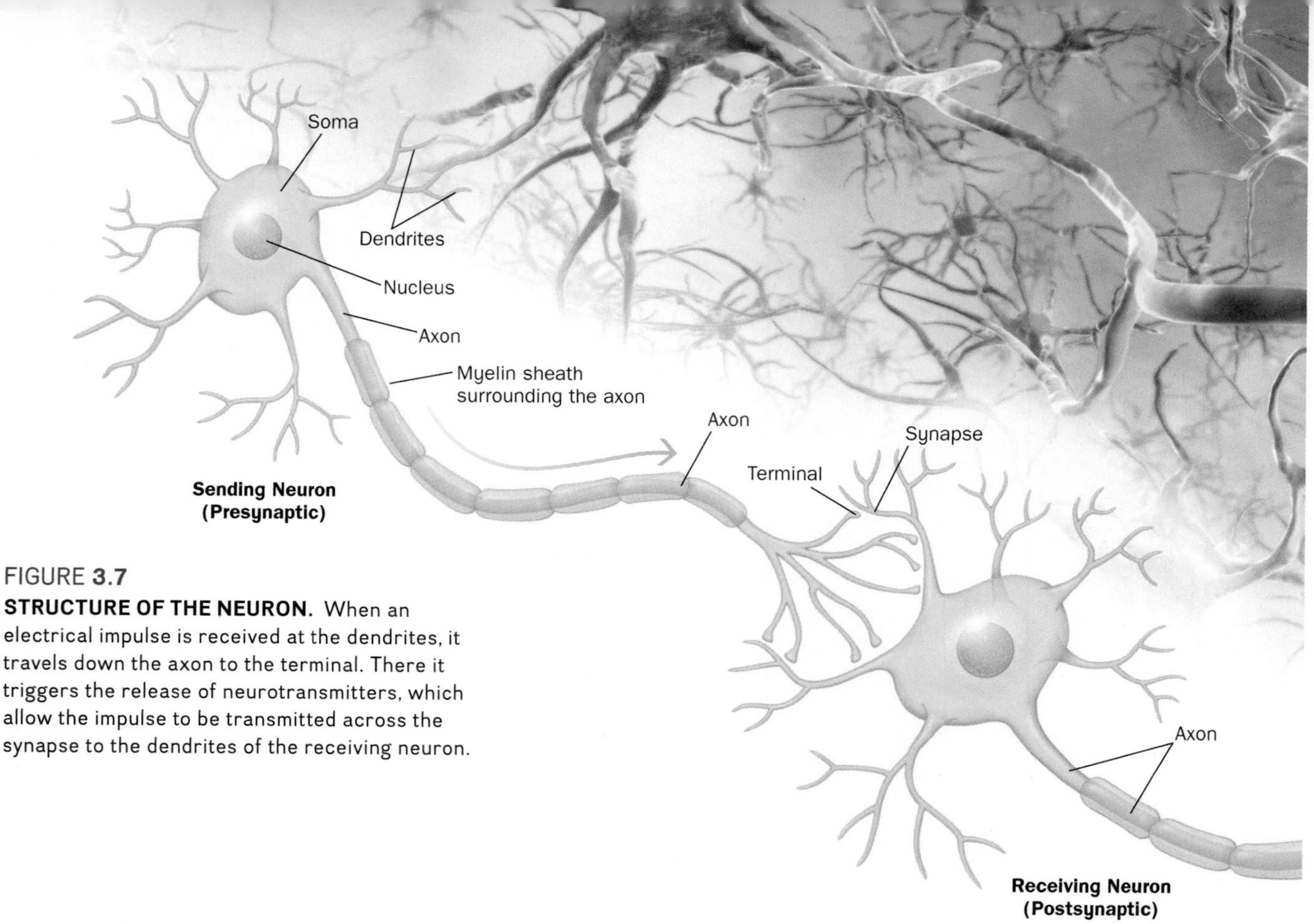

FIGURE **3.7**

STRUCTURE OF THE NEURON. When an electrical impulse is received at the dendrites, it travels down the axon to the terminal. There it triggers the release of neurotransmitters, which allow the impulse to be transmitted across the synapse to the dendrites of the receiving neuron.

soma
the cell body of the neuron.

dendrites
finger-like projections from a neuron's soma that receive messages from other neurons.

axon
a long projection that extends from a neuron's soma; it transmits electrical impulses toward target neurons.

myelin sheath
the fatty substance wrapped around some axons, which insulates the axon, making the nerve impulse travel more efficiently.

oligodendrocyte
a type of glial cell that myelinates axons in the CNS.

Schwann cell
a type of glial cell that myelinates axons in the PNS.

As in other cells, the cell body, or **soma,** of the neuron contains a *nucleus* and other components needed for cell maintenance and function (see Figure 3.7). Within the nucleus itself are the genes that direct neural change and growth. Extending from the soma are the **dendrites,** finger-like projections that receive incoming messages from other neurons. On the opposite side of the soma is a long projection called the **axon,** which transmits electrical impulses toward the adjacent neuron. Although messages can be received at the soma or axon, the dendrites, with their branched shape, are the best equipped at receiving messages.

The axons of some neurons are wrapped in a fatty **myelin sheath,** which insulates the axon at regular intervals along its length. Myelin is made by two types of glial cells: **oligodendrocytes** found in the CNS (Tomassy & Fossati, 2014) and **Schwann cells** found in the PNS (Beirowski, 2013). The uninsulated gaps, called **nodes of Ranvier,** are situated between segments of myelin and together they allow the neuronal impulse to travel more quickly down the axon. Since the electrical impulse cannot travel along the myelinated segments of axon, the impulse skips from node to node, allowing the impulse to travel more quickly to target neurons. Myelin is white in colour, so the term *white matter* refers to parts of the nervous system that contain myelinated axons while *grey matter* refers to those made up of cell bodies, dendrites, and small unmyelinated neurons. The process of *myelination* is a gradual one that starts before birth and continues into early adulthood (Fields, 2008). The neurological disorder multiple sclerosis is a result of the body's immune system mistakenly destroying myelin, which interferes with the transmission of electrical signals along neurons. This results in symptoms such as muscle weakness, dizziness, and problems with vision.

The specialized junction between the axon and the adjacent neuron is known as the **synapse,** and is the site of communication between a neuron and its target.

At the end of the axon, at each synapse, is a **terminal** (also called a *terminal button*) containing tiny sacs of neurotransmitters. When an electrical impulse reaches the terminal, it triggers the release of neurotransmitter molecules into the gap between neurons, known as the *synaptic cleft*. This gap is tiny, only 20 nm wide, which is 0.00002 mm (Lucić et al., 2005; Zuber et al., 2005). (Keep in mind that 1 mm is about the thickness of the side of dime). It is here at the synaptic cleft where the neurotransmitter carries the signal to the next neuron. The neuron *before* the synaptic cleft is called the **presynaptic neuron** and it releases neurotransmitter. The neuron *after* the synaptic cleft is referred to as the **postsynaptic neuron** and its membrane contains receptors that bind to released neurotransmitter.

There are three kinds of neurons: sensory neurons, motor neurons, and interneurons. **Sensory neurons** receive incoming sensory information from the external environment via the sense organs (eyes, ears, skin, tongue, and nose). Anything you see, hear, touch, taste, or smell activates sensory neurons, which take the message to the CNS for processing. **Motor neurons** take commands from the brain and carry them to the muscles and glands of the body. Each time you move any muscle in your body, intentionally or unintentionally, motor neurons are at work. Motor neurons are also responsible for initiating hormone release from endocrine glands.

Interneurons communicate only with other neurons. Most interneurons connect neurons in one part of the brain with neurons in another part. Others receive information from sensory neurons and transmit it to motor neurons for action. So if you touched a sharp object, interneurons in the spinal cord would receive pain information from sensory neurons in your fingers and communicate it to motor neurons in the muscles of your arm so that you could pull your hand away. Interneurons are the most common kind of neuron in the brain, outnumbering sensory and motor neurons by at least ten to one (Nauta & Feirtag, 1979).

nodes of Ranvier
uninsulated gaps between segments of myelin; the neuronal impulse travels by skipping from node to node, increasing the speed of conduction.

synapse
the junction between an axon and the adjacent neuron, where information is transmitted from one neuron to another.

terminals
little knobs at the end of the axon that contain tiny sacs of neurotransmitters.

presynaptic neuron
the neuron on the sending side of a synapse, it releases neurotransmitter.

postsynaptic neuron
the neuron on the receiving side of the synapse, neurotransmitters bind to receptors on its membrane.

sensory neurons
nerve cells that receive incoming sensory information from the sense organs (eye, ear, skin, tongue, nose).

motor neurons
nerve cells that carry commands for movement from the brain to the muscles of the body.

interneurons
neurons that communicate only with other neurons.

LO7 Neuronal Communication

Most neuronal connections are arranged in networks, with many axons travelling together to common targets. Some networks are quite complex, involving thousands of neurons located across the CNS and PNS. Some are much simpler, such as the spinal network responsible for the pain-withdrawal reflex just described. Regardless, information always travels in one direction in the neuron—from the dendrites to the soma to the axon to the synapses.

All neurons essentially have two important jobs: (1) to transmit a message to its target neuron across synapse and (2) to transmit message along the neuron itself. These two distinct tasks involve two special types of electrochemical signals, **graded potentials,** which result from chemical communication at the synapse and **action potentials,** which allow the signal to travel from the neuronal dendrites and soma, along the axon and to the terminal. Chemical messengers, called **neurotransmitters,** are released from the terminal into the synaptic cleft and generate graded potentials in postsynaptic neurons. These graded potentials can in turn trigger action potentials, which stimulate neurotransmitter release from the terminal. In a normally functioning nervous system, these processes are happening continuously as messages get passed along the length of the neuron and then from one neuron to another. Therefore, it is possible to think of these processes as a cycle (see Figure 3.8).

The whole neuron, like any other cell, is enveloped by a fatty cell membrane. Membranes of neurons are specialized in that they contain special channels that allow the passage of charged particles, called **ions,** which are present in fluid inside and outside of the cell. Ions are important because they are the basis of electrical signalling in neurons; the movement of these ions through membrane channels is how charge is propagated throughout the nervous system. Although

graded potential
small electrical signals generated at the synapse by neurotransmitters; can trigger action potentials.

action potential
electrical signal that travels along the length of the neuron; stimulates neurotransmitter release.

neurotransmitters
chemicals that transmit information between neurons.

ions
particles that carry electrical charge; found both inside and outside cells.

Sensory and motor neurons make this Frisbee catch possible, while improvement in performance after extensive practice is dependent upon interneurons in the brain.

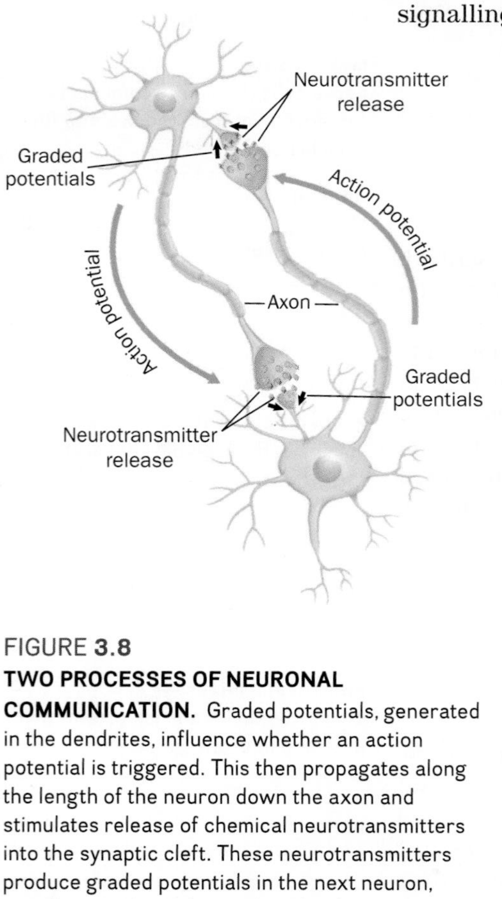

FIGURE **3.8**
TWO PROCESSES OF NEURONAL COMMUNICATION. Graded potentials, generated in the dendrites, influence whether an action potential is triggered. This then propagates along the length of the neuron down the axon and stimulates release of chemical neurotransmitters into the synaptic cleft. These neurotransmitters produce graded potentials in the next neuron, usually at synapses located on dendrites.

there are many different types, there are five particularly important in neuronal signalling. Positively charged sodium ions (Na^+) and negatively charged chloride (Cl^-) ions are more abundant in the fluid outside the cell, while positively charged potassium (K^+) and negatively charged protein molecules (A^-) are more abundant inside the cell. Calcium (Ca^{2+}) is more concentrated outside the cell and is important at the terminal for neurotransmitter release (see Figure 3.9(a)). The unequal distribution of these ions across the neuronal cell membrane creates a force called a **concentration gradient,** which promotes movement of the ions to equalize their distribution. When opportunities to cross the membrane occur, ions will move along their concentration gradients from areas of high concentration to low concentration.

In addition to the force created by the concentration gradient, the uneven distribution of ions also creates an **electrical gradient,** which promotes the movement of ions in a direction that equalizes the charge across the membrane. There is a difference in charge inside the cell compared to outside the cell at all times. In the resting state—that is, when no impulse is being transmitted—there is an excess of negatively charged particles inside the axon. The fluid outside the axon has a positive charge. This charge difference between the inside and outside of the neuron is known as a *potential.* When a neuron is in the resting state, the electrical charge difference between the inside and the outside of the axon is −70 millivolts (mV), where the minus sign indicates that the difference in charge is negative. This value is the **resting potential** of the neuronal membrane.

Since ions cannot pass directly through the fatty interior of the membrane, ion movement only occurs with the opening of specialized pores in the membrane, called *ion channels* (see Figure 3.9(b)). Most channels remain closed at the resting potential, and therefore the combined driving forces of the concentration and electrical gradients cannot result in ion movement. Some channels, called *transmitter-dependent*

(a)

Substance	Symbol	Charge	Location
Proteins	A^-	negative	inside
Potassium	K^+	positive	more inside
Sodium	Na^+	positive	more outside
Chloride	Cl^-	negative	more outside
Calcium	Ca^{2+}	positive	more outside

(b)

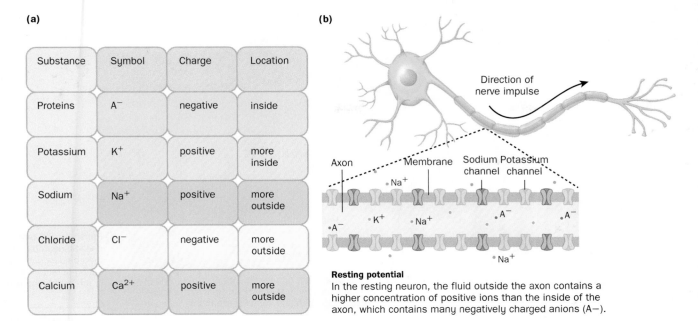

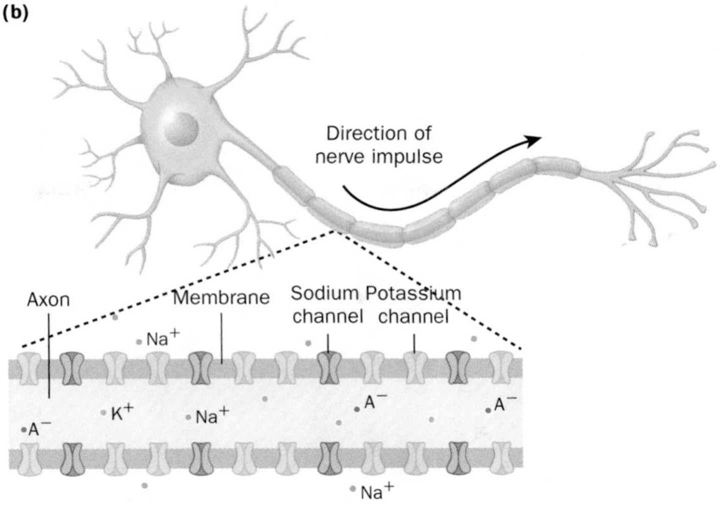

Resting potential
In the resting neuron, the fluid outside the axon contains a higher concentration of positive ions than the inside of the axon, which contains many negatively charged anions (A−).

FIGURE **3.9**

DISTRIBUTION OF IONS ACROSS THE NEURONAL MEMBRANE. (a) Ions are differentially distributed across the membrane. The resting potential of the neuron is −70 mV, meaning that the inside is slightly more negative than the outside of the cell. (b) Cross-section of an axon depicting the ion channels for sodium and potassium. Note that most of the ion channels are closed at rest.

channels, will open when a specific neurotransmitter binds to a site on the channel. Others, called *voltage-dependent channels,* open when there is a change in the electrical potential across the neuron. As you will learn in the next two sections, each of these have their own unique role in controlling the ion movement necessary for neurons to talk to each other.

concentration gradient
the difference in the concentration of different ions across the neuronal cell membrane; creates a driving force for ion movement.

electrical gradient
the difference in charge across the neuronal cell membrane; it creates a driving force for ion movement.

resting potential
the difference in electrical charge between the inside and outside of the axon when the neuron is at rest.

synaptic vesicles
tiny sacs in the terminal that contain neurotransmitters.

Communication between Neurons: Graded Potentials

The transfer of a message between neurons begins with neurotransmitter release from the presynaptic neuron. Although presynaptic terminals can form synapses with any part of the postsynaptic neuron, such the soma and axon, they are mostly found on the branches of dendrites. Neurotransmitters are packaged in sacs called **synaptic vesicles** in the presynaptic terminal, and are released into the synaptic cleft, where they bind to receptors on the dendrites of adjacent neurons (Schwartz, 2000). There are different types of neurotransmitters, each of which binds only with a specific receptor. For example, some receptors bind only with the neurotransmitter acetylcholine. If other neurotransmitters come in contact with acetylcholine receptors, they will not bind to them and no signal will be transmitted. Many receptors contain transmitter-gated ion channels, and once bound to a neurotransmitter that "fits" its shape, will open ion channels in the postsynaptic membrane (see Figure 3.10).

Depending upon the type of receptor on the postsynaptic dendrite, there are two possible changes that occur in the neuron's cell membrane—excitation or inhibition. Excitatory receptors allow the passage of ions that make the inside of the neuron more positive than its resting potential of −70 mV, a change referred to as **depolarization.** Receptors for the neurotransmitter glutamate are excitatory and allow ions like Na^+ and Ca^{2+} to enter the cell along their concentration and electrical gradients. When they enter the cell, they bring their positive charge with them. Inhibitory receptors, such as those for the neurotransmitter GABA, allow the passage of ions such as Cl^-, making the inside of the cell more negative than its resting potential, referred to as a **hyperpolarization.**

depolarization
a change in the membrane potential of a neuron so that the inside of the cell becomes less negative.

hyperpolarization
a change in the membrane potential of a neuron so that the inside of the cell becomes more negative.

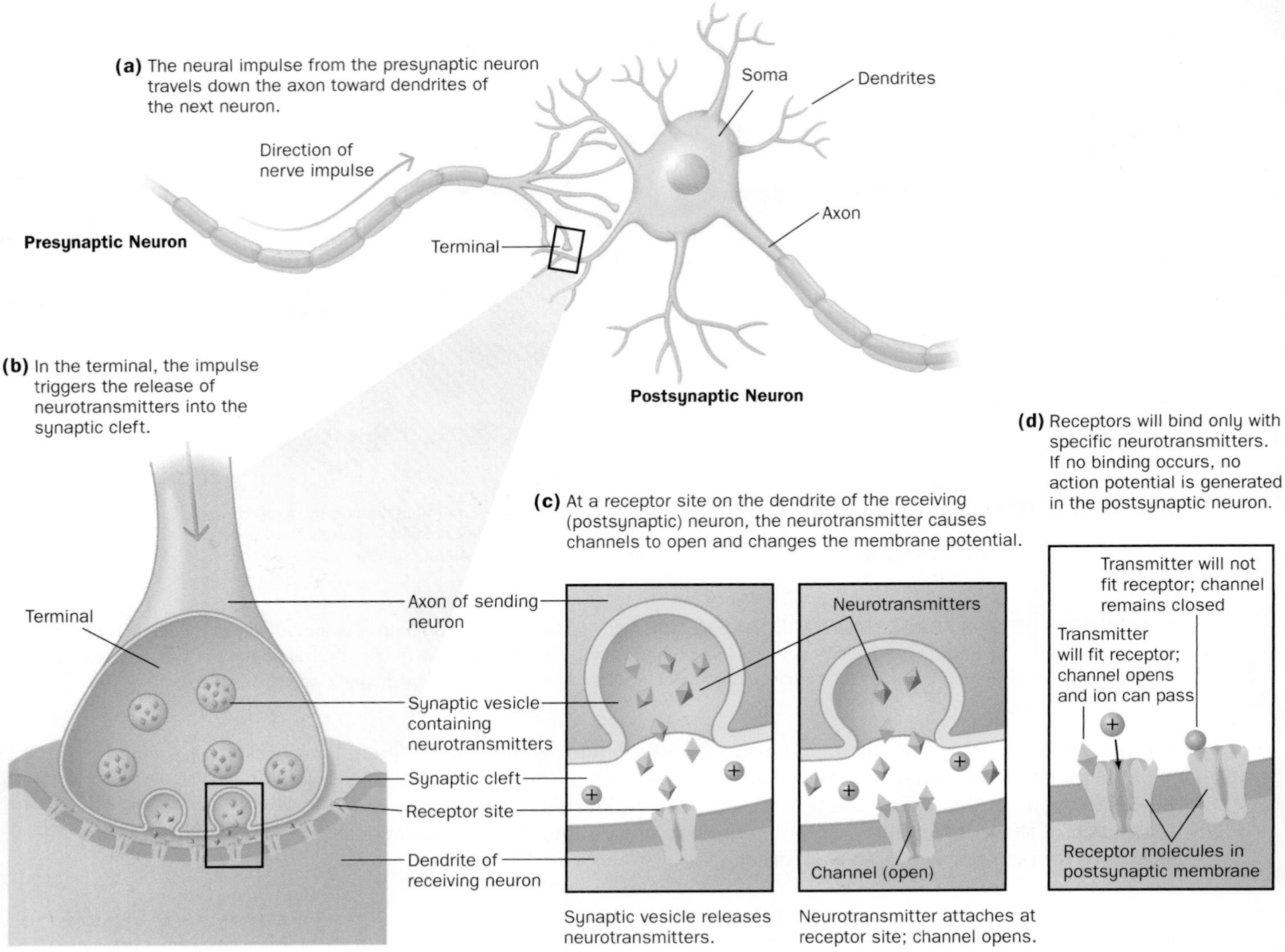
(a) The neural impulse from the presynaptic neuron travels down the axon toward dendrites of the next neuron.
Direction of nerve impulse
Soma
Dendrites
Axon
Presynaptic Neuron
Terminal
Postsynaptic Neuron
(b) In the terminal, the impulse triggers the release of neurotransmitters into the synaptic cleft.
Terminal
Axon of sending neuron
Synaptic vesicle containing neurotransmitters
Synaptic cleft
Receptor site
Dendrite of receiving neuron
(c) At a receptor site on the dendrite of the receiving (postsynaptic) neuron, the neurotransmitter causes channels to open and changes the membrane potential.
Neurotransmitters
Channel (open)
Synaptic vesicle releases neurotransmitters.
Neurotransmitter attaches at receptor site; channel opens.
(d) Receptors will bind only with specific neurotransmitters. If no binding occurs, no action potential is generated in the postsynaptic neuron.
Transmitter will not fit receptor; channel remains closed
Transmitter will fit receptor; channel opens and ion can pass
Receptor molecules in postsynaptic membrane

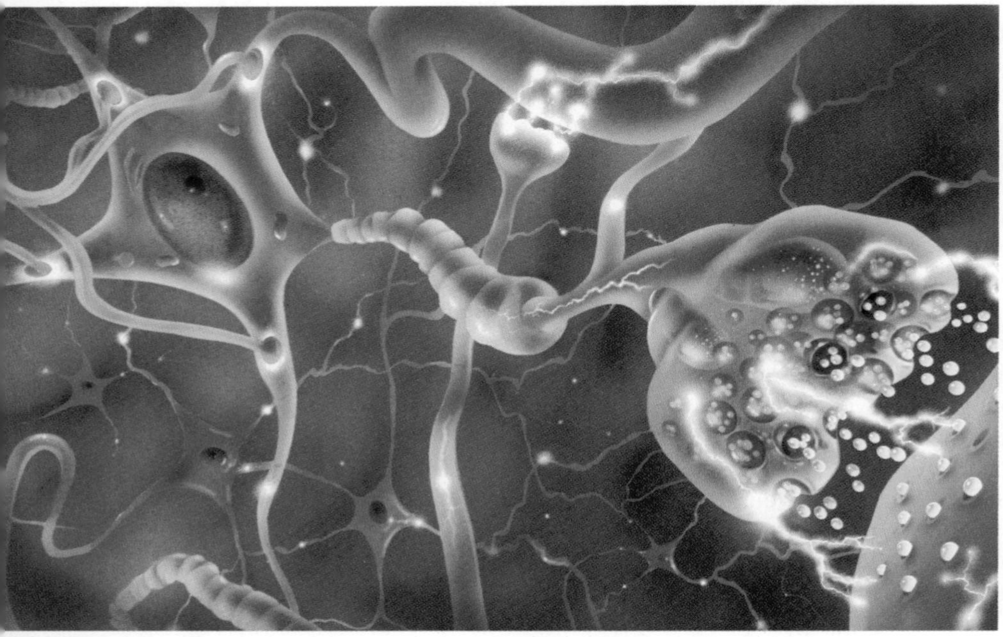

FIGURE **3.10**
HOW SYNAPSES AND NEUROTRANSMITTERS WORK. In (a) the presynaptic neuron forms a synapse with the postsynaptic neuron; however, the neurons do not touch at the synaptic cleft. In (b) the synapse has been enlarged to show the synaptic vesicles that carry neurotransmitters. They release neurotransmitters into the cleft where they bind to receptor sites on the postsynaptic neuron. In (c) we see a further enlargement of the neurotransmitters being released into the synaptic cleft and binding to receptor sites in the postsynaptic neuron. To the left is a three-dimensional artistic interpretation of neurons in the brain.

The small changes in the membrane potential that occur from transmitter-dependent channels are graded potentials and on their own make only very small changes in the postsynaptic cell. However, neurotransmitter release results in many molecules binding to many postsynaptic receptors. The combined effect of many graded potentials can alter the membrane potential enough so that an action potential is generated and the message can be relayed down the axon to the terminal, and therefore on to the next neuron. Graded potentials increase or decrease the likelihood of an action potential occurring by influencing whether or not the resting membrane potential reaches its **threshold** of −55 mV (Kole & Stuart, 2008). The excitatory potentials bring the neuron closer to threshold (by making the potential more positive), while the inhibitory potentials bring it further away from threshold (by making the potential more negative). The soma in the postsynaptic neuron *integrates* the graded potentials that the postsynaptic neuron receives from its many synapses. If the integrated message from these graded potentials depolarizes the axon enough to cross the threshold, then an action potential will occur.

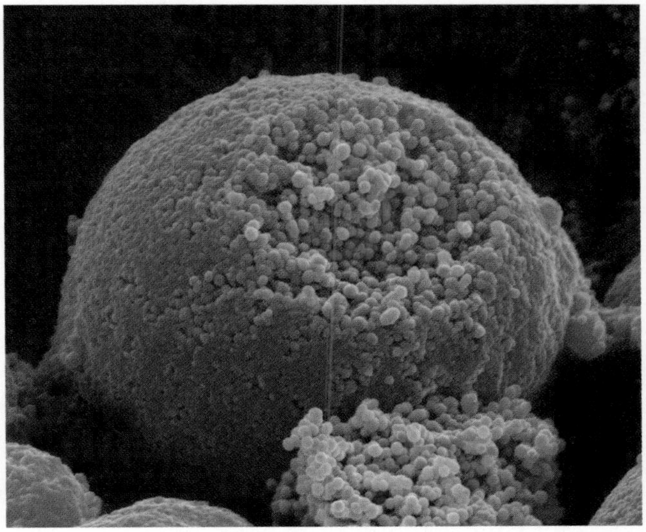

In this image taken by a scanning electron microscope, we see an axon terminal that has been broken to show vesicles (coloured balls). Neurotransmitters reside in the vesicles.

LO8 LO9

Communication within Neurons: The Action Potential In order for a message to get passed on to the next neuron in a network, a signal received at the dendrite must travel to the neuron's terminal. In some neurons, like the motor neuron that runs from your spinal cord to your big toe, this can be up to a metre away. Therefore, graded potentials generate a different type of electrical signal to send information across great distances. Action potentials are waves of depolarization followed by hyperpolarization, which travel at full strength along the length of the neuron. Unlike graded potentials, which can vary in size depending upon the number of receptors activated by neurotransmitter, action potentials are fixed in size. Therefore stronger signals are reflected by a higher number of action potentials, rather than in size of the signal itself (Hodgkin & Huxley, 1939).

threshold
membrane potential of −55 mV, necessary for the generation of an action potential.

The link between graded potentials and action potentials is the presence of voltage-dependent sodium channels present on the axon. These channels are the basis of the neuron's threshold, since they are sensitive to a voltage change and open when the membrane potential rises to −55 mV. If incoming graded potentials depolarize the neuron enough to reach this threshold, the neuron becomes *depolarized* and fires an action potential. The opening of sodium channels in the axon allows positively charged sodium ions pour into the cell, which move along their concentration and electrical gradients (see Figure 3.11a). The influx of sodium leads to a brief spike in positive charge, raising the membrane potential from −70 mV to +40 mV. This surge in positive charge is the first part of the action potential (see Figure 3.11c).

Two important changes occur at this point in the action potential; at a membrane potential of +40 mV, the sodium channels close and voltage-dependent potassium channels open (see Figure 3.11b). At this positive membrane potential, there is pressure from both the concentration and electrical gradients to drive potassium out of the cell. As positively charged potassium ions flow out of the cell, the membrane potential becomes hyperpolarized and returns to its resting state of −70 mV. While the neuron is returning to its resting state, it temporarily becomes super negatively charged. During this brief period, known as the **refractory period,** the neuron cannot generate another action potential.

refractory period
the span of time, after an action potential has been generated, when the neuron is returning to its resting state and the neuron cannot generate an action potential.

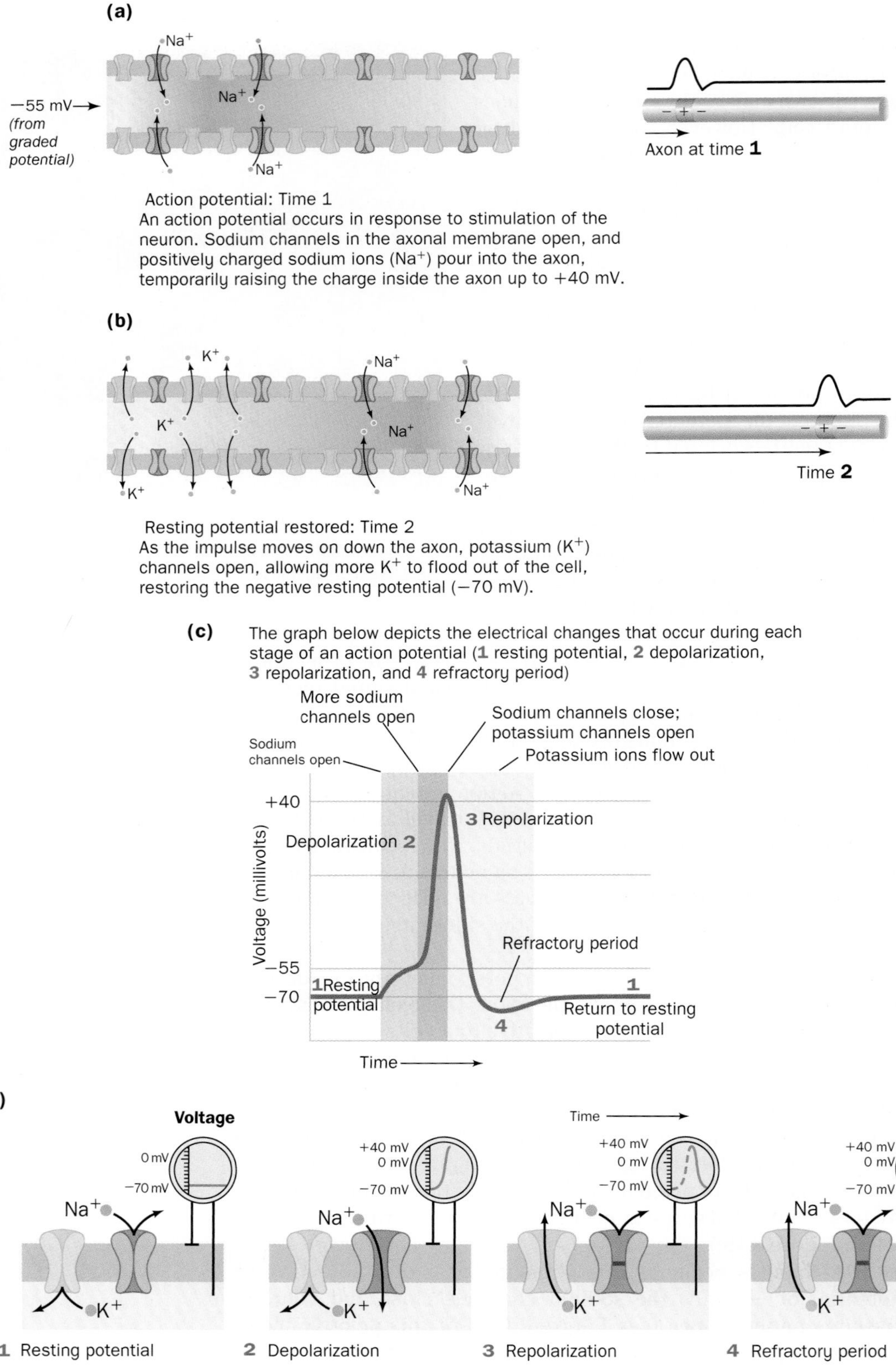
(a)
Na+
Na+
Na+
−55 mV
(from graded potential)
Axon at time 1
Action potential: Time 1
An action potential occurs in response to stimulation of the neuron. Sodium channels in the axonal membrane open, and positively charged sodium ions (Na+) pour into the axon, temporarily raising the charge inside the axon up to +40 mV.
(b)
K+
K+
K+
Na+
Na+
Na+
Time 2
Resting potential restored: Time 2
As the impulse moves on down the axon, potassium (K+) channels open, allowing more K+ to flood out of the cell, restoring the negative resting potential (−70 mV).
(c)
The graph below depicts the electrical changes that occur during each stage of an action potential (1 resting potential, 2 depolarization, 3 repolarization, and 4 refractory period)
More sodium channels open
Sodium channels close; potassium channels open
Sodium channels open
Potassium ions flow out
+40
3 Repolarization
Depolarization 2
Voltage (millivolts)
Refractory period
−55
−70
1 Resting potential
1
Return to resting potential
4
Time
(d)
Voltage
Time
0 mV
−70 mV
+40 mV
Na+
K+
1 Resting potential
2 Depolarization
3 Repolarization
4 Refractory period

FIGURE 3.11

MEMBRANE AND VOLTAGE CHANGES DURING AN ACTION POTENTIAL. Each change in membrane potential corresponds to specific changes in the axonal membrane. In (a), a change in voltage from graded potentials in the dendrites and cell body allow the neuron to reach threshold. Voltage-dependent sodium channels open. In (b), the incoming sodium brings the membrane potential to +40 mV and voltage-dependent potassium channels open. (c) The change in the membrane potential across the entire action potential. (d) Changes in the voltage-dependent sodium channels across the action potential.

Lidocaine is a drug that is commonly used to block pain sensations during dental procedures, and works by blocking sodium channels in neurons. What effect would you expect lidocaine to have on an action potential?

We can summarize the electrical changes in the neuron from resting to action potential to refractory period and back to the resting state as follows (see also Figure 3.11d):

1. Resting potential is −70 mV.
2. If incoming graded potentials cause sufficient depolarization, voltage-dependent sodium channels open and sodium ions flood into the neuron.
3. The influx of positively charged sodium ions quickly raises the membrane potential to +40 mV.
4. When the membrane potential reaches +40 mV, the sodium channels close and potassium channels open. The outward flow of positively charged potassium ions restores the negative charge inside the cell.

Action potentials begin their journey towards the terminals at the portion of the axon next to the cell body. Voltage-dependent sodium channels located on the neighbouring segment of axon are sensitive to the positive charge resulting from the incoming sodium ions. When the membrane potential in this portion of the axon reaches −55 mV, these sodium channels open. This depolarizes the next portion of membrane, causing sodium channels to open there, and continuing or *propagating* the action potential. This process is repeated all along the axonal membrane, as the impulse moves toward the synapse. Like a wave, the action potential travels along the axon, until it reaches the terminal.

How fast are action potentials anyway? In the 1920s, Edgar Douglas Adrian measured and recorded individual action potentials of sensory neurons and confirmed a speed of about 30 metres per second (Kandel, 2006). Myelinated neurons conduct action potentials much faster than unmyelinated ones, as depolarization occurs only at gaps in the myelin sheath and the action potential skips from gap to gap. Adrian's work also confirmed the existence of thresholds—a point of no return; once the charge inside the neuron exceeds this threshold, the action potential fires and it always fires with the same intensity. This is known as the **all-or-none principle.** Since the opening of voltage-dependent sodium channels set up a wave of propagation, an action potential either fires or it does not; there is no halfway. If the depolarization threshold is not reached, there is no action potential.

all-or-none principle
the idea that once the threshold has been crossed, an action potential either fires or it does not.

Once the action potential reaches the terminal, a third ion channel comes into play. Embedded in the membrane of the terminal are voltage-dependent calcium channels, which open when the depolarizing phase of the action potential arrives. Calcium flows into the cell along its gradient and triggers neurotransmitter release by enabling synaptic vesicles to fuse together with the membrane at the synapse with the next neuron. There the neurotransmitter binds to receptors, and causes excitation or inhibition in the postsynaptic cell. The process then starts all over again.

Once a neuron has passed its message on to its postsynaptic target, it is important that the released neurotransmitter is deactivated. If neurotransmitter stayed in the synapse indefinitely, it would be able to continually bind to receptors and generate graded potentials. Two processes control the end of neuronal signalling: enzymatic degradation and presynaptic reuptake. **Enzymatic degradation** involves chemical breakdown of the neurotransmitter molecule by enzymes present in the synapse. The second method, called **presynaptic reuptake,** returns excess neurotransmitter via special proteins to the neuron that released it. This neurotransmitter can then be repackaged in vesicles for future use.

enzymatic degradation
a way of deactivating neurotransmitter from the synapse, whereby specific enzymes alter the neurotransmitter so that it can no longer bind to receptors.

presynaptic reuptake
a way of removing excess neurotransmitter from the synapse, whereby neurotransmitter is returned to the presynaptic neuron for storage in vesicles for future use.

Common Neurotransmitters

Within the past century, over 100 distinct neurotransmitters have been identified in the nervous system, and descriptions of these could easily fill the rest of the pages of this textbook. This section is devoted to just seven of the best-characterized

	Major function
Acetylcholine	Slows ANS activity; eating, drinking, neuromuscular junction; involved in learning, memory, sleeping, and dreaming
Dopamine	Plays an important role in arousal, mood (especially positive mood); oversupply correlates with schizophrenia; voluntary muscle control
Epinephrine	Increases ANS activity; flight-or-fight response
Norepinephrine	Affects CNS activity; plays role in increasing alertness, attention
Serotonin	Plays role in mood, sleep, eating, temperature regulation; undersupply correlates with anxiety and depression
GABA	Is the major inhibitory neurotransmitter in the brain; slows CNS function; correlates with anxiety and intoxication
Glutamate	Is the most common excitatory neurotransmitter in the brain; involved in learning and memory; may be involved in schizophrenia.

FIGURE **3.12**
NEUROTRANSMITTERS AND THEIR FUNCTIONS. Neurotransmitters can be excitatory, increasing the likelihood of an action potential, or inhibitory, decreasing the likelihood of an action potential.

neurotransmitters (see Figure 3.12). Neurotransmitter effects depend on the type of receptors to which they bind. Recall that glutamate receptors produce excitation through depolarization, while GABA receptors produce inhibition through hyperpolarization. Most neurotransmitters, however, bind to many different receptor types that can have excitatory or inhibitory effects.

GABA (gamma-aminobutyric acid) the major inhibitory neurotransmitter in the brain that inhibits postsynaptic neurons.

Gamma-aminobutyric acid, or **GABA,** is the major inhibitory neurotransmitter in the brain, and therefore tells the postsynaptic neurons *not* to fire and slows CNS activity. Without GABA the central nervous system would have no "brakes" and could run out of control. In fact, one theory about epilepsy is that GABA does not function properly in people who suffer from the disorder (Laschet et al., 2007). Many drugs classified as depressants, such as alcohol and anxiety drugs like diazepam (Valium), increase GABA activity in the brain and lead to relaxing yet ultimately uncoordinated states. Because GABA inhibits much of the CNS activity that keeps us conscious, alert, and able to form memories, large amounts of alcohol consumption can lead to memory lapses, blackouts, loss of consciousness, and even death (White, 2003).

glutamate the major excitatory neurotransmitter in the brain that excites postsynaptic neurons; important in learning, memory, neural processing, and brain development.

Glutamate is the brain's major excitatory neurotransmitter and is important in learning, memory, and neural processing. Glutamate is also important during nervous system development since it facilitates growth and change in neurons and the migration of neurons to different sites in the brain (Nadarajah & Parnavelas, 2002). It also amplifies certain neural signals, making some stimulation more important than others. For example, which is more important? To notice a car skidding out of control in front of you or that your shoes are still the same colour they were when you put them on this morning? Glutamate boosts the signals about the car.

acetylcholine (ACh) a neurotransmitter that controls muscle movement and plays a role in learning, memory, attention, sleeping, and dreaming

The neurotransmitter **acetylcholine (ACh)** is involved in the neural control of muscle and plays a role in mental processes such as learning, memory, attention, sleeping, and dreaming. Furthermore, researchers have discovered that the degenerative memory disorder called Alzheimer's disease results at least partly from a decrease in ACh activity and that drugs that enhance ACh aid memory.

Dopamine is released in response to behaviours that feel good or are rewarding to the person or animal. Eating a good meal, doing well on an exam, having an orgasm, or drinking a glass of water when really thirsty—each of these behaviours stimulates dopamine activity in the brain (Hamer & Copeland, 1998). Because dopamine activity is rewarding, many drug addictions involve increased dopamine activity. For instance, cocaine blocks the reuptake of dopamine into the presynaptic neuron, leaving it in the synaptic cleft for a longer period of time before it binds to receptors in the postsynaptic neuron (Bradberry, 2007). The result is a feeling of euphoria and intense wanting.

Dopamine is also involved in voluntary motor control. One of the more dramatic examples of the effects of dopamine is Parkinson's disease. People who suffer from Parkinson's disease gradually lose the ability to control their muscles and shake involuntarily. Dopamine-producing neurons die in Parkinson's disease, and eventually the loss of motor control can cause death when muscles involved in swallowing shut down. Most treatments for Parkinson's include drugs that replace or mimic the effects of dopamine.

Epinephrine and **norepinephrine** primarily have energizing and arousing properties. (Epinephrine is also called "adrenaline," a term that is still widely used in everyday speech—"Wow! What an adrenaline rush!") Both epinephrine and norepinephrine are produced in the brain and by the adrenal glands that rest on the kidneys. Epinephrine tends not to affect mental states, whereas norepinephrine does increase mental arousal and alertness. When you are alert and paying attention, norepinephrine levels are elevated. Norepinephrine activity also leads to physiological arousal such increased heart rate and blood pressure.

Serotonin has some of the most wide-ranging effects on behaviour of any of the neurotransmitters. It is involved in dreaming and in controlling emotional states, especially anger, anxiety, and depression. People who are generally anxious and/or depressed often have low levels of serotonin (Caspi et al., 2003; Kendler et al., 2005). Thus, drugs that block the reuptake of serotonin are widely used to treat anxiety and depression.

People who are consistently angry and/or aggressive (especially males) often have abnormally low levels of serotonin. Researchers have shown that when

Connection

ACh enhancers are used to treat memory disorders such as Alzheimer's disease, and they seem to slow the progression of memory loss.

See Chapter 6, LO9.

dopamine
a neurotransmitter released in response to behaviours that feel good or are rewarding to the person or animal; also involved in voluntary motor control.

epinephrine
also known as adrenaline, a neurotransmitter that arouses bodily systems (such as increasing heart rate).

norepinephrine
a neurotransmitter that plays an important role in the sympathetic nervous system, energizing bodily systems and increasing mental arousal and alertness.

serotonin
a neurotransmitter with wide-ranging effects: involved in dreaming and in controlling emotional states, especially anger, anxiety and depression.

The street drug known as ecstasy stimulates the release of high levels of the neurotransmitter serotonin, which makes people temporarily feel euphoric and affectionate. By interfering with the body's ability to produce serotonin, however, ecstasy eventually may cause depression in some people.

Connection

Common treatments for depression, which may result in part from a deficiency of the neurotransmitter serotonin, block the reuptake of serotonin at the synapse, making more of it available for binding with postsynaptic neurons.

See Chapter 16, LO5.

drugs that increase serotonin are given to monkeys who are aggressive, their aggressive tendencies diminish (Suomi, 2005). Likewise, the street drug ecstasy (MDMA), which makes people feel social, affectionate, and euphoric, is known to stimulate extremely high levels of serotonin. Ironically, however, ecstasy ultimately interferes with the brain's ability to produce serotonin, and so depression can be an unpleasant side effect of the drug (de Win et al., 2004).

Summary of the Steps in Neural Transmission

The steps in the process of neural communication are outlined in Figure 3.13. Most neurons receive thousands of inputs, but for the sake of simplicity, only two are shown here: one excitatory and one inhibitory synapse. In a typical neuron, the graded potentials from many synapses are integrated in the soma, where a "decision" is made to fire an action potential if the threshold is reached.

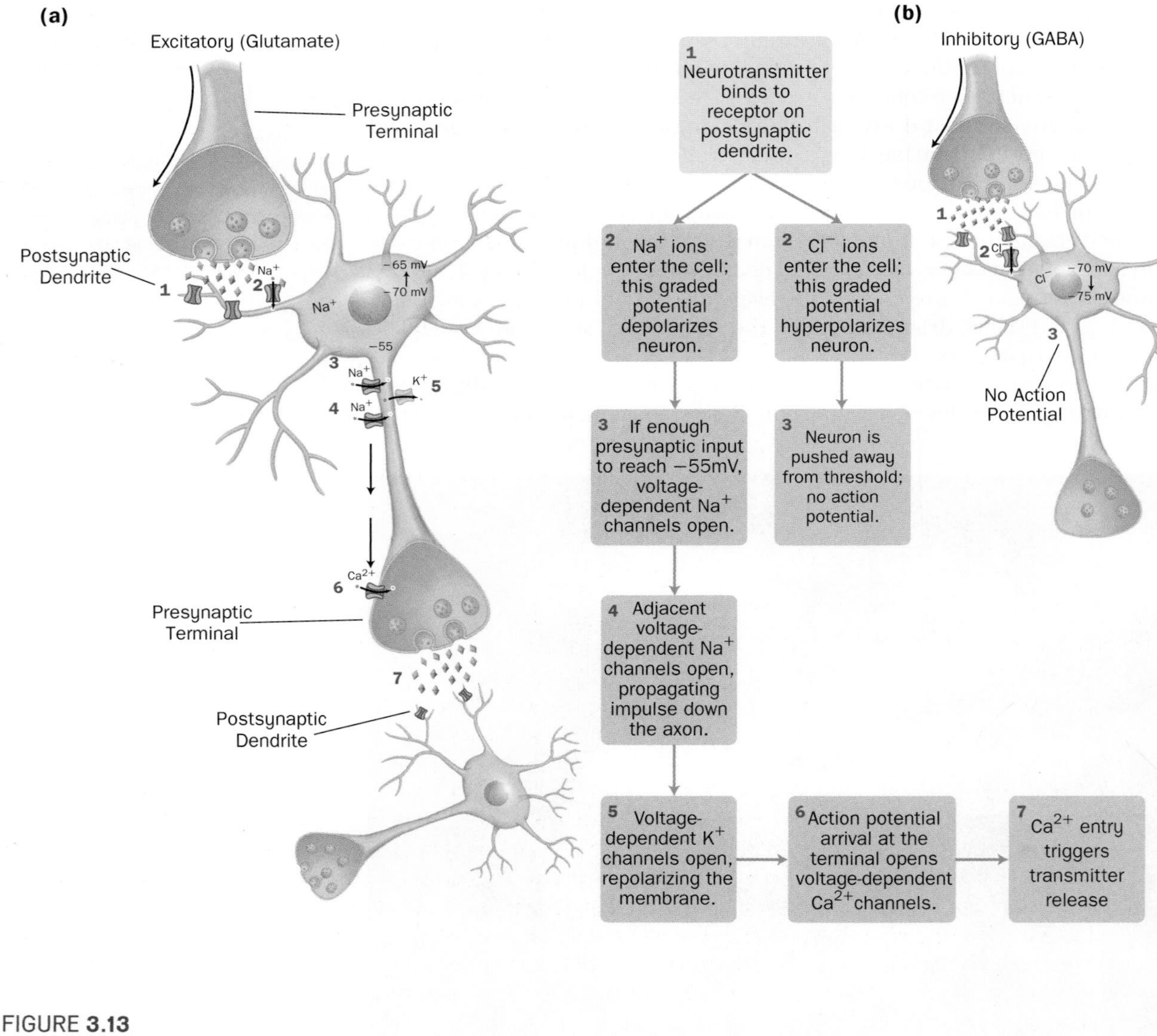

FIGURE **3.13**

STEPS IN NEURAL TRANSMISSION. The sequence of events from binding of neurotransmitter at the dendrites, to the release of neurotransmitter from the terminal. The diagram in (a) outlines the sequence of events that occur at an excitatory synapse, and that in (b) outlines an inhibitory one.

Quick Quiz 3.2: The Nervous System

1. Which branch of the nervous system is responsible for the fight-or-flight response?
   a. the parasympathetic nervous system
   b. the somatic nervous system
   c. the central nervous system
   d. the sympathetic nervous system
2. The finger-like projections on neurons that receive input from other neurons are called
   a. dendrites.
   b. nuclei.
   c. axons.
   d. terminals.
3. Graded potentials differ from action potentials in that graded potentials
   a. maintain their strength along the length of the neuron; action potentials do not.
   b. either depolarize or hyperpolarize the neuron; action potentials do both.
   c. open voltage-dependent calcium channels in the terminal.
   d. are all-or-none.
4. What is the most common excitatory neurotransmitter in the brain?
   a. GABA
   b. serotonin
   c. glutamate
   d. acetylcholine

Answers can be found at the end of the chapter.

THE BRAIN

Philosopher Susan Blackmore has said about the brain: "This huge organ is dangerous and painful to give birth to, expensive to build and, in a resting human, uses about 20 per cent of the body's energy even though it is just 2 per cent of the body's weight. There must be some reason for all this evolutionary expense" (Blackmore, 1999). From a biological viewpoint, we devote enormous energy and effort to our brain, since it has the important task of not just allowing us to *do* but also simply *be*. This jelly-like mass at the top of the spine has been mapped and described in astonishing detail. At this point, the picture is still far from complete; however, neuroscientists continue to piece it together. Here we consider the evolution of the brain, look at key brain regions, and explore what is currently known about their specialized functions.

Evolution of the Human Brain

Across species as diverse as squid, rats, rabbits, and humans, neurons are remarkably similar in how they conduct electrical impulses (Schwartz et al., 1995). However, the arrangement of individual neurons into structures and networks in the nervous system can differ dramatically across species. For instance, primates have relatively large amounts of brain cortex compared to other mammals, birds, reptiles, and fish. The large primate cortex is thought to be an important adaptation, enabling unique cognitive abilities. As we discussed in Chapter 1, over long periods of time, nature selects traits and behaviour that work well in a given environment. These differences are thought be have been guided by natural selection and over time led to big changes in living forms and structures, particularly in the brains.

The human brain has been shaped, via natural selection, by the world in which humans have lived. It is worth noting here that brains do not fossilize to allow a present-day analysis, but the skulls that hold them do. By looking at the size and shape of skulls from all animals and over very long time periods, scientists can glean something about how and when human brains evolved. The evolution of the human brain is a fascinating story. Although the details lie well beyond the scope of this book, we can consider a general outline of brain evolution (Dunbar, 2001; Jerison, 2000; Klein, 1999).

Connection

Examination of Neanderthal DNA has revealed a human-like form of a gene called FOXP2, which is important in speech production and comprehension. Therefore, Neanderthals might have been capable of some form of language.

See Chapter 8, LO2.

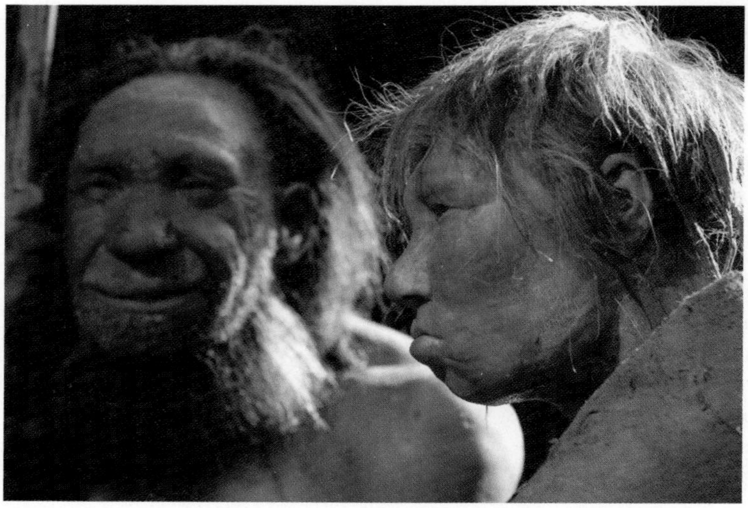

From Neanderthal fossils, scientists have determined that this close ancestor had distinctive anatomical features and a different lifestyle than early humans.

The earliest ancestors of humans appeared in Africa about 6 million years ago. One of our closest evolutionary relatives, the Neanderthals (*Homo neanderthalensis*) lived from about 350 000 to 28 000 years ago, when they were replaced by our species (*Homo sapiens*). Neanderthals had brains slightly larger on average than those of modern humans (see Figure 3.14), and genetic evidence suggests that they may have possessed very rudimentary language. Nevertheless, they did not produce highly complex tools or symbolic pieces of art, at least none that have been found. In other words, their brains were modern in size but probably not modern in function. It is possible, therefore, that the human brain took up to 100 000 years to become fully wired and complex, all the while staying the same overall size.

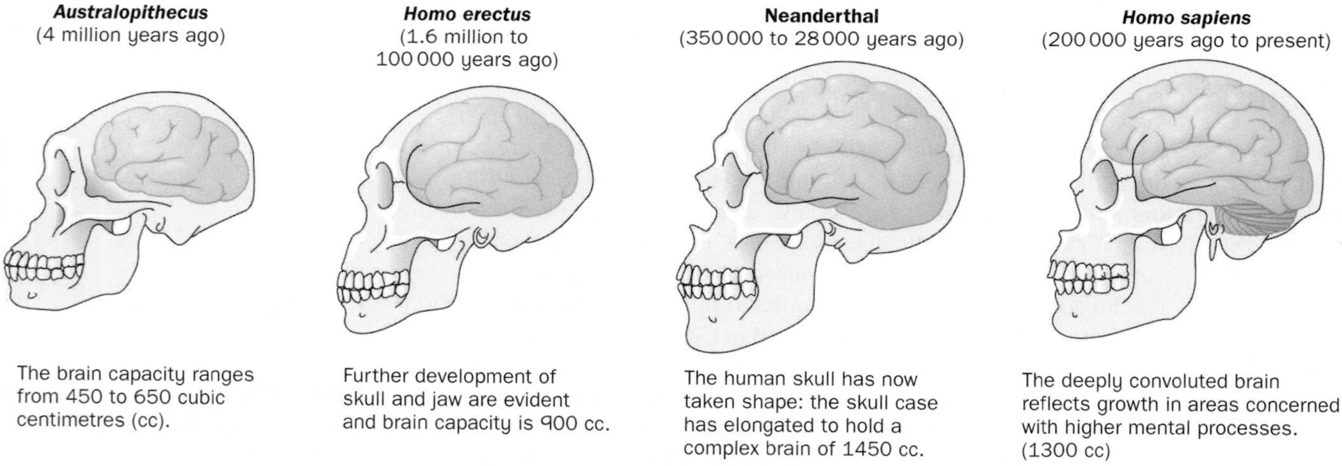

Australopithecus
(4 million years ago)
Homo erectus
(1.6 million to 100 000 years ago)
Neanderthal
(350 000 to 28 000 years ago)
Homo sapiens
(200 000 years ago to present)
The brain capacity ranges from 450 to 650 cubic centimetres (cc).
Further development of skull and jaw are evident and brain capacity is 900 cc.
The human skull has now taken shape: the skull case has elongated to hold a complex brain of 1450 cc.
The deeply convoluted brain reflects growth in areas concerned with higher mental processes. (1300 cc)

FIGURE **3.14**

EVOLUTION OF THE HUMAN BRAIN OVER THE LAST 4 MILLION YEARS. An early form of prehuman, Australopithecus, had a brain about one-third the size of the modern human (*Homo sapiens*) brain. In general, the overall brain size has grown over the course of 4 million years. But note that Neanderthal's brain size was slightly larger than ours. Just as important as overall size for modern human thought and behaviour is the relative enlargement of the frontal lobe area. This can be seen in the less sloped forehead of modern humans compared to their earlier ancestors.

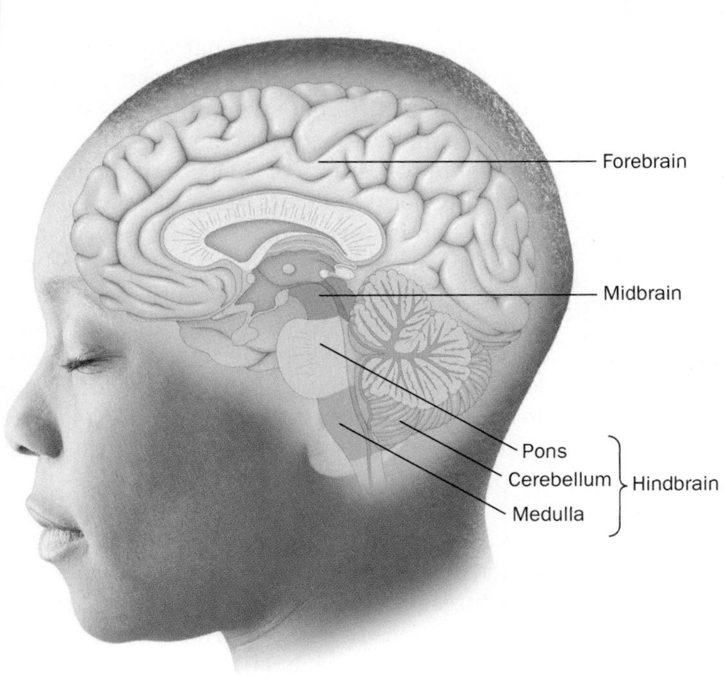

FIGURE **3.15**

THREE MAIN BRAIN STRUCTURES: HINDBRAIN, MIDBRAIN, AND FOREBRAIN. The hindbrain regulates breathing, heart rate, arousal, and other basic survival functions. The midbrain controls eye muscles, processes auditory and visual information, and initiates voluntary movement. The forebrain controls cognitive, sensory, and motor function and regulates temperature, reproductive function, eating, sleeping, and emotions.

LO10 Overview of Brain Regions

In evolutionary terms, then, the human brain is the result of a few hundred million years of natural selection. The three major regions of the brain, in order from earliest to develop to newest, are the hindbrain, the midbrain, and the forebrain (see Figure 3.15). By comparing the relative size of each region in distinct kinds of animals that vary in evolutionary age (see Figure 3.16), we gain an appreciation of how these regions evolved. When we compare brains from these different groups, we see an increase in size of the forebrain in humans and other primates (Jerison, 2000).

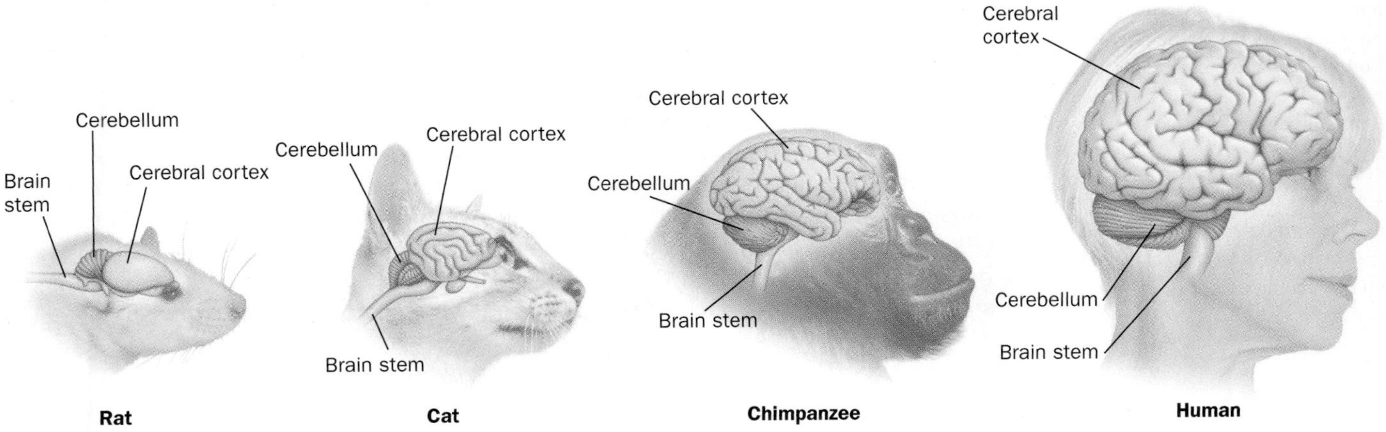

FIGURE **3.16**

BRAIN STRUCTURE OF MAMMALS. Mammals have many of the same brain structures, but of different relative sizes. Notice how much larger the cerebral cortex is in humans than in chimpanzees, cats, and rats.

What other differences can you notice between the brains of these different species?

Swallowing is one of a number of inborn reflexes.

The study of neuroanatomy can be overwhelming; the spinal cord and brain can be subdivided into hundreds of different structures. It is beyond the scope of this chapter to examine neuroanatomy in fine detail. However, the study of behaviour benefits immensely from a general understanding of how the brain is organized. For instance, most structures in the brain are *bilateral,* meaning that there is a left and right version of each brain area. When describing brain geography, neuroanatomists use terms to indicate location in the nervous system. *Posterior* refers to structures that are located near the back of the head, while *anterior* refers to structures located nearest to the nose. The next section will discuss the brain starting at its posterior end, working up to the anterior region.

Hindbrain The oldest brain region is the hindbrain, the region directly connected to the spinal cord. Hindbrain structures regulate breathing, heart rate, arousal, and other basic functions of survival. There are three main parts of the hindbrain: the medulla, the pons, and the cerebellum.

medulla
a hindbrain structure that extends directly from the spinal cord; regulates breathing, heart rate, and blood pressure.

reflexes
inborn and involuntary behaviours—such as coughing, swallowing, sneezing, or vomiting—that are elicited by very specific stimuli.

pons
a hindbrain structure that serves as a bridge between lower brain regions and higher midbrain and forebrain activity.

cerebellum
a hindbrain structure involved in body movement, balance, coordination, fine-tuning motor skills, and cognitive activities such as learning and language.

reticular formation
a network of nerve fibres that runs up through both the hindbrain and the midbrain; it is crucial to waking up and falling asleep.

Extending directly from the spinal cord, the **medulla** regulates breathing, heart rate, and blood pressure. It also is involved in various kinds of reflexes, such as coughing, swallowing, sneezing, and vomiting. **Reflexes** are inborn and involuntary behaviours that are elicited by very specific stimuli (Amaral, 2000). **Pons** means "bridge," and the pons indeed serves as a bridge between lower brain regions and higher midbrain and forebrain activity. For instance, information about body movement and various sensations gets relayed from the cortex via the pons to the cerebellum. The **cerebellum,** or "little brain," contains more neurons than any other single part of the brain. It is responsible for body movement, balance, coordination, and fine motor skills like typing and piano playing. The cerebellum is also important in cognitive activities such as learning and language (Murdoch, 2010).

Midbrain The next brain region to evolve after the hindbrain is the smallest of the three major areas, the midbrain. Different parts of the midbrain control the eye muscles, process auditory and visual information, and initiate voluntary movement of the body. People with Parkinson's disease have problems with midbrain functioning, due to the loss of neurons that use dopamine there, and so they shake uncontrollably. The midbrain, the medulla, and the pons together are sometimes referred to as the *brainstem.*

Running through both the hindbrain and the midbrain is a network of nerves called the **reticular formation.** (Reticular means "netlike.") The reticular formation is crucial to waking up and falling asleep. In other words, it is involved in arousal. Among the first neuroscientists to study the reticular formation were Giuseppe Moruzzi and Horace Magoun. In a classic study, Moruzzi and Magoun (1949) electrically stimulated the reticular formation of a sleeping cat, and it immediately awoke. When they *lesioned,* or cut, its connection to higher brain systems, the cat went into a deep coma from which it could not be aroused.

Forebrain The last major brain region to evolve was the largest part of the human brain, the forebrain. It consists of the highly folded outer surface, called the cerebral cortex, and numerous other structures, including the thalamus and the limbic system. Collectively, the structures of the forebrain control cognitive, sensory, and motor function and regulate temperature, reproductive functions, eating, sleeping, and the display of emotions.

thalamus
a forebrain structure that receives information from the senses and relays it to the cerebral cortex for processing.

From the bottom up, the first forebrain structure is the **thalamus,** which receives input from the ears, eyes, skin, or taste buds and relays sensory information

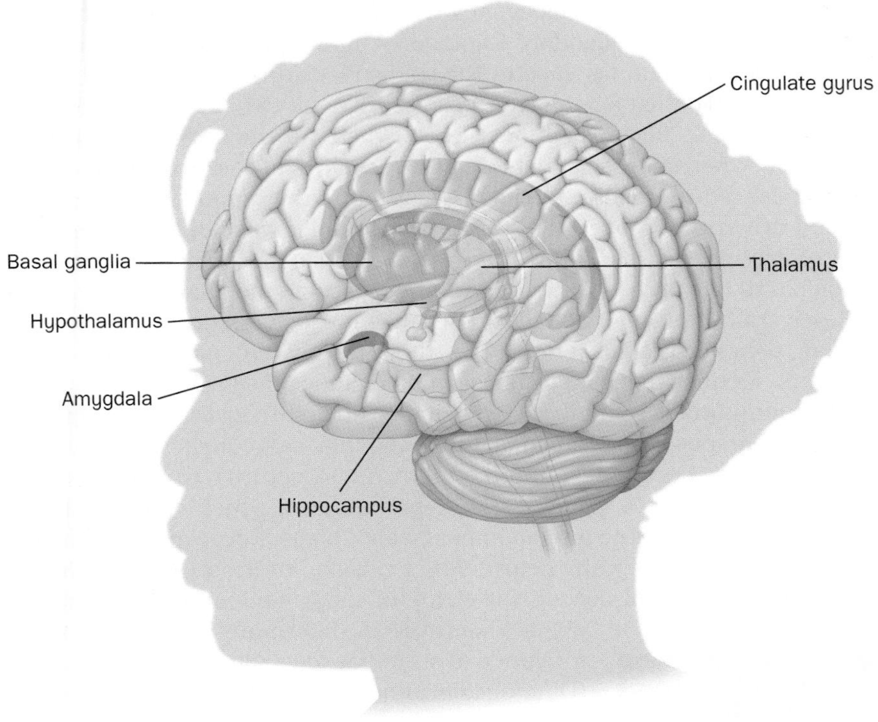

FIGURE **3.17**
THE LIMBIC SYSTEM. The limbic system controls motivation and emotion. It includes the hypothalamus, hippocampus, amygdala, and cingulate gyrus.

to the part of the cerebral cortex most responsible for processing that specific kind of sensory information. For this reason, the thalamus is often called a sensory relay station. In fact, olfaction (the sense of smell) appears to be the only sense that does not have a thalamic relay (Kay & Sherman, 2007).

The Limbic System In the middle of the brain directly around the thalamus lies a set of structures that typically are referred to as the *limbic system* (see Figure 3.17). These are the hypothalamus, the hippocampus, the amygdala, and the cingulate gyrus. Together, the limbic system structures are important in emotion and motivation. However, there is some debate as to whether these structures work together as a system, so some neuroscientists suggest the term limbic system should be abandoned (LeDoux, 2003).

The structure directly below the thalamus is the hypothalamus. In fact, *hypo* simply means "below." The **hypothalamus** is the master regulator of almost all major drives and motives we have, including hunger, thirst, temperature, and sexual behaviour. It also controls the pituitary gland, which is responsible for controlling most of the hormones our body produces. Researchers in the 1940s discovered the role the hypothalamus plays in eating: lesioning one part of it produced overeating and obesity in animals, whereas lesioning another part of the hypothalamus led to undereating (Kupfermann, Kandel, & Iversen, 2000). The hypothalamus is also involved in sexual arousal (Karama et al., 2002).

Wrapped around the thalamus is the **hippocampus,** which plays a vital role in learning and memory. Sensory information from the sense organs goes to the hippocampus. If these events are important enough, they are processed in the hippocampus and eventually established as lasting memories.

As we will see throughout this book, it is well established that learning and memory change the brain. The brain structure most open to change is the hippocampus. It changes with learning and experience. To get a feel for the kind of

How does this picture make you feel? The structures of the limbic system play a key part in emotion and motivation.

hypothalamus
a limbic structure; the master regulator of almost all major drives and motives we have, such as hunger, thirst, temperature, and sexual behaviour; also controls the pituitary gland.

hippocampus
a limbic structure that wraps itself around the thalamus; plays a vital role in learning and memory.

Challenge Your Assumptions

True or False? Learning increases the number of neurons in your brain and alters their structure.

True: Whenever we learn and retain information long term, neurons in our brains actually grow and change.

Connection

Psychologists learned how essential the hippocampus is in memory and learning through a case study of "H.M.," who had this structure surgically removed on both sides of the brain.

See Chapter 6, LO8.

research that demonstrates this capacity, let's look at recent research conducted with taxi cab drivers in London, England. Why study taxi drivers in London? They are an ideal group because of the tremendous amount of spatial and geographic knowledge they must have to pass a difficult cab driving test (Maguire, Woollett, & Spiers, 2006). They must know where all the streets are relative to other streets. When neuroscientists examined images of the hippocampus of taxi drivers compared to non–taxi drivers, they found the hippocampus was larger in the taxi drivers. Moreover, the researchers found it was not the stress and frequency of driving that led to this increase in the size of the hippocampus. When they compared bus drivers to taxi drivers, they still found a larger hippocampus in taxi drivers (Maguire et al., 2006). Because bus drivers drive the same route every day, they need to learn much less about the spatial layout of the city than taxi drivers. As this study suggests, learning changes the brain.

The **amygdala** is a small, almond-shaped structure located directly in front of the hippocampus. Anatomically, the amygdala has connections with many other areas of the brain, including the following structures, which appear to be involved in emotion and memory: the hypothalamus, which controls the autonomic nervous system; the hippocampus, which plays a crucial role in memory; the thalamus, which contains neurons that receive information from the sense organs; and the cerebral cortex. By virtue of its prime location, the amygdala plays a key role in determining the emotional significance of stimuli, especially when they evoke fear (Öhman, 2002; Phelps & LeDoux, 2005).

One of the special functions of the amygdala is to recognize situations for which fear is an appropriate response.

What would happen if humans were not able to experience fear?

Studies in animals and humans show how important the amygdala is to emotions, especially fear. Electrical stimulation of the amygdala in cats makes them arch their backs in an angry-defensive manner, a response suggesting that anger and aggression involve the amygdala. Moreover, when aggressive monkeys had this region of the brain surgically lesioned, they became tame and non-aggressive. They also became fearless; for instance, rather than fleeing from snakes, they approached them (Klüver & Bucy 1937; Meunier & Bachevalier, 2002). Similarly, in cases of disease, injury, or surgery to the human amygdala, people often lose their aggressive tendencies. They become mild-mannered and non-hostile, yet they also become fearless. Additionally, our ability to recognize certain emotional expressions on other people's faces—especially fear—involves the amygdala (Adolphs et al., 2005; Morris et al. 1996). Without the amygdala, we cannot learn appropriate emotional responses, especially to potentially dangerous situations. The amygdala, along with the hypothalamus and other brain structures, is also activated during sexual arousal (Hamann et al., 2004; Karama et al., 2002).

The **cingulate gyrus,** meaning "belt ridge" in Latin, is a belt-like structure in the middle of the brain. Portions of the cingulate gyrus, in particular the anterior part, play an important role in attention and cognitive control (Botvinick, Cohen, & Carter, 2004). For instance, when people are first trying to figure out a difficult problem and preparing to solve it, parts of the cingulate gyrus are activated (Kounios et al., 2006). In contrast, this area seems to malfunction in people with schizophrenia, who do have major difficulties in focusing their attention (Carter et al., 1997).

The **basal ganglia** are a collection of interconnected structures involved in voluntary motor control. These structures are located below the cingulate gyrus and surround the thalamus and have connections with the cerebral cortex,

amygdala
a small structure located directly in front of the hippocampus; has widespread connections and is important for processing emotional information, especially that related to fear.

cingulate gyrus
a belt-like structure in the middle of the brain that plays an important role in attention and cognitive control.

basal ganglia
a collection of structures surrounding the thalamus involved in voluntary motor control.

thalamus, and brain stem (Kopell et al., 2006). Several movement-related neurological disorders, including Parkinson's disease and Huntington's disease, affect the functioning of neurons in this region. Individuals who have these disorders suffer from jerky, often incontrollable movements.

Because voluntary movement is an important part of emotional and motivated behaviour, the basal ganglia are often considered part of the limbic system. In the 1950s at McGill University, James Olds and Peter Milner made a groundbreaking discovery: Animals would deliver stimulation to electrodes placed in a certain region of the basal ganglia, called the **nucleus accumbens** (Olds & Milner, 1954). The animals appeared to find the electrical *self-stimulation* rewarding, and later studies showed that this part of the brain is activated by natural rewards such as food or sex. This part of the basal ganglia appears to be an important link between the emotional aspects of reward and the redirection of voluntary behaviour towards it.

Connection

The amygdala plays a significant role in emotion.

See Chapter 11, LO10.

nucleus accumbens
basal ganglia structure involved in reward.

LO11 LO12

The Cerebral Cortex At the most anterior end of the brain is the **cerebral cortex** (plural *cortices*), which makes up approximately 80 percent of the human brain. In Latin, *cortex* means "tree bark," which the cerebral cortex resembles. When most of us think about the human brain, we typically envision this highly folded structure. The cortex is so large that it covers most of the other brain regions we have discussed so far in this chapter; in fact, these other parts are not visible unless the brain is dissected. The cortex is the where much of human thought, planning, perception, and consciousness take place. In short, it is the site of all brain activity that makes us most human.

cerebral cortex
the folded outer layer of brain matter in which much of human thought, planning, perception, and consciousness takes place.

The cortex is divided by a large groove along the midline of the head into the left and right hemispheres, and each hemisphere contains four anatomically distinct *lobes*. The four lobes are the frontal, temporal, parietal, and occipital (Figure 3.18), and each carries out distinct functions. The *frontal lobes*, in the front of the brain, make up one-third of the area of the cerebral cortex. One important region of the frontal lobe is a strip of cortex running from the top of the head down along the side, called the *primary motor cortex*. One of the earliest discoveries about the brain's frontal lobes involved the motor cortex. In the 1860s, the German physiologist Eduard Hitzig had noticed while caring for wounded soldiers that touching the surface of a specific side of the brain caused the soldier's body to twitch on the opposite, or **contralateral,** side. From these medical observations, Hitzig and his colleague Gustav Fritsch decided to more systematically test the idea that stimulating distinct parts of the brain would cause the body to move. They found a strip of the frontal cortex in dogs where mild electrical stimulation caused different parts of the body to move. And, indeed, as in the soldiers, stimulating one side of the brain caused the opposite part of the dog's body to move.

Hitzig and his colleagues also found that as they moved the stimulation along this strip of cortex and stimulated one small region at a time, different parts of the body would move. More importantly, they were the first researchers to discover and study

contralateral
an anatomical term meaning opposite side.

Lobes of the brain

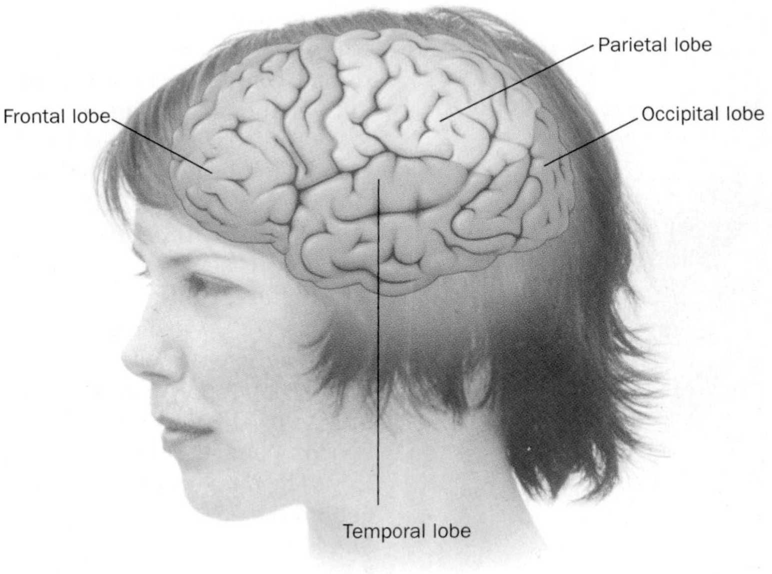

FIGURE **3.18**
FOUR LOBES OF THE CEREBRAL CORTEX. Each of the four lobes has a counterpart on the opposite side of the brain. Most important for thinking, planning, and integrating the brain's activity are the frontal lobes. The parietal lobes integrate the sensation and perception of touch. Hearing is the main function of the temporal lobes, and visual information is processed in the occipital lobes.

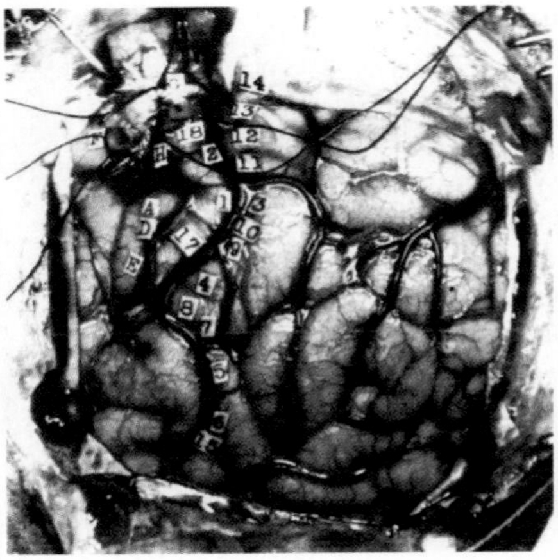

FIGURE **3.19**
MAPPING OF THE PRIMARY MOTOR CORTEX. This photograph is of the brain of a boy who had part of his cortex removed as a treatment for epilepsy. The surgeons stimulated the indicated brain regions (displayed as numbers), and made observations of the patient's experience. (From Penfield, W., and Boldrey, E. (1937). Somatic motor and sensory representation in the cerebral cortex of man as studied by electrical stimulation. *Brain, 60,* 389–443.)

something that few believed: Different parts of the cortex are responsible for different functions—a phenomenon known as *cortical localization.* They were also the first to study localization in a lab (Finger, 1994). In the 1930s, Wilder Penfield and Edwin Boldrey at the Montreal Neurological Institute famously mapped the primary motor cortex in epilepsy patients undergoing brain surgery (Penfield & Boldrey, 1937). Since these surgeries were carried out without general anesthesia, patients were conscious and could report movements and sensations they experienced. The surgeons then recorded the location of the brain region responsible (see Figure 3.19).

The frontal lobe carries out many important functions, including attention, planning, abstract thinking, control of impulses, creativity, and social awareness (Miller & Cummings, 1999). The frontal lobes are more interconnected with other brain regions than any other part of the brain and therefore are able to integrate much brain activity. This integration allows for insight and creative problem solving (Furster, 1999). For example, connections between the frontal lobes and the hippocampus and temporal lobe facilitate tasks involving language and memory, respectively.

Probably the most famous story in neuroscience comes from the first case study of frontal lobe involvement in impulse control and personality (Macmillan, 2000). In September 1848, a 25-year-old railroad foreman, Phineas Gage, was laying railroad ties. While hammering a tamping iron (an iron bar), Gage accidentally ignited gun powder used to lay the track and it exploded. The iron bar shot upward, entered Gage's left cheek, and exited through the top of his skull after passing through his frontal lobe (see Figure 3.20). The iron bar was travelling so fast that it moved cleanly through Gage's head and landed over 7 metres away. Miraculously, not only did Gage survive—but he never even lost consciousness!

Although not severely injured physically (other than the hole in his brain), Gage suffered immediate and obvious changes to his personality. Before the accident, he had been a mild-mannered but clever businessman. After the accident he was stubborn, impulsive, and argumentative, and at times he would say offensive things. Gage's accident was one of the first documented cases of marked personality change following an injury to the frontal lobes.

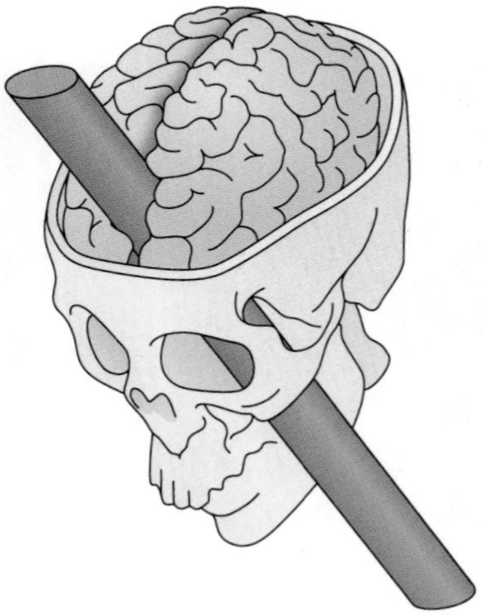

FIGURE **3.20**
PHINEAS GAGE'S ACCIDENT. Miraculously, Gage survived, but his personality changed dramatically as a result of the injury to his frontal lobe.

The *parietal lobes,* which make up the top and rear sections of the brain, play an important role in the sensation and perception of touch. In the most anterior part of the parietal lobe is the *primary somatosensory cortex.* Electrical stimulation of this area produces sensations in different regions of the body. The somatosensory cortex lies directly behind the motor cortex of the frontal lobe. In fact, Penfield and Boldrey's careful observations revealed that these two regions are "twins." The areas of the motor and somatosensory cortex that govern specific parts of the body are parallel to and directly next to each other (see Figure 3.21). For example, the part of the motor cortex involved in moving the lips is directly opposite the region of the sensory cortex where we sense that our lips are being touched (Penfield & Boldrey, 1937).

The *temporal lobes* lie directly below the frontal and parietal lobes and right behind the ears. The temporal lobes have many different functions, but the main one is hearing. The temporal lobes house the *primary auditory cortex,* where sound information arrives from the thalamus for processing. The temporal lobes also house and connect with the hippocampus and amygdala, and so are also involved in memory and emotion.

In the rear of the brain lie the *occipital lobes.* The optic pathway travels from the eye to the thalamus and then to the occipital lobes—specifically, to the *primary visual cortex,* involved in the processing of visual information. Neuroscientists have discovered that individual neurons are specialized for the many different aspects of vision, including shape, colour, shadow, light, and orientation.

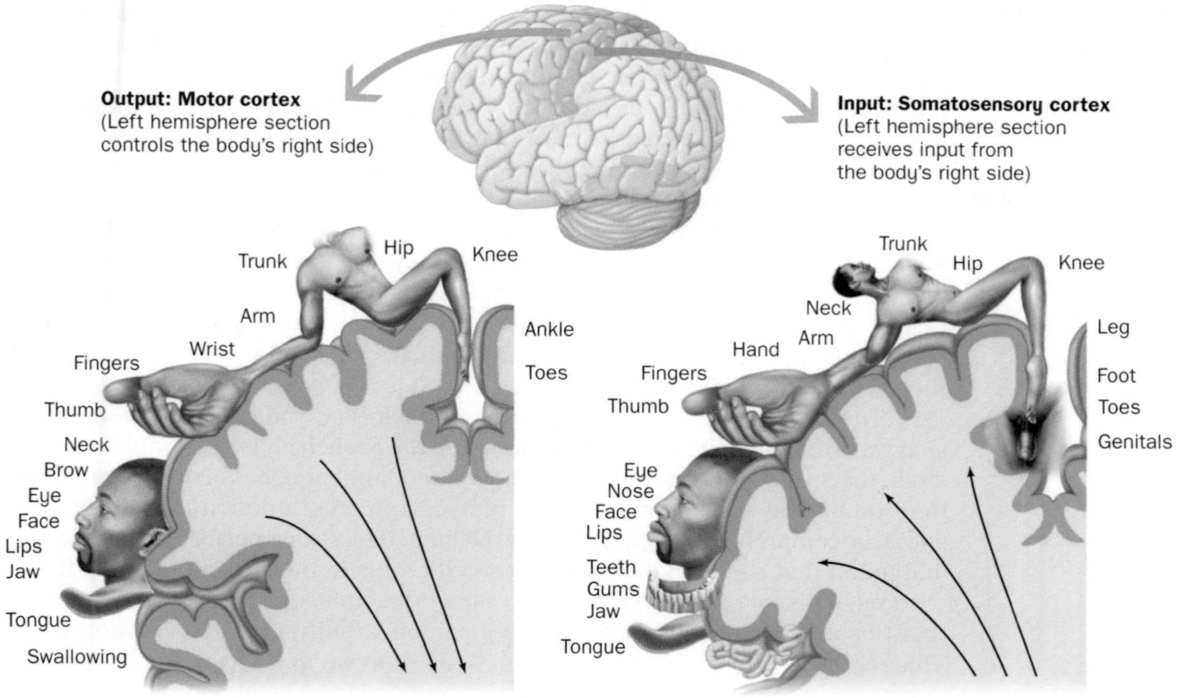

FIGURE 3.21

MOTOR AND SOMATOSENSORY CORTICES OF THE BRAIN. Note that the regions of the motor and somatosensory cortices are "twins." The face, lips, or toes, for example, activate the same areas of both cortices. The arrows going down into the lower brain region represent motor output and the arrows coming up into the somatosensory cortex correspond to input from the sense of touch.

Why do you think the size of some body parts is distorted on these cortical maps? Are there some body parts missing?

Different neurons in the visual cortex are activated when we see horizontal lines, diagonal lines, and vertical lines (Wurtz & Kandel, 2000).

The **insula** is a small structure that resides deep inside the cortex, in the area that separates the temporal lobe from the parietal lobe. The insula is active in the perception of bodily sensations, emotional states, empathy, and addictive behaviour (Damasio, 2000; Naqvi et al., 2007). It communicates with structures of the limbic system and higher brain areas involved in decision making. The insula also plays a key role in our awareness of our body as our own (Tsakiris et al., 2007).

insula
a small structure inside the cortex that plays an important role in the perception of bodily sensations, emotional states, empathy, and addictive behaviour.

Cerebral Asymmetry The cortical stimulation studies by Hitzig and Penfield revealed that some regions of the cortex have a contralateral relationship with the body. For instance, the primary motor cortex controls movement on the opposite side of the body. The primary sensory areas also share this arrangement; the left somatosensory cortex in the parietal lobe responds to the sense of touch on the right side of the body. These areas also have a *topographic,* or map-like, relationship with the rest of the body, such that the body retains its spatial order in the brain. In other words finger neurons are located next to hand neurons. However, the majority of the cortex is not directly associated with primary motor and sensory information, such that stimulation does not result in movement or physical sensation in the body. These "silent" areas are referred to as **association cortex,** and are involved in the integration of information that comes from other cortical areas and the rest of the brain.

association cortex
cortical areas that do not produce movement or sensation when stimulated; involved in complex perception and thought.

Association cortex differs from primary motor and sensory areas in that there is a large degree of asymmetry between the hemispheres. Studies have shown that damage to a particular region of association cortex produces profoundly different deficits based upon which hemisphere is affected. In general, the left hemisphere association cortex processes information in a more focused and analytic manner, whereas the right hemisphere integrates information in a broader, more holistic manner (Beeman & Bowden, 2000). Perhaps the best-described asymmetry between the hemispheres is their involvement in language and visuospatial tasks. Brain imaging shows that people typically recruit their left hemisphere for language comprehension and production, and their right hemisphere for tasks involving spatial arrangements, such as deciphering facial expressions (Hellige, 1996). These functions are said to be *lateralized* because they are biased toward one side of the brain.

The importance of the left hemisphere in speech and language comprehension was first described in the early 1860s by the French physician Paul Broca. He studied a stroke patient who could understand language, but he could not speak in grammatical sentences. He had a type of **aphasia,** a deficit in the ability to speak or comprehend language. After the man died, Broca performed an autopsy and found that a cyst had damaged a small region in the left frontal lobe. Broca went on to discover similar damage in eight other aphasia patients, so he inferred that this area must be responsible for a person's ability to speak (Pinker, 1994). This region is commonly referred to as **Broca's area,** and this type of aphasia is known as Broca's aphasia. These clinical findings have been confirmed by modern brain imaging techniques: people with aphasia often have damage or lesions in the same region of the left frontal lobe.

aphasia
deficit in the ability to speak or comprehend language.

Broca's area
an area in the left frontal lobe responsible for the ability to produce speech.

About 20 years after Broca found the area of the brain now named for him, a German physiologist, Carl Wernicke, discovered that damage to another region of the left hemisphere created a different language problem. This area of the left temporal lobe, now called **Wernicke's area,** is responsible for speech comprehension. Wernicke's aphasia, in contrast to Broca's aphasia, results in fluent, grammatical streams of speech that lack meaning. For instance, a patient with this disorder who was asked why he was in the hospital responded: "Boy, I'm sweating. I'm awfully nervous, you know, once in awhile I get caught up, I can't mention the tarripoi, a month ago, quite a little, I've done a lot well, I impose a lot, while, on the other hand, you know what I mean, I have to run around, look it over, trebbin and all that sort of stuff" (as quoted in Pinker, 1994, p. 316).

Wernicke's area
an area deep in the left temporal lobe responsible for language comprehension.

In contrast to the left hemisphere's role in speech and language, the right hemisphere specializes in spatial processing. The ability to perceive the location of objects in relation to other objects is an important skill, without it simple tasks such as walking into a classroom and finding a place to sit would be impossible. Damage to association cortex in the right parietal lobe can cause a condition called **contralateral neglect,** where individuals ignore the left side of their world (Mort, 2003). Eating from only one side of the plate and dressing only one half of the body are common symptoms of this disorder.

contralateral neglect
a condition in which individuals do not respond to one side of space, usually caused by damage to the right parietal lobe.

Different regions of the right hemisphere control other aspects of spatial ability, such as face processing. Processing information about faces requires fine discrimination of the spatial layout of a person's features. The right occipital and temporal lobes appear to play a dominant role in facial recognition, since damage to these areas of can result in a condition known as **prosopagnosia** (Barton, 2008). This is sometimes also referred to as *face blindness,* since affected individuals have extreme difficulty in recognizing people from their faces. In many cases individuals are unable to even recognize their own face in the mirror.

prosopagnosia
a condition in which individuals do not recognize faces, often caused by damage to the right cortex.

Although the findings we have just described point to specialized roles of the hemispheres, the degree of asymmetry between the left and right sides of the cortex is not fixed. Language is strongly left dominant in the majority of people, but not in many left-handed individuals, whose language function is often housed in the right hemisphere or is equally distributed across both hemispheres (Szaflarski et al., 2002). There are also significant sex differences in hemispheric asymmetry. Although most women are left dominant for language, they tend to use parts of their right hemisphere during language tasks, whereas men rely mainly upon the language areas in the left hemisphere (Shaywitz et al., 1995).

As we have seen, the two hemispheres of the brain appear to specialize in distinct cognitive processes. However, the cerebral hemispheres do not operate independently. A thick band of nerve fibres connecting the two hemispheres of the brain, called the **corpus callosum,** provides a channel for extensive communication between the hemispheres.

In the early 1960s a former prisoner of war from World War II developed epileptic seizures as a result of a failed parachute jump. The seizures were so severe that his doctor approached Roger Sperry, a local researcher who had begun to do research on the corpus callosum, for help (Finger, 1994). Previous medical evidence had suggested that cutting the bundle of nerves between the two hemispheres could stop epileptic seizures. Because the war veteran's seizures had become life threatening, he underwent the surgery under Sperry's guidance and it was very successful. Not only did the man's seizures stop, but there was also no noticeable change in his personality or intelligence. However, Sperry and his colleagues soon discovered a fascinating problem. The man could not name things that were presented to his left visual field, but he could do so with things presented to his right visual field. Even more puzzling was that, despite his inability to name objects on the left, he was easily able to identify these objects by touch. Why?

The representation of visual space in the hemispheres is contralateral, in that information from our right visual field (the right portion of the visual scope of each eye) goes to the left occipital cortex, while information from the left visual field (the left portion of the visual scope of each eye) goes to the right occipital cortex (see Figure 3.22). But, because the war veteran had had his corpus callosum cut, the information from the left visual field could not get transferred to the language centres in the left hemisphere. He could, however, consistently pick up with his *left* hand the image he saw! Thus, because the right hemisphere (where the image was projected) controls spatial ability, he was able to identify the object based upon its shape (see Figure 3.23). The hemispheres normally share language and spatial information, but in *split brain* syndrome, as this condition became known, these processes become isolated from each other (Sperry, Gazzaniga, & Bogen, 1969).

Challenge Your Assumptions

True or False? People can be classified as left brained or right brained, depending on whether they are more analytical or artistic.

False: Although the brain's association cortex is asymmetrical, with most people relying heavily on the left hemisphere for language and the right hemisphere for spatial tasks, people use *both* halves of their brain to function. Brain damage to one hemisphere results in specific deficits, which is evidence that each hemisphere plays an important role.

corpus callosum
the nerve fibres that connect the two hemispheres of the brain.

LO13 Brain Plasticity and Neurogenesis

When scientists began mapping the brain in the late 19th century, they did so by stimulating various brain regions in animals and observing the behavioural changes that such stimulation caused; they then diagrammed the locations of functions in the cerebral cortex (Kandel, 2006). Such mapping contributed to the notion that brain function was fixed. Certain brain regions had certain functions and that was that. But as far back as the early 20th century, researchers had stimulated different places on the motor cortex in several different monkeys and had found that maps generated from such stimulation varied from monkey to monkey. They were as individual as fingerprints.

A decade or so later, other neuroscientists mapped the motor cortices of several monkeys many times during a four-month period. They found that neural areas corresponding to the movement of specific fingers changed to reflect changes in the animal's patterns of movement over that time period (Jenkins et al., 1990).

These findings were only the tip of the iceberg. Since the 1990s, numerous principles of brain plasticity have emerged (Perry, 2002). First and most generally, **neuroplasticity** is the brain's ability to adopt new functions,

neuroplasticity
the brain's ability to adopt new functions, reorganize itself, or make new neural connections throughout life, as a function of experience.

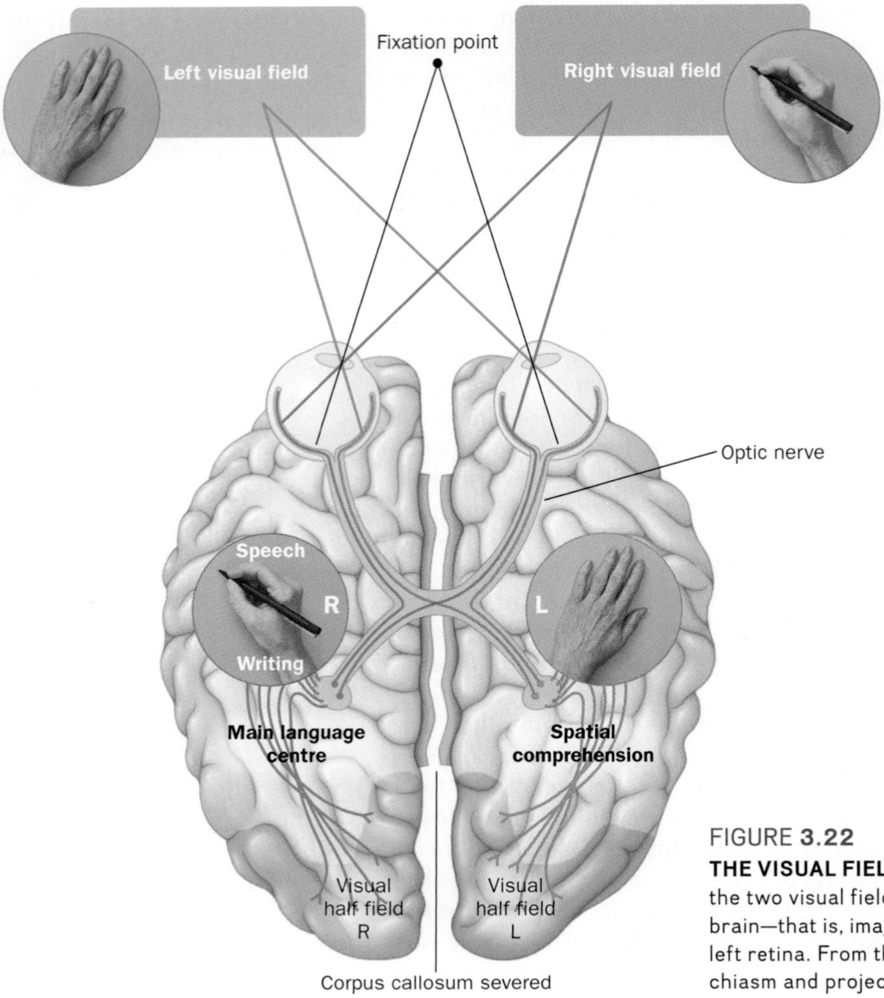

FIGURE **3.22**

THE VISUAL FIELD AND THE BRAIN. Information from the two visual fields is processed in the opposite side of the brain—that is, images from the right visual field stimulate the left retina. From the retina the optic nerves cross at the optic chiasm and project to the visual cortex in the occipital lobes.

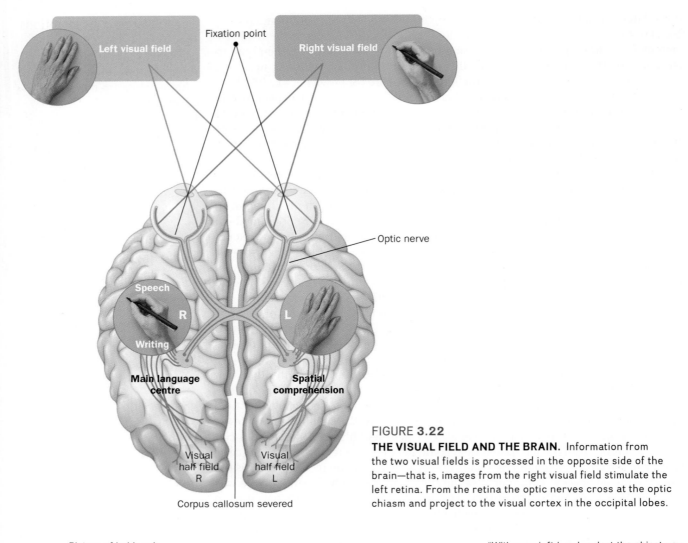

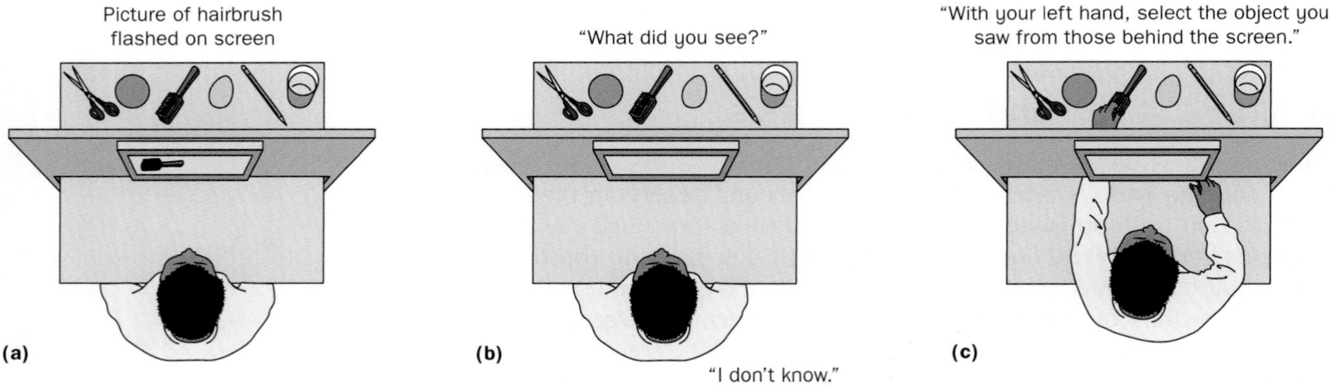

FIGURE **3.23**

PERCEPTION AND LANGUAGE IN A SPLIT-BRAIN PATIENT. In (a), a person who has had an operation to cut the corpus callosum is shown an object (hairbrush) to her left visual field. In (b), when asked what she saw, she cannot say, because her language production centre (Broca's area) is in her left hemisphere. Because the image is shown to her left visual field, only her right visual cortex perceives it. With a split corpus callosum, there is no way for that information to cross from the right hemisphere to the left. So she is unable to say what she saw. In (c), however, she is able to pick up the object she saw with her *left* hand. Why her left hand? Because it is controlled by her right hemisphere, which did in fact perceive the brush.

reorganize itself, or make new neural connections throughout life, as a function of experience. Second, almost every major structure of the neuron is capable of experience-based change. Third, not all regions of the brain are equally plastic. For example, a part of the brain heavily involved in learning and memory, the hippocampus, is more plastic than just about any other part of the brain. And fourth, brain plasticity varies with age, being strongest in infancy and early childhood and gradually decreasing with age. Yet, at no time in our lives does the brain lose its ability to grow new neurons, though the different parts of the brain are not equally plastic at all times.

Connection

If a person is not exposed to language much before mid to late childhood, the ability to speak is limited because the brain loses some of its plasticity as we age.

See Chapter 8, LO3.

Experience-based change in the nervous system occurs in several ways. Most common are the formation of new neurons, the growth of dendrites in existing neurons, and the formation of new synapses. The process of developing new neurons is known as **neurogenesis.** The growth and formation of new dendrites is called **arborization** (from the Latin *arbor,* or "tree"), because dendrites are like branches on a tree. Probably the best-known example of neuroplasticity, however, is the process known as **synaptogenesis,** the formation of entirely new synapses or connections with other neurons that is the basis of learning.

neurogenesis
the development of new neurons.

arborization
the growth and formation of new dendrites.

synaptogenesis
the formation of entirely new synapses or connections with other neurons

Although these principles of neuroplasticity are universal—that is, apply to everyone—some of the strongest evidence for them comes out of research on people with different kinds of sensory deficits, such as blindness or deafness. It is in deafness and blindness that we see most clearly how flexible the brain really is.

In most hearing people, the area that is called the *auditory cortex* processes sound. Although it is labelled by its function, anatomically the auditory cortex is actually a section of the temporal lobe. It is called the auditory cortex because the sensory neurons from the inner ear come here. But if those neurons don't pick up any sounds, what does this area of the brain do? Nothing? What a waste of brain tissue that would be. As it turns out, brain function and localization vary considerably on the basis of the experience of the individual.

For centuries scientists and ordinary people have observed that deaf people see better than hearing people and that blind people hear better than sighted people. Neuroscientist Helen Neville always thought there must be truth to these observations. In the process of testing these assumptions, she discovered that—overall—blind people are not better at hearing. They are not more sensitive to softer sounds than sighted people. Similarly, deaf people do not excel at all kinds of vision, nor are they able to see fainter images than do hearing people.

What Neville found, however, was that deaf and blind people are more expert in peripheral sensory experiences. That is, deaf people have better *peripheral* vision than sighted people—they are better at seeing things "out of the corner of their eyes" (Bavelier et al., 2000). They have better motion detection as well, and this also seems to be processed by the auditory cortex. Just as deaf people see better at the periphery, those who are blind don't hear better overall, but their *peripheral* hearing—hearing for things around the edges of a sound field (rather than the centre)—is better than that of sighted people. These peripheral

To compensate for deafness or blindness, the brain reorganizes and rewires the part of the brain normally dedicated to hearing or vision for other uses. Legendary blues and jazz guitarist Jeff Healy went blind at eight months of age from cancer of the eye.

Challenge Your Assumptions
True or False? In people who are blind, vision areas of the brain do not function.

False: The visual cortex takes on new functions, such as processing auditory information, in blind people.

sounds are actually processed by the visual cortex (Bavelier et al., 2000). In short, by virtue of its natural plasticity, the brain compensates for deficits in one sensory modality by reorganizing and rewiring unused regions to take on new functions. This neuroplasticity can be a problem for amputees, since the loss of a limb results in new vacancies in the motor and somatosensory maps in the cortex, leading to sensations of a *phantom limb.* The "Psychology in the Real World" section highlights some innovative, yet simple, neuroplastic treatments for phantom limbs.

Quick Quiz 3.3: The Brain

1. Posterior brain structures are those found nearest the
   a. thalamus.
   b. forebrain.
   c. back of the head.
   d. hypothalamus.
2. Which limbic structure plays a crucial role in fear?
   a. hypothalamus
   b. basal ganglia
   c. amygdala
   d. hippocampus
3. Where is the somatosensory cortex?
   a. in the occipital lobes
   b. in the frontal lobes
   c. in the temporal lobes
   d. in the parietal lobes
4. Split brain syndrome is caused by a last resort treatment for epilepsy. Which structure is severed in this treatment?
   a. corpus callosum
   b. left hemisphere
   c. right hemisphere
   d. both b and c
5. Research indicates that blind people
   a. are more sensitive to softer sounds than sighted people.
   b. process peripheral sounds in their visual cortex.
   c. have better peripheral vision than sighted people.
   d. all of the above.

Answers can be found at the end of the chapter.

Psychology in the Real World

Using Mirrors to Treat Phantom Limb Pain

One of the most puzzling phenomena in clinical medicine is the vivid sensation of a missing limb *after* amputation. Historical accounts of "spirit limbs" by the French military surgeon Ambroise Paré in the 16th century were based on reports of soldiers who lost limbs after being wounded in battle. American Civil War physician Silas Weir Mitchell later coined the term *phantom limb,* to refer to the ghostly perceptions of amputated limbs described by his patients (Ramachandran & Blakeslee, 1998, Doidge, 2007).

Almost all amputees experience the feeling of a phantom limb and can provide detailed descriptions of its perceived physical characteristics, sensations, and apparent movements. These sensations usually appear shortly after removal of the limb and can persist for many years (Hunter et al., 2008). Roughly half of patients with phantom limbs report distressing symptoms of paralysis and pain in their missing limb, particularly if they experienced these sensations before amputation (Melzack et al., 2001). Phantom pain can be extremely debilitating and it is extremely difficult to treat—how can you relieve pain in a limb that no longer exists?

Early explanations of phantom pain focused on damaged nerve endings in the stump, called *neuromas.* Since they were thought to be the cause of phantom pain, the goal of treatment was to deal with this troublesome sensory input by a number of different surgical approaches: removal of neuromas, further amputations, or cutting the sensory nerves to the spinal cord (Ramachandran & Blakeslee, 1998). Unfortunately, these treatments were largely ineffective, so this led researchers to investigate the central nervous system in a search for the origin of the phantom limb sensations. Studies in both humans and animals have revealed a rewiring of the primary somatosensory cortex after amputation (Flor et al., 1995; Melzack et al., 2001). This cortical reorganization is similar to what happens with the loss of vision or hearing: Neurons from neighbouring parts of the cortex appear to invade the territory vacated by the loss of the limb.

Neurologist and researcher V.S. Ramachandran decided to test the rewiring hypothesis in several patients suffering from phantom limb pain after arm amputation. By simply stroking different areas of the body with a cotton swab, Ramachandran discovered that sensations in the phantom arm could be triggered by simply touching the patient's face and jaw (Ramachandran & Altschuler, 2009). If you remember Penfield's map of the somatosensory cortex (see Figure 3.21), the face-sensitive neurons are located right next to the hand- and arm-sensitive neurons. Ramachandran reasoned that the somatosensory face map invaded the area once occupied by the map of the missing arm and hand, and that this remapping was causing sensations in both the face as well as the phantom limb.

These findings shed new light the origin of phantom limbs, but did not solve the puzzle of why so many patients experience aversive sensations like pain and paralysis. One hypothesis points to a disintegration of the signals between motor intention and feedback from the joints and visual system. When we execute a motor command from control centres in the CNS, it is guided by feedback from the muscles, skin, and joints. This way, we move just the right amount to carry out the desired task. People with amputated limbs still have motor intentions, but because they lack important feedback information, their motor control centres do not turn the command off. In fact, many amputees describe their phantom pain as cramping due to over-clenching the non-existent muscles (Harris, 1999). Since the somatosensory map for the amputated limb is activated by other neurons from the maps of neighbouring body parts, the patient experiences the clenching sensations as "real" pain originating from the original limb (Ramachandran & Blakeslee).

In the early 1990s Ramachandran decided to test this feedback hypothesis by providing his phantom limb patients with artificial visual feedback from their phantom limbs by using a simple mirror box. In this procedure, the patient is instructed to move

Mirror therapy provides virtual visual feedback from the phantom limb.

the intact limb while looking at its reflection in the mirror, and simultaneously attempting to copy the motion with their phantom. The visual feedback from Ramachandran's mirror box was immediately successful in the first patient who tried it—a man who experienced relief from phantom pain and paralysis for the first time in 11 years! Since then, many more patients have benefitted from this therapy with a reduction in perceived pain and paralysis by simply practising in front of a mirror for a few minutes a day (Ramachandran & Blakeslee, 1998; Ramachandran & Alschulter, 2009). Other researchers have extended discoveries from Ramachandran's case studies using controlled experiments, and have also reported immediate improvement in some patients (Chan et al., 2007). Furthermore, pain relief is correlated with a reduction in cortical invasion from neighbouring areas on the somatosensory map (Foell et al., 2014). In other words, reducing the neuroplasticity is linked to a reduction in phantom pain. Although not all patients respond to mirror therapy, it has been a simple, cheap, and effective breakthrough for many who have been plagued by their phantom limbs.

Groundbreaking Research

Neurogenesis in the Adult Brain

Neurons are unique cells in the body. Unlike many other cells, including hair, blood, or skin cells, nerve cells are not continually replaced. Based on his observations over 100 years ago, Spanish physician and Nobel Prize winner Ramón y Cajal concluded that neurons are incapable of growth, at least after early childhood. Until the 1990s, researchers and physicians alike accepted the idea that once a region of the brain was damaged, its function was lost forever. All neural growth and change were understood to be limited to fetal and childhood development, and the adult brain did not change.

EVIDENCE OF NEURON GROWTH

By the early 1960s, an accumulation of evidence began to suggest that adult brains do change. Perhaps the first empirical demonstration of neurogenesis occurred when neuroscientists detected evidence of cell division (evidence of growth) in the brains of adult rats (Bryans, 1959).

In the early 1960s, Joseph Altman published a series of ground-breaking studies with adult rats and cats in scientific journals. Armed with a new cell-labelling technique, Altman found evidence of the growth of new neurons—neurogenesis—in several brain areas that are crucial for learning and memory (Altman & Das, 1966; Gross, 2000). Even though these appeared in prestigious journals, however, Altman's findings were almost completely ignored or discounted. Why? He was working alone and he was a little-known researcher who violated the dogma, or strongly accepted view.

Animals reared in naturalistic settings have higher rates of neurogenesis than those reared in cages.

What could explain these differences?

As often happens with ideas that radically challenge basic assumptions and long-held beliefs, neuroscientists and others either trivialized or ignored Altman's findings of adult neurogenesis. What does it take for a movement to change a well-entrenched, century-old idea? Three scientific events took place during the 1980s and 1990s that finally turned the tide of belief. First, a series of studies on birds showed exceptional neuronal growth in many areas of the adult avian brain, including the hippocampus (Nottebohm, 1985). Second, there was increasing evidence for the formation of new synaptic connections in the brains of rats when they were raised in enriched environments, more so than normally occurs with development (Comery et al., 1996). For example, rats that lived in cages with playmates and wheels to run on and toys showed more dendritic growth than those who lived alone in sparse cages (Rosenzweig & Bennett, 1969). Third, in the 1990s, researchers began to find solid evidence for neurogenesis in one particular region of the hippocampus in adult rats, monkeys, and humans. Neurogenesis was no longer something seen only in birds and rats. There was no more denying that neuronal growth occurs in humans.

ENVIRONMENTAL EFFECTS ON NEURON GROWTH

One of the key figures in demonstrating new neural growth in adult primates has been Elizabeth Gould. She and her colleagues have compared rates of neurogenesis and synaptic growth in the brains of primates living in naturalistic settings with those living in lab cages. The naturalistic settings simulated a wild environment, with natural vegetation where the animals could search for food, among other activities. As you learned in Chapter 2, the brains of the animals that lived in these environmentally complex settings showed brain growth in areas important for thinking and feeling. They also had higher rates of neurogenesis and more connections between neurons than the animals reared in cages. In other studies, Gould and her colleagues found that stress and impoverished environments resulted in less neurogenesis in mammals (Mirescu & Gould, 2006; Mirescu et al., 2006).

Challenge Your Assumptions

True or False? Nerve cells cannot regenerate like other cells in the body.

False: The growth of new neurons has been observed in many species, including humans.

The person most responsible for demonstrating neurogenesis in humans is Fred "Rusty" Gage (a cousin of the famous Phineas Gage) (Gage, 2002). How? You can guess that researchers cannot train humans and then slice open their brains to see if neural growth occurred. Furthermore, brain imaging techniques that we currently use cannot detect the growth of new cells. One technique, however, lends itself to testing whether new nerve cells grow in the human brain. It involves injecting people with a substance called BrdU, which is incorporated into dividing cells so that they can be identified.

Although it is not legally ethical to inject healthy people with BrdU, Gage and his colleague Peter Erikkson knew that some cancer patients receive this injection as part of their therapy. Because it identifies new cells, it is used to track how aggressively cancerous tumours are growing. After some patients who had been injected with BrdU died, Gage and Erikkson examined their hippocampus tissue. Based on the presence of BrdU, they found new cells in the adult human hippocampus (Begley, 2007; Erikkson et al., 1998). In fact, it was the same part of the hippocampus that earlier had shown the greatest neuronal growth in rats and monkeys.

Because of the onslaught of findings demonstrating neurogenesis in adult animals during the 1990s, the dogma of no new neural growth finally died. Now we know that neurons and their dendrites and synapses change, grow, and die in both young and old animals—including humans—depending on the kind of stimulation they receive from the outside world.

Quick Quiz 3.4: Neurogenesis in the Adult Brain

1. The brain's ability to adopt new functions, reorganize itself, and make new neural connections is known as
   a. neuroplasticity.
   b. neurogenesis.
   c. the neuron doctrine.
   d. localization of function.

2. In what region of the human brain is there the most evidence of neurogenesis?
   a. hypothalamus
   b. frontal cortex
   c. amygdala
   d. hippocampus

Answers can be found at the end of the chapter.

LO14 MEASURING THE BRAIN

To be able to look into the brain as it is working was a long-time dream of philosophers and scientists. In the last few decades, a number of new techniques have made this a possibility. This section will cover three techniques now commonly used to measure human brain activity, as well as research strategies used in animal models.

Electroencephalography

Researchers use **electroencephalography (EEG)** to record electrical activity of the brain from electrodes placed on a person's scalp. The electrodes, metal disks attached to wires, are usually mounted in a fabric cap that fits snugly over the head. Typically, the person is conducting certain tasks while electrical activity is recorded (see Figure 3.24).

electroencephalography (EEG) a method for measuring brain activity in which the electrical activity of the brain is recorded from electrodes placed on a person's scalp.

event-related potential (ERP) a special technique that extracts electrical activity from raw EEG data to measure cognitive processes.

magnetic resonance imaging (MRI) brain imaging technique that uses magnetic fields to produce detailed images of the structure of the brain and other soft tissues.

The **event-related potential (ERP)** is a special technique that extracts electrical activity from raw EEG data to measure cognitive processes. To examine ERPs, one gathers electrical recordings from an EEG cap on research participants who are performing cognitive or emotional tasks, such as trying to attend to an object on a computer screen, remember a list of words, or view emotionally charged slides. Typically, raw EEG data provide a summary of all the electrical activity in the brain that happens at a particular time. Generally, this level of detail is fine for measuring states of wakefulness, for example. But you need more temporal precision if you want to see a brain reaction, say, to a particular stimulus, such as a flashing light or a line. To examine ERPs, researchers use a special averaging process that allows them to filter out all electrical activity except the activity that is related to the stimulus the person is processing in a controlled experiment.

Because they are based on EEG, ERPs provide excellent temporal resolution (they show brain activity linked with behaviour almost immediately) but poor spatial resolution (activity cannot be localized to a precise area). Therefore EEG is superior to other brain imaging techniques in showing *when* brain activity occurs. It is not very accurate at indicating precisely *where* activity occurs. Two other techniques provide better spatial resolution than EEG: MRI and PET.

FIGURE **3.24**
ELECTROENCEPHALOGRAPHY (EEG). One of the authors (Jennifer Stamp) in an EEG cap for a study on brain activity and word categorization.

Magnetic Resonance Imaging (MRI) and Functional MRI (fMRI)

MRI stands for **magnetic resonance imaging.** MRI uses magnetic fields to produce very finely detailed images of the structure of the brain and other soft tissues. In MRI, the patient lies on a platform or bed that slides into a tube surrounded by a circular

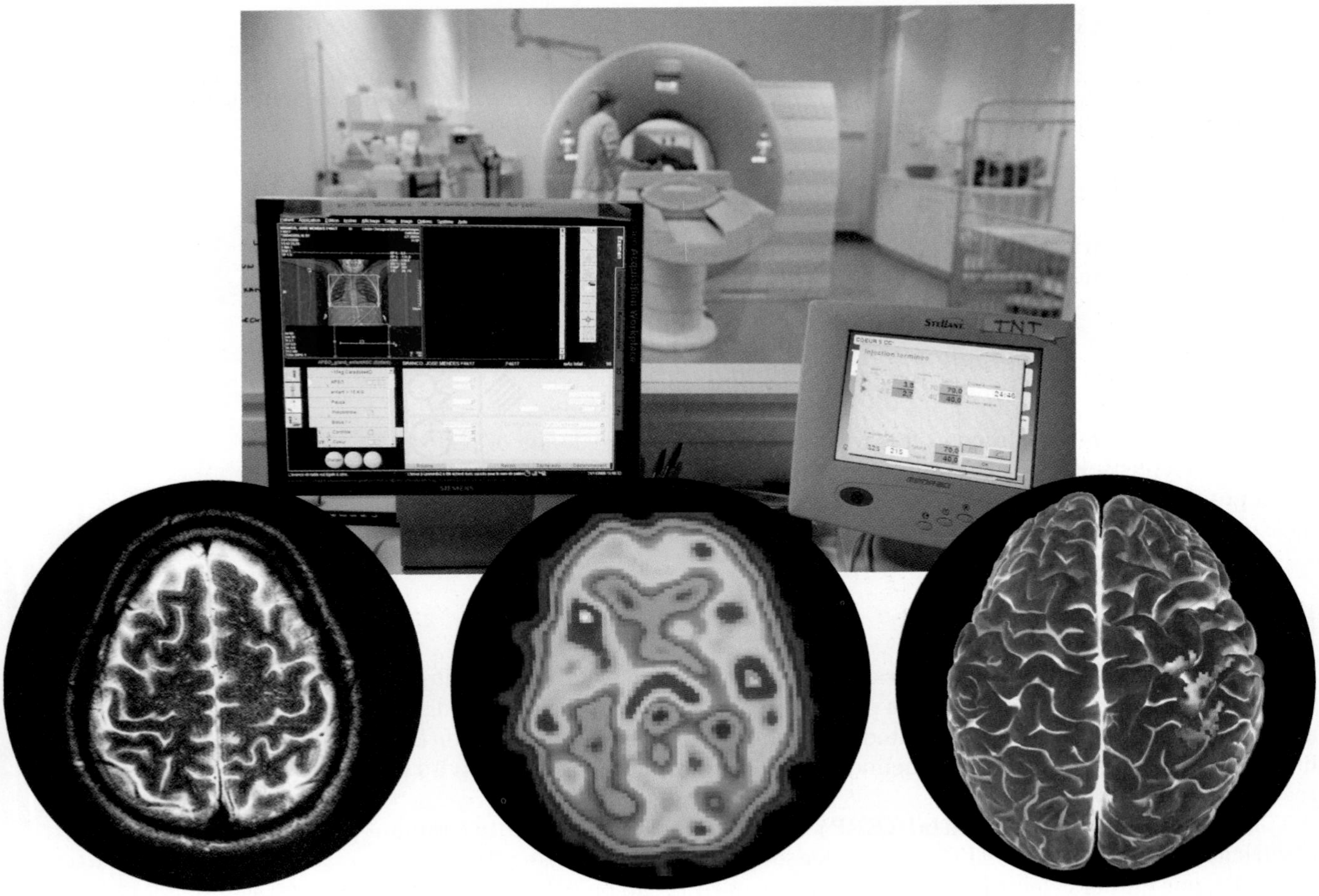

MRI SCAN   PET SCAN   FMRI SCAN

FIGURE **3.25**

BRAIN IMAGING TECHNOLOGY. MRI equipment (right) takes very clear, detailed images of soft tissue, including the brain, but it doesn't record brain activity. Both PET scans and fMRI, in contrast, highlight brain activity.

Which of these techniques gives the most precise location of brain activity?

magnet. The magnet, along with radio waves, is used to produce a signal that is then processed by computer. The computer then produces an image with an amazing level of detail (see Figure 3.25). MRI provides static pictures, and it is very useful for looking at structures and abnormalities in structures, such as when someone is injured. MRI does not tell us anything about activity, just structures.

functional magnetic resonance imaging (fMRI)
brain imaging technique that uses magnetic fields to produce detailed images of activity in areas of the brain and other soft tissues.

A variation on MRI, **functional MRI (fMRI),** does, however, tell us about brain activity. Images from fMRI tell us where activity in the brain is occurring during particular tasks by tracking blood oxygen use in brain tissue, as shown in Figure 3.25. In this way, researchers can see which areas of the brain are using the most oxygen (and presumably are most active) during certain tasks (Casey, Davidson, & Rosen, 2002; Lagopoulos, 2007). When people perform different tasks while they are being scanned, the researchers can distinguish from high-resolution images in which areas "light up" or are active during the task. To be sure, they are indirect images of activity based on how the brain uses oxygen rather than a direct "readout" of nerve impulses.

Although fMRI provides a much better measure of *where* activity occurs than EEG does, it is not without drawbacks. For one thing, it is very expensive. Also, it does not provide very precise measures of *when* activation occurs in response to a particular stimulus or task. It is not entirely clear exactly how directly fMRI images reflect underlying neural activity (Lagopoulos, 2007). Some studies suggest a fairly direct correlation with processing in certain cortical areas (Logothetis et al., 2001). As such, fMRI findings should always be interpreted with care.

Positron Emission Tomography (PET)

Positron emission tomography (PET) measures blood flow to brain areas in the active brain (see Figure 3.25). From these measurements researchers and doctors can determine which brain areas are active during certain situations. PET involves injecting the participant or patient with a harmless radioactive form of oxygen (or glucose). The brain then takes up the oxygen during cell metabolism. Thanks to the radioactive *label* on the oxygen, scanners and computers can be used to create images of the brain regions using that oxygen during a certain task. Although the results are very informative, the use of radioactive substances means PET is not risk-free. fMRI is a much safer way to image metabolism in the brain.

positron emission tomography (PET)
brain imaging technique that measures blood flow to active areas in the brain.

Invasive Techniques in Animals

Technologies allowing a glimpse into the human brain have been key tools in studying the biology of behaviour. However, there are a number of limitations in the conclusions that can be drawn from this type of research. For instance, it is difficult to measure events at the human synapse, since dissection of brain tissue is usually required for close contact with a neuron. Therefore, researchers often turn to animal models in order to ask these types of questions. Electrical recordings of graded and action potentials are predominantly performed in animals, quite often in invertebrates such as insects and squid. **Electrophysiology** is the study of electrical activity in the body and is used to assess electrical changes in groups of cells or individual neurons. Neurotransmitter release can be measured by a technique called **microdialysis,** in which a small probe is placed in the brain area of interest to collect samples of fluid. Released neurotransmitter can then be measured using biochemical techniques. Sometimes researchers use toxic chemicals or strong electrical currents to damage or **lesion** a brain area in order to determine what effect its absence might have on behaviour. This is often done to follow up findings from human brain damage case studies, but researchers have control over the brain area damaged and can make firmer conclusions about function.

electrophysiology
the study of electrical activity in the body.

microdialysis
technique to measure released neurotransmitter by implanting a probe in the brain.

lesioning
intentionally damaging the brain with chemicals or electricity in order to determine the role in behaviour.

Quick Quiz 3.5: Measuring the Brain

1. Which brain measurement technique best shows *when* neural activity has occurred?
   a. PET
   b. MRI
   c. EEG
   d. fMRI

2. Which form of brain measurement requires the use of radioactive substances?
   a. PET
   b. MRI
   c. EEG
   d. fMRI

Answers can be found at the end of the chapter.

Evaluating Connections in the Biology of Behaviour

What Esref Armagan's Story Reveals about the Brain

This chapter opened with a profile of the blind artist Esref Armagan. Besides being a fine example of someone creatively overcoming a disability, Armagan's story offers us a way to connect much of the material in this chapter. Let's take a closer look.

When Armagan paints, he uses a Braille stylus (writing instrument) to sketch out his drawing by laying down bumps on paper. With his other hand, he follows the raised bumps to "see" what he has put down (Motluk, 2005). He then transfers this sketch to canvas and applies acrylic paint with his fingers, one colour at a time. Armagan waits for each colour to dry before applying another so that they will not blend or smear too much. No one helps him when he paints, and his paintings are entirely his own creations.

Armagan has learned much from talking with other people, such as what the typical colours of certain objects are. He always keeps his paints lined up in the same order so that he can find the right colour. His sense of perspective is harder to explain. He portrays perspective with uncanny realism, far beyond what any other blind painter has ever achieved (Kennedy & Juricevic, 2006). He says he learned this from talking with others as well as from feeling his way in the world (*Biography*, n.d.).

Armagan's skill appears to have at least some inborn basis, given how early he started without receiving any instruction. Before age six, he would draw in dirt and scratch drawings on the furniture in his home. His parents, wanting to save their furniture, finally gave him drawing materials (Kennedy & Juricevic, 2006; Motluk, 2005)—something not usually offered to blind children. This early, automatic, and almost compulsive behaviour suggests that something about how his brain was wired drove young Esref to draw, and genetics likely played a role.

What senses does Armagan use while painting? Like many blind people, Armagan relies mostly on his sense of touch. Interestingly, he needs total silence while working. In many blind people, the so-called "visual" centres of the brain are used to process hearing (Röder, 2006). Maybe Armagan needs silence because he cannot afford to devote the precious resources of his mind's eye to hearing.

How can we explain Armagan's act of painting in the context of the nervous system? As Armagan moves the stylus to create bumps on paper and moves his fingers over those bumps, the sensations from his fingertips stimulate his sensory neurons. These neurons, in turn, stimulate interneurons in different regions of the brain (discussed on the following page), which eventually

Esref Armagan with some of his paintings.

stimulate motor neurons to move his hands and fingers in precise ways to execute his painting.

Throughout this entire process, millions of neurons are firing. As Armagan moves his hands and fingers and begins to paint, the neurons send impulses to other neurons. Some of the messages are excitatory; some are inhibitory. If a neuron receives a preponderance of excitatory impulses and the membrane potential changes sufficiently, it will fire in an all-or-none fashion. At this point, the cell membrane opens channels letting potassium out and sodium in. The wave of opening and closing channels moves the impulse down the axon and stimulates the release of neurotransmitters in vesicles that are in the terminal buttons. The neurotransmitters are released into the synaptic cleft where they bind with receptor sites in postsynaptic neurons, get taken back up into the presynaptic neuron, or degrade. The message is then relayed to the next (postsynaptic) neurons.

There is activity throughout his brain, in brain stem structures as well as in the forebrain. As Armagan paints, as is true for anything he does, his breathing, heart rate, body temperature, and even consciousness are regulated by the medulla (see Figure 3.26). Armagan's thalamus transfers and relays most of the sensory information coming into various parts of the brain for different kinds of processing. And there is so much information to process!

In order to paint, Armagan needs to plan and execute the actions of painting. The frontal lobes play a key role in planning and keeping in mind the tasks needed to paint. His motor cortex controls movement of his legs, arms, hands, and fingers. His basal ganglia help carry out the commands to move the various parts of his body. Perhaps Armagan decides to put his fingers in the paint container to his left. The parietal lobes get involved in orienting his body in space, and the frontal lobes plan the action to reach for the paint pot to his left. When he is ready to move his hand, the signal from these cortical areas travels to the cerebellum to control fine movement, then to the pons, medulla, and finally to the spinal cord to the nerves that control the muscles in his hand and arm. All this occurs in an instant. His brain gets feedback on the position of the hand and makes needed adjustments: a complex interplay among the somatosensory cortex (which receives sensory input from his fingers and arms as he paints), the insula, and the cerebellum.

Armagan is one of the few blind people with the ability to accurately portray depth and perspective in his drawings and paintings. When asked to draw a cube and then rotate it once and then once again, he draws it in perfect perspective, with horizontal and vertical lines converging at imaginary points in the distance (Kennedy & Juricevic, 2006). This ability to render perspective accurately in three dimensions is processed in the parietal lobes near the top and back of his brain. The visual images that Armagan forms from his sense of touch activate the same region of the brain that is active when sighted people see something: the occipital lobe.

When sighted people imagine something, their visual cortex (in the occipital lobe) is active—but in a much weaker way than when they actually look at something. When Armagan imagines an object, his visual cortex is even less active than that. But when he paints, his occipital cortex becomes so active that it cannot easily be distinguished from a sighted person's visual cortex as he actually sees something (Begley, 2007; Motluk, 2005). Armagan's brain appears to be seeing.

Because Armagan has been blind since birth, his visual cortex has never received any visual input (light). But that part of his brain didn't merely die or stop functioning. In many blind people, the visual cortex takes on hearing functions, enabling them to hear certain types of sounds better than sighted people can (Röder, 2006). Armagan's

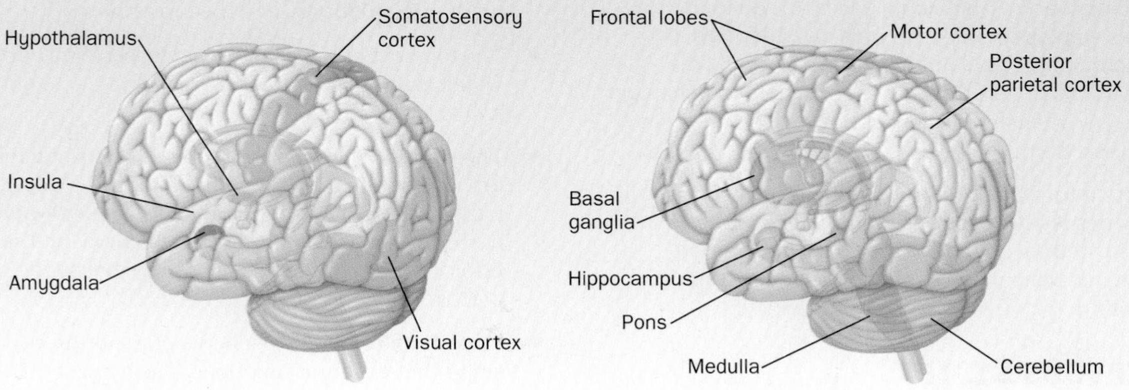

FIGURE **3.26**

SOME OF THE BRAIN REGIONS INVOLVED WHEN ESREF ARMAGAN PAINTS. When he is drawing or painting, Armagan uses many different regions of his brain. Most interestingly, Armagan's visual cortex is active in forming images of what he paints. These images do not stem from his visual system (eyes) but rather from his sense of touch (fingers). When Armagan touches something, his occipital lobes are as active as a sighted person's occipital lobes are when seeing something. In other words, he forms visual images, but they come from touching rather than seeing.

occipital cortex indeed is very active when he paints, but he is receiving tactile (touch) and not visual input.

Furthermore, in most blind people who read Braille, the visual cortex is active in processing tactile and verbal memory function. But Armagan can't read Braille and his visual cortex is not recruited for any aspect of language. In fact, his memory for language is rather poor. He is a very "visual" person, but his visual images are built from tactile information. There is evidence from neuroscientists who study blind people in general that this plasticity of the occipital lobes is the norm—it usually processes tactile information, verbal information, or both for blind people (Amedi et al., 2005). Armagan's life, abilities, and brain illustrate that the brain is both highly plastic *and* specialized (Begley, 2007). The so-called visual part of his brain found something to do.

Chapter Review

GENES AND BEHAVIOUR

- At least three principles of behavioural genetics are important for psychology: (1) The relationship between specific genes and behaviour is complex since most behaviours derive from many genes. (2) Behavioural genetics employs studies of twins and adoptees, or gene manipulations in animals, to disentangle the contributions of heredity and environment to behaviour. (3) The environment influences how and when genes affect behaviour.
- The extent to which a characteristic is influenced by genetics is known as heritability. Researchers use twin studies, adoption studies, twin-adoption studies, and gene-by-environment designs to study heritability.

THE NERVOUS SYSTEM

- There are two kinds of cells in the central nervous system: glial cells and neurons. Glial cells provide structural support, among other important functions.
- Presynaptically released neurotransmitter is received by the branchlike dendrites and cell bodies of postsynaptic neurons. This creates changes, called graded potentials, in the membrane of the postsynaptic neuron. If the right conditions are met, that neuron fires an action potential in an all-or-none fashion.
- Action potentials move down the length of the axon as channels in the membrane open and close, allowing ions to move in and out of the axon. The action potential stimulates the release of neurotransmitters from the terminals, into the synaptic cleft.
- Neurotransmitters bind to receptor sites on the dendrites of postsynaptic neurons, allowing an action potential to be generated if the charge threshold is surpassed. Excess neurotransmitter is either taken back into the original neuron or broken down in the synaptic cleft.

THE BRAIN

- The brain is divided into three major regions: the hindbrain, midbrain, and the forebrain.
- The topmost brain structure is the cerebral cortex, which is the seat of abstract reasoning, planning, and higher-order thought.
- The cortex comprises four lobes: The frontal lobes are involved in abstract reasoning, self-control, and motor control. The temporal lobes house the auditory cortex; the parietal lobes process tactile and spatial information; and the occipital lobes house the visual cortex.
- The left and right hemispheres of the brain carry out somewhat different functions. The biggest difference between the hemispheres is language, which is usually controlled by the left hemisphere.
- One major shift in our understanding of the brain over the last 15 to 20 years is how much neurons and brain

structures are shaped by experience. New neurons form, new dendrites grow, and new synapses are created across the life span, especially in infancy and early childhood.

MEASURING THE BRAIN

- Various methods offer glimpses into the brain and its functions. Electroencephalography (EEG) measures electrical activity from scalp readings. Magnetic resonance imaging (MRI) measures blood flow changes in the brain without the added risk of the radioactive dyes used in PET scans. The adaptation of MRI to functional MRIs (fMRI) allows researchers to determine which brain areas are active during specific tasks.

EVALUATING CONNECTIONS IN THE BIOLOGY OF BEHAVIOUR

- The story of Esref Armagan offers a glimpse of the brain in action. For example, as Armagan moves his hands and fingers and begins to paint, the neurons send impulses to other neurons. Activation occurs in many regions of the brain. The cerebellum fine-tunes his movements by attending to whether his body is moving appropriately with the right amount of effort. The visual images that Armagan forms from his sense of touch activate the same region of the brain that is active when seeing people see something: the occipital lobe.

Quick Quiz Answers

Quick Quiz 3.1: 1. b 2. c 3. a **Quick Quiz 3.2:** 1. d 2. a 3. b 4. c **Quick Quiz 3.3:** 1. c 2. c 3. d 4. a 5. b **Quick Quiz 3.4:** 1. a 2. d **Quick Quiz 3.5:** 1. c 2. a

CHAPTER

4

Sensing and Perceiving Our World

CHAPTER OUTLINE

Challenge Your Assumptions

True or False?

- ☐ Seeing is done as much with the brain as with the eyes.
- ☐ Different regions of the tongue contain taste buds for specific types of taste, such as sweet or bitter.
- ☐ The experience of "seeing sounds" or "hearing colours" occurs only under the influence of drugs.
- ☐ Cultural background can influence how people perceive the world.

LEARNING OBJECTIVES

- **LO1** Explain what is meant by sensation and perception.
- **LO2** Describe basic sensory processes such as adaptation and transduction.
- **LO3** Discuss the principles of psychophysics.
- **LO4** Describe the structure and cell types involved in vision.
- **LO5** Explain how we perceive depth in vision.
- **LO6** Explain the Gestalt laws of grouping.
- **LO7** Explain how we perceive colour.
- **LO8** Describe how physical properties of sound waves are represented perceptually.
- **LO9** Identify the main parts of the auditory system and what role each plays in hearing.
- **LO10** Explain how the sensations of touch and pain are relayed to the brain.
- **LO11** Explain how chemical information is conveyed to the brain for the senses of smell and taste.
- **LO12** Describe synesthesia.

Mike May lost his vision at age three. Four decades later, he had surgery to repair his eyes, in which doctors replaced the corneas (the clear outer layer of the eye) and other tissues. The surgery gave Mike working eyes. But it takes more than working eyes to see. Mike May could not miraculously "see" right after his surgery. He could barely make out vague shapes, colours, and light. It took him months to learn how to see again. Finally, three years after the surgery, Mike's vision started to approach normal. Many formerly blind people whose vision is restored never fully recover their vision, especially if they have been blind since birth (Kurson, 2007).

The case of Mike May shows how seeing takes place as much in the brain as in the eyes. After the surgery on his eyes, Mike May's brain did not know how to interpret the new visual information. As discussed in Chapter 3, neurons in the visual cortex often process other kinds of sensory information, such as touch and sound, in people who have no vision. It is possible that after he went blind at age three, Mike's visual cortex took on different functions. Now his brain had to learn to see again by reorganizing itself and developing new neurons. Seeing requires the right environmental stimulation (in this case, light) and neurons specialized for vision (Maurer et al., 2007). It requires both sensation and perception, which involve a complex dance of environmental input and biology, of nature and nurture.

Every moment of every day we are bombarded with stimulation—sights, sounds, tastes, smells, and textures. In this chapter we examine the interface between the outside world and our inner experience by looking at how we sense and perceive external stimuli. It is a long journey from light entering the eye to the experience of seeing something, and as Mike May's story suggests, it is by no means a straightforward process. For each of the major sensory systems, we will examine how physical information is transformed into neural signals, how the brain processes that information, and how our knowledge and expectations can shape our sensory experiences.

LO1 THE LONG STRANGE TRIP FROM SENSATION TO PERCEPTION

The better animals can sense what is happening in the world around them, the better they can survive and reproduce. Yet the apparently simple act of knowing that the sound vibrations hitting your ear represent someone calling your name, for example, is a complex process involving the sense organs and the brain. The sense organs transform information from its physical form (whether light or sound waves or chemicals) into a "language" that the brain can understand, in the form of nerve impulses. The brain then organizes and manipulates that information, interprets it, and then initiates a response. And it all happens in an instant.

This interplay between taking in information from the outside world and interpreting it is what sensation and perception are all about. **Sensation** is the response of our sense organs to stimulation by the outer world. Our sense organs detect different features of our surroundings: Eyes are sensitive to light waves, ears to sounds, skin to touch and pressure, tongues to tastes, and noses to odours.

sensation
a physical process: the stimulation of our sense organs by features of the outer world.

Yet sensing does not automatically translate into perceiving. Our brains have to receive the sensory input and then compare it to everything else it already knows, remembers, feels, and thinks. **Perception** is the act of organizing and interpreting sensory experience. It is how our psychological world represents our physical world. If you, for example, had not been taught to read, the words on this page would not be words. They would be shapes. You read and make sense

perception
a psychological process: the act of organizing and interpreting sensory experience.

of them because you spent years learning to speak English and then to read it. Your brain transforms the raw sensory experience of black and white marks into meaningful concepts that—we hope—will inspire you to learn and investigate further.

As we mentioned in Chapter 3, the brain organizes and interprets sensory experience to give it meaning. Before the brain can create meaning from sensory information, our sense organs transform physical stimuli from the outer world to a form that the brain can use—neuronal activity. Let's consider how basic sensory processes transform stimuli into neural information.

Is there a rainbow at the end of this road? We depend on sensation and perception together to detect, organize, and interpret stimuli in the world around us.

LO2 Basic Sensory Processes

Imagine that you were constantly aware of the sensations that bombard your sense organs, such as the sound of the air conditioner, clock, traffic, and radio; the sight of the chair you're sitting on, the ceiling light, the rug on the floor; the smells in the air; and the feel of your clothing against your skin. If you were constantly sensing all this, you would suffer from sensory overload. Our sensitivity diminishes when our senses are constantly stimulated, a process we know as **sensory adaptation.** Sensory adaptation ensures that we notice changes in stimulation more than stimulation itself. Changes in our environment, rather than steady states, are more likely to indicate events of importance. Therefore, sensory adaptation essentially acts as a filter to direct our attention to the most relevant sensory information. Notice how your gaze is automatically redirected towards a fast-moving object in your visual field compared to the background objects. A quickly moving hockey puck is more likely to grab your attention than the ice that it is travelling across (especially if it is moving quickly towards the direction of your head!).

sensory adaptation
the process by which our sensitivity diminishes when our senses are constantly stimulated.

Once we know that a physical stimulus is something to attend to, the sense organs convert it into action potentials. This conversion of physical into neural information is called **transduction.** Transduction happens when cells in the retina change light waves to neural energy, when hair cells in the inner ear change sound waves to neural energy, when chemicals in the air bind to receptors in the nose, when food chemicals stimulate taste receptors on the tongue, and when pressure and temperature stimulate touch receptors in the skin.

transduction
the conversion of physical into neural information.

LO3 Principles of Perception

Some of the earliest experiments in psychology were in the field of **psychophysics,** the study of how people psychologically perceive physical stimuli such as light, sound waves, and touch. Some basic principles of perception have emerged from over a century of research in this area. We outline these principles briefly in this section.

psychophysics
the study of how people psychologically perceive physical stimuli such as light, sound waves, and touch.

Absolute Thresholds

What is the smallest object you can see from a distance? What is the softest sound that you can hear? These questions refer to **absolute thresholds,** defined by psychologists as the lowest intensity level of a stimulus we can detect half of the time. A common way to assess absolute thresholds is for a researcher to present stimuli (sounds, for example) of different intensities to a research participant. The intensity level that the participant

absolute threshold
the lowest intensity level of a stimulus a person can detect half of the time.

can hear 50 percent of the time is that person's absolute threshold for sound. For example, imagine that five sound intensities, 20, 40, 60, 80, and 100 decibels (dB), are presented ten times each. A 100 dB sound is the loudness of heavy automobile traffic, and is therefore likely to be heard each time, while the 20 dB sound corresponds to the loudness of a soft whisper, and might be detected only infrequently. Of these values, the participant detects the 40 dB value 50 percent of the time and therefore 40 dB is this person's absolute threshold for this sound stimulus (Goldstein, 2007).

Psychologists have made some general conclusions about thresholds of perception (see Figure 4.1). For example, researchers determined under ideal laboratory conditions that an average person on a very clear night could detect a single candle from 50 kilometres away or could distinguish 8 litres of water with only one teaspoon of sugar as being different from 8 litres of pure water (Galanter, 1962).

Signal Detection There are a few problems, however, with measuring absolute thresholds. First, when a sensory stimulus is near absolute threshold, some people are more likely to say, "Yes, I perceive it" and others more likely to say, "No, I don't." Put differently, detecting sensations is a matter not only of intensity of the stimulus, but also of the decision-making process of the person in a particular context. **Signal detection theory** takes into account both stimulus intensity and the decision-making processes people use in detecting a stimulus.

signal detection theory
the viewpoint that both stimulus intensity and decision-making processes are involved in the detection of a stimulus.

Consider the situation in which there are serious consequences if you miss detecting a visual or auditory stimulus. A nurse in emergency medicine, for example, would not want to miss a slight change in a vital sign of a severely injured patient. An air-traffic controller would not want to miss a bleep on his or her screen—it might make the difference between averting a mid-air collision or not. In such situations, people may be more sensitive to sensory input, so much so that they might say they saw or heard something that was not there.

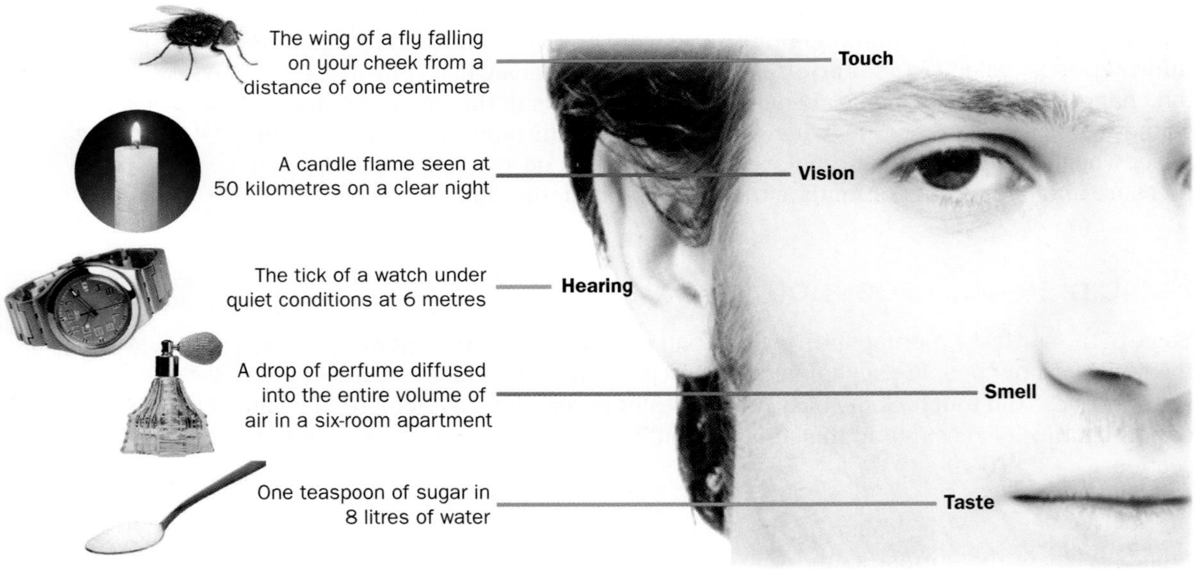

The wing of a fly falling on your cheek from a distance of one centimetre
Touch
A candle flame seen at 50 kilometres on a clear night
Vision
The tick of a watch under quiet conditions at 6 metres
Hearing
A drop of perfume diffused into the entire volume of air in a six-room apartment
Smell
One teaspoon of sugar in 8 litres of water
Taste

FIGURE **4.1**
ABSOLUTE SENSORY THRESHOLDS. These are the smallest amounts of a stimulus that most humans can perceive. (*Source:* Smith, B.D. (1998). *Psychology: Science and understanding.* New York, NY: McGraw-Hill.)

Why is it important for certain jobs to have people with more awareness of low-intensity signals, and what does it say about how we measure absolute thresholds?

In signal detection research, a low-intensity stimulus is presented on some occasions and not presented on other occasions (Green & Swets, 1974; Swets, 1964). Instead of having a 50 percent detection line, signal detection experiments present only a single low-intensity stimulus. Let's use hearing as an example. A participant has 100 chances to detect a soft tone. During the 100 chances, the tone is either present or not. In signal detection, there are four possible outcomes: a *hit* is correctly detecting a stimulus that is there; a *miss* is failing to detect a stimulus that is there; a *false alarm* is saying that a stimulus exists when it does not; and a *correct rejection* is not reporting a stimulus that is not there. Figure 4.2 summarizes the possible outcomes in signal detection experiments. In a signal detection study, the participant's responses create a profile of hits, misses, false alarms, and correct rejections. Using the classic method of absolute threshold, a person's threshold is assumed to be constant (e.g., sound intensity of 40 db). But in signal detection, it is assumed that a person's absolute threshold fluctuates, sometimes being more sensitive and other times being less sensitive. Moreover, because the stimulus is often presented in the context of other stimuli (noise for example), signal detection techniques are more like the real world, where many stimuli occur at once and where people's expectations can bias their response.

	Participant's Response	
	"Yes"	"No"
Stimulus Present	Hit	Miss
Stimulus Absent	False alarm	Correct rejection

FIGURE **4.2**

POSSIBLE OUTCOMES IN SIGNAL DETECTION RESEARCH. In signal detection research, the participant's responses create a profile of hits, misses, false alarms, and correct rejections.

Connection

Attention helps prevent sensory overload by filtering out sensory stimuli that aren't important.

See Chapter 5, LO3.

Difference Thresholds In addition to the question of absolute threshold, there is a second question: What is the smallest amount of change between two stimuli that a person can detect half of the time? This threshold is known as a **difference threshold.** Difference thresholds are also referred to as *just noticeable differences* (JND) because they involve the smallest difference that is noticeable. Being able to perceive slight differences is essential to a piano tuner, for example, who has to be able to distinguish the slightest change in pitch to tune it.

difference threshold
the smallest amount of change between two stimuli that a person can detect half of the time.

Weber's law
the finding that the size of a just noticeable difference is a constant fraction of the intensity of the stimulus.

The laws of just noticeable differences in sensory perception go back to Ernst Weber, who in 1834 discovered that the size of the JND is a constant fraction of the intensity of the stimulus. This is known as **Weber's law.** To put this more concretely: If you are given two weights, and one weighs 100 grams and the other weighs 103 grams, you would probably be able to say, "Yes, these two objects are different in weight." But you might not be able to detect the difference between a 100-gram object and a 102-gram object. In this case, 3 grams, or 3 percent, is the JND. In fact, 3 percent is the JND for weight perception (Canter & Hirsch, 1955). This means, then, that even if you had much heavier objects, say of 100 and 102 *kilo*grams, you would not perceive a difference in the weight of these two.

bottom-up processing
assembling a perceptual experience from its basic elements.

top-down processing
perception of the whole based on our experience and expectations, which guide our perception of smaller elemental features of a stimulus.

perceptual set
the effect of frame of mind on perception; a tendency to perceive stimuli in a certain manner.

Perceptual Set We have already made clear that perception happens in the brain, after transduction of the stimulus at the sense organ. So our experience of seeing or hearing or tasting is primarily a result of processing of incoming stimuli by the brain. Building a perceptual experience from basic elements of sensation is known as **bottom-up processing.** However, other things going on in the brain at the time of sensory processing can influence perceptual experience and can override our perception of the stimulus elements. Processing in which perception of the whole guides perception of smaller elemental features is called **top-down processing.** For instance, our frame of mind, which is ultimately coded in the brain, can impact how we perceive things. The effect of frame of mind on perception is known as **perceptual set.** Figure 4.3 reproduces an image from a classic study of perceptual set. Bruner and Minturn (1955) showed two groups of research participants this image. The two groups, however, each saw a different set of items before viewing this image. One group saw a series of numbers; the other saw a series of letters. Of those who saw the numbers first, the vast majority said that this image was the number "13." For those who saw letters first, the vast majority saw the figure as a "B." Since both groups viewed the same stimulus, they likely used the same bottom-up processes to assemble the basic elements, but they employed different top-down processes to interpret the experience. What people had seen prior to the test image created an expectation, or perceptual set, for how they perceived what came next. As you will learn later in this chapter, perceptual sets can arise from many different sources, including mood, health, knowledge of how the world works, and cultural upbringing.

FIGURE **4.3**
A DEMONSTRATION OF PERCEPTUAL SET. People who saw this figure after a series of letters perceived it as a "B." Those who saw it after a series of numbers perceived it as a "13." (Bruner & Minturn, 1955)

What conditions might lead to people having different perceptions of this image?

Quick Quiz 4.1: The Long Strange Trip from Sensation to Perception

1. The conversion of physical into neural information is called
   a. transduction.
   b. conduction.
   c. perception.
   d. adaptation.

2. Which of the following may act as a perceptual set in constructing our visual experience?
   a. mood
   b. expectation
   c. knowledge of how the world works
   d. all of the above

Answers can be found at the end of the chapter.

VISION

Most mammals rely on smell over all other senses, but humans are visual creatures. We rely so much on our sense of sight that we often ignore other types of information. Why is vision so important? Evolutionarily, being able to see helps us know where we are, what other people might want from us, and whether there is danger nearby. We evolved as hunter-gatherers. In hunting, vision is critical for locating prey and avoiding danger. So is hearing, which is our next-most-relied-upon sense. In gathering food, we use vision to locate the foods we can eat, but we also rely on our sense of smell to know whether a food is safe. But vision is king, and it starts with the eye.

The Physics of Light and the Psychology of Vision

Light consists of tiny particles, called photons, which travel in waves. The lengths of the waves are measured in nanometres (nm), or billionths of a metre. Humans are sensitive to wavelengths from 350 to 750 nm, so this range is referred to as visible light (see Figure 4.4). Other wavelengths of energy, such as ultraviolet, infrared, and microwaves, are invisible to us, but can be seen by other organisms. For instance, snakes can see into the infrared portion of the electromagnetic spectrum while vision in the ultraviolet range appears to be important for courtship displays in many birds (Hausmann et al., 2003).

What does the eye do? It bends light, converts light energy to neural energy, and sends that information to the brain for further processing. The eye is the gateway to vision, but very little of what we experience as vision actually happens in the eye. Visual experience happens in the brain, as we learned from Mike May's story. Before we explore the more complicated matter of how the brain

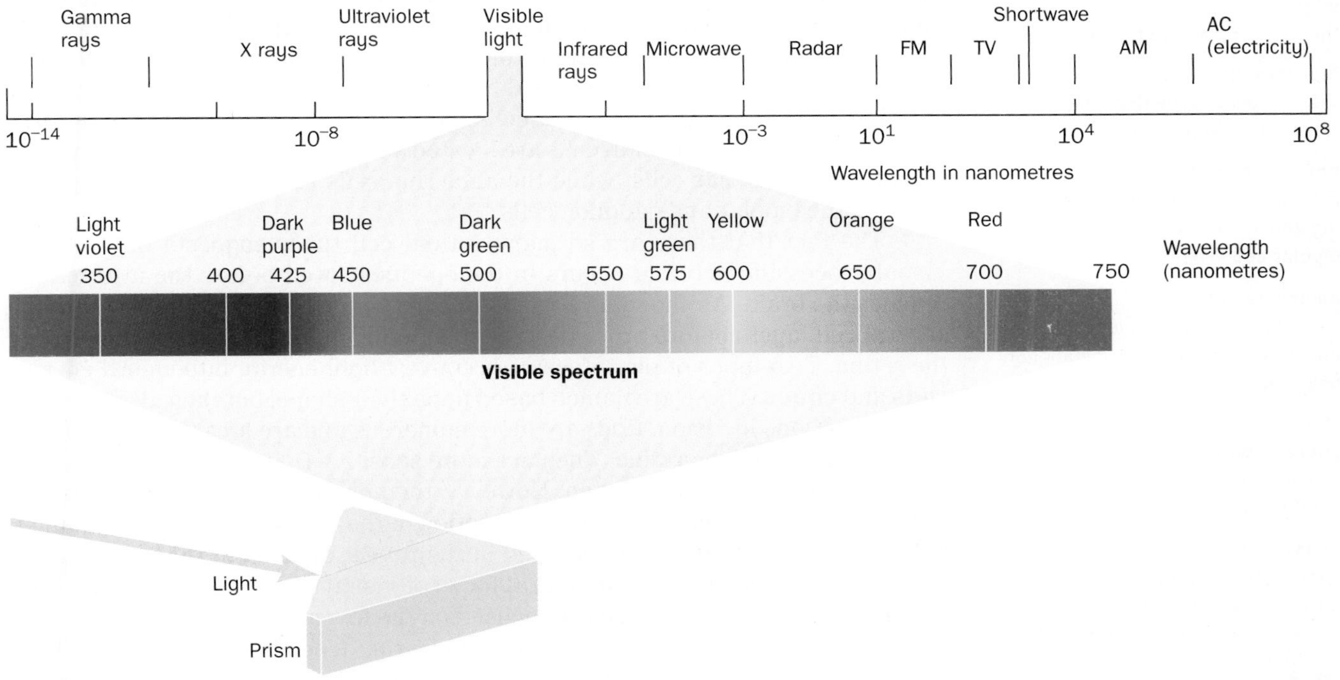

FIGURE **4.4**

LIGHT WAVES AND THE ELECTROMAGNETIC SPECTRUM. The entire electromagnetic spectrum ranges from gamma waves at the smallest end to AC current at the largest end. Between these two extremes is a very narrow band of wavelengths visible to the human eye. Visible light ranges from about 300 nanometres (violet) to about 750 nanometres (red).

cornea
the clear hard covering that protects the lens of the eye.

pupil
the opening in the iris through which light enters the eye.

iris
the muscle that forms the coloured part of the eye; it adjusts the pupil to regulate the amount of light that enters the eye.

lens
the structure that sits behind the pupil; it bends the light rays that enter the eye to focus images on the retina.

retina
the thin layer of nerve tissue that lines the back of the eye.

accommodation
the process by which the muscles control the shape of the lens to adjust to viewing objects at different distances.

photoreceptors
cells in the retina (called rods and cones) that convert light energy into nerve energy; they are transducers.

ganglion cells
the retinal cell type that carries visual information from the eye to the brain; their axons make up the optic nerve.

bipolar cells
the retinal cell type that links the photoreceptors with the ganglion cells.

horizontal cells
retinal cells responsible for modulating activity at the photoreceptor–bipolar cell synapse.

amacrine cells
retinal cells responsible for modulating activity at the bipolar–ganglion cell synapse.

rods
photoreceptors that function in low illumination and play a key role in night vision.

cones
photoreceptors that are responsible for colour vision and are most functional in conditions of bright light.

fovea
spot on the back of the retina that contains the highest concentration of cones in the retina; place of clearest vision.

visual acuity
the ability to see clearly.

sees, let's look briefly at the organ of the eye itself and how it converts light energy to neural energy.

LO4 **Vision and the Eye** Light enters the eye at the **cornea,** a clear hard covering that protects the lens. It then passes through liquid until it reaches a hole called the **pupil.** Light enters the interior of the eye through the pupil. The coloured part of the eye, the **iris,** adjusts the pupil to control the amount of light entering the eye. The light then passes through the **lens,** which bends the light rays to allow the large area of visual space to be represented in the much smaller area in the eye. Muscles around the lens alter its shape, depending on the distance of an object, to allow it to focus light on the **retina,** a thin layer of nerve tissue that lines the back of the eye. The process by which the muscles control the shape of the lens to adjust to viewing objects at different distances is known as **accommodation.** When light enters the eye, the lens bends the light in such a way that the image is upside down compared to the orientation of the object in the outside world. In Figure 4.5, you will notice that the image of the butterfly is flipped on the retina. The brain reorients the inverted image so that our world is right-side up.

Transduction in the visual system occurs in the retina, which consists of several layers of cells that are quite different from the cells that make up the other parts of the eye. In fact, the cells in the retina are actually neurons, and therefore the retina can be considered as an extension of the brain. The arrangement of the cells layers is somewhat unusual in that the **photoreceptors,** which convert light energy into neural impulses, are located in the deepest cell layer (see Figure 4.5). The photoreceptors are the only retinal cell type responsive to light; the other cells types are responsive to neurotransmitters and therefore act like typical neurons. The most superficial cell layer contains the **ganglion cells,** whose axons form the optic nerve that carry the information from the eye to the brain. The next deepest layer consists of **bipolar cells,** which form synapses with both the ganglion cells and the photoreceptors. Therefore the bipolar cells link the cells that transduce the light stimulus (the photoreceptors) with those cells that transmit the information from the eye to the brain (the ganglion cells). Two other cells types, the **horizontal** and **amacrine cells,** are located in an orientation perpendicular to the other cells types, and they integrate the activity of the other cells. The horizontal cells are located at the synapses between the photoreceptors and bipolar cells, while the amacrine cells are located at the synapse between the bipolar and ganglion cells.

The fact that there are so many retinal cell types suggests that a lot of visual processing actually occurs in the eye itself, well before the information reaches the brain. As shown in Figure 4.5, light entering the eye travels through several cell layers before processing begins in the photoreceptors at the back of the retina. Two types of photoreceptors convert light energy into neural energy, **rods** and **cones.** These are named based upon their shape, but they also have different functions in vision. Rods are more numerous and are located mainly in the outer periphery of the retina. They are more sensitive to light, so they work well in conditions of low illumination. However, they do not allow for finely detailed or colour vision, which is instead the function of the cones. Cones are less numerous than rods and are mainly located in the **fovea,** an area in the centre of the retina that corresponds to our central focus of visual space. We see images with the greatest clarity when they are focused on the fovea.

Visual acuity, or our ability to see clearly, depends on our cones. Those animals with the best acuity have the most cones. Most mammals only have two kinds of cones. Primates—humans included—have three. Birds have four kinds of cones (Goldsmith, 2006). Not only do birds see more colours than we do, but they also far surpass humans in visual acuity. This gives the saying "to see like a hawk" new meaning.

Embedded in the cell membranes of rods and cones are proteins with light-sensitive photochemicals. When light interacts with these photochemicals, it

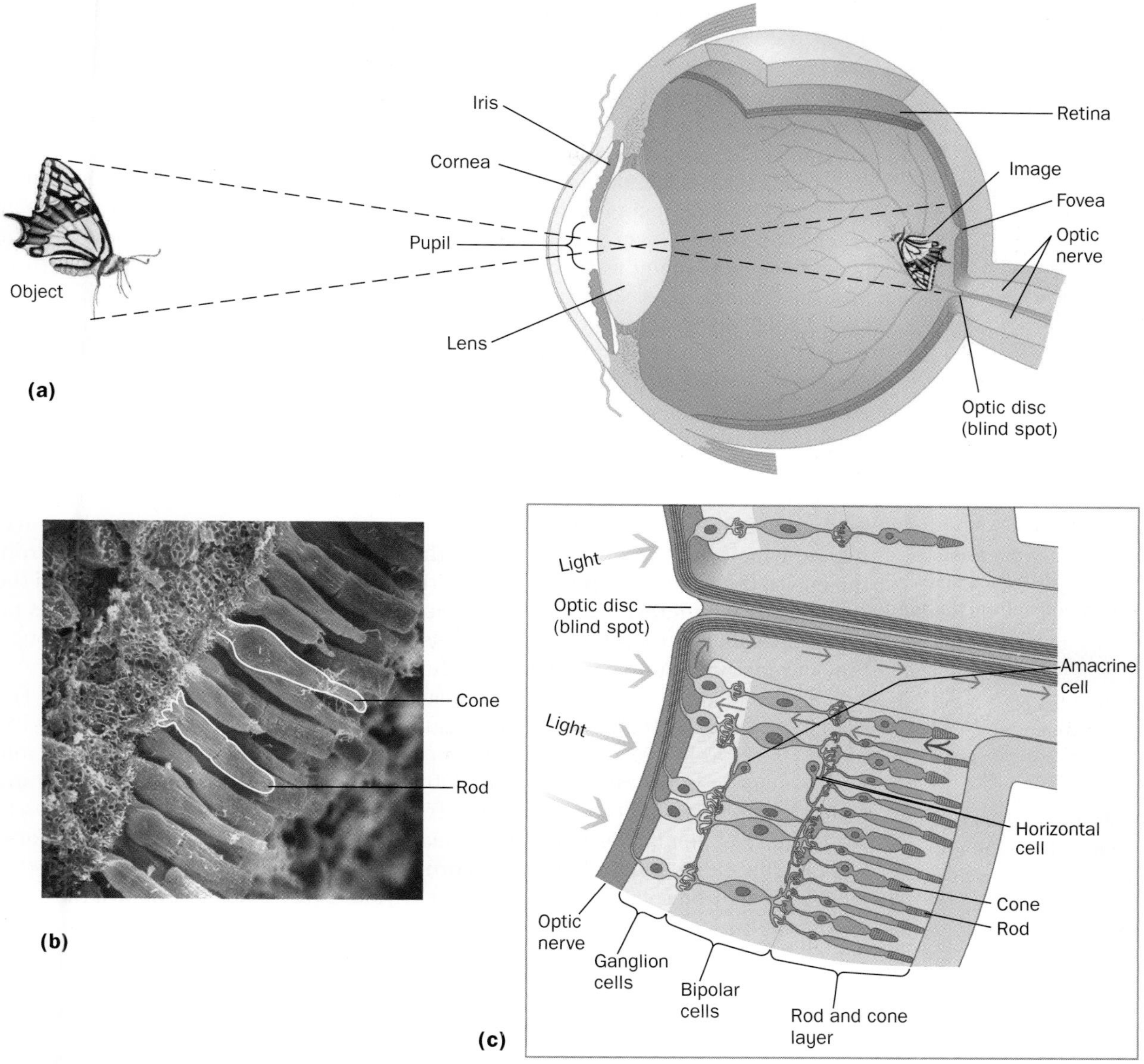

FIGURE **4.5**

THE EYE AND ITS RECEPTOR CELLS. In (a) we see all the main structures of the eye. Notice that the image of the butterfly is projected upside down on the retina in the back of the eye. In (b) we see the layers of cells in the retina, including the photoreceptors (rods and cones). In (c), an enlarged view of the retina shows the layers of the cells involved in processing light. Light hits the retina and is processed first by the photoreceptors (deepest layer), then by the *bipolar cells,* which send it to the ganglion cells. Horizontal and amacrine cells modulate the activity of the other cell types.

results in a change in the shape of the protein. This in turn alters the flow of sodium across the photoreceptor membrane and alters release of neurotransmitter at the synapse with bipolar cells. The protein found in rod cells is called **rhodopsin,** and it is particularly sensitive to light. Under conditions of bright illumination, it is said to be *bleached,* a term used to describe the inactivation of this protein after maximal stimulation. In fact, under typical daytime lighting conditions, we rely exclusively on our cones for vision since the rhodopsin in rods is totally bleached. Cones contain **photopsins,** which are less sensitive and do not bleach under conditions of bright light. In humans, cones contain one of three different photopsins, which respond to light at different ranges in the colour spectrum. As you will learn later in this chapter, these photopsins in cones enable us to see colour.

rhodopsin
the light-sensitive protein responsible for transduction in rods.

photopsins
the light-sensitive proteins responsible for transduction in cones; different photopsins are sensitive to different wavelengths of light.

Humans can see under a huge range of light intensities, although the quality of the visual experience is quite different between dim and bright light. We are not often aware of this with gradual changes in illumination, although we have all experienced a dramatic shift in visual function when light levels suddenly change. Consider what happens when someone turns out the lights. At first everything is completely dark. Then, after about five minutes, you begin to see shapes and forms, which is a result of the unbleaching of photopsins in the cones. Rods, whose rhodopsin is maximally bleached under normal lighting conditions, react much more slowly than cones and can take up to 30 minutes to respond. The process of adjustment to seeing in very dim light is known as **dark adaptation,** and reflects the photochemicals in cones and rods readjusting to low illumination. **Light adaptation** is the opposite process, and is most pronounced when we are suddenly exposed to bright light after our eyes have adjusted to the dark (Rushton, 1961). You have experienced how sensitive rod-based vision is if you've ever had the lights suddenly turned on in the dark; normal indoor lighting seems glaring because rods are unbleached and supersensitive.

dark adaptation
process of adjustment to seeing in dim light.

light adaptation
process of adjustment to seeing in bright light.

Vision and the Brain After transduction at the photoreceptor layer, visual information is processed by different layers of cells in the retina. The **optic nerve,** which arises from the axons of the ganglion cells, transmits signals from the eye to the brain. The point at which the optic nerve exits the eye is called the **optic disc,** which forms a *blind spot* on the retina because this location has no receptor cells and therefore nothing is seen (see Figure 4.5). A demonstration of how our visual system deals with the blind spot is shown in Figure 4.6.

optic nerve
structure composed of the axons of ganglion cells from the retina that carry visual information from the eye to the brain.

optic disc
the point at which the optic nerve exits the eye; it contains no photoreceptors so forms a *blind spot.*

optic chiasm
the point at which strands of the optic nerve from half of each eye cross over to the opposite side of the brain.

Exactly what happens when visual information arrives in the brain? The optic nerve carries impulses to the thalamus and, ultimately, to the visual cortex of the occipital lobes. This journey is *not* straightforward. As you can see from Figure 4.7, the information from the left visual field is processed in the brain's right hemisphere, and the information from the right visual field is processed in the brain's left hemisphere. How the visual information gets to these hemispheres is a bit complicated. Let's look at this process more closely.

In Figure 4.7, notice that in each eye, each half of the retina (the area at the back) sends out its own axons. So each optic nerve has two strands. One strand from each eye contains axons that travel from the retina to the thalamus and on to the visual cortex of the *same* side of the brain as the eye from which the axons come. The other strand crosses to the *opposite* side of the brain in an area called the **optic chiasm.**

The first stop in the brain for most of the fibres of the optic nerve is the thalamus. If the pathways to the thalamus are cut, visual perception is not possible, beyond some crude ability to detect the presence of a stimulus (Wurtz

FIGURE **4.6**

TEST YOUR BLIND SPOT. Locate the blind spot in your left eye by shutting the right eye and looking at the upper cross with the left eye. Position your head about 30 cm from the image and move it slightly closer and farther until the circle on the left disappears. At this point the circle occupies the blind spot in the left eye. If you then look at the lower cross, the gap in the black line falls on the blind spot and the black line will appear to be continuous. (From Wurtz & Kandel, 2000a, who adapted it from Hurvich, 1981)

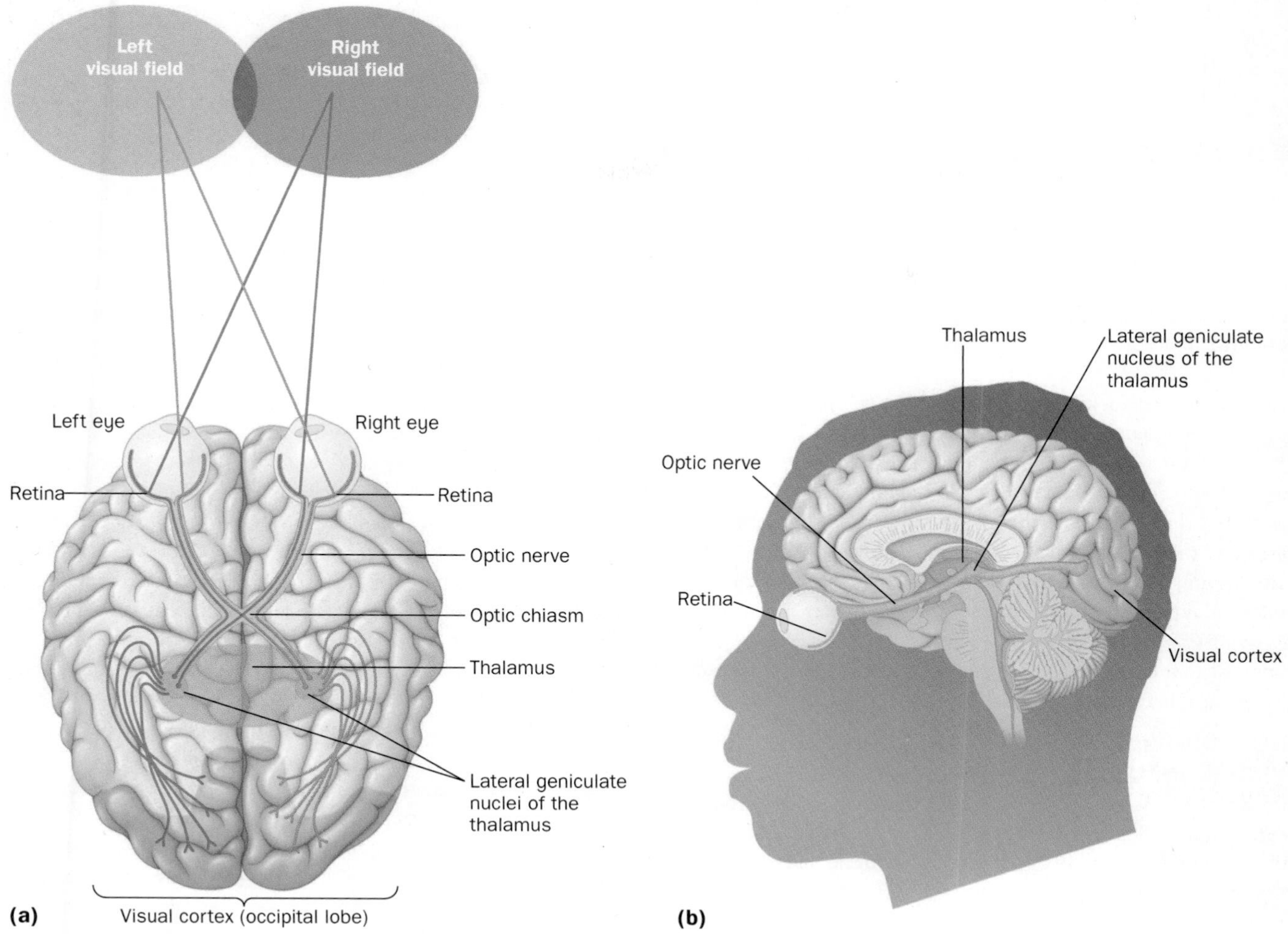

FIGURE **4.7**

THE VISUAL PATHWAYS IN HUMAN VISION. In (a) we see how input from the right visual field is sensed by the left side of the retina of each eye. This input then travels along the optic nerve to the optic chiasm and then to the thalamus (lateral geniculate nucleus). The same happens to input from the left visual field, except it is sensed by the right side of the retina of each eye (blue). From the thalamus, nerve fibres transmit visual information to the visual cortex of the occipital lobes (green). In (b) we see a side view of the path that visual stimulation takes from the retina via the optic nerve and the thalamus to the visual cortex.

& Kandel, 2000a). As we discussed in Chapter 3, the thalamus serves as a relay station for most of the major sense inputs to the brain, taking information from the sense organs and sending it to the relevant area of the cerebral cortex for processing. The thalamus does more than just relay information, however. Real visual processing occurs there. A cluster of the neuron cell bodies in the thalamus form the *lateral geniculate nucleus* (LGN). Visual information creates a point-by-point representation on the tissue of the LGN. What this means is that patterns of neural firing that correspond to the shape projected on a specific region of the retina affect a similar layout of cells in the LGN. So the retina and the LGN represent visual information in similar ways (Wurtz & Kandel, 2000a).

Fibres from the LGN in the thalamus then travel to the visual cortex in the occipital lobes. Neurons in the visual cortex analyze the retinal image in terms of its various patterns, contrasts, lines, and edges. Different cortical cells handle different aspects of this analysis. A breakthrough discovery in neuroscience showed just how specific the functions of certain cortical cells can be.

Groundbreaking Research

Functions of Individual Neurons in Vision

For centuries, a common belief was that nerves and the brain worked together as one structure to accomplish specific tasks, such as speech, vision, hearing, and thinking. Toward the end of the 1800s, however, many cases of brain injury demonstrated that injury to different parts of the brain resulted in different speech and behaviour disabilities. We saw this in Chapter 3 with Broca's area and speech. These cases provided some of the earliest evidence that different parts of the brain performed different functions.

Until the mid-20th century, however, scholars studying vision focused mostly on the eye. It had long been known, for instance, that rods and cones were the primary photoreceptors and that nerve fibres from each eye crossed at the optic chiasm and projected into the brain. But researchers did not fully understand or appreciate the importance of the brain in vision (Finger, 1994). No one was prepared for the new findings that two neuroscientists, Canadian David Hubel and Swedish Torsten Wiesel, reported in the 1950s and 1960s.

HOW INDIVIDUAL NEURONS RESPOND TO VISUAL INPUT

Researchers had known for decades that after leaving the retina, optic fibres synapse with neurons in the visual portion of the thalamus (the LGN), which then send the information to the visual cortex in the occipital lobes. Hubel and Wiesel's research—for which they won the Nobel Prize in 1981—showed something astounding. By implanting electrodes into the visual cortex of cats, they were able to record activity of individual neurons. Their work showed us that individual neurons fire only because of very specific visual information. They provided the first evidence that the neurons of the visual cortex are highly specialized for detecting specific regions of visual space, called **receptive fields.** They subsequently discovered that neurons only respond to specific features of visual stimuli in their receptive fields. As a result, they discovered neurons called **feature detectors** in the visual cortex, which analyze the retinal image and respond to specific aspects of shapes, such as angles and movements (Hubel & Wiesel, 1962, 1979).

receptive field
the area of visual space that stimulates activity of a particular neuron.

feature detectors
neurons in the visual cortex that analyze the retinal image and respond to specific aspects of shapes, such as angles and movements.

More specifically, Hubel and Wiesel described three types of neurons in the visual cortex that act as feature detectors. *Simple cells* respond to very specific information, such as a bar of light oriented at a particular angle. Some simple cells respond to only one angle or orientation, other simple cells respond to other angles of orientation, and still others to edges. As seen in Figure 4.8a, a particular simple cell might only respond to a diagonal line of a particular orientation. As seen in Figure 4.8b, recordings from this one simple cell show activity only to lines that match its receptive field, which in this case is a diagonal line from about 11 o'clock to 5 o'clock (\). The cell begins to fire more often as the stimulus (line) approaches the angle to which the cell is most responsive. As the stimulus passes that orientation on its way back to horizontal, the cell fires less and less often. This is the activity of just one simple cell. Other simple cells are responsive to other orientations, shapes, and sizes of lines.

A simple cell responds only to visual stimuli that stay still or are in the middle of its receptive field. Other cells, called *complex cells,* receive input from many different simple cells and are receptive to particular stimuli in different parts of the receptive field. Unlike simple cells, complex cells are also sensitive to movement. *Hypercomplex cells* receive inputs from many complex cells, and so they fire in response to patterns of lines. To give a concrete example: If some simple cells are responsive to / and others to \, then the hypercomplex cells are sensitive to the entire configuration of \/\/.

If the images and objects are broken up into horizontal and vertical lines, edges, colours, faces, hands, and shapes by the visual cortex, how is it that we ever see whole and integrated images? Reassembling the pieces occurs partly in hypercomplex cells in the visual cortex, but integration mostly happens when the visual cortex sends the images to other parts of the brain, such as the frontal or parietal lobes (Perry & Zeki, 2000; Wurtz & Kandel, 2000b). Thus, the cortex does not passively accept the nerve impulses from the retina and thalamus. The cortex actively transforms the signals by first breaking them down and then putting them back together.

Hubel and Wiesel made an even more monumental discovery when they closed one eye of a newborn cat. In the first weeks in a cat's life, when its brain is growing the most, visual experience is critical for brain structures to develop all the necessary neural connections needed to see well. If a cat is blinded or has its eyes closed for a week or more during this important stage of development, its visual cortex does not develop properly and the animal's vision is forever stunted. If one eye is closed early in life for an extended period of time, the part of the brain receiving messages from the closed eye soon begins to receive and process visual messages from the one good eye. Moreover, it is not merely light that the developing brain needs if vision is to properly develop, but also lines, shapes, and colours—the full visual experience. We see because our brains learn to see.

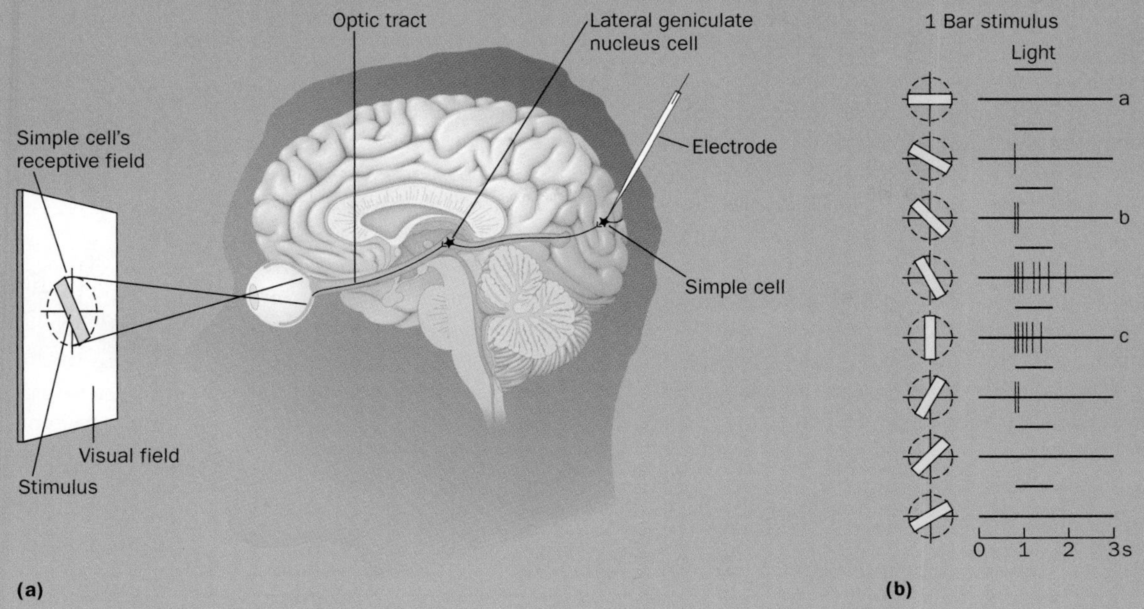

FIGURE **4.8**

NEURAL ACTIVITY OF A SIMPLE CELL THAT IS RECEPTIVE TO ONE PARTICULAR DIAGONAL ORIENTATION. In (a) we see the stimulus on a visual field and how this particular simple cell is receptive to lines tilted from about 11 o'clock to 5 o'clock as if it were a clock face. In (b) each vertical line to the right of the stimulus represents a neural impulse. The cell begins to fire more often as the stimulus (line) approaches the angle to which the cell is the most responsive. As the stimulus passes that orientation on its way back to horizontal, the cell fires less and less frequently. Otherwise, this particular cell does not fire. (Adapted from Wurtz & Kandel, 2000a, p. 534)

HOW THESE FINDINGS CHANGED PSYCHOLOGY

The implications of Hubel and Wiesel's findings are quite profound. For instance, we can better understand the case of Mike May, who regained vision as an adult after going blind as a three-year-old child. If the cortex and other parts of the brain have missed the window of opportunity to fully learn how to reassemble images, as in the case of Mike May, it may be impossible or very difficult to learn it later. After his operation, his brain almost immediately was able to take in colour and motion, but not three-dimensional space, depth, faces, and gender (Kurson, 2007). These more complex activities require more than visual training and experience to achieve. His eyes were fine, but his brain had missed the critical period for visual cortical growth and had forgotten how to see. Studies of restored vision have allowed researchers a unique glance into the importance of experience in visual development. Daphne Maurer and Terri Lewis of McMaster University have been studying recovery of visual function in children with congenital cataracts, which render them essentially blind at birth. Remarkably, these infants show recovery of visual function within the *first hour* of restored vision after surgery. Although this rapid "catch-up" demonstrates the amazing adaptability of the brain, typically these children do not regain full recovery of all aspects of visual function. For instance, previously blind patients show normal face detection (they can easily distinguish a face from a non-face object) but they have persistent impairments in face recognition (recognizing a specific face from other similar faces) (Maurer et al., 2007).

After Hubel and Wiesel's work, other researchers continued to find other cortical cells that fire in response to certain visual stimuli. Some, for example, respond to faces. If some cells fire when they are stimulated with faces in general, what happens

Connection

In many areas of development, such as language and learning, there are sensitivity periods when the brain is optimally receptive to environmental stimulation. One researcher found this out when newly hatched goslings (geese) mistook him for their mother.

See Chapter 7, LO10; and Chapter 8, LO3.

Challenge Your Assumptions

True or False? Seeing is done as much with the brain as with the eyes.

True: We integrate and make sense of visual information only if our brains have been stimulated with visual information. In this sense, we "see" as much with our brains as with our eyes.

when cells are stimulated with a specific face? Believe it or not, scientists have found evidence of cortical cells in the temporal lobe that respond only to images of certain individuals—for example, images of Bill Clinton, Jennifer Aniston, and Halle Berry (Quiroga et al., 2005). The so-called "Halle Berry neuron" that one individual displayed responds not just to photos of Berry, but also to line drawings of her and to her name printed in white letters against a black background!

This consistency of response by single cells to different types of stimuli—with very different physical features (colour photos, lines on paper, and typeface)—associated with Halle Berry shows that individual cells are responsive to abstract categories, rather than simple stimulus properties. Although the temporal lobe is not part of visual processing in most people, the specificity of cell response is very compelling. Does that mean we are born with Halle Berry neurons? No. What it does mean is that based on our exposure and interest in certain things or people, *single cells* can come to represent a category of things, such as all things Halle Berry-ish.

Do you have a Halle Berry neuron?

Quick Quiz 4.2: Sensing Visual Stimuli

1. Neurons called _____ in the visual cortex analyze the retinal image and respond to aspects of shapes, such as angles and movements.
   a. subjective contours
   b. shape responsive cells
   c. feature detectors
   d. horizontal cells

2. How did Hubel and Wiesel discover that some cortical neurons responded to seeing lines of a specific orientation?
   a. by using fMRI to study cat brain function during visual tasks
   b. by inserting electrodes into single cells in the visual cortex
   c. through surgical removal of cortical tissue
   d. with EEG

Answers can be found at the end of the chapter.

Perceiving Visual Stimuli

So far we have followed visual information from light entering the eye to impulses sent to the thalamus and then on the visual cortex, where cells fire in response to very specific features of a visual stimulus. How do we move from detecting edges to perceiving shapes, from noticing lines to identifying objects? A number of processes work together to help us recognize objects in the world. These involve motion, depth, size, grouping, and colour perception.

Perceiving Motion As we view any scene, several factors contribute to how we perceive movement. One factor is the background against which an object moves, and another factor is the size of the object. When an object moves across a complex background, it appears to move faster than when it moves across a simple background. For example, a deer running across a field with mountains and trees in the background will seem to move faster than one running across a wide open plain, simply because the background objects provide references that help us note the change of position in the deer. The human visual system is quite sensitive to changes in the position of objects, a sensitivity that appears to decline a bit with age (Bennett, Sekuler, & Sekuler, 2007). Size matters too. Smaller objects appear to move faster than larger objects, when all else is equal. If we see a domestic rabbit and a mule deer run across a wide open plain, the rabbit will appear to be running at a faster speed because of its size. In fact, these two animals run at about the same speed.

We can sometimes be fooled into thinking something is moving when it is not. We refer to this illusion as *apparent motion* because our brains interpret images that move across our retinas as movement. The "moving" lights on a movie theatre marquee are a rapid succession of bulbs lighting up in a row. Even though we know the lights are not moving, we still interpret this illusion as movement. Here's another interesting question. If you press on your eyelid when your eye is open and look straight ahead, you will notice the image shaking around. Yet, you do not perceive this effect as an earthquake. Why? According to research on monkeys, there are neurons that respond only when the image itself moves and not when the eye moves. So when you press on your eye, these neurons that detect image movement, called *real movement neurons,* do not fire. When the image itself moves without eye movement, they do fire (Galletti & Fattori, 2003). This is one way the brain can determine the difference between real and false movement.

LO5 **Depth Perception** We take for granted that we see things in three dimensions and can discriminate what is near from what is far, or what we call **depth perception.** This skill is remarkable, given that the image projected on the retina is two-dimensional. So how does this work? Two major aspects of human visual anatomy and processing allow for depth perception: binocular and monocular depth cues.

depth perception
the ability to see things in three dimensions and to discriminate what is near from what is far.

binocular depth cues
aids to depth perception that rely on input from both eyes.

convergence
a binocular depth cue; the way in which the eyes move inward as an object moves closer to you.

Binocular Depth Cues. **Binocular depth cues** rely on input from both eyes. One key binocular cue to depth comes from the fact that the eyes are separated by some space, so the images from each eye provide slightly different viewpoints. The difference, or *binocular disparity,* in these retinal images plays a key role in our ability to perceive depth. To see how this works, hold a finger out in front of you. Close one eye, and then close the other eye: You will see how the image shifts slightly to one side relative to the background scene, depending on which eye is closed and which eye is opened. If you hold your finger farther from your eyes, the image of your finger will appear to shift less. The brain integrates these two slightly different two-dimensional images apparent at different depths into a single three-dimensional image. This is the basis of 3-D movies; we are able to experience three dimensions because the left and right lenses present a slightly different image to each eye (see Figure 4.9).

Another binocular depth cue comes from information provided by the muscles that move the eyeballs around. Put your right finger out in front of you at arm's length. As you move the finger closer to your nose, your eyes come together or move inward. When you move the finger away from you, they move outward. This way that your eyes move inward as an object moves closer to you is known as **convergence.** During convergence of the eyes, the muscles that move the eyeball contract, and the brain makes use of the feedback from these muscles to perceive distance. Convergence is most effective as a depth cue for stimuli that are fairly close to us—that is, within three metres, but we rely upon binocular disparity to judge distances greater than this (Goldstein, 2007).

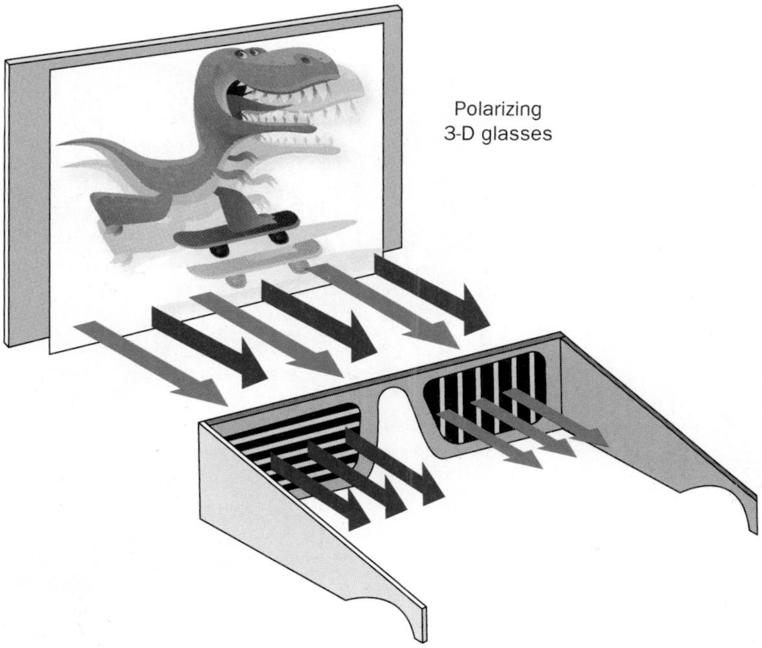

FIGURE **4.9**
HOW 3-D GLASSES WORK. Two cameras are needed for making 3-D films. Each camera records with a differently angled polarizing filter—either horizontal or vertical—and the viewer wears polarizing glasses when watching the final product. One lens filters out the vertical image and leaves only the horizontal one; the other lens filters out the horizontal image and leaves only the vertical one. Each eye, therefore, sees only one image. The brain then integrates these two slightly different images, so that we see them as being three-dimensional (Brain, 2003).

monocular depth cues
aids to depth perception that do not require two eyes.

Monocular Depth Cues. We derive a great deal of information about depth from the numerous **monocular depth cues** (*monocular* meaning "one eye") that do not require two eyes to be effective. One of these is *motion parallax,* which works in a similar manner to binocular disparity. This can be demonstrated by closing one eye and holding your finger in front of your face while slowing moving your head from side to side. You will notice that the closer your finger to your eye, the more it appears to move relative to the objects in the background. This cue allows people who are blind in one eye to perceive some depth.

Monocular depth cues can also be used to assess three-dimensions in two-dimensional representations such as pictures and photographs. Our knowledge of many of these cues derives from the seminal work of James Gibson (1950, 1966). Let's discuss some of the most common ones. Parallel lines, such as the railroad tracks in Figure 4.10a, appear to converge in the distance, a cue referred to as *linear perspective.* The farther away the lines are from the viewer, the more they converge and the greater distance we perceive. *Texture gradient* is a monocular depth cue that causes the texture of a surface to appear more tightly packed together and denser as the surface moves to the background. These changes in textural information help us judge depth. Notice in Figure 4.10b that the red poppies are more tightly packed at the top of the picture, which makes us think that those flowers are farther away. Also evident from Figure 4.10b is *relative image size.* If we know that two (or more) objects are the same size, such as the poppies, then different image sizes on the retina means that the smaller objects are farther away. Another cue, *atmospheric perspective,* comes from looking across a vast space into the distance in the outdoors. When we are looking through air and particles in the air (especially when the air is polluted), and objects farther away appear more blurred (see Figure 4.10c). *Interposition,* the partial blocking

(a) Linear perspective

(b) Texture gradient

(c) Atmospheric perspective

(d) Interposition

FIGURE **4.10**
MONOCULAR CUES TO DEPTH. It isn't necessary to have vision in both eyes to perceive depth using monocular cues.

of objects farther away from the viewer by objects closer to the viewer, happens when objects closer to the viewer often overlap with those farther away. This is a reliable cue to depth. Look at the image in Figure 4.10d of the lemons. The closer lemons hide part of the one behind them. Another monocular depth cue obvious from this image is the influence of *light and shading.* Light hits the closest objects and makes them appear brighter (like the pointy part of the lemon on the left) and casts objects that are further away into shadow.

Perceptual Constancy We know what familiar objects look like, and we know that when they change position or distance in relation to us, they remain the same. Nevertheless, the images on our retinas change shape and size as objects move through space. The ability of the brain to preserve perception of such objects in spite of the changes in retinal image is known as **perceptual constancy.** We will look at two types of perceptual constancy: those of size and shape.

perceptual constancy
the ability of the brain to preserve perception of objects in spite of changes in retinal image when an object changes in position or distance from the viewer.

Size Constancy. We see things as the same size regardless of the changing size of the image on the retina, because we know what the size of the object is. For example, if you see your friend Jayson, who is quite tall, walking away from you, the size of his image on your retina shrinks. Yet you do not suddenly think, "Oh no, Jayson is shrinking!" Rather, your knowledge of Jayson's height and your knowledge that people maintain their height even when they move away from you prevent you from interpreting the smaller retinal image as a smaller person. Also, distance cues, such as linear perspective, indicate that the road Jayson is walking on is in the distance and your brain makes use of this information *plus* your knowledge of Jayson's size to keep his size constant in your mind.

A stunning demonstration of distortions in the perception of size is the Ames room. In Figure 4.11a, the child on the right looks enormous compared to the one on the left. It turns out, however, that the room is not rectangular (as we expect it to be) but rather trapezoidal and the girl on the right is actually standing much closer to the peephole through which the viewer looks (as depicted in Figure 4.11b).

(a)

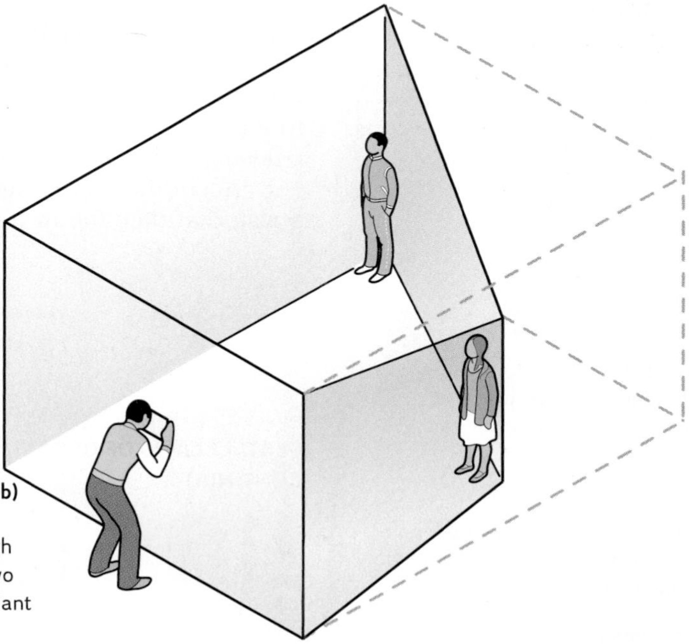

(b)

FIGURE **4.11**

THE AMES ROOM. (a) The Ames room was designed to distort perceptions of size. (b) When a person looks into the room through a peephole, it appears to be a normal rectangular room but the two people seem to be very different sizes: The one on the right is a giant compared to the one on the left.

These two children are about the same size, so why does the child on the right appear enormous compared to the child on the left? What does the Ames room demonstration show about perceptual constancy?

So the distance cues that we tend to rely on are not available, and we perceive the two people as equally far away, which makes the child on the right appear enormous.

Shape Constancy. People know the shapes of common things just as they know their sizes. The brain uses this knowledge to override changing retinal images that might make the world very confusing indeed. Take a look at Figure 4.12. When we see a door that is closed, it looks like a rectangle (and this is what the 2-D image on our retina looks like). A door that is partially open looks like a trapezoid. Still, we would not think that the door has suddenly changed shape. Again, the brain corrects based on previous knowledge that doors retain their shape when they change position.

FIGURE **4.12**

SHAPE CONSTANCY. Even though the two-dimensional retinal image of the door changes in shape from rectangular to trapezoidal when the door is opened, we know the door's shape hasn't changed.

LO6 Organizing Visual Information: Gestalt Laws of Grouping

How is it that we recognize a set of black marks on a white page as a letter or a shape rather than just a bunch of markings? We know, for example, that the letter "E" is more than just one long vertical line segment plus three shorter horizontal line segments. The Gestalt psychologists recognized that often we perceive wholes as more than merely the sum of their parts. *Gestalt* is a German word that means "form," "pattern," or "shape." German researchers Max Wertheimer, Kurt Koffka, and Wolfgang Köhler studied visual perception in the early 20th century and described a set of principles or laws by which people organize elements of figures or scenes into whole objects. These laws are most easily demonstrated with visual examples, though we can apply them to sounds. For example, when we hear notes strung together in certain patterns, we hear a musical phrase or tune, not just individual notes. Let's examine the major Gestalt laws of visual organization: similarity, continuity, proximity, closure, and figure-ground.

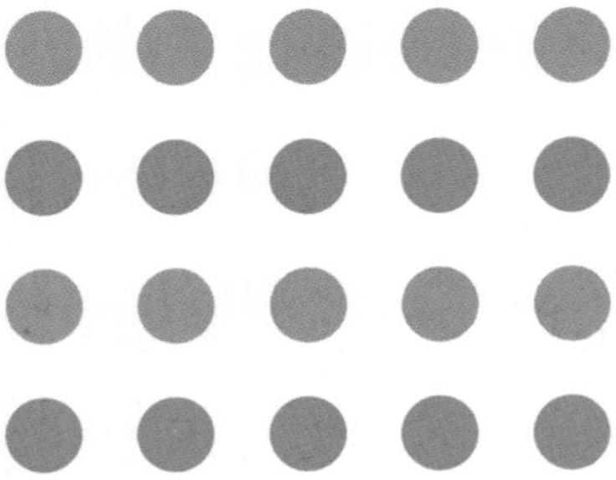

FIGURE **4.13**

GESTALT LAWS OF ORGANIZATION: SIMILARITY. People are more likely to see this figure as two rows of blue dots and two rows of red dots than as 20 dots, some red, some blue.

What do you see when you look at Figure 4.13? Most people with normal colour vision would report seeing two lines of blue dots alternating with two lines of red dots. You would not say, "Oh, 20 dots; some are red and some are blue." Instead, we group the elements that are like one another together into a perceptual unit—the red dots go together and the blue dots go together. This Gestalt tendency to group like objects together is as known **similarity.**

According to the Gestalt law of **continuity,** we see points or lines in such a way that they follow a continuous path. This sounds rather abstract, so let's look at an example. Consider the first drawing in Figure 4.14. We see a straight line running through a curved line. We do *not* see the first drawing as a result of combining the two pieces from the second drawing.

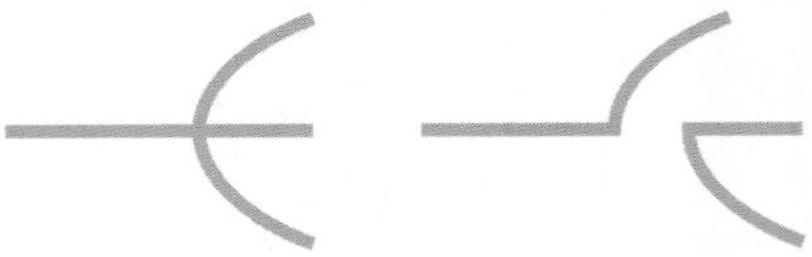

FIGURE **4.14**

GESTALT LAWS OF ORGANIZATION: CONTINUITY.

The Gestalt law of **proximity** says that we tend to group together objects that are near one another. Figure 4.15 shows a series of blue boxes. How would you describe what you see here? Most people say that they see four pairs

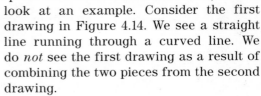

FIGURE **4.15**

GESTALT LAWS OF ORGANIZATION: PROXIMITY.

How would you describe what you see here? Four pairs or eight single boxes? Which do you think most people see, and why?

similarity
the Gestalt tendency to group like objects together in visual perception.

continuity
the Gestalt tendency to see points or lines in such a way that they follow a continuous path.

proximity
the Gestalt tendency to group objects together that are near one another.

of boxes, rather than eight boxes, because of the spacing. The first two are closer together than the second and third, and the third and fourth are closer together than the fourth and fifth, and so on.

Take a look at Figure 4.16a. Most human observers see these figures as distinct shapes (a circle and two triangles) rather than as lines, curves, and spheres, even though they are incomplete. The law of **closure** occurs when we perceive a whole object in the absence of complete information. The drawing in Figure 4.16b provides another example of how our perceiving brain completes the drawing to see a duck.

Another key Gestalt notion concerns how we separate things into *figure* and *ground,* where the figure is the thing that stands in front of a somewhat unformed background. Gestalt psychologists pointed out that we readily separate a figure from its background in order to perceive it. Perhaps the most famous example of figure-ground effects is the face-vase figure, a version of which is shown in Figure 4.17a. Notice that you can view the figure either as a blue vase against a light background or as two facial profiles (with blue space in between them). It is impossible to see both the vase and the faces at the same moment. Dutch painter M.C. Escher regularly used figure-ground effects in his paintings, one of which is also depicted in Figure 4.17b.

Connection

The Gestalt law of proximity makes use of the short-term memory technique called "chunking."

See Chapter 6, LO3.

closure
the Gestalt tendency to see a whole object even when complete information isn't available.

(a) (b)

FIGURE **4.16**

GESTALT LAWS OF ORGANIZATION: CLOSURE. We see the figures (a) as distinct shapes. We see (b) as a duck, not as a bunch of curved line segments.

How and why do you view these images as whole?

FIGURE **4.17**

FIGURE-GROUND EFFECTS.

In (a), is it a vase or two faces? In (b), M.C. Escher's *Sky and Water I*, do you see fish or geese?

Numerous visual illusions stem from Gestalt figure-ground principles, many of which have hidden figures as in Figure 4.18. Once you know what to look for in the picture, the hidden object becomes figural and you cannot help but see it. Try it for yourself.

Other visual illusions make use of the way our brain interprets depth cues (see Figure 4.19). Which line is longer, the one on the right or the one on the left? If you take a ruler to the page you will find that both line segments are identical in length, but many people report that the one on the right looks longer. Why do we see it that way? This illusion, known as the Müller-Lyer illusion, results from our tendency to see the right line as the inside corner of a room and the left one as the outside corner of a room or building, making use of the monocular depth cue of linear perspective.

Another commonly experienced illusion results from monocular depth cues. The *moon illusion* occurs when the moon is closer to the horizon. At that time, it appears to be much larger than when it is in the sky. Of course, the moon is not any larger, so why does this happen? Scientists offer several different explanations for the moon illusion, and although no answer provides one true cause for the illusion, nearly all explanations involve cues to depth perception (Goldstein, 2007). One explanation is that when the moon is near the horizon, we see it against other cues that indicate we are looking off into the distance (such as buildings interposed on the moon, possibly roads that offer cues to linear perspective, and so on). You can see this in Figure 4.20. Another way to look at it is this: When the moon is in the middle of the night sky, there are no cues to distance, no objects with which to compare it, and it is surrounded by a huge sky. Relative to the sky, the moon does not look so big. When the moon is on the horizon, however, we view it against objects whose size we know. Relative to those earthly objects, the moon looks enormous, which it is (Baird, Wagner, & Fuld, 1990).

FIGURE **4.18**
FIGURE AND GROUND EFFECTS IN SCENE PERCEPTION. What do you see in this image? See the end of the chapter to find out what you may have missed.

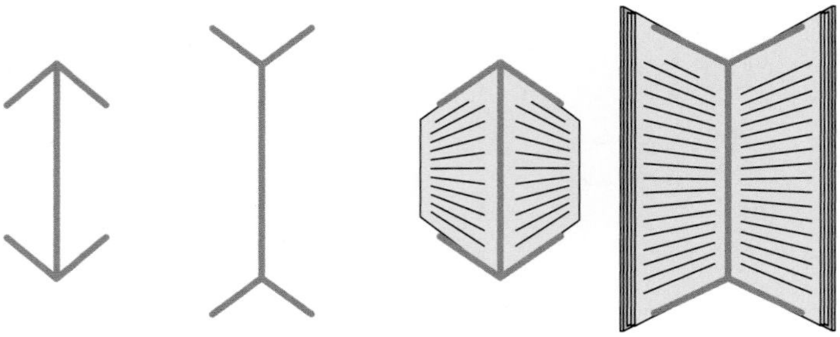

FIGURE **4.19**
THE MÜLLER-LYER ILLUSION. Which line is longer?

Visual Perception: Bottom-Up or Top-Down?

Feature detection research suggests that visual perception is a process of building a visual experience from smaller pieces, an example of bottom-up processing. We put the pieces together, and then we "see" the whole. Yet we have also looked at how perceptual set and Gestalt principles can guide how we make visual sense of information, a clear example of top-down processing. These two processes would seem to work in opposition, so which is correct? It depends on the nature of the information being processed. Reading, for example, relies on both bottom-up and top-down processing. To recognize a vertical line segment intersected by a shorter line segment as a "t," some building up of elemental features is required. But to make sense of the meaning of a "t" next to an "o" as the word "to," some top-down processing takes over, including your knowledge of English and the meaning of a preposition in a sentence (Johnston & McClelland, 1974; Pelli, Farell, & More, 2003).

FIGURE **4.20**
MOON ILLUSION. Distance cues make the moon look bigger at the horizon.

LO7 **The Perception of Colour** We tend to think of colour as a property of the objects we see. "That rose is red" or "The sky is blue." But colour is not a property of objects—it is a property of us. Our perception of colour depends on our photoreceptors, our brains, and the physical characteristics of the stimulus we look at. Let's start with the physical stimulus. Colour perception is partly determined by wavelength, measured in billionths of a metre or nanometres (nm). The spectrum of colour visible to humans ranges from 350 nm, which most of us perceive to be the colour blue, to 750 nm, which most of us perceive as red. Light that we perceive as green is at 550 nm.

Two Theories of Colour Vision. Psychological science has offered two main theories of colour perception, each of which explains different aspects of how most humans see colour. Let's consider the aspects of perception that each explains.

Young and Helmholtz developed their theory of colour vision around the idea that people have three kinds of cones: red, green, and blue. We now know this is anatomically correct, but Young and Helmholtz did not. They inferred it from their experiments on colour perception. They reasoned that all colour that we experience must result from a mixing of these three colours of light, so they called their theory the **trichromatic colour theory.** But mixing light is not like mixing paints. Mix red, green, and blue light together in equal amounts and you get white; with paints, you get a brownish muck. Light colour mixing actually occurs inside the eye, in terms of how different kinds of cones respond to different wavelengths of light.

The human retina contains three kinds of receptor cones, each sensitive to different wavelengths of light. The red cones are so named because they are most responsive to wavelengths of light in the longer end of the visual spectrum. Green cones are most responsive to medium-wavelength light, while blue cones respond mostly to shorter-wavelength light. Different firing patterns of these various kinds of photoreceptors combine to help create our experience of a wide array of colours. How much each cone is stimulated determines the colour we will see. For instance, for most people, the perception of yellow occurs with equal stimulation of red and green cones plus a smidgen of blue cone stimulation (see Figure 4.21).

Even though trichromatic colour explains how photoreceptors process coloured light, it cannot explain some aspects of colour vision. Take, for example, colour afterimages. **Afterimages** are visual images that remain after removal of the stimulus. Figure 4.22 demonstrates a popular colour afterimage. Stare at the white spot in the middle of the green-and-black flag for about ten seconds and then stare at the black dot in the white rectangle, where you will see, very briefly, a regular red-and-white Canadian flag. Trichromatic colour theory cannot account for this afterimage, but opponent-process theory can.

Ewald Hering (1878) proposed **opponent-process theory** to explain colour vision. He said that cones are

trichromatic colour theory
the theory that all colour that we experience results from a mixing of three colours of light (red, green, and blue).

afterimages
visual images that remain after removal of or looking away from the stimulus.

opponent-process theory
the theory that colour vision results from cones linked together in three opposing pairs of colours so that activation of one member of the pair inhibits activity in the other.

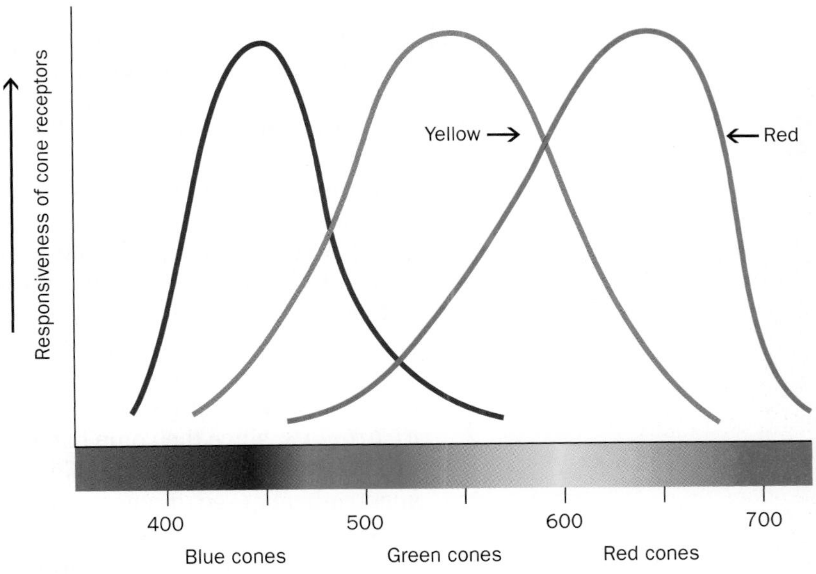

FIGURE **4.21**
RELATIVE ACTIVITY OF CONES. The wavelength indicated in the figure corresponding to our perception of yellow activates red (long wavelength) and green (medium wavelength) cones equally. The wavelength of light corresponding to our perception of red also activates the red cones to the same extent, but since it does not activate green cones, our visual system can distinguish between these wavelengths. People who lack the green cones have trouble making this distinction.

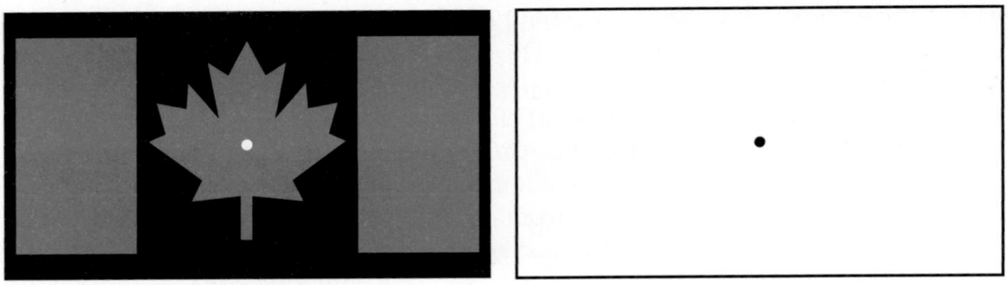

FIGURE **4.22**

COLOUR AFTERIMAGE. Stare at the white spot in the middle of the green-and-black flag for about ten seconds and then stare at the black dot in the white rectangle on the right. You will see, very briefly, a regular red-and-white Canadian flag. Trichromatic colour theory cannot account for this afterimage, but opponent-process theory can.

linked together in three opposing colour pairs: blue/yellow, red/green, and black/white. Cone signals combine at other levels in the retina so that opposing colour pairs have opposite effects on activity of retinal ganglion cells. For instance, in the case of red/green opponency, the long-wavelength, red cones have an opposing effect on retinal ganglion cell activity. In other words, the members of the colour pairs oppose one another, such that activation of one member of the pair inhibits activity in the other (Dacey, 2000; Solomon & Lennie, 2007). This theory helps to explain why we never experience some colours, such as reddish-green or yellowish-blue.

Current research indicates that both theories account for how human colour vision works. The trichromatic theory explains processing at the level of the cones, and explains why we can see so many shades of colour. The relative activity of the three different types of cones acts as a code for each particular shade that we perceive. Opponent process theory explains other characteristics of colour vision, such as afterimages and rules of perceptual colour blending. The opponent process organization of retinal ganglion cells is also retained in neurons of the LGN and cortex. In these brain areas, some cells are excited by red, for example, and inhibited by green stimuli (Lennie, 2000).

Deficiencies in Colour Vision. There are many types of colour blindness. Only about 10 people in a million actually fail to see colour at all (Goldstein, 2007). More commonly, colour blindness refers to a weakness or deficiency in perception of certain colours. Usually this results from an inherited photopsin deficiency in the photoreceptors making cones less sensitive than they should be, and is most often observed in men and boys due to the pattern of inheritance. The most common form of colour blindness results from a deficiency of the green (medium-wavelength) sensitive cones (Neitz et al., 1996). These people are called *dichromats*, since they only have two functional photopsins. People with this disorder have trouble distinguishing shades in the red to green region of the colour spectrum, may see greens, yellows, and reds as similar. The relative activities of cones depicted Figure 4.21 can help explain this. For instance, in normal colour vision, light in the deep red portion of the spectrum (around 700 nm) will activate the red cones only, while light in the green portion of the spectrum (around 525 nm) will also activate these red cones to the same degree. The reason that we can distinguish between these two colours is that the green (medium-wavelength) cones are also activated by green light, and therefore these cones distinguish red from green. These green cones essentially act as a "tie-breaker," since the red cones are equally active by red and green light. Since dichromats are missing the photopsin usually present in the green cones, they essentially have no means to distinguish the two. Figure 4.23 presents a colour blindness test that taps into red–green weaknesses. Yellow–blue deficiencies are less common.

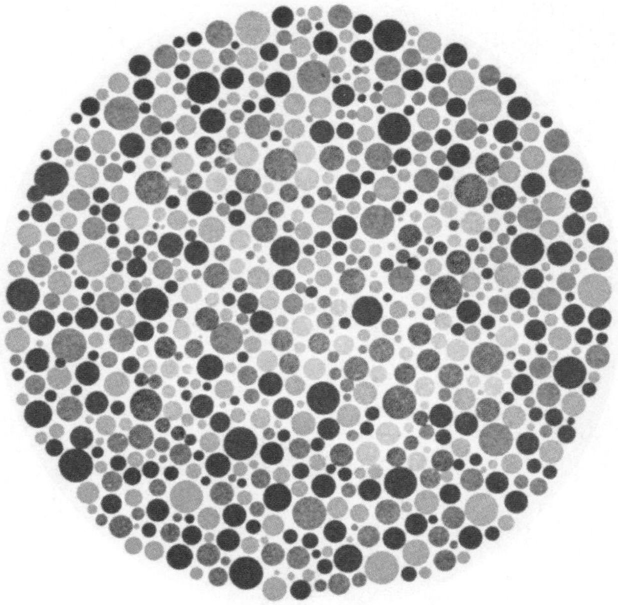

FIGURE **4.23**
EXAMPLE OF THE ISHIHARA COLOUR BLINDNESS TEST. People with normal colour vision can see the number embedded among the dots of this picture. People with red-green colour blindness cannot see the "74" embedded in the circle.
Why do some people have colour blindness?

Quick Quiz 4.3: Perceiving Visual Stimuli

1. What fibres make up the optic nerve?
   a. axons from ganglion cells of the retina
   b. axons from rods
   c. axons from thalamus
   d. occipital neuron axons
2. After leaving the retina, what is the first stop in the brain for processing of visual information?
   a. the occipital cortex
   b. the parietal lobe
   c. the hypothalamus
   d. the thalamus
3. Which of the following is *not* a monocular depth cue?
   a. linear perspective
   b. convergence
   c. texture gradient
   d. interposition
4. The ability of the brain to preserve perception of objects in spite of the changes in retinal image is known as
   a. interrelative consistency.
   b. proximity.
   c. visual stability.
   d. perceptual constancy.

Answers can be found at the end of the chapter.

HEARING

We could clearly make the case that for humans seeing is the most important sense. So much of our lives revolves around what we see. The science of vision is much more developed than the science of any other sense. And yet people who are both blind and deaf beg to differ. The deaf and blind American author Helen Keller put it most eloquently when she wrote:

> I am just as deaf as I am blind. The problems of deafness are deep and more complex, if not more important, than those of blindness. Deafness is a much worse misfortune. For it means the loss of the most vital stimulus—the sound of the voice that brings language, sets thoughts astir and keeps us in the intellectual company of man. (Helen Keller, as quoted in Ackerman, 1990, p. 191.)

Theatres and concert halls are designed to reflect and absorb sound so that wherever you sit, you can hear the performance. For musicians, however, constant exposure to loud music can cause hearing loss.

Just as vision starts when we sense light waves, hearing begins when we sense sound waves. Sound waves can move through fluid or air, but most of the time we hear sound waves that travel through air. Sound waves travel much more slowly than light waves, which is why you hear thunder after you have seen lightning.

LO8 The Physics of Sound and the Psychology of Hearing

We perceive different physical properties of sound waves as different attributes of sounds. Hearing is affected by three physical properties of the sound wave: its amplitude, frequency, and purity. The height, or *amplitude,* of the sound wave determines what we perceive as loudness. The taller the wave is, the louder the sound. The scale for a sound's loudness is decibels (dB). The scale starts with 0, which is the threshold for normal human hearing. The scale has no upper limit, but sounds above 150–170 dB are seldom registered anywhere. To give you markers for loudness: A whisper is about 30 dB, a regular human conversation is about 55–60 dB, a jackhammer is about 90 dB, a very loud bar or nightclub is around 100–110 dB, a very loud rock concert is about 110–120 dB, and a jet airplane is about 130–140 dB. If you were to ever hear a sound at 160 dB, your eardrum would burst. Where might you hear such an incredibly loud noise? Believe it or not, car sound system competitions, such as "dB Drag Racing" regularly achieve sound in the 150–160 dB range. The record stands at 171 dB. Needless to say, these levels are strictly for competition and no one is in the car during the competition.

The *frequency* of the sound wave, or how many waves occur in a given period of time, we perceive as the sound's pitch. Frequency is measured in units called *hertz (Hz),* which is how many times the wave cycles per second. The higher the frequency, the higher the pitch. The higher keys on a piano—those further to the right—are of higher pitch than the lower keys, for example. The range for human pitch perception is from about 20 Hz to about 20 000 Hz, but most people cannot hear sounds at either extreme. Sounds below 20 Hz are called *subsonic* and those above 20 000 Hz are called *ultrasonic*. Most sounds we hear are in the range of 400 to 4000 Hz. The human voice generally ranges from 200 to 800 Hz, and a piano plays notes ranging from 30 to 4000 Hz. Other animals have frequency ranges that differ from humans; elephants communicate with sounds in the subsonic range, while dogs and rodents can hear into the ultrasonic range.

The third property of sound waves, *purity*, refers to the complexity of the wave. Some sound waves are pretty simple, made of only one frequency (see Figure 4.24). Most, however, are almost always a mixture of frequencies and how much of a mixture defines its purity. We perceive purity as timbre (pronounced "tamber"). Musicians often refer to timbre as the "colour" of sound. Timbre allows us to distinguish a middle C (256 Hz) as being from either a piano or from a violin. They both are 256 Hz and may even be of equal loudness, but we have no trouble telling them apart because they produce waves of different purities.

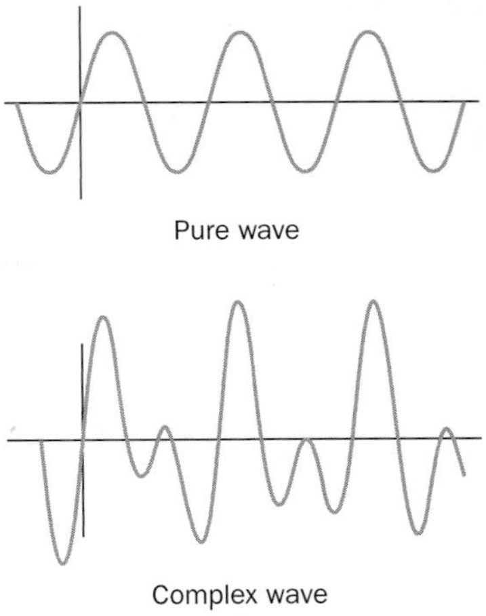

FIGURE 4.24
PURE AND COMPLEX SOUND WAVES. A pure wave consists of only one wave, whereas a complex wave is a mixture of more than one wave.

LO9

The Ear

The anatomy of the ear is relatively straightforward. First off, as the structures on the sides of our head, our ears have very little to do with hearing itself. These structures, called *pinnae* (singular = *pinna*), collect and funnel sounds into the passage called the *auditory canal*. Once inside this canal, sound vibrations travel to the eardrum, or **tympanic membrane.** The auditory canal and tympanic membrane make up the *outer ear*. The sound waves on the tympanic membrane set into motion the bones of the *middle ear:* the hammer, anvil, and stirrup (see Figure 4.25). These bones do more than just vibrate—they amplify the waves 20 times compared to when they entered the ear. The hammer hits the anvil and the anvil moves the stirrup. The vibration of the stirrup, in turn, sets into motion a series of important changes in the *inner ear*.

The inner ear includes the semicircular canals and the cochlea. The **semicircular canals** play a key role in maintaining a sense of balance. The **cochlea** is a bony tube, curled like a snail's shell and filled with fluid, and is the site of transduction in the auditory system. As the stirrup vibrates, it moves a membrane that covers the inner ear, called the *oval window*. The vibrations on the oval window send movement through the fluid-filled cavity of the cochlea. The **basilar membrane** runs through the cochlea and contains the **hair cells,** which are the sensory receptors for sound just as the photoreceptors are for vision. Hair cells are so named because they have tiny hair-like structures called *cilia* arranged in rows extending from the top of the cell into the cochlear fluid. As the vibrations move through the cochlear fluid, the basilar membrane vibrates, and this makes the cilia bend. The bending of the cilia opens up ion channels in the membrane of the hair cell, which alters its electrical properties and results in transmitter release at the synapse with **cochlear nerve cells.** The axons of the cochlear nerve cells make up the **auditory nerve,** which transmits auditory information to the brain.

The cochlea uses two methods to code the frequency of sounds: *phase locking* and *place coding*. For lower-pitched sounds (those with a frequency less than 3000 Hz) the hair cell cilia bend at the same frequency as the sound wave. In other words, a sound with a frequency of 1000 Hz will result in cilia bending at a rate of 1000 times per second. However, at sounds greater than 3000 Hz, the cilia on the hair cells do not have time to close before the next cycle of the wave arrives. At these higher frequencies, the sound is coded depending upon which hair cells are activated. Hair cells vary in size depending on where in the cochlea they are with the smallest hair cells are nearest the oval window and the largest hair cells are in the coiled-up centre part of the cochlea. The size of a hair cell is related

tympanic membrane
the eardrum.

semicircular canals
structure of the inner ear involved in maintaining balance.

cochlea
a bony tube of the inner ear, which is curled like a snail's shell and filled with fluid.

basilar membrane
a membrane that runs through the cochlea; contains the hair cells.

hair cells
inner ear sensory receptors that transduce sound vibrations into neural impulses.

cochlear nerve cell
the neuron that synapses with hair cells; its axons make up the auditory nerve.

auditory nerve
the nerve that transmits auditory information to the brain.

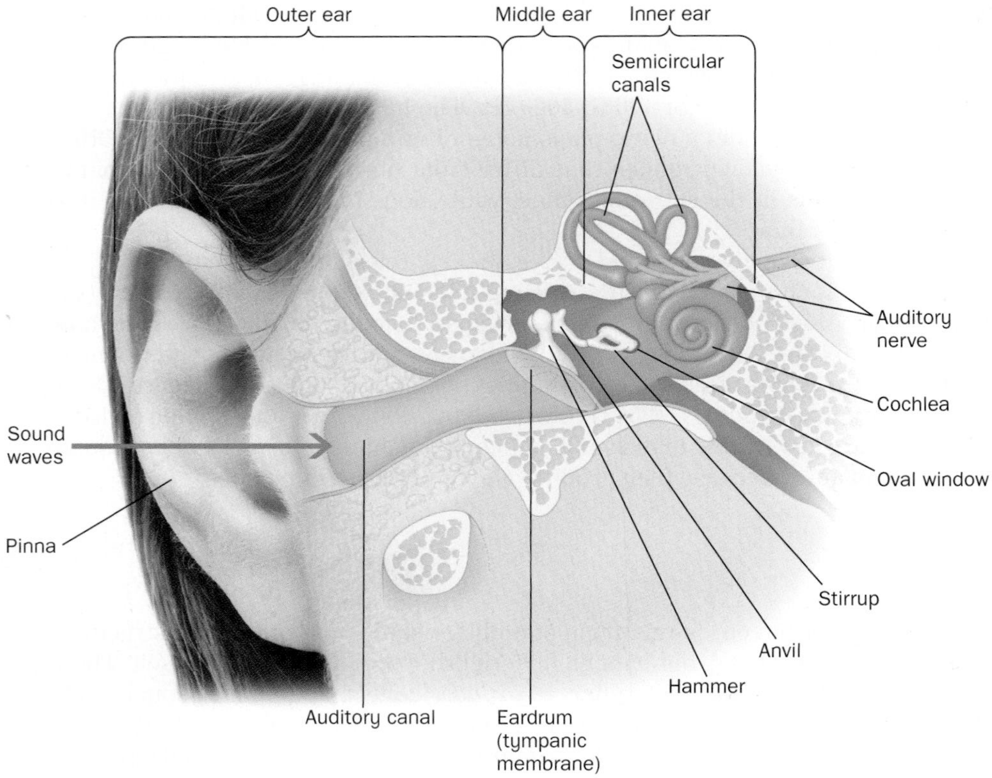

FIGURE **4.25**

ANATOMY OF THE HUMAN EAR. Sound waves hit the outer ear and travel down the auditory canal, where they vibrate the eardrum, which sets in motion the bones of the middle ear (hammer, anvil, and stirrup). The bones vibrate and amplify the waves, where they vibrate the oval window. The vibrations cause fluid in the cochlea to bend the hair cells. Stimulation of the hair cells transduces sound vibrations into electrical impulses. These electrical impulses can generate an action potential in the auditory nerve, which is then sent to the brain's auditory cortex for processing and interpreting.

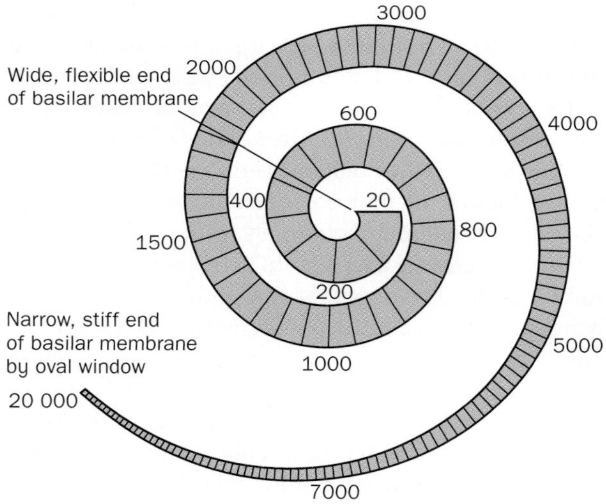

FIGURE **4.26**

DIFFERENT PARTS OF THE COCHLEA PROCESS DIFFERENT FREQUENCIES OF SOUND. The highest frequencies of sound stimulate the narrowest region of the cochlea. The small hair cells here are sensitive to high-frequency (high-pitch) sounds in the range of 15 000 to 20 000 cycles per second (Hertz). The largest hair cells are in the wide centre portion of the cochlea. These hair cells respond to low-frequency (pitch) sounds in the range of 100 to 20 cycles per second.

to its sensitivity to different frequencies of sounds. The smallest cells are sensitive to the highest frequencies (up to 20 000 Hz), and the largest hair cells are sensitive to the lowest frequencies (down to 20 Hz) (see Figure 4.26). The louder the sound, the bigger the vibration in the cochlear fluid, the more stimulation of the hair cells, the faster the rate of action potentials in the auditory nerve, and louder the sound we perceive.

If the hair cells in the inner ear become damaged, as can happen when a person is exposed to very loud noises once or moderately loud noises (such as machines) over long periods of time, the person can suffer irreparable hearing loss. For more information about hearing loss, see "Psychology in the Real World."

Hearing Loss in the Age of the iPod

Most people take their hearing for granted, but there is a good chance that at some point in your lifetime you will suffer some degree of hearing loss. It could be minor or it could be major. Studies often divide the causes of hearing loss into categories of age-related and noise exposure, but in fact, these two are related. Being exposed to loud noise levels over long periods of time leads to a loss of hearing after 10 to 15 years.

Noise often leads to age-related hearing loss, especially in the high-frequency range of 5000–15 000 Hz (Lutman & Spencer, 1991) (see Figure 4.27). For example, in a large-scale study of exposure to noise at work, middle-aged to older men (ages 45 to 70) have their threshold for hearing high-frequency sounds (4000 Hz and higher) raised by 10 dB compared to men not exposed to such noise at work (Tambs et al., 2006). A 10 dB increase is sound that is 10 times as intense, which we perceive as twice as loud. Factory or machine workers exposed to noise at the 90 dB level for eight hours a day, five days a week, suffer permanent hearing loss after ten years on the job (Bauer et al., 1991; Lutman & Spencer, 1991). Similarly, rock musicians—exposed to noise levels from 95 dB to 107 dB—when tested before and after concerts, showed both temporary and permanent hearing loss (Gunderson, Moline, & Catalono, 1997).

Because of this well-documented loss of high-frequency hearing with age, cell phone users, especially young students, have discovered a way to hear calls during class that their older teachers cannot: Have the ring tone be at a frequency higher than what most older people can hear. The best-known high-pitched ringtone is called *mosquito,* and falls within the 16 000–18 000 Hz range. Mosquito technology was actually invented by a company to disperse young people in a crowd (because they find it annoying), while leaving the older people unaffected (they cannot hear it). The irony is that some younger people copied the tone and turned it into a ringtone for their cell phone that they can hear, although older people supposedly cannot (Vitello, 2006). However, it doesn't always work as expected. Some 30- and 40-year-olds can, in fact, hear the mosquito ringtone. To hear these high-pitched tones yourself, try searching "mosquito ringtones" online.

But don't think that hearing loss does not affect younger people. MP3 players, like the iPod, have maximum decibel levels of around 115–120 dB, about the loudness of a rock concert. Here are some guidelines for listening to music without causing long-term damage to your ears (Knox, 2007):

- Limit earphone listening to an hour a day, at a setting no greater than 6 on a 10-notch scale.
- If someone can hear earphone "leakage" from a few metres away, it is too loud.
- If someone has ringing in the ears or a feeling of fullness in the ear, or if speech sounds muffled after a listening session, the music was too loud.

FIGURE **4.27**
HEARING HIGH TONES. Due to age-related hearing loss, the highest-pitched sounds we can hear decline as we get older. Sounds in the mosquito ringtone range cannot be heard by most people beyond their teenage years.

Hearing in the Brain

After the sound energy is changed to neural energy in the cochlea, the hair cells synapse with auditory neurons that transmit the sound impulses to the thalamus in the brain. The auditory pathways go from the cochlea to the *inferior colliculus* in the brain stem and from there to the *medial (middle) geniculate nucleus (MGN) of the thalamus,* and from there to the auditory cortex in the temporal lobe. The auditory cortex also receives inputs from several other cortical regions, including the visual cortex and regions involved in perceiving speech. There are also hemispheric differences in auditory perception: the right auditory cortex is more active in processing non-verbal stimuli, whereas the left auditory cortex is more active in processing speech and language (Zatorre, Evans, & Meyer, 1994).

Quick Quiz 4.4: Hearing

1. The _____ of a sound wave determines what we perceive as loudness.
   a. frequency
   b. shape
   c. amplitude
   d. width

2. Which structure is responsible for the transduction of sound vibrations into action potentials?
   a. the tympanic membrane
   b. cochlea
   c. stapes
   d. hair cells

Answers can be found at the end of the chapter.

LO10 THE BODILY SENSES

We feel things on our skin and in our bodily organs. The largest contact surface area any sensory input has with our bodies is the skin, and it is carefully mapped in the somatosensory cortex in the parietal lobe of the brain (Blakeslee & Blakeslee, 2007). Bodily senses also include knowing where our body parts are. In addition, we also sense things inside our bodies—organ pain, levels of heart rate, depth of breathing, to name a few. The senses based in the skin, body, or any membrane surfaces are known as the **bodily senses.** There are at least six distinct bodily or somatic senses: touch, temperature, pain, position/motion, balance, and interoception (perception of bodily sensations). Of these six senses, we will discuss touch and pain.

bodily senses
the senses based in the skin, body, or any membrane surfaces.

Connection
Figure 3.21 shows how the somatosensory cortex maps to specific regions of the body.
See Chapter 3, LO11.

Touch

Imagine your eyes are closed and someone puts an object in your left hand. You feel it for a minute. You feel its weight, shape, hardness, and temperature. Then the person puts something in your right hand. You conclude, with eyes still shut, that the first was a screwdriver and the second was a pen. How were you able to do this?

The top layers of skin have receptor cells that are sensitive to different tactile qualities—some to shape, some to grooves, some to vibrations and movements. These receptor cells are known as **mechanoreceptors,** and they are like the photoreceptors in the eye or the hair cells in the ear (Goldstein, 2007). There are, in fact, four different kinds of mechanoreceptors, each of which has a unique profile of sensitivity. Some of the mechanoreceptors adapt slowly while others are fast to change with variations in tactile stimulation. Some are sensitive to fine details, whereas others are less so. For example, slowly drag your fingertip

mechanoreceptors
receptor cells in the skin that are sensitive to different tactile qualities, such as shape, grooves, or vibrations.

over a quarter. You can feel the bumps and grooves, thanks to fine-detail receptors in your skin. If you were to run your elbow over the surface of that same quarter, you would find that the degree of sensitivity is greatly reduced. Some mechanoreceptors also sense movement and vibration, such as when someone runs fingers over your forearm. It is important to point out, however, that different areas of skin have different numbers of mechanoreceptors. If someone put a screwdriver and a pen against your feet, for example, you might have trouble telling them apart. You have far fewer mechanoreceptors on the soles of your feet than on your fingertips. This is probably a good thing—it would be overwhelmingly uncomfortable to have extremely sensitive soles.

Like photoreceptors in the eye, mechanoreceptors mark only the beginning of the journey from sensation to perception. The sensory qualities (shape, size, hardness, and temperature) of the screwdriver and pen stimulate different kinds of mechanoreceptors in the skin, but the resulting sensory impulses must travel to the brain to be processed and interpreted. When something touches our fingertips, forearm, or shoulder, a dedicated region of cortex becomes active, and we perceive the sensation of being touched. Tactile sensations from our skin travel via sensory neurons to the spinal cord and up to the brain. The first major structure involved in processing bodily sensations is the thalamus, which relays the impulses to the somatosensory cortex in the parietal lobes.

Connection

What are the benefits of touch for premature and low-birth-weight newborns?

See Chapter 10, LO6.

Repeated sensory and motor tactile experience changes the amount of cortex involved in processing that particular sensation or movement. The general location in the somatosensory cortex stays the same, but areas of the cortex devoted to that experience or function grow (Jenkins et al., 1990). The more one body region is touched or stimulated, the more sensory or motor cortex is used to process information from the mechanoreceptors. For instance, musicians who play stringed instruments such as violins use the right hand to bow and the left hand to play the notes. Researchers have found that experienced violinists have larger representations, or *brain maps,* of the hand and finger regions of the somatosensory cortex than do non-musicians (Pantev et al., 2001). Athletes who practise the same movement over and over, whether it is hitting a tennis ball or shooting a basketball, no doubt have similarly well-developed sensory and motor cortices.

Pain

Pain is no fun, but we need it to survive. People born with no pain receptors can be severely injured or killed, because they don't know they have been harmed (Watkins & Maier, 2003). **Pain** is a complex emotional and sensory experience associated with actual or potential tissue damage (Merskey & Bogduk, 1994). It is usually very unpleasant, but people vary widely in their experiences of pain, what they think is painful, and whether they might even enjoy pain (Schwerdtfeger, 2007). In fact, some people feel no pain during great injury, such as soldiers in battle situations. Others feel pain without obvious tissue damage, which is often classified as *psychogenic* or *psychosomatic* pain. This type of pain is difficult to treat since it is unclear if the pain is purely psychological or rather that the biological cause has not been identified (Rashbaum & Sarno, 2003). Pathological pain is characteristic of a number of disorders, such as *chronic pain* and *fibromyalgia,* and sufferers might be so sensitive to tactile stimulation that even taking a shower can be excruciating (Watkins & Maier, 2003). Another peculiar condition is *phantom limb pain,* when people who have lost a limb feel pain in the missing arm or leg. Such cases dramatically show how pain is not just a direct result of tissue damage, but an experience in the brain as well. Pain also is enhanced by one's reaction to the injury. Often the emotional reaction to pain creates as much suffering as the actual tissue damage. In fact, physical and emotional pain involve many of the same brain structures (Singer et al., 2004).

pain
a complex emotional and sensory experience associated with actual or potential tissue damage.

Connection

Phantom limb pain can be treated using mirror therapy, which tricks the brain into thinking that the missing limb has been restored.

See Chapter 3, LO13.

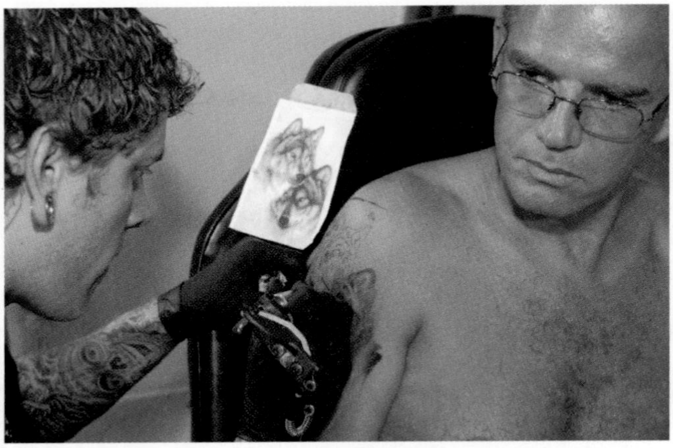

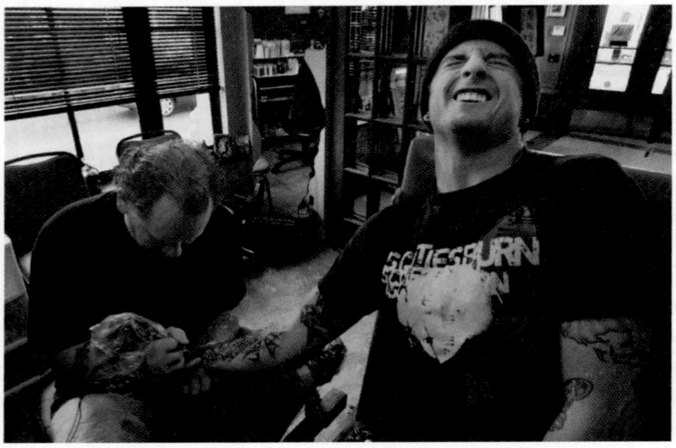

Pain is subjective, and the perception of pain varies from one person to another. Some people may perceive the experience of getting a tattoo as moderately uncomfortable. Others might find it to be quite painful.

Are there certain types of pain that you can tolerate better than others? How would you feel about the pain of getting a tattoo?

Pain Perception How do we sense and perceive pain? It's not merely touch gone too far. In fact, damage to the skin is only one kind of pain. Other forms include organ tissue and nerve damage as well as joint inflammation. Pain from tissue damage is called *nociceptive pain*. Pain receptors that are sensitive to heat, cold, chemical irritation, and pressure are all types of *nociceptors* (Basbaum & Jessell, 2000). Heat, frostbite, chemical burns, and cutting or hitting your thumb with a hammer all hurt because these events stimulate nociceptors in our skin. The nociceptors send signals to the spinal cord and then to the brain, signalling that damage has occurred. Your brain can then initiate an appropriate response, such as pulling your hand away from the hot burner. You can now see why it is so dangerous not to experience pain! In fact, sensory experiences early in life affect responses to pain later in adulthood. In a series of classic experiments by Ronald Melzack at McGill University, dogs reared in environments of sensory deprivation were much less responsive to pain compared to littermates raised in normal sensory environments (Melzack & Scott, 1957).

Many brain structures are involved in the perception of damage. A partial list of brain structures activated by skin-based pain includes the thalamus, hypothalamus, limbic system, insula, and anterior cingulate cortex (see Figure 4.28; Goldstein, 2007). A recent and somewhat surprising finding is that some of the same brain regions activated when we experience physical pain also are activated during emotional pain—especially when we are rejected by others or see others receive shocks (Eisenberger, Lieberman & Williams, 2003; Singer et al., 2004). The brain regions active in both physical and emotional pain are the anterior cingulate cortex (ACC) and the insula (see Figure 4.28). Even more fascinating, as Singer and colleagues (2004) showed, when we observe a loved one being given a mild shock, only the ACC and the insula become active, not the somatosensory cortex, which is activated when we ourselves are shocked. So when we see someone we love hurt, the aspects of the pain circuit involved with emotion are active, but not the entire circuit.

gate control theory of pain
idea that the spinal cord regulates the experience of pain by either activating or suppressing neural networks, called gates, that transmit pain sensations to the brain.

Explaining Pain One of the more influential explanations for pain is the one proposed by Ronald Melzack and Patrick Wall (1965, 1988). Their **gate control theory of pain** proposes that the spinal cord regulates the experience of pain by either activating or inhibiting neural networks, called *gates*, involved in pain sensations that get sent to the brain. Some networks are dedicated to pain sensations, and when they are activated, pain messages get sent to the brain. Activation of other neural networks can inhibit the transmission of pain impulses to the brain. This theory was influential since it helped to explain why a tactile stimulus can be extremely painful under some conditions and barely noticed under other conditions. In fact, acupuncture or even rubbing one's skin can relieve sensations of pain. The signals from acupuncture may override other, even more intense sensations of pain, such as chronic pain from injury (White, 2006).

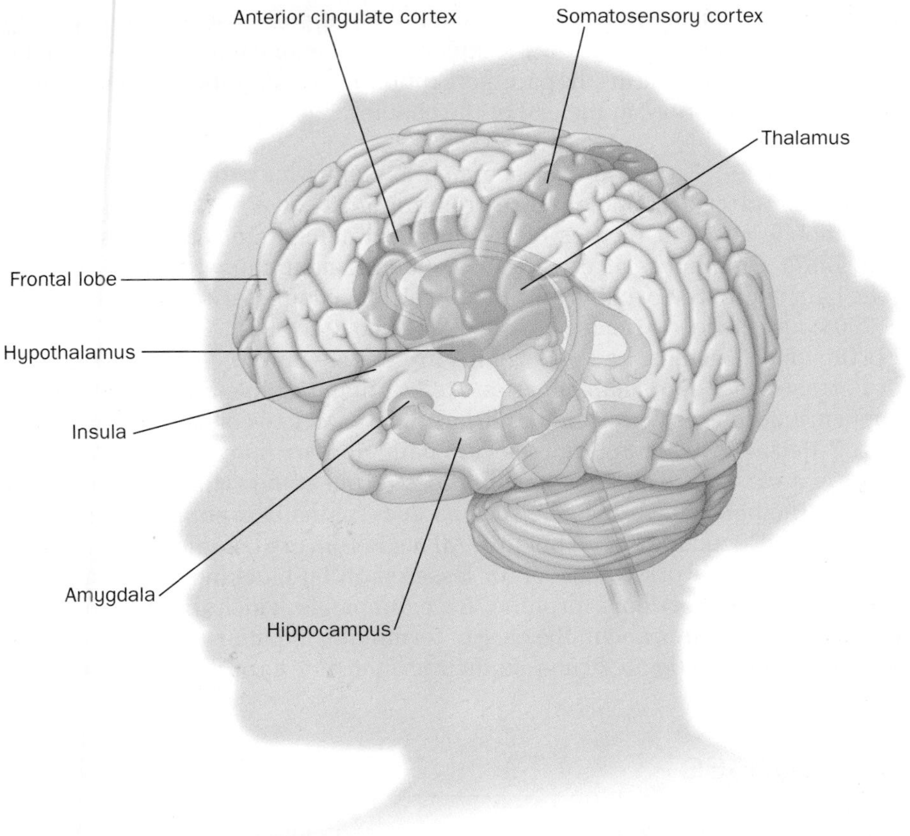

FIGURE **4.28**

THE BRAIN AND PAIN. The structures shown are activated during the perception of physical pain. The anterior cingulate cortex and the insula (located deep within the temporal lobe) are also activated by emotional pain.

One key region of the central nervous system important in the gate control theory of pain is the spinal cord, which appears to play an active rather than passive role in pain perception. That is, the spinal cord does not simply relay the pain messages from the sensory neurons to the brain; it also can suppress or enhance those messages. Pain suppression can be achieved by the body's natural painkillers; the best characterized of these are *endorphins* (for endogenous morphines), which belong to a class of neurotransmitter called **opioids.** When we get hurt or are experiencing conditions of danger, our body responds by releasing these substances (Fields, 2005). Endorphins work by stimulating the release of neurotransmitters that interfere with pain messages in the spinal cord as well as the brain. Pain enhancement usually occurs under conditions of illness, when elevated pain signals are thought to be beneficial so that an organism can rest and recuperate. Most surprisingly, it is not neurons in the spinal cord that enhance the pain signals, but rather the glial cells wrapped around the axons (Watkins & Maier, 2003). Once the pain messages get sent and even enhanced by the spinal cord, they move on to the brain.

opioids
neurotransmitters involved in reducing the response to pain.

What is most interesting about the gate control theory of pain is the idea that pain facilitation and suppression can actually come from the brain as well as the body. Messages sent by the brain itself can close channels in the spinal cord involved in pain sensations. Thoughts, feelings, and beliefs can influence pain sensations, which is one reason why people vary so much in their perception of pain. Different people experiencing the same level of pain may have completely different experiences of their pain. We explore this phenomenon in more detail by examining the role of culture in pain perception in "Evaluating Connections in Sensation and Perception" at the end of the chapter.

Controlling Pain Endorphin release may explain why people initially experience no pain after a horrible injury from an accident. For example, soldiers and automobile accident victims often report no immediate sensations of pain (Warga, 1987). Only hours afterward or maybe the next day while in a hospital does the pain begin. Endorphins also play a role in acupuncture-based pain relief (Han, 2004) and placebo effects (Amanzio & Benedetti, 1999).

Connection

Why do opiates have a high potential for abuse?

See Chapter 5, LO10.

If thoughts, feelings, and endorphins are not enough to control pain, there are drug treatments. For small aches and pains, many people take aspirin, acetaminophen, ibuprofen, or other similar drugs. These work to control inflammation (Loeser & Melzack, 1999). For more severe pain, doctors may prescribe opiates. Opiates are a class of drug known as *analgesics* (meaning "without pain"), and they mimic the body's own opioids, such as endorphins. Morphine, heroin, oxycodone, and hydrocodone are all opiates. All but heroin are commonly prescribed for pain relief. They work to deaden or lessen pain by blocking neural activity involved in pain perception. Morphine, for example, is widely used before and after medical procedures and in the care of terminally ill patients. There is a high risk of dependency on opiate drugs, so their use must be carefully monitored.

Quick Quiz 4.5: The Bodily Senses

1. The receptor cells for touch that reside in the skin are called
   a. tactile cilia.
   b. mechanoreceptors.
   c. interoceptors.
   d. receptive fields.

2. Our bodies have natural painkillers called
   a. analgesics.
   b. opiates.
   c. endorphins.
   d. acetaminophens.

Answers can be found at the end of the chapter.

LO11 THE CHEMICAL SENSES: SMELL AND TASTE

Smell and taste are chemical senses, because they respond to contact with molecules from objects we encounter in the world. Smell and taste are very important survival-related senses, for they govern our choices about what we take into our bodies. As such, these senses are very sensitive, are heightened during pregnancy, and can trigger emotional reactions (Profet, 1992; Rolls, 2004).

Unlike receptors for other senses, receptors for chemical molecules are regularly replaced, because they are constantly exposed not only to the chemicals in food but also to dirt and bacteria that can impair function (Goldstein, 2007). Smell and taste receptors are replaced every few weeks.

Smell (Olfaction)

olfactory sensory neurons the sensory receptors for smell that reside high up inside the nose.

A small area high in the lining of the nasal cavity contains the **olfactory sensory neurons,** which are the receptors for smell (see Figure 4.29). These neurons contain hair-like projections called *cilia,* which are similar to the hair

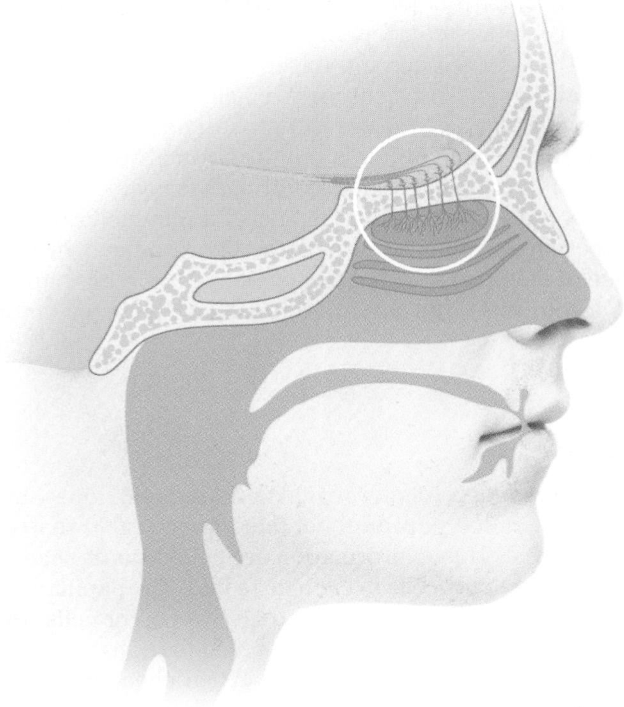

FIGURE **4.29**

OLFACTORY RECEPTORS IN THE NASAL CAVITY. The receptors in the nasal cavity, called cilia, are like the hair cells in the ear. They change chemical stimulation received from smells to nerve signals that are sent to the brain for processing and interpreting.

olfactory bulb
a forebrain structure that sends information either directly to the smell-processing areas in the cortex or indirectly to the cortex by way of the thalamus.

cells in the inner ear. The cilia convert chemical information in odour molecules into neural impulses.

When chemicals come in contact with receptors on the cilia, transduction occurs via changes in ion flow, and the olfactory message travels to the **olfactory bulb** in the forebrain. The olfactory bulb sends information either directly to the smell-processing areas in the cortex or indirectly to the cortex by way of the thalamus (Buck, 2000). The *primary olfactory cortex* resides in the temporal lobe; the *secondary olfactory cortex* is in the frontal lobe near the eyes.

Some fibres from the olfactory bulb go directly to the amygdala, which sends smell information to the hypothalamus, thalamus, and frontal cortex. You may recall that the amygdala plays a key role in emotional responses and also connects to memory areas like the hippocampus. These connections may explain why smells can instantly evoke an emotional memory (Herz, 2004). The smell of menthol cough drops, for example, immediately transports one of us (J. Stamp) to her grandmother's home in Newfoundland.

Just as there are specific photoreceptors for different primary colours, different odours stimulate different olfactory neurons. In fact, there may be as many as 1000 different olfactory sensory receptors (Buck, 2000). Greater concentrations of odours will stimulate a greater number of sensory neurons, and this can lead us to perceive the same odour presented at different concentrations as being an entirely different smell.

People differ considerably in their ability to sense odours. Some people lose the ability to sense smell with infection or injury, but usually this is short

African giant pouched rats can be easily trained to signal, by scratching the ground, when they have detected the odour of explosives. They are rewarded with treats such as peanuts or bananas.

term. Many mammals have a heightened sense of smell compared to humans. Grizzly bears can locate dead animals from kilometres away and will readily feed on them. Sharks can detect one drop of blood in 100 litres of water (Marks, 2006). Dogs have been long used in law enforcement to sniff out suspects and illegal drugs. The risky task of clearing landmines in former conflict zones has benefited from the olfactory capabilities of animals such as dogs, pigs, and rats. These animals can be trained to use their sense of smell to detect landmine explosives much better than even the most sophisticated artificial device. In Mozambique, African giant pouched rats have been used in landmine detection and they offer several advantages over dogs. They have a superior sense of smell, are native to the climate, and are significantly smaller (less than 4 kilograms) and are therefore less likely to detonate the mines (Habib, 2007).

papillae
textured structures on the surface of the tongue that contain thousands of taste buds.

taste buds
structures inside the papillae of the tongue that contain the taste receptor cells.

taste receptor cells
sensory receptors for taste that reside in the taste buds.

Taste

A close look at the human tongue reveals all kinds of ridges and bumps. These textured structures, called **papillae,** contain about 10 000 **taste buds.** The cells on the buds that process taste information are called **taste receptor cells.** There are dozens of taste receptor cells in each taste bud. The papillae in the central part of the tongue contain no taste buds and no taste receptor cells, so we do not taste from that region. Human experience of taste results from stimulation of taste buds on the front, sides, and rear of the tongue. When chemicals from food or liquid come into contact with the tips of these taste buds, a chain of events unfolds that lead to the experience of taste.

Challenge Your Assumptions

True or False? Different regions of the tongue contain taste buds for specific types of taste, such as sweet or bitter.

False: Recent evidence shows taste receptor cells are distributed throughout the tongue.

Different tastes use different mechanisms to stimulate an impulse in a taste cell. In general, chemicals alter the membranes of taste receptor cells in ways that make them more likely to generate action potentials. Such signals from taste receptor cells in various regions of the tongue then travel down fibres to the brain stem. From the brain stem, taste information travels to the thalamus and frontal lobe. Neurons from the thalamus project taste information to the *taste cortex* in the insula and other regions of the frontal-parietal cortex (Ogawa et al., 2005).

Humans distinguish at least five basic taste qualities: bitter, sweet, salty, sour, and savoury (called *umami*, a word borrowed from the original Japanese term). It used to be thought that receptors for the different tastes resided only in certain regions of the tongue (see Figure 4.30), but we now know that these taste receptor cells are distributed in many regions (Buck, 2000; Chaudhari & Roper, 2010; Huang et al., 2006). Although specific receptors exist for each type of taste, the umami experience comes from the combined sensory experience of monosodium glutamate (MSG, a flavour enhancer, traditionally used in many Asian foods) and the perception of savoury odours (Kawamura & Kare, 1987; McCabe & Rolls, 2007). The combined influences that produce the umami flavour highlight the interaction between taste and smell in our experiences of flavour in general.

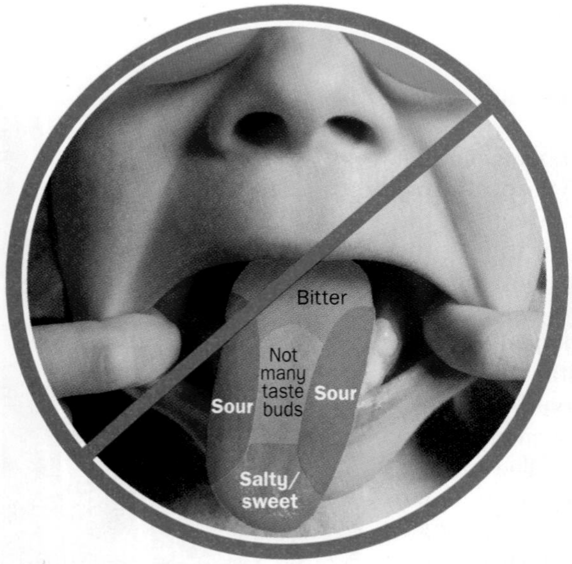

FIGURE **4.30**
LOCATION OF TASTE RECEPTORS ON THE HUMAN TONGUE. Until recently, it was thought that distinct regions of the tongue had receptors for specific types of taste. We now know that the entire tongue is involved in each taste sensation.

Simply put, the experience of flavour results from the combination of taste plus smell (Goldstein, 2007). Have you ever noticed how dull food tastes when you have a cold? This is because your sense of smell is impaired. Try squeezing your nostrils shut while tasting an apple or any other food. Notice the flavour. Then release your nostrils and take another bite.

You will notice more intense "apple-ness" with your nostrils open, because food aromas contribute greatly to the experience of flavour (Lawless et al., 2004). When the nose is shut, olfactory receptors in the passage that connects the oral and nasal cavities do not get stimulated. As a result, less olfactory information is available and taste is impaired. Also, the region of the brain most involved in flavour perception, namely the orbitofrontal cortex (OFC), receives inputs from brain areas involved in olfaction and taste, as well as from areas involved in touch and vision (Rolls, 2000). The OFC is where signals from taste and smell meet. Indeed, this brain area plays a key role in both perception of flavour and satisfaction of appetite, which relies on many senses (Rolls, 2006).

The experience of flavour showcases the brain's ability to combine sensory information to produce a unique sensory experience. Our unique sensory experiences can in turn influence behaviour—for instance, by affecting our food preferences. Research by Linda Bartoshuk at Yale University has identified individuals who are "supertasters"—those who experience particularly intense tastes. These individuals actually possess more taste receptors on the tongue and experience a more intense burn from the chemicals found in hot peppers. They are also less likely than "normal" tasters to smoke or drink alcohol. The particularly strong taste sensations are not necessarily pleasant, and supertasters are generally thinner than normal tasters (Bartoshuk, 2000).

In some people, sensory experiences sometimes combine in even more unusual ways. The next section, which deals with synesthesia, focuses on these cases.

Quick Quiz 4.6: The Chemical Senses: Smell and Taste

1. The primary olfactory cortex resides in which lobe of the brain?
   a. frontal lobe
   b. temporal lobe
   c. parietal lobe
   d. occipital lobe

2. Humans have taste receptor cells for what flavours?
   a. sweet, sour, bitter, salty, sharp
   b. sweet, sour, salty, sharp, savoury
   c. sweet, sour, bitter, salty, savoury
   d. sweet, sour, salty, sharp

Answers can be found at the end of the chapter.

LO12 SYNESTHESIA

Many of us use expressions such as "he was green with envy" or "her anger was red hot." We use these colours metaphorically, knowing full well he is not really green and her anger is not really red. But what if we literally experienced numbers as colours or touch as tastes? A surprisingly large segment of the population, roughly 4–5 percent, can do just that. They experience what is known as **synesthesia,** which occurs when a person experiences sensations in one sense when a different sense is stimulated (Cytowic, 1989; Ramachandran & Hubbard, 2003). In short, synesthesia occurs when the senses get mixed up and don't stay separate. For example, some people with this condition experience yellow when they hear a tone such as middle C. Still others experience numbers as colours, such as 5s as green and 2s as red. People with synesthesia, called *synesthetes* (SIN-ess-theets), describe these sensations as automatic and involuntary, and many value their unique abilities as a sort of "superpower." Many famous

synesthesia
an unusual sensory experience in which a person experiences sensations in one sense when a different sense is stimulated.

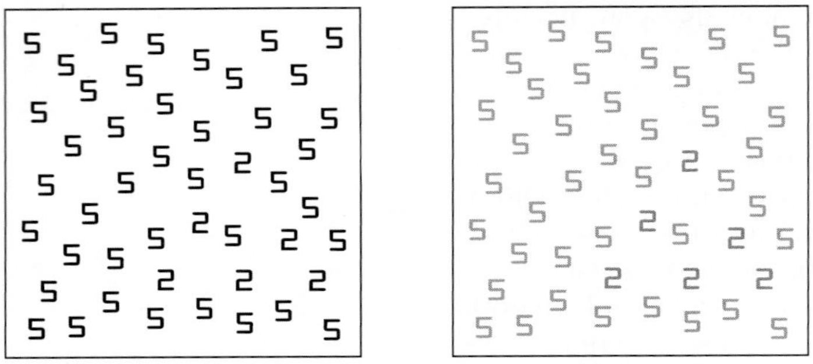

The way a person without synesthesia sees it

The way a person with synesthesia sees it

FIGURE **4.31**

SYNESTHESIA. People who perceive numbers as colours would have no trouble distinguishing the numbers 5 and 2 in the square on the left. They would see the numbers in colour as shown in the example on the right. (From Ramachandran & Hubbell, 2003)

musicians, including classical composers Franz Liszt and Jean Sibelius as well as modern pop artists Tori Amos and Billy Joel, experience coloured hearing, so that music is perceived with both hearing and vision.

The most common form of synesthesia is when people experience numbers or sometimes letters as colours (Ramachandran & Hubbard, 2003). One way that scientists were able to discover that synesthesia was a real perceptual phenomenon and not just a learned association or merely an overly active sense of metaphor was to administer perceptual tests such as the one in Figure 4.31 (5s and 2s). In the figure on the left, there are a few 2s within the 5s. For most of us they are hard to pinpoint and it takes us a while to determine how many there are. But a person who sees 5s as blue and 2s as red, as shown on the right, has no trouble seeing that there are six 2s forming a triangle.

How does synesthesia happen? One explanation is that synesthesia results from a cross-wiring or cross-activation of sensory neurons in various parts of the brain (Hubbard & Ramachandran, 2005; Ramachandran & Hubbard, 2003). Cross-activation occurs when two areas of the brain, normally kept separate, get activated at the same time by the same stimulus. So brain regions involved in colour perception get cross-activated with sensations of numbers. As it turns out, one region of the temporal lobe is active in processing both colour sensations and numbers and is therefore the most likely area of cross-activation in this form of synesthesia (Hubbard & Ramachandran, 2005; Ramachandran & Hubbard, 2003). Similarly, the orbitofrontal cortex in the frontal lobes has many so-called bimodal neurons (Rolls, 2000). Bimodal neurons respond to more than one sense—such as taste, smell, touch, and vision—and may become cross-activated in synesthesia (Radeau & Colin, 2004). Certain hallucinogenic drugs can temporarily create synesthetic experiences, but the brain mechanisms responsible for this kind of synesthesia are not well described (Weil & Rosen, 1998).

Challenge Your Assumptions

True or False? The experience of "seeing sounds" or "hearing colours" occurs only under the influence of drugs.

False: About 4 percent of the population has a crossover of sensory experience where they "see sounds" or "hear colours."

But how does synesthesia arise? Research shows that multisensory perceptions in adult synesthetes were present in childhood, and remain very consistent throughout life. Based upon studies of the development of visual perception in children, Daphne Maurer of McMaster University proposes that the cross-sensory associations are evident in all children, but become refined as we grow up (Spector & Maurer, 2009). In other words, *everyone* has synesthesia, at least as children, until our brains prune our sensory pathways so that they respond to only one sensory modality. According to this view, synesthetes have not had extensive neural pruning of their sensory pathways and are left with "superpowers" that the rest of us lose. These tendencies appear to be shaped by our early life experiences. One large-scale survey of over 6500 participants found that the letter–colour associations in a subset of synesthetes exactly matched a coloured-letter fridge magnet toy popular between the late 1960s and early 1990s (Witthoft et al., 2015). This correlational research cannot determine whether the magnet toy *caused* the adult letter–colour association, but the coincidence has sparked interest in whether certain aspects of synesthesia can be learned by early life experiences.

Differences across Cultures

Throughout this chapter we have touched on ways in which people differ in sensory perception. For example, some people are more sensitive to bitter tastes than others. Individual differences in perception may result from differences in perceptual set, or frame of mind. Thus, it stands to reason that growing up in a certain environment, with particular beliefs, ways of viewing things, and physical settings might impact how one perceives the world. Culture and place can serve as perceptual sets. Most research on cultural influences on perception has focused on three sense systems: vision, olfaction, and pain.

FIGURE **4.32**
PICTURE FOR DEPTH PERCEPTION TASK TESTED ON BANTU. **Is the hunter after the elephant or the gazelle? How might your explanation of this scene depend on your cultural perspective?** (Based on Hudson, 1960)

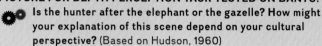

Cultural Variation in Visual Perception

Differences exist across cultures in response to certain visual images that use monocular cues to depth. Look again at the Müller-Lyer line illusion in Figure 4.19. Recall that linear perspective explains why people see the line on the right as longer than the one on the left, when the lines are in fact equal. The drawing on the right looks like the inner corner of a room, and the one on the left looks like the outer corner of a building. Do people who grow up in a world with no corners view these drawings the same way we do? Researchers have studied the effects of living in a *carpentered world*—an environment with constructed buildings with many right angles—on various people's perceptions of depth. Navajos who have lived at least ten years in round huts are much less likely to see the lines of Figure 4.19 as differing in length, for they are not accustomed to rooms with edges (Pederson & Wheeler, 1983). A similar effect has been reported in studies of children living in Zambia, in a rural setting with few modern buildings (Stewart, 1973). But Navajos and Zambians who have lived in the presence of corners do experience the Müller-Lyer illusion (Matsumoto & Juang, 2004). Experience modifies perception.

Moreover, Hudson (1960) studied the perception of depth cues in the Bantu people of the Niger-Congo region of Africa. He showed people the picture depicted in Figure 4.32 and others similar to it. He then asked them to explain what was going on in the scene. When people from the United States, Europe, and India viewed such a picture, they said the hunter is going after the gazelle, as the elephant is clearly in the distance. Bantu people, however, said the hunter is attacking the elephant. So the Bantu do not appear to use relative size differences as cues to depth because they don't see the elephant as being in the background. Why? The Bantu people's response may result from not having much experience with two-dimensional drawings like the figure. Interestingly, Bantu who had been educated in European schools say the hunter is going for the gazelle (Matsumoto & Juang, 2004).

As we have just seen, different cultural backgrounds can impact how people make sense of and perceive their world. This is true not just for illusions and depth perception, but also for perceiving and attending to foreground and background. People from Eastern cultures tend to perceive the world more as a whole, with people, objects, and the context being connected and belonging together. Westerners, however, tend to focus most on foreground objects and less on background and the periphery (Nisbett et al., 2001). Figure 4.33 describes research on this question that found cultural influences in how people perceive and recall figural versus background information in visual scenes (Masuda & Nisbett, 2001). These findings are consistent with the more established observation that Eastern people view themselves as embedded in the larger world rather than as independent entities (Markus & Kitayama, 2001). In another example of top-down processing, one's orientation toward life and the world can shape visual perception and memory.

Research Process

Japanese participant in perception study

FIGURE **4.33**
HOW CULTURE AFFECTS PERCEPTION OF FOREGROUND BACKGROUND. Culture influences the perception of visual information. Japanese people view themselves as more embedded in the larger world and notice backgrounds more than Americans, who feel more independent from their settings. (*Source:* T. Masuda & R.E. Nisbett (2001). Attending holistically versus analytically: Comparing the context sensitivity of Japanese and Americans. *Journal of Personality and Social Psychology 81,* 922–934.)

1 Research Question

Do people from an Eastern culture (Japan) focus more on and have better recall for objects in the background and periphery of a scene than people from a Western culture (United States)?

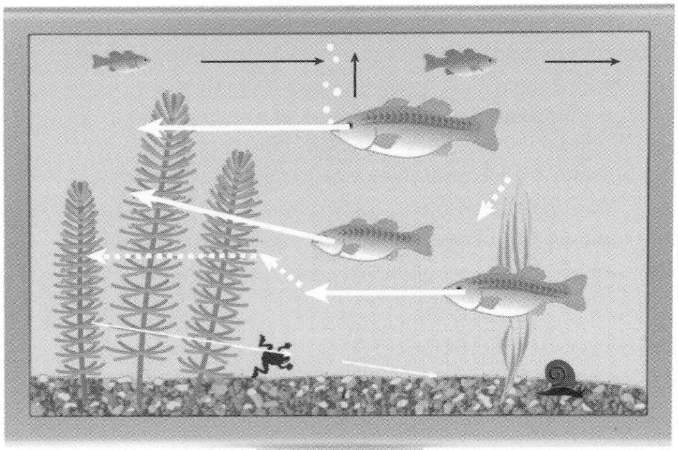

2 Method

For this quasi-experimental study by Masuda and Nisbett (2001), participants came into the laboratory individually and sat down at a computer. They watched a 20-second video of the scene depicted here. The large fish are considered foreground. Plants, small fish, and the other non-moving animals (rocks and snail) are considered background. Arrows indicate the direction in which the fish and other objects moved during the scene. After viewing the video, participants orally described what they had seen. Trained coders rated the number of statements they made about various aspects of the scene, such as foreground and background fish, the small stationary animals, and the plants.

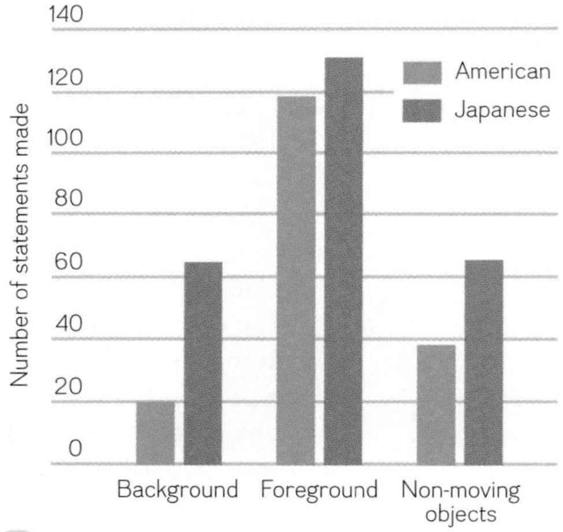

3 Results

As predicted, and consistent with cultural values and attitudes, the Japanese commented much more on the background and non-moving animals (snail and frog) than the Americans did. There was no significant difference in how much people from each culture commented on the large fish in the foreground.

4 Conclusion

How we perceive everyday scenes is influenced by our culture. Our brains have been shaped by the assumptions and values of our society. In this case, people in Eastern cultures, such as Japan, tend to focus on background, foreground, and non-moving objects, whereas those in Western cultures, such as the United States, tend to focus more on the foreground and moving objects only. This research is consistent with the more established observation that Eastern people view themselves as rooted in the larger world rather than as independent individuals.

Cultural Variation in Olfactory Experience

Smell is an interesting sense to compare across cultures in part because it is a highly emotional sense. Because smells elicit emotions so readily, cultures often develop strong rules or norms about which smells are okay and which ones aren't. That is, cultures differ widely on the acceptability of odours based on experience, climate, and cuisine. Also, different places vary in their ideas of cleanliness and acceptable body odour (Hannigan, 1995). Do people raised so differently with respect to what is typical to smell or what it is okay to smell like show differences in scent detection in controlled experiments?

A highly controlled experiment on scent detection with participants from the United States and Japan suggests remarkable similarity across these two cultures in ability to recognize a wide variety of scents (Kobayashi et al., 2006). There were a few distinct differences, however, that appear to be culturally based. Japanese were much better than Americans at detecting 3 of the 13 smells in final testing. Does that mean the Japanese have superior smell ability? Probably not. Each of these scents (such as condensed milk) is more common in Japan and therefore these results help us to understand that smell recognition is a perceptual process guided by experience with the substances to which we are exposed.

Other aspects of smell may be less susceptible to cultural effects. Consider gender differences in smell perception. Overall, women tend to be more sensitive to smells than men (Brand & Millot, 2001). Scientists at the University of Pennsylvania wanted to know whether such gender differences in smell perception held across cultures and ethnic backgrounds. They tested how well native Japanese and Americans of African, European, and Korean descent could identify odours in a controlled laboratory setting (Doty et al., 1985). Korean Americans performed better than African Americans and white Americans on the odour detection tasks, and both of these groups performed better than the native Japanese. Across all the groups, however, women outperformed men.

Cultural differences in pain perception are evident in this photo, taken during the Hindu festival of Thaipusam in Malaysia.

So the gender differences observed in previous research held for a diverse set of cultural and ethnic backgrounds. Perhaps this is a case where evolutionary pressures override the more subtle effects of ethnic culture or subculture. Women may have more highly developed olfactory perception because they are the ones who bear children. Remember, both olfaction and taste play gatekeeper roles for keeping harmful things out of the body. The sense of smell is greatly enhanced during early pregnancy, which might be because it helps keep the mother from ingesting toxins that might harm the developing baby (Profet, 1992).

Challenge Your Assumptions

True or False? Cultural background can influence how people perceive the world.

True: Our culture and life experiences can lead to different perceptions. People who grow up without constructed buildings do not see the Müller-Lyer illusion. Also, people who do not have experience with two-dimensional drawings or pictures have difficulty using monocular cues to gauge depth.

Cultural Variation in Pain

Given the large role that subjective factors play in pain perception, many researchers have looked at cultural and ethnic differences in pain. As we have discussed, there are big differences among people in pain tolerance, and we can even experience pain in the absence of any real tissue damage—remember phantom limb pain? As the startling photograph from the Hindu festival of Thaipusam shows, there are clear cultural differences in tolerance for pain!

In one of the most painful of human experiences, childbirth, we see widely differing perceptions of how painful it is. For example, the Yap who live in the South Pacific consider childbirth to be simply a part of everyday life. Yap women routinely work in the fields right up until childbirth and are often back at work the next day. What is even more interesting is that Yap fathers experience the pain of childbirth, and they are the ones who stay in bed to recover after the birth of the child (Kroeber, 1948).

Quick Quiz 4.7: Evaluating Connections in Sensation and Perception

1. People who grow up in environments with few or no right angles and corners are less likely to be fooled by the _____ illusion.
   a. Ishihara colour blindness
   b. moon
   c. Müller-Lyer
   d. apparent motion

2. Cultural differences in various kinds of sensory perception, which may stem from differences of belief and physical environments, point to the role of _____ in perceptual experience.
   a. top-down processing
   b. bottom-up processing
   c. elementalism
   d. perceptual constancy

Answers can be found at the end of the chapter.

Chapter Review

THE LONG STRANGE TRIP FROM SENSATION TO PERCEPTION

- Sensation is the stimulation of our sense organs by the external world. Perception is the process by which the brain organizes and interprets sensory experience.
- Stimulation of the sense organs involves taking in sensory energy from the outside world, whether it be sound waves, light waves, chemicals, or pressure. Our sensory system transforms the physical energy into neural energy in a process known as transduction. The brain then organizes the transformed information, interprets it, and initiates a response.
- Absolute thresholds are the lowest level of a stimulus that humans sense. Difference thresholds are the smallest amount of change in stimulus that a person detects. According to Weber's law, the smallest detectable change is a constant proportion of the intensity of the original stimulus.
- The effect of our frame of mind affects our perception of objects and is known as our perceptual set.

VISION

- The eye bends light, converts light energy to neural energy, and sends that information to the brain for further processing.
- Vision happens in the brain, in the lateral geniculate nucleus (LGN) of the thalamus, and in the visual cortex in the occipital lobes.
- Hubel and Wiesel demonstrated that single cells in the visual cortex act as feature detectors—of which there are three kinds for vision: simple cells, complex cells, and hypercomplex cells. Integration of this feature information occurs in the parietal and temporal cortices.
- Depth perception is the ability to figure out how far or near objects are. One cue for depth perception is binocular disparity, the fact that our two eyes provide slightly different viewpoints that our brains integrate into a single 3-D image. Monocular depth cues include linear perspective, texture gradient, atmospheric perspective, and interposition.
- The brain organizes visual sensations with Gestalt laws of similarity, continuity, proximity, and closure.
- Separating figures from backgrounds helps us organize visual sensations, but also makes us vulnerable to illusions.
- The retina contains two types of photoreceptor cells called rods and cones. Cones are sensitive to different wavelengths of light and mediate colour vision, whereas rods are responsible for vision in dim lighting conditions.
- The trichromatic theory of colour vision states that we perceive the full range of colours as different combinations of three colours. The opponent-process theory says that cones are linked together in three opposing colour pairs: blue/yellow, red/green, and black/white.

HEARING

- Humans respond to three different properties of sound waves: We perceive amplitude as loudness, frequency as pitch, and purity as timbre.
- The receptor hair cells in the cochlea are sensitive to different frequencies of sound waves and convert the mechanical energy of sound into neural energy for processing in the auditory cortex.

THE BODILY SENSES

- The bodily senses include sensations of touch, temperature, pain, balance, position/motion, and interoception.
- The brain regions most involved in touch are the thalamus and the somatosensory cortex in the parietal lobes. Pain sensations are processed mainly by the insula and the anterior cingulate cortex in the frontal lobes.

THE CHEMICAL SENSES: SMELL AND TASTE

- Smell receptors in the nose contain olfactory sensory neurons, which convert chemical information into neural information. The olfactory message goes to the olfactory bulb and then to the primary olfactory cortex in the temporal lobe.
- Information about taste is processed by taste receptors on the tongue. Humans distinguish five basic taste qualities: bitter, sweet, salty, sour, and savoury.

SYNESTHESIA

- Synesthesia occurs when one sensory system is activated by stimulation of a different sensory system, and the neurons are cross-activated in the brain.
- In the most common form of synesthesia, people experience letters or numbers as colours.

EVALUATING CONNECTIONS IN SENSATION AND PERCEPTION

- Variations in experience across cultures influence the way people see, smell, and feel pain. Ethnic and cultural differences aside, women are more sensitive to smells than are men.

Quick Quiz Answers

Quick Quiz 4.1: 1. a 2. d **Quick Quiz 4.2:** 1. c 2. b
Quick Quiz 4.3: 1. a 2. d 3. b 4. d **Quick Quiz 4.4:** 1. c 2. d
Quick Quiz 4.5: 1. b 2. c **Quick Quiz 4.6:** 1. b 2. c
Quick Quiz 4.7: 1. c 2. a

Solution to Figure 4.18:

Consciousness

CHAPTER

5

CHAPTER OUTLINE

Challenge Your Assumptions

True or False?

- ☐ People in comatose states cannot communicate with others.
- ☐ Talking on a hands-free phone while driving is as distracting as talking on a hand-held phone.
- ☐ You can make up for lost sleep.
- ☐ You can't drink yourself to death.

LEARNING OBJECTIVES

- **LO1** Identify and describe the two dimensions of consciousness.
- **LO2** Identify the different states of consciousness and describe how behaviour and brain activity differ for each.
- **LO3** Give examples of how attention influences consciousness.
- **LO4** Describe the effects of meditation on consciousness.
- **LO5** Discuss the rhythmic nature of sleep and describe the changes that happen during sleep.
- **LO6** Discuss theories of sleep and dreaming by describing the supporting evidence.
- **LO7** Describe the different disorders of sleep.
- **LO8** Outline how different parts of the brain control different aspects of sleep and wakefulness.
- **LO9** Describe the effects of hypnosis on consciousness.
- **LO10** Describe the mechanisms of major drugs of abuse at their target receptors and compare their effects on behaviour and brain activity.

On Sunday, January 30, 1994, our lives changed forever. David, the brother of one of this book's authors, was hit by a car while riding his bicycle home from work. He first crashed onto the windshield and then landed on the street. He was not wearing his helmet. Fortunately for David, within just a few minutes emergency workers whisked him off to one of the top trauma centres in the country. David had suffered a severe traumatic brain injury.

When we arrived at the hospital, David was in a coma. We asked the trauma nurse to explain just how comatose he was. She explained that they use a special scale to rate the degree of coma and non-responsiveness. Scores range from 3 to 15. "Where was David on this scale?" we asked. She said David was a "4." We asked what a "4" meant in practical terms. The nurse picked up the small bottle of saline solution (basically saltwater) from David's bedside table. "You see this?" she asked. "This is a 3." David was barely alive.

Two weeks after the accident, David opened his eyes. Five months later, he emerged from his vegetative state and began responding to input from the outside world. Witnessing David's near miraculous recovery over the next year not only pushed the limits of our concepts of life and death but also illustrated just how delicate states of consciousness can be. Thankfully, David's coma was temporary but for some unfortunate individuals, disorders of consciousness are permanent. The treatment of these individuals has sparked complicated medical and ethical debates, as highlighted with the right-to-live versus right-to-die case of Terri Schiavo. She was in a "permanent vegetative state" for 15 years and died in 2005 after a long battle between her husband and family over the removal of the feeding tube that kept her alive. This tragic case illustrated that understanding consciousness is more than just a philosophical exercise.

For a long time, the topic of consciousness—something that occupies the centre of our psychological experience—was a neglected area in psychology. Thanks to the cognitive revolution, evolutionary psychology, and neuroscience—which returned mental phenomena to the forefront of psychological research—the scientific study of consciousness is back. In this chapter, we review what the science of psychology has to say about consciousness. In particular, we'll explore what consciousness is, examine how we know the contents of our own minds, look at how psychologists have studied the conscious mind, and consider how meditation, sleep, drugs, and mental exercises can modify consciousness. Finally, we take a look at hypnosis (what is it and how is it different from other levels of consciousness?) before returning to the consciousness-altering effects of brain injury.

LO1 WHAT IS CONSCIOUSNESS?

LO2 Consider what happens if you walk out of a dark house onto a sunny porch. Many signals assault your brain: The bright light from the sky hits your eyes, which send information to visual processing areas. The heat from the sun bathes your skin, and temperature sensors there send impulses to the somatosensory cortex. Your brain processes these many sensory signals instantaneously and simultaneously, and they come together into the experience of right now being on the front porch in the sun. They come together in your consciousness. Consciousness acts as a stage for the "main event" of your brain at a given moment in time. When the connections among the various processing areas of the brain areas become strong enough, a conscious experience occurs (Engel, Debener, & Kranczioch, 2006). The various sensory elements are brought together in what has been called the *global workspace* of consciousness (Baars, 1997; Baars & Franklin, 2003).

In spite of its central role in our experience, consciousness is not easily defined. Most simply, **consciousness** is an awareness of one's surroundings and of what is in one's mind at a given moment. It is our experience of a moment as we move through it. However, our awareness of our surroundings is biased towards our current tasks and desires. Much of what happens around us is filtered out in order to focus only on stimuli that are relevant to the task at hand. For instance, if we are scanning a newspaper looking for the winning lotto numbers, we are probably not really paying much attention to how the paper feels in our fingers. Conscious experiences are guided by past experiences and current desires, which is why two people can experience the same set of stimuli and have unique conscious experiences.

What do you think this woman is consciously aware of? The rain? Is she looking for someone? Do you think her dog is conscious of the same things?

Many of the psychological processes that contribute to the experience of consciousness having been examined using objective scientific measures. Throughout this text you will learn about the study of perception, sensation, memory, awareness, wakefulness, and sleep. However, the subjective aspect of being a conscious human—*what it feels like* to be in love, see red, or have an idea—has eluded science. The focus of this chapter is psychology's contribution to understanding conscious processes, and to the development of methods that may bring the subjective aspect of consciousness into clearer view.

Connection

How much information can we hold in consciousness before it is processed further, stored, or forgotten?

See Chapter 6, LO3.

Two Dimensions of Consciousness: Wakefulness and Awareness

We defined consciousness as the extent to which we are aware of our surroundings and of what's in our mind at a given moment. But consciousness can be viewed as having two key features: the degree to which we are awake and the degree to which we are aware. **Wakefulness** refers to the degree of alertness, whether a person is awake or asleep. **Awareness** refers to the monitoring of information from the environment and from one's own thoughts, and is closely tied to attention (Brown & Ryan, 2003).

consciousness
an awareness of one's surroundings and of what's in one's mind at a given moment; includes aspects of being awake and aware.

wakefulness
degree of alertness reflecting whether a person is awake or asleep.

awareness
monitoring of information from the environment and from one's own thoughts.

Variations in consciousness can be explained in terms of degrees of wakefulness and awareness (Laureys, 2007). According to this theory, each component ranges from low to high and all states of consciousness exist somewhere in this two-dimensional space (see Figure 5.1). Coma, for example, is one extreme of consciousness and is characterized by very low wakefulness and awareness. In contrast, the vegetative state is wakeful but not very aware. Psychologists often study levels of consciousness by measuring differences in behaviour and brain activity that accompany different states. As you will learn in this section, although this approach to studying consciousness is useful, one must be extremely cautious in defining features of consciousness.

Minimal Consciousness If you have ever fainted, you have experienced a loss of consciousness. **Coma,** in which the eyes are closed and the person is unresponsive, is a much more severe and enduring loss of consciousness than fainting. People cannot be roused from a coma as they can be roused from sleep. Coma generally results from illness or brain injury that damages areas of the brain that control wakefulness—in particular, the reticular formation and the

coma
a state of consciousness in which the eyes are closed and the person is unresponsive and unarousable.

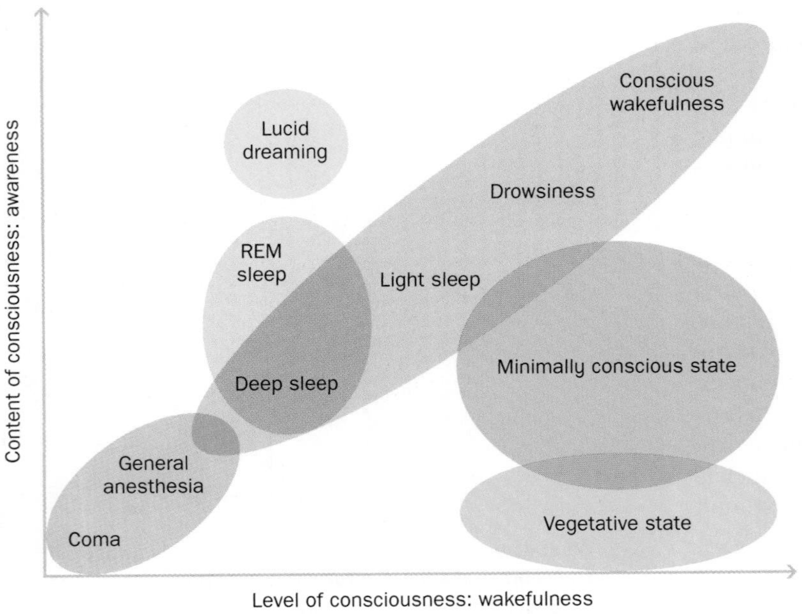

FIGURE **5.1**

TWO DIMENSIONS OF CONSCIOUSNESS. Consciousness can be considered on a continuum from low to high wakefulness and from little to high awareness. Each state of consciousness exists somewhere in this two-dimensional space. (*Source:* Laureys, 2007.)

Looking at this figure, what is the difference between a coma and a vegetative state? Between deep sleep and lucid dreaming? Between light sleep and full wakefulness?

thalamus (Bernat, 2006; Fernandez-Espejo et al., 2010). At least some brain activity is evident in comatose people, but there is a lot of variation. People whose brains show normal sleep patterns are more likely to regain consciousness than are those who do not exhibit these patterns (Fischer, 2004).

The medical community distinguishes different degrees of coma with the Glasgow Coma Scale (Teasdale & Jennett, 1976), the instrument used to assess David's level of consciousness (see Figure 5.2). The scale classifies people as suffering from severe, moderate, or mild brain injury based on their degree of eye opening, verbal responsiveness, and motor responsiveness. The scores are used to predict an individual's chances of recovery (Jain, Dharap, & Gore, 2008). Recall that David's initial score (from a total of his score on the three subscales) was a 4. His chances of any kind of meaningful recovery were slim.

In another form of minimal consciousness, the **vegetative state,** the eyes might be open, but the person is otherwise unresponsive (Owen et al., 2006). The vegetative state has been defined as "wakefulness without awareness" (Bernat, 2006, p. 1181). Physicians used to think that anyone who was vegetative did not react to stimuli from the environment, primarily because of the lack of a behavioural response. We now know that this is not always the case.

vegetative state
a state of minimal consciousness in which the eyes might be open, but the person is otherwise unresponsive.

A highly publicized case study offers insight into the responsiveness of the brain in a vegetative state (Owen et al., 2006). Researchers asked a young woman who was in vegetative state to imagine a few things, such as walking through her house and playing tennis. As they asked her to imagine these things, they scanned her brain using fMRI. Surprisingly, her brain showed activation in the same areas as did the brains of people who were conscious and asked to imagine the same things. Not only does this mean that this woman was responsive while in a vegetative state—she was responding with her brain—but it also showed that she could exhibit intentional thought because she followed the researchers' instructions (see Figure 5.3). Clearly, the absence of behavioural responses does not guarantee that people in vegetative states cannot process information from the outside world. The fact that one person in a so-called vegetative state could be this responsive forces a rethinking of the ethical implications of labelling someone vegetative. In fact, studies show that patients who show signs of brain activity are more likely to transition from a vegetative state to a *minimally*

Eye opening	
spontaneous	**4**
to speech	**3**
to pain	**2**
no response	**1**
Verbal response	
alert and oriented	**5**
disoriented conversation	**4**
speaking but nonsensical	**3**
moans/unintelligible sounds	**2**
no response	**1**
Motor response	
follows commands	**6**
localizes pain	**5**
withdraws from pain	**4**
abnormal limb flexion	**3**
abnormal limb extension	**2**
no response	**1**

FIGURE **5.2**

GLASGOW COMA SCALE. This scale is used to classify brain injuries as severe, moderate, or mild. Scores on each of the three sections are summed to provide a total score, which is used to predict chances of recovery in people with traumatic brain injury. (*Source:* Teasdale & Jennett, 1976.)

FIGURE **5.3**
MEASURING CONSCIOUS AWARENESS IN THE VEGETATIVE STATE. By using brain responses rather than bodily movements, researchers were able to determine that a patient who was presumed to be in a deep coma could voluntarily respond to instructions. (*Source:* Owen, A.M., Coleman, M.R., Boly, M., Davis, M., Laureys, S., & Pickard, J.D. (2006). Detecting awareness in the vegetative state. *Science, 313,* 1402.)

1 Research Question

Can brain imaging be used to detect conscious awareness in patients who are assumed to be in a vegetative state, but still have intact cognitive abilities? Adrian Owen and colleagues (2006) devised a relatively simple experiment to test this hypothesis.

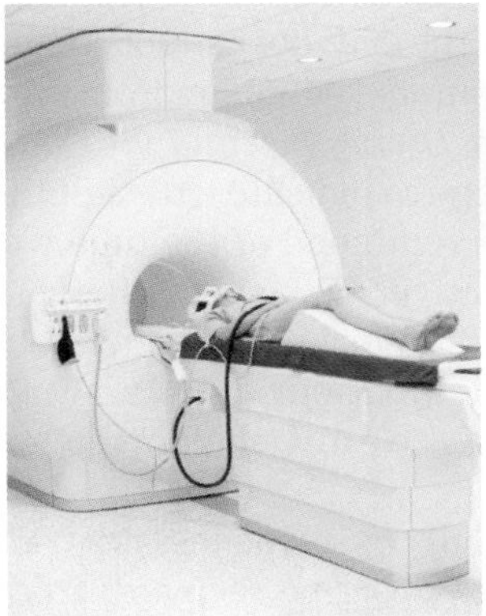

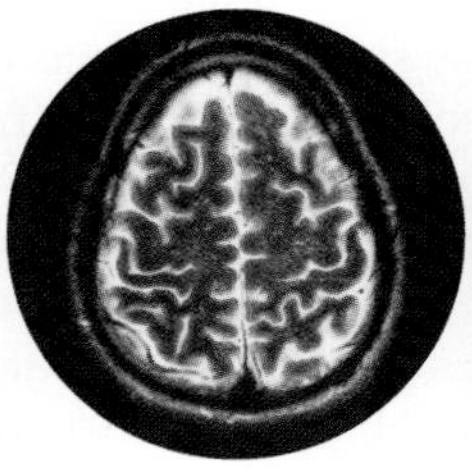

MRI SCAN

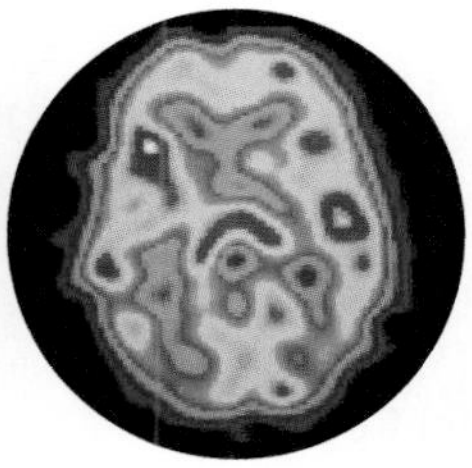

PET SCAN

2 Method

Participants included a 23-year-old woman, presumed to be in a vegetative state after sustaining a traumatic head injury from a car accident, and 12 healthy controls for comparison. Participants were asked to use mental imagery to visualize themselves either playing tennis or walking through their home while their brains were imaged using fMRI. Engaging in mental imagery when asked by researchers involves both conscious awareness of one's environment as well as voluntary control of thought. These tasks were chosen because they produce distinct patterns of brain activity, with the tennis imagery activating areas involved in motor planning, and the navigation imagery activating areas involved with spatial relationships.

3 Results

When the vegetative patient pictured herself playing tennis, the supplementary motor area (SMA) became active and when she pictured herself walking around her home, her posterior parietal cortex (PPC), parahippocampal gyrus (PPA), and premotor cortex (PMC) became active. These activation patterns were virtually identical to those observed in healthy controls when they did the same mental imagery tasks.

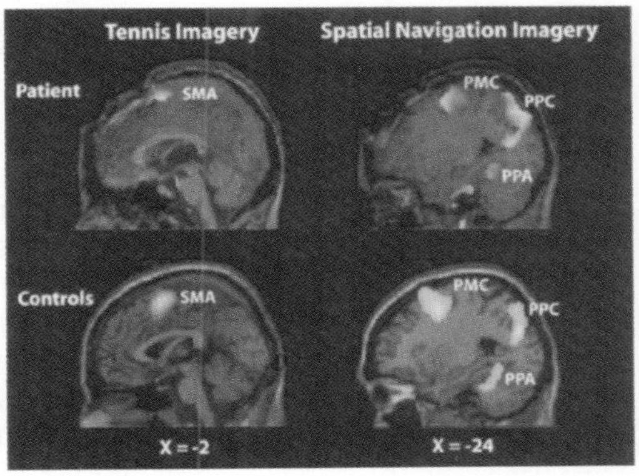

4 Conclusion

Using fMRI to measure brain responses during mental imagery can be used to detect conscious awareness in patients who have retained their cognitive abilities, but are unable to make behavioural responses.

conscious state in which the person is barely awake or aware but shows some deliberate movements (Laureys, 2007). For example, whereas a vegetative person cannot intentionally track a person with the eyes, a minimally conscious person can.

The use of fMRI and other brain imaging techniques to assess the responsiveness of patients in minimally conscious or vegetative states has led to concerns about widespread use of behaviourally based tools like the Glasgow Coma Scale. Have a look at the scoring system for the scale in Figure 5.2. If you were conscious but could not make any movements, what would your score be? What conclusions would your medical specialists likely make? Most cases of minimal consciousness arise from extensive damage to the brain, which can impair motor responses used to make clinical diagnoses (Gawryluk et al., 2010). *Locked-in syndrome* is a condition of severe muscle paralysis in otherwise cognitively intact individuals, usually as a result of damage to the pons in the brainstem. Typically these individuals can make only small movements of the eyes but cannot communicate verbally. Jean-Dominique Bauby, who suffered from locked-in syndrome after a stroke, wrote of his experiences in his memoirs, *The Diving Bell and the Butterfly.* He communicated the entire text by blinking his left eye to indicate letters of the alphabet (Bauby, 1997).

Challenge Your Assumptions

True or False? People in comatose states cannot communicate with others.

False: Some people believed to be comatose have been able to respond to instructions by using mental imagery. This produces specific patterns of brain activity that can be viewed with fMRI.

Personally, we are reminded of the time we spent with David when the doctors said he was vegetative. We asked whether David could hear us; they said probably not, but they did not know. We tried to reach him anyway. We played music for him, told him about our days, and moved his arms and legs. Was his brain taking in some of it? We always thought so, but we couldn't be certain.

Full Consciousness Full consciousness is a tricky concept to define. In medicine, this term is often used to describe recovery from anaesthesia or coma. However, what does full consciousness mean in everyday life? We spend most of our waking lives relatively alert and aware. Still, alertness waxes and wanes throughout the day. Sometimes we are sharp, and other times we lose focus. Some of these fluctuations in alertness stem from a normal daily sleep–wake rhythms, which we will discuss later in the chapter. But even normal wakefulness ranges from drowsiness to full focus. When people are awake but understimulated and not very aroused by their environment, they may be *bored.* When they are awake but have the impulse and need to sleep, they are *drowsy.* Ask your professors: They know only too well that not everyone who is awake is fully present and paying attention. As we will see in the discussion of sleep, when we are drowsy our brains exhibit a unique pattern of brain wave activity that is different from a fully awake and alert brain.

There are also periods when we are more alert and present than normal. We may be stimulated and even excited. Or we may become so involved in what we are doing that we lose a sense of time and forget where we are. Some psychologists have called this state *flow* (Csíkszentmihályi, 1990). Flow exists when we thrive in our ability to rise to the occasion of challenging tasks. Think of a sport or craft you really love to do and do well. Think of the times when you were involved in such an activity and everything "clicked" all at once—everything you did was just right. This is the flow state. Our attention is so focused and everything goes so smoothly that an hour may feel like a minute or a minute like an hour. We are so engaged with the experience that time does not matter at all.

mindfulness
a heightened awareness of the present moment, whether of events in one's environment or in one's own mind.

Another state of full consciousness is **mindfulness,** a heightened awareness of the present moment, of events in one's environment and events in one's own mind. For example, when you are talking with a friend, you can be aware of what your friend is saying, how he looks, and how his words and tone of voice affect how you feel (Brown & Ryan, 2003). The more mindful person attends to all of these things; the less mindful person might notice only the friend's words. As we will discuss later in the chapter, people can develop their mindfulness skills using techniques such as meditation.

A great deal of mental activity occurs in the areas between a complete lack of consciousness and full consciousness. Although it may seem that our behaviour

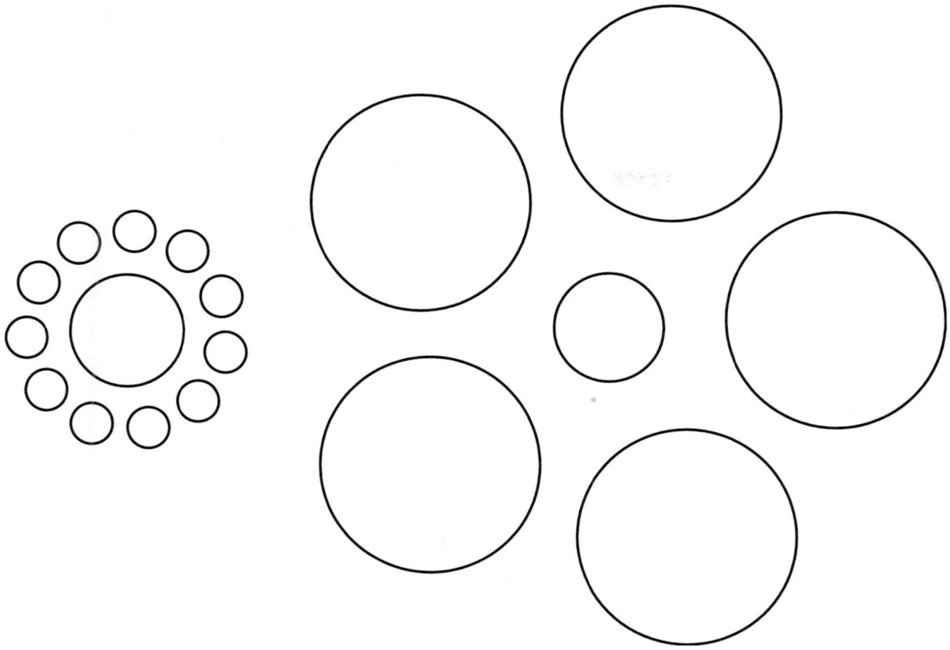

FIGURE **5.4**
THE EBBINGHAUS ILLUSION. Although the centre circles are identical in size, the one of the left appears larger. However, if participants are instructed to pick up the central circle, the distance between their thumb and forefinger is the same for both circles (*Source:* Haffenden and Goodale, 1998.)

is controlled by our conscious commands, many complex mental processes operate outside the boundaries of awareness (Bargh & Ferguson, 2000). For example, whereas visual perception of objects appears to operate within conscious awareness, visual control of our motor response to these objects operates outside of it. The dissociation between "controlled" versus "automatic" visual processing was demonstrated in an elegant experiment by Haffenden and Goodale (1998) at the University of Western Ontario. They used the Ebbinghaus illusion (see Figure 5.4) in which identical disks appear to be different sizes because of the stimuli that surround them. Participants were shown the stimuli and then made a perceptual evaluation of disk diameter by indicating the size with their fingers, or a motor evaluation by actually grasping the object itself. The participants indicated that the disk on the left was larger when asked to indicate the size manually, demonstrating that they were fooled by the illusion. However, when they grasped the disk, the grip distance between their thumb and forefingers was the same for each central disk, indicating that visual control of motor behaviour was guided by the true size of the objects rather than the illusion. Brain imaging studies suggest that consciously guided motor behaviours, like newly learned tasks, are mainly under control of the cortex, while automated motor behaviours are carried out at subcortical levels (Ramnani, 2009).

Quick Quiz 5.1: What Is Consciousness?

1. The two main dimensions of consciousness are
   a. unconsciousness and consciousness.
   b. preconsciousness and consciousness.
   c. wakefulness and sleepiness.
   d. wakefulness and awareness.
2. _____ is a heightened awareness of the present moment, which can be applied to events in one's environment and events in one's own mind.
   a. Wakefulness
   b. Attention
   c. Mindfulness
   d. Optimism
3. Locked-in syndrome is usually caused by damage to which brain area?
   a. prefrontal cortex
   b. pons
   c. reticular formation
   d. thalamus

Answers can be found at the end of the chapter.

LO3 ATTENTION: FOCUSING CONSCIOUSNESS

Being conscious—that is, being awake and aware—involves attending to particular parts of our world. So attention is a key aspect of consciousness; it is how we direct the spotlight of awareness.

We can be aware of only a finite amount of material at a time. **Attention** is the limited capacity to process information that is under conscious control (Styles, 2006). For example, when you are in class, it is not possible to type a text message to your friend and also to pay attention to the lecture. If you are typing your thoughts to a friend, you cannot also hear what the professor is saying. There are several different types of attention. We will examine two attentional processes that help determine the contents of consciousness at any given moment in time: selective attention and sustained attention.

attention
the limited capacity to process information that is under conscious control.

Selective Attention

Imagine being in a crowded room where several people are talking, although you want to listen to just one person. You filter out unwanted noise to focus on the person you want to hear. If attention is a general process, then focusing conscious attention even more narrowly is selective attention. **Selective attention** is the ability to focus awareness on specific features in the environment while ignoring others. When your professor asks for your "undivided attention," then, she is really interested in your selective attention.

selective attention
the ability to focus awareness on specific features in the environment while ignoring others.

The classic scientific evidence for selective attention came from research on the dichotic listening task (Broadbent, 1954). In these studies, a participant received one message in one ear and another message in the other ear. Typically, researchers presented several messages to both ears and then told the participant to pay attention to just one ear (the attended ear). They then measured recall for items presented to both ears. Recall was much better for the attended ear. If, for example, people were instructed to attend to the left ear message, they showed little to no memory of the message presented to the right (unattended) ear (Broadbent, 1954; Styles, 2006).

Later studies showed that if the material presented to the unattended ear is meaningful in some way, it can make its way into consciousness (Treisman, 1964). For instance, if you were at a large party trying to listen to a conversation in spite of a lot of background noise and someone in another part of the room mentioned your name, you would immediately become aware of the other conversation. Somehow you tuned out the background noise so that you could follow the first conversation, but now you cannot push that background information out of your awareness. The ability to filter out auditory stimuli and then to refocus attention when you hear your name is called the *cocktail party effect* (see Figure 5.5; Moray, 1959).

Connection
The psychological disorder schizophrenia is marked by an inability to selectively attend to only the most relevant information in one's surroundings.
See Chapter 15, LO5.

Selective attention creates gaps in attention and perception. When we selectively attend, we focus so much on certain things that we are blind to other things. As a result of paying attention to some parts of our environment, we may miss other parts. In one study that clearly demonstrates gaps in attention, researchers showed people a video of two basketball teams, with one team dressed in white T-shirts and the other in black shirts. They asked participants simply to count the number of times the players on the team wearing white T-shirts passed the ball. About half the participants were dumbfounded to learn afterward that they completely missed seeing a person dressed in a gorilla suit walk into the game, pause for a second to beat his chest, and then walk off screen. They were so focused on counting passes made by people wearing white shirts that they ignored everything else (see Figure 5.6). Attending closely to one thing can blind us to other

FIGURE **5.5**
THE COCKTAIL PARTY EFFECT. The cocktail party effect is the ability to filter out auditory stimuli and then to refocus attention when you hear your name.
When this effect is most likely to occur?

events, even gorillas walking into a basketball game (Simons & Chabris, 1999). This phenomenon by which we fail to notice unexpected objects in our surroundings is referred to as *inattentional blindness.*

If we can be inattentive in spite of efforts to attend, does that mean we can prevent the intrusion of unwanted information during concentration? For example, if you are reading an engrossing novel, is it possible to tune out the sounds of your roommate's TV? Can you apply your attention so intensely that nothing else can get in? The *perceptual load model* states that we do not notice potential distracters when a primary task consumes all of our attentional capacity (Lavie et al., 2004). When a primary task is minimally demanding, however, distracters can capture your awareness. In a laboratory experiment on this phenomenon, participants were asked to view a drawing of a cross on a computer screen. The two arms of the cross were different colours, and one arm was subtly shorter than the other. In the low-perceptual-load condition, participants had to name the colour of the arm. In the high-perceptual-load condition, participants had to say which arm was longer, a more difficult task. The researchers then introduced an irrelevant stimulus (a square) and looked at which group was more likely to see it. Those who were less busy—that is, the people in the low-perceptual-load condition—were more likely to see the square than those in the high-perceptual-load condition (Lavie, 2007). Perceptual load theory might explain why it is easier to ignore the TV when you are lost in an engrossing novel than when you are reading a boring chapter in a textbook. It might also explain why we might miss certain things when our mind is too busy. Tuning out information is not always a good thing. What might happen if you missed seeing a pedestrian while driving because you were involved in a cell phone conversation? See "Psychology in the Real World" for a discussion of the effects of cell phone use on attention in drivers.

FIGURE **5.6**
MISSING THE OBVIOUS. How could anyone miss the gorilla in the middle of this picture? If you were asked to watch a video and count the number of people wearing white shirts, you might be one of the 50 percent who wouldn't notice the gorilla.

Psychology in the Real World

Hazards of Cell Phone–Induced Driver Distraction

All Canadian provinces and most territories have enacted laws banning the use of hand-held devices while driving, but the practice of talking and texting while driving is still widespread. Phone conversations while driving are distracting, since talking on the phone diverts attention from the demanding tasks of safely operating and navigating a car. With such distraction, performance declines and safety is compromised. Think of all the things one has to manage while driving: scanning the road, operating the pedals and gears, watching for other cars and pedestrians, and remembering directions. There is much to attend to without the added task of having a phone conversation.

Is a cell phone conversation, even a hands-free one, any more distracting than having a conversation with someone in the car? Studies have shown that people talking with a friend in the car perform better in a simulator than can those on the phone. Why would real-life conversation be significantly less distracting than phone conversation? Passengers also attend to the driving environment and understand pauses in conversation due to driving demands, and they may assist the driver with directions, road obstacles, and other driving tasks (Strayer & Drews, 2007). In fact, using a phone while driving is similar to drunk driving in that the drivers follow other cars too closely, show slower braking reactions, and have more accidents (Strayer, Drews, & Couch, 2006).

The most direct evidence of the dangers of cell phone use while driving comes from controlled studies using driving simulators. Strayer and Drews (2007) did several experiments in which some participants wore a hands-free headset and engaged in a conversation while doing a driving task, and others had no cell phone and simply drove (see Figure 5.7). Later they were tested on recognition of objects present during the driving simulation. People talking on a cell phone saw half as many objects as those not on the phone; they were not fully paying attention to the driving situation. In another study, the researchers varied the objects inserted into the driving scene in terms of how important they were for driving safety. The hypothesis was that people talking on the phone simply do not attend to things that have little relevance to safety, but they do attend to things that matter. Some of the objects inserted into the driving scene were irrelevant to safety (such as billboards), and others were quite relevant (traffic signs, pedestrians). Later, when drivers were tested on memory for seeing the objects, they were just as likely to miss safety-relevant objects as safety-irrelevant objects.

In a large meta-analysis of 33 studies on over 2000 participants, cell phone use during driving was found to be just as dangerous in terms of slowing down reaction times, whether the callers were using hand-held or hands-free devices (Caird et al., 2008). Although most provincial laws allow the use of hands-free devices while driving, studies have shown that the dangers to driving are similar for hand-held and hands-free phones (Ishigami & Klein, 2009).

Texting while driving has an even worse impact on performance. One driving simulation study showed that using the phone, texting, and eating while driving all impaired performance, but texting led to significantly slower reaction times than the other distracting activities (Cobb et al., 2010). Compared to a control condition, new drivers, while texting, made substantially more errors in shifting out of their lane and noticing traffic signs in a driving simulator task (Hosking, Young, & Regan, 2006). Even more frightening was that they spent 400 percent more time with their eyes off the road!

Clearly, using the phone while driving, even with a hands-free device, seriously impairs driver performance (Beede & Kass, 2006). Such effects may be particularly problematic for new drivers, who are less experienced, have more accidents, and tend to engage in more distracting activities while driving (Neyens & Boyle, 2007). This is one area in which psychological science has clarified a problem for the real world. It might make you think twice about using a phone while driving.

Challenge Your Assumptions

True or False? Talking on a hands-free phone while driving is as distracting as talking on a hand-held phone.

True: Driving while talking on a hands-free phone slows reaction time and interferes with attention to the driving situation, similar to driving while talking on a hand-held phone.

FIGURE **5.7**

RESEARCH PARTICIPANT IN A COMPUTERIZED DRIVING SIMULATOR. The simulator provides a 180-degree city street interactive driving display in a realistic car interior. The "driver" is wearing a hands-free cell phone headset.

Can you pay attention to both driving and your phone conversation at the same time? What does the research say?

Sustained Attention

Staying focused on a task is difficult, especially if the task both requires a high degree of concentration and can have life-and-death consequences. For example, as we discussed in Chapter 4, air-traffic controllers must focus on an airplane on a visual display. To do so, they must coordinate with other airplanes, controllers, and pilots to make sure that each plane lands where it should without crossing the paths of other planes that are landing or taking off. This ability to maintain focused awareness on a target is known as **sustained attention.**

sustained attention the ability to maintain focused awareness on a target or idea.

What are the limits of people's abilities to sustain their focused attention on one task? The airlines need to know this, as do many other industries that require careful attention on the part of their employees. Pilots often face long working hours and yet must stay alert for the safety of their crew and passengers. Many pilots consume caffeine to sustain attention; one study of helicopter pilots showed that caffeine consumption increased by a whopping 42 percent on their flight days compared to their days off (Gander et al., 1998). But does caffeine really work to enhance sustained attention? Or does it simply delay drowsiness without affecting performance? If you've ever used caffeine to pull an all-nighter to get a term paper finished, you might have had the opportunity to observe these effects first hand. Research in this area is mixed, with some reports of improvement and others suggesting no change in attention as a result of caffeine (McKim, 2007). One study, however, revealed that a combination of caffeine and sugar produced improvement on sustained attention and verbal memory tasks compared to caffeine or sugar given alone (Adan & Serra-Grabulosa, 2010). However, as you will learn later in this chapter, a good night's sleep is a much better remedy for fatigue.

One tool that researchers use to study sustained attention is the Continuous Performance Test (CPT). Imagine having to detect the letter Y, among other letters shown very rapidly, one by one on a computer screen. The CPT requires that the participant maintain attentional focus for an extended period of time.

For air-traffic controllers, the ability to sustain attention for long stretches of time is fundamental to the safety of air travellers. Yet research suggests that most people have difficulty focusing attention on a continuous performance task for more than 15 minutes. What does this suggest about highly focused occupations like air-traffic controller?

Most people cannot perform well on CPT tasks for more than about 15 minutes, and their accuracy in detecting targets declines considerably after five to seven minutes (Nuechterlein & Parasuraman, 1983; Parasuraman, 1998). The CPT has been used extensively to assess the effects of stimulant drugs, since they are commonly used to enhance attention and alertness. Drugs used to treat disorders of attention, such as attention-deficit hyperactivity disorder (ADHD), have been shown to enhance performance on the CPT. In particular, methylphenidate (also known as Ritalin) has been consistently shown to reduce errors both in healthy adults and in children with ADHD (Riccio et al., 2001).

Quick Quiz 5.2: Attention: Focusing Consciousness

1. What term best describes not perceiving a person in a gorilla suit when asked to count the number of people playing basketball?
   a. inattentional blindness
   b. not paying attention
   c. absent-mindedness
   d. minimally conscious state

2. You are at a loud party talking to a friend. The noise of the chatter is nearly deafening, but all of sudden you hear your name rise above the noise. This is known as the
   a. self-recognition effect.
   b. cocktail party effect.
   c. attentional effect.
   d. divided attention effect.

Answers can be found at the end of the chapter.

LO4 TRAINING CONSCIOUSNESS: MEDITATION

meditation
practices that people use to calm the mind, stabilize concentration, focus attention, and enhance mindfulness.

Any time you read, reason, solve problems, or learn something new, you are sharpening your mental skills. Some age-old techniques, however, are designed specifically to train the conscious mind. **Meditation** refers to a wide variety of practices that people use to calm the mind, stabilize concentration, focus attention, and enhance awareness of the present moment.

There are many different types of meditation techniques with different goals. To improve concentration, for example, meditators might spend minutes or even hours sitting still, relaxed yet alert, focusing their attention on the breath moving in and out of their mouths and noses, noticing how it moves in and out. This simple, but powerful ancient practice calms the mind and stabilizes attention (Wallace, 2006). Many forms of meditation develop mindfulness, a fully conscious state of heightened awareness of the present moment. Unlike concentration techniques, mindfulness meditation encourages attention to the details of momentary experience, such as all the thoughts, feelings, and sensations available in the moment (Baer et al., 2006).

Connection
Every time you make a memory or learn something new, you change your brain by strengthening synaptic connections or growing new neurons.
See Chapter 6, LO7.

People with high scores on questionnaire measures of mindfulness have higher scores on measures of well-being and optimism, are more in tune with their emotional states, and are less self-conscious and anxious. Also people who practise meditation consistently have higher mindfulness scores than those who do not (Brown & Ryan, 2003). Mindfulness meditation training appears to enhance well-being, reduce stress, decrease depression, and improve physical health (Anderson et al., 2007; Kabat-Zinn et al., 1998; Teasdale et al., 2000). Mindfulness training has shown promising results in reducing pain associated with a number of medical conditions (Ludwig & Kabat-Zinn, 2008).

Meditation can also improve attentional skills (Jha, Krompinger, & Baime, 2007). In the first true experiment on this question, 64 experienced meditators were randomly assigned to a control group or to receive intensive training in concentration meditation (similar to the breathing technique described at the beginning of this section), which they practised for several hours a day for three months straight. They were assessed before, during, and after the three-month training. One of the questions the researchers asked was whether concentration meditation practices improve attention. The results suggest that, compared to the control condition, concentration meditation allowed participants to distinguish differences in the length of lines with greater sensitivity (MacLean et al., 2010). It is akin to having sharper vision or better hearing. In this case, meditation sharpened attention to detail.

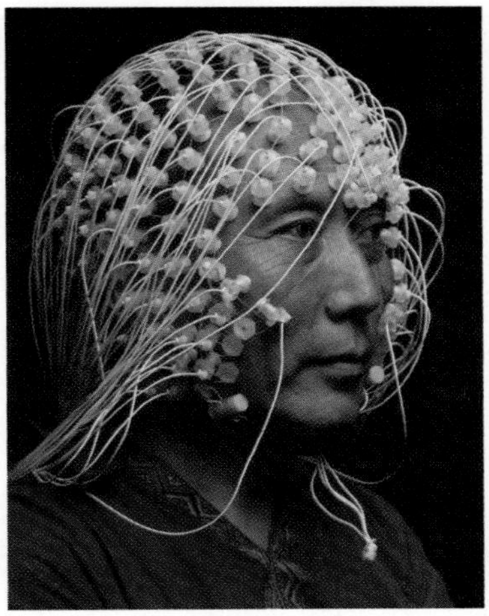

Meditation, an integral part of the Buddhist spiritual practice for thousands of years, develops concentration and mindfulness. Here, a Buddhist monk is being outfitted with EEG electrodes for monitoring his brain during meditation.

Connection

What aspects of experimental designs allow for conclusions about cause and effect?

See Chapter 2, LO5.

Meditation may also change brain function and structure. For instance, after eight weeks of mindfulness meditation training, people who had no previous meditation experience showed significant increases in EEG activity in the left frontal cortex (an area associated with positive mood) and decreases in negative mood, compared to those who received no training (Davidson et al., 2003). These EEG changes persisted for at least four months after training. In another study, MRI revealed thicker brain tissue in areas of the cortex associated with attention, sensitivity to bodily sensations, and the processing of external sensory information, in experienced meditators versus a comparison group of non-meditators (Lazar et al., 2005). Also, those who had meditated the longest showed the greatest cortical thickness in certain areas. A true experimental design is needed to uncover a causal link between meditation training and brain thickness; however, these correlational findings suggest a potential benefit of meditation on brain growth.

Quick Quiz 5.3: Training Consciousness: Meditation

1. Which of the following does meditation appear to improve?
   a. mindfulness
   b. attention
   c. well-being
   d. all of the above

2. A brain imaging study of experienced meditators and a comparison group of non-meditators found that the experienced meditators' brains showed evidence of
   a. thicker cortex in brain areas associated with attention and sensitivity to sensory information.
   b. more diverse synaptic connections throughout the cerebellum.
   c. cortical thinning throughout motor areas, but thickening in frontal areas.
   d. less synaptic death than non-meditators.

Answers can be found at the end of the chapter.

LO5 SLEEPING AND DREAMING

LO6 Meditation offers specific practices for working with consciousness. Yet consciousness varies constantly on a daily basis without much intervention, by virtue of our degree of wakefulness or our moods. In this section, we discuss two major sources of variation of consciousness: sleeping and dreaming.

A five-year-old boy once described sleep as "when I go to my bed and I think about nothing." Typically, we think of sleep as a time of rest and relaxation, when we put out of our minds the day's events. Although our conscious experience of sleep may be of nothing and no time passing, it is in fact a very active process. We behave while we sleep—we move, we dream, and sometimes we even talk and walk. The sleeping brain is very active, but it is only partially processing information from the outside world. Sleep has two essential features: There is a perceptual wall between the conscious mind and the outside world, and the sleeping state can be immediately reversed (Dement, 1999). Awareness of the outside world is greatly diminished in sleep, but not completely. The mind is still able to filter relevant from irrelevant stimuli: a baby's cry may awaken a parent, but much louder sounds (like a TV blaring in the room) may not. Although many of us use alarm clocks to rouse ourselves out of bed in the morning, research suggests that we can even track the passage of time while sleeping (Born et al., 1999).

Rhythmic Nature of Sleep

circadian rhythms
the variations in physiological processes that cycle within approximately a 24-hour period, including the sleep–wake cycle.

Sleep occurs in the context of a daily sleep–wake cycle, which follows a pattern known as a circadian rhythm (from the Latin, *circa*, meaning "about," and *dian*, meaning "day"). **Circadian rhythms** are the variations in physiological processes that cycle within approximately a 24-hour period. Many physiological systems, including the sleep–wake cycle, feeding, hormone production, and cellular regeneration, vary on a circadian basis (Refinetti, 2006). In Figure 5.8 we see how three different bodily processes—body temperature, the hormone melatonin, and alertness—each fluctuate on a circadian cycle. Body temperature, for instance, peaks a few hours before bed and soon after waking up, and then drops during sleep.

free-running rhythm
the internally generated rhythm observed in individuals living in the absence of time cues.

Although circadian rhythms appear to follow the external cycle of day and night, in fact these rhythms are generated internally. In the absence of time cues such as the regular appearance of daylight, individuals' temperature, hormone, and sleep rhythms will follow a pattern close to, but not exactly, 24 hours. After a period of days or weeks of living in a "time-free" environment, individuals will display the **free-running rhythms** of their own biological clock (Lavie, 2001). Free-running rhythms in humans are typically observed under artificial laboratory conditions, such as specially designed underground facilities without access to daylight cues. However, free-running rhythms have been documented in Arctic researchers living in constant daylight (Steel et al., 1995) and in the blind (Lockley et al., 2008). The reason that we do not free run is because our rhythms are reset each day by light, ensuring that our internally generated rhythms are synchronized to our environment. Shortening or lengthening our days by travelling across time zones or working night shifts throws off this synchronization, and it takes time for the body to readjust to the new daily cycle.

For many years, it was assumed that the brain was fairly inactive during sleep. Since a major feature of sleep is a dramatic reduction in movement, psychologists had few tools to study sleep. The brain, as it turns out, is very active during sleep. With EEG technology, scientists have

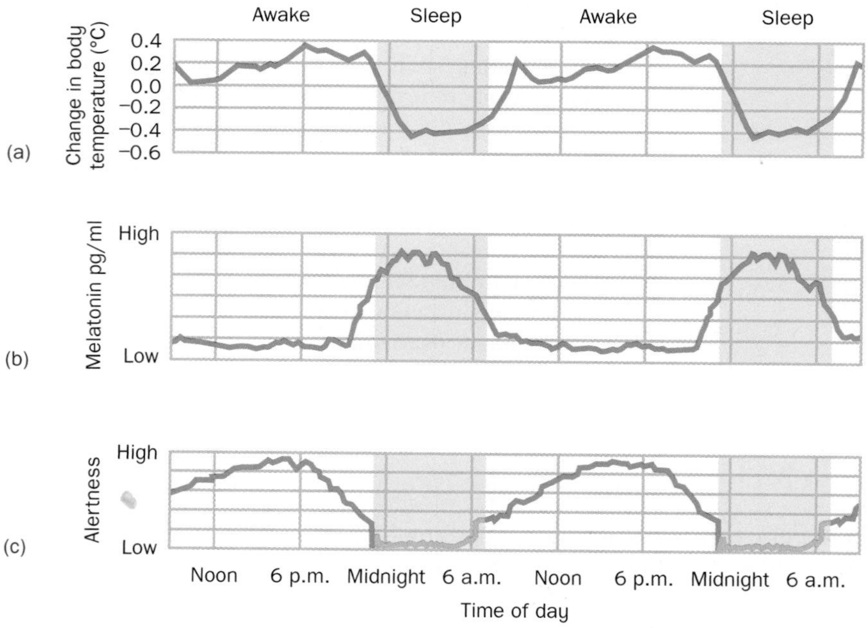

FIGURE **5.8**
HUMAN CIRCADIAN CYCLES. Our body temperature (a), melatonin levels (b), and alertness (c) fluctuate regularly on 24-hour circadian cycles.

learned that the sleeping brain undergoes predictable changes throughout the night (Loomis et al., 1936; Bulkeley, 1997; Dement, 1999). Brain EEG activity follows regular rhythmic pattern of activity cycles typically lasting about 90 minutes (Le Bon et al., 2009). These are considered **ultradian rhythms,** meaning that their cycles are less than a day in length.

Another breakthrough in the scientific study of sleep came in the 1950s. Nathaniel Kleitman and Eugene Aserinsky were studying attention in children and noticed that when children lost attention and fell asleep, their eyes moved rapidly underneath their eyelids (Bulkeley, 1997). They suspected these movements were important in sleep and, after further research, discovered that they occurred in everyone throughout the night (Aserinsky & Kleitman, 1955). They coined the phrase **rapid eye movements (REM)** to describe these eye movements (Dement, 1999). Further research revealed that periods of REM were accompanied by a specific pattern of rapid EEG activity as well as extremely low muscle tension (Dement & Kleitman, 1957). These discoveries revolutionized the study of sleep and dreaming since it allowed psychologists to take objective measures of these subjective states of consciousness. We now know that each stage of wakefulness and sleep has its own pattern of brain activity. When we are awake, brain activity is characterized by rapid waves known as **beta waves.** When we are awake but relaxed and drowsy, our brain activity switches to slower waves known as **alpha waves.** These types of waves also occur during REM sleep, which is why REM sleep is also called paradoxical sleep (Kryger et al., 2005).

Only 15–20 percent of a typical night is spent in REM sleep; the rest is characterized by sleep with relatively few eye movements, called **non-REM.** There are four stages of non-REM sleep, each marked by different arousal levels and unique brain wave patterns (see Figure 5.9). When we enter Stage 1 of sleep, our

ultradian rhythms
the variations in physiological processes that repeat in a cycle of less than 24 hours; sleep stages follow this type of rhythm.

rapid eye movements (REM)
quick movements of the eye that occur during sleep, thought to mark phases of dreaming.

beta waves
pattern of brain activity when one is awake; a rapid, low-energy wave.

alpha waves
pattern of brain activity when one is relaxed and drowsy; slower than beta waves.

non-REM
form of sleep with few eye movements, which are slow rather than fast.

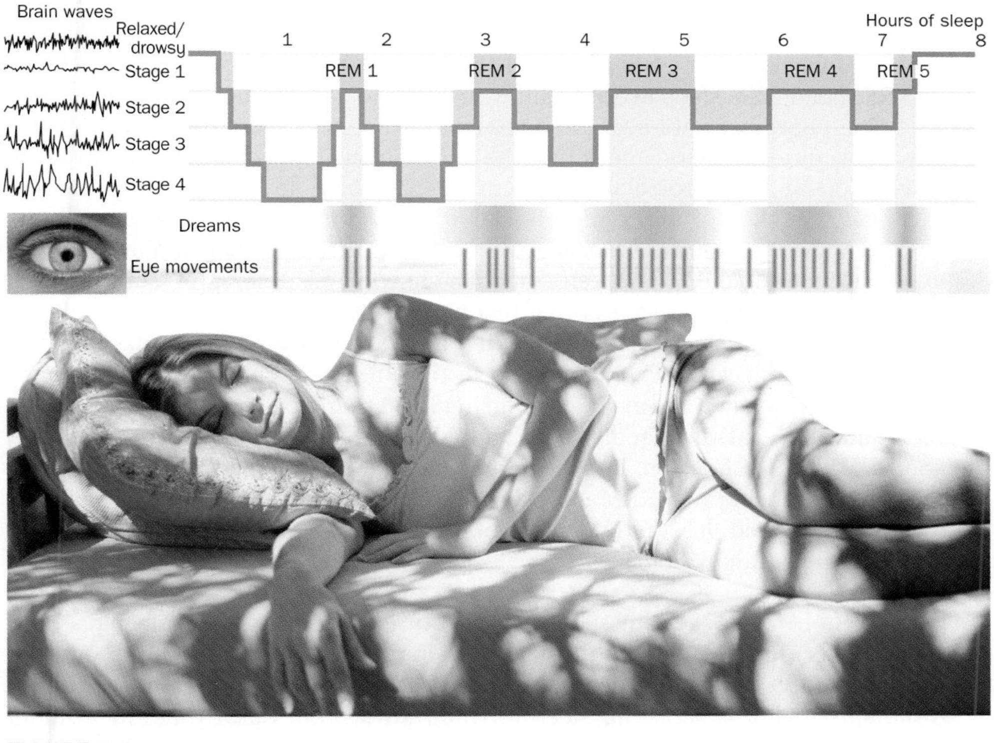

FIGURE **5.9**

TYPES OF BRAIN WAVES AND DIFFERENT STAGES OF CONSCIOUSNESS AND SLEEP. Each stage of wakefulness and sleep is marked by a unique pattern of brain wave. For the typical seven-hour night of sleep for an adult, there are about five cycles of sleep.

What happens to the amount of dreaming as the night progresses?

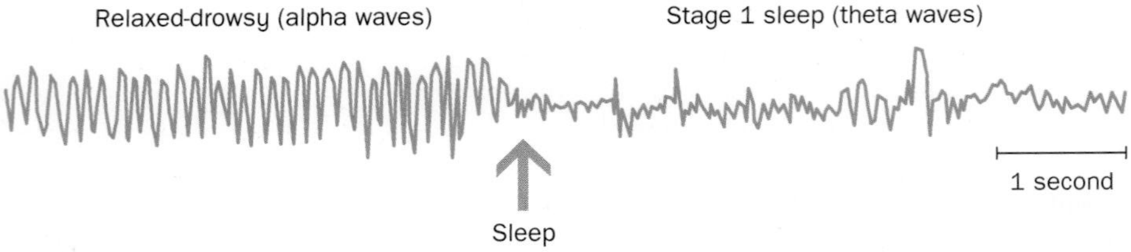

FIGURE **5.10**

THE ONSET OF SLEEP. An EEG shows the abrupt transition from alpha waves typical of the drowsy but awake state to the slower theta waves of Stage 1 sleep. This transition occurs in a period of less than ten seconds.

theta waves
pattern of brain activity during Stage 1 sleep; slower than alpha waves.

delta waves
type of brain activity that dominates Stages 3 and 4 sleep; slower than theta waves.

brain waves change to **theta waves,** which are slower than alpha waves. The precise moment when we fall asleep is readily apparent on an EEG readout—we move from alpha to slower theta wave activity (see Figure 5.10). Stage 1 sleep starts when the sensory curtain drops and we are much less responsive to the outside world. However, Stage 1 sleep is a light sleep, and not much stimulation is needed to awaken us. After about five to seven minutes, we move to Stage 2 sleep, a deeper stage requiring more intense sensory stimulation for arousal than Stage 1. Stage 2 EEG is predominantly theta waves but it also includes short periods of extremely fast and somewhat higher-energy *sleep spindles.* The other unique markers of Stage 2 sleep are sudden high-energy *K-complexes.* After a short period of time, we move from Stage 2, deeper into Stage 3 sleep. Stage 3 initially consists of theta waves with much slower **delta waves.** As we progress through Stage 3, more and more delta waves appear and there are fewer and fewer sleep spindles and K-complexes. When the latter disappear completely, we have entered our deepest stage of sleep, Stage 4. Sleep Stages 3 and 4, which contain the highest proportion of slow delta waves, are often referred to *slow-wave sleep.* Shortly after entering Stage 4 sleep, we start going back to sleep spindles and K-complexes of Stage 3 and then theta waves of Stages 2 and 1. When we return to Stage 1, our eyes begin to move rapidly underneath the eyelids. We are now in REM sleep and are actively dreaming. The night's first episode of REM sleep lasts for only about eight to ten minutes before the whole process starts over. With each progressive cycle, the non-REM periods are shorter and the REM periods are longer (Dement, 1999). Adults move through about four to six different cycles of non-REM and REM sleep every night, which fit into a 90-minute ultradian cycle.

The characterization of particular patterns of EEG activity during sleep has allowed researchers a peek into the unconscious mind since particular brain waves appear to be correlated with different behavioural states. The amount of sound required for awakening is called the *acoustic arousal threshold,* and has been used to characterize sleep depth in the different stages. For instance, takes a louder sound to awaken someone showing EEG signs of Stage 4 sleep than the other sleep stages. Another technique that has enabled the study of consciousness during sleep is simply waking a person during a particular stage of sleep and asking what was happening in their mind. People are more likely to report dreams if they are awakened during REM than non-REM sleep (Dement & Kleitman, 1957; Takeuchi et al., 2003). Full-blown dreams are less common during non-REM than REM sleep, but they do occur regularly during non-REM stages. The dreams during non-REM sleep are different from REM dreams: They tend to be less detailed, less active, and more like regular thinking (Bulkeley, 1997; Foulkes, 1996; Kahan, 2001).

Development of Sleep over the Life Span In humans, REM sleep declines rapidly over the life span, as illustrated in Figure 5.11. Newborns of many species, especially humans, spend more time in REM sleep than in non-REM sleep. Although newborns typically sleep for only a few hours at a time, they might spend a total of eight hours in REM sleep and another eight hours in non-REM sleep *per day.* The percentage of total sleep that is REM stays close to 50 percent for the first three months of life. By eight months it falls to 33 percent, and by age one it drops to about 28 percent. During adolescence and adulthood, the amount of sleep that involves REM steadily decreases.

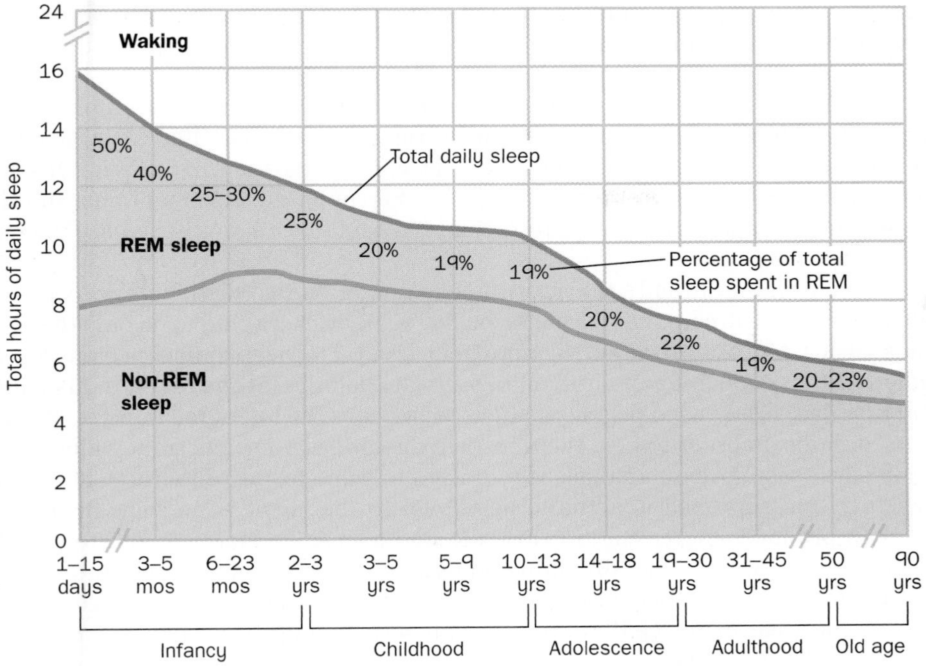

FIGURE **5.11**

SLEEP ACROSS THE LIFE SPAN. As this graph shows, infants and young children not only need more hours of sleep than do older children and adults, but also spend significantly more time in REM sleep. It may be that REM sleep supports brain growth and development.

The fact that newborns and infants spend so much more time in REM sleep than adults has led some researchers to hypothesize that the main function of REM sleep is to assist in brain growth and development. The amount of REM sleep over the life span does correspond to the degree of brain plasticity and neural growth (Dement, 1999). Our brains are most plastic in infancy and childhood and less so in adulthood—precisely the pattern we see in REM sleep. REM sleep, just like new neural growth, continues throughout our lives—it just decreases with age.

Dreaming

Dreams are one of the most fascinating and curious features of consciousness, as well as one of the most puzzling. But what are dreams exactly? **Dreams** are the succession of images, thoughts, and feelings we experience while asleep. The succession of images is loosely connected by unusual associations and not well recalled afterward. The content of our dreams, however, is related to events during our waking life, which is known as the *continuity hypothesis*. Comparison of dream diaries with daily experiences reveal that particular types of activities are more likely to show up in dreams compared to others. For instance, talking with friends and family is a much more common occurrence in dreams than more cognitive activities such as working on a computer (Schredl & Hofman, 2003). Most of us dream numerous times each night, and yet we rarely recall our dreams on waking. When people in sleep labs are awakened, they report dreaming almost always if they were in REM sleep and somewhat regularly if they were in non-REM sleep (Bulkeley, 1998; Dement, 1999).

dreams
images, thoughts, and feelings experienced during sleep.

Do dreams have real meaning or do they simply reflect random activity of a complex brain? Psychologists from different perspectives disagree on what dreams are and what they mean. In this section, we will consider two prominent perspectives on dream theory.

Psychoanalytic Theory In *The Interpretation of Dreams*, Sigmund Freud wrote that dreams are "the royal road to the unconscious" (1900/1953, p. 608). He argued that impulses, thoughts, feelings, and drives that threaten the waking mind are released in distorted and disguised form by the sleeping mind. In this view, each dream is an attempt to fulfill unacceptable desires or satisfy unconscious wishes.

According to Freud's theory, dreams operate on two distinct levels of consciousness. The dream that we consciously recall after waking up is only the surface level, which Freud called the **manifest level.** The deeper, unconscious level, where the true meaning of a dream lies, he labelled the **latent level.** In his clinical practice, Freud used psychoanalysis to uncover the latent meaning of his clients' dreams, in order to help them resolve the hidden conflicts from which their problems arose. Dream analysis is still used in some forms of therapy, although whether this approach is actually beneficial to the client is unclear. Recalling dreams produces increases in heart rate and arousal, which is consistent with Freud's interpretation that dreaming houses our unconscious desires, and dream recall appears to enhance insight and self-awareness in psychotherapy. However, there is no clear evidence that dream recall actually improves clients' symptoms (Pesant & Zadra, 2004).

manifest level
Freud's surface level of dreams, recalled upon waking.

latent level
Freud's deeper, unconscious level of dreams; their meaning is found at this level.

Memory Consolidation Theory According to cognitive psychologists, dreams are not that different from everyday thinking. Research shows that some of the standard processes that we use during our waking life, such as imagery, memory, and problem solving, operate in a similar manner during dreaming (Cavallero & Foulkes, 1993; Kahan, 2001). Several lines of evidence support a role for dreaming in supporting memory functions. First, the amount of time spent in REM sleep is longer after a period of new learning, an effect that has been observed in both humans and animals. Selective deprivation of REM sleep appears to produce impairment in certain types of memory tasks, even if participants are allowed to experience non-REM sleep episodes. Furthermore, REM sleep deprivation can block synaptic plasticity that accompanies new learning (Frank & Benington, 2006). Although these lines of evidence provide a convincing case for the memory consolidation hypothesis, it is not universally accepted amongst sleep researchers. Some experiments have found no memory impairment as a result of REM sleep deprivation, while others have found a stronger role for non-REM sleep and memory. The strongest evidence against the memory consolidation hypothesis comes from observations of the REM-suppressing effects of many types of drugs. Most antidepressants, for example, drastically reduce REM sleep, yet produce no measurable effects on memory in people who take them for depression (Vertes & Eastman, 2000).

Connection

Free association is another therapeutic technique used in Freudian psychoanalysis.

See Chapter 16, LO1.

Functions of Sleep

Our need for sleep is one of the biggest mysteries in psychology. To date, all animals that have been studied show some period of sleep or rest, though there is a great degree of variation between species in the amount and timing of sleep. Despite widespread consensus that sleep serves some vital function, there is yet no agreement on what specific role it serves (Leksu et al., 2009). A common approach to determine the function of sleep is to observe what happens during sleep deprivation. The most consistent finding in both animals and human experiments is that moderate periods of sleep deprivation result in longer sleep time characterized by proportionally more time spent in Stages 3 and 4 (Endo et al.,

1997; Rechtschaffen et al., 1999; Armitage et al., 2001). This certainly suggests that humans and animals have a strong need for sleep, but sheds no light on why we sleep. In rats, prolonged sleep deprivation, up to three weeks, leads to an overall physical deterioration and eventually leads to death. These rats typically have skin lesions and show impairment in metabolism and temperature regulation (Everson et al., 1989). Therefore sleep indeed appears to be necessary, but given the diverse set of symptoms after prolonged deprivation, it is not clear exactly what sleep is necessary for.

The necessity of sleep is obvious; we cannot live without it. Therefore one prominent theory, the restoration theory, proposes that sleep is necessary for physical restoration of cells in the body. When our bodies use energy through the process of metabolism, some cells are damaged. Specifically, when we metabolize oxygen, by-products of this process known as *free radicals* damage cells, including brain cells (Harmon, 2006). In fact, sleep deprivation has been shown to inhibit the growth of new neurons in rats (Guzman-Marin et al., 2003)—something to think about next time you consider staying up all night to cram for a test. Sleep supports cell function by triggering the production of enzymes that fight cell damage (Ramanathan et al., 2002). Similarly, sleep slows metabolism itself, thereby slowing the rate of cellular damage (Wouters-Adriaens & Westerterp, 2006). Since sleep appears to fight cell damage, prolonged sleep deprivation might prevent the body from repairing itself of the damage accumulated while awake.

Another prominent theory, the memory consolidation theory, proposes that sleep helps us learn and remember things (Karni et al., 1994; Payne & Nadel, 2004; Stickgold & Walker, 2007). In a study of the effects of sleep deprivation on performance in a perceptual skills task, participants who had normal amounts of REM sleep performed better on the task afterward than did participants who were roused during REM sleep and missed some normal REM cycles (Karni et al., 1994). Neuroimaging studies of people learning to navigate a virtual maze show increases in activation in the hippocampus, the brain structure that is central to memory formation and learning (see Chapters 3, 5, and 6). If people sleep after this training, the same kind of hippocampal activity resurfaces during slow-wave sleep. The more hippocampal activation shown during slow-wave sleep, the better the person performs on the task the next day (Peigneux et al., 2004; Stickgold & Walker, 2007). In short, task learning is replayed in the brain during sleep, and then this brain practice helps performance the next day.

Sleep Restriction and Sleep Debt Do you get enough sleep? How much sleep is enough? We are often told to get eight hours of sleep per night, yet recent surveys show that the typical adult gets only about six hours and 40 minutes of sleep on weekdays and seven hours and 25 minutes on weekends (National Sleep Foundation, 2008). However there is a large degree of variability between individuals (Webb & Agnew, 1970), and there is no evidence to suggest that the standard eight hours a night is necessary for a good night's sleep (Kripke et al., 2002). So how can you tell if you're getting enough sleep? You might be sleep deprived if you need an alarm clock to wake up, if you sleep longer on the weekends than on weekdays, or if you fall asleep during lectures (Maas, 1998). Although we rarely skip a whole night's sleep, many of us regularly restrict our sleep by staying up late even though we are tired, or waking up with an alarm before our night's sleep has finished. This type of chronic sleep restriction is very common and can produce impairments in attention and cognition. In fact, restricting sleep to four hours per night for a period of two weeks results in deficits in sustained attention and memory similar to that observed in people who have not slept for two days (Van Dongen et al., 2003). Not surprisingly, sleep habits are strongly correlated with academic performance in both high school and university students: Reduced sleep quality and quantity are associated with daytime sleepiness and lower grades (Curcio et al., 2006).

A good night's sleep before an exam may do more for your performance than an all-night cram session.

Challenge Your Assumptions
True or False? You can make up for lost sleep.

True: It is possible to make up for lost sleep by getting extra sleep. Most people, however, do not pay back their "sleep debt," and it continues to negatively affect their thinking and behaviour.

Sleep expert William Dement (1999) developed the concept of *sleep debt* to represent the amount of sleep our brains owe our bodies. It is like a monetary debt that must be "paid back." Sleeping longer on weekends is a way to pay back a little bit of sleep debt accumulated during the week. However we do not usually pay back our sleep debt minute per minute, in fact only a fraction of lost sleep time is added to the next night's sleep. It appears that we compensate for lost sleep more by changes in sleep structure rather than increases in sleep time (Rechtschaffen et al., 1999). A central feature of the restoration theory of sleep is that it is important to conserve a certain amount of slow wave sleep (sleep containing delta waves), which occurs primarily in Stages 3 and 4 (Benington, 2000). People whose sleep is restricted to four hours per night spend the same amount of time in slow wave sleep as those who sleep six or eight hours (Van Dongen et al., 2003). Furthermore, slow-wave sleep in daytime napping is subtracted later from nighttime sleep (Feinberg et al., 1992).

LO7 **Disorders of Sleep** For most people, sleeping six to eight hours a day is a relaxing experience, notwithstanding the occasional nightmare or restless night. For an estimated 20 percent of the population, however, nighttime is often fraught with problems (Dement, 1999). Let us consider five disorders of sleep: insomnia, sleep apnea, sleepwalking, narcolepsy, and hypersomnia.

insomnia
a sleep difficulty characterized by difficulty falling and staying asleep, as well as not feeling rested.

Insomnia is defined as taking more than 20 minutes to fall asleep, having trouble staying asleep, and/or not feeling rested after a night's sleep for two or more consecutive weeks (Krystal, 2005). Somewhere between 15 and 20 percent of adults suffer from insomnia (Pearson, Johnson, & Nahin, 2006). Some sleep experts consider insomnia more a symptom of other maladies than a disorder in its own right, although there is some debate on this matter (Dement, 1999). There are many possible causes of insomnia—for instance, restless leg syndrome, erratic hours, medical conditions, psychological disorders such as depression, and excessive use of alcohol and other drugs (Dement, 1999; Roehrs, Zorick, & Roth, 2000). Iron deficiency may also cause insomnia. This fact might explain why women, who are more likely to be iron deficient, show higher rates of insomnia than men (Lee, 2006; Mizuno et al., 2005). Most drug treatments for insomnia work by increasing the effects of the neurotransmitter GABA (gamma-aminobutyric acid), which decreases central nervous system activity. In this way, they produce a general feeling of relaxation, however one significant problem with these drugs is that the brain adapts to the inhibitory effects of sedative drugs and counteracts their effects by making neurons more excitable. This can lead to problems once the drug is no longer taken, since it can produce additional sleep problems in the form of *rebound insomnia* (Voderholzer et al., 2003). Therefore, there has been a lot of interest in developing non-drug treatments for insomnia. One promising treatment involves giving instant feedback about EEG arousal in an attempt to have the insomniac try to reduce central nervous system arousal to a level that is appropriate for sleep. This technique is called *neurofeedback* and has been shown reduce the number of nighttime wakenings and lengthen total sleep time in insomnia sufferers (Cortoos et al., 2010).

Loud snoring may be due to **sleep apnea,** a temporary blockage of the airway (Dement, 1999). In sleep apnea, the person literally stops breathing for a short amount of time. (*Apnea* means "without breath.") It is more common in men than women (4 percent versus 2 percent) and in obese people. Because people with apnea seldom fall into deep and REM sleep, they are consistently sleep-deprived and often suffer from insomnia. Not only can apnea be disruptive, but in some cases it is also fatal. Apnea sufferers are at increased risk for automobile accidents, diabetes, and heart disease. Treatments for apnea aim to reduce throat blockage either by weight loss, surgery, or devices that keep the throat open. The most effective treatment is use of a device during sleep that pushes air into the throat at high enough pressure to keep the throat open (American Sleep Apnea Association, 2006).

sleep apnea
sleep difficulty that results from temporary blockage of the air passage.

sleepwalking
sleep difficulty characterized by activities occurring during non-REM sleep that usually occur when one is awake, such as walking and eating.

narcolepsy
sleep disorder characterized by excessive daytime sleepiness and weakness in facial and limb muscles.

orexin
a neurotransmitter important for arousal; it is absent in the narcoleptic brain.

Sleepwalking occurs when a person gets out of bed during sleep, usually during the first third of the sleep cycle, and engages in activities that normally occur during wakefulness, such as walking, eating, dressing, or bathing. People who sleepwalk are difficult to rouse and do not remember having been up after waking in the morning. Since the brain inhibits muscle activity during REM sleep, sleepwalking occurs during non-REM sleep, so the sleepwalker is not likely to be acting out a dream. Sleepwalking occurs in about 4–15 percent of children and about 1.5–2.5 percent of adults (Guilleminault et al., 2005).

The main feature of **narcolepsy,** another sleep disorder, is excessive daytime sleepiness. People with this condition may fall asleep at inopportune times throughout the day, often with little to no warning. They may also experience *cataplexy*, a weakness of facial muscles and muscles in limbs (Nishino, 2007). The origin of narcolepsy may lie in a deficiency of **orexin,** since levels of this neurotransmitter are absent in the brains of narcoleptic humans and dogs (Nishino et al., 2010). Narcolepsy is often a function of insomnia; EEG studies reveal that people who suffer from narcolepsy show some abnormality in sleep spindles and disruption of REM sleeping patterns. Narcolepsy appears to have a genetic basis. It is most often treated with amphetamines, which help prevent daytime sleepiness, and antidepressants, which can help with cataplexy. Neither treatment addresses the nighttime sleep disruptions (Nishino, 2007; Tafti, Dauvilliers, & Overeem, 2007).

Sleepwalking is more common in children than in adults, possibly because it occurs during non-REM sleep and adults spend less time in non-REM sleep than children do.

hypersomnia
sleep difficulty characterized by sleeping more than ten hours a day for two weeks or more; includes urge to nap during inappropriate times.

Hypersomnia exists when a person sleeps more than ten hours a day for two weeks or more. Hypersomnia involves strong urges to nap throughout the day, often at inappropriate times such as during meals or in the middle of conversations. It can be caused by other sleep disorders such as apnea, brain injury, or depression. Adolescents who commit suicide are more likely to have suffered from hypersomnia than those who do not commit suicide (Goldstein, Bridge, & Brent, 2008).

LO8 Neuroanatomy of Sleep

The body has an internal timekeeper located in the hypothalamus, called the suprachiasmatic nucleus. The *suprachiasmatic nucleus (SCN)* regulates physiological activity on daily cycles (Moore & Eichler, 1972; Weaver, 1998). When the retina in the eye senses light in the morning, and it stimulates the SCN, which in turn signals the nearby *pineal gland* to decrease the amount of melatonin it releases (Itri et al., 2004). *Melatonin* is a hormone that plays a role in relaxation and drowsiness. In the evening, decreased activity in the SCN prompts the secretion of melatonin, which increases relaxation. Because of its role in relaxation, melatonin can be taken as a drug to combat the effects of jet lag. Research suggests for some people it can be effective in reducing these disruptive effects of jet travel, but more when we travel ahead in time (east) than backward in time (west) (Atkinson, Reilly, & Waterhouse, 2007).

Although the neural mechanisms of the circadian timing of sleep are well understood, the role of the brain in controlling the different sleep stages is more complex and not as well understood. A number of brain regions appear to have specific roles in particular sleep processes. The basal forebrain contains neurons that produce the neurotransmitter *acetylcholine,* which produces the rapid pattern of EEG activation observed during both waking and REM sleep. These *basal forebrain* neurons are themselves activated by signals arriving from a collection of structures in the brainstem. Sleep-promoting neurons containing the neurotransmitter GABA are found in the *preoptic area,* while wake-promoting orexin neurons are located in the *posterior hypothalamus* (Rosenwasser, 2009). These are interconnected and also communicate with the SCN to regulate the timing, duration, and intensity of sleep.

Quick Quiz 5.4: Sleeping and Dreaming

1. Delta waves occur during which stage of sleep?
   a. REM
   b. Stage 3
   c. Stage 4
   d. both b and c.
2. Dreaming is most likely to occur during which stage of sleep?
   a. non-REM
   b. REM
   c. Stage 3
   d. Stage 4
3. The sleep disorder narcolepsy is thought be caused by a deficiency in the neurotransmitter
   a. melatonin.
   b. acetylcholine.
   c. orexin.
   d. GABA.
4. What brain region is important in the timing the daily cycle of sleep and waking?
   a. basal forebrain
   b. the preoptic area
   c. the posterior hypothalamus
   d. none of the above

Answers can be found at the end of the chapter.

LO9 HYPNOSIS

Although the Greek word root *hypnos* means "sleep," hypnotized people are very much awake. Yet they have little voluntary control over their own behaviour. **Hypnosis** is a state of mind that occurs in compliance with instructions and is characterized by focused attention, suggestibility, absorption, lack of voluntary control over behaviour, and suspension of critical faculties of mind (Raz & Shapiro, 2002; Stewart, 2005). People may be more easily hypnotized if they are relaxed, but they can be hypnotized without relaxation (Raz & Shapiro, 2002).

hypnosis
state characterized by focused attention, suggestibility, absorption, lack of voluntary control over behaviour, and suspension of critical faculties; occurs when instructed by someone trained in hypnosis.

People vary considerably in the degree to which they can be hypnotized, largely because they are not equally suggestible. About 65 percent of the population is mildly to moderately responsive to hypnotic suggestion, with about 15 percent being highly hypnotizable (Song, 2006; Hilgard, 1965). The rest are resistant to hypnosis.

The mention of hypnosis conjures up images of a performer putting audience volunteers into sleep-like trances and then instructing them to behave in ways that are out of character. Yet hypnosis is a clinical tool and should not be confused with stage techniques. Numerous studies support the effectiveness of hypnosis for pain relief during childbirth, dental procedures, and surgery. Further, hypnosis may be effective in treating nicotine addiction, nausea and vomiting related to chemotherapy, and anxiety associated with certain medical procedures (Lang et al., 2006; Montgomery, DuHamel, & Redd, 2000; Patterson, 2004; Stewart, 2005). The therapeutic benefits of hypnosis are not fully understood, but the availability of brain imaging techniques has motivated efforts to document its effectiveness and to learn how it works to reduce pain (Flammer & Bongartz, 2003; Stewart, 2005).

It is not easy to offer a general explanation for how hypnosis works. Even studies of brain activation and brain function during hypnosis cannot reveal whether the way hypnosis works to relieve pain is different from how it works to decrease anxiety. Recent research in cognitive neuroscience offers new insight into how the brain operates during hypnosis, however, and in the process expands our understanding of basic mechanisms of attention and consciousness. Let's consider what these researchers are finding.

Hypnosis therapy has helped people to quit smoking. This group of smokers is being hypnotized to believe that cigarettes taste like vomit.

Groundbreaking Research

The Cognitive Neuroscience of Hypnosis

Is hypnosis a special psychological state? Or is it a role people adopt in reaction to situational demands? The ground-breaking research of a few pioneers shows that hypnosis may provide a model for understanding attention and the brain.

PREVIOUS RESEARCH ON HYPNOSIS

Early theories regarded hypnosis as a special state with dissociation of the conscious mind from the events that happen during hypnosis. Stanford University's Ernest Hilgard (1977) showed that under hypnosis one aspect of a person's mind can remain aware and open to stimulation from the outside (such as the hypnotist's voice), while other parts are cut off from external input. Hilgard hypnotized a man and told him he was deaf. While in the hypnotic state, the man did not respond to loud noises nearby. Next, Hilgard told the man to raise a finger if he could hear him. The man raised his finger! The man demonstrated both responsiveness to the hypnotic instruction (he was "deaf" as he did not respond to noises) and an ability to attend selectively to important external input. Hilgard called this phenomenon the *hidden observer effect.*

A second theory maintains that hypnosis does not alter consciousness, nor do hypnotized individuals give up control of their behaviour. Instead, they behave the way they think a hypnotized person would behave, according to the social context and expectations of the situation. In short, they are role-playing (Orne, 1959). That is not to say that hypnosis cannot have significant effects on behaviour and physiology. The late Nicholas Spanos, a leading hypnosis expert at Carleton University in Ottawa, was a strong proponent of the social context and expectation model of hypnosis, yet his research showed that hypnotic suggestion can shorten the time course of viral infections, such as warts (Spanos et al., 1990).

HOW HYPNOSIS AFFECTS THE BRAIN

Neuroscientist Amir Raz and his colleagues have studied whether hypnosis might help to eliminate the Stroop effect (Raz, Fan, & Posner, 2005). The Stroop task tests visual selective attention; it measures how people deal with conflicting verbal and colour information. In a typical Stroop test, participants view the names of colours, such as *green, red,* and *blue,* printed in different colours and must name the colour in which the word is printed. People are slower to identify the colour of words that are printed in a different colour from the meaning of the word (such as when the word *blue* is printed in yellow ink) than words that are printed in the same colour (*blue* printed in blue). The delay in reaction time caused by mismatching colour words and the colour in which the words are printed is known as the **Stroop effect** (Stroop, 1935; see Figure 5.12).

Stroop effect
delay in reaction time when colour of words on a test and their meaning differ.

Raz and his colleagues hypnotized 16 people—8 who were highly hypnotizable and 8 less hypnotizable (Raz et al., 2005). While hypnotized, the participants received instruction on a Stroop test that they would perform a few days later in an fMRI scanner. After the hypnosis session, all participants received a posthypnotic suggestion, which is a suggestive statement that a particular behaviour will occur sometime in the future. Participants were told that during the test they would see gibberish words in different colours and they would have the task of pushing a button corresponding to the actual colour of the letters. In fact, the words they saw during the test were names of colours.

Highly hypnotizable people who received the "gibberish" suggestion identified the colours faster than the less hypnotizable people who received the same suggestion. Brain scans taken during the Stroop test showed that highly hypnotizable people had turned off the areas of the brain that normally process word meaning, and so these areas did not interfere with colour recognition. The anterior cingulate cortex is an area that is usually activated when people experience the conflict in the Stroop test (Carter et al., 1997). In highly hypnotizable people, there was less activation in the anterior cingulate cortex during the Stroop test than in the less hypnotizable people, who were not able to suppress the Stroop effect. It is important to emphasize that participants were not in a hypnotic state while in the brain scanner. In response to the posthypnotic suggestion, the highly hypnotizable people saw real words as gibberish and therefore attended only to identifying the colour of the letters.

The studies on the Stroop effect lend support to the idea that consciousness can be divided in hypnosis. They don't address the issue of role-playing, but another set of studies does. In these studies, a group of researchers used brain imaging techniques to compare perceptions of hypnotically induced pain, physically induced pain, and imagined pain in highly hypnotizable people (Derbyshire et al., 2004; Raij et al.,

FIGURE **5.12**

THE STROOP EFFECT. Participants will name the colour of the letters more rapidly when their colour matches the meaning of the word compared to when there is a mismatch.

Why do you think this is?

2005). The researchers induced real pain by touching participants' skin with a hot metal rod, activating a well-known pain brain circuit. They contrasted this pattern of activation with that of participants who imagined pain. The imagined pain did not activate the same brain areas. However, hypnotically induced pain activated the same brain circuit as the real pain did. Also, participants reported actually feeling pain for both real and hypnotically induced pain, but not for imagined pain. So hypnotic and real pain activate the same brain regions and produce the same subjective feelings. Imagining pain does not have the same effects. Hypnotic pain, then, is not just an imitation of the real thing. It is more like real pain.

Where do these studies leave us? There is some evidence for the special state hypothesis, both in studies of cognition with the Stroop task as well as pain perception. However, it is difficult to rule out role playing so the effect of hypnosis is far from straightforward. One word of caution: the studies described used participants who were easily hypnotized, and therefore these findings might not apply to everybody. However, the possibility of using suggestion to deprogram automatic behaviours in highly hypnotizable people offers promise for the treatment of problematic behaviour that has become automatic, such as drug abuse and eating disorders. Smoking behaviour is largely under control of automatic processes, so smokers quite often reach for a cigarette without thinking. Hypnosis has long been used as an alternative treatment for quitting smoking, but due to the small number of controlled scientific studies to demonstrate its efficacy, this treatment remains controversial. However, recent research indicates that hypnosis results in improved quit rates when combined with nicotine replacement therapy, and it is particularly effective for people who have a history of depression (Carmody et al., 2008).

Quick Quiz 5.5: Hypnosis

1. Research has recently demonstrated that under hypnosis
   a. hypnotically induced pain creates a subjective experience similar to real pain.
   b. people had turned off the areas of the brain that normally process the meaning of words.
   c. hypnotically induced pain activated the same brain circuit as real pain did.
   d. all of the above.
2. According to recent research, hypnosis used in conjunction with nicotine replacement therapy is particularly useful for quitting smoking in people who have a history of
   a. warts.
   b. role-playing.
   c. depression.
   d. pain.

Answers can be found at the end of the chapter.

LO10 ALTERING CONSCIOUSNESS WITH DRUGS

Psychoactive drugs are naturally occurring or synthesized substances that, when ingested or otherwise taken into the body, reliably produce qualitative changes in conscious experience. Psychoactive drug use is universal among humans. Every culture in every recorded age has used mind-altering substances. People use psychoactive drugs for many reasons: to aid in spiritual practice, to improve their health, to explore the self, to regulate mood, to escape boredom and despair, to enhance sensory experience, to stimulate artistic creativity and performance, and to promote social interaction (Weil & Rosen, 1998).

psychoactive drugs
naturally occurring or synthesized substances that, when ingested or otherwise taken into the body, reliably produce qualitative changes in conscious experience.

Most people who use consciousness-altering drugs only use them occasionally and do not experience significant harm from their use. The majority of adult Canadians drink caffeinated beverages daily in order to heighten arousal. According to a Statistics Canada report, 20 percent of men and 15 percent of women over the age of 30 consume more than the recommended daily allowance of 400 mg of caffeine (Garriguet, 2008). Habitual use of caffeine rarely causes significant health problems, although prolonged use of other psychoactive drugs can lead to abuse.

Repeated use of a psychoactive drug usually leads to *tolerance*, a reduction in the effects experienced by the user. This is due to enhanced breakdown of the drug, mainly in the liver, as well as decreased responsiveness of the drug's target neurons in the brain. In order to experience the same state of consciousness,

Psychoactive drugs, such as alcohol, can produce profound changes in perception and consciousness.

the user often increases the drug dose and frequency of use. Tolerance to some types of drugs results in bodily changes that can make the user feel ill once the drug is no longer present. These *withdrawal symptoms* can make quitting the drug quite difficult, and the user is said to be *physically dependent* on the drug. Alcohol withdrawal for an alcoholic, for example, creates many unpleasant side effects—such as delirium tremens (often referred to as the DTs), the symptoms of which may include tremors, insomnia, irritability, seizures, confusion, hallucinations, nausea and vomiting, and agitation. In some cases the DTs lead to death. Not all abused drugs produce physical dependence, although most addictive drugs, such as cocaine, produce significant craving after prolonged use, a state known as *psychological dependence.* This is thought to be due to compensatory changes in brain areas that process rewards which can long outlast the physical withdrawal symptoms. Drug addiction is most often defined as a loss of control over drug use despite negative consequences, and can occur for many types of drugs, whether or not they produce physical withdrawal symptoms (McKim, 2007). In fact, withdrawal symptoms typically disappear after a few days, yet addicts can often relapse after long drug-free periods. Managing craving associated with psychological dependence is therefore an important goal in addiction treatment.

Connection

Tolerance to drug effects can actually protect the user from overdose.

See Chapter 7, Figure 7.19.

In this section we survey the behavioural, psychological, and neurological effects of the major classes of psychoactive drugs: depressants, stimulants, and hallucinogens. As outlined in Figure 5.13, psychoactive drugs affect various neurotransmitter systems, though all influence signalling at synapses in the nervous system. **Agonist** drugs, such as nicotine, mimic the action of a neurotransmitter at its receptors, while **antagonist** drugs, such as caffeine, block the effects of neurotransmitters. We will consider illegal substances as well as the most commonly used and abused legal ones, and explore explanations as to why attempts by the user to alter consciousness can lead to uncontrolled and problematic drug use.

agonist
drug that mimics the effect of a neurotransmitter at its receptors.

antagonist
drug that blocks the effect of a neurotransmitter at its receptors.

depressants
substances that decrease or slow down central nervous system activity.

Depressants

Depressants, which include drugs such as alcohol, sedatives, and opiates, work by decreasing or slowing down central nervous system activity. In low doses, these drugs generally produce relaxation and promote sedation; in high doses, they can slow down heart rate and brain activity to dangerously low levels. The most commonly prescribed sedatives are the benzodiazepines, which include drugs such as diazepam (Valium) and lorazepam (Ativan). The benzodiazepines increase the activity of GABA, the main inhibitory neurotransmitter in the brain, and are used to reduce feelings of anxiety and promote sleep. Alcohol, which also enhances GABA activity, produces similar changes in consciousness as sedative drugs. Alcohol additionally affects signalling of other neurotransmitters; it decreases the activity of glutamate, the main excitatory neurotransmitter in the brain, and enhances activity at certain types of serotonin receptors (Feldman et al., 1997). If taken during pregnancy, alcohol can destroy developing neurons in the fetus's brain, leading to learning disabilities, poor judgment, or intellectual disability (Farber & Olney, 2003). Additionally, combining alcohol with sedatives can be lethal. The opioids work differently, as we will see, but they can be equally dangerous. Let's look in more detail at each type of depressant.

psychoactive drugs

Drug classification	Effects on consciousness	Drug mechanism
Depressants Alcohol	Relaxation, depressed brain activity, slowed behaviour, reduced inhibitions	↑ effect of GABA and serotonin ↓ effect of glutamate
Sedatives	Relaxation, sleep	↑ effect of GABA
Opiates	Euphoria, pain relief, bodily relaxation	↑ effect at opioid receptors (mu, delta, and kappa types)
Stimulants Caffeine	Alertness, nervousness, increased heart rate	↓ effect of adenosine
Nicotine	Arousal, stimulation, increased heart rate	↑ effect at acetylcholine receptors (nicotinic type)
Cocaine	Exhilaration, euphoria, irritability	↓ synaptic reuptake of dopamine, serotonin, and noradrenaline
Amphetamines	Increased alertness, excitability, difficulty concentrating	↑ release of synaptic dopamine, serotonin, and noradrenaline
Ecstasy (MDMA)	Mild amphetamine and hallucinogenic effects, high body temperature and dehydration; sense of well-being and social connectedness	↑ release of serotonin (as well as noradrenaline and dopamine)
Hallucinogens Marijuana	Euphoric feelings, relaxation, mild hallucinations, time distortion, attention and memory impairment, fatigue	↑ effect at cannabinoid receptors
LSD	Strong hallucinations, distorted time perception, synesthesia	↑ effects at some types of serotonin receptor

FIGURE **5.13**

COMMON PSYCHOACTIVE DRUGS, THEIR PRIMARY EFFECTS ON CONSCIOUSNESS, AND MECHANISM AT THE TARGET NEURONS IN THE BRAIN.

Which drugs have similar mechanisms? Do they also produce similar effects on consciousness?

Alcohol Alcohol is the most widely used depressant. How quickly alcohol is absorbed in the bloodstream depends on a variety of factors, including how much food is in the stomach and how much body mass a person has. The amount of alcohol in the bloodstream is the common measure of inebriation known as blood alcohol concentration (BAC). BAC is measured in milligrams of alcohol per 100 millilitres of blood (milligrams percent), so a BAC of .10 means that one tenth of 1 percent, or 1/1000th of one's blood content is alcohol. Figure 5.14 shows the amount of alcohol one must consume to reach .05 BAC (which is currently the legal limit for driving in most Canadian provinces) for various body weights. The figure includes various effects for different BACs.

The more alcohol a person consumes, the more obvious the depressant effects become, sometimes leading to blackouts. These effects are counterintuitive to the loose feeling that many people get in the early stages of drinking alcohol. This apparently stimulating effect occurs because alcohol suppresses the

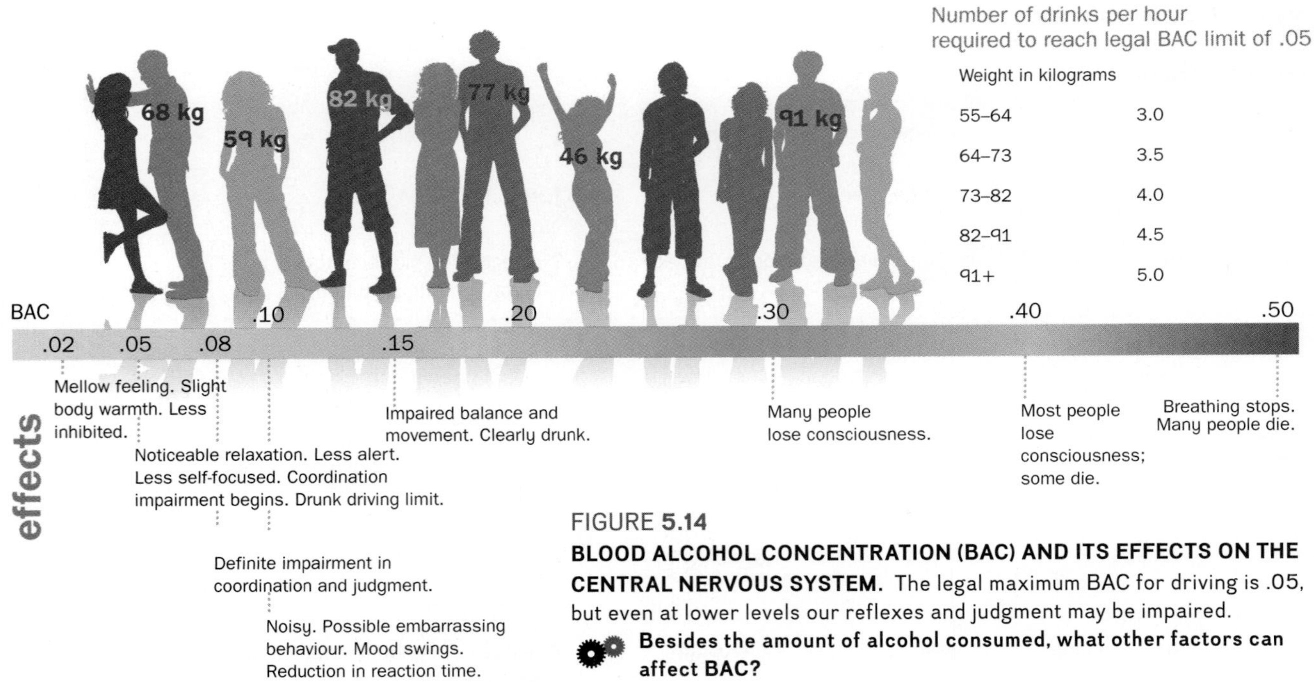

FIGURE **5.14**

BLOOD ALCOHOL CONCENTRATION (BAC) AND ITS EFFECTS ON THE CENTRAL NERVOUS SYSTEM. The legal maximum BAC for driving is .05, but even at lower levels our reflexes and judgment may be impaired.

Besides the amount of alcohol consumed, what other factors can affect BAC?

Challenge Your Assumptions

True or False? You can't drink yourself to death.

False: Once blood alcohol concentration exceeds .40, it can be lethal.

higher social regulatory functions of the cerebral cortex, thereby lowering inhibitions. Perhaps the most startling and most devastating physical effect of heavy drinking is that over a prolonged period it actually shrinks the brain. Neurons die from excessive alcohol use and therefore brain tissue is lost, creating widespread deficits in cognition and behaviour (Mechtcheriakov et al., 2007; Oscar-Berman & Marinkovic, 2003) (see Figure 5.15). For example, frontal lobe damage leads to deficits in planning, working memory, and abstract reasoning; and damage to the hippocampus leads to deficits in learning and memory. How exactly excessive alcohol shrinks the brain is unclear, but malnutrition and cirrhosis of the liver are two likely candidates. With abstinence from alcohol the brain recovers much of its lost volume, especially in the first month of abstinence (Gazdzinski, Durazzo, & Meyerhoff, 2005; Kubota et al., 2001).

Research indicates that the risks of brain shrinkage from drinking may be greater for adolescents than adults, given the amount of development still occurring in the frontal cortex and other areas (Clark, Thatcher, & Tapert, 2008). As we have discussed elsewhere, the brain undergoes substantial development in adolescence, and that process can be disturbed by any kind of substance abuse. Brain shrinkage due to alcoholism is a serious reminder of how the brain not only affects behaviour but also is affected by behaviour. Excessive drinking is more common in men than in women; one survey of Canadian undergraduate students found that 38 percent of undergraduate men and 21 percent of undergraduate women reported drinking more than 15 alcoholic beverages per week (Gliksman et al., 1997). A particularly harmful pattern of excessive drinking in adolescents and young adults is *binge drinking,* which is usually defined as at least five to seven drinks in a row for men and four to six for women (Jackson, 2008; Read et al., 2008; Wechsler, Lee, & Kuo, 2002). Frequent episodes of consuming many drinks in a short period of time is an unhealthy pattern of behaviour, and one that is becoming increasingly common in university students. How prevalent is it? About 40 percent of college students binge drink, and the numbers are rising (National Institute on Alcohol Abuse and Alcoholism, 2005; Wechsler et al., 2002). One of the more serious risks of binge drinking is blacking out (Wechsler et al., 2002). *Blacking out* is a loss of memory of specific events. If anyone has ever told

FIGURE 5.15

BRAIN REGIONS MOST AFFECTED BY EXCESSIVE DRINKING. The main regions of the brain most affected by long-term and excessive drinking include the frontal lobes (planning and abstract thinking and reasoning); the hippocampus (learning and memory); the hypothalamus (hunger, thirst, and sexual motivation); and the cerebellum (movement and coordination).

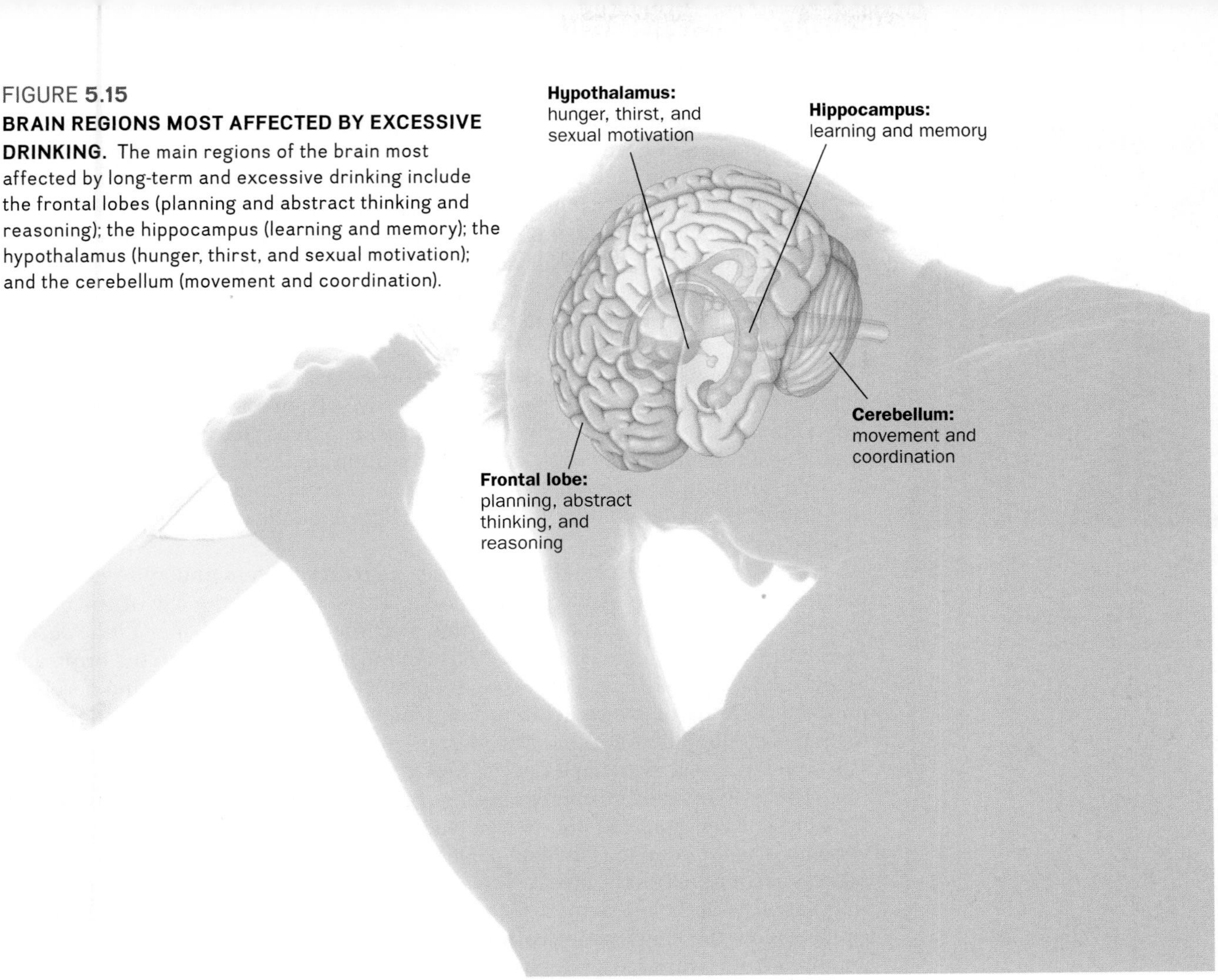

you of something you did the night before at a party when you were drunk and you have absolutely no recollection whatsoever of having done that, then you have blacked out.

As dangerous and deadly as alcohol can be, numerous studies show that mild to moderate alcohol intake provides protective effects for cardiovascular health. Moderate alcohol consumption is generally defined as no more than two drinks a day. Moderate alcohol use raises the amount of the beneficial form of cholesterol (HDL) in the blood, which has protective effects on the cardiovascular system (King, Mainous, & Geesey, 2008). Although these cardiovascular benefits were initially linked to red wine only, research now shows that many forms of alcohol convey the same advantages (Hines & Rimm, 2001; Sacco et al., 1999).

Connection

What is special about the adolescent brain?

See Chapter 10, LO9.

Sedatives Sedative drugs are most commonly taken to reduce arousal, and are usually prescribed clinically to treat states of hyperarousal—namely, anxiety and insomnia. Prescription sedatives such as benzodiazepines reduce anxiety and also slow the heart rate and relax skeletal muscles. There are numerous types of benzodiazepine drugs, which differ in how quickly they produce effects and how long these effects last. Long-acting benzodiazepines, such as diazepam (Valium), are often used to treat anxiety, since the inhibitory effects are required for a prolonged period of time throughout the day. Shorter-acting preparations, such as triazolam (Halcion), are preferred for the treatment of insomnia since the sedative effects are only required during sleep. These short-acting drugs reduce

Michael Jackson died in June 2009 from a combination of long-term drug abuse and an anesthetic administered illegally by his personal physician.

the time it takes to fall asleep and also increase total sleep time, making them an appealing treatment for insomnia. However, they also reduce the amount of time spent in deeper stages of sleep, and therefore the increase in sleep time might not necessarily result in improved sleep quality (Hindmarch et al., 2005). Given the similar effect that these drugs have on the GABA system, it is not surprising that they create a feeling of stupor similar to that of alcohol intoxication. These drugs have the potential for both physical and psychological dependence, particularly in people with a previous history of drug abuse (Farré et al., 1998), and they can be lethal at high doses if used in combination with other drugs.

Opiates Opiate drugs are taken for two reasons: to reduce the perception of pain and to elevate mood. These drugs are derived from opium or chemicals similar to opium. They may be derived from natural sources (like morphine), may be partially synthetic (like heroin), or may be entirely synthetic (such as methadone). Modern synthetic opiates include oxycodone (Percocet or Percodan), which is prescribed for moderate to severe pain, and hydrocodone (Vicodin), which is prescribed for milder pain.

Opiates have been used for centuries as pain relievers and still remain the most effective pain-relieving drugs known. These drugs make use of the body's own naturally occurring opiate systems. Our own bodies produce *endorphins*, opiate-like proteins, called *opioids*, that bind to opioid receptors in the brain and act as natural painkillers. The stronger opiates—opium, morphine, and heroin—produce feelings of overwhelming bliss, euphoria, and bodily relaxation. The feeling is so good that nothing else matters. As one intravenous heroin user said, "It's so good. Don't even try it once" (Weil & Rosen, 1998).

Because of their strong euphoric properties, opiates have a high potential for abuse. Even some of the newer, widely prescribed synthetic opiates have become drugs of abuse (Paulozzi, 2006). Contrary to the popular image, not all addicts are junkies on the street. Some people inadvertently develop an addiction to opiates while being treated for chronic pain (Gallagher & Rosenthal, 2008). Opiates slow the heart and breathing; high doses can kill by stopping the heart and breathing (Hayes, Klein-Schwartz, & Doyon, 2008). For many of these drugs, the amount required to feel an effect may not be that much less than the amount that can be deadly, especially in people who have developed tolerance. Some newer therapeutic opiates, such as buprenorphine, can be taken at higher doses with less risk of overdose (Johnson, Fudala, & Payne, 2005).

Stimulants

stimulants
substances that activate the nervous system and produce arousal.

Stimulants activate the nervous system and produce arousal. Two of the most widely used psychoactive drugs are the stimulants caffeine and nicotine. Cocaine and amphetamines also enhance psychomotor or behavioural stimulants since they have much more pronounced effects on motor behaviour than caffeine or nicotine (Kolb & Wishaw, 2001).

Caffeine If you drink coffee, tea, cocoa, or certain soft drinks (including energy drinks), you are a stimulant user (see Figure 5.16). Caffeine is the world's most commonly consumed psychoactive drug, ingested by 90 percent of North American adults on a daily basis (Lovett, 2005). The effects of mild to moderate caffeine intake are increased alertness, increased heart rate, loss of motor coordination, insomnia, and nervousness. Too much caffeine can make people jittery and anxious.

If regular caffeine users stop consuming caffeine, they can experience withdrawal symptoms, the most common of which is headache. Giving up caffeine can also lead to fatigue and decreased energy, depressed mood, and difficulty

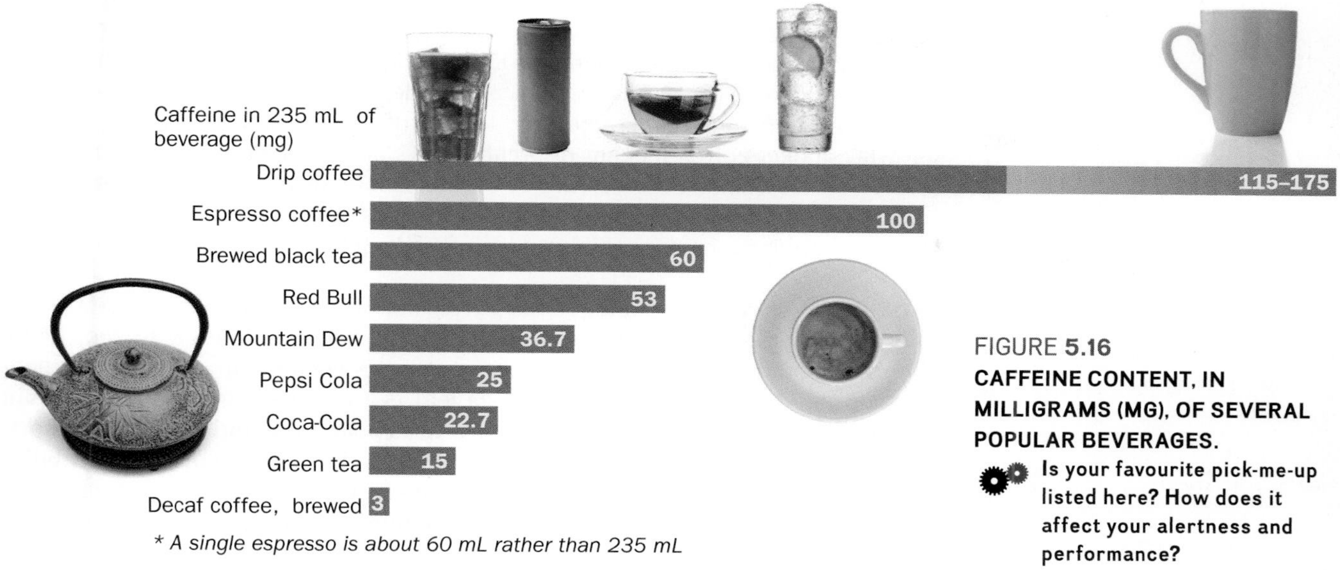

FIGURE **5.16**
CAFFEINE CONTENT, IN MILLIGRAMS (MG), OF SEVERAL POPULAR BEVERAGES.

Is your favourite pick-me-up listed here? How does it affect your alertness and performance?

concentrating (Juliano & Griffiths, 2004). These withdrawal effects show that caffeine creates physical dependence. To eliminate these negative withdrawal effects, people who want to stop using caffeine should gradually reduce their consumption.

Traditionally, coffee, tea, and soft drinks have been the most common sources of caffeine. However, the recent surge in popularity of energy drinks is changing the way that many people consume caffeine, especially young adults. In addition to caffeine, energy drinks contain the amino acid taurine, and the effects of the combination of these substances are not well studied. This is of some concern since energy drinks are often combined with alcohol. One recent study at Dalhousie University showed that undergraduate university students drank significantly more alcohol with energy drinks, compared to when they drank alcohol alone (Price et al., 2010).

Nicotine Tobacco is one of the most widely used recreational drugs worldwide. In 2009, 17 percent of Canadians over the age of 15 reported that they smoked cigarettes regularly (Health Canada, 2009). The active drug in tobacco, nicotine, acts as a stimulant and is thought to be responsible for the addictive properties of tobacco.

Smoking tobacco puts nicotine in the bloodstream almost immediately; within eight seconds of inhalation it reaches the brain. As a stimulant, nicotine increases heart rate and rate of respiration, and it creates a feeling of arousal. Over time, the cardiovascular arousal associated with nicotine use increases the risk of high blood pressure and heart disease. Ironically, many nicotine users report that cigarettes calm them down. This perception may stem from the fact that nicotine relaxes the skeletal muscles even as it arouses the autonomic nervous system.

Nicotine is extremely addictive. It creates high tolerance and unpleasant withdrawal symptoms. The high that heroin creates is more intense than the feeling of arousal from cigarettes, and the disruption to daily life of the heroin addict is more extreme than that of the smoker; but in terms of how difficult it is to quit, nicotine ranks higher than heroin (Keenan et al., 1994).

There are many known health risks of smoking. Cigarette smoking reduces life expectancy on average by ten years, increases the risk for lung cancer more than tenfold, and triples the risk of death from heart disease in both men and women

(CDC, 2001; Doll et al., 2004). The U.S. Surgeon General has reported that smoking is also conclusively linked to leukemia, cataracts, pneumonia, and cancers of the cervix, kidney, pancreas, and stomach. Tobacco smoke contains many cancer-causing agents that trigger severe damage to DNA and can inhibit DNA repair in lung cells. Tobacco smoke also contains carbon monoxide, a toxic substance that displaces oxygen in the bloodstream, depriving tissues of needed oxygen. This is one reason why smokers often feel out of breath (CDC, 2001; Doll et al., 2004; Feng et al., 2006; Health & Human Services, 2004). Carbon monoxide from smoking also makes people look older than they are, because it reduces the blood supply to skin tissue. Tobacco smoking increases skin wrinkles even in young smokers (Koh et al., 2002).

Connection

Dopamine is released when we feel good, and serotonin affects how sociable and affectionate we feel.

See Chapter 3, "Common Neurotransmitters."

Cocaine For centuries, indigenous peoples of South America have chewed the coca leaf for its stimulant and digestion-aiding properties (Weil & Rosen, 1998). The most notable component in the coca plant is cocaine, a psychoactive substance that when isolated from the coca leaf is a much stronger stimulant than chewed coca. When snorted, cocaine increases heart rate and produces a short-lived, but intense rush of euphoria. It also can lead to a sense of invulnerability and power. Physiologically, cocaine induces a sense of exhilaration by increasing the availability of the neurotransmitters dopamine, serotonin, and noradrenaline (Mateo et al., 2004).

The brevity of the cocaine high helps explain why people abuse it—they keep chasing after a short-lived euphoria with even more cocaine. Some people inject (free-base) cocaine or smoke crack cocaine, a form of cocaine that is sold on the streets in pellets. Along with being extremely addictive, cocaine can cause other health problems, including increased heart rate and irregular heartbeat, increased risk of heart attack, and, occasionally, death (Weil & Rosen, 1998).

Amphetamines Amphetamines are synthetically produced compounds that produce long-lasting excitation of the sympathetic nervous system, the part of the nervous system that keeps us ready for action. There are three main forms, all of which are pills: methamphetamine (Meth), dextroamphetamine (Dexedrine), and amphetamine sulfate (Benzedrine or "speed"). Methamphetamine is highly addictive. The street drug called crystal meth is a crystallized form of methamphetamine that is smoked. Most people who abuse amphetamines get them from health care providers. Common medical uses of amphetamines are to suppress appetite and to treat symptoms of attention deficit hyperactivity disorder.

Amphetamines raise heart rate, increase motivation, and elevate mood. The effects vary with dosage and manner of use, but other short-term effects may include insomnia, stomach distress, headaches, decreased libido, and difficulty concentrating. Long-term use can lead to severe depression, paranoia, loss of control over one's behaviour, and, in some cases, amphetamine psychosis, a condition marked by hallucinations. Withdrawal from chronic amphetamine use creates unpleasant symptoms, such as fatigue, anxiety and depression, hunger, overeating, and disordered thought and behaviour.

Ecstasy The psychoactive drug MDMA, also known as ecstasy, is chemically similar to both methamphetamine and the active ingredient in hallucinogenic mushrooms, making it both a stimulant and a mild hallucinogen. At moderate to high doses, MDMA produces mild sensory hallucinations as well physiological arousal. It is sometimes called "the love drug" because it produces feelings of euphoria, warmth, and connectedness with others. Among friends, it dissolves interpersonal barriers and produces feelings of affection and a desire to touch and hug. This effect may be why MDMA became popular in dance clubs.

The popularity of this drug has been of particular concern since MDMA is known to be toxic to several organs, including the heart, liver, and brain (Turillazzi et al., 2010). MDMA destroys serotonin and, to a lesser extent, dopamine neurons in several regions of the brain, which may lead to long-term behavioural, cognitive, and mood changes (Yamamoto et al., 2010). The dangers of prolonged MDMA use include increased risk of depression, slower processing times on cognitive tasks, and greater impulsivity (Halpern et al., 2004; Thomasius et al., 2006). Despite compelling evidence of its neurotoxicty in both animal models and human users, there is still much controversy surrounding the safety of ecstasy use. Many popular websites suggest that MDMA toxicity is a result of contaminants from "dirty" batches of ecstasy, and commercially available drug-testing kits are promoted so that users can test the purity of their pills. Although some contaminants are certainly more harmful than MDMA, the evidence that this drug is safe is misleading.

Hallucinogens

The third major class of psychoactive drugs is the hallucinogens. As the name implies, **hallucinogens** create distorted perceptions of reality ranging from mild to extreme. Sometimes, they also alter thought and mood. There are numerous hallucinogens, but we will discuss only marijuana and LSD.

hallucinogens
substances that create distorted perceptions of reality ranging from mild to extreme.

Marijuana Marijuana comes from the blossoms and leaves of the *Cannabis sativa* plant and has been used for thousands of years to alter consciousness and for its medicinal properties. The active ingredient in cannabis is tetrahydrocannibinol (THC), which affects the brain and body by acting at *cannabinoid* (CB) receptors in the brain and body. These receptors also bind to naturally occurring neurotransmitters called **endocannabinoids,** the body's own marijuana-like chemicals. Marijuana alters mood to create euphoria and changes perception, especially one's perception of time and food. It makes time appear to slow down and makes food more desirable (Crystal, Maxwell, & Hohmann, 2003; Nicoll & Alger, 2004). Marijuana is often classified as a hallucinogen, although people rarely experience hallucinations when using low or moderate doses. Such experiences occur more readily when people eat it.

endocannabinoids
natural, marijuana-like substances produced by the body.

Marijuana does not produce physical dependence; that is, it does not lead to physical dependence and withdrawal symptoms the way that nicotine and heroin do. But in the course of long-term habitual use, people develop cravings for marijuana when they are without it and this craving has a physiological basis (Wölfling, Flor, & Grüsser, 2008). People can become psychologically dependent on marijuana or use it compulsively.

Marijuana has long been known to cause memory impairment, which is probably the most commonly reported harmful effect of this drug (Kanayama et al., 2004). While under the influence of the drug, people have more difficulty storing information for later recall, although previously stored information appears to be unaffected (Ranganathan & D'Souza, 2006). Of greater concern are the lingering memory impairments observed in chronic users, who show memory impairments outside of the period of marijuana intoxication (Lundqvist, 2005). In fact, marijuana causes neuronal loss in parts of the brain involved in memory, although this loss appears to be reversible once drug use is discontinued (Chan et al., 1998). Recent research also suggests that regular marijuana use is common in adolescents who later develop schizophrenia, which has led some people to suggest a link between marijuana use and schizophrenia in people who might be genetically predisposed to this disorder (Arseneault et al., 2004). Given that the most common route of ingestion is smoking, heavy marijuana smoking does increase the likelihood of a variety of respiratory illnesses, and can cause immune system impairment (Tashkin et al., 2002).

In contrast to these harmful effects, marijuana also offers promise for medical treatment of various medical disorders. For instance, marijuana is known for its effective prevention and treatment of nausea. As such, it has been

In 2001 the Canadian government passed regulations allowing legal access to marijuana for certain conditions, such as multiple sclerosis and epilepsy. Although not part of the federal medical marijuana program, many "compassion clubs" provide marijuana to registered users.

recommended and prescribed for people who suffer chemotherapy-related nausea or the involuntary weight loss due to AIDS. Research shows that marijuana may help people eat not by increasing appetite, but by making food appear more appealing (Nicoll & Alger, 2004). Additionally, marijuana and its derivatives may be helpful for the treatment of pain. Marijuana-activated receptors in brain areas modulate pain and thus marijuana may work more safely and more effectively than opioids (Hohmann et al., 2005). Marijuana's inhibitory effects at its receptors also enable it to reduce excessive neuronal activity characteristic of epilepsy and muscle spasms associated with multiple sclerosis.

LSD LSD (lysergic acid diethylamide-25), or "acid," is a synthesized form of lysergic acid, which is derived from the grain fungus ergot. People notice dramatic changes in conscious experience when they ingest LSD. These experiences include altered visual perceptions (such as seeing the tracks that your hand makes when you move it through the air or the lines dance about on a page), enhanced colour perception, hallucinations, and synesthesia, which is when we "see" sounds or "hear" visual images. At high doses, LSD produces subjective effects that are profoundly different from our typical states of consciousness. Users may feel as if their experiences are disconnected from their physical selves. Because it can temporarily separate a person from reality, for some people LSD use can lead to panic and negative experiences, known as bad trips. For other people, it can have the opposite effect and lead to very profound, life-altering experiences (Weil & Rosen, 1998). In one controversial study, terminally ill patients were administered LSD to enhance psychotherapy. Most patients became less anxious about death and required less pain medication than prior to their LSD administration (Pahnke et al., 1970). The use of LSD as a treatment for alcoholism was also explored in Canada in the early 1950s. Unfortunately, these early studies received negative media attention so our understanding of the benefits, and risks, of LSD's use in medicine remains unclear (Nichols et al., 2004). Still, more so than any other drug, LSD has highlighted the important connection between brain function and consciousness.

Neurochemically, LSD appears to work by stimulating a particular subtype of serotonin receptor, which in turn increases the excitatory neurotransmitter glutamate in the cortex, which may play a role in creating hallucinations (Marek & Aghajanian, 1996; Scruggs, Schmidt, & Deutch, 2003). The known side effects from LSD include increased body temperature, increased blood pressure, insomnia, and psychosis-like symptoms in some people (Strassman, 1984).

Quick Quiz 5.6: Altering Consciousness with Drugs

1. Benzodiazepines, used to treat anxiety and insomnia, have a mechanism of action *most* similar to that of
   a. alcohol.
   b. heroin.
   c. cocaine.
   d. marijuana.

2. Which of the following drugs is most likely to produce hallucinations?
   a. marijuana
   b. LSD
   c. heroin
   d. morphine

Answers can be found at the end of the chapter.

Evaluating Connections in Consciousness

Brain Injury Revisited

Remember David? Today, more than a decade after his brain injury, David functions pretty well. His most profound deficits are problems with consciousness that affect attention, memory, and learning. By revisiting David's situation and the effects of brain injury on consciousness in general, we can integrate many of the topics addressed in this chapter.

David moved through various stages of conscious awareness in his first year of recovery. He went from comatose to vegetative to responsive in five months, but even when he was responding to the outside world, he was minimally conscious. In some cases of brain injury this is a transitional state to full consciousness; sometimes it is a permanent state. Fortunately, in David's case, minimal consciousness eventually led to full consciousness. His brain gradually became more and more responsive. How does this happen? We do not know for sure. What we do know is that people with damage to lower brain regions that control basic functions, such as sleep–wake cycles, are less likely to regain consciousness than are people with damage to the cerebral cortex (Laureys, 2007). David had cortical damage.

David's consciousness bears permanent scars from his injury. For example, when he is working on a task, David can suddenly become distracted and forget what he is doing. We all experience this kind of distraction from time to time, but for David it can be disabling. He might be emptying the dishwasher and overhear someone saying something about baseball. Hearing the word *baseball,* David might look up and—as a fanatic about baseball statistics—suddenly have some thought about baseball. He will then ask his brother Greg if he knew, say, that Joe DiMaggio had a lifetime fielding percentage of .978. Then he'll head to his room to send an email to his other brother about the same topic. Meanwhile, the dishwasher remains unemptied. By the time he's finished sending the email, David has forgotten all about the dishwasher.

Some researchers attribute such distractibility to problems with selective attention. Indeed, David has a hard time staying on task and filtering out or setting aside information to deal with at a later time. As soon as he heard "baseball," David thought of Joe DiMaggio and simply had to talk about him. He couldn't set the topic aside briefly. As a result, he lost the ability to continue unloading the dishwasher. Distractibility is a common problem for people with brain injury. People with brain damage, especially to the frontal lobes, have trouble blocking out extraneous information and using selective attention to stay on task (Ries & Marks, 2005). Some studies show that such individuals perform poorly on the Stroop test, for example, possibly because it takes them longer to process information overall (Mathias & Wheaton, 2007). For David, a related problem is an inability to concentrate on one thing for any extended period of time. That is, he shows deficits in sustained attention. Research confirms that, in general, people with traumatic brain injury have deficits in sustained attention (Mathias & Wheaton, 2007).

Sleeping and dreaming may also change with brain injury. In fact, how people sleep while comatose or vegetative may be an important predictor of recovery. People in a coma, who show more organized EEG patterns during sleep, have less disability later and a greater likelihood of survival than those whose brain patterns are less organized while sleeping (Valente et al., 2002). After they have regained consciousness, sleep and wakefulness may be disrupted. David's sleep is not normal. He suffers from hypersomnia, or excessive sleeping. Sometimes he sleeps 14 hours a day; other times he has trouble sleeping at night and naps frequently throughout the day. Insomnia and chronic fatigue are also common in people with traumatic brain injury (Ouellet & Morin, 2006; Ouellet, Beaulieu-Bonneau, & Morin, 2006).

Brain injury can also lead to disruptions in dreaming, probably as a consequence of disordered sleep, though this doesn't seem to be a problem for David. It may depend on the location of the brain injury. Some people who sleep normally following traumatic brain injury nevertheless have problems with dreaming, indicating that different areas of the brain may be responsible for sleeping and dreaming. People with damage to the association cortex and the limbic system and areas around it or the links between these areas show the greatest dreaming deficits and, in some cases, a total absence of dreaming (Domhoff, 2001; Solms, 2000). Although not dreaming might seem insignificant, often people who experience a total lack of dreaming due to brain injury also lack "initiative, curiosity, and fantasy" in waking life (Domhoff, 2001, p. 16).

Lastly, drug use and abuse can occur in people who are coping with the challenges of a brain injury. It is most common among those who experience depression and anxiety (Anson & Ponsford, 2006).

Quick Quiz 5.7: Evaluating Connections in Consciousness

1. Since his accident, David, like many people with brain injury, experiences an overwhelming need for sleep called
   a. somnambulism.
   b. night terrors.
   c. circadian flux.
   d. hypersomnia.

2. People with brain damage, especially to the frontal lobes, have trouble with selective attention. This problem leads to much _____ in daily life.
   a. fatigue
   b. distractibility
   c. amnesia
   d. confabulation

Answers can be found at the end of the chapter.

Chapter Review

WHAT IS CONSCIOUSNESS?

- Consciousness is an awareness of one's surroundings and of what's in one's mind at a given moment. It is also that limited portion of the mind of which we are aware at any given moment, sometimes called a global workspace.
- Consciousness has two aspects: the degree to which we are awake and the degree to which we are aware.
- Different levels of consciousness stem from these two dimensions. Minimal consciousness refers to states when people are barely awake or aware, such as coma and vegetative states. Full consciousness is a high degree of wakefulness and awareness and ranges from normal waking states to states of flow and mindfulness.

ATTENTION: FOCUSING CONSCIOUSNESS

- Attention is focused awareness. Selective attention is the process by which we filter out unwanted stimuli while focusing on other stimuli. Selective attention can result in inattentional blindness, the failure to notice the unexpected. Sustained attention is the ability to stay focused on one thing.

TRAINING CONSCIOUSNESS: MEDITATION

- Meditation is a form of mental training that can be used to calm the mind, stabilize concentration, or enhance awareness of the present moment.
- Evidence from brain-imaging studies suggests that meditation has lasting effects on mood, concentration, and learning.

SLEEPING AND DREAMING

- Four stages of sleep are characterized by different EEG patterns. We move through sleep Stages 1–4 roughly once every 90 minutes during the night. Rapid eye movement (REM) sleep occurs only during Stage 1 sleep, when most dreaming occurs. Most sleep consists of non-REM sleep.
- Sleep is important for three major restorative processes: neuronal growth, memory consolidation, and the formation of enzymes that protect against cellular damage.
- Sleep disorders affect about 20 percent of the population. Insomnia, apnea, sleepwalking, and hypersomnia are the most common sleep disorders.
- Dreams consist of images, thoughts, and feelings that we experience while we sleep. Freud maintained that dreams are attempts to fulfill unconscious wishes. More recent research supports a role for dreaming in memory consolidation.

HYPNOSIS

- Hypnosis is a state of mind that occurs naturally and is established by compliance with instructions. It is characterized by focused attention, suggestibility, absorption, lack of voluntary control over behaviour, and suspension of critical faculties of mind.

- Research not only shows that hypnosis has a real physiological and neurological basis, but also points to ways that hypnosis may serve as a model for understanding attention.

ALTERING CONSCIOUSNESS WITH DRUGS

- A psychoactive drug is a naturally occurring or synthesized substance that produces qualitative changes in conscious experience. The three major categories of psychoactive drugs are depressants, stimulants, and hallucinogens.
- Depressants decrease central nervous system activity. Alcohol, sedatives, and opiates are all depressants. Typically, people develop tolerance for these drugs quickly, withdrawal is unpleasant, and the risk of overdose is high.
- Stimulants increase central nervous system activity. The most commonly used stimulants are caffeine and nicotine. Cocaine, amphetamines, and ecstasy all have stronger stimulant properties than caffeine and nicotine and carry a high risk of abuse and physical and psychological problems.
- Hallucinogens create altered sensations and perceptions. The two most widely known examples are marijuana and LSD. Heavy marijuana smoking increases the risk of respiratory ailments, impairs immune system functioning, and can lead to memory problems. Marijuana mimics the effects of endocannabinoids, pain-relieving substances produced in the body.

EVALUATING CONNECTIONS IN CONSCIOUSNESS

- Brain injury can affect many different aspects of consciousness, depending on the location and extent of the damage.
- As happened to David, brain damage interferes with selective attention, creating difficulties with staying on task, as well as with sleep and dreaming.

Quick Quiz Answers

Quick Quiz 5.1: 1. d 2. c 3. b **Quick Quiz 5.2:** 1. a 2. b **Quick Quiz 5.3:** 1. d 2. a
Quick Quiz 5.4: 1. d 2. b 3. c 4. d **Quick Quiz 5.5:** 1. d 2. c **Quick Quiz 5.6:** 1. a 2. b
Quick Quiz 5.7: 1. d 2. b

Memory

CHAPTER 6

CHAPTER OUTLINE

Challenge Your Assumptions

True or False?

- ☐ Getting a good night's sleep strengthens memory.
- ☐ Emotional memories are easier to recall than non-emotional memories.
- ☐ Eyewitness memories are usually accurate.
- ☐ Only complex organisms are capable of forming memories.

LEARNING OBJECTIVES

- **LO1** Explain the difference between explicit and implicit memory.
- **LO2** Describe the memory stores of Atkinson and Shiffrin's three-stage model and discuss how information is transferred between them.
- **LO3** Describe the different components of Baddeley's model of working memory.
- **LO4** Describe the different types of long-term memory.
- **LO5** Compare processing theories of memory.
- **LO6** List the factors that interfere with memory retrieval.
- **LO7** Describe how neurons store memory.
- **LO8** Describe the types of memory controlled by different brain regions.
- **LO9** Explain the biological factors that lead to memory loss.

When he was nine years old, a boy known as H.M. was hit by a bicyclist, which resulted in a brain injury that caused severe epileptic seizures. To stop these seizures, doctors removed part of the temporal lobe on both sides of H.M.'s brain, which resulted in the loss of several brain structures, including most of his hippocampus and amygdala (Figure 6.1). The seizures stopped, but at quite a cost: H.M. lost the ability to form new memories. He lived forever in the present. Brenda Milner, the Canadian neuropsychologist who examined H.M. regularly for more than 30 years, had to introduce herself each time they met! However, most of the memories he had formed prior to the surgery remained intact. For instance, H.M. could recognize himself in pictures that were taken before his surgery, but not after. Post-surgery he could not even recognize himself in the mirror, since he could not form a new memory of his appearance as his face changed with aging (Kandel, 2006).

What probably makes H.M.'s story most remarkable is the specific nature of his memory deficits. Despite his inability to form new memories of events in his life, H.M. was capable of learning new motor skills. This was an important demonstration of the existence of more than one type of memory.

Moreover, since H.M.'s memory problems stemmed from the precise removal of a particular portion of his brain, researchers were able to link his memory problems with specific neuroanatomical regions. The study of both H.M.'s memory abilities *and* inabilities sparked a whole new field of research and discovery on the role of the specific brain regions in different types of memory (Milner et al., 1998). It was only after his death in 2008 at the age of 82 that H.M. became known by more than his initials. Henry Molaison, after donating his time to the research of memory for more than 30 years, also agreed to donate his brain upon his death (*New York Times,* 2009). The brain dissection, a 53-hour procedure carried out at the Brain Observatory in San Diego, California, was broadcast live, and hundreds of thousands of people tuned in online to watch (Brain Observatory, 2009). The entire brain was sliced into 2041 ultra-thin sections, and a high-resolution image of each section was captured for a virtual, Web-accessible brain atlas available to other scientists to use for research (Annese et al., 2014).

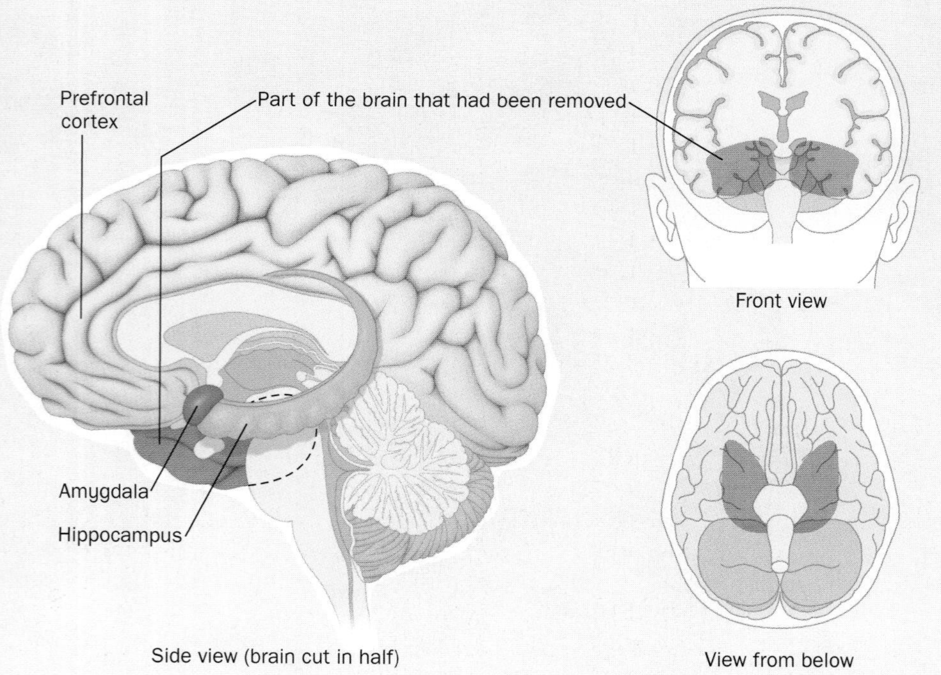

FIGURE **6.1**
PORTIONS OF H.M.'S BRAIN REMOVED DURING SURGERY. Patient H.M. had most of his hippocampus and adjacent tissues in the medial temporal lobe removed from both hemispheres of his brain (Carey, 2008).

In this chapter, we will explore different types of memory, how we form memories, the nature of forgetting, and how the brain controls these processes. Without memory we would be, like H.M., stuck forever in the present, unable to store away new experiences or to adapt to a changing environment. The ability to remember not only makes us who we are, but is also the foundation of intelligence, learning, and thought. Although there is still much to learn about memory and the mechanisms involved in making and retaining memories, researchers agree on at least three attributes of memory:

1. There are multiple types of memory that differ in their capacity for information, duration that information can be held, and degree to which the information enters conscious awareness.
2. We reconstruct memories from our past experiences, rather than recording accurate images of what has happened.
3. Different memory processes involve different areas of the brain.

We will explore each of these attributes in turn.

LO1 MULTIPLE TYPES OF MEMORY

Brenda Milner

Brenda Milner's (1962) work with H.M. provided the first documented evidence of distinct kinds of memory in operation. For example, she gave H.M. a standard learning task, in which he had to trace inside the outline of a star while looking at the star in a mirror (see Figure 6.2). This task is particularly difficult because the mirror image of every movement is reversed. True to Milner's expectations, H.M. had no recollection of doing this task even though he had been trained on it for days, sometimes completing up to ten trials of the task. Each time he did it, H.M. said that it was a completely new task. Yet some part of his brain knew and remembered the task, because the drawings improved the more often he worked on them. Although H.M. may have lost the ability to form new memories of his experiences, some type of memory formation had to have occurred, or he would not have improved on the task.

How might one explain this contradictory finding? As H.M.'s case illustrates, being unable to consciously recall experiences doesn't mean there is no memory of an event. In fact, we humans are incapable of intentionally bringing into awareness much of what we remember, such as memories that have been put away for some time or memories for how to do things, like tie one's shoes or ride a bike. Many things we know are outside of conscious awareness. Most generally, **memory** is simply the ability to store and use information. It need not be a conscious recollection.

At the broadest level, there are two types of memory: implicit and explicit. **Explicit memory** is the conscious recall of facts and events and is sometimes called *declarative* memory because it refers to memories that can be deliberately accessed or declared. When we know or remember something but don't consciously know we remember it, we are tapping into **implicit memory.** Implicit memory is also known as *non-declarative memory,* because this type of memory is not easily described using words. For instance, the fact that you can understand the words on this page indicates that you have a memory for the cognitive skills involved in reading. However, if asked to describe *how* you can read these words, you will likely find it quite difficult to do. Although we can perform many skills automatically, we don't have ready access to the memory of the many steps they require (Kandel, Kupfermann, & Iversen, 2000).

Although most researchers agree with the distinction between explicit and implicit memory, there are many different views on exactly how many different types of memory there are (White & McDonald, 2002). Furthermore, researchers often disagree on how information moves from one memory store to another. Therefore, the study of memory requires an examination of the prominent theories and a clear understanding of the methods used to demonstrate different types of memory.

memory
the ability to store and use information; also the store of what has been learned and remembered.

explicit memory
knowledge that consists of the conscious recall of facts and events; also known as declarative memory.

implicit memory
kind of memory made up of knowledge based on previous experience, such as skills that we perform automatically once we have mastered them; resides outside conscious awareness.

Research Process

1 Research Question

Can a person who cannot form new long-term memories learn to do a new task?

2 Method

As part of her case study of H.M., who lost the ability to form new memories following the removal of his medial temporal lobe, the neuropsychologist Brenda Milner (1962) asked H.M. to perform a mirror tracing task. The goal was to trace within the two lines of the star, while viewing only the reverse image of the star in a mirror. In other words, the image was inverted, so each time H.M. moved his hand in one direction, the movement of his hand in the mirror went in the opposite direction. H.M. was asked to perform this task up to ten times each day for three days. An error was counted each time H.M. went outside the lines. H.M.'s drawings improved with time, even though he could not recall ever doing the task before.

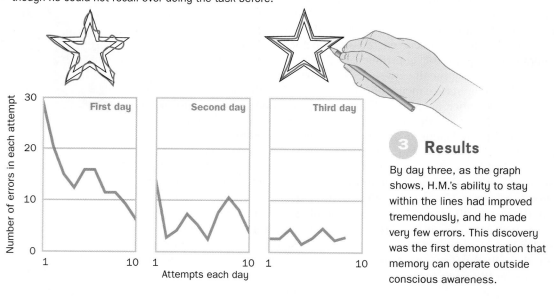

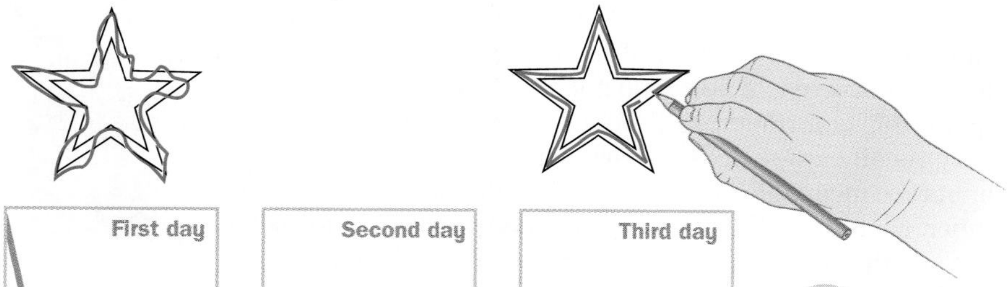

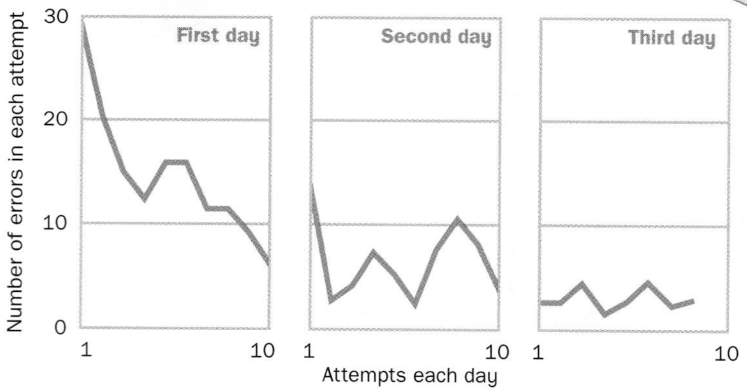

3 Results

By day three, as the graph shows, H.M.'s ability to stay within the lines had improved tremendously, and he made very few errors. This discovery was the first demonstration that memory can operate outside conscious awareness.

4 Conclusion

Many different parts of our brain are involved in learning, and conscious awareness is not required for all learning.

FIGURE **6.2**

A CASE STUDY OF MEMORY WITHOUT RECOLLECTION. Although H.M.'s memory problems prevented him from recalling ever having completed this star-tracing task, some part of his brain clearly did "recall" the task. He got better and better at it over time. (*Source:* Kandel, Kupferman, & Iverson [2000]. Learning and memory. In E. Kandel, J.H. Schwartz, & T.M. Jessell [Eds.]. *Principles of neural science,* 4th ed., pp. 1227–1246, McGraw-Hill.)

Memory Stores

One way of studying memory is to consider the mind as having many storage compartments. Clear evidence for multiple storage systems came from studies of patients like H.M., but different memory stores can also be observed in people without profound memory problems, provided the research question is carefully designed and tested under the appropriate experimental conditions. Most early psychological theories of memory focused on memory as storage, and described memory in terms of its structure. Many classic experiments in psychology have come from this perspective and will be considered in this section.

Sensory Memory As we interact with the world, our brains are bombarded by an enormous amount of information from multiple sensory systems—we may smell, taste, feel, see, or hear different aspects of an experience. In order to form memories of the experiences arriving through our senses, we first must select and store information about specific features of an event. The term **sensory memory** refers a part of memory that holds information in its original sensory form for a very brief period of time, usually for a few seconds or less. Because vision and hearing are key sources of information for humans, the two kinds of sensory memory that have received the most attention from memory researchers are visual and auditory memory (Craik, 1979).

sensory memory
the part of memory that holds information in its original sensory form for a very brief period of time, usually about a half a second or less.

Iconic memory is a brief record of a visual scene, whereas *echoic memory* is short-term retention of sounds. Testing these types of memory is tricky, because in an experimental testing situation, bringing attention to a visual or auditory stimulus makes it more likely that these sensory traces will end up being rehearsed in short-term memory. Therefore psychologists have devised elegant procedures to isolate sensory memory traces. In a classic experiment, George Sperling (1960) tested visual sensory traces by presenting stimuli for a very brief duration, long enough for conscious perception, but not long enough to make it into short-term memory stores. Participants were shown three rows of four digits on a screen for 50 milliseconds (a millisecond is a thousandth of a second), followed by a blank screen. If asked immediately, most participants could correctly report only about four or five of the total number of items shown. Sperling modified the test by introducing a delay after showing the digits, followed by a tone that indicated the row participants were to recall (Figure 6.3). In other words, the array was not visible during the participants' recall, and therefore they had to rely upon the entire image that was briefly stored in memory. Under these conditions, participants could recall the letters in the indicated row with perfect accuracy. However, if the tone was presented after a delay of about a third of a second, participants' performance dropped dramatically. This suggests that we have the ability to "hold" an entire visual scene in mind, but only for a brief period of time.

Similar to the iconic memory store for visual images, the echoic memory store acts as a temporary buffer for sounds; however, the echoic store has a significantly longer duration, on the order of seconds rather than milliseconds. The echoic store can be demonstrated experimentally by having participants listen to two different categories of auditory stimuli, such as digits and words, and performing a task that

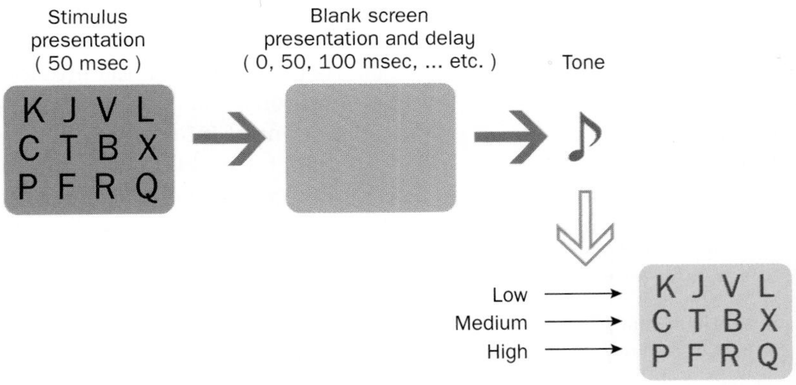

FIGURE 6.3
TESTING ICONIC MEMORY. An array of letters is flashed on a viewing screen, followed by a blank screen. After a delay, a tone is played that indicates the row that the participant should recall. Short delays result in almost perfect memory recall, but if the delay is more than 300 milliseconds, the accuracy drops dramatically.

Iconic memory enables us to write with a trail of light, what we see is actually a brief memory of visual space.

requires careful listening to only one. The "ignored" sounds cannot be processed by short-term memory stores and therefore recall is thought to rely on memory for sensory features. If the delay between the ignored sounds and the recall test is greater than about five seconds, memory declines dramatically (Cowan et al., 2000). Our ability to hold sounds in this temporary buffer is thought to be critically important for language comprehension since speech is often interrupted by coughs, car horns, and many other sorts of non-speech sounds, yet we have no trouble filling in the gaps. In fact, we generally do not realize that a sound is missing from a word since the surrounding speech in echoic memory provides a context to decipher the word (Sivonen et al., 2006).

LO2 **The Three-Stage Model** One of the most influential attempts to explain multiple memory stores and the interactions between them was proposed by Atkinson and Shiffrin (1971). Their **three-stage model of memory** (also called the *multistore* or *modal model*) classifies three types of memory stores—sensory memory, short-term memory, and long-term memory—based on how long the memories last. As you learned in the previous section, sensory memory has a large capacity but duration of only a few seconds. **Short-term memory** temporarily stores a limited amount of information before it is either transferred to long-term storage or forgotten. Information stays in short-term memory for 2 to 30 seconds—about long enough to remember a phone number before you dial it. **Long-term memory** has the capacity to store a vast amount of information for as little as 30 seconds and as long as a lifetime. This is where memories of your first pet and how to read reside.

three-stage model of memory
classification of memories based on duration as sensory, short-term, and long-term.

short-term memory
the part of memory that temporarily (for 2 to 30 seconds) stores a limited amount of information before it is either transferred to long-term storage or forgotten.

long-term memory
the part of memory that has the capacity to store a vast amount of information for as little as 30 seconds and as long as a lifetime.

rehearsal
the process of repeatedly practising material so that it enters long-term memory.

According to the three-stage model, memory formation starts with sensory input from the outside world (see Figure 6.4). If we do not pay attention to it, the sensation vanishes and the information is lost. If we pay attention to it, the sensation becomes a short-term memory. Once the sensation enters short-term memory, either it makes the transition to long-term memory within a short period of time or it disappears. If we repeat or rehearse the information actively, the original sensation becomes a long-term memory. **Rehearsal** is the process of reciting or practising material repeatedly. Storing and recalling a shopping list is an everyday example of this. If we want to remember the list long enough to use it, we typically rehearse it by repeating it to ourselves. If we continue rehearsing

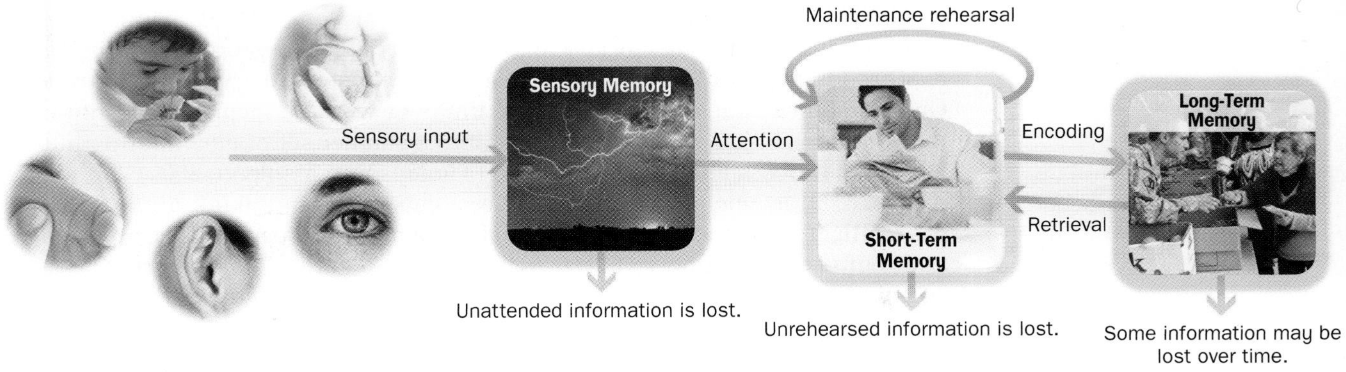

FIGURE **6.4**

THE THREE-STAGE MODEL OF MEMORY. When our senses are stimulated, the nervous system forms a very brief trace of what we saw, heard, tasted, felt, or smelled (sensory memory). If we pay attention, the information is passed on to short-term memory. Here, if we attend to it only briefly, it will remain in short-term memory as long as we need it, but then will be forgotten. If we rehearse it over and over, the information is encoded and passed on to long-term memory, which can be retrieved back into short-term memory at a later time (*Source:* Atkinson & Shiffrin, 1971.)

it, after more than a minute or two, the information might make the transition to long-term memory. The process by which we attend to, take in, and process new information is called **encoding,** while the recovery of information stored in memory is called **retrieval.**

encoding
the process by which we attend to, take in, and process new information.

retrieval
the recovery of information stored in memory.

Working Memory We often need to stay focused on something temporarily to solve a problem or perform a task, such as getting to a restaurant after just hearing the directions on the phone. To do so, we put our short-term memory to work. In fact, we rely upon short-term memory for many other skills that demand our present attention, such as reading, talking, and listening to someone speak. The number of items that can be held in short-term memory is called short-term memory capacity, and for most people, it is between four and nine units of letters, digits, or chunks of information; however, there are substantial individual differences (Feldman-Barrett, Tugade, & Engle, 2004; Baddeley, 2003, Cowan, 2001). It is not a coincidence that local phone numbers typically contain seven digits. Cognitive psychologist George Miller famously referred to this capacity as the "magical number seven, plus or minus two" to reflect the average capacity as well as the degree of variation between individuals (Miller, 1956).

The duration of short-term memory, as its name suggests, is remarkably short, although we are not often aware of it. Without active rehearsal, we can keep information in short-term memory only a briefly. If you've ever forgotten someone's name only seconds after being introduced, you have likely experienced the fleeting duration of short-term memory. This was demonstrated by a classic experiment by Peterson and Peterson (1959), where research participants were given lists of three-letter combinations and were asked to recall the items after different delay periods. Participants were prevented from rehearsing the letters by performing simple mental arithmetic during the delay. If the delay was greater than six seconds, participants recalled slightly less than half of the items. After a delay of 18 seconds, only 10 percent of the items were correctly recalled.

Because short-term memory is a place to temporarily store information we need while working on a problem, psychologists commonly refer to it as working memory. **Working memory** is the part of memory required to attend to and solve a problem at hand. Bear in mind that the term *short-term memory* emphasizes

working memory
the part of memory required to attend to and solve a problem at hand; often used interchangeably with *short-term memory*

the duration of this type of memory, while the term *working memory* emphasizes its function. Working memories can be transferred to long-term memory if they capture attention or if they are consciously practised; otherwise, they are lost. One of the best ways to overcome the limits of working memory capacity is to transform what you want to remember into a smaller set of meaningful units or chunks, a process known as **chunking** (Thompson & Madigan, 2005). For example, 09112001 is much more difficult to remember than the chunks of 09–11–2001, especially if you notice that these groupings of numbers represent the month, day, and year of the September 11 attacks in the United States. Chunking enables us to combine items into larger units and can improve later recall of the information.

chunking
the process of breaking down a list of items to be remembered into a smaller set of meaningful units.

LO3 **Baddeley's Model of Working Memory** Working memory is critical for our ability to draw upon previous experiences and to incorporate new ones yet it has a limited capacity for information and a very short duration. So you might wonder how we are ever able to perform any complex tasks, especially those that require juggling and processing different types of information. The three-component model's short-term memory store does not adequately explain how we are able to carry out complicated and demanding tasks such as reading or having a conversation. In an attempt to test the limits of working memory, Alan Baddeley and Graham Hitch had participants complete two tasks simultaneously: a primary memory task, such memorizing word lists, and a secondary task, like rehearsing sequences of numbers. Surprisingly, they found only modest memory errors when participants were heavily loaded with cognitive demands. This led Baddeley to propose a multi-component model of working memory, in contrast to the unitary short-term memory store of Atkinson and Shiffrin (Baddeley, 1986, p. 43).

Baddeley's model of working memory consists of a number of distinct components that cooperate to allow an otherwise limited capacity mechanism to excel in information holding and processing. According this model, working memory is made up of three temporary storage systems, one for sounds and language (phonological), one for images and spatial relations (visuospatial), and one that connects the two storage systems, interacts with long-term memory, and provides temporary storage for specific events (episodic buffer) (see Figure 6.5). These stores are managed by an attentional control system, called the *central executive,* which focuses, divides, and shifts attention and also communicates with long-term memory systems (Baddeley, 2003, 2007).

Baddeley proposed that working memory operated via three distinct processes: *attending* to a stimulus, *storing* information about the stimulus, and *rehearsing* the stored information to help solve a problem. According to

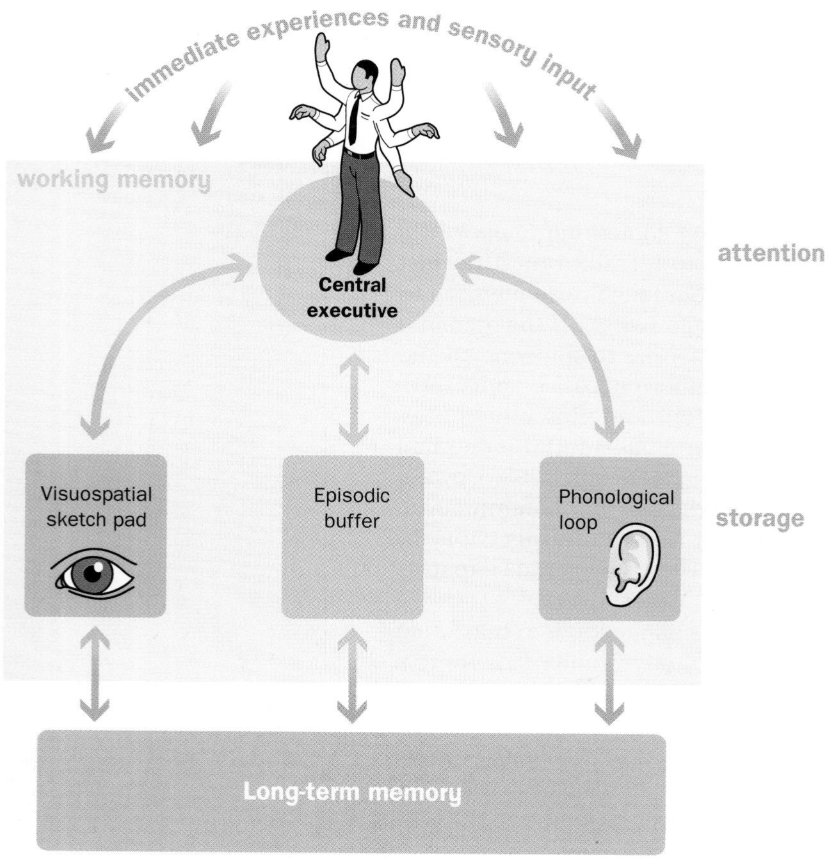

FIGURE 6.5
BADDELEY'S MODEL OF WORKING MEMORY. The four components of working memory are the central executive, which focuses attention, and three storage systems (visuospatial sketch pad, episodic buffer, and phonological loop). Once our attention is focused on something, we need places to temporarily store the relevant information. Images and spatial relations are stored in one storage centre; events and experiences in another; and language and sounds in another. (*Source:* Baddeley, 2003.)

this model, the first process, focusing and switching attention, is carried out by the central executive, which decides where to focus attention and selectively hones in on specific aspects of a stimulus. Attention allows us to focus on the task at hand and develop a plan for solving a problem. We are bombarded by dozens of sensations every second. How do we know which are important and deserve our attention and which we can ignore? The central executive is responsible for making these decisions.

Joe Martin. Used with permission.

Once information is taken in and we attend to it, it is sent to a temporary store: the *phonological loop* if it is sound or linguistic information, the *visuospatial sketch pad* if it is visual or spatial information, or the *episodic buffer* if it is a specific event or experience involving multisensory information. The *phonological loop* assists the central executive by providing extra storage for a limited number of digits or words for up to 30 seconds at a time. The *visuospatial sketch pad,* as the name implies, briefly provides storage for visual and spatial sensations, such as images, photos, scenes, or three-dimensional objects. Normally, we can hold a small number of images (three or four) in short-term storage. Information that enters either of these memory stores lasts only seconds before it fades—unless we attend to it and process it more deeply. Therefore, the loop and sketch pad are distinct in that they handle different types of material. Furthermore, they also appear to operate independently since working on a verbal task, such as remembering words or digits, does not affect performance on a simultaneous visuospatial task, such as spatial pattern recall (Oberauer & Göthe, 2006). Studies of brain-damaged patients suggest that these two components of working memory might recruit different parts of the brain, since one system can be selectively impaired while the other is unaffected (Baddeley, 2003). The episodic buffer is less well understood than the other components of working memory, but it is thought to be a temporary store critically important for information that will become long-term memories of specific events. Tasks that require integration of different perceptual features or require coordination of information between working and long-term memory rely upon this component of working memory (Karlson et al., 2010).

Distinguishing Working from Long-Term Memory Working memory is all about thinking in the here-and-now, keeping information in an active state long enough to transform and manipulate it. This can mean attending to incoming sensory information and forming a new long-term memory, as outlined by the three-stage model, or it can involve retrieving prior long-term memories into the mental workspace. With all of the cross-talk and sheer amount of information, it means that we often use working memory and long-term memory at the same time. So how can we distinguish between these memory stores?

In the late 19th century, Mary Whiton Calkins observed an interesting memory phenomenon to shed some light on this issue. When learning a list of items, people are better able to recall items at the beginning and end of the list; they tend to forget the items in the middle (Calkins, 1898; Madigan & O'Hara, 1992). This effect is known as the **serial position effect.**

serial position effect
the tendency to have better recall for items in a list according to their position in the list.

In studies of the serial position effect, participants might be presented with a list of 15 words read at one-second intervals. They would be told in advance that they would be asked to recall as many as they could, in any order. Typically, about 50 percent of the participants recall the first two words on the list, about 50–75 percent recall words near the end of the list, and about 90–95 percent of participants recall the last two words on the list. So recall for the beginning and

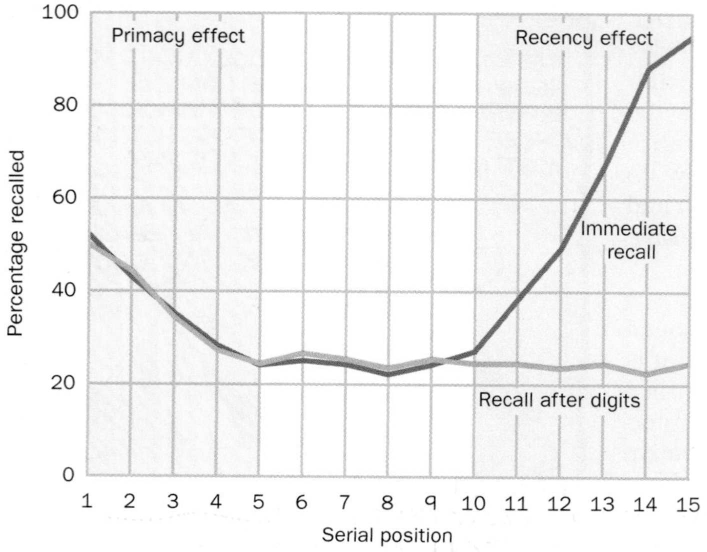

FIGURE **6.6**
SERIAL POSITION EFFECTS AND RECALL. People have the best recall of items that are in the beginning of a series (primacy) or at the end of a series (recency). The recency effects go away if people are given a distracting task such as having to recall digits before recalling the words in a list. (From R. Thompson and S. Madigan, 2007, *Memory: The Key to Consciousness*, p. 30. Princeton University Press. Reprinted by permission of Princeton University Press.)

end of the list is pretty good, but only about 25 percent of the participants recall words in the middle of the list. The tendency to preferentially recall items at the beginning of a list is known as the *primacy effect*, whereas recall for items at the end of a list is known as the *recency effect* (see Figure 6.6).

The main explanation offered for the primacy effect is that the items in the beginning of the list are quickly rehearsed and transferred to long-term memory storage. So they are remembered. Most of the items in the middle of the list haven't made that trip to long-term memory yet, and are therefore less likely to be recalled. The items in the middle cannot be rehearsed as more and more items are being added to the list. These new items interfere with rehearsal of those presented before, which can prevent long-term storage. The recency effect results from those items at the end still being held in working memory, so they are easily accessible. If rehearsal is prevented by having participants engage in a verbal task after the 15 words have been presented, the performance for the last two items on the list is no better than those in the middle. In other words, the recency effect disappears if working memory is immediately engaged in some other task. Recall for the items at the beginning of the list are unaffected by the interfering task, which suggests that these items made it into long-term memory stores (Thompson & Madigan, 2005). Recent neuroimaging data show that early and late items activate different brain regions during recall, suggesting that these stimuli recruit different neural processes (Talmi et al., 2005).

LO4 **Long-Term Memory** In April 2006, on the centennial of the 1906 San Francisco earthquake, a 109-year-old survivor reported these two memories from that disaster: "I remember the smell of the smoke [from the fires afterward] . . . and the cow running down California Street with its tail in the air" (Nolte & Yollin, 2006). Memories that are 100 years old definitely qualify as long-term memories! Yet, recalling our definition of long-term memory as "any information that is stored for at least 30 to 40 seconds and up to a lifetime," things that you remember from earlier today—the topic of a psychology lecture, for example—are also in long-term storage. So is information you remember for only a few weeks, such as material for your next midterm exam. Will you remember the material you learned in this course 20 years from now? That depends on a number of factors, but primarily it depends on how often you use or rehearse the information.

Once learned, skills for riding a bicycle become implicit memories that we recall without effort.
What other types of skills can you remember without conscious effort?

Types of Long-Term Memory Unlike working memory, long-term memory has an incredibly long duration. For most people, memories of significant personal events will usually last a lifetime. Long-term memory also has a seemingly unlimited capacity; we continually acquire and store new information until we die. Long-term memory is similar to working memory in that it can also be subdivided into different types, each unique in its processing of information and how well it is retained in the long term. People often forget specific things such as people's names or birthdays, but they typically do not forget how to tie their shoes, ride a bike, or how even to add 6 to 12. How is it possible that a person could forget names but almost never forget skills such as simple arithmetic? The short answer is that there is more than one type of long-term memory, and the types operate differently. H.M.'s case, described at the beginning of the chapter, is important partly because it helped psychologists see the distinction between implicit and explicit memory.

Although the three-stage model explains explicit memory performance, such as free recall of word and digit lists, it struggles to explain the existence of long-term implicit memories. This model places emphasis on two processes that do not seem to be engaged in implicit tasks: attention (necessary for the transfer of information from sensory to working stores) and rehearsal (required to keep information in working memory). Therefore, researchers use different types of tasks to test implicit memory. With explicit tests, participants are usually asked to *remember* something, whereas with implicit tasks participants are generally asked to *do* something. (Richardson-Klavehn & Bjork, 1988). If done properly, people engaged in implicit tasks do not even know they are performing a memory task at all (Roediger, 1990).

Some examples of implicit memory are procedural memory and priming. **Procedural memory** refers to knowledge we hold for almost any behaviour or physical skill we learn, whether it is how to play golf, ride a bike, drive a car, or tie a shoe. The star-tracing task that H.M. worked on (see Figure 6.2) is another example of procedural memory. Part of his brain enabled him to remember the mirror task because his performance improved each time he did it; however, the brain regions responsible for conscious recall did not remember the task.

Priming is a kind of implicit memory that occurs when recall is improved by prior exposure to the same or similar stimuli. In one laboratory demonstration of priming, people with memory problems (amnesia group) were compared to individuals without such problems (comparison group) on a word-learning task. When asked to recall a list of words they were exposed to, people in the amnesia group demonstrated much less recall than the comparison group (see Figure 6.7). But when they were given the first three letters of the words as a prime, or memory aid, the amnesia group performed at least as well

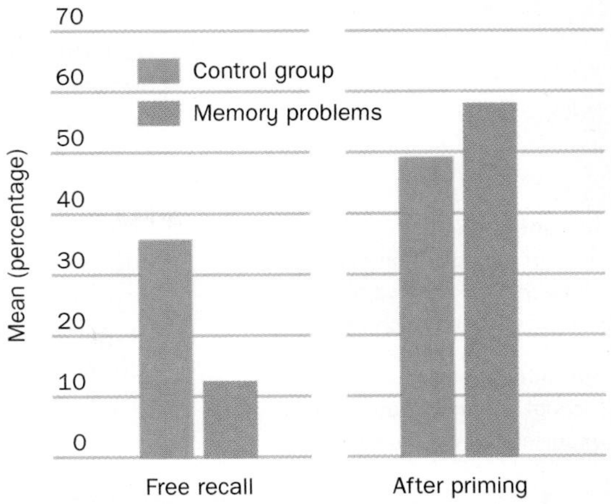

FIGURE 6.7
RECALL OF WORDS WITH AND WITHOUT PRIMING. With no priming, recall by people with memory problems is impaired. They recall only about 10 percent of the words, compared to about 35 percent for those without memory problems. Those with memory problems, however, outperform those without memory problems after they have been primed (given the first three letters of the word). (*Source:* Squire, 1987.)

procedural memory
kind of memory made up of implicit knowledge for almost any behaviour or physical skill we have learned.

priming
a kind of implicit memory that arises when recall is improved by earlier exposure to the same or similar stimuli.

How do you spell . . .? This spelling bee contestant is relying on her semantic memory to spell challenging words correctly.

as the comparison group (Squire, 1987). What is intriguing about this outcome is that the amnesia group had no conscious recollection of having seen the words before. Like H.M., who was primed by his previous learning of the star-tracing task, people with severe long-term memory problems show a remarkable ability to recall words if they have been primed.

semantic memory
form of memory that recalls facts and general knowledge, such as what we learn in school.

episodic memory
form of memory that recalls the experiences we have had.

There are two distinct kinds of explicit memory: semantic and episodic (Tulving, 1972, 1985). **Semantic memory** is our memory for facts and knowledge, such as what we learn in school. **Episodic memory** is our memory for the experiences we have had. Remembering that Fredericton is the capital of New Brunswick is an example of semantic memory, whereas remembering your high school graduation would be an episodic memory. Episodic memories are therefore more personal than semantic memories.

Images associated with events like high school graduation are stored temporarily by the visuospatial sketch pad in short-term memory before making the trip to long-term memory. The emotions that accompany such occasions increase the likelihood that our memories of them will last a lifetime.

Stages in Long-Term Memory Obviously, not all the information entering working memory becomes permanently stored. As you have learned from the three-stage model, cognitive processes are important in the memory formation. Attention and rehearsal act to keep pertinent events at the forefront of the mind and can become successfully stored for the long-term by a process called encoding. Encoded memories can be accessed at some time in the future through the process of retrieval. However, what the three-stage model fails to consider are events that happen *after* the original information is encoded into long-term stores. In fact, the overall strength of a memory is largely dependent upon events that happen after encoding, a process called *consolidation.* Once information is encoded and consolidated, the brain organizes the information for availability in the future by a process called *storage.* Understanding long-term memory necessarily involves looking at these processes and how they fit together.

The first stage in long-term memory is encoding. As the three-stage model points out, attention is important in driving the encoding process; if we fail to pay attention or try to multitask, an experience is not likely going to be processed deeply enough to be stored for a long period. Explicit and implicit memories are quite unique in their recruitment of attentional resources since explicit tasks require conscious awareness while implicit tasks do not. Therefore the encoding processes are also thought to be quite different. These two classes of memory also differ in how well they encode different types of information. For explicit memory tests, such as free recall, visual images are encoded more easily than verbal descriptions, while the reverse is true for implicit tasks, such as priming (Weldon & Roediger, 1987).

mnemonic device
a method devised to help remember information, such as a rhyme or acronym.

A common way to encode information deeply is to devise mnemonic (pronounced neh'-mon-ik) devices. A **mnemonic device** is a scheme that helps people remember information. Rhyming, chunking, and rehearsal are types of mnemonic devices. Others include imagery and acronyms. For example, imagery can be used to remember a set of words or a list of objects in a set order. Simply form a mental image of each word or object in a specific place along a route you know very well, such as from your home to your school. Rehearse this a few times. Then when you need to recall the word or object list, take a mental stroll along the familiar path and the visual images of the list should be relatively easy to recall (Thompson & Madigan, 2005).

Daniel Tammet, who can recall the number pi (π) to 22 514 digits, is a mnemonist (someone who displays extraordinary memory skills). Like most mnemonists, Daniel uses his own mnemonic device: For him it is the ability to see each number as a shape in a landscape. He then simply "strolls" through that landscape and reads off the numbers, such as the digits of pi, as he sees them. However, you need not be a mnemonist to benefit from this technique. Research shows that using visualization to encode verbal material greatly enhances later recall. In one experiment, journalism students could better recall details of written news articles when they were accompanied by descriptive pictures, compared to text-only articles (Prabu, 1998). One influential theory to explain this type of memory enhancement is the **dual coding theory** proposed by Allan Paivio of the University of Western Ontario. His theory suggests that visual and verbal information are processed and stored independently by the brain, and therefore using both systems essentially brings "two minds" to the memory task (Paivio, 1986). This theory has been influential since it complements Baddeley's division of working memory into the phonological loop for verbal information and the visuospatial sketch pad for visual information. The use of both verbal and visual processes to enhance memory has been useful in real-world applications for improving memory, such as during foreign language vocabulary learning, education, and marketing.

dual coding theory
theory proposing that visual and verbal information are processed by independent, non-competing systems.

Acronyms are another type of mnemonic device. We usually create acronyms by combining the first letters of each word or object we need to remember. Acronyms work best when they form a word we can pronounce or some other meaningful unit. For example, in school you may have used the acronym HOMES to remember the names of the five Great Lakes or "ROY G. BIV" to remember the colours of the rainbow. (And remember OPTIC from Chapter 2? That's another mnemonic device.) You might have your own favourite mnemonic devices to help you encode material that you need to know for an exam. If you have never tried this approach to studying, you might be surprised at how much it improves memory.

Challenge Your Assumptions

True or False? Getting a good night's sleep strengthens memory.

True: Sleep enhances memory through consolidation while sleep deprivation impairs memory.

The second stage of long-term memory formation is **consolidation,** the process of establishing, stabilizing, or solidifying a memory (Kandel, 2006; McGaugh, 2000). A consolidated memory is resistant to distraction, interference, and decay (Dubai, 2004). As we'll discuss in some detail shortly, new proteins are manufactured in the brain during long-term memory formation, and consolidation provides time for these proteins to develop. Sleep plays an important role in memory consolidation. Psychologists have long known that we recall information better after we "sleep on it" than after the same amount of time if we stay awake. Recent findings indicate that not only does sleep stabilize the memory, but it also enhances memory and makes it stronger (Walker & Stickgold, 2006). Moreover, sleep deprivation has been shown to have a detrimental effect on memory (Stickgold, 2005). We can conclude, then, that cramming all night before an exam is not the best study strategy. (We'll consider better alternatives in the "Evaluating Connections in Memory" section at the end of this chapter.) In fact, research shows that learning over long periods of time and evenly spaced sessions leads to better recall (Kornell & Bjork, 2007).

Connection

New learning is associated with an increase in rapid eye movement (REM) sleep, and blocking REM sleep impairs performance on certain types of memory tasks.

See Chapter 5, LO6.

consolidation
the process of establishing, stabilizing, or solidifying a memory; the second stage of long-term memory formation.

Once memories have been encoded and consolidated, they are ready to be stored. **Storage,** the retention of memory over time, is the third stage of long-term memory formation. We organize and store memories in at least three distinct ways: in hierarchies, schemas, and networks.

storage
the retention of memory over time; the third stage of long-term memory formation.

We use **hierarchies** to organize related information from the most general feature they have in common to the most specific. An example of a hierarchy for song titles is depicted in Figure 6.8. This type of arrangement was used in a memory experiment by Andrea Halpern (1986). She found that presenting song titles in a logical hierarchy such as this one improved memory for these items in free recall tests, compared to presentation of the hierarchy in an illogical order. Although the study participants did not arrange the hierarchy themselves, they

hierarchies
a way of organizing related pieces of information from the most specific feature they have in common to the most general.

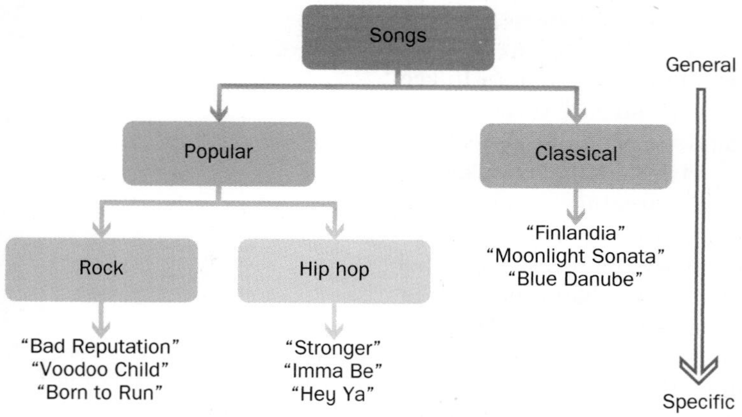

FIGURE **6.8**

AN EXAMPLE OF A HIERARCHY FOR SONG TITLES, SIMILAR TO THE ONE USED IN THE EXPERIMENT BY HALPERN AND HER COLLEAGUES (1986). Arranging the titles in a logical hierarchy improved participants' recall, whereas an illogical hierarchy did not.

were all able to use the organization to improve storage of song titles. **Schemas** are mental frameworks based upon our experiences with particular objects or events and, like hierarchies, they help us organize information and improve memory. They act as a filter through which we encode and organize information about our world. One way to investigate the influence of personal schemas on memory is to test participants who differ in their experience with the items to be memorized. One French study (Huet & Mariné, 2005) administered a memory test for bar beverages to experienced waiters, beginner waiters, and non-waiters. The experienced waiters outperformed the other groups in recalling the items, presumably because they had a richer schema to organize the information.

schemas
mental frameworks that develop from our experiences with particular people, objects, or events.

associative network
a chain of associations between related concepts.

Hierarchies and schemas bring order and organization to our perceptions and experiences. The psychological process that binds concepts together is *association*. Associations are linked together in networks by their degree of closeness or relatedness (Hopfield, 1982). An **associative network** is a chain of associations between related concepts. Each concept in a network is referred to as a *node*. The links between the nodes are associations. When people think of a concept, and its node is activated, they are more likely to make an association to a nearby concept or node (Collins & Loftus, 1975). Figure 6.9 illustrates an associative network for the concept of fire engine. "Fire engine" activates both vehicle and colour networks of association, and it may well activate others not shown here (such as emergency).

Research in computer science has advanced theories about how networks might be organized in the nervous system. *Neural networks* are computer models that imitate the way neurons talk to each other (Chappell & Humphreys, 1994). Neural networks have nodes too, but their nodes are not single concepts like a colour or a vehicle. Rather, these nodes are information-processing units. Based on the analogy of the nervous system, the nodes in a network of neurons are single cells (neurons) that can process information. The more the nodes in a neural network communicate with each other, the stronger the link between nodes. As we will discuss later in this chapter and in the next, repeated connection between neurons leads to stronger connections, and stronger memories and learning (Hebb, 1949).

The work of encoding, consolidating, and storing memories would be wasted if we could not retrieve information when we needed it. Retrieval is the last stage in long-term memory and

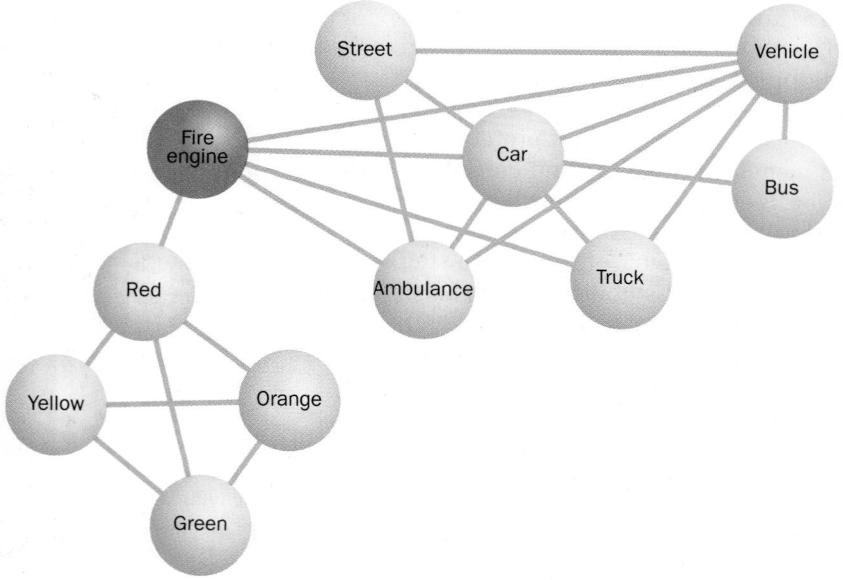

FIGURE **6.9**

ASSOCIATIVE NETWORK. Associative networks are chains of association between related concepts or nodes that get activated. The closer concepts are to each other, the more directly related they are and the more likely they are to activate the other node. The network for "fire engine" consists of a rich associative network of related concepts. (*Source:* Collins & Loftus, 1975.)

Create an associative network for the concept "ice cream." Have a friend create one as well and compare your results. How are your associative networks different? How are they similar?

allows you to remember where you put that birthday gift when it comes time to give it to your friend. The ease of retrieval and the time frame over which we can recall a particular event or piece of knowledge is determined by the previous stages of memory. How did we encode it? Did we consolidate it? Did we store it where we can access it? Additionally, whenever we retrieve a memory, we need to focus our attention on remembering, which requires working memory. Factual information is not always properly encoded and stored, and we cannot always retrieve it at will. A common retrieval problem is the inability to remember the name of a person only minutes after meeting him, even if we repeated his name immediately after hearing it. What most likely happens in this situation is that we fail to pay enough attention to the person's name when we first hear it and focus instead on the whole social interaction. Consequently, we do not encode, consolidate, and store the name very deeply. When we try to retrieve it, we cannot. We'll explore retrieval problems in more detail when we talk about forgetting, and later the "Evaluating Connections in Memory" section outlines some strategies for improving retrieval.

LO5 Memory as Process

The storage view of memory helps to explain the existence of multiple types of memory; however, it is limited in that it doesn't fully address the powerful role that memory processes play. Modern theories of memory are based on a much more process-oriented approach to the study of memory. As you have learned already, we have a number of different encoding strategies to choose from, with huge effects on our ability to later remember. At the most basic level, psychologists describe two kinds of encoding processes: one that happens with little effort and one that takes significant effort (Hasher & Zacks, 1979). **Automatic processing** happens with little effort or conscious attention to the task. Episodic memory involves this kind of automatic processing. For instance, you probably did not try to consciously memorize what you ate for breakfast this morning, although the fact that you can recall is evidence that this information was encoded. Implicit memories, such as priming, also require only minimal attention in order for information to be encoded (Newell et al., 2008).

automatic processing
encoding of information that occurs with little effort or conscious attention to the task.

effortful processing
encoding of information that occurs with careful attention and conscious effort.

Now think about what you learn in your courses. You read the textbook, attend lectures, take notes, and study those notes—usually multiple times. Before an exam, you then go over these materials again and again. Needless to say, this kind of learning takes work. **Effortful processing** occurs when we carefully attend to and put conscious effort into remembering information. Effortful processing is the basis of semantic memory. Effortful processing usually involves rehearsal of the information, so that it goes from working to long-term memory. Interestingly, advancing age tends to lessen recall for events and experiences that require effortful processing but not automatic processing (Hasher & Zacks, 1979).

Associating images with information we want to remember, such as vocabulary words, helps to encode the material more deeply.

Levels of Processing The connection between encoding and remembering is at the core of the levels-of-processing approach to memory (Craik & Lockhart, 1972). The idea

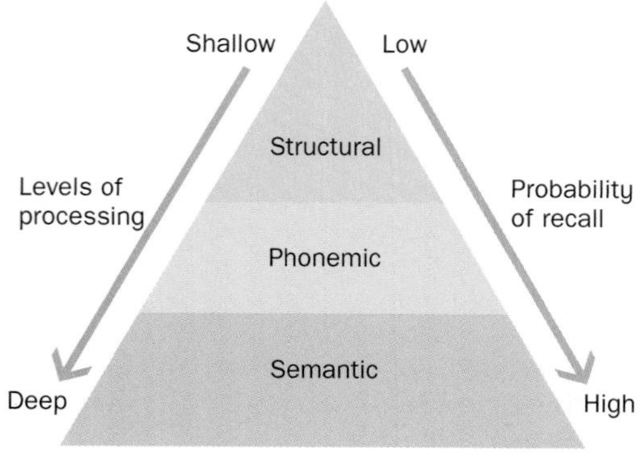

FIGURE **6.10**
LEVELS-OF-PROCESSING MODEL OF MEMORY AND RECALL. The level at which we process information affects the probability of explicit recall. The deeper we process information, the more likely we are to recall it. Structural processing is the shallowest level of processing and also the least likely to be recalled. Semantic processing is both the deepest and the most likely to be recalled. (*Source:* Craik & Lockhart, 1972.)

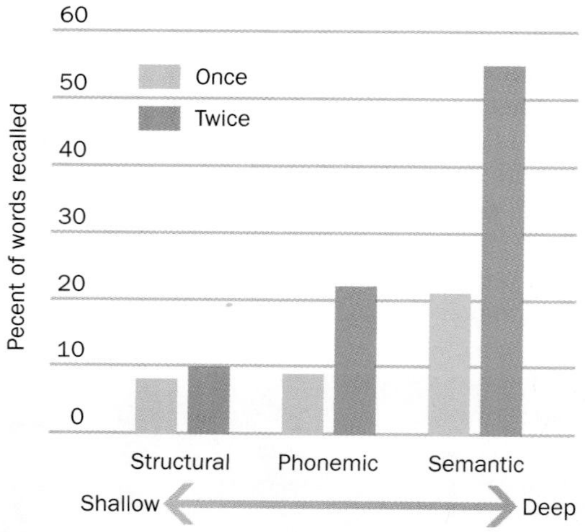

FIGURE **6.11**
RESULTS OF LEVELS OF PROCESSING AND RECALL. These results show that the more deeply people process information, the better they recall it. If people are presented the word list twice, the effect of depth of processing on recall is even stronger. (*Source:* Craik & Tulving, 1975.)

behind **levels of processing** is that the more deeply people encode information, the better they will recall it. Thomas Hyde and James Jenkins (1973) created a standard procedure for manipulating depth of processing in which they typically presented a list of about 28 words with a five-second interval between words. To eliminate primacy and recency effects, the researchers ignored participants' recall of the first two and the last two words on the list. Excluding these four words left 24 possible words to be recalled. Participants heard beforehand that they would be given a list of words and should focus on a specific aspect of the words. Participants were not told that they would be asked to recall as many words as possible, so they were somewhat surprised when they were asked to name them.

Using this experimental procedure, researchers have identified three different levels of processing: structural, phonemic, and semantic (Craik & Tulving, 1975; Hyde & Jenkins, 1973; see Figure 6.10). *Structural processing* is the shallowest level of processing. When studying structural processing, researchers direct participants to focus on the structure of the word by asking questions such as "Is the word in capital letters?" To study *phonemic processing,* or mid-level processing, they ask questions to focus participants' attention on the sound of the word, such as "Does the word rhyme with _____?" *Semantic processing* is the deepest level of processing. Participants in studies of semantic processing are asked to think about the meaning of the words and answer questions such as "Would the word fit the sentence: 'He met a _____ in the street'?"

Results across many studies find the best recall when words are encoded more deeply and worse recall for words that are processed less deeply (Craik & Tulving, 1975; Hyde & Jenkins, 1973; Lockhart & Craik, 1990). Craik and Tulving (1975) conducted classic experiments in the 1970s at the University of Toronto to demonstrate this phenomenon. In a series of ten different experiments, they manipulated the participants' level of processing for target words and found that the deeper the level of processing required, the better the recall (see Figure 6.11). This is not always the case for implicit memory tasks, such as priming on a word completion test, and therefore depth of encoding is does not enhance all types of memory (Roediger, 1990; Schacter & McGlynn, 1989). The take-home message here is that for explicit tasks that require effortful processing, the more deeply information is encoded, the better you will remember it. We will come back to this point in our discussion of the role of memory in studying at the end of this chapter.

Encoding Specificity The levels of processing view emphasizes encoding as the major player in laying down strong memories. However, memory testing necessarily involves retrieval as well as encoding, so other theories consider the interaction between these two processes. The **encoding specificity principle** states that memory for stored information is strongest when the conditions at retrieval match those that were present during encoding of the original information (Tulving & Thomson, 1973). In other words, it's the similarity of the encoding and retrieval environments, rather than the depth of processing, that influences memory performance. A closely related idea is *transfer-appropriate processing,* which states that recall is best if the cognitive processes used during encoding are the same as those for retrieval. This perspective focuses less on the memory environment, and more on the similarity of thought processes recruited to work on encoding and retrieving information (Blaxton, 1989; Lockhart, 2002; Morris et al., 1977). Both theories predict that the more similar the conditions during encoding and retrieval, the better the

levels of processing
the concept that the more deeply people encode information, the better they will recall it.

encoding specificity principle
the idea that memory is strongest when the conditions at recall match those present during encoding.

retrieval will be. In one study, participants were shown either pictures or words for common objects and asked to categorize them. Afterwards, they were given a list of words as a recognition test for the items they previously categorized. Recognition was better for the words they have previously seen as words, compared to words they had previously seen as pictures, in line with both transfer-appropriate processing and the encoding specificity principle (Vaidya et al., 2002).

Encoding specificity helps to explain why memory performance is best if our remembering environment matches our initial learning environment. It turns out that reminder cues don't have to be connected to the information to be remembered. The context in which the information is presented can support encoding specificity, a phenomenon known as *context-dependent memory*. One classic study by Godden and Baddeley (1975) attempted to address this by using very distinct encoding and retrieval environments, as well as a special population of participants. They recruited scuba divers to learn word lists either underwater or on dry land and then later tested recall in the same environment (water-water or land-land) or different environments (water-land, land-water). They found the highest recall when the environments were matched rather than mismatched. Other research has looked at context-dependent memory in the classroom, since students often learn material in environments (e.g., classroom or library) distinctly different from the testing environment (e.g., examination room). While some early studies showed clear benefits to matching the testing and learning environments in the classroom, others did not. More recently, Smith and Vela (2001) performed a meta-analysis looking at 75 studies of context-dependent effects and found a small but significant effect of matching the learning and testing environments. So, should you be studying in the same room where you'll be writing your exam? This is not always possible, and the effects are small, so it's probably best to use other memory-enhancing techniques, which are discussed at the end of the chapter.

Emotional Memory

Most of the research you've learned about so far is based on memorization of word lists, which is something that we rarely need to do. In everyday life, memories of our personal experiences are processed automatically, with some types of information much easier to encode than others. Why is it that you can remember in great detail the events of your first date but cannot recall what you ate for breakfast yesterday morning? Generally speaking, emotional memories are easier to recall than are factual ones, since emotions help us encode and retrieve memories without requiring effortful processing. When emotions occur—especially negative ones—attention is focused and details are noted, because emotions usually are connected with events that have important implications for the individual. As such, these events may be important to recall.

In a study that demonstrates the role of emotion in both the encoding and retrieval of memories, researchers brought nine women into the lab and showed them a series of pictures. Some pictures had potentially emotional content—such as spiders, snakes, graphic violence, nudes, nature, beauty—while others were neutral, such as a picture of a city street. A year later they saw the same images. Both times their brains were scanned. One year later, the women showed better recognition of the pictures with emotional content than the neutral pictures. Also, their scans showed enhanced brain activity when they saw the emotional, remembered items (Dolcos, LeBar, & Cabeza, 2005). What is interesting about these findings is that the brain regions that were active during encoding of emotional stimuli were also active during retrieval of those memories, indicating that emotion helped both stages of the memory process.

The relationship between emotion and memory is far from perfect. Sometimes, emotions distort our memories. In terms of autobiographical memories, when people look back over their lives they preferentially recall pleasant times over the negative. So there is a positive bias in autobiographical memory recall. The "good ole' days"

Challenge Your Assumptions

True or False? Emotional memories are easier to recall than non-emotional memories.

True: Memories involving emotions capture our attention and help with both encoding and retrieval of information.

Not all battle scars are physical. Post-traumatic stress disorder (PTSD), a condition that forces sufferers to relive terrifying events over and over, makes readjusting to civilian life difficult for an increasing number of war veterans. After returning from witnessing the genocide in Rwanda, Roméo Dallaire, former commander of the United Nations peacekeeping force, struggled to deal with PTSD.

are good partly because we remember the good more readily than we remember the bad (Walker, Skowronski, & Thompson, 2003). In fact, negative emotions themselves can result in memory impairment; refugees who have endured extreme emotional stress show impaired recall of specific episodic memories and some cancer survivors show impaired semantic memory (Moradi et al., 2008). However, extremely negative events can sometimes enhance memory for trauma, as with the case of post-traumatic stress disorder (PTSD). This is a condition in which a person who has experienced an extremely traumatic event, such as being a crime victim or a soldier in a war, relives the event over and over. Not everyone who experiences trauma develops PTSD. In fact, this condition only occurs in a minority of trauma victims. Research consistently points to prior stressful experience as a reliable predictor of the development of PTSD after trauma (Ozer et al., 2003; Delahanty & Nugent, 2006; Bronner et al., 2010). Therefore, stressful emotions may both enhance the encoding of information and impair the retrieval of emotional memories (Buchanan & Tranel, 2008).

Emotions and the events that trigger them are often remembered with a special clarity that is missing from more mundane episodic memories. It's not uncommon for someone to remember a significant life event "like it happened yesterday," even though decades have passed. The term **flashbulb memory** refers to a vivid memory for an emotionally charged event, usually for something that is unexpected and of great consequence. Although any strong emotion can produce a flashbulb memory, they tend to be associated with negative events such as those involving accidents or death. Despite the vividness of these recollections, research suggests that these memories might not be as accurate as they seem. In one study by Hirst and colleagues (2009), participants' memories of the September 11, 2001, terrorist attacks were tested one week, 11 months, and 35 months after the event. Despite high ratings of confidence for their memories of this event, participants did not give consistent ratings across the different time points. Furthermore, the recollections of the details of the event itself (the non-emotional content such as the number of planes involved) were recalled *more* consistently than the emotions themselves.

flashbulb memory
a vivid memory for an emotional event of great significance.

Quick Quiz 6.1: Multiple Types of Memory

1. H.M. had damage to which structure crucial for memory?
   a. insula
   b. hippocampus
   c. thalamus
   d. hypothalamus
2. The brief traces of a touch or a smell left by the firing of neurons in the brain are examples of
   a. perceptual memory.
   b. long-term potentiation.
   c. implicit memory.
   d. sensory memory.
3. What kind of memory do we use to keep someone's phone number in mind right after we've learned it?
   a. working memory
   b. iconic memory
   c. long-term memory
   d. sensory memory
4. What sort of memory allows us to perform skills, such as tying our shoes automatically, once we have mastered them?
   a. explicit memory
   b. declarative memory
   c. procedural memory
   d. echoic memory
5. For sensory input to make the transition from sensory memory to working memory to long-term memory, it must go through what four processing stages?
   a. encoding, consolidation, storage, and retrieval
   b. encoding, reconstruction, storage, and retrieval
   c. encoding, consolidation, storage, and remembering
   d. encoding, reconstruction, storage, and remembering

Answers can be found at the end of the chapter.

LO6 FORGETTING AND MEMORY LOSS

Many of us have vivid memories from when we were very young. Jean Piaget, the renowned child psychologist whose work is discussed in Chapter 10, recalled a harrowing experience from when he was only two. This is his recollection:

> I was sitting in my pram [carriage], which my nurse was pushing in the Champs-Élysées, when a man tried to kidnap me. I was held by the strap fastened around me while my nurse bravely tried to stand between me and the thief. She received various scratches, and I can still see vaguely those on her face. Then a crowd gathered, a policeman with a short cloak and a white baton came up, and the man took to his heels. I can still see the whole scene. . . . (Piaget, 1962, p. 187)

Piaget recalled this event from his childhood clearly, but it never happened. No one ever tried to kidnap him. Apparently, Piaget had been told about this situation by his parents and his nurse (who was like a nanny). When Piaget was 15, the nurse confessed that she had made up the whole thing; she had told his parents the story to improve their opinion of her. Meanwhile, Piaget had made it part of his own recollections, with vivid sensory details of the sights and sounds of the event, as though he had experienced every moment of it.

How is it that we can remember something that probably never happened? Furthermore, if memory can fool us into thinking we had an experience we didn't have, how reliable are our memories of real events and important information? We will come to understand, as Piaget's false memory attests, that memory is not like a photographic image of the things we have experienced. Memory and forgetting are much more of a subjective and reconstructive process than an objective one. It is all too easy to think of the mind as an objective recorder of events. But human memory is not an objective recorder of experience. In the process of remembering, we select, distort, bias, and forget events. What we generally think of as **forgetting** is the weakening or loss of memories over time.

One reason why we forget is **interference,** which occurs when other information competes with the information we are trying to recall. Interference can happen in one of two ways (Jacoby, Hessels, & Bopp, 2001). First, **retroactive interference** occurs when new experiences or information causes people to forget previously learned experiences or information. Memory's vulnerability to interference from information that follows immediately after an event has profound applications in the real world. For example, recall of a crime by an eyewitness, even if testimony is given only minutes after the event (which it usually is not), will be distorted by the events that occurred in those few minutes (or hours or days or weeks) after the crime occurred. A second type of interference, **proactive interference,** occurs when previously learned information interferes with the learning of new information. Perhaps the serial position effect occurs because the process of remembering the first words interferes proactively with recall of the middle words.

forgetting
the weakening or loss of memories over time.

interference
disruption of memory because other information competes with the information we are trying to recall.

retroactive interference
disruption of memory because new experiences or information cause people to forget previously learned experiences or information.

proactive interference
disruption of memory because previously learned information interferes with the learning of new information.

The Seven Sins of Memory

Throughout this chapter, you've learned about several theories explaining multiple types of memory, yet there are few unified theories on different types of forgetting. This is surprising given that much of what we know about memory comes from examining people's memory failures. Memory researcher Daniel Schacter attempted to organize memory errors into a unified framework in his book *The Seven Sins of Memory* (2001). Schacter summarizes the imperfections of memory in a list of seven "sins," falling into one of two categories: errors of omission, which involve failures of recall, and errors of commission, which occurs when recall is distorted, incorrect, or unwanted.

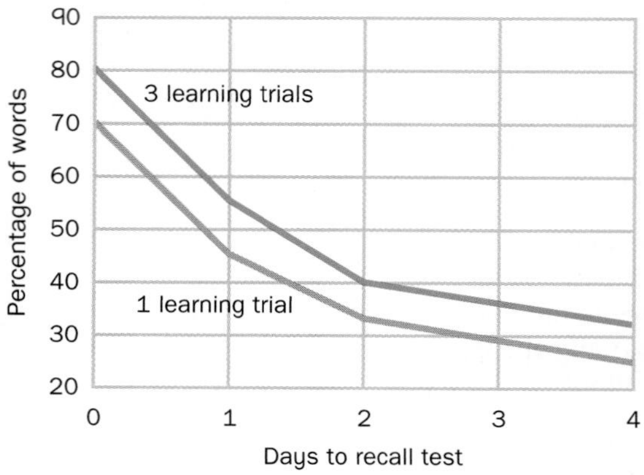

FIGURE **6.12**

THE FORGETTING CURVE. Forgetting happens in a predictable way over time, known as the "forgetting curve." With each passing day, we remember less, but the rate of decline slows. (*Source:* Slameck & McElree, 1983.)

transience
loss of information over time, the most common type of forgetfulness.

absent-mindedness
a form of forgetfulness that results from inattention.

blocking
the inability to retrieve some information once it is stored.

Connection

Can we really multitask? How does talking on the cell phone affect your attention to driving?

See Chapter 5, LO3.

"Sins of Omission": The Act of Forgetting

Transience, Schacter's first sin of omission and the most common type of forgetting, simply refers to loss of information over time due to the fleeting nature of some memories. Another term often used to describe how memories fade with time is *decay.*

Research on forgetting began in the 1880s with Herman Ebbinghaus, who found that recall shows a steady decline over time. This decline is what we now call Ebbinghaus's *forgetting curve.* A modern demonstration of the forgetting curve comes from the work of Norman Slamecka and Brian McElree (1983). Participants in their research were given a long list of words to learn. Some saw the list once and others saw it three times. Moreover, some were asked to recall the list either immediately or one, two, three, or four days later. When Slamecka and McElree plotted the results, they produced the classic forgetting curve. Recall was between 70 and 80 percent immediately, but it declined steadily for each additional day between learning and recalling the word list (see Figure 6.12). It is noteworthy that seeing the list three times, compared to once, increased recall only a little bit.

Forgetting sometimes occurs because we don't pay close attention when we first learn or experience something, and therefore we never encode or consolidate the memory very well. **Absent-mindedness,** Schacter's second sin of omission, is a form of forgetfulness that stems from not paying adequate attention. Consider this: Sandra is distraught over not being able to find her keys. After spending ten minutes looking all over the house in all of the obvious places, she finally goes out the front door to the car only to discover the keys are still in the lock to the house. Such experiences happen when we do not pay close attention or divide our attention among different tasks. Talking on your phone while writing an email can only lead to poor encoding of either the phone conversation or the email, or both. Absent-mindedness increases with age, but it typically is not a significant problem until people reach their 70s, though there are vast differences among individuals. Some people show little memory decline into their 90s, and others begin to experience it in their 60s (Schacter, 2001).

The third of Schacter's "sins of omission" is **blocking,** the inability to retrieve some information that we once stored—say, a person's name or an old phone number. It simply won't resurface despite our efforts. One example of blocking is the frustrating *tip-of-the-tongue* phenomenon in which we can almost recall something but the memory eludes us. We might even know that the word begins with a particular letter. We say to ourselves: "I know it! It's right there. I can even see the person's face. Her name begins with _____." More often than not, it does begin with that letter.

Another form of blocking is *repression,* in which retrieval of memories that have been encoded and stored is actively inhibited. Memories of a traumatic experience are more likely to be repressed than other memories. The implication is that under the right circumstances—during psychotherapy, for instance—the person may suddenly remember the repressed event. We will come back to this topic in our discussion of false memories.

Have you ever lost your keys?

"Sins of Commission": Memories as Reconstructions of the Past Whereas sins of omission are all forms of forgetting, sins of commission consist of distorting, reconstructing, or falsely remembering events. The first sin of commission is **misattribution,** which occurs when we wrongly believe the memory came from one source when it fact it came from another—for instance, when we believe a friend told us something that we actually read in the newspaper.

misattribution
assigning memory to the wrong source.

A curious form of misattribution, dubbed *cryptomnesia* by Schacter (2001), happens when a person unintentionally plagiarizes someone else's ideas, believing that an idea is original or new when in fact it originated with someone else. Writers sometimes plagiarize other writers, but in cryptomnesia the writer is truly convinced he or she is the author of those words, having long forgotten the original source. Cryptomnesia, therefore, is unwitting and unconscious—which may or may not avoid legal problems involving plagiarism. A relatively widely publicized example of cryptomnesia occurred not long ago when a 19-year-old Harvard student unconsciously lifted text from a book she had known well—not for a class paper, but rather for a novel published by a major publishing house. Kaavya Viswanathan published her novel *How Opal Mehta Got Kissed, Got Wild and Got a Life* a few years after she had read Megan McCafferty's book *Sloppy Firsts*. Viswanathan was very impressed by McCafferty's book and so internalized the dialogue that a few years later when she wrote her own book, she used almost identical situations and language, not recalling that she had first read these situations in McCafferty's book (Smith, 2006).

Another of Schacter's "sins of commission" is **consistency bias,** or selective recall of past events to fit our current beliefs, such as when we edit or rewrite our memories of past events based on what we now know or believe. These revisions often tell us more about who we are now than who we were then. When people, for example, are asked to recall their political views from ten years ago, they often remember them in ways that are more consistent with their current beliefs than with their beliefs as they were ten years earlier (Schacter, 2001).

consistency bias
selective recall of past events to fit our current beliefs.

A third sin of commission is **persistence,** which is the repeated recall of pleasant or unpleasant experiences even when we actively try to forget them. Persistence explains how some of the effects of emotion on memory work. For example, persistent memories may play over and over in our mind some embarrassing or traumatic event that we'd really rather forget. Pleasant experiences—an unexpected great first date, being accepted to one's first-choice university—can pop into our minds over and over, against our will. Because they are so pleasant, they aren't at all problematic. When the event is negative or traumatic, then persistence becomes a problem. The most extreme form of persistence is PTSD, wherein the person might relive a traumatic experience over and over again. More often persistence takes a milder form: for example, when we lie awake at night thinking about an embarrassing blunder we made or when we think about how a former lover rejected us. What these kinds of memories have in common—the pleasant and unpleasant, the mild and the traumatic—is that they are created with strongly felt emotions.

persistence
the repeated recall of pleasant or unpleasant experiences even when we actively try to forget them.

The final sin of commission is **suggestibility,** which occurs when memories are altered or implanted in our minds based on leading questions, comments, or suggestions from someone else or some other source. A classic study by memory researcher Elizabeth Loftus indicates how changing the wording of a question impacts people's recall for events. Participants watched a video of a staged car accident and were then asked questions about it. They estimated higher speeds of travel when asked "How fast were the cars going when they *smashed* into each other?" rather than "How fast were the cars going when they *hit* each other?" (Loftus, 2003). With the first question, participants were also more likely to report seeing broken glass at the scene, simply because one word in the question was different. This effect is unconscious: People have no idea and will even deny

suggestibility
problem with memory that occurs when memories are implanted in our minds based on leading questions, comments, or suggestions by someone else or some other source.

Leading questions might influence how an eyewitness recalls a car accident.

If you were a police officer, how could you ask a witness how fast the cars were going without biasing their response?

that they responded differently to the different wording in the questions. Suggestibility is an important issue in law enforcement and legal proceedings since evidence for crimes often comes from eyewitnesses whose memories could be altered by the way police officers and lawyers word their questions. This issue will be discussed in detail in next section.

False Memories

false memories
memories for events that never happened, but were suggested by someone or something.

The most fascinating, controversial, and disturbing issue concerning memory is probably the phenomenon of **false memories**—memories for events that never happened, but were suggested by someone or something. A false memory is not simply a lie; the person develops an actual memory, sometimes very elaborate and detailed, based on false information. In one experiment, Canadian psychologist Stephen Porter found that over half of his undergraduate participants formed a distorted memory of a fabricated story they believed was provided to the researchers by their parents (Porter et al., 1999). What is amazing is that the fabricated stories involved very emotional and stressful events, such as an animal attack or a serious injury—incidents you would not expect to be misremembered. Further research by Porter showed that vulnerability to false memories is actually stronger when using emotionally negative images, compared to positive ones (Porter et al., 2010).

Why is it seemingly so easy to implant memoires? What sorts of factors make this more likely? It appears that visual imagery plays an important role, since mental images or actual pictures appear to boost the likelihood of false memories (Schacter, 2001, p. 125). One study found that almost half of participants formed a false memory of a fabricated story, but this jumped to a whopping 78 percent if the participants were shown a class photograph at the age when the false memory was supposed to have happened (Lindsay et al., 2004).

Probably the strongest evidence about how false memories arise comes from Elizabeth Loftus's research on eyewitness memory. The reliability of eyewitnesses is a central concern for judges, lawyers, and jurors. Loftus has shed light on how fragile eyewitness testimony can be, which is critically important since this type of testimony is often the deciding evidence presented at a trial. Loftus and her colleagues were among the first memory researchers to demonstrate that people's memories of events, even under the best of circumstances, are not very accurate. Furthermore, they are susceptible to suggestion, particularly in the interval between the original experience and recall of the event (Loftus, 1996, 2003). In a classic study, participants watched a video and answered questions, some of which contained direct misleading suggestions about the event they had just witnessed. A misleading suggestion, for instance, might be about what a person in the video was wearing. After answering these questions, participants were asked to recall specific details about the event they saw. Participants were likely to incorporate suggestions about the wrong clothing into their memory and even elaborate on them. This alteration of memory by misleading information presented between encoding and recall is known as the **misinformation effect.**

misinformation effect
alteration of memory by misleading information presented between encoding and recall.

Even without deliberate misleading information, eyewitness memory is not as always reliable, especially in children. Young children tend to make less accurate eyewitness identifications compared to older children and adults (Pozzulo & Lindsay, 1998), a finding that has prompted interest in research into the factors that contribute to these age-related differences. Research by Carole Peterson of Memorial University of Newfoundland has identified several factors affecting children's recall of events, such as language skill, temperament, and stress. In one study, Peterson investigated recall of hospital emergency room visits by children of different ages and found that young children (aged two to four) who were highly distressed had poorer recall about details of their injury compared to older children. This effect was not found if children had low levels of stress regarding their experience (Peterson, 2010).

Challenge Your Assumptions

True or False? Eyewitness memories are usually accurate.

False: Eyewitness memories are prone to errors, especially if people are exposed to misleading information.

The research surrounding false memories is controversial and there is much debate distinguishing false memories from traumatic memories that people have repressed. A **recovered memory** is one that was encoded and stored, though not retrieved for a long period of time. It is then is later retrieved after some event brings it suddenly to consciousness. The reason recovered memories are so controversial is that sometimes they are triggered while a person is under the care of a psychotherapist. The controversy arises when it is not clear whether a psychotherapist has helped a patient to recover a memory of an actual event or has unwittingly suggested an event that the client "remembers." If the event involves traumatic experiences such as physical or sexual abuse and people's lives are at stake, you can see why recovered memory became such an explosive topic when the phenomenon first came to light in the early 1990s. The so-called memory wars often pitted academic memory researchers against psychotherapists. The debate has died down somewhat, partly because everyone recognizes the truths on both sides: Many really did experience abuse in childhood, and unprofessional suggestions by therapists can also lead to falsely recovered memories (Ost, 2003).

recovered memory
a memory from a real event that was encoded and stored, but not retrieved for a long period of time until some later event brings it suddenly to consciousness.

Quick Quiz 6.2: Forgetting and Memory Loss

1. The most common type of forgetting, the fleeting nature of some memories, is known as
   a. absent-mindedness.
   b. decay.
   c. transience.
   d. blocking.
2. _______ occurs when we wrongly believe the memory came from one source when in fact it came from another.
   a. Misattribution
   b. Interference
   c. Decay
   d. Consistency bias
3. The fact that changing the wording of a question impacts people's recall for events illustrates which sin of memory?
   a. persistence
   b. traceability
   c. rephrasing
   d. suggestibility
4. Selective recall of past events to fit our current beliefs is known as
   a. memory binding.
   b. consistency bias.
   c. faulty rendering.
   d. persistence.

Answers can be found at the end of the chapter.

THE BIOLOGICAL BASIS OF MEMORY

Memory is a complex process. It's clear that the brain is critically involved with memory, as cases like H.M. clearly demonstrate, but how? What neural mechanisms enable us to remember the name of our first teacher or a song that we haven't heard for years, or how to calculate our GPA? After decades of research by many people, we are beginning to answer some of these questions. The following section outlines major advances in the biology of memory, from neuron to brain.

LO7 Memory in Neurons

Imagine you decided to document every meal you have for the rest of your life by taking a picture of breakfast, lunch, and dinner each day. In order to store these images permanently, you could save them on a hard drive, or alternatively you could print off hard copies and organize them into a physical album. Over time, you'd have to increase the size of your hard drive or buy more albums to store the tens of thousands of images. In contrast, building up a lifetime of memories doesn't change the overall size of our heads, even with years and years of new experiences.

How is it possible to continually add new items to our memory stores without dramatically increasing the size of our brains? The answer resides in the billions of cells that make up our nervous system—neurons. By studying how our neurons change in response to new experiences, we can better understand our memory processes. In the first half of the 20th century, much of psychology ignored the biological basis of memory and learning, focusing instead on observable behaviour. However, a number of psychologists believed that biology was not just an important factor, but the *foundation* of all learning and memory. Based on his studies of brain anatomy and behaviour, Canadian psychologist Donald Hebb developed a theory to explain the permanence of memory, using neurons as his building blocks.

Hebb's theory of memory storage in neurons can be summarized in two steps. First, when one neuron repeatedly fires and excites another neuron, there is a temporary memory trace that reverberates across the synapse for a short time. Second, if this memory trace persists, it is followed by a permanent change in the receiving neuron, the excitatory neuron, or both, which strengthens the synaptic connection. In Hebb's own words, "When an axon of cell A is near enough to excite a cell B and repeatedly or persistently takes part in firing it, some growth process or metabolic change takes place in one or both cells such that A's efficiency, as one of the cells firing B, is increased" (Hebb, 1949, p. 62). The repeated stimulation of a group of neurons in this way leads to the formation of *cell assemblies*, networks of neurons that persist even after stimulation has stopped. The more times synapses in these assemblies fire together, Hebb stated, the stronger the network becomes, increasing the likelihood that they will fire together again (see Figure 6.13). The shorthand version of this theory is this: *neurons that fire together, wire together.* What is now referred to as the Hebb rule led to another important conclusion from his theory: *Use it or lose it.* If the cell assemblies are not stimulated repeatedly, eventually the synaptic connections weaken and we forget (Cooper, 2005).

When Hebb introduced his model, little was known about the inner workings of the brain, and there was no way to test the model in humans. However, many researchers turned to simpler nervous systems to test Hebb's ideas, since neurons work in a very similar way across species.

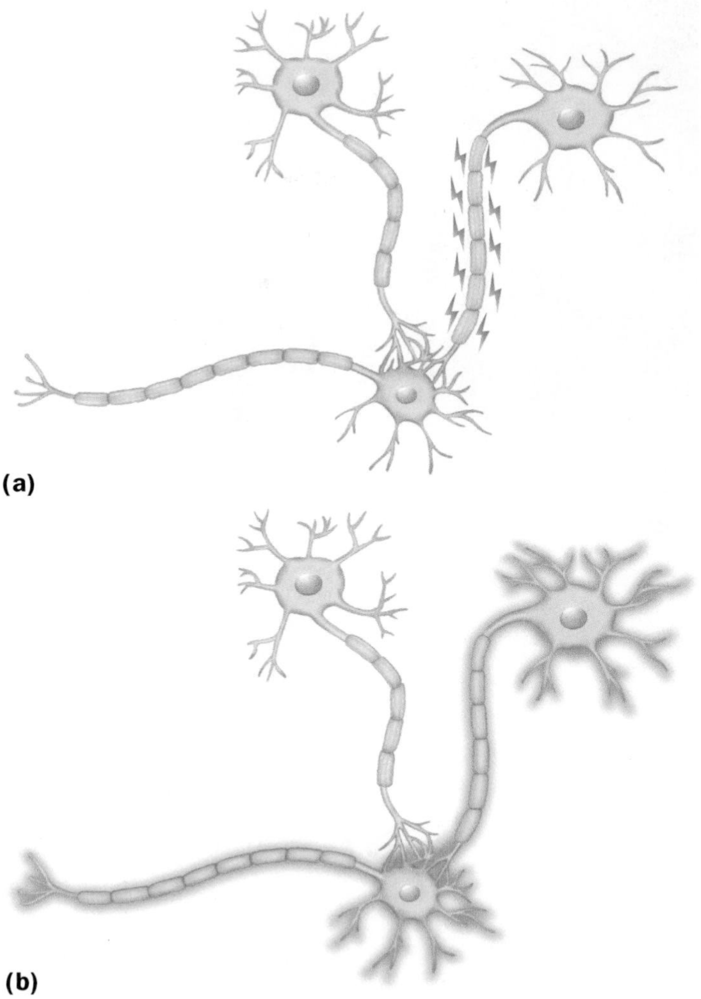

FIGURE **6.13**
THE HEBB RULE. (a) If a neuron repeatedly stimulates another neuron at a synapse, (b) a change occurs to one or both neurons to strengthen communication at that synapse in the future.

Long-Term Potentiation If forming memories involves changes in neurons, then one obvious place to look for these changes is in areas of the brain important for memory function. The hippocampus, which was removed from H.M.'s brain, is one such area. Its anatomical organization and role in memory is very similar to other animals and so has long been a hot spot of memory research (Jacobs, 2003). In the early 1970s two researchers, Timothy Bliss and Terje Lømo, made a remarkable discovery in the rabbit hippocampus. They found that by repeatedly stimulating a neural pathway leading to the hippocampus, they could produce long-lasting activity in the postsynaptic target neurons (Bliss & Lømo, 1973). This activity trace can persist for hours to days, long after the stimulation is over, and so fits in well with Hebb's idea of a memory trace. This strengthening of a synaptic connection when one neuron repeatedly fires and excites another became known as **long-term potentiation (LTP).** Further research revealed the occurrence of LTP in other areas of the brain involved with memory (Sjöström et al., 2008). One important player in the process of LTP is the excitatory neurotransmitter glutamate, since blocking a particular type of glutamate receptor prevents LTP and interferes with memory (Malenka & Nicoll, 1999).

long-term potentiation strengthening of a synaptic connection when one neuron repeatedly fires and excites another neuron.

Molecular Biology of Memory Storage Another important finding about the neuronal storage of memory came from studies of a very unusual animal, the sea slug *(Aplysia)*. Sea slugs have far fewer neurons than humans (about 20 000 compared to a trillion) and their neurons are large enough to be seen with the naked eye. Also, they are capable of simple behavioural reflexes controlled by simple neural circuits (Kandel, 2004). It was for these reasons that Eric Kandel decided to use the *Aplysia* as a model animal to search for the neuronal basis of memory. When Kandel's group administered a shock to the tail of the sea slug, it responded with a defensive posture. If the researchers administered the

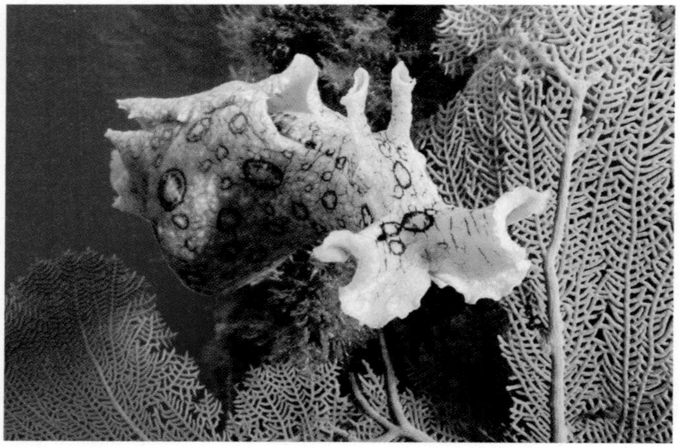

In Kandel's study, the sea slug (*Aplysia*) created a long-term memory of how to react to shock.

Why did Kandel want to use a sea slug to study human memory?

shock only once, the sea slug's defensive response persisted for only about ten minutes. If administered four or five times in close succession, the sea slug exhibited the same defensive response to the shock days later. The sea slug had created a long-term memory of how to react to a shock (Pinsker et al., 1973). Kandel's conclusion: "Conversion from short-term to long-term memory storage requires spaced repetition—practice makes perfect, even in snails" (Kandel, 2001, p. 294).

Following up on these findings, Kandel set out to learn just *how* repeated experience changes the brain. Kandel and his colleagues discovered that repeated stimulation of a neuron actually sends signals to the nucleus of the cell, where its DNA is stored. These signals trigger the production of *CREB,* a protein that switches on genes responsible for the development of new synapses. Repetition brings about the growth of new synapses that stabilize a new memory (see Figure 6.14). By repeatedly pulling away from a shock, the sea slug rehearsed and remembered a defensive behaviour. Thus, experience from the outside world (repeated stimulation) changes genes and the way in which they are expressed. These neuronal mechanisms of memory storage were later demonstrated in more complex nervous systems, like those of rats and mice (Kandel, 2006). This work was so significant that Kandel was awarded the 2000 Nobel Prize in Physiology or Medicine.

LO8

Memory in the Brain

Challenge Your Assumptions
True or False? Only complex organisms are capable of forming memories.
False: Even animals with very simple brains, like the sea slug, can form memories based on experiences.

At the beginning of this chapter we introduced H.M., who lost the ability to make new long-term memories after having his temporal lobes removed. Why was he still able to retrieve memories stored before the surgery? And how was he able to learn the star-tracing task more and more rapidly each time it was presented, even though he didn't remember learning it before? The reason is that structures within the temporal lobe, such as the hippocampus, transfer explicit memories to long-term stores. As you will learn in this section, encoding of procedural tasks into the long-term and retrieval of previously stored memories are processed by structures outside of the temporal lobe. Since H.M. did not have damage to these areas, these abilities were unimpaired.

H.M.'s unusual case illustrates how much we can learn from the damaged brain. In fact, much of what we know about the role of the human brain in memory is a result of careful observations of patients with brain dysfunction from disease or injury. The cognitive impairments suffered by these patients are life-changing and often devastating, and therefore their contributions to science should be greatly appreciated. It is important to keep in mind, however, that our ability to tease apart the neuroanatomy of memory from these case studies is limited for a number of reasons. Patients often have damage to several brain regions, making it difficult to pinpoint the area responsible for the memory deficit. Also, brain damage is often due to accident or disease, and those events could themselves be responsible for cognitive impairments. Therefore, researchers use other strategies to study the biology of memory. Neuroimaging of the undamaged human brain and animal lesioning studies have helped to fill in the gaps.

Connection
Why do smells evoke particularly strong and specific memories?
See Chapter 4, LO11.

Sensory Memory: The Sensory Cortices Our sensory memory system is fairly straightforward. As we saw in Chapter 4, sensory neurons carry

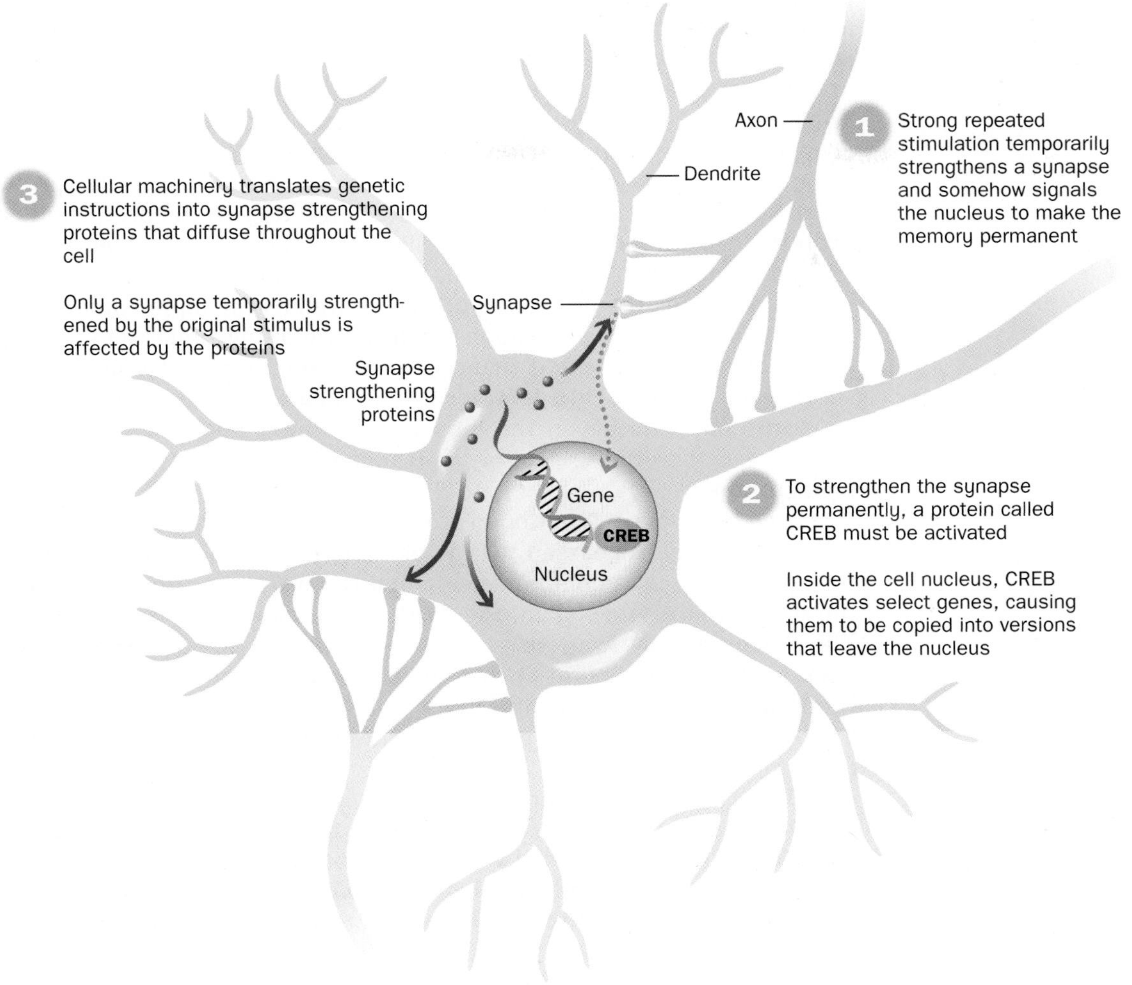

Axon
Dendrite
1 Strong repeated stimulation temporarily strengthens a synapse and somehow signals the nucleus to make the memory permanent
3 Cellular machinery translates genetic instructions into synapse strengthening proteins that diffuse throughout the cell
Only a synapse temporarily strengthened by the original stimulus is affected by the proteins
Synapse
Synapse strengthening proteins
Gene
CREB
Nucleus
2 To strengthen the synapse permanently, a protein called CREB must be activated
Inside the cell nucleus, CREB activates select genes, causing them to be copied into versions that leave the nucleus

FIGURE **6.14**

HOW MEMORIES STICK. When we experience something emotionally important or an experience is repeated over and over, synapses fire repeated neural impulses as if to say, "this is important; remember this event." (1) These repeated neural firings in turn strengthen the synapse by activating a protein called CREB (2). CREB then turns on certain genes that set into motion a process that builds other proteins that strengthen the synaptic connection (3). This process makes memories last in our minds, in effect "tattooing" the event in our brain. (*Source:* Fields, 2005.)

information about external stimuli from our sense organs to different parts of the brain. First, the sensation travels to the thalamus, which then relays the sensory information to the cerebral cortex for further processing. Each sensory system has a dedicated sensory cortex for processing sensory stimuli. The visual cortex is located in the occipital lobes, the auditory cortex is in the temporal lobes, and the somatosensory cortex (touch) is in the parietal lobes, the gustatory cortex (taste) spans the frontal and temporal lobes, and the olfactory cortex (smell) in the olfactory bulbs. The sensory stimuli that activate specific cortical regions are also activated by memories of those sensations (Wheeler et al., 2000).

Working Memory: The Prefrontal Cortex and Hippocampus From the evidence presented in this chapter so far, it is clear that working memory is a busy place. It should not be surprising that working memory is not localized to just one area of the brain. Rather, research suggests that specific brain areas seem to have important roles in particular working memory processes. The prefrontal cortex is the front-most region of the frontal lobes and plays a crucial role in working memory. It determines what information in the environment is worthy of our attention. When we speak, read, solve problems, or make some other use of working memory, we rely on the prefrontal cortex to keep the crucial information accessible (Baddeley, 1998; Kandel, 2006; Miller & Cummings, 1999; Miyake et al., 2000). The encoding stage of memory formation activates the prefrontal cortex as well as the hippocampus, where the memory is consolidated through rehearsal and repetition (Fields, 2005; Kandel et al., 2000). The repeated firing of neural impulses necessary to convert a short-term memory to a long-term one occurs mostly in the hippocampus. Memory consolidation in the hippocampus may take hours, days, or sometimes weeks before the memory is transferred back to the cortex for permanent storage.

The other main function of working memory is rehearsal. Auditory input is processed and rehearsed via the phonological loop from the prefrontal cortex to the language comprehension centre (Wernicke's region) in the rear of the left parietal lobes (Paulesu, Frith, & Frackowiak, 1993; Schacter, 2001). The processing pathway for visual information of the visuospatial sketch pad goes from the prefrontal cortex to the temporal lobes (for spatial information) and then to the occipital lobes (for visual information; Baddeley, 2003). Figure 6.15 highlights the regions of the brain that play a role in short-term (working) memory.

From human brain damage studies, it is clear that the temporal lobe is critical in the ability to encode explicit, episodic memories for the long term. Initially, many researchers concluded that the hippocampus is responsible for this process; however, Brenda Milner herself cautioned against this interpretation, since H.M.'s surgery included removal of other temporal lobe structures (Scoville &

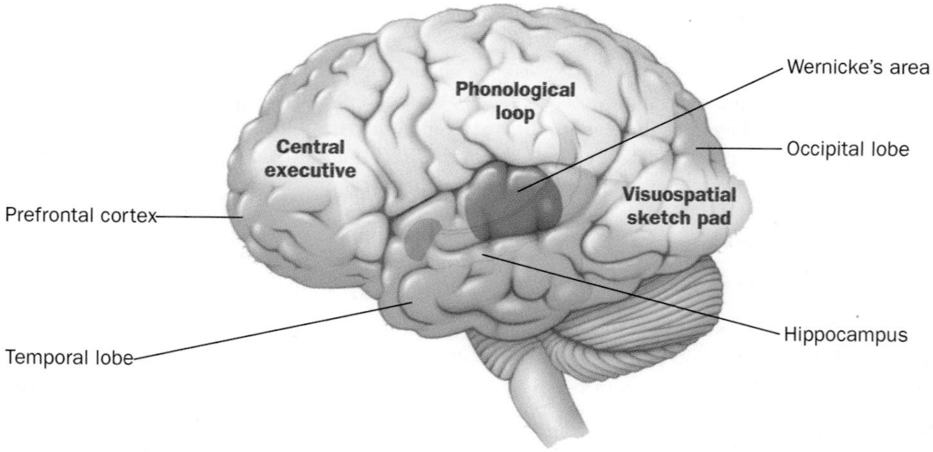

FIGURE **6.15**

BRAIN REGIONS INVOLVED IN WORKING MEMORY. The prefrontal cortex focuses attention on sensory stimuli and holds information long enough for us to solve a problem, then transfers information to the hippocampus for memory consolidation. The temporal and occipital lobes, as well as Wernicke's area, are active in rehearsal of auditory and visuospatial information needed by working memory.

Milner, 1957). More precise lesions in animals have pointed to a more specific role of the hippocampus in encoding episodic memories. Damage to the hippocampus in laboratory animals impairs the ability to encode new locations, such as an escape from a maze, even though *previously* learned locations can be accessed without problems (Steffenach et al., 2002). In healthy humans, storing spatial memories certainly involves activity of the hippocampus. Taxi drivers in London, England, have to learn the location of approximately 25 000 street names as well as the locations of many tourist destinations. One study showed that regions of the hippocampus in London taxi drivers are actually larger than those of London bus drivers, who only have to remember the streets of their particular route (Maguire et al., 2006).

Long-Term Memory Storage in the Brain Most memories begin and end in the cortex, but in between, as we have seen, they are processed in the temporal lobe, where some are converted to long-term memory. Because long-term memory is the most permanent form of memory, it is also the most complex when it comes to brain activity and location.

We store the different types of long-term memory in different places in the brain. Explicit long-term memories are stored in the cortex, specifically in the area where the original sensation was processed (Ji & Wilson, 2007). Retrieving information that requires attention and focus involves working memory, which is predominantly an activity of the prefrontal cortex. For instance, when we actively try to recall information, especially words, from long-term memory, we use the prefrontal cortex (Gershberg & Shimamura, 1995; Mangels et al., 1996; Thompson & Madigan, 2005). Implicit memories are mainly stored in structures in the subcortex, specifically in the striatum (part of the basal ganglia), amygdala, and cerebellum (Kandel, 2006; see Figure 6.16). Priming occurs mostly in the cortex, while procedural memories for skills and habits involve the striatum. Tasks that require memory for precise movements, like playing a musical instrument, involve the cerebellum. In fact, the cerebellum of a trained pianist is actually larger than that of someone who does not play (Han et al., 2009). The amygdala is crucial for associating particular events with emotional responses such as happiness or fear. As you will learn in the next section, the amygdala is involved specifically with memories with emotional content.

Emotional Memory: The Amygdala As you learned earlier in this chapter, people have superior memory for events with strong emotional content. But *how* does emotion help memory? Emotional events activate many areas of the brain, but one structure in particular has a special relationship with emotional memory, a structure located deep in the temporal lobes called the amygdala (Phelps & LeDoux, 2005).

Emotion acts as a powerful memory booster. In fact, people remember the visual details of an object better if negative emotions were aroused while viewing it (Kensinger, Garoff-Eaton, & Schacter, 2007). An imaging study of healthy human volunteers showed that the degree of activation in the amygdala was positively correlated with the recall of emotionally distressing videos, depicting scenes such as violent crime. Interestingly, there was no association between amygdala activity and recall of emotionally neutral videos, displaying scenes such as court proceedings (Cahill et al., 1996). People with damage to the amygdala do not display a memory boost from emotions; they do not recall emotional events better than non-emotional events (Adolphs et al., 1997). Amygdala damage specifically impairs memories for the overall feeling of an event, but not for details. In other words, the details are still there, but the emotional accent is gone (Adolphs, Tranel, & Buchanan, 2005).

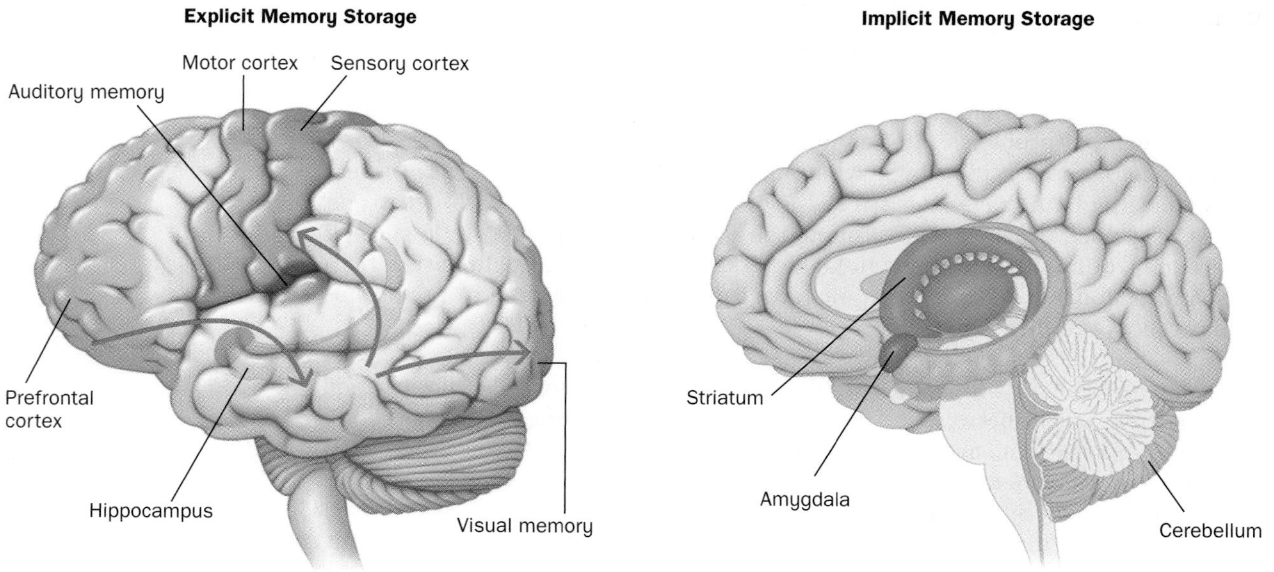

FIGURE **6.16**
BRAIN REGIONS INVOLVED IN LONG-TERM MEMORY. Many different brain areas are involved in memory. The hippocampus is involved in laying down and retrieving memories, particularly personal ones and those related to finding your way about. After being processed in the hippocampus, explicit long-term memories are returned to the cortex for storage in the area where the sensory information was processed originally. Implicit memories are processed and stored in the cortex, the striatum, and the amygdala. (*Source:* Kandel, 2006.)

Groundbreaking Research

The Brain's "Inner GPS" and Spatial Memory

Knowing how the brain represents space is one of the first steps in piecing together how we store meaningful life events, because places and locations act as anchors for our episodic memories. The 2014 Nobel Prize in Physiology or Medicine was awarded to three researchers, John O'Keefe, Edvard Moser, and May-Britt Moser, whose careful experiments and meticulous work have begun to solve the puzzle of how the brain deals with space and incorporates it into memories of our personal experiences.

THE HIPPOCAMPUS: ENCODING THE MAP

John O'Keefe's motivation for searching for the brain's navigator is best summed up in his own words: "Space plays a role in all our behaviour. We live in it, move through it, explore it, defend it" (O'Keefe & Nadel, 1978, p. 5). He started his search in the hippocampus, since cases like H.M. showed that structures in the medial temporal lobe are important in memory, and damage to this area in laboratory animals impairs their ability to form spatial memories. The hippocampus is also a hotbed of LTP activity, which is one of the ways that memories are thought to be stored in neurons.

By listening in on rat hippocampal neurons with electrodes, O'Keefe's research group made an interesting discovery about neurons in the rat hippocampus: these neurons became electrically active when the rat was in a particular location, regardless of what was happening there or what the animal was doing. They called these neurons *place cells* and the spatial areas that activated them *place fields* (O'Keefe & Dostrovsky, 1971). Place cells map out the animal's space entirely, in other words, every location is totally represented in the hippocampus. Further studies showed that the activity of place cells is tied to the context in which they were encountered, since changing the dimensions of the testing environment from a square to a rectangle resulted in a similar change in the shape of the place fields (O'Keefe & Burgess, 1996). Therefore, place cells appear to use landmarks and shift their place field to accommodate differently shaped environments. In fact, rats make different hippocampal maps for different environments; one study recorded 11 distinct activity patterns for 11 different environments (Alme et al., 2014). This flexibility of the hippocampus means that it can be used to represent any space an individual encounters. In rats, hippocampal place cells "replay" activity of locations of routes taken to find food rewards, which happens during pauses in training as well as during sleep (Gupta et al., 2010). Many believe that this is evidence of memory consolidation, the third stage in long-term memory.

From left to right, John O'Keefe, May-Britt Moser, Queen Silvia and King Carl XVI Gustaf, Edvard Moser, and Eileen O'Keefe during the 2014 Nobel Prize awards ceremony. May-Britt Moser's gown is decorated with a pattern of the grid cell neurons she co-discovered, created by British fashion designer Matthew Hubble.

THE ENTORHINAL CORTEX: NAVIGATING SPACE

In the 1990s, Norwegian scientists Evard and May-Britt Moser spent several months training in John O'Keefe's lab at University College in London. Building upon what John O'Keefe learned about hippocampal place cells and spatial maps, they set off on their own quest to dig deeper into the brain to find out where the hippocampus gets its information about space. Upon returning to Norway, they themselves made an amazing discovery about how the brain codes space. They recorded from a part of the brain called the entorhinal cortex, which is a major input to the hippocampus. Whereas hippocampal place cells fire at a specific spatial location, these entorhinal cortex cells increased their firing activity at many locations, arranged in regularly spaced intervals (Hafting et al., 2005). This activity was organized in a grid-like pattern, so these neurons were called *grid cells* (see Figure 6.17). Another big difference between grid cells and place cells is that grid cells do not change their firing pattern in different environments (Fyhn et al., 2007) and so they are able to provide information about distance and direction, essentially acting as the brain's own global positioning system.

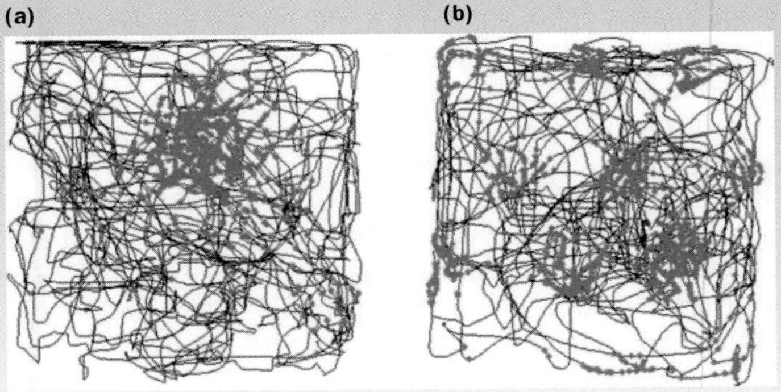

FIGURE **6.17**

MAPPING SPACE IN THE BRAIN. The black lines in the figures above show the movement path of a rat. The red indicates increased neuronal activity of a place cell in the hippocampus in (a) and a grid cell in the entorhinal cortex in (b). (From Moser et al., 2008.)

PUTTING IT ALL TOGETHER IN EPISODIC MEMORY

So how are these findings important for the study of episodic memory? From this research we know that grid cells in the entorhinal cortex provide the raw coordinates of space, which can then be used by the hippocampus to create numerous, customized maps of the locations of landmarks, objects, or events of interest. Grid cells have recently been discovered in the brains of epilepsy patients travelling through a virtual environment, and the pattern of activity is very similar to that observed in rats travelling through real mazes (Jacobs et al., 2013). Knowledge about how we code space could someday help people with temporal lobe damage, who live forever in the present because of their inability to store new experiences. It is no wonder that H.M. had difficulty in forming new episodic memories since he had most of his hippocampus and entorhinal cortex removed. Without his inner GPS and map maker, he had no way to store reference points for his experiences.

amnesia
memory loss due to brain injury or disease.

anterograde amnesia
the inability to remember events and experiences that occur after an injury or the onset of a disease.

retrograde amnesia
an inability to recall events or experiences that happened before the onset of a disease or injury.

LO9 **The Biology of Memory Loss** When people forget due to injury or disease to the brain, we refer to the condition as **amnesia.** Two types of amnesia associated with organic injury or disease are anterograde amnesia and retrograde amnesia. **Anterograde amnesia** is the inability to remember events and experiences that occur *after* an injury or the onset of a disease. People with anterograde amnesia fail to make new long-term memories. They recall experiences for only a short period of time, perhaps ten minutes or less. H.M., whose case we recounted earlier in the chapter, had anterograde amnesia after his temporal lobes had been removed. **Retrograde amnesia** is an inability to recall events or experiences that happened *before* the onset of the disease or injury. The memory loss in this type of amnesia might involve only the incident that preceded it or might include years of memories. Accidents almost always result in retrograde amnesia of the event itself. Car accident victims, for instance, will usually say that they do not remember the accident.

A severe form of age-related memory loss occurs in the organic brain disease known as Alzheimer's disease. Although it can affect people as earlier as their 40s or 50s, Alzheimer's disease usually strikes people over the age of 60. It results in progressive memory loss, ending with complete memory loss. In people who suffer from Alzheimer's disease, both transience and absentmindedness are evident. For instance, forgetting the death of a spouse is common among people who suffer from moderate to severe forms of Alzheimer's. They may go through the whole grieving process over and over, as if each time someone reminds them that their loved one is gone, they are hearing the news for the first time. Although the causes of Alzheimer's disease are uncertain, most research points to the abnormal accumulation of a protein called beta-amyloid, which is thought to be toxic to the certain populations of neurons that contain the neurotransmitter *acetylcholine.* These *cholinergic* neurons send their axon terminals to memory regions such as the hippocampus and cortex (Coulson et al., 2009).

Milder forms of memory loss are observed with marijuana use, which is thought to be due to the active ingredient, Δ^9-tetrahydrocannbinol (THC) (McKim, 2007). One perplexing question is why the human brain would have neuronal receptors for THC in the first place. It turns out that the receptors that bind to marijuana also bind to naturally occurring neurotransmitters called *endocannabinoids,* which are the brain's own marijuana-like compounds. These receptors are particularly abundant in memory-related structures in the brain, such as the hippocampus, amygdala, and cortex (Iverson, 2003). Activation of these receptors in both animals and humans promotes the forgetting of irrelevant information and has led to speculation that endocannabinoids might help to refine memories by getting rid of useless information (Lutz, 2007). Although most of what you have read in this chapter has focused on memory recall as desirable, forgetting irrelevant information is equally important. If you could not inhibit the memory of where your parked your car yesterday, it might interfere with your ability to form a new memory of where you parked it today. Some disorders, such as PTSD, are characterized by persistent, vivid memories of unpleasant events, and there has been interest in the endocannabinoid system as a potential target for treatment. To learn more about how commonly used drugs that affect memory, see "Psychology in the Real World."

Manipulating Memory with Drugs

We have learned a lot in this chapter about how memories are formed, stored, and retrieved. Clearly we have come a long way from the early days of memory research—the Nobel Prizes for Physiology and Medicine in 2000 *and* 2014 were awarded to researchers working on unravelling the mysteries of memory at the neuronal level. But has this wealth of knowledge allowed us to tweak our brains to boost memory? Have you ever wished for a better memory? This section will highlight some ways that drugs can boost, and block, our memory powers.

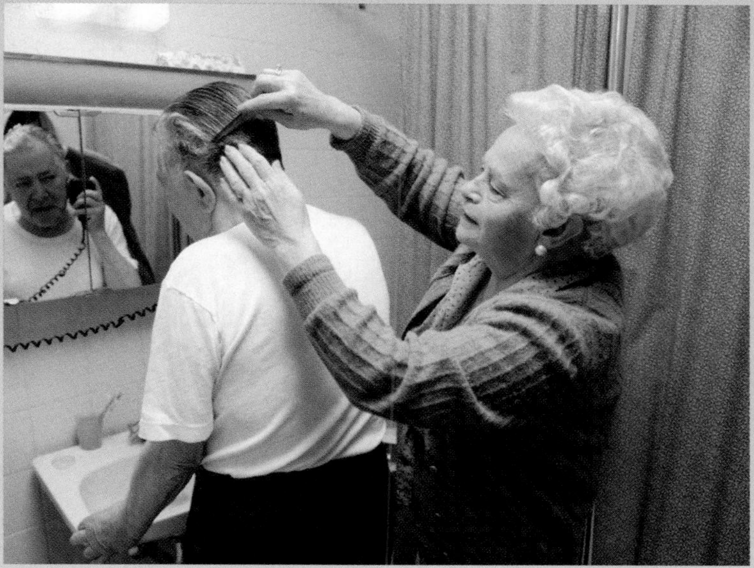

Although drugs can slow the rate of decline in Alzheimer's disease, they are not a cure. In later stages of the disease, simple tasks such as grooming require help.

Forgetting things we once had no trouble recalling, especially as we age, is one of the more frustrating experiences in life. For some people memory loss represents the loss of identity, the loss of self, and ultimately the loss of life. Alzheimer's disease, for instance, robs people in their later years of their most valued treasure—their memories. Ultimately, this fatal disease destroys the brain's ability to maintain basic functioning. Therefore, there is a real medical need, as well as a psychological need, for therapeutic help for people with Alzheimer's and other severe memory deficits. The two most widely prescribed drugs for Alzheimer's disease are donepezil and galantamine, which both enhance the levels of the acetylcholine in the brain by preventing its breakdown in the synapse. Unfortunately, these drugs do not cure the disease; rather, they help treat symptoms and slow the patient's rate of decline. Therefore, the search for treatments that can halt or even reverse memory decline is the aim of intensive research.

Interest in memory-boosting drugs is not confined to those with memory problems. Drugs are sometimes used as a tool by those looking improve their memory skills. There is mixed evidence that prescription stimulants, such as amphetamine (Adderall) and methylphenidate (Ritalin), improve memory (Ilieva, Boland, & Farah, 2013). The positive effects of these drugs happen only in low doses (Mehta, Sahakian, & Robbins, 2001). Higher doses of prescription stimulants can actually interfere with and block memory formation (Devilbiss & Berridge, 2008). The stimulant drug caffeine, alone or in combination with taurine as found in energy drinks, has small but reliable effects in enhancing memory (Giles et al., 2012; Howard & Marczinski, 2010).

So there is certainly no magic pill available to boost memory ability, but there are plenty of readily available drugs that impair memory, and the most common is certainly alcohol. No surprise that alcohol affects encoding of new memories, which explains why people can completely forget what happens during a period of drinking, yet previous memories are intact and working memory still functions (Pressman & Caudill, 2013). Sometimes encoding is completely blocked, as with a blackout, or partially blocked so that people have fuzzy memories of their drinking episode, or can recall them with triggers (Goodwin, 1995). Severe alcoholism can lead to increased risk of Korsakoff syndrome, which is caused by thiamine (Vitamin B1) deficiency and is characterized by both retrograde and anterograde amnesia for episodic memories, even if the person is not drunk. Memory impairments from Korsakoff syndrome are permanent and irreversible and are thought to be due to damage to various parts of the cortex, particularly the frontal lobes, and the thalamus (Brion et al., 2014).

Another recreational drug that impairs memory is marijuana, although research on this topic has produced many conflicting findings. One of the most consistent findings is that marijuana impairs encoding of information presented while high; however, recall of information that was encoded while sober appears relatively unaffected (Ranganathan & D'Souza, 2006). Of more concern, perhaps, is the effect of chronic marijuana use on memory beyond the period of intoxication, which has been the subject of much debate. It appears that heavy marijuana use does lead to mild memory impairments, even when the user is not high (Block et al., 2002; Lundqvist, 2005).

There is intensive medical research directed toward developing drugs that block or dampen the process of memory formation. Why would anyone want to do that? The most obvious application of this kind of drug is to prevent traumatic experiences—such as abuse, car accidents, or war experiences—from developing into post-traumatic stress disorder (PTSD), a condition in which a person who has experienced an extremely traumatic event, such as being a crime victim or a soldier in battle, relives the event over and over. Alain Brunet and his colleagues at McGill and Harvard have shown some promising results with propranolol, a heart medication that blocks certain receptors for the neurotransmitters epinephrine and norepinephrine. They used a technique called trauma reactivation, where the sufferer gives a vivid description of the event that caused his or her PTSD. Treatment with propranolol dramatically reduced PTSD symptoms, and several patients no longer met the diagnostic criteria after six treatment sessions (Brunet et al., 2011).

Quick Quiz 6.3: The Biological Basis of Memory

1. When we actively try to recall information, especially words, from long-term memory, we use the
   a. occipital cortex.
   b. prefrontal cortex.
   c. parietal cortex.
   d. parahippocampal gyrus.
2. Rehearsal makes memories stick. So does what kind of experience?
   a. drunkenness
   b. storage
   c. emotion
   d. fatigue
3. Complete this phrase: Neurons that _____ together _____ together.
   a. grow; sow
   b. lie; die
   c. synapse; degrade
   d. fire; wire
4. CREB is a(n) _____ that switches on genes responsible for the development of new synapses.
   a. amino acid
   b. protein
   c. neurotransmitter
   d. enzyme
5. _____ is the inability to remember events and experiences that occur *after* an injury or the onset of a disease.
   a. Anterograde amnesia
   b. Retrograde amnesia
   c. Post-traumatic amnesia
   d. Selective amnesia

Answers can be found at the end of the chapter.

Evaluating Connections in Memory

How to Study

One of the most common questions students have while learning about memory in introductory psychology is: "How can I use this material to study more efficiently?" This question may come up after the first exam, especially from students who expected an A but got a C. "What did I do wrong? I reread my notes, highlighted the book; how come I didn't do better?" It turns out that the things that worked for you in high school might not work anymore. To really master a lot of complex new material, you may have to adopt new study strategies. You can make psychological science work for you by using the years of research about memory to optimize how to learn new material and prepare for exams (Bjork, 2001; Kornell & Bjork, 2007).

Consider that anything you hear in a lecture or read in the book—after a brief stint in sensory memory—is in that vulnerable place called short-term memory. Your job is to move this information into long-term memory and to then retrieve it for an exam. In particular, the material you learn in any class—new facts, terms, processes, and so on—is semantic memory. Like all long-term memories, how well you remember this material begins with encoding.

1. *Go to class and pay attention.* Attending and paying attention in lectures is a first, very important step. If there is something you don't understand when the instructor first mentions it, ask a question about it right away. If you are too shy to do so in class or you can't get a word in edgewise with your instructor, note it in the margin of your notes so you can come back to it later. Consider that if you do not attend to it now, you will forget it by the end of class. Why? Interference of new material presented afterward, the fact that your stomach is growling, and thoughts of getting to your next class in time will make it difficult for you to remember what you wanted to ask. By being in class and hearing in more detail what was posted on the

lecture outline and what you read in the book, you give yourself another context in which to work with the material: engaging your attention. Avoid creating sources of interference, like talking with a friend, text messaging, or emailing during lectures. These activities will interfere with encoding and make it likely that you are not paying attention.

2. *Read the book before class.* To increase the odds of learning and remembering the material for a long period of time, it is important to read the material in the book. Reading the chapter before class helps you to establish a network of associations in which to fit the new material, so that when you hear your instructor talk about it, you have a place to put the information—you can make the associations. A related encoding tool is relating the new material you learn to things you have already experienced, so you begin to build more associations. What else can help at the encoding stage? Many professors post lecture outlines electronically before class, which, like reading the book in advance, gives you the opportunity to begin encoding and storing material from the upcoming lecture before you get there.

3. *Study deep, not shallow.* In addition to the lecture and book information, you can improve the way you study the material outside of class. What you have learned from levels of processing theory can help you learn how to approach studying. According to depth of processing theory and research, the more deeply you process material, the better it is recalled. Rereading notes and highlighting the book are both examples of shallow processing. They involve rote rehearsal. You want to process the material semantically, to work with the meaning of the material, which enhances your depth of processing and memory. Simply reading a definition of a term like *storage* over and over again is not all that different from repeating a list of nonsense words over and over. But if you attempt to work with the meaning of the material, you will remember it better. Think about it. *Storage* is a word we use a lot, and you only recently saw it related to memory. What does it mean in our everyday speech? To put something away and keep it there. Like storing your memorabilia from high school in the attic of your parents' house. You put your yearbooks, varsity jacket, and track trophies into a box and bring them to the attic. Memory storage is just like this. It is the process of putting something away and leaving it there for future use. If you can elaborate your understanding of concepts like storage in this way, you don't have to remember the word-for-word definition, because you understand what it means. That's good semantic processing.

   Recent research on student study habits shows that spacing out study activities is also important. Students tend to cram right before an exam, and they often think this is the most effective approach to learning. Yet spacing things out and covering topics or chapters in separate study sessions, using both studying and self-testing of that material, is much more effective for long-term memory (Kornell & Bjork, 2007).

4. *Form a study group.* Another way to increase depth of processing is to form a study group. Getting together with a few other students to review and discuss material before an exam can be enormously helpful, as long as you prepare before getting together. Meeting with your peers to discuss course material adds new information, fills in gaps, and helps build up new semantic networks, but most importantly, it offers a context in which to talk about the material. This is an excellent opportunity to see if you know the material—by talking about it with others. You might also have a peer who can explain a concept in a way that your instructor did not. Study groups foster discourse, social interaction, and the need to make another person understand you. This requires semantic processing, preparation, and some emotional charge, because you don't

Paying attention during class is an important first step in successfully encoding new course material.

want to look like an idiot in study group. It is also important to have time between meeting with the study group and taking the test, so that you can go over any lingering questions that may have arisen during study group and consolidate your learning. To be sure that the material you are studying becomes consolidated or firmly established, make a point of sleeping well after studying.

5. *Devise meaningful mnemonics.* Will you be able to access the information you learned when you need it? What can you do while studying to facilitate retrieval? Reviewing material with the study group is like a practice test, which is a nice evaluation of retrieval ability. Also, using an easy-to-remember mnemonic device during encoding may make it easier to retrieve information later. If you make a concept personally relevant and integrate it into a semantic network, you can provide yourself with labels or tags as memory prompts. So, for example, to remember the meaning of memory *storage*, you can just think *attic* and you will activate that whole network of associations.

Quick Quiz 6.4: Evaluating Connections in Memory: How to Study

1. In terms of studying your course material, rereading notes and highlighting the book are both examples of _____ processing.
   a. depth of
   b. staged
   c. shallow
   d. retroactive
2. Which of the following study approaches is most effective for long-term memory?
   a. rote rehearsal
   b. studying large amounts of material in a few sessions
   c. rereading the chapter
   d. spacing out your study sessions to cover different topics in several sessions
3. Which of the following helps you process new material more deeply?
   a. making the material personally relevant
   b. building up associations with new concepts
   c. discussing the material
   d. all of the above

Answers can be found at the end of the chapter.

Chapter Review

- Memory, the ability to store and recall information, is the foundation of all intelligence, learning, and thought.
- Three major principles of memory state that (1) memories persist for different lengths of time; (2) memories are processed and stored in different parts of the brain; and (3) memory is very much a reconstructive process.

MULTIPLE TYPES OF MEMORY

- Memory systems are classified as implicit and explicit. These types of memory can be further subdivided into separate memory stores based upon function, duration, and capacity.
- Atkinson and Shiffrin's three-stage model organizes memory into three stores: sensory memory, short-term memory, and long-term memory. Sensory memory is a brief trace of a sensory experience that lasts from less than a half a second to two or three seconds. Short-term memory holds a limited amount of information between two and 30 seconds, or as long as we continue to rehearse it. Short-term memories can be transferred

to long-term memories by the process of encoding, and long-term memories can be brought into short-term memory by the process of retrieval.

- Baddeley's model of working memory describes how we are able to hold information in short-term memory while solving a problem. This model divides working memory into three temporary storage systems, one for sounds and language (phonological loop), one for images and spatial relations (visuospatial sketchpad), and one that connects the two storage systems, interacts with long-term memory, and provides temporary storage for specific events (episodic buffer), all managed by an attentional control system (the central executive).
- The serial position effect is a phenomenon of short-term memory whereby we most likely remember information that comes first and last in a series. It may be due to retroactive or proactive interference.
- Long-term memory is the repository of any material that we retain for between 30 seconds and a lifetime. It includes implicit memory, where skills, behaviours, and procedures that we don't consciously retrieve are stored, and explicit memories of events and facts stored for conscious recall.
- Long-term memory is divided into four stages: encoding, consolidation, storage, and retrieval. Encoding involves acquiring new memories. During consolidation, memory becomes firmly established and resistant to distraction, interference, and decay. Storage is the retention of information over time. Information can be stored via hierarchies, schemas, or association networks. Retrieval is the recall of stored information from long-term memory.
- Unlike the storage models, process-oriented models of memory emphasize *how* we remember information rather than *where*. Automatic processing requires little conscious attention, while effortful processing involves deliberate effort to remember. The levels of processing approach suggests that the deeper we encode information, the better our recall. The encoding specificity principle states that recall is best when the conditions during encoding are similar to those during retrieval.
- Memories with strong emotional content are better recalled than those with less emotional content. One symptom of PTSD involves enhanced memories for traumatic life events.

FORGETTING AND MEMORY LOSS

- Daniel Schacter's "seven sins of memory" are categorized as sins of omission or sins of commission. Sins of omission include forgetting or transience, absent-mindedness, and blocking. The sins of commission are misattribution, consistency bias, persistence, and suggestibility, all of which can distort the way we recall past events.
- The two most serious effects of suggestibility are false memories and recovered memories. A false memory is a recollection of an event that never happened, whereas a recovered memory resurfaces after it was completely forgotten.

THE BIOLOGICAL BASIS OF MEMORY

- Different memories are processed in different areas of the brain. Sensory memories are processed primarily by their respective sensory cortices. Working memories are processed mostly by the hippocampus and frontal lobes. Long-term memories are stored for the most part in the areas of the cortex where they were processed as sensory memories. Emotional memories are processed by the amygdala.
- Repetition and sometimes strong emotion initiate neural activity that converts short-term memories to long-term memories. In long-term memory formation, proteins activate genes that turn on the production of new dendrites and synapses.
- Encoding memories of spatial layout involves grid cells in the entorhinal cortex and place cells in the hippocampus.

EVALUATING CONNECTIONS IN MEMORY

- Going to class and paying attention to lectures help you to encode lecture material deeply.
- Reading the book before a lecture will help build a richer network of associations of the lecture material.
- You can process the material deeply by rehearsing and spacing out your studying.
- Forming a study group also facilitates deeper processing of the material because you have to learn by generating information, not simply reading or hearing it.

Quick Quiz Answers

Quick Quiz 6.1: 1. b 2. d 3. a 4. c 5. a **Quick Quiz 6.2:** 1. c 2. a 3. d 4. b
Quick Quiz 6.3: 1. b 2. c 3. d 4. b 5. a **Quick Quiz 6.4:** 1. c 2. d 3. d

Learning

CHAPTER

7

CHAPTER OUTLINE

Challenge Your Assumptions

True or False?

- ☐ Phobias can be learned.
- ☐ Negative reinforcement is the same as punishment.
- ☐ Children are not affected by watching violent cartoons or movies.
- ☐ Learning strengthens connections in the brain.

LEARNING OBJECTIVES

- **LO1** Define what is meant by learning.
- **LO2** Explain how learning occurs through classical conditioning.
- **LO3** Explain how learning occurs through operant conditioning.
- **LO4** Explain how reinforcers and punishers influence behaviour.
- **LO5** Describe the effects of different schedules of reinforcement on behaviour.
- **LO6** Describe biological constraints on learning.
- **LO7** Explain how latent learning and conditioned taste aversion challenge conditioning models of learning.
- **LO8** Explain how learning occurs through observation.
- **LO9** Explain the role of the brain in learning processes.

It was a beautiful August morning at the Santa Cruz Yacht Harbor, and I (Erika) was about to embark on an ocean adventure. This time I would conquer my motion sickness. I had, after all, cutting-edge medical knowledge on my side. My doctor had given me a scopolamine patch. Scopolamine is a drug that sometimes prevents or relieves nausea. (Astronauts use scopolamine for motion sickness in space.)

I was so sure I would not get seasick that I had agreed to go on a deep-sea fishing trip with my boyfriend and his co-workers. At 9 A.M. we boarded the boat. Someone had brought a big box of doughnuts. I grabbed an old-fashioned chocolate doughnut, my favourite kind, and downed it in a few seconds. About 30 minutes later we set sail. Before our boat had even cleared the harbour, I was turning green. Soon I was vomiting off the side of the boat. The remaining three or four hours of the trip seemed like an eternity, as the sickness continued. I thought about jumping overboard, because surely death would have been better than this. Finally, the boat returned to the harbour. For ten years afterward, I could not eat chocolate doughnuts.

What happened? Exactly how did a chocolate doughnut, which had not caused my seasickness, become a source of queasiness for years to come? Why did I suddenly associate the taste and smell of chocolate doughnuts with the conditions that had made me sick? By associating the doughnut with nausea, I had *learned* to avoid chocolate doughnuts.

Later we will see why this one experience made such an impression on me. First, we need to understand what learning is. In this chapter, we will discuss three major theories of learning—classical conditioning, operant conditioning, and social learning theory—as well as the role of evolution in learning. We will also explore how learning both emerges from and changes the brain.

LO1 BASIC PROCESSES OF LEARNING

learning
enduring changes in behaviour that occur with experience.

As we try things out in the world, changes in sensation, perception, behaviour, and brain function alter who we are, what we know, and what we can do. Psychologists define **learning** as enduring changes in behaviour that occur with new experiences. Learning is therefore dependent upon storing information about past experience and using this information to alter behaviour in the future, so learning and memory work together. Without learning and memory, we could not process, retain, or make use of new information. Learning occurs when information moves from short-term to long-term memory. During this process, new knowledge is stored in networks in the brain. For this reason, we don't have to learn to ride a bicycle every time we want to go for a spin. Once we have mastered the skill of riding a bicycle, that knowledge can be retrieved from memory, and we can pedal away without thinking about it.

As you learned in Chapter 6, there are multiple types of memory. It should be no surprise that psychologists also make distinctions between different types of learning—from making a connection between motion sickness and a chocolate doughnut to mastering a musical instrument or a foreign language. Throughout this section we will explore the different types of learning and the conditions under which they occur.

Some phenomena fit the definition of learning as "enduring changes in behaviour that occur with experience" much more clearly than others. For example, if a dim light were presented to you in a dark room, you would look at it immediately. This automatic shift of attention toward a new stimulus is known as the *orienting response.* After a while, if the brightness and location of the light remained the same, you would no longer respond to it. In fact, you might not notice it at all. This phenomenon, called *habituation,* is a sensory process by which individuals adapt to constant stimulation. The result is a change in your response (from seeing a spot of light to not seeing it) stemming from experience. The change is a fairly short-lived one, however. As soon as the stimulus is varied even slightly, the orienting response occurs, and the process begins again. Habituation is often regarded as learning in its simplest form (Carew & Kandel, 1973).

Connection

Right now you are habituated to dozens of stimuli—including the feel of clothing on your skin. Now you are sensitized to it. How so?

See Chapter 4, LO2.

Association

Every time we feed our cat, Spalding, we first take the can opener out of the drawer in the kitchen. As a kitten, Spalding would hear the sound of someone opening a drawer at feeding time. So the sound of the drawer opening signalled to Spalding that he was going to be fed. Now, every time anyone opens a kitchen drawer, Spalding comes running and meowing eagerly. Frequently it is a false alarm (sometimes the drawer is opened for other reasons), but the connection, or association, between the sound of a drawer opening and being fed are very strong for him.

An **association** occurs when one piece of information from the environment is linked repeatedly with another and the individual begins to connect the two sources of information. Associations form simply as a result of two events occurring together, whether or not the relationship between them makes any sense. For instance, there is nothing inherently delicious about the opening of a drawer, but Spalding comes looking for food when he hears the sound. Eventually, the repeated association results in the events becoming linked in the individual's memory. By virtue of their association, one event may come to suggest that the other will occur. Learning by association is a simple but powerful form of learning.

association
process by which two pieces of information from the environment are repeatedly linked so that we begin to connect them in our minds.

CONDITIONING MODELS OF LEARNING

conditioning
a form of associative learning in which behaviours are triggered by associations with events in the environment.

classical conditioning
form of associative learning in which a neutral stimulus becomes associated with a stimulus to which one has an automatic, inborn response.

Conditioning is a form of associative learning in which a behaviour becomes more likely because the individual links that behaviour with certain events in its environment. Spalding the cat, for example, is *conditioned* to the sound of the drawer opening because he has come to associate the sound with food. Sometimes the sound means that food will come; sometimes it does not. But the association is strong because feeding is always preceded by the sound of a drawer opening.

Psychologists distinguish between two types of conditioning: classical and operant. Both are forms of associative learning. In classical conditioning, individuals learn from the relations between stimuli. In operant conditioning, individuals learn from the consequences of their behaviour. Let us look at these two forms of learning in more detail.

Pavlov and his dogs.

LO2 Classical Conditioning

In **classical conditioning,** learning occurs when a neutral stimulus becomes associated with a stimulus to which the learner has an automatic, inborn response. Exactly how this works will become clearer if we consider the pioneering example of Ivan Pavlov and his dogs.

Pavlov's Dogs Ivan Pavlov received the Nobel Prize in Medicine in 1904 for his research on saliva and digestion. While he was studying digestion in dogs, Pavlov (1906, 1928) discovered classical conditioning quite accidentally. As often happens, luck, keen observation, and serendipity (making important discoveries by accident) led to this important scientific discovery.

In order to examine digestive enzymes in the dogs' saliva, Pavlov and his technicians placed tubes in their mouths to collect their saliva. Then they placed meat powder in their mouths, which naturally produces salivation. After doing this for a while, he noticed that the dogs would begin to salivate even before the meat powder was presented, when the laboratory technician who fed them prepared the apparatus to collect their saliva. It was as though the sounds of the technician manipulating the apparatus signalled to the dogs that meat powder was about to come (Fancher, 1996). Pavlov guessed that the dogs had formed an association between the sounds of the apparatus and the meat powder, just as Spalding formed an association between the sounds of a drawer opening and being fed.

Pavlov reasoned that the dogs had formed an association between a stimulus that had no inherent food value (the sound of the apparatus) and one that did (the meat powder). Could he teach a dog to salivate to something else? He designed a laboratory experiment that mimicked the conditions in which the dogs salivated to sounds made by the technician. Working with different dogs, Pavlov presented a neutral stimulus (such as a bell sound) just before showing them the meat powder. The dogs had no previous experience with the bell, but they salivated to the meat powder, because dogs always salivate to meat powder, from the first time they smell it. Salivation is a reflex, an automatic response to a particular stimulus (food) that requires no learning.

Pavlov presented the bell along with the meat powder to the dogs over and over again. The dogs salivated. Then he tried presenting the bell alone to see if the dogs might now link the bell with the meat powder in the way the first dogs linked the noise of the apparatus with the meat powder. Bingo! The dogs salivated to the bell alone. By virtue of the association made during repeated pairings with meat powder, the non-appetizing bell had come to signal "meat powder" to the dogs. The dogs had learned that they would get meat powder after the bell sounded.

How Classical Conditioning Works Pavlov called the kind of learning he'd observed the *conditioning of reflexes*, and we now call it *classical conditioning*. He coined the term **unconditioned response (UR)** to describe the automatic, inborn response to a stimulus. In this case, salivation is the UR. *Unconditioned* simply means "unlearned." Pavlov used the term **unconditioned stimulus (US)** to refer to the stimulus (meat powder) that always produced the same unlearned response (salivation). Without learning, the US always produces the UR; in Pavlov's experiment, meat powder—the US—always leads to salivation—the UR.

unconditioned response (UR) the automatic, inborn reaction to a stimulus.

unconditioned stimulus (US) the stimulus that always produces the same unlearned response.

Food makes you salivate, pressure on your eye makes you blink, and a tap just below your kneecap will cause your leg to jerk forth. These reflexes are unlearned, fixed responses to specific types of environmental stimuli. Pavlov defined reflexes, such as salivation in response to food, as fixed stimulus–response patterns. Classical conditioning is the modification of these stimulus–response (S–R) relationships with experience.

Pavlov presented the neutral stimulus (bell) right before the US (meat powder). Salivation in the presence of meat powder was the UR. After repeated pairings of the bell with meat powder, when the bell alone led to salivation, the bell would be called a conditioned stimulus. A **conditioned stimulus (CS)** is a

conditioned stimulus (CS) a previously neutral stimulus that an individual learns to associate with the US.

previously neutral stimulus that an individual learns to associate with the US. If salivation occurred in response to the CS (as it did in Pavlov's experiment), it would then be called a conditioned response. A **conditioned response (CR)** is a behaviour that an individual learns to perform when presented with the CS alone. Figure 7.1 shows how classical conditioning works.

conditioned response (CR) a behaviour that an individual learns to perform when presented with the CS.

Notice that Figure 7.1 shows the neutral stimulus being presented just before the US. This process is known as *forward conditioning.* One can also present the neutral stimulus and the US simultaneously. When the neutral stimulus follows the US, a process called *backward conditioning,* conditioning is less successful. An example of backward conditioning would be sounding the bell after presenting the food to Pavlov's dogs. Based on repeated, painstakingly careful experimentation, Pavlov laid out certain criteria for stimulus–response conditioning to succeed (Pavlov, 1906, 1928). Two of the most fundamental criteria are as follows:

1. Multiple pairings of US and neutral stimulus (CS) are necessary for an association to occur and for the CS to produce the conditioned response.
2. The US and CS must be paired or presented very close together in time in order for an association to form.

When a behaviour has been conditioned to occur in the presence of a given stimulus (such as Spalding's meowing whenever he hears the kitchen drawer opening), it may also increase in the presence of similar stimuli. Spalding comes running to the kitchen not only when he hears the kitchen drawer opening, but also when he hears us open a cabinet or make almost any sound related to food preparation. This phenomenon, known as **stimulus generalization,** is the extension of the association between US and CS to a broad array of similar stimuli. The opposite of stimulus generalization is **stimulus discrimination,** which occurs when a CR (such as salivation) occurs only to the exact CS to which it was conditioned. For example, if Pavlov's dogs did not salivate to a buzzer but only to a bell, they would discriminate the conditioned stimulus (bell) from other stimuli (buzzers, clicks, and so on). Or take Erika's aversion to chocolate doughnuts: She was only unable to eat chocolate doughnuts. Glazed or sprinkled doughnuts were fine. Her conditioning was specific to chocolate doughnuts.

stimulus generalization extension of the association between US and CS to include a broad array of similar stimuli.

stimulus discrimination restriction of a CR (such as salivation) to the exact CS to which it was conditioned.

Can a conditioned response be unlearned? Would you expect Pavlov's dogs to continue salivating indefinitely in response to the bell alone? It turns out that the dogs gradually stopped salivating to the bell (CS) once they learned that the bell wasn't accompanied by meat powder (US). This weakening and disappearance

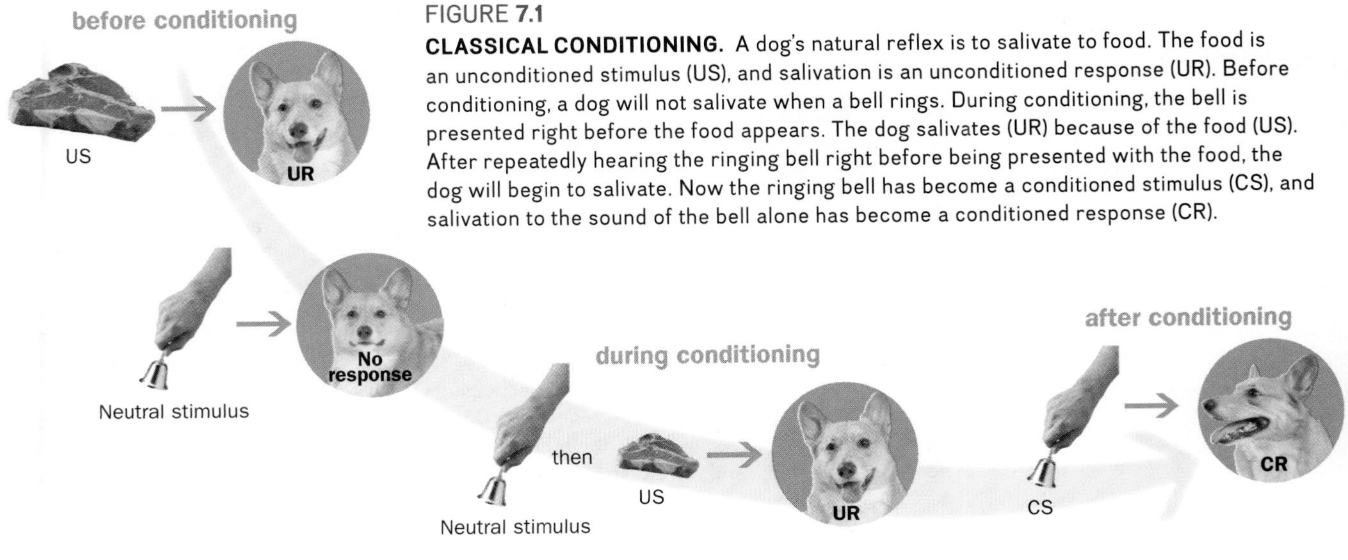

FIGURE 7.1
CLASSICAL CONDITIONING. A dog's natural reflex is to salivate to food. The food is an unconditioned stimulus (US), and salivation is an unconditioned response (UR). Before conditioning, a dog will not salivate when a bell rings. During conditioning, the bell is presented right before the food appears. The dog salivates (UR) because of the food (US). After repeatedly hearing the ringing bell right before being presented with the food, the dog will begin to salivate. Now the ringing bell has become a conditioned stimulus (CS), and salivation to the sound of the bell alone has become a conditioned response (CR).

extinction
the weakening and disappearance of a conditioned response, which occurs when the US is no longer paired with the CS.

of a conditioned response is called **extinction,** and it occurs when the US is no longer paired with the CS (see Figure 7.2). It can be difficult to extinguish some behaviours, especially if they are associated with fear (LeDoux, 1996). As you will learn in the next section, the process of extinction is often the target of treatments for phobias. Although extinction to fearful stimuli appears to be more resistant than other types of learned associations, our life experiences can make a difference in how quickly we "unlearn" fear. In one recent experiment, participants showed faster extinction to a stimulus paired with an electric shock if they had a night's sleep, compared to those who underwent extinction training after the same period of wakefulness (Pace-Schott et al., 2009; see Figure 7.3).

Just because a conditioned response is extinguished, it does not mean that the relationship between the CS and US has disappeared. In fact, the simple

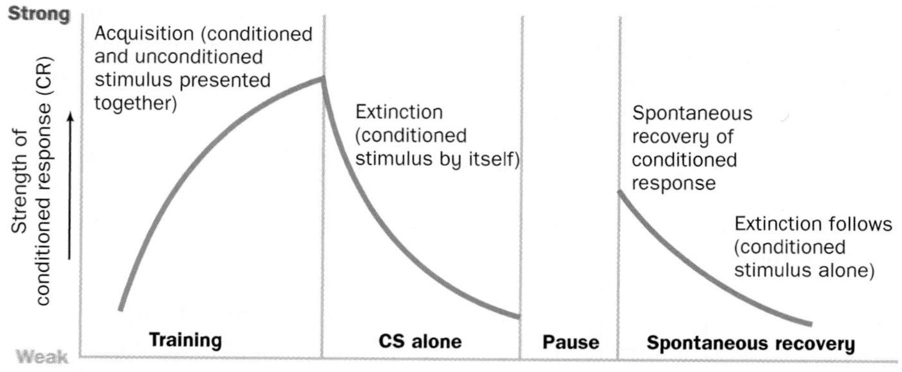

FIGURE **7.2**

ACQUISITION, EXTINCTION, AND SPONTANEOUS RECOVERY IN CLASSICAL CONDITIONING. The graph shows how a conditioned response (CR) gradually becomes stronger during conditioning, then weakens when the conditioned stimulus (CS) is no longer paired with the US, and then disappears (extinction). Following a pause during which the CS is not presented, spontaneous recovery of the CR may occur briefly before it is extinguished again.

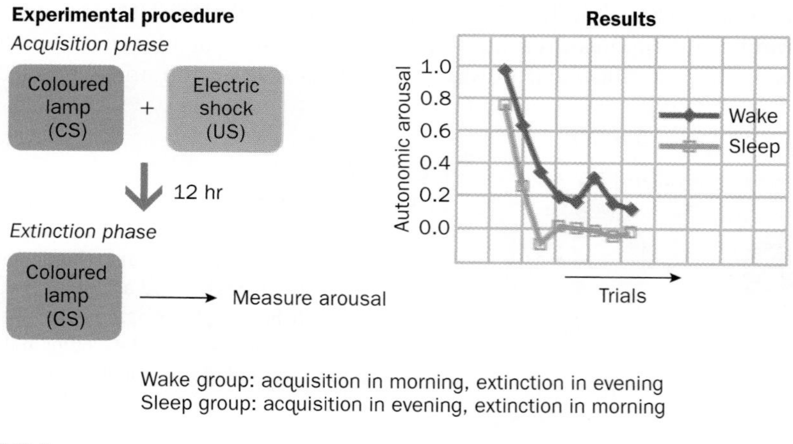

FIGURE **7.3**

SLEEP PROMOTES EXTINCTION OF CONDITIONED FEAR. Acquisition of a conditioned fear response, autonomic arousal, to a coloured light (CS) was achieved by presentation with a mild electric shock (US). After a 12-hour delay, participants were shown the CS alone for several trials. Half of the participants experienced the CS–US pairing in the morning and were tested for extinction in the evening, while the other half experienced the pairing in the evening, had a normal night's sleep, and were tested in the morning (*Source:* Pace-Schott, E.F., Milad, M.R., Orr, S.P., Rauch, S.L., Stickgold, R., Pitman, R.K. (2009). Sleep promotes generalization of extinction of conditioned fear. *Sleep,* 32, 19–26.)

passage of time can lead to the reappearance of a conditioned response, a phenomenon known as **spontaneous recovery** (see Figure 7.2). One real example of spontaneous recovery comes from a colleague who was involved in a car accident. His car was sideswiped as he was making a blind turn from a campus parking lot. After the accident, he would have a panic attack whenever he passed that parking lot, and so he couldn't park there. Several months later, the attacks stopped, and he started parking in the lot again. Then, one day as he approached the parking lot, he had an unexpected panic attack. A learned response he thought had been extinguished suddenly came back. It is clear from recent research on spontaneous recovery that extinction never completely eliminates the response, but only suppresses it (Moody, Sunsay, & Bouton, 2006). After the response has been extinguished, it is quite common for the response to reappear spontaneously if a person returns to the original setting where the conditioning took place.

spontaneous recovery
the sudden reappearance of an extinguished response.

Once conditioning has been established, the CR can be elicited by pairing the CS with a new neutral stimulus, a process known as **higher-order conditioning.** For instance, Pavlov first demonstrated this by presenting the sound of a metronome with meat, and then pairing the metronome with a black square. Even though the black square was never directly paired with the meat, it was capable of eliciting salivation (Gewirtz & Davis, 2000). This type of conditioning is commonly used by advertisers; they often show products (such as beer) with other conditioned stimuli (such as the Canadian flag) in the hopes that their products can trigger the same positive emotions.

higher-order conditioning
a form of conditioning whereby a neutral stimulus is paired with a CS.

Why does classical conditioning work? It may be adaptive in an evolutionary sense. We need to be able to associate certain types of stimuli with potential harm and to respond quickly to new stimuli that present threats. For instance, we might not be hardwired to see long, sharp metal objects as dangerous; but once we see that pressing one of them against the skin causes bleeding, then we know it is dangerous. Most animals can learn such things readily, and it helps them survive and reproduce. It is by virtue of experience and association that many objects acquire their meaning for us. That knives are dangerous is something we learn. The fact that classical conditioning is a powerful learning device for nearly all creatures suggests that it has advantages for survival.

The Conditioning of Little Albert Pavlov's work caught the attention of young psychologists in the early 20th century. They saw in Pavlov's research the first systematic account of a scientific procedure for studying behaviour. One American psychologist, John Watson, felt strongly that classical conditioning could be used to shape human behaviour:

> Give me a dozen healthy infants, well-formed, and my own specified world to bring them up in and I'll guarantee to take any one at random and train him to become any type of specialist I might select—doctor, lawyer, artist, merchant-chief, and yes, even beggarman and thief, regardless of his talents, penchants, tendencies, abilities, vocations, and race of his ancestors. (Watson, 1925, p. 82)

Watson's complete faith in the ability to mould human behaviour seems naïve today, and some would even call it dangerous. Yet Watson and his view of the infant as a blank slate helped push psychology—which Watson defined as "the study of behaviour"—forward as a science. To Watson, classical conditioning offered a model for transforming the field.

In a classic study of the power of conditioning techniques, Watson conditioned a baby known as Little Albert to fear white rats and other white fluffy objects. When Watson and his colleague Rosalie Rayner first met Albert, they brought out a white rat and showed it to Albert. He was curious, but not afraid of it.

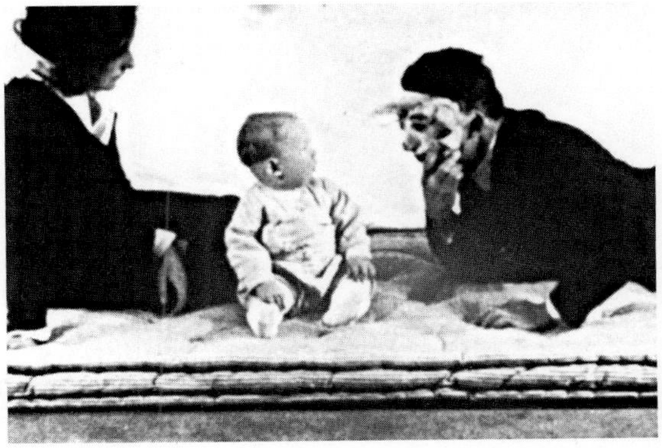

Little Albert with Rosalie Rayner and John B. Watson.

Then Watson and Rayner (1920) paired the presentation of the rat with a very loud noise (the sound of a hammer striking a steel bar right behind Albert's head). Naturally, the loud sound (a US) startled Albert (the UR), and he got very upset.

After repeated pairings of the loud sound with the rat, seeing the rat alone (the CS) upset Albert. Upon further testing, Albert's fear grew to include an intense emotional response not only to white rats but also to many other white, fluffy items, including John Watson's fake white beard—an example of stimulus generalization.

Regrettably, Little Albert did not undergo deconditioning (Watson & Rayner, 1920). Controversy surrounded this case for years, and it is still not clear what happened to Little Albert. We see in this case that psychology in its infancy lacked clear ethical guidelines for research. Watson's "experiment" raised many ethical issues, particularly about the need to safeguard the rights of individuals who cannot give informed consent to participate in research. Still, Watson is remembered as the father of behaviourism for his role in establishing psychology as the study of behaviour. His experiment with Little Albert clearly showed that human fear can be learned, which led to the idea that it can also be unlearned. Using principles of classical conditioning, psychologists have developed behavioural-based treatments for fear disorders such as phobias. For example, consider the case of someone who had a bad experience with a bee sting at four years old. Thereafter, that person had an extreme reaction to the sight of bees. Psychologists can treat this kind of abnormal fear reaction using extinction. Exposing the woman repeatedly to bees in situations in which she does not get stung helps her learn that they will not always sting. This experience reduces the extreme fear reaction she has to bees (see Figure 7.4).

Connection

Could Watson do research on Little Albert in today's world?

See Chapter 2, LO9.

Challenge Your Assumptions

True or False? Phobias can be learned.

True: Watson's experiment with Little Albert demonstrated that phobias can be learned by associating frightening experiences with objects or events that were not initially feared.

LO3 Operant Conditioning

The examples of learning described so far have involved experience-dependent changes in involuntary behaviours, such as nausea, salivation, and fear. However, deliberate behaviours can also be changed by experience. In the late 19th century, Edward L. Thorndike (1905) noted that rewarding consequences can make a voluntary behaviour more likely to occur again. He found, for example, that a cat would escape from a specially designed cage if left to its own devices for a while, not

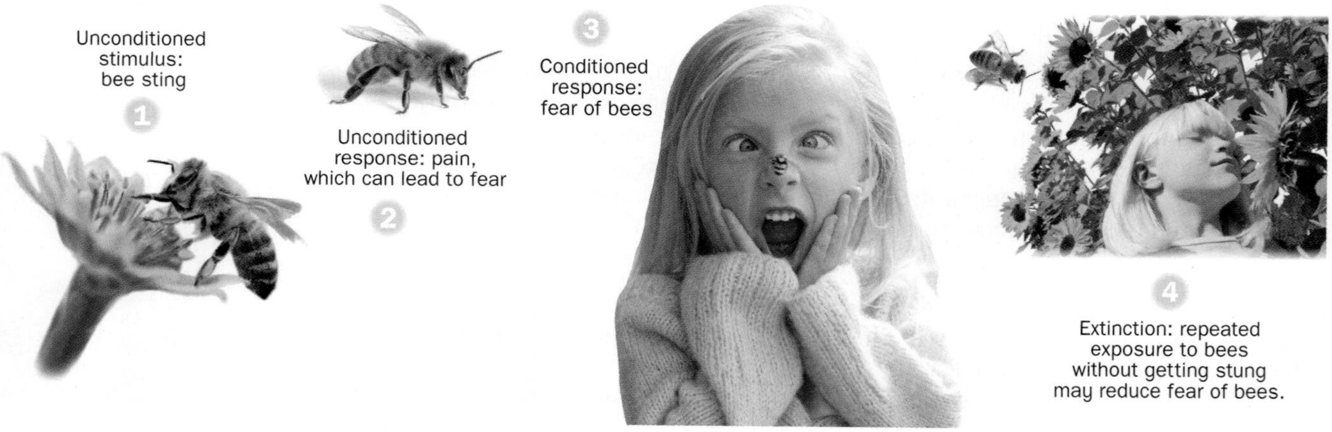

FIGURE 7.4

CLASSICAL CONDITIONING IN THE REAL WORLD. A person who suffered a painful bee sting continues to fear all bees for a long time. After enough exposure to bees without being stung, however, the person can learn to not react with fear. At this point, the conditioned response (fear) is extinguished.

necessarily because it figured out how to get out, but because certain motions eventually were rewarded by the door opening (see Figure 7.5). This reward made it more likely that the specific behaviour that led to the door opening would happen again if the cat were again confined in the same cage. In the same way, you might come back to a café you casually walked into if you found out that it had free wireless Internet service and gave out tasty samples of its pastries. Thorndike labelled this principle the **law of effect.** Briefly, the law of effect means that the consequences of a behaviour increase (or decrease) the likelihood that the behaviour will be repeated.

Like Thorndike, B.F. Skinner viewed the consequences of an individual's actions as the most important determinants of behaviour (Skinner, 1938, 1953). Skinner set out to explain the environmental factors that led Thorndike's cat to learn to open the cage (or you to return to the Internet café). Skinner wanted to know how disorganized, spontaneous behaviour becomes organized. And exactly what role do the consequences of an action play in the organization of the response? Figure 7.6 shows how consequences may increase behaviour in real-life examples.

Skinner (1938) coined the term *operant* to refer to behaviour that acts—or operates—on the environment to produce specific consequences. **Operant conditioning** is the process of learning based upon the consequences of behaviour. According to Skinner, a behaviour that is rewarded is more likely to occur again. For example, if a hungry animal does something that is followed by the presentation of food, then the animal is more likely to repeat the behaviour that preceded the food presentation. If a café gives you free wireless access, you might come back. In contrast to classical conditioning, which modifies an involuntary behaviour (such as salivation), operant conditioning works when voluntary behaviour is made more likely by its consequences.

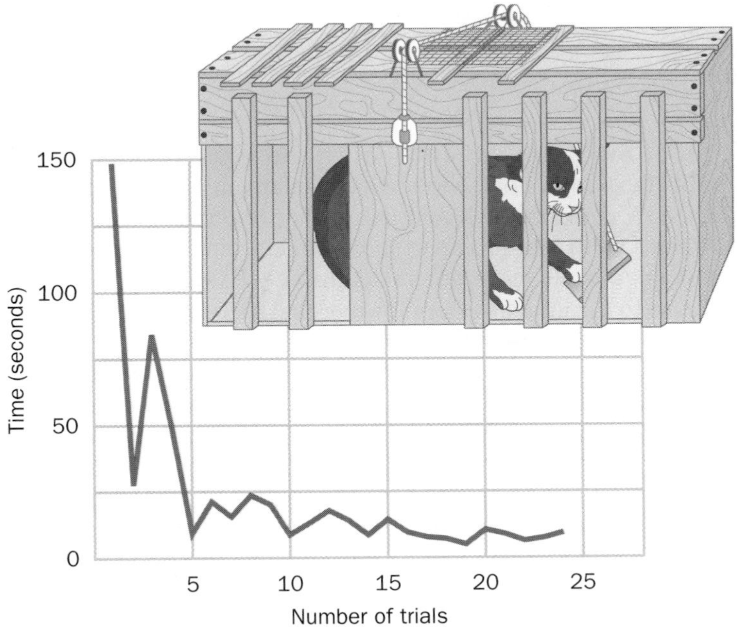

FIGURE **7.5**

THE LEARNING CURVE. Depicted here is the box from which Thorndike's cats learned to escape. Thorndike found that a cat would escape from a specially designed cage if left to its own devices for a while, not necessarily because it figured out how to get out, but because certain motions eventually were rewarded by the door's opening. This reward of the opening door made it more likely that the specific behaviour that led to the opening door would happen again if the cat were again confined in the same cage. The graph shows the amount of time it would take the cat to escape. Initially, it took more than two minutes, but after just a few trials, the cat could consistently escape in about ten seconds.

Connection

Behavioural treatments for phobias, such as systematic desensitization, involve exposing sufferers to their fears, with the aim of extinguishing the fear response.

See Chapter 16, LO3.

law of effect
the consequences of a behaviour increase (or decrease) the likelihood that the behaviour will be repeated.

operant conditioning
learning based upon the consequences of behaviour.

B.F. Skinner

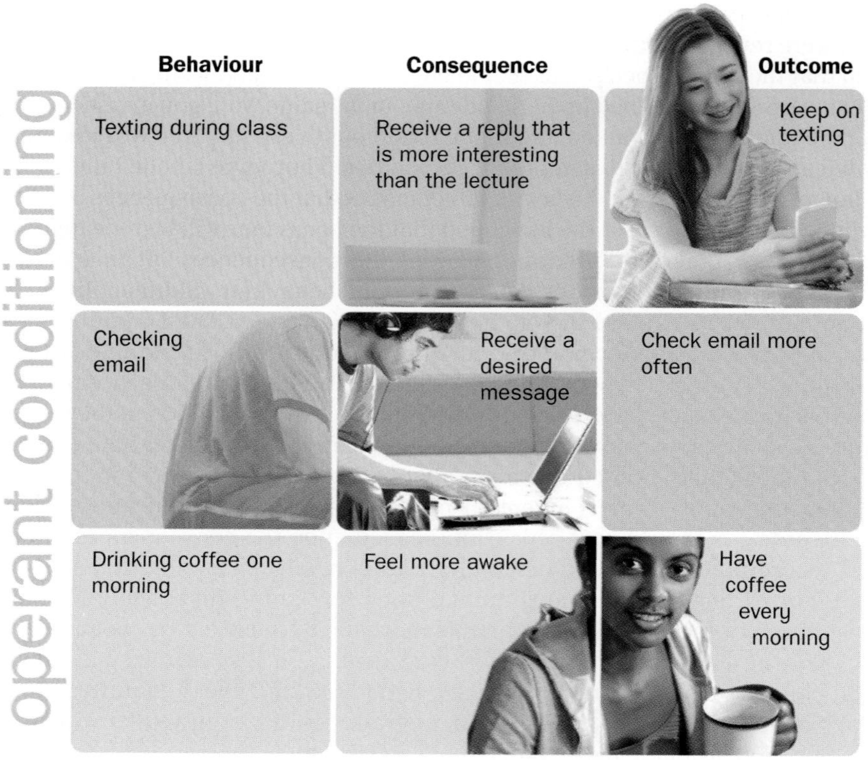

operant conditioning
Behaviour
Consequence
Outcome
Texting during class
Receive a reply that is more interesting than the lecture
Keep on texting
Checking email
Receive a desired message
Check email more often
Drinking coffee one morning
Feel more awake
Have coffee every morning

FIGURE **7.6**

THREE EXAMPLES OF HOW CONSEQUENCES CAN INCREASE OR REINFORCE BEHAVIOUR.

Can you think of other everyday examples of operant conditioning?

reinforcer
an internal or external event that increases the frequency of a behaviour.

primary reinforcers
innate, unlearned reinforcers that satisfy biological needs (such as food, water, or sex).

secondary (or conditioned) reinforcers
reinforcers that are learned by association, usually via classical conditioning.

LO4 **Reinforcement and Punishment** When the consequences of a behaviour increase the likelihood that a behaviour will occur again, the behaviour is reinforced, or strengthened. A **reinforcer** is any internal or external event that increases a behaviour. When a baby sees he can get a big smile from his mother when he smiles at her, he is likely to smile more often (Adamson & Bakeman, 1985). The mother's smile in response to the infant's is a reinforcer that increases the frequency of smiling by the baby, because parental smiles are inherently rewarding to babies. This is a key point. Reinforcers have to be things that the learner wants in order for them to influence the likelihood that a behaviour will occur again. For example, you will continue getting paid on a regular basis if you do your job. You want the money, so you keep working hard. But if your employer gave you paper clips for your hard work, you'd quit. Similarly, if your credit card company suddenly offered iTunes credits for using your card, you might use it more often. This last case shows how corporations apply principles of operant conditioning to make a profit. All of these examples differ from classical conditioning in which two things become linked because they occur together, whether or not they are inherently rewarding.

There are two kinds of reinforcers: primary and secondary. **Primary reinforcers** are not learned. They are innate and satisfy biological needs. Food, water, and sex are primary reinforcers. **Secondary (or conditioned) reinforcers** are learned by association, usually via classical conditioning. Money, grades, and peer approval are secondary reinforcers. A potential reinforcer may acquire pleasant characteristics if it is associated with something that is inherently reinforcing (such as food or sex). Advertisers regularly take advantage of this fact and pair attractive images and celebrities with their products, with the hope of changing our consumer decision making. But does it work? Research using classical conditioning procedures have shown that pairing fictitious product brands, such as Brand L Toothpaste (CS), with pleasant pictures (US) not only enhanced participants' attitudes of the brand, but also enhanced the likelihood of buying the product in the future (Stuart et al., 1987). These findings suggest that these advertising strategies could actually influence our operant behaviour while we are shopping. Most of us might think that we are immune to marketing strategies, but research suggests otherwise. We seem to be particularly influenced by celebrity product endorsements, as demonstrated in research by Till and colleagues (2008). The researchers induced conditioning by pairing photos of actress Jennifer Aniston with an imaginary brand of hair styling gel. If the celebrity photos were presented immediately before the styling gel, participants rated the product more favourably than if the photos and products were presented randomly. Furthermore, the product ratings did not decline with extinction training.

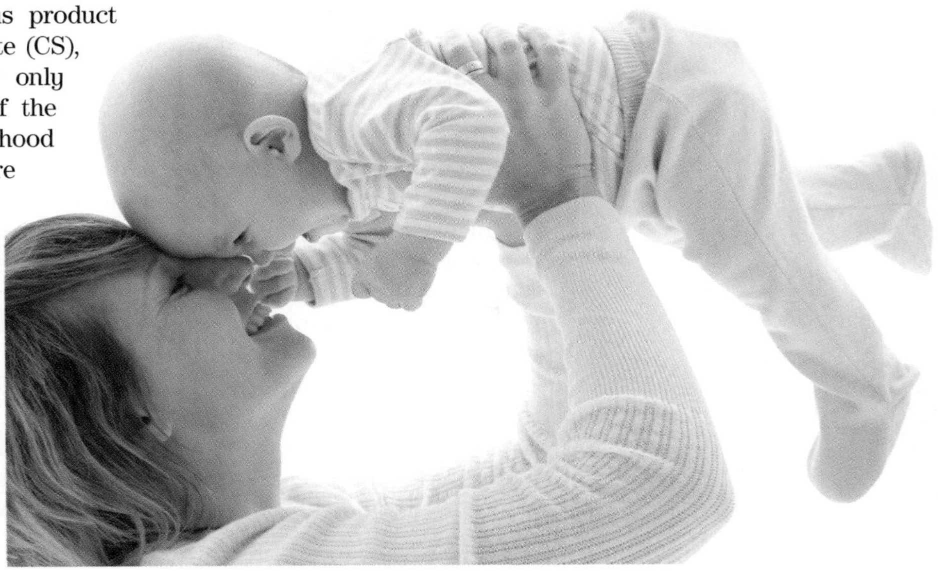

A smile is inherently rewarding for babies. According to the principles of operant conditioning, the more often the baby is rewarded with a smile for smiling at mom, the more likely he will continue to smile at her.

Reinforcement can be positive or negative—not in terms of being good or bad, but in terms of whether a stimulus is added to a situation (positive) or taken away (negative). **Positive reinforcement** occurs when the presentation or addition of a stimulus to a situation increases the likelihood of a behaviour. Giving extra credit points for turning in homework on time would be positive reinforcement if it led to students submitting their assignments on time. We use the term **negative reinforcement** to refer to the removal of a stimulus to *increase* behaviour. Frequently, the stimulus removed is something unpleasant. As an example, consider the many ways we try to reduce pain. If you have a painful headache, you might take ibuprofen to try and get rid of it. The headache is painful and taking medication can remedy this, so in this case, the *removal* of the painful stimulus is negative reinforcement for taking ibuprofen.

positive reinforcement
the presentation or addition of a stimulus after a behaviour occurs that increases how often that behaviour will occur.

negative reinforcement
removal of a stimulus after a behaviour to increase the frequency of that behaviour.

Is the distinction between positive and negative reinforcement important? Some behavioural psychologists have argued that it is unnecessary and, at times, difficult to make (Baron & Galizo, 2006; Michael, 1975). Here is an illustration of how this distinction can be confusing. Let's say you drink coffee to wake up. From one perspective, the wakefulness induced by the caffeine is positive reinforcement for drinking coffee. But are you really increasing wakefulness or decreasing fatigue (which would be negative reinforcement for drinking coffee)? Either way, the consequence for behaviour is the same—you drink more coffee.

Negative reinforcement is often confused with **punishment,** which is any stimulus that *decreases* the frequency of a behaviour. Like reinforcement, punishment can be positive or negative. Remember, however, that punishers *decrease* the frequency of behaviour. By definition, negative reinforcers *increase* desired behaviours, and so they cannot be punishers.

punishment
stimulus, presented after a behaviour, that decreases the frequency of the behaviour.

Typically, when most people think of punishment, they think of **positive punishment,** the addition of a stimulus that decreases behaviour. A classic example of a positive punisher is spanking. Spanking a child (adding a stimulus) is positive punishment if it decreases the undesirable behaviour. **Negative punishment** decreases behaviour by removing a stimulus, usually a desirable

positive punishment
the addition of a stimulus that decreases behaviour.

negative punishment
the removal of a stimulus to decrease behaviour.

stimulus. For example, revoking a child's TV-watching privileges for repeatedly hitting a sibling is a form of negative punishment if it stops the hitting. Figure 7.7 summarizes positive and negative forms of punishment and reinforcement.

Skinner emphasized that reinforcement is a much more effective way of modifying behaviour than is punishment (Skinner, 1953). Specifically, using reinforcement to increase desirable behaviours works better than using punishment in an attempt to decrease undesirable behaviours. Let's say a girl hit her brother because she said he took away her toy. Instead of punishing the girl for hitting her brother, the parents could reinforce more desirable behaviours for dealing with the stolen toy—such as the girl's telling her brother that it upset her that he took the toy and suggesting that if he would please give it back, they could share it for a while. When the little girl acts in this preferable way, the parents could commend her—perhaps give her special privileges (like more play time). This, in turn, would increase the likelihood of the girl's using something more appropriate than physical retaliation to deal with theft. Punishment, as it focuses on decreasing or eliminating behaviours, doesn't tell kids what they should be doing—only what they shouldn't be doing. Reinforcement offers them an alternative.

Challenge Your Assumptions
True or False? Negative reinforcement is the same as punishment.
False: All reinforcement, including negative, *strengthens* behaviour, whereas all punishment *weakens* behaviour.

How Operant Conditioning Works The basic idea behind operant conditioning is that any behaviour that is reinforced becomes strengthened and is more likely to occur in the future. Behaviours are reinforced because they are instrumental in obtaining particular results. Understanding operant conditioning is therefore crucial to the psychological study of motivation. Motivated behaviour is usually adaptive, since it directs us to benefits, like food, and keeps us away from dangers, such as pain. However, when motivated behaviour becomes excessive, as the case with drug addiction, it can be problematic. As you will learn by the end of the chapter, the rules of operant conditioning have been helpful in understanding normal *and* abnormal behaviour and have resulted in innovative treatments for psychological disorders.

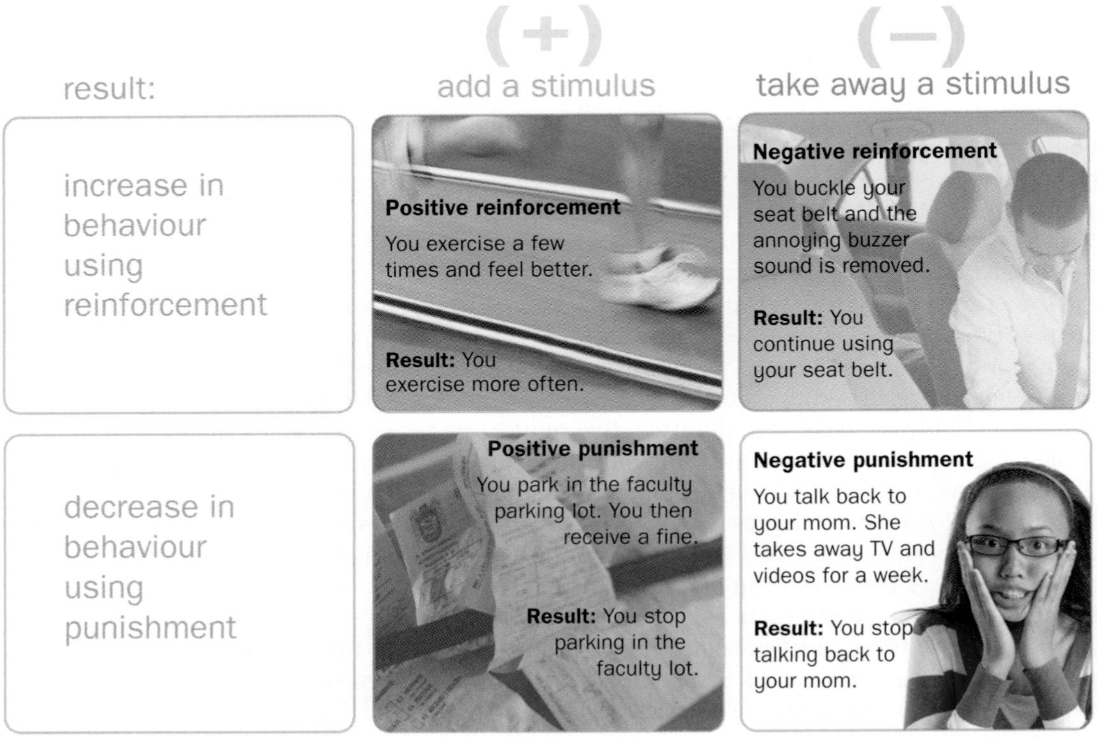

(+)
(−)
result:
add a stimulus
take away a stimulus
increase in behaviour using reinforcement
Positive reinforcement
You exercise a few times and feel better.
Result: You exercise more often.
Negative reinforcement
You buckle your seat belt and the annoying buzzer sound is removed.
Result: You continue using your seat belt.
decrease in behaviour using punishment
Positive punishment
You park in the faculty parking lot. You then receive a fine.
Result: You stop parking in the faculty lot.
Negative punishment
You talk back to your mom. She takes away TV and videos for a week.
Result: You stop talking back to your mom.

FIGURE 7.7
POSITIVE AND NEGATIVE REINFORCEMENT AND PUNISHMENT IN OPERANT CONDITIONING.

To test his conditioning principles, Skinner created the **Skinner box,** a simple chamber in which a small animal can move around, with a food dispenser and a response lever to trigger food delivery (see Figure 7.8). This simple apparatus offered several advantages over Thorndike's puzzle box (see Figure 7.5), mainly because animals tested in a Skinner box could make many responses to obtain reinforcement, compared to only one response (escape) in Thorndike's puzzle box. Therefore, it is possible to determine the effort the animal is willing to make for a particular consequence, allowing a direct measurement of motivation. For instance, we know that a food-deprived animal will make more operant responses for food than a recently fed one (Moscarelloa et al., 2009). The Skinner box itself has been modified in recent years to allow for the delivery of a variety of reinforcers, both positive and negative, as well as computer collection of responses, but many laboratories still use chambers very similar to Skinner's original device.

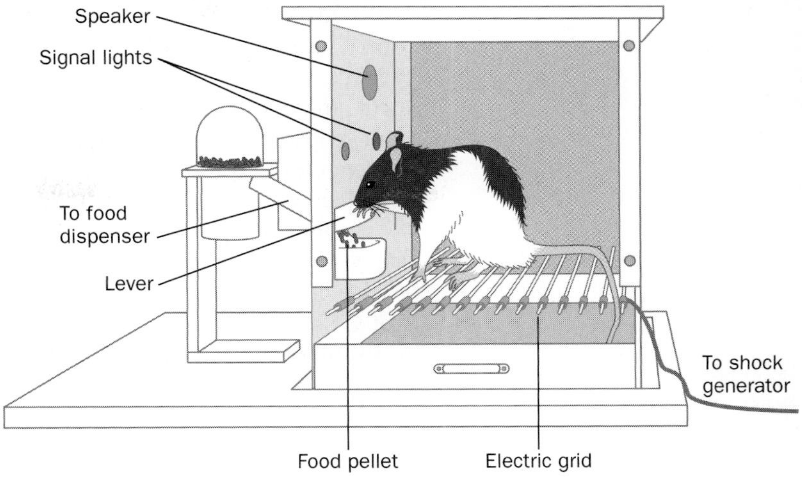

FIGURE **7.8**

THE SKINNER BOX. This modern Skinner box provides a small space in which the rat can move and a lever to press that delivers food as a reinforcer. A small region of the floor can be set up to deliver a shock as a punisher. The rats learn through punishment to avoid that region of the floor.

Skinner box
simple chamber used for operant conditioning of small animals.

How exactly does someone study operant conditioning? How can you get a rat to press a lever? Not surprisingly, rats have no inherent interest in lever pressing. You might give the rat a food pellet for pressing the lever, but how do you get the animal to press the lever in the first place?

Skinner trained a rat to perform a desired behaviour (such as lever pressing) by reinforcing behaviours that occurred when the rat came closer and closer to pressing the lever. If you put a rat in a Skinner box, sooner or later in its exploration of this new environment, it will come close to the lever. If you reinforce that behaviour by giving it some food, the rat makes an association between getting closer to a particular region of the chamber and food appearing. More specifically, the rat learns that the appearance of food seems to be contingent on getting over to that region of the chamber. Gradually reinforcing behaviours that come closer and closer to the target behaviour will eventually produce the target behaviour. For example, you could then increase the requirements for food presentation, such that brushing up against the lever will be reinforced with a food pellet. Finally, the rat has to press the lever to get the food. The reinforcement of successive approximations of a desired behaviour is called **shaping.**

shaping
the reinforcement of successive approximations of a desired behaviour.

Professional trainers rely on shaping to get animals to perform tricks or to assist people with handicaps. But does shaping work with humans? You have probably used shaping if you've ever tried to teach someone a new task. Let's say you are trying to teach your friend how to drive a car with a stick shift. The first time he tries, even if he makes a few mistakes and stalls a few times, you might give him lots of encouragement and praise. Later, when you are trying to get him to master changing gears smoothly, you give praise only when each movement is done correctly. You are reinforcing successive approximations of the desired behaviour, and as your student gets closer and closer to the goal, the criteria for reinforcement become more stringent. By the 15th attempt, bucking forward a couple of metres before stalling gets no praise.

Through shaping and reinforcement, pigeons can learn to discriminate colours.

Just like in classical conditioning, an operant response will also undergo extinction if the learned association is weakened. In operant conditioning, extinction occurs when a behaviour stops being reinforced. So if a rat presses the lever and repeatedly gets no food, the lever-pressing behaviour will decrease and eventually disappear. If you keep leaving phone messages for someone you want to ask on a date, but he or she never returns your calls, eventually you will stop calling. The phone calling behaviour has been extinguished. Figure 7.9 compares classical and operant conditioning.

Operant conditioning offers a powerful method for modifying behaviour in the treatment of clinical disorders in humans, such as phobias (severe, specific fears), addictions, and learning disabilities (Anthonisen et al., 2005; Lamb et al., 2004; Lovaas, 1987). A notable and beneficial application of operant conditioning is in the treatment of autism. (See "Psychology in the Real World.")

	Classical conditioning	Operant conditioning
basic principle	Learning to associate a conditioned stimulus (CS) and a conditioned response (CR).	Reinforcement increases the frequency of a behaviour. Punishment decreases the frequency of a behaviour.
nature of behaviour	The behaviour is based on an organism's involuntary behaviour: its reflexes. The behaviour is elicited by the unconditioned stimulus (US) or conditioned stimulus (CS).	The behaviour is based on an organism's voluntary action. The consequence of the behaviour creates the likelihood of its increasing or decreasing the behaviour.
order of events	Before conditioning occurs, a US leads to a UR. After conditioning, a CS leads to a CR.	Reinforcement leads to an increase in behaviour. Punishment leads to a decrease in behaviour.
example 	 A bee stings a child (US). The child feels pain (UR) from the sting. The child then develops a strong fear (CR) when the child sees bees (CS).	 **Negative reinforcement** Buckling a seat belt removes the annoying buzzer, so you're more likely to buckle the seat belt again. 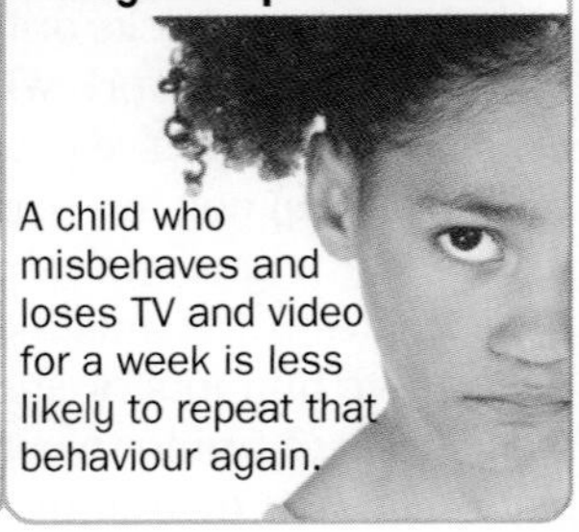 **Negative punishment** A child who misbehaves and loses TV and video for a week is less likely to repeat that behaviour again.

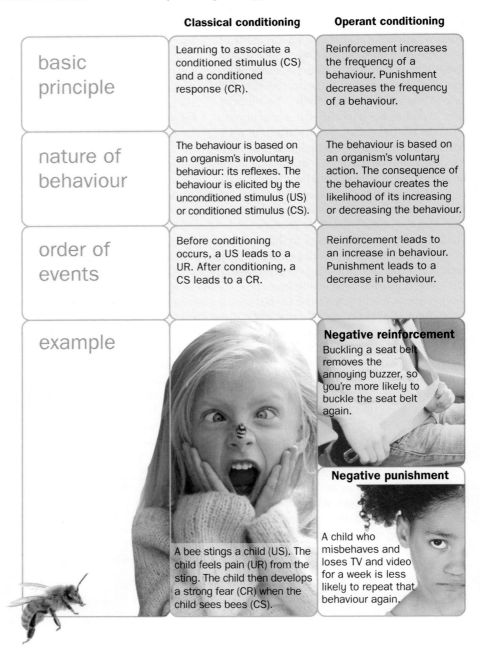

FIGURE **7.9**
DIFFERENCES BETWEEN CLASSICAL AND OPERANT CONDITIONING.

Psychology in the Real World

Treating Autism with Applied Behaviour Analysis

Autism is a debilitating developmental disorder that usually appears in the first few years of life. It is characterized by drastic deficits in communication and language, social interaction with others, emotional expression and experience, and imaginative play (Kanner, 1943). At one time, autism was considered relatively rare, but with greater awareness and diagnosis, it has become a major mental health concern. Recent estimates suggest that autism affects anywhere from 41 to 45 out of every 10 000 children between the ages of five and eight and that the rate is four times higher in boys than in girls (Fombonne, 2003).

It was long assumed that autism was untreatable. Because many children with autism are unresponsive to social interaction, psychotherapy is largely ineffective. Yet certain behavioural strategies offer the promise of modifying inappropriate social responses. The best-known behavioural treatment for autism is applied behavioural analysis (ABA), developed by Ivar Lovaas at UCLA.

Based on operant conditioning theory, ABA uses reinforcement to increase the frequency of adaptive behaviours in autistic children and, in some cases, punishment to decrease the likelihood of maladaptive behaviours. The intensive program involves ignoring harmful or undesirable behaviours such as hand flapping, twirling, or licking objects, as well as aggressive behaviours. It also involves reinforcing desirable behaviours, such as interaction with others, simple speech, and appropriate toy play. Typically, the program involves at least two years of treatment for 35–40 hours per week.

In his original study of ABA in 39 children, Lovaas (1987) found that almost half of the autistic children who started treatment at about 30 months of age went on to perform normally in Grade 1. Only 2 percent of the controls did. Also, intelligence test scores of children in the experimental group were significantly higher by age seven than in the control group. Follow-up studies of these children at about 13 years of age showed that these gains endured (McEachin, Smith, & Lovaas, 1993). Apparently, ABA can produce long-lasting beneficial effects for young autistic children.

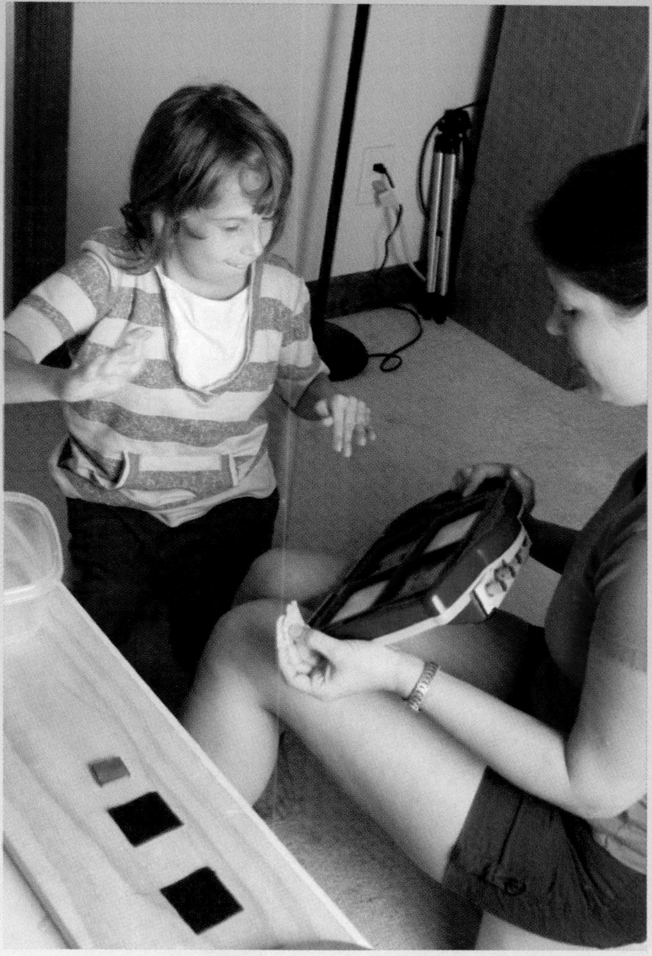

The behaviour strategies taught in ABA have been most effective in improving language skills and communication, reducing violent behaviours, and enhancing school performance. Recent reports suggest, however, that behavioural programs for autism such as ABA and others do not effectively treat the social and emotional deficits of autism (Lord & McGee, 2001). Nevertheless, ABA remains the most effective treatment for autism, especially in terms of school performance and life skills (Beadle-Brown, Murphy, & Wing, 2006).

LO5 **Schedules of Reinforcement** So far we have only considered examples where reinforcement follows every operant response (such as giving a dog a biscuit *every* time he sits), an arrangement termed **continuous reinforcement.** However, reinforcers can be arranged (or scheduled) to follow behaviour under a variety of conditions or rules. It is unlikely that you are rewarded with a "Hello" every time you call a friend's phone number, yet this behaviour does not extinguish the first time you get a voice message or busy signal. **Intermittent reinforcement**

continuous reinforcement
reinforcement of a behaviour every time it occurs.

intermittent reinforcement
reinforcement of a behaviour—but not after every response.

schedules of reinforcement patterns of reinforcement distinguished by whether reinforcement occurs after a set number of responses or after a certain amount of time has passed since the last reinforcement.

fixed ratio (FR) schedule pattern of intermittent reinforcement in which reinforcement follows a set number of responses.

variable ratio (VR) schedule pattern of intermittent reinforcement in which the number of responses needed for reinforcement changes.

(also called *partial reinforcement*) does not occur after every response. As you will learn in this section, both the timing and consistency of reinforcement have substantial effects on behaviour.

Intermittent reinforcement produces a stronger behavioural response than continuous reinforcement does. Why? The explanation has to do with memory and expectation. If an animal gets a food pellet every time it hits the lever, it will likely remember and expect that food will appear each time it presses the lever. But if it sometimes receives food after one lever press and other times it takes five or ten presses, the animal will not learn a predictable pattern. It will keep responding as fast as possible in hope that eventually it will receive food, because it is not sure when food will come.

It is well documented that intermittent reinforcement produces stronger responses—both in terms of rate of responding and resistance to extinction—than does continuous reinforcement (Ferster & Skinner, 1957). Think about your own behaviour: How often do you check email each day? Maybe you check it several times a day. Some people are essentially "addicted" to email and check it dozens of times a day. This behaviour is very easy to explain in terms of operant conditioning. Occasionally, a very important or interesting (reinforcing) email arrives. But we don't know when the next one will come (intermittent), so we check and we check, each time hoping for that important email. This behaviour is shaped by intermittent reinforcement.

Skinner identified four patterns of intermittent reinforcement, which he called **schedules of reinforcement** (see Figure 7.10). These schedules can be distinguished on the basis of whether reinforcement occurs after a set number of responses or after a certain amount of time has passed since the last reinforcement.

In a **fixed ratio (FR) schedule,** reinforcement follows a set number of responses. The pattern becomes predictable, and so the response rate is not steady. Typically, there will be a pause in response immediately after reinforcement occurs, and then the response rate will increase. The FR schedule produces a steep, step-wise pattern of response, as shown in Figure 7.11. An example is being paid by the number of units a worker produces, whether the units are pajama sets or pizzas delivered. A worker whose wages or tips depend on the number produced will work faster to make more money.

A **variable ratio (VR) schedule,** in which the number of responses needed for reinforcement varies, produces a very steady rate of response, because the individual is not quite sure how many responses are necessary to obtain reinforcement (see Figure 7.11). VR schedules produce reinforcement around a mean number of responses, but the exact ratio differs for each trial. So the mean may be set at 10 responses, but some trials may require 10 responses for reinforcement, some 20, some 5, some 7, and so on. An example of a device that delivers reinforcement on a VR schedule is the slot machine. The player cannot know how many pulls of the slot machine arm it will take to win. On one occasion it might take just one pull to win a small jackpot. Other times dozens of quarters might be spent before winning. Casinos

FIGURE **7.10**

SCHEDULES OF REINFORCEMENT. Workers who are paid for the number of units produced are reinforced on a fixed ratio schedule. Winnings from playing slot machines vary in amount and in the interval between payoffs (variable ratio). An example of fixed interval reinforcement would be going to class right before a scheduled exam and not attending lecture after taking an exam. Continuing to redial a friend who doesn't respond to "call waiting" until you get an answer illustrates a variable interval reinforcement schedule, because the number of times you have to redial varies over time.

What schedule of reinforcement does Tim Hortons' "roll up the rim" follow?

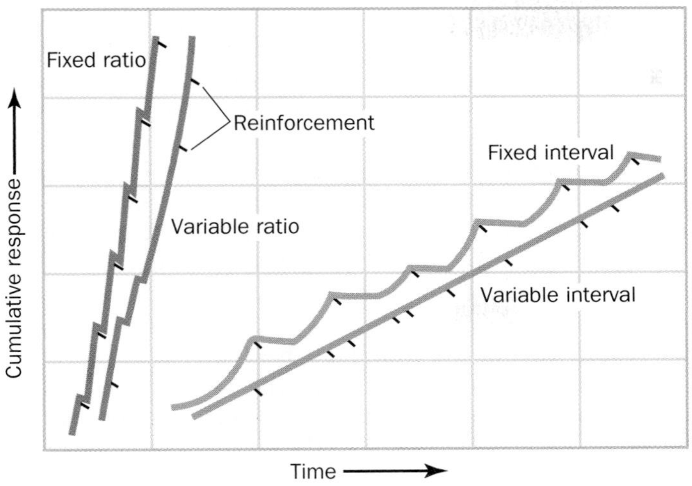

FIGURE **7.11**

EFFECT OF DIFFERENT SCHEDULES OF REINFORCEMENT ON LEARNING. Different schedules of reinforcement lead to different rates of response. Each hatch mark indicates when a reinforcer is administered. Ratio schedules of reinforcement result in more of the reinforced behaviour being performed over a given amount of time (the two steep slopes) than interval schedules of reinforcement (the two flatter slopes). Also, the fixed interval schedule leads to the classic "scallop" effect, which indicates that responses decrease immediately after the reinforcer is administered and then increase again as the next reinforcer draws near.

make a lot of money capitalizing on the steady rate of response produced by a variable ratio schedule—gamblers do not.

In a **fixed interval (FI) schedule,** reinforcement always follows the first response after a set amount of time, say, every four seconds. This produces a response pattern in which the rate of response immediately following reinforcement is low. The response rate accelerates as the time of reinforcement approaches. A graph of the FI schedule produces a scalloped pattern, as seen in Figure 7.11. An example of the effects of a fixed interval schedule of reinforcement might be studying behaviour before and after a test. If tests are given every four weeks, students learn that immediately after the test their performance will not be evaluated, so we would expect to see a drop in rate of studying at that time. The same is true of class attendance before and after exams.

fixed interval (FI) schedule pattern of intermittent reinforcement in which responses are always reinforced after a set period of time has passed.

In a **variable interval (VI) schedule,** the first response is reinforced after time periods of different duration have passed. The researcher sets a mean interval length around which the intervals will vary. For example, the mean interval may be five seconds, but sometimes reinforcement occurs after ten seconds, sometimes after one second, sometimes after five seconds, and so on. The variable nature of the interval makes it difficult for the subject to predict when reinforcement will occur. Variable interval schedules therefore produce a steady, moderate rate of response (see Figure 7.11). Suppose, for example, you are trying to reach a good friend on the phone, but every time you call you get her voice mail. You can tell she is on the line already. So you keep calling back every few minutes to see if she is off. Her conversation can last only so long. Eventually, she will pick up the phone (your reward), but the wait time is unpredictable. In other words, reinforcement follows a variable interval schedule.

variable interval (VI) schedule pattern of intermittent reinforcement in which responses are reinforced after time periods of different duration have passed.

Looking again at Figure 7.11, we can see that fixed schedules show pauses in response after reinforcement. (Note the scalloped pattern for FI and step-wise pattern for FR.) In contrast, variable schedules tend to yield a steadier rate of responding and greater resistance to extinction. (Note the smoother lines for the VR and VI schedules on the right.) Also, ratio schedules tend to produce more rapid responses than interval schedules, as seen in the steep slopes of the FR and VR curves.

Challenges to Conditioning Models of Learning

Traditional learning theory assumes that the principles of conditioning are universal. That is, classical conditioning and operant conditioning each work pretty much the same way in different species of animals. In fact, Skinner maintained that given the proper reinforcement, almost any animal could be taught to do almost anything.

Skinner's faith in universal principles of learning was so strong that he was convinced that what he learned about a rat or pigeon in a conditioning chamber was representative of most species' learning in any context. In one sense Skinner was correct. The biochemical processes involved in learning and memory are the same in slugs as in humans (Kandel, 2006). Skinner was also suggesting that we could understand learning by training behaviour, not because it is inherently interesting to us or to the animal, but rather because trained behaviour is easily observed. The specific species or the behaviour does not make a difference. As we are about to see, however, some of the basic assumptions of conditioning models of learning did not go unchallenged.

LO6 **Biological Constraints on Conditioning** Are species really interchangeable? And is learning to press a bar equivalent to learning to play the piano? Over many years, it has become clear that the notion of the equivalence of species and tasks is problematic. As it turns out, there are limits to what different species will learn and how they will learn it.

Ironically, this conclusion first appeared from the research of two of Skinner's students, Keller Breland and Marian Breland. Initially, the Brelands (1961) successfully applied traditional operant conditioning principles to shaping all kinds of behaviours in many kinds of animals. In fact, they successfully conditioned 38 different species and more than 6000 animals. When they turned their attention to species whose learning behaviour had not been studied, however, they began to experience failures. For example, when they tried to condition different animal species to insert poker chips into a vending machine, raccoons rubbed them instead of putting them in the slot machine, pigs rooted them with their snouts, and chickens pecked at them. When describing the raccoons' "problematic behaviour," Breland and Breland wrote, "The rubbing behaviour became worse and worse as time went on, in spite of non-reinforcement. . . . These egregious failures came as a rather considerable shock to us, for there was nothing in our background in behaviourism to prepare us for such gross inabilities to predict and control the behaviour of animals with which we had been working for years" (Breland & Breland, 1961, p. 683).

Initially, the Brelands considered such behaviour misguided and even titled their article "The Misbehaviour of Organisms." Eventually, however, they became convinced that these behaviours were not "misbehaviours" but normal expressions of innate instincts. It seems that raccoons naturally wash, pigs root, and chickens peck. Breland and Breland (1961) called this effect **instinctive drift,** which they defined as learned behaviour that shifts toward instinctive, unlearned behaviour tendencies.

instinctive drift
learned behaviour that shifts toward instinctive, unlearned behaviour tendencies.

biological constraint model
view on learning proposing that some behaviours are inherently more likely to be learned than others.

Instinctive drift challenges the behaviourist conviction that learning always results either from associating an event with an unconditioned stimulus or from shaping by reinforcement or punishment. The Brelands' findings imply that there are biological limitations, or constraints, on learning. According to the **biological constraint model** of learning, some behaviours are inherently more likely to be learned than others (Garcia, McGowan, & Green, 1972; Seligman & Hager, 1972). In other words, biology constrains, or limits, options so that the adaptive ones are more likely to occur than the maladaptive ones.

Connection

What is innate about language learning?

See Chapter 8, LO5.

Constraints on learning have positive evolutionary implications: They guide individuals in a direction that speeds up learning and aids survival or reproductive success. This model serves to explain instinctive drift. Humans are geared to learn language—one could say we "instinctively drift" toward speaking. It is very easy for us to learn to speak, assuming we are simply exposed to language early in infancy and childhood. Reading, writing, and arithmetic, however, are not so easily learned, which is one reason why we need to go to school to learn these skills.

Imprinting Not all forms of learning depend on reward and reinforcement. A good example is **imprinting,** the rapid and innate learning of the characteristics of a caregiver within a very short period of time after birth (Lorenz, 1935, 1937). Mammals and birds, which are born helpless, need to form a strong bond to a caregiver almost immediately after birth to avoid getting lost or being killed by a predator. We know this from **ethology,** the scientific study of animal behaviour, and especially from the work of Austrian ethologist Konrad Lorenz, who won the 1973 Nobel Prize in medicine. Lorenz studied imprinting extensively in birds. He observed that soon after they hatched, ducklings and goslings (baby geese) would learn to follow whomever they saw most, be it a mother duck or goose or, surprisingly, a human. This parent figure tends to be the first moving object the young animal sees within the first few days of life. Usually, this figure is the animal's mother, but it need not be, as Lorenz found out when he became an imprinted parent to a flock of goslings.

imprinting
the rapid and innate learning of the characteristics of a caregiver very soon after birth.

ethology
the scientific study of animal behaviour.

Imprinting provides clear evidence of a *sensitive period* in learning: a period when a particular type of learning occurs very readily if an animal is exposed to a particular stimulus or situation. The brain seems to be primed at a particular time for a particular kind of learning. Once the animal has moved beyond that sensitive period, it becomes much harder, if not impossible, to learn certain skills or make use of certain kinds of information. Once a "parent" has been imprinted on young ducks or geese, that learning is permanent and cannot be unlearned. Imprinting, in other words, can be learned soon after birth—or not at all. After a certain age, imprinting cannot be learned, unlearned, or relearned—it cannot be modified at all.

Although imprinting does not occur in humans, young babies do develop an important attachment with their primary caregivers that serves much the same function (see Chapter 10). Imprinting and sensitive periods in learning remind us that the mind is not a blank slate, able to learn anything at any time, given the right reinforcers and stimuli. The brain is structured in such a way that certain kinds of experiences are more or less easily learned at different periods in life; language learning by humans is one example, as discussed in Chapter 8.

Biological constraints provide an excellent example of the limits nature places on nurture. Biology makes it possible for humans, but not chimpanzees, to talk. Experience interacting with the capacity for speech determines not only whether an individual learns to talk, but also the language learned. Later in the chapter, we explore some groundbreaking research that revises traditional thinking about classical conditioning within the limits of biology.

LO7 **Latent Learning** Even before the Brelands studied biological constraints and learning, other psychologists challenged some of the basic assumptions of learning theory. One was Edward Tolman. Like many other learning researchers, Tolman ran rats through mazes. In one key study, hungry rats were randomly assigned to one of three groups (Tolman & Honzick, 1930). Rats in Group 1 were rewarded with food if they reached the end of the maze. Rats in this group became better and better at maze running, thanks to the reliable reinforcement of a food reward. Rats in Group 2 received no food for their work, and not surprisingly, they never ran the maze very well. They had no reinforcement. These results are what standard behaviourism would predict.

The rats in Group 3, however, received no reinforcement for running the maze—at least not at first. Like

Konrad Lorenz and goslings.
Why are these goslings following Konrad Lorenz?

Group 2, they did not run the maze very well. But after a set of non-reinforced trials, they started being reinforced with food for their maze running. Suddenly, these rats started running the maze really well. It was as if they had been learning all along. In fact, the Group 3 rats even started performing better than the rats in Group 1.

latent learning
learning that occurs in the absence of reinforcement and is not demonstrated until later, when reinforcement occurs.

How might we explain this outcome? Tolman argued that the rats in Group 3 had been learning all along—they just didn't show it before they started being reinforced. This type of learning is called **latent learning,** which is learning that occurs in the absence of reinforcement and is not demonstrated until later, when reinforcement occurs. Tolman reasoned that these rats had formed internal *cognitive maps*—like pictures in their minds—of the maze from all the practice they had received. When they finally had rewards waiting for them, the rats could use these maps to run the maze more efficiently. Although it is impossible to determine if the rats really had formed mental maps of the maze, it is clear from these findings is that learning can occur in the absence of reinforcement. Running the maze, even without rewards, helped the rats in Group 3 run much better when reinforcement was available.

Connection
How can people with severe long-term memory problems learn if they cannot remember?

See Chapter 6, LO1.

Tolman's work was very important because it set the stage for future work on the role of thought in learning, something that Skinner (1990) and other behaviourists deemed irrelevant. Tolman's work also showed that prior experience—whether reinforced or not—aids future learning. Further, it suggested that motivation plays a part in learning. The idea of latent learning implies that learning sometimes stays hidden until the learner is motivated to perform.

Quick Quiz 7.1: Basic Processes and Conditioning Models of Learning

1. Using the definition provided in the text, which is the best example of learning?
   a. A plant moves toward the sun in order to get the best sunlight.
   b. A newborn baby automatically grabs a finger that is placed in her palm.
   c. A cat perks up its ears and looks toward the sound after a bell has rung.
   d. Ten-year-old Jerry can snowboard down the mountain after practising for a week.
2. Because we always use a can opener to open his food, Spalding the cat runs into the kitchen each time he hears someone open the drawer where the can opener is kept. According to the text, Spalding has
   a. remembered what cat food is.
   b. made an association between the drawer opening and being fed.
   c. habituated to noises in the kitchen.
   d. none of the above.
3. A rat presses a lever, resulting in food delivery. The rat then presses the lever more frequently. This is an example of
   a. punishment.
   b. higher-order conditioning.
   c. reinforcement.
   d. extinction.
4. In a typical classical conditioning experiment, a neutral stimulus is
   a. repeatedly paired with the UR.
   b. not paired with any other stimulus.
   c. repeatedly paired with the CS.
   d. repeatedly paired with the US.
5. A reinforcer is anything that _____; a punisher is anything that _____.
   a. makes a behaviour less likely; makes a behaviour more likely
   b. makes a behaviour more likely; makes a behaviour less likely
   c. is positive; is negative
   d. is shaped; is extinguished
6. A slot machine player cannot know how many pulls of the slot machine arm it will take to win. On one occasion it might take just one pull to win a small jackpot. Other times dozens of quarters might be spent before winning. This payout schedule is what kind of schedule of reinforcement?
   a. fixed interval
   b. fixed ratio
   c. variable interval
   d. variable ratio
7. Because Konrad Lorenz was the first and only animal they knew for the first few weeks of their life, baby geese thought Lorenz was their "mother." This kind of association is known as
   a. reinforcement.
   b. imprinting.
   c. learning.
   d. conditioning.

Answers can be found at the end of the chapter.

Groundbreaking Research

Conditioned Taste Aversion

Remember our story about an aversion to chocolate doughnuts caused by an episode of seasickness after eating a doughnut? This was a case of **conditioned taste aversion,** the learned avoidance of a particular taste when nausea occurs at about the same time as the food. Whether or not the food actually causes the sickness, it is experienced that way in future encounters. In the 1960s, experimental psychologist John Garcia made a remarkable discovery. His groundbreaking research went beyond the limits of conditioning to explain how we learn aversion to tastes.

conditioned taste aversion
the learned avoidance of a particular taste or food.

John Garcia

THE TRADITIONAL LEARNING MODEL

Traditional learning theory would explain conditioned taste aversion as a special case of classical conditioning, in which a neutral or even pleasant taste is linked with the unconditioned causes of nausea. This learned association (say, between a doughnut and nausea) is not much different from the one made by Pavlov's dogs (see Figure 7.12). The catch is that classical conditioning requires repeated pairings of the CS and the US to create and maintain a conditioned response. But in the case of the chocolate doughnut, the doughnut (the CS) acquired the ability to induce nausea (CR) after a brief pairing with the motion of the boat (US), more than 30 minutes after the doughnut was eaten. Garcia's work helped explain how the CR could last for years without repeated pairings of the CS with the US.

REFINING THE LEARNING MODEL

Garcia had always been curious about taste aversion because his mother had a lifelong aversion to chocolate due to one bad experience (Garcia, 2003). Yet he began studying taste aversion almost by accident. In research designed for other purposes, he noticed that rats receiving frequent low doses of radiation ate and drank less than normal. Garcia wondered whether the rats had developed a taste aversion for the food and water they had consumed during the radiation period. He and his colleagues (1955) at the U.S. Naval Laboratory decided to look more closely at this phenomenon. They would try to condition rats to develop an aversion to a taste they liked—saccharin water. They began with the following questions:

1. Could taste aversion to saccharin water occur by pairing the taste with radiation (a US for nausea)?
2. How long would the taste aversion last without repeated exposure to radiation (the US)?

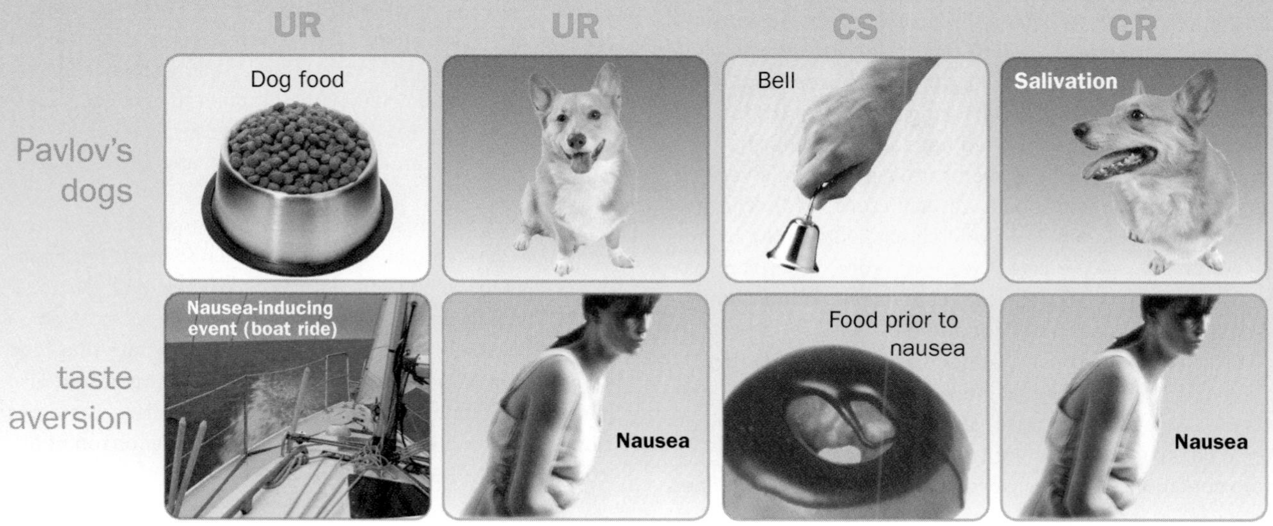

FIGURE 7.12
CLASSICAL CONDITIONING MODEL OF TASTE AVERSION.

Garcia's team varied the type of fluid presented during a radiation period (plain water or saccharin water) and the radiation exposure level (none, low, or moderate dose). One control group had access to plain water during a six-hour period of exposure to radiation (irradiation). Another control group received saccharin water and no radiation. In the experimental conditions, rats received saccharin water during periods of low or moderate irradiation. According to traditional classical conditioning, US and CS must be paired very closely in time—typically no more than a few seconds apart. But in some cases, several minutes passed between the time when the rats were irradiated (US) and when they drank the fluid (CS).

Following the conditioning period in which rats were irradiated or not, all rats were housed in cages with two drinking bottles, one containing plain water and one with saccharin water. At this time, taste aversion was measured, and the dependent variable was how much saccharin water the rats consumed.

There were no changes in the control groups' water preferences, but in the two experimental groups aversion occurred. Regardless of radiation level, rats that had been drinking saccharin water during irradiation consumed significantly less saccharin water after conditioning (see Figure 7.13). This result answered the first question the researchers posed: Rats could be conditioned to avoid a taste they previously liked. Also, the drop in intake of saccharin water lasted for at least 30 days. This finding answered the second question about how long such conditioning might last.

Garcia's subsequent research derailed another assumption of traditional learning theory: that reflexive responses (such as nausea) could be conditioned to any kind of stimulus. Garcia and Koelling (1966) varied the type of aversive stimulus (US) to which rats were exposed and the type of neutral stimulus (CS). Nausea (the UR) was induced by exposure to X-rays, whereas pain (the other UR) was induced by electrical shocks sent through the floor of the cage. When the rat licked the drinking tube, it received the CS of either saccharin water or "bright-noisy water" (plain water accompanied by a light and a buzzer that went on when the rat touched the drinking tube). The US for half the rats was irradiation-induced nausea. The other half received a shock. The irradiated rats avoided the sweet water but not the bright-noisy water (Figure 7.14), whereas rats that received a mildly painful shock avoided the bright-noisy water but not the sweet water (Figure 7.14). The researchers described the first response as "conditioned nausea" and the second as "conditioned fear."

The key finding here is that contrary to the predictions of traditional learning theory, an individual cannot be conditioned to respond to just any "neutral" stimulus paired with an unconditioned stimulus. We can learn certain things only under certain conditions. In other words, nausea can be conditioned to a taste but not to a light, because taste is relevant to eating and light is not.

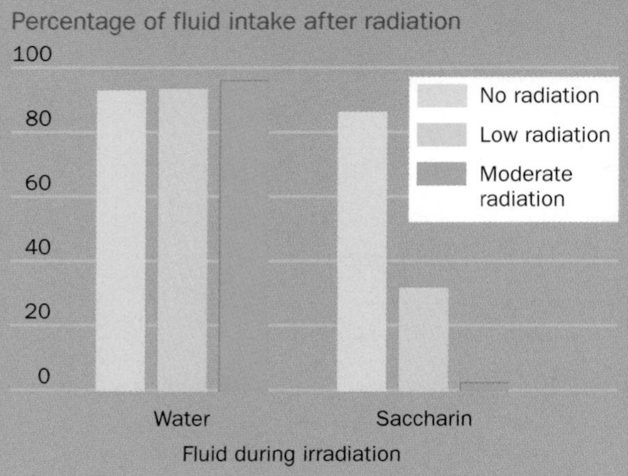

FIGURE **7.13**

CONDITIONED TASTE AVERSION. Compared to rats that received no radiation, rats exposed to radiation (US) while drinking saccharin water (CS), developed a long-lasting aversion to saccharin water (CR). Water intake did not vary much among the control and experimental groups, but the amount of saccharin water consumed by the irradiated rats was significantly less than the amount consumed by the control group. (*Source:* Garcia, Kimeldorf, & Koelling, 1955.)

In sum, Garcia's research on taste aversion undermined two key assumptions of classical conditioning: (1) that conditioning could happen only if an individual was exposed repeatedly within a brief time span to the US and CS together and (2) that individuals can learn to associate any two stimuli. With respect to the first assumption, Garcia showed in other research that the CS and US could be separated by as much as 75 minutes and still lead to conditioned taste aversion (Garcia, Ervin, & Koelling, 1966). With respect to the second assumption, the "bright-noisy water" findings showed that only certain stimuli could be conditioned to produce nausea (Garcia & Koelling, 1966). More specifically, you cannot make someone be nauseated by a sound or a sight as easily as by a taste.

Garcia's findings fit with an evolutionary perspective on taste aversion. In this view, it is very important for organisms to learn which tastes might make them sick. Nausea may follow ingestion of a food by several minutes, even hours. It is valuable to learn quickly to associate that food with nausea in order to avoid contact with the potentially harmful substance again. From this perspective, taste aversion is a distinct evolutionary adaptation (Jacobson et al., 2006; Profet, 1992).

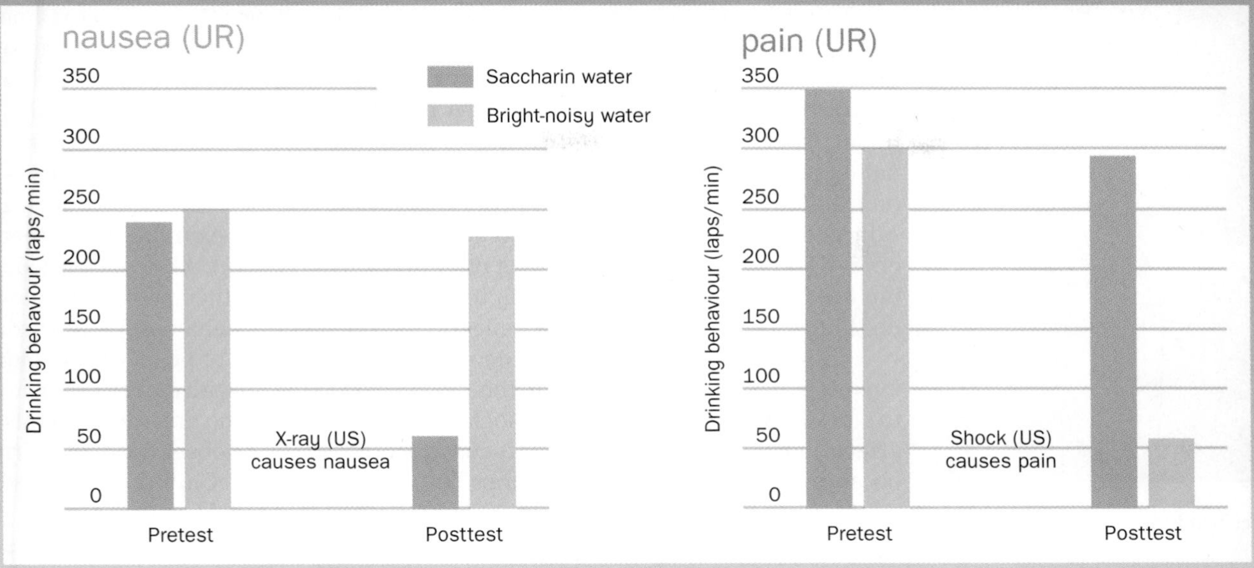

FIGURE **7.14**

LIMITS ON CONDITIONED TASTE AVERSION. Contrary to predictions from traditional learning theory, taste aversion conditioning depends on the stimulus. Conditioned taste aversion occurs only to the kind of stimulus that makes biological sense. For example, nausea produces aversion to taste, but not to noise and light, as shown in the graph on the left. Pain produces aversion to frightening stimuli, such as noise and bright lights, but not to saccharin water, as shown in the graph on the right. (*Source:* Garcia & Koelling, 1966).

LO8 SOCIAL LEARNING THEORY

We all look to others for clues on how to behave. Think about how you first learned to tie your shoes or even to swim. Did someone just explain the way to do it? Or did you try random motions and then get praise from your teacher every time you did something that was right? There may have been some random success, but chances are you learned the right movements by copying what your swim teacher or parent did. There is more to learning than associating one thing with another or doing something and then being reinforced for it. Classical and operant conditioning explain many aspects of learning, but they neglect the powerful role of modelling in the learning process.

Obviously, people learn from their own experience, from their own successes and failures, and from trial and error. But if we had to learn everything that way, not only would the process take much, much longer, but it would also require reinventing what others have already learned, over and over again. Learning by observing others is much more efficient. Canadian psychologist Albert Bandura proposed that we learn both by doing and by observing. Bandura (1986) called learning by doing **enactive learning** and learning by watching the behaviour of others **observational learning.** Bandura's **social learning theory** (1986) goes beyond traditional conditioning approaches to include observation and modelling as major components of learning. **Modelling** is Bandura's term for the process of observing and imitating behaviours performed by others. Modelling is everywhere. Younger children mimic the behaviour of their older siblings. We pick up figures of speech and mannerisms from our closest friends.

enactive learning
learning by doing.

observational learning
learning by watching the behaviour of others.

social learning theory
a description of the kind of learning that occurs when we model or imitate the behaviour of others.

modelling
the imitation of behaviours performed by others.

Albert Bandura

Connection

Do you think watching violence in movies and TV leads to aggressive behaviour? Overwhelmingly, the answer seems to be yes.

See Chapter 14, LO10.

Modelling is only one aspect of social learning theory. According to Bandura (1986), social learning also works through reinforcement. Remember from operant conditioning that the consequences of our behaviour influence whether we repeat those behaviours. People learn best those things they are rewarded for doing, whether the rewards are external (such as praise, money, candy) or internal (such as joy and satisfaction). Bandura noted that reinforcement matters not only for the person carrying out the behaviour, but also for those who watch. Advertisers make use of this phenomenon all the time. For example, when teenagers see young adults getting a lot of attention and having fun while they are drinking beer, they might be more likely to want to drink beer themselves. People will do things they see others doing, especially if the model's behaviour is rewarded.

Bandura and his colleagues demonstrated the power of observational learning in a series of classic studies in the 1960s. They came up with clever experiments to show how two key elements of social learning—modelling and reinforcement—affect behaviour. The first study focused on the power of observational learning on aggressive behaviour (Bandura, Ross, & Ross, 1961). Children observed an adult either being aggressive or not with an inflatable doll, called a Bobo doll. Half saw the adult play politely with the Bobo doll. The others saw the adult sock the Bobo doll hard, hit it with a rubber mallet, and kick it around. Afterwards, one at a time the kids entered a room filled with toys (including the ones the model played with) and were allowed free play. Children who saw the adults act aggressively with the doll were much more likely to be aggressive when they had the chance to play with the Bobo than those who saw the adults play pleasantly with the doll. In fact, they adopted many of the same actions the adults used. So these initial studies demonstrated the power of modelling in the learning of aggression.

Another key study showed how reinforcement works with modelling to lead to learning (Bandura, Ross, & Ross, 1963). Again using an experimental design, this time the researchers introduced another variable: What happened to the models after they behaved aggressively? Here's how they set it up. The children saw one of four films: one with no models, one with two adult men who interacted in a non-aggressive manner, and two films with adult men who played aggressively with each other, but in one the aggressive man was punished whereas in the other he was rewarded. The first two films (no model and non-aggressive models) were control conditions, whereas the last two (aggression) were experimental conditions. In the films shown to the experimental groups, one man was aggressive toward the other man. The aggressive man hit the non-aggressive man with a rubber mallet and shot darts at him. He also roughed up the inflatable Bobo doll. A key element of this study is that the films also showed what happened to the

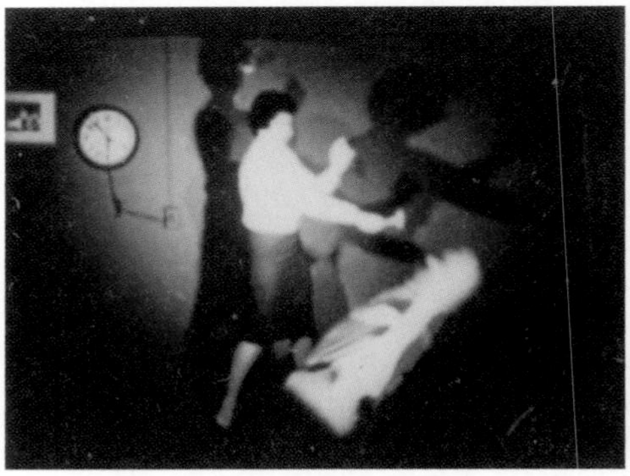

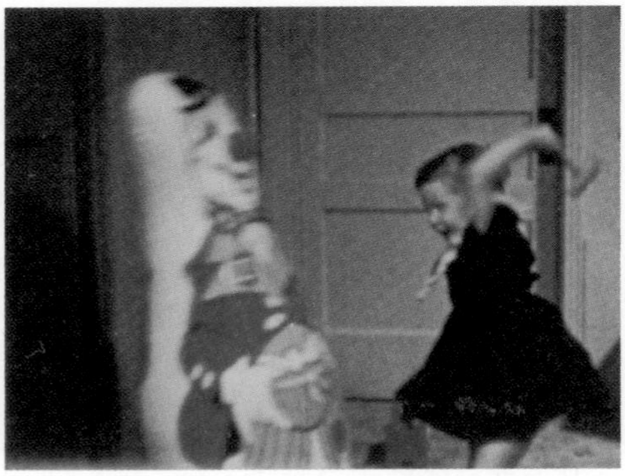

Children who observed an adult model being aggressive with a Bobo doll (top) in a study by Bandura tended to behave aggressively when given the opportunity to play with the doll (bottom).

What kind of learning is this? What conditions might increase the likelihood of children modelling this adult behaviour?

aggressive adult after the interaction. There were two possibilities. The aggressive adult was either punished (he lost the conflict and ended up cowering in the corner) or rewarded (he won the conflict and got to play with all the toys) for his aggression. The research design is summarized in Figure 7.15.

After seeing the film, the children had an opportunity to play with the Bobo doll and other toys they saw in the film. Just as in the previous set of studies, how the kids acted with the doll and other toys was the main dependent variable. The primary finding from the previous study was replicated: Those who viewed aggression were more aggressive with the doll than those who did not see aggression (see Figure 7.16). But the consequences for the model also mattered. The children who saw the aggressive adult rewarded for his aggression were more violent with the toys and Bobo doll than those who saw the aggressive adult get punished. Those who did not see an aggressive model did not show much aggression with the toys, nor did those who saw the adult punished. These studies show how modelling and reinforcement can work together to influence behaviour. Kids are more likely to copy behaviour that they see others being rewarded for.

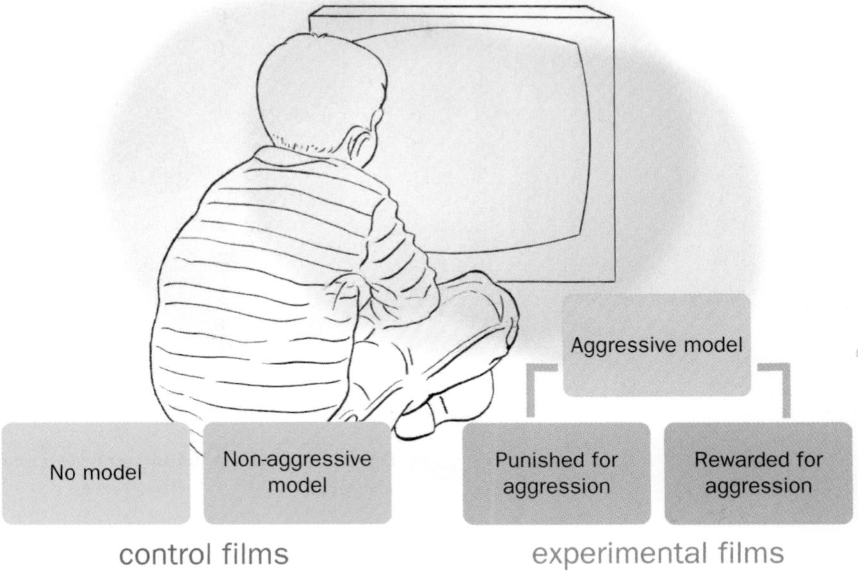

FIGURE **7.15**

EXPERIMENTAL DESIGN FOR BANDURA'S STUDY OF OBSERVATIONAL LEARNING AND AGGRESSION. Children viewed one of four films: one with no model, one with non-aggressive adult models, or one of two with an aggressive adult model where the model is either rewarded for being aggressive or punished for it. (*Source:* Bandura, Ross, & Ross, 1963)

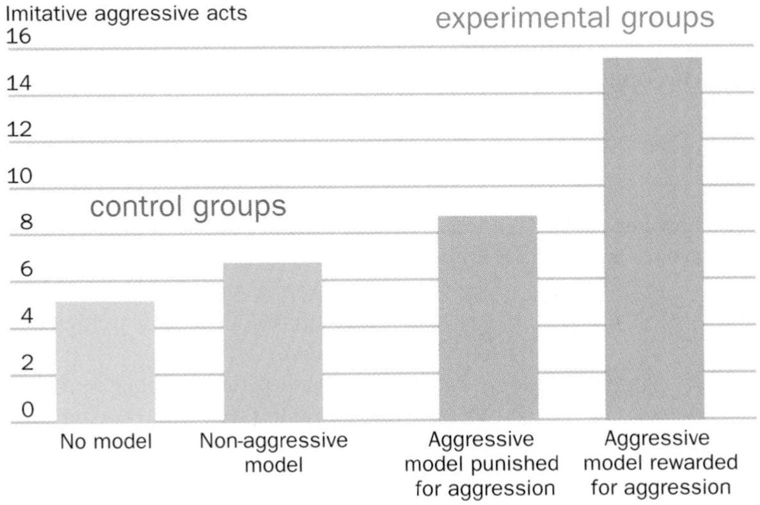

FIGURE **7.16**

EFFECT OF MODELLING AND REWARD ON LEARNED AGGRESSIVE BEHAVIOUR. This graph depicts the number of imitative aggressive acts by children who viewed one of four film conditions. The children who saw the aggressive adults get rewarded for their aggression showed more aggressive acts, such as hitting the Bobo doll with a hammer or punching it, than did the children in the other three categories. (*Source:* Bandura, Ross, & Ross, 1963)

Challenge Your Assumptions

True or False? Children are not affected by watching violent cartoons or movies.

False: Experimental research shows that watching violent films increases aggressive behaviour in children.

Do you think there is too much violence on TV? What effect might this have on viewers?

Connection

Even very brief exposure to violent video games can make people less responsive when watching films of real-life violence.

See Chapter 14, LO10.

The Bobo doll studies were pivotal in showing how children learn aggression and other violent behaviours from viewing aggression in others. The results, of course, have implications for the effect of violence on television, in movies, and in video games on children and teens. Numerous studies have demonstrated that kids behave more violently after exposure to violence in the media (Bushman & Anderson, 2001). Consider this startling real example: Two teenage lovers, Ben Darras and Sarah Edmondson, apparently under the influence of drugs and Oliver Stone's movie *Natural Born Killers*, went on a killing spree. The movie depicted two young lovers, on a wild and drug-filled rampage, callously killing and robbing people. After the copycat killers were arrested, they claimed they had also taken drugs and played Stone's movie in a continuous loop all night ("Natural Born Copycats," 2002).

Quick Quiz 7.2: Social Learning Theory

1. Barbara just started a new job, and she watches how her colleagues dress and act. The type of learning Barbara is doing is known as
   a. observational learning.
   b. enactive learning.
   c. operant conditioning.
   d. reinforcement.
2. The major finding(s) from Bandura's so-called Bobo doll experiments were that
   a. children learn to be aggressive by watching other people be aggressive.
   b. children learn to be aggressive by observing whether aggression in others is reinforced.
   c. children learn to be aggressive only if they see someone of the same sex be aggressive.
   d. both a and b are correct.
3. Research generally shows that children
   a. are not at all likely to be aggressive after watching aggression on TV or in movies.
   b. are likely to be aggressive after watching aggression on TV or in movies.
   c. are more aggressive after watching aggression on TV or in movies only if they are from impoverished backgrounds.
   d. know the difference between movies and real life and are not influenced by movie violence.

Answers can be found at the end of the chapter.

LO9 THE BIOLOGICAL BASIS OF LEARNING

The early behaviourists refused to study anything that could not be directly observed, including mental processes and any potentially relevant biological structures. Watson and Skinner, in particular, took the position that all learning was a function of either stimuli (classical conditioning) or consequences (operant conditioning), both of which come from the outside environment. Although Skinner acknowledged the role of genetics in behaviour, he and Watson ignored the role of cognitive and brain processes in learning, because these could not be observed (Skinner, 1938, 1990). Likewise, the behaviourists did not consider any form of instinctive behaviour worthy of scientific study.

As we have seen, behaviourism sprang in part from a desire to study behaviour in a measurable way. In behaviourism's heyday, there simply was no technology available for observing brain function or measuring its activity. When such technologies began to appear in the 1950s, the behaviourist model was challenged from various angles. Learning, it turns out, is not just an environmental process. It results from the constant interaction of the brain and the environment. Biology makes learning possible and learning changes biology. Extreme forms of behaviourism paint a picture of learning resulting primarily from the experiences one has. It is an extreme environmental, or nurture-only, view. Few modern behaviourists agree with such a one-sided view.

Neuroanatomy of Classical and Operant Conditioning

It is impossible to confine the associative learning processes discussed in this chapter to a single brain region, since the methods used to study learning involve multiple perceptual, memory, and motor systems. However, certain brain regions appear to have unique roles in classical and operant conditioning. As you learned in Chapter 6, the amygdala is active during both encoding and retrieval of emotional memories. Most of the examples of classical conditioning discussed in this chapter have involved USs that evoke strong emotions, such as pleasure or fear, so it should not be surprising that the amygdala is involved.

Classical conditioning to emotional stimuli has been studied in both humans and animals using a procedure called fear conditioning, a technique quite similar to the experiments with Little Albert. Typically, individuals are presented with a neutral stimulus (such as a tone) immediately before an aversive stimulus (such as an electric shock). Later if the tone is presented alone, individuals show fear responses such as changes in heart rate and blood pressure. Human imaging studies consistently reveal an association between activation of the amygdala and the acquisition of conditioned fear (Sehlmeyer et al., 2009). Animal lesioning studies confirm the importance of the amygdala in fear conditioning. A common measure of conditioned fear in laboratory rodents is a defensive behaviour called freezing, whereby the animal stops all movement in response to a CS (Le Doux, 1996). In one study, when control mice were conditioned to associate a tone (CS) with an electric shock (US), they showed enhanced freezing behaviour when the tone was later presented alone. Mice with amygdala damage showed very little freezing behaviour, suggesting that an intact amygdala is necessary to make the new association (Desmedt et al., 1998). In addition to its role it fear conditioning, the amygdala also appears be important in classical conditioning to positive USs, such as tasty foods. In fact, distinct neuronal populations are activated during conditioning of CSs to positive and negative emotional stimuli (Paton et al., 2006).

Classical conditioning can have powerful effects on motivated behaviour. For instance, if a food deprived rat is associates a CS with food, later presentation of the CS alone promotes feeding in the rats, even after they have been fed enough to regain pre-deprivation weights. This effect involves the amygdala as well as parts of the hypothalamus and frontal lobes (Holland & Petrovich, 2005). CSs associated with addictive drugs, such as cocaine, also activate these brain areas, and can trigger drug-seeking behaviour (Stewart, 2008). One region of the brain that has a unique role in reward-seeking behaviour is the nucleus accumbens, a small forebrain region with connections to the amygdala and motor systems. Human imaging studies show that this part of the brain becomes activated by stimuli that are associated with rewards, such as money (Knutson et al., 2001). The neurotransmitter dopamine plays an important role in the nucleus accumbens, since blocking dopamine in this area reduces the amount of effort that rats will make in order to receive food (Salamone et al., 2007) or addictive drugs such as cocaine (Thomsen et al., 2009). Figure 7.17

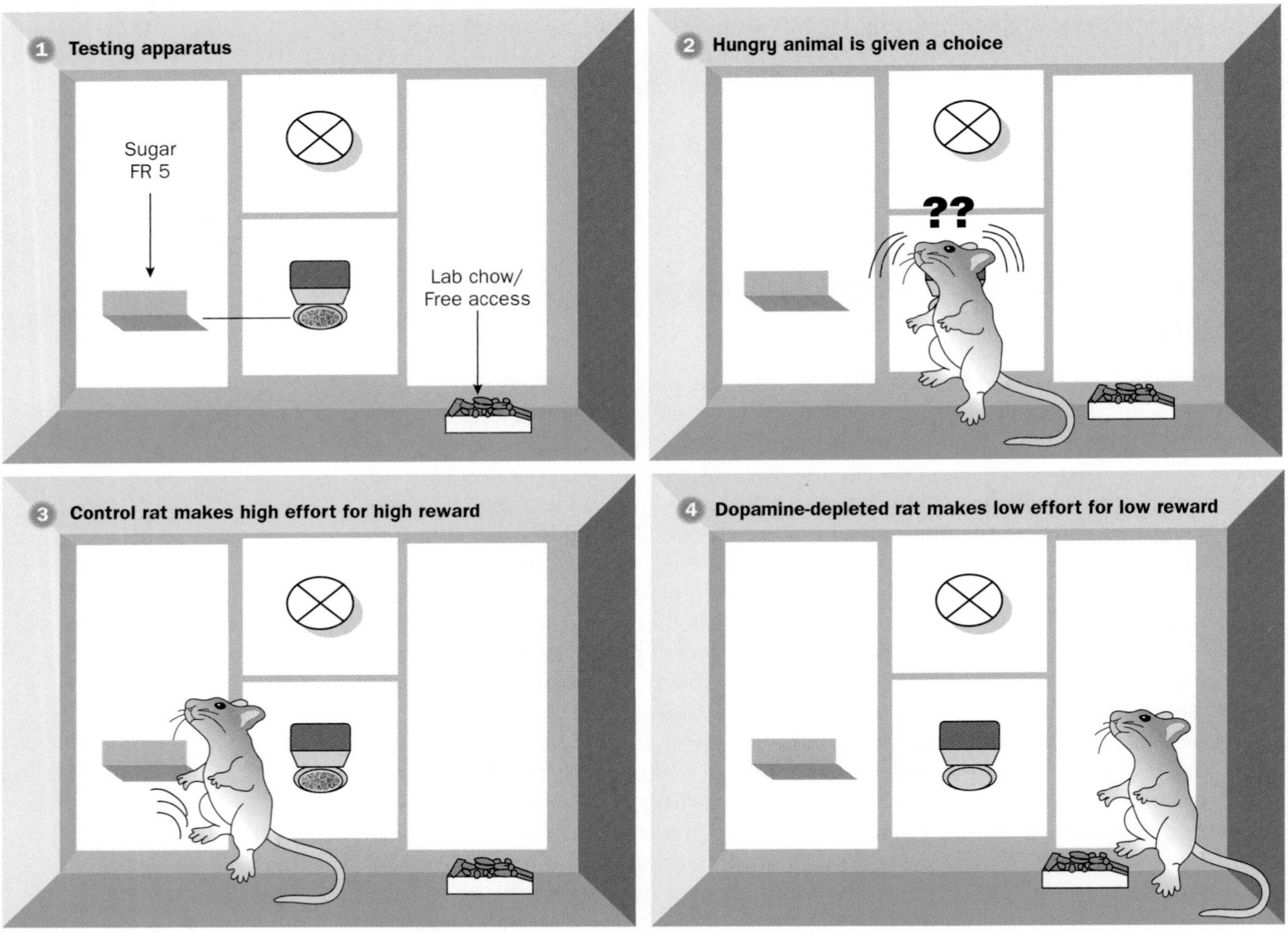

FIGURE **7.17**

THE EFFECT OF BLOCKING DOPAMINE ON MOTIVATED BEHAVIOUR. Rats with an intact dopamine system work harder for a tasty food reward compared to standard lab chow. (1) Methods used to test the effort for reinforcement; lab chow is provided freely, whereas five lever presses (FR5) results in a more palatable food reinforcer. (2) Food-deprived rats are introduced into the Skinner box and allowed to choose a reinforcer. (3) Control rats will make the extra effort to obtain the palatable food. (4) Rats that have had their dopamine depleted will choose the less effortful task, even if it means a less desirable reinforcer. (*Source:* Figure re-drawn by J.D. Salamone and M. Correa, based on Salamone, J.D., Correa, M., Farrar, A., and Mingote, S.M. (2007). Effort-related functions of nucleus accumbens dopamine and associated forebrain circuits. *Psychopharmacology, 191(3);* Fig.2, 461–82.)

shows the effect of dopamine blockade on responding for food reinforcement.

Imitation, Mirror Neurons, and Observational Learning

Like father, like son. We learn by observing and imitating others.

Humans imitate one another. Imitation is fundamental to the way in which human and non-human primates learn. As we discussed in the section on social learning theory, classical and operant conditioning do not take into account the powerful role of imitation in the learning process. Infants begin copying the behaviour of adults and other children almost immediately. Babies as young as seven hours old imitate simple adult facial expressions (Meltzoff & Moore, 1977, 1983).

Imitation by infants may be a result of mirror neuron systems in the brain (Lepage & Théoret, 2007). As discussed in Chapter 3, humans and other primates have mirror neurons that respond in much the same way while watching an action as they do while performing an action (Iacoboni & Mazziota, 2007; Rizzolatti et al., 1996; see Figure 7.18).

Simply put, for some neurons in the frontal lobe of the cerebral cortex, the experience of watching someone else do something is like doing it yourself. When a monkey observes another monkey or a human grab a peanut, the same neurons fire in the frontal lobe as fire when the observing monkey actually grabs a peanut (Fogassi & Ferrari, 2006). It is likely that mirror neuron systems are involved in imitation and social learning (Filimon et al., 2007; Iacoboni et al., 1999). Autistic children, who have trouble imitating others' gestures, may have deficits in mirror neuron systems (Oberman & Ramachadran, 2007; Williams et al., 2006).

Connections

Do mirror neurons explain newborns' ability to imitate grown-ups who stick out their tongue?

See Chapter 10, LO8.

Are mirror neurons behind much imitation seen in social interaction?

See Chapter 15, LO3.

Synaptic Change during Learning

If you've ever tried to learn a second language, you know that if you don't use it for a while, you forget what you've learned. Similarly, you will probably forget much of the material you learn in this class soon after the exam, even if it is learned well to begin with. Why is that?

In Chapter 6 we saw what Hebb's work on learning and memory revealed about the plasticity of the brain: "Neurons that fire together wire together" and "Use it or lose it." We also discussed Kandel's studies on the sea slug *Aplysia*. Both areas of research provided experimental evidence of the neural basis of learning and memory (Kadel, 2006; Pinsker et al., 1973). Specifically, certain proteins become activated in short- and long-term memory formation and learning. These proteins change pre-existing synaptic connections and cause the growth of new synapses (Fields, 2005; Kandel, 2001). What this means is that learning, in a real sense, *is* the growth of new synapses. Synaptic connections between neurons become stronger and even grow during long-term associative learning (Leuner et al., 2003). The brain literally grows and changes as we learn, through the development and frequent use of new synaptic connections.

Yet these same synaptic connections will weaken if they aren't used regularly, resulting in forgetting and the loss of learning. So when we stop using learned information, the synapses that support our knowledge weaken and ultimately degrade. Practice, use, and rehearsal are important in retaining what we have learned. If you play a musical instrument, you know that the more you

Research Process

1 Research Question

Rizzolatti and colleagues (1996) were studying neurons involved in hand movements in monkeys, when they made an accidental discovery: The same motor neurons fired when the monkey observed an experimenter grabbing an object as when the monkey made a similar action itself. It made the researchers wonder: Does the brain contain neurons that rehearse motor actions during observational learning?

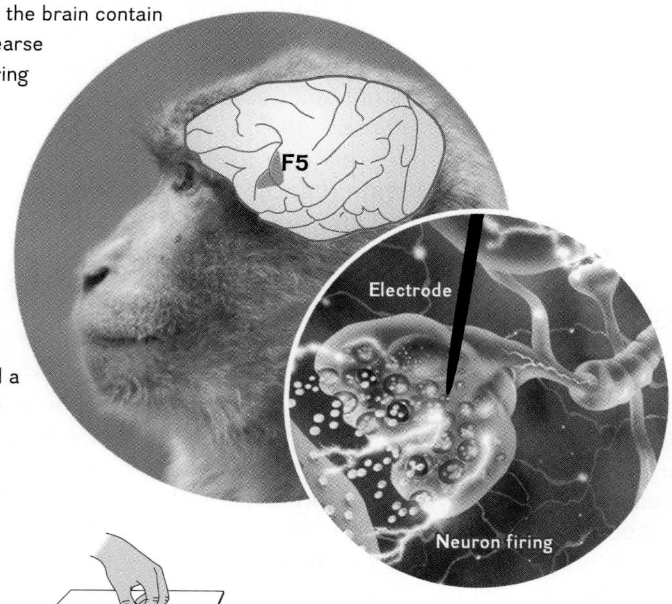

2 Method

In a descriptive study of two monkeys, the researchers monitored activity of individual neurons in the motor cortex. They implanted a wire electrode in the motor cortex (area F5) and measured the firing rate of a single neuron while the monkey either grasped a piece of food itself or saw the experimenter pick it up.

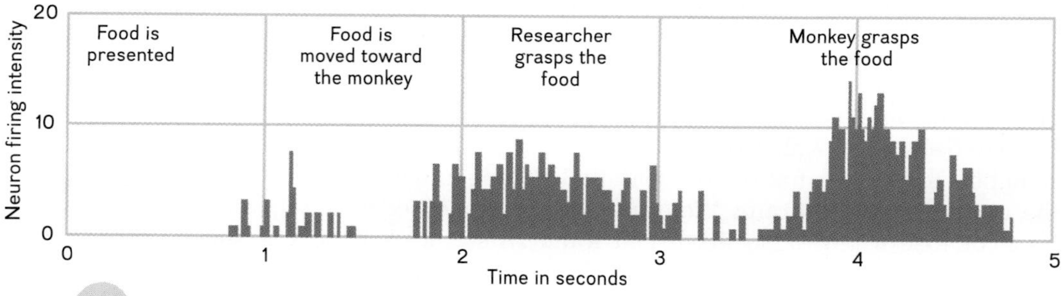

FIGURE **7.18** **THE DISCOVERY OF MIRROR NEURONS.** Mirror neurons in the brain respond in much the same way while watching an action as they do when performing an action. (*Source:* Rizzolatti, G., Fadiga, L., Gallese, V., & Fogassi, L. (1996). Premotor cortex and the recognition of motor actions. *Cognitive Brain Research, 3,* 131–141.)

3 Results

The graph shows the results of firing patterns in area F5 when food is presented, when it is moved toward the monkey, when the researcher grasps food, and when the monkey grasps food. The peaks of the graph are taller when the firing rate in area F5 is faster. They are shorter when the firing rate is slower. Notice that there is minimal firing when the monkey simply looks at the food. The firing rates increase during observation of grasping and during grasping itself. More importantly, the pattern of firing is similar when action is observed and when action is made by the monkey itself. Neurons that fire during action and observation of similar actions are called mirror neurons.

4 Conclusion

Mirror neurons support the function of rehearsal during learning. By watching others' actions, we "exercise" the motor regions of the brain involved in making those actions. This, in turn, allows us perform the same behaviour more readily.

practise the scales on your piano or guitar, for example, the easier they are to play. The sensations and movements associated with the increased experience of playing occupy a greater area of your motor cortex and, in effect, change the mapping of touch information in your brain (Pascual-Leone, 2001). If you stop practising, those connections weaken, the brain map changes, and the scales are harder to recall the next time you try to play.

What effect does regular practice have on synaptic connections?

Experience, Enrichment, and Brain Growth

As we have seen again and again, experience changes the brain. Recall the discussion in Chapter 2 of the classic work demonstrating that rats reared in enriched or normal environments grow more neural connections and learn to run mazes faster than genetically identical rats raised in impoverished environments (Bennett et al., 1964; Rosenzweig et al., 1962).

Building on this research, later experiments showed that animals did not have to be raised from birth in an enriched environment to benefit. Laboratory mice, for example, can have identical "childhoods" (the first 21 days of their lives) and then be randomly assigned to three different environments: no enrichment, short enrichment (68 days), and long enrichment (six months). The longer they live in an enriched environment, the more neural growth there is in the hippocampus (Kempermann & Gage, 1999). More importantly, however, simply being in an enriched environment is not even the best way to stimulate the growth of new neurons: Being in an enriched environment that continues to have new and novel forms of stimulation is even better (Kempermann & Gage, 1999). Similar enrichment effects on neuron growth occur in other species besides rats, including birds, primates, and humans (Doetsch & Scharff, 2001; Eriksson et al., 1998; Gould et al., 1994).

Connection

Can experience generate new neurons in an elderly person?

See Chapter 10, LO12.

Challenge Your Assumptions

True or False? Learning strengthens connections in the brain.

True: New experiences stimulate the growth of new neurons in many brain areas, including the hippocampus.

Quick Quiz 7.3: The Interaction of Nature and Nurture in Learning

1. Damage to the _____ results in impairment in _____.
   a. amygdala; observational learning
   b. amygdala; fear conditioning
   c. nucleus accumbens; observational learning
   d. nucleus accumbens; fear conditioning
2. The neurotransmitter dopamine acting on neurons in the nucleus accumbens is important in
   a. making associations between CSs and aversive USs.
   b. making associations between CSs and pleasurable USs.
   c. controlling how hard an animal will work for a positive reinforcer.
   d. habituation to an aversive stimulus.
3. Research on learning and the brain has shown that rats raised in impoverished environments
   a. learn just as quickly as rats raised in enriched environments.
   b. have the same number of neurons in the hippocampus as the rats raised in enriched environments.
   c. learn more slowly but have the same number of neurons and synaptic connections as rats raised in enriched environments.
   d. learn more slowly and have fewer neurons and synaptic connections as rats raised in enriched environments.

Answers can be found at the end of the chapter.

Evaluating Connections in Learning

Addiction as a Learning Disorder?

A national survey by the Canadian Centre on Substance Abuse in 2004 estimated that the annual prevalence rate for use of alcohol was almost 80 percent and was close to 50 percent for other types of recreational drugs (such as cannabis, hallucinogens, and cocaine). However, when asked about the consequences of alcohol and drugs, only 9 percent of respondents reported harm from alcohol use and 18 percent reported harm from other drug use (Canadian Centre on Substance Abuse, 2004). A more recent global study in 2007 revealed that in Canada, drugs with comparatively low rates of prevalence (such as cocaine and opiates) were the drugs most often used by people treated for drug dependence (United Nations Office on Drugs and Crime, 2009). These statistics highlight two issues: First, there is a distinction between recreational drug *use* and problematic drug *abuse,* and second, some drugs have a stronger abuse potential than others. Drug abuse is not restricted to illegal substances: The most common addictions are to legal drugs such as alcohol and tobacco, and many prescription drugs, like morphine and oxycodone, also have high abuse potential.

Understanding why some individuals have difficulty controlling drug intake is a topic of intense debate and controversy. The definition of the term "addiction" itself is contentious; however, most definitions include two key criteria—a loss of control over intake and continued use despite negative consequences (McKim, 2007). Given that addiction involves impaired control over a voluntary behaviour, some consider it to be a disorder of excessive motivation (West, 2001). Drug-seeking behaviour appears to follow the same principles of conditioning that govern food-reinforced behaviour and therefore some researchers consider addiction a "hijacking" of brain processes that ordinarily control typical reward-related learning (von der Goltz & Kiefer, 2009). Here we will explore how the basic processes of associative learning can aid us in understanding addiction.

Addiction is not an immediate result of first drug use; in fact, addiction usually occurs after prolonged drug exposure in three distinct stages: acquisition, maintenance and relapse. Positive reinforcement is critical in the acquisition phase of addiction. Most addictive drugs, whether they are prescription medications or illegal narcotics, produce a subjective experience of euphoria or "high." This high, or pleasurable experience upon initial administration, strongly promotes the likelihood that the user drug will take the drug again. However, the desirable effects of some drugs appear to be more social rather than physical. Think about it: The actual sensory qualities of cigarette smoking on first experience are anything but pleasant—coughing, dizziness, and nausea. But most smokers start smoking as teenagers, and most teens start smoking because they seek some of the rewards that appear to come with smoking: coolness, peer acceptance, looking like an adult. Kids see that others who smoke get some of these rewards for smoking. Thus, they might copy smoking behaviour from their role models in order to obtain these rewards themselves, as Bandura's social learning theory would predict (Bandura, 1969, 1986). Generally speaking, if drugs offer us some reward or benefit, we are more likely to take them again in the future.

In some individuals, behaviour is excessively influenced by the positively reinforcing properties of drugs and leads to continuous use. With persistent drug use, the body's physiology attempts to adapt to the continued presence of the drug by counteracting the way that the body reacts to it, a phenomenon known as *tolerance.* For instance, alcohol acts as a depressant and inhibits neuronal activity, so after prolonged exposure to alcohol, neurons compensate by producing more excitatory receptors. Heavy drinkers are susceptible to seizures when they stop drinking because their brains are made much more excitable by chronic alcohol exposure (Feldman et al., 1997). At this stage in the addiction process, negative reinforcement processes can strongly promote drug-seeking behaviour, since continued drinking can alleviate unpleasant physical withdrawal symptoms. Not all addictive drugs produce severe physical withdrawal symptoms, but most heavy drug users will experience withdrawal in the form of unpleasant cravings once they stop using the drug. Therefore, negative reinforcement is a powerful process in the maintenance phase of addiction.

Having friends who smoke increases the likelihood of smoking.

The negatively reinforcing properties of addictive drugs last as long as the period of withdrawal, usually only a week at the most. Yet, former drug users can relapse years after they successfully quit. For example, after many pairings of cigarette smoke with the presence of nicotine in the blood, the smell of smoke can later act as a trigger because it comes to represent nicotine. Just as Pavlov's dogs made associations between neutral cues and the presentation of food, drug users make associations between cues in their environment and the effects of the drug. Pavlov's dogs reflexively reacted to the anticipation of food by salivating, whereas a drug user reflexively reacts to the anticipation of the onslaught of high levels of the drug by reducing the effect of the drug at the neuron. Neurons will rapidly reduce the number of receptors available to respond to the drug as well as the neurotransmitters to which they bind, resulting in diminished effects (Martini & Whistler, 2007). The result of this process is craving and withdrawal, which makes relapse more likely.

Although associations between a drug's effects (US) and classically conditioned cues (CS) are long-lasting and act as powerful triggers for relapse, they can also be protective. Neuronal receptors that mediate the mood-altering effects of addictive drugs also mediate their lethal effects. A classic experiment performed by Shepard Siegal and his colleagues at McMaster University showed that classical conditioning can protect rats against overdose from heroin. On alternate days, rats were given injections of heroin in their home colony room and control injections (without heroin) in a different room with white background noise. Another group of rats had the same injection schedule, except that the heroin was given in the white-noise room and the control injections in the home colony. A third group of rats was given control injections in both rooms. After one month of injections, enough time to establish addiction to heroin, all rats were given an overdose injection of heroin in one of the two rooms. Rats that received the overdose injection in the environment where they did not get the drug (the unpaired environment) and rats without a history of heroin injections were more likely to die of the overdose. Rats that had an overdose injection of heroin in the environment previously paired with the drug were most likely to survive (Siegel et al., 1982; see Figure 7.19). Although this type of experiment would be unethical to carry out in humans, there have been case studies of heroin overdose resulting from injecting a usual dose in an unusual environment (Gerevich et al., 2005). Without classically conditioned cues to prepare neurons for the arrival of heroin, the user is more susceptible to the lethal effects of the drug, so a typical dose effectively becomes lethal.

Knowledge of the role of associative learning in addiction has led to the development of novel treatments. Certain drugs, like heroin and alcohol, produce withdrawal after prolonged use and therefore become strongly negatively reinforcing because of their ability to alleviate

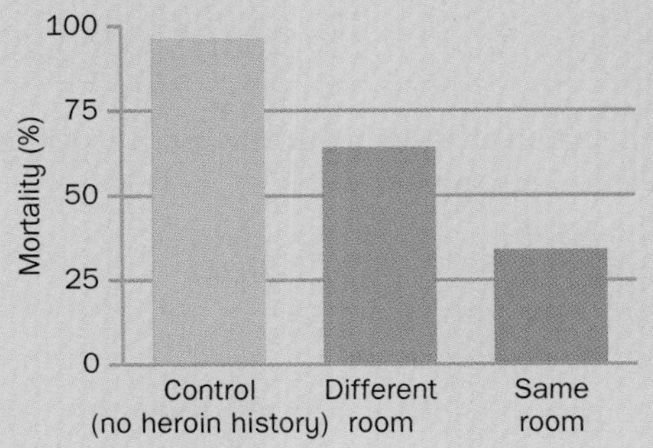

FIGURE **7.19**

CLASSICAL CONDITIONING CAN PROTECT AGAINST OVERDOSE. Experiencing drug effects in a particular environment can result in classically conditioned compensatory responses to the drug. Rats that had an overdose injection of heroin in the same environment as previous injections were most likely to survive compared to rats that received heroin in a different environment, or rats without previous injections.

withdrawal symptoms. **Drug replacement therapy** is often used to avoid withdrawal by providing the user with a less harmful form of the drug or route of ingestion. Methadone is a drug similar to heroin that is often prescribed to addicts because it can be taken orally rather than intravenously and its prolonged action in the body prevents the abrupt appearance of withdrawal symptoms (McKim, 2007). **Behaviour modification** techniques, which apply principles of operant conditioning to changing behaviour, have also been particularly effective in helping people quit drugs, especially when combined with replacement therapies. Smokers who participate in such programs are likely to live longer than those who don't (Anthonisen et al., 2005).

drug replacement therapy a treatment for addiction that involves a less harmful form of the drug to avoid withdrawal.

behaviour modification the application of operant conditioning principles to change behaviour.

If learning processes are important in the addiction process, then why are there such large differences between individuals? Do people who *use* drugs differ in some fundamental way from those who *abuse* drugs? Research shows that personality style predicts drug choices and patterns of abuse, and that certain "addictive" personalities are at particular risk. Four addictive personality types have been well characterized: anxiety sensitive, hopeless, sensation seeking, and impulsive. The first two types use drugs to relieve anxiety and depression symptoms, respectively, and therefore their motivation is based upon negative reinforcement. Sensation seekers use drugs for the thrill or buzz, and so are motivated by positive reinforcement. Impulsive types appear to be less able to control behaviour when presented with reward and punishment cues (Woicik et al., 2009). Personality-based psychological treatments that target motivations behind substance use have been shown to reduce drinking in adult alcoholics and to prevent problem drinking in adolescents (Conrod et al., 2000; Conrod et al., 2008).

Quick Quiz 7.4: Evaluating Connections in Learning

1. The acquisition phase of addiction is dependent upon which learning process?
   a. withdrawal
   b. relapse
   c. positive reinforcement
   d. negative reinforcement
2. A heroin user regularly injects the drug in his bathroom at home. As a result, going to the bathroom at home now triggers a craving for heroin. In this situation, the bathroom has become a
   a. US.
   b. CS.
   c. UR.
   d. CR.
3. Drug use for which personality type is motivated by positive reinforcement?
   a. anxiety sensitive
   b. hopeless
   c. sensation seeking
   d. impulsive

Answers can be found at the end of the chapter.

Chapter Review

BASIC PROCESSES OF LEARNING

- Learning is an enduring change in behaviour that results from experience. It involves changes in sensation, perception, behaviour, and brain function.
- Learning by association is a simple form of learning that links two pieces of information from the environment with one another because, in our experience, they repeatedly occur together.

CONDITIONING MODELS OF LEARNING

- Classical conditioning centres on stimulus–response (S–R) relationships. It involves the modification of reflexes with experience. A conditioned response occurs when a neutral stimulus (such as a bell) elicits what was previously an unconditioned response (such as salivation) to an unconditioned stimulus (such as food) when it is presented alone. After conditioning, the neutral stimulus is called a conditioned stimulus.
- In operant conditioning the consequences of spontaneous behaviour are manipulated in order to elicit the desired behaviour. According to Skinner, certain consequences make a behaviour more likely to occur again. When the consequences of a behaviour increase the likelihood that a behaviour will occur again, we say that the behaviour has been reinforced. Reinforcement can be positive (something added) or negative (something subtracted). In contrast, punishment decreases the likelihood that a behaviour will occur again. The stimuli used for reinforcement and punishment are unrelated to the target behaviour. Shaping is the reinforcement of successive approximations of a desired behaviour.
- Reinforcement may be presented every time a behaviour occurs or only occasionally. Intermittent reinforcement, reinforcement that does not occur after every response, produces a stronger behavioural response than does continuous reinforcement. There are four schedules of reinforcement that dictate how an intermittent reinforcement might be implemented: fixed ratio, variable ratio, fixed interval, and variable interval.
- Biology limits behavioural options in order to make the adaptive ones more likely. The biological constraint

model of learning suggests that some behaviours are inherently more likely to be learned than others. Instinctive drift, in which an organism fails to learn the target behaviour because it conflicts with a stronger instinctive behaviour, is a type of biological constraint.

- Latent learning occurs in the absence of reinforcement and is not demonstrated until later, when reinforcement occurs.

GROUNDBREAKING RESEARCH: CONDITIONED TASTE AVERSION

- Conditioned taste aversion, the learned avoidance of a particular taste or food if sickness occurs at the same time as or shortly after exposure to it, can develop after only one exposure. The time lapse between exposure and getting sick may be an hour or more.
- Biological constraints limit the development of a conditioned response to a neutral stimulus that is relevant to the situation. For example, you cannot make someone be nauseated by a sound or a sight as easily as by a taste.

SOCIAL LEARNING THEORY

- Social learning theory takes into account the role of social influence in learning. Imitation or modelling plays a key role in how we learn, and it can work together with reinforcement to shape behaviour. Bandura proposed that reinforcement makes learning more likely not only for the person doing the behaviour but also for observers.
- Modelling is the process of observing and imitating behaviours performed by others, particularly behaviours that are rewarded in others.

THE BIOLOGICAL BASIS OF LEARNING

- Certain brain regions have distinct roles in associative learning: the amygdala is important in classical conditioning, while the nucleus accumbens influences the amount of effort applied to an operant response, mirror neurons in the cortex are thought to be critical in observational learning.
- Learning strengthens synaptic connections, but these synaptic connections will weaken if they aren't used regularly.
- Living in an enriched environment enhances learning and increases neuron growth in the brain, while living in an impoverished environment has the opposite effects.

EVALUATING CONNECTIONS IN LEARNING

- Drug addiction involves three distinct phases: acquisition, maintenance, and relapse.
- Applications derived from models of learning, such as behaviour modification, may help people unlearn unwanted or undesirable addictive behaviours.
- Particular addictive personality types engage distinct learning processes in their motivations for drug use.

Quick Quiz Answers

Quick Quiz 7.1: 1. d 2. b 3. c 4. d 5. b 6. d 7. b **Quick Quiz 7.2:** 1. a 2. d 3. b
Quick Quiz 7.3: 1. b 2. c 3. d **Quick Quiz 7.4:** 1. c 2. b 3. c

Language and Thought

CHAPTER

8

CHAPTER OUTLINE

Challenge Your Assumptions

True or False?

- ☐ Learning grammar is easy only for highly educated people.
- ☐ Critical thinking involves seeing only the weaknesses and flaws in ideas.
- ☐ People are generally rational in their decision making.
- ☐ People who learn to speak a second language before their early teens are more likely to speak without an accent.
- ☐ Children raised from infancy with two languages (bilingually) seldom confuse the two languages.

LEARNING OBJECTIVES

LO1 Define and differentiate morpheme, phoneme, semantics, syntax, grammar, and pragmatics.

LO2 Explain how human language differs from animal communication as a result of evolution.

LO3 Describe the stages in language development.

LO4 Explain what is meant by a sensitive period in language development.

LO5 Explain and contrast the theories of language acquisition.

LO6 Describe evidence of language learning in non-human species.

LO7 Compare evidence to support the theories of linguistic determinism and linguistic relativity.

LO8 Describe the ways that we represent thoughts in our minds.

LO9 Explain the difference between deductive and inductive reasoning and the relationship to biased thinking.

LO10 Compare and contrast critical thinking, scientific thinking, and metacognitive thinking.

LO11 Describe errors that can arise when using heuristics to solve problems.

As they awaited the birth of their first child, Mike and Lisa had a decision to make: In what language should they raise their child? Mike was born in Greece but had moved to Toronto at age 11, so he was fluent in both Greek and English. Lisa was born and raised in Vancouver; she was fluent in English and conversationally fluent in Greek. They never questioned wanting their daughter to be bilingual in both Greek and English—partly because they believed her thinking would be more flexible from the different language structures (e.g., verbs are in different places). They weren't even aware of the research that confirms this hunch and shows that being bilingual facilitates cognitive and intellectual development and enables flexible, creative thinking; it even appears to delay the onset of dementia later in life (Bialystok & Craik, 2010; Bialystok, Craik, & Ryan, 2006). In short, raising their child bilingually made sense for both cultural and cognitive reasons.

Yet how would Lisa and Mike go about raising their daughter, Zoé, to be bilingual? Would one parent speak one language and the other another language? They chose a different route: They decided they would both speak to her only in Greek from the day she was born. They reasoned that raising Zoé in Canada guaranteed her ease in picking up English quickly from grandparents, aunts, uncles, cousins, neighbours, and playmates. Indeed, research shows that children pick up a culturally dominant language outside the home very quickly and often prefer it (as it is the language of most of their friends), so Greek would need strong support at home. Mike and Lisa would speak only Greek during Zoé's infancy and early childhood, taking annual trips to Greece to visit family.

Some family friends and relatives wondered whether not teaching Zoé the language of her larger environment (English) would confuse her and put her at a disadvantage. Also, wouldn't she try to speak Greek to people who spoke only English? After all, young children don't even have a concept of "English" or "Greek"—they just speak.

Zoé ended up having little trouble in both languages. She is now nine years old and has spoken fluent Greek from toddlerhood and by age five was fluent in English. Given that English is her second language, it is not unusual for her to become fluent later than English-only—speaking children. Most importantly, she intuitively knows who understands which language and never tries to speak Greek to her Canadian relatives or English to her Greek relatives. Interestingly, Zoé had decided by age four or so, however, that at home she wanted to speak English, so now the primary language at home is English. She attends a Greek school once a week and takes long visits with family in Greece, which helps maintain her fluency. Whether coincidence or not, she is quite artistic and creative.

Language is so much a part of being human that we forget it is possible to think without words. However, when we dream, visually imagine something, or experience a strong sensation such as a touch or a smell, our thoughts are not initially word-bound. And surely the thoughts of young babies are not verbal. Still, most of our thoughts are translated into words. Even a smell is quickly labelled as a rose or a cake in the oven, and so it becomes a verbal experience as well as a sensory one. Language and thought appear to develop side by side, with few exceptions. One is not possible without the other, at least in adult humans. Some linguists, in fact, have argued that abstract thought can only have evolved in the context of complex language (Perlovsky & Ilin, 2013).

This chapter introduces the psychology of language and thought, both separately and together. First we look at language by exploring its nature, evolution, and development in humans. Then we turn to current psychological research and theory concerning how we represent our thoughts visually and verbally. We will look at how people reason, form judgments, and make decisions. Finally, we bring all these topics together by examining how and when learning a second language changes our brain and affects our ability to reason, solve problems, and think flexibly. We will continue the discussion of thought in Chapter 9, where we discuss the nature of intelligence, problem solving, and creativity.

THE NATURE OF LANGUAGE

If you lived 300 000 years ago, before language was fully developed, how would you think? How would you communicate if everyone you met could only grunt and groan? Much like the other primates on the planet, you would communicate with other humans only about immediate, concrete states. Everything you knew would be experienced directly through smell, taste, hearing, sight, or touch. Your ability to communicate would be limited chiefly to events in the present; culture and civilization as we know it could not exist without language. Without language, your ways of thinking, understanding, and transmitting knowledge would be very different, since language is more than just a means of communication. To quote linguist Steven Pinker (2000), language is the "jewel in the crown of cognition." As you will see in this chapter, language helps us organize our thoughts.

Bonobos do communicate with one another—not with words, but by using facial expressions and leaving scent markers on the floor of the tropical forests where they live.

If bonobos (pygmy chimps) could speak, what would these two be talking about?

LO1 Language Defined

Linguists define **human language** as an open and symbolic communication system that has rules of grammar and allows its users to express abstract and distant ideas (Bickerton, 1995). *Open* means that the system is dynamic and free to change. One aspect of the "openness" of the English language is exemplified in the addition of several thousand new words every year to the Oxford English Dictionary. *Symbolic* means that there is no real connection between a sound and the meaning or idea associated with it. For instance, nothing about the word "cat" links it to the four-legged meowing creature it represents. Linguists estimate that there are over 7000 different human languages; each is distinct from the other in that native speakers of one cannot understand native speakers of another (Lewis, Simons, & Fennig, 2014). However, each of these languages is also similar enough to one another, and different enough from animal communication, for example, that we can refer to them in the singular as *human language* (Pinker & Bloom, 1992).

human language
a communication system specific to *Homo sapiens;* it is open and symbolic, has rules of grammar, and allows its users to express abstract and distant ideas.

All languages are organized in a hierarchical structure (see Figure 8.1). The smallest units of meaning in a language are called **morphemes,** which are represented by basic consonant and vowel sounds called **phonemes.** For instance, the word *balls* contains two morphemes, the word *ball* and the suffix *-s,* while it contains four phonemes, the sound units represented by "b," "a," "ll," and "s." Languages vary in number of phonemes, with some having as few as 15 and others having more than 80. The English language has about 40 phonemes that can

morphemes
the smallest units of meaning in a language.

phonemes
the smallest units of sound in a language

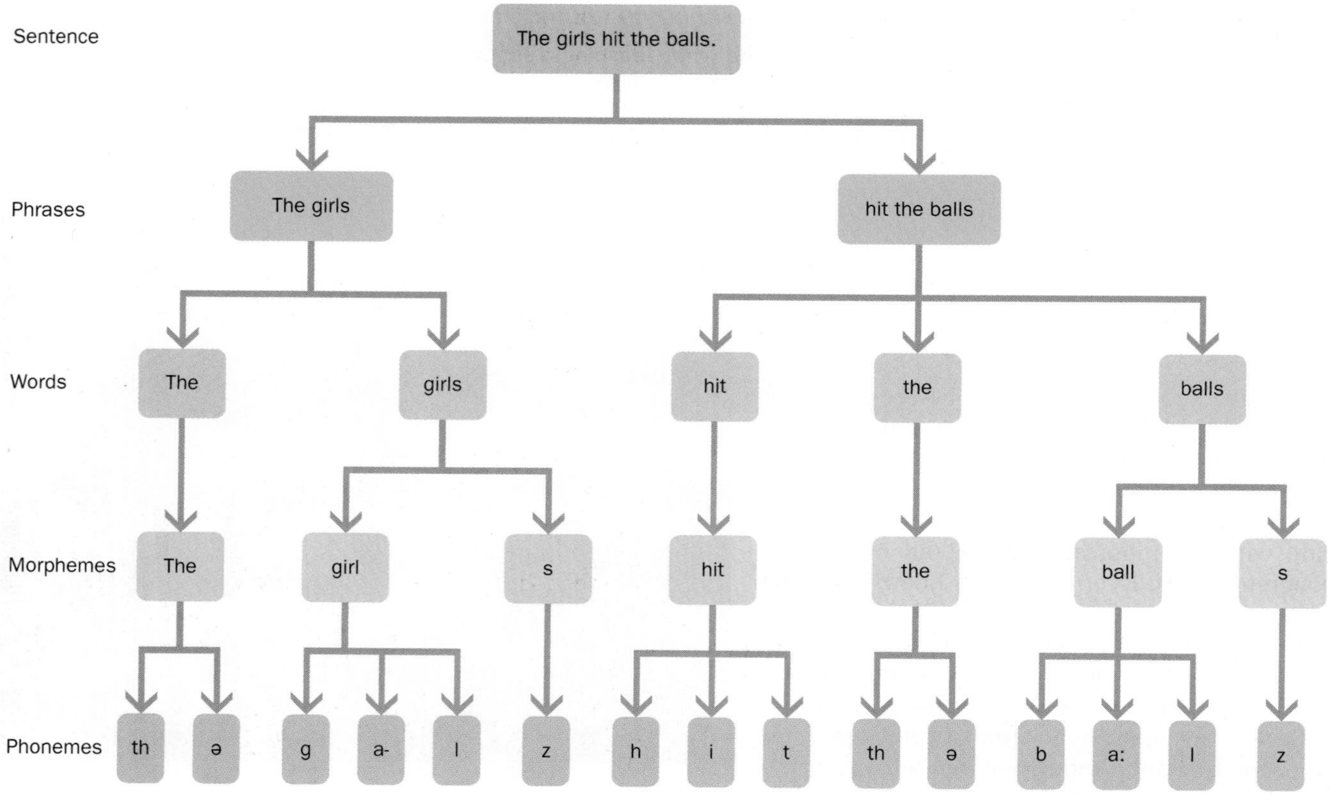

FIGURE **8.1**

THE HIERARCHICAL STRUCTURE OF LANGUAGE. Every spoken language can be broken down into these five levels, with phonemes as the most basic unit. In the row of phonemes, you can see some of the symbols used by linguists to represent specific sounds.

semantics
the meaning derived from words and combinations of words in a language.

syntax
the rules for arranging words and symbols to form sentences or parts of sentences in a particular language.

grammar
the entire set of rules for combining symbols and sounds to speak and write a particular language.

pragmatics
the rules associated with the use of language across social situations.

protolanguage
very rudimentary language, also known as pre-language, used by earlier species of *Homo.*

be combined to form 100 000 morphemes. In turn, these morphemes can be combined to form over 500 000 words. **Semantics** refers to the meaning of words and combinations of words in a language, whereas **syntax** refers to the rules for arranging words and symbols in sentences (or parts of sentences). Consider the following sentences: "Shirin juggled the balls" and "The balls were juggled by Shirin." Both sentences convey the same semantic meaning but they differ in syntax (i.e., in the arrangement of nouns and verbs). **Grammar** comprises the entire set of rules for combining symbols and sounds to speak and write a particular language and includes such matters in English as subject–verb agreement, plurals, and use of possessives.

The symbolic nature of language allows for a great deal of flexibility in expressing meaning. For instance, there are probably hundreds of ways to combine phonemes into morphemes to greet someone: "Hi," "Hello," and "Welcome" all convey a greeting message but have slightly different meanings. Waving your hand to greet someone, a non-verbal gesture, is a much more limited form of communication. The arbitrary nature of the connection between sound and meaning is evident when we consider that we can say the exact same sentence in almost every language in the world. For example, "I am reading the book" can also be "*Je lis le livre*" in French and "Я читаю книгу" in Russian. Although each language has its own distinct sounds for saying the same thing, these sounds are arranged according rules of syntax and grammar, which allow for the expression of meaningful relationships, such as who did what to whom, at what time, and where (Pinker & Jackendoff, 2005).

Social context also influences the meaning of language. **Pragmatics** refers to the practical aspects of language that are required for effective and appropriate communication in many different situations. Pragmatics involves knowing how to take turns in a conversation or how to speak differently to different people, for example. Consider four-year-old Susie who sees her mother's friend reach for a cookie and says, "Better not take that, or you'll get even bigger." If you're Susie's mother, you are probably horrified by your daughter's rude remark. However, before you reprimand Susie, you should consider whether she meant harm by the comment or she just does not have a complete grasp of the "politeness" rules of language. Given Susie's age, the latter explanation is likely. Being able to communicate effectively in a language includes knowing when and how to use the language appropriately across social situations (Gleason, 2013).

Human language is unique because it is the only system capable of transmitting abstract ideas. Although most animals communicate, for the most part they are able to signal to other members of their species only their immediate and concrete states, such as being angry, threatened, hungry, hurt, or eager to reproduce (Deacon, 1997). Some forms of animal communication share certain features with human language—for instance, the songs of many birds appear to follow rules of syntax. However, birdsong does not have the flexibility to convey infinite meaning (Doupe & Kuhl, 1999). In contrast, using language, humans can discuss not only immediate feelings and needs but also abstract and remote ideas or states of being, such as infinity, the afterlife, the universe—or whether Macs are better than PCs.

New technologies, such as mobile devices, have influenced the way we use language to communicate.

How does the language you use in texting your friends differ from the language you use when emailing your professors? (Hint: If the language you use in these two contexts doesn't differ, it probably should.)

LO2 The Evolution of Language in Humans

As far as we know, earlier species of humans, such as *Homo erectus* and *Homo neanderthalensis*, had, at most, very rudimentary language, called **protolanguage,** or pre-language (Arbib, Liebal, & Pika, 2008; Givón & Malle, 2002; Johansson, 2013). A protolanguage differs from true human language in that it is thought to consist of words without syntax (Bickerton, 1990). No one knows for sure when fully grammatical language first appeared, but archaeologists and linguists suggest that probably only our species *(Homo sapiens)* has used grammatical and syntactical language. If so, language is less than 150 000 years old.

The most dramatic difference between human language and the forms of communication among other animals is that human language can easily represent ideas that are not tied to the present moment or location. The content of most animal communication focuses on immediate events related to mating, survival, and social identity (like dominance rank) and usually prompts an immediate response from the listener (Bickerton, 2008). Therefore, the development of fully grammatical language that can transcend the present is a big and unusual step, and many scientists think that evolution of language and evolution of the brain were intertwined. That is, as our ancestors moved from protolanguage to grammatical language, they required brains with greater working memory and the ability for abstract thought (Deacon, 1997; Dunbar, 2001). In fact, human language relies upon other neural circuits than those used in the production and comprehension of animal calls (Rizzolatti & Arbib, 1998). Increases in the size of human social groups may have triggered increased brain size and specialization as well. The more complex a group is, the greater the need for its members to communicate (Dunbar, 2001).

Canadian-born linguist and cognitive scientist Steven Pinker argues that human language is an instinct that evolved through natural selection, as an adaptation to our communication needs.

THE DEVELOPMENT OF LANGUAGE

Language Development in Individuals

If you have ever travelled to a country where you don't speak the language, you know that a foreign language can seem like a single, continuous string of sounds. It is hard to know where one word ends and the next one begins unless you have been hearing and speaking that language since childhood. As children develop their understanding of language, they learn that the sounds coming from the mouths of the people around them are meaningful units that form words.

In a child's language development, the ability to understand words develops before the ability to produce words (Fenson et al., 1994). We can easily observe that comprehension comes first because babies can do many things that are asked of them, such as pointing to their nose, long before they can say the words associated with those actions. Language comprehension, as we saw in Chapter 3, occurs in the left hemisphere of the brain, in the region called Wernicke's area, whereas language production is associated with the left-hemisphere region called Broca's area (see Figure 8.2). The fact that infants understand language before they start speaking suggests that Wernicke's area develops earlier than Broca's area.

LO3

cooing
the first sounds humans make other than crying, consisting almost exclusively of vowels; occurs during the first six months of life.

babbling
the sounds made as a result of the infant's experimentation with a complex range of phonemes, which include consonants as well as vowels; starts around five or six months of age.

Stages of Language Development The first speech sounds humans make consist almost exclusively of vowels, such as "aah, ee, ooh." Most infants begin uttering repeated vowel sounds, called **cooing,** during the first six months. Cooing sounds are universal: They vary little from hearing to deaf babies or among babies from all over the world.

Babbling overlaps with cooing, and it starts at around five or six months of age. **Babbling** refers to the infant's experimentation with a complex range of phonemes, which include consonants as well as vowels. In babbling, however, the sounds are not yet recognizable as words. At first, babies babble single syllables, such as "buh" and "duh"; later they utter "gibberish," which is simply a string of single syllables, such as "da, buh, ma, wee. . . ."

At first, babbling babies make many more sounds than they hear in their native language. Before babies' brains have been fully shaped by their native language, they can make many more sounds than their parents can. They can also hear more sounds than their parents (Jusczyk, 1997; Plunkett, 1997). Adults who speak Asian languages, which do not distinguish between the phonemes "r" and "l," for example, do not perceive a difference between these two sounds. Their toddler children do, which suggests that the ability to discriminate sounds declines at some point in development. In a series of classic experiments, Canadian researchers Janet Werker and Richard Tees were able to determine the age at which this ability disappears. They exposed English-speaking children of different ages to phonemes from English, Hindi, and Salish (a language native to south central British Columbia). Children from six to eight months of age could easily discriminate between non-English phonemes that adults could not. However, this ability was lost in children by the time they reached the age of one year (Werker & Tees, 1984). As children progress through the babbling stage, and with repeated exposure to the subset of sounds in their native language, they "prune" away sounds that are not used in that

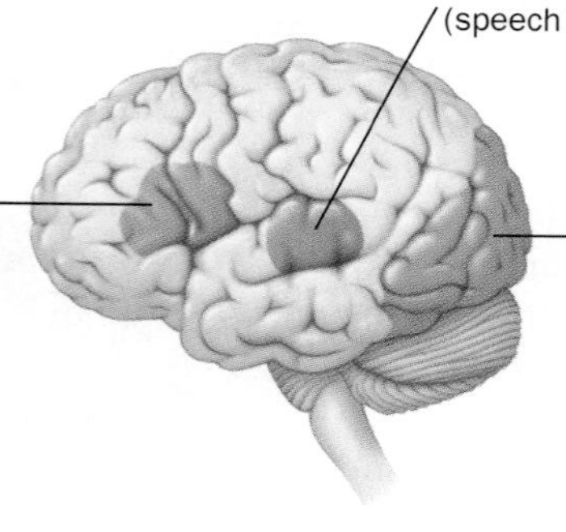

FIGURE **8.2**
WERNICKE'S AND BROCA'S AREAS AND THE OCCIPITAL LOBES. The occipital lobes are home to the visual cortex. As we'll see later, thinking involves both verbal and visual representations.

language and lose the ability to say or perceive non-native sounds (Goto, 1971; Kuhl, Stevens, & Hayashi, 2006).

At the end of the babbling stage, usually at around 12 months, **one-word utterances** emerge. Now children first speak such classic words as "mama," "dada," "more," and the all-important "no!" One-word utterances are likely descended from protolanguage. Like toddlers, our ancestors probably made up sounds for objects (nouns) and actions (verbs) before they developed more complex sentences (Goldfield, 2000).

one-word utterances
single words, such as "mama," "dada," "more," or "no!"; occurs around 12 months of age.

Whether a word is at the beginning, middle, or end of a sentence seems to be related to how likely young children are to learn that word. Children tend to acquire words that are spoken at the ends of sentences first. For example, in languages that are structured in the order of subject-verb-object, such as English, children acquire nouns earlier than verbs because nouns are objects and therefore tend to appear at the end of sentences. In languages that are structured subject-object-verb, such as Japanese and Mandarin, children acquire verbs earlier than nouns (Chan, Brandone, & Tardif, 2009; Clancy, 1985; Tardif, Gelman, & Xu, 1999). In English, for example, we say, "Maria read the book," whereas in Japanese people say, "Maria the book read." English-speaking children learn *book* before *read,* whereas Japanese-speaking children learn the Japanese version of *read* before *book.* This tendency to learn the last word in a sentence first may reflect the memory phenomenon called the *recency effect,* discussed in Chapter 6.

Starting around 18 months, children make **two-word utterances** such as "my ball," "mo wawa" (more water), or "go way" (go away). During this phase of language development, parents often find themselves serving as translators because their children create unique ways of saying things. For instance, our youngest son, Evan, would say "ba" for any kind of water. Why? Because he had learned to say "ba" to mean "bottle of water." He extended "ba" to other types of water, such as a lake, pool, or bathtub, which we easily understood. Our babysitters did not, however, so we had to translate "Evanese" for them.

two-word utterances
phrases children put together, starting around 18 months, such as "my ball," "mo wawa," or "go way."

sentence phase
the stage when children begin speaking in fully grammatical sentences; usually age two-and-a-half to three.

By age two-and-a-half or three, most children enter the third phase of language development—the **sentence phase**—in which they begin speaking in fully grammatical sentences. This transition happens so quickly that linguists usually have a tough time studying it. Linguist Steven Pinker uses Adam as an example. At age two, Adam would say, "Play checkers. Big drum. I got horn." Less than a year later, at age three, he would say, "I going come in fourteen minutes. You dress me up like a baby elephant. You know how to put it back together" (Pinker, 1994, pp. 273–274). These sentences may not always be what adults consider grammatically correct, but they are grammatical sentences.

Although there is a large degree of individual variability in the age at which children reach each of these language milestones, girls slightly outperform boys in the acquisition of language skills, particularly vocabulary. This is true regardless of the language spoken and geographical area (Bornstein et al., 2005; Bouchard et al., 2009). Whether this is due to a specific female advantage in language ability, or rather general differences in the rate at which boys and girls develop is not clear, since the female advantage is not as apparent by the age of six and gender differences in language ability in adults are not as clear (Wallentin, 2009).

In sum, children go through a very predictable sequence in acquiring language: from cooing to babbling, one-word utterances, two-word utterances, and finally, adult-like sentence structure—a stage that is reached around age three. These stages in speech development map remarkably well onto the growth in the child's overall brain size (see Figure 8.3). There is a steep rise in both

By age three, children begin to speak in full grammatical sentences. Their brains are also nearly adult size.

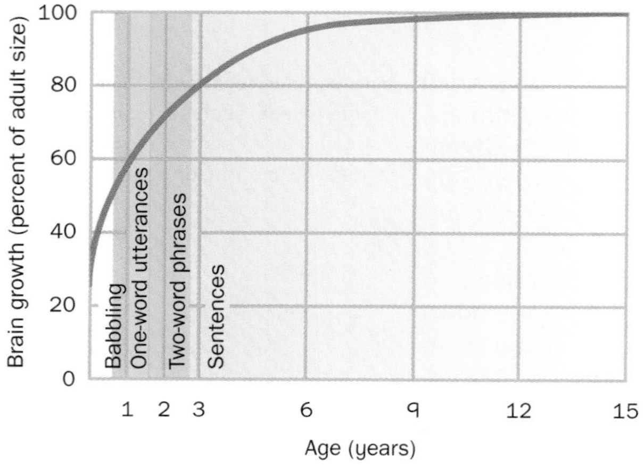

FIGURE **8.3**

ASSOCIATION BETWEEN BRAIN GROWTH AND LANGUAGE DEVELOPMENT. As the child's brain approaches its final adult size, the onset and rapid development of language matches the rapid growth of the brain. At age one, when the child's brain is less than 50 percent of its adult size, the infant is babbling and perhaps saying a few words. By age three, when the brain is 75–80 percent of its adult size, the child has progressed to two-word phrases and short sentences. (*Source:* Sakai, 2005.)

brain growth and language between the ages of one and three. The brain of a three-year-old child has reached about 80 percent of adult size. At about this age, children can form adult-like sentences.

LO4

The Sensitive Period An important principle of language development is that if children are not exposed to any human language before a certain age, their language abilities never fully develop (Lenneberg, 1967; Newport, 2003; Uylings, 2006). This sensitive period for language acquisition begins in the first years of life and ends at about age 12. It is the optimal time for learning language. Severe neglect and lack of exposure during this period cause permanent problems in language development. As Uylings (2006) points out, sensitive periods end after neural pruning and neural wiring have reached their peak, at which point the plasticity of neural connections becomes less flexible.

One of the most dramatic examples of the importance of the sensitive period in language development is the case of an abused and severely neglected girl known as "Genie." When she was two years old, a family doctor diagnosed Genie as being mildly retarded (Rymer, 1993). Her father, who was mentally unstable, interpreted this to mean that she was severely retarded and needed "protection." He tied her to a chair all day long and caged her in a crib at night. Moreover, he beat her every time she tried to speak and barked at her like a dog. This abuse lasted until Genie was 13½, when her mother finally ran away, taking Genie with her. The local social worker whose help they sought thought Genie was six or seven years old because she was only 1.4 metres tall and weighed 27 kilograms. The social worker arranged for the state of California to take temporary custody of the child. At that time, Genie could speak only a few words, such as *stopit* or *nomore*.

Connection

Early life experiences are also crucial in the development of sensory systems, such as vision.

See Chapter 10, LO3.

At age 17, after four years of language training, Genie's language skills were still extremely delayed. She could communicate simple ideas, but her speech was limited mainly to ungrammatical sentences. She would say things like "Spot chew glove" or "Applesauce buy store" (*Transcripts*, 1997). In this sense, her language ability was on par with that of a young child. Her language comprehension, however, was much better than her language production. She understood much of what was said to her. Brain imaging revealed something most unusual about Genie's brain activity while speaking or listening: The activity was located mostly in her right hemisphere (Curtiss, 1977). Recall that language ability is located in the left hemisphere. The case of Genie suggests that left hemisphere speech development requires stimulation from the environment during a certain sensitive period if it is to develop properly.

As tragic as Genie's story is, it reveals something very important about language: We need verbal stimulation from others, and we need it while we are young children if we are to develop fully and completely the ability to speak. Now in her 50s, Genie lives in supportive foster care. The movie *Mockingbird Don't Sing*, released in 2001, is based on her life.

LO5 Theories of Language Acquisition

Unless they suffer from some sort of disease or deficit, all humans learn to speak, including those who were born deaf. Many children who can't hear learn spoken language in order to communicate with hearing individuals, but many rely heavily on sign language as well, which is every bit as complex and communicative as spoken language. This suggests that we have innate, genetically based structures in the brain that enable us to learn language. Yet the vast differences in how well each of us learns to speak illustrate the importance of environmental stimulation. Different theories of language acquisition emphasize contributions of nature and nurture to language differently, but they all agree that both are involved.

Socio-Cultural Theories We learn language from the people around us. We acquire vocabulary by hearing others speak, and we figure out what they mean by the context (Hoff, 2006; Zhang, Jin, Shen, Zhang, & Hoff, 2008). Children who hear more total and unique words, and more complex sentences, develop their language faster and more richly than those who do not (Gathercole & Hoff, 2007; Hart & Risley, 1992, 1995; Huttenlocher, Vasilyeva, Cymerman, & Levine, 2002; Pan, Rowe, Singer, & Snow, 2005). In a review of the evidence for how environment shapes and moulds language acquisition, Erika Hoff (2006) provides a partial list of the environmental influences on language. They include culture, socioeconomic status, birth order, school, peers, television, and parents. Each of these influences has a rich research history demonstrating how socio-cultural forces shape language development, particularly the timing of vocabulary development.

The richness of a child's vocabulary is very much a function of how many words are spoken in the family. Hart and Risley (1992, 1995) examined language development in 42 families with young children from three different economic and educational groups: professional, middle and working class, and unemployed (welfare). Each month for over two years (from when the children were ten months to three years of age), the researchers tape-recorded and analyzed in-home verbal interactions.

One major finding was that the children all started to speak around the same time and they developed good structure and use of language. Yet children from professional families heard an average of 2153 words per hour, those from middle- and working-class families heard an average of 1251 words per hour, and those from unemployed (welfare) families heard an average of 616 words per hour. Extending these numbers to total words heard in a year, by age four, the children from the unemployed families would have heard about 32 million fewer words than the children from professional families.

These differences in number of words heard translated into differences in the child's own vocabulary (see Figure 8.4). By age three, the average vocabulary of the children from unemployed (welfare) families was around 500 words, whereas for professional families it was around 1100 words. The children from the professional families also heard more encouragement words than discouragement words than did the children from either the working-/middle-class or welfare-recipient families.

Much of what we learn comes from imitating family members. Imitation is doing exactly what you see someone else do, and with certain behaviours imitation is evident immediately after birth. Newborns as young as 50 minutes old will stick out their tongues or open their mouths when they see an adult do so (Meltzoff & Moore, 1983). At a slightly older age, babies try to imitate the speech sounds they hear (Kuhl & Meltzoff, 1997). Adults, in turn, do many things to encourage imitation. For example, they speak in a higher pitch, raise and lower the volume of their voice, use simpler sentence structures, emphasize

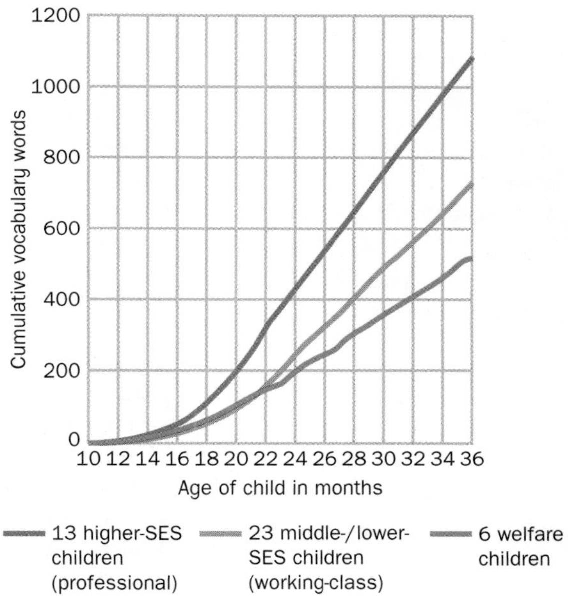

FIGURE **8.4**

DEVELOPMENT OF VOCABULARY AS A FUNCTION OF SOCIOECONOMIC STATUS OF THE FAMILY. Given the differences between families in the numbers of words spoken to children, it is not surprising that these differences would translate into differences in the children's vocabulary. In this graph, we see the development of total vocabulary size over a two-and-a-half-year period in children in three socioeconomic status (SES) groups: professional, middle-/working-class, and unemployed (welfare). By age three, children from professional families are using more than twice as many different words as children from welfare families. (*Source:* Hart & Risley, 1995.)

child-directed speech changes in adult speech patterns—apparently universal—when speaking to young children or infants; characterized by higher pitch, changes in voice volume, use of simpler sentences, emphasis on the here and now, and use of emotion to communicate messages.

the here and now, and use emotion to communicate their messages (Fernald & Morikawa, 1993; Rice, 1989). These changes in adult speech patterns—which appear to be universal—are referred to as **child-directed speech.**

Although these are very social processes we have been discussing, they also demonstrate profound interdependence with brain processes, which is yet another example of the interplay between nature and nurture. Mirror neurons, the clusters of brain cells that fire not only when an individual performs some task (such as sticking out one's tongue), but also when an individual observes another person do the same task, facilitate social learning and imitation (Rizzolatti & Arbib, 1998; Rizzolatti & Craighero, 2004). Although initially discovered in monkeys, humans have an equivalent mirror neuron system that becomes active during both language and imitation tasks, suggesting an important relationship between the two (Corballis, 2010).

Another line of evidence underlining the interplay of socio-cultural experience and brain processes is observed in speakers of signed languages, like American Sign Language (ASL). Spoken languages rely upon auditory input and oral output, while signed languages use visual input and manual output. Despite these differences in modality, signed languages like ASL are true languages and recruit the same left hemisphere language areas used in spoken languages. However, using signed language also involves regions of the right hemisphere, which has a strong role in spatial cognition. The degree of right hemisphere activation in signers is strongly influenced by early life experience, since individuals who learned ASL before puberty show much more right hemisphere involvement than signers who learned after puberty (Newman et al., 2001).

Connection

One reason newborn infants are capable of imitating behaviour immediately after birth is that humans and other animals have "mirror neurons." These were detected first after a chance observation in laboratory monkeys.

See Chapter 7, Figure 7.18.

Conditioning and Learning Theory B.F. Skinner (1957) believed that language is like any other behaviour: something that exists because it is reinforced and shaped. He proposed that we speak not because we want to convey an idea or a feeling, but rather because we have been reinforced for doing so. What are the conditions that bring about or reinforce verbal behaviour? According to Skinner, children learn to speak a particular language because when they say anything that even comes close to a word, the parents smile and say things like "Wow! She said 'mama'!" The parents' reaction has a reinforcing effect, making the child more likely to say that word; that is, the reaction shapes her behaviour.

As we just discussed, young children begin language development by cooing, then babbling, then uttering one and two words until they begin to say short phrases and sentences. Skinner explained this progression in terms of shaping, successive approximations, and reinforcement: The first approximation of a complex behaviour will be reinforced. When, for instance, a toddler utters "mama," she gets more of her mother's attention and smiles than she does when she utters "baba." The child learns first that the word *mama* matters and soon thereafter learns what it means. In a short while the child is saying "mama go bye-bye." Each step is subsequently reinforced until the child reaches the final behaviour, which, in this case, would be speaking in fully grammatical sentences—"Mommy is going away."

Nativist Theory There is little doubt that language development, such as the acquisition of certain words, is shaped partly by parental responses. When a child correctly names an object for the first time—such as "doggy"—the parents lavish much praise and encouragement: "Yes, that's right! Spot is a doggy!" However, such reinforcement does not as consistently occur for other aspects of language development, such as syntax and grammar rules. Still, children seem to learn these aspects with little difficulty. In fact, children tend to overgeneralize language rules; for example, they may add *ed* to *run* to form the past tense because adding *ed* is the typical way of forming the past tense in English. Instead of saying "Spot ran," then, the child says "Spot runned." Reinforcement cannot explain this formation, because children most likely have never heard "runned" from their parents and so have not been reinforced for using it. In other words, it is impossible to learn novel utterances through imitation and reinforcement. One cannot use shaping to teach someone to say something no one has ever said. So Skinner's explanation of language acquisition cannot fully explain how we learn language.

Some linguists contend that we discover language rather than learn it, that language development is "native," or inborn. This is the main assumption of the **nativist view of language.** In this view, the brain is structured, or "wired," for language learning; indeed, as we saw earlier, Broca's and Wernicke's areas are dedicated to speech production and comprehension, respectively. The linguist Noam Chomsky (1972, 1986) has argued that humans are born with a **language acquisition device (LAD)**—an innate, biologically based capacity to acquire language. Just as birds are biologically built to fly, humans are biologically built to speak. We are not born with a capacity to learn a particular language, such as Chinese or English, but rather we are simply born with a capacity to learn "language." Further, Chomsky (1972, 2000) has suggested that there is essentially a single universal grammar underlying all human languages; each individual language is simply a specific expression of this universal grammar.

nativist view of language
the idea that we discover language rather than learn it, that language development is inborn.

language acquisition device (LAD)
an innate, biologically based capacity to acquire language, proposed by Noam Chomsky as part of his nativist view of language.

Chomsky argues for a built-in language acquisition device (LAD) partly because of how easily and automatically humans learn to do this most complex and difficult thing: speak in complete and grammatical sentences. It is universal and it develops intuitively in children in about the same way and at the same time all over the world, regardless of which language they learn. Any child can learn equally easily any language as her or his native language. If you grew up in certain regions of Africa, you would be speaking Swahili; certain parts of Asia, Mandarin; certain parts of Europe, German. Where we are born and what language we are exposed to is the one we learn, and we have no trouble learning it.

Challenge Your Assumptions

True or False? Learning grammar is easy only for highly educated people.

False: Learning the grammar of one's native language is an automatic and relatively effortless skill for humans.

Chomsky also argues that our biologically based language acquisition device must have *principles* of universal grammar that allow a child to learn any language as her or his native language (Chomsky, 2000; Radford, 1997). Universal grammar follows universal principles. For instance, a universal grammar principle might be "Languages have subjects, objects, and verbs." All languages have these components of speech, but they vary in where they can be put in sentences. As we saw earlier in the chapter, English is a subject-verb-object (S-V-O) language, whereas Japanese is a subject-object-verb (S-O-V) language. So when an English speaker says "Maria read the book" and a Japanese speaker says "Maria the book read," the principles are the same, but the rules or word order are different.

Noam Chomsky

Nature, Nurture, and Language Learning As we have seen, different theorists emphasize different contributions of nature and nurture. Social and learning theorists argue for the importance of social input and stimulation, whereas nativist theorists argue for the importance of brain structures and genetic factors. Both perspectives are needed to fully explain language. Most scholars of language agree that acquiring language involves natural abilities which are modified by the language learner's environment (Hoff, 2006; Lidz & Gleitman, 2004; MacWhinney, 1999). The phrase *innately guided learning* captures the interaction between nature and nurture very well (Elman et al., 1996). We learn to speak, but in doing so we are guided by our innate capacity for language learning. The importance of both nature and nurture is starkly illustrated by the case of Genie: She could speak, and even learned a few words as a child, but her environment was so barren that her language development was severely stunted.

Still, genetic factors and innate structures have a stronger influence on some aspects of language development, while environmental conditions have a greater influence on other aspects. For instance, grammar is more innate and

According to Noam Chomsky, regardless of where we are born or what language we are exposed to, we have no trouble learning it.

genetically influenced than vocabulary, which is more strongly shaped by input from the environment (Dale et al., 2000; Hoff, 2006). Recall that one common way to determine how much of a trait is due to genetic influence is by comparing identical twin pairs to fraternal twin pairs (see Chapter 3). If a trait is strongly genetically influenced, it will show much stronger correlations in identical twins than in fraternal twins because identical twins are more genetically alike than fraternal twins. Dale and colleagues (2000) compared vocabulary and grammar skills in 1008 identical twin pairs to those same skills in 1890 fraternal twin pairs; all were about two years old. The children's parents assessed their vocabulary and grammar skills by completing questionnaires dealing with the kinds of words and sentences their children could say. Identical twin pairs were more similar in vocabulary and grammar than were fraternal twin pairs. Figures from the study show us that about 25 percent of vocabulary development and about 40 percent of learning about grammar are genetically influenced (Dale et al., 2000).

Studies of twins, like these identical twins, suggest that grammar is influenced more by genetics than the environment, whereas vocabulary is influenced more by the environment than by genetics.

The genetic contribution to vocabulary and grammar has raised a number of important questions about the origins of language. What genes play a role in language? Do we share these genes with other animals? Although it is unlikely that we will ever discover a single gene that is responsible for all the complex perceptual, motor, and cognitive processes necessary for human language, one gene has been the focus of much research, and debate. FOXP2 is a gene involved in both understanding and producing speech; abnormalities in this gene were discovered in an English family with an inherited form of language disorder (Watson et al., 2002). Variants of the FOXP2 gene are found in all mammal species, but the human form of this gene differs from that of the chimpanzee, our closest living relative (Corballis, 2010). Recently, the human form of this gene was discovered in Neanderthal DNA, suggesting that they too may have been capable of some form of human language (Krause et al., 2007).

LO6 Can Other Species Learn Human Language?

Animals of all kinds communicate with members of their own species. Birds sing songs to tell other birds where they are, that they want to mate, or that a predator is nearby; sometimes they sing just for the fun of it (Rothenberg, 2005). Whales sing long, melancholic (to human ears) tones that other whales hear from great distances. Bees dance to tell other bees where nectar can be found. But do these forms of animal communication represent the ability to use language as humans do? For centuries it was argued that the capacity for language is what separates humans from other animals. Yet, if humans share almost all of their genes with chimps, and humans and apes share a common ancestor from roughly 6 million years ago, an obvious question is: Is it possible for apes to learn human language?

Chimps do not have a vocal apparatus that allows them to speak, so are physically incapable of making the same range of sounds as humans (see Figure 8.5). However, apes can be taught to communicate using a non-vocal sign language, most often ASL. A number of captive apes have learned ASL to different degrees and have been able to communicate with humans. Allen and Beatrix Gardner, for instance, have compiled more than 400 ASL signs that three chimps named Dar, Tatu, and Moja acquired in the course of extensive training (Gardner, Gardner, & Van Cantfort, 1989). Their first chimp, Washoe, learned to sign almost 200 distinct words. Another chimp, Sarah, developed a vocabulary of about 100 words (Premack, 1971). Perhaps the most linguistically gifted ape to date is Kanzi, a bonobo chimp (Cohen, 2010; Rumbaugh, Beran, & Savage-Rumbaugh, 2003).

Kanzi was the son of Matata, who had been caught wild in Zaire. When Matata was an adult, linguist Sue Savage-Rumbaugh attempted to teach her sign language, with limited success. Kanzi was present during these training sessions but was not formally taught any signs. Savage-Rumbaugh soon discovered, however, that Kanzi had been paying attention to the signs they were teaching his mother. Moreover, he learned more quickly and developed a larger vocabulary than his mother. The research team decided to compare Kanzi's language comprehension to that of a two-and-a-half-year-old human child, Alia. At the time, Kanzi was seven years old. Both Kanzi and Alia were given 660 spoken requests to see whether they understood them well enough to carry them out. The requests were things like "Take the shoe to the bathroom," or "Give Karen an apple," and

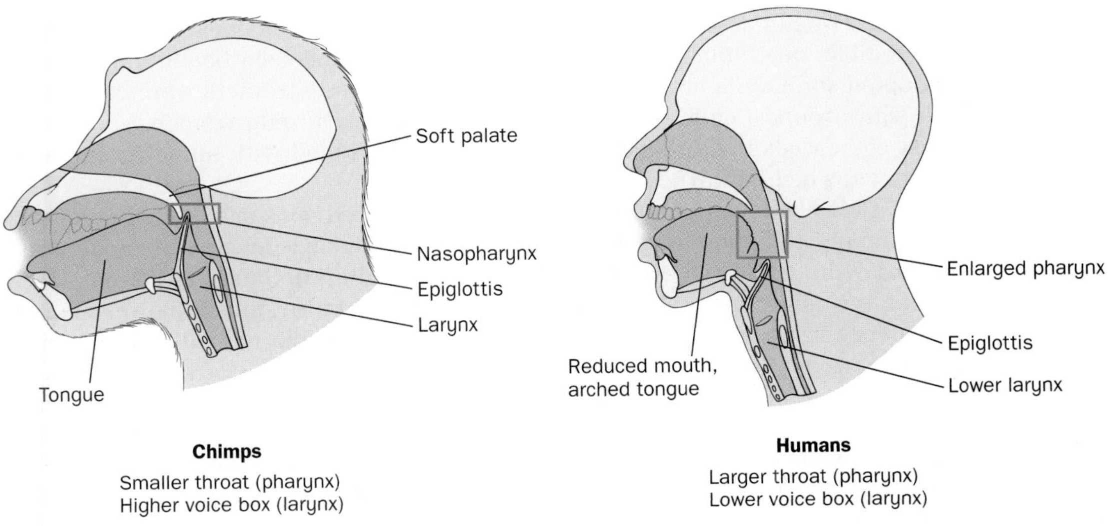

FIGURE **8.5**

VOCAL ANATOMY OF CHIMPS AND HUMANS. Vocal structures (throat, voice box, tongue) determine the kinds of sounds chimps and humans are capable of making. (*Source:* Deacon, 1997.)

Kanzi, a bonobo who understands at least 3000 English words, uses symbols to communicate with his teacher, linguist Sue Savage-Rumbaugh.

reversals such as "Make the doggie bite the snake" then "Make the snake bite the doggie" (Rumbaugh, Beran, & Savage-Rumbaugh, 2003, p. 411). Alia and Kanzi performed these commands at very similar levels of success—about 70 percent. Since then, Kanzi, now over 30 years old, has learned to comprehend as many as 3000 English words (Raffaele, 2006).

If apes can learn sign language, do they use it to talk with each other? The answer seems to be: Sometimes, in some circumstances, and in some species of ape. So what do apes sign to one another about? Fouts and colleagues (1984) analyzed the types of conversations five signing chimpanzees had among themselves. They found that 88 percent of the conversations were about social interaction, play, and reassurance, whereas the other 12 percent were about feeding, grooming, cleaning, discipline, and chimps signing, or "talking," to themselves (just as we humans talk to ourselves) (Fouts, Fouts, & Schoenfeld, 1984). More incredibly, one chimp, also named Washoe, spontaneously began teaching her adopted son Loulis how to sign (Fouts, 1997). Human trainers were careful not to sign around Loulis to ensure that he would learn only from Washoe. After just eight weeks with Washoe, Loulis regularly signed with humans, and after 18 months he had learned about 20 signs.

However, even the most linguistically talented apes are limited compared to humans, although they do appear to have some basic level of metacognition, or knowing what they know and do not know (Beran, Smith, & Perdue, 2013). First, the developmental sequence in which they acquire signs is slower than the sequence in which humans do so. For instance, a gorilla named Koko acquired signs at about half the speed of very young human children (Parker & McKinney, 1999), and Loulis learned only about one sign a month during his first 18 months of learning. In addition, apes seldom progress beyond two- or three-word combinations, which means that their highest level of language learning is equivalent to the level achieved by a toddler in terms of vocabulary and sentence structure. Adult apes may have vocabularies of 100 to 300 words, compared to the 60 000-word vocabulary of an average high school student (Hauser, Chomsky, & Fitch, 2002; Parker & McKinney, 1999). Finally, primates seldom either understand or consistently use correct word order (syntax). For example, one chimp, named

Nim Chimsky after linguist Noam Chomsky, would alternate among "Banana give Nim," "Give Nim banana," and "Banana Nim give" (Terrace, 1987).

Whether or not these apes truly use language as humans do, the discovery that they can learn to use arbitrary symbols to express themselves was surprising. We may, in fact, have overlooked the linguistic abilities of other animals. Though no species appears to *produce* speech in the way that humans do, there is ample evidence many species can *understand* words that humans use. A border collie living in Germany, named Rico, has a vocabulary of about 200 words, similar to that of a human toddler. Not only can Rico successfully fetch objects based upon their spoken name, if Rico is asked to retrieve an object using a word that he has never heard before, he will choose a novel object over more familiar ones. This suggests that he can make the link between a novel, arbitrary sound and a novel object, a process important in language development in human children (Kaminski, et al. 2004). Language learning might not even be restricted to living beings. Fred Popowich and Anoop Sarkar of the Natural Language Lab at Simon Fraser University create computer programs that can learn, understand, and translate language. Advances in computer science have produced software capable of linguistic feats such as language translation, an ability that is not necessarily easy even for multilingual humans.

LO7 Language, Culture, and Thought

Does the language we speak cause us to see the world in a particular way? Can people who speak vastly different languages communicate effectively, even in translation? After we learn our native language, can we still learn about concepts that do not exist in our language but only in other languages?

According to the *Whorf-Sapir hypothesis,* language creates thought as much as thought creates language (Whorf, 1956). Anthropologists Benjamin Whorf and Edward Sapir, the authors of the Whorf-Sapir hypothesis, suggested that language shapes our thoughts and perceptions to such an extent that people who speak languages that lack a common foundation, such as English and Chinese, have difficulty directly communicating and translating their ideas from one language to the other. Taken to its logical conclusion, the Whorf-Sapir view leads to the **linguistic determinism hypothesis,** which states that our language determines our way of thinking and our perceptions of the world. In this view, if there are no words for certain objects or concepts in one's language, it is not possible to think about those objects or concepts.

linguistic determinism hypothesis the proposition that our language determines our way of thinking and our perceptions of the world; the view taken by Sapir and Whorf.

An example offers support for the linguistic determinism hypothesis. The Pirahã, a very small tribe of only about 200 people living in the Amazon area of Brazil, are challenging some of science's most basic notions of language, numbers, memory, perception, and thought (Everett, 2005). The Pirahã have no words for the numbers higher than two. As a result, it is nearly impossible for them to learn concepts such as ten. They even have difficulty learning simple arithmetic relationships, such as "3 + 1" (Gordon, 2004). This difficulty occurs not because they are unintelligent, but rather because their language so strongly works against such concepts. They function very well without these concepts and by adulthood learning them is rather difficult.

Support for the linguistic determinism hypothesis comes from studies of the Pirahã tribe in Brazil.

Think what it would be like to try to understand an idea or a concept for which you had no word.

Linguists studying the Pirahã claim that the Pirahã have no way to include one clause within another. They can construct only independent clauses. For example, they cannot say something like "When I finish eating, I want to speak to you." Instead, they must say two things: "I finish eating. I speak to you" (Bower, 2005). This claim is radical because it directly challenges the concept of a universal grammar. According to Chomsky, a cornerstone of universal grammar is that all languages embed clauses within clauses. The Pirahã, however, do not do this; they do not construct sentences that start with words like *when*, *before*, or *after*, and as a result they are limited to talking about the here and now and only about what is directly observable. Not surprisingly, they lack stories about the ancient past—they have no stories, for instance, of how the world began, and they refer only to known, living relatives.

Nonetheless, the view that language determines our thinking is almost certainly overstated. Most research on the topic shows how language influences rather than determines our thinking (Boroditsky, 2001; Newcombe & Uttal, 2006; Regier & Kay, 2009; Regier, Kay, Gilbert, & Ivry, 2010). This position is known as *linguistic relativism*. If languages differ in the words they use to define categories, one might expect a cognitive advantage with a larger number of categories. For instance, languages vary in the words used to define colour boundaries. Russian, for example, has distinct words for lighter blues (*goluboy*) and darker blues (*siniy*), while English has only "blue." Since the Russian language designates a boundary within the blue end of the colour spectrum, a native Russian speaker might perform differently on a colour-discrimination task than a native English speaker (Winawer et al., 2007; see Figure 8.6).

Connection

Damage to certain regions of the left hemisphere can cause aphasia, an impairment in producing or understanding speech.

See Chapter 3, LO12, LO13.

As these examples illustrate, thought, memory, number, and perception are all tied to language. In humans, language is important for organizing, storing, and communicating ideas. Our ability to think, reason, and make decisions often takes verbal form. However, much of our mental world is not rooted in language, as Jill Bolte Taylor describes vividly in her book *My Stroke of Insight* (2006). Dr. Taylor is a neuroscientist who suffered a left hemisphere stroke due to a brain hemorrhage, which resulted in severe language impairment. Since her right hemisphere was undamaged, her experience of the world was radically different in the absence of the input from the "chatter" of the logical, sequential, language-based left hemisphere. She has made a dramatic recovery, but has shared her experiences of her non-verbal, intuitive perspective of the world through her book, lectures, and television appearances.

Quick Quiz 8.1: Language

1. A language's particular rules for arranging words and symbols in a sentence or parts of a sentence is called
   a. grammar.
   b. semantics.
   c. syntax.
   d. pragmatics.
2. During which stage of language development do babies make many more sounds than they hear in their native languages?
   a. babbling
   b. cooing
   c. one-word utterances
   d. telegraphic speech
3. According to Skinner, children learn to speak a particular language because
   a. they possess an inherent ability to speak.
   b. they engage in imitation of what they hear.
   c. they have a language acquisition device.
   d. they get reinforcement from their parents for various utterances.
4. Which theory of language argues that if there are no words for certain objects or concepts in one's language, one is unable to think about those objects or concepts?
   a. nativist theory
   b. theory of innately guided learning
   c. linguistic determinism hypothesis
   d. Skinnerian theory of language

Answers can be found at the end of the chapter.

Research Process

1 Research Question

Is people's ability to discriminate colours altered by language? Unlike English, Russian has two distinct words for lighter blues (*goluboy*) and darker blues (*siniy*); English does not. Does knowledge of these different colour categories affect how quickly a person can discriminate between different shades of blue?

English speakers

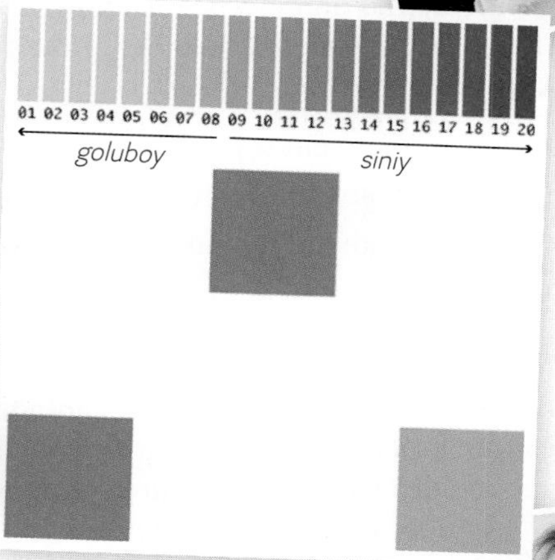
01 02 03 04 05 06 07 08 09 10 11 12 13 14 15 16 17 18 19 20
goluboy
siniy

Russian speakers

2 Method

The prediction was that the Russian speakers should be faster at making colour matches to the target if the sample stimuli were from different categories of blue compared to trials when the samples were from the same category. For English speakers, there would be no differences in discrimination time. Twenty colour stimuli spanning the Russian *siniy/goluboy* range were used. The participants viewed colours arranged in a triad as shown above. Their task was to indicate as quickly and accurately as possible which of the two bottom colour squares was identical to the top square.

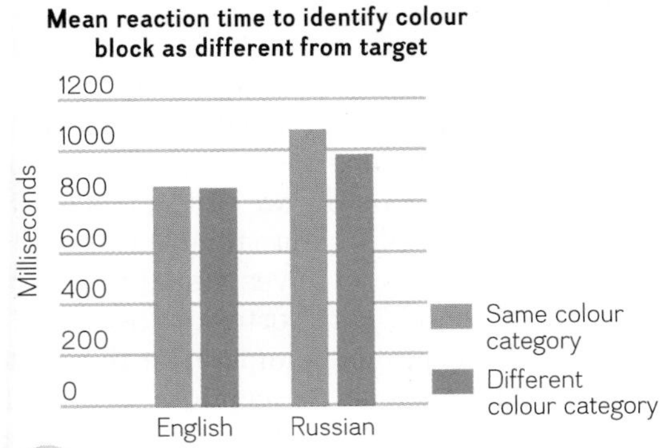
Mean reaction time to identify colour block as different from target
1200
1000
800
600
400
200
0
Milliseconds
English
Russian
Same colour category
Different colour category

3 Results

Although there were no differences in colour discrimination accuracy, Russian speakers were faster at discriminating blues that came from different colour categories than at discriminating blues that came from within the same category. For English speakers, response time did not differ for same versus different category of blue, because there is only one category of blue in English.

4 Conclusion

Knowledge of words for different categories of blue does affect how quickly people can discriminate between examples of blue. Notice, however, that the English speakers performed very well overall—in fact, they were faster than Russian speakers—but their performance was not affected by the different language categories. Language knowledge can influence thought.

FIGURE **8.6**

LANGUAGE AND COLOUR DISCRIMINATION Words for colour influence our perception of and thinking about those colours. (*Source:* Winawer, J., Witthoft, N., Frank, M.C., Wu, L., Wade, A.R., & Boroditsky, L. (2007). Russian blues reveal effect of language on colour discrimination. *Proceedings of the National Academy of Science, 104,* 7780–7785.)

LO8

THINKING, REASONING, AND DECISION MAKING

What does it mean to know something? For instance, if our bodies just do something automatically, like breathing or digesting food, could we say that we know how to breathe and digest or that we just do it?

These questions and examples suggest that knowledge is distinct from instinct, and certainly it is. Psychologists use the word **cognition,** which means "to know," to refer to mental processes involved in acquiring, processing, and storing knowledge. **Cognitive psychology** is the science of how people think, learn, remember, and perceive (Sternberg, 2006).

cognition
the mental processes involved in acquiring, processing, and storing knowledge.

cognitive psychology
the science of how people think, learn, remember, and perceive.

In this section, we will consider three fundamental questions about cognition and reasoning:

1. How do we represent thoughts in our minds?
2. How do we reason about evidence?
3. How do we make judgments and decisions?

How Do We Represent Thoughts in Our Minds?

Even with the most up-to-date brain imaging technology, we cannot actually see inside the brain as it conjures up an image or comes up with a solution to a problem. Imaging techniques can only measure changes in blood flow, which suggest brain activity. We cannot and probably never will be able to actually *see* thoughts and ideas. Yet it is clear that we all have thoughts, memories, and ideas, so the question arises: How do we use our brains to store and maintain these mental processes?

Connection

The occipital and parietal lobes of the brain develop before the temporal and frontal lobes. This pattern of growth partly explains why we see before we can talk.

See Chapter 10, LO3.

Cognitive psychologists approach this question by proposing that we represent ideas, knowledge, or memories as *mental representations.* A **mental representation** is a structure in our mind—such as an idea or image—that stands for something else, such as the external object or thing (Thagard, 1995). Mental representations allow us to think about and remember things in the past or imagine things in the future. They also allow us to think about abstract ideas that have no physical existence, such as love, truth, or justice. For the most part, we represent ideas and thoughts in our minds visually and verbally.

mental representation
a structure in our mind—such as an idea or image—that stands for something else, such as an external object or thing sensed in the past or future, not the present.

visual imagery
visual representations created by the brain after the original stimulus is no longer present.

Visual Representation We think both in images and in words. The visual system, located mostly in the occipital lobes (see Figure 8.2), is older in evolutionary terms than the verbal system. It also develops before verbal ability (Givón, 2002): We see before we talk. Consider how babies respond to picture books before they learn to talk.

How does the brain store and maintain mental processes?

Every animal with eyes perceives visual images, but only those animals with significant cortex are better able to keep and store visual sensations in mind after the sensory stimulation stops. Indeed, visual perception occurs while the stimulus is still present, as we learned in Chapter 4. **Visual imagery,** however, involves visual representations created by the brain after the original stimulus is no longer present (Kosslyn, 2005). The brain is active in much the same way during visual imagery as it is during visual perception. Thus, you would have a hard time distinguishing between a brain image of someone actually perceiving something and a brain image of someone imagining seeing the same thing (Thompson & Kosslyn, 2000).

Being able to imagine things that are not currently being perceived is a very useful and complex skill, although about 2 percent of the population cannot do it at all (Kosslyn,

Many successful athletes use visual imaging to improve their performance. Visualizing success can help to make it happen.

2002). People clearly differ in their ability to imagine an event or object in their "mind's eye" (Ganis, Thompson, & Kosslyn, 2009; Kosslyn, Van Kleeck, & Kirby, 1990). If you have the ability to imagine outcomes, you can make them more likely to happen. For instance, if you first form a mental image of an ideal performance, such as hitting a home run or playing a piece of music without errors, you are more likely to perform that activity better (Hale, Seiser, & McGuire, 2005). Performance may be improved because the brain is primed by the images of success; that is, the pathways are activated in advance. Neuroscientists have shown that the brain is activated in much the same way while imagining a task as it is while performing that task (Bonnet et al., 1997). So, next time you are getting ready to play a game of tennis or perform a Mozart sonata, imagine doing your best. It can help you succeed.

Visual imagery and visual imagination can also be critical to many creative accomplishments, in both art and science (A. Miller, 1996). For example, Albert Einstein made it quite clear that words were not involved or came after the fact when he was developing his most creative ideas. When describing how he came up with his ideas for the theory of relativity, Einstein said, "These thoughts did not come in any verbal formulation. I rarely think in words at all. A thought comes and I may try to express it in words later" (quoted in Wertheimer, 1959, p. 228). He often visually imagined certain thought experiments, such as riding on a light beam or travelling at the speed of light in an elevator. Other physicists have argued that Einstein's great creativity dried up when he could no longer produce such visual images (Feist, 2006).

Visual imagery is crucial for some cognitive tasks, particularly those concerned with interpreting spatial relationships. The process of imagining an object rotating in three-dimensional space is known as **mental rotation.** Look at the shapes in Figure 8.7. The pairs are either the same or different, and your task is to decide which is which. If you are like most people, it will take you about 2.5 seconds for each pair to determine whether it is the same (a and b) or different (c). In order to do this task, you not only have to conjure up a mental picture of the geometric figure, but also manipulate the image to make a judgment about its spatial properties.

mental rotation
the process of imagining an object turning in three-dimensional space.

Researchers examining gender differences in the performance of mental rotation tasks have reported moderate to large gender effects, with boys

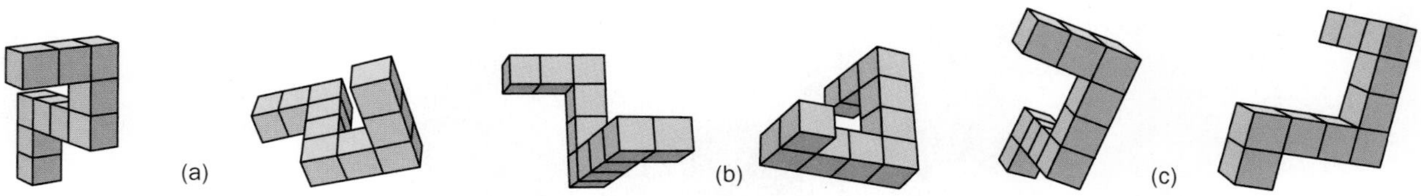

FIGURE **8.7**

MENTAL ROTATION. In this example, figures on the right are always rotated 80 degrees compared to the figures on the left. It takes most people about 2.5 seconds to mentally rotate the figures. The pairs in (a) and (b) are the same, whereas the pair in (c) is different. (*Source:* Shepard & Metzler, 1971.)

and men generally doing better than girls and women (Geary & DeSoto, 2001; Halpern, 2004; Hyde, 1990). Cross-cultural research has shown that these effects also appear in China, Ecuador, Ireland, and Japan (Flaherty, 2005; Geary & DeSoto, 2001; Silverman, Choi, & Peters, 2007). It may not only be gender directly that leads to differences in spatial ability but also one's gender role identification. That is, in a meta-analysis of 12 studies, girls and women and boys and men who self-identify as "masculine" have higher spatial ability scores than those who identify as "feminine" (Reilly & Neumann, 2013).

One possible cause of this gender difference in spatial ability appears to be levels of the male sex hormone testosterone (Kimura, 2007). Female rats injected with testosterone during development perform better than non-injected female rats on spatial tasks (maze running; Berenbaum, Korman, & Leveroni, 1995). The relationship in humans, however, among testosterone, gender, and spatial ability is complex and not linear (Ceci & Williams, 2010). In humans, it is females with relatively high levels and males with relatively low levels of testosterone who perform best on spatial tasks. So it is too simple to say that high levels of testosterone alone result in better spatial skills. In humans, this is true only for women. For men, having low levels of testosterone leads to better spatial skills (Ceci & Williams, 2010; Hines et al., 2003).

Verbal Representation A major function of thought is to organize and classify our perceptions into categories. One way in which humans organize their environment is by naming things and giving them labels. We organize our sensory experience by putting like with like and then distinguishing that group of things from other groups of things. We do this by first finding similar features and then forming concepts and building categories based on those similarities. The most basic unit of knowledge is a **concept,** which is a mental grouping of objects, events, or people. The concept "fruit" includes yellow, red, blue, orange, and green fruit, as well as large and small fruit, but what an apple and banana have in common defines the concept "fruit": the edible part of a plant that contains seeds.

concept
a mental grouping of objects, events, or people.

Concepts help us organize our perceptions of the world. We can store and process these concepts in at least two ways: in a hierarchy and by parallel distributed processing. A **concept hierarchy** lets us know that certain concepts are related in a particular way, with some being general and others specific. In so doing, it helps us order and understand our world. A particular dog, Goldie, is a "Golden Retriever," which is a "dog," which is an "animal," which is a "living thing."

concept hierarchy
an arrangement of related concepts in a particular way, with some being general and others specific.

A more complex model of how we store and organize knowledge in our brain is *parallel distributive processing* (PDP). The PDP model proposes that associations between concepts activate many networks or nodes at the same time (McClelland, 1988; McClelland & Rogers, 2003; McClelland & Rumelhart, 1985). Concepts are activated in the network based on how strongly associated or connected they are to each other. They are also arranged by similarity as well as hierarchy. For instance, animals such as bird and fish are closer to each other and farther away from plants such as trees and flowers. The location of a concept is based on its relation to other concepts. In the example in Figure 8.8, "living thing" is the most general conceptual category, of which there are two particular examples, "plants" and "animals." The relationship between nodes takes the form of "CAN," "HAS," or "IS A." An animal, for instance, CAN move, HAS skin, and IS A bird or fish, whereas a plant HAS roots and IS A flower or tree. A fish, in turn, HAS scales and gills, IS A salmon, and CAN swim. We can use these relationships and networks to reason about things: If a bird can fly and a robin is a bird, then a robin can fly.

A **category** is a concept that organizes other concepts around what they all share in common. For instance, all things that move and eat can belong to the category "animals," whereas all living things that grow out of the earth and do not eat are in the category "plants." Categories can be either *concrete* (e.g., triangles, cars) or *abstract* (e.g., good, consciousness). In addition, some examples of a category fit that category better than others. "Robin," for example, fits and represents the category "bird" better than does "ostrich," as ostriches cannot fly, are big, and have long legs. We refer to the best-fitting examples of a category as **prototypes** (Rosch, 1973). Thus, a robin is a better prototype for the category "bird" than an ostrich is.

category
a concept that organizes other concepts around what they all share in common.

prototypes
the best-fitting examples of a category.

Now that we have developed concepts and categories to help organize our mind's representations, how do we use them to make sense of our world and to reason about them? In the next section, we'll consider an answer to this question as we talk about humans' reasoning ability.

LO9 How Do We Reason about Evidence?

Almost anytime we use the word *because*, we are reasoning (e.g., "He is smiling at me because he likes me.") **Reasoning** is the process of drawing inferences or conclusions from principles and evidence (Sternberg, 2006). Sometimes reasoning

reasoning
the process of drawing inferences or conclusions from principles and evidence.

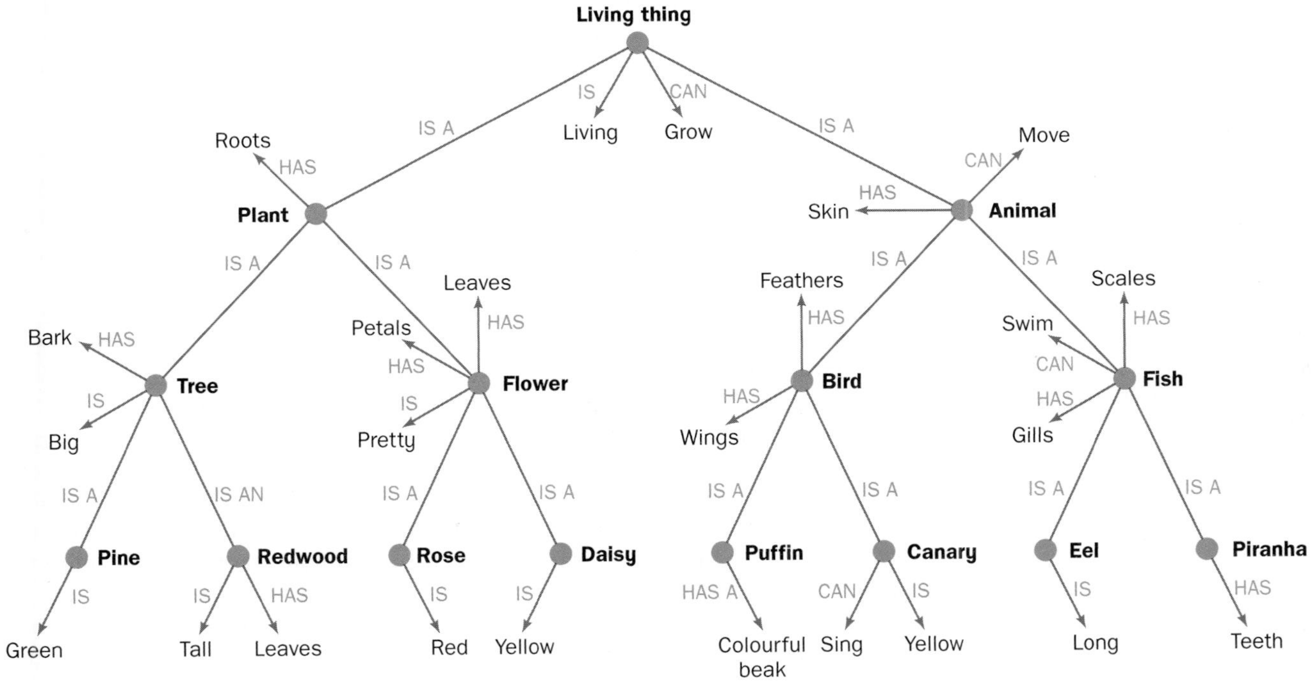

FIGURE **8.8**
PARALLEL DISTRIBUTED NETWORK OF THE VERBAL CONCEPT "LIVING THING." Concepts, printed in bold type, are represented by circles, or nodes, and are interconnected. Properties of concepts are depicted by arrows, which represent statements. Relationships are shown in CAPS. The concept Flower, for instance, HAS petals and leaves, IS pretty, IS a plant, and IS a rose or a daisy. The concept Plant is more general than Rose and Daisy. (*Source:* McClelland & Rogers, 2003.)

allows us to draw sound, correct conclusions, yet this is not always the case. Consider the statement, "The FBI and CIA are both out to get me because I always see people looking at me." The conclusion is not a sound one, for it is based only on the evidence that people are looking at you. In fact, it's probably not correct, either.

deductive reasoning
reasoning from general statements of what is known to specific conclusions.

Cognitive psychologists distinguish between two kinds of reasoning drawn from formal logic: deductive and inductive. **Deductive reasoning** occurs when we reason from general statements of what is known to specific conclusions. The specific conclusion is always correct if the general statement is true. For instance:

All humans are mortal (premise A).
Socrates is human (premise B).
Therefore, Socrates must be mortal (conclusion).

That Socrates is mortal is a logical conclusion that has to be true if the two premises are true. This form of reasoning, of course, leads to correct conclusions only when the general premises on which they are based are true. Consider the following:

All humans are green (premise A).
Socrates is a human (premise B).
Therefore, Socrates must be green (false conclusion).

This reasoning obviously leads to a false conclusion because it is based on false premise A. Even though the structure of the two arguments is exactly the same, one leads to a correct conclusion and the other does not. When scientists make specific predictions from their general theories, they are engaging in deductive reasoning.

inductive reasoning
reasoning to general conclusions from specific evidence.

Inductive reasoning draws general conclusions from specific evidence. Such conclusions are less certain than those drawn from deductive reasoning because many different conclusions might be consistent with a specific fact. With deduction we can reach certain and necessarily correct conclusions. With induction, however, the best we can hope for are highly likely conclusions. An example of inductive reasoning is "All peaches I have eaten have been sweet; therefore, all peaches are sweet." All it takes is one unsweet peach to undermine that conclusion. A better inductive conclusion would be that *most* peaches are sweet. When scientists develop theories, they employ inductive reasoning because they offer general statements that explain many specific facts or observations. When we use inductive reasoning we often use **causal inferences,** judgments about whether one thing causes another thing (Koslowski, 1996). "Every time I get chilled, I catch a cold. So getting chilled must cause colds."

causal inferences
judgments about causation of one thing by another.

confirmation bias
the tendency to selectively attend to information that supports one's general beliefs while ignoring information or evidence that contradicts one's beliefs.

Inductive reasoning and causal inferences are related to a phenomenon that is often seen in most people, including scientists: confirmation bias. **Confirmation bias** is the tendency to selectively attend to information that supports one's general beliefs while ignoring information or evidence that contradicts one's beliefs. In the 1960s, Peter Wason conducted classic research to demonstrate the pervasiveness of the confirmation bias. Wason (1960) decided to find out whether people propose and test hypotheses systematically and, more to the point, whether they would be more likely to falsify or to confirm their own theories.

Wason gave students the task of determining the hidden rule behind a sequence of three numbers, known as a *triplet*. The students were asked to guess at the rule by writing down triplets that they thought conformed to it and the reason they selected them. They could make as many guesses and explanatory statements as they wished, until they thought they knew the rule. Then they wrote down what they thought the rule actually was. The experimenter, who knew the hidden rule, could answer only "yes" or "no" to the students' guesses, and was not allowed to say whether their reasons were correct or incorrect. For instance, if the experimenter gave the students the triplet "2–4–6," the students might guess a triplet of "6–8–10" and state that the hidden rule is "continuous series of even numbers." In this case, the guess is right but the rule is incorrect, so the experimenter would say "yes" to the guess but "no" to the rule. The students would then have to keep proposing triplets to test other reasons until they come up with the specific rule.

The actual rule was that the numbers in the triplet must increase in value, and of the 29 participants in the study, 23 made an incorrect first guess at the rule. This in itself is not surprising, as the students could make as many guesses as they liked and, therefore, might need a few tries in order to guess the rule. What was surprising, however, was that the participants who made an initial incorrect guess at the rule were more likely to rephrase this rule in subsequent guesses, rather than come up with an entirely new one. Correct answers were much more likely to arise when students tried to disconfirm the rule. For instance, the best way to test the rule "a continuous set of even numbers" would be to generate a triplet that does *not* conform to this rule, such as 6–7–10, instead of a conforming triplet such as 6–8–10. This experiment shows that people are so inclined to test only ideas that confirm their beliefs that they forget that one of the best ways to test an idea is to try to tear it down—that is, disconfirm it. This is the foundation of the scientific method. Most people, though, look only for information that confirms what they already believe and seldom look for information that disconfirms what they think; that is, they fall prey to confirmation bias (see Figure 8.9).

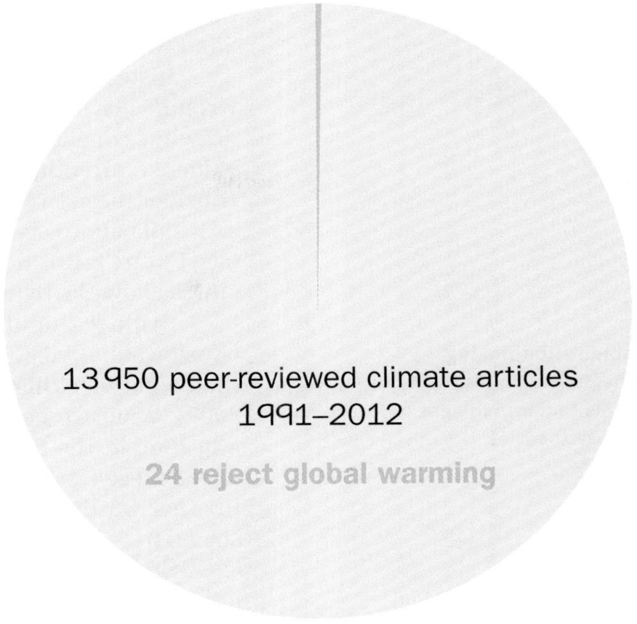

FIGURE **8.9**

AN EXAMPLE OF CONFIRMATION BIAS? A recent analysis of peer-reviewed scientific articles on climate published between 1991 and 2012 reveals that over 99 percent support evidence for global warming (Powell, 2012). Yet despite this overwhelming scientific consensus, some people still deny the existence of climate change.

How does confirmation bias explain this? Can you think of other examples of confirmation bias in operation in our daily lives?

LO10 Critical Thinking

You've probably heard about "critical thinking" quite often, first in high school and now in university. Teachers are always talking about getting their students to think critically. So what exactly is critical thinking?

We can answer this question in part by examining the origin of the word *critical*. It comes from the ancient Greek word *kritikos* and means "to question, to make sense of, and to be able to analyze; or to be skilled at judging" (Chaffee, 1999, p. 32). Educator Paul Chance has provided a more complete definition of **critical thinking:** "The ability to analyze facts, generate and organize ideas, defend opinions, make comparisons, draw inferences, evaluate arguments, and solve problems" (Chance, 1986, p. 6). The essence of strong critical thinking is to be objective and skeptical in solving problems. It requires evaluation of evidence and arguments independently of one's prior beliefs and opinions. As you just learned from Wason's study of the confirmation bias, it is often quite difficult for us to challenge our own opinions.

critical thinking
the process by which one analyzes, evaluates, and forms ideas.

In the late 1980s a group of educators, philosophers, psychologists, and biological and physical scientists organized a conference around the topic of critical thinking in education, and there they arrived at a consensus on what it means to be a good critical thinker. They were almost unanimous in identifying three factors that define critical thinking, analyzing, evaluating, and making inferences, and more than three-quarters of them agreed on interpreting, explaining, and self-regulating (Facione, 1990). If you become skilled in these qualities, or at least in most of these qualities, you will be able to think critically. In particular, you will be able to counter assertions that have little basis in reality, and you will know the difference between sound and faulty reasoning. For instance, the following argument was made by Charles Johnson, a former president of the International Flat Earth Research Society: "Nobody knows anything about the true shape of the world. The known, inhabited world is flat. Just as a guess, I'd say that

Challenge Your Assumptions

True or False? Critical thinking involves seeing only the weaknesses and flaws in ideas.

False: Critical thinking involves seeing both strengths and weaknesses in claims and evidence.

the dome of heaven is about 4,000 miles away, and the stars are about as far as San Francisco is from Boston."

Instead of simply saying, "That's silly" or "That's stupid" or "That's just wrong," a critical thinker would examine the claim by analyzing, evaluating, and drawing conclusions based on the facts and evidence at hand. A great deal of evidence directly and clearly contradicts the belief that the Earth is flat. Just consider these two pieces of evidence: (1) The top of a ship is the last thing we see as it sails out to sea because it is sailing on a sphere rather than on a flat surface (see Figure 8.10), and (2) images and photographs taken from spaceships and satellites show Earth as a round sphere with half of it shining in the light of the sun.

scientific thinking
the process of using the cognitive skills required to generate, test, and revise theories.

Critical thinking is closely related to scientific thinking and reasoning (Koslowski, 1996; Kuhn, Amsel & O'Loughlin, 1988). **Scientific thinking** involves the cognitive skills required to generate, test, and revise theories (Zimmerman, 2007). What we believe or theorize about the world and what the world is actually like, in the form of evidence, are two different things. Scientific thinking keeps these two things separate, whereas non-scientific thinking confuses them. In other words, scientists keep in mind that belief is not the same as reality. Non-scientists, on the other hand, tend to assume that what they believe is true.

metacognitive thinking
the process that includes the ability first to think and then to reflect on one's own thinking.

Critical and scientific reasoning also involves being able to think metacognitively. **Metacognitive thinking** requires the ability first to think and then to reflect on one's own thinking (Feist, 2006; Kuhn & Pearsall, 2000). People who can think metacognitively are able to question their own thinking (see Figure 8.11). This ability is not universal, however. Without specific training, many people find

FIGURE **8.10**
EVIDENCE THAT THE EARTH IS NOT FLAT. The drawing on the left shows how a ship would appear as it comes into view if Earth were flat. On the right we see the ship coming into view on a round Earth.
Which view is correct?

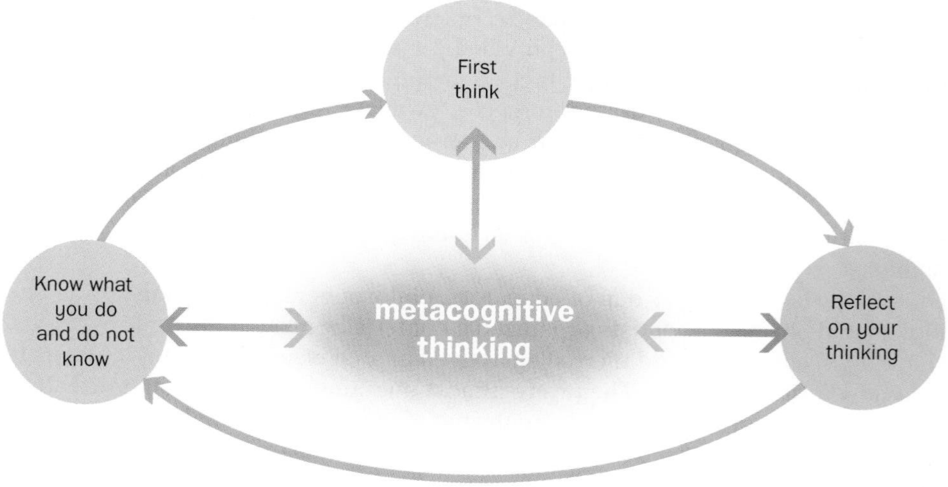

FIGURE **8.11**
METACOGNITIVE THINKING. In an era marked by 24/7 information overload, we often leap to overly simplistic or incorrect conclusions based on what we think we "know."
Can you think of a time when you were surprised by what you didn't know even though you felt confident in your knowledge beforehand, such as on an exam or for some other experience?

Psychology in the Real World

Applying Critical Thinking beyond the Classroom

Critical thinking is a necessary skill in almost every walk of life. We can apply it to any domain in which we form beliefs and opinions. Here is just a partial list: deciding whether someone committed a crime; evaluating the claims of a company advertising a product; deciding whether what we read or hear in the classroom, in the newspaper, in politics, or in our work environment is valid and what evidence it is based on.

To apply critical thinking skills we should ask ourselves, What is the evidence for this conclusion, and is it valid? Let's take just one example. Suppose you are on a jury in a murder trial. The primary evidence on which the case is based is eyewitness testimony: two people picked out the defendant from a line-up. The Crown offers no other concrete evidence, such as DNA findings, fingerprints, bloodstains, or ballistic (bullet) matching. Your job is to decide whether the defendant committed the murder. You will want to draw on your critical thinking skills, because in this situation ignoring evidence and basing judgments on bias can have serious consequences.

Canadian politicians have to weigh a wide range of issues and options in oil pipeline construction, such as the Keystone XL or the Northern Gateway. On the one hand, the building of such pipelines could benefit the Canadian economy. On the other hand, such pipelines could have adverse effects on the environment. Critical thinking is essential in weighing the possible costs and benefits in taking any action.

Unfortunately, many people, including adults, sometimes are lacking in critical and scientific reasoning (Ransdell, 2010). Deanna Kuhn studied the connection between scientific and informal (everyday) reasoning in adults (Kuhn, 1993). She asked 160 people (teenagers and people in their 20s, 40s, and 60s) their theories on three topics: what causes prisoners to return to a life of crime, what causes children to fail in school, and what causes unemployment. After stating their theories, participants were asked for evidence on which they based their ideas. Only 40 percent of the participants could give actual evidence, that is, information that is based on actual observations that bear on the theory's correctness. For instance, a man in his 20s who theorized that poor nutrition causes children to fail in school answered the question, "What would show that?" with "[They would get poor grades because] they are lacking something in their body." This is false evidence because it does not explain why poor nutrition might affect school failure. When asked to come up with reasons their thinking may be wrong, many actively resisted. As one participant said, "If I knew from the evidence that I'm wrong, I wouldn't say what I am saying." Others were even more stubborn, saying things like, "They'll never prove me wrong." Critical thinking requires that we be open to evidence that bears on whether our ideas are correct or not, even if we are not happy with the evidence.

it difficult to question their own thinking. If one were able to do so as a matter of course, one could more readily dismiss a line of thinking as wrong when it is not supported by evidence. In fact, the ability to think openly and flexibly might be as important as more standard measures of cognitive ability, such as mathematical skill. Keith Stanovich at the University of Toronto has shown that flexible and open-minded thinking in undergraduate participants shows a stronger correlation with performance on reasoning tasks than mathematical background (Stanovich & West, 1998). See the "Psychology in the Real World" feature to learn how to develop critical thinking outside the classroom.

LO11 How Do We Make Judgments and Decisions?

Should I wear the red shirt or the brown one? Paper or plastic? Should I go to class or not? Can I make it across the street without getting hit by that car? Should I have a glass of water or a Coke? We make hundreds of decisions every day, and each of those decisions is based on many different assumptions, judgments, and estimates. We also make judgments countless times each day. Every time we say things like "I decided . . .," "Chances are . . .," "It is unlikely . . .," or "She probably did that because . . .," we are judging how likely something is to happen.

As it turns out, most often we use mental shortcuts to make decisions. These shortcuts, known as **heuristics,** are methods for making complex and uncertain decisions and judgments (Kahneman & Tversky, 1972). Consider, for example, the thought processes involved in deciding how to avoid being hit by a car when crossing a busy street. Instead of reasoning out each step systematically, we check oncoming traffic in both directions and quickly judge how fast the cars are moving and how fast we can get across. We base the decision of whether to step off the curb on our quick judgment of the pace of the oncoming cars. We usually don't debate with ourselves for very long before making that decision. Heuristics allow us to come to quick and efficient decisions.

heuristics
mental shortcuts; methods for making complex and uncertain decisions and judgments.

We use many types of heuristics. Here we look briefly at the two most common types: the representativeness heuristic and the availability heuristic.

The Representativeness Heuristic Consider this information about Joe: He is friendly, often works weekends, and knows his way around town very well. Now we ask you to answer this question: Is Joe more likely to be a real estate agent or a doctor? You are likely to process this information about Joe and come to the conclusion that he is a real estate agent. After all, friendliness is an asset in any sales industry, and any successful realtor would be well acquainted with the neighbourhoods where they list properties. Making a classification decision based upon how well available evidence "fits" into a category is an efficient mental shortcut, and can quickly generate an accurate answer. This type of heuristic is called the **representativeness heuristic,** a strategy used to estimate the probability of one event based on how typical or representative it is of another event (Tversky & Kahneman, 1974).

representativeness heuristic
a strategy we use to estimate the probability of one event based on how typical it is of another event.

The problem with using the representativeness heuristic is that we tend to rely upon this strategy in the face of other types of evidence. For instance, what if you were given additional information about Joe—that he was chosen randomly from a group of 70 doctors and 30 real estate agents. When given the proportions of each occupation in the group, estimating the likelihood of Joe's profession should be easy—the correct answer is 30 percent that he is a real estate agent (and 70 percent that he is a doctor). Kahneman and Tversky (1973) performed a similar set of experiments and found that personality descriptions that fit certain occupations were used to make probability judgments even when the base rates were given to participants. This type of error is not unusual when many of us make quick decisions.

The Availability Heuristic The second major type of heuristic is the **availability heuristic,** which is a strategy we use when we make decisions based on the ease with which estimates come to mind or how available they are to our awareness (Tversky & Kahneman, 1974). For instance, the availability heuristic is often used when people make judgments about the aggressiveness of dog breeds. Pit bulls certainly have a bad reputation, and many North American cities, such as Ottawa, have banned the breed altogether. Although pit bulls are sometimes involved in fatal dog attacks, German shepherds are actually more likely to be involved in fatalities (Gladwell, 2006). However, media coverage of pit bull attacks tends to be very vivid and thoughts of a snarling pit bull are easily called to mind. Vividness and availability lead us to overestimate how likely certain events are.

availability heuristic
a device we use to make decisions based on the ease with which estimates come to mind or how available they are to our awareness.

In a series of experiments, Stuart McKelvie (1997) had participants listen to a list containing an equal number of men's and women's names. In one version of the list, the male names were all examples of famous men, while in another version only the female names were famous. When later tested, participants reported

Finding one item in a large supermarket is made easier by heuristics. If you're looking for cold juice, you can narrow your search to a few places where cold beverages are stored and ignore all the other aisles. Deciding on a specific juice drink might be harder.

that there were more men on the list if they heard the version with famous men, while the reverse was true for the famous women list. Presumably, the names of famous people stand out and become more prominent in memory, and therefore the participants had better recall for them. The more available information is to our recall, the more likely we are to be biased towards it.

Heuristics and their importance in decision making and judgments are relatively new concepts in psychology. These notions developed from research in the early 1970s by Daniel Kahneman and Amos Tversky. How they came up with the idea for carrying out this groundbreaking research provides an interesting glimpse into how psychologists make discoveries by challenging assumptions held by other scientists.

Groundbreaking Research

Non-rational Decision Making

Are the mental processes you use to make decisions based on reasonable, rational thought? Are you sure? Most of us like to think we are always reasonable and rational, and yet a Nobel Prize was awarded in 2002 for findings showing that not all decisions are rational and reasonable, especially economic decisions.

RATIONAL CHOICE THEORY

For much of the 20th century, cognitive scientists and economists who studied human decision making believed that people generally make rational decisions. Specifically, it was thought that when given a choice between two or more options, humans will choose the one that is most likely to help them achieve their particular goals—that is, the rational choice. Economists called this *rational choice theory* (Scott, 2000). They based this theory on principles of behaviourism. For decades, theorists held that people base financial decisions on a *cost-benefit analysis*. They ask themselves, "Do the costs outweigh the benefits? If yes, we don't buy; if no, we do buy." Think, however, about how you actually purchase items. How often do you buy things when you know you shouldn't because you really can't afford them—that is, the cost outweighs the benefits? If the rising levels of credit card debt are any indication, many of us are not rational consumers. But what does research tell us about how rational our decisions and judgments are?

Many of us are not rational consumers. The fact that we cannot afford to buy three pairs of shoes at a time does not mean that we do not buy them.

EVIDENCE AGAINST RATIONAL CHOICE THEORY

As we saw in the case of confirmation bias, not all reasoning is rational. In the 1970s, Amos Tversky and Daniel Kahneman began to challenge rational choice theory with their research on human judgment and decision making. Their collaboration began when both were at the Hebrew University in Israel, where Kahneman was teaching a graduate seminar in applied psychology. "In what turned out to be a life-changing event," Kahneman writes, "I asked my younger colleague Amos Tversky to tell the class about what was going on in his field of judgment and decision-making" (Kahneman, 2002). In the seminar, Tversky demonstrated how people make judgments about the probability of events. He combined red and white poker chips in two different bags and in two different ratios as an example. He explained that people are generally rational in their judgments; that is, they take into account differences in base rates. Using his bags of poker chips, he demonstrated that the odds are higher that a red chip will come from a bag with a base rate of 70/30 red to white chips than from a bag with a base rate of 30/70 red to white chips.

Amos Tversky

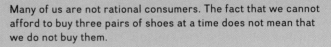

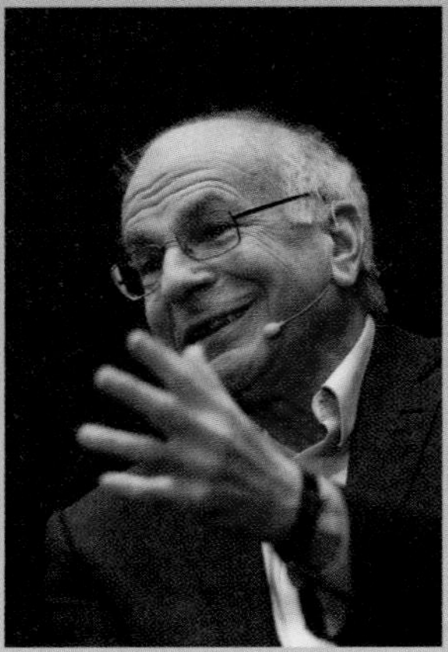

Daniel Kahneman

Tversky's conclusion that people are rational and make use of base rate information, however, started a lively debate in the seminar, as Kahneman later described: "The idea . . . did not seem to fit with the everyday observation of people commonly jumping to conclusions. [Tversky] went in to the seminar believing in his findings that people are relatively rational judges but left with that belief shaken" (Kahneman, 2002). This seminar exchange was the beginning of the research collaboration between Kahneman and Tversky.

In 1974, they published a paper that summarized the results of 13 of their studies on "judgments under uncertainty" (Tversky & Kahneman, 1974). In it, they presented several principles that would change the fields of psychology, economics, and even philosophy. We have already discussed two of them: the availability and representativeness heuristics.

Additional research by Kahneman and Tversky revealed other areas in which people are less than rational in their decision making and judgments. For example, if people were rational they would realize that the odds of two events can never be higher than the odds of one of those events alone. To put it most simply, the odds of A and B occurring together can never exceed the odds of either A or B occurring separately. Let's consider a specific example: The odds of your both (A) winning the lottery and (B) getting a promotion on the same day can never be greater than the odds of either one of these events happening alone. Sometimes, though, we get information that can be so representative of a stereotype that it biases us and we are likely to forget this simple rule of logic and make an error in our judgment. Take the classic example of Linda offered by Tversky and Kahneman (1983):

> Linda is 31 years old, single, outspoken, and very bright. She majored in philosophy. As a student, she was deeply concerned with issues of discrimination and social justice, and participated in anti-nuclear demonstrations.

Now you are asked the odds of each of the following: (A) that Linda is active in the feminist movement, (B) that Linda is a bank teller, and (C) that Linda is a bank teller and is active in the feminist movement. It is clear that A is more likely than B.

But what about B compared to C? Remember that the combination of two events cannot be more likely than either event separately. Yet because what we are told about Linda is representative of feminists (A) and not of bank tellers (B), we are likely to say what 85 percent of the participants said—namely, that (C) is more likely than (B). In this case, the representativeness heuristic has led to an error known as the **conjunction fallacy**, which occurs when people say the combination of two events is more likely than either event alone.

These findings and others like them point to the conclusion that people sometimes ignore base rates, sometimes are biased by stereotypes, and sometimes use shortcuts to arrive quickly, but not completely rationally, at their decisions and conclusions. In short, Kahneman and Tversky demonstrated that people bypass fully rational decision making and make use of automatic shortcuts in their reasoning and judgments.

conjunction fallacy
an error in logic that occurs when people say that the combination of two events is more likely than either event alone.

HOW THESE FINDINGS CHANGED PEOPLE'S MINDS

To some psychologists, these conclusions about less than rational reasoning were not surprising—after all, psychologists know just as much as anyone else about irrational thought and biased behaviour. Yet to others, as well as to many economists and philosophers, Kahneman and Tversky's findings were nothing short of revolutionary, although not everyone appreciated them. A well-known American philosopher once told Kahneman, who had started to describe some of his findings at a dinner party, "I am not really interested in the psychology of stupidity" and walked away (Kahneman, 2002).

As a sign of how revolutionary their research was, in 2002 Kahneman won the Nobel Prize in Economics (Tversky had died in 1996). In so honouring Kahneman, the Nobel committee wrote in its press release:

> Traditionally, much of economic research has relied on the assumption of a "homo-economicus" [economic human] motivated by self-interest and capable of rational decision-making. Daniel Kahneman has integrated insights from psychology into economics, thereby laying the foundation for a new field of research. Kahneman's main findings concern decision-making under uncertainty, where he has demonstrated how human decisions may systematically depart from those predicted by standard economic theory. Kahneman has also discovered how human judgment may take heuristic shortcuts that systematically depart from basic principles of probability. His work has inspired a new generation of researchers in economics and finance to enrich economic theory using insights from cognitive psychology into intrinsic human motivation. (*The Prize*, 2002)

Challenge Your Assumptions
True or False? People are generally rational in their decision making.
False: Research on heuristics shows that people do not always come to rational conclusions and decisions.

Quick Quiz 8.2: Thinking, Reasoning, and Decision Making

1. Structures in our mind—such as an idea or image—that stand for something else, such as an external object or thing, are known as
   a. memories.
   b. mental representations.
   c. mental rotation.
   d. visions.
2. Which of the following would be considered a prototype for fruit?
   a. rhubarb
   b. tomato
   c. avocado
   d. apple
3. When we reason from general statements of what is known to specific conclusions, we are engaging in
   a. hypothesis testing.
   b. inductive reasoning.
   c. deductive reasoning.
   d. logic.
4. What distinguishes scientific thinking from non-scientific thinking?
   a. the ability to separate belief from evidence
   b. the ability to reason
   c. concept formation
   d. the use of heuristics
5. __________ are mental shortcuts for making complex and uncertain decisions and judgments.
   a. Categories
   b. Schemas
   c. Calculations
   d. Heuristics
6. Even though the odds of dying in a car crash (1 in 85) are greater than dying in a plane crash (1 in 5682), many people believe they are more likely to die in a plane crash than a car crash. This example illustrates
   a. the conjunction fallacy.
   b. the availability heuristic.
   c. the confirmation bias.
   d. the representativeness heuristic.

Answers can be found at the end of the chapter.

Learning a Second Language

Learning a second language involves many of the linguistic and cognitive principles we reviewed in this chapter. As we saw with Mike, Lisa, and Zoé at the beginning of the chapter, bilingualism, or fluency in more than one language, is not uncommon in Canada. The provinces Quebec and New Brunswick have the highest proportion of French–English bilingualism in the country (Statistics Canada, 2001). Vocabulary tests often reveal higher vocabulary in monolingual children than bilingual children, but the latter have better executive functioning skills than the former (Bialystok, Barac, Blaye, & Poulin-Dubois, 2010; Hoff et al., 2012). As we consider bilingualism and how we can apply it to the topics in this chapter, we'll think about these questions: Is learning a second language essentially the same as learning one's first language? How much does it matter how old we are when we learn the second language? Finally, does learning a second language actually make you more creative and more able to think about your thinking (metacognitive)?

Sensitivity Periods and Second-Language Acquisition

What is the best way to master a second language? Most experts agree: The earlier an individual is exposed to a language, the better. Janet Werker of the University of British Columbia has shown that bilingual infants begin to learn about the properties of their two languages very early in life, long before they actually begin to speak. Werker's research suggests that humans appear to be as capable of learning two languages as one (Werker & Byers-Heinlein, 2008). Even if children are not exposed to a bilingual environment from infancy, they can still easily learn a second language early in life. In fact, exposure to a second language later in childhood is a common experience for many Canadian children. English-speaking children enrolled in Canadian French-immersion schooling seem to benefit from exposure to French; after about a year of second language exposure, strong grammatical knowledge in French is correlated with reading skills in both English and French (Deacon, 2006).

Second language instruction is not always beneficial, however, especially for minority language speakers. A study of Inuit children in northern Quebec compared early schooling in culturally dominant languages (either English or French) to their native Inuktitut. Researchers found that the children who were taught in English or French for the first three years of school had poorer language skills in their own native Inuktitut language, even after only one year of school (Wright et al., 2000). This loss of language fluency with second language learning is called *subtractive bilingualism,* and it can be avoided if the minority language is supported at home and school (Shanley, 2007).

There is a sensitive period for second-language acquisition: Children learn second languages more quickly than adults do and speak them more fluently (Birdsong, 2006; DeKeyser & Larson-Hall, 2005; Kim et al., 1997; Sakai, 2005; Uylings, 2006). A strong negative correlation exists between the age of learning the second language and the proficiency of speaking that language (DeKeyser & Larson-Hall, 2005). The younger a person is when he or she acquires the second language, the more proficiently the person speaks that language. By around age seven, learning a second language starts to become a little more difficult, and proficiency is reduced; and by early adolescence (around ages 13 to 15), the sensitive period for learning to speak a second language without an accent appears to end (Birdsong, 2005; Flege, Munro, & MacKay, 1995a, 1995b; Long, 1990; Jiang, Green, Henley, & Masten, 2009; Oyama, 1976; Sakai, 2005). For example, native English speakers evaluated the strength of the accent in English spoken by Italian immigrants to the United States (Oyama, 1976). The length of time the immigrants had been in the United States did not affect the strength or thickness of their accent, but the age at which they had moved to the United States did. If they were six when they immigrated

What advice would you give to parents to support second-language development in their children?

Challenge Your Assumptions

True or False? People who learn to speak a second language before their early teens are more likely to speak without an accent.

True: The window for learning to speak a second language with no trace of one's native language seems to be early to mid-adolescence.

and had been in the country for only two years, they had much less of an accent than if they were 30 years old when they learned the language but had been in the United States for ten years. A systematic review of the literature by Long (1990) confirmed this finding from dozens of studies. Thus, as a time for learning to speak a second language without an accent, childhood is better than adolescence and adolescence is better than adulthood. Although the finding is robust that age of second-language acquisition affects the accent level of non-native speakers, numerous social factors lessen this effect, such as continued education, the amount of second language that is used, and gender (Flege, 1999; Flege et al., 1995a, 1995b; Hakuta, Bialystok, & Wiley, 2003).

Second-Language Learning and the Brain

People who are fluent in two languages apparently are capable of more efficient cognitive processing than those who speak only one language. Psychologists examined the ability of speakers of one and two languages to perform cognitive tasks (Bialystok et al., 2006). They found that those who spoke two languages performed better on these cognitive tasks and continued to do so later in life.

Learning another language may also have a long-term beneficial effect on the brain. When matched for age, gender, and other qualities, elderly speakers of two languages develop dementia more than four years later than do elderly speakers of only one language (Bialystok, Craik, & Freedman, 2007). What is most interesting about these results is they once again support the view that stimulation from the environment—in this case, learning another language—can enrich our brains and enable them to process information more efficiently.

Neuroscientists have begun to demonstrate even more directly the long-lasting effects of learning two languages. First, compared to single-language speakers, bilingual speakers have a greater density of neurons in the language centres of the brain (Mechelli et al., 2004). Not only that, but neural density is proportional to the age at which the person learned the second language. The earlier the second language is learned, the greater the neural density (Mechelli et al., 2004). These findings demonstrate yet again how the brain is shaped by experience.

Second, bilingual people exhibit differences in brain activation depending on when they learned their second language (Kim et al., 1997). What is most fascinating is that the brains of people who learn a second language early in life are more efficient at language processing and more similar when speaking in both languages than are the brains of people who learn a second language late in life. If someone learns a second language early in life, essentially at the same time that they learn their first language, the brain regions that are active during speech (production) overlap almost completely. On the other hand, if a person learns a second language years after learning the first language, the brain regions that are active during speech (production) are next to each other but hardly overlap (see Figure 8.12).

What is equally fascinating is that the same pattern does not hold for comprehension or listening. The brains of both early and late second-language learners show the same areas of activation when the learners are listening to their first and second languages (Kim et al., 1997). Thus, the age at which a person learns a second language is reflected in differences in the brain, but only in areas involved in producing rather than understanding speech.

Reasoning in a Second Language

It is difficult enough to get through a university exam in one's native language. Imagine doing it in a second language in which you are not perfectly fluent. In research that compared students' deductive reasoning in their native language and their deductive reasoning in a second language, not surprisingly the students performed better in their native language (D'Anglejan, 1979). Therefore, it is quite possible that the validity of these tests for non-native speakers is somewhat questionable and that the scores do not accurately portray the aptitude of the test takers.

Second Language Acquisition and Metacognition

Remember the concerns that Mike and Lisa's family and friends had about raising Zoé in Greek only and letting others teach her English? One of the concerns was how Zoé would know when to speak which language with whom. Her Canadian relatives didn't know Greek, and her Greek relatives didn't know English very well. One explanation for why children do not confuse which language to speak to which group of people is "theory of mind," a topic we will explore in Chapter 10. By about age four, children understand that other people's thoughts and ideas are different from their

Connection

"Theory of mind" refers to our knowledge and ideas about how other people's minds work, especially knowing and understanding what other people are thinking, wanting, or feeling. Psychologists use the *false-belief* task to determine when children develop theory of mind and come to know that others can believe something that is false.

See Chapter 10, LO4.

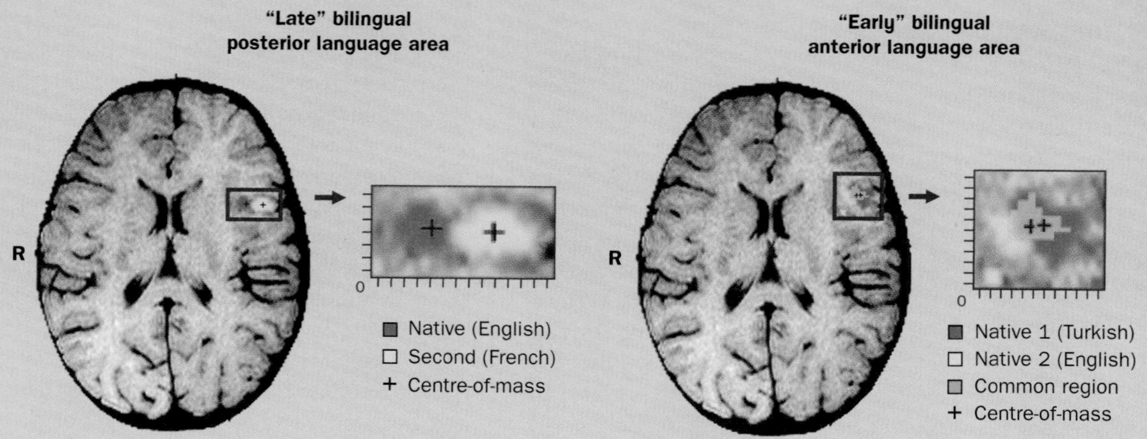

FIGURE **8.12**

ACTIVATION IN BROCA'S AREA FOR LATE LEARNERS AND EARLY LEARNERS OF A SECOND LANGUAGE. People who learn a second language later in life (after the age of 16) use different areas of the brain to produce speech in two languages, as shown by the images on the left. People who learn a second language in childhood show activation in overlapping areas of the brain when producing speech in two languages, as shown on the right. In other words, the brain of the early learner responds almost identically when speaking either language. Perhaps the reason why late learners are less fluent is that the brain treats the two languages differently. (*Source:* Kim et al., 1997.)

Challenge Your Assumptions

True or False? Children raised from infancy with two languages (bilingually) seldom confuse the two languages.

True: Probably because they are sensitive to what other people know and don't know, bilingual children seldom mix up languages or speak the wrong language to someone.

own. Research shows that bilingual children are more skilled in theory of mind tasks than are monolingual children, suggesting that they are aware of what the person they are speaking to knows and does not know (Kovács, 2009; Tare & Gelman, 2010).

Accurately knowing what you do and do not know and the ability to monitor your thinking as you work on a problem are two hallmarks of metacognition. Because learning a second language requires one to think about one's thinking, some linguists and psychologists have proposed that bilingual children should be better at knowing what they know and monitoring their thinking than monolingual children (Barac & Bialystok, 2012; Jimenez, Garcia, & Pearson, 1994; Ruan, 2004; Tobias & Everson, 2002; Wenden, 1998). The findings of research on this question are mixed. It may be, however, that metacognitive thinking is more pronounced when one is first learning a second language than later, when one is rather fluent (Tobias & Everson, 2002).

Other studies have also reported at least partial support for the idea that speaking two languages facilitates creative, flexible, and original problem solving (Kovács & Mehler, 2009; Landry, 1973; Lasagabaster 2000; Ricciardelli, 1992; Zhang, 2010). In a quantitative review (meta-analysis) of a large body of research, Ricciardelli reported that 20 out of 24 published studies had found that bilingual students scored higher on creativity tasks than did monolingual students. Flexible and creative thinking thus are closely aligned with metacognitive thinking (Sternberg, 2004).

Quick Quiz 8.3: Evaluating Connections in Language and Thought

1. The sensitive period for learning to speak a second language without an accent appears to end at what stage of life?
   a. early childhood
   b. early teens
   c. young adulthood
   d. middle age

2. Compared to those of single-language speakers, the brains of bilingual speakers have
   a. greater density of neurons in the brain.
   b. larger right hemispheres.
   c. larger left hemispheres.
   d. fewer axons in the corpus callosum.

Answers can be found at the end of the chapter.

Chapter Review

THE NATURE OF LANGUAGE

- Human language is an open symbolic communication system that follows rules of syntax and grammar.

THE DEVELOPMENT OF LANGUAGE

- Individuals develop language in a four-stage sequence, beginning with cooing and babbling in infancy. At about 12 months of age, toddlers start making their first one-word utterances. At around 18 months, babies progress to two-word utterances. By age two-and-a-half to three, most children enter the short-sentence phase. Continued language development requires stimulation from other people during a sensitive period between about the first six years of life and age 12.
- There are three major theories of language. Socio-cultural theories propose that we learn vocabulary by hearing others speak and figure out what they mean by the context. Conditioning and learning theories argue that language is like any other learned behaviour, something that occurs because it is reinforced and shaped. Nativist theories argue that humans possess a language acquisition device (LAD), an innate, biologically based capacity to acquire language that comes with a general and universal grammar.

THINKING, REASONING, AND DECISION MAKING

- Cognitive psychology is the scientific study of how people think, learn, remember, and perceive.
- We use visual and verbal representations in our mind as mental structures or processes for an image or idea. Concepts and categories are mental representations that we use to organize our world. Prototypes are the best-fitting examples of a category.
- We use reasoning to draw inferences or conclusions from principles and evidence. In deductive reasoning, we start with a general statement of what is known and draw specific conclusions from it. We use inductive reasoning to draw general conclusions from specific evidence. These conclusions are less certain because many different conclusions might be consistent with a specific fact.
- Confirmation bias is the tendency to selectively attend to information that confirms one's general beliefs while ignoring information or evidence that contradicts one's beliefs.
- Critical thinking uses sound reasoning when analyzing facts, generating and organizing ideas, defending opinions, making comparisons, drawing inferences, evaluating arguments, and solving problems.
- Scientific thinking is metacognitive thinking that is used to generate, test, reflect upon, and revise theories.
- Heuristics are shortcuts that we use in making judgments. We use the representativeness heuristic when we estimate the probability of one event based on how typical it is of another event. We use the availability heuristic to make estimates based on the ease with which we can bring an event or object to mind.

EVALUATING CONNECTIONS IN LANGUAGE AND THOUGHT

- Children who learn a second language early, during a sensitive period that ends around age 15, speak it more fluently, without an accent, and with greater proficiency than do older teens or adults.
- Bilingualism appears to enhance cognitive processing and is associated with a lower rate of dementia in the elderly.
- People who learn a second language in childhood process both languages in roughly the same area of the brain, whereas in later learners, processing of the two languages occurs in two scarcely overlapping areas.
- At least initially, learning a second language may enhance metacognition, knowledge of what we know and don't know, and foster flexible thinking and creative problem solving.

Quick Quiz Answers

Quick Quiz 8.1: 1. c 2. a 3. d 4. c **Quick Quiz 8.2:** 1. b 2. d 3. c 4. a 5. d 6. b **Quick Quiz 8.3:** 1. b 2. a

Intelligence, Problem Solving, and Creativity

CHAPTER 9

CHAPTER OUTLINE

Challenge Your Assumptions

True or False?

- ☐ Intelligence is a single, general capacity.
- ☐ People with high IQs have larger brains.
- ☐ People with very high IQs are geniuses.
- ☐ Intelligence is strongly linked to creativity.

LEARNING OBJECTIVES

LO1 Define intelligence and summarize the various theoretical perspectives.

LO2 Describe how intelligence is measured, the characteristics of a good test, and problems with test bias.

LO3 Describe the extremes of intelligence.

LO4 Explain how nature and nurture affect intelligence.

LO5 Summarize the controversy surrounding group differences in intelligence scores.

LO6 Describe how culture affects intelligence.

LO7 Discuss the primary types of problems, strategies for forming solutions, and obstacles to reaching effective solutions.

LO8 Define creativity, describe factors that contribute to creativity, and explain the role of creativity in problem solving and intelligence.

LO9 Explain what is meant by genius and describe its relationship to intelligence and creativity.

Like many people, Josh Tiessen of Stoney Creek, Ontario, loved arts and crafts as a young child. What makes Josh exceptional is that he became a world-class artist at a very young age, winning countless awards and selling his first painting at age 11. His artistic talent caught the attention of celebrated Canadian artist Robert Bateman, who mentored Josh and encouraged him to pursue a career as a professional artist. Presently, his work hangs in galleries all over the world. For years, his younger brother Zac lived in his shadow; however, at the age of 13, Zac became interested in playing the guitar. In a very short period of time, Zac became an accomplished musician, composer, and producer (Ruf, 2013).

Josh and Zac's accomplishments are clearly quite extraordinary. In addition to their artistic talents, the Tiessen brothers also excelled academically. Both boys finished high school early and enrolled in university courses to further their interests and training, all while still in their teens. When American psychologist and child prodigy expert Joanne Ruthsatz studied the Tiessen brothers, she found they have exceptional working memory and a high level of attention to detail, traits that are found universally in other child prodigies (Ruthsatz et al., 2014).

What does it mean when we say someone is gifted? Does painting beautiful images or mastering a musical instrument make someone smart? The Tiessen brothers' story raises important questions about what it means to be smart or talented. Are we born smart or do our abilities develop with training? Being brothers, Josh and Zac share similar genes, so perhaps their talent is innate—coded in their DNA. But what role does the environment play? They grew up in the same home with the same parents, so maybe the family environment provided ample opportunity to develop their abilities to their full potential.

Psychologists agree that there are three capacities that shape how smart people are: intelligence, problem solving, and creativity. Here we will discuss what intelligence is, how it is measured, and the role of genes and the environment. We will also look at the skills of problem solving and creativity and how they influence our definitions of intelligence. Throughout the chapter, we will see how these topics overlap, yet also reveal distinct capabilities of the human mind.

LO1 INTELLIGENCE

Many people consider intelligence the primary trait that sets humans apart from other animals. But what is intelligence? Is it the same as being generally smart, or is it more complicated than that? Is it a single ability or many different abilities? Intelligence can be defined in a number of ways, and even the experts cannot agree on a definition. Over the years, groups of intelligence experts have convened for the purpose of defining intelligence (Neisser et al., 1996; Snyderman & Rothman, 1987; Sternberg & Detterman, 1986). Let's see what they have come up with.

Defining Intelligence

intelligence
a set of cognitive skills that includes abstract thinking, reasoning, problem solving, and the ability to acquire knowledge.

Intelligence may be our inherent potential for learning, how fast we are able to learn, or the body of knowledge we possess. It may also include the ability to do things in ways that other people have never tried. The definition of intelligence that we will use in this book encompasses all these qualities. According to the experts, **intelligence** is a set of cognitive skills that includes abstract thinking,

Question	Theory	Summary
How intelligent are you?	Spearman's general intelligence (g)	Intelligence is a single general capacity.
How are you intelligent?	Thurstone's multiple factors	Intelligence consists of seven primary mental abilities, including spatial ability, memory, perceptual speed, and word
How are you intelligent?	Cattell–Horn–Carroll (CHC) hierarchical intelligence	Intelligence can be broken down into three levels of ability: general, broad, and narrow.
How are you intelligent?	Sternberg's triarchic theory	Intelligence is made up of three abilities (analytical, creative, and practical) necessary for success.
How are you intelligent?	Gardner's multiple intelligences	Intelligence includes at least eight distinct capacities, including musical intelligence, interpersonal intelligence, and bodily-kinesthetic intelligence.

FIGURE **9.1**
THEORIES OF INTELLIGENCE. There are two principal views of intelligence. One considers intelligence as a single, measurable ability. The other looks at intelligence as comprising several distinct abilities.

reasoning, problem solving, and the ability to acquire knowledge. Other less-agreed-on qualities of intelligence include mathematical ability, general knowledge, and creativity (see Figure 9.1).

Theories of Intelligence

Theories of intelligence started sprouting up in the early 1900s, soon after the first modern intelligence tests appeared. Two distinct views of intelligence have come to dominate these theories. One view says that intelligence is a single, general ability; the other says that intelligence consists of multiple abilities.

Intelligence as One General Ability Charles Spearman (1904, 1923) developed the first theory of intelligence. He proposed that human intelligence is best thought of as a single general capacity, or ability. Spearman came to this conclusion after research consistently showed that specific dimensions, or factors, of intelligence—namely, spatial, verbal, perceptual, and quantitative factors—correlated strongly with one another, suggesting that they were all measuring much the same thing. In other words, people who achieve high scores on the verbal section of an intelligence test are also likely to have high scores on the spatial, perceptual, and quantitative sections.

Spearman's theory is now known as a **g-factor theory** of intelligence because it describes intelligence as a single *general* factor made up of specific components. This theory strongly influenced intelligence test construction for most of the 20th century. A person's overall intelligence score is determined by his or her specific scores on subtests. Thus, the g-factor theory implies that a single number can accurately reflect a person's intelligence. A person who scores 115 on an intelligence test is generally more intelligent than a person who scores 100, for example. This perspective is illustrated by the question: "How intelligent are you?" (See Figure 9.1.)

g-factor theory
Spearman's theory that intelligence is a single general (g) factor made up of specific components.

Intelligence as Multiple Abilities Critics of Spearman's theory argue that it does not do justice to the complexity of intelligence. They do not dispute that moderately high correlations among subtests of intelligence exist, but they disagree on how they should be interpreted. Early critics noted that the correlations are low enough to support arguments that verbal, quantitative, and other abilities are distinct dimensions of intelligence (Thurstone, 1938). Moreover, they insisted that test scores by themselves ignore important aspects of intelligence that the traditional tests don't measure. This view, the **multiple-factor theory of intelligence,** holds that the different aspects of intelligence are distinct enough that multiple abilities must be considered, not just one. This perspective is illustrated by the question: "*How* are you intelligent?" (See Figure 9.1.) The key difference, then, between g-factor and multiple-factor theorists is that g-factor theorists say a single test score accurately reflects a person's overall intelligence, whereas multiple-factor theorists say that it doesn't.

multiple-factor theory of intelligence
idea that intelligence consists of distinct dimensions and is not just a single factor.

One of the first people to "break intelligence in two" was Raymond Cattell, with his notion of fluid and crystallized intelligence (Horn & Cattell, 1966). **Fluid intelligence** involves raw mental ability, pattern recognition, and abstract reasoning and is applied to a problem that a person has never confronted before. Problems that require finding relationships, understanding implications, and drawing conclusions all require fluid intelligence. Neither culture nor vocabulary influence fluid intelligence. One commonly used measure of fluid intelligence is the *Raven's Progressive Matrices Test* (see Figure 9.2). Matrix reasoning is fluid intelligence because it does not depend on acquired knowledge and involves the ability to find patterns. Fluid intelligence measures are *culture-fair* because their solutions do not require culturally acquired experience.

fluid intelligence
the ability to think through a problem one has never confronted before and recognize patterns that may lead to a solution.

Knowledge that we have gained from experience and learning, education, and practice, however, is called **crystallized intelligence.** This form of intelligence is influenced by how large your vocabulary is as well as your knowledge of your culture. Being asked, for example, whether Dalmatian is to dog as oriole is to bird is an example of a problem that requires crystallized intelligence.

crystallized intelligence
the kind of knowledge that one gains from experience and learning, education, and practice.

John Carroll (1993) further subdivided intelligence when he reviewed and integrated more than 450 sets of intelligence data published from the 1930s to the mid-1980s and concluded that the Cattell-Horn model of fluid and crystallized intelligence best fit the existing evidence. Carroll extended the model, however, arguing that intelligence actually consists of *three* levels, arranged in a hierarchy.

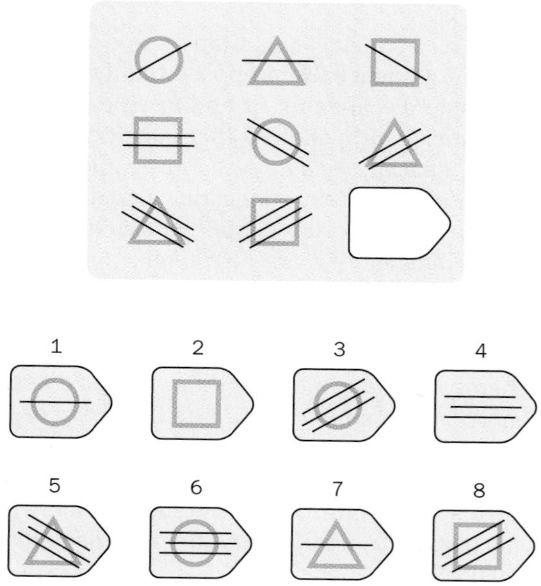

FIGURE **9.2**
EXAMPLE FROM RAVEN'S PROGRESSIVE MATRICES TEST. This sample problem requires fluid intelligence. It is non-verbal and requires pattern recognition, not prior acquired knowledge. For this reason, this test is often considered a "culture-fair" test of intelligence. (Simulated items similar to those in the Raven's Progressive Matrices. Copyright © 1998 by NCS Pearson, Inc. Reproduced with permission. All rights reserved. "Raven's Progressive Matrices" is a trademark in the US and/or other countries, of Pearson Education, Inc. or its affiliates.)

Can you figure out which of the numbered bottom figures would be next in the series of nine above?

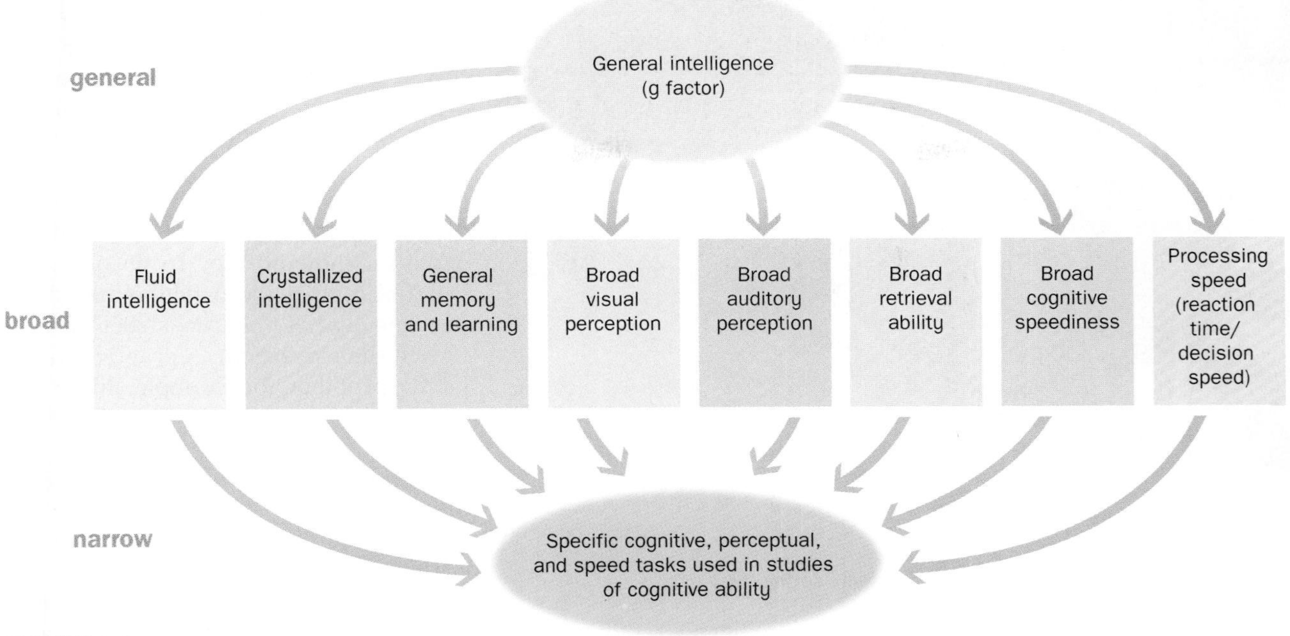

FIGURE **9.3**

THE CATTELL-HORN-CARROLL (CHC) MODEL OF INTELLIGENCE. This hierarchical model integrates the concept of a general intelligence with several broadly defined abilities, including fluid and crystallized intelligence. The broad categories consist of more specific abilities, such as speed of reasoning (fluid intelligence) and language comprehension (crystallized intelligence).

At the top of the hierarchy is general intelligence, at the middle is broad intelligence, and at the bottom is narrow intelligence. **General intelligence** is very similar to Spearman's concept of "g." **Broad intelligence** consists of abilities such as crystallized and fluid intelligence, as well as memory, learning, and processing speed. **Narrow intelligence** consists of nearly 70 distinct abilities, such as speed of reasoning and general sequential reasoning for fluid intelligence and reading, spelling, and language comprehension for crystallized intelligence (see Figure 9.3). Because this model includes Cattell and Horn's crystallized and fluid intelligences, it has become known as the *Cattell-Horn-Carroll (CHC) model of intelligence.*

Robert Sternberg and Howard Gardner have proposed even more radical theories of multiple intelligence. Sternberg argues for a broader view of intelligence than is found in traditional g-factor theories. Most important, he focuses not simply on intelligence but on **successful intelligence,** which he defines as an integrated set of information-processing and cognitive abilities needed for life success (Sternberg, 2005, p. 104). Three interrelated but distinct abilities make up successful intelligence: analytic, creative, and practical intelligence (Sternberg, 1985, 2006). Sternberg's three-part theory is known as the **triarchic theory of intelligence.**

The first type of intelligence, *analytic intelligence,* involves judging, evaluating, or comparing and contrasting information (Sternberg, 1998). Analytic intelligence resembles the kind of academic intelligence that leads to high scores on tests of intelligence. For example, an analytic problem might require a person to figure out an uncommon word from its context in a sentence, or it might ask the person to determine the next number in a series of numbers (Sternberg, 2003). The second form of intelligence is *creative intelligence.* Creative intelligence is involved in coming up with fresh and useful ideas for solving problems.

general intelligence
one of Carroll's three levels of intelligence; very similar to Spearman's concept of "g."

broad intelligence
one of Carroll's three levels of intelligence that includes abilities such as crystallized and fluid intelligence, as well as memory, learning, and processing speed.

narrow intelligence
one of Carroll's three levels of intelligence that includes many distinct abilities.

successful intelligence
according to Sternberg, an integrated set of abilities needed to attain success in life.

triarchic theory of intelligence
Sternberg's three-part model of intelligence, including analytic, creative, and practical intelligence.

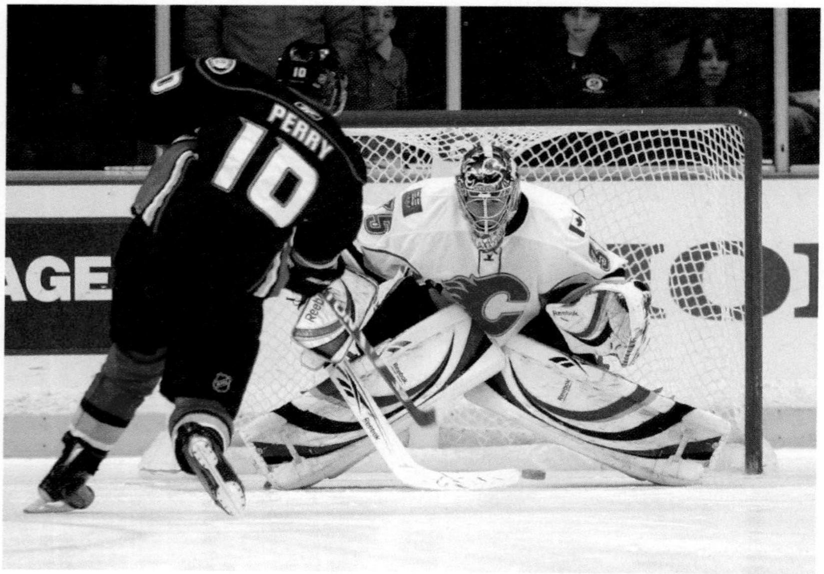

Athletes use practical intelligence to solve problems during the game.

For example, a person might be given a number of cartoon images and then be asked to come up with a caption for each (Sternberg, 2006). Traditional measures of intelligence do not measure creative intelligence well. The third processing skill, *practical intelligence,* is the ability to solve problems of everyday life efficiently. Practical intelligence plays a role in knowing how to do one's job well and requires knowledge and skills that one learns "on the street" rather than in the classroom. A practical intelligence problem, for example, might ask people to come up with three solutions to a real everyday problem they are currently experiencing in their life (Sternberg, 2003).

Another scholar who has focused on the multifaceted view of intelligence is Howard Gardner. Gardner (1983, 1993) argues that intelligence comprises at least eight distinct capacities: linguistic, mathematical–logical, musical, bodily–kinesthetic, spatial, intrapersonal, interpersonal, and naturalistic. *Naturalistic intelligence,* for instance, is the ability to recognize, classify, and understand the plants and animals in one's environment. In cultures that have formal science, highly skilled people in this domain of intelligence are likely to become biologists, botanists, and animal scientists or veterinarians. In cultures without formal science, they are the most talented hunters, gatherers, and farmers. *Interpersonal intelligence* is the ability to perceive and understand other people's intentions, motives, and behaviours. Interpersonally intelligent people therefore work well with others and know how to get along with others. See Figure 9.4 for a complete listing and definitions of Gardner's eight intelligences.

Challenge Your Assumptions

True or False? Intelligence is a single, general capacity.

False: Although some early theories of intelligence viewed it as a single ability, more modern views of intelligence recognize specific domains of intelligence.

Scholars are strongly divided, however, over Gardner's theory. Those who have the most problems with it tend to be psychologists. They see little value in calling skills like music, movement, and social skills "intelligence" and argue that Gardner has not provided tests of these intelligences (Eysenck, 1994a; Scarr, 1985; Sternberg, 1991). Moreover, there have been few direct empirical tests on Gardner's theory, and therefore some argue his ideas are more theory than science (Klein, 1998). For some psychologists and more educators, however, Gardner's ideas address two real problems: (1) Different students learn in different ways, and (2) some students who have demonstrated ability in some areas fail academic subjects and do poorly on traditional intelligence tests (Kornhaber, Fierros, & Veenema, 2004). They may even drop out of school.

How should teachers nurture and teach these failing students—indeed, all students—given the fact that different students learn different material differently? Entire schools have been designed to enhance the "intelligences" of students. We describe one of these programs in "Psychology in the Real World."

Howard Gardner

LO2 Measures of Intelligence

Like different theories of intelligence, tests of intelligence, commonly called IQ tests, are controversial. Some of the questions they raise are "How does someone interpret a person's score on an intelligence test?" "Where does a person stand compared to everyone else?" and "How do we know that a given test is any good at all?" There have been numerous attempts to answer these questions over the

Intelligence	Definition	Representative Professions
linguistic	Ability to learn, understand, and use both spoken and written language	Poets, writers, lawyers, politicians
logical-mathematical	Ability to analyze information and problems logically and to perform mathematical operations	Scientists, engineers, accountants
musical	Ability in performing, composing, or appreciating musical patterns	Musicians, dancers, songwriters
bodily-kinesthetic	Ability to use one's body or parts of it to solve problems or create products	Athletes, dancers, mechanics, craftspeople
spatial	Ability to think about and solve problems in three-dimensional space	Navigators, pilots, architects, sculptors
interpersonal	Ability to understand and be aware of other people's intentions, motivations, thoughts, and desires; also the ability to work well with and get along with others	Psychologists, social workers, teachers, politicians
intrapersonal	Ability to be aware of, understand, and regulate one's own behaviour, thoughts, feelings, and motivations	Psychologists, monks, priests
naturalistic	Ability to recognize, classify, and understand the plants and animals in one's environment	Naturalists, biologists, botanists, veterinarians, hunters, farmers

FIGURE **9.4**
GARDNER'S MULTIPLE INTELLIGENCES. The far-right column lists professions that are well served by each ability.

years. All of them have been based on the way intelligence was understood at the time the tests were devised, and so we begin our discussion with a bit of history.

The development and history of intelligence testing has been marked by three distinct periods. For the first period of 70 years or so, from about 1910 to about 1980, people constructed tests around practical and clinical concerns rather than any theory and understanding of intelligence. That began to change during the second period in the 1980s, when the first theory-driven intelligence tests were developed. Then, during the third period in the 1990s, in a major shift, some creators of intelligence tests acknowledged that intelligence may be many things rather than just one. Integrating theory and measurement, they developed intelligence tests that assess several aspects of intelligence.

Intelligence tests were among the first psychological tests. Sir Francis Galton, a cousin to Charles Darwin, was the first person to suggest the idea of intelligence testing in a paper, published in 1865 in England (Fancher, 2009). Galton believed that intelligence was inherited and he set out to demonstrate that people who were more socially and occupationally successful would perform better on a series of tasks designed to assess mental ability. To test his theory, Galton set up a laboratory at the 1884 London International Health Exhibition. Several thousand volunteers took his tests of reaction speed, muscular strength,

Psychology in the Real World

Bringing Multiple Intelligences to School

The chief motivation behind bringing multiple intelligences (MI) to the school setting is to avoid some of the limitations of traditional testing and teaching that discourage students who do not do well. Gardner (1999) realized that testing in the usual sense would have to be abandoned and classrooms would have to be arranged and equipped with materials that stimulate and foster each of the different forms of intelligence. Under this model, classrooms may be arranged with areas meant for dance, exercise, and construction. The materials may include board games, art and music materials, nature specimens (e.g., a fish tank), and natural objects.

An educational principle based on MI theory is that children should have some freedom to choose activities on their own. If they ignore certain kinds of activities, their teachers provide encouragement and "bridges" for them to try the neglected activities. For instance, if students are reluctant to tell stories, a teacher might encourage them to build a diorama (a three-dimensional model). The teacher would then ask the students to tell a story about what is happening to the people and animals in the diorama.

More than 40 schools in the United States have been designed to put into practice the development of all Gardner's forms of intelligences (Kornhaber et al., 2004). Many schools in Canada also implement MI theory. One example is Banded Peak School in Bragg Creek, Alberta, a public elementary school for children in kindergarten through Grade 8. Students at Banded Peak are encouraged to do the most with what they have, whether that means in academics, sports, leadership, or citizenship (McLaren, 2009). Assessment takes place many times throughout the year and can take on many forms. For example, students may demonstrate one of their multiple intelligences by presenting a project as a performance, such as a play, poetry reading, or artistic interpretation. They may also write papers on what they have learned. These presentations are often videotaped and put into the student's portfolio, which serves as a record of each student's cognitive and emotional development. Students still must take Alberta's province-wide standardized achievement tests in Grades 3 and 6, and when they do, they do at least as well as students from other schools (McLaren, 2009). In general, many of the schools adopting this model report that the MI approach helps decrease disciplinary problems and increase parent participation. Often, the performance of students with learning disabilities improves markedly when they attend MI schools (*Key Learning Community*, n.d.; Kornhaber et al., 2004).

In short, the MI schools teach to different learning styles and to their students' different intellectual talents. For some students at least, this alternative fosters academic achievement that might not occur in a traditional setting.

Should naturalistic intelligence be nurtured in the same way as mathematical skills, verbal ability, and at least five other kinds of intelligence?

and sensory acuity. He even measured people's head circumferences, presumably because he thought bigger heads reflected bigger and more powerful brains! To his disappointment, performance on each of these measures wasn't related to much of anything, including social and occupational success. So although Galton can be credited with generating interest in testing mental abilities, he wasn't really successful in developing a useful measure of intelligence.

The person who deserves the most credit for developing the first true "practical" test of intelligence is the French scholar Alfred Binet. In the early 1900s, the government hired Binet to identify students who would benefit most from special instruction techniques. For this purpose, Binet and a colleague, Theodore Simon, developed a test containing 30 problems of increasing difficulty. Their idea that ability to solve increasingly difficult problems depends on age became widely influential and has since become known as mental age. **Mental age** is the equivalent chronological age a child has reached based on his or her performance on an intelligence test. Children are given a mental age not according to how old they are in years, but rather according to the level or age group at which they can solve problems. Mental age is a norm or average because it is based on what most children at a particular age level can do.

Sir Francis Galton took measurements of head circumference as part of his early intelligence tests.

Do you think that head size is related to intelligence? Why or why not?

A few years after Binet developed the concept of mental age, a German psychologist, William Stern, introduced the *intelligence ratio,* in which mental age (MA) is divided by chronological age (CA) and multiplied by 100 to determine an intelligence score. The ratio of mental age over chronological age is commonly known as a person's *intelligence quotient* or IQ. In other words, if a child had a mental age of 10 and was 10 years old, she had an IQ of 100 ($10 \div 10 \times 100$). But if she had a mental age of 12 and was only 10 years old, she had an IQ of 120, whereas if she had a mental age of 8 and was 10 years old, her IQ was 80. This ratio was very useful in the early years of IQ testing with children, but it is no longer used. Part of the problem with Stern's intelligence ratio formula is that it doesn't work very well with adults. Typically by age 16, people's performance on IQ tests, or their mental age, starts to level out (Eysenck, 1994b) while their chronological age continues to increase. As a result, Stern's intelligence ratio yields increasingly lower IQ scores as people get older! Thus, today IQ scores are based on how well a child does on tests relative to norms or standards established by testing children of the same age.

mental age
the equivalent chronological age a child has reached based on his or her performance on an intelligence test.

About ten years after Binet published his first test, Lewis Terman, an American psychologist, translated the test for American students. Because Terman taught at Stanford University, he named the test the *Stanford-Binet test.* The most significant changes Terman made were to establish national norms and to adopt and apply the ratio score of $MA \div CA$ to a widely used IQ test.

In the 1930s, David Wechsler created new intelligence tests to measure adult intelligence. Wechsler's test became known as the *Wechsler Adult Intelligence Scales* (*WAIS*, Wechsler, 1944, 1958). Later he developed a test for children, the *Wechsler Intelligence Scales for Children (WISC).* At present, these two tests are the ones most frequently administered in Canada and the United States (Wasserman & Tulsky, 2005). To sample the kinds of problems included on one of these IQ tests, see Figure 9.5. The current versions of both the Stanford-Binet and the WAIS are based on modern theories about intelligence, which we discuss in the "Groundbreaking Research" feature.

Reliability and Validity of IQ Tests

Tests are meaningful only if they are both reliable and valid. Recall from Chapter 2 that *reliability* refers to consistency of results. There are many different forms of reliability. If a test has good **test-retest reliability,** a person who takes the same test on two different occasions will obtain very similar scores on both occasions. IQ tests tend to be extremely reliable, with test-retest correlations of +.90 or higher. Questions on a given subtest also tend to correlate very highly with other items on the subtest, meaning that the test's **internal consistency** is very high. So, overall, test makers have done a good job of creating reliable IQ tests (Gregory, 2007).

test-retest reliability
the extent to which scores on a test are similar over time.

internal consistency
the extent to which items within a test correlate with one another.

As we saw in Chapter 2, *validity* requires that the tests really measure intelligence and not something else. One indicator of a test's validity is the ability of verbal subscales

Similarities

An individual must think logically and abstractly to answer a number of questions about how things might be similar.

Example: "In what ways are boats and trains the same?"

Comprehension

This subscale is designed to measure an individual's judgment and common sense.

Example: "Why do individuals buy automobile insurance?"

non-verbal subscales

Picture Arrangement

A series of pictures out of sequence is shown to an individual, who is asked to place them in their proper order to tell an appropriate story. This subscale evaluates how individuals integrate information to make it logical and meaningful.

Example: "The pictures below need to be placed in an appropriate order to tell a story."

Block Design

An individual must assemble a set of multicoloured blocks to match designs that the examiner shows. Visual-motor coordination, perceptual organization, and the ability to visualize spatially are assessed.

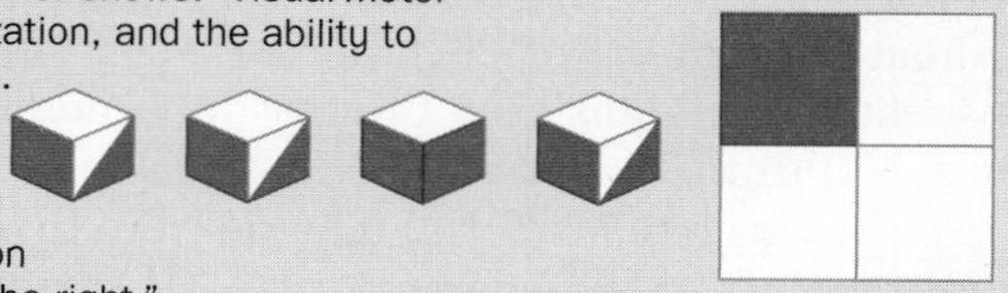

Example: "Use the four blocks on the left to make the pattern at the right."

FIGURE **9.5**

IQ TEST PROBLEMS SIMILAR TO THE ONES IN THE WECHSLER ADULT INTELLIGENCE SCALES (WAIS). The WAIS and the Wechsler Intelligence Scale for Children are the most widely administered intelligence tests in Canada and the United States. Simulated items similar to those found in the Wechsler Adult Intelligence Scale—Revised (WAIS-R). Copyright © 1981, 1955 by NCS Pearson, Inc. Reproduced with permission. All rights reserved. "Wechsler Adult Intelligence Scale" and "WAIS" are trademarks, in the US and/or other countries, of Pearson Education, Inc. or its affiliates.

Connection

The strength of the relationship between two variables can be measured using a correlation coefficient. The closer it is to +1.00 or −1.00, the stronger the relationship between variables.

See Chapter 2, LO4.

its test scores to predict real-world outcomes. The validity of a test is more difficult to establish than is its reliability. Although there is a great deal of evidence that the Wechsler and Stanford-Binet tests, among others, do provide valid measures of intelligence, many intelligence experts, notably Sternberg and Gardner, have argued that they measure only verbal, spatial, and mathematical forms of intelligence. The other forms that Gardner identified—social, emotional, musical, bodily, practical, and natural history—are not measured at all.

construct validity
the degree to which a test measures the concept it claims to measure, such as intelligence.

predictive validity
the degree to which intelligence test scores are positively related to real-world outcomes, such as school achievement or job success, and thus have predictive value.

There are at least two distinct forms of validity: construct and predictive. **Construct validity** refers to what we have just discussed: that a test measures the concept, or *construct,* it claims to measure. **Predictive validity** addresses the question of whether the construct is related positively to real-world outcomes, such as school achievement or job success. IQ tests do predict certain real-world outcomes, the first and foremost being academic performance. IQ scores predict

Groundbreaking Research

Changing Intelligence Tests

Because IQ tests were first created for practical purposes in the early part of the 20th century, they were not based on a clear understanding of the nature of human intelligence. In the 1980s, however, there was a shift in the way intelligence tests were developed. Now all major IQ tests have some basis in theories of intelligence.

OLD ASSUMPTIONS ABOUT THE NATURE OF INTELLIGENCE

For 50 years IQ tests were based on the assumption that intelligence is a single quality. The developers of both the Stanford-Binet and Wechsler tests failed to take into account Jean Piaget's work on cognitive development and newer findings from neuroscience.

As we will discuss in Chapter 10, Piaget found that the cognitive abilities of young children and adolescents are fundamentally different and that cognitive development occurs in stages rather than gradually over time. Adolescents can reason abstractly, for example, but young children cannot. Yet IQ tests continued to give very similar problems to young children, teenagers, and adults, changing only the level of difficulty.

Moreover, until the 1980s, IQ test developers ignored advances in neuroscience indicating that even though the two hemispheres of the brain work together, they process information differently, with the right hemisphere integrating the overall message and the left hemisphere analyzing the specific pieces of information in a message (Kaufman, 1979). Consistent with these findings, new evidence showed that some children learn best when information is taught piece-meal, one step at a time, whereas others learn best when information is presented visually all at once (Das, Kirby, & Jarman, 1975). In the late 20th century, a new approach to intelligence testing incorporated Piaget's ideas, findings from neuroscience, and learning style differences.

INTELLIGENCE TESTS BASED ON MODERN PSYCHOLOGICAL THEORY

As advances in neuroscience led to greater understanding of how the brain solves problems, psychologists became increasingly aware of the limits of existing IQ tests. In the late 1970s, when Alan and Nadeen Kaufman were on a family outing with their young children, they found themselves discussing the need for an intelligence test that would reflect current neuroscientific theories of the brain and information processing. They talked about what such a test would look like. By the time they reached their destination, they agreed that their plan was unrealistic and they wouldn't attempt it. As luck would have it, however, a test developer telephoned the next day to ask Alan, "Would either you, or Nadeen, or both of you want to develop a new intelligence test to challenge the Wechsler?" In this way the Kaufman-Assessment Battery for Children (K-ABC) was born (*Test Developer Profiles*, 2001).

Nadeen and Alan Kaufman

The K-ABC differed from the Stanford-Binet and Wechsler tests in four ways. First, it was the first IQ test to be guided by theories of intelligence, in particular Cattell and Horn's concepts of fluid and crystallized intelligence and Piaget's theory of cognitive development. Second, influenced by Piaget, the Kaufmans included fundamentally different kinds of problems for children of different ages, as well as problems at varied levels of difficulty. Third, unlike older tests, the K-ABC measured several distinct aspects of intelligence. Finally, influenced by neuroscience and information processing theory, the K-ABC assessed different types of learning styles. In this sense, the K-ABC was the first of many intelligence tests informed by contemporary ideas about how the brain worked and developed (Kaufman & Kaufman, 1983).

The K-ABC test was the first theory-based IQ test and one of two major shifts in the field of intelligence testing that took place in the 1980s. Raymond Cattell, John Horn, and John Carroll (who developed the CHC model of intelligence) led the second one (the "CHC shift"). This second ground-breaking shift began when Cattell and Horn served as consultants on another cognitive test—the second edition of the Woodcock-Johnson Tests of Cognitive Ability (WJ-R; Woodcock & Johnson, 1989). The new test was designed entirely based on Cattell and Horn's theory of crystallized and fluid intelligence. Subsequently, Carroll analyzed all known intelligence tests using the Cattell-Horn theory and extended the model so that it linked models of intelligence as a single quality with multidimensional models (see Figure 9.3; McGrew, 2005). The result was a rapid shift in all major intelligence tests. Now test makers became focused on creating intelligence tests that measured intelligence on more than one dimension (McGrew, 2005).

The Aftermath of the Shift in Intelligence Tests

Both the Kaufman and CHC shifts led to fundamental changes in intelligence tests, including the Stanford-Binet and the Wechsler scales. Tests may still produce an overall IQ score, but now they also yield scores on as many as seven dimensions of intelligence.

Influenced by the CHC model, the newest versions of both the WAIS (WAIS-IV) and the WISC (WISC-IV) include scores on four dimensions: verbal comprehension, perceptual reasoning, working memory, and processing speed (Hogan, 2007). Verbal comprehension measures general verbal skills, such as verbal fluency (for sample items, see the Similarities and Comprehension subscales in Figure 9.5). The perceptual reasoning dimension assesses the ability to examine a problem, drawing upon visual—motor and visual—spatial skills (see the Block Design subscale in Figure 9.5 for a sample item). Processing speed assesses how quickly a person can focus attention and quickly scan, discriminate between, and sequentially order visual information. Working memory, which holds information in mind for a short period so that it can be used to solve a problem at hand, is one of the dimensions that were missing before 1985. For examples of working memory tasks included in the Wechsler scales, see Figure 9.6.

Also influenced by the CHC model, the fifth edition of the Stanford-Binet assesses five different factors of general intelligence, each with verbal and non-verbal dimensions (Roid & Pomplun, 2005). In addition to assessing fluid and crystallized intelligence, the newest version of the Stanford Binet assesses quantitative reasoning (dealing with knowledge and the application of numerical concepts), visual–spatial processing (involving timed tasks such as completing a puzzle), and working memory.

Connection

How much information can most people keep in mind while working on a problem? Is working memory the same as short-term memory?

See Chapter 6, LO3.

In sum, current intelligence tests reflect contemporary thinking about intelligence as a general quality with many dimensions. Since the development of the CHC model and publication of the first version of the K-ABC, all other major IQ tests have followed suit and developed more theory-driven and complex tests of at least five aspects of intelligence rather than just two or three.

Digit span

Examiner says: 6 - 2 - 9	Examinee repeats it back
Examiner says: 7 - 4 - 6 - 1 - 4 - 8 - 3 - 9	Examinee repeats it back

Letter-number sequencing

Examiner says: L - 7 - C - 3	Examinee has to repeat the sequence with numbers in ascending order and then letters in alphabetical order 3 - 7 - C - L

FIGURE **9.6**
SIMULATED EXAMPLES OF WORKING MEMORY TASKS ON THE WECHSLER SCALES OF INTELLIGENCE. The latest version of the WISC and the WAIS also assess verbal comprehension, perceptual reasoning, and processing speed. Simulated items similar to those in Wechsler Intelligence Scale for Children—Fourth Edition (WISC-IV).

students' grades, school performance, and class rank in high school quite well, with correlations typically falling between +.50 and +.60 (Deary et al., 2007; Zhu & Weiss, 2005). That is, after all, what they were meant to predict. For example, preschool scores on two IQ tests taken by children in the American preschool intervention Head Start Program accurately predicted the children's academic achievement scores from kindergarten to Grade 6 (Lamp & Krohn, 2001). Moreover, scores from the WAIS predict both one's academic class rank in high school and one's college grade point average (Gregory, 2007). IQ scores also predict people's occupations and job performance within their chosen occupations fairly well (Schmidt & Hunter, 2004). People scoring higher in intelligence are more likely to end up in more prestigious occupations (Strenze, 2007). And people with higher intelligence perform better across a wide variety of occupations, with the typical correlation being +.51 (Schmidt & Hunter, 1998). However, even though IQ can predict the kind of job you get, how much money you make (Schmidt & Hunter, 2004), and how well you will do in your job, it cannot predict how happy and satisfied you are with your life or job (Gow et al., 2005).

Are IQ Tests Biased? Did you know that Canadians tend to perform slightly better than Americans on intelligence tests (Saklofske, Patterson, Gorsuch, & Tulsky, 2001)? Given such differences among groups in average

IQ scores, it is tempting to conclude that IQ tests are biased and unfair. Whether a test is either biased or unfair or both involves two separate, though related, issues. Let's first be clear about what each term means and then examine the evidence for each. The general public attaches a different meaning to *bias* than scientists do. The general public may use the term *bias* to refer to the notion that group differences in IQ scores are caused by different cultural and educational backgrounds, not by real differences in intelligence. This view is expressed in the **cultural test bias hypothesis** (Reynolds, 2000). Scientists, however, distinguish between test bias and test fairness. When scientists refer to **test bias** in an IQ test, they refer to whether a test predicts outcomes equally well for different groups. A test is biased if it is a more valid measure for one group than for another. For example, if an IQ test predicts academic achievement better for Hispanics than for Asians, it is biased. Researchers have found, however, very little evidence for the existence of this kind of bias in contemporary IQ tests (Brown, Reynolds, & Whitaker, 1999; Hunter & Schmidt, 2000; Reynolds, 2000). Intelligence tests are developed using norms that reflect the makeup of the general population—a process called **standardization.** Often, separate norms are established for the use and interpretation of intelligence tests within different countries. For example, Canadian norms have been published for the WAIS-III (Salofske et al., 2005). Just because different groups score differently on a given test does not automatically mean that it is biased. If the test is equally valid for different groups and they still score differently on it, the test is not biased. It may be unfair, but it's not biased.

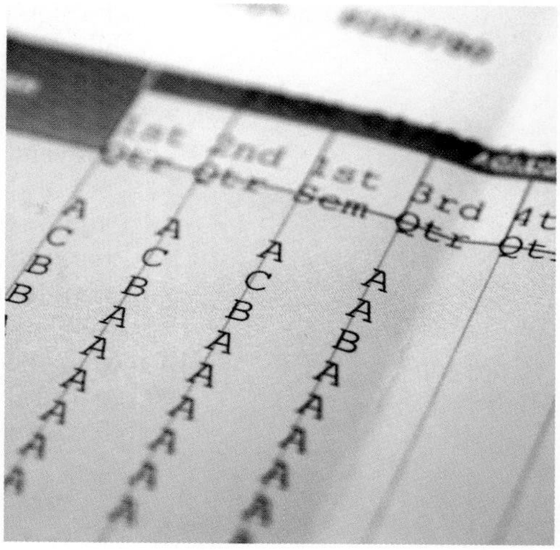

How well do school grades reflect someone's intelligence? Is there a better way to represent academic achievement?

Test fairness, on the other hand, reflects values, philosophical differences, and the ways in which test results are applied (Gregory, 2007). Test results, especially IQ test results, are meant to be applied—often by people in education, the military, and business. Problems arise when people use IQ test results unfairly to deny certain groups access to universities or jobs. So test fairness, in this sense, concerns the application of the test results rather than the test itself. An unbiased test result could be applied unfairly.

An extreme example of test unfairness is revealed in the case of an Alberta woman, Leilani Muir (Wahlsten, 1997). In 1995, Muir was awarded almost a

Are IQ tests unfair to a particular group of individuals?

cultural test bias hypothesis
the notion that group differences in IQ scores are caused by different cultural and educational backgrounds, not by real differences in intelligence.

test bias
characteristic of a test that produces different outcomes for different groups.

standardization
the process of giving a test to a large group of people to establish norms or standards by which all other people who take the test are compared.

test fairness
judgment about how test results are applied to different groups based on values and philosophical inclinations.

million dollars in damages by the Alberta government for her involuntary sterilization. When Muir was 14, she was labelled as mentally deficient based on her low score on an IQ test, and was subsequently sterilized. Her sterilization was a result of the Alberta Sexual Sterilization Act of 1928—a program intended to prevent the reproduction of members of the population considered to be carriers of defective genetic traits, such as low intelligence. When her IQ was tested again several years later, Muir scored almost 20 points higher, suggesting that her initial performance on the IQ test was not a valid indicator of her underlying cognitive ability. Sadly, Muir's case was not unique. It is estimated that nearly 3000 people were rendered sterile by Alberta's Sexual Sterilization Act, many of them deemed "mentally defective" on the basis of an IQ test. Clearly, the issue of cultural test bias and test fairness is not to be treated lightly—"bad" testing can have huge consequences.

LO3 Extremes of Intelligence

Intelligence varies in a very predictable way, which is most easily seen in the frequency of different IQ scores in the population. When one plots the scores on a graph, one sees a very clear bell curve, with most people falling in the middle and a few people at the high and low ends of the curve. This shape is referred to as a *bell curve* because it is shaped like a bell. Looking at the bell curve for IQ scores in Figure 9.7, we can see that 68 percent of test-takers will score between 85 and 115 and almost all—99.7 percent—will score between 55 and 145. It is at the two ends of the curve, or distribution, that we find "extremes of intelligence"—specifically, intellectual disability and giftedness.

intellectual disability
significant limitations in intellectual functioning as well as in everyday adaptive behaviour, which start before age 18.

Intellectual Disability To meet the criteria for **intellectual disability,** formerly referred to as *mental retardation,* an individual must show significant limitations in intellectual functioning as well as in everyday adaptive behaviour, and these deficits must start before age 18 (American Association on Intellectual and Developmental Disabilities, 2010; American Psychiatric Association, 2000). Historically, intellectual disability was defined and diagnosed solely on the basis of IQ, with 70 being the most common cutoff score. Leilani Muir was labelled as mentally defective because she scored 64 on her initial IQ test. There are four

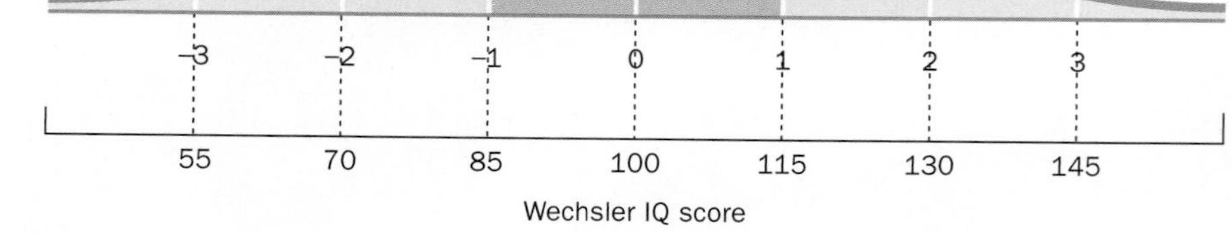

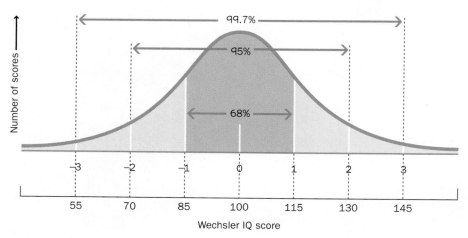

FIGURE **9.7**
NORMAL DISTRIBUTION OF IQ TEST SCORES (BELL CURVE). The vast majority of people (95 percent) achieve scores between 70 and 130 on the Wechsler IQ scales. The norm or mean is 100; the standard deviation is 15. Only a small percentage of people score at the extremes.

levels of intellectual disability, depending on how adaptive the behaviour or thinking is: mild (IQ of 50–70), moderate (35–50), severe (20–35), and profound (below 20). More recently, however, a different criterion, adaptive behaviour, has been added to IQ as a determinant of intellectual disability. **Adaptive behaviour** is defined as how well a person adjusts to and copes with everyday life (Hogan, 2007). For example, how well can the person feed or dress himself or herself? Does the person have the ability to understand the time, make change, or read simple words? At a more complex level, one might ask whether the person can take a bus or subway or follow the news on TV. If the criteria of adaptive behaviour had been applied to Leilani Muir, it is unlikely that she would have been labelled as "mentally deficient." Most current diagnoses of intellectual disability emphasize adaptive functioning over IQ scores. They therefore measure a person's everyday abilities more than their academic performance.

Like this happy couple, many people with Down syndrome have full, productive lives in spite of their intellectual limitations.

The origins of intellectual disability vary. In about 50 percent of cases, the cause of intellectual disability is *organic,* meaning that it is genetic or the result of brain damage. **Down syndrome,** a disorder that results from a condition known as trisomy-21, in which a person has three rather than two number 21 chromosomes, is an example of organic intellectual disability. The genetic cause of Down syndrome is not fully known, but it is related to maternal age. Children born to older women are more likely to develop trisomy-21 and Down syndrome (*What Causes Down Syndrome,* 2007). In other cases, in which the cause is not clearly biological, environmental factors, such as neglect and poor nutrition, may be to blame. Sometimes called *familial-cultural intellectual disability,* this type is more prevalent among people of low socioeconomic status, it tends to occur in more than one family member, and it tends to be mild (Kerig & Wenar, 2006).

adaptive behaviour
adjustment to and coping with everyday life.

Down syndrome
a chromosomal disorder characterized by mild to profound intellectual disability.

Giftedness Giftedness lies at the high end of the intelligence spectrum. Students who do very well in school and also do well on standardized tests of intelligence are sometimes placed in "gifted" programs. In most schools, children are admitted to such a program if they score 130–140 or above on a standardized IQ test like the WISC or Stanford-Binet. Extreme giftedness usually takes various forms, two of which are prodigies and savants.

Prodigies. A **prodigy** is a young person who is extremely gifted and precocious in one area, such as math, music, art, or chess, and is at least average in intelligence (Feldman, 2004). Most often, prodigies are people under the age of 20. Sometimes they possess extreme talent in more than one domain, such as math and language. Probably the world's most famous child prodigy was Wolfgang Amadeus Mozart, who was playing the piano by age three and composing symphonies by age eight. Another more recent example is Tiger Woods, who started playing golf at age three and was winning tournaments and making holes-in-one by age six. Although they are relatively rare, some people display extreme early talent in visual arts, like Josh Tiessen, whose story is outlined at the beginning of this chapter.

prodigy
a young person who is extremely gifted and precocious in one area and at least average in intelligence.

In addition to documenting individual cases of intellectual prodigies, researchers have conducted large-scale studies of mathematical prodigies. The best-known of these is the Study for Mathematically Precocious Youth (SMPY; Stanley, 1996). Begun in the United States in 1971, the SMPY is a 50-year

Josh Tiessen is a gifted young artist who has been painting and drawing since he was a small child.

longitudinal study of extremely talented people, especially in math. One of the main criteria for participation is a score of 500 or higher (out of 800) on the Scholastic Aptitude Test (SAT)-Quantitative before age 13. The SAT is a standardized test for college admissions in the United States. A score of 500 on the SAT-Quantitative by age 13 occurs in about one in 100 cases, meaning that the person scores higher than 99 percent of his or her peers.

A subset of the study focuses on an even more select group: those who score 700 on the SAT-Quantitative and 630 or higher on the SAT-Verbal *before* their 13th birthday. Only about one in every 10 000 test-takers achieves a score this high (Lubinski et al., 2006). Students in this precocious group go on to have very successful careers. Follow-up research 25–35 years later shows that many of them attended top universities at both the undergraduate and graduate levels and then went on to become successful scientists, mathematicians, engineers, and doctors (Lubinski & Benbow, 2006).

Savants. Since at least the 1700s, there have been reports of people with **savant syndrome,** a very rare condition characterized by serious mental handicaps and isolated areas of ability or remarkable giftedness (Treffert, 2006). Savants (the word *savant* comes from the French word for "knowing") have low overall intelligence, typically with an IQ below 70, and an incredible ability for calculating numbers, recalling events, playing music, or drawing. Often these individuals cannot speak at all or speak poorly.

By some estimates, there are only about 100 savants in the world today, about 50 percent of whom suffer from autism and the other 50 percent from some other kind of psychological disorder, such as brain injury, epilepsy, or intellectual disability (Treffert, 2006). Savant syndrome occurs most often in five major areas of talent: music (usually piano), art, math, calendar calculations, and spatial/mechanical skills (Treffert, 2006). A relatively common form is seen in individuals who can immediately calculate the day of the week on which a particular date in history fell. For example, if asked what day of the week June 15, 1899, was, they would correctly answer "Thursday." Others with savant syndrome can take apart clocks, toys, bicycles, and other machines and rebuild them with expert precision.

savant syndrome
a very rare condition in which people with serious mental handicaps also show isolated areas of ability or brilliance.

In Chapter 6, we met Daniel Tammet, whose uncanny memory skills enable him to recall pi to 22 514 digits and calculate complex mathematical problems almost instantaneously. Tammet has savant syndrome as well as synesthesia, which, as you might recall from Chapter 4, occurs when a person experiences sensations in one sense when a different sense is stimulated. In Tammet's case, he sees each number as a distinct colour and shape, and this is the secret behind his uncanny memory for numbers and calculations. For example, when he is reciting pi out to 22 500 digits, he does not think in numerals but rather he simply sees in his mind's eye a rolling landscape of coloured shapes.

Connection

Daniel Tammet used mnemonic devices, a memory tool, to help him remember the value of pi. How do mnemonic devices aid memory?

See Chapter 6, LO4.

Another person with savant syndrome is Kim Peek. Although Peek may be most famous as the inspiration for the movie *Rain Man,* starring Dustin Hoffman, his abilities go much further than the movie suggests. He is one of the world's only true speed-readers—he can read a page in about three seconds and retain essentially every word. Incredibly, Peek has memorized about 9000 books after reading them only *once.* He can immediately provide biographical information about any of the U.S. presidents; tell you the zip code of any city or borough in the United States; and identify who composed almost any piece of classical music, where it was composed, and when it was first performed. Like some other savants, he also can tell you more or less instantly the day of the week on which any date in history fell.

Given his phenomenal abilities, it is easy to forget that Peek is unable to do many basic things—such as dress himself. Indeed, his tested IQ is 73, which is in the range for people with autism. Socially he is very awkward, and he likes to repeat certain phrases, saying over and over again how great is the person he has just met. He also does not understand metaphors like "get hold of yourself."

Instead, he interprets everything literally. His adaptive functioning skills are poor, and his father continues to take care of him on a daily basis. A scan of his brain revealed that Peek, like some other savants, has no corpus callosum and very little cerebellum (Treffert & Christensen, 2005). The absence of a corpus callosum means that information processed in one of the brain's hemispheres cannot be communicated to the other hemisphere. Lacking a functional cerebellum also means that Peek lacks coordinated movement and balance.

LO4 The Nature and Nurture of Human Intelligence

If you want to start an argument, all you need to do is take a strong stance on one of the following positions: (1) A person's intelligence is determined almost completely by genetics, or (2) a person's intelligence is determined almost completely by the environment in which he or she is raised. Most people realize that intelligence results from a combination of "being born that way" and "being brought up that way" by our family and teachers. What is most remarkable is the complexity of the interaction between these two forces.

One way we see the interaction between environment and biological forces is in how the brain responds differently to different kinds of problems, intelligence problems among them. The region most often involved in various IQ tasks is the prefrontal cortex (Duncan et al., 2000; Haier et al., 2004). For instance, when a person is working on verbal tasks, only the left prefrontal region of the brain is activated. When an individual is working on spatial tasks, however, the prefrontal cortices of both the left and right hemispheres, as well as the occipital cortex, are activated (see Figure 9.8; Duncan et al., 2000; Haier et al., 2004).

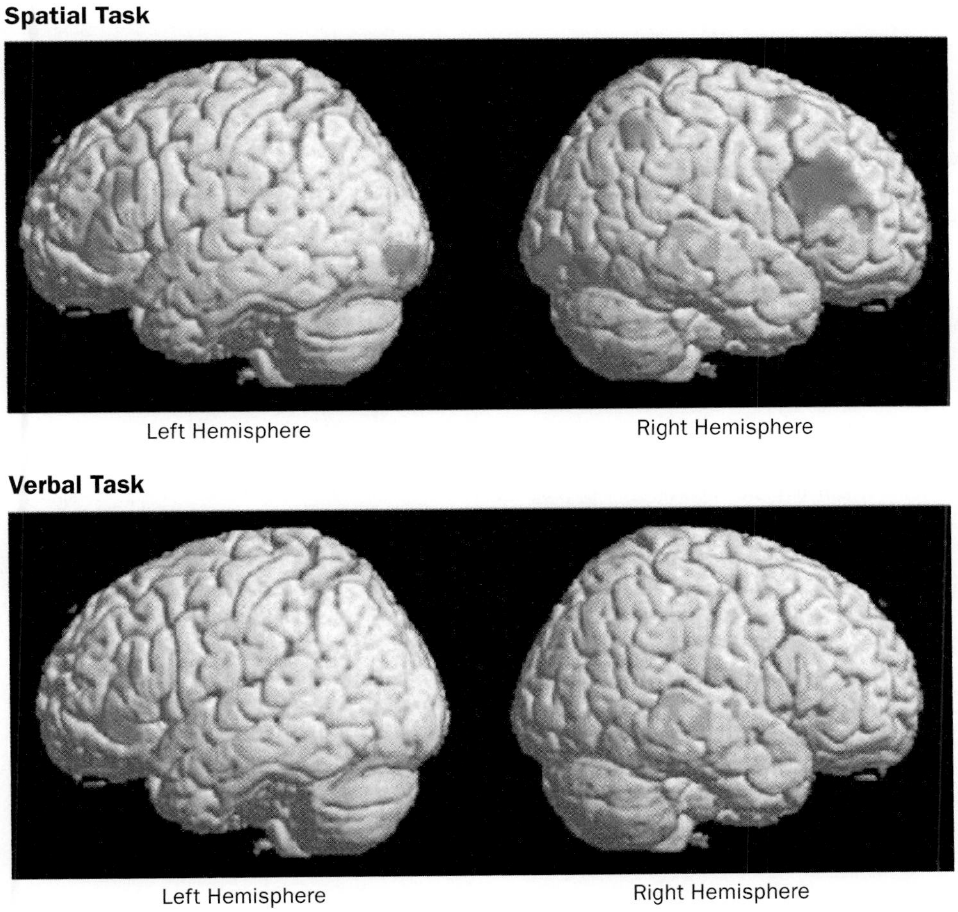

FIGURE **9.8**
BRAIN ACTIVATION WHILE WORKING ON IQ PROBLEMS. Red areas show activation during two different IQ tasks, a verbal task and a spatial task. The spatial task activates the frontal lobe in both the right and left hemispheres, whereas the verbal task activates only the left frontal lobe region (Broca's area). (*Source:* Duncan et al., 2000.)

Moreover, the frontal lobe is more involved when an individual is performing fluid intelligence tasks, such as pattern recognition, than when the person is performing tasks that involve crystallized intelligence and learned experiences (Gray & Thompson, 2004).

Challenge Your Assumptions

True or False? People with high IQs have larger brains.

True: Brain volume, especially in the regions of the brain that control working memory and executive function, is increased in people with high IQ compared to those with average IQ.

The brains of highly intelligent people have a surprising and unique characteristic. There is a positive relationship (a correlation between .30 and .40, on average) between brain size and intelligence, meaning that highly intelligent people actually have more brain volume than less intelligent people (McDaniel, 2005; Miller & Penke, 2007). This relationship seems to be strongest in the areas of the brain associated with working memory, executive functioning, and attention (Frangou, Chitins, & Williams, 2004).

Twin-adoption and family studies demonstrate the interconnectedness of nature and nurture in intelligence. As we saw in Chapter 3, these kinds of studies allow researchers to hold one factor constant, while varying the other one. The more genetically related people are, the more similar they are in IQ, even if reared apart (see Figure 9.9). Identical twins reared apart are more similar in their levels of intelligence than fraternal twins reared together. Similarly, dozens of studies have shown that adopted children's overall intelligence is more similar to that of their biological parents than to that of their adoptive parents (Munsinger, 1975). Yet adoption—hence, the environment—can also enhance a child's IQ (van IJzendoorn & Juffer, 2005). Compared to orphans not adopted, adopted children tend to have higher IQs. In sum, genetic factors ("nature") account for about 50 percent of the variability in intelligence among individuals; environment ("nurture") accounts for about 40 percent; the remaining 10 percent is, as yet, unexplained (Grigorenko, 2000; Lynn, 2006; Plomin & Petrill, 1997).

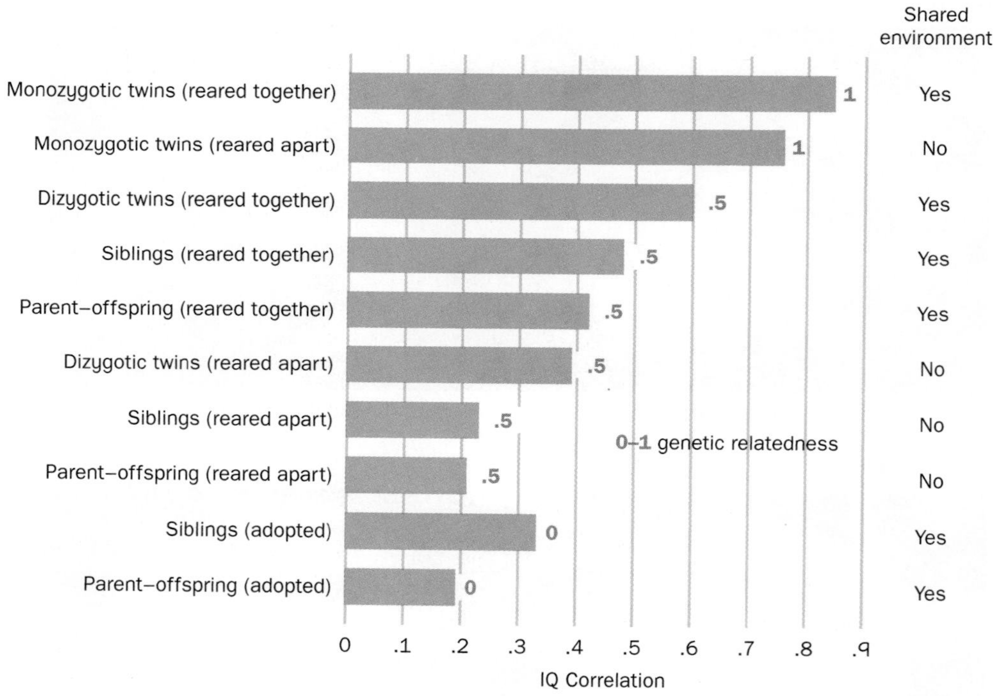

FIGURE **9.9**

GENETIC AND ENVIRONMENTAL EFFECTS ON IQ. Numbers in orange represent genetic relatedness. Genetic relatedness of 1 means 100 percent genetic similarity; .5 means 50 percent genetic similarity; and 0 means no genetic similarity. (*Source:* Adapted from Grigorenko, 2000; Plomin & Petril, 1997.)

The concept of reaction range provides further evidence for the interaction of biology and environment in determining a person's intelligence. A **reaction range** is the genetically determined range within which a given trait, such as intelligence, may fall; that trait's exact value, however, depends on the quality of the individual's environment (Scarr, 1981; Weinberg, 1989). For most people in most environments, the reaction range for IQ is about 25 points—meaning that a given person may end up scoring anywhere in a 25-point range on an IQ test, depending on the kind of environment in which he or she is raised (Weinberg, 1989). Being raised in an enriched environment means someone is likely to obtain an IQ score near the upper limit of his or her reaction range; being raised in an impoverished environment means one is likely to obtain a score near the lower limit; and being raised in a normal environment means one is likely to obtain a score in the middle of his or her reaction range (see Figure 9.10). The important point here is that genes do not determine behaviour but, rather, establish the range of possible behaviours.

reaction range
for a given trait, such as IQ, the genetically determined range of responses by an individual to his or her environment.

Environment, however, is a complex thing. Only part of the environmental influence on intelligence comes from being in the same household and sharing experiences. The other part comes from experiences that are not shared by family members—that is, the individual's unique environmental experiences. One such experience is the prenatal environment and what happens to the fetus during pregnancy. Toxins ingested by the mother, either intentionally or unintentionally, may influence the child's intelligence. Alcohol, drugs, and viral infections in a pregnant woman can seriously lower her child's overall intelligence (Jacobson & Jacobson, 2000; Ruff, 1999; Steinhausen & Spohr, 1998). For example, heavy alcohol consumption during pregnancy can lead to intellectual disability in the

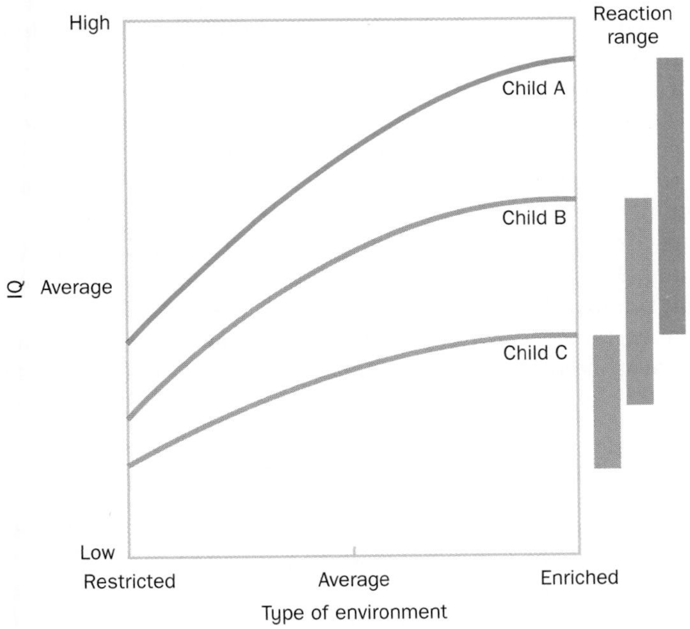

FIGURE **9.10**
REACTION RANGE AND INTELLIGENCE. The concept of reaction range suggests that heredity places upper and lower limits on an individual's potential, but environment determines whether the individual reaches the upper limit or a point somewhere between the upper limit and the lower limit. This graph shows hypothetical reaction ranges for three children (A, B, and C) and how their surroundings could shape their IQs. With enriched environments, all three could reach their individual upper limit, as shown on the right side of the graph. (*Source:* Seifert et al., 2000.)

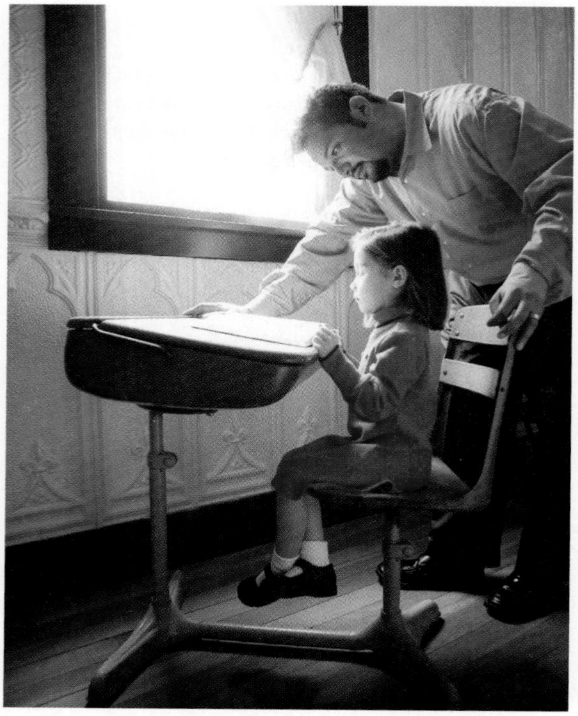

Reading to children regularly from the time they are very young as part of an enriched environment may actually enhance their IQ.

child (Streissguth et al., 1989). Prenatal exposure to high levels of lead, mercury, or manganese may lead to serious impairments in a child's intelligence (Dietrich et al., 1991; Jacobson & Jacobson, 2000).

Another environmental effect on intelligence is *birth order.* Recent research has reported that first-born children have a slight advantage over second-born children, who have a smaller advantage over third-born children (Kristensen & Bjerkedal, 2007). Analysis of these results showed that these advantages must be caused by differences in family interactions due to birth order, not prenatal environment, because the effect held only in situations in which no older sibling died in infancy. In other words, if a biological second-born has an older sibling who dies in infancy, that second-born child becomes, in effect, a first-born and displays a slight increase in IQ.

In the 1980s, James Flynn, a political scientist, observed that IQ scores in the Western world had increased substantially over the last century (Flynn, 1984, 1987). The **Flynn effect,** as this mysterious phenomenon has been labelled (Hernstein & Murray, 1994), suggests that IQ scores have increased by almost three IQ points per decade, leading to IQs that are a full 15 points higher than those of our grandparents who lived 50 years ago! What accounts for this change? Are we really smarter than our grandparents?

Flynn effect
the trend of increasing IQ scores over the past century.

Most psychologists agree that these gains are far too rapid to result from genetic changes (Flynn, 1998; Neisser, 1998). Rather, they are more likely the result of environmental influences on IQ. One suggestion is that we haven't actually gotten any smarter (Flynn, 1987). Rather, this gain is due to our increased test-taking sophistication and motivation to score well. In other words, today's generations score higher because they have learned how to write tests and they care enough about the outcome to try hard! Others suggest that improvements in health and nutrition have fuelled the IQ increase (Lynn, 2009). It may also be the case that recent generations' exposure to a more technological and complex visual world through toys, games, television, and computers has increased performance on IQ tests (Schooler, 1998). We are also spending more time in school than our grandparents did (Bronfenbrenner, McClelland, Wethington, Moen, & Ceci, 1996). Many studies have shown that school attendance can raise IQ scores (Ceci & Williams, 1997). Whatever the cause of these IQ gains, their occurrence means that IQ tests are now routinely re-standardized on a regular basis to ensure the average remains 100.

Connection

Teratogens are harmful environmental agents that can interact with fetal growth to produce negative outcomes.

See Chapter 10, LO2.

LO5 Group Differences in Intelligence Scores

Given the importance of intelligence to success in life, the question of whether there are group differences in intelligence is bound to stir up controversy (Fancher, 1985). Research on this topic necessarily has political and social implications, and from time to time scientists who have studied group differences in intelligence have been harassed or threatened. If there are differences in intelligence between racial–ethnic groups, what should we do as a society to compensate for those differences to level the playing field? Can that even be done?

In the 1960s and 1970s Arthur Jensen received death threats for publishing research that not only reported differences in IQ among racial–ethnic groups, but also argued that because IQ is under genetic influence, racial–ethnic differences in IQ must be at least partly genetic in origin (Jensen, 1969). Canadian psychologist J. Philippe Rushton also caused a stir when he reported racial–ethnic differences on a number of measures, including intelligence, social behaviour, and physical attributes such as brain size (Rushton, 1991, 1995; Rushton & Jensen, 2005). In his research, Rushton reported that Asians scored highest on measures of intelligence and individuals of black African descent scored lowest. Whites of European descent scored in the middle. Like Jensen, Rushton argued that these racial–ethnic differences in IQ are largely due to heredity. Many people were outraged by his claims, calling him a racist, and demanding that he be fired from the University of Western Ontario. For a time, the university was forced to cancel his classes, fearing for his safety ("Western's Controversy," 2006).

But it was a highly controversial book published in the mid-1990s that most recently ignited an academic, political, and cultural firestorm over intelligence. The book was called simply *The Bell Curve,* but its subtitle hinted at the more controversial contents: *Intelligence and Class Structure in American Life.* The book's authors, Richard Herrnstein and Charles Murray (1994), summarized the results of a study on racial–ethnic group differences, social class, and intelligence among 12 000 individuals. They concluded what many others had before and since: First, racial–ethnic groups vary on IQ scores; second, differences in IQ contribute to a large extent to differences in education and income (Gottfredson, 1997). Their carefully worded conclusion suggested that group differences in IQ, and hence in education and income, can be explained in part by genetics. Herrnstein and Murray tried to avoid some of the more blatant racial–ethnic arguments of Jensen and Rushton, but to little avail. The controversy swept through universities and social circles very quickly (Sternberg, 1995).

When all of the smoke cleared and tempers settled down, there was still no widely accepted and agreed-on explanation for racial–ethnic differences on IQ scores. There are a few schools of thought (in addition to a partly genetic one). Some experts maintain that racial–ethnic differences in IQ result from biases in IQ tests that favour people from certain cultural backgrounds over others (Reynolds, 2000). For example, Claude Steele (1997) has demonstrated that culturally held stereotypes of intellectual ability (e.g., certain ethnic minority groups are intellectually inferior to others) can have an adverse impact on the test performance of members of such groups—an effect that has become known as **stereotype threat.** The threat occurs when people become worried that they will confirm the stereotype about their group in their test performance. Their self-doubt and anxiety may then actually worsen their test performance, and thus, confirm the stereotype (Steele & Aronson, 1995). Others have argued that a finding of differences in IQ scores according to race–ethnicity is meaningless because race is mostly a social construct with little scientific support or biological foundation (Sternberg, Grigorenko, & Kidd, 2005). In addition, these psychologists also point out that heritability findings apply only within the group of people studied, not between groups. So it is a misinterpretation of heritability to argue that group differences are due to genetics even if IQ is heritable (see Figure 9.11). Moreover, most of the research conducted on heritability and IQ has come from European Americans and therefore is not applicable among the different racial–ethnic groups (Sternberg et al., 2005).

stereotype threat
the process whereby anxiety about culturally held group stereotypes impacts negatively on individual test performance.

The conclusion that genetics influence intelligence is often interpreted—or misinterpreted—as implying that IQ levels are determined at birth or conception. If this were so, then trying to change IQ levels with preschool intervention programs, such as U.S. Head Start or Canadian Aboriginal Head Start, would likely be unsuccessful (Herrnstein & Murray, 1994). Yet, such a conclusion is faulty for two reasons. First, genes interact with environmental forces, and therefore

Difference between average plant heights is due to different environments.

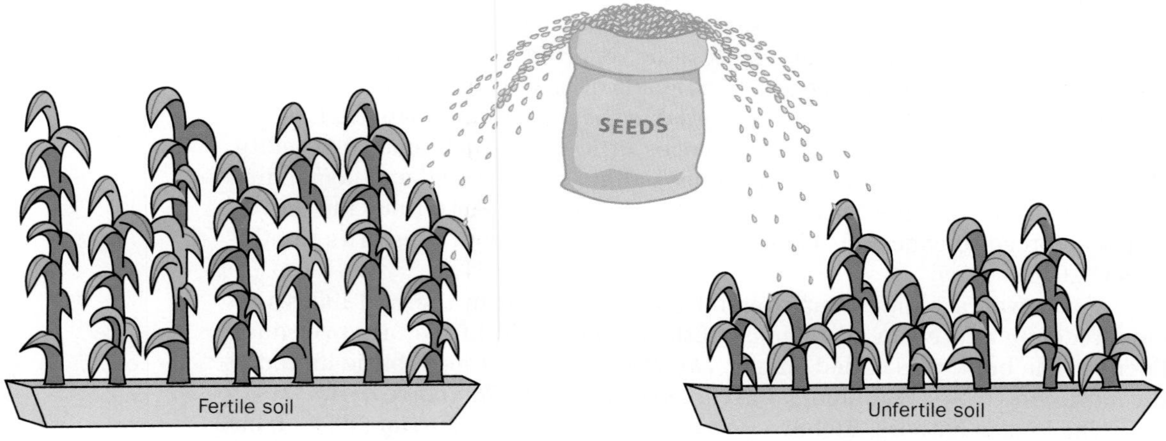

Within-group difference in heights of plants is due to genetic variability in seeds.

Within-group difference in heights of plants is due to genetic variability in seeds.

FIGURE **9.11**

HERITABILITY AND BETWEEN-GROUP DIFFERENCES. Even if variation within a group on a trait is largely due to heredity, the differences between groups may be due to environmental factors. For example, suppose you plant corn seeds from the same seed bag in two different soils—fertile and unfertile. While differences in plant height within each soil environment may be largely due to genetic factors (seed differences), it says nothing about differences in average plant height between the groups, which are largely environmental (due to soil differences). (*Source:* Lewontin, 1976.)

environment can shape gene expression. We saw this in Chapter 3 with the concept of epigenetics. Similarly, the concept of a reaction range makes clear the connection between genes and environment. Second, interventions have succeeded in changing IQ levels. As we will see in more detail in Chapter 15, children raised under conditions of severe neglect and abuse who are adopted within the first few years of life showed tremendous growth in brain size and gains in IQ scores. Those adopted later in life or not adopted at all do not show increases in IQ scores (Perry, 2002). Moreover, one longitudinal study randomly assigned infants to either an early educational intervention program or to a control group. All children were from socially disadvantaged households. The intervention program lasted up until age five and focused on language, social, emotional, and cognitive stimulation. The children from both groups were studied again at ages 12, 15, and 21. The findings were clear: During adolescence and early adulthood, those who had been in the intervention program had higher IQ scores, performed better in school, and obtained higher-paying jobs than those in the control condition (Campbell & Ramey, 1995; Campbell et al., 2002). In short, both genetic and environmental forces play important roles in determining IQ scores.

LO6 Non-Western Views of Intelligence

Ask Canadian university students to list their ideal of an intelligent person and who do you think tops their list? Most popular choices include Albert Einstein, Leonardo da Vinci, Isaac Newton, Stephen Hawking, William Shakespeare, and Bill Gates (Paulhus & Landolt, 2000). But what if you posed this question to people in Kenya, China, Malaysia, and Bolivia? Would you get similar answers? Probably not. Research suggests that people's conceptions of intelligence vary according to their culture. Western cultures emphasize verbal and cognitive skills first, whereas many African cultures see social skills, such as being socially responsible, cooperative, and active in family and social life, to be crucial aspects of intelligence (Ruzgis & Grigorenko, 1994; Serpell, 1982). Asian cultures have traditionally emphasized humility, awareness, doing the right thing, and mindfulness as important qualities of intelligence (Sternberg, 2000). For example, Japanese college students identify traits of being sympathetic, modest, and seeing another's point of view as important characteristics of an intelligent person (Okagaki & Sternberg, 1993). Doing well in school and being quick to learn are not universally acknowledged to be essential qualities of intelligence. Sternberg and his colleagues have examined practical intelligence in cultures where academic intelligence is not valued as highly as it is in Western cultures. They have found that children in Kenya and Tanzania, for example, may not do well at solving "bookish" analytic problems but do very well at solving everyday practical problems (Sternberg, 1998).

Problems that require intelligence are just one kind of problem we face. Problem solving pervades almost everything we do, from our choice of a major in university to our choice of friends, where we live, how we vote, and so on. Next we look at the psychology of problem solving.

Quick Quiz 9.1: Intelligence

1. Which of the following skills is *not* part of the definition of intelligence?
   a. abstract reasoning
   b. problem solving
   c. acquiring knowledge
   d. remote associations
2. Historically, a child's IQ was calculated by dividing ______ by chronological age and multiplying by ______ (Pick the best pair of words/numbers.)
   a. perceptual skill; 100
   b. mental age; 50
   c. perceptual skill; 50
   d. mental age; 100
3. The Kaufmans broke new ground in intelligence testing by developing an IQ test that
   a. could be universally applied.
   b. was grounded in psychological theory and knowledge of the brain.
   c. was reliable and valid.
   d. was culture-fair.
4. ______ involves raw mental ability, pattern recognition, and abstract reasoning and is applied to a problem that a person has never confronted before.
   a. Crystallized intelligence
   b. Narrow intelligence
   c. Fluid intelligence
   d. General intelligence
5. Someone who is good at detecting whether or not a person is lying would be said to have high
   a. interpersonal intelligence.
   b. naturalistic intelligence.
   c. practical intelligence.
   d. creative intelligence.

Answers can be found at the end of the chapter.

LO7 PROBLEM SOLVING

None of us goes through a day without having to solve a problem, because every time we face a task that we do not know how to carry out, we are confronted with a problem (Simon, 1978). On any given day, you may have to budget your time so that you can study for your test and go to a party with friends or figure out the most efficient route to drive to a place you have never visited.

Psychologists have examined how people go about solving problems, often by presenting research participants with problems and studying how they solve them. Take a few minutes to work on each of the following problems. Some are easy and others not so easy, but give them a try. We will return to each problem later in the section.

FIGURE **9.12**

PROBLEM SOLVING. (a) Remove one match to make seven squares. (b) Connect all nine dots with four straight lines—without lifting your pencil. (Answer to b appears at the end of the chapter.)

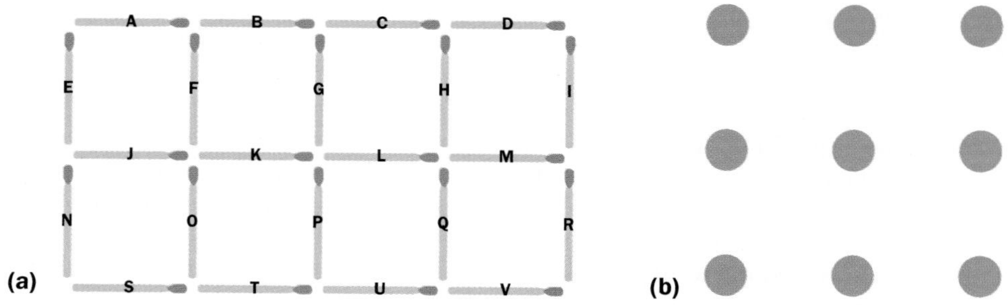

FIGURE **9.13**

TWO STRING PROBLEM. How do you connect two strings if you can't reach the second one without dropping the first one? (Answer appears at the end of the chapter.)

- How are a dog and a lion alike?
- How would you solve the problem of rising world temperatures?
- In Figure 9.12a, remove one match to make seven squares.
- Look at the nine dots in Figure 9.12b. Connect all the dots using only four straight lines without lifting up your pen or pencil from the paper once you've started.
- Figure 9.13 is a picture of a person in a room with two strings hanging from the ceiling. Also in the room are a book of matches, a pair of pliers, and some cotton. The task is to tie the two pieces of string together. The strings are too short for the person to hold on to one and grab the other. How would you go about tying the strings together?
- Pretend you have three jars (A, B, and C), each containing a set amount of water. Add or subtract the given amounts in each jar to come up with a set final amount. For instance, Jar A holds 21 units of water, Jar B holds 127 units, and Jar C holds 3 units. Using any of the jars, discard or add water as needed to end up with 100 units of water. Figure 9.14 shows some variations you can try.

Types of Problems

convergent thinking problems problems that have known solutions and require analytic thinking and crystallized intelligence to come up with the correct answer.

Convergent thinking problems have known solutions, which can be reached by narrowing down a set of possible answers. Intelligence tests and college entrance exams include convergent problems. Figuring out how to operate a new coffee maker is another convergent problem. There is one right way to brew coffee with a given machine. Convergent problems require analytic thinking and crystallized intelligence—the problem solver has to analyze the problem and then apply learned strategies and knowledge to come up with the answer.

divergent thinking problems problems that have no known solutions and require novel solutions.

Some problems, however, may not have a known solution. Consider the problem: "How would you solve the problem of rising world temperatures?" There are many possible solutions to these problems, some of which work better than others. These kinds of problems are known as **divergent thinking problems.** To solve them, we must break away from our normal problem-solving strategies and make unusual associations to arrive at novel ways of thinking about a problem. Imagine that your new roommate snores so loudly you can't sleep. How would you solve this problem? Divergence may lead to redefining the problem in a way that makes finding a solution more likely. These kinds of problems require fluid and creative intelligence.

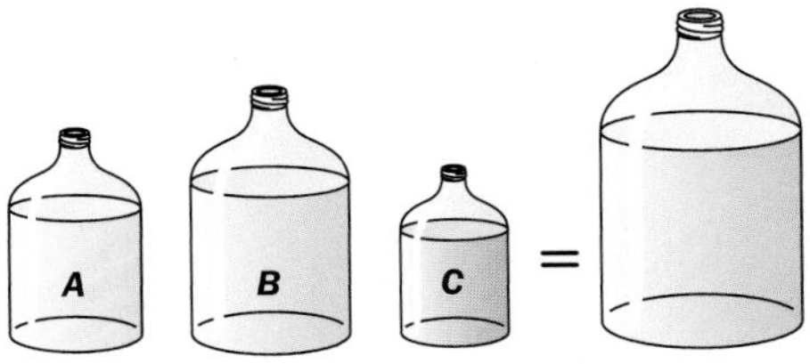

FIGURE **9.14**
WATER JAR PROBLEMS AND MENTAL SET. The task is to use any combination of jars A, B, and C, subtracting or adding jars of "water" to obtain the desired amount. Try it. (*Source:* Luchins & Luchins, 1970.)

Problem	Jar A	Jar B	Jar C	Obtained the amount
1	21	127	3	100
2	14	163	25	99
3	18	43	10	5
4	9	42	6	21
5	20	59	4	31
6	23	49	3	20
7	15	39	3	18

Solution Strategies

Psychologists describe three kinds of strategies that people use to solve different kinds of problems: algorithms, insight, and thinking outside the box. When you were solving the water jug problems in Figure 9.14, did you realize that the last two could be solved much more easily than the first five? If you are like about 75 percent of the population, you continued to use the solution pattern or algorithm you may have discovered in solving the first few problems. **Algorithms** are step-by-step formulas or procedures for solving problems. In this case, the algorithm is "Jar B − Jar A − Jar C (twice)." For this problem, this algorithm also helped you create a **mental set,** which is a tendency to continue to use problem-solving strategies that have worked in the past, even if better solutions are available (Luchins & Luchins, 1970). This mental set probably made you miss the easier solutions to Problems 6 and 7: Jar A − Jar C and Jar A + Jar C, respectively. Luchins and Luchins (1970) found that if Problems 1 to 5 were not given first, 100 percent of adults saw the direct solution. In contrast, if they first received Problems 1 to 5 and had to develop an algorithm, only 24 percent found the more direct solutions to Problems 6 and 7. Figure 9.15 depicts the research process for a jar study that demonstrated that groups are better able to break out of their mental set than individuals (Luchins & Luchins, 1969).

algorithm
a step-by-step procedure or formula for solving a problem

mental set
a tendency to continue to use problem-solving strategies that have worked in the past, even if better solutions are available.

Not all solutions involve algorithms. Some occur with a flash of insight. One of the best-known examples of insight occurred in ancient Greece, when the philosopher-scientist Archimedes solved the problem of how to determine whether a crown contained anything besides gold. The solution came to him in a flash when he saw the water level rise as he entered the public baths. Because gold is heavier than other metals, it will displace more water, so by seeing how much water it displaced, Archimedes would be able to determine whether the crown was pure gold without melting it down. The insight excited him so much that without pausing to dress, he ran out of the baths yelling *"Eureka!"* (in Greek, "I have found it!"). In honour of Archimedes, these kinds of sudden solutions are referred to as either **Eureka insights** or **insight solutions.**

Eureka insight or insight solutions
sudden solutions that come to mind in a flash.

A modern version of such a "Eureka solution" happened to George de Mestral, a Swiss engineer (*How a Swiss invention hooked the world,* 2007). De Mestral would often go on hikes in the Alps with his dog. When they came home he noticed that his clothes and his dog's fur caught thistle burrs, which he found on close inspection to have hooks on the ends. The dog's fur and his clothes contained loops that snagged the plants. In a flash, de Mestral realized that a fastener could

Research Process

FIGURE **9.15**
GROUP VERSUS INDIVIDUAL SOLUTIONS TO THE JAR PROBLEM. Group problem solving takes advantage of the group's "collective intelligence" and people are better able to break out of a mental set when solving a simple quantitative problem. All it takes is one person to come up with the more direct solution and the whole group benefits. (*Source:* Luchins, A.S., & Luchins, E.H. (1969). Einstellung effect and group problem solving. *The Journal of Social Psychology*, 77, 79–89.)

1 Research Question

Are individuals or small groups better at breaking out of their mental sets to solve the water jar problem?

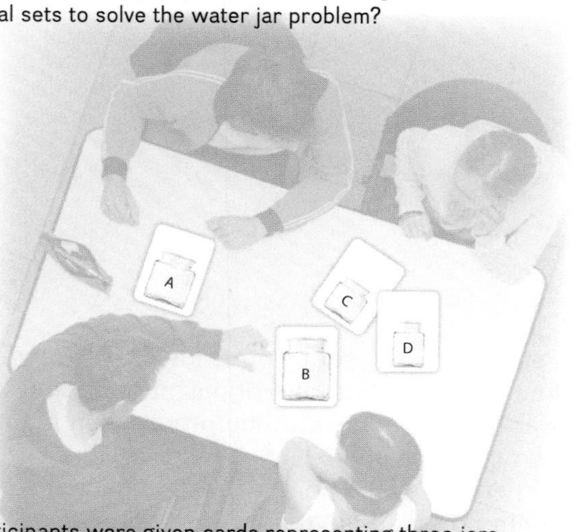

2 Method

As with the jar problem presented in Figure 9.14, participants were given cards representing three jars (A, B, C). Each card had different amounts of water and they had to add or subtract any combination of the cards to obtain a final amount. The problems were identical to those in Figure 9.14, with two exceptions. First, a fourth jar was added, and second, two additional problems were administered that could be solved without the mental set algorithm established by the first five problems (B – A – 2C). In this study there were four problems (problems 6 through 9) that gave participants an opportunity to break their mental set and solve the problem more directly. In addition to being tested individually, some participants were assigned to be tested in small groups of four people. In the group condition, each group member was given only one jar amount and the group then had to work together to solve the problem. As was true of individuals, each group had 2.5 minutes to solve the problem.

3 Results

In all of the last six problems, groups outperformed individuals in the ability to solve the problem by breaking out of the mental set algorithm suggested by the first three problems (B – A – 2C). More than 80 percent of individuals, however, had figured out how to break out of the mental set by the time they were given the last two problems (8 and 9), but groups still outperformed individuals.

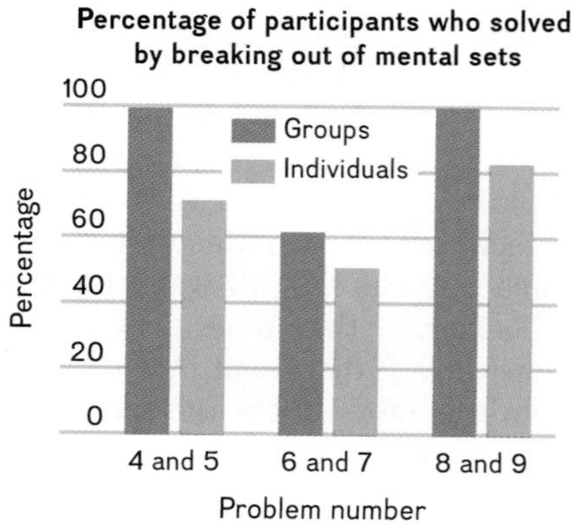

4 Conclusion

Mental sets are ways of thinking that help in some situations but blind us to simpler ways of solving problems in other situations. Because each person in the group received only one jar amount, the group had to cooperate in order to solve the problems. All jars had to be considered in the group in a way that was not true for individuals working on the problem.

be made to connect to loops. The best part about the hook and loop system was it was easily reversible and could be fastened over and over again. De Mestral invented Velcro, which is now a common fastener of such things as shoe straps, backpacks, and clothing. George de Mestral's Eureka insight produced one of the most versatile fasteners in history.

The solution to the two-string problem in Figure 9.13 often comes as a Eureka insight (Maier, 1931). You might have suddenly realized that the pliers could be used as a weight at the end of one string and then swung into motion. As you stand holding the other string, the weighted string swings over and you grab it and tie the two together.

The third problem-solving strategy is turning a problem around and thinking about it from a different perspective. If you have ever heard the phrase "thinking outside the box," you now know where it comes from—the nine-dot problem (Figure 9.12b). **Thinking outside the box** requires you to break free of self-imposed conceptual constraints and think about a problem differently in order to solve it. If you came up with a solution, it required that you go outside the self-imposed "box" that the nine dots create in your mind. There is no such box there in reality, but you perceive one. Once you think outside the box, a couple of solutions may come to you rather easily (see the end of the chapter for the solution). Creative thinkers regularly think flexibly and differently about problems (Feist, 1999).

thinking outside the box
approach to problem solving that requires breaking free of self-imposed conceptual constraints and thinking about a problem differently in order to solve it.

Obstacles to Solutions

The difficulties people encounter in solving the nine-dot problem point to some of the common obstacles we face in solving all kinds of problems. One of the biggest blocks to solving a problem is **fixation,** or the inability to break out of a particular mind-set in order to think about a problem from a fresh perspective. Fixation prevents many people from seeing possible solutions to the seven-square match problem (Figure 9.12a). It is difficult, for example, to see that one can simply remove match B, C, T, or U. If one takes away match B, for instance, there are only seven squares but the continuity in the upper row of squares is broken. This solution may not be obvious because people become fixated on a self-imposed mental set in which "all the squares must continue to touch each other." Note that the instructions do not require this—people unconsciously impose such rules themselves.

fixation
the inability to break out of a particular mind-set in order to think about a problem from a fresh perspective.

As we saw earlier, mental sets are a kind of fixation. A mental set provides solutions to problems but can also stand in the way of new ideas and novel solutions. Education and training create mental sets. When we learn solution strategies in school and in the workplace, we learn how to solve problems. Sometimes these solutions are algorithms, sometimes insights, and sometimes they are heuristics. But strategies can blind us to more novel, efficient, and even creative solutions. It becomes hard to step back and see the problem from a fresh perspective.

Connection
Heuristics are mental shortcuts we use in making decisions and judgments.
See Chapter 8, LO11.

Another obstacle to successful problem solving is our tendency to be blind to unusual uses of common everyday things or procedures: This is known as **functional fixedness** (Duncker, 1945). A good example of functional fixedness occurs when people try to solve the two-string problem. People are used to thinking of pliers as tools for cutting or bending metal wire. But pliers can also be used as a weight at the end of a string that causes it to swing like a pendulum. Figuring out a new way to use a set of pliers is an example of thinking outside the box to find a creative solution to a problem. As mentioned earlier, creative thinkers often think differently about how to solve a problem. We discuss this type of creative thinking and creativity in general next.

functional fixedness
mind-set in which one is blind to unusual uses of common everyday things or procedures.

Quick Quiz 9.2: Problem Solving

1. In what kind of problems must the person trying to solve them narrow down the range of possible solutions to arrive at the correct answer?
   a. simple problems
   b. convergent thinking problems
   c. algorithms
   d. divergent thinking problems
2. A child discovers that 2×2 is the same as $2 + 2$. He therefore wrongly concludes that 3×3 is the same as $3 + 3$. What tendency is affecting this child's problem-solving strategies?
   a. mental set
   b. divergent thinking
   c. test bias
   d. response bias
3. An inability to break out of a particular frame of mind in order to think about a problem from a fresh perspective is known as
   a. perpetuation.
   b. mental set.
   c. fixation.
   d. functional fixedness.

Answers can be found at the end of the chapter.

LO8 CREATIVITY

What was it about Leonardo da Vinci that made him so versatile as an artist and inventor? What was going on in the mind of Isaac Newton when he realized the significance of the apple falling from a tree? Why are some people able to paint magnificent landscapes while others can hardly draw a straight line? The answer is that these individuals are more creative than the average person.

The ability to think or act creatively is highly prized in our society (Feist, 1999; Sawyer, 2006; Simonton, 1999). All of society's advances—artistic, musical, industrial, governmental, legal, and scientific—happen because a person or group of people came up with a creative idea. Creative thinking is related to, yet distinct from, both intelligence and problem solving. To fully appreciate the nature of human creativity, we define what psychologists mean by it, discuss its connection to genius and intelligence, define its stages, review the brain systems involved in creative thought, and finally discuss the cognitive mechanisms involved in creative thinking.

WHAT IS CREATIVITY?

Read the following two paragraphs, written by different people, and think about what each one means and whether they are equally "creative."

Can you think of other creative geniuses who changed society in some important way?

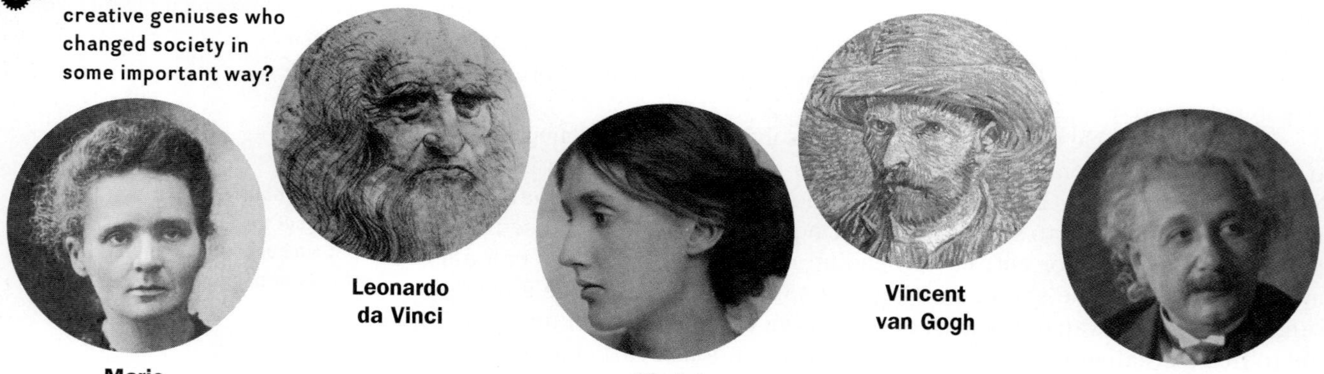

Marie Curie · Leonardo da Vinci · Virginia Woolf · Vincent van Gogh · Albert Einstein

They're all so different Boylan talking about the shape of my foot he noticed at once even before he was introduced when I was in the DBC with Poldy laughing and trying to listen I was waggling my foot we both ordered 2 teas and plain bread and butter I saw him looking with his two old maids of sisters when I stood up and asked the girl where it was what do I care with it dropping out of me and that black closed breeches he made me buy takes you half an hour to let down wetting all myself always with some brand new fad every other week. . . .

This creation in which we live began with the Dominant Nature as an Identification Body of a completed evolutionary Strong Material creation in a Major Body Resistance Force. And is fulfilling the Nature Identification in a like Weaker Material Identification creation in which Two Major Bodies have already fulfilled radio body balances, and embodying a Third Material Identification Embodiment of both.

The first paragraph is an excerpt from James Joyce's great novel *Ulysses*. The second paragraph was written by a person who is schizophrenic and is an example of what is called *word salad*, a collection of words that are mixed up in sentences with no real meaning (White, 1964). These two paragraphs demonstrate an essential point about what creativity is and what it is not. It is not simply original thinking, for the paragraphs are equally original. They are both unusual, and both give voice to sentences that probably had not been uttered or written before these writers penned them. For something to be deemed creative, however, it not only has to be original but must also be useful or adaptive and solve a problem. Joyce's paragraph does that because it's part of solving the problem of telling a story. The second paragraph is not creative because it is not useful and it does not solve a problem.

Creativity, then, is thought or behaviour that is both novel-original and useful or adaptive (Amabile, 1996; Feist, 1999; MacKinnon, 1970; Simonton, 1999). The usefulness criterion requires that someone at some time sees real value and usefulness in the creative accomplishment. Truly creative works are often appreciated in the creator's lifetime, but not always. For instance, Vincent van Gogh sold very few of his paintings while alive. But his creative genius is now fully appreciated by novices and experts alike, and his paintings are worth millions.

creativity
thinking and/or behaviour that is both novel–original and useful–adaptive.

One of the challenges facing researchers in the study of creativity has revolved around how to measure it. If creativity involves novel thinking, then we should not necessarily expect people to express their creativity in the same way. Some of the earliest measures of creativity focused on divergent problem solving (Guilford, 1962). One of the most widely used divergent measures is the Torrance Tests of Creativity (TTCT, Torrance, 1966; Khatena, 1989). Figure 9.16 shows a sample item from these tests. Other tests of creativity focus on personality characteristics, such as intuitiveness and high energy, that are associated with the generation of novel ideas (Amabile, 1996). Still other researchers have turned to the study of eminent people, such as Charles Darwin and Albert Einstein, to elucidate the nature of creativity (Simonton, 1997). As you read about creativity in the next few pages, you will see the many different, "creative" ways that researchers measure creativity.

Connection

Psychologists sometimes use a psychobiography to examine the lives of historically important people.

See Chapter 2, LO3.

Creativity and the Brain

Imagine what was going on in Newton's brain when he "discovered" gravity or in Einstein's when he came up with the theory of relativity. Of course, we'll never know what was going on in the minds of these geniuses from the past. But neuroscientists are beginning to uncover what happens in the brain when a typical person has a Eureka insight or when creative people solve problems compared to

FIGURE **9.16** **MEASURING CREATIVITY.** Suppose you were given five minutes to complete each of the pictures on the left. What would you produce? The completed drawings on the right would be scored for originality, evidence of motion, emotion, humour, and visual perspective, among other things.

less creative people. The research has revealed three consistent findings: Creative insight increases frontal lobe activity, insights are processed more strongly in the right hemisphere rather than the left, and creative people solving creative problems show more balanced activity between their right and left frontal lobes.

Creative Insight Results in Results in Increased Frontal Lobe Activity The frontal lobes are active in abstract reasoning, planning, focused working memory, and the integration of sensory input. Creativity involves integrating ideas in novel and valuable ways. It is not surprising, therefore, that modern neuroscience supports the conclusion that creative problem solving and insights involve frontal lobe activity (Carlsson, Wendt, & Risberg, 2000; Chow & Cummings, 1999; Feist, 2004; Folley & Park, 2005; Mell, Howard, & Miller, 2003; Takeuchi et al., 2010). Recent research examined whether greater neural connection in the frontal lobe is associated with greater levels of creativity. Takeuchi and colleagues (2010) measured creativity and neural connectivity in 55 college students. The creativity tasks involved generating unique ideas for how to use everyday objects. For example, students were asked such questions as "Other than reading, how can we use newspapers?" Neural connectivity was measured with an MRI technique that assesses white matter connections in the brain. Takeuchi and colleagues found a direct and positive relationship between the students' creativity scores and their neural connectivity, especially in the frontal lobe. Greater connectivity suggests more myelinated neurons and hence more efficient communication between the neurons. Recall from Chapter 3 that axons are often covered with myelin, which facilitates neural transmission. It may be that more creative people have both more connections between neurons and more myelin. Further research, however, is needed to confirm this idea.

Creative Insight and the Right Hemisphere It's not easy to undertake brain research related to creativity. The main way to study creativity and the brain is to administer a creativity problem to a person while she or he is either lying down in a brain scanner or sitting down hooked up to an EEG machine. One kind of problem that has been used in such research is a *remote associate* word problem (Mednick & Mednick, 1967). Remote associate problems display three words at one time to the participant, who must then come up with a single word that could be used with all three of the words. The single word could be added to each of the words to create a compound word or it could modify one of the displayed words in some way. This requires the participant to form a non-obvious or "remote" association in order to solve the problem. For example, if the three words were *French, shoe,* and *car,* what one word could you think of that could be used with the other three? What if the three words were *pine, crab,* and *sauce?* (The answers appear at the end of the chapter.) Interestingly, people often solve these kinds of problems with Eureka insights.

In one set of studies, researchers presented remote association tests to either the right or left visual fields of participants. These participants were not selected for high or low levels of creativity. The researchers presented the information to the individual visual fields because they wanted to control which hemisphere of the brain processed the information. Recall from Chapter 3 that information presented to the left visual field is processed in the right hemisphere of the brain and information presented to the right visual field is processed in the left hemisphere of the brain. When the problem was presented in the left visual field and processed in the right hemisphere, insight into the problems occurred much more frequently than when the problem was presented to the right visual field and processed in the left hemisphere (Beeman & Bowden, 2000; Bowden & Jung-Beeman, 2003). Moreover, when researchers took brain images using fMRI and EEG while people were solving insight problems, they found that sudden insights consistently activated the right hemisphere more than the left (Bowden et al., 2005). Similarly, patients with damage to the frontal region of their right hemisphere are less able to solve problems requiring insight than people without damage to their right hemisphere (Miller & Tippett, 1996).

Connection

People who have had their corpus callosum severed cannot say what they see if the information is presented to their left visual field but can verbally label it if it is presented to their right visual field. Why?

See Chapter 3, LO12.

Creativity and Balanced Activity between the Hemispheres The third consistent finding from the neuroscience of creativity is that when solving problems, creative people have more balanced brain activity between the hemispheres than less creative people. In particular, while solving problems they show equally active areas in their right and left frontal lobes, which translates into a widening rather than a narrowing of attention and a greater flexibility in moving from one way of thinking to another (Carlsson, Wendt, & Risberg, 2000; Goel & Vartanian, 2005). Widening attention and being able to shift ways of thinking easily and flexibly are hallmarks of creative thinking (Feist, 2004; Martindale, 1999). Let's take one study as an example: Carlsson and colleagues (2000) selected participants who during earlier testing scored either high or low on creativity problems. Participants in each of these two groups were each given a non-creative and creative task to complete while in a brain scanner. Brain scans compared the two conditions. Results showed more left than right frontal lobe activity in the less-creative participants. Highly creative participants, however, showed a balance in right and left frontal lobe activity. See the orange regions in Figure 9.17.

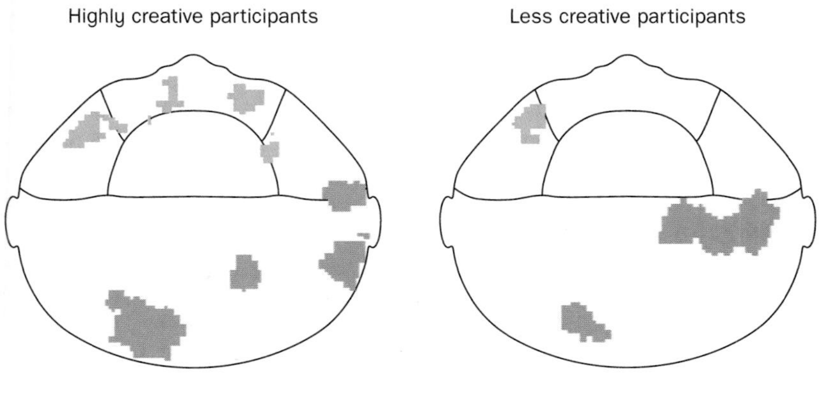

FIGURE **9.17**

BRAIN ACTIVITY WHILE SOLVING CREATIVE PROBLEMS. Orange regions show areas of increased activity while solving creative problems compared to non-creative problems. Green regions show areas of decreased activity. The more creative participants use both left and right hemispheres (frontal region) while working on creative problems, while the less creative participants show increased activity only in their right frontal lobe. (*Source:* Carlsson et al., 2000.)

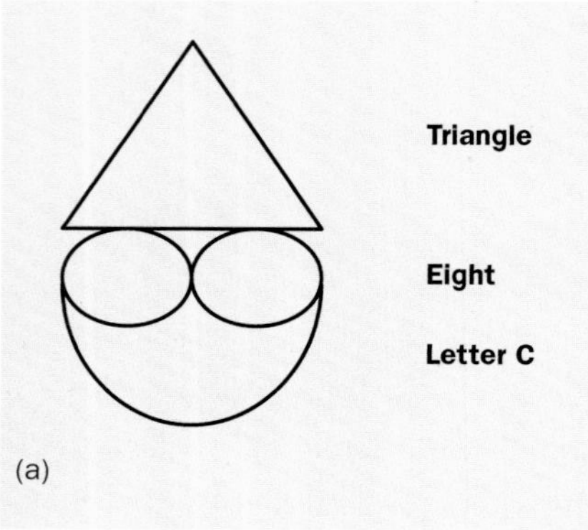

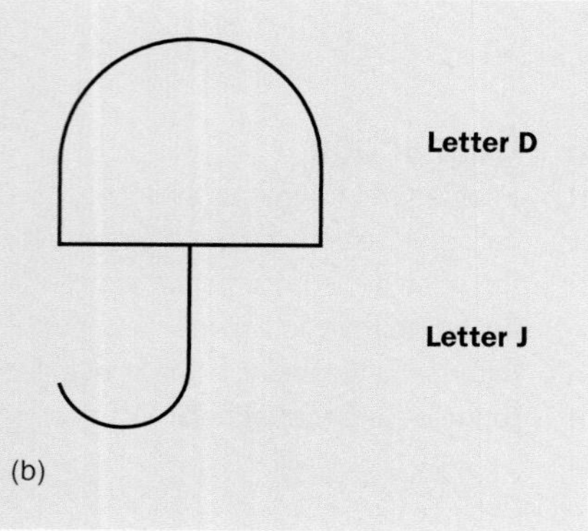

FIGURE **9.18**
CREATIVE PROBLEM SOLVING USING MENTAL IMAGERY. (a) Participants are given simple stimuli (letters, numbers, and shapes) and asked to combine them in any way to produce a single image or object. (b) These are some of the solutions created using stimuli the shapes in (a). (*Source:* Finke et al., 1992.)

What kind of images can you create using the stimuli shown above? Do you find this task difficult or easy to do?

This finding may appear to contradict what we just said about the importance of the right hemisphere in creative problem solving, but it does not. The right hemisphere findings are from non-creative participants who are coming up with insight solutions. The balanced hemisphere result comes from comparing creative to less creative people. In both cases, right hemisphere activity is more pronounced in creative people than in less creative ones.

Cognitive Processes in Creative Thinking

Creative thinking entails unique cognitive processes. Psychologists who study the cognitive aspects of creative thought have focused on visual thinking, fluency, flexibility, and originality. Visual imagery occurs when we see a solution in our "mind's eye." Many scientists, artists, and writers solve problems by using creative mental images (A. Miller, 1996). Einstein, for example, often visualized a situation, such as riding in an elevator travelling at the speed of light. Imagining such a scenario and then thinking about what would happen to a light beam he emitted led to his discovery of the theory of relativity.

Cognitive psychologists have developed clever experiments to test people's ability to come up with creative mental images. They display images of letters or geometric shapes and ask participants to combine some of them in a creative way (Finke, Ward, & Smith, 1992). Figure 9.18a contains a set of such objects. Three of these images are chosen at random during each trial, and the participant's task is to assemble them in such a way as to create a recognizable shape or pattern. Various solutions are presented in Figure 9.18b.

ideational fluency
the ability to produce many ideas.

flexibility of thought
the ability to come up with many different categories of ideas and think of other responses besides the obvious one.

The ability to produce many ideas is central to creative thought. This ability is termed **ideational fluency** (Guilford, 1967). Highly creative people usually come up with more ideas for a given problem than less creative people do. Not all the ideas will be equally useful, but having a large number of ideas increases the chance that any one of them will be a useful or adaptive solution to the problem at hand. J.P. Guilford developed the *Alternate Uses* test to measure creativity. In this test, participants are given a common object such as a brick or a pencil and asked to write down all the possible uses they can think of for the object within a limited amount of time. An ideationally fluent person can list many alternate uses for the object within a short period.

The ability to produce many ideas does not by itself guarantee that one can break out of one's mental set and think of unusual uses. A creative person can also come up with many different categories of ideas and think of other responses besides the obvious one. This ability is called **flexibility of thought** (Guilford, 1967). In the *Alternate Uses* test, flexibility of thought is gauged by the number of categories of response a person offers. For instance, if all the answers for the uses of a brick involve building something, the person is not displaying flexible thinking but remaining within one rather obvious category. In contrast, coming up with uses that involve building, painting, writing, weights, step stools, and ballasts means a person is a flexible thinker because those uses cut across many different categories. As we saw with the nine-dot problem, creative people "think outside the box" and break out of mental sets more easily than less creative people do.

originality
the ability to come up with unusual and novel ideas.

A third cognitive process involved in creative thought is **originality,** which means thinking of unusual and novel ideas. In the *Alternate Uses* test, the test taker's originality is scored by comparing his or her responses to a set of norms developed from the answers given by thousands of respondents who have taken the test previously. A person's answer is scored as original if it is rare or uncommon compared to the norms. Again using the brick as an example, a higher originality score is given to "step stool" than to "paperweight" because there are fewer instances of "step stool" in the norms. In this sense, an original response is the same as an infrequent response. But originality in itself is not enough to explain creative thought. Creative thinking occurs when a person combines all three cognitive processes at once—fluency, flexibility, and originality.

Quick Quiz 9.3: Creativity

1. Creative thinking or behaviour is both novel and
   a. interesting.
   b. artistic.
   c. useful.
   d. unusual.
2. When compared to less creative people, creative people show what pattern of brain activity while solving problems?
   a. asymmetry between the hemispheres
   b. balance between the hemispheres
   c. parietal lobe activation
   d. occipital lobe activation
3. What is measured by the task in which participants are asked to think of as many different uses for a brick as they can?
   a. originality
   b. flexibility of thought
   c. functional fixedness
   d. both a and b

Answers can be found at the end of the chapter.

LO9

Evaluating Connections in Intelligence, Problem Solving, and Creativity

Genius, Intelligence, and Creativity

Intelligence, creativity, and problem solving are abilities used by people in every walk of life, including art, science, cooking, teaching, parenting, inventing, and engineering. Indeed, humans are distinguished from other animals by our well developed intellectual, problem solving, and creative abilities. For many people, finding out that someone has an extremely high IQ (140 and above) is enough to call him or her a "genius," but are all very smart people necessarily geniuses? Moreover, does having extremely high IQ mean the person will be creative? These are fascinating and important questions and they beg two other questions:

1. What is genius?
2. Is intelligence necessary and sufficient for creativity?

What Is Genius?

What makes someone a genius? Is superior intelligence enough? Consider Marilyn vos Savant. Most people have not heard of her, although she writes a weekly nationally syndicated column for *Parade* magazine. She has the world's highest recorded IQ ever—an off-the-chart 228—yet she has not created master works of note. Genius is not, as some have claimed, simply being smart or having a very high IQ (Simonton, 1999). Having an IQ of 130 or 140, which puts someone in the top 1 percent of the population, does not guarantee producing creative works of lasting influence.

Something other than intelligence must go into the making of a genius. **Genius** is high

genius
High intelligence combined with creative accomplishments that have a tremendous impact on a given field.

intelligence combined with creative accomplishments that have a tremendous impact on a given field (Simonton, 1999). The paintings, plays, buildings, novels, and scientific discoveries of geniuses change their respective fields. Literature was never the same after Shakespeare or Virginia Woolf. Physics has not been the same since Newton, Einstein, and Marie Curie. Art has not been the same since van Gogh and Picasso. Music has not been the same since Bach and Beethoven. If people's accomplishments change their field, other people appreciate their importance sooner or later. Having a major impact and being appreciated for one's accomplishments is what distinguishes genius from genius-like IQ. For every Shakespeare, Beethoven, and Einstein, there are many more people with equally high intelligence who make no significant contributions to society. Moreover, there have been people of truly monumental creative accomplishment whose intelligence was only somewhat above average. Charles Darwin, was—by his own admission—of only modestly high intelligence (Simonton, 1999), but his accomplishments have had as much impact on science and culture as those of just about any other person. By this standard, he was a genius.

Is Intelligence Necessary and Sufficient for Creativity?

Genius, by definition, and creativity are closely related, but what about intelligence and creativity? Does being really smart make a person more creative? Surprisingly, however, IQ and creativity are not very strongly related (Albert & Runco, 1989; Sternberg & O'Hara, 1999). For example, a meta-analysis of 21 studies that included more than 45 000 participants reported an average correlation between creativity and intelligence of only +.17 (Kim, 2005). That is, knowing an IQ score tells us only a little bit about how creative someone may be.

Clearly the relationship between intelligence and creativity is not a simple one. Starting in the 1950s and 1960s, creativity researchers concluded there was a threshold on intelligence, which assumes that above-average intelligence is *necessary* for high-level creativity (Guilford, 1967). This is usually assessed statistically by comparing people's IQ scores with measures of creativity and then looking at how the relationship changes with increasing IQ (see Figure 9.19). A threshold is the point at which the relationship changes; below the threshold, intelligence and creativity are positively correlated, but above the threshold there is no clear pattern. For many years, the threshold IQ was widely accepted as a score of 120, since many studies showed a positive relationship between creativity and intelligence below 120, but no relationship above this threshold. This would imply that intelligence is a necessary condition, but not a sufficient one, for creativity.

Challenge Your Assumptions

True or False? People with very high IQs are geniuses.

False: IQ alone does not determine genius; genius requires creative accomplishments that change some aspect of society.

More recent investigations, however, have shown a more complex relationship between intelligence and creativity (Jauk et al., 2013; Jung et al., 2009; Karwowski & Gralewski, 2013; Kim, 2005; Preckel, Holling, & Wiese, 2006). It appears that the nature of the relationship may depend on the aspect of creativity being measured. Jauk and colleagues (2013) report different thresholds for different components of creative potential (doing well on tests of creativity). If the number of ideas (fluency) is the measure of creative potential, the threshold is only an IQ of 85; however, if originality of ideas is the measure of potential, then support for the threshold of 120 is reported (see Figures 9.19a and 9.19b). In other words, high intelligence predicts original ideas more than just quantity or number of ideas. Moreover, when the measure of creativity is achievement (actually producing creative works in art, music, or science), there is no threshold whatsoever (see Figure 9.19c). Intelligence is positively related to creativity—meaning that, the more intelligent people are, the more likely they are to produce creative works.

Challenge Your Assumptions

True or False? Intelligence is strongly linked to creativity.

False: Although there appears to be some link between intelligence and creativity, the relationship is weak and depends upon the way creativity is measured.

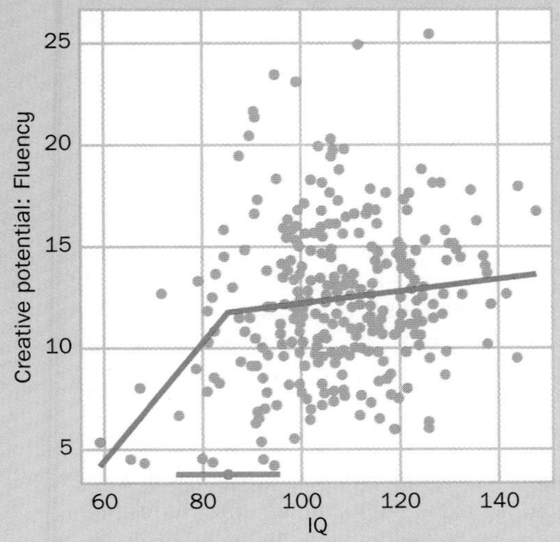

(a) An IQ of 85 is the breakpoint, or threshold, for the relationship between IQ and fluency/number of ideas (creative potential).

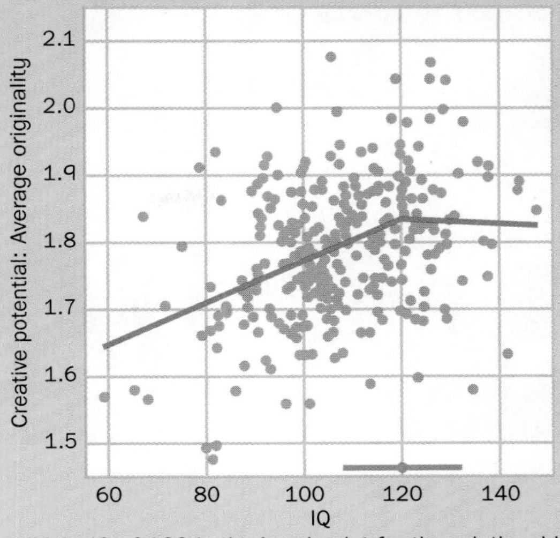

(b) An IQ of 120 is the breakpoint for the relationship between IQ and originality of ideas (creative potential).

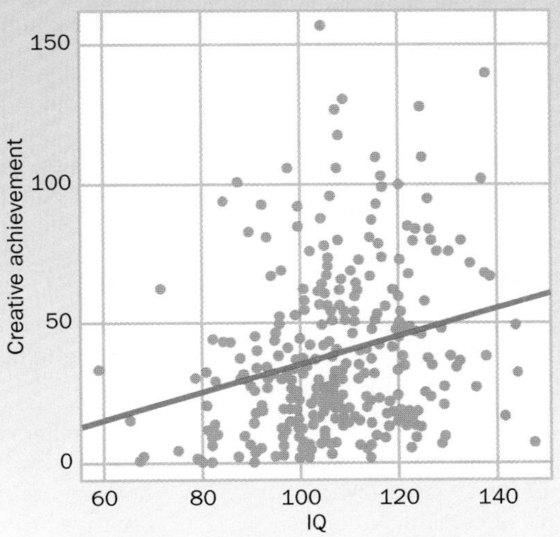

(c) There is no threshold for the relationship between IQ and creative achievement.

FIGURE **9.19**

IQ THRESHOLDS FOR CREATIVE POTENTIAL (FLUENCY AND ORIGINALITY) AND CREATIVE ACHIEVEMENT. In these scatterplots, each dot represents a person's IQ score and his or her score on a different measure of creativity (Jauk et al., 2013). The line through the dots represents the slope of the relationship. A diagonal line is a significant relationship, but a flat line is no relationship. The sharp change in direction of the line is the threshold, or breakpoint.

Quick Quiz 9.4: Evaluating Connections in Intelligence, Problem Solving, and Creativity

1. Genius is the combination of superior intelligence and
   a. talent
   b. practice.
   c. creative accomplishments that have a significant impact.
   d. ideational fluency.

2. Research on the threshold hypothesis of creativity shows that there is no threshold for IQ and
   a. genius.
   b. creative achievement.
   c. originality of ideas.
   d. number of ideas.

Answers can be found at the end of the chapter.

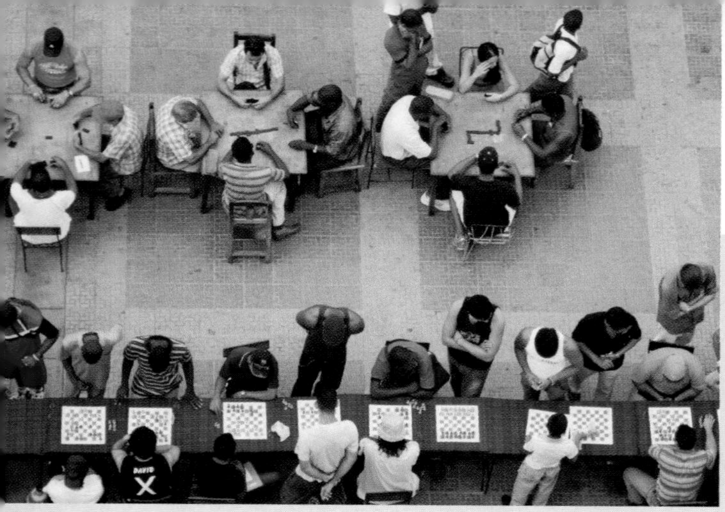

Chapter Review

INTELLIGENCE

- Intelligence is a set of cognitive skills that include abstract thinking, reasoning, problem solving, and the ability to acquire knowledge.
- There are two major theories of the nature of intelligence. The single-factor or general-factor theory argues that intelligence at its core is one overall ability. The other theory, the multifactor theory, says that intelligence consists of multiple abilities.
- Some of the factors of intelligence in the multifactor theory are crystallized and fluid intelligence, as well as analytic, practical, musical, and bodily–kinesthetic intelligence.
- Measures of intelligence, including the Stanford-Binet and the Wechsler Adult Scales of Intelligence (WAIS), tend to be reliable and predictive of certain outcomes (school achievement, type of occupation, and job performance), but not others (happiness or satisfaction with one's job).
- Intelligence ranges widely on a continuum from very low to very high. On the extreme low end is intellectual disability and on the extreme high end is giftedness.
- Nature and nurture interact to influence intelligence. The concept of reaction range suggests that heredity places upper and lower limits on an individual's intellectual potential, but environment determines where an individual's IQ falls within that range of potential. IQ scores have been steadily rising over the past century; this phenomenon is known as the Flynn effect.
- Group differences in IQ do exist for race, and yet there is much debate concerning possible explanations for these differences.
- Definitions of what it means to be intelligent vary according to culture.

PROBLEM SOLVING

- Two distinct kinds of problem exist. Convergent thinking problems have known solutions, which can be reached by narrowing down a set of possible answers. Divergent thinking problems have no known solution, and require breaking away from our normal problem-solving strategies and making unusual associations to arrive at novel ways of thinking about a problem.
- People use different kinds of strategies to solve problems. Algorithms are formulas that guarantee correct solutions to particular problems. Thinking outside the box requires one to break free of self-imposed conceptual constraints and think about a problem differently in order to solve it. Eureka insights involve a sudden understanding of a solution.
- Obstacles to solutions include fixation, or inability to break out of a particular mind-set in order to think about a problem from a fresh perspective, and functional fixedness, which is the tendency to be blind to unusual uses of common everyday things or procedures.

CREATIVITY

- Creativity is thought or behaviour that is both novel and useful or adaptive. It is measured in many different ways.
- Researchers have uncovered two principles of creative thinking and the brain: Insights occur more in the right hemisphere than the left, and creative people solving creative problems show more balanced activity between their right and left frontal lobes than less creative people.
- Cognitive processes commonly associated with creative thinking are visual imagery, flexibility (coming up with many different categories of ideas), ideational fluency (the ability to produce many ideas), and originality (thinking of novel solutions).

EVALUATING CONNECTIONS IN INTELLIGENCE, PROBLEM SOLVING, AND CREATIVITY

- Genius is closely related to creativity in that it combines high intelligence with achievements that change entire fields (art, music, science, technology, business).
- Intelligence, genius, and creativity are related but distinct concepts. Intelligence appears to be necessary but not sufficient for both genius and creativity.

Quick Quiz Answers

Quick Quiz 9.1: 1. d 2. d 3. b 4. c 5. a **Quick Quiz 9.2:** 1. b 2. a 3. c **Quick Quiz 9.3:** 1. c 2. b 3. d **Quick Quiz 9.4:** 1. c 2. b

Solution to first remote association is "horn" and the second is "apple."
SOLUTIONS TO FIGURES 9.12b AND 9.13: Can you think of any others?

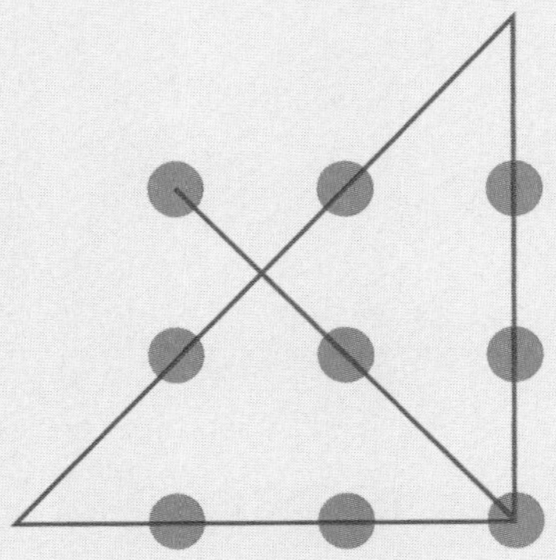

Human Development

CHAPTER 10

CHAPTER OUTLINE

Challenge Your Assumptions

True or False?

- ☐ The heart is the first major organ to develop.
- ☐ Schizophrenia in an offspring is more likely if the mother is exposed to a virus while pregnant.
- ☐ Babies are born able to see and hear as well as adults.
- ☐ Being regularly touched as a newborn increases both physical and mental health later in life.
- ☐ Parents are the main social influence on development through late adolescence.
- ☐ Alzheimer's disease is limited to problems of memory.

LEARNING OBJECTIVES

LO1 Define developmental psychology and describe the types of research designs developmental psychologists use.

LO2 Describe the stages and processes of prenatal development and discuss some of the problems that may arise from teratogens.

LO3 Describe the important events and features of infant and childhood physical development, including how researchers measure infant perception.

LO4 Describe and explain Piaget's stage theory of cognitive development, comparing it to Vygotsky's theory and theory of mind.

LO5 Present an overview of Kohlberg's stage theory of moral development, describing the characteristics of each level, and summarizing the criticisms surrounding this theory.

LO6 Define attachment and explain the contributions of Bowlby, Ainsworth, and Harlow to our understanding of this aspect of emotional development.

LO7 Define temperament and discuss how infant temperament relates to personality.

LO8 Discuss the development of emotion from infancy to childhood, distinguishing between social referencing, social competence, and the role of peers.

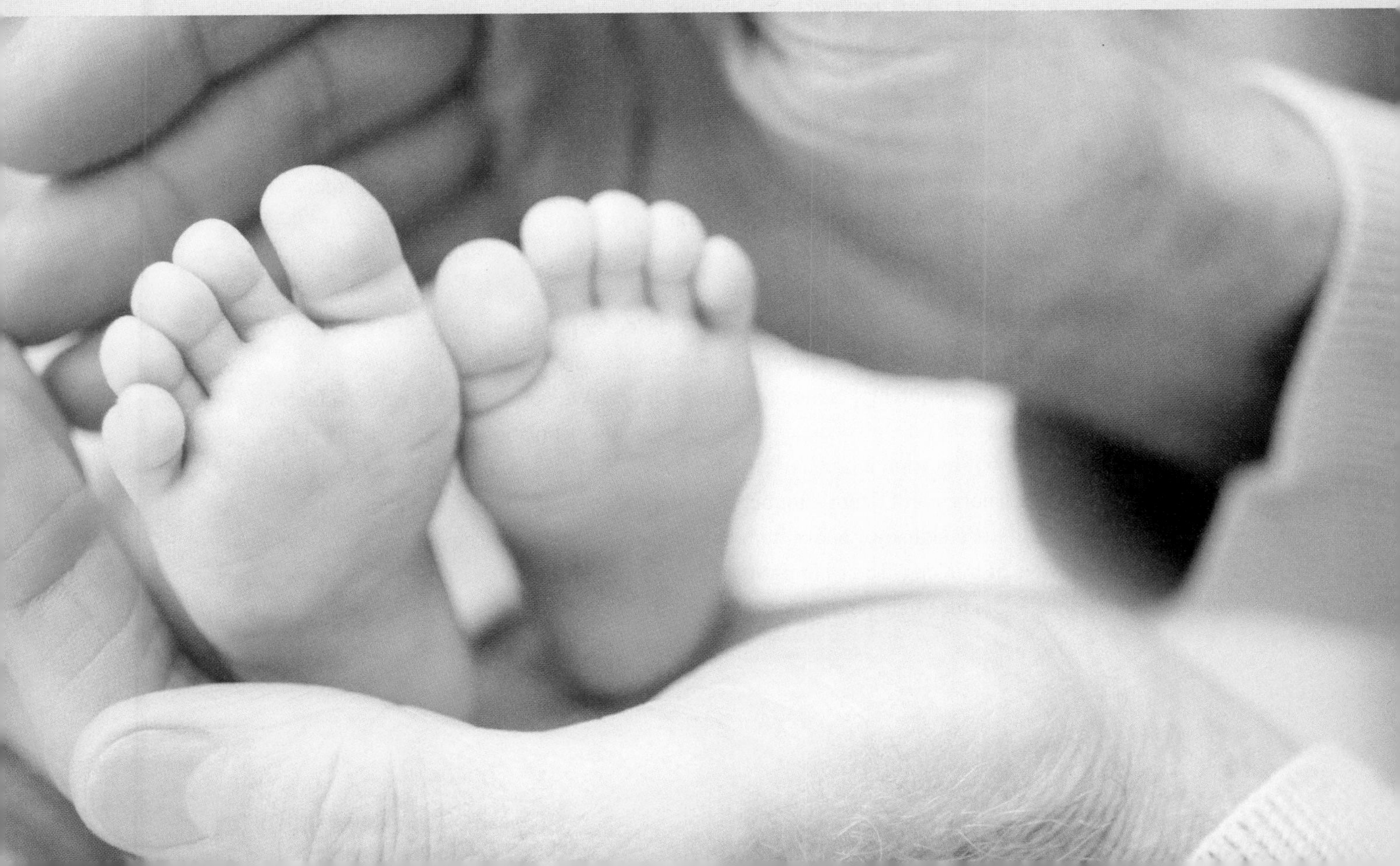

LO9 Describe the development of gender identity, differentiating between gender constancy and gender roles.

LO10 Define adolescence and summarize the main physical, cognitive, and social-emotional changes that occur during this period.

LO11 Explain when adulthood begins in our culture, emphasizing the impact of marriage and parenthood.

LO12 Describe the important developmental issues of middle adulthood, including the concept of generativity versus stagnation.

LO13 Discuss how brain function and cognition changes in late adulthood, including the onset of diseases such as Alzheimer's.

At age 21, George and Brent were identical strangers. Each knew he had been adopted. In fact, George was raised with someone he thought was his fraternal twin, Marcus. Imagine then the shock and disbelief of finding out in early adulthood that there is someone else just like you—your identical twin! And in George's case, finding out that the twin you thought was your brother really isn't biologically related to you at all!

George and Brent first met at a lounge at Ottawa's Carleton University in the fall of 1991. Brent was a student there and he was also a member of the Strategy Club—a university group whose members played board games, cards, and chess. George was working as an usher at a local theatre at the time, but like Brent, he also liked games and had friends in the Strategy Club whom he would often visit at the university. One day, George's friend Sasha greeted who she thought was her friend "George." She was shocked when the young man replied, "My name is Brent, not George" (Segal, 2005, p. 30). She explained that her friend George looked just like Brent and suggested that they meet. Their first meeting came several days later—Brent was in the same lounge and everyone stopped and stared when George entered. In Brent's words, "I was surprised to see someone who looked so much like me, although his hair was a bit different. It was eerie—for both of us" (Segal, 2005, p. 30).

As with other pairs of identical twins reared apart, George and Brent were remarkably similar. When they first met, they found that they shared the same ideas and sense of humour. They liked the same actors, the same old films, and the same kind of music. Although neither one was athletic, they were both obsessed with football statistics.

Yet, despite being identical, there were also some differences in the twins. Brent had worn braces on his teeth to prevent him from developing an overbite. George hadn't had braces, and lisped slightly as a result. Brent finished high school, whereas George was one credit shy of graduation. Brent enrolled in a number of college programs although he never finished them. In contrast, George never attended college but he tried a number of temporary jobs.

The life paths of George and Brent support both the nature and nurture assumptions of development. On the nature side, they share common looks and interests. They share many identical mannerisms and ways of thinking. Their life paths, however, are different enough to also lend support to the assumption that nurture helps mould individuals.

LO1 STUDYING HUMAN DEVELOPMENT

Researchers in human development are interested in studying age-related changes in behaviours and mental processes across the life span in three major domains—physical, cognitive, and social-emotional development. In general, research and theory in human development seeks to answer three questions:

1. Does development unfold in distinct, discontinuous stages (i.e., is our growth punctuated by sharp, sudden changes in our abilities?), or is it a gradual, continuous process?
2. How do nature (our genes) and nurture (our environment) interact to make us who we are?
3. To what extent do we stay the same over time (i.e., remain stable) versus change?

Although these theoretical issues guide the basic direction of research, most developmental psychologists prefer to adopt an *interactionist approach*, believing that development incorporates all of these ideas.

To study age-related change, developmental psychologists employ several types of research designs. A **cross-sectional design** allows researchers to examine individuals of different ages at the same point in time. Suppose we were interested in studying differences in the intellectual abilities of a group of 10-year olds, 30-year-olds, 50-year-olds, and 70-year-olds. We could measure each individual within each age group on a number of measures of intellectual ability and then compare the differences between age groups. One of the advantages of this type of design is that it allows researchers to collect data fairly quickly and relatively inexpensively. However, it has the disadvantage that participants in each age group (or *cohort*) grew up in different historical contexts, so we can't be certain whether any observed differences between groups are due to age or due to the different social and political conditions experienced by each group (a *cohort effect*). For example, although our 70-year-olds may score lower on tests of intellectual ability than our 30-year-olds, such a finding may be due to group differences in formal education, access to technology, or nutrition—not necessarily aging.

cross-sectional design
a research design in which different people of various ages are studied at one point in time to find age-related differences.

To avoid the problem with the cohort effect, researchers may conduct a **longitudinal design,** where they repeatedly test the same group of people (or cohort) over a number of years. Starting now, we could test the intellectual abilities of a group of 10-year-olds and then retest the same group 20 years later when they are 30 years old, and then retest them again when they are 50 years old, and so forth. One of the advantages of this type of design is that it allows researchers to look at *real* age-related changes because they are able to compare the *same* individuals at different ages. As such, longitudinal designs tend to be more sensitive to developmental influences than cross-sectional designs (Magnusson & Stattin, 1998). However, longitudinal research is also more costly and time-consuming to conduct because it takes a number of years to complete. Participant drop-out (or *selective attrition*) is also a problem when over time the people in the study may lose interest or move away. As a result, you may end up with a sample that is a lot smaller and not quite as representative of the population that you want to draw conclusions about. Moreover, even though you are studying the same people over time,

longitudinal design
a research design in which the same people are studied over time at various ages to find age-related changes.

How has access to mobile devices impacted the development of today's cohort of children?

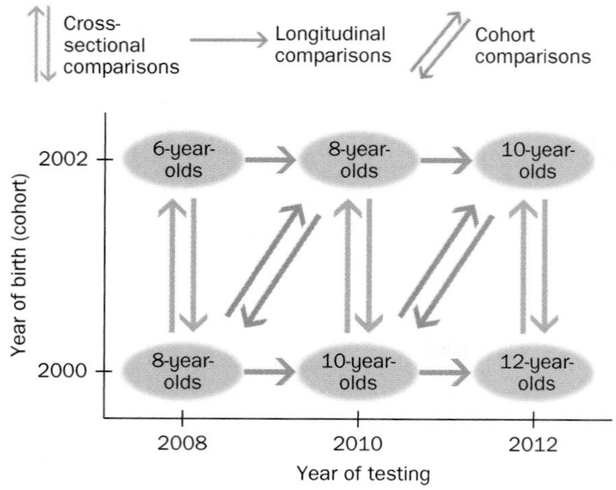

FIGURE **10.1**

THE LONGITUDINAL-SEQUENTIAL DESIGN. The longitudinal-sequential design addresses some of the limitations of the cross-sectional and longitudinal approaches. Suppose researchers are interested in age-related changes in children's Internet usage. Beginning in 2008, the researchers study a group of six-year-olds and a group of eight-year olds and then follow each group longitudinally over a period of four years, retesting each group every two years. Employing a longitudinal-sequential design allows researchers to examine cross-sectional age differences in Internet usage between cohorts (brown arrows), age-related changes in Internet usage over time among different cohorts (blue arrows), and comparisons in Internet usage between cohorts at the same age (green arrows).

you still can't be sure whether changes in intellectual ability, for example, are due to aging and occur for everyone, or are unique to this particular cohort (a *history effect*).

To address the problem of cohort and history effects, many developmental researchers employ a **longitudinal-sequential design**—a combination of the cross-sectional and longitudinal designs (von Eye & Mair, 2005). As shown in Figure 10.1, this type of design allows researchers to repeatedly test two or more age cohorts as they grow older. Thus, researchers can compare different cohorts at the same age to see if they exhibit the same behaviours, as well as determine whether the different cohorts follow a similar developmental pattern. The longitudinal-sequential design has the advantage of being a very comprehensive design, but its complexity also makes it costly and time-consuming.

Let us now turn to examine how people grow and develop. This process begins before birth, in the prenatal environment of the mother's womb. And so we open the discussion of development at the time of conception.

LO2 THE DEVELOPING FETUS

From conception until birth, we grow from a single cell to a fully formed, but still developing, human. The brain is the first major organ to form. The heart develops about a week later. (It is strange to think we have a brain before we have a heart!) A little more than eight months later, when we are born, the brain has more than 100 000 000 000 (100 billion) cells.

We pass more biological milestones before birth than we will in the rest of our lives. Development in the womb is incredibly fast and complex and includes not only physical growth, but psychological development as well.

longitudinal-sequential design
a research design in which two or more age groups of people are studied repeatedly over time.

Challenge Your Assumptions
True or False? The heart is the first major organ to develop.
False: The brain develops before the heart.

Stages of Prenatal Development

Life before birth is commonly divided into three distinct stages: the germinal, embryonic, and fetal stages. The **germinal stage** begins at conception and lasts for two weeks. At conception, the fertilized egg is a single-celled **zygote.** This single cell starts dividing rapidly around 36 hours after conception. By the seventh day, the multi-celled organism—now called a *blastocyst*—travels down the mother's fallopian tube and attaches to the uterine wall (see Figure 10.2). This process is far from risk-free: between 30 percent and 50 percent of the blastocysts do not implant properly and the pregnancy ends without the woman having known she was pregnant (Gupta et al., 2007).

germinal stage
the first prenatal stage of development, which begins at conception and lasts two weeks.

zygote
the single cell that results when a sperm fertilizes an egg.

embryonic stage
the second prenatal stage, from two weeks to eight weeks after conception, when all of the major organs form.

If implantation is successful, the second stage of prenatal development begins, at about two weeks after conception. At this point, the growing bundle of cells is officially an *embryo.* The **embryonic stage** is marked by the formation of the major organs: the nervous system, heart, eyes, ears, arms, legs, teeth, palate and external genitalia. Embryonic development continues until about eight weeks after conception.

In Figure 10.3, we see the timetable for prenatal development. Each bar in Figure 10.3 shows when major structures develop and how long it takes. Notice that the central nervous system (brain and spinal cord) takes the longest amount of time to develop. Most major abnormalities occur only in the early stages of

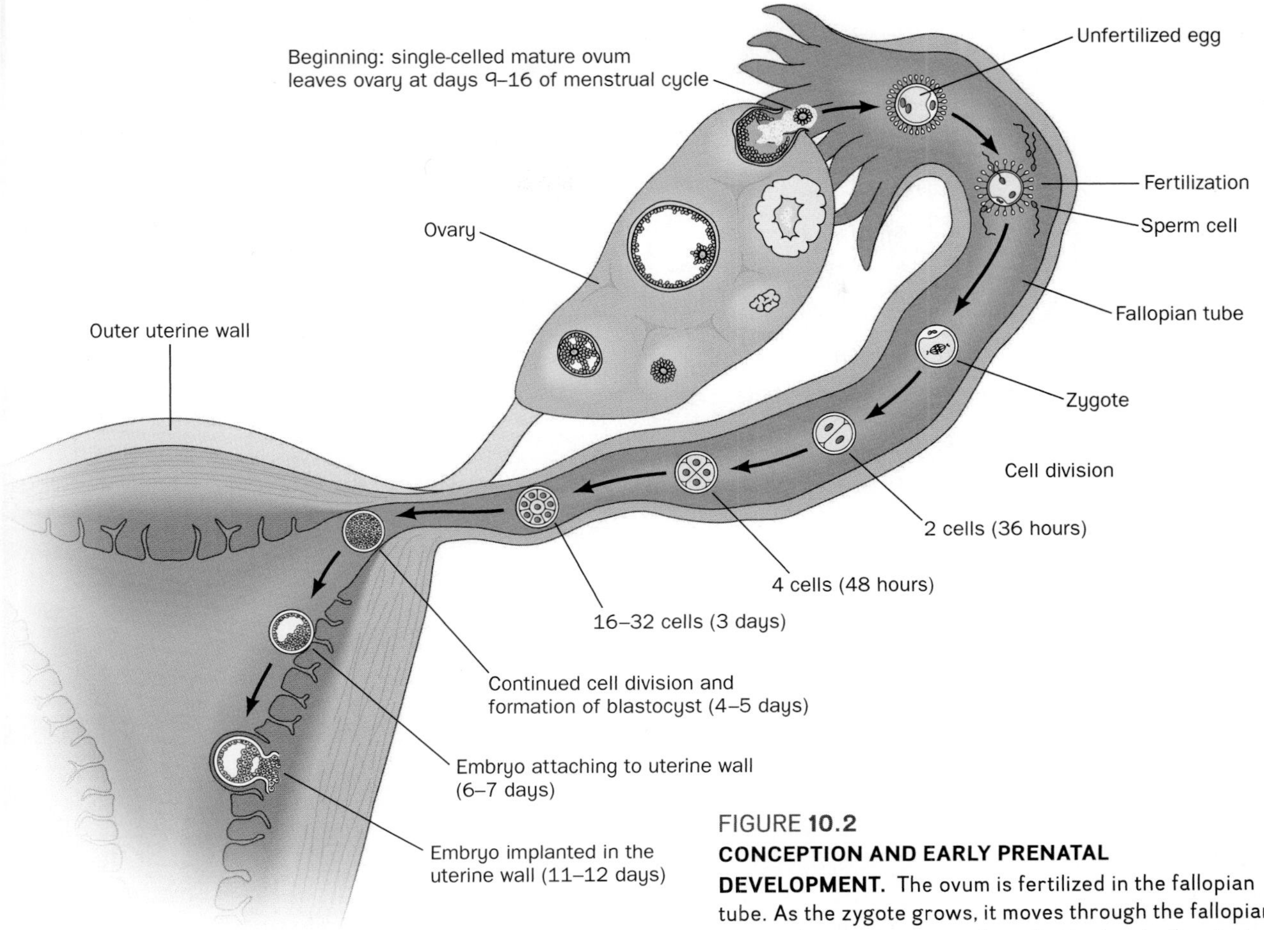

FIGURE **10.2**
CONCEPTION AND EARLY PRENATAL DEVELOPMENT. The ovum is fertilized in the fallopian tube. As the zygote grows, it moves through the fallopian tube and into the uterus, where it attaches to the uterine wall and implants there. (*Source:* Patterson, 2008.)

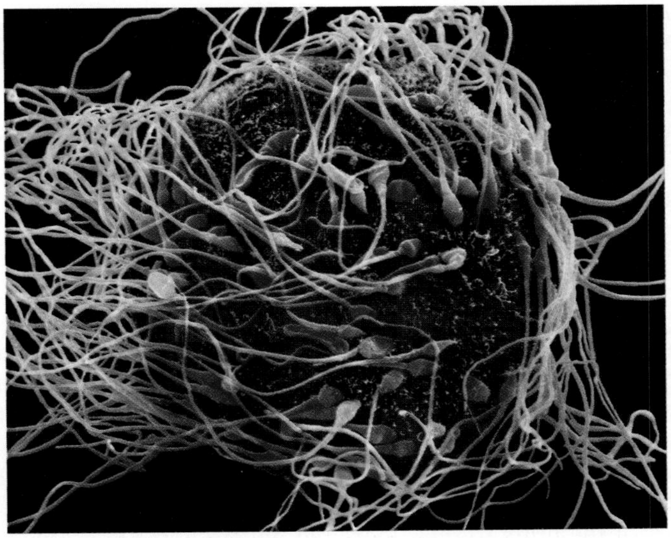

Life begins with the fertilization of an egg. In this highly magnified image, many sperm surround a single egg. Only one sperm will succeed in penetrating the egg.

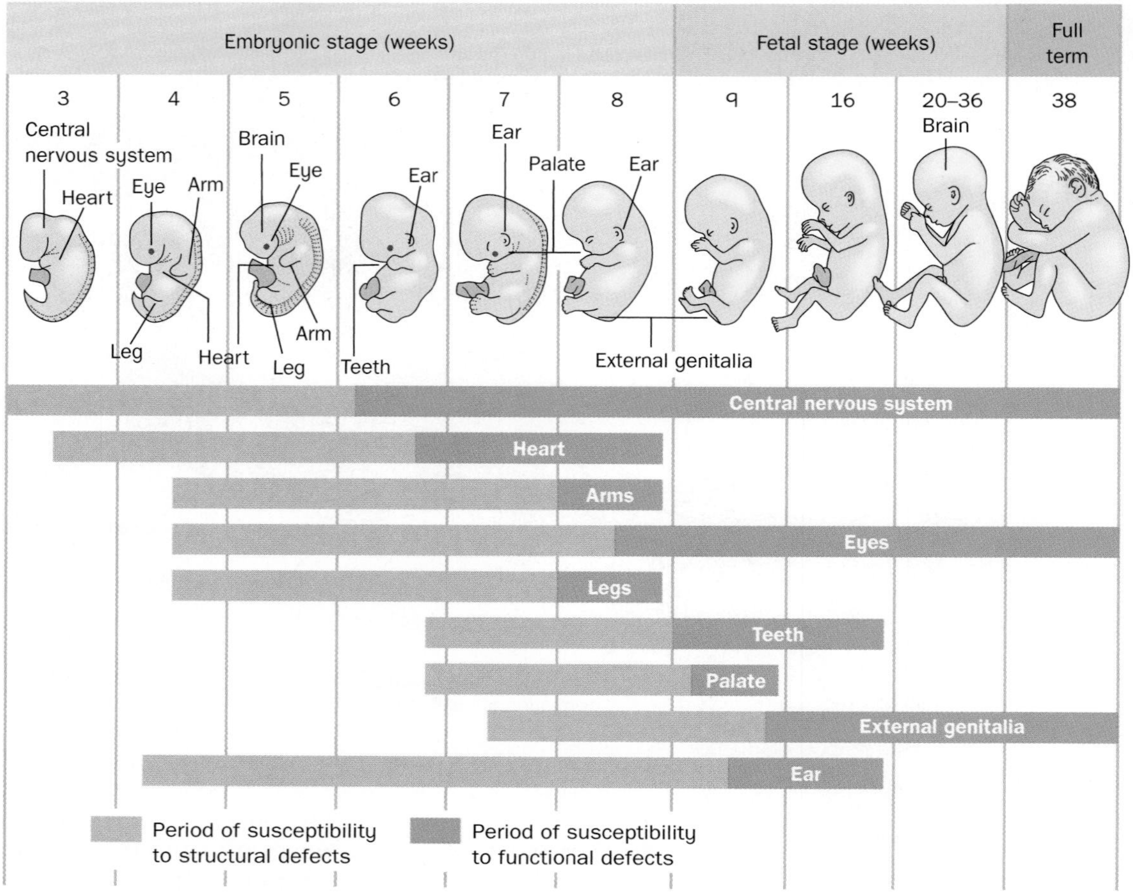

FIGURE **10.3**

PRENATAL DEVELOPMENT TIMELINE. Each bar shows when major structures develop and how long it takes for development to be completed. Note that the central nervous system begins developing in the third week after conception and continues to develop nearly the entire time we are in the womb. The blue section of each bar indicates when major abnormalities can occur if growth goes awry. After that crucial period, minor abnormalities can still occur.

development, when exposure to environmental hazards, such as drugs or illness, can cause serious defects.

fetal stage
the third prenatal stage, which begins with the formation of bone cells eight weeks after conception and ends at birth.

The key event that distinguishes the embryonic stage from the third stage, the **fetal stage,** is the formation of bone cells at eight weeks after conception. By this time, all of the major organs have already begun to form. Between 8 and 12 weeks into development, the heartbeat can be detected with a stethoscope. Organs continue to grow and mature while the fetus rapidly increases in size.

Brain and Sensory Development before Birth

neural migration
the movement of neurons from one part of the fetal brain to their more permanent destination; this occurs during the third to the fifth month of pregnancy.

As mentioned earlier, the brain is the first major organ to develop, and it is still growing rapidly at birth (see Figure 10.4). By the time an infant is born, its head has grown to 25 percent of its adult weight, whereas its body is only 5 percent of its adult weight (see Figure 10.5). During the fetal stage, the rate of new neural growth can be approximately 3 million neurons per minute at its peak (Purves & Lichtman, 1985). From the third to the fifth month of pregnancy, neurons move from one part of the brain to their more permanent home in a process known as **neural migration** (Nadarajah & Parnavelas, 2002). Factors that interfere with normal neural migration, such as prenatal exposure to certain toxins or viruses,

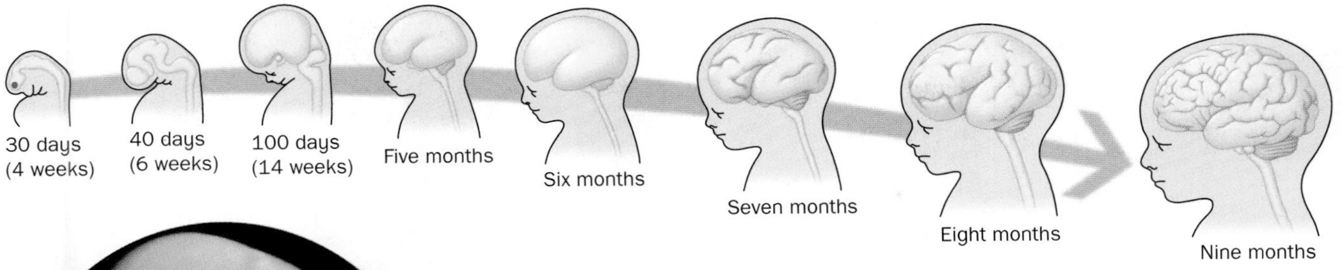

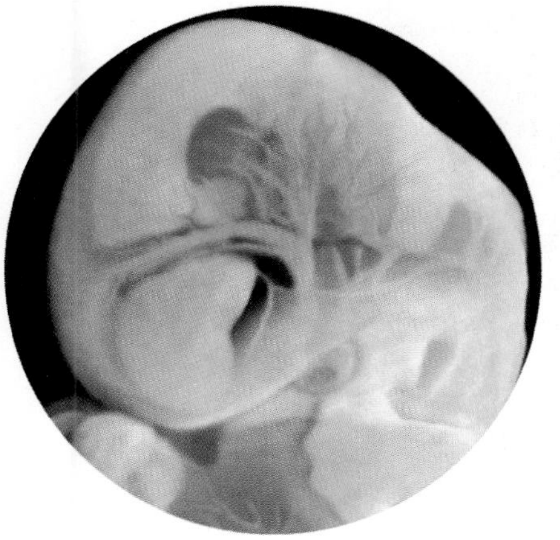

FIGURE **10.4**

PRENATAL BRAIN DEVELOPMENT. The size and complexity of the brain increase dramatically in the weeks and months following conception. At birth, the baby's brain weighs about 25 percent what an adult brain weighs. For comparison, a newborn weighs only about 5 percent as much as an adult. The photograph shows the brain at 44 days after conception. Note the well-developed blood vessels, which provide blood and oxygen to the rapidly developing brain.

	Newborn	2 years	4 years
Percentage of total weight			
Brain	25%	75%	90%
Body	5%	20%	30%

FIGURE **10.5**

NEWBORN AND CHILD BRAIN AND BODY AS PERCENTAGE OF ADULT WEIGHT. The size and complexity of the brain increase dramatically in the weeks and months following conception. By comparison, the body grows at a much slower pace.

What implications does this brain growth pattern have for child-rearing practices?

can increase the risk of psychological disorders (Kandel, 2006).

Soon after the nervous system has started to form, the embryo begins to move. By four to six months after conception, the fetus's movements are noticeable (DiPietro et al., 1996). Mothers can feel the fetus moving as early as 16 weeks into pregnancy, although it may feel a little like abdominal gas or "butterflies." Generally, male fetuses are more active than females, suggesting their greater activity levels after birth may be inborn (DiPietro et al., 1996).

The major sensory systems develop at different times and at different rates. The neurons connecting the ear to the brain are complete around 18 weeks after conception and the fetus begins to respond to sound around 26 weeks (six months) after conception (Kisilevsky, Muir, & Low, 1992). A few weeks later, fetuses find their mother's voice soothing, and they prefer the sound of their mother's voice to others (DeCasper & Fifer, 1980; DeCasper & Spence, 1986; Kisilevsky et al., 2003). How can researchers possibly know what a fetus *prefers?* The researchers monitor the fetus's heart rate. Research has shown that a slowed heart rate indicates attention, interest, or orienting response, whereas an increased heart rate indicates fear or distress (Groome et al., 2000). Moreover, particular sounds and music to which fetuses are exposed change their neural networks and these sounds and music are retained in memory for at least four months after birth (Partanen et al., 2013; Partanen, Kujala, Naatanen, & Huotilainen, 2013). In other words, learning already occurs prior to birth!

Kanye West or Mozart—can a fetus hear the difference? How do you think researchers monitor its reactions to the different music styles?

Taste and odour-related chemicals from the mother's diet are present in amniotic fluid (Manella, Johnson, & Beauchamp, 1995). In turn, fetuses are sensitive to odours in the amniotic fluid before birth, and they remember these smells. When pregnant mothers consumed anise-flavoured foods during the last stages of pregnancy, their newborns liked the smell of anise more than babies whose mothers did not consume the anise flavour (Schaal, Marlier, & Soussignan, 2000).

Such studies suggest that our taste preferences may start in the womb (Beauchamp & Manella, 2009; Hopson, 1998). By 13 to 15 weeks after conception, the taste buds of a fetus look very much like an adult's (Bradley, 1972). Researchers do not know whether the fetus uses the taste buds, but babies born prematurely—who would otherwise still be developing in the womb—prefer sweet flavours to other flavours, suggesting that this taste preference exists in the womb (Beauchamp & Manella, 2009; Mennella & Beauchamp, 1996).

The least-well-developed sense in the fetus is vision (Hopson, 1998). Fetuses do not open their eyes. Also, as discussed in Chapters 3 and 4, vision perception occurs in the brain. The brain needs visual stimulation to develop the sense of sight (Ptito & Desgent, 2006). Because it is not receiving visual stimulation, the fetus's brain is not developing the appropriate neural connections in the visual cortex to respond to visual imagery. Thus, at birth, infants are near-sighted and cannot see things clearly unless they are close to their face. Infants cannot see as well as adults until they are at least six months old, whereas their hearing is almost adult-like soon after birth.

Environmental Influences on Fetal Development

To a fetus, the mother's womb is its only "environment." Thus, what a pregnant mother eats, drinks, smokes, feels, and experiences plays an important role in fetal development. **Prenatal programming** refers to the process by which events in the womb alter the development of physical and psychological health (Coe & Lubach, 2008). For instance, chemical substances the mother takes in or is exposed to may shape the development of the brain and other bodily systems in the fetus

prenatal programming
the process by which events in the womb alter the development of physical and psychological health.

during the time when they are developing rapidly (Coe & Lubach, 2008). Common factors involved in prenatal programming are maternal nutrition and substances that can cause permanent damage, known as **teratogens.**

teratogens
substances that can disrupt normal prenatal development and cause lifelong deficits.

Maternal Nutrition Doctors know that what a pregnant woman eats and drinks is important for the health of the fetus and even for the infant and child for years after birth. For instance, they prescribe folic acid and other vitamins to women who are pregnant or trying to become pregnant because they reduce the rates of abnormalities in the nervous system, which starts developing only 19 days after conception (Ryan-Harshman & Aldoori, 2008).

If the mother does not eat well or eat enough, the risk of various types of problems increases for the unborn child. For example, both schizophrenia and antisocial personality disorder are more likely to occur if the mother is malnourished during pregnancy (Neugebauer, Hoek, & Susser, 1999; Wahlbeck et al., 2001). Iron deficiency in the mother's diet and maternal stress predispose the infant to anemia, or low red blood cell count. This condition affects how well the body functions. In addition, iron deficiencies in children can lead to cognitive impairment, motor deficiencies, and poor emotional functioning (Lozoffet al., 2006).

As it turns out, the body may have a built-in toxin detector. It's called pregnancy sickness, commonly referred to as "morning sickness." Pregnant women often develop aversions to certain foods, and some women get nauseated and even vomit regularly during pregnancy (Profet, 1992). Pregnancy sickness is worst during the first three months of pregnancy, when the fetus's major organs develop and the embryo is most vulnerable to teratogens. Pregnancy sickness occurs most commonly with exposure to foods susceptible to moulds (such as aged cheeses and mushrooms) and to bitter substances (such as coffee), possibly because these foods can cause birth defects (Keeler, 1983).

Maternal nutrition is also one of the most important examples of epigenetics, the study of how the environment affects gene expression (see Chapter 3). Diet is an environmental event. Certain kinds of maternal diet can lead to obesity not only in the person or animal eating a particular diet but also in her offspring. In one study of this phenomenon, researchers took two genetically identical strands of female laboratory mice and randomly assigned them to receive two different kinds of diet while pregnant (Dolinoy & Jirtle, 2008). One group received a diet rich in substances that turn on a gene that causes weight gain. The other group received a diet rich in nutritional supplements (folic acid and B12) that protect against such weight gain. Results showed that the offspring of the pregnant mice that received the diet that turned on the weight gain gene became obese. The diet of the mother while pregnant, not the diet of the animal after birth, led to obesity. Equally noteworthy: The diets of pregnant mice that are rich in vitamin B12 and folic acid protect against obesity in offspring (Dolinoy & Jirtle, 2008; Waterland & Jirtle, 2003).

Challenge Your Assumptions

True or False? Schizophrenia in an offspring is more likely if the mother is exposed to a virus while pregnant.

True: The odds increase four-fold (from 1 percent to 4 percent) of developing schizophrenia if the mother is afflicted with a viral illness, such as the flu, while pregnant.

Teratogens Substances and chemicals that come from the external environment also have an impact on fetal and infant development. Because all major body parts are forming and growing during the embryonic and fetal stages, the fetus is quite susceptible to birth defects during these stages. Known teratogens include viruses, such as those that cause rubella (measles) and the flu; alcohol; nicotine; prescription drugs, such as the antidepressants Prozac and Zoloft; and radiation. Viruses may have a major impact early in pregnancy and relatively little effect toward the end of pregnancy. If a pregnant woman develops an infection, such as the flu, especially during the fourth to sixth month of pregnancy, the risk of schizophrenia increases for the child later in life (Brown, 2006; Khandaker, Dibben, & Jones, 2012; Koenig, 2006).

Connection

How does having the flu while pregnant influence the way neurons grow in the developing fetus and increase vulnerability to schizophrenia later in life?

See Chapter 15, LO5.

Maternal substance use can also cause serious prenatal and postnatal problems. Pregnant women who drink alcohol take chances with their developing baby, as there is no known safe level of alcohol consumption during pregnancy

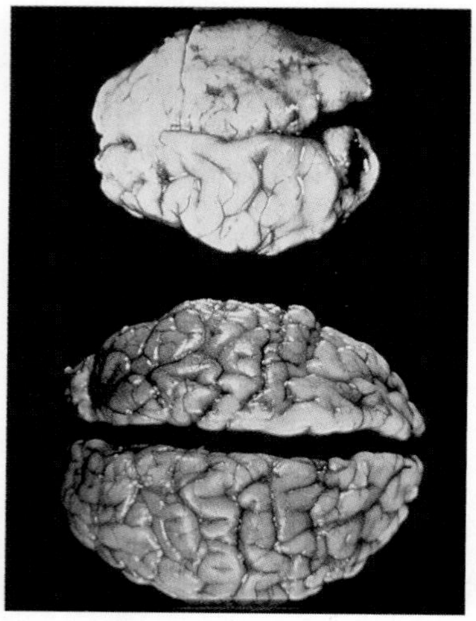

Compared with the brain of a typical child (bottom), the brain of a child with FASD (top) is clearly underdeveloped. Brain abnormalities caused by maternal alcohol use before giving birth result in intellectual disability and behaviour problems.

What would cause such underdevelopment? Knowing these effects, what advice would you give to pregnant women about alcohol consumption during pregnancy?

fetal alcohol spectrum disorder a consequence of prenatal alcohol exposure that causes multiple problems, notably brain damage and intellectual disability.

(Centers for Disease Control and Prevention, 2007, May 31). The most serious effect of prenatal alcohol exposure is **fetal alcohol spectrum disorder (FASD),** which causes damage to the central nervous system; low birth weight; physical abnormalities in the face, head, heart, and joints; intellectual disability; and behavioural problems (Burd, Roberts, Olson, & Odendaal, 2007; Moore et al., 2007; Sen & Swaminathan, 2007; Uylings, 2006). Brain damage from fetal alcohol exposure may explain many of the problems of FASD (Medina & Krahe, 2008). The effect of fetal alcohol exposure is described as a spectrum of disorders because the types and degrees of deficits can vary tremendously among individuals. In Canada, it is estimated that nine in every 1000 children born suffer from FASD, or more than 3000 babies a year (Public Health Agency of Canada, 2006). FASD is the leading cause of intellectual disability in the Western world (Synthesis on Fetal Alcohol Spectrum Disorder, 2007). FASD has been reported in babies of women who drink excessively as well as in infants whose mothers have only occasionally had drinks during pregnancy, although binge drinking and heavy drinking appear to increase the severity of FASD (May et al., 2008).

Nicotine exposure from maternal smoking interferes with the oxygen supply to the fetus. It can lead to premature and low-birth-weight babies as well as increased risk for stillbirth (delivery of a dead fetus) (Centers for Disease Control, 2007, August 8; Zigler, Finn-Stevenson, & Hall, 2002). In addition, if pregnant women smoke, the risk of the child developing bipolar disorder later in life doubles (Talati et al., 2013).

Recall from Chapter 5 that caffeine is the most commonly consumed psychoactive drug in the world. Studies examining the effects of caffeine on fetal development have yielded mixed results (Kuczkowski, 2009). Although there is limited evidence that caffeine consumption during pregnancy leads to birth defects, some studies do suggest a link between heavy caffeine consumption (i.e., consuming more than 300 mg or three cups of coffee per day) and increased risk of miscarriage or delivering a low-birth-weight baby (Boylan et al., 2008). The Motherisk Program at Toronto's Hospital for Sick Children currently advises women that they don't need to stop drinking coffee during pregnancy, but should avoid overindulging (Koren, 2000).

Prescription drugs also pose risks for the developing fetus. Many women take prescription drugs during pregnancy, especially if they were taking them before they learned they were pregnant. Research on animals and humans generally indicates that the antidepressants Zoloft and Prozac can cause respiratory problems, increased risk of premature birth, and short-lasting effects on motor development, but others suggest there are few risks to the developing fetus (Huang, Coleman, Bridge, Yonkers, & Katon, 2013; Maschi et al., 2008; Moses-Kolko et al., 2005). The safest course of action is to avoid these drugs prior to pregnancy, if at all possible.

Quick Quiz 10.1: The Developing Fetus

1. Life before birth is commonly divided into three distinct stages: the _____, embryonic, and fetal stages.
   a. gestational
   b. seminal
   c. germinal
   d. cellular
2. How can researchers tell which sounds a fetus prefers to hear?
   a. By measuring the position of the fetus in the womb.
   b. By measuring changes in fetal heart rate in response to sounds.
   c. By taking a reading of fetal respiration.
   d. It is not possible to measure fetal preferences.
3. Teratogens are
   a. substances that can cause birth defects.
   b. genes that turn on or off with exposure to viruses.
   c. inborn fetal taste preferences.
   d. factors that influence the generation of fetal brain tissue.

Answers can be found at the end of the chapter.

LO3

THE DEVELOPING INFANT AND CHILD

Because it's still developing, the newborn human brain is more responsive than that of other animals to its surroundings. This distinction allows nurture to shape human nature more than is the case for most animals.

Physical Development in Infancy and Childhood

Adults take for granted the ability to act at will, and yet when first born, humans are completely incapable of acting intentionally. Motor and sensory systems develop substantially in newborns. In this section, we explore how physical growth, motor skills, and sensory capacities develop in infancy and early childhood. We examine how experience and the brain interact to shape early human development.

Early Motor Development When we speak of motor development, we are referring to changes in physical movement and body control. In general, children's motor development follows a *cepholocaudal trend,* meaning that development proceeds from the head downwards. Babies gain control of their heads first, then their arms, and then their legs. Motor development also follows a *proximodistal pattern* in which growth proceeds from the centre of the body outwards. For example, children gain control of their arms before their hands; and their hands and feet before their fingers and toes.

Figure 10.6 outlines the major milestones of motor development during the first 15 months. Like any list of milestones we might present in this chapter, the sequence is predictable, but the exact age at which children reach each milestone

FIGURE **10.6**
MAJOR MOTOR DEVELOPMENT MILESTONES IN INFANCY AND TODDLERHOOD. Some children reach these milestones earlier than others, but most achieve them within the range indicated by the purple bars.

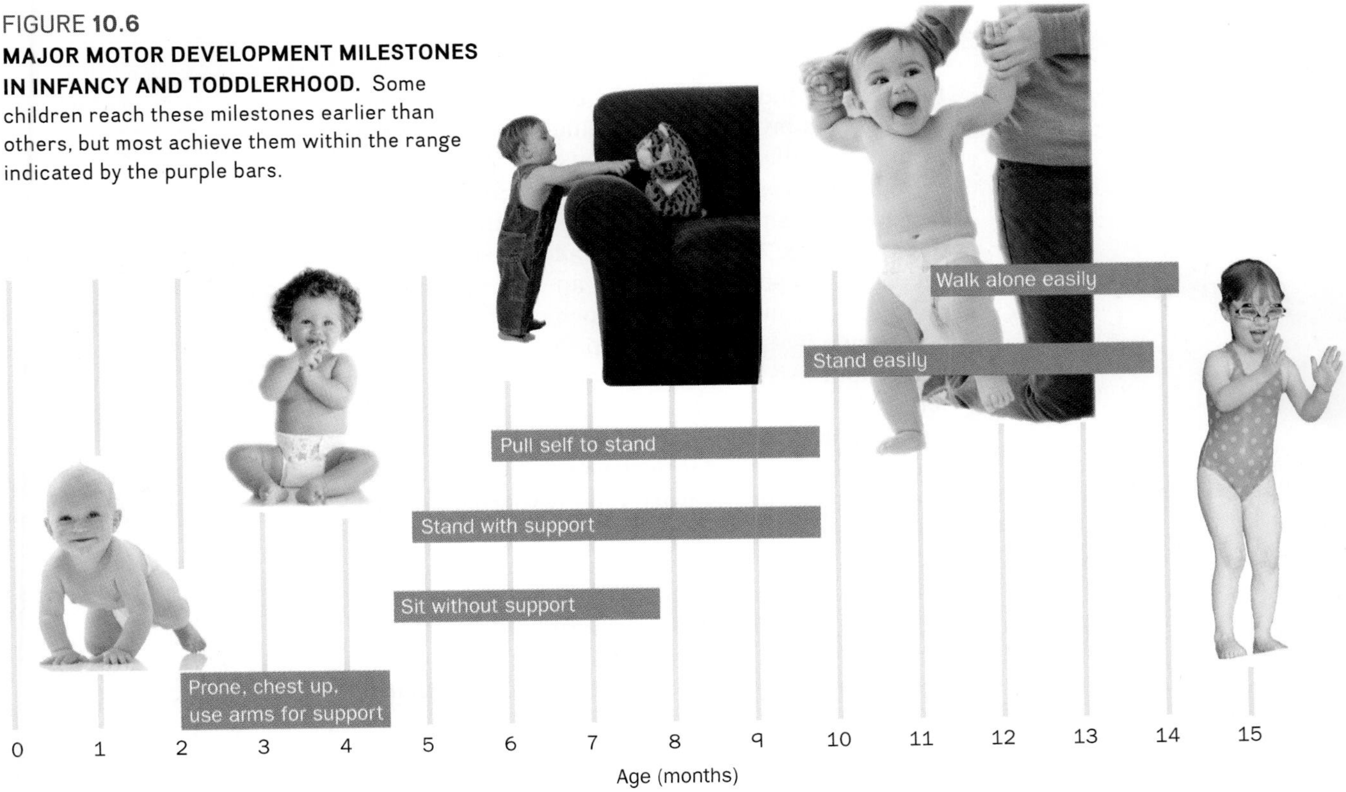

varies. For example, our son Jerry did not crawl until he was nine months old, but he walked at ten months. Our son Evan, on the other hand, crawled at seven-and-a-half months and then started walking at about 12 months.

Early in infancy, babies start to show intentional movements. First, they look at their mother with their unfocused gaze, and then they turn their heads to look at her. By about two months of age, babies lying on their stomach can lift their heads. A three-month-old who is fascinated by a stuffed ring dangling in front of him will suddenly, though not very smoothly, grab for it. At four months, babies can hold objects. By six months, many babies can sit by themselves, without any help. By seven months, babies can pull themselves up and hold on to furniture, and at about eight to nine months, they walk from sofa to coffee table by holding on to the furniture. Many babies take their first steps before their first birthday, though it may be some time—at about 17 months of age—before they settle into walking on their own (Patterson, 2008).

Other motor responses are more specific. If you give a newborn baby your finger, she will grasp it tightly. If you stroke her cheek, she will turn her head, open-mouthed in expectation of a breast, a reflex called *rooting*. If you place something in a baby's mouth, she will suck. Grasping, rooting and sucking are among several reflexes present at birth—involuntary responses to very specific stimuli.

It takes a while before young children can turn knobs and pick up tiny objects. These *fine motor skills* involve the coordination of the actions of many smaller muscles, along with information from the eyes, in the service of some task. Fine motor skill development shows up, for example, in children's drawing skills. Two-year-olds typically show very crude crayon scribbles, but by age three or four children can make crude drawings of people, and by age five most kids can print letters, dress alone, and use silverware (Gardner, 1980; Patterson, 2008). In fact, training in fine motor skills actually aids kindergarteners' attention, especially in girls, showing just how joined cognition and action can be (Stewart, Rule, & Giordano, 2007).

FIGURE **10.7**
VISUAL ACUITY IN INFANTS. These are computer simulations of what a picture of a human face looks like to a one-month-old, two-month-old, three-month-old, and one-year-old (top to bottom).

Challenge Your Assumptions

True or False? Babies are born able to see and hear as well as adults.

False: Newborn vision is only 20-600 and becomes adult-like (20–20) only around age three; hearing becomes adult-like by about age six months.

Early Sensory Development As noted earlier, the five major senses develop at different rates. Hearing is almost fully developed at birth, but a newborn's vision is only about 20-600, meaning that infants see an object that is 20 feet (6 metres) away as indistinctly as an adult with normal vision would see an object 600 feet (183 metres) away (see Figure 10.7).

Visual sharpness, or acuity, continues to improve during infancy, and by six months of age, vision is 20-100. By age three or four, a child's vision is similar to an adult's (Banks & Salapatek, 1983). You may be surprised to learn that newborns do not see colours very well and are best able to see black and white edges and patterns (Fantz, 1961). Colour vision approximates that of adults by four months of age (Kellman & Arterberry, 2006).

How do we know infants have these sensory abilities? It's not as if we can ask them their preferences. Researchers have developed numerous techniques to study babies' sensory capabilities. One method, known as the **habituation-dishabituation paradigm,** is used to determine if an infant can detect the difference between a familiar and novel stimulus (Miller, 2007). This technique relies on the fact that people tend to prefer novelty and pay less and less attention, or *habituate,* to a stimulus when it is repeatedly presented. For example, if you present a baby with a photo of another baby, she will initially look at the face for a few minutes but then over time, she will become bored and stop looking. However, if you then presented the baby with a stimulus that she can discern as different, such as a photo of an old woman, she will initially spend more time looking at it, or *dishabituate* to the new photo. The baby's dishabituation to the new stimulus tells the researcher that the baby can see the differences between the two photos. The habituation-dishabituation paradigm can be used to study babies' abilities not only to distinguish between sights, but also sounds, tastes, touches, and smells.

Another technique used to study infants' preferences for certain visual stimuli is known as **preferential looking.** In this method, an infant is shown two stimuli and the researcher measures how long the infant spends gazing at each. If the infant spends more time looking at one stimulus than another, researchers infer that she can distinguish between the stimuli and finds one stimuli more pleasurable, more interesting, or more complex to look at than the other one (Spelke, 1985). Robert Fantz (1961), an early pioneer of this research method, found that babies as young as four months old preferred looking at complex objects, rather than simple ones, and at whole faces rather than faces with features in disarray (see Figure 10.8).

Experience is crucial in the development of vision, as it is in all aspects of human development. The occipital cortex of the brain has to be stimulated by visual input in order to develop the proper synaptic connections needed to process visual information. It is for this reason that young infants respond chiefly to visual stimuli within 20 to 30 centimetres of their face. For full development of the visual sense, these early months are a **critical period,** one of several in human development, when individuals are biologically most receptive to a particular kind of input from the environment.

Can all babies who have normal vision in both eyes and can crawl see the world in three dimensions? In a study that has become a classic, Gibson and Walk (1960) examined this question by creating the *visual cliff* to test depth perception in babies who have learned to crawl (see Figure 10.9). They placed clear Plexiglas (hard plastic) over one end of a crawl area to make it look as though there was a steep drop in the middle. They put a baby on one end of the crawl area and asked the mother to stand at the end with the drop. The mother's role was to encourage the baby to crawl across the clear plastic surface to her. Mothers were able to convince their six-month-olds to wiggle over the visual cliff; but ten-month old babies stopped crawling when they reached the cliff, indicating that at least by the time

habituation-dishabituation paradigm
a research method used to test babies' abilities to discriminate between a novel and familiar stimulus.

preferential looking
a research technique used to test an infant's perceptual abilities by measuring which stimulus an infant gazes at longest.

critical period
a specific period in development when individuals are most receptive to a particular kind of input from the environment (such as visual stimulation and language).

Connection

Language acquisition depends on exposure to a language-stimulating environment during the first 12 years of life when the brain's neural connections are forming. Limited exposure to language during this *sensitive period* can lead to permanent problems in language development.

See Chapter 8, LO4.

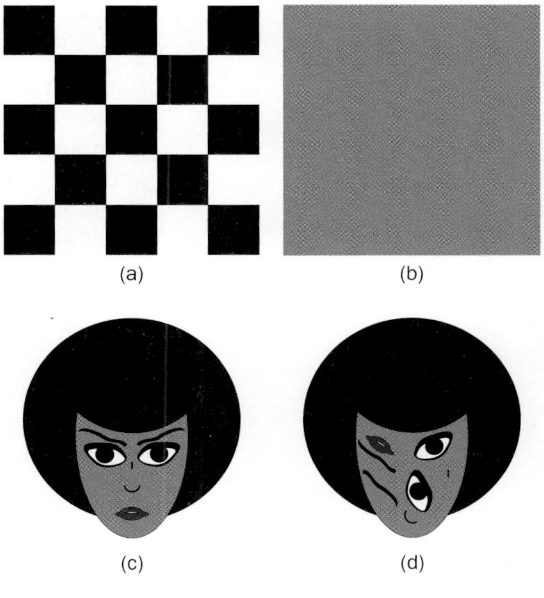

FIGURE **10.8**
VISUAL PERCEPTION IN INFANTS. Early research (based on Fantz, 1961) suggests that young infants prefer looking at complex stimuli, like a checkerboard pattern (a), than simple stimuli, like a solid square (b). Infants also prefer face-like patterns (c) compared to faces with jumbled features (d).

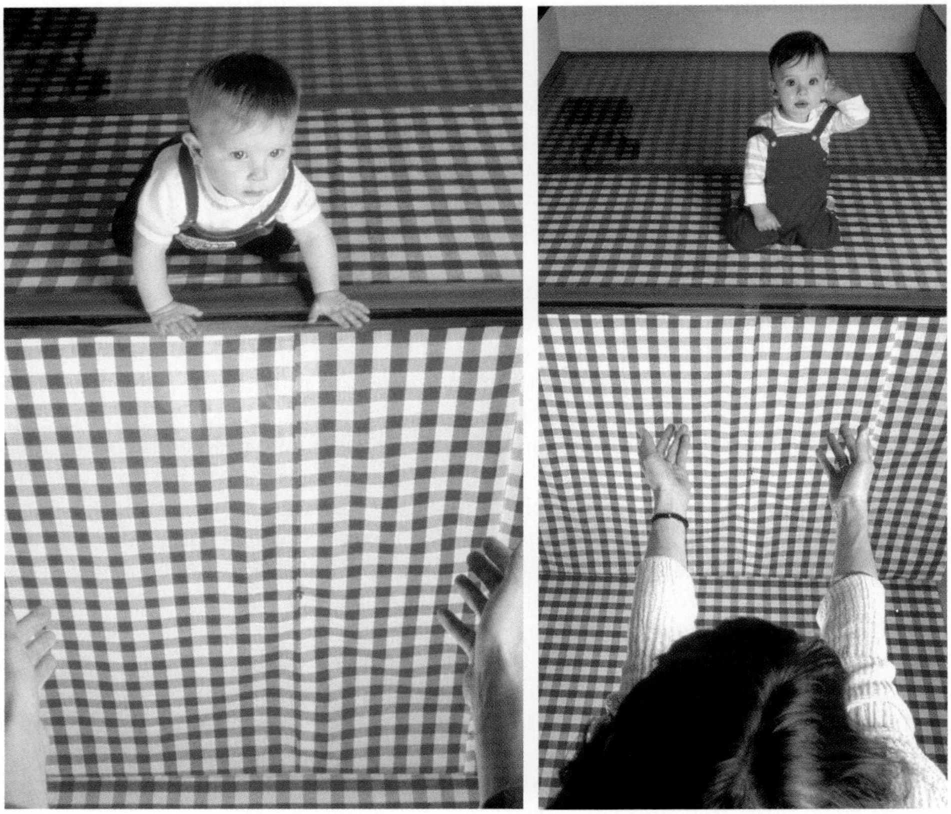

FIGURE **10.9**

THE VISUAL CLIFF. In a demonstration of depth perception, babies will stop at the edge of a clear sheet of plastic, rather than crawling over what appears to be a cliff.

they learn to crawl, babies can perceive depth. Follow-up studies revealed that babies as young as one-and-a-half months notice the difference between the deep and shallow sides of the crawl area, but only babies who are crawling are actually afraid of the deep side (Campos, Hiatt, Ramsay, Henderson, & Svejda, 1978). In other words, it is the babies' experience of crawling in addition to the development of the visual system that seems to be important for the development of depth perception.

As we have seen, children's sensory systems mature rapidly in early infancy. After two years, sensory development slows down, although some physical changes continue to occur during the elementary school years. For example, physical changes in the eye can lead to children needing glasses; changes in the physical structure of the ear can lead to a reduction in ear infections, a risk factor for hearing loss.

synaptic pruning
the degradation of synapses and dying off of neurons that are not strengthened by experience.

Early Brain Development Experiences such as eating, exercising, and learning mould our brains throughout life, but especially in infancy and childhood. With learning and experience, certain synaptic connections become stronger, whereas those that do not receive stimulation from the environment die off—a process, known as **synaptic pruning,** nature's way of making the brain more efficient (Baltes, Reuter-Lorenz, & Rösler, 2006; Greenough, Volkmar, & Juraska, 1973; Perry, 2002). Pruning is not only about creating a more efficient brain but is also required for normal brain development. Research shows that problems with neural pruning are associated

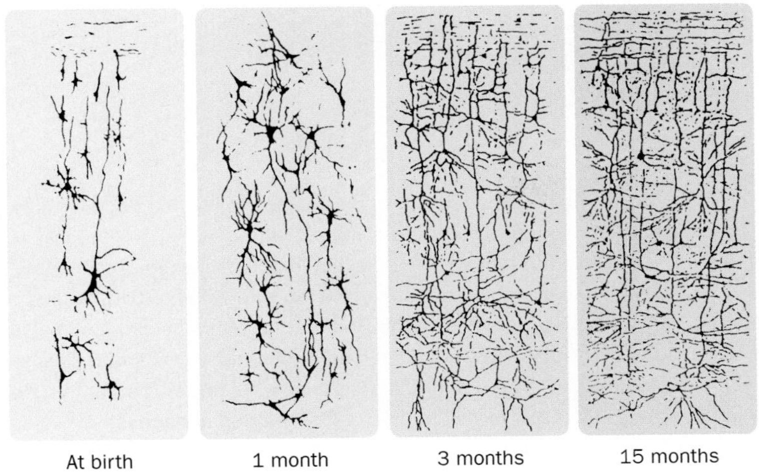

FIGURE **10.10**

NEURAL GROWTH DURING THE FIRST 15 MONTHS OF LIFE.

What changes are happening in the cerebral cortex of an infant during the first 15 months of life?

(*Source:* Reprinted by permission of the publisher from The Postnatal Development of the Human Cerebral Cortex, Vols. I–VIII by Jesse LeRoy Conel, Cambridge, Mass.: Harvard University Press, Copyright © 1939, 1975 by the president and Fellows of Harvard College.)

with neurological disorders, such as autism or schizophrenia (Cusack, Swahari, Hampton, Ramsey, & Deshmukh, 2013; Rapoport, Chavez, Greenstein, Addington, & Gogtay, 2009).

After birth, the brain continues to grow new neurons and we see a proliferation in the growth of new synapses over the first two years of life (see Figure 10.10). After age two, some neurons and synapses begin to die off. The rate of change slows down considerably after the age of six, increases in early adolescence, and then settles again after adolescence (Chechik, Meilijson, & Ruppin, 1999; Sakai, 2005).

In some nine-year-old children showing early signs of puberty, grey matter in the prefrontal and parietal regions of the brain surprisingly *decreases* somewhat in volume (Giedd et al., 1999; Peper et al., 2009). Such decreases in grey matter volume suggest that pruning is still occurring late in childhood. Recall that grey matter consists of the cell bodies; white matter is made up of the axons and myelin (see Figure 10.11). The number of neurons (grey matter) starts to decline in adolescence, but white matter (axons and connectivity) continues to grow into one's 40s (Westlye et al., 2010).

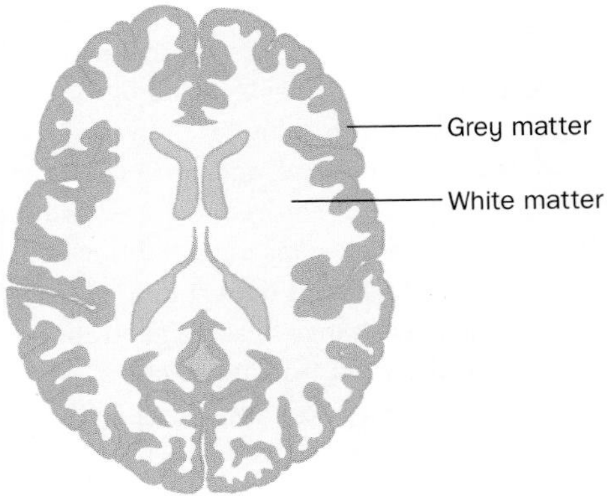

FIGURE **10.11**

WHITE AND GREY MATTER IN THE HUMAN BRAIN.

Because pruning is based on input from the environment, the quality of the environments in which we are raised influences how our brains develop. Normal and enriched environments create more complex neural connections, while abusive, neglectful, and impoverished environments create less developed neural connections and fewer of them (Mirescu & Gould, 2006). An example of how experience can positively shape the brain is seen in the findings that physically fit children are also more cognitively fit; that is, they do better in reasoning tasks and school in general (Castelli et al., 2007; Hillman, Buck, Themanson, Pontifex, & Castelli, 2009). "Psychology in the Real World" looks at another type of experience—musical training—that influences brain growth and cognitive development.

Connection

Experience is crucial in the formation of synaptic connections (*synaptogenesis*) and the growth of new neurons (*neurogenesis*) in the brain throughout the life span.

See Chapter 3, LO13.

Psychology in the Real World

Musical Training Changes the Brain

The brain develops throughout life, yet it is most responsive to stimulation during infancy and childhood. In other words, early in life there is more opportunity for experience to leave its mark on the brain (Cicchetti, 2001).

Learning to play a musical instrument is a fascinating example of how experience changes the brain, or of how nature and nurture work together to create who we are. If you want to learn to play guitar, for example, you must learn how to finger on the neck, how to hold your fingers and press the strings firmly enough to get a clear sound, and how the fingering movements relate to the notes on different musical scales. In Chapter 3, "The Biology of Behaviour," we discussed how monkeys trained in a finger-tapping task showed substantial increases in the amount of somatosensory cortex devoted to the fingertips compared to both the amount they had before training and the amount in untrained monkeys (Jenkins et al., 1990). Can we see similar effects in the brains of string instrument players?

Researchers who were curious about this question applied a slight pressure to each finger on each hand of right-handed musicians and non-musicians of various ages. Using fMRI, they mapped the brain's responses to this pressure. For musicians, the area on the somatosensory cortex devoted to those fingers on the side of the brain that controls the fingering left hand was bigger than the area that controls the non-fingering right hand, and musicians who started playing before the age of 12 showed the most pronounced effects. The somatosensory maps did not differ between sides in the brains of non-musicians (Elbert et al., 1995). So musical training may change brain organization, especially for people who start training as children.

Musical training appears to shape the structure of the brain, as well. People who have had intensive musical training have a thicker corpus callosum and more brain growth in regions associated with music-related skills than do non-musicians, and the difference is even greater if they started their training before age seven (Schlaug et al., 1995). A thicker corpus callosum makes for greater communication between the two sides of the brain. Also, musicians have larger cerebellums (an area involved in motor coordination) than do non-musicians (Hutchinson et al., 2003). Other research shows that the earlier musical training begins, the greater the degree of activation of the music-processing areas of the brain (left auditory cortex) when listening to music (Ohnishi et al., 2001), and evidence indicates significant growth in brain regions of six-year-old children after just 15 months of musical training compared to those without training (Hyde et al., 2009).

Moreover, as the brain regions involved in moving muscles and processing sound grew, the better the children's musical performance became. Recent evidence points to musical training enhancing neural activity in the hippocampus, which is the brain region most involved in learning and memory (Herdener et al., 2010). Most impressive, perhaps, is the finding that these neuroplastic effects of musical training last well into adulthood (Skoe & Kraus, 2012).

The findings discussed so far are correlational. Recall a lesson from Chapter 2: Correlation is necessary but not sufficient for causation. Correlational findings suggest that musical training can shape the brain, but they do not lead to the conclusion that musical training *causes* brain growth. One way to address the problem of correlation is to do an experiment. Pascual-Leone taught people who had never before played piano a one-hand, five-finger exercise. They repeated the exercise in two-hour practice sessions for five days, and then they were given a test. The test involved 20 repetitions of the exercise (responses measured by computer for speed, etc.). As skill improved, cortical representation for the finger muscles involved in the task increased (Pascual-Leone, 2001). Next, participants were randomly assigned to either continue daily practice of the exercise for four more weeks or to stop practising. For those who stopped practising, within one week, brain maps returned to the way they were before training. For those who continued practising, brain map changes continued. In short, if you don't use it, you lose it!

How can learning to play a musical instrument in childhood impact your brain's development?

Neglect exists when caregivers fail to provide basic sensory experience and stimulation to a child during key periods of development (Perry, 2002). Again, timing is critical. A dramatic instance of the effect of neglect and abuse on the development of the human brain comes from research on children who spent their early years in Romanian orphanages, where they were confined much of the time to cribs and had very limited stimulation. Figure 10.12 shows a PET scan from one of the orphans alongside one from a typically developing child. The red to yellow areas in Figure 10.12a represent the active regions in the brain of a normal child. Figure 10.12b shows the brain activity of a Romanian orphan who was neglected from birth. As you can see, brain activity is greatly diminished in the orphan (Cicchetti, 2001). Similarly, research shows decreases in brain size in children raised in severely neglectful homes. These deficits can be made up if the children are removed from the neglectful environment—sooner rather than later, however. The longer they stay in the deprived environment, the less likely it is that they will recover (Perry, 2002).

Findings in neuroscience suggest that children's brains are more plastic and more sensitive to stimulation from the outside world than are the brains of older people. Part of the reason is that young brains are more flexible because they have less myelin, which makes neural transmission more efficient but at a cost to neuroplasticity. In Chapter 3 we noted that many axons are covered with a myelin sheath, the fatty insulation that makes nerve impulses travel faster. Few neurons are myelinated at birth: With age, more and more neurons become myelinated (Fields, 2008). Figure 10.13 shows the relative increases in myelin over time from age four to age 20 (Fields, 2008; Peper et al., 2009). Scientists have identified specific protein molecules in myelin that stop axons from sprouting and forming new connections. Thus, myelination may close the window on the critical periods for such skills as learning language (Fields, 2008). We return to this issue later in the chapter when discussing adolescence.

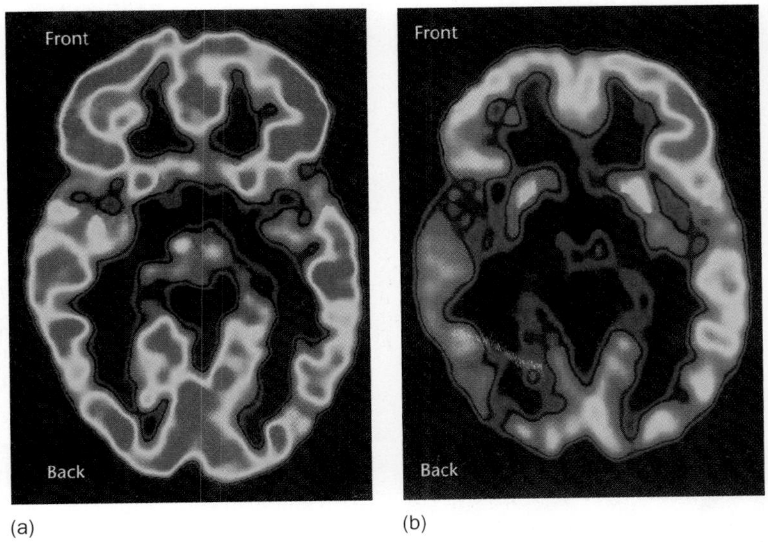

FIGURE **10.12**

BRAIN DEVELOPMENT IN A NORMAL CHILD COMPARED TO A DEPRIVED AND NEGLECTED CHILD.

If red represents high levels of brain activity and blue relatively less brain activity, what do these two images tell you about the brain of (a) a typically developing child and (b) a child who experienced deprivation and neglect in an orphanage? (*Source:* Cichetti, 2001.)

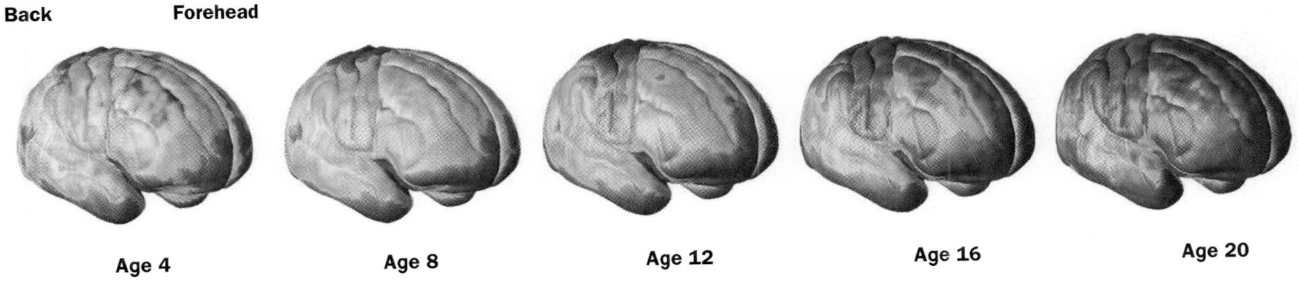

FIGURE **10.13**

MYELINATION IN THE DEVELOPING BRAIN. In the figure, unmyelinated neurons appear yellow and orange. Myelinated neurons appear purple. (*Source:* Fields, 2008.)

What does myelin do for developing brains? Can you provide some examples of age-related changes in behaviour that may reflect underlying change in brain myelination?

LO4 Early Cognitive Development

With brain growth comes cognitive development—advances in the ability to think, pay attention, reason, remember, learn, and solve problems. How do cognitive skills grow and how can we study them in babies who cannot speak? As we saw earlier in infant perception, researchers rely on infants' ability to pay attention to new and unfamiliar stimuli as their primary means of studying infant thought.

When infants from four to seven months pay attention to something that interests them for more than a few seconds, brain activity narrows from many brain regions to more specific brain regions (Richards, Reynolds, & Courage, 2010). This finding suggests that the brain is becoming more organized and efficient during the first six months of life and this increased brain organization leads to increased ability to pay attention and focus on one thing during the first year of life (Richards et al., 2010).

If there is one important thing that developmental psychologists have learned about infants over the last 20 years, it is that infants are smarter than we ever thought. Alison Gopnik summarized these findings in her book, *The Philosophical Baby* (2009). Infant perception, knowledge of the world, and even problem-solving skills are much more sophisticated than previously believed. For example, eight-month-old infants understand the basics of statistics and probability. Not the kind that might give you fits in your university-level statistics class, but they do become surprised by very unlikely events. In one experiment, researchers put mostly white and a few red ping-pong balls into a box and then reached into the box and pulled out a few white balls but many red balls (Xu & Garcia, 2008). The babies registered that this event was very unlikely; they looked longer at this situation than when the researchers pulled out many white and only a few red balls (much more likely) (Xu & Garcia, 2008). Psychologists therefore call babies "intuitive statisticians"—without any training they know some events are very unlikely.

So we have learned from developmental science that infants and young children have many perceptual and cognitive skills that develop rapidly over time. Are there any limits on how and when these skills develop?

Jean Piaget

assimilation
the process by which people incorporate new information into already existing schemas.

accommodation
the process by which people change existing schemas to incorporate new information.

Connection

Stereotypes are a specific type of schema that people have about how others are likely to behave based on group membership.

See Chapter 14, LO2.

Piaget's Theory of Cognitive Development Perhaps the person who has most influenced our understanding of how children's thinking develops from birth throughout childhood is Swiss psychologist Jean Piaget. In his early work administering intelligence tests at the Binet Laboratory in Paris, Piaget noticed that young children consistently gave wrong answers to certain questions. Piaget was intrigued not so much by the wrong answers, but by the characteristics of children's thinking that led to the wrong answers. He observed that young children consistently made types of mistakes that older children and adults did not, leading him to theorize that young children's cognitive processes are inherently different from those of adults (Evans, 1973).

Piaget viewed children as actively constructing knowledge about their world. When children encounter a new situation or event, they form a *schema*, or mental representation, about it. For example, if mom points to a picture of a dog and says, "Look at the doggie," her child, Shannon, will form a schema for "doggie" that looks similar to that picture. In essence, schemas provide a framework for understanding our world; they are the building blocks of cognitive development. Piaget considered two mechanisms as important for schema formation—**assimilation** and **accommodation.** When children encounter something new, they will first try to *assimilate* that experience into an already existing schema. For example, suppose little Shannon points and says "doggie" when she sees a horse. She has assimilated the new information about the animal into her already existing schema for dogs. When mom and others correct her—"No, that's a horse"—Shannon has to create a new schema for horse, a type of animal that is bigger than a dog, that you don't usually see walking down the street, that doesn't bark, and so on. In other words, Shannon has to modify or restructure her existing schema about dogs and develop a new schema for horses to accommodate the new information (Piaget, 1954, 1962).

Relying primarily on careful observations of his own three children, Piaget also outlined four distinct phases of cognitive development from birth through adolescence, which he called the sensorimotor, preoperational, concrete operational, and formal operational stages. Figure 10.14 summarizes Piaget's theory of cognitive development.

Piaget called the first stage of cognitive development the **sensorimotor stage** because it characterizes the way infants learn about the world through their senses and their own movements. Young children sense more than they "think" and come to understand the world by manipulating and moving through it. Piaget observed that during the first eight or nine months, a child has no concept of **object permanence,** which is the ability to realize that objects still exist when they are not being sensed (Piaget, 1954). In other words, it is "out of sight, out of mind" for young infants. When an object is hidden from them, they will not look for it, even if they see someone hide it. Around nine months of age, however, infants will move a cloth or look under something to find the hidden object because they have begun to remember that objects

How does love of the game peek-a-boo demonstrate that a baby has acquired object permanence?

sensorimotor stage
Piaget's first stage of cognitive development (from birth to age two), when infants learn about the world by using their senses and moving their bodies.

object permanence
the ability to realize that objects still exist when they are not being sensed.

	Approximate age (years)	Core cognitive capacities
Sensorimotor	0–2	Knowledge is through senses (tasting, seeing, smelling, touching, hearing) Object permanence develops between four and nine months
Preoperational	2–5	Verbal and egocentric thinking develop Can do mentally what once could only do physically Conservation of shape, number, liquid not yet possible
Concrete operational	6–11	Conservation of shape, number, liquid are now possible Logic and reasoning develop, but are limited to appearance and what is concretely observed
Formal operational	12 and up	Abstract reasoning—principles and ideals develop Systematic problem solving is now possible (no longer just trial and error) Ability to think about and reflect upon one's thinking (metacognition) Scientific reasoning

FIGURE **10.14**
PIAGET'S STAGES OF COGNITIVE DEVELOPMENT

continue to exist even when they are not directly sensed. Mastering object permanence is a hallmark of the sensorimotor stage.

Quebec-born psychologist Renée Baillargeon and her colleagues conducted intriguing research using a different technique that challenged Piaget's argument that infants develop object permanence at about nine months (Baillargeon & DeVos, 1991). They developed and used a *violation-of-expectation paradigm,* based on the principles of habituation-dishabituation discussed earlier. They measured infants' responses to both expected and impossible events (see Figure 10.15). First, infants were shown an inclined track and a screen that was lowered or raised in front of the track. They learned that when a car rolls down the track, the car keeps rolling behind the lowered screen and appears on the other side of it. They were not surprised to see the car, even though it was hidden for a short time by the lowered screen. They were shown this event many times, until they got used to it—that is, until it became expected. In the next sequence, everything was the same except that the researchers placed a toy mouse behind the track while the babies watched. Again, they were not surprised to see the car roll behind the lowered screen and appear on the other side of it.

Then something impossible happened. The researchers placed the mouse *on* the track while the infants watched. When the screen was down, hiding the mouse from the infants' view, the experimenters removed the mouse. The researchers found that, when the car rolled down the track and kept rolling (impossible if the mouse was still on the track), the infants were quite surprised, which Baillargeon and DeVos were able to tell by studying the infants' eyes. When things go as expected, infants get bored and stop looking at the event, but when they witness an impossible event, their eyes widen and they keep looking. Infants as young as four months of age, not nine months, realize objects still exist even when they do

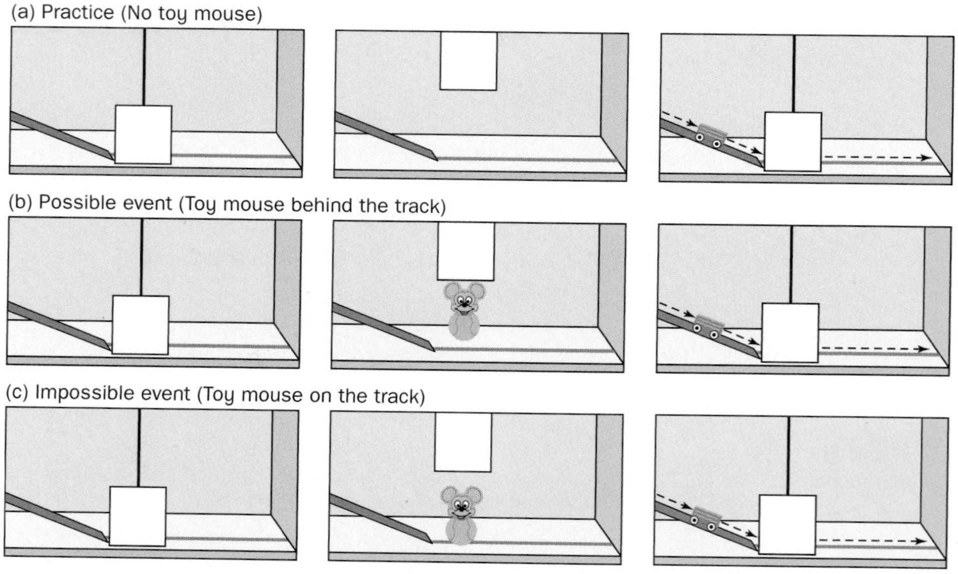

FIGURE **10.15**

THE DEVELOPMENT OF OBJECT PERMANENCE. In the practice sessions (a), children learn that cars can still roll all the way to the wall, because the screen is in front of the track, not blocking the car's path. In the possible session (b), they are not surprised to again see the car roll all the way to the wall, because the mouse was behind, not on, the track. But in the impossible session (c), the infants were surprised to see the car roll all the way to the wall, because the mouse should have blocked it (unbeknownst to the children, the mouse had been removed while the screen was down). (*Source:* Baillargeon & DeVos, 1991.)

How do the researchers know whether the young child was surprised or not?

not see them. Piaget was right about object permanence but wrong about the age at which it first happens.

At around age two, with the emergence of symbolic thought, children move into Piaget's second stage of cognitive development—the **preoperational stage,** a period that lasts until about age five or six. Symbolic thinking involves using symbols, such as words or letters, to represent ideas or objects. The cognitive limitations of the preoperational stage include animistic thinking, egocentrism, and lack of conservation.

preoperational stage
the second major stage of cognitive development (ages two to five), which begins with the emergence of symbolic thought.

Animistic thinking refers to the idea that inanimate objects are alive. For example, Piaget reported on a child in this stage who was asked whether the sun moved. The child answered, "Yes, when one walks, it follows." When the child was asked why it moves, he responded, "Because when one walks, it goes too." Finally, when the child was asked whether the sun was alive, he responded, "Of course, otherwise it wouldn't follow us; it couldn't shine" (Piaget, 1972b, p. 215).

animistic thinking
a belief that inanimate objects are alive.

Egocentrism is the tendency to view the world from one's own perspective and not see things from another person's perspective. Piaget and Inhelder (1967) designed the *three mountains task* to measure young children's egocentrism (see Figure 10.16). For this demonstration, three mountains are placed on a small table. Each mountain is slightly different in shape and has a small distinguishing reference object on top (e.g., a cross, a house, or a snow-capped peak). The child sits on one side of the table and a doll is placed in a chair on the other side of the table. The experimenter asks the child to describe how the doll sees the three mountains. Typically, the three possible perspectives are drawn on a board and the child has to choose the correct perspective. Egocentric, preoperational children will choose the perspective from which *they* see the mountains—they cannot visualize them from the doll's point of view. For example, as shown in Figure 10.16, the doll can "see" a house on top of the left mountain but this house is obscured in the child's view. The child would mistakenly say that the doll can only see the snow and cross, and not the house.

egocentrism
viewing the world from one's own perspective and not being capable of seeing things from another person's perspective.

Conservation is the ability to recognize that when some properties (such as shape) of an object change, other properties (such as volume) remain

conservation
the recognition that when some properties (such as shape) of an object change, other properties (such as volume) remain constant.

FIGURE **10.16**
PIAGET'S THREE MOUNTAINS TASK: EGOCENTRIC PERCEPTION OF PREOPERATIONAL CHILDREN. When asked to describe what the doll could see from the other side of the table, children in the preoperational stage can't visualize the scene from any perspective other than their own. (*Source:* Patterson, 2008.)

After a four- or five-year-old child (preoperational) sees liquid poured from a short, fat container to a tall, thin one, does the child think the amount of liquid is more than or is the same as when it was in the short container? What did Piaget's research tell us?

constant. During preoperational thinking, the child cannot yet recognize that amounts stay the same when shapes change. They are unable to conserve. Piaget used many different objects and situations to examine conservation. Figure 10.17 shows a number of them.

Let's look at the conservation of liquid as an example. This task involves filling two glasses of the same shape and size with equal amounts of water. The child confirms that the two glasses contain the same amount of water. Then the child pours one of the glasses of water into a third container that is wider but shorter than the first two. The child does nothing to the second glass. When asked whether the two glasses contain the same amount of water, the child will say no if he or she lacks the ability to conserve. Usually, the child will say the tall, thin container has more water than the short, wide one.

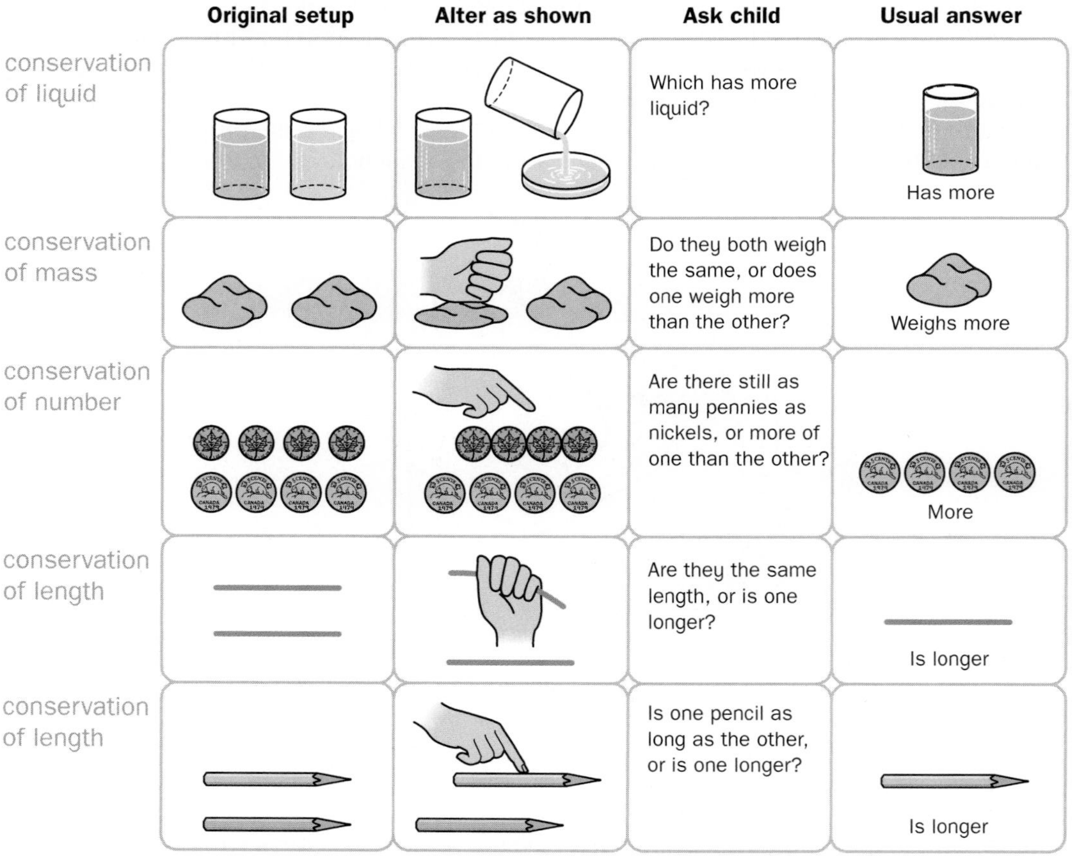

FIGURE **10.17**

DIFFERENT KINDS OF CONSERVATION TASKS. Children in the preoperational stage don't realize that the quantity of something doesn't change if it is rearranged. (*Source:* Seifert et al., 2000.)

During Piaget's third stage, called the **concrete operational stage** (ages 6 to 11), children can perform mental operations—on real, or concrete, objects and events—but they still have trouble with abstract ideas and reasoning. The ability to reverse events is one type of operation a child masters in this stage. One of the benchmarks that indicates whether a child has moved from preoperational to concrete operational thinking is the ability to conserve. For example, the child can mentally pour the liquid back into the original container in the conservation of liquid task and realize that pouring liquid from one container into another doesn't change the amount. Notice that this conclusion is also a logical conclusion: "It has to be same—the amount of liquid does not change when the shape of the container changes." In this stage, logic remains concrete and limited to objects that a child directly observes. The child can reason that the amount of liquid she or he sees going from one glass into the other must remain the same, but would have trouble solving a problem of this type: "If Susan is half as old as Robert, and Robert is twice as old as Samantha, then how old is Samantha compared to Susan?"

concrete operational stage
Piaget's third stage of cognitive development, which spans ages 6 to 11, during which the child can perform mental operations—such as reversing—on real objects or events.

With the onset of adolescence, children gain the ability to reason about abstract concepts and problems. Piaget called this phase of cognitive development the **formal operational stage** (Inhelder & Piaget, 1958; Piaget, 1972a). During this stage, formal logic becomes possible. Here is an example: "If Maria is a woman, and all women are mortal, then Maria is mortal." In addition, adolescents develop scientific reasoning and hypothesis-testing skills. We'll go into more detail about this stage of cognitive development in our discussion of adolescence.

formal operational stage
Piaget's final stage of cognitive development, from age 11 or 12 through adulthood, when formal logic is possible.

Although Piaget's theory remains important for our understanding of cognitive development (Flavell, 1996; Lourenco & Machado, 1996), it is limited in some respects. Some researchers disagree with the idea that cognitive development proceeds through distinct stages (Siegler, 1994, 2006). For example, if you study the everyday learning of children at any given age, you will probably notice that a child may use several different strategies to solve a problem, some being more complex and accurate than others. Such a pattern is inconsistent with making a sudden leap from one stage to another. In addition, as we saw in more recent research on object permanence, Piaget appears to have underestimated young children's cognitive abilities. His theory has also been criticized for undervaluing the impact of culture on children's cognition.

Lev Vygotsky

Vygotsky's Theory of Cognitive Development In contrast to Piaget's view that children are the most important constructors of their own knowledge, Russian psychologist Lev Vygotsky (1978) emphasized how children learn through their social interactions with others. These social interactions occur within a particular cultural context and help children to internalize the cognitive ways of their culture, including speech patterns, written language, and more sophisticated mental processes. For example, consider how culture might impact the type of memory strategies we develop. In our North American culture where formal education is emphasized, children often learn to make a list or take notes to aid memory. However, children in preliterate societies who don't have access to pen and paper must clearly develop other strategies, such as tying knots in string to remember, or carrying pebbles. In Vygotsky's view, culture plays an active role in shaping the ways in which children think.

Connection

According to the Whorf-Sapir hypothesis, language creates thought as much as thought creates language.

See Chapter 8, LO7.

According to Vygotsky, each child has a **zone of proximal development (ZPD)**—a range of tasks too difficult for the child to perform alone but possible with the help of adults and more skilled peers. Suppose, for example, that eight-year-old Rashid loves to play games. Over the years, he has developed the skills and knowledge necessary to play a variety of games. Now, he wants to learn to play the card game Wizard, a game he has never played before. He knows his older sister, Ranjeet, plays the game very well, so he asks her for

zone of proximal development (ZPD)
a range of tasks too difficult for a child to perform alone but possible with the help of others.

help. She helps him, guiding him through the play of the game, and teaching him the rules. He is learning the game in his ZPD. His sister helps him less and less as they play the game and he masters the rules. Vygotsky used the term **scaffolding** to refer to this changing level of support. These concepts of ZPD and scaffolding underlie Vygotsky's view of cognition as developing first in a social context and then gradually shifting to come under a child's independent control.

scaffolding
adjusting the level of support to fit a child's current level of performance on a task.

Theory of Mind Knowing and understanding what other people are thinking, wanting, or feeling is a critical skill in human society. The term **theory of mind** refers to our knowledge and ideas of how other people's minds work. The important questions from a development perspective are when and how does such a skill emerge, and how does it change with age?

theory of mind
ideas and knowledge about how other people's minds work.

Most adults—especially those who learn to think critically—know that people believe things that sometimes are not true. They may even come to realize that their own beliefs may not always be true. Children under the age of four are cognitively incapable of understanding that people may believe things that are not true. Psychologists created the *false-belief* task to explore children's theory of mind and the stage at which they come to know that others may hold false beliefs (Wimmer & Perner, 1983). They discovered that age four is commonly when children understand that other people can believe something different from their own beliefs (see Figure 10.18).

Canadian researchers Victoria Talwar and Kang Lee (2008) have examined the relationship between children's lie-telling and theory of mind development. They use a method called the *temptation-resistance* paradigm to create a lie-telling opportunity for children. Children sit with their backs to the researcher and are asked to identify some toys by the sound that they make. Before the last toy (a Barney doll) is presented, the researcher is called out of the room. Before she leaves, the researcher tells the child that the toy will be left on the table with its' sound playing but requests that the child not turn around to peek at it. The sound that the Barney doll emits has actually been altered so that the child cannot correctly identify the toy. A hidden camera records the child's behaviour while the researcher is out of the room for one minute. When the researcher (who is unaware if the child peeked or not) returns, the researcher covers up the Barney doll. Then, requesting that the child tell the truth, the researcher asks, "When I was gone did you peek at the toy?" and "Who do you think the toy is?" Children who correctly identify Barney are also asked, "How did you know who the toy was?"

Talwar and Lee (2008) found that starting around ages three to four, most children peeked at the forbidden toy and 64 percent lied about their peeking to the researcher. Not surprisingly, children who demonstrated false-belief understanding were more likely to lie, as telling a lie successfully requires being able to create a false belief in another. However, younger lie-tellers had difficulty in "keeping their stories straight." They were more likely to correctly identify the toy as Barney after claiming not to have peeked at the toy and they failed to provide a reasonable explanation for why they knew the toy's identity. Consistency between the initial lie and subsequent responses was associated with higher level false-belief understanding (e.g., Simon knows that Mary knows it is raining) in children seven years and older. Thus, it seems that theory of mind development plays an important role in children's lying abilities.

Connection

Autism is a childhood disorder characterized by severe language and social impairment combined with repetitive habits and inward-focused behaviours. How is autism related to theory of mind?

See Chapter 15, LO3.

As shown in Figure 10.19, false belief understanding appears to develop at the same time for children across different cultures (Callaghan et al., 2005). Such *culturally universal* findings suggest that theory of mind development is more heavily influenced by biological maturation than cultural practices.

Research Process

1 Research Question

At what age can children first realize that other people can believe something different from their own beliefs?

2 Method

For the false-belief task, a child between the ages of three and five sits with an experimenter at a table. The experimenter has cardboard cutouts of a story. In the first cutout, Sally puts her marble in a basket. In the next picture, Sally goes away. In the next scene, Ann takes the marble from the basket and puts it in a box. In the final scene, Sally returns. The researcher asks this critical false-belief question: Where will Sally look for her marble, in the box or the basket?

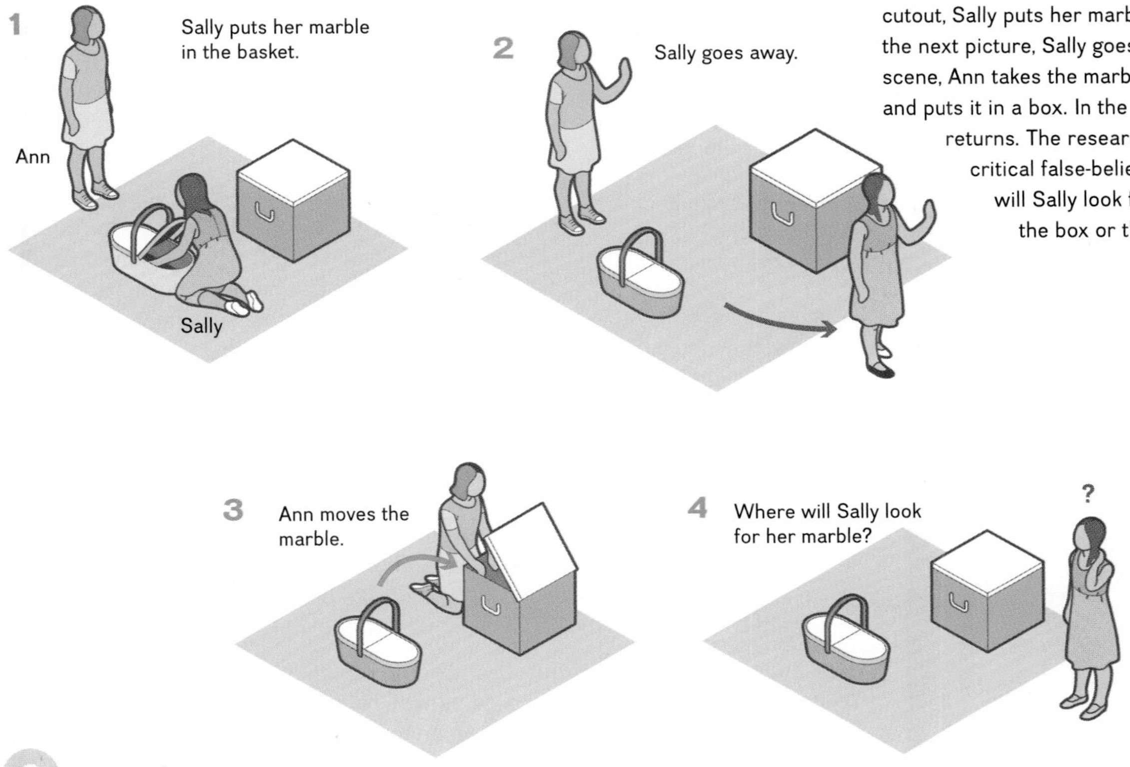

1
Sally puts her marble in the basket.
Ann
Sally
2
Sally goes away.
3
Ann moves the marble.
4
Where will Sally look for her marble?
?

3 Results

A three-year-old will say that Sally will look in the box, because a three-year-old cannot distinguish what she or he knows from what Sally knows. Around age four, however, children can disentangle their own beliefs from other people's beliefs and say, "Sally will look in the basket," because they understand that Sally doesn't know that Ann moved the marble (Gopnik, Meltzoff, & Kuhl, 1999; K. Sullivan, Zaitchik, & Tager-Flusberg, 1994; Wimmer & Perner, 1983).

4 Conclusion

Children learn to untangle their own beliefs from other people's at around age four.

FIGURE **10.18**

FALSE-BELIEF TASK. Children under age four will say that Sally will look for the marble in the box because they saw Ann put it there and can't distinguish between what they know and what Sally knows.

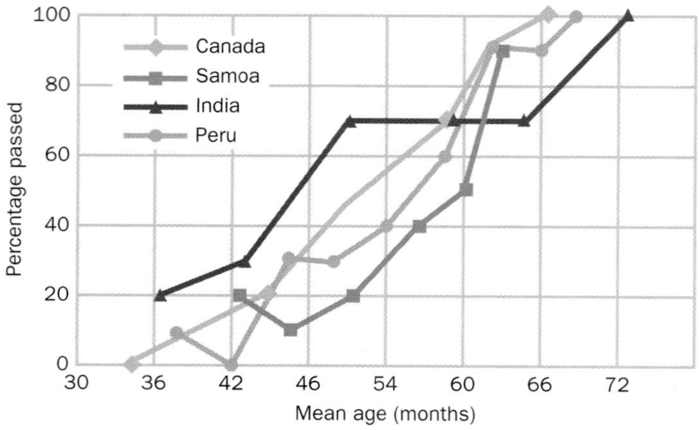

FIGURE **10.19**

FALSE-BELIEF TEST ACROSS CULTURES. Similar percentages of children pass the false-belief test at similar ages across cultures. (*Source:* Callaghan et al., 2005. Synchrony in the onset of mental-state reasoning: Evidence from five cultures. *Psychological Science*, 16(5), 378–384. Reprinted by permission of SAGE Publications.)

What conclusions about theory of mind can you draw from this graph?

Lawrence Kohlberg

preconventional level
the first level in Kohlberg's theory of moral reasoning, focusing on avoiding punishment or maximizing rewards.

conventional level
the second level in Kohlberg's theory of moral reasoning, during which the person values caring, trust, and relationships as well as social order and lawfulness.

LO5 Development of Moral Reasoning

As children develop cognitive, social skills, and theory of mind, they also develop a sense of right and wrong. Most likely, social and cognitive skills work together to help the child make sense of the workings of the world.

The most well-known account of the development of moral reasoning comes from Lawrence Kohlberg (1981), who studied the development of moral reasoning in children and adults by giving them a moral dilemma and recording the reasons they provided for their responses. Their responses were less important to him than was the reasoning behind them.

The dilemma Kohlberg commonly presented to his participants was the "Heinz Dilemma," as follows:

> A woman was near death from a special kind of cancer. There was one drug that the doctors thought might save her. It was a form of radium that a druggist in the same town had recently discovered. The drug was expensive to make, but the druggist was charging ten times what the drug cost him to produce. He paid $200 for the radium and charged $2,000 for a small dose of the drug. The sick woman's husband, Heinz, went to everyone he knew to borrow the money, but he could only get together about $1,000, which is half of what it cost. He told the druggist that his wife was dying and asked him to sell it cheaper or let him pay later. But the druggist said: "No, I discovered the drug and I'm going to make money from it." So Heinz got desperate and broke into the man's store to steal the drug for his wife. Should Heinz have broken into the laboratory to steal the drug for his wife? Why or why not? (Kohlberg, 1981)

After analyzing the reasoning that people of different ages gave, Kohlberg proposed a three-stage theory of moral reasoning. He found that moral reasoning moves from being focused on the self to being increasingly focused on others, with a basis in clear personal principles of morality and ethics (see Figure 10.20). In the first and least-developed level of moral reasoning, the **preconventional level,** the responses tend to be something like this: "Heinz should not steal the drug because he will get in trouble and go to jail." The reasoning behind the answer has to do with avoiding punishment or maximizing reward. Children obey rules because their parents tell them to comply. In the second level, the **conventional level,** the person might respond with "Heinz should not steal the drug because stealing is wrong. Society cannot function if people steal all the time." At this level, the person values caring, trust, and relationships as well as social order and lawfulness. In the third level of moral reasoning—the **postconventional level**—a person might respond, "Although it is legally wrong, Heinz should steal the drug to save his wife's life. But he also has to be willing to suffer the consequences and go to jail if need be." In this case, the person acknowledges both the norm and the law, but argues that there are universal moral rules that may trump unjust or immoral local rules. Therefore, disobeying the more local rule or law may be necessary. This is the principle of *civil disobedience* embraced by great moral leaders from Henry David Thoreau to Mahatma Gandhi to Martin Luther King,

	Motive–reasoning
pre-conventional	To avoid punishment Judgments are based on personal needs
conventional	Rules are rules and they are not to be broken Judgments are based on needs of society; individual needs serve group needs
post-conventional	Willing to break the law—and suffer the consequences—if it is perceived as unjust or immoral Judgments balance the needs of society with personal convictions

FIGURE **10.20**
SUMMARY OF KOHLBERG'S STAGES OF MORAL REASONING. Kohlberg saw a possible progression through three stages of moral reasoning, but not everyone reaches the postconventional stage.

Why is that the case?

Jr. These individuals exhibited well-developed moral codes for which they were willing to sacrifice their lives, if need be, to set right unjust and immoral laws and societies.

Research supports Kohlberg's argument that children tend to reason preconventionally and adults conventionally (Carroll & Rest, 1981; Lapsley, 2006). Moreover, research on moral reasoning in different cultures from all over the world offers support for the first two stages of Kohlberg's model, but not for the third. Snarey (1985) reviewed 45 studies on the development of moral reasoning in 27 different countries and found universal support for the preconventional and conventional levels of moral reasoning. The postconventional level, however, appears to be limited more to Western cultures. When one realizes that Western cultures place a strong emphasis on individualism and individual values, this finding makes sense, because postconventional moral reasoning is heavily based in a personal moral code. In contrast, many non-Western cultures emphasize the group and community, and so the highest level of moral reasoning would be

postconventional level
the third level in Kohlberg's theory of moral reasoning, in which the person recognizes universal moral rules that may trump unjust or immoral local rules.

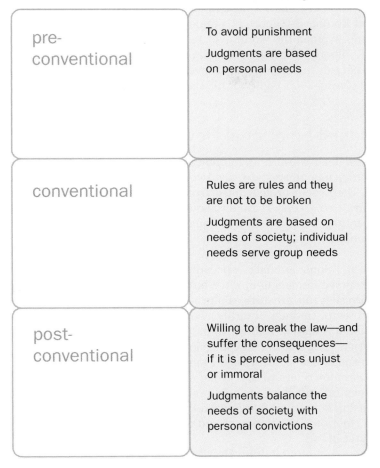

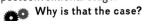

likely to involve compassion and caring for others, altruism, and family honour—values that Kohlberg did not measure (Matsumoto & Juang, 2004). Other scholars say that Kohlberg's theory is a male-oriented perspective that values justice above caring. Women the world over tend to put more emphasis on caring than men, and Kohlberg's theory, in effect, penalizes such an emphasis by including care for others in the conventional level, rather than in the higher postconventional level (Carlo, 2006; Gilligan, 1982).

Early Social-Emotional Development

All mammals need warmth and contact to survive and flourish. Human babies, born in a very immature state, need constant care in order to survive to early childhood. They seem programmed from birth to form close relationships with their primary caregivers. Thanks to some pioneering research that began in the mid-20th century, we know that the quality of those relationships can have lifelong implications.

imprinting
the rapid and innate learning of the characteristics of a caregiver very soon after birth.

attachment
the strong emotional connection that develops early in life between infants and their caregivers.

separation anxiety
the distress reaction babies show when they are separated from their primary caregiver (typically shown at around nine months of age).

LO6 **Attachment** Some animals, especially birds, follow and imitate the first large creature they see immediately after birth. This behaviour is called **imprinting.** The newborn sees this creature as a protector. Usually this creature also happens to *be* the protector (mother or father), so it is a good strategy (Lorenz, 1935, 1937). Newborn humans cannot follow around the first large creature they see, so they do not imprint. They *attach* (Kirkpatrick, 2005).

In everyday usage, *attachment* means "connectedness." In human development, **attachment** refers to the strong emotional connection that develops early in life to keep infants close to their caregivers. Attachment is a way to describe the relationship between infant and caregiver. This relationship shapes the child's social and emotional development and may form the foundation for social relationships later in life.

British psychologist John Bowlby (1969) described how infants become emotionally attached to their caregivers and emotionally distressed when separated from them. He proposed that the major function of this affection-based bonding system is to protect infants from predation and other threats to survival. In his observations of human infants and primates, Bowlby noted that they went through a clear sequence of reactions—from protest, to despair, to detachment—when separated from their caregiver. Bowlby defined **separation anxiety** as the distress reaction shown by babies when they are separated from their primary caregiver (typically shown at around nine months of age).

On the basis of such observations, Bowlby (1969, 1973, 1980) developed his attachment theory, which rests on two fundamental assumptions. First, a responsive and accessible caregiver (usually the mother) must create a secure base for the child. The infant needs to know that the caregiver is accessible and dependable. With a dependable caregiver, the child can develop confidence and security in exploring the world. The bonding relationship serves the critical function of attaching the caregiver to the infant, thereby making survival of the infant, and ultimately the species, more likely.

Baby geese imprinted on Canadian inventor Bill Lishman after he hatched them in an incubator. He wondered whether geese could be taught new migration patterns by following ultra-light aircraft flown by him. In 1993, he successfully led a flock of Canada geese on a winter migration from Ontario to Northern Virginia. His story was the basis for the film *Fly Away Home*.

The second assumption of attachment theory is that infants internalize the bonding relationship, which provides a mental model on which they build future friendships and love relationships. Therefore, attachment to a caregiver is the most critical of all relationships. In order for bonding to take place, an infant must be more than a mere passive receptor to the caregiver's behaviour. It is a bidirectional relationship—the infant and the caregiver respond to each other and influence each other's behaviour.

Influenced by Bowlby's work, Canadian psychologist Mary Ainsworth and her associates (1978) developed a technique for measuring the attachment of infant and caregiver. This procedure, known as the *strange situation,* consists of a 20-minute laboratory session that creates a mildly stressful situation for the baby. The strange situation is designed to see how much the caregiver (usually the mother) is a safe haven when the infant is distressed and a "secure base" from which to explore.

Here is how the strange situation works: After a one-minute introduction, the mother and her 12-month-old infant are left alone in a playroom. Then a stranger comes into the room, and after a few minutes the stranger begins a brief interaction with the infant. The mother then leaves for two separate three-minute periods. During the first period, the infant is left alone with the stranger. During the second period, the infant is left completely alone. The critical behaviour that Ainsworth and her colleagues rated was how the distressed infant reacted when the caregiver returned. They presumed that the infant's reaction would reflect the way the baby learned to respond to his or her caregiver and that these reactions would be based on the history of comfort and reassurance the caregiver provided.

secure attachment
an attachment style characterized by infants who will gradually explore new situations when the caregiver leaves and initiate contact when the caregiver returns after separation.

anxious-avoidant attachment
an attachment style characterized by infants who stay calm when their primary caregiver leaves and who ignore and avoid her when she returns.

anxious-resistant attachment
an attachment style characterized by infants who are very distressed when separated from their caregiver and seek and reject contact with their caregiver on reunion.

From the behaviour in this context, Ainsworth et al. (1978) described three attachment styles: secure, anxious-resistant, and anxious-avoidant. In a **secure attachment,** infants show low to moderate distress when the mother leaves but they are happy and initiate contact when the mother returns. They will go over to her and want to be held. After they've been reunited with their mothers, they return to their play. Securely attached infants are confident in the accessibility and responsiveness of their caregiver, and this security and dependability provides the child with the foundation for play and exploration when the caregiver is absent. Worldwide, about 65 percent of infants are classified as securely attached (van IJzendoorn & Kroonenberg, 1988; van IJzendoorn & Sagi-Schwartz, 2008).

The other two types of attachment represent insecure attachment. Insecurely attached infants lack the ability to engage in effective play and exploration. In **anxious-avoidant attachment,** an infant often shows little to no distress in separation episodes, although physiological measures suggest that the infant is indeed under stress (Gunner, Brodersen, Nachmias, Buss, & Rigatuso, 1996; Spangler & Grossman, 1993). When the mother returns, the infant tends to ignore and avoid her. The infant's avoidance on reunion may reflect the expectation that a bid for more contact would be followed by the parent's rejection. The avoidant classification is most common in Western cultures (15–20 percent in North America and Europe). In cultures such as Africa and Japan, where infant care practices involve almost constant physical contact between mother and infant, the classification is rare (True, Pisani, & Oumar, 2001). In an **anxious-resistant attachment** style, infants are ambivalent. When their mother leaves the room, they become unusually upset, and when their mother returns they seek contact with her but reject attempts at being soothed. These infants give very conflicted messages. On the one hand, they seek contact with their mother; on the other hand, they squirm to be put down and may throw away toys that their mother has offered them. The infant's ambivalence and distress during the reunion may reflect the infant's lack of confidence in being comforted. On average, about 10–15 percent of infants are classified as anxious-resistant (van IJzendoorn & Sagi-Scwartz, 2008).

Babies form attachments with many different people in their lives—mothers, fathers, siblings, grandparents, daycare providers, and others.

How can caregivers facilitate secure attachments?

Connection

Attachment styles are stable throughout life and may set the blueprint for love relationships in adulthood.

See Chapter 14, LO15.

disorganized attachment
an insecure attachment style characterized by infants who appear disoriented in the strange situation and show inconsistent reactions to the caregiver's departure and return.

A third category of insecure attachment—**disorganized attachment**—was subsequently added by Ainsworth's colleague Mary Main. Infants with disorganized attachment show odd, confused behaviours in the strange situation. They might approach the mother on reunion, but they do so with their heads awkwardly averted. Or they might freeze in place for 50 seconds in the mother's presence (Main & Solomon, 1990). Theory and research suggest that these infants are frightened (Main & Hesse, 1990). Kids who have been maltreated are more likely to be insecure-disorganized, and home observations suggest they are afraid of their parents. Not all parents of infants classified as disorganized maltreat their infants (Hesse & Main, 2006). This classification is considered the most insecure because infants' fear of their attachment figures inhibits the development of a strategy for effective regulation of stress.

The infant–caregiver relationship provides the first context for the development of love in the baby's life. Some research suggests that this initial relationship helps shape adult romantic love relationships (Hazan & Shaver, 1987; Bartholomew & Horowitz, 1991) in that the attachment style from infancy brings something to bear on the ways one connects with a romantic partner (or not). We return to this issue in Chapter 14.

Groundbreaking Research

How Touch and Comfort Influence Development

Up until the 1950s, most people—and most psychologists, for that matter—assumed that if children were well fed and well sheltered they would grow and develop normally. Physical touch and contact were considered nice but not necessary for normal, healthy development. As it turns out, this assumption was wrong.

THE IMPORTANCE OF COMFORT AND PHYSICAL CONTACT

Harry Harlow thought there might be more to infants' desire for contact than a need for nourishment. In his early work, Harlow (1958) noticed that baby monkeys whom he had separated from their mothers became very attached to cloth diapers that lined their cages. This strong attachment to cloth made Harlow think that a baby primate needs something soft to cling to. It reminded him of the attachment babies have for their blankets.

To test his hunch that the need for something soft to hold is as fundamental as the need for nutrition, Harlow and his colleagues carried out a series of studies with newborn monkeys whom they separated from their mothers. They housed them with surrogate mothers constructed of wire and wood (see Figure 10.21). One was just a wire frame with a crude head. The other was a wire frame covered with soft terry cloth. Both "mothers" were heated and either could be hooked up to a bottle of milk.

In the first study, Harlow removed eight monkeys from their mothers shortly after birth. Cloth and wire mothers were housed in cubicles attached to the infants' cages. Half the monkeys were randomly assigned to get milk from the wire monkey; the other half got their milk from the cloth monkey. Harlow used the amount of time spent with a surrogate mother as a measure

FIGURE **10.21**
THE CLOTH AND WIRE MOTHERS FROM HARLOW'S RESEARCH.
Which surrogate does the baby spend more time with, and why?

contact comfort
comfort derived from a baby's physical contact with his or her caregiver.

of the affection bond. He found that **contact comfort** was much more important than the source of food in determining which surrogate mother the monkeys preferred. Regardless of whether a baby monkey nursed from the cloth mother or the wire mother, it spent most of its time with the cloth mom (see Figure 10.22). Monkeys fed by wire surrogates quickly got milk from the wire mom and then ran over to the cloth mom to cuddle. Harlow's findings thus challenged the belief that feeding was the basis for the bond between babies and mothers. He went so far as to say that contact is as essential a function of nursing in humans as is nutrition.

However, having a cloth surrogate was clearly not as good as having a real mother. In follow-up research, Harlow found that monkeys raised without mothers (including some raised with cloth surrogates) were negligent and abusive mothers when they had their own babies. They failed to give their babies proper contact or even to feed them correctly (Arling & Harlow, 1967). One possible conclusion, then, is that they did not know how to behave with their offspring because they hadn't had a live mother themselves. So real-life moms are more than a source of physical contact and nutrition. It seems they are role models for future social relationships, especially caregiving.

TOUCH THERAPY

Because of Harlow's work, physical contact came to be considered central to optimal human development, but not all babies get enough of it. As researcher Tiffany Field noted, preterm human babies who spend weeks or months in special hospital beds where they were kept warm, protected from infection, and monitored by the latest technology, are rarely touched.

What might be the effects of this deprivation among the neediest babies? To explore this question, Field and her colleagues (1986) tested the impact of touch on tiny premature infants. She randomly assigned 40 preterm infants from a hospital's newborn intensive care unit to either receive touch therapy (experimental group) or not (control group). All of the premature infants lived in isolettes, plastic-covered bassinets designed to prevent infection. This touch therapy involved gently stroking the baby with warmed hands (no gloves) through portholes in the isolette for 15 minutes, three times a day for ten days. What Field and her colleagues found was truly surprising: The regularly touched babies, who had the same diets as those who were not regularly touched, gained significantly more weight and were released from the hospital sooner (see Figure 10.23). Weight gain is crucial for preterm infants as they struggle to adjust to life outside the womb. Later research showed the same effect in weight gain when mothers touched their preterm infants (Field et al., 2004). Additional research found that touch

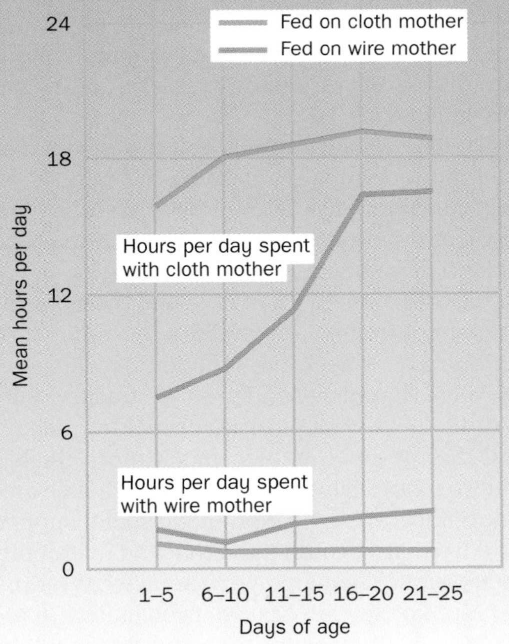

FIGURE **10.22**
TIME MONKEYS SPENT ON CLOTH VERSUS WIRE SURROGATE "MOTHERS." Whether or not the baby monkeys were fed by the wire mother or the cloth mother, all of them preferred the comfort of the cloth mother. (*Source:* Harlow, 1958.)

Connection

The frequency of licking a rat mother gives her pup changes the chemistry of the DNA in certain genes involved in the offspring's stress response, a process known as epigenetics.

See Chapter 3, LO2.

Challenge Your Assumptions

True or False? Being regularly touched as a newborn increases both physical and mental health later in life.

True: The simple act of regularly stroking and touching a newborn facilitates physical and mental growth and well-being.

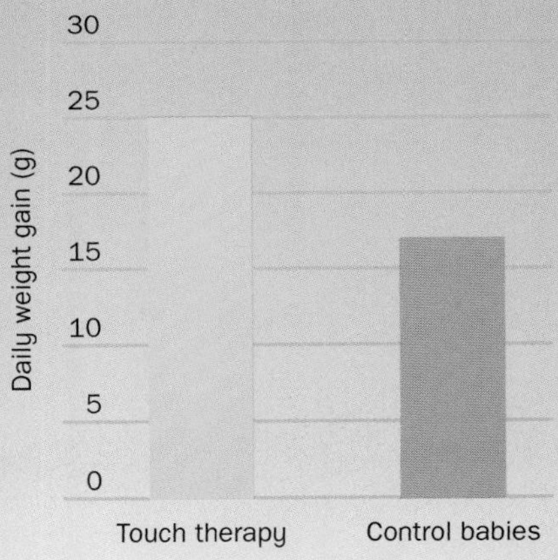

FIGURE **10.23**
WEIGHT GAIN IN PREMATURE INFANTS WHO DID OR DID NOT RECEIVE TOUCH THERAPY. The graph shows the amount of weight gained per day, in grams. Over time, the difference in the weights of the two groups could be expected to increase. Along with the added weight, the massaged babies gained better overall health. (*Source:* Field et al., 1986.)

also leads to reduced stress levels in premature babies and to less diarrhea (Diego, Field, Hernandez-Reif, 2007; Jump, Fargo, & Akers, 2006).

Touch therapy has also been used to improve motor skills in children with *cerebral palsy*, a movement disorder caused by brain damage at birth (Hernandez-Reif et al., 2005). Moreover, it helps children with autism. A study of Qigong (a Chinese touch therapy) showed improvements in sensory, social, and basic living skills in autistic children (Silva, Cignolini, Warren, Budden, & Skowron-Gooch, 2007). Finally, massage therapy improves the well-being, motor dexterity, sleeping, and overall health in kids with other disabilities (Barlow, Powell, Gilchrist, & Fotiadou, 2008). In short, touch is more than just comforting—it makes for better health.

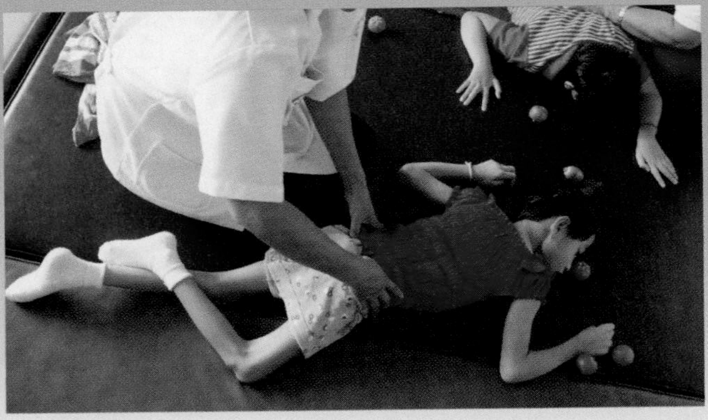

What benefits would touch and massage therapy provide for children with cerebral palsy?

LO7

Developing Temperament and Personality After birth, some infants soon settle into a predictable routine. Others do not. Some are generally happy; others are not. And some infants have lower thresholds for stimulation than others. The biologically based tendency to behave in specific ways from the beginning of life is what psychologists call **temperament** (Gonzalez, Hynd, & Martin, 1994; Rothbart, Ahadi, & Evans, 2000). Based on their classic study of such differences, Alexander Thomas and Stella Chess (1977) developed a model of temperament with three general categories that is still widely accepted: the easy child, the difficult child, and the slow-to-warm-up child. The *easy child* is predictable in daily functions, is happy most of the time, and is adaptable. About 40 percent of children fell into this category. The *difficult child* is unpredictable in daily functions, is unhappy most of the time, and is slow to adapt to new situations. About 10 percent fell into this category. The *slow-to-warm-up child* is mildly intense in his or her reactions to new situations and mildly irregular in the daily patterns of eating, sleeping, and eliminating. Although his or her first response to new situations might be negative, after repeated exposures, he or she develops an approaching style. About 15 percent of the children fell into this category. About 35 percent of the children were not classified by these three dimensions.

temperament
the biologically based tendency to behave in particular ways from very early in life.

What does early childhood temperament predict about adult personality and behaviour? One longitudinal study evaluated 1000 New Zealand children over 18 years to try to answer this question. The children were assessed on many temperamental, cognitive, medical, and motor dimensions at age three and then again about every two or two-and-a-half years until they were 21 years old (Caspi, 2000). Ratings by parents of their children at age three revealed three basic types of temperament: well-adjusted, undercontrolled, and inhibited.

Eighteen years after the initial assessment, the individuals whose parents had classified them as undercontrolled (impulsive and prone to temper tantrums) at age three were impulsive and likely to engage in thrill-seeking behaviours. Compared to well-adjusted kids, this group was also much more likely to be aggressive and hostile, to have more relationship conflict, and to abuse alcohol.

At age 21, the inhibited children were less likely to have social support and were more likely to avoid risk and harm, to be non-assertive and overcontrolled, and to suffer from prolonged depression. They also were somewhat more likely than well-adjusted individuals to attempt suicide or have problems with alcohol. Further, they were about as likely as well-adjusted types (and less likely than the undercontrolled individuals) to have committed a criminal offence. Finally, as adults, inhibited children reported the least amount of social, emotional, and financial support from others. In sum, our temperament at age three seems to have power over our personalities into adulthood (Kagan, 2003).

A separate study assessed three- and four-year-old children for *openness to new experiences*—that is, how curious, exploratory, creative, and imaginative

Are children born with different temperaments and personality, or do they only learn to be different from experience?

they were. These individuals were assessed again at ages 18 and 23 (Gjerde & Cardilla, 2009). Interestingly, the open and imaginative young boys tended to become self-assured, flexible, and resilient young adults. The results were rather different for the open and imaginative young girls. They tended to become relatively anxious and self-doubting young women. The authors suggest this finding may be explained by socialization differences: "bright girls may be less encouraged than bright boys to make full use of their cognitive potentials" (Gjerda & Cardilla, 2009, p. 1461). Regardless of the explanation, the fact remains that who we are as young children does foreshadow—sometimes in predictable ways and other times in unpredictable ways—who we become as adults.

LO8 **Developing Social Relationships and Emotions** It is no doubt frustrating at times to be a baby. Think about it: There are things you need and want, and you are not yet able to ask for them, other than by crying. Yet babies learn other ways to communicate their needs to their caregivers, even before they can talk. One way in which they do so is by facial expression. At just seven hours old, newborns can imitate, or *mimic,* simple adult facial expressions (Meltzoff & Moore, 1977, 1983). By imitating others, infants learn to make certain facial expressions that help them to communicate their needs (Iacoboni & Mazziota, 2007; Lepage & Théoret, 2007).

Babies also seem to know at a very young age what the facial expressions of others mean. Four-month-olds show different patterns of visual attention to angry, fearful, and sad facial expressions in a peek-a-boo game (Montague & Walker-Andrews, 2001). Moreover, older babies know how to look to their primary caregiver, whom they know they can trust, for information about emotion and situations.

The visual cliff discussed earlier as a way of testing babies' depth perception has also been used to study whether babies look to their caregivers for information about safety (Sorce, Emde, Campos, & Klinnert, 1985). If the mother showed fear or anger on her face, the baby did not move over the cliff, but most babies went willingly over the cliff when the mom smiled. What this means is that by the age of one, children can make sense of their mother's emotional facial expressions and use them to know what to do. This ability to make use of social and emotional information from another person, especially a caregiver, is known

Connection

One way we learn is by imitating someone else's behaviour. This type of learning, seen also in infant mimicry, may be based on mirror neuron systems in the brain.

See Chapter 7, LO9.

social referencing
the ability to make use of social and emotional information from another person—especially a caregiver—in an uncertain situation.

as **social referencing** (Campos & Stenberg, 1981). Babies also rely on parental vocal information (such as changes in the pitch and loudness of a voice) for social referencing (Vaish & Striano, 2004).

The research on social referencing shows that babies understand the meaning of some different facial expressions of emotion much earlier than age one. On the basis of studies measuring visual preference and brain activity, we know that by seven months babies can discriminate between fearful and happy faces. Babies of this age also understand the emotional meaning of the voice (intonation changes) that tends to go with certain emotional states, such as happy, angry, or sad (Grossman, Striano, & Friederici, 2006). Well before one year of age, then, babies possess a basic ability to interpret other people's emotions.

Development of Emotions. Babies show their own emotions very early in life—though not with the subtle variations that adults do. They start with pleasure and pain after birth, and somewhat later they respond to mom's voice or face with a smile. This transition occurs between two and three months of age (Lavelli & Fogel, 2005). A month later, they laugh in response to playful social interaction.

Signs of anger in facial expression occur as early as four months. How do you make young babies angry? One way is to restrain their movement, simply by holding their arms firmly. Between the ages of four and seven months, infants begin to show facial expressions similar to adult expressions of anger when restrained, and the more frustrated they get, the more they show it (Stenberg, Campos, & Emde, 1983).

Other studies tell us that babies may not be able to differentiate their emotions the way adults can (Bridges, 1932). There is evidence, for example, that babies use "anger faces" in situations where they might feel fear, such as when they see a noisy toy gorilla head. So it is not clear whether the anger faces at this age are specific to situations that provoke anger (Camras et al., 2007; Oster, 2005). With further development and experience, babies refine their emotional expressions.

emotional competence
the ability to control emotions and know when it is appropriate to express certain emotions.

Learning to regulate and control emotion is not easy for most children. **Emotional competence** is the ability to control emotions and know when it is appropriate to express them (Saarni, 1999; Trentacosta & Izard, 2007). The development of emotional competence starts as early as preschool and continues throughout childhood (Feng et al., 2008; Grolnick, McMenamy, & Kurowski, 2006; Saarni, 1984). Moreover, the better children do in school and the fewer stressful and dysfunctional situations they have at home, the more emotionally skilled and competent they become (Feng et al., 2008; Spinrad et al., 2006).

One aspect of emotional competence is learning to regulate emotion. By the age of nine, children become more aware of the impact of their reactions on other people's feelings. Carolyn Saarni (1984) conducted a classic series of studies to uncover how children learn to modify their emotional expressions in the presence of others. She gave Grade 1 (age seven), Grade 3 (age nine), and Grade 5 (age 11) children a task to complete and told them that afterward they would get a very desirable toy. The children, however, received a less-than-desirable toy either alone or in the presence of the experimenter. When alone, kids readily showed their disappointment. In the presence of the experimenter, the young children (age seven) readily showed their disappointment, but by the age of nine they tried to inhibit facial expressions of negative emotion when receiving an undesirable gift so as not to hurt the experimenter's feelings. Such social smiling comes only with age and maturity (Simonds et al., 2007).

Peer Interaction. As children get older, their social world expands from the intimate environment of the home to include play with other children. Although attachment to the primary caregiver is important for the baby and young child, relations with other children have a big impact after early childhood (Harris, 1998). Indeed, in early childhood, children do not even interact much with other children, even if other children are playing nearby. Children begin to interact socially during play at about age three (Howes & Matheson, 1992).

Most people assume that parents are the biggest influence in a child's life, so they are surprised to learn that, by mid- to late childhood, **peers** are probably an even bigger influence than parents on a child's development. Why? Peers share equal standing or status, in terms of age, gender, skill, or power, so they are important role models. How early does peer influence start? A study of over 100 British children shows that even five-year-olds are sensitive to criticism. Kids who are more attuned to social and emotional information are more likely to display this sensitivity. Researchers have evaluated children's skills with social and emotional information by giving them tasks such as identifying facial expressions of emotion and determining what a puppet in an acted-out scene or a character in a story might do or feel (Cutting & Dunn, 2002).

peers
people who share equal standing or status and are at the same level, in terms of age, gender, skill, or power.

Across cultures, research shows that boys engage in rough-and-tumble play with each other.

In peer interactions, children tend to sort themselves out by gender. First, even when not pressured by adults to do so, children will flock to same-sex playmates (Maccoby & Jacklin, 1987). Second, these gender differences in play occur all over the world—in Europe, North America, Asia, and Africa (Omark, Omark, & Edelman, 1973; Whiting & Edwards, 1988). Eleanor Maccoby (2000) has attributed this same-sex interaction preference to shared preferences for certain types of play. Boys prefer rough-and-tumble play, whereas girls opt for cooperative play (Green & Cillessen, 2008; Maccoby, 2000). Only in adolescence do boys and girls begin to move toward opposite-sex interactions.

gender identity
the perception of oneself as male or female.

gender roles
the behaviours, attitudes, and personality traits that are associated with being female or male.

LO9 **Developing Gender Identity** At what age do children develop a sense that they are a boy or a girl? Is it innate or the result of social influences in the culture that they grow up in?

Children's development of a **gender identity,** their perception of themselves as male or female, is an important aspect of their self-understanding. Studies using preferential looking designs show that babies as young as three or four months display knowledge of gender. They can distinguish between male and female faces (Quinn, Yahr, Kuhn, Slater, & Pascalils, 2002) and prefer to look at gender-traditional toys, with male babies preferring to look at trucks, and female babies preferring to look at dolls (Alexander, Wilcox, & Woods, 2009). By 21 months, most children develop a basic gender identity; they can label themselves and others as being a girl or a boy (Zosuls et al., 2009). This is around the same time that they show an increased preference for playing with gender-traditional toys (Serbin, Poulin-Dubois, Colburne, Sen, & Eichstedt, 2001; Zosuls et al., 2009). For example, girls generally like to play with kitchen sets and dolls, whereas boys prefer blocks, and vehicles (Caldera, Huston, & O'Brien, 1989).

Why do many little girls go through a pink, frilly dress phase?

Between three and four years, children continue to develop knowledge about gender categories, and specifically, **gender roles**—the behaviours, attitudes, and personality traits that are typically attributed to, expected from, or preferred in boys and girls. They increasingly view their gender as a very important and positive aspect of themselves (Ruble et al., 2007). However, to the horror of many parents, they can become quite rigid in their beliefs about the types of activities boys and girls are allowed to engage in (Martin, Ruble, & Szkrybalo, 2002), as well as in what clothes they are allowed to wear (Halim et al., 2014). For example, a little girl might insist on wearing pink, frilly dresses, even in the most inappropriate of circumstances, like horseback riding or on a family hike. She also might tell you that "girls can't be doctors" even though her own mother is one! By five or six years of age, this rigid thinking lessens, as children begin to recognize that both sexes "can" do most activities. And the flexibility of these beliefs continues to increase throughout the elementary school years (Trautner et al., 2005).

These rigid beliefs may be related to the development of **gender constancy**—the understanding that being male or female is a permanent part of

gender constancy
the realization that gender is fixed and does not change over time.

a person. Before five to seven years, children tend to believe that gender is something that can change if a person puts on clothing or makes other superficial changes that are characteristic of the opposite sex (deVries, Kreukels, Steensma, & McGuire, 2014). Consider a three-year-old who came home crying inconsolably. The problem? She thought her mother was a girl, like her, but now she knew her mother wasn't really a girl. Why not? Because her mother had short hair! As we saw earlier, children's thinking becomes more logical around age six or seven, and consistent with this change in thinking comes the certainty that they will be a boy or girl for the rest of their lives across all contexts.

What factors influence the development of gender identity? One view is that children actively construct knowledge about their gender based on their interactions with their social world (Martin & Ruble, 2004). Once children recognize that there are two gender categories, information about their own gender and about differences between boys and girls becomes extremely important to them. In essence, they become "gender detectives." Important people, like parents, may also subtly influence children's perceptions about gender by conveying cultural stereotypes. Research reveals that these processes begin early in life with parents rating their newborn girls as more feminine and delicate and less strong than their newborn boys (Karraker, Vogel, & Lake, 1995). Somewhat surprisingly, however, the development of gender identity also seems to be guided by biological forces. Research shows that nonhuman primates, who are *not* influenced by parents' gender biases, exhibit the same play preferences for gender-traditional toys as human babies (Alexander & Hines, 2002; Hassett, Siebert, & Wallen, 2008). Specifically, when toys are placed in cages, girl monkeys tend to play with dolls and pots whereas boy monkeys tend to choose balls and cars (Alexander & Hines, 2002). It seems then that toy preferences may reflect biologically based predispositions towards certain types of play, such as aggressiveness or caregiving. Clearly, as in other areas of development, nature interacts with nurture to influence our gender identity.

Quick Quiz 10.2: The Developing Infant and Child

1. In the newborn infant, the sense of _____ is almost fully developed, but the sense of _____ continues to change and improve over the first few years of life.
   a. taste; hearing
   b. vision; taste
   c. vision; hearing
   d. hearing; vision
2. With learning and experience, certain synaptic connections grow stronger, while those that are not strengthened by experience degrade and die off. This process is known as
   a. neural efficiency.
   b. honing.
   c. pruning.
   d. reductionism.
3. People who have had intensive musical training have _____ than non-musicians.
   a. thicker finger pads
   b. a thicker corpus callosum
   c. a smaller cerebellum
   d. a thicker caudate nucleus
4. Piaget's _____ stage of cognitive development begins when the child can conserve—that is, knows that the amount of a liquid or substance stays the same even when it changes shape.
   a. sensorimotor
   b. abstract–ideational
   c. logical operations
   d. concrete operations
5. The biologically based tendency to behave in a specific way is what psychologists call
   a. temperament.
   b. personality.
   c. response bias.
   d. attachment.
6. A little boy insists that boys drink coffee and girls drink tea. He becomes quite upset when his dad drinks tea. This little boy is exhibiting
   a. rigid gender role beliefs.
   b. gender constancy.
   c. confused gender identity.
   d. negative peer influence.

Answers can be found at the end of the chapter.

LO10 THE DEVELOPING ADOLESCENT

Adolescence is the transition period between childhood and early adulthood, beginning at about age 11 or 12 and lasting until around age 18. Adolescence is a tumultuous time, made both exciting and difficult by all the changes that have to take place in a relatively short period to turn a girl into a woman and a boy into a man.

adolescence
the transition period between childhood and adulthood.

Physical Development in Adolescence

Puberty, the period when sexual maturation begins, marks the beginning of adolescence. During puberty, major hormonal changes prepare the body for reproduction and stimulate changes in body size and proportions. On average, girls reach puberty at about age 11 and boys at about age 13. The changes that mark the beginning of puberty stem from the release of sex hormones. First, the pituitary gland sends hormonal signals to the sex glands, telling them to mature. The sex glands, or *gonads,* then release sex hormones (see Figure 10.24). The male gonads are called *testes;* the female gonads are the *ovaries.* The testes release the male sex hormone *testosterone,* which initiates the physical changes we associate with male maturation, such as facial and pubic hair, deepening of the voice, widening of the shoulders, and growth of the penis. The release of the female sex hormone *estradiol* from the ovaries transforms girls into women, with the growth of breasts, widening of hips, and an increase in body fat.

puberty
the period when sexual maturation begins; it marks the beginning of adolescence.

In girls, breast development can start as early as age ten. The next major change is the onset of menstruation, known as **menarche.** You may be surprised to learn that menstruation is not solely a biological event; indeed, it is also affected by cultural and environmental events. The age of menarche is highly variable, but it often occurs by age 12. In most Western cultures, the age of menarche has dropped from about age 16 during the 1800s to 12 or 13 today, a phenomenon known as the *secular trend.* The beginning of menstruation marks the beginning of fertility for a young woman, so this is an important developmental milestone.

menarche
the first menstrual period.

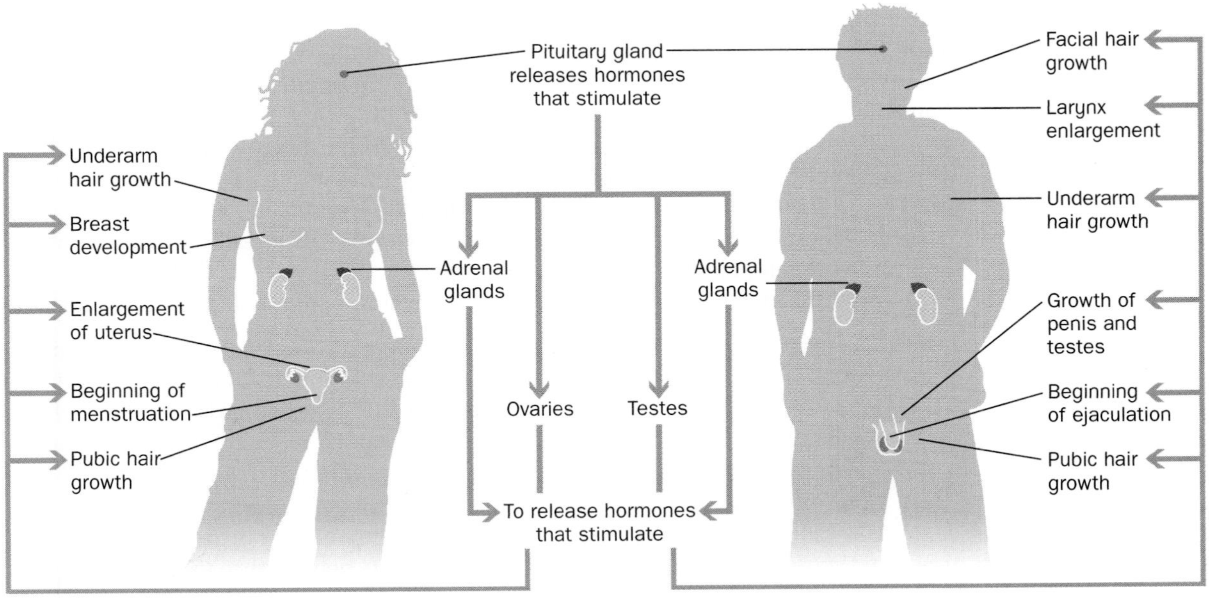

FIGURE **10.24**
PHYSICAL DEVELOPMENT OF MALES AND FEMALES DURING PUBERTY.

spermarche
the first ejaculation.

Girls start puberty about two years earlier than boys. Recent research suggests that the average age of menarche for girls in Canada is 12.72 years (Al-Sahab et al., 2010). Age of menarche varies across provinces, with fewer girls attaining early menarche (i.e., onset occurring before 11.53 years) in British Columbia and the highest proportion of girls maturing late (i.e., menarche occurring after 13.91 years) living in Ontario.

Can you explain the differences?

In boys, the event that signals readiness to reproduce is **spermarche,** or the first ejaculation. Usually the first ejaculation is unexpected, and it occurs as a *nocturnal emission* or "wet dream." Once a male has ejaculated, technically he can father a child. This presents a primary problem of adolescence: In boys and girls, the body is ready for parenthood far earlier than the mind is.

Cognitive and Brain Development in Adolescence

As the body undergoes this dramatic transformation, changes continue to unfold in the brain. During adolescence, children gain the ability to reason about abstract concepts and problems. Recall that Piaget called this stage, *formal operational,* when teens begin to think abstractly and may show the ability to engage in scientific reasoning and hypothesis testing.

Adolescents and even adults do not all develop this reasoning ability to the same degree (Klahr, 2000; Kuhn, Amsel, & O'Loughlin, 1988; Kuhn & Pearsall, 2000; Wilkening & Sodian, 2005). The extent to which people develop scientific reasoning skills is related to their ability to think and solve problems systematically, rather than relying on the trial-and-error method that children use. It is also related to the ability to distinguish one's thoughts about how the world works from the evidence for how it really works (Kuhn & Pearsall, 2000). For example, believing that the position of the planets affects human personality does not make it so. Good scientific thinkers realize the world may or may not operate the way they think it does, so they devise step-by-step ways of testing their ideas. This requires the ability to think about alternatives and to question their own thinking.

With adolescence and formal operations, young people begin to ask abstract philosophical, religious, and political questions and form their own beliefs. Moreover, with abstract thinking comes the ability to consider alternatives—not just how things are, but how they could be. For instance, science fiction and Internet gaming appeal to adolescents because they involve abstract, imaginative, and alternative forms of thinking.

The cognitive developments of adolescence, such as abstract reasoning and logical thinking, are linked with the dramatic brain development occurring during this period. The frontal lobes are the last areas of the brain to fully develop, and they continue to mature until late adolescence or early adulthood (Fuster, 2002; Miller & Cummings, 1999; Sowell et al., 2001). They are involved in planning, attention, working memory, abstract thought, and impulse control. The onset of formal operational and scientific thinking occurs after the frontal lobes have developed more fully (Kwon & Lawson, 2000).

It is not so much that the frontal lobes and other brain regions are growing in size—but rather they are growing in neural complexity. In adolescence, complexity is seen in more myelin and white matter, greater neural coordination or synchrony, and neural pruning. In general, there is a direct relationship between cognitive development and brain development.

A multitude of changes occur in brain development throughout adolescence:

- The brain develops more myelin around the axons as well as more neural connections (Fields, 2008; Perrin et al., 2009; Sabbagh, 2006; Sakai, 2005; Shaw et al., 2006). And as we saw in Figure 10.13, myelination proceeds from the back of the brain to the frontal lobes during the period from childhood to adolescence. The rate and locations of myelination differs between boys and girls (Fields, 2008; Perrin et al., 2009; Schmithorst, Holland, & Dardzinski, 2008). In girls, this increased white matter organization is in the right hemisphere; in boys it is in the left hemisphere (Schmithorst, 2008; Schmithorst et al., 2008). This is one of numerous examples of how development of boys' and girls' brains between childhood and the teen years shows both similarities and differences.

- *Neural synchrony,* or the ability of certain types of brain waves to work together to allow for coordinated activity in the brain also increases throughout adolescence and possibly into early adulthood (Ulhaas et al., 2009). Abnormal neural synchrony appears to play a role in such disorders as autism and schizophrenia (Ulhaas & Singer, 2006, 2010).
- *Synaptic pruning* reaches its final stages, whereby rarely used synapses are allowed to die off to make the brain more efficient (deGraaf & Hadders-Algra, 2006; Paus, Keshavan, & Giedd, 2008).

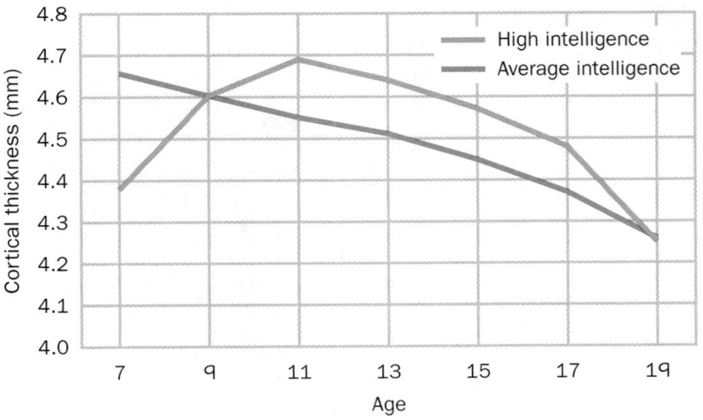

FIGURE **10.25**

THE DEVELOPING BRAIN: CORTICAL THICKNESS AND INTELLIGENCE. (*Source:* Shaw et al., 2006.)

Can you think of any reasons highly intelligent children at age seven have a thinner cortex but between the ages of 11 and 17 they have a thicker cortex than average intelligent children?

How the brain develops and, in particular, how the cortex develops affects intelligence. Philip Shaw and colleagues (2006) periodically scanned the brains of more than 300 participants during childhood and adolescence and discovered something surprising. At age seven the highly intelligent children had thinner frontal cortices, but by mid-adolescence their cortices had become thicker than those of the children with average intelligence. Moreover, by age 19, the thickness of the cortex in the two groups was the same (see Figure 10.25). So the cortex grows thicker into adolescence, and the brains of highly intelligent people are more elastic and trace a different developmental path.

If so much brain growth is occurring, why do teens often seem really absent-minded and/or prone to risky and impulsive behaviour? Research on other mammals offers some clues to this question. "Teen" mice taught how to learn a maze perform much slower than both prepubescent and adult mice. They also have an increased abundance of GABAnergic receptors in the hippocampus at that time, which impairs learning (Shen et al., 2010). Impaired hippocampus functioning, therefore, may be responsible for questionable and risky behaviour seen in teen mice and, by extension, teen humans.

In teens, the frontal lobes become overloaded during complex and demanding tasks, whereas the workload is distributed more evenly throughout the brain in adults (Sabbagh, 2006). Moreover, although teenagers have the same basic reasoning skills as adults, more sophisticated cognitive skills, such as the ability to plan ahead or evaluate the possible consequences of a decision, do not develop until late adolescence or young adulthood (Steinberg, 2005). The tendency of teenagers to engage in impulsive and risky behaviour, such as driving at excessive speeds and fighting, can be partly explained by these findings.

The active development of the teen brain—the growing brain structures, increased myelination, neural synchrony, and synaptic pruning—also helps explain why people are more vulnerable to brain-related dysfunctions and disorders during adolescence (Paus et al., 2008). When so many changes are happening in the brain, it is more vulnerable to toxins and disease that affect the nervous system.

Social Development in Adolescence

The changes to the brain during adolescence influence social as well as cognitive behaviour. Areas of the brain involved in how we interpret other people's faces, our understanding of emotion, and "theory of mind" are still developing into the

Can you recall a time when you felt lonely and rejected during adolescence? Why are adolescents more vulnerable to these feelings?

teen years. These areas include the amygdala, portions of the temporal lobe, and the medial prefrontal cortex (mPFC) (Sebastian, Viding, Williams, & Blakemore, 2010). For instance, teens use slightly different brain regions to process certain emotions than do adults, indicating that further change occurs during the teen years (Burnett, Moll, Frith, & Blakemore, 2008).

Teens are also more sensitive than adults to rejection. In a laboratory task in which a teen is left out of simulated group play (a computer game with unseen partners) and then ostracized for it, the omitted teens showed a much stronger response to rejection than did adults in the same situation. It may be that the sensitivity to rejection in the teen years is related to the extended period of development in the prefrontal cortex that occurs over the course of adolescence, but more research is needed to confirm this hypothesis (Sebastian et al., 2010).

With the onset of puberty and adolescence, children begin to focus on the questions of who they are. Just as we try on clothes to see what fits, adolescents try on identities to see what looks good and feels comfortable. One way teens experiment with identity is in how they relate to groups, which groups they identify with, and how they present themselves to others more generally. Group identifications can be very important and long-lasting, and quite distressing to teens if they are challenged (Lemay & Ashmore, 2004). For instance, one of this book's authors (J.P.) performed in musical theatre productions in high school. Being a performer—an actor—became an important part of her identity, as did relating to the community of theatre performers at school. This identification lasted well through adulthood. Although identity development occurs across the life span, teens are more self-conscious about the changes associated with them and experience changes more intensely than do children or adults (Steinberg, 2005, 2010).

Puberty brings profound changes not only in the body but also in relationships. Family becomes less central, and peer relationships become the focus of life. Having close, intimate friends during adolescence is associated with many positive social and emotional outcomes, such as self-confidence, better relationships with parents and authority figures, better performance in school, and even better overall adjustment and feelings of self-worth in adulthood (Bagwell, Newcomb, & Bukowski, 1998). In contrast, feeling isolated and lacking close peer relationships during adolescence is associated with poorer performance in school, more conflict with parents and authority figures, and lower self-esteem.

In the teen years, peers start to replace parents as a source of identification (Bukowski & Sippola, 2001; Pugh & Hart, 1999). In the search for who they are, adolescents look to their friends for answers. The values and social rules operating within different peer groups give teens "identity templates" that they use to define themselves (Pugh & Hart, 1999). Moreover, perceived pressure and criticism from others (mother and friends, for instance) foretells whether or not disordered eating might emerge in both male and female teens (Shomaker & Furman, 2009). Reactions from parents and peers also play a role in whether teens end up using alcohol and/or cigarettes (Kristjansson et al., 2010).

Challenge Your Assumptions

True or False? Parents are the main social influence on development through late adolescence.

False: Peers begin to be the primary social influence on teens.

Compared to childhood, however, the most obvious change in adolescent social development is the emergence of sexual interest and sexual relationships. In Canada, the average age for first sexual intercourse for men and women is about 17.5 years old (Rotermann, 2012), although there is quite a bit of variability. Contrary to the common assumption that recent cohorts of teens are more likely to have had intercourse than cohorts of teens from the past, research suggests the percentage of Canadian youth who have experienced sexual intercourse has not increased (Boyce et al., 2006; see Figure 10.26). A recent study (McKay & Barrett, 2010) indicates that Canadian teen pregnancy rates have dropped by 37 percent over the last decade, perhaps due to better sex education and access to birth control. Paradoxically, teen rates for sexually transmitted infections have not dropped and continue to be a concern for health educators (Maticka-Tyndale, 2008). As teens become sexually active, many switch from using condoms to birth control pills, leading to increased risk of infection.

The teen years are also the time of sexual identity formation. Roughly 88 percent of teenagers describe themselves as predominantly *heterosexual* (interested

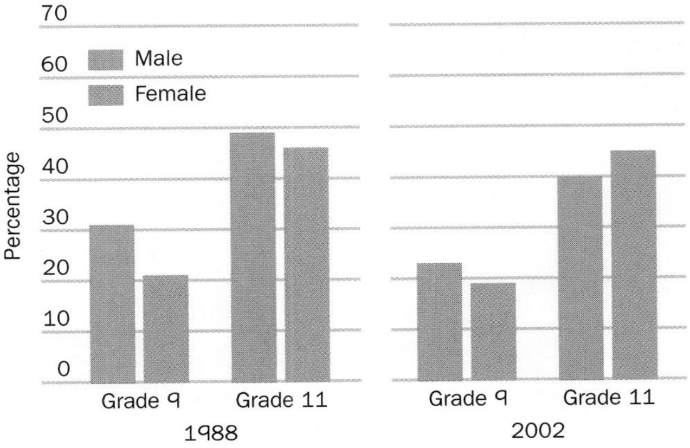

FIGURE **10.26**
PERCENTAGES OF GRADE 9 AND GRADE 11 STUDENTS REPORTING THAT THEY HAVE HAD SEXUAL INTERCOURSE AT LEAST ONCE. This data comes from the *Canada, Youth and AIDS Study* conducted in 1988 and the *Canadian Youth, Sexual Health and HIV/AIDS Study* conducted in 2002. (*Source:* Boyce et al., 2006.)

Experimenting with different styles of dress appeals to adolescents in the midst of identity formation.

FIGURE **10.27**

ERIKSON'S EIGHT STAGES OF PERSONALITY DEVELOPMENT. Each stage has a core strength (shown in bold type) and a crisis to resolve. (*Source:* Feist & Feist, 2009.)

only in the opposite sex), while about 1–4 percent see themselves as predominantly *homosexual* (interested only in the same sex) or *bisexual* (interested in both sexes). About 10 percent of teens say they are confused about their sexual orientation (Remafedi et al., 1992). Another survey conducted in Montreal showed that about 6 percent of teens are heterosexual with same-sex attraction/fantasy or behaviour (Zhao et al., 2010).

Finally, some adolescents explore their identity through experimenting with drugs and alcohol (Duncan, Duncan, & Strycker, 2006; Tang & Orwin, 2009). Both parental and peer behaviour influence whether someone will start drinking and how his or her drinking behaviour develops.

Developing Temperament and Personality

Although many aspects of temperament and personality are stable over time, our personalities also grow and change as we age. Erik Erikson (1968) proposed a model of personality development with eight stages, each defined by an identity crisis or conflict (see Figure 10.27). According to Erikson, an identity crisis is an opportunity for adaptive or maladaptive adjustment. Each stage consists of a conflict from which a person may develop a strength or a weakness. Adolescence interested Erikson first and foremost, likely because of his own issues when growing up and trying to fit in as the son of a Jewish mother and non-Jewish, Danish father (Hunt, 2007). The patterns that Erikson theorized about during adolescence were the bases for his thinking about all the other stages (Boeree, 2006).

Erikson (1968) saw *identity versus identity confusion* as the conflict during adolescence. Testing, experimenting, and trying on identities are the norm during adolescence. Experimenting allows a person to find out which identities work and which ones don't. The three primary areas of identity formation during adolescence are dating and sexual orientation, religious and political belief systems, and career decisions. The basic strength that develops in adolescence is *fidelity,* a sense of faith and commitment to an identity. Erikson's theory has generated a large body of research on identity development (Marcia, 1966, 2002; Schwartz 2001) despite criticisms that it is difficult to generate operational definitions from his ideas (Côté & Levine, 1987).

Quick Quiz 10.3: The Developing Adolescent

1. What event marks the beginning of adolescence?
   a. puberty
   b. formal operations
   c. growth of body hair
   d. symbolic thinking

2. In which area of the brain does significant development occur during adolescence?
   a. occipital lobes
   b. hippocampus
   c. frontal lobes
   d. cerebellum

Answers can be found at the end of the chapter.

THE DEVELOPING ADULT

As adolescence draws to a close and people enter their 20s, the transition from high school to university or college and work increases independence. Many changes to behaviour occur with the transition from the teens to the 20s, and even across the life span. We will look at adulthood in terms of three phases: early, middle, and late.

LO11 Early Adulthood

Major changes in thinking, feeling, and behaviour occur during childhood and adolescence, but what happens when you turn 18? Are you suddenly a grown-up? Most young people in industrialized nations, like Canada, would probably reply, "Not by a long shot." In fact, as Figure 10.28 shows, only in their late 20s and early 30s do a clear majority of people indicate that they feel they have reached adulthood (Arnett, 2000).

By the time most young people have reached sexual maturity, their lives are still in great flux. As we saw with our twins, George and Brent, at the beginning of the chapter, young adults start experimenting with being a grown-up. Further changes associated with assuming responsibilities for one's own finances, housing, clothing, and career shape the time between adolescence and young adulthood. Although some reliance on parents persists throughout university, when a person reaches adulthood, some threshold has been crossed. This threshold, however, is not defined by landmarks in physical and psychological development, as is the case for childhood and adolescence. Rather, the movement into adulthood entails successful passage through certain life transitions, which end in nearly complete independence from one's parents.

emerging adulthood
the transitional phase between adolescence and young adulthood; it includes ages 18–25 years.

Emerging Adulthood Arnett (2004) uses the term **emerging adulthood** for the phase between adolescence and young adulthood, which spans ages 18–25. Emerging adulthood is a phase of transition between the teen years and adulthood. Teens rely on their parents for food, clothing, and housing. At about age 18, things change. Young people in their late teens know that soon they will have to assume greater responsibility for keeping themselves alive, and this has broad-reaching implications for behaviour and thought.

As young people enter university, college, or the workforce, financial responsibility starts to shift to their shoulders. They continue to try on many behaviours and self-concepts (just as teens do), but this experimentation is tinged by the realization that soon they will have to stabilize a bit and assume more responsibility for their own livelihoods. Not all young people go to university or college, of course, but many more do so today than did even 25 years ago (Employment and Social Development Canada, 2015).

The key changes during emerging adulthood centre on coping with increased responsibility and recognizing the need to make decisions about some of the things one has been exploring (Arnett, 2006). Figure 10.29 shows the key features of emerging adulthood. Although much brain development has happened by the time of emerging adulthood, the brain continues to change and grow. The prefrontal cortex continues to develop and fibres there are increasingly myelinated, which facilitates neural communication. Brain structure changes as well (de Graaf-Peters & Hadders-Algra, 2006). For example, brain areas that organize incoming sensory information and help generate emotional responses change significantly from the early to late teen years (Bennett & Baird, 2006).

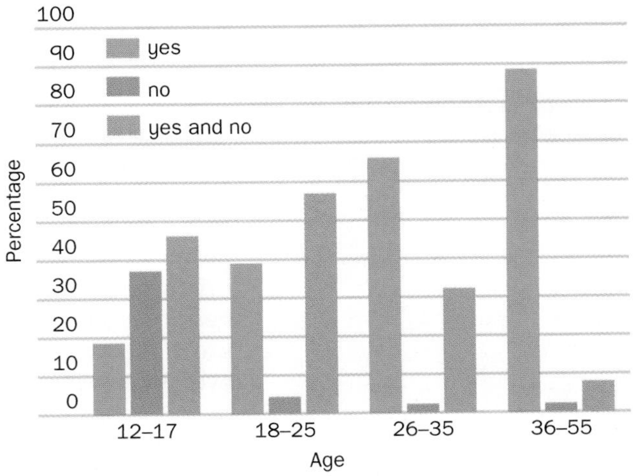

FIGURE 10.28
DO YOU FEEL THAT YOU HAVE REACHED ADULTHOOD? Age differences in young people's answers to this question suggest that reaching adulthood is a process that occurs over many years. (*Source:* Adapted from Arnett, 2000, Figure 2, p. 472.)

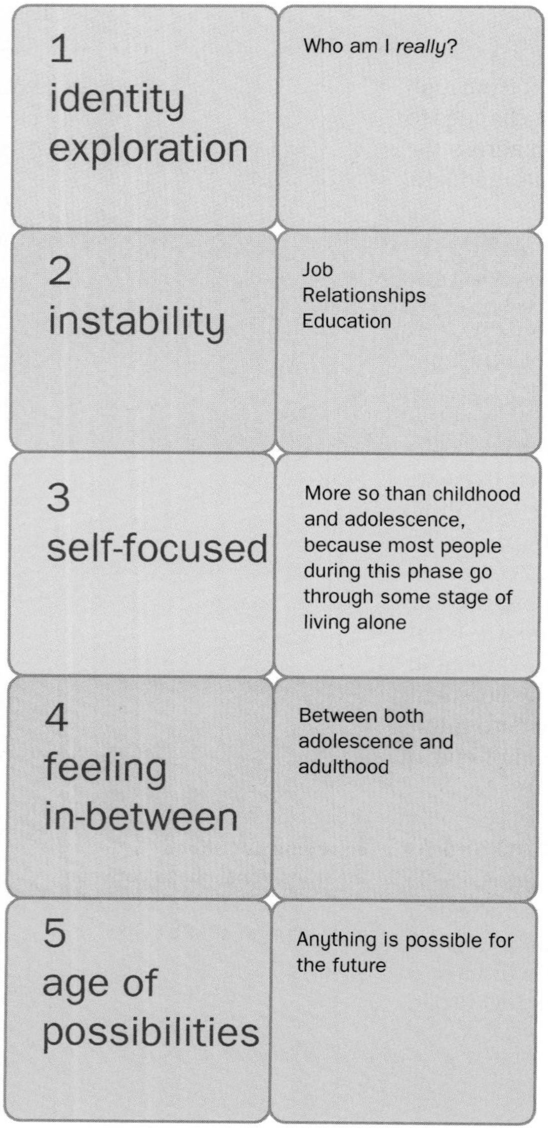
1
identity
exploration
Who am I *really*?
2
instability
Job
Relationships
Education
3
self-focused
More so than childhood and adolescence, because most people during this phase go through some stage of living alone
4
feeling
in-between
Between both adolescence and adulthood
5
age of
possibilities
Anything is possible for the future

FIGURE **10.29**
STATE OF EMERGING ADULTHOOD.
What factors figure into identity formation of emerging adulthood? (*Source:* Arnett, 2004.)

An emerging adult necessarily has an emerging identity. Numerous issues figure into identity formation, but we will discuss three: career identity, sexual identity, and ethnic identity.

Career Identity. By the time young people are finishing high school, they need to start looking for a job or go to university or college to train for a career. These choices involve a great deal of soul searching about such questions as how to spend their time, what are their life goals, and what, exactly, might they offer the world (Porfeli & Skorikov, 2010). For many young people, transitioning from school to the working world can be especially challenging (Kenny & Sirin, 2006). Social support from family and friends appears important in facilitating a smooth transition from college to career (Murphy, Blustein, Bohlig, & Platt, 2010). Emerging adults perceive their first jobs more positively and report more satisfaction when they hold more realistic and well-informed expectations (Murphy et al., 2010).

Sexual Identity. The age of first sexual experience varies by culture, ethnicity, and education, among other factors (Jordahl & Lohman, 2009). In Canada, most people become sexually active during adolescence. While less than half of Canadian young people report having intercourse before age 18, more than two-thirds do so before age 20 (Rotermann, 2012). Although sexual behaviour begins in the teens, issues surrounding psychological sexual maturation and experience also occur in the late teens and extend well into the early 20s (Zimmer-Gembeck, Hughes, Kelly, & Connolly, 2011). Adolescents experiment with relationships and partners. Fifty years ago, young people were expected to settle down with a single partner by their early 20s. Today, if you make a commitment to someone you have dated for a while in high school, it is considered a mistake (Arnett, 2004).

Those who readily know they are heterosexual may have a hard enough time developing a sense of sexual identity during adolescence and emerging adulthood, but for those who are either confused about their orientation or identify as lesbian, gay, bisexual, or transgendered (LGBT), it is even harder. The additional pressure from and challenge of dealing with other people's negative attitudes toward their orientation and attempts to fit into a heterosexual identity that is not theirs are linked with depressed mood and even higher incidences of suicide than in heterosexual students (Spencer & Patrick, 2009). These young adults often experience a unique kind of "minority stress" that is different from the pressures experienced by other minorities: There's no guaranteed familial support. Hence, the support from friends becomes even more important.

Gay couples still struggle with even more identity and acceptance issues than heterosexual couples.

Ethnic Identity. Approximately 18.5 percent of adolescent and emerging adults living in Canada are members of ethnic minority groups (Statistics Canada, 2009) and this proportion is expected to steadily rise over the next few decades (Malenfant, Lebel, & Martel, 2010). These groups include Canada's First Nations, Asian Canadians, Hispanic Canadians, and African Canadians. For young people in these groups, the development of an ethnic identity—a sense of belonging to their group and learning their cultural heritage—becomes important (Phinney & Ong, 2007). Exploration and acceptance of one's ethnic identity increases from adolescence to emerging adulthood (French, Seidman, Allen, & Aber, 2006; Pahl & Way, 2006; Syed & Azmitia, 2010).

Ethnic identity in youth is associated with many positive outcomes. For example, individuals with a stronger sense of ethnic identity generally report higher levels of self-esteem (Schwartz, Zamboanga, & Jarvis, 2007; Umaña-Taylor, 2004). They are also happier and worry less (Kiang, Yip, Gonzales-Backen, Witkow, & Fuligni, 2006). In addition, feeling attached to one's ethnic group promotes cooperative and prosocial behaviour (Armenta, Knight, Carlo, & Jacobson, 2011). Moreover, ethnic identity can become stronger in reaction to, and serve as a buffer against, discrimination (Armenta & Hunt, 2009).

Olympic and World Championship sprinter Donovan Bailey was born in Jamaica and emigrated to Canada at age 13. He is one of Canada's most highly decorated track athletes.

How does ethnic identity influence development? How can a strong sense of ethnic identity be encouraged in young people?

Some youth develop a strong ethnic identity for both their minority and mainstream cultures. For example, many Chinese Canadians embrace both Chinese and Canadian cultures (Hiller & Chow, 2005; Costigan & Su, 2004). However, problems can arise when parents maintain strong feelings of ethnic identity for the minority culture that their children do not share. In one study by Catherine Costigan and her colleagues at the University of Victoria, children of Chinese immigrants had more conflict with their parents and were less interested in school when they strongly identified with Canada but their parents did not (Costigan & Dokis, 2006). Research on immigrant youth in Canada, the United States, Norway, and the Netherlands suggests that young people adapt better to their new country when they maintain their cultural heritage from their country of origin (Berry, Phinney, Sam, & Vedder, 2006).

Young Adulthood

How do you know when you are an adult? At a certain point, some threshold has been crossed, but the criteria for adulthood vary from culture to culture (Cheah & Nelson, 2004). Though some cultures still have rituals of transformation, most modern technological societies rely on the assumption that certain responsibilities occur when the person reaches a certain age. Usually, the transition to **young adulthood** occurs in the 20s, though certain life transitions represent more significant markers than does age (Arnett, 2004; see Figure 10.30). In young adulthood, financial and living arrangements have settled down, and many people marry or form other long-term partnerships (though this, too, is changing). These tasks all push the person to become increasingly engaged with the outside world (Burt & Masten, 2010).

young adulthood
the development stage that usually happens by the mid-20s, when people complete the key developmental tasks of emerging adulthood.

Aberg and colleagues (2009) studied over a million Swedish men who had enlisted for military service at age 18, and they examined data on intelligence, cardiovascular fitness, and muscular strength outcome measures. They found a positive correlation between cardiovascular fitness (but not muscular strength) and better cognitive scores. Further, people whose cardiovascular fitness had improved from 15 to 18 years of age had higher intelligence scores at age 18 years than those whose cardiovascular fitness had declined over that time. This research suggests that physical fitness and cognitive functioning are linked in young adulthood. Not only the middle-aged and elderly can benefit cognitively from being physically fit. Young adults can too.

Marriage. Over the past 40 years, the average age at which Canadians marry has increased from the early to mid-20s to late 20s to early 30s for both men and women, though women tend to marry a bit earlier overall (see Figure 10.31; Statistics

1 Do you accept responsibility for yourself?
2 Do you make independent decisions about major life events?
3 Are you financially independent?

FIGURE **10.30**
ARE YOU AN ADULT? (*Source:* Arnett, 2004.)

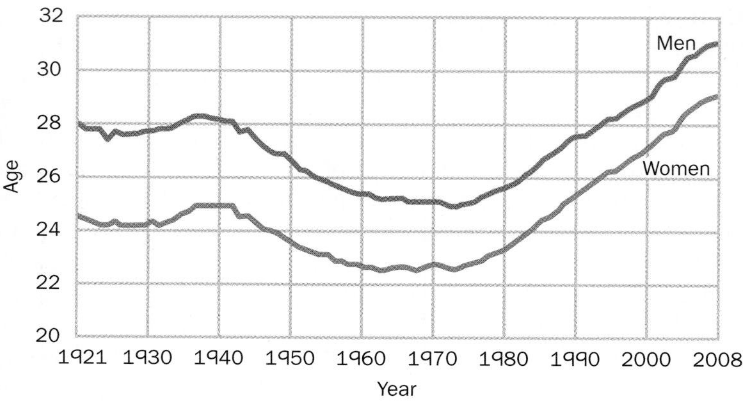

FIGURE **10.31**
CANADIAN AVERAGE AGE AT FIRST MARRIAGE, 1921–2008. The average age of first marriage has always been higher for Canadian men than women. (*Source:* For 1921 to 1987: Statistics Canada. *Marriage and conjugal life in Canada.* Ottawa: Statistics Canada, 1992. (Cat. No. 91-534E); for 1988 to 1999: Statistics Canada, Demography Division; for 2000 to 2004: Statistics Canada. *Mean age and median age of males and females, by type of marriage and marital status, Canada, provinces and territories, annual* (CANSIM Table 101-1002). Ottawa: Statistics Canada, 2008; and for 2005–2008: Statistics Canada. Canadian Vital Statistics, Marriage Database and Demography Division (population estimates), Ottawa: Statistics Canada, 2011. Table from: http://www4.hrsdc.gc.ca/.3ndic.1t.4r@-eng.jsp?iid=78#M_2)

What are some of the reasons the average age of marriage in Canada is now higher than it has been in more than 75 years?

Canada, 2011). Why is marriage being delayed? More people are pursuing higher education, a trend that accounts for the lengthening of young adulthood generally (Arnett, 2004). In addition, more people are living together prior to marriage, though according to survey research, living together before engagement does not predict better marital satisfaction down the line (Rhoades, Stanley & Markman, 2009).

Parenthood. One clear marker of reaching adulthood is having a child, although about 15 percent of adults never have children and many people consider themselves to be adults before they become parents (Goodwin, McGill, & Chandra, 2009). The age at which people have their first child has increased steadily over the years, primarily because time spent in university and other training means it takes longer to settle down in industrialized societies (Kokko, Pulkkinen, & Mesiäinen, 2009).

Personality may also play a role in whether and when people become parents. For instance, shy men become fathers later than men who are not shy. By contrast, shy women are more conventional and thus are even more likely to become parents early—and less likely to be moving into the world into careers (Caspi, Elder, & Bem, 1988). Both men and women who tend to avoid harm and risk are less likely to have children at all (Jokela, Hintsa, Hintsanen, & Keltikangas-Jarvinen, 2010).

Early Adult Personality Development Having a solid sense of self and identity is important for early adulthood—the period during one's 20s. In this stage, Erikson believed the primary conflict is between intimacy and isolation (see Figure 10.27). Erikson defined **intimacy** as the ability to fuse one's identity with another's without the fear of losing it (Erikson, 1968). If an individual does not develop a relatively secure sense of identity as an adolescent, forming intimate

intimacy
as defined by Erikson, the ability to fuse one's identity with another's without the fear of losing it.

relationships may not be possible during young adulthood. Before they have completely figured out who they are, people may develop very close love relationships and then let the relationship define who they are. Their identity gets lost in the relationship. Then, years later, the relationship may end—because as each person develops his or her own identity, differences surface. The core strength to emerge in young adulthood is love, which involves commitment, passion, cooperation, competition, and friendship (Erikson, 1982).

Consistent with Erikson's theory, a number of studies have identified intimacy as an important social goal in the dating experiences of adolescents and young adults (Sanderson & Cantor, 1995; Zimmer-Gembeck & Petherick, 2006). There is some evidence that young people who do not successfully negotiate early stages, such as identity versus role confusion, experience more difficulty with later intimacy versus isolation (Marcia et al., 1993; Stein & Newcomb, 1999). However, there is also evidence to suggest that identity and intimacy develop simultaneously during adolescence and emerging adulthood (Meeus, Iedema, Helson, & Vollebergh, 1999; Paul & White, 1990).

Erik Erikson

LO12 Middle Adulthood

After establishing one's career, settling down in long-term relationships, and often having children, one moves into middle adulthood—generally acknowledged to be the ages between 40 and 60 or 65 (Santrock, 2010). Like all developmental stages, middle adulthood has its own unique challenges, two of which involve sensory and physical development.

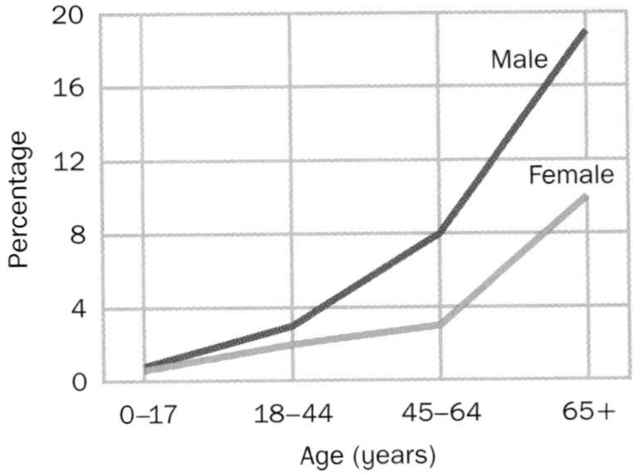

FIGURE **10.32**
PREVALENCE OF HEARING LOSS BY AGE GROUP AND GENDER. From childhood to middle age, men and women are equally likely to suffer hearing loss. After middle age, men far outnumber women in suffering from hearing loss.

Sensory and Brain Development Many people experience some loss of vision or hearing by middle adulthood. Most people need reading glasses sometime in their 40s, as the lens of the eye loses flexibility (Goldstein, 2007). For those who already wear glasses or contacts as adults, bifocals may become necessary as they enter their late 40s.

On average, about 10 percent of adults suffer from normal hearing loss, defined as difficulty in hearing normal conversation, but age, gender, and profession are the three biggest predictors of hearing loss (see Figure 10.32). A recent large-scale study found that as many as 50 percent of older adults (mean age of 67) experience some degree of hearing loss (Chia et al., 2007). Certain professions are more prone to suffering hearing loss than others, with farming/agriculture, mining, construction, manufacturing, and certain forms of music being highest on the list (*Work-related hearing loss*, 2001). By age 50, 49 percent of miners have significant hearing loss, and by age 60 the figure is 70 percent (*Work-related hearing loss*, 2001). Exposure to loud sounds throughout life, such as rock concerts, heavy machinery, and overuse of headphones accounts for many hearing problems in people over 40 (Wallhagen et al., 1997). Age-related hearing deficits can stem from problems with the ears, the auditory nerve, or various brain areas and are more common in men than women (Pearson et al., 1995; Tremblay & Ross, 2007). High-pitched, high-frequency sounds become harder to hear as people get older. Some people report that as they age, they can hear conversations but they cannot always understand them.

Some people also experience a loss of sensitivity to taste and smell, though these changes vary considerably among individuals. Taste buds lose sensitivity, although the ones affected—sweet, salty, bitter, or savoury—vary from person to person. These changes do not seem to adversely affect appetite, however (Kremer et al., 2007). As many as half of the people over 65 demonstrate significant loss of smell (Doty et al, 1984).

Connection

Mosquito ringtones for cell phones were developed by young people to exploit older adults' decreasing ability to hear high-pitched sounds. Why can't older adults hear this frequency?

See Chapter 4, LO8.

In spite of the potential for sensory losses, the brain remains quite plastic and generative throughout adulthood (Leuner & Gould, 2010). Although the rate of neurogenesis tapers off in middle adulthood compared to young adulthood, new neurons still form, particularly in the hippocampus. The amount of neurogenesis depends on a number of factors. Opportunities for continued learning throughout life appear to aid neurogenesis, while stress and anxiety hinder it (Leuner & Gould, 2010; Morgenstern, Lombardi, & Schinder, 2008).

Personality Development during Middle Adulthood Erik Erikson proposed that in midlife we confront the crisis between *generativity versus stagnation* (see Figure 10.27). He defined **generativity** as the creation of new ideas, products, or people (Erikson, 1982). Parenting, starting a business, and creating a work of art are different ways of being generative. **Stagnation** occurs when the adult becomes more self-focused than oriented toward others and does not contribute in a productive way to society or family. The core strength of adulthood is *care*—being committed to and caring for the people, ideas, and products one has generated.

generativity
a term Erik Erikson used to describe the process in adulthood of creating new ideas, products, or people.

stagnation
a situation in which an adult becomes more self-focused than oriented toward others and does not contribute in a productive way to society or family.

A very popular notion of midlife is that nearly everyone goes through some kind of "midlife crisis"—quitting their jobs, getting divorced, buying a sports car, contemplating the meaning of life, and becoming painfully aware of the passage of time and impending death. These ideas are in fact based on psychological theory, like that of Erikson. Indeed many people experience crises and major life changes during middle adulthood, but the scientific evidence for a crisis being universal or widespread is lacking (Freund & Ritter, 2009; Lachman, 2004). Most people do not change careers or take some other drastic action to change the direction in their lives.

LO13 Late Adulthood

The last stage of life begins around age 65 and is labelled "late adulthood." Of the many significant developmental changes occurring during late adulthood, we will focus only on brain development, cognition, and personality development.

Brain Development and Cognition Normal changes in the brain occur with age. Just as body mass gradually decreases with age, so does brain mass (Enzinger et al., 2005). Most normal cognitive decline with aging results in brain changes to the frontal lobes, the part of the brain most involved in working memory, planning, and abstract reasoning (Braver & Barch, 2002; Raz, 2000).

The older brain does not change as rapidly as the younger brain, but it remains dynamic (Baltes et al., 2006). New experiences and mastery of new skills continue to give rise to neural branching and growth throughout life (Kemperman, 2006). Learning new skills, such as a new language, a new game, or a new computer activity, can lead to new neural growth (Cotman et al., 2007). Taking up a musical instrument can also stimulate brain growth (Pascual-Leone, 2001; see "Psychology in the Real World" earlier in this chapter).

People often complain about memory problems as they get older. Yet cognitive decline in adulthood is a complex topic. Some abilities, such as expertise in a given area, take time to develop and reach a peak in middle adulthood (Kim & Hasher, 2005). Verbal memory actually peaks after 50 (Schaie, 1996). Declines do occur in other kinds of memory, however, especially the kind involved in processing information and maintaining information while making decisions. The rate of decline does not become noticeable until people reach their 60s or 70s. Even then, healthy older people in their 70s who receive training in memory skills show improvements not only in cognitive performance, but also in their ability to manage the tasks of daily living, such as shopping, food preparation, managing finances, and household tasks (Willis et al., 2006).

One of the clearest developmental changes in adult intelligence is the gradual decline in fluid intelligence beginning in middle adulthood, but the strengthening of crystallized intelligence (Schaie, 1996; see Figure 10.33). Recall from Chapter 9 that fluid intelligence involves the ability to solve new problems whereas crystallized intelligence refers to the knowledge we have obtained from experience. Only in very late adulthood do we see a levelling off in acquired knowledge and crystallized intelligence. How quickly one processes information, keeping things in mind while solving problems (working memory), and how well one recalls events are key components of fluid intelligence. These skills reach a peak in one's 20s and 30s and then begin to decline (Basak, Boot, Voss, & Kramer, 2008; Hedden & Gabrieli, 2004; Nilsson, 2003; Schaie, 1996).

One way to stave off, or at least reduce, cognitive decline with aging is to exercise (Bherer, Erickson, & Liu-Ambrose, 2013). Older people who were previously inactive improved significantly in a wide range of cognitive tasks after aerobic exercise training compared to a control group that did not exercise (Colcombe & Kramer, 2003). Similarly, engaging in meaningful, challenging work can make a huge difference for thinking and the brain.

One cognitive benefit of aging is *wisdom*—the ability to know what matters, to live well, and to show good judgment (Baltes & Smith, 2008). Wisdom comes with learning from the situations in which we find ourselves. The more we experience, the more we learn about what is important and how to manage our time (Carstensen, 2006). Wisdom also comes from learning not to take things too seriously.

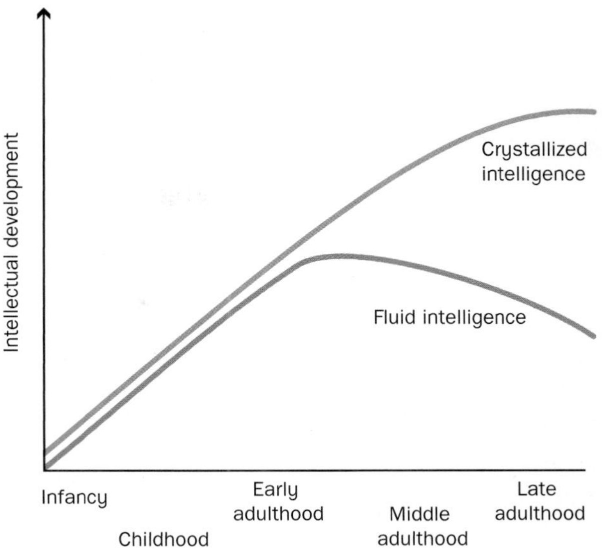

FIGURE **10.33**

COGNITIVE DEVELOPMENT OVER THE LIFE SPAN. (*Source:* Schaie, 1996.)

What is crystallized intelligence, and what is fluid intelligence? Why does crystallized intelligence level off at a much later stage than fluid intelligence?

Most normal cognitive decline with aging results in brain changes to the frontal lobes, the part of the brain most involved in working memory, planning, and abstract reasoning (Braver & Barch, 2002; Raz, 2000). Normal changes in the brain occur with age. Just as body mass gradually decreases with age, so does brain mass (Enzinger et al., 2005).

Sometimes more than just normal forgetting occurs with aging. **Dementia** is an unusual loss in cognitive functions and includes memory problems and

dementia
a loss of mental function, in which many cognitive processes are impaired, such as the ability to remember, reason, solve problems, make decisions, and use language.

For these aging Japanese ballplayers, an active lifestyle has cognitive and social benefits as well as physical benefits.

difficulty reasoning, solving problems, making decisions, and using language. Age is a risk factor for dementia, but in and of itself, aging does not cause dementia (Fratiglioni, Winblad, & von Strauss, 2007).

Alzheimer's disease
a degenerative disease marked by progressive cognitive decline and characterized by a collection of symptoms, including confusion, memory loss, mood swings, and eventual loss of physical function.

Several neurological conditions, including stroke and **Alzheimer's disease,** can lead to dementia in the elderly. It may be impossible to determine which condition is responsible for dementia because they share symptoms. A *stroke* occurs when a blood vessel that serves the brain is blocked or ruptures. As a result, the brain tissue served by that vessel does not receive the oxygen and nutrients it needs, and it dies. Multiple strokes are a common source of dementia in the elderly (Schneider, Arvanitakis, Bang, & Bennett, 2007). Dead brain tissue after a stroke makes for many little (or sometimes big) cognitive impairments, such as memory loss and confusion.

Challenge Your Assumptions

True or False? Alzheimer's disease is limited to problems of memory.

False: Alzheimer's disease ultimately affects the whole body, not just memory.

Alzheimer's disease is a degenerative disease marked by progressive cognitive decline and characterized by a collection of symptoms, including confusion, memory loss, mood swings, and eventual loss of physical function (see Figure 10.34). Alzheimer's accounts for 60–70 percent of the cases of dementia among the elderly (Fratiglioni et al., 2007). Today, women represent 72 percent of all cases (Alzheimer Society of Canada, 2010). Usually Alzheimer's affects older people, but not always. *Early-onset Alzheimer's* affects people younger than 65 (Alzheimer's Association, 2008).

Currently, the only way Alzheimer's can be diagnosed definitively is by examining brain tissue after death, although recent progress in brain imaging (such as MRI) may help identify early risk factors (Schmand, Eikelenboom, & van Gool, 2011; Wermke et al., 2008). For the most part, physicians diagnose Alzheimer's by noting a collection of symptoms and structural brain changes (from brain imaging) that they cannot attribute to anything else.

One of the challenges in this area of research is trying to distinguish between the deficits and changes associated with normal aging as opposed to those indicating early impairment (Dixon et al., 2007). The Victoria Longitudinal Study (Hultsch, Hertzog, Dixon, & Small, 1998) has yielded numerous studies documenting the changes in the cognition of healthy, community-dwelling older adults. Recent findings suggest that one predictor of compromised neurological systems may be the consistency with which an individual performs across numerous tasks that require a quick response. Specifically, inconsistency in an individual's performance across similar tasks that measure reaction time may reflect the beginnings of a mild neurocognitive impairment (Hultsch, Hunter, MacDonald, & Strauss, 2005; Hultsch & MacDonald, 2004).

The defining anatomical feature of Alzheimer's is the presence of patches of dead tissue in the brain, especially in the hippocampus and areas of the cortex (Kalat, 2007). As a result, the affected person experiences lapses in memory, confusion, and other cognitive impairments. In addition, low levels of the neurotransmitter acetylcholine inhibit

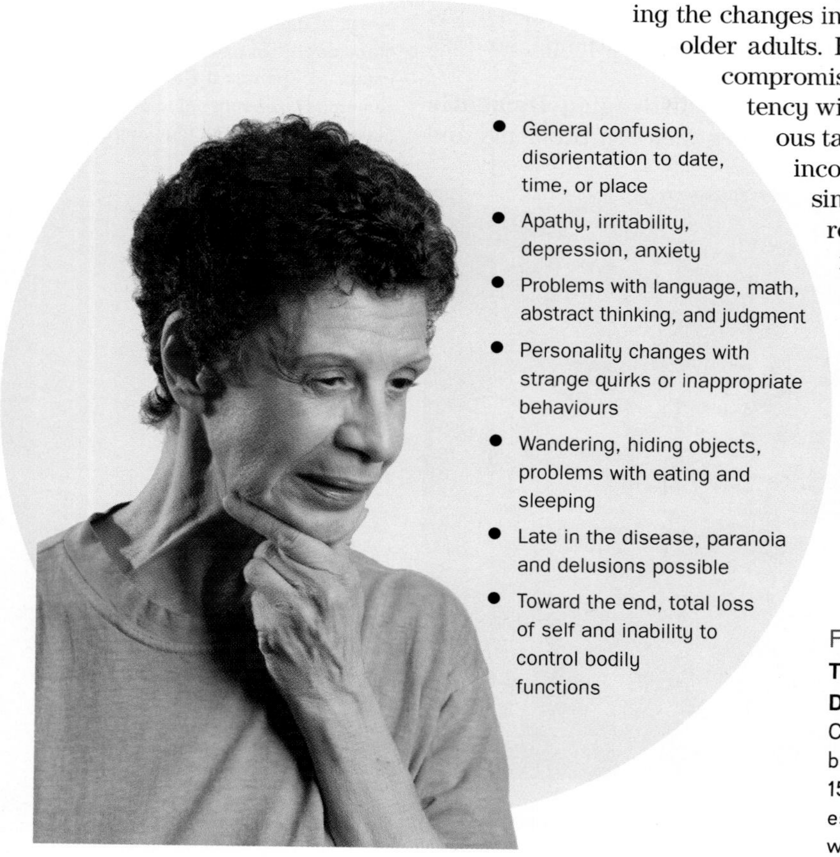

General confusion, disorientation to date, time, or place
Apathy, irritability, depression, anxiety
Problems with language, math, abstract thinking, and judgment
Personality changes with strange quirks or inappropriate behaviours
Wandering, hiding objects, problems with eating and sleeping
Late in the disease, paranoia and delusions possible
Toward the end, total loss of self and inability to control bodily functions

FIGURE **10.34**
TYPICAL SIGNS AND SYMPTOMS OF ALZHEIMER'S DISEASE. According to the Alzheimer Society of Canada (2010), as many as 500 000 Canadians may be living with this fatal disease, with approximately 15 percent of them being under the age of 65. It is estimated that this number will more than double within 25 years.

memory formation in people with Alzheimer's (Akaike, 2006). Alzheimer's is progressive, which means that it worsens over time and eventually is fatal. Currently there is no cure for Alzheimer's, although some drugs do seem to slow the progression of the disease (Hansen et al., 2007). There have been recent advances in developing vaccines that may one day protect people against the disease (Lambracht-Washington & Rosenber, 2013).

What are the benefits of aerobic exercise in preventing mental decline in old age?

Some evidence suggests that neurogenesis, the growth of new neurons, in the adult brain might offset or even prevent the kind of neural degeneration seen in Alzheimer's and other age-related brain disorders, such as Parkinson's disease (Kaliman et al., 2011; Petzinger et al., 2013). One of the benefits of aerobic exercise—brisk physical activity that causes the heart and lungs to work harder to meet the body's increased need for oxygen—is that it appears to protect against a decline in higher mental processing and may actually make the brain grow (Bherer et al., 2013; Colcombe et al., 2006; Kaliman et al., 2011; Petzinger et al., 2013). Recent evidence suggests that changes in gene expression (epigenetic influences) may be responsible for the effect that exercise has on neural growth (Kaliman et al., 2011). Environmental enrichment is known to improve memory and learning, improve brain plasticity, and interact with genetic factors to reduce progressive degenerative diseases of the nervous system in rodents (Nithianantharajah & Hannan, 2006). It can also stimulate neurogenesis in humans and help counteract the cognitive effects of neural degeneration (Kemperman, 2006; Steiner, Wolf, & Kemperman, 2006).

Personality Development in Late Adulthood The final stage of Erikson's theory of personality development is old age, starting around age 60 or 65. The conflict of old age is between *integrity and despair*. Integrity is the feeling of being whole and integrated. It is the sense that all one's life decisions are coming together. The core strength of old age is *wisdom*. Erikson defined wisdom as being informed and knowledgeable about life and yet having a detachment from it that comes only with old age, when one is no longer in the throes of establishing a family and career. Meeting the challenges of this final stage is important for psychological well-being. Consistent with Erikson's theory, research has revealed that elderly adults who fail to accept the past with all its faults and missed opportunities are more susceptible to depression and anxiety (James & Zarrett, 2006; Rickwood & Rylands, 2000). Moreover, elderly adults who view the world as meaningful and manageable more easily accept their life experiences, including limitations and failures (Dezutter, Wiesmann, Apers, & Luyckx, 2013).

Quick Quiz 10.4: The Developing Adult

1. Which of the following enhances neural growth in adulthood?
   a. gingko biloba
   b. diet
   c. caffeine
   d. physical exercise
2. According to Erikson, the identity crisis during middle adulthood is between
   a. identity and identity confusion.
   b. integrity and despair.
   c. intimacy and isolation.
   d. generativity and stagnation.
3. What is necessary for a definitive diagnosis of Alzheimer's disease?
   a. an fMRI
   b. an autopsy
   c. EEG
   d. psychological testing

Answers can be found at the end of the chapter.

Impact of Technology across the Life Span

Today computers, the Internet, video games, cell phones, iPods, social networking sites, and tablets like the iPad pervade daily life. From the moment we're born to the moment of our death, technology shapes who we are, how we behave, and with whom we interact. Some people see these trends quite negatively, believing that they have ruined attention spans and greatly diminished face-to-face contact. Others, however, see these developments with unbridled enthusiasm—there's no such thing as too much technology! In this section, we will look at some of the ways in which electronic technology has influenced and changed how humans develop.

Infancy and Toddlerhood

If there is one important lesson we have learned from neuroscience over the last 20 years, it is that the brain is incredibly plastic, especially in infancy and early childhood. As we saw in Chapter 6, learning happens *because* our brains change—synaptic connections get strengthened and sometimes even new neurons, dendrites, and synapses form as a result of long-term learning and memory. A recent survey suggests that 4 percent of infants/toddlers have used a computer (Vandewater et al., 2007). How does technology impact this brain development early on in life?

Cognitive and Brain Development and Technology

Many technological tools have been developed and marketed to aid in preschool cognitive development and learning, from LeapPad and LeapFrog to Baby Einstein. There are even some online programs for teaching infants and toddlers how to use the computer.

Data show that early computer use can help and hinder cognitive development. There is some evidence that infants who learn to use the computer *and* do tasks other than play games are more likely to be able to read later on than children who use the computer just to play games (Calvert, Rideout, Woolard, Barr, & Strouse, 2005; Castles et al., 2013). Other findings, however, suggest that early media use is associated with having attention deficits later in childhood (Christakis, Zimmerman, DiGiuseppe, & McCarty, 2004). In one recent Quebec study, researchers found that higher TV exposure for toddlers at 29 months corresponded to less achievement in math at age ten (Pagani et al., 2010). Recently, Disney has been required to revoke its claims that Baby Einstein is educational, because there are no data indicating it helps infants in any way (Lewin, 2009).

Childhood

Most parents want more than anything for their children to be good learners—to learn to speak well, to learn to read, to learn to do math, to learn to make friends, and to learn about their world in general. Sixty-six percent of Canadian parents say education is the biggest benefit of their children being on the Internet (Media Awareness Network, 2010). Not surprisingly, 94 percent of Canadian children between the ages of 9 and 16 report that they have Internet access at home (Steeves, 2014; Steeves & Wing, 2006). Whereas most students accessed the Internet by desktop computers at home in 2005, today students are more likely to use portable devices for access, such as mobile phones, tablets, and laptops (Steeves, 2014).

Cognitive and Brain Development and Technology

Certain kinds of video training may have positive effects on the brains of young children. With a simple attention-training computer program, children's brains show more efficient processing in the frontal lobes, where executive planning and attention and focus are most active (Posner & Rothbart, 2007). Four- to six-year-old children were randomly assigned to be either in experimental or control conditions. The experimental group learned to control a cat on a computer screen and had to keep it out of the rain or go to grass rather than mud. They did this for 30 minutes a day for just five days. The control group watched and responded to interactive videos. After only five days of training, the children in the attention-training group showed attention patterns in their frontal lobes similar to adults, and these skills also boosted their scores on IQ tests. This finding is consistent with other research showing that video games can enhance cognitive skills, such as mental rotation, visual tracking, and even certain kinds of problem solving (DeLisa & Wolford, 2002; Dye & Bevelier, 2004; Schmidt & Vandewater, 2008). It is not clear, though, how these improvements on laboratory tasks and games might translate into better academic performance or real-world problem solving.

The news on technology and cognitive development, however, is not all positive. Researchers report that kids who use TV, DVDs, and computers heavily tend to have problems with paying attention and keeping focus (Schmidt & Vandewater, 2008; Shank & Cotton, 2014). More than ten hours a week of electronic media use correlates with a lack of physical exercise and poor school performance (Schmidt & Vandewater, 2008; Shields, 2006; Williams et al., 1982). In 2004, over a third (36 percent) of Canadian children aged 6 to 11 logged more than two hours of "screen time" (i.e., watching television, playing video games, or using the computer) each day (Shields, 2006). These children were twice as likely to be overweight or obese (35 percent) as were those whose daily viewing amounted to an hour or less (18 percent). In another study, heavy amounts of video gaming—but not TV viewing—were associated with being overweight in children (Vandewater, Shim, & Caplovitz, 2004). A study of Grade 5 children in Alberta revealed that access to and night-time use of electronic devices, such as computers and smartphones, is associated with shortened sleep duration, excess body weight, poorer diet quality, and lower physical activity levels (Chahal, Fung, Kuhle, & Veugelers, 2013). This latter finding is concerning given that 39 percent of students in Grades 4–11 report sleeping with their cell phone in case they receive calls or messages in the night (Steeves, 2014).

Adolescence

If there is an age group that has been most influenced by technology, it is adolescents. They are even referred to as the Net Generation ("NetGeners") or Digital Natives. Twenty-four percent of Canadian teens report being online three hours per day (Ipsos Reid Corporation, 2012). How do they spend their time online? Research suggests that online media is primarily used for communication with friends and family, as well as for entertainment, and that such usage increases through the teen years (see Figure 10.35; Steeves, 2014). Canadian teens use texting (54 percent) and online social networking (48 percent) the most to communicate on a daily basis (Ipsos Reid Corporation, 2012).

Social-Emotional Development and Technology

The effects of online interaction on various psychological measures have changed over the years, possibly as a result of improvement in the online mediums. For instance, research conducted in the 1990s reported that the more time teens spent in online interaction, the lower their degree of social connectedness and well-being (Valkenburg & Peter, 2009). Research conducted in the 2000s, however, suggests that online communication mostly bolsters and strengthens already existing friendships more than it provides a venue for forming new relationships. Most adolescents use the Internet to talk to friends rather than strangers. Moreover, communicating online with friends increases closeness between friends (Valkenburg & Peter, 2007). Yet, the same amount of communication does not increase closeness of strangers. In fact, when teens form relationships with people they first meet over the Internet, they are more likely to come from families where they have lots of conflict and troubled communication with their parents (Wolak, Mitchell, & Finkelhor, 2002).

Just as is true in face-to-face friends, online relationships can both enhance and lower a person's overall well-being and esteem. Take feedback on your profile as a case in point. When teens receive negative feedback on their online

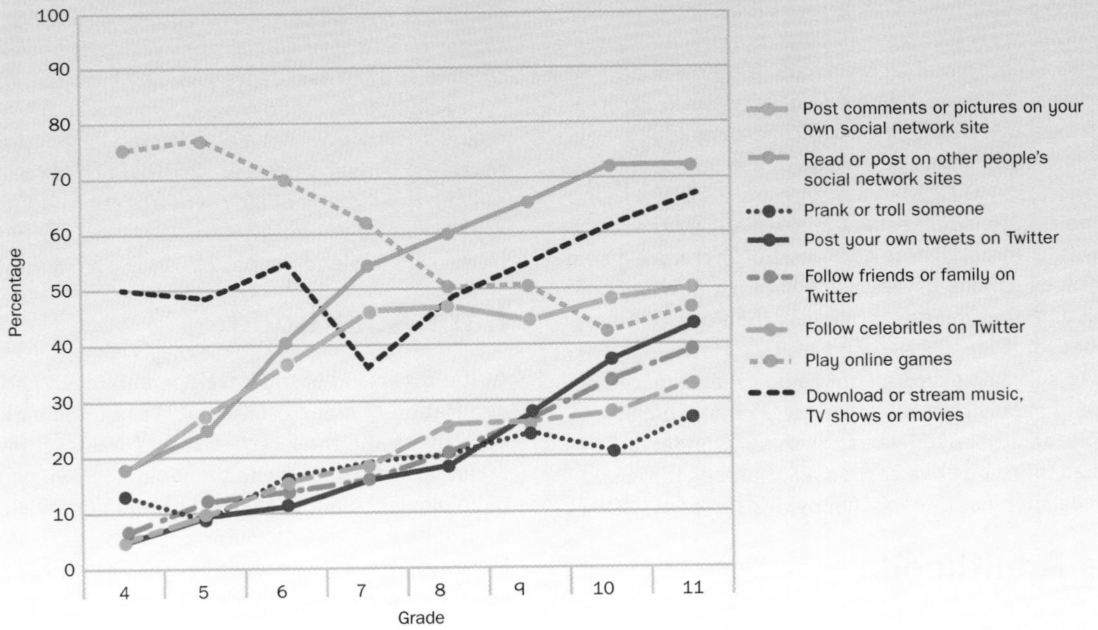

FIGURE **10.35**

WHAT ARE STUDENTS DOING ONLINE? As indicated from this national survey of 5436 Canadian students in Grades 4–11, teens engage in numerous online activities to stay "connected," and these activities increase with age. (*Source:* Steeves (2014). *Young Canadians in a Wired World, Phase III: Life Online,* p. 20. Ottawa: MediaSmarts.)

profiles, they experience lower self-esteem, but they feel good about themselves when they receive positive feedback. Such changes in self-esteem, in turn, affect a person's overall sense of well-being (Valkenburg, Peter, & Schouten, 2006). Interestingly, introverted and socially anxious teens do prefer to disclose personal information more online than offline and seem to use the Internet to compensate for face-to-face social skills to form new relationships (Peter, Valkenburg, & Schouten, 2005; Pierce, 2009; Valkenburg & Peter, 2009). Extraverted teens, on the other hand, use online communication to enlarge their already large social network—to use the words of one group of researchers "the rich get richer" (Peter et al., 2005).

Early Adulthood

Today's generation of emerging adults (those aged 18–25) are labelled "millennials" and like all generations seem to have their own characteristics. When asked what makes their generation unique, the top answer was "technology use" (*The Millennials,* 2010). To back that up, 75 percent have profiles on a social networking site and 83 percent sleep with their cell phone near or on the bed. Among Canadians, older adolescents and emerging adults report the highest level of social networking site use (see Figure 10.36; Statistics Canada, 2013a).

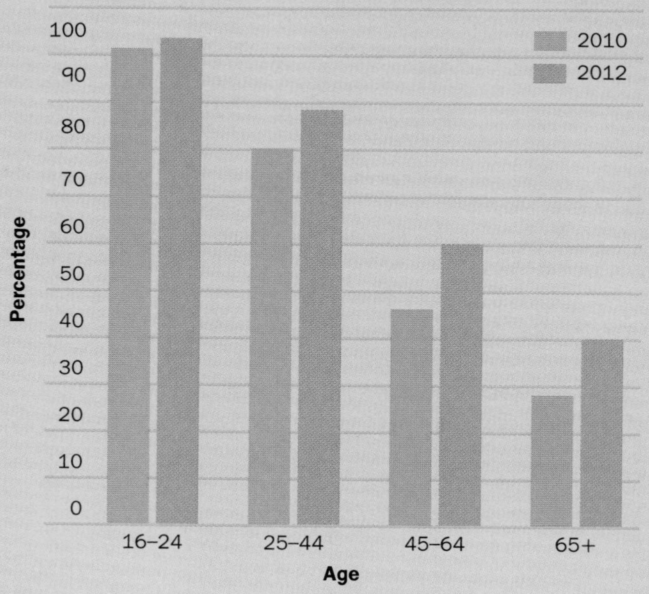

FIGURE **10.36**

SOCIAL NETWORK USE IN CANADA, 2010, AND 2012. Older teens and emerging adults use social networks more than other age groups, but the gap is closing with those in their mid-20s to mid-40s. (*Data source:* Statistics Canada. (2013a). Canadian Internet use survey, Internet use, by age group, Internet activity, sex, level of education and household income, occasional (percent), CANSIM Table 358-0153. Retrieved from http://www5.statcan.gc.ca/cansim/a47)

Social-Emotional Development and Technology

Traditional ways of meeting potential life partners have begun to change over the last generation or two. Although work, school, family, and friends still are the most common ways in which people meet life partners (Madden & Lenhart, 2006), the Internet is gaining in popularity with each passing year. Roughly 11 percent of all adults and 18 percent of the millennial adults used online dating services in 2006 (Madden & Lenhart, 2006). By 2010, emerging adults were the most likely of all age groups to use online dating (Donn & Sherman 2002; Madden & Lenhart, 2006).

Online relationship seekers share many things in common with traditional date seekers, but there are also a few differences. Online daters place higher value on communication and physical attractiveness than offline daters (Rosen, Cheever, Cummings, & Felt, 2007). How much emotion and self-disclosure an online ad reveals increases the chance of receiving a response (at least in women). For example, ads that used words such as "wonderful," or "excited" had more positive responses than ads that used milder words such as "fine" or "happy" (Rosen et al., 2007).

Middle Adulthood

This age group is also opening up to technology. In 2009, those from 35 to 55 years old were the fastest-growing group on Facebook (Smith, 2009).

The literature on the use of social networks by middle-aged adults clearly points to the positive effects of having both face-to-face and electronic networks (Christakis & Fowler, 2009; Hogeboom, McDermott, Perrin, Osman, & Bell-Ellison, 2010; Lubben & Gironda, 1996). The bigger one's social support network, the better able one is to cope with stress, depression, and relationship difficulties. Additionally, middle-aged adults who have the largest online social networks also have the largest face-to-face networks (Hogeboom et al., 2010). Perhaps a little later, but like their young adult counterparts, middle-aged adults are turning to the Internet for social networks and dating (Alterovitz & Mendelsohn, 2009; Thayer & Ray, 2006).

Late Adulthood

At the other end of the developmental life span is the generation of older adults that did not come of age with computers and the Internet. Nevertheless, they too have taken up the call of these technologies, even if they have been slower to adopt them. A recent survey suggests that Internet usage by Canadians aged 65 years and older has increased from 24 percent in 2005 to 48 percent in 2012 (Statistics Canada, 2010, 2013b).

Cognitive and Brain Development and Technology

By age 65, many people notice some degree of cognitive decline, especially in memory and selective attention, planning, and cognitive control. Training programs that stimulate the brain and help it to resist or at least slow down normal cognitive decline have become very popular (McArdle & Prindle, 2008; Willis et al., 2006). For example, in one study, 70-year-old participants were trained for seven to eight weeks to learn a video game steeped in strategy and, hence, one that required the executive functioning skills of planning, reasoning, attention, and working memory (Basak et al., 2008). Not surprisingly, those in the experimental group improved their cognitive skills compared to a control group. They got faster at playing the game; their problem solving was more flexible and capable of change; and the skills that increased with cognitive training tended to be those that were trained specifically. For instance, if memory is trained, then it improves, but language, attention, and problem solving do not (Ball et al., 2002; Basak et al., 2008; McArdle & Prindle, 2008).

Internet searching can keep the brain nimble, as well. Small and colleagues (2009) measured brain activation (using fMRI) during Internet searching and a text reading task. For experienced "searchers," Internet searching activated more brain areas than did simple reading, especially those areas involved in decision making and reasoning.

In sum, there is no denying that technology has an impact on our development. Based on recent research, it appears that technology can both facilitate growth and present challenges. Understanding these will aid us in navigating our wired world successfully!

Quick Quiz 10.5: Evaluating Connections in Development

1. Research on the impact of technology on children's cognitive development suggests that
   a. parents see no benefit to their children using the Internet.
   b. video training can improve processing in the frontal lobes.
   c. too much technology use is not a problem.
   d. playing computer games can lead to better academic performance.
2. Adolescents primarily use technology to
   a. study.
   b. stay connected.
   c. bully others.
   d. listen to music.

Answers can be found at the end of the chapter.

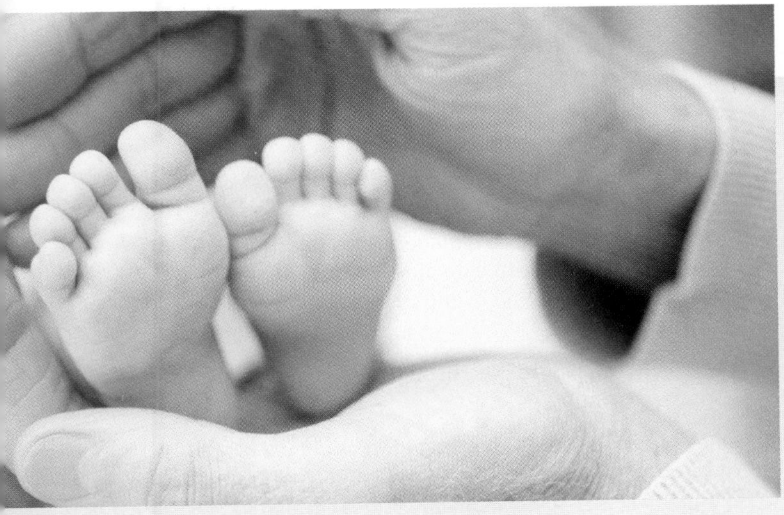

Chapter Review

STUDYING HUMAN DEVELOPMENT

- Human development is the study of change and continuity in the individual across the life span. To study age-related change, developmental psychologists typically use one of three types of research design: cross-sectional, longitudinal, or longitudinal-sequential.

THE DEVELOPING FETUS

- Life before birth is divided into the germinal, embryonic, and fetal stages.
- Prenatal programming refers to a change in developmental trajectory for certain health outcomes that are established in the womb.
- Two common sources of prenatal programming are maternal nutrition and substances known as teratogens, which can harm the developing fetus. Mild to profound changes in the brain and body of the fetus can result from diet and chemicals the pregnant mother takes into her body.

THE DEVELOPING INFANT AND CHILD

- The five major senses develop at different rates. Hearing is almost fully developed at birth, but vision is not. Researchers have developed numerous techniques to study babies' sensory capabilities, such as the habituation-dishabituation paradigm and preferential looking.

- Learning and experience strengthen certain synaptic connections. Synaptic connections that are not reinforced and strengthened by experience degrade and ultimately die off. This process is known as pruning.
- Piaget proposed four major stages of cognitive development. The first stage of cognitive development is the sensorimotor stage. The major accomplishment during the sensorimotor stage is object permanence. In the second stage, the preoperational stage, young children begin to think symbolically. The third stage is the concrete operational stage, when school-age children master conservation, the knowledge that the total amount of something stays the same even when its shape or arrangement changes. The fourth stage is the formal operational stage. In this stage, adolescents begin to think logically and abstractly.
- Vygotsky emphasized how children learn through their social interactions with others.
- The ability to know and understand what other people are thinking, wanting, or feeling is called theory of mind. Typically this skill develops around age four, when children recognize that other people's beliefs may be different from their own. Theory of mind is associated with children's ability to tell lies.
- Kohlberg proposed three stages of moral reasoning: preconventional, conventional, and postconventional.
- In human development, attachment refers to the strong emotional connection that develops early in life to keep infants close to their caregivers. Comfort and touch in infancy are crucial to healthy development.
- Temperament refers to the biologically based tendency for infants and young children to behave in certain ways. Research has shown links between a child's early temperament and later adolescent and adult personality characteristics.
- Babies show their emotions very early in life. The development of emotional competence starts as early as preschool and continues throughout childhood.
- Gender identity refers to a person's sense of being male or female. Young babies appear able to distinguish male and female categories and nonhuman primates show play preferences for gender-traditional toys suggesting that gender identity development results from biological factors, in addition to social influences.

THE DEVELOPING ADOLESCENT

- For girls, a major change during adolescence is the first menstrual period, known as menarche. For boys, the equivalent change is spermarche, the first ejaculation.
- Brain development continues in adolescence, with the frontal lobes being the last part of the brain to mature.
- Social relationships become paramount in adolescence. Peers begin to replace parents as a source of identification. Sexual maturity brings sexual behaviour, with Canadian adolescents engaging in first sexual intercourse, on average, around age 17.5.
- Erik Erikson proposed a life span theory of psychosocial development to describe how our personalities also grow and change as we age. Each stage has a core strength and a crisis to resolve.

THE DEVELOPING ADULT

- The period of emerging adulthood, from age 18 to 25, is a time of transition when individuals take full control of their own life. Developing a career identity, sexual identity, and ethnic identity are an important focus of the emerging adult.
- Young adulthood is marked by a series of life transitions, such as marriage and parenthood.
- Most sensory systems (e.g., vision and hearing) gradually decline after middle age.
- Cognitive decline is complex and not inevitable in adults. Most decline begins in the late 60s or early 70s.
- Age is a risk factor for dementia, a loss of mental function in which many cognitive processes, such as the ability to remember, reason, solve problems, make decisions, and use language, are impaired.
- Alzheimer's disease is a degenerative condition marked by progressive cognitive decline, confusion, memory loss, mood swings, and eventual loss of physical function.
- Healthy aging is possible through physical exercise and cognitive training.
- One cognitive benefit of aging is wisdom, or the ability to know what matters, to live well, and to show good judgment.

EVALUATING CONNECTIONS IN DEVELOPMENT

- Technology affects development from cradle to grave.
- Many technological programs have been developed to aid infants' and toddlers' cognitive development, although there are mixed findings about the benefits of such use.
- Certain kinds of video training may have positive effects on young children's brain development.
- Adolescents mainly use new forms of technology, such as the Internet, for socialization.
- Social networking sites help foster friendships and relationships.
- Young adults use online dating to help them find and maintain close intimate relationships.
- Middle-aged adults benefit from having both face-to-face and online social networks.
- Elderly adults are increasingly turning to computer training to stave off memory and cognitive decline.

Quick Quiz Answers

Quick Quiz 10.1: 1. c 2. b 3. a **Quick Quiz 10.2:** 1. d 2. c 3. b 4. d 5. a 6. a
Quick Quiz 10.3: 1. a 2. c **Quick Quiz 10.4:** 1. d 2. d 3. b **Quick Quiz 10.5:** 1. b 2. b

Motivation and Emotion

CHAPTER

11

CHAPTER OUTLINE

Challenge Your Assumptions

True or False?

- ☐ Craving sweet, fatty, and salty foods is a socially and culturally determined preference.
- ☐ Men and women have similar attitudes about casual sex.
- ☐ People in different cultures express emotion differently on their faces.
- ☐ More money leads to greater happiness.

LEARNING OBJECTIVES

LO1 Define motivation, drives, needs, and incentives.

LO2 Describe the different models of motivation.

LO3 Describe the biological, psychological, and cultural influences on hunger and feeding.

LO4 Describe the biological, psychological, and cultural influences on sexual behaviour.

LO5 Explain the difference between emotions, moods, and affective traits, and list the basic and self-conscious emotions.

LO6 Explain the roles that appraisal, emotional regulation, and reappraisal play in the emotion process.

LO7 Describe the physiological, behavioural/expressive, and subjective changes of the emotional response.

LO8 Compare the James-Lange, Cannon-Bard, and Schachter and Singer theories of emotion.

LO9 Describe the role of the brain in emotion.

Beck Weathers was finally doing what he had long dreamt of doing: climbing Mt. Everest. A successful pathologist and amateur mountaineer, Weathers had already accomplished much in his 49 years. His passion for climbing grew as a way to deal with crippling depression, as he found the challenge of mountain climbing an effective way of coping (Weathers, 2000).

Weathers and his team spent two months on Mt. Everest adjusting to the altitude until finally the conditions were right to attempt to summit the 29 029-foot (8848 metre) peak. Unfortunately, Weathers had to stop just short of the 28 000-foot mark; completely exhausted, depleted of oxygen, and literally blinded by weather conditions, he could not continue. He promised his guide, Rob Hall, he would wait for his return from summiting with another client. Not knowing that his guide and the other client would wind up in trouble, Weathers waited for hours alone. Beck finally joined a few others going down the mountain, but it was too late. They got caught in a fierce storm and had to spend the night in nearly 160 km/h winds and temperatures of −35°C.

The next morning Anatoli Boukreev, a Russian guide, came upon Beck's five-person group. The storm was still blasting at full force, so Boukreev could only take a few climbers at a time down to the 26 000-foot (7925 metre) Camp Four. He sent a rescue team for two of the remaining stranded climbers, one of whom was Weathers. The rescue team found them lying in the snow, both still breathing but close to death. It would be dangerous to try to take them down the mountain, so the pair were left for dead. Word got back to camp, and a phone call was made to his wife in Dallas, informing her of Beck's death.

Weathers remained in the subzero temperatures and snow for more than 12 hours, but "for some unknowable reason a light went on in the reptilian core of Beck's inanimate brain and he floated back to consciousness" (Krakauer, 1999, p. 841). When he first woke up in the snow, Weathers thought he was in a dream. He was no longer cold, and he was motivated to survive: "I was overwhelmed by an enormous, encompassing sense of melancholy. That I would not say good-bye to my family, that I would never again say 'I love you' to my wife, that I would never again hold my children, was just not acceptable. 'Keep moving' I said to myself again and again" (Weathers, 2000, p. 95).

After finding his way back to Camp Four, using wind direction as his only guide, and getting into a sleeping bag, the people there were still convinced that he would be dead by morning and was left alone to die—yet again! However, Jon Krakauer, author of *Into Thin Air,* decided to check on Weathers as others prepared to leave the camp the next day and "was shocked to discover that Beck was still alive" (Krakauer, 1999, p. 853).

After another day of horrifically difficult climbing, being guided footstep by footstep, Weathers finally made it to a lower camp at around 20 000 feet (6100 metres), but it was still unclear how he would make it off the mountain. The answer was one, beyond-belief act of heroism: the highest helicopter rescue ever performed by Madan Khatri Chhetri. At that elevation, helicopters can't get enough lift. The pilot risked his own life, but he succeeded, and Beck Weathers survived beyond all expectation and reason.

Weathers's survival is not only one of miraculous drive and motivation but also one that demonstrates how emotion can often fuel motivation. The thought of never seeing his wife and children again gave Weathers the strength and perseverance to make it back down to camp. Although he was left for dead three times and ended up losing both hands and his nose to frostbite, Weathers survived and became a better husband and father (Weathers, 2000). Motivation and emotion are important forces of survival, and in this chapter we explore how these two forces shape human thought and behaviour.

LO1 MOTIVATION

Consider what the following situations have in common:

- a baby seeking a nipple
- a boy studying for a math exam
- a homeless person searching for food in a garbage can
- a scientist conducting research
- a musician learning a new piece
- a couple making love

These are all examples of motivated behaviours. **Motivation** can be defined as the urge to move toward one's goals, whatever they may be. Motivation gives us an energetic push toward accomplishing tasks, such as getting dinner, getting rich, and getting lucky. Babies seek the nipple because they need nutrition; a boy might study for a test because he finds the material fascinating. There might be various reasons for a behaviour, but each involves motivation.

motivation
the urge to move toward one's goals; to accomplish tasks.

Needs, drives, and incentives all contribute to motivation. **Needs** are states of cellular or bodily deficiency that compel drives. They are inherently biological. Examples include the needs for water, food, and oxygen. **Drives** are the perceived states of tension that occur when our bodies are deficient in some need. Such a deficiency creates a drive (thirst or hunger) to alleviate the state—to drink or eat. In this way, needs and drives push us. On a very hot day when we are extremely thirsty, we simply *must* get a drink of water! All our physiological needs have drive components. Figure 11.1 shows the drive components associated with various physiological and psychological needs. Motivated *behaviours*, therefore, result from needs and drives.

needs
inherently biological states of deficiency (cellular or bodily) that compel drives.

drives
the perceived states of tension that occur when our bodies are deficient in some need, creating an urge to relieve the tension.

If drives *push* us into action, then incentives *pull* us into action. An **incentive** is any external object or event that motivates behaviour. In general, drives come from the body, whereas incentives come from the environment. For some people, money is a primary incentive, but for others winning a gold medal at the Olympics or getting a university degree might be the main incentive behind their training or studying.

incentive
any external object or event that motivates behaviour.

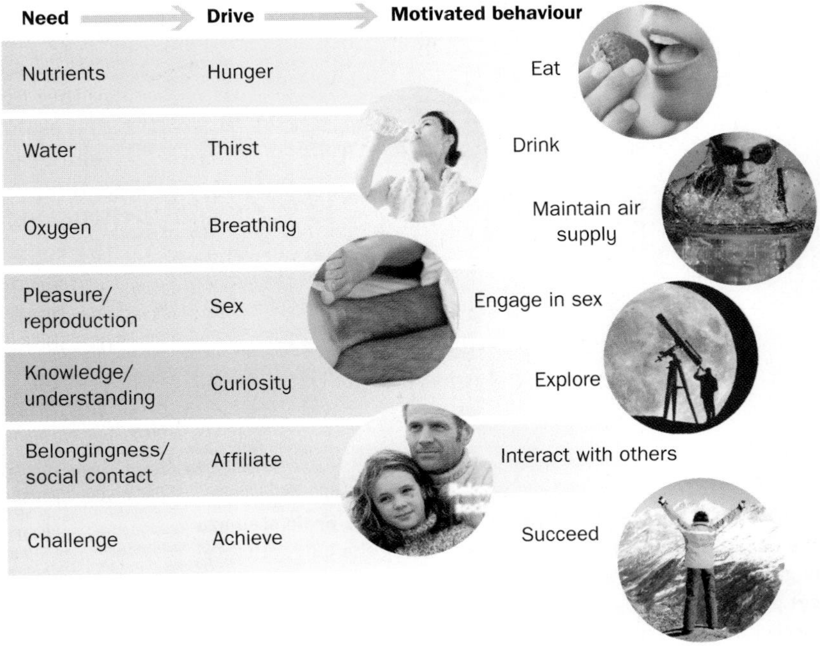

Need
Drive
Motivated behaviour
Nutrients
Hunger
Eat
Water
Thirst
Drink
Oxygen
Breathing
Maintain air supply
Pleasure/ reproduction
Sex
Engage in sex
Knowledge/ understanding
Curiosity
Explore
Belongingness/ social contact
Affiliate
Interact with others
Challenge
Achieve
Succeed

FIGURE **11.1**
NEEDS, DRIVES, AND MOTIVATED BEHAVIOURS.
As humans, we have a strong need for belongingness and social contact. Can you think of motivated behaviours from your own life that fulfill this need?

LO2 Models of Motivation

Psychologists propose many models, or explanations, for motivation. Some models of motivation focus more on internal drives, some more on external incentives, and others on both.

The Evolutionary Model Evolutionary theory looks at internal drives to explain why people do what they do. Biologically speaking, the purpose of any living organism is to perpetuate itself. The processes of natural and sexual selection have shaped motivation over time to make all animals, including humans, want those things that help them survive and reproduce (Buss, 2003). As a result, the major motives all involve basic survival and reproduction needs and drives: hunger, thirst, body-temperature regulation, oxygen, and sex. Our bodies "know" they want food, water, oxygen, and—after adolescence—sex. In fact, sexual behaviour in humans appears to be enhanced at times when the chance of conception is most likely. In a study of sexual motivation, Schwarz and Hassebrauck (2008) had women keep a diary of their clothing style across the menstrual cycle, and found that they reported dressing more provocatively during their most fertile phase. Researchers also had the women take a picture every day, which were later rated by men who also rated clothing as sexier and the women more attractive during the fertile phase.

instinct
an inherited behavioural tendency that has been preserved within a species because it helped ensure survival.

homeostasis
the process by which all organisms work to maintain physiological equilibrium or balance around an optimal set point.

set point
the ideal fixed setting of a particular physiological system, such as internal body temperature.

Desires, wants, and needs have been shaped over the course of evolution to guide behaviour either toward adaptive or away from maladaptive actions (Buss, 2003; Miller, 2000). An inherited behavioural tendency of a species is referred to as an **instinct,** and implies that internal drives are constant amongst members of a species because they serve adaptive functions for survival. In most cases, we are unaware that our behaviour is related to these instincts. We know only that we do something because it feels good and that we stop doing something if it feels bad. So one answer to the question of why we do what we do is that we do it to please ourselves or to remove some undesirable state.

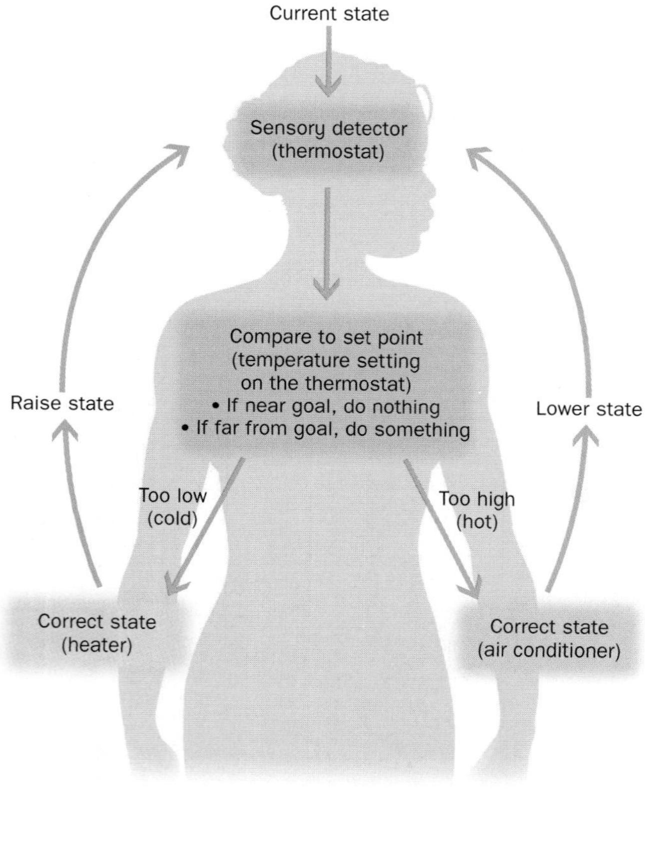

FIGURE 11.2
MODELS OF HOMEOSTASIS. Detectors in the brain stabilize the body's psychological state by comparing the current state (e.g., blood sugar level, body fluids, body temperature) to a set point. If the body is far from the set point, the organism is motivated to correct the imbalance (e.g., by seeking food or putting on a sweater). Sensory feedback to the brain tells it when the set point has been achieved, and the brain then tells the body to stop correcting. This feedback system keeps the body's physiological systems at their ideal set point. (*Source:* Berridge, 2004.)

The Drive Reduction Model Other psychologists argue that when our physiological systems are out of balance or depleted, we are driven to reduce this depleted state (Hull, 1943; McKinley et al., 2004; Weisinger et al., 1993). That's what drive is—the perceived internal state of tension that arises when our bodies are lacking in some basic physiological capacity. Central to drive reduction is the idea of maintaining physiological balance, or **homeostasis** (Cannon, 1929). The term implies that all organisms are motivated to maintain physiological equilibrium around an optimal **set point,** defined as the ideal fixed setting of a particular physiological system. We have set points for hunger, thirst, respiration, and many other drives. For example, compare the normal human body temperature of 37°C to a thermostat that is set to keep a temperature in a room constant (see Figure 11.2). When the thermometer in the thermostat senses that the temperature in the room has fallen more than a degree or two lower than the set point, it switches on the heater. If it senses that it's too hot, the air conditioner comes on. Once the temperature has been brought back within the ideal set-point range, the thermostat turns off the heater or air conditioner. Our body behaves in a similar fashion: If we get too hot, we sweat to cool off. If we get too cold, we shiver to warm up.

For this system to work, our bodies must have sensors that detect its current state and any changes that cause it to deviate from the set point. Most of these sensors are located in the brain. If our bodily states move too far from the set point, these sensory detectors trigger mechanisms that motivate us to take action—to raid the refrigerator, for example. In other words, certain brain mechanisms evaluate the options and decide what to do to meet a biological need based on the information the brain is getting from our organs and tissues. *Homeostasis* is the term we use to describe this feedback loop.

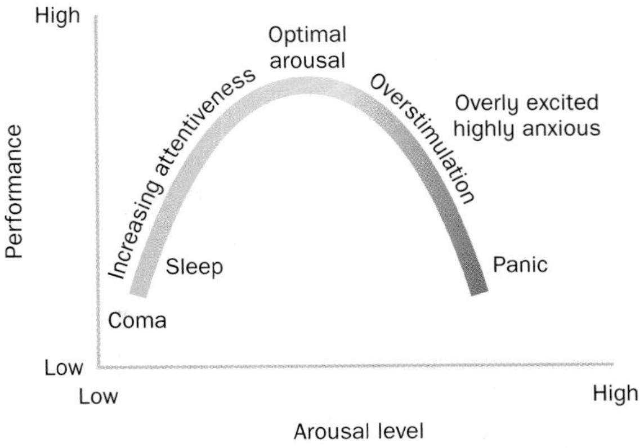

FIGURE **11.3**

YERKES-DODSON LAW. The Yerkes-Dodson law states that performance is best when we are optimally aroused. To be optimally aroused is to be moderately aroused. Performance is worst when we are not very aroused (asleep or not paying attention) or overly aroused (highly excited or anxious). (*Source:* Smith, 1999.)

The Optimal Arousal Model Another model of motivation proposes that we function best at an "optimal level of arousal." This model rests on classic research by Yerkes and Dodson (1908), who showed that both low arousal and high arousal lead to poor performance, whereas moderate levels of arousal lead to optimal performance (Yerkes & Dodson, 1908). The finding is so common that it is now referred to as the **Yerkes-Dodson law** (see Figure 11.3).

The optimal arousal model of motivation argues that humans are motivated to be in situations that are neither too stimulating nor not stimulating enough. We know this, for instance, from research on sensory deprivation. Sensory deprivation research involves having a person lie down on a bed or in a sensory deprivation (salt water) tank. Classic research from the 1950s demonstrated that people could not remain in sensory deprivation for more than two to three days even if they were paid double their daily wage for each day they remained in the tank (Bexton, Heron, & Scott, 1954). Moreover, when they stayed for only a few days, "pathology of boredom" developed (Heron, 1957). After long periods of sensory deprivation, people begin to hallucinate, their cognitive ability and concentration suffer, and they develop childish emotional responses. Long-term sensory deprivation in rats actually shrinks the brain regions most involved in the senses that have been deprived—yet another example of the plasticity of the brain (Cheetham et al., 2007; Finnerty, Roberts, & Connors, 1999).

Yerkes-Dodson law
the principle that moderate levels of arousal lead to optimal performance.

In the 1990s, Mihály Csíkszentmihályi introduced the concept of *flow* to describe the fact that people perform best and are most creative when they are optimally challenged relative to their abilities (Csíkszentmihályi, 1990, 1996). Others have applied a similar model to explain learning and motivation (Day, 1982). According to this school of thought, needs such as curiosity, learning, interest, beauty-aesthetics, competence, challenge, flow states, and optimal experiences are motivated by the desire to be optimally aroused (Berlyne, 1960; Csíkszentmihályi, 1990; Deci & Ryan, 1985; Silvia, 2006).

Connection

What are some of the qualities of self-actualizing people?

See Chapter 13, LO5.

The Hierarchical Model Another model of motivation, which combines drives and incentives, is Abraham Maslow's hierarchy of needs (Maslow, 1970). The essence of Maslow's hierarchy is simple: Needs range from the most basic physiological necessities to the highest, most psychological needs for growth and fulfillment (see Figure 11.4). At the lowest level of the hierarchy are *physiological needs,* such as the needs for food, water, oxygen, and adequate body temperature. The next level are *safety needs,* which include the needs for physical security, stability, dependency, protection, and freedom from threats such as war, assault, and terrorism. We need to be fed and out of danger's way before we can pay attention to higher-level needs.

The third level in the hierarchy consists of the *love and belongingness needs,* including the desire for friendship, sex, a mate, and children, as well as the desire to belong to a family or social group. The fourth level in Maslow's hierarchy of needs is the *need for esteem,* that is, the need to appreciate oneself and one's worth and to be appreciated and respected by others. The top level in the hierarchy is the need

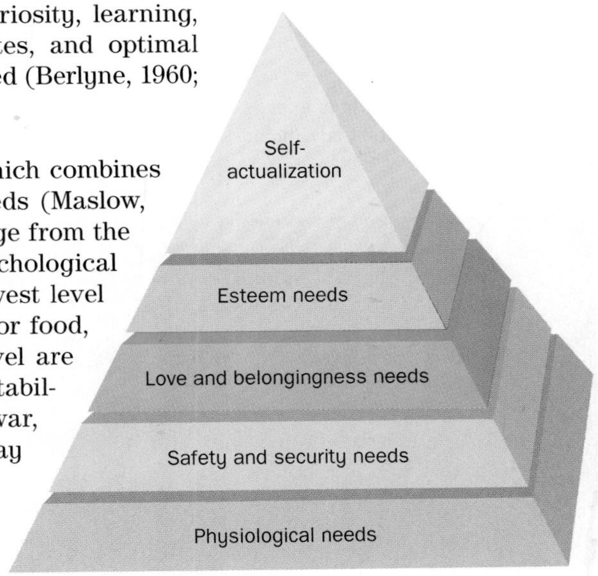

FIGURE **11.4**

MASLOW'S HIERARCHY OF NEEDS. According to this model, lower-level needs must be satisfied before we can focus on achieving self-actualization.

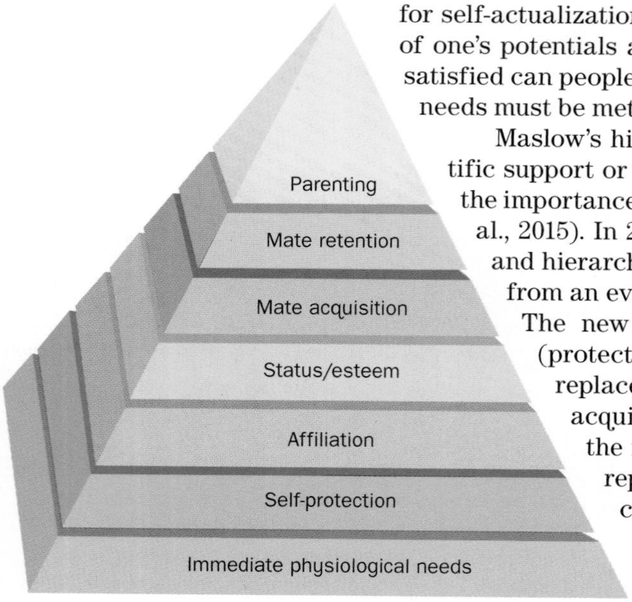

FIGURE **11.5**

EVOLUTIONARY UPDATE TO MASLOW'S HIERARCHY OF NEEDS. An evolutionary revision of Maslow's hierarchy of needs conceptualizes the stages as overlapping, rather than replacing, previous stages.

What are the major differences between Maslow's original hierarchy and Kenrick's updated model?

for self-actualization. Maslow defined **self-actualization** as the full realization of one's potentials and abilities in life. Only when lower-level needs have been satisfied can people focus on higher-level needs. For example, hunger and safety needs must be met before self-actualization needs can be fulfilled.

Maslow's hierarchy, although influential, has had relatively little scientific support or updating. Although the majority of psychologists recognize the importance of self-actualization, it can be tricky to measure (D'Souza et al., 2015). In 2010, Doug Kenrick and colleagues bridged the evolutionary and hierarchical models of motivation by modifying Maslow's hierarchy from an evolutionary perspective (Kenrick et al., 2010; see Figure 11.5). The new model builds on the basic needs—physiological, safety (protection), love and belongingness (affiliation), and esteem—and replaces self-actualization with three types of reproductive goals: acquiring a mate, retaining a mate, and parenting. In addition, in the new model, the levels self-actualization overlap rather than replace earlier needs, clarifying that they do not go away but can be activated when necessary.

Now we are ready to turn our attention to two very basic drive states: hunger and sex. In evolutionary terms, there is nothing more basic than the survival of the individual and the species.

Hunger: Survival of the Individual

LO3

All animals need to replenish the energy continuously being used by their bodies. The rate at which we consume energy is known as *metabolism*. When our energy has been depleted, hunger drives us to replenish it by eating. Hunger is not just an internal biological process, however. It is the product of biological processes interacting with external, environmental ones.

self-actualization
the inherent drive to realize one's full potential.

The Biology of When We Eat Internal signals control the desire to eat or stop eating. From a drive reduction perspective, being hungry depends not only on how much food we have consumed recently but also on how much energy is available for organ function. Hunger has four biological components: the stomach, the blood, the brain, and hormones and neurochemicals.

glucose
a simple sugar that provides energy for cells throughout the body, including the brain.

We've all noticed that when we get hungry, our stomach starts to growl. "Growling" results from gastric secretions that are activated by the brain when we think of, see, or smell food. Hunger can also cause the stomach to contract. Contractions occur when the stomach and small intestine have been relatively empty for about two hours. Although stomach contractions correspond with hunger pangs, they do not cause hunger: Humans who have their stomachs removed for medical reasons still feel hunger, as do rats in whom the nerves between the stomach and the brain have been severed (Brown & Wallace, 1980; Cannon & Washburn, 1912). So the stomach does not act by itself to produce feelings of hunger.

Hunger is a basic drive we share with other animals.

Blood is another important player in hunger. The most important source of energy for the body is cellular glucose. **Glucose** is a simple sugar in the blood that provides energy for cells throughout the body, including the brain. Although fat and protein provide their own forms of energy, some organs, including the brain, can use only glucose. Our blood sugar level drops when we go without eating for long periods. If this happens, the hypothalamus, which monitors glucose levels, triggers the drive to obtain food.

As with almost all behaviour, many regions of the brain are involved in eating behaviour. The hypothalamus regulates most basic physiological needs, including hunger. The hypothalamus is unique in that certain regions lack an effective blood brain barrier, which enable neurons to detect blood-borne nutrients, such as glucose (Delaere et al., 2010). In this way, it acts as hunger's sensory detector. Different parts of the hypothalamus, in turn, send signals to different brain regions to either start or stop eating (Berthoud, 2002; Stellar, 1954).

The **lateral hypothalamus** is often considered one of the main hunger centres in the hypothalamus. In rats, destruction of this area leads to a reduction in feeding, while stimulation promotes feeding—even in overfed animals. Lesioning of this area has also been performed in humans as a controversial treatment for obesity. In one study, surgeons first stimulated the lateral hypothalamic area in order to ensure that the lesion would target the hunger centre. Stimulation immediately triggered feelings of hunger. In fact, one patient stated, "I am so hungry that I could eat a whole fried chicken with chips" (Qaade et al., 1974). Subsequent destruction of this area reduced caloric intake and body weight in these patients. Although these results were promising, results were temporary, suggesting that other areas are also likely involved in hunger (Qaade et al., 1974). The **ventromedial hypothalamus** plays the complementary role of promoting satiety (feeling full). Destruction of this area leads to overfeeding and weight gain, while stimulation has the opposite effect (Kiba, 2002). Weight gain as a result of a ventromedial lesion is not solely due to overeating, since visceral organs, such as the stomach, small intestine, liver, and pancreas, grow more cells in the absence of ventromedial input. The ventromedial hypothalamus inhibits the parasympathetic nervous system, so when it is destroyed, the "rest and digest" activities of the visceral organs become more pronounced (Kintaka et al., 2009).

lateral hypothalamus region of the hypothalamus that promotes feeding.

ventromedial hypothalamus region of the hypothalamus that promotes satiety.

Hormones and neurochemicals also play a role in hunger, either by stimulating or suppressing appetite (Rowland, Li, & Morien, 1996; Williams et al., 2004). Neuropeptide Y (NPY), orexin, ghrelin, melanin, and the endocannabinoids all stimulate feeding (Williams et al., 2004). *Neuropeptide Y (NPY)* is released in the hypothalamus when an animal is hungry or underfed, and it stimulates appetite. *Ghrelin* is a hormone released from the digestive system; levels rise when we are hungry and fall drastically after we eat. It sends signals of hunger to the brain and also stimulates feeding. The endocannabinoids are naturally occurring neurochemicals that can increase appetite. Blocking receptor sites for endocannabinoids leads to a decrease in eating and to weight loss (Kirkham, 2005; Nicoll & Alger, 2004).

Connection

Endocannabinoids and their relative, marijuana, are used medically to treat cancer patients who are on chemotherapy, because they stimulate appetite.

See Chapter 5, LO10.

At least four hormones suppress appetite: insulin, leptin, peptide YY (PYY), and cholecystokinin (CCK; Williams et al., 2004). For example, one of the most important hormonal effects on hunger comes from *insulin,* which is produced by the pancreas. Rising glucose levels stimulate insulin production; insulin, in turn, transports glucose out of the blood and into the cells. As a result, hunger decreases.

The Psychology of What We Eat What we eat is shaped by both nature and nurture. We crave foods that are essential to our bodies but that were scarce during early periods of human evolution, but we also learn to like and crave particular foods common in our culture.

Food preferences are very much shaped by evolutionary forces. Without realizing it, most humans crave the basic nutrients that our bodies require and that were scarce during ancestral times: sugar, salt, and fat. The fast-food industry capitalizes on this fact by creating foods that are rich in these substances (Moss, 2013). Companies conduct research to determine precisely the optimal

Would you eat raw blubber? How about brains? What do you think guides your food preferences?

levels of flavours that people crave—the so-called bliss point. Sweets and fats are no longer scarce in industrialized society, and their easy access and over-consumption contribute to increasing problems of obesity.

Our choice of what we eat is also driven by culture. That some people eat cows and others eat worms is, for the most part, culturally determined. Different cultures expose children to different flavours. Exposure does not immediately lead to preference, however (Pliner, 1982; Rozin, 1996). It often takes multiple exposures, perhaps eight to ten, before children will come to like a food that they initially disliked (Birch & Fischer, 1996; Birch & Marlin, 1982). Different cultures expose children to their unique flavour combinations, which means that different cultures shape food preferences while people are young. For instance, people in very cold climates commonly eat raw animal fat: Icelanders eat raw whale blubber pickled in whey; the Inuit eat raw seal fat. In contrast, cow brains and tongue are commonly eaten in Mexico. The more often people eat certain foods, the more they like them. Once people develop a preference for a kind of food, they are motivated and even driven to eat that kind of food. If, for example, you develop a strong liking for Mexican food, but then spend a year studying in Europe or Asia, where there is little Mexican food, you will probably be driven to seek out and find any kind of burrito.

Challenge Your Assumptions

True or False? Craving sweet, fatty, and salty foods is a socially and culturally determined preference.

False: The fact that we crave basic foodstuffs is heavily influenced by evolutionary forces.

The Psychology of When and How Much We Eat Ever wonder why late-night television food ads make you want to snack? Although we may feel that our eating behaviour is controlled by feelings of how hungry or full we feel, signals outside the body have a very strong impact on the timing and size of our meals. Visual or auditory cues associated with food through classical conditioning can trigger feeding, even in individuals who have just eaten a meal (Weingarten, 1983). Research by Brian Wansink at Cornell University suggests that we rely upon our eyes, not our stomachs, to tell us when we are full. In one clever experiment, participants were instructed to eat as much tomato soup as they liked, either from a normal bowl or a secretly self-refilling bowl. Those who had soup from the self-refilling bowl consumed more calories than the control group, even though they estimated that they ate the same amount (Wansink et al., 2005). In other words, participants relied upon what their eyes told them to gauge portion size. Further research by Wansink has shown that changing the appearance of food portions might be useful as a strategy for weight control. In another experiment, participants were given a 400-calorie portion of crackers, either in a single package or four 100-calorie packages. Participants given the smaller packages actually ate less than those given the same calories in one large portion, possibly because by pausing to open a new package, they were more aware of how much they were eating (Wansink et al., 2011).

The Motive to Be Thin and the Tendency toward Obesity Fat provides a store of energy for future use. In our evolutionary past, this was important, in case food became scarce. But in modern industrialized societies with abundant food, fat is a liability. We no longer need to consume large quantities of food against the day when there isn't enough to eat. Moreover, because our lifestyle is sedentary compared with earlier times, we need less food to be healthy. Even our ideas about beauty have been transformed as a result of having more food available than we need. Thinness has come to define attractiveness, and being thin has become a cultural obsession. Surveys indicate that roughly half of Canadians are currently dieting (Pérusse-Lachance et al., 2010; Health Canada, 2002). Although most dieters aim to lose weight, only a minority maintain long-lasting weight loss. Furthermore, dieting is associated with other problems such as mood and cognitive disturbances, and is a significant risk factor for the development of eating disorders (Polivy & Herman, 1992).

Sometimes a person's relationship with food can become maladaptive. The two most prevalent eating disorders are anorexia nervosa and bulimia nervosa. People diagnosed with **anorexia nervosa** cannot maintain 85 percent of their ideal body weight for their height, have an intense fear of eating, and have a distorted body image (American Psychiatric Association, 2000). Moreover, they do not recognize that they are unusually thin or that they have an eating disorder. The other major eating disorder is bulimia nervosa. A person suffering from **bulimia nervosa** is prone to binge eating and feeling a lack of control during the eating session. Binge eating involves eating much more food at one time than the average person would, such as having a full tub of ice cream as a late-night snack. A person with bulimia regularly engages in either self-induced vomiting, use of laxatives or diuretics, strict dieting, or fasting in order to prevent weight gain.

anorexia nervosa
an eating disorder in which people cannot maintain 85 percent of their ideal body weight for their height, have an intense fear of eating, and have a distorted body image.

bulimia nervosa
an eating disorder characterized by binge eating and a perceived lack of control during the eating session.

The causes of anorexia are unknown, although a number of factors have been identified that put people at risk for this disorder, such as reactivity to stress, genetics, and personality. Women are much more likely than men to develop anorexia or bulimia (Nolen-Hoeksema, 2008). Women with eating disorders show higher physiological reactivity to stress. A study of more than 31 000 fraternal and identical twin pairs (both male and female) from Sweden examined the genetics of anorexia nervosa (Bulik et al., 2006). By comparing twins raised apart to twins raised together, one can estimate how much of a trait is attributable to genetics and how much to environment. This study reported that 56 percent of the variability in whether or not people develop anorexia nervosa is

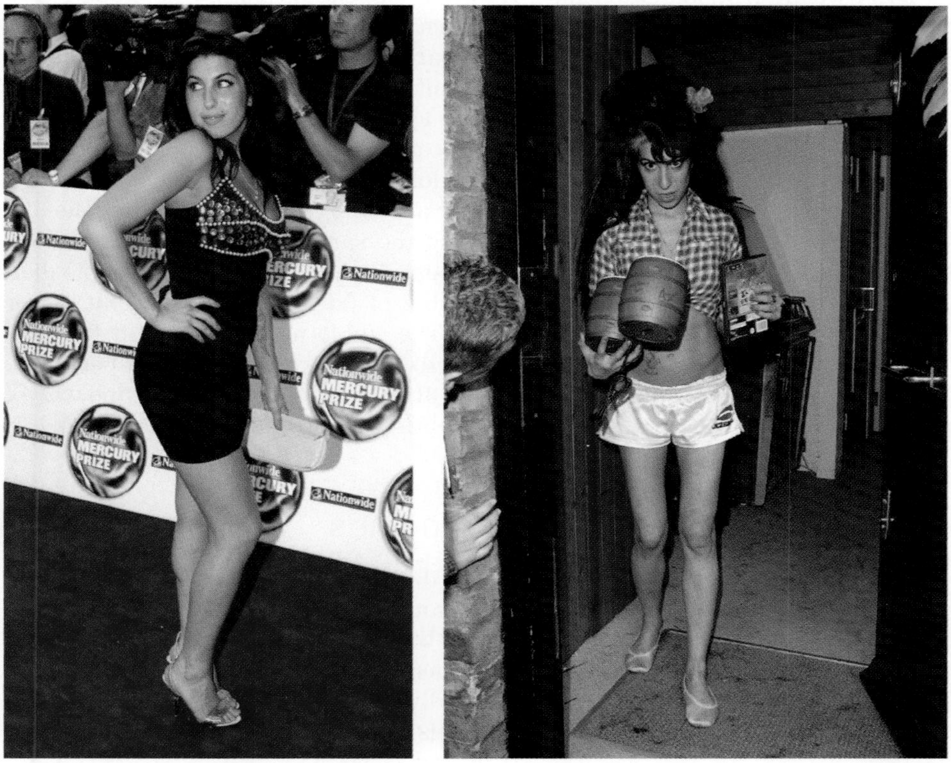

Singer-songwriter Amy Winehouse suffered a very public battle with substance abuse, but she also struggled with bulimia throughout her life.

attributable to genetic influence, with most of the remaining influence (38 percent) being attributable to the common environments shared by family members. Moreover, people who had demonstrated a proneness to anxiety, depression, and low self-esteem (as measured by the trait of neuroticism) later were more likely to develop anorexia. Other studies have found that many personality traits distinguish anorexics from other people: In addition to being higher in neuroticism, anorexics are also more conscientious, more introverted, and less open to new and novel situations than are non-anorexics (Bollen & Wojciechowski, 2004).

At the other end of the spectrum is obesity, which has increased dramatically in the population over the past several decades. How do we define obesity? Any definition of being overweight must consider both height and weight. Therefore, in evaluating an individual's weight we use a measure termed the *body mass index (BMI)*. BMI is determined by dividing weight by height to yield a weight-to-height ratio. The healthiest BMI range is between 20 and 25, with 26 to 29.9 considered overweight and 30 or above considered obese. In 2004, the Canadian Community Health Survey reported that over one-third of adult Canadians were overweight and roughly 23 percent were obese. Moreover, rates of obesity have climbed over the last 30 years—from 14 percent in the late 1970s (Statistics Canada, 2008). Adverse health outcomes associated with obesity are strongly linked to distribution of fat in the abdominal region (Blüher, 2010); therefore, many studies have specifically focused on abdominal obesity as a major health concern. A recent national survey showed that the percentage of Canadians with abdominal obesity has increased dramatically over the past 20 years (Janssen et al., 2010). Unhealthy weight gain has also risen dramatically in groups that traditionally showed low rates of obesity, such as in children and adolescents.

As discussed earlier, weight gain is clearly subject to environmental influence. This is not to say, however, that biological factors play no role in being overweight or obese. They do, as genes appear to be responsible for about 70 percent of adult weight (Allison et al., 1994; Hamer & Copeland, 1998). One study found that adults who had been adopted as children were much closer in weight to their biological parents than to their adoptive parents (Maes, Neale, & Eaves, 1997). Certain types of obesity are caused by a mutation to the gene that produces the leptin hormone, which normally suppresses appetite (Hamer & Copeland, 1998).

Genes also control the number of fat cells a person has: The number of fat cells a person has is set by childhood and adolescence and does not change much after that (Spalding et al., 2008). Each year about 10 percent of our fat cells die, but they are replaced by roughly the same number of new fat cells (Spalding et al., 2008). Dieting does not change this. When people diet, they are not decreasing the number of fat cells they have, but rather how much fat each cell stores. The stable number of adult fat cells may explain why it is so difficult to keep off weight that has been lost. Indeed, a recent meta-analysis of 31 studies reported that losing weight is relatively easy, but keeping it off is very difficult (Mann et al., 2007).

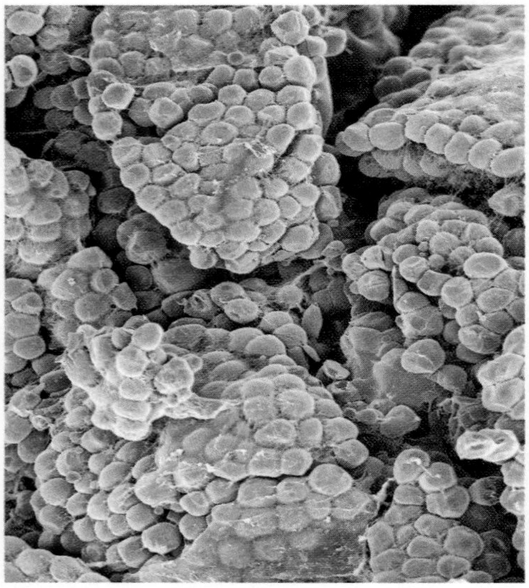

Fat cells.

Sex: Survival of the Species

LO4

Without food, we would starve to death. Without sex, individuals would not die, but if everyone went without sex, our species would die. So the simplest answer to the question "Why do we have sex?" would be "To propagate the species." Such an answer is useful at the species level but not at the individual level. As individuals we have sex for the simple reason that it is enjoyable and feels good.

Human Sexual Response Like many basic questions, "What is sex?" is more complex than it would appear. For the sake of clarity, we define **sexual behaviour** as actions that produce arousal and increase the likelihood of orgasm.

sexual behaviour
actions that produce arousal and increase the likelihood of orgasm.

Masters and Johnson (1966) were the first scientists to study the human sexual response systematically and directly. One of their major findings was that men and women go through four phases of sexual arousal, but do so somewhat differently (see Figure 11.6). The four phases are excitement, plateau, orgasm, and resolution. The major signs of the initial excitement phase are vaginal lubrication in the female and erection in the male. In the second phase, plateau, excitement level remains high but is pre-orgasmic. In men, the plateau phase might be rather short, but orgasm almost always follows. In women, the plateau phase often lasts longer than in men and is not necessarily followed by orgasm. In fact, some women stay in the plateau phase for a while and then pass to the resolution phase without achieving orgasm. These women also have a gradual resolution phase. An even more striking gender difference is the ability of some women to have multiple orgasms. Men always have a refractory period immediately following orgasm in which erection is lost and orgasm is not possible, but some women may go on to have multiple orgasms.

Updated models of female sexual arousal suggest that the initial sexual response in women involves more psychological processes than simply arousal and desire (Basson, 2001). Desire and arousal do not happen spontaneously in many women, who often require the right balance of thoughts and feelings dealing with intimacy, closeness, trust, and lack of fear and anxiety. Only if these conditions are met will arousal happen. These thoughts and feelings play off and feed arousal, which in turn leads to deeper feelings of intimacy and closeness. Arousal continues to increase and may or may not lead to orgasm, but arousal and excitement are important and meaningful even without orgasm (Basson, 2001).

The Biology of Sexual Behaviour This newer model of sexual response matches well with brain imaging research on sexual arousal, including orgasm. Many brain regions involved in emotion, which we will discuss shortly, are also involved in the earlier stages of sexual arousal, prior to orgasm. As is true of

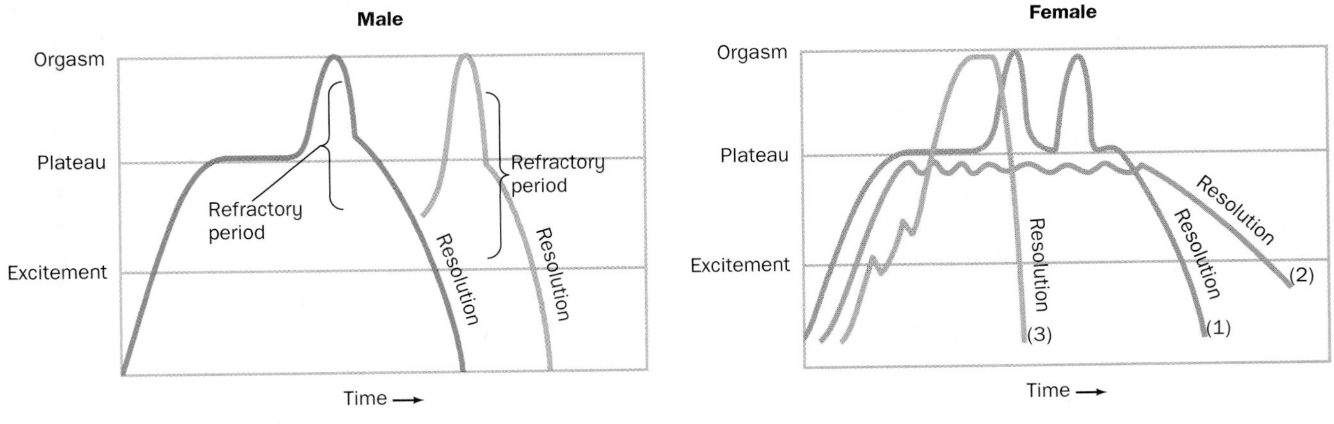

FIGURE **11.6**
THE SEXUAL RESPONSE CYCLE IN MEN AND WOMEN. The four phases are excitement, plateau, orgasm, and resolution. Women are more varied in their sexual response than men. There are at least three distinct types of response in women. In (1) we see a response pattern much like men's, except that there is the possibility of multiple orgasm. In (2) we see a woman who gets aroused and stays at the plateau level, never reaching orgasm. In (3) we see a pattern where the woman gets aroused and excited, skips the plateau phase and has a quick resolution phase. In men, there is only one pattern, though sometimes second orgasm can occur after a refractory period. (*Source:* Passer & Smith, 1998.)

Testosterone, the primary male sex hormone, also controls women's sex drive.

many physiological drives, such as hunger, the hypothalamus plays a crucial role in sexual behaviour (Dominguez & Hull, 2005; Melis & Argiolis, 1995). In humans, lesions to parts of the hypothalamus lead to a decrease in sexual behaviour, whereas electrically stimulating the same regions leads to an increase in sexual behaviour, especially in males (Baird et al., 2007; Dominguez & Hull, 2005). In addition, the part of the hypothalamus involved in sexual behaviour is larger in men than in women (Allen & Gorski, 2007).

As you might expect, brain activity changes during orgasm—surprisingly, certain brain regions actually shut down. Gert Holstege and colleagues from the Netherlands took brain images of women while they were having an orgasm (being manually stimulated by their partners) and while they were faking it (Georgiadis et al., 2006). Achieving a real orgasm always involved deactivation of brain regions involved with fear and anxiety in the amygdala and hippocampus as well as parts of the cortex involved in consciousness. During faked orgasms, however, these brain regions remained activated. Men too show brain deactivation during orgasm, but only in the left amygdala (Holstege et al., 2003).

Testosterone, the major male sex hormone, controls sex drive in both men and women (Morris et al., 1987; Persky et al., 1978). The role of testosterone in the female sex drive was discovered accidentally when women whose adrenal glands were removed lost their sex drive (Waxenberg, Drellich, & Sutherland, 1959). The adrenal glands produce testosterone in both males and females, as well as other hormones. Younger women have both higher levels of male sex hormones and more frequent sexual activity than do older women (Persky et al., 1982). Indeed, males and females with high baseline levels of testosterone are more sexually active at earlier ages and engage in sex more frequently than those with low baseline levels of testosterone. Similarly, testosterone treatments appear to increase sex drive in women (Bolour & Braunstein, 2005).

In most species, females are not continually receptive to males. Although women are not nearly as cyclical in their sexual desire as are females of other species, there is, in fact, some regular cyclical activity and interest in the course of the 28-day menstrual cycle. Female-initiated sexual behaviour peaks around ovulation and again before and after menstruation (Bullivant et al., 2004; Ford & Beach, 1951; Udry, Morris, & Waller, 1973). The strongest cyclical effect for women, however, occurs in relation to their fantasies involving men other than their regular sex partner (Buss, 2003). As women approach ovulation, the frequency and intensity of their fantasies involving sex with men other than their partner increase (Bullivant et al., 2004). Such an increase in sex drive makes sense from an evolutionary perspective, because a woman is most likely to become pregnant during ovulation.

In restrictive societies, sex is typically forbidden outside of marriage.

Culture and Sexual Behaviour What is acceptable and normal sexual behaviour varies from culture to culture. In a classic study of sexual behaviour and culture, Clellan Ford and Frank Beach (1951) studied attitudes toward sex before and after marriage in 190 different cultures. They identified three kinds of societies in terms of sexual attitudes: *restrictive societies* restrict sex before and outside of marriage; *semirestrictive societies* place formal prohibitions on pre- and extramarital sex that are not strictly enforced; and *permissive societies* place few restrictions on sex. Thirty years later, Broude and Greene (1980) conducted a similar study of 141 non-Western cultures and found that for women, premarital sex was mildly to moderately disapproved of in 30 percent of the societies and strongly disapproved of in 26 percent. Extramarital sex was common among men in 69 percent of the cultures and among women in 57 percent of the cultures.

Challenge Your Assumptions

True or False? Men and women have similar attitudes about casual sex.

False: Women are, in fact, less willing to engage in casual sex with a stranger than are men.

Gender and the Drive for Casual Sex The belief that men are more promiscuous than women is widespread, but is it true? In a word, yes. Research consistently shows that men are more willing and interested in casual sex than are women (see, for example, Bailey, Kirk, et al., 2000; Buss, 2003; Clark & Hatfield, 1989; Maticka-Tyndale, Harold, & Opperman, 2003). For instance, in a meta-analysis of 177 studies of gender and sexual attitudes and behaviour published between 1966 and 1990, Oliver and Hyde (1993) reported that men, on average, have much more positive attitudes toward casual sex and are slightly more likely to approve of premarital or extramarital sex. Russell Clark III and Elaine Hatfield (1989, 2003) conducted a classic study on the question of gender differences and casual sex. Research assistants approached strangers of the opposite sex and asked them whether they would be willing to either go on a date, come over, or go to bed with them. As you can see in Figure 11.7, the results were striking. Three-quarters of the men responded that they were willing to have sex with a stranger of the opposite sex, but not one woman was willing to do so!

The huge gender difference in attitudes about casual sex is often explained using *parental investment theory*. If pregnancy results, the cost of having sex is quite different for men and women (Trivers, 1972). Biologically speaking, for men the only assured contribution to parenthood is the act of sex itself. If a woman becomes pregnant, however, her contribution includes nine months of carrying the fetus and many years of caring for the child. It follows, therefore, that women would be less motivated to have sex with little emotional commitment—a single sexual encounter could have consequences that endure a lifetime. On the surface, this theory appears to make a lot of sense, since it provides a tidy, biologically based explanation for these large gender differences. However, this perspective has been harshly criticized for being too narrow and failing to consider other equally plausible explanations (Meynell, 2012). Despite the differences in attitudes toward casual sex, research shows that men and women show remarkably similar attitudes about love (Fehr et al., 2001). Although some consistent gender differences in romantic relationships have been well documented, they can be easily explained by social factors, such as culture and early socialization experiences which reinforce very different behavioural norms for girls and boys (Sprecher et al., 2007).

Boys and girls are often given different toys to play with from an early age. How could this contribute to gender differences in behaviour?

Sexual Orientation What drives most people to be attracted predominantly to the opposite sex, yet a significant minority to be attracted to the same sex? **Sexual orientation** is our disposition to be attracted to either the opposite sex (heterosexual), the same sex (homosexual), or both sexes (bisexual). Historically, sexual orientation was thought of as an either–or proposition—a person was either heterosexual or homosexual. But in the 1940s Alfred Kinsey

sexual orientation
the disposition to be attracted to either the opposite sex (heterosexual), the same sex (homosexual), or both sexes (bisexual).

Research Process

1 Research Question

Are there differences between men and women in their interest in casual sex? The researchers hypothesized that men are more eager for casual sex than are women.

2 Method

Clark and Hatfield (1989) developed a brief survey to address the research question. Research assistants who were college students approached students of the opposite sex. After a brief introduction, the research assistant would ask each student one of these questions: "Would you go out with me tonight?" "Would you come over to my apartment tonight?" or "Would you go to bed with me tonight?"

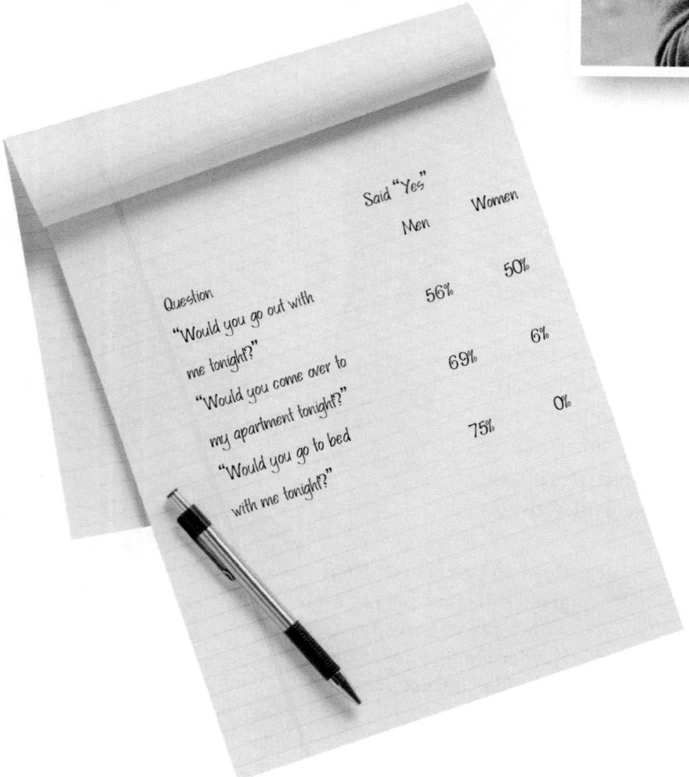

Said "Yes"
Men
Women
Question
"Would you go out with me tonight?"
56%
50%
"Would you come over to my apartment tonight?"
69%
6%
"Would you go to bed with me tonight?"
75%
0%

3 Results

This table gives responses to the various questions, by gender.

4 Conclusion

Men and women were equally likely to agree to go on a date with someone they didn't really know. As the proposal became increasingly intimate, however, women backed off. Consistent with the hypothesis, men were much more likely than women to agree to have sex.

FIGURE **11.7**

GENDER AND CASUAL SEX. A simple survey revealed gender differences in the interest in casual sex. When approached, most men will agree to casual sex with an opposite-sex stranger, while most women will not. (*Source:* R.D. Clark III & E. Hatfield. 1989. Gender differences in willingness to engage in casual sex. *Journal of Psychology and Human Sexuality, 2,* 39–55.)

Can you think of reasons why women are less accepting of casual sex than men?

proposed a now-standard view of sexual orientation: It exists on a continuum from exclusively heterosexual to exclusively homosexual (Kinsey, Pomeroy, & Martin, 1948). After interviewing thousands of individuals, Kinsey and his colleagues realized that sexual orientation was not either–or and devised a seven-point scale extending from 0 to 6. Zero was exclusively heterosexual and 6 exclusively homosexual. Most people fall between 0 and 2 but a consistent minority of people exist on the homosexual end of the scale. Between 1 percent and 5 percent of the adult male population and 1 percent and 3.5 percent of the adult female population classify themselves as predominantly homosexual (LeVay & Hamer, 1994; Tarmann, 2002). For men, sexual orientation tends to be either–or, producing a dip between 2 and 4 on Kinsey's seven-point scale (the "bisexual" range). For women, however, there is a more gradual decrease from exclusively heterosexual to exclusively homosexual, with more women than men identifying themselves as bisexual (Diamond, 2008; Hamer & Copeland, 1998; Rahman, 2005).

Many people wonder what causes a person to be sexually attracted to someone of the opposite sex or the same sex. The age-old nature–nurture question inevitably arises: Is sexual orientation more a result of biology or of upbringing and environment? Both are involved in sexual orientation, and in complex ways (Bailey, Dunne, & Martin, 2000). There is evidence that our first biological environment—the womb—exerts a long-term effect on our sexual orientation. Research has revealed that, to some extent, individuals exposed to relatively high levels of testosterone in the womb are more likely to be attracted to women, whereas those exposed to relatively low levels of testosterone are more likely to be attracted to men (Cohen, 2002; Ellis & Ames, 1987; Rahman, 2005). These findings are not fully replicated and more research is needed before people can draw conclusions about the role of prenatal testosterone exposure in sexual orientation.

Genetic research suggests that sexual orientation is partly under genetic influence, at least in men. Studies of twins indicate that genetics plays a bigger role in determining sexual orientation in men than in women. For women, environmental factors seem to have a strong influence on sexual orientation. Female twins raised in the same household are much more likely to have the same sexual orientation than are females twins raised in different households, regardless of whether they are identical or fraternal twins. For males, degree of genetic relationship seems to matter most in twin sexual orientation (Bailey, Dunne, & Martin, 2000; Demir & Dickson, 2005; Hamer & Copeland, 1998; Hyde, 2005; Rahman, 2005).

Scholars have also proposed a number of social-environmental theories to explain the origins of sexual orientation. These theories argue that sexual orientation is a social construction (Bell, Weinberg, & Hammersmith, 1981; Van Wyk & Geist, 1984). Some social-environmental theories of sexual orientation have argued, for example, that child play, early peer relations, differences in how parents treat boys and girls, and gender identity are important factors in the development of sexual orientation, both heterosexual and homosexual. For instance, many studies report that engaging in play more typical of the opposite sex early in childhood predicts a homosexual orientation later in life, in both men and women (Bailey & Zucker, 1995; Cohen, 2002). These environmental theories are quite

Acceptance of the diversity of sexual orientation is promoted during Pride week celebrations across Canada.

consistent with biological ones. Biology could start the development of sexual orientation, which in turn would be strengthened or discouraged by environmental factors. The two sets of explanations work best in cooperation rather than competition.

The Needs to Belong and to Excel

As we saw in Maslow's hierarchy of needs, human needs extend beyond the physiological needs of hunger and sex. The need for social contact and belonging is a powerful and universal need. Psychologists call this the *need for affiliation*. The need to excel, achieve, and be competitive with others is also a powerful and universal one. Psychologists call this the *need for achievement*.

achievement motivation
a desire to do things well and overcome obstacles.

Connection

Affiliation with others is so important that social exclusion physically hurts and activates pain regions in the brain involved in physical pain.

See Chapter 14, LO7.

The Need to Belong: Affiliation Humans are inherently social creatures. We depend on other people our entire lives, especially at life's beginning and end. It is not surprising, therefore, that our need to belong and to be accepted by others is one of the strongest of all human needs (Adler, 1956; Baumeister & Leary, 1995; Murray, 1938/1962). Almost every close relationship in our lives is driven by this need.

The opposite of being accepted is being rejected, which can be one of the more painful experiences in life. Baumeister and Leary (1995) reviewed evidence that lack of belongingness and being rejected lead to both physical health and psychological problems, ranging from having more health problems to developing eating disorders, from being more depressed to being more likely to commit suicide. Moreover, being rejected also makes people more prone to get angry and lash out and be aggressive toward others (Leary et al., 2006). Many explosive violent episodes are preceded by the person's being fired from work or being rejected by peers, a lover, or a spouse (Williams & Zudro, 2001). For example, many of the school shootings, such as École Polytechnique in Montreal and Columbine High School and Virginia Tech in the United States, have been carried out by boys and men who were teased and rejected by their peers (Leary et al., 2003).

Despite falling short of his goal to run across Canada, Terry Fox's 143 day, 5373 km Marathon of Hope from St. John's to Thunder Bay inspired Canadians and millions of others across the world to support his cause to fight cancer. Terry's determination and motivation live on through the Terry Fox Foundation, which has raised hundreds of millions for cancer research.

The Need to Excel: Achievement Some people have a tremendous need to excel and to be the best at what they do. Many successful athletes, businesspeople, and politicians, for example, are driven by such a need. But in truth, almost everyone strives to overcome shortcomings and imperfections (Adler, 1956). In the process, some people compete fiercely with other people, whereas others compete more with themselves simply to do the best they can.

The motivation to succeed raises the question of how to define achievement and success. McClelland and his colleague Atkinson emphasized that **achievement motivation** is a desire to do things well and overcome difficulties and obstacles (McClelland, 1985). However, those obstacles can be measured only in terms of one's goals. When David (the brother of one of the authors, whom you met in Chapter 5) was coming out of his vegetative state following his bicycle accident, lifting a finger was a tremendous achievement. Yet, for a highly driven, accomplished, and motivated athlete, a silver medal at the Olympics might be a crushing defeat.

Atkinson (1964) argued that the tendency to achieve success is a function of three things: motivation to succeed, expectation of success, and the incentive value of the success (see also McClelland, 1985). Let's apply Atkinson's model to a familiar example: your motivation to obtain a good grade in this introductory psychology course. Your *motivation to succeed* is the extent to which you really want to be successful. In a course such as introductory psychology, success will have different meanings for different students. For some, an A– might be a horrible failure, whereas for others a B+ might be a great accomplishment.

Expectation of success is an individual's evaluation of the likelihood of succeeding at a task. Your evaluation of your performance in this course consists of two different beliefs: whether you have the ability to do well and what the actual outcome is likely to be. These two beliefs may not match. For instance, some students may see themselves as quite capable, but due to other circumstances, such as missing several classes, they may not obtain a high grade for the course.

Incentive value stems from two factors. First, success at the task has to be important to you. Second, the more difficult the task and the lower the odds of succeeding at it, the more it will mean to you if you do succeed. Applied to taking this course, the incentive value for doing well differs depending on what a good grade in the course means to you. If you are a psychology major and the GPA in your major plays an important role in your class standing or whether you keep your scholarship, the grade in Intro Psych might have a higher incentive value than it would if you were a physics major taking the course to satisfy a general education requirement. In addition, the difficulty of a task plays a role in its incentive value. Succeeding at something that is very difficult means more to most people than succeeding at something they consider easy, because the easier task does not provide much feedback about ability. Likewise, failing at a difficult task may not provide much useful feedback concerning your abilities. Intuitively most people shy away from tasks that they perceive as very easy or very difficult and seek to tackle tasks that are moderately challenging.

Quick Quiz 11.1: Motivation

1. Which model of motivation can be compared to the thermostat in your house?
   a. evolutionary
   b. drive reduction
   c. optimal arousal
   d. hierarchical

2. Which of the following hormones does *not* stimulate hunger?
   a. orexin
   b. ghrelin
   c. neuropeptide Y
   d. cholecystokinin

3. Most research on weight loss has reported that
   a. losing weight is very difficult for most people.
   b. losing weight is relatively easy, but keeping it off is very difficult.
   c. keeping weight off is relatively easy for most people.
   d. losing weight is relatively easy and so too is keeping it off.

4. Brain imaging research has found that during orgasm
   a. some parts of the brain "shut down" and become deactivated.
   b. most of the brain becomes very active.
   c. only the brain stem is active.
   d. the insula becomes very active.

Answers can be found at the end of the chapter.

LO5 EMOTION

Not all of our actions stem from basic drives or higher motivations. Sometimes we are motivated to do something simply because it makes us happy. In this sense, emotions are motivators too.

Basic drives such as hunger and sex differ from emotions in important ways. First, drives are linked with very specific needs, whereas emotions are not (Tomkins, 1962, 1981). Hunger comes from a need for food, thirst from a need for water, lust from a need for sex. But joy can be associated with just about anything: smelling a rose, visiting a friend, reading a good book, or seeing a beautiful sunset. Also, emotions can override biological drives (Tomkins, 1962). For instance, the emotion of disgust can easily override the fundamental drive of hunger. A sandwich is less appealing after a fly lands on it or if, on closer contact, it smells bad.

How can the emotion of disgust override a drive as strong as hunger? Disgust is important for survival. It arises when we have come across something that is potentially toxic or harmful. Sometimes disgust can override drives if we just think something is disgusting, even if we know it is not. Consider how you would react if you were asked to hold a piece of rubber that is joke vomit between your lips. How about a rubber eraser? Studies show that most people are disgusted by the fake vomit but would willingly put the eraser between their lips (Rozin & Fallon, 1987). We know they are made of the same substance and are equally sanitary, but the basic need to avoid contamination overwhelms our sense of reason. This fear of contagion appears in cultures all over the world (Nemeroff & Rozin, 1994; Rozin & Fallon, 1987).

Other negative emotional states can also enhance hunger. For instance, depressed mood enhances appetite and preference for sweet foods. In one study, negative mood was induced in participants by having them solve arithmetic problems while listening to loud white noise. Mistakes were punished with an increase in the noise volume, producing a stress reaction and reductions in mood. After the stress task, participants reported feeling hungry and had greater cravings for sweet foods (Verschoor et al., 2010). Stress reduces brain serotonin levels, and can therefore lower mood. Since brain serotonin levels are controlled by diet, eating carbohydrate-rich foods boosts serotonin release. Therefore an enhanced preference for sweets is thought to be one way to counteract the mood-altering effects of stress (Wurtman & Wurtman, 1995).

In this part of the chapter we explore what emotions are, why we have them, and how they affect our thoughts and bodily systems.

Defining Emotion

Emotions emerge from our interactions with the world around us. They are triggered by situations that are relevant to our personal goals, physical safety, or well-being. Because emotions stem from situations that are important to us, they reveal much about what makes us tick.

emotions
brief, acute changes in conscious experience and physiology that occur in response to a personally meaningful situation.

moods
affective states that operate in the background of consciousness and tend to last longer than most emotions.

affective traits
stable predispositions toward certain types of emotional responses such as anger.

Types of Affect Psychologists use the term *affect* to refer to a variety of emotional phenomena, including emotions, moods, and affective traits. **Emotions** are brief, acute changes in conscious experience and physiology that occur in response to a meaningful situation in the person's environment. Emotions make us pay attention, forcing us to set priorities and deal with life-relevant situations (Ekman, 1992; Lazarus, 1991; Levenson, 1994). They occupy the foreground of our consciousness, often dominating our awareness. In fact, emotions can impact memory, perception, attention, and decision making (Cohen, 2005; Phelps, 2006).

Moods are transient changes in affect that fluctuate throughout the day or over several days. We experience moods both physiologically and psychologically, and they tend to last longer than most emotions (Ekman, 1984; Davidson, 1994; Hedges, Jandorf, & Stone, 1985). Moods make certain emotions more likely to occur than others. An irritable mood, for instance, makes people more easily angered than usual. A slight inconvenience that would not ordinarily bother you, such as having to wait in line at the supermarket checkout, might cause you to act rudely toward the clerk.

Affective traits are enduring aspects of our personalities that set the threshold for the occurrence of particular emotional states (Ekman, 1984;

Judging from her expression, what do you think this woman is feeling?

Connection

We tend to remember emotional events better than non-emotional events.

See Chapter 6, "Emotional Memory."

Lazarus, 1991; Rosenberg, 1998). Consider the example of being cut off in traffic. People who have the affective trait of hostility are most likely to feel anger. They aren't always angry, but they have hair triggers. For several minutes or likely even longer, these people will continue focusing on the event—how they were wronged—and they feel the emotion of anger. Then the event recedes from consciousness, and the feelings of anger go with it. Nonetheless, they may remain in a more diffuse, less focused, less pressing irritable mood. By the end of the day, they may still be in a bad mood but not even realize it.

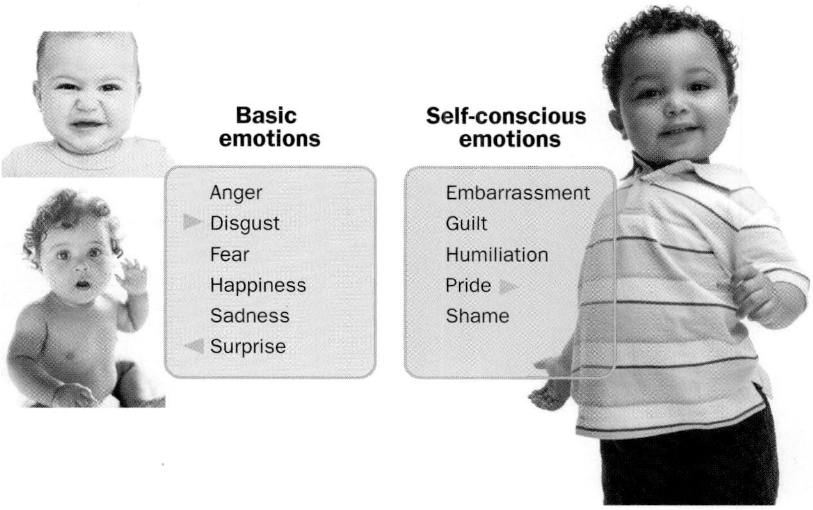

Basic emotions
Anger
Disgust
Fear
Happiness
Sadness
Surprise
Self-conscious emotions
Embarrassment
Guilt
Humiliation
Pride
Shame

FIGURE 11.8
BASIC AND SELF-CONSCIOUS EMOTIONS. (*Source:* Ekman, 1992; Tracy, Robins, & Tangney, 2007.)

Emotions, Basic Emotions, and the Dimensions of Affect A small set of emotions seems to be common to all humans and a product of our evolutionary past (Ekman, 1992). These **basic emotions** are anger, disgust, fear, happiness, sadness, and surprise (see Figure 11.8). These emotions reflect fundamental emotional states that play a role in essential life tasks, such as protecting oneself and loved ones from harm (fear), progressing toward the realization of a goal (happiness), or experiencing irrevocable loss (sadness) (Ekman, 1992; Lazarus, 1991). Basic emotions are only a small set of the infinite variety of emotional states humans can experience.

basic emotions
set of emotions that are common to all humans; includes anger, disgust, fear, happiness, sadness, and surprise.

The basic emotions are not single states; rather, they are categories or groups of related emotions. Ekman (1992) describes such a grouping as an *emotion family*. For instance, the fear family may arise in response to a threat to physical safety. This family includes such emotions as anxiety, trepidation, and nervousness. The happiness family of emotions includes joy, contentment, elation, amusement, and exhilaration, among others.

Other theorists argue that all emotions are states that vary in their degree of pleasantness and arousal (Clark, Watson, & Leeka, 1989; Russell, 1980; Watson & Tellegen, 1985; Woodworth & Schlossberg, 1954). Figure 11.9 shows how these underlying dimensions of pleasantness and arousal might explain a number of emotions.

self-conscious emotions
types of emotion that require a sense of self and the ability to reflect on actions; they occur as a function of meeting expectations (or not) and abiding (or not) by society's rules.

Self-Conscious Emotions The feeling of pride a child feels at learning how to ride a bike and the shame of being caught in a lie are examples of **self-conscious emotions,** which are emotions that occur as a function of how well we live up to our expectations, the expectations of others, or the rules set by society (see Figure 11.8; Tracy, Robins, & Tangney, 2007; Tangney, Stuewig, & Mashek, 2007). These emotions require a sense of self and the ability to reflect on one's own actions. They include shame, guilt, humiliation, embarrassment, and pride.

Self-conscious emotions are displayed by distinct and recognizable expressions. Displaying pride involves specific body movements, a smile, head tilted upward, with slightly expanded chest. People show elements of this behaviour when in situations that produce pride, such as winning medals at the Olympics (Tracy & Matsumoto, 2008). This expression is recognized as pride by children and adults in North America and by people in a preliterate, socially isolated tribe in West Africa (Tracy & Robins, 2008). This cross-cultural recognition data from very diverse groups suggest that this pride expression may be common across the globe, and may be a way to signal our successes to others.

Embarrassment, on the other hand, is a self-conscious emotion that we display when we have violated some social rule. People often get giggly when embarrassed and act as if they want to make amends for some sort of social

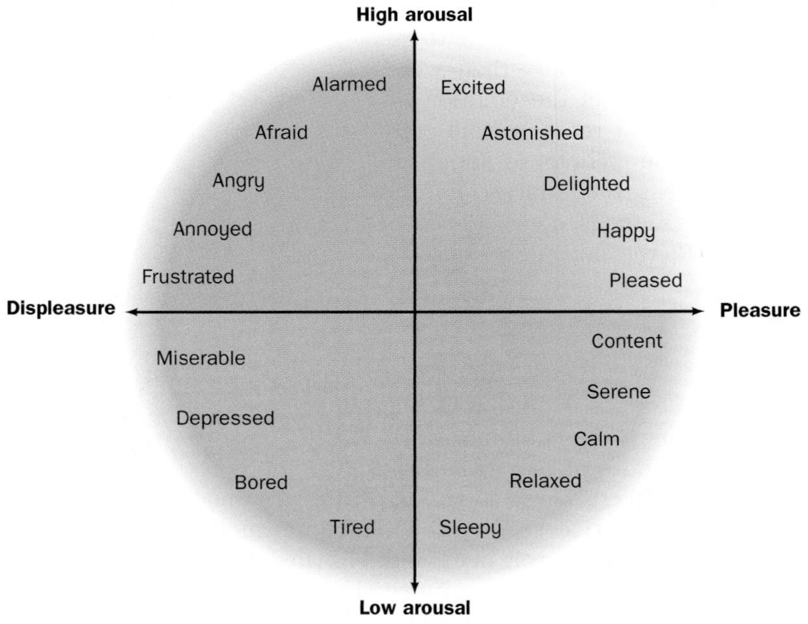

FIGURE **11.9**

MODEL OF EMOTIONS AS COMBINATIONS OF AROUSAL AND PLEASURE. According to Russell's (1980) model of emotion, all emotions can be placed in two dimensions, arousal and pleasure–displeasure. For example, being afraid is a state of high arousal and displeasure, whereas being happy is a pleasant and moderately aroused state. (*Source:* Russell, 1980) transgression (Keltner, 1995; Tangney et al., 2007). Keltner (1995) describes the facial expression of embarrassment, which he argues serves to appease and placate those who have seen one's mistake. The embarrassment expression involves a sequence of facial and gestural actions, each of which may correspond to some sort of social function (see Figure 11.10).

Emotions as Evolutionary Adaptations Why do we have emotions? From an evolutionary perspective, emotions are adaptations. That is, they evolved because they solved a particular problem in our ancestral past and thus contributed to survival and reproductive success (Tooby & Cosmides, 1990). According to one evolutionary view, emotions bring our physiological systems together to help us deal efficiently with critical situations (Levenson, 1988; Mauss et al., 2005; Rosenberg & Ekman, 1994). For example, when danger approaches, the heart pumps blood to the skeletal muscles to enable quick movement in case escape is necessary, the respiratory system works harder to bring in more oxygen, and the brain prioritizes attention so that we can figure out what we need to do to escape the dangerous situation. This view of emotions as *organized responses* illustrates the adaptive value of negative emotions, which enable people to respond efficiently to a significant challenge or obstacle.

Positive emotions, such as contentment, happiness, love, and amusement, solve different kinds of adaptive problems. According to the **broaden-and-build model,** positive emotions widen our cognitive perspective, making our thinking more expansive and enabling the acquisition of new skills (Fredrickson, 1998, 2001). Compared to negative emotions, which promote a narrow, vigilant way of

broaden-and-build model
Fredrickson's model for positive emotions, which posits that they widen our cognitive perspective and help us acquire useful life skills.

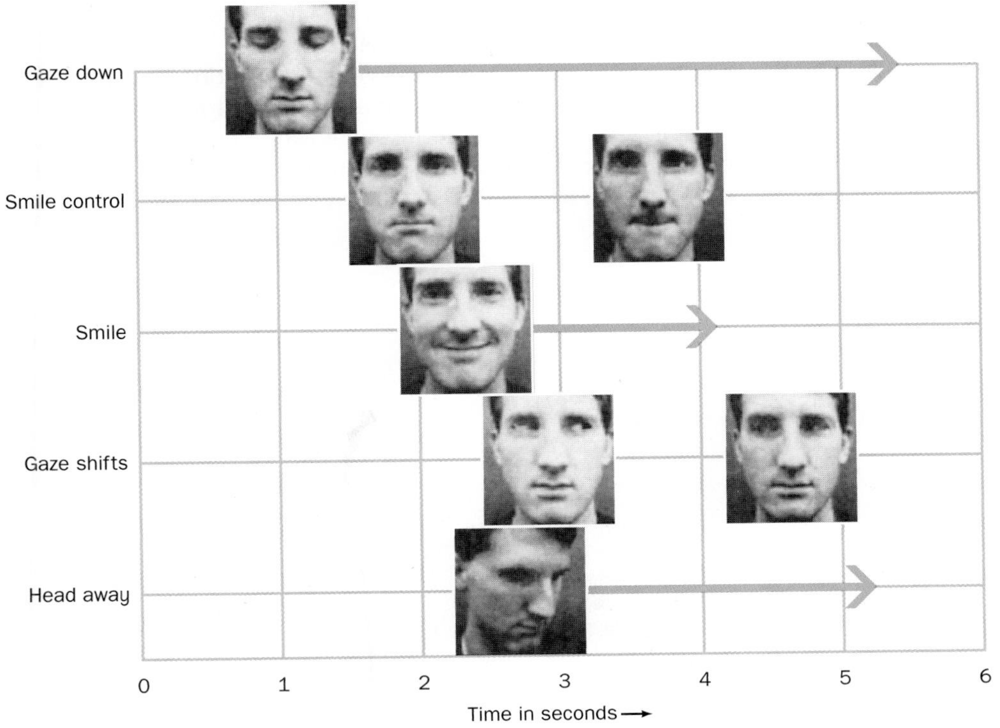

FIGURE **11.10**
TYPICAL FACIAL EXPRESSIONS OF EMBARRASSMENT. The display of embarrassment involves a sequence of actions, each of which might serve a social function. First there is a smile, which may reflect amusement at one's own transgression. Then the eyes gaze away, as if to indicate a desire to escape the awkward situation. Smile control is an attempt to dampen the amusement, as well as looks downward and turning the head away. (*Source:* Keitner, 1995.)

looking at the world, positive emotions help us see the possibilities for new ways of responding to situations, which helps us to *build* new skills (Derryberry & Tucker, 1994). Play, for example, especially the rough-and-tumble play of animals and young children, helps develop physical and strategic skills that may be useful for hunting, escaping, or defensive fighting.

Several studies show that positive emotions broaden one's focus (Fredrickson & Branigan, 2005). For instance, when people are in positive moods they perform poorly on tasks of selective attention that require a narrow focus compared to people in sad or neutral moods, and they perform better on tasks that require a broader attentional focus (Rowe, Hirsch, & Anderson, 2007). For instance, in a task in which people were instructed to think of as many uses as they could for a brick, people who had been put in a positive mood thought of more uses and more creative uses than those experiencing negative emotion (Rowe et al, 2007; Isen, Daubman, & Nowicki, 1987). In a perceptual task, positive emotions also enhance attention to visual information in the outer edges of a visual display, compared to the centre (Wadlinger & Isaacowitz, 2006). This finding indicates that positive emotions might enable people to take more information from any given visual scene.

LO6 Emotion as a Process

Emotions create changes in experience, thought, physiology, and behaviour. For decades psychologists debated which component of emotion best defines or exemplifies what an emotion is, be it a facial expression, an experience, or a physiological change. Researchers now recognize that we can best understand emotions by considering how the various aspects of emotion unfold—that is, by viewing emotion as a *process* (Lazarus, 1991; Levenson, 1994).

antecedent event
a situation that may lead to an emotional response.

An emotion begins with an **antecedent event,** a situation that may lead to an emotional response (see Figure 11.11). We use the word *may* because not everyone responds to the same situation in the same way. The person evaluates the event to determine whether it is potentially harmful or beneficial. Depending on the results of that appraisal, he or she may experience an emotional response.

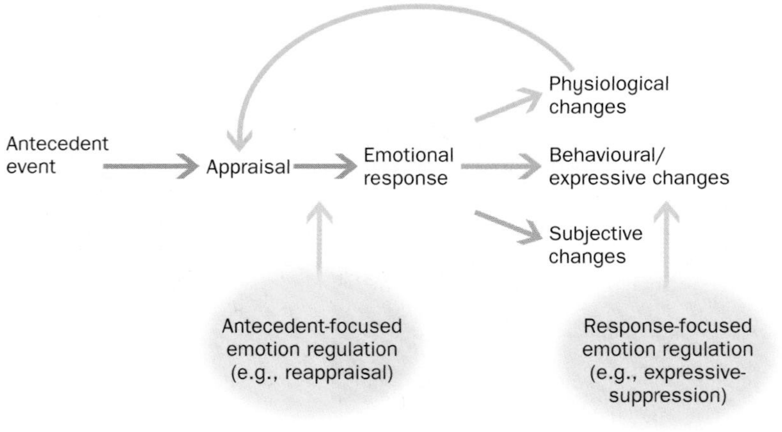

FIGURE **11.11**

THE EMOTION PROCESS. Emotions start with an event that is appraised as relevant to one's goals. If deemed relevant, an emotional response begins, which consists of physiological changes, behavioural and expressive changes, and subjective changes in feelings. Changes in the body's physiology, behaviour, and subjective feelings then feed back to the appraisal process and become inputs for experiencing new emotions. Attempts to regulate (modify, change, or suppress) emotion can occur early or late in the emotion process.

The emotional response, in turn, produces changes in physiology, behaviour and expressions, and subjective experience of the event. The direction of the arrows moving from left to right in Figure 11.11 is only part of the story. As the reverse-curved arrow suggests, the process can move in the other direction as well. That is, the activation of facial and physiological responses might enhance the emotion, becoming yet another kind of input for a new emotional experience. Levenson (2003) points out that in addition to the antecedent events that are external to us, there may be internal inputs into the emotion process, inputs provided by facial and physiological changes. In addition, once we generate emotions, we sometimes attempt to modify them, regulate them, or make them go away, which in turn involves new appraisals and new responses. To some extent, then, the emotion process moves in a loop rather than in a single direction.

Appraisal in the Emotion Process Whether an event or situation leads to an emotion depends on how the person appraises it. **Appraisal** is the evaluation of a situation with respect to how relevant it is to one's own welfare (Lazarus, 1991). Appraisal need not be a conscious, deliberate thought process. Most of the time it probably occurs automatically, well outside awareness, and it may occur in an instant (Barrett, Ochsner, & Gross, 2007).

appraisal
the evaluation of a situation with respect to how relevant it is to one's own welfare; it drives the process by which emotions are elicited.

Appraisal drives the process by which emotions are elicited (Roseman, 1984; Scherer, Dan, & Flykt, 2006). It explains why, for example, the level of happiness expressed by Olympic athletes can be greater for winners of the bronze medals (third place) than for winners of the silver medal (second place) (Medvec, Madey, & Gilovich, 1995). Bronze medalists could easily imagine an alternative outcome: They may not have even placed. Compared to that outcome, third is great. Silver medalists, on the other hand, could easily imagine and hope for an alternative outcome: Winning first place! Compared to that outcome, second is somewhat disappointing. Our own beliefs clearly influence the way in which we appraise our situation, as do our personalities, personal histories, and goals.

The type of appraisal that occurs determines the type of the emotion generated. Fear, for instance, comes from situations of uncertainty and over which we feel we have little control (Ekman, 2003; Lazarus, 1991). In one study, students completed appraisal and emotion questionnaires before and immediately after taking a midterm exam. Students who reported appraisals of unfairness and uncertainty and the idea that others were in control of the situation after the exam were more likely to experience fear than those who did not report such

What frightens you? Many people are afraid of potentially threatening situations over which they have little control.

appraisals (Ellsworth & Smith, 1988; Smith & Ellsworth, 1987). Although it might be impossible to study automatic appraisals as they happen, research on people's understanding of situations and their responses to them can inform us indirectly about appraisal.

emotion regulation the cognitive and behavioural efforts people make to modify their emotions.

reappraisal an emotion-regulation strategy in which one re-evaluates an antecedent event so that a different emotion results.

expressive-suppression a response-focused strategy for regulating emotion that involves the deliberate attempt to inhibit the outward manifestation of an emotion.

Regulation of Emotion People can intentionally or unintentionally change their emotions or the extent to which they experience certain emotions. The term **emotion regulation** refers to the cognitive and behavioural efforts people use to modify their emotions.

Looking at the emotion process as depicted in Figure 11.11, you can see that attempts to regulate emotions may occur at the beginning or end of the emotion process (Gross, 1998; Gross, Richards, & John, 2006). An example of emotion regulation that can occur early in the emotion process is **reappraisal,** in which people re-evaluate their views of an event so that a different emotion results. For example, rather than seeing your next midterm as an opportunity for failure, an outlook that might create fear or anxiety, you might reappraise the exam as a challenging opportunity to prove to yourself and others how much you have learned, an outlook that would lead to eager anticipation.

Another kind of emotion regulation operates when people want to make an unpleasant feeling go away. An example of this kind of strategy for regulating emotion is **expressive-suppression,** the deliberate attempt to inhibit the outward display of an emotion (Gross et al., 2006). For instance, in order to avoid a confrontation, you might literally bite your lip rather than tell your roommates that they are slobs for letting the dishes pile up and waiting for you to wash them. Instructing people to suppress their negative emotions like this can decrease the experience of negative emotion, but it increases activation of the sympathetic nervous system and sustains the emotional response (Gross & Levenson, 1997).

In an important application of emotion research to the real world, researchers have taught schoolchildren strategies for regulating emotion in order to reduce maladaptive behaviour and improve academic performance (see "Psychology in the Real World"; Conduct Problems Prevention Research Group, 1999a, 1999b; Kam, Greenberg, & Kusché, 2004). The idea that emotional skills are linked to success in life was popularized in the mid-1990s by Daniel Goleman (1995). Goleman's book, *Emotional Intelligence,* summarizes research on how the ability to recognize emotions in oneself and others, the development of empathic understanding, and skills for regulating emotions in oneself and others may be at least as important to one's success in life as academic achievement. Goleman drew heavily on research by Peter Salovey and John Mayer, who introduced the concept of emotional intelligence in 1990 (Salovey & Mayer, 1990).

LO7

emotional response the physiological, behavioural/expressive, and subjective changes that occur when emotions are generated.

The Emotional Response Whether processed consciously or automatically, emotional responses emerge from events appraised as relevant to one's safety or personal goals. As shown in Figure 11.11, the **emotional response** includes physiological, behavioural/expressive, and subjective changes. Here we will discuss each type of change.

Physiological Changes. Emotions produce physiological changes, such as increases in heart rate and rate of respiration. The physiological system responsible for changes during an emotional response is the autonomic nervous system (ANS). The ANS governs structures and processes over which we have little conscious control, such as changes in heart rate and blood pressure and the release of hormones. The ANS plays a crucial role in emotional response because it activates other systems that are needed for action, including the circulatory system and the respiratory system.

Psychology in the Real World

Social and Emotional Learning in Schools

If you ask most people what you are supposed to learn in elementary school, they might say, "Reading, writing, math, science, history. . . ." How many people would say, "I learned how to regulate my anger"? Yet today many schools are teaching just that. Psychologists and educators argue that the development of skills for recognizing and regulating emotions is just as important to success in life as is academic achievement. And new research backs up this assertion. The past decade or so has seen the development and implementation of programs designed to teach young children skills for managing their emotions and promoting social adjustment. These social-emotional learning (SEL) programs constitute an important application of the psychology of emotion to the real world.

Mark Greenberg, director of the Prevention Research Center for the Promotion of Human Development at Penn State University, initiated much of the research on SEL. Through applied psychological research, he and his colleagues have evaluated the effectiveness of the prevention programs developed by the centre. One of those programs is PATHS (Providing Alternative THinking Strategies), a groundbreaking program developed by Greenberg and Carol Kusché (Greenberg & Kusché, 1998; Kusché & Greenberg, 1994). The PATHS program gives teachers a detailed curriculum for improving children's emotional awareness and regulation skills and enhancing their social competence.

An example of an exercise in the PATHS program is the turtle story and lesson, which is aimed at developing self-control. Children are told about a turtle that gets into trouble with other turtles in various situations because he does not stop to think. He gets some help from "wise old turtle," who tells him that when he just can't handle his anger and feels aggressive, he should go into his shell and consider what the best way to respond might be.

The PATHS program uses a modified version of the turtle story to teach children the technique of pulling back and mulling over options when they are upset in order to gain self-control and reduce aggressive behaviours. Kids learn to time themselves out when they get upset by "playing turtle" and thinking about what to do next. Other exercises are designed to help children identify their feelings, develop empathic understanding, and recognize that it's okay to have all feelings but that not all behaviours are okay.

Research using controlled intervention trials in which classrooms were randomly assigned to receive the PATHS curriculum or not (thereby continuing as usual) has shown that PATHS leads to improvements in social and emotional skills in high-risk children, reduction of aggressive behaviours in both normal and special-needs children, fewer depressive symptoms in special-needs kids, and improvements in classroom functioning (Conduct Problems Prevention Research Group, 1999a, 1999b; Kam, Greenberg, & Kusche, 2004). Other prevention programs, such as Head Start, have also applied the theory and methods of emotion research to decrease behaviour problems in schools, and initial results are promising (Izard et al., 2004).

Now, more than a decade after the implementation of major SEL programs, it is possible to see how the development of socio-emotional learning might be linked to academic success. A large-scale meta-analysis of more than 500 studies shows that SEL programs significantly improve children's academic performance (Durlak et al., 2007). Specifically, children who participate in these programs have better attendance and less disruptive classroom behaviour; they like school more and have higher GPAs.

Once elicited, emotions engage the ANS almost immediately. For emotions that are concerned with survival and protection from harm, such as fear, the sympathetic branch of the ANS is activated. Sympathetic activity mobilizes body resources into an organized response to a real or imagined environmental threat. The heart pumps blood rapidly to the muscles; oxygen intake in the lungs increases; and processes that are not immediately necessary for action, such as digestion, shut down so that energy is conserved for more urgent body functions.

The patterns of ANS activity can vary, depending on the emotion elicited. Anger increases heart rate more than fear does; disgust slows the heart (Ekman, Levenson, & Friesen, 1983; Levenson, Ekman, & Friesen, 1990). Such autonomic nervous system changes appear to be common to people all over the world

(Levenson et al., 1992; Tsai et al., 2002; Tsai, Levenson, & Carstensen, 2000). Such cross-cultural data on the physiology of emotion supports the view of emotions as evolutionarily old, as does evidence of emotion in non-human primates, other mammals, birds, and even fish (Paul, Harding, & Mendl, 2005).

Positive emotions engage the parasympathetic branch of the ANS. They apparently serve to return the body to a more relaxed, responsive state (Levenson, 2003). For example, Fredrickson and Levenson (1998) showed participants a fear-eliciting film and followed it with film clips known to elicit sadness, amusement, or contentment—or no emotions at all. They measured cardiovascular activity while participants viewed the films and again afterward. Cardiovascular activation elicited by the negative film returned to baseline levels more quickly in people who saw a pleasant film (amusement or contentment) after the fear film, than in those who saw films leading to sad or non-emotional conditions. This ability of positive emotions to "undo" the effects of negative emotional arousal by helping to return the body to a state of relaxation may result from parasympathetic nervous system activation.

Connection
The autonomic nervous system both activates and relaxes physiological systems.
See Chapter 3, LO4.

Behavioural-Expressive Changes. Emotions create expressive changes in the face and voice, as well as behavioural tendencies toward particular types of action (Frijda, 1986). People show their emotions—knowingly or not—through both verbal and non-verbal means, such as changes in facial behaviour and vocal intonation. Although researchers have studied both facial and vocal expressions of emotion, the most extensive body of research has focused on facial expressions.

Humans are predisposed to respond to faces. Newborn babies mimic the facial expressions of adults; at five months they can discriminate between different types of facial expressions of emotion; and by one year of age they rely on the faces of their caregivers to convey important information about how they might act (Meltzoff & Moore, 1977; Schwartz, Izard, & Ansul, 1985; Sorce et al., 1985). There are specialized neurons in the brain for responding to faces, and certain brain areas are specialized for particular facial expressions, such as fear (Adolphs et al., 1994, 2005; Kanwisher, 2000).

Facial Action Coding System (FACS)
a widely used method for measuring all observable muscular movements that are possible in the human face.

How do psychologists study spontaneous facial expressions? The **Facial Action Coding System (FACS)** is a widely used method by which coders score all observable muscular movements that are possible in the human face (Ekman & Friesen, 1978). Using FACS, researchers have found that many different facial expressions recognized across cultures—such as anger, disgust, fear, happiness, sadness, and surprise—are also shown when people spontaneously experience emotions (Ekman & Rosenberg, 2005).

Duchenne smile
a smile that expresses true enjoyment, involving both the muscles that pull up the lip corners diagonally and those that contract the band of muscles encircling the eye.

The most recognizable facial expression of emotion is the smile of happiness. Yet research using FACS shows that not all smiles are created equal. Only certain smiles indicate truly felt enjoyment. Other smiles are used for a variety of interpersonal reasons, such as to be polite in conversation, to mask negative emotions, or to pretend that one is feeling happy when, in fact, one is not. A smile that both pulls up the lip corners diagonally and contracts the band of muscles that circle the eye to create crow's feet and raise the cheeks is known as a **Duchenne smile,** named after the French anatomist who first described it. A Duchenne smile is a genuine smile that expresses true enjoyment. When we smile for social reasons and are not genuinely happy, we use only the lips and not the band of muscles around the eye, which is called a non-Duchenne smile (Davidson et al., 1990; Ekman, Davidson, & Friesen, 1990). Figure 11.12 shows a Duchenne smile and a non-Duchenne smile.

The human voice also expresses emotion. Have you ever noticed how your voice can betray you? Consider the first time you ever gave a speech. You may have had your hair and clothes in fine order; perhaps your facial expressions showed great composure; and you knew your speech well, having practised it many times. But when the time came to start speaking, your voice quivered or even squeaked! Why did this happen? The voice is very sensitive to emotional fluctuations because the vocal cords are innervated by the autonomic nervous system. So nervousness leaks through the voice (Bachorowski, 1999; Scherer et al., 1991).

The same vocalization can sound different, depending on the speaker's facial expression. This happens because lip movements affect vocal characteristics. For example, you can actually hear a smile or a frown. When listening to recordings, people can reliably distinguish between laughs produced while smiling and while frowning (Bachorowski, 1999).

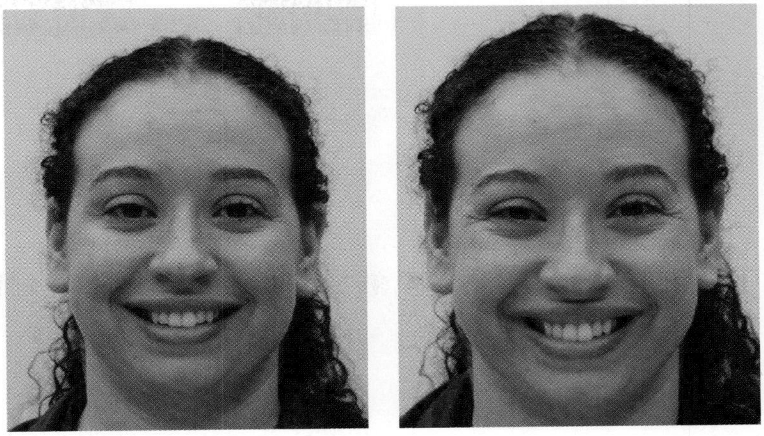

FIGURE 11.12
DUCHENNE SMILE VERSUS NON-DUCHENNE SMILE. Both photos depict a smile of the same intensity, but they differ in the involvement of muscles around the eye.
Which one is a Duchenne, or true enjoyment, smile?

LO8 **Subjective Changes in Emotion.** The third component of the emotional response is referred to as the **subjective experience of emotion,** which is the quality of our conscious experience during an emotional response. When people talk about how an emotion *feels,* they are referring to subjective experience. Each emotion creates a unique feeling: Anger feels different from sadness, which feels different from happiness. The subjective aspect of emotion draws on a person's experience of body changes as well as the effects emotions have on cognition, for emotions can activate associations with images and memories of significant events.

Is Leonardo da Vinci's *Mona Lisa* smiling out of pleasure or merely posing a smile in her portrait?

What produces subjective feelings of emotion? Perhaps the most influential theory was proposed by William James (1884) and Carl Lange (1885/1992). The **James-Lange theory of emotion** says that it is our perception of the physiological changes that accompany emotions that creates the subjective emotional experience. Without the perception of body changes, they argued, there is no emotional experience. Moreover, these changes that accompany different emotional states are unique. We experience fear as feeling different from sadness, for example, because we perceive different body changes for each emotion. In short, "I am trembling, and therefore I am afraid; or I feel a lump in my throat, therefore I am sad."

Several lines of evidence support the James-Lange view. First, when people in many cultures are asked to identify the body sensations associated with emotions, they differentiate among several emotional states. For instance, "stomach sensations" are associated most strongly with disgust, far more so than with other emotions, and sadness with a lump in the throat (Breugelmans et al., 2005). Figure 11.13 presents an overview of the sensations that people participating in research studies report are associated with each emotion. In support of the idea that feedback from body sensations creates the subjective experience of emotion, people who pose on their faces the muscular movements of some emotion expressions report feeling that emotion (Strack, Martin, & Stepper, 1988). Additionally, the better people pose facial expressions of emotion, the more intense the feeling (Ekman et al., 1983; Levenson et al., 1990).

Despite this support for the James-Lange theory, there are several findings that are inconsistent with this view. For instance, people with spinal cord injuries have very little feedback about physiological changes from the body, yet their subjective experience of emotion is no less intense than that of an uninjured individual (Chwalisz et al., 1988). In the 1920s, Walter Cannon proposed an alternative to the

subjective experience of emotion the changes in the quality of our conscious experience that occur during emotional responses.

James-Lange theory of emotion the perception of the physiological changes that accompany emotions that produces the subjective emotional experience.

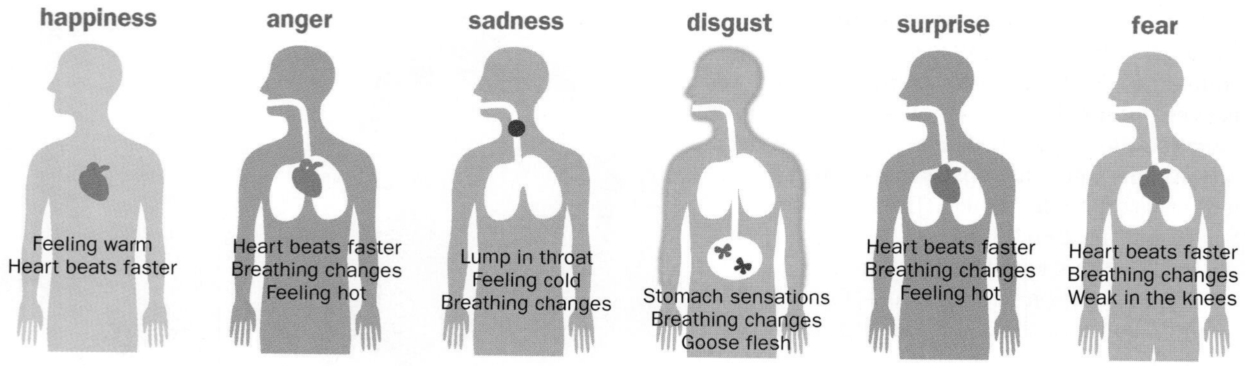

FIGURE **11.13**
BODILY SENSATIONS ASSOCIATED WITH DIFFERENT EMOTIONS. (*Source:* Breugelmans et al., 2005.)

Cannon-Bard theory of emotion theory that incoming emotional sensory stimuli travel to the thalamus, where the signal gets divided into a descending pathway to control body arousal and an ascending cortical pathway to control emotional experience.

two-factor theory of emotion theory that the subjective experience of emotion is determined by awareness of physiological arousal as well as a cognitive process to assess the most plausible emotional state.

James-Lange theory, which was later extended by Philip Bard. The **Cannon-Bard theory of emotion** suggests that the subjective experience of emotion as well the physiological changes in the body are parallel processes, mediated by two distinct neuronal pathways. According to this theory, incoming sensory signals from emotional stimuli travel to the thalamus, and are then relayed through a descending pathway to the body to regulate physiological changes, and through an ascending cortical pathway to control subjective experience. Most modern theories of emotion incorporate a role for bodily feedback, as outlined in the James-Lange view, as well as parallel brain processes proposed by the Cannon-Bard perspective.

Probably one of the most influential theories of emotion is Schachter and Singer's **two-factor theory of emotion.** This theory states that our conscious experience of emotion is determined by both an awareness of bodily arousal paired with a cognitive appraisal of the situation. In other words, we make a decision about which emotion we are experiencing based upon the explanation that best fits the circumstances (Aronson et al., 2004). Schachter and Singer (1962) tested this theory by artificially manipulating participants' arousal levels and then placing participants in emotionally charged situations. This way they could test whether high arousal influenced the type and intensity of their subjective emotional experience. Participants were told that they would be given an injection of a vitamin, but were in fact given epinephrine, a hormone produced by the sympathetic (or "fight or flight") nervous system. Participants in the control condition were given a placebo. They then filled out a questionnaire with another participant (working for the experimenter) who, in one experimental condition, became offended and angry at the questions being asked. In another condition, the other participant acted in a playful and happy manner, throwing balls of paper and paper airplanes into the trash. Compared to control participants, those that were given epinephrine reported feeling emotions that matched those of the other individual. These results suggest that the high physiological arousal from epinephrine was used as a cue to explain their current emotional state.

This theory, like the James-Lange view, ascribes an important role to changes in physiological arousal that accompany emotional states. However, like the Cannon-Bard theory, it also distinguishes physiology and cognition as separate processes in emotion. It differs from the Cannon-Bard theory in that it proposes that these processes are connected.

Detecting Deception

The ability to distinguish between physiological, behavioural, and subjective changes associated with emotions has revealed that these components are under different degrees of voluntary control. This is particularly important since humans hide emotional displays for a variety of reasons. For instance, if you are upset with your professor about a low grade, you might not want this to be obvious if you are meeting with her to discuss it. Therefore, you might alter your facial expression to appear pleasant and easy-going, rather than hostile and angry. However, the physiological changes controlled by the autonomic nervous system are not as easy to suppress.

Knowledge about our ability, or lack thereof, to hide emotions is of great interest in the study of lie detection. Most technologies developed for the purpose of detecting deception are based upon the premise that people feel tension when telling a lie, and this heightened emotional arousal can be used to catch liars. The oldest and best-characterized method for lie detection is the polygraph, which monitors changes in autonomic nervous system activity, such as heart rate, blood pressure, respiration, and skin conductance (which provides information about sweating). An equally important part of the polygraph test is the method used to elicit lying in the participant. Traditionally, this is done in one of two ways—by using the control question test or the guilty knowledge test. The *control question test* basically measures physiological reactions when participants are asked questions relevant to the lie (for example, "Did you cheat on your final exam?") and compares this response to responses obtained to neutral questions (such as "Are you wearing glasses?"). The *guilty knowledge test* measures responses to questions whose answers would only be known to the guilty party (such as questions about items left at the crime scene) (Wolpe et al., 2010).

The use of the polygraph in lie detection has been hotly debated for decades. One problem is that, although reliability in correctly detecting lying ranges from 70 to 85 percent, there is an alarming proportion of *incorrectly* identified lies, somewhere in the range of 7 to 15 percent. This means that 7 to 15 percent of the time, an honest person is incorrectly identified as a liar. This might be due to the fact that the polygraph actually measures arousal, and therefore will detect general anxiety associated with being questioned as well as tension associated with the deception itself (Wolpe et al., 2010). Newer methods of detecting deception rely upon signatures of brain activity rather than relying upon sympathetic nervous system changes. Although there has been much hype regarding the sensitivity of techniques such as *brain fingerprinting*, based upon EEG, there is mixed evidence regarding their accuracy (Hyman, 2010).

Not surprisingly, there is a growing demand for quick and efficient lie detection techniques for use in criminal and terrorist investigations. Setting up a polygraph is time-consuming and cumbersome for use in real-life situations requiring lie detection, such as in airports and courtrooms. Furthermore, newer technologies based upon measuring brain activity changes are expensive and impractical in field settings. Therefore, another approach to lie detection has focused on the behavioural, rather than physiological, component of emotions. Contrary to popular belief, there is no single telltale sign that someone is lying. Common misconceptions about the significance of fidgeting and averting gaze have not been supported by scientific evidence (Kassin, 2008). The most reliable behavioural changes associated with deception are rigid posture, reduction of hand and arm movements, long pauses in speech, and lower rates of blinking. Furthermore, liars are more likely than truth-tellers to repeat words, phrases, and details related to the fabricated information (Porter & ten Brinke, 2010).

Most people think that they can tell when people are lying to them. According to the research, however, most of us are not effective lie detectors. Most people perform no better than chance—which means no better than randomly guessing between the two alternatives of lying or truthfulness—in detecting deception from the way people act. Why are we unsuccessful at catching liars? Most of us rely on misleading cues. We put too much weight on what people are saying, over-interpret ambiguous non-verbal cues (thinking any sign of nervousness means a person is lying), ignore relevant non-verbal information, and get fooled by signs of warmth and competence (Ekman & O'Sullivan, 1991).

So who makes a good lie detector? Are some people better than others? Psychologists with a special interest in deception have also been shown to do much better than others in detecting deceit (Ekman, O'Sullivan, & Frank, 1999). You might also expect professionals such as police, parole officers, and judges to be skilled in catching liars. However, many studies show that they tend to perform no better, or worse, than undergraduate students, despite being more confident in their judgments (Kassin et al., 2005). These findings are alarming, since the accused liar could face severe consequences based upon others' decisions of their trustworthiness. Fortunately, lie-detection skills can be learned and many evidence-based training programs have been shown to increase accuracy (Porter et al., 2000).

Quick Quiz 11.2: Emotion

1. Stress-induced negative mood enhances preference for sweet foods, since they contain carbohydrates that boost brain levels of
   a. serotonin.
   b. insulin.
   c. orexin.
   d. neuropeptide Y.
2. Which of the following is *not* a self-conscious emotion?
   a. pride
   b. embarrassment
   c. resentment
   d. shame
3. According to the view of emotions as a process, _____ drive(s) the process by which emotions are elicited.
   a. emotional responses
   b. expressive changes
   c. physiological changes
   d. appraisal

Answers can be found at the end of the chapter.

Groundbreaking Research

The Universality of Facial Expressions of Emotion

If you were to visit an exotic place, such as the Amazon rain forest, could you expect your smile to be greeted with a smile from the local inhabitants? Or might they do something else? More generally, can we expect facial expressions of emotion to mean the same thing to people from different cultures? In the late 1960s, Paul Ekman went to a remote culture to find out whether facial expressions of emotion were universal or culturally specific. His research broke new ground, not just in our understanding of expression, but in helping launch the field of emotion research in psychology as well.

EMOTION EXPRESSION: CULTURALLY DETERMINED OR UNIVERSAL?

In the 1960s, most social scientists believed that behaviour was strongly determined by a person's environment. Anthropologists, for instance, proposed that facial expressions of emotion were **culturally relative;** that is, expressions varied across cultures and could be understood only in their cultural context. After all, anthropologists in the field had observed cultures in which people acted playfully at funerals and those in which people showed expressions of fierce anger at joyous festivals (Ekman, 1973).

cultural relativism
the idea that behaviour varies across cultures and can be understood only within the context of the culture in which they occur.

Trained as a behaviourist who emphasized the effects of environment on behaviour, a young psychologist named Paul Ekman thought the anthropologists were right. By the mid-1960s, however, he was beginning to question that view. Ekman's mentor, Silvan Tomkins, showed research participants numerous photographs of European Americans posing different emotions and asked them to decide which emotion the person in the picture may have been feeling. He obtained pretty strong evidence of agreement on the emotional meaning of those facial expressions (Tomkins & McCarter, 1964). Then Ekman and his colleague, Wallace Friesen, showed Tomkins's pictures to people in the United States, Japan, Argentina, and Chile and found a high degree of consensus on the meanings of a core set of facial expressions of emotion (Ekman & Friesen, 1969). At about the same time, Carroll Izard (1969) did a similar study and obtained similar results. Such high level of consensus on the meaning of facial expressions of emotion across numerous cultural groups in several studies supported Darwin's (1872) assertion that the facial expressions of certain "basic" emotions are **universal,** that is, common to all human beings (see Figure 11.14).

universal
term referring to something that is common to all human beings and can be seen in cultures all over the world.

One problem with these studies on emotion recognition, however, is that all participants lived in literate, industrialized cultures. Maybe the findings of cross-cultural consistency in facial expression recognition reflected the spreading influence of the popular media rather than the existence of a universal human skill. That is, people in Japan and the United States might have agreed on the emotional meaning of certain expressions because they had seen portrayals of actors in movies. About this time Ekman (Ekman, 1972; personal communication, March 28, 2006) read Charles Darwin's (1872) book *The Expression of the Emotions in Man and Animals,* in which Darwin described in detail how people and animals display emotions through their faces and bodies and offered a theory for the evolution of emotion expression. Ekman knew he needed to collect data from preliterate people who were isolated from Western culture, if he wanted to show that consistency in certain facial expressions of emotion occurred universally and was not a product of culture. This approach

FIGURE **11.14**
DRAWINGS AND PHOTOGRAPHS OF ANGER/AGGRESSION ACROSS SPECIES FROM DARWIN'S 1872 BOOK. Darwin asserted that expressions of emotion are universal across human cultures. His book *The Expression of the Emotions in Man and Animals* influenced Ekman's research. (*Source:* Darwin, 1998.)

Do facial expressions of emotion have the same meaning in different cultural groups? What do you think this child is feeling?

to disproving a rival hypothesis in order to rule out an alternative explanation of one's findings represents an important step in the process of doing science. In this case, the rival hypothesis was that cross-cultural consistency in the understanding of facial expressions reflected the spread of media influence.

EVIDENCE OF UNIVERSALITY IN EMOTION EXPRESSION

Thanks to an anthropologist friend, Ekman had the chance to study just such an isolated, preliterate group: the Fore tribe from Papua New Guinea. His plan was to show members of this tribe pictures of facial expressions of emotion and find out which emotions, if any, they saw in those faces. But how could he gather such data from a culture without a written language? He decided to ask the people to make up stories to explain why the person in a picture would make such a face. To Ekman's dismay, the New Guineans found it very difficult to make up stories about the pictures, so he was not able to get a large sample of data. Ekman says that after collecting these data, he sat alone on a hill, listening to "The Fool on the Hill" by the Beatles, and felt disappointed. Nonetheless, the data were promising, and he published them, but they did not yield the high consensus he had expected (Ekman, Sorenson, & Friesen, 1969).

Paul Ekman with children in Papua New Guinea, circa 1967. The boys are wearing Western clothing that they accepted as gifts for participating in Ekman's research.

Ekman was fairly convinced that the people in New Guinea knew what the expressions meant, but he believed that his method was flawed. Instead of giving up, Ekman decided to try another approach. He chose a technique that had been used in studies of children's ability to recognize emotion in facial expressions. The method involved presenting stories about emotional situations to New Guineans and showing them a set of three photographed faces per story. Examples of stories include "He [she] is angry and about to fight" (which should lead participants to pick an "angry" face) or "She [he] is looking at something that smells bad" (for disgust). Then the experimenter would ask the listener which of the three faces matched the story. When Ekman used this method, the degree of consensus was much higher. Both children and adult New Guineans consistently discriminated the "correct" face from other faces; that is, they consistently matched a given story with the face that would have been predicted, and the results matched the data from studies of people in literate cultures (Ekman & Friesen, 1971). Results of these two early studies from both literate and preliterate cultures show that the range of agreement was relatively high for five of the six basic emotions (Ekman et al., 1969; Ekman & Friesen, 1971). Follow-up research conducted 20 years later showed similar high-level agreement across ten literate cultures (Ekman et al., 1987). For summaries of facial recognition data across several studies, see Figure 11.15.

EMOTION RESEARCH AFTER THE FINDINGS ON UNIVERSALITY

Ekman's findings showed that the face contained reliable information about emotion that was common to all humans. It brought the subjective state of emotion into the realm of science and made it a topic of objective study. By the late 1980s and throughout the 1990s, emotion became one of the most widely studied topics in all of psychology (Rosenberg, 2005). Moreover, spurred by the knowledge that the face contained reliable information about emotion, Ekman and his colleagues developed the objective coding system of the face, FACS, that we discussed earlier in the chapter (Ekman & Friesen, 1978). And finally, the findings from New Guinea led to an integration of the two competing perspectives, culture differences and universality. Soon after returning from New Guinea, Ekman (1972) proposed the **neurocultural theory of emotion** to account for the fact that certain aspects of emotion, such as the facial expressions and physiological changes of basic emotions, are similar in all humans, whereas other aspects, such as how people appraise situations and regulate their emotional expressions in front of others, vary from one culture to another.

neurocultural theory of emotion
Ekman's explanation that some aspects of emotion, such as facial expressions and physiological changes associated with emotion, are universal and others, such as emotional regulation, are culturally derived.

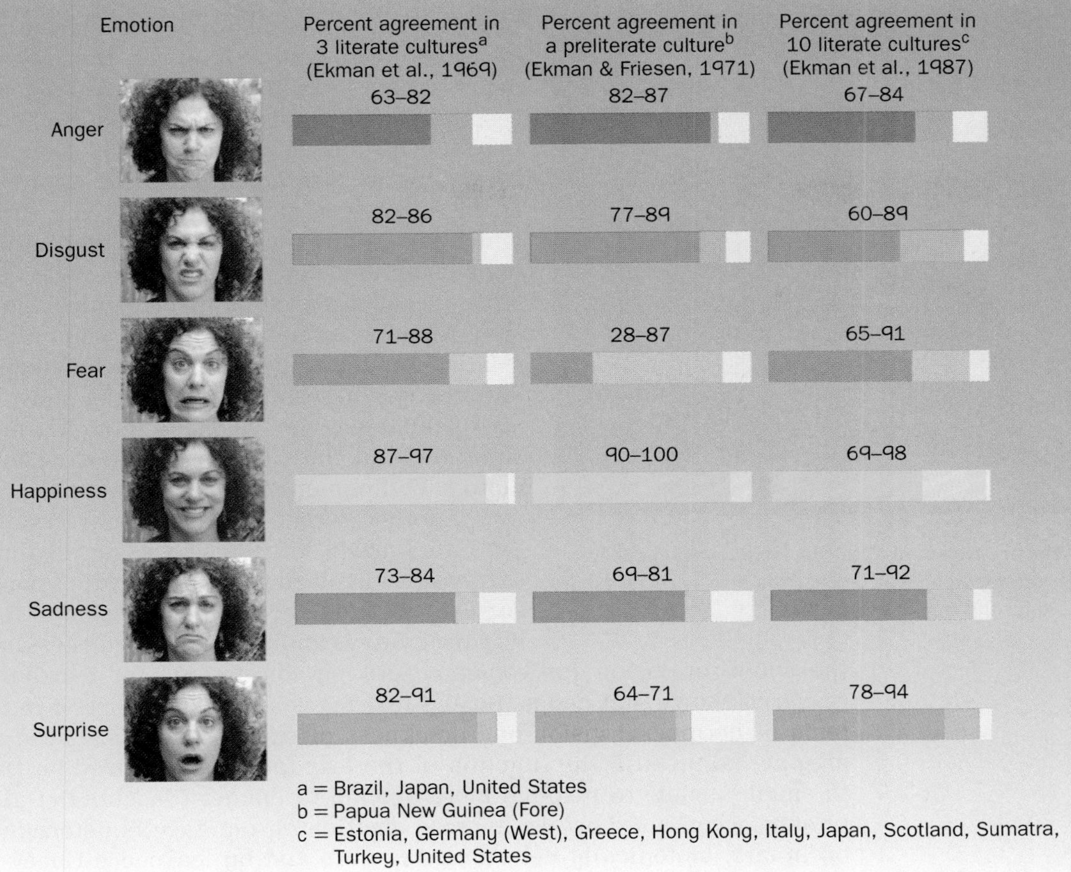

Emotion
Percent agreement in 3 literate cultures[a] (Ekman et al., 1969)
Percent agreement in a preliterate culture[b] (Ekman & Friesen, 1971)
Percent agreement in 10 literate cultures[c] (Ekman et al., 1987)
Anger
63–82
82–87
67–84
Disgust
82–86
77–89
60–89
Fear
71–88
28–87
65–91
Happiness
87–97
90–100
69–98
Sadness
73–84
69–81
71–92
Surprise
82–91
64–71
78–94
a = Brazil, Japan, United States
b = Papua New Guinea (Fore)
c = Estonia, Germany (West), Greece, Hong Kong, Italy, Japan, Scotland, Sumatra, Turkey, United States

FIGURE **11.15**
CONSISTENCY IN EXPRESSIONS OF BASIC EMOTION ACROSS LITERATE AND PRELITERATE CULTURES.

How Culture Impacts Emotion Expression

Anthropologists have offered numerous examples of cultural variability in emotion expression—such as the case of Samurai women who smiled broadly after learning that their husband or son had died in battle (Ekman, 1973). Such examples suggest that facial expressions of happiness and sadness are not universal. How can the findings on universality of facial expressions jibe with the fact that there are cultural differences in emotions? Friesen and Ekman (1972; Friesen, 1972) proposed the concept of display rules to address this dilemma. **Display rules** are learned norms or rules, often taught very early, about when it is appropriate to show certain expressions of emotion and to whom one should show them. As it turns out, Samurai women were expected to be proud of a son or husband who had been killed in battle, and the society required them to display joy at the news. More mundane examples from daily life in Canada include the requirements that winners should not boast, losers should not mope, and men should not cry in public (although this last norm is changing).

The first empirical support for display rules came from a study comparing disgust expressions in American and Japanese students (Ekman, 1972; Friesen, 1972). Both groups viewed a film showing a very graphic medical procedure, but in two different conditions: in the presence of an authority figure and alone. When alone, both groups felt perfectly comfortable expressing the

Challenge Your Assumptions

True or False? People in different cultures express emotion differently on their faces.

False: The expression of basic emotions on the human face is remarkably similar across cultures.

display rules
learned norms or rules, often taught very early, about when it is appropriate to express certain emotions and to whom one should show them.

obvious response—disgust. When in the presence of an authority figure, however, the Japanese students did not show disgust, and they masked their responses with non-Duchenne (fake) smiles. American students, however, showed about the same level of disgust in both conditions. The expressive differences between groups emerged in a situation in which the cultures had very different norms about expression, but not in the solo viewing condition. More recent research on display rules and expression support and extend these original findings (Matsumoto et al., 2008). Overwhelmingly, however, people across many cultures show remarkably similar emotion displays in highly emotional situations—in the Olympics, for example (Matusmoto & Willingham, 2006).

In some cultures, men are expected to refrain from crying in public. Sometimes, though, strong emotions can override display rules, as they apparently have for the man in this picture.

Another recent finding on universality goes back to Darwin (1872), who asserted that facial expressions evolved due to their functional role in survival. For instance, the expression of fear, with its raised brows and widely opened eyes, increased the scope of vision for someone looking for options for escape. Recent research shows that people posing fear faces actually see better in terms of tests of peripheral vision and quickness of eye movements. These changes may actually fulfill the function of the fear face hypothesized by Darwin—to enable people to respond more quickly to danger (Susskind et al., 2008). In sum, when and how we express emotion on our face is determined both by innate, biologically determined factors and by learned influences, such as display rules, that may vary from one culture to another. The evidence strongly suggests that all humans share a core set of basic facial expressions of emotion.

LO9 Emotion and the Brain

So far we have examined the emotion process in detail, from the eliciting event to the appraisal mechanisms that bring forth the emotional response to the resulting changes in physiology, expression, and experience. Missing from this picture is the brain, which participates in every aspect of the emotion process.

Affective neuroscience, the field devoted to studying the brain's role in emotion, is a rapidly growing area of research. Most current evidence tells us that emotional information is processed in brain circuits that involve several brain structures, and emotional processing is highly interlinked with cognitive processing (Pessoa, 2008). Although there is no main emotion centre in the brain, we can identify some key areas for emotion processing, including the amygdala and the prefrontal cortex, as well as other brain regions (see Figure 11.16).

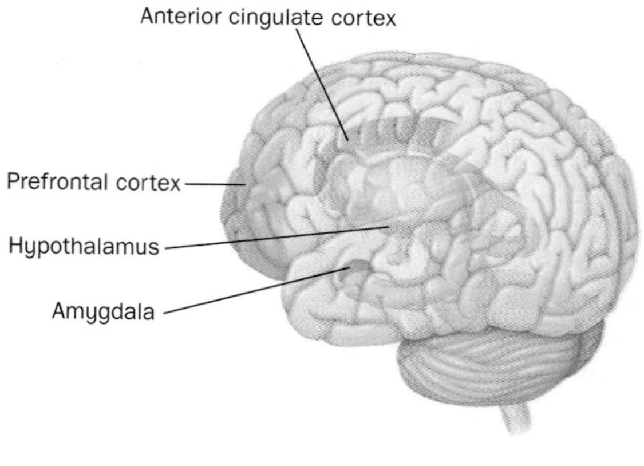

FIGURE **11.16**
FOUR MAIN REGIONS OF THE EMOTIONAL BRAIN. No single area of the brain is responsible for emotion, but the amygdala, prefrontal cortex, anterior cingulate cortex, and the hypothalamus play key roles in the way we experience emotion and remember emotional experiences.

The Amygdala Anatomically, the amygdala has connections with many important brain regions, including structures that appear to be involved in emotion and memory: the hypothalamus, which controls the ANS; the hippocampus, which plays a crucial role in memory; the thalamus, which receives information from the sense organs; and the cerebral cortex. The amygdala appears to play a very important role in appraisal of the emotional significance of stimuli, with a specialized function for noticing fear-relevant information (Öhman, 2002; Phelps & LeDoux, 2005).

Much of the research on the amygdala has centred on its pivotal role in quick appraisals during threatening or fear-inducing situations (LeDoux, 1996, 2000). Along these lines, Joseph LeDoux and his colleagues have used classical conditioning of fear in rats as a model for studying emotion in the human brain (Wilensky et al., 2006). In their experiment, a rat is exposed to a tone, which is emotionally neutral at first. Then the tone is repeatedly paired with an aversive stimulus, an electric shock (the unconditioned stimulus, or US). After repeated pairings with the shock, the tone itself becomes a fear-eliciting stimulus (the conditioned stimulus, or CS). When the researchers examined the circuitry of fear conditioning in the rat brain, they found that the certain regions of the amygdala are most active in learning to be afraid of the tone (Wilensky et al., 2006).

A number of studies of the amygdala's role in fear in humans have yielded findings consistent with those of studies using rats. People with damaged amygdalas do not show normal physiological reactions under fear conditioning. They tend to trust faces that most people find to be untrustworthy and have trouble recognizing facial expressions of fear, especially in the eyes (Adolphs et al., 1994, 2005; Adolphs, Tranel, & Damasio, 1998; Phelps & LeDoux, 2005). Brain imaging studies of people with intact brains reveal increased amygdala activation when they are exposed to fear faces, while the amygdala is not active when people view other facial expressions of emotion (Breiter et al., 1996). Finally, although certain regions of the amygdala are more involved in fear, other regions are more involved in anger and rage (Panksepp, 2000). In fact, tumours of the amygdala have been found in violent criminals, such as in Charles Whitman, who climbed the tower at the University of Texas in 1966 and in a 90-minute shooting spree killed 19 people and wounded 38 (Charles J. Whitman Catastrophe, Medical Aspects, Report to Governor, September 8, 1966).

The Prefrontal Cortex Phineas Gage, whose case is described in Chapter 3, was a 19th-century railroad worker who survived a severe injury to his prefrontal cortex, only to be transformed from a relatively mild-mannered man into an impatient, easily enraged individual. This was the first indication to scientists of the importance of the prefrontal cortex in emotion and personality. Since then, researchers have discovered that the prefrontal cortex is one of the more active regions of the brain in the experience and appraisal of emotions. Damage to the left prefrontal cortex results in depression (Morris et al., 1996; Sackheim et al., 1982). According to EEG studies that measure cortical activity, clinically depressed people show less activity in the left prefrontal cortex than do non-depressed people (Davidson, 2001). Moreover, due to its involvement in planning, impulse control, and working memory, the prefrontal cortex plays a role in the appraisal and reappraisal of emotion (Miller & Cummings, 1999; Miyake et al., 2000). Kevin Ochsner and his colleagues (2002) reported that the amygdala is more involved in determining whether a situation merits an emotional response at all, while the prefrontal cortex may be more involved in determining options for response or reappraisal. Given that there are neural connections between the prefrontal cortex and the amygdala, this finding and others like it may indicate that certain regions of the prefrontal cortex influence the emotional responses produced by the amygdala (Davidson, 2004; Pessoa, Padmala, & Morland, 2005; Pessoa, 2008).

Connections

The prefrontal cortex plays a key role in working memory by evaluating sensory information and designating it for storage or disposal.

See Chapter 6, LO8.

Other Brain Regions in Emotion Other regions of the brain are involved in emotions as well (Dalgleish, 2004). A meta-analysis of more than 55 brain imaging studies reports that the *anterior cingulate cortex* (ACC) is active when people either recall or imagine emotional experiences (Phan et al., 2002; also see Figure 11.16). The ACC is also the region of the brain that is active both in physical pain and in the pain of rejection or exclusion (Eisenberger et al., 2003).

What areas of the brain are active when we experience positive emotions? Several studies suggest that the left prefrontal cortex is more involved in positive emotions than the right (Davidson, 2004; Davidson et al., 1990). Other work suggests that these regions are primarily involved in emotions that have approach components (emotions that impel the organism to move toward something or someone), which includes the negative emotion of anger as well as positive emotions (Harmon-Jones, 2003). The hypothalamus also appears to be a pleasure or reward centre, because animals will forgo food and drink to receive stimulation there (Olds & Milner, 1954). Similarly, humans report feeling pleasure when this region is stimulated (Heath, 1975).

Connection

When you see another person you care about get hurt physically, it creates activity in the insula similar to what you experience with feelings of your own physical pain.

See Chapter 14, LO12.

Finally, the insula is the brain structure most involved in *interoception,* or the perception of sensations arising within the body. As such, it plays an important role in emotional experience. In fMRI studies, the insula is active during the experience of pain and empathy for another's pain (Singer et al., 2004). Visualizing disgusting scenes also leads to activation of the insula as well as the ACC (Schienle, Shafer, & Vaitl, 2008). Insular activity is reduced when women attempt to regulate their disgust with reappraisal (Goldin et al., 2008).

Gender and Emotion

Are there sex differences in emotion? People all around the world think women are more emotional than men (Fischer & Manstead, 2000). Women do outperform men in accurately recognizing facial expressions of emotion (Brody & Hall, 2000; Hall & Matsumoto, 2004; Merten, 2005). But if you study emotions as they are actually happening, men and women's ratings of their emotional experience look similar (Barrett et al., 1998). The sexes differ most in how they describe their emotional experiences in words and in the frequency of smiling.

Women talk more about emotions than men do. In a study of married couples discussing an area of conflict in their marriage, women were more likely to use words expressing distress and anger, whereas men were more likely to withdraw from conflict. Furthermore, men reported feeling negative when they were physiologically aroused, while there was no relationship between mood and arousal in women (Levenson, Carstensen, & Gottman, 1994). Furthermore, women are more likely to describe their reactions to a particular experience with more refinement than men, using phrases such as "I felt angry and upset" rather than the more general phrase "I felt bad" (Barrett et al., 2000).

Women tend to talk about emotions more than men do, but there is little difference in the facial expressions of men and women during emotional experiences.

In general, women smile more often than men (LaFrance, Hecht, & Paluk, 2003). And exposure to pictures of animal or human attacks provokes greater amygdala activation in men than in women, possibly reflecting a greater tendency toward aggressive action in men (Scheinle et al., 2008). Otherwise, studies of facial behaviour during emotional experiences find no consistent differences between men and women (Gross & John, 1998). Likewise, the similarities between the sexes in terms of emotion and the brain are far more impressive than the differences (Wagner & Ochsner, 2005).

Quick Quiz 11.3: Culture, the Brain, and Gender in Emotion

1. Which of the following is *not* a basic emotion?
   a. fear
   b. happiness
   c. disgust
   d. shame
2. The social norm set forth by our culture that says that winners should not gloat is an example of a(n)
   a. display rule.
   b. human universal.
   c. affective trait.
   d. antecedent event.
3. The _____ appears to play a very important role in appraisal of the emotional significance of stimuli, with a specialized function for noticing fear-relevant information.
   a. amygdala
   b. hypothalamus
   c. prefrontal cortex
   d. insula
4. Which kind of emotion phrases are women more apt to use than men?
   a. more general comments, such as "I feel bad"
   b. more specific comments, such as "I am upset and angry."
   c. more affective imagery, such as "my fear is blue and cold"
   d. phrases such as "I will blow my top!"

Answers can be found at the end of the chapter.

Evaluating Connections in Motivation and Emotion

Living a Happy Life

The idea that emotion and motivation are intertwined seems obvious when we're faced with hunger, thirst, sexual attraction, or social isolation. As Beck Weathers's story at the beginning of the chapter clearly illustrates, when our very survival is threatened, these two powerful psychological forces join together. Certainly we all have a strong will to survive. But what do we really want in our day-to-day lives? Not surprisingly, most people would answer that they simply want to be happy. But what does it mean to be happy and how do we achieve happiness in our lives? In this section we discuss the pursuit of happiness in the context of motivation and emotion.

Life Satisfaction around the World

Throughout this chapter, the word *happiness* was used to describe a brief, emotional state, but it can also be used to mean a long-term sense of satisfaction with life. In order to capture this broader meaning, researchers usually measure **life satisfaction,** the overall evaluation we have of our lives (Diener et al., 1999). Psychologists consider life satisfaction to be a subset of **subjective well-being,** which also includes satisfaction in different domains, such as career, family, finances, and social networks.

life satisfaction
the overall evaluation we make of our lives and an aspect of subjective well-being.

subjective well-being
state that consists of life satisfaction, domain satisfactions, and positive and negative affect.

Most countries measure their wealth in terms of a statistic called the *gross national product* (GNP), the value in goods, services, and income produced by a country in one year. Often evaluated on a per-person basis, a high GNP is considered a sign of a country's economic success. So why, in 1972, did the King of Bhutan decide to measure the wealth of his nation differently? In response to criticism that his country was poor, King Jigme Singye Wangchuk argued that, on the contrary, Bhutan is rich. This tiny Himalayan kingdom is steeped in spiritual practices that promote happiness and freedom from suffering for all beings.

As an alternative to the GNP, King Wangchuk created a new metric, the *GNH*. GNH is an indicator of *gross national happiness*. It reflects things like access to health care, a clean environment, the amount of free time available for family, and other non-monetary measures of well-being. GNH per person is measured by having people complete a survey to measure their sense of well-being in different contexts, from the workplace to the home. This small nation actively encouraged others to follow, and in 2011 the United Nations passed a resolution proposed by the prime minister of Bhutan, inviting member countries to measure the happiness of their people. This culminated in the first *World Happiness Report*, which was released in 2012.

One of the consistent findings from the original *World Happiness Report* and subsequent updates is that life satisfaction varies widely across the globe (see Figure 11.17). Ratings are measured on a scale called the Cantril ladder, which asks participants to evaluate their lives from 0 (worst possible life) to 10 (best possible life). The countries reporting the highest life satisfaction in are mainly in northern Europe, particularly Nordic countries, and those reporting lowest life satisfaction are almost exclusively in sub-Saharan Africa. The data show this divide to be substantial, with a full four point difference on the Cantril ladder between the happiest and unhappiest countries (Helliman et al., 2012; 2013; 2015). (Incidentally, Canada consistently ranks fifth or sixth in the world).

So what's different about happy and unhappy countries? In general, the higher a country's GNP, the higher its well-being. On the surface, this makes a lot of sense because poverty generally brings problems that interfere with life satisfaction (Diener & Seligman, 2004). But there are many exceptions to this trend, especially in Latin America. Mexico and Costa Rica are just as happy as countries like Sweden and the Netherlands, in spite of having only a *fifth* of their per-person GNP. Other non-monetary factors, such as social support and life expectancy, also contribute to life satisfaction and well-being (Helliwell et al., 2015).

Can Money Buy Happiness?

Basic needs must be met for a person to be relatively satisfied with life. Accordingly, affluent countries have higher levels of well-being than poorer countries. Maslow's hierarchical model of motivation offers a useful framework for a discussion of motivation and happiness. After all, basic needs are met with money to buy food, clothes, and shelter. For nations with at least $12 000 per-person, per-year GNP, close relationships matter most for overall levels of happiness (Headey, 2008). At the individual level, there is a modest, yet complex relationship between income and overall life satisfaction as well. Having more money does make people slightly happier, but this is true only for those driven by money (Diener et al., 1999; Nickerson et al., 2003).

You might be thinking, of course money can't buy everything, but it can certainly make life easier, and doesn't that make people happier? It turns out this might not be so simple. In a now famous study, Brickman and colleagues (1978) surveyed two groups of people who should differ dramatically in their self-reports of life

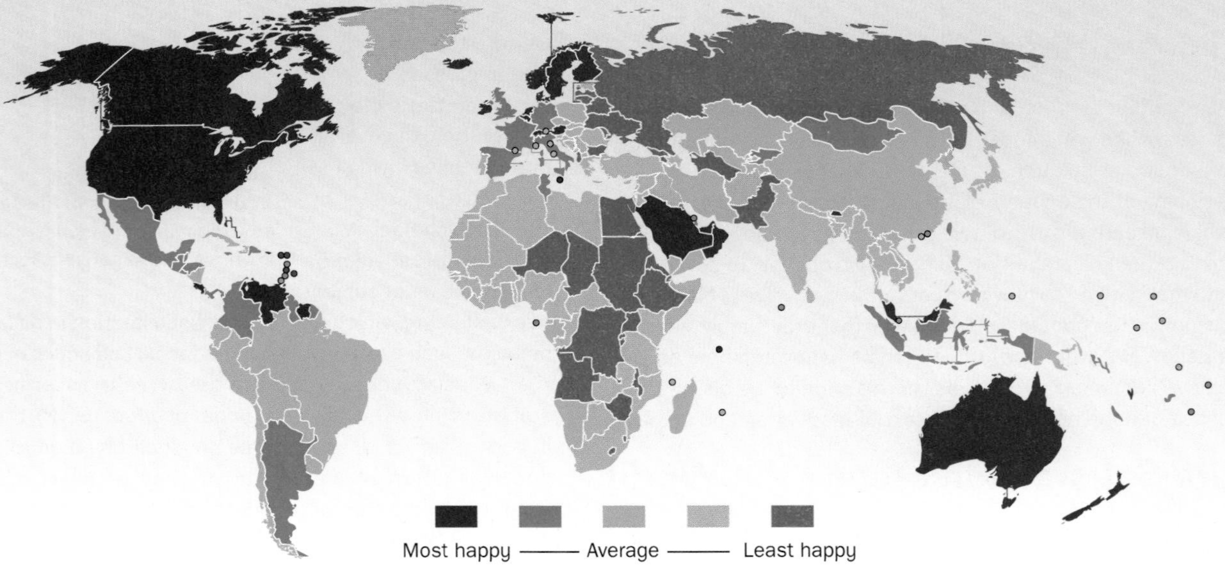

FIGURE **11.17**

WORLD HAPPINESS MAP. This map of subjective well-being closely matches projections based on poverty and national income.

satisfaction: new lottery winners and quadri- or paraplegics who were recent victims in serious accidents. Surprisingly, they found no difference in ratings of happiness between the two groups! In fact, more recent research suggests that it isn't how much money we make, but how we spend it that matters. Elizabeth Dunn of the University of British Columbia and collaborator Michael Norton of Harvard University have shown that spending money on *others*, not ourselves, is associated with happiness (2008). This line of research shows that not only does spending on others make us feel happier, but it also improves work satisfaction in Australian bank employees, leads to higher sales in pharmaceutical sales teams in Belgium, and improves performance in players on a Canadian dodge ball team (Anik et al., 2013). Paying-it-forward makes us happy and appears to be universal: Four-year-old human children and adult monkeys will reward others with gifts if they have just received a gift themselves (Leimgruber et al., 2014).

So what should we do to do in order to fulfill our drive for a happy life? According to research, Maslow's higher-level needs are most likely to lead to happiness. Bruce Headey (2008) reported in a 20-year longitudinal study that people who value non-competitive goals, such as spending time with a spouse, children, and friends, tend to become happier and more satisfied with life over time. People, however, who most value competitive achievement goals, such as career advancement and material gains, actually decrease in happiness over time. Another higher-level need is the cognitive need to explore and understand the world. People who are curious and interested in exploring novel and challenging situations tend to be happier than people who would rather stick with what they know and not challenge themselves with new tasks and experiences (Diener et al., 1999; Gallagher & Lopez, 2007; Headey, 2008). This finding is consistent with the broaden-and-build model of positive emotion we discussed earlier, which assumes that positive emotional states lead to expansive thoughts and behaviour rather than to a narrow focus. The connection between curiosity, openness to novel experiences, and life satisfaction is also consistent with the optimal arousal theories of motivation, which assert that people seek out challenging and moderately arousing situations for optimal performance.

Emotions, Happiness, and Meaning in Life

A sense of well-being and satisfaction in life consists of the right balance of many different positive and negative emotions. In particular, the positive emotions can act as a buffer against long-term negative emotions. Happiness and life satisfaction are not about avoiding negative emotions, but rather about not dwelling on them. Sadness, anger, disgust, and even depression happen to everyone. Psychological science shows that if we bring some degree of life satisfaction and positive emotions with us as we go through our more challenging life experiences, we are more likely to emerge happier and healthier than if we don't. Fostering positive emotion, even in the face of tragic and trying experiences, can reap long-term psychological and emotional benefits (Fredrickson & Joiner, 2002). Similarly, people who find meaning in their lives in general and even in negative and tragic experiences are likely to be happier in life than those who do not see meaning and purpose in life's difficult and unpleasant experiences (King et al., 2006). Psychologists propose that positive emotion can enhance meaning in life by broadening one's way of thinking and connecting experiences.

Challenge Your Assumptions

True or False? More money leads to greater happiness.

Somewhat True, Somewhat False: Modest gains in income lead to higher levels of happiness; after that, there is no increase. Research shows that money *can* make people happy if it's spent on others.

Quick Quiz 11.4: Evaluating Connections in Motivation and Emotion

1. According to research, what is the relationship between money and happiness?
   a. Money is linked to happiness in countries of the northern hemisphere, but not the southern hemisphere.
   b. Receiving large sums of money, such as winning the lottery, increases people's happiness for a long period of time.
   c. In general, countries with the lowest GNP report the greatest life satisfaction.
   d. In general, countries with the highest GNP report the greatest life satisfaction.

2. People who are curious and interested in exploring novel and challenging situations tend to be
   a. about as smart as everyone else.
   b. happier than those who have a narrow perspective.
   c. smarter than narrow-minded people.
   d. alienated from others.

Answers can be found at the end of the chapter.

Chapter Review

MOTIVATION

- The psychology of motivation addresses the question of why people do what they do.
- Motivation encompasses needs, drives, and motivated behaviour. Motives involve anything that energizes or directs behaviour.
- Needs are states of cellular or bodily deficiency that compel drives, such as the need for water, food, and oxygen, while drives are the perceived state of tension that occurs when our bodies are deficient in some need—thirst, hunger, breathing.
- Maslow organized the various forces that drive human behaviour in a vertical fashion, creating a hierarchy in which lower-level biological needs are subordinate to higher-level needs. More recent updates to this theory have incorporated evolutionary perspectives.
- Hunger is a basic drive that ensures that we take in sufficient nutrition to survive.
- Internal signals of hunger include sensations of the stomach and blood glucose levels, both of which are coordinated by sensors in the brain; external signals for hunger include the sight and smell of food as well as culturally influenced preferences.
- Eating disorders are complex and dangerous outcomes of a culture obsessed with thinness. At the same time, rates of obesity have increased dramatically over the last 50 years.
- Like all human motives, sexual desire results from a complex interplay of both biological and social forces.
- The hypothalamus plays an important role in sexual arousal.
- Hormones, especially testosterone, regulate sexual drive.
- Research on gender differences and casual sex tends to consistently find that males are more likely than females to engage in casual sex.
- Sexual orientation is a motive that involves both biological and social influences.
- One's tendency to achieve success is a function of three things: motivation to succeed, expectation of success, and the incentive value of the success.

EMOTION

- Unlike the longer-lasting moods and affective traits, emotions are acute, multifaceted responses to important events in our environment. Emotion can best be understood as a process that unfolds over time, beginning with exposure to an antecedent event, then appraisal. Appraisals determine whether an emotion occurs. Emotional responses include changes in behaviour/expression, physiology, and subjective experience.
- Emotion regulation is an umbrella term for anything we do to try to change or otherwise manipulate the emotions we experience.
- From an evolutionary perspective, emotions function to organize body systems for a quick and efficient response to an important environmental event. This model applies best to negative emotions. Positive emotions, according to the broaden-and-build model, expand our thinking and help us develop knowledge and skills.
- The facial expressions of a set of basic emotions—anger, disgust, fear, happiness, sadness, and surprise—are recognized universally and appear to have evolutionary significance.
- Self-conscious emotions are a function of how well we live up to our expectations, the expectations of others, or the rules set by society and require a sense of self and the ability to reflect on one's own actions. Shame, guilt, humiliation, embarrassment, and pride are examples of self-conscious emotions.
- Display rules show how cultural factors can lead to differences in expression of emotion. Cultural variability is less apparent in the physiological changes associated with emotions.
- Physiological changes of negative emotions tend to be associated with higher arousal and activation of the sympathetic branch of the autonomic nervous system. Many physiological changes of positive emotions engage the parasympathetic nervous system to relax the body.
- Scientists are not sure what produces the subjective experience of emotion. The James-Lange theory holds that the perception of body changes plays an important role in a person's emotional experience. The Cannon-Bard theory states that subjective emotional experience

and physiological changes occur simultaneously via parallel brain pathways. Schachter and Singer's two-factor theory of emotion suggests that conscious emotional experience is determined by both an awareness of bodily arousal paired with a cognitive appraisal of the situation.

- The brain is involved in every aspect of the emotion process, from appraisal to regulation. Although many brain structures appear to be crucial to emotions, the amygdala and the prefrontal cortex are major players.

EVALUATING CONNECTIONS IN MOTIVATION AND EMOTION

- Happiness, life satisfaction, and subjective well-being are not directly related to income. People who find meaning in their lives in general and even in negative and tragic experiences are likely to be happier in life.

Quick Quiz Answers

Quick Quiz 11.1: 1. b 2. d 3. b 4. a **Quick Quiz 11.2:** 1. a 2. c 3. d **Quick Quiz 11.3:** 1. d 2. a 3. a 4. b
Quick Quiz 11.4: 1. d 2. b

Stress and Health

CHAPTER

12

CHAPTER OUTLINE

Challenge Your Assumptions

True or False?

- ☐ Adrenaline is also known as the "stress hormone" and is responsible for most body responses to prolonged stress.
- ☐ Stress is always bad for your health.
- ☐ Stress can make your hair suddenly turn grey.
- ☐ People with Type A behaviour patterns react to stress with hostility, and this puts them at risk for heart disease.

LEARNING OBJECTIVES

- **LO1** Define what is meant by stress and give examples of different types of stressors.
- **LO2** Explain the role of appraisal in the stress response.
- **LO3** Explain the roles of the adrenal-medullary system and HPA axis during stress.
- **LO4** Describe the three stages of the general adaptation syndrome.
- **LO5** Describe how stress affects health.
- **LO6** Describe behaviours that promote and prevent disease.
- **LO7** Describe problem-focused and emotion-focused coping.
- **LO8** Explain how social support can help an individual cope with stress.
- **LO9** Give examples of how positive emotions and traits benefit health and well-being.

It seems that every semester when final exams roll around something happens to Dora's health. One year she had a huge canker sore under her tongue and could hardly talk for a few days. Another time she had horrific headaches. Both problems occurred shortly after the most intense studying period of the semester, making it hard for her to concentrate on her exams, and sometimes ruining the beginning of her break.

Kyle has herpes, a virus that often remains dormant in the body but occasionally causes very painful and itchy sores. His outbreaks always seem to occur when he's been stressed out. Moreover, the more he worries about the possibility of an outbreak, the more likely he is to get one.

Estelle, 52, takes care of her 75-year-old mother, who has advanced Alzheimer's disease. It is exhausting work, because her mother is losing the ability to perform many daily tasks, such as preparing food and bathing. It's made even worse because her mother's emotions have become very unpredictable. Confused from the disease, she yells at Estelle frequently and blames her daughter for her problems. Estelle has a hard time coping with this stress and finds herself drinking vodka for relief, far more often than she knows she should.

As a new recruit in the military, George was exhausted from the daily physical challenges and sleep deprivation (less than five hours a night) that were part of the rigorous, challenging, and stressful training program. George, however, had always been driven and disciplined and stuck to his goals and interests. He was determined to make it through training, even though a relatively large number of recruits did not. He not only finished, he thrived and was one of the highest ranked trainees at graduation.

Each of these real-life cases highlights a kind of life stress and shows how stress might affect health. What causes stress, and what effects does stress have on us? Why do some people manage to see a situation as challenging rather than burdensome, whereas others don't? Can stress really make us sick?

In this chapter we examine the psychological and physiological nature of stress and the related topic of coping. We then survey some major topics in the field of health psychology, a discipline that emerged from an interest in the effects of stress on physical health. We will highlight how stress emerges from and modifies mental and physical processes, how differences in people's ability to deal with life's challenges influence the functioning of their bodies, as well as how these bodily responses can affect how people think and feel. Few other topics in psychology illustrate as clearly the interdependence of nature and nurture.

LO1 WHAT IS STRESS?

We all know what it feels like to be stressed. But the term *stress* can refer to a wide variety of phenomena. We speak of having a stressful life when we consider the pressures or demands that make our lives difficult or interfere with our ability to maintain a feeling of well-being. Sometimes people talk about "feeling stressed," as if stress were an emotional state, one that involves anxiety and exhaustion. Some people are "stressed" by minor events such as a parking ticket or a missed train, whereas others seem to sail through life amid a great number of demands—work, family, school—all the while maintaining a sense of well-being and balance.

Stress is part of a dynamic interplay between people's interpretations of events in their lives and their reactions to those interpretations. **Stress** occurs when a situation overwhelms a person's perceived ability to meet the demands of that situation. As with emotions, we continually evaluate our experiences of stressful situations and attempt to cope with the challenges they pose. Suppose, for example, you are doing poorly in a class, and you have the final exam in one week. You feel stressed at first, but then you realize that with more review of the material, meeting with a study group, and more sleep, you could do better. You resolve to make these changes to improve your chances for a good final exam grade.

stress
a state when a situation overwhelms a person's perceived ability to meet the demands of that situation.

Stress has different meanings in different contexts. Stress can be external to us. We can think of stress as something that happens *to* us—that is, as situations that push us to the limit or threaten our safety or well-being. Or stress can be the relentless onslaught of difficulties, such as being late on a term paper, the car breaking down, realizing there is no money in bank, and then getting into a fight with a roommate all in one week. We call these events that push us to the limit or exceed our ability to manage the situation at hand **stressors.** The focus on the situations that cause stress is known as the *stimulus view of stress.*

stressors
events that trigger a stress response.

In contrast, stress can be internal to us; we can think of it as the feeling we experience when events are too much to handle. The *response view of stress* has focused on the physiological changes that occur when someone encounters an excessively challenging situation. Later we will explore Hans Selye's work on looking at stress as a physiological response.

Clearly stress is much more than being in certain situations, and it is much more than physiological responses. It exists within the relationship between the

Driving, particularly in high-traffic urban areas, can elicit a stress response.
What events in your day-to-day life would you consider stressful?

Life Event	Value
Death of spouse	100
Divorce	73
Marital separation	65
Jail term	63
Death of close family member	63
Change in financial state	38
Death of a close friend	37
Change to a different line of work	36
Foreclosure of mortgage	30
Change in responsibilities at work	29
Change in sleeping habits	16
Change in eating habits	15
Vacation	13
Christmas	12
Minor legal violations	11

FIGURE **12.1**
SOCIAL READJUSTMENT RATING SCALE. Developed by Holmes and Rahe, this scale quantifies stress in terms of major life changes. The higher the value, the greater the stress associated with an event.

external events and the internal responses. Stress emerges from people's interpretations of the relevance of certain stressors to their lives and their ability to deal with them. This *relational view of stress* holds that stress is a particular relationship between the people and the situations in which they find themselves.

We will look briefly at the view of stress as a stimulus, which has dominated psychological research for many years. Then we will explore the relational view, before turning to the research on stress as a physiological response, which sets a foundation for our understanding of how stress can affect health.

Stress as a Stimulus

Generally, stressors fall under two classes: *systemic* and *processive.* Systemic stressors are those that pose a direct physical threat to survival, such as injury or lack of oxygen. Processive stressors, on the other hand, are psychological in nature and do not pose a direct threat to survival. Rather, they are associated with threats based on an individual's prior experience and include most of the stressors we are faced with in our daily lives, such as financial troubles and relationship difficulties (Herman & Cullinan, 1997). Processive stressors tend to persist for a longer period of time and therefore are most likely to have a significant impact upon health and well-being.

Psychologists typically measure stress as a stimulus by quantifying the number of stressors a person experiences during a given period, ranging from daily hassles to major life events. Any situation that creates a major upheaval in a person's life could potentially lead to stress, so one approach to measuring stress as a stimulus focuses on major life events. In the late 1960s, Holmes and Rahe (1967) developed an instrument called the "Social Readjustment Rating Scale" (SRRS) to quantify stress in terms of major life changes. The scale consists of a list of 43 events that might be considered life-changing; each is assigned a corresponding life change value (a selection of items from this scale is shown in Figure 12.1). After a person has responded to the questions on the scale, a researcher can calculate the total amount of stress the respondent is experiencing by adding up relative stress values, which were derived on the basis of previous research, known as Life Change Units (Holmes & Rahe, 1967).

The SRRS is easy to administer and score, but it has some drawbacks. First, it ignores the fact that people view similar events differently, and while some people might find marriage more stressful than a major work change, for others it may be vice versa (Scully, Tosi, & Banning, 2000). Second, by measuring stress in terms of life events, the SRRS fails to consider differences in people's emotional responses to stressors. Nevertheless, the SRRS is still widely used in research on stress and health, showing positive correlations with measures of mental and physical health (Gottlieb & Green, 1984).

Connection

Like stress, emotions are generated by our appraisals of events in our lives.

See Chapter 11, LO6.

Often it's the little things that really bother us rather than major life events. An alternative to the SRRS is the "Hassles and Uplifts Scale," which measures the frequency and intensity of minor irritations (hassles) and positive events (uplifts) of daily life (Kanner et al., 1981). The accumulation of minor irritations—traffic, too much homework, relationship troubles—might wear us down, both mentally and physically. On the other hand, life's little pleasures, such as spending time with friends and family, can lessen the impact of negative experiences. A number of studies report positive correlations between the frequency of daily hassles and self-reported health symptoms (DeLongis, Folkman, & Lazarus, 1988; Feist et al., 1995; Kohn, Lafreniere, & Gurevich, 1991). In fact, some data indicate that hassles are more strongly related to health outcomes than are major life events (Kohn, et al., 1991; Weinberger, Hiney, & Tierney, 1987).

But we have said that stress is complex, involving situations, interpretations, and physiological responses. Given such a perspective, what are the limitations of measuring stress only in terms of stressors, or situations? A major limitation to measuring both major life events and hassles is that not all people view situations in the same way. What is a stressor to one person might not be a stressor at all to another. For example, a poorly prepared student might dread an exam, but a student who has studied thoroughly might welcome it as a challenge. This example points to the ways in which people differ in how they respond to situations. Using this logic, Lazarus and Folkman (1984) argued that because people do not view similar situations in the same way, it is misleading to examine stress solely in terms of the situations that may call it forth. We have to look at the person in relation to the situation.

Do you consider moving a major stressor? Do you think everyone feels the same way as you do?

LO2 Relationship between Person and Situation

As we saw with emotion, when we first encounter a situation in our environment, we quickly appraise its significance to us. Lazarus and Folkman (1984) talk about two kinds of appraisal. **Primary appraisal** is an assessment of what a situation means to us. The outcome of this appraisal determines whether an emotional response might occur. If we view the event as not personally relevant, we feel no emotion. If we consider it personally relevant, we appraise its significance as either contrary to or consistent with our goals or welfare. If we appraise it as contrary to our well-being, we feel a negative emotion, which might cause stress. If we appraise it as consistent with our well-being, we feel a positive emotion. Figure 12.2 depicts the process by which different appraisals lead to different emotional outcomes. Even though both pleasant and unpleasant events might lead to stress, stress emerges from negative emotional responses to events that we cannot get under control. Any kind of event—pleasant or unpleasant—might be fodder for such emotional reactions. For example, a wedding is a pleasant event that can be stressful, as is a new relationship or a busy social calendar.

primary appraisal
quick assessment of the meaning of a given environmental event for the individual.

Emotional events may escalate into stress when we cannot deal with the demands that the event entails. According to Lazarus and Folkman, we assess the resources available to cope with stress in a process they term **secondary appraisal.** When we find ourselves in a stressful situation, we try to figure out what to do about that situation, how to resolve it, or how to make the unpleasant feeling it creates go away.

secondary appraisal
self-assessment of the resources available to cope with stress.

LO3 The Physiology of the Stress Response

When stressful situations lead to negative emotions, physiological changes occur in the autonomic nervous system (ANS), the endocrine system, and the brain. As discussed in Chapter 3, the sympathetic, or "fight or flight," division of the ANS mediates arousal and action in the face of threat, and therefore plays a crucial role in response to stress. The sympathetic nervous system is made up of neurons that influence organs and glands, and its activation has widespread effects on physiology. For instance, it stimulates the circulatory system to pump blood to large muscle groups during times of emergency, and the respiratory system to provide the oxygen required so that those muscles can function.

Whether the body is in a state of "fight or flight" or "rest and digest" is strongly influenced by the release of **hormones,** chemical messengers that

Connections

The sympathetic branch of the ANS activates the body; the parasympathetic branch calms the body. Both play a role in stress and emotion.

See Chapter 3, LO4; and Chapter 11, LO7.

hormones
chemicals, secreted by glands, that travel in the bloodstream and carry messages to tissues and organs all over the body.

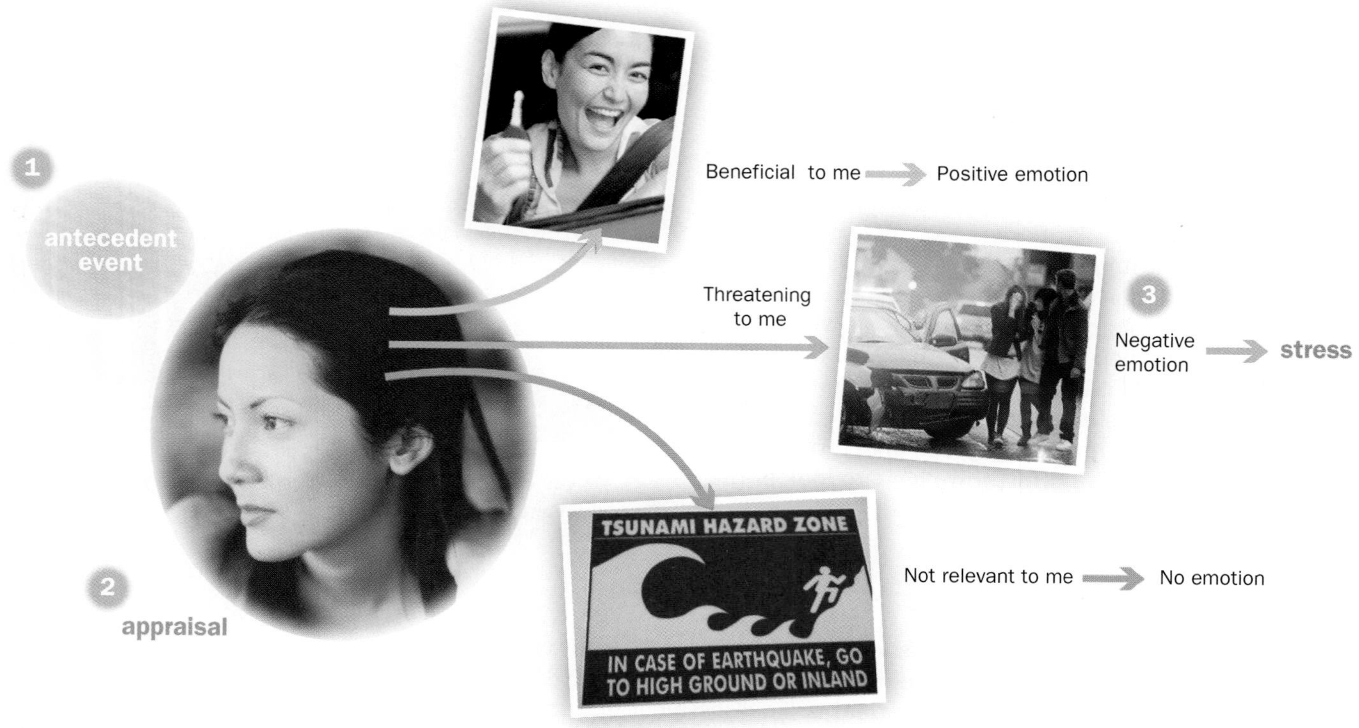

FIGURE **12.2**

THE EMOTION/STRESS PROCESS. When events are appraised as threatening, negative emotions occur. In this model, stress occurs only when negative emotion is sustained.

According to this model, under what conditions does stress occur?

travel through the bloodstream to tissues and organs all over the body and regulate body functions. Hormones play a crucial role in regulating metabolism, growth, reproduction, mood, and other processes. Hormone release is controlled by glands of the **endocrine system.** Figure 12.3 depicts some of the major endocrine glands of the body.

endocrine system
system of glands that secrete and regulate hormones in the body.

The *thyroid* gland sits in the neck region and releases hormones that control the rate of metabolism, the process by which the body converts nutritional substances into energy. The *pancreas* releases hormones, including insulin, that play a vital role in regulating the blood sugar levels. The sex glands (ovaries and testes) release sex hormones that lead to development of sex characteristics (such as body hair and breast development), sex drive, and other aspects of sexual maturation.

Emotional states brought about by the limbic system, can have profound effects on release of certain types of hormones. The limbic system has strong connections with the endocrine system, particularly via the hypothalamus. It controls the **pituitary gland,** also called the body's master gland, because it secretes hormones that control the release of hormones from glands elsewhere in the body. The **neuroendocrine system** refers to hormonal systems whose activity is regulated by the nervous system. The hypothalamus is the site of unique neurons known as *neurosecretory cells,* whose terminals release their chemical messengers into bloodstream rather than into a synapse (Brown, 1994).

pituitary gland
the master endocrine gland that controls the release of hormones from glands throughout the body.

neuroendocrine system
the hormonal systems whose activity is regulated by the nervous system.

The key structures involved in the neuroendocrine regulation of stress responses include the hypothalamus, the pituitary gland, and the adrenal glands. The hypothalamus serves as a major link between the nervous system and the parts of the endocrine system relevant to emotions: It releases chemicals that stimulate the release of hormones from the pituitary gland, which sits just

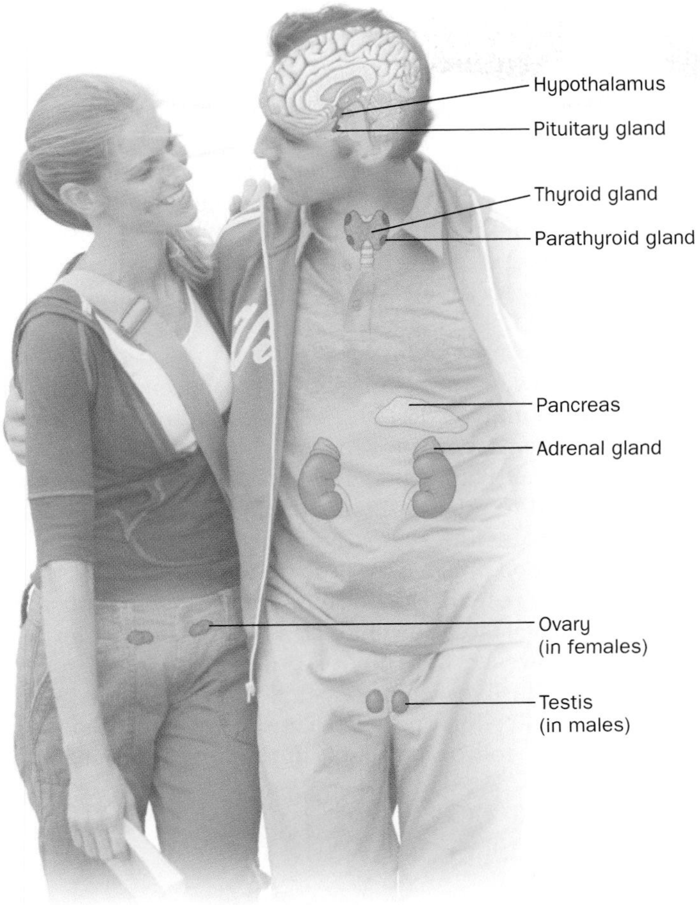

FIGURE 12.3
THE ENDOCRINE SYSTEM. The endocrine system consists of numerous glands found throughout the body. The pancreas, for example, releases insulin, which is important in transporting sugars (glucose) from the bloodstream into the cells. Cells then use the glucose as their energy source. The thyroid gland regulates metabolism.

beneath it, and it is connected to brain stem structures that control the ANS. The pituitary releases hormones that play a key role in the stress response.

The **adrenal glands,** which sit atop the kidneys, release hormones in response to stress and regulate heart rate, blood pressure, and blood sugar.

adrenal glands
endocrine structures that release hormones important in regulating the stress response and emotions.

Physiological changes that enable us to respond quickly during an emergency can take a toll on our bodies if stress persists.

catecholamines
chemicals released from the adrenal glands that function as hormones and as neurotransmitters to control ANS activation.

adrenal steroids
fat-soluble hormones released from the adrenal gland; they have widespread and long-lasting effects.

glucocorticoids
steroid hormones released by the adrenal glands; responsible for maintaining the activation of bodily systems during prolonged stress.

adrenal-medullary system
a major neuroendocrine pathway stimulated during stress in which the hypothalamus activates the sympathetic nervous system.

norepinephrine
a neurotransmitter that activates the sympathetic response to stress, increasing heart rate, rate of respiration, and blood pressure in support of rapid action.

The adrenal glands release numerous different hormones, but they fall into one of two classes: the fast-acting **catecholamines** and slower acting **adrenal steroids.** The catecholamines released from the adrenal glands include norepinephrine, and epinephrine, which are also released as neurotransmitters in the brain. When released into the bloodstream as hormones, they control ANS activation and arousal in the body. The adrenal steroids are synthesized from cholesterol and are therefore fat-soluble, which enables their widespread distribution throughout the body and brain. Like the catecholamines, adrenal steroids called **glucocorticoids** are released during stress. They act over a longer time period to maintain the activation of many bodily systems during prolonged stress.

When activated by an emotional event, the hypothalamus initiates a series of endocrine events that have a profound effect on the body. Two major neuroendocrine pathways are stimulated: the adrenal-medullary system and the hypothalamus-pituitary-adrenal axis (see Figure 12.4). First in line is the **adrenal-medullary system,** in which the hypothalamus sends instructions to the brain stem to activate sympathetic neurons. Then, sympathetic neurons tell the adrenal gland to release the important catecholamine **norepinephrine.** Norepinephrine activates the sympathetic response, increasing heart rate, rate of respiration, and blood pressure in order to support rapid action by the body.

The sympathetic response evolved because rapid mobilization of the body's resources in emergency situations had clear survival and reproductive benefits. In cases of stress, however, we cannot regulate this emergency response. Moreover, if we continually live with stress-inducing situations, our body remains in "emergency mode" for long periods. Thus, a response that is adaptive in the short term can take a toll on the body in the long term, leading, for example,

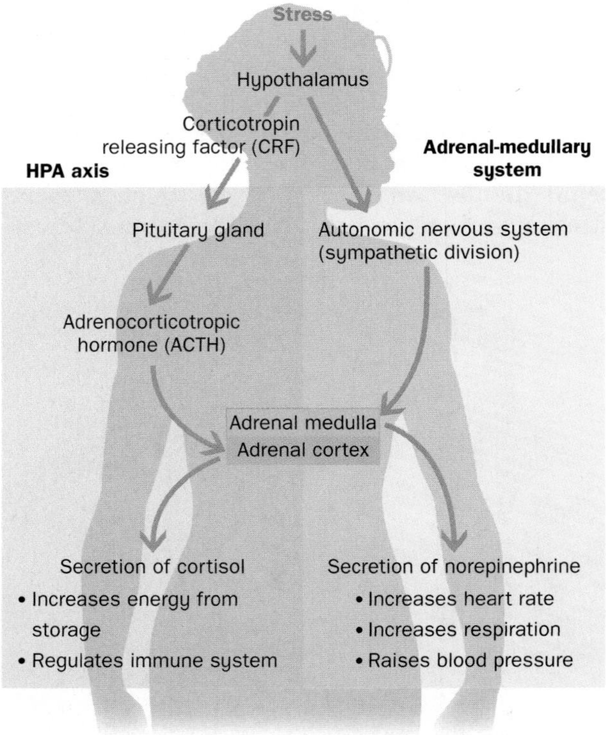

FIGURE **12.4**
THE HPA AXIS AND THE ADRENAL-MEDULLARY SYSTEM. During emotional arousal and stress, the hypothalamus activates the neuroendocrine system to prepare the body's response. The hypothalamus releases CRF, which stimulates the pituitary to release ACTH. ACTH then stimulates the cortex of the adrenal gland to release the "stress hormone" cortisol.

to sustained increases in blood pressure and heart rate. Think about how you feel when something startles you: Your heart races; you start breathing heavily; you're in a state of high alert. Now imagine what it would be like to remain in that condition for a period of days.

The other major neuroendocrine pathway that is relevant to the stress response is known as the **hypothalamic-pituitary-adrenal (HPA) axis.** Recall that the hypothalamus releases substances, called releasing factors, which tell the pituitary when to release various hormones. During emotional arousal and stress, the hypothalamus releases a substance called corticotropin releasing factor (CRF), which stimulates the pituitary to release adrenocorticotropic hormone (ACTH). ACTH then stimulates the cortex of the adrenal gland to release **cortisol,** the major glucocorticoid produced in humans, which is commonly known as the "stress hormone." When the level of cortisol in the blood adequately meets the body's metabolic needs, the hypothalamus stops releasing CRF, thereby reducing the release of cortisol. This kind of negative feedback occurs throughout the neuroendocrine system.

Cortisol has many important functions. It plays a role in the breakdown of complex molecules into simpler ones to release energy and so plays an important role in ensuring that more glucose is available for fuel in the bloodstream. Cortisol also has a regulatory effect on the immune system. It often acts to reduce the number of immune cells in the bloodstream, thus suppressing the immune system's ability to protect the body against infection (Segerstrom & Miller, 2004).

hypothalamic-pituitary-adrenal (HPA) axis
a major neuroendocrine pathway relevant to the stress response involving the hypothalamus, pituitary gland, and the adrenal cortex.

cortisol
hormone produced by the body to mobilize the body's energy resources during stressful situations.

Challenge Your Assumptions

True or False? Adrenaline is also known as the "stress hormone" and is responsible for most body responses to prolonged stress.

False: Although adrenaline (also called epinephrine) is released as part of the early sympathetic, or "fight or flight" response to stress, it is cortisol that maintains body responses to prolonged stress. Cortisol, not adrenaline, is referred to as the "stress hormone."

LO4

The General Adaptation Syndrome (GAS)

Canadian physiologist Hans Selye is credited with first identifying the importance of the HPA axis in responding to stress. Selye was fascinated by what happens to the body when it cannot cope with extreme stressors. Based upon experiments on rats carried out at McGill University in the 1930s, he discovered that stress exposure produces a series of physiological changes, including release of hormones from the adrenal gland (Selye, 1936, 1937). Selye is credited with first demonstrating the universality of this stress response, since he documented similar changes in animals exposed to a range of stressors such as extreme temperature change, severe electrical shock, radiation, or heavy exercise. In 1946, he proposed a three-stage model to explain the changes in physiology that occur during exposure to severe stressors. Selye believed that attempts to adapt to overwhelming stressors cause the body to wear down and eventually get sick. He used homeostasis as his starting point, and he viewed the changes that the body goes through when confronted with extreme situational demands as manifestations of adaptation to stress (Selye, 1976).

Selye proposed that although an infinite range of circumstances elicit stress, all stress causes a generalized, non-specific set of changes in the body. He measured hormones, metabolism, organ function, and other variables that change in response to stressors and observed a consistent pattern of responses regardless of the stressor. Selye coined the term **general adaptation syndrome (GAS)** to describe this general pattern of responses. In Selye's words, "The general adaptation syndrome is the sum of all the nonspecific, systemic reactions of the body which ensue upon long continued exposure to stress" (1946, p. 119).

The GAS consists of three stages: alarm, resistance, and exhaustion (see Figure 12.5). Upon exposure to a stressor, an animal enters into a state of physiological shock, called the **alarm stage,** which is the body's emergency response to an environmental threat. The alarm stage mobilizes the body's resources to act via the effects of adrenal-medullary activation of the sympathetic nervous system. During this stage the HPA axis is active as well, and the sustained release of cortisol from the adrenal glands may move from being helpful (by making more fuel available) to being harmful in the long run (by suppressing certain aspects of immune function).

Connections

Do you think an ethics review board would allow Selye to conduct his research on extreme stressors in animals today?

See Chapter 2, LO9.

general adaptation syndrome (GAS)
as defined by Hans Selye, a generalized, non-specific set of changes in the body that occur during extreme stress.

alarm stage
the phase of the general adaptation syndrome in which all of the body's resources respond to a perceived threat.

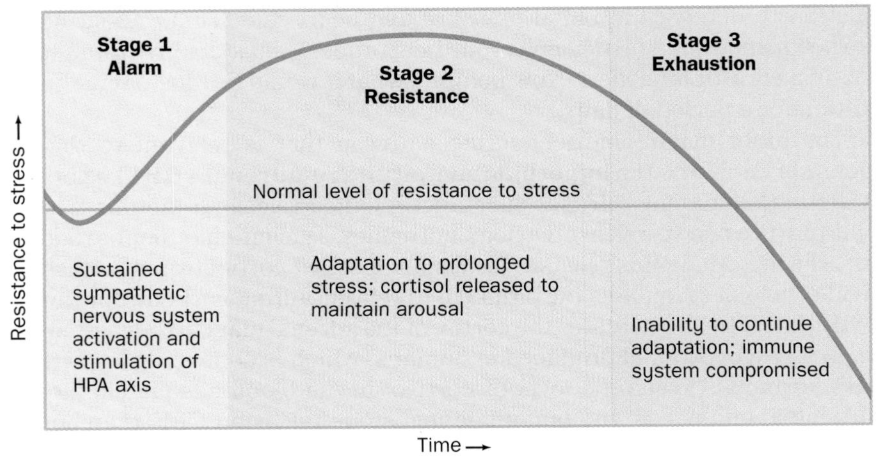

FIGURE **12.5**

SELYE'S GENERAL ADAPTATION SYNDROME (GAS). In the alarm stage, the body's resources are mobilized in response to a stressor. Resistance occurs when the body can no longer sustain the emergency response, and the organism must find other ways to ward off the threat. If the threat persists, eventually the body's resources become depleted, physical exhaustion occurs, and illness becomes much more likely.

resistance stage
in the general adaptation syndrome, extended effort by the body to deal with a threat.

exhaustion stage
the phase of the general adaptation syndrome when all resources for fighting the threat have been depleted and illness is more likely.

Animals, however, can persist in the alarm stage for only so long. With continued exposure to the stressor, they eventually either die or find other ways of coping with the enduring threat. When they develop other ways to cope, they enter the second stage of adaptation, the **resistance stage.** Resistance implies that the organism maintains efforts to fight off or manage the threat. This extended effort, however, takes its toll physically and psychologically by diverting resources from maintenance of normal body functions.

Resistance cannot be maintained indefinitely. With repeated or continuous exposure to a stressor, animals enter the **exhaustion stage.** At this stage, their resources for fighting off threats have been depleted, and illness becomes much more likely. Have you ever come down with a cold or other illness a week or so after final exams?

Selye's model laid the groundwork for research on the physiology of stress, but it soon became clear that his GAS model did not apply to all stress responses. First, Selye studied extreme physical stressors, such as nearly freezing an animal to death or repeatedly exposing it to severe electrical shock, and subjected animals to these stressors for prolonged periods. Questions arose as to whether the body changes that occurred in response to such severe demands provided a good model for enduring the stress of, say, divorce or financial troubles. Second, some researchers questioned the idea that a syndrome of body responses to stress occurred regardless of the type of stressor.

In the 1970s, John Mason conducted research that seriously challenged Selye's assumption that the stress response is a general one. Mason (1971, 1975) showed that an animal's response to a stressor differed depending on its psychological state. If the animal could anticipate a stressor, for example, it showed a less severe physiological response than an animal that could not anticipate a stressor (Mason, 1971). Further, research conducted during the 1980s showed that different emotions produce different patterns of ANS activation, casting further doubt on Selye's idea of a generalized physiological response to any environmental demand (Ekman, Levenson, & Friesen, 1983). Despite these findings, Selye's discovery of HPA axis activation as a physiological response common to all stressors has remained essentially unchallenged. In fact, HPA hormones are often used in both human and animal research as a stress indicator.

How We Adapt to Stress Most accounts of the physiology of stress (such as Selye's) think of stress as a deviation from balance. Recovery from stress occurs when all systems return to normal. This view is based on the notion of homeostasis—the idea that unless we are being provoked by something, we are operating at a state of balance, humming along at an even-keeled *baseline* state, and we return to that same state after the stress. Moreover, homeostasis implies that just one system in the body struggles to return to the baseline at a time (*homeo-* means "same"). For example, suppose you are walking in a desert: The homeostasis view says that you would sweat to cool your body to return to an ideal temperature. In doing so, you would also become dehydrated (Sapolsky, 1998). If you think about it for a minute, you'll realize that it's not just your sweat glands that need to adapt to the desert. So a new concept was needed to explain the more complex and dynamic changes that occur when the body is stressed.

Connections

The concept of homeostasis is key to drive theories of motivation.

See Chapter 11, LO2.

Some researchers have offered an alternative explanation: Rather than a state of balance, our normal state is one of actively responding to the world around us. This more dynamic, responsive "resting" state is known as **allostasis,** which means that the body achieves stability through change (Schulkin, 2005; Sterling & Eyer, 1988). *Allo* means "different" or "changing." In other words, body systems actively work to adjust to challenges. Allostasis is better able to account for the widespread changes in body systems during stress, compared to the more passive response described by homeostasis.

allostasis
process by which the body achieves stability through physiological change.

If we think of the baseline state as one of dynamic responsiveness rather than a fixed baseline, it's easier to understand the effects of stressful challenges on the body. To return to the example of walking in the desert: The concept of allostasis emphasizes that your body would respond in many ways, not simply by sweating. Your kidneys would start producing less output; mucous membranes in your eyes and skin would dry out; even your veins and arteries would constrict to maintain blood pressure with a smaller volume of blood. The concept of allostasis makes clear that our bodies can adaptively respond to challenge for only a short period of time. If we are pushed too long, and the kinds of active attempts the body makes to adapt are sustained, we are taxed, and the body starts to wear down. This is how stress causes illness.

The distinction between short-term and prolonged stress is an important one because it's chronic exposure to stressors that makes us sick. But what precisely constitutes acute stress and how do we distinguish it from chronic stress? How brief is brief? One researcher in this area, Firdhaus Dhabhar (2009) suggests that acute stress is stress that lasts minutes to hours (such as anxiety in the preparation for a final exam), whereas chronic stress lasts months to years (such as having to stay in an abusive relationship).

An increasingly large body of research shows that acute stress may not be harmful to health at all; it might actually be beneficial. Recall Hans Selye's work on the GAS, which argued that, in the short term, stress is an adaptive response by our bodies to deal with emergency. In this new area of work, we are seeing that responding to some challenges with stress may confer benefits to health—more so than not responding at all! How could that be?

Recent research shows that acute stress may actually *promote* healing (Dhabhar, 2014). In one key study, mice were randomly assigned to a control or stress condition (being restrained in a plastic tube), then received repeated UV radiation, which can initiate squamous cell carcinoma, a type of skin cancer (Dhabhar, 2010). Researchers repeated this stressor several times during the middle of a ten-week irradiation period and measured immune responses and tumour incidence in these mice. Compared to no-stress controls, the short-term stress group showed fewer tumours, more immune cells, and better immune cell function. Research in humans also supports the idea that acute stress can be beneficial. A study of people undergoing knee surgery showed that those with

Challenge Your Assumptions

True or False? Stress is always bad for your health.

False: Not all stress is the same. Acute (short-lived) stress can, in fact, can boost the immune system and improve healing.

strong immune cell activation to stress had better post-operative mobility compared than those who did not (Rosenberger et al., 2009). In other words, mild stress helped them heal faster.

Stress and the Brain So far we have emphasized how stress affects a wide array of physiological responses, most of which involve systems outside the central nervous system. But what about the brain? We tend to think of stress as being caused by processes within the brain, for it is our interpretations of the events in the world around us that trigger emotions. In another example of the bidirectional relationship between nature and nurture, the physiological activation triggered by stress also affects the brain. Cortisol has a profound effect on the hippocampus, a brain structure that plays a pivotal role in memory. It turns out that the hippocampus contains one of the greatest concentrations of cortisol receptors in the brain (McEwen, De Kloet, & Rostene, 1986). Why? Because this brain structure—which plays a crucial role in the transformation of short-term to long-term memories—also plays a part in terminating the activation of the HPA axis via a negative feedback mechanism (Kim & Yoon, 1998).

Acute stress seems to enhance memory, particularly if stress-related cortisol levels are low (Buchanan & Tranel, 2008; Duncko et al., 2009). One study exposed rats to a brief period of stress and found better retention of fear memory compared to control rats. Furthermore, these researchers found much higher rates of neurogenesis in the hippocampus of stressed rats (Kirby et al., 2013). Unfortunately, prolonged stress actually reduces neurogenesis in the hippocampus, and stress-related cortisol release over a long period of time can cause neuronal dendrites to wither and shrink. This can interfere with several types of memory and may inhibit synaptic plasticity, impacting learning and memory formation (Artola, 2008; Wang et al., 2008). Clearly, the effects of stress on the brain strongly depend upon the amount of stress exposure.

Connections

The hippocampus, located deep inside the brain, is critical for memory formation.

See Chapter 3, LO12; and Chapter 6, LO8.

A fascinating set of studies by Elissa Epel and her colleagues reveals some of the connections between biology and environment that play a role in people's responses to stress and their effects on health. In "Psychology in the Real World" we describe how Epel and her colleagues (2004) demonstrated that stress can literally affect aging at the cellular level.

Psychology in the Real World

Effects of Chronic Stress on Aging

Stress often makes people look worn out. As mentioned earlier, this is one of Selye's main ideas: Physiologically, long-term stress wears out or wears down the body, making a person more vulnerable to illness (the exhaustion stage). People often refer to the stresses of life as wearing them out or causing grey hairs. Is there any evidence, however, that this everyday logic has any basis in the physiology of aging? Can stress actually make you age more quickly?

Contrary to common wisdom, there is little evidence that stress or trauma can suddenly turn a person's hair grey overnight. Most scientific and medical evidence points to purely genetic explanations for hair greying (Nishimura, Granter, & Fisher, 2005; Van Neste, D. & Tobin, 2004). However, mounting evidence has accumulated that stress is linked to other, more troubling signs of aging, particularly at the level of DNA.

In an innovative study of the physiological effects of stress, psychologist Elissa Epel and her colleagues examined indicators of cellular aging in healthy women who were biological mothers of either normal or chronically ill children. The mothers reported on the amount of stress they perceived in their daily lives, using a standard questionnaire. The researchers derived indicators of cellular aging from tests on blood samples collected from each woman. In particular, they examined the telomeres of chromosomes in the DNA of certain white blood cells. *Telomeres* are part of the chromosome involved in replication during the process of cell

Ask any mother of young children how she feels. Chances are she'll tell you she's exhausted. Long-term stress that is perceived as severe can speed up the process of cellular aging.

division. With age, telomeres shorten; moreover, the activity of telomerase, an enzyme that protects telomeres, decreases with age. Both of these variables are good measures of aging.

Epel and her colleagues measured stress not in terms of life conditions per se but in terms of the duration of stress and the perceived severity of stress experienced by the women. They found that the more stress a woman perceived in her life, the shorter the telomeres and the lower the level of telomerase activity in her blood, conditions that imply older cells. In practical terms, these women's cells were "the equivalent of 9–17 additional years" older than those of women who perceived less stress (Epel et al., 2004, p. 17314). A different analysis of the same sample found a positive relationship between measures of cellular aging and the stress-relevant hormones norepinephrine and cortisol (Epel et al., 2006). Even though we do not yet know how cellular aging translates into body age and health changes, this research provides a fascinating example of how stress can wear down the body.

Challenge Your Assumptions

True or False? Stress can make your hair suddenly turn grey.

False: Most research shows that psychological stress plays little to no role in premature greying of hair.

Quick Quiz 12.1: What Is Stress?

1. According to the definition provided in the text, which of the following is the best example of stress?
   a. Maria is studying for one exam.
   b. Maria is studying for three exams on the same day, but she has a handle on all three.
   c. Maria is studying for two exams on the same day and feels unprepared for both of them.
   d. Maria is angry at her boyfriend.
2. The ________ view of stress focuses on the physiological changes that occur when someone encounters an excessively challenging situation.
   a. stimulus
   b. response
   c. relational
   d. situational
3. The model of adaptation that says there is stability through change is the
   a. functional view.
   b. physiological view.
   c. homeostatic view.
   d. allostatic view.
4. The stress hormone cortisol is released from the
   a. adrenal glands.
   b. hypothalamus.
   c. pituitary gland.
   d. limbic system.

Answers can be found at the end of the chapter.

LO5 HOW STRESS AFFECTS HEALTH

Our discussion so far has implied that stress increases a person's susceptibility to disease. This idea is one of the oldest expressions of the interplay between nature and nurture, and it forms the central tenet of **psychosomatic theory.** Even though people tend to use the term *psychosomatic* to refer to an illness that is "all in the head" or, by implication, "made up," this is a

psychosomatic theory
the idea that emotional factors can lead to the occurrence or worsening of illness.

Eating in response to stress may make us feel good, but it may also make us more susceptible to certain diseases.

misconception of the actual theory. Rather, *psychosomatics* deal with how emotional factors can increase the likelihood of certain disorders occurring or worsening.

The field of health psychology grew out of psychosomatic medicine. **Health psychology** is the study of psychological factors related to health and illness. It includes disease onset, prevention, treatment, and rehabilitation and involves clinical practice as well as research. Research in health psychology ranges from studies of how psychological variables enhance health or increase susceptibility to disease to the role of social factors in doctor–patient communication.

health psychology the study of psychological factors related to health and illness.

There are two primary ways of explaining the relationship between stress and illness: Both illustrate the dynamic interplay among environmental situations, people's interpretations of them, and changes in body functioning. The **physiological reactivity model** examines how the sustained physiological activation associated with the stress response can affect body systems in such a way as to increase the likelihood that illness or disease occurs. As such, this model is rooted in psychosomatic medicine. By contrast, the **health behaviour approach** focuses on the behaviours in which people engage, such as diet, exercise, or substance abuse, that may make them more susceptible to illness or may enhance health. These explanations are not mutually exclusive. For example, a person might experience sustained blood pressure elevation due to stress and drink heavily during a time of intense stress, both of which would affect the person's health.

physiological reactivity model explanation for the causal role of stress-related bodily changes in illness.

health behaviour approach explanation for illness or health that focuses on the role of behaviours such as diet, exercise, and substance abuse.

Figure 12.6 depicts the physiological reactivity model. (We discuss the health behaviour approach later in the chapter.) You will notice similarities between this and the emotion/stress process diagram in Figure 12.2: Each begins with the elicitation of negative emotion and stress. In the physiological reactivity model, however, the activation of the sympathetic nervous system persists and creates sustained physiological arousal. Recall Selye's notion that the physiological effects of sustained stress contribute to the wearing out of the body. This is the exhaustion stage, which may create a greater susceptibility to illness. A wide array of body systems may be affected by sustained stress, but a few key systems have been the focus of much research.

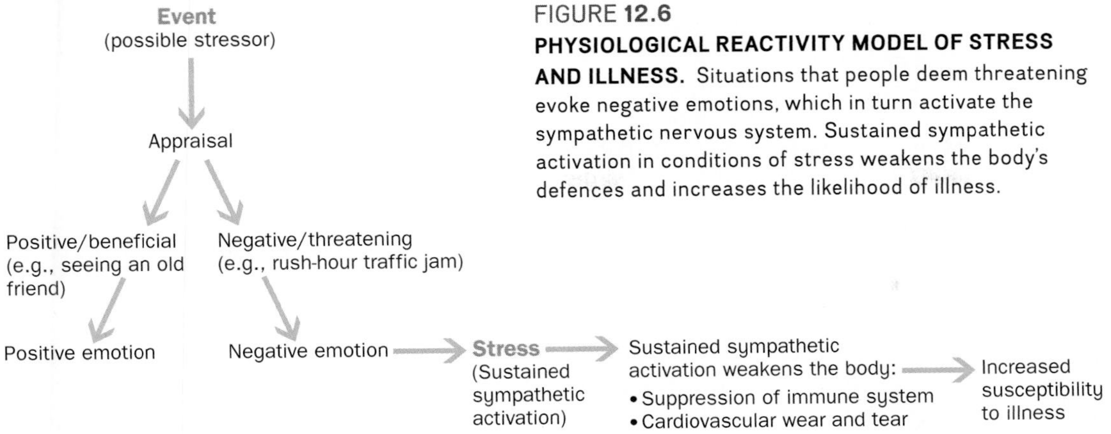

FIGURE **12.6**

PHYSIOLOGICAL REACTIVITY MODEL OF STRESS AND ILLNESS. Situations that people deem threatening evoke negative emotions, which in turn activate the sympathetic nervous system. Sustained sympathetic activation in conditions of stress weakens the body's defences and increases the likelihood of illness.

Let's consider what we mean by sustained physiological arousal and why it can be harmful to health. Earlier we said that the sympathetic branch of the autonomic nervous system activates organ systems to enable an animal to respond to emergency situations. So the effects of sympathetic arousal on the heart and lungs (increasing pumping and oxygen intake) help the animal act quickly and thus survive. From an evolutionary perspective, these physiological effects were advantageous because of their ability to enable a quick and efficient response. However, the same type of emotional response occurs in daily life, in most cases without an outlet for action—for example, when you are stuck in traffic or annoyed with a co-worker. So the activation persists for hours or days, or is elicited repeatedly in similar situations over many years. Under such conditions, you can become ill as a result of the recurring arousal produced by stress-related body changes (Sapolsky, 1998).

cardiovascular system
the heart, blood, and all the blood vessels.

psychoneuroimmunology (PNI)
the science of how psychological factors relate to changes in the immune system.

Especially susceptible to the effects of sustained arousal is the **cardiovascular system,** which consists of the heart and all the blood vessels of the body. During activation of the sympathetic nervous system, heart rate and blood pressure increase. In sustained physiological activation, heart rate and blood pressure remain elevated or are activated repeatedly over extended periods. Frequent blood pressure elevations can damage arteries by reducing their elasticity and increasing the likelihood of fatty build-up. These processes set the stage for heart disease.

Also subject to the effects of sustained arousal is the immune system—whose impaired function increases susceptibility to many kinds of disease. Sustained activation of the HPA axis leads to sustained release of cortisol, which inhibits the production of certain immune cells. In the short term, suppression of immune cell production makes sense, because in an emergency these immune cells might not be immediately necessary. Over the long term, however, immune suppression makes a person more susceptible to certain diseases. Interest in this possibility, and its implications for health care, has given rise to a field of study known as **psychoneuroimmunology (PNI),** the science of how psychological factors relate to immune changes. The story of the birth of PNI illustrates groundbreaking work that showed for the first time the link between psychological states and immune function.

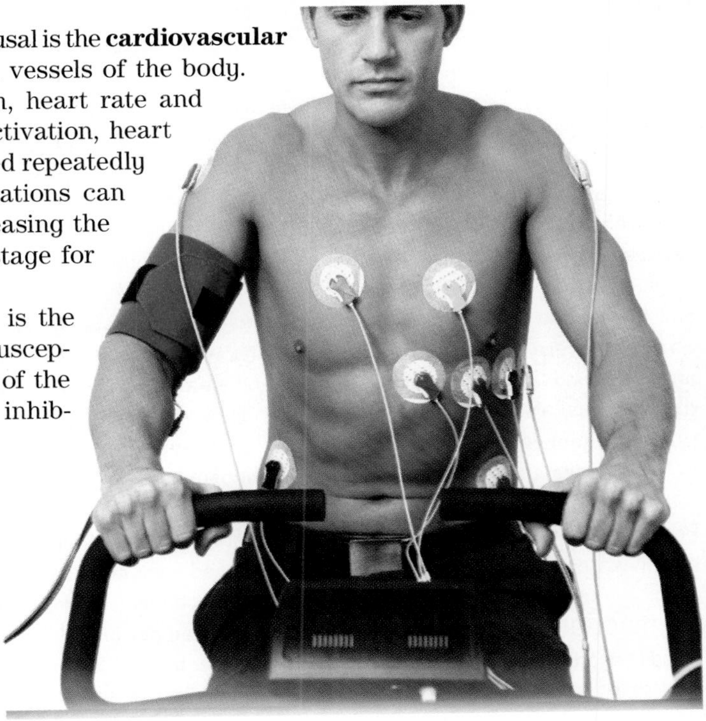

One way of assessing the risk of heart disease is to take a stress test, aptly named because it subjects the cardiovascular system to increasing physiological activation.

Groundbreaking Research

Psychological Processes and the Immune System

With the general adaptation syndrome, Hans Selye provided a framework for thinking about how stress might make the body vulnerable to disease, and he suggested that this vulnerability might be due to the effects of stress on the immune system. As we will see, however, no one knew if psychological factors could affect the immune system until some groundbreaking research of the 1970s.

IMMUNE SYSTEM AS AN AUTONOMOUS DEFENCE SYSTEM

The job of the immune system is to defend the body against foreign substances. Before the 1970s, the prevailing view was that the immune system operated quite independently of the central nervous system. In other words, everyone believed the immune system was invulnerable to thoughts, feelings, and stress. As far as anyone knew at the time, there were no anatomical or chemical connections between immune system structures and any aspect of the nervous system that would allow them to communicate. Even though most physicians believed that stress could make people sick, or at least sicker, they did not consider it physiologically possible for psychological conditions to have any effect on the immune system. But that was about to change.

CONNECTING THE BRAIN AND THE IMMUNE SYSTEM

Robert Ader was replicating some classic experiments on conditioned taste aversion. Recall from Chapter 7 that conditioned taste aversion is a form of classical conditioning in which a neutral taste, after repeated pairing with an agent that can induce nausea and vomiting, will come to produce those characteristics when it is presented alone. In the early research, saccharin water was paired with radiation, which causes nausea (Garcia, Kimeldorf, & Koelling, 1955). In his work, Ader paired a chemical that induces nausea with saccharin water to create taste aversion to the saccharin water. Some rats were exposed to a lot of saccharin water even after they had learned to associate it with nausea. And something unusual was happening to those rats. They were dying! But why? Ader remembered that the toxin he was using to induce nausea also happened to be an immunosuppressant; that is, something that suppresses immune system function. Perhaps, he reasoned, in addition to learning to avoid saccharin water, the rats were acquiring conditioned immunosuppression from the repeated pairing of the saccharin solution with the immunosuppressant.

Connection

Conditioned taste aversion is a type of learning similar to what happened when Pavlov's dogs learned to salivate to the sound of a bell (classical conditioning).

See Chapter 7, LO7.

To suggest any connection between psychological processes and immune system functioning ran counter to the view in medicine that the immune system operates independently of the central nervous system (Boorboor, 2002). Nevertheless, Ader and his colleague, Nicholas Cohen, embarked on a series of experiments to determine whether immunosuppression could be classically conditioned in rats (Ader & Cohen, 1975). They conditioned nausea or "illness-induced" taste aversion in an experimental group by pairing saccharin water with injections of the immunosuppressant. They also created two control groups: a group that was injected with a placebo around the time they drank saccharin water (which served as a control for the stress-inducing effects of injection in the absence of conditioning) and a group that received the immunosuppressant and plain water (a non-conditioning control group).

Ader and Cohen needed a way to test whether the immune system was suppressed in rats with immunosuppressant-induced conditioned taste aversion. They reintroduced the conditioned stimulus, in this case saccharin, and then introduced an **antigen**, a substance foreign to the body. They injected the antigen, sheep blood cells, into the bloodstreams of all the rats. In healthy animals, exposure to a foreign substance like this should cause certain immune cells to release chemicals called antibodies. If immune suppression had been conditioned to the taste of saccharin water, the taste of saccharin water should impair the antibody response to the antigen. Because it takes a while for the body to manufacture an antibody response to an antigen, the experimenters waited a few days and then sacrificed the rats to collect their blood. They found that the blood of rats that had been conditioned to avoid saccharin via the immunosuppressant showed a much weaker antibody response to the sheep blood cells than did rats injected with the placebo. That is, the blood from rats with conditioned immunosuppression showed a weaker defence against a foreign substance.

antigen
any foreign substance that triggers an immune response.

THE BIRTH OF PSYCHONEUROIMMUNOLOGY

Some scientists were amazed by these results. By demonstrating that one could classically condition the suppression of an antibody response to an antigen, Ader and Cohen had shown that there must be connections between the CNS and the immune system. How else could a change in immune system functioning be learned? There was now solid behavioural and biological evidence for what Selye and others had believed all along—that psychological processes and immune processes interact. In this way, the field of psychoneuroimmunology was born.

Stress and Immune Function

Today, the field of psychoneuroimmunology (PNI) examines the relationships among the brain, thought, feeling, endocrine changes, and immune system functioning. As a discipline, PNI is concerned with any kind of connection between psychological processes and the immune system. For instance, there are chemical linkages between psychological processes and immune system changes. Chemicals involved in the stress response, such as cortisol and norepinephrine, influence the number of immune cells produced in the body. This is a means by which stress can affect the immune system.

Furthermore, connections between the central nervous system and immune system are bidirectional. That is, just as stress can change immune function, certain immune changes (such as the release of chemicals called *cytokines*, which regulate immune response) can feed back and influence brain areas involved in mood regulation (Nishida et al., 2002; Miller, Capuron, & Raison, 2005).

A newborn's immune system is still developing. Antibodies present in the mother's breast milk protect the baby from infection until the baby's own immune system has matured.

Overview of the Immune System The human immune system defends the body against invasion by disease, inspects the body for cells that may take on dangerous mutations, and performs basic housekeeping functions such as cleaning up cellular debris after an injury. There are two basic lines of defence: natural immunity and acquired immunity. **Natural immunity** consists of a number of inborn processes that help remove foreign substances from the body. These responses typically are very quick, and they provide the first line of defence upon exposure to antigens. *Inflammation* is a process by which tissues are restored following injury. After you cut your finger, for example, blood vessels at the injured area contract and dilate to increase blood flow to the area, creating warmth and redness. The dilated vessels then release inflammatory chemicals, and damaged cells release enzymes to destroy invading microorganisms.

natural immunity form of immunity that is the first response to antigens.

acquired immunity immunity provided by antibodies or cells produced in the body in response to specific antigens.

Acquired immunity involves a number of endocrine and cellular processes that recognize specific antigens and then reproduce specialized cells or circulating proteins to fight those antigens. Acquired immunity is so called because it involves experience—an effective immune response occurs only after prior exposure to a particular antigen. For instance, every cold we have leads to a learned or acquired immune response, and as a result we are less likely to get sick if we are exposed to that particular virus again. This latter fact forms the basis for how vaccination protects against disease.

Research on Stress, Immune Function, and Health The physiological reactivity model predicts that the physiological effects of stress, when sustained over time, will eventually weaken the immune system. Theorists have extended the model a step further, reasoning that *immunosuppression* increases susceptibility to disease by reducing the body's ability to fight invading bacteria or viruses or its ability to fight off potentially cancerous cells, or both. This is why psychologists, in collaboration with medical researchers, began conducting

Research on the effects of stress on the human immune system often makes use of natural stressors, such as exams.

studies of stress and immune function. The basic idea is simple: If researchers can show that stress affects immune variables, it should follow that such immune system changes would leave the organism more susceptible to disease. In reality, many studies have shown linkages between prolonged stress and numerous immune system measures, but very few have shown that these reductions actually affect susceptibility to disease. Let's look at some of the major research on stress and immune function in both animals and humans.

Results from animal research show that a variety of experimental stressors can weaken responses to antigens, reduce the numbers of certain immune cells, and impair immune cell functions such as responses to vaccines (Glaser & Kiecolt-Glaser, 2005). Some of the stressors tested in animal studies are maternal separation, inescapable shock, abrupt temperature change, and loud noise. A few studies have manipulated stress in humans by randomly assigning people to participate in a stressful task, such as public speaking, or an emotion-evoking task, such as writing about a traumatic event (Pennebaker, Kiecolt-Glaser, & Glaser, 1988). A more common approach in human research, however, is to rely on naturally occurring stressors such as final exams, sleep deprivation, loud noise, bereavement, and divorce. Although the major finding in studies of humans is that stressors are associated with changes in various kinds of immune function, it is often difficult to know whether the observed immune changes have meaningful effects on health.

Sheldon Cohen and his colleagues (1993, 2003) have studied the interplay of stress and social connectedness in people's susceptibility to the common cold, an infectious illness mediated by the immune system. Susceptibility is the key issue here, as exposure to the cold virus does not guarantee a person will get sick. For example, you and your roommate might both spend time with a friend who is sick, but only one of you might catch the cold. In these studies, Cohen and his colleagues exposed people to a virus and collected information about people's stress experiences and social resources in managing stress. Later, they clinically verified whether or not people got sick. They found that perception of stress—rather than the number of stressors to which people had been exposed—predicted whether or not they develop a cold (Cohen, Tyrell, & Smith, 1993). Further, having more meaningful social interactions in one's daily life reduces susceptibility to colds (Cohen et al., 2003). Perceiving oneself as lower in socioeconomic status also predicts susceptibility to the common cold in people exposed to the virus, independent of one's actual socioeconomic status (Cohen et al., 2008).

In terms of the relationship between stress and illness, then, it is not the situation as much as how the individual evaluates that situation that drives the stress and its effects. Notice that in terms of susceptibility to the common cold, *perceived* stress mattered more than actual exposure to stressors; *perceived* low socioeconomic status mattered more than actual socioeconomic status. These results remind us of the importance of defining and measuring stress not just as a stimulus (number of stressors), but also in terms of how people respond to the stressors and cope with possible stress. As discussed earlier, social support and social connectedness might buffer the effects of stress by providing interpersonal resources for emotional support and problem solving (Cohen & Wills, 1985).

Psychological Risk Factors for Heart Disease

Heart disease is the number one killer of both men and women in Canada (Statistics Canada, 2006). We saw earlier that the physiological changes associated with negative emotions and stress influence the cardiovascular system. Research has identified a number of psychological risk factors for heart disease. In this section we tell the story of how this research began and describe the main areas of research on psychology and cardiovascular health.

Time urgency is a component of the Type A behaviour pattern that does not predict heart disease after all.

Type A and Anger For centuries scientists have argued that personality and emotion might play a role in the development of heart disease, but research on this topic did not begin until the middle of the 20th century. In fact, it began in the waiting room of cardiologist Meyer Friedman's office in San Francisco. A janitor pointed out to Friedman that the upholstery on the chairs in his waiting room was wearing out much more quickly than that on chairs in other waiting rooms. He wondered whether Friedman's patients fidgeted a lot. Friedman said "yes." In fact, he had noticed that many of his patients were tense and impatient. Friedman and his colleague Ray Rosenman decided to study the effects of such an emotional style on a person's risk of developing heart disease. They described a set of psychological characteristics that they believed put people at risk for heart disease: impatience, competitiveness, hostility, and time urgency. They named it the **Type A behaviour pattern (TABP)** and explained that this pattern emerges when under conditions of challenge or stress. That is, Type A people are not always impatient and hostile, but when they find themselves in high-pressure situations they exhibit this pattern of behaviour. Friedman and Rosenman hypothesized that people who exhibit the TABP *under provocation* are at greater risk for heart disease than those who do not.

Type A behaviour pattern
a way of responding to challenge or stress, characterized by hostility, impatience, competitiveness, and time urgency.

Friedman and Rosenman embarked on an ambitious research program to see if they could measure the Type A pattern and determine whether it increases risk for heart disease. They developed an interview to measure Type A behaviour and distinguish it from Type B behaviour, which is a more relaxed, laid-back style. Then they designed a study in which healthy men were evaluated on psychological and health-related variables and then assessed periodically over a number of years (Rosenman et al., 1964). In their original study, they found that Type A behaviour predicted the incidence of coronary heart disease eight years later, over and above such traditional risk factors as blood pressure, cholesterol, and age. This finding shocked the medical world, for no one had anticipated that something psychological could affect heart disease.

Soon other major studies replicated the finding that the presence of Type A behaviour predicted the incidence of heart disease and extended it to women (French-Belgian Collaborative Group, 1982; Haynes et al., 1978). Twenty-two years later, Rosenman and Friedman conducted a follow-up study on their original participants. Surprisingly, Type A did *not* predict death from heart disease in this group. Then another major study of men and women produced null findings (Shekelle et al., 1985). People began to question whether psychological factors could put anyone at greater risk for heart disease.

But could it really be that Type A did not affect the incidence of heart disease after all? Karen Matthews wondered if the concept just needed to be refined. After all, Type A is a collection of various characteristics. She took a closer look at the follow-up interviews from Friedman and Rosenman's original sample to see how each component of the Type A pattern (hostility, time urgency, competitiveness, and impatience) related to coronary outcomes (Matthews et al., 1977). She found that *hostility* was the only component that predicted death from heart disease at a 22-year follow-up. As a result of Matthews's findings, the measurement of global Type A has been abandoned, for the most part, in favour of more specific measures of hostility.

Challenge Your Assumptions

True or False? People with Type A behaviour patterns react to stress with hostility, and this puts them at risk for heart disease.

True: Reacting with hostility is a component of Type A behaviour, and is linked to increased risk of mortality from heart disease.

Matthews's findings stimulated numerous studies on the relationship between hostility and a number of measures of cardiovascular health. Redford Williams and his colleagues (1980) measured Type A behaviour, hostility, and other psychological variables in 400 patients who were about to undergo angiography, a procedure that enables physicians to see the inside of the coronary arteries, which supply the heart muscle with oxygen-rich blood. As coronary artery disease develops, the openings of these arteries narrow due to the accumulation of fatty deposits, and the risk of coronary heart disease increases. Measures of hostility positively correlated with the degree of arterial blockage in those patients, much more so than overall Type A behaviour did. Hostility also correlates with a number of other cardiovascular conditions that are relevant to coronary health, such as blood pressure reactivity in situations that provoke anger (Suarez et al., 1993; Suarez & Williams, 1989) and increases in fats in the bloodstream (Suarez, Bates, & Harralson, 1998).

Research indicates that anger affects health-relevant cardiovascular outcomes. Anger can lead to heightened and prolonged blood pressure reactivity (Schuler & O'Brien, 1997; Siegman et al., 1992). In coronary patients, the risk of heart attack increases significantly during the hour following an outburst of anger (Moller et al., 1999). A study of coronary patients undergoing the Type A Structured Interview found that episodes of insufficient blood supply to the muscle of the heart were more likely to occur when those patients displayed facial expressions of anger (Rosenberg et al., 2001).

Stress and Mental Illness

Stress has been implicated as a contributing cause to most types of mental illness, particularly depression (Sapolsky, 1998). Although the major symptoms of depression include feelings of profound sadness and hopelessness, this disorder is also associated with impairments in motivation and cognition, and sleep disturbances. There is much debate regarding what causes depression; however, most instances of depression are preceded by a stressful life event (Brown et al., 2010), and high levels of cortisol also increase the risk of a depressive episode (Harris et al., 2000).

Depression is not solely a mental health problem. It is also associated with increased severity of symptoms and increased risk of death from coronary heart disease (Geerlings, et al., 2002; Glassman & Shapiro, 1998). A large-scale meta-analysis reported that for people with diagnosed coronary heart disease, being clinically depressed more than doubles the risk of death from the disease (Barth, Schumacher, & Hermann-Lingen, 2004). Also, chemicals involved in inflammation that present a risk for coronary heart disease are present at higher levels in people who are depressed than in others (Barth et al., 2004; Empana et al., 2005). As both of these diseases represent major health problems in Canada, further work is needed to better understand the causal pathways linking heart disease and depression.

Post-traumatic stress disorder (PTSD) is an anxiety disorder triggered in some individuals by an intensely stressful event, such as a natural disaster, motor vehicle accident, or a sexual assault. It is associated with a low cortisol response to stress, activation of the sympathetic nervous system, and enhanced memory for the traumatic event itself (Delahanty & Nugent, 2006; Bronner et al., 2010). Research on combat veterans from the wars in Iraq and Afghanistan showed that PTSD is associated with changes in the way the brain processes information. When shown pictures relevant to combat trauma, war veterans with PTSD showed enhanced activation of in the brain's emotional processing areas, such as the amygdala, compared to veterans who did not develop the disorder after combat. The traumatic stimuli also interfered with performance on working memory tasks in the PTSD veterans, suggesting that the emotional activation brought on by memories of the trauma can interfere with information processing (Morey et al., 2009).

LO6 Research on Health-Relevant Behaviour

Earlier we mentioned another pathway to illness called the *health behaviour approach.* People engage in behaviours that increase risk for disease or help to prevent disease. Some health behaviours are conscious lifestyle choices, such as how and what to eat or whether or not to exercise. Others may begin as conscious choices but over time become habits that have serious health implications, such as smoking, drinking alcohol, and taking other drugs. Sometimes, when under stress, people drink or take drugs to change their mood. This is emotion-focused coping. They may turn to tobacco, alcohol, or food to calm themselves down or cheer themselves up. Long-term use of some of these substances can create health problems and may increase the likelihood of major, sometimes fatal, illnesses.

Smoking Many smokers say that they have a cigarette when they are stressed because it calms them down. Yet nicotine, the drug component of cigarette smoke, is not a relaxant. Nicotine is a stimulant that activates the sympathetic nervous system, increasing heart rate and blood pressure. Nicotine relaxes the skeletal muscles, however, which is probably why some people find it calming. This calming effect is one reason that smokers tend to have a cigarette when stressed—they use nicotine for emotion regulation. But cigarette smoking is harmful to health in many ways. In fact, it is the single most preventable cause of death in Canada (Makomaski Illing & Kaiserman, 2004). Cigarette smoking reduces life expectancy by an average of ten years, increases one's risk for lung cancer more than ten-fold, and triples the risk of death from heart disease in both men and women (Centers for Disease Control and Prevention, 2001; Doll et al., 2004). Smoking is also a risk factor for many other cancers, stroke, lung disease, emphysema, and male impotence (USDHHS, 2004).

The tremendous health care costs associated with smoking, as well as the difficulty many people have with stopping or reducing cigarette consumption, have prompted governments to implement policies to promote quitting. For instance, many countries have implemented mandatory warning labels on cigarettes packages in order to trigger negative thoughts and emotions about smoking. Studies show that the more graphic the warnings, the greater the impact on health behaviour. Canada's warnings on packages are among the most successful in triggering negative emotions and reduction in smoking (Hammond, 2004; Borland et al., 2009).

Drinking Alcohol People often drink alcohol to calm down or loosen up. Alcohol is a depressant, which means it slows down central nervous system functions. Heavy alcohol consumption can cause liver damage, such as cirrhosis, and also increases the likelihood of liver cancer and cancers of the digestive tract, not to mention an increased risk for accidents due to alcohol's effect on motor and cognitive performance. Binge drinking, defined as five drinks for men and four drinks for women on a single occasion, is prevalent among university students and is linked to significant alcohol-related problems (Wechsler et al., 1999). Students who binge drink are more likely to suffer from alcohol poisoning, unintentional injuries, sexually transmitted diseases, and sexual assaults. Not all the news regarding alcohol is bad, however. Considerable data indicate that regular

A healthy diet rich in fruits, vegetables, and whole grains and low in fat may protect against heart disease and certain cancers and prevent conditions associated with obesity, such as adult-onset diabetes.

but moderate alcohol consumption (one to two drinks), especially with food, may reduce the risk of coronary heart disease, the number one killer in the developed world (Guiraud et al., 2008; Renaud & de Lorgeril, 1992).

Diet and Eating Eating well promotes health. Eating saturated fats, such as those found in meats and dairy products, increases risk for heart disease, while eating other essential fats, such as those found in certain kinds of fish and nuts, may have protective effects (Schaefer, Gleason, & Dansinger, 2005). The consumption of ample high-fibre, less fatty foods, such as whole grains and plenty of leafy green vegetables, may help protect against cancers of the colon and rectum, although the data are somewhat inconclusive (Cummings et al., 1992). A healthy diet also appears important for a healthy brain. In a study of Grade 5 students in Nova Scotia, low-quality diet was associated with poor performance on standardized tests of literacy (Florence et al., 2008). Food choices and food portions also affect body weight, and it is well known that excessive weight gain is risky. Obesity increases a person's risk for heart disease, high blood pressure, adult-onset diabetes, and certain cancers (McTiernan, 2005).

Eating and Stress. Some people eat as a way of coping with stress. In fact, sugary foods in particular actually help some people feel better and calm down. Research now supports the connection between eating and stress reduction: Stress increases eating and, in turn, eating reduces stress reactivity in the HPA axis (Dallman, Pecoraro, & la Fleur, 2005). When a person eats in response to stress, stress-related physiological activity decreases. So eating relieves stress for some people, which makes it likely they will continue to do such eating. When people eat in response to stress (especially sugary foods), reward pathways in the brain are stimulated. These areas release endorphins that make people feel better. So people eat under stress because they get a "good feeling" reward—like a drug high—from the brain (Adam & Epel, 2007).

But stress-induced eating is risky, as it increases fat in the abdominal area (compared to other places), which is a predictor of heart disease in men and women (Epel et al., 2000; Rexrode et al., 1998; Rexrode, Buring, & Manson, 2001). This is especially true if the stress-induced eating includes sugary junk foods (Kuo et al., 2007).

Exercise Besides not smoking, one of the best things you can do for your health is exercise regularly. Regular exercise reduces the risk of heart disease, stroke, and certain types of cancer (Noda et al., 2005; Thune & Furberg, 2001). Exercise helps keep diabetes under control and also slows the rate of bone loss in older women (Cussler et al., 2005). Recent data show that moderate exercise, even as little as walking 20–25 minutes a day three or four times per week, can extend life by three to four years (Franco et al., 2005). In addition, exercise offers a healthy way to regulate mood, as it reduces anxiety and depression (Barbour & Blumenthal, in press; Binder et al., 2004).

Like a healthy diet, exercise can also help your brain. One correlational study found that children in Grades 3 and 5 who were the most physically fit also performed the highest on standardized math and reading tests (Hillman, Erickson, & Kramer, 2008).

Other research more directly suggests exercise promotes the birth of new neurons (neurogenesis) in the hippocampus, the area of the brain most involved in learning and memory (Pereira et al., 2007). Compared to mice that did not exercise, mice that exercised had increased brain activity in their hippocampus after exercising for two weeks. They also developed new neurons in the same region of the hippocampus. Increased activity is directly related to neural growth. Similar effects have been found with humans as well (see Figure 12.7). Being physically fit appears to make the brain fit, too.

Meditation for Stress Reduction Given the harmful effects of stress, strategies designed to reduce stress can benefit both mental and physical health. One such strategy is meditation. Mindfulness meditation involves both paying attention to the present moment and being aware that everything that may arise in one's mind, be it a thought, an emotion, or a sensation, will eventually fade away. The meditator is trained to note experiences as they occur, without clinging to or ascribing value to them. These skills allow one to keep thoughts and emotions in perspective and help prevent an unhealthy obsession with negative emotions (Kabat-Zinn, 1990).

Connection

Mindfulness meditation can improve well-being, cognition, and brain function.

See Chapter 5, LO4.

Researchers have applied mindfulness meditation training to the treatment of stress reduction, pain relief, and physical disorders. Kabat-Zinn and his colleagues have examined the effectiveness of a program called Mindfulness-Based Stress Reduction (MBSR) for treating a variety of physical and psychological conditions. MBSR training reduces self-reported pain and pain-related behaviours in people suffering from chronic pain (Kabat-Zinn, Lipworth, & Burney, 1985). Also, Kabat-Zinn and colleagues (1992) found that MBSR training led to significant and substantial reductions in anxiety, depression, and fear in people who have various types of anxiety disorders.

Mindfulness training also improves the rate of skin healing in people with psoriasis (Kabat-Zinn et al., 1998). Psoriasis is an annoying and often painful rash that can be exacerbated by stress. Mindfulness meditation techniques appear to be effective in reducing the stress-related immune changes underlying skin outbreaks. Mindfulness meditation has also been linked to enhanced immune response to a vaccine (Davidson et al., 2003).

Mindfulness training through meditation can help counteract the effects of stress.

Research Process

1 Research Question

Will exercise increase brain activity and stimulate neural growth in humans?

2 Method

Having found that exercise was correlated with neural growth in the hippocampus of mice, Pereira and colleagues (2007) conducted a study to look for the same effects in humans. They recruited eleven adults (ages 21–45) with below-average cardiovascular fitness to take part in an exercise program four times a week for 12 weeks. Each session lasted about one hour and consisted of a combination of stretching, aerobic training, and cooling down. Brain images were made before and after the training with MRI to measure changes in blood volume, an indirect measure of neural growth.

The hippocampus is the brain region most involved in learning and memory, so participants' memories were tested before and after the program with a list of 20 words read by the experimenter, to find out whether there was any change in memory capacity. Participants were distracted with another word list and were then asked to recall as many words from the original list as they could.

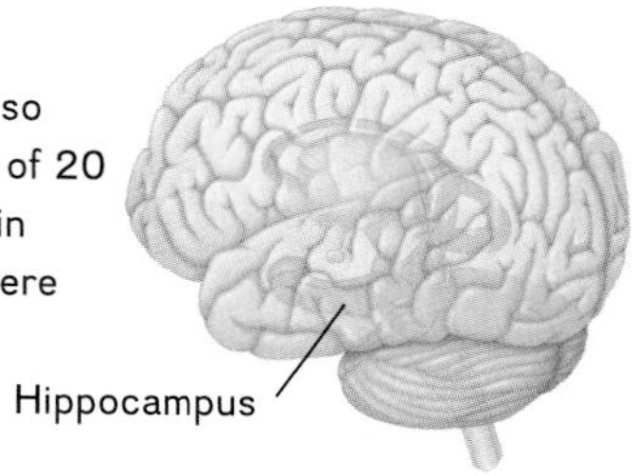

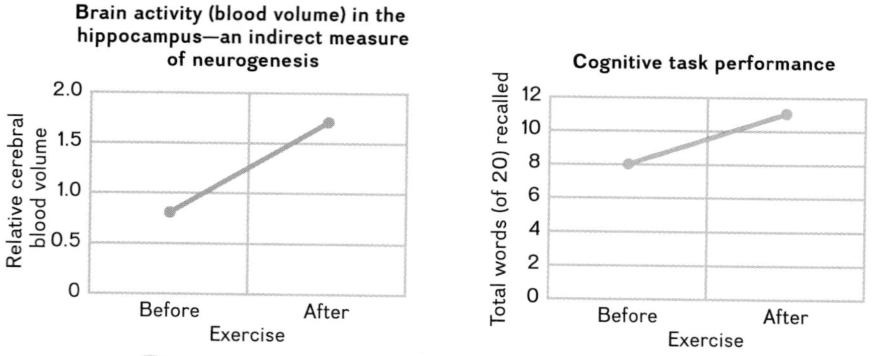

FIGURE 12.7 **EFFECTS OF EXERCISE ON THE BRAIN.** Physical exercise is as good for the brain as it is for the body. (*Source:* A.C. Pereira, D.E. Huddleston, A.M. Brickman, A.A. Sosunov, R. Hen, G.M. McKhann, R. Sloan, F.H. Gage, T.R. Brown, & S.A. Small (2007). An in vivo correlate of exercise-induced neurogenesis in the adult dentate gyrus. *Proceedings of the National Academy of Sciences, 104,* 5638–5643.)

3 Results

MRIs performed before and after the exercise program revealed that cerebral blood flow increased after the program. In addition, participants improved their performance on a cognitive test after 12 weeks of exercise.

4 Conclusion

After exercising regularly, people who had been out of shape showed improvement in memory. This improvement is correlated with—and perhaps a consequence of—new neural growth in the region of the brain most involved in learning and memory, the hippocampus. Although we cannot conclude from the correlations revealed by this study that physical exercise causes improvements in memory, these findings suggest that exercise not only makes the body more fit, but it also makes the brain more fit.

Quick Quiz 12.2: How Stress Affects Health

1. If a psychologist studies how diet and sleep affect overall health, which view would best match her research?
   a. physiological reactivity
   b. general adaptation syndrome
   c. health behaviour approach
   d. homeostasis view
2. Martin is very prone to anger, impatient, and competitive; he is always in a hurry and feeling rushed. We would say Martin probably suffers from
   a. Type A behaviour pattern.
   b. Type B behaviour pattern.
   c. hostility.
   d. high drive disorder.
3. Which personality trait is most strongly related to the development of heart disease?
   a. anxiety
   b. hostility
   c. depression
   d. introversion
4. Exercise helps
   a. improve cardiovascular health.
   b. decrease stress.
   c. stimulate neural growth.
   d. all of the above.

Answers can be found at the end of the chapter.

COPING

If a person clearly cannot cope with the demands created by a situation, stress escalates to the point where it wears down body systems. Whether or not a person can cope depends on how well he or she adapts psychologically to the situation by modifying either the situation, his or her interpretation of the situation, or the feelings it creates. Such is the domain of coping. Coping plays a big role in the duration of stress responses and whether they develop sufficiently to become harmful.

Even though stress results from situations in which we feel that we cannot manage or cope with the challenges we face, we are probably coping with those challenges in some way whether we realize it or not. Generally, **coping** refers to anything people do to deal with or manage stress or emotions. When we walk away from someone who is making us angry, or complain about our boss to a friend, we are coping with stresses in our lives. In this section we explore various ways people cope with stress.

coping
act of dealing with stress or emotions.

LO7 Coping Strategies

People don't like feeling bad. So they try to get out of situations that create unpleasantness or look for ways to change their negative feelings. Psychologists Richard Lazarus and Susan Folkman (1984) differentiated between these two types of coping strategies, labelling them *problem-focused* and *emotion-focused* coping. Social support combines problem-focused and emotion-focused coping strategies. Figure 12.8 provides an overview of these three coping strategies.

Problem-Focused Coping

Problem-focused coping involves strategies that aim to change the situation that is creating stress. For example, if your roommate plays a stereo loudly while you are sleeping, you might choose to discuss it with her, buy earplugs, or cut the speaker wires. Each of these choices is a form of problem-focused coping, as each is geared toward changing the situation that created the stress. Examples of problem-focused coping strategies include devising a plan to solve the problem, seeking social support as a way to gather information, and taking assertive action. Problem-focused coping tends to focus attention on the stress-provoking situation, and we are most likely to use it when we feel that we can do something to change the situation.

problem-focused coping
way of dealing with stress that aims to change the situation that is creating stress.

	Strategy	Example
problem-focused strategy	Solve the problem Seek social support Take assertive action	Roommate's stereo too loud: Focus on how to make it quiet. An assertive act might be to cut the stereo speaker wires.
emotion-focused strategy	Reappraise Distancing Use escape-avoidance Seek social support Exercise self-control Emotional disclosure Accept responsibility	Breakup with a partner: Focus on how to feel better. An escape-avoidance act may be to take a vacation to get away from the former partner. Write about it to unburden emotions.
social support strategy	Combines problem-focused and emotion-focused strategies Develop social connectedness Seek advice from or talk with friends and loved ones	Support groups: Giving and showing support to other people may increase longevity.

FIGURE **12.8**
COPING STRATEGIES. We tend to apply problem-focused coping strategies to change a stressful situation and emotion-focused coping strategies in situations that we feel we cannot control.

emotion-focused coping
way of dealing with stress that aims to regulate the experience of distress.

Emotion-Focused Coping In contrast, **emotion-focused coping** aims to regulate the experience of distress. Lazarus and Folkman describe several forms of emotion-focused coping, including *reappraisal,* the emotional regulation strategy of re-evaluation of a situation in light of new information or additional thought; *distancing,* or attempting to separate oneself from an emotional experience; *escape-avoidance,* wishful thinking or doing something to get one's mind off the situation (such as going to the movies); *seeking social support* by talking with friends for purposes of emotional support; *self-control,* or trying to regulate one's feelings or actions regarding the problem; and *accepting responsibility,* acknowledging one's role in the stress-eliciting situation (Lazarus & Folkman, 1984).

Connection

Emotion regulation is another term for the strategies we use to alter our emotional state and is similar to emotion-focused coping.

See Chapter 11, LO6.

Emotion-focused coping may be beneficial when a situation is beyond one's control, and certain types of emotion-focused coping—especially reappraisal—can be helpful in regulating the emotional aspects of stress. But it can also be problematic. Willful suppression of upsetting emotions, which is a form of self-control, can lead to chronic physiological arousal and is associated with poor psychological adjustment (Gross & Levenson, 1993; Gross, Richards, & John, 2006). Moreover, some strategies that we use to reduce the experience of distress, such as drinking, smoking, and other forms of drug use, may be maladaptive (Hien & Miele, 2003).

emotional disclosure
way of coping with stress through writing or talking about the situation.

It is widely believed that a good way to cope with stress is to vent, or "let it all out." The implication is that relieving ourselves of a burden can be beneficial. James Pennebaker has developed and tested a technique known as **emotional disclosure** that enables people to unburden (Pennebaker, 1995). In a typical emotional disclosure task, people are instructed to write for about 15 minutes about a recent emotional experience—in particular, one that they have found troubling, that still bothers them from time to time, and that they haven't discussed much with other people. Participants in the control condition write for a similar amount of time about non-emotional events, such as what they did the day before. Emotional disclosure consistently improves a number of health outcomes, including health variables related to HIV/AIDS, immune function, and cancer (O'Cleirigh et al., 2008; Petrie et al., 2004; Smyth, 1998; Stanton et al., 2002).

How might writing about one's emotional experiences, especially traumatic ones, benefit health? There are several possible explanations. People in both Western and non-Western cultures believe that confession is beneficial. For the Ndembu of West Africa, for instance, public confession allows for the transformation of negative feelings into positive ones in the community, thereby promoting social harmony (Georges, 1995). It is also thought that *not* working through difficult emotions taxes the body, as research on the association between emotional suppression and ANS arousal suggests (Gross & Levenson, 1993). When confession or disclosure occurs, then, one should observe a decrease in sympathetic nervous system activation or a return to a more relaxed state. In fact, numerous laboratory studies have found that just talking about a traumatic event creates noticeable reductions in autonomic measures such as blood pressure and sweating (Pennebaker, 1995).

Writing about a stressful experience is one way of working through the negative emotions associated with it.

LO8

Social Support

A coping strategy that combines problem- and emotion-focused coping is seeking social support. Our friends and loved ones provide advice, give hugs, or simply listen when we are under stress. Social support not only is one of the most frequently used ways of coping but also can benefit physical health. The *direct effects hypothesis* states that social support is beneficial to mental and physical health whether or not the person is under stress. Cohen (2004) has pointed out that being part of a social network guarantees the availability of certain resources. Our social network may offer guidelines for health-related behaviours, help us regulate our emotions, and give us a sense of identity. We may learn from friends, for instance, that running or jogging can help us feel better when we're stressed. Examples of social connectedness include being married, belonging to social groups such as churches or clubs, and having many friends. Friends provide an outlet for sharing emotional distress, offering comfort as well as advice.

Alternatively, social support may serve as a buffer against the impact of stress. This is known as the *buffering hypothesis,* which states that social support works as a buffer only under certain conditions, such as a highly stressful life. In fact, one influential study found that regular participation in a support group in which members talked about their emotional difficulties improved well-being and extended survival in women with advanced breast cancer (Spiegel et al., 1989), though this finding has not replicated consistently (Edelman et al., 1999; Edmonds, Lockwood, & Cunningham, 1999; Goodwin, 2004; Goodwin et al., 2001).

The extent to which a person is integrated into a *social network* influences whether social resources are beneficial to health. A social network is simply a cluster of related people, such as family members, spouses, friends, co-workers, or neighbours. When people are well integrated into a social network, social support can buffer the effects of stress by providing interpersonal resources for emotional support and problem solving (Cohen & Wills, 1985). This is why people with close friendships have an easier time dealing with stressful events than do "loners," who have no one to turn to when they feel overwhelmed.

The health benefits of social connectedness include longer life and reduced susceptibility to colds (Berkman & Glass, 2000; Cohen et al., 2003). A recent study that followed more than 12 000 people over 32 years examined the influence of social networks on quitting smoking (Christakis & Fowler, 2008). Social networks influenced the likelihood that a person would stop smoking, but not all social connections had the same effect. If a spouse stopped smoking, the chance the other spouse would also stop went up by 67 percent; if a friend stopped smoking, the chance another friend stopped went up by 36 percent; and if a co-worker stopped smoking, the chance another worker stopped went up by 34 percent. So the effect of the other person's behaviour on any given person depended to some extent on how close they were to each other.

Social networks may be harmful to health as well. For instance, researchers looked at the influence of obesity in the same social network study of 12 000 people. The risk of obesity spread among people who were socially connected. In other words, if a person became obese (that is, had a body mass index greater than 30), his or her friends, family members, spouse, or neighbours were more likely to become obese. As was true with smoking, however, not all social connections had the same effect. For instance, if a person's friend became obese over a given period of time, that person's chance of becoming obese increased 57 percent; if a sibling became obese, the chance increased 40 percent; and if a spouse became obese, the chance increased 37 percent (Christakis & Fowler, 2007). Moreover, gender mattered. Individuals of the same gender in a social network influenced same-sex individuals more than opposite-sex individuals.

Social resources clearly play a role in health-related behaviour and how we manage stress, but so do our own personal resources. Life is not just a course in stress management, but rather a daily journey through a series of joys as well as challenges.

LO9 Positive Psychology of Coping

Traditionally, research on stress and coping has focused on how people respond to threatening situations and manage the distress associated with them. For years, however, some psychologists have argued that it is an oversimplification to assume that stress involves only negative emotions and their management (Folkman & Moskowitz, 2000; Lazarus, Kanner, & Folkman, 1980; Seligman & Csíkszentmihályi, 2000). This section discusses various ways in which positive psychological states have been studied in relation to stress and coping.

Positive Traits, Positive Emotions Some people approach the world in a positive way, and as a result their interpretation or experience of distress is reduced compared to that of others. *Optimists* tend to emphasize the positive, see the glass as "half full" rather than "half empty," and believe that things will turn out well (Scheier, Weintraub, & Carver, 1989). *Pessimists,* by contrast, emphasize the negative; for them, the glass is always half empty and the future is bleak. Optimists are less likely to feel helpless or depressed, adjust better to negative life events than do pessimists, and show better general mental health than pessimists (Chang, 1998; Smith, Young, & Lee, 2004).

Are you the type of person who sees this glass as half full? Would you consider yourself an optimist or a pessimist?

Optimism may also benefit physical health (Kubzansky et al., 2001). By seeing the world positively, optimists may appraise events in such a way that negative emotions are less likely and positive emotions more likely. They may be more likely to see potentially stressful situations as challenges rather than threats. People with terminal illnesses who notice beauty amidst their pain and find opportunities for positive experience in their lives are happier than those who don't, and they may even live longer (Folkman, 1997; Moskowitz, 2003).

Having a positive outlook is linked to psychological health.

Positive emotions may facilitate recovery from the physiological effects of negative emotions. For example, Fredrickson and Levenson (1998) showed participants a fear-eliciting film and followed it with either a sad, a pleasant, or a neutral film. The researchers measured cardiovascular activity throughout the film-viewing and post-film-viewing period. Cardiovascular activation elicited by the fear film returned to baseline levels more quickly in people who saw the pleasant film after the fear film, but not in people in the sad or neutral conditions. So positive emotions may help the body return to a state of calmness.

The power of positive thinking may also be a benefit when adjusting to new situations. The adjustment from high school to university is a challenging time for most students. One study of Canadian university students showed that the highest levels of stress were reported during the beginning of the first term of the university year. Students whose stress levels decreased during the second term showed the most emotional, social, and academic adjustment (Friedlander et al., 2007). But what enables some students but not others to reduce their levels of stress? It turns out that schoolwork tasks described as most stressful are the same ones that students feel least confident about (Zajacova et al., 2005). Confidence in one's own ability to succeed is called *self-efficacy* and it is associated with academic performance in university (Chemers et al., 2001). Self-efficacy was first defined by Canadian psychologist Albert Bandura as a central part of his social-cognitive theory, and it has an important influence on how we approach challenges (Bandura, 1997).

Connection

Self-efficacy is an important part of Bandura's theory of human personality.

See Chapter 13, LO6.

Believing that you have some control over situations in life, especially traumatic situations, can also improve your psychological health (Taylor, 1989). Health psychologist Shelley Taylor has studied various groups of people suffering from chronic, debilitating, and often fatal diseases such as breast cancer, heart disease, and HIV/AIDS. She has found that people who believe they have some control over their illness—in spite of medical evidence to the contrary—are actually happier and less stressed than less optimistic people with the same diseases (Hegelson & Taylor, 1993; Reed et al., 1994; Taylor, 1989). As it turns out, these perceptions of control provide the greatest benefits in situations that are severe or uncontrollable (Taylor et al., 2000).

Resilience is a personality trait that means being more flexible and able to bounce back from difficult situations. Resilient people experience quicker recovery from stress-induced cardiovascular arousal, in part because they are more likely to find some positive meaning in a difficult situation (Tugade & Fredrickson, 2004). People who suffered from childhood physical and sexual abuse are less likely to suffer from depression as adults if they are highly resilient (Campbell-Sills & Stein, 2007). Resilience appears to reduce the likelihood of addictive behaviours such as smoking and other drug use (Goldstein et al., 2012). In the wake of the 9/11 terrorist in the United States, resilient people who managed to experience positive moods amidst their despair were more likely to thrive and less likely to fall into depression than those who were less resilient (Fredrickson et al., 2003). Therefore, stress appears to have less of an impact on resilient people, which might help explain why some people are much less affected by traumatic events than others.

Quick Quiz 12.3: Coping

1. You buy earplugs so you can sleep when your roommate plays loud music at 1:00 A.M. You have used what kind of coping?
   a. problem-focused
   b. emotion-focused
   c. stimulus-focused
   d. meaning-focused
2. Research has found that having a well-connected social network of friends, family, neighbours, and co-workers is ________ for health outcomes.
   a. never beneficial
   b. sometimes beneficial
   c. sometimes beneficial and sometimes harmful
   d. always beneficial
3. Seeing the "glass as half full," or being optimistic, is likely to have what kind of an effect on a person's response to stress and illness?
   a. no real effect
   b. negative effect
   c. a positive effect
   d. the same effect as being pessimistic would
4. Who would be most likely to bounce back quickly from a very stressful experience?
   a. a young person
   b. a pessimist
   c. someone who holds in his or her feelings and pretends the event did not happen
   d. a resilient person

Answers can be found at the end of the chapter.

Evaluating Connections in Stress and Health

Social Support, Caregiver Burnout, and the Power of Belief

Although stress can significantly impact health, it is an inevitable part of life. We all have to juggle multiple stressors every day—some of them predictable and manageable, others sudden and seemingly overwhelming. Throughout this chapter we've discussed a number of things that can help us cope with stressors, including the powerful resource of social support. It seems that we're biologically programmed to seek out others in times of need. In fact, the parts of the brain that signal threats to basic survival, like pain or injury, are some of the same areas involved in processing threats to social connections (Eisenberger, 2013).

Social Support and the Benefits of Marriage

There has long been an interest in marriage as a source of social support, since it is linked to positive health outcomes like lower depressive symptoms, fewer alcohol problems, and higher income (Horwitz et al., 1996). According the Canadian National Public Health Survey, which asked over 15 000 Canadians about their marital status and health, cohabitation confers similar health benefits as marriage (Averett et al., 2013). Does this mean the way to deal with stress is for everyone to find someone to marry or live with?

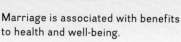

Marriage is associated with benefits to health and well-being.

Although large population studies consistently report higher well-being with marriage or cohabitation, there is much variation. Some marriages provide more social support than others, which has important health consequences. Research by Janice Kiecolt-Glaser at Ohio State University has shown a link between the way couples interact and immune system function. In one study, researchers inflicted suction wounds on the forearms of married couples and then had the couples talk for ten minutes about their relationship. Researchers monitored the couples' behaviour during the interaction to document the degree of hostility, support, and humour the couples showed toward each other. They found couples that interacted with hostility had slower wound healing and higher levels of inflammatory cytokines in their blood (Kiecolt-Glaser et al., 2005).

Social Support and Caregiver Burnout

The benefits of social support are particularly important during times of illness, especially for diseases with significant physical or cognitive impairment. Alzheimer's disease, as you learned in Chapter 10, is a progressive neurodegenerative disorder characterized initially by memory impairment, and later followed by cognitive and physical decline and eventually death (Mortimer et al., 2005). In the advanced stages, most Alzheimer's patients require daily care, sometimes around the clock. Social support is typically provided by family members, usually a spouse or adult child, and is usually referred to as "informal" caregiving. This form of caregiving is a critical part of medical care for Alzheimer's patients and has a significant impact on patient quality of life (Roth et al., 2015). Family members who provide this essential service are usually unpaid and often endure extreme stress. In addition to facing the general health decline and eventual death of their loved one, Alzheimer's caregivers also face unique challenges because as cognitive decline worsens, patients sometimes act maliciously towards their caregivers, or engage in potentially dangerous behaviours, such as wandering off (Dura et al., 1990).

Given the stress associated with caregiving can last for years, it should not be surprising that caregivers often face significant, personal, financial, and health costs (Do et al., 2015). The most common adverse health effects are symptoms of depression and feelings of loneliness (Robinson-Whelen et al., 2001)—symptoms that often persist years after the loved one has died. There is evidence that caregiving influences physical health as well, which might be due to effects of stress on the immune system (Damjanovic et al., 2007). In a study of people caring for Alzheimer's patients, caregivers and a matched control group received small puncture wounds. They then returned to the laboratory for wound healing assessments and blood tests to measure immune variables. Compared to the control group, the caregivers showed substantially slower healing of puncture wounds and reductions in immune regulators involved in healing (Kiecolt-Glaser et al., 1995). One study showed that caregivers face a 63 percent higher mortality risk that non-caregiving controls (Schulz et al., 1999), making caregiving stress an important public health issue with the aging population.

The mental, physical, and emotional exhaustion experienced by caregivers is often called *caregiver burnout.* Although these findings paint a grim outlook for the future of Alzheimer's patients as well as their caregivers, some

Caregiving can involve helping with basic activities of daily living.

recent research has shown that not all caregiver experiences are negative or overly burdensome. Most research on caregiving has focused on the negative, but some recent large-scale population studies have shown significant benefits from caregiving. In fact, a recent meta-analysis showed that caregivers actually live *longer* than non-caregiving controls (Roth et al., 2015). Research into the positive aspects of caregiving is relatively new, but results look promising and suggest that caregiver burnout is not inevitable (Cassidy et al., 2015). Having strong social support from and friends is associated with positive caregiving experiences, while perceived stress and burden are linked to negative outcomes.

Beyond Social Support: The Power of Belief

So far, this section has outlined the importance of others in coping with stress and promoting health and well-being. But what if you don't have a strong social network? Many of us are fortunate enough to have supportive relationships through our family and friends, but some people are not so lucky. This is a common problem in the elderly, since longevity means outliving your social support network. What can we do to ensure well-being if we only have ourselves to rely on?

We have discussed concepts in this chapter that point to how the "goodness" or "badness" of stress depends on whether you perceive or believe that something (a stressor) is overwhelming or not. The question, therefore, is: If you change your mind about stress, can you change how your body responds to it? Research shows that thoughts and beliefs can change the effects of stress on health.

Stress in many ways is more subjective than objective—the same experiences will be considered stressful or not by different people. Earlier in the chapter, we questioned the value of viewing "stress" simply in terms of the stimulus we encounter (e.g., work, marriage, illness, exams) or the response (e.g., physiological activation, immune changes). You might also recall the role of appraisal in determining whether a given situation is stressful. Once we have appraised something as threatening and too much to handle and the stress response ensues, how we cope with the stress matters. Coping strategies, such as reappraisal of the situation, can turn something from a stressor into a non-stressor. In this way, not all stress is equal, and certainly not all stress produces illness.

The belief that stress makes you sick has become almost accepted as a truism in our society, even though—as we have already discussed—the data show that the relationship is not particularly strong and not really clear. A surprising study by Keller and colleagues (2012) revealed that people's beliefs about the relationship between stress and illness were an important predictor of life span. This finding was based on a survey conducted by the National Center for Health, which asked over 30 000 Americans about stress: how much stress they experienced, whether they had done anything to reduce stress, and most importantly, how much they *believed* stress affected their health. Not surprisingly, those with the highest stress were most likely to die within eight years. What is most surprising, however, was that it was not how much "stress" they had in life but whether they believed stress could make them sick. Specifically, those who reported the most stress and believed stress could make them sick were the most likely to be dead after eight years! This finding is alarming but also hopeful, as it shows that we can change our beliefs, and therefore our longevity.

Quick Quiz 12.4: Evaluating Connections in Stress and Health

1. One of the effects of marriage on health and well-being is
   a. lower depressive symptoms.
   b. impaired wound healing.
   c. lower income.
   d. all of the above.
2. Research shows that caring for a loved one is associated with positive experiences if
   a. the loved one only lives for a short time.
   b. caregiving is viewed as a burden and plans are made to deal with it.
   c. caregivers are paid a fair wage for their unpaid work.
   d. the caregiver has strong social support from others.

Answers can be found at the end of the chapter.

Chapter Review

WHAT IS STRESS?

- Stress results when we appraise the demands of a situation as exceeding our ability to cope with or manage those demands. Researchers often define stress in terms of events or our physiological responses to certain events.
- Primary appraisal is the initial evaluation of how threatening a situation is. Secondary appraisal involves evaluation of resources to manage the stressful situation or the feelings it generates.
- Most stress-related physiological changes are observed in the autonomic nervous system (ANS), especially the sympathetic branch.
- In the endocrine system, glands secrete chemicals called hormones, which travel in the bloodstream to tissues and organs all over the body. The pituitary gland, called the master gland of the body, controls the release of hormones from other glands in the body. The adrenal glands secrete hormones involved in sympathetic nervous system responses and stress.
- The adrenal-medullary system controls the release of catecholamines, chemicals that activate heart rate, respiration, and other responses that prepare the organism to deal with emergency situations.
- The hypothalamic-pituitary-adrenal (HPA) axis releases the hormone cortisol, which frees up glucose as a source of energy.

- The stress response is beneficial in short term, emergency situations but not over the long term. When sustained over time, the stress response can weaken the body.
- Hans Selye proposed a three-stage model, the general adaptation syndrome (GAS), to describe how the body reacts and adapts to chronic, extreme stress. In the alarm stage, the body is in emergency mode and all body systems are activated for quick response. In the resistance stage, the body gradually adjusts to the high level of stress created by the demands of its environment. In the exhaustion stage the body is unable to sustain the response and becomes more susceptible to illness.

HOW STRESS AFFECTS HEALTH

- There are two major approaches to studying how stress leads to illness: the physiological reactivity model and the health behaviour model.
- The physiological reactivity model examines how the psychological effects of sustained stress make illness more likely.
- Psychoneuroimmunology (PNI) encompasses research on any type of connection between the CNS and the immune system. The work of Ader and Cohen on classically conditioned immunosuppression showed a relationship between psychological processes and changes in immune function.
- The immune system defends the body against disease. When antigens are present, lymphocytes either release antibodies into the blood or bind directly with the antigen to disable it.
- Numerous studies have demonstrated the effects of stress on regulation of the immune system. The most convincing argument for a meaningful stress-immune connection comes from studies that measure the experience of stress, immune measures, and related illness outcomes.
- The Type A behaviour pattern, a characteristic way of responding to demanding situations with hostility, time urgency, and competitiveness, can predict the later development of heart disease. The hostility component of the Type A pattern best predicts coronary heart disease.
- People engage in behaviours that enhance health as well as those that make them more susceptible to illness. Behaviours such as smoking and drinking alcohol increase risk for major illness such as heart disease, cancer, and liver disease. Eating in response to stress also imposes risks.
- Healthy diet and exercise can extend life and enhance brain function.

COPING

- Some strategies for coping are problem-focused, in that they address how to remedy or change the situation that called forth the stress response. Others are emotion-focused, aimed at reducing the emotional distress or unpleasant experience created by a stressful situation.
- Social support can profoundly improve mental and physical health. Social networks influence health behaviour, both positively and negatively.
- Some people are more likely than others to believe that they have control over situations, and this belief may make them healthier.
- Some people experience positive affect, even in dramatically stressful situations. Positive affect, in turn, may facilitate recovery from the negative emotional arousal of stress.

EVALUATING CONNECTIONS IN STRESS AND HEALTH

- Social support is a powerful resource for coping with stress. Caregivers of people with debilitating diseases, such as Alzheimer's, often suffer from stress-related health concerns and impaired immune responses. Caregivers are more likely to view caregiving as a positive experience if they have strong social support. Believing that stress causes illness is associated with mortality.

Quick Quiz Answers

Quick Quiz 12.1: 1. c 2. b 3. d 4. a **Quick Quiz 12.2:** 1. c 2. a 3. b 4. d **Quick Quiz 12.3:** 1. a 2. c 3. c 4. d
Quick Quiz 12.4: 1. a 2. d

Personality: The Uniqueness of the Individual

CHAPTER 13

CHAPTER OUTLINE

Challenge Your Assumptions

True or False?

- ☐ Personality is unrelated to genetics.
- ☐ Many different kinds of animals have personality in the sense that humans do.
- ☐ Your personality predicts future success in your career better than letters of recommendation, educational credentials, or interviews.
- ☐ Facebook "likes" reliably predict your personality traits.

LEARNING OBJECTIVES

- **LO1** Define personality.
- **LO2** Discuss how nature and nurture contribute to personality development.
- **LO3** Describe Freud's psychoanalytic theory of personality, including the key criticisms of his theory.
- **LO4** Compare Freud's theory to that of his followers, Adler, Jung, and Horney.
- **LO5** Discuss the humanistic-positive theories of psychology, comparing the approaches of Maslow and Rogers.
- **LO6** Compare and contrast the social-cognitive theories of personality of Bandura and Mischel.
- **LO7** Summarize the trait approach to personality and compare the Big Five theory to Eysenck's biological theory.
- **LO8** Describe the main methods of personality assessment.
- **LO9** Discuss the degree to which personalities can change.

Still at the hospital and in only his second day of life, Jerry received a needle stick in his heel for a routine blood test. As the needle pricked his skin, Jerry let out a typical newborn cry. Almost four years later, Jerry's new brother, Evan, went through the same procedure. He hardly flinched, at which the nurse predicted, "He's going to be a tough one!" The two brothers differ physically in other ways besides their response to pain, even though they share obvious similarities in hair colour, eyes, face, and physical size.

Jerry is now 16 and Evan is 12. They have similar yet distinct personalities. Both are curious, intelligent, verbal, full of energy, and active. Jerry, is quiet much of the time (except around his best friends) and is prone to being mildly anxious, especially around spiders. He would not go up and talk to a stranger if his life depended on it. Jerry loves sports and is physically very active, having ridden multiple 100 km bike rides and climbed a 4000 metre mountain (Mt. Shasta) before his 16th birthday.

Evan, by contrast, is very expressive, artistic, dramatic, energetic, aggressive, and fearless. He loves breaking rules just for the fun of it and, without a shred of shyness, will ask a stranger a question or strike up a conversation. Moreover, he can easily tell you what he is thinking and feeling and describe the details of why something bothers him. All you get from Jerry is an "I don't know" or "Nothing" when he's asked what's bothering him or "good" and "fine" when he's asked how he liked something. Often during play, even if alone, Evan will pose intense anger and scowl at pretend enemies. Evan is not interested in sports, but he can and does spend hours upon hours making and editing videos.

We, the first two authors of this textbook, know these two children very well: They are our children! Although we highlight them here, Jerry and Evan could be any pair of brothers. This kind of contrast is more the rule than the exception among siblings. If you have brothers or sisters, this description, at least in outline form, probably rings true. How is it that two people—reared in similar environments by the same parents—can have such different personalities? To answer this question, we must address what personality is, examine classic and current research on the nature and nurture of personality, review the major theoretical explanations for what personality is and how it develops, and describe how personality is measured. Lastly, we connect many of these topics by reviewing the issue of personality change.

LO1 DEFINING PERSONALITY

personality
the unique and relatively enduring set of behaviours, feelings, thoughts, and motives that characterize an individual.

When psychologists use the term **personality,** they are referring to the unique and relatively enduring set of behaviours, feelings, thoughts, and motives that characterize an individual (Feist & Feist, 2009; Roberts & Mroczek, 2008). There are two key components to this definition. First, personality is what distinguishes us from one another and makes us unique. Second, personality is relatively enduring, or consistent. Let's consider these key components in more detail.

Connection

Would you shock someone to unconsciousness if an authority figure told you that you had no choice? Extreme situations can push people to behave in ways we would not expect from their personalities.

See Chapter 14, LO6.

The first major component of personality is the uniqueness of an individual's thoughts, feelings, and behaviour. The fact is that in almost every situation, people will behave somewhat differently from each other. Consider what happens when one driver cuts in front of another. Some people react to such an incident with "road rage," while others are able to take it in stride. A characteristic of personality—hostility—may determine whether someone responds with road rage or not. Personality, therefore, is about uniqueness, or *individual differences.* The concept of personality would not exist if everyone acted and thought alike. Personality psychology is concerned with the fact that some people do and some people don't act in a particular way in the same situation.

A second part of the definition of personality is its relatively enduring consistency, of which there are two kinds: consistency across different situations and consistency over time. *Consistency across situations* refers to the notion that people behave the same way in different situations and carry who they are into almost every situation. *Consistency over time*, in contrast, is the extent to which people behave the same way throughout their lives.

Bringing these two components of personality together, we label a person as "friendly," for example, only if we observe her behaving in a friendly manner in situations in which most others might not act friendly and she does so consistently over time and in many different situations. A friendly person might behave in a friendly manner at a party, while having coffee with friends, or when meeting someone for the first time. We would say that this person's friendly behaviour is unique and consistent.

Friendliness is a personality **trait,** or a disposition to behave consistently in a particular way. Although traits make up a large part of an individual's personality, they are not quite synonymous with it. Personality is the broader term because it comprises not only traits but also motives, thoughts, self-concept, and feelings.

trait
a disposition to behave consistently in a particular way.

One important principle of personality traits is that they, like intelligence, are normally distributed in the population. Recall from Chapter 9 (Figure 9.7) that a normal distribution exists when the graph of all the scores is symmetrical and bell-shaped. A few people exist at both the extreme low and extreme high end of the distribution, but most people are average. Consider the trait of neuroticism, which is a tendency to experience negative emotional states, such as fear and sadness. A few people tend to react positively regardless of their situation, while others are extremely moody or irritable most of the time, but most people are somewhere in the middle (see Figure 13.1). The same is true for other traits, such as extraversion, warmth, and conscientiousness.

Another important principle of traits is they are directly connected to behaviour.

Can you think of anyone you know that has a low threshold for laughter? How would you describe that person's personality?

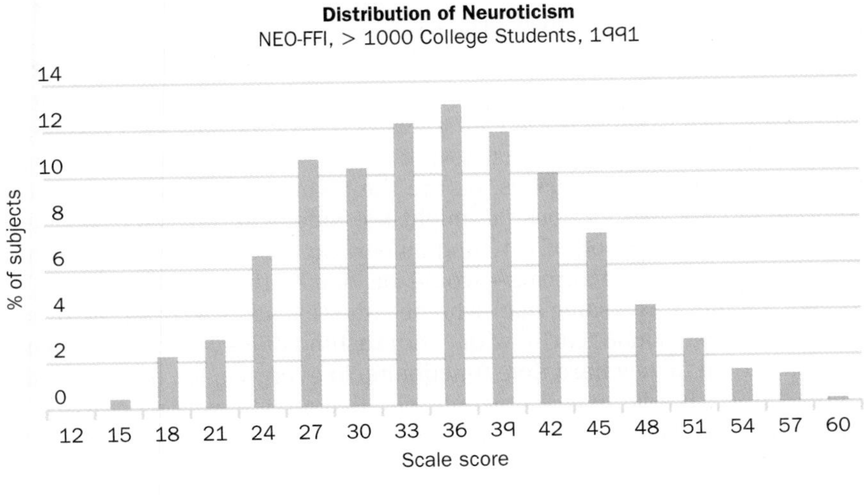

FIGURE **13.1**
DISTRIBUTION OF NEUROTICISM IN THE POPULATION. When we measure personality traits like neuroticism (tendency toward negative emotions) and then plot the number of people at all scores from low to high, we end up with a normal—or bell-shaped—distribution. Most people score in the middle, with a few on the extremes. (*Source:* https://bspace.berkeley.edu/access/content/group/0f4d90d8-c107-467d-000e-28cb28b3815b/Lecture%20 Supplements/stats_meths/images/neuroticism.gif).

Where might you be on the distribution?

behavioural thresholds the point at which a person moves from not having a particular response to having one.

They lower **behavioural thresholds,** or the point at which you move from not having a particular response to having one (Allport, 1937; Feist & Barron, 2003; Rosenberg, 1998). A low threshold means you are very likely to behave in a particular way, whereas a high threshold means you are not. To illustrate: Carlos is shy, which means he has a low threshold for feeling awkward, or is very likely to feel awkward. If he were introduced to a group of strangers, he would likely feel uncomfortable. In the same situation, however, Karen, who is outgoing, would probably feel comfortable because she has a much higher threshold for social awkwardness. Their optimal levels of arousal—or thresholds—are different. In short, traits lower behavioural thresholds and are directly connected to behaviour.

Quick Quiz 13.1: Defining Personality

1. Two characteristics of personality include
   a. uniqueness and instability in behaviour.
   b. uniqueness and consistency in behaviour.
   c. consistency in behaviour and identity formation.
   d. uniqueness and change in behaviour.

2. A statistical property of most personality traits is that they are
   a. unreliably measured.
   b. randomly distributed.
   c. normally distributed.
   d. skewed distributions.

Answers can be found at the end of the chapter.

LO2 THE NATURE AND NURTURE OF PERSONALITY

Personality is shaped by the forces of both nature and nurture. The interaction between the two can be seen in at least four lines of reasoning and research: evolutionary theory, genetics, temperament and fetal development, and cross-cultural universality.

The Evolution of Personality Traits

Human personality traits evolved as adaptive behavioural responses to fundamental problems of survival and reproduction. Certain behaviours were useful for survival or reproductive success during early periods of human evolution, and these behaviours have been shaped by natural selection (Buss, 2008; Buss & Greiling, 1999; McCrae & Costa, 1999). The tendency to be sensitive to threats, for instance, may well have been adaptive in dangerous environments like those in which our ancestors lived. Heightened anxiety would provide a signal of danger and threat; its absence would quickly lead to extinction of the species. Consider a hunter on the savannah. He hears the growl of a large animal and becomes fearful. He drops back behind the bushes, before the animal becomes aware of his presence. If he did not feel anxious, he might not hide, with dire consequences for his safety and his likelihood of catching dinner. By the same token, the other extreme—hypersensitivity to threats—would be debilitating and disruptive to everyday functioning. If the same man who became fearful at hearing the growl of a large animal also became fearful with every rustling of leaves or every sound of the wind, he would have a hard time functioning in everyday life. Having some degree of fearfulness is adaptive, and people with that quality were more likely to survive, reproduce, and pass on that disposition.

Naturally selected traits are favoured if they increase one's chances of survival and reproductive success. Sexually selected traits, on the other hand, make one more attractive to the opposite sex. For example, a recent study of over 400 individuals, many of whom were creative artists and poets, revealed a positive correlation between creativity and sexual success. That is, more creative people were also more sexually active (Nettle & Clegg, 2005). The authors argue that this finding supports the theory, first proposed by Darwin and more recently by Geoffrey Miller (2000), that human creative ability is a sexually selected trait because it is a quality that increases one's attractiveness to members of the opposite sex.

Being anxious when faced with a threat, like an angry grizzly bear, is adaptive since it promotes survival.

Genetics and Personality

Recall from Chapter 3 that complex traits are almost never the result of a single gene and that our genome is the starting point, not the end point, for how our genes are expressed (our phenotype). There is no "smart" gene, "shy" gene, or "aggressive" gene. We discuss these two themes in detail later in this section, but first let's look at how *behavioural geneticists* study the relationship between genes and personality.

When studying behavioural genetics, researchers use two major methods to examine the relationship among genetics, behaviour, and personality. The first method, called the **quantitative trait loci (QTL) approach,** is a technique that looks for the locations of specific bits of DNA (called loci) that might be associated with particular behaviours. In essence, it is a search for "genetic markers" of behaviour. Some personality types display a lot of a specific behaviour, while others might show this behaviour much less often, and therefore these behaviours are considered *quantitative* traits. For example, anxiety is a quantitative trait because some people are not at all anxious, most people are average, and a few are very anxious. The QTL method uncovers locations on particular genes that are associated with high or low levels of a trait. These locations are also known as "markers." QTL research has uncovered genetic markers for several basic personality traits, such as novelty- or thrill-seeking, impulsivity, and neuroticism/anxiety (Benjamin et al., 1996; Hamer & Copeland, 1998; Lesch et al., 1996; Plomin & Caspi, 1999; Rutter, 2006).

As discussed more fully in Chapter 3, the second method for examining the effect that genetics play in behaviour and personality is the study of twins, both identical and fraternal, who have been raised together or apart. Twin studies have found that most basic personality traits have heritability estimates of between 40 and 60 percent. For instance, the trait of extraversion or outgoingness often correlates around .50 for identical twins and around .20 to .25 for fraternal twins, which leads to a heritability estimate of between 50 and 60 percent (see Figure 13.2). Likewise, between 50 and 55 percent of population differences in neuroticism and conscientiousness are due to genetics, and about 40 percent of differences in openness and agreeableness are due to genetics (Bouchard & Loehlin, 2001; Caspi, Roberts, & Shiner, 2003; Loehlin et al., 1998; Plomin & Caspi, 1999; Tellegen et al., 1988).

Such a figure leaves roughly 50 percent of the differences in personality in a population to be explained by three non-genetic sources: shared environment, unshared environment, and error. Shared environment consists of what siblings share in common, such as parents or household, whereas unshared environment consists of things like birth order, different friends, different teachers, and different social groups. The surprising conclusion from research is that most of the environmental effects are of the unshared kind, and almost no variance is explained by shared environment (see Figure 13.2). The environment that seems to matter most is the "unshared" environment—differences in birth order or peer

Connection

Many people think genes affect behaviour by means of a single gene—a gene for "aggression," for example. Any given behaviour or personality trait, however, is never the result of single genes but rather many genes.

See Chapter 3, LO1.

quantitative trait loci (QTL) approach
a technique in behavioural genetics that looks for the location on genes that might be associated with particular behaviours.

Challenge Your Assumptions

True or False? Personality is unrelated to genetics.

False: Although genes are not the only source of influence on personality, research shows a moderately strong relationship between genes and personality traits.

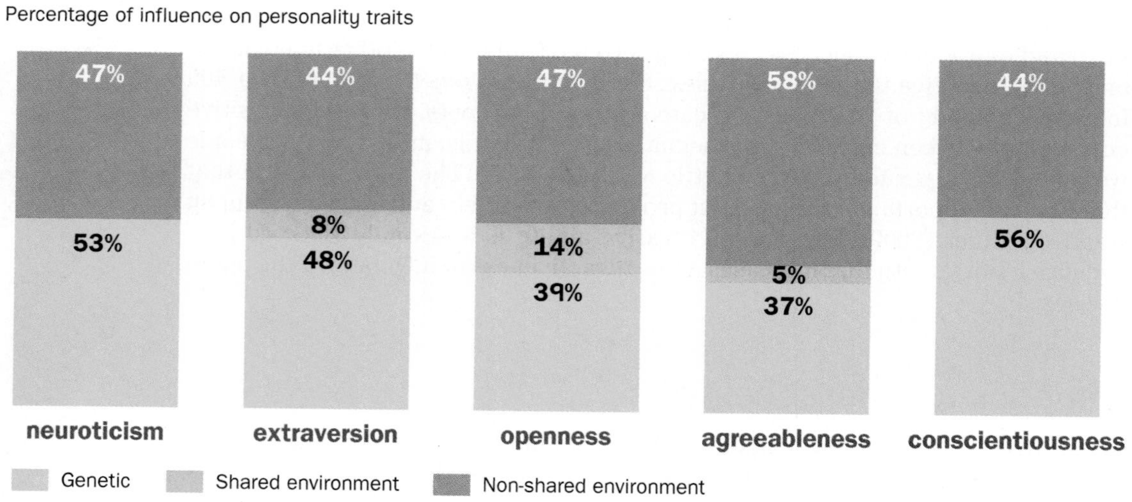

FIGURE **13.2**

NATURE AND NURTURE OF PERSONALITY: HERITABILITY OF FIVE TRAITS. Twin studies indicate that heredity (genetics) accounts for roughly 40 to 60 percent of the variance in most traits. What's surprising is that the influence of the shared environment (home and family) on these traits is small, compared with the influence of the non-shared environment. (*Source:* Plomin & Caspi, 1999.)

groups or even changes in parenting style and attitudes over time (Arseneault et al., 2003; Bouchard & Loehlin, 2001; Hamer & Copeland, 1998; Plomin & Caspi, 1999; Rutter, 2006). In short, personality is influenced by our environment, but more by the experiences we do not share in common with our family members, such as peer group influences.

Temperament and the Fetal Environment

Connection

Are some babies and toddlers temperamentally fussy and more difficult to care for than others?

See Chapter 10, LO7.

Recall from Chapter 10 that temperament is the biologically based disposition to behave in certain ways, which lays the foundation for later personality traits. Evidence suggests that temperament and personality differences are manifest even *before* birth. Apparently, fetal activity and heart rate can reveal something about temperament differences over the first year of life. In particular, a high heart rate at 36 weeks gestation (nearly full term) foreshadowed less predictable eating and sleeping habits three and six months after birth and less emotionality at six months after birth. Having high activity levels at 36 weeks' gestation predicted being slow to adapt to new people or situations and having more irregular eating and sleeping habits at three and six months and being more difficult or fussy at six months (DiPietro et al., 1996).

The prenatal environment may play an important role in shaping personality. In fact, the amount of stress the mother experiences during pregnancy changes the infant's permanent stress response. That is, infants born to mothers who have experienced an unusual amount of stress during pregnancy tend to have impaired stress function, higher baseline levels of stress hormones, and a faster, stronger, and more pronounced stress response, all of which persist into childhood (Barbazanges et al., 1996).

Personality and Culture: Universality and Differences

Additional evidence that both nature and nurture shape personality comes from cross-cultural research on personality traits. If personality dispositions are part of

In Japan and other Asian cultures, respect for others and an emphasis on harmonious interpersonal relationships takes precedence over individual concerns. Interpersonal relatedness as a dimension of personality is rare in the West.

our biology, we would expect the same personality dimensions or traits to appear in cultures all over the world. Environment and culture, however, might modify temperament and make certain traits more likely in some societies than in others. Indeed, there is evidence for both of these perspectives.

Researchers have investigated many personality traits across cultures, including extraversion, neuroticism, agreeableness, openness to experience, conscientiousness, and psychoticism. Research confirms the existence of these personality traits not only in Western cultures (the United States, the United Kingdom, Germany, Australia, Iceland, Spain, Portugal), but also in Asian (China, Japan, South Korea), African (Zimbabwe), Middle Eastern (Iran, Israel), and Pacific Rim (Malaysia and the Philippines) cultures (Benet-Martinez & Oishi, 2008; McCrae, 2002; McCrae & Allik, 2002; McCrae & Costa, 1997). One common measure of personality is the NEO-Personality Inventory (or NEO-PI), which has been translated into more than 40 languages. It assesses five major dimensions of personality, called the "Big Five," and research has revealed these same personality dimensions in every cultural group tested (Rolland, 2002). In other words, people from vastly different cultural backgrounds universally exhibit these traits—which suggests there might be a biological basis. We will return to a discussion of the Big Five factor model of personality later in this chapter.

Yet people in different cultures also differ on certain dimensions of personality. In particular, people in Asian cultures exhibit qualities that fit a dimension of "interpersonal relatedness" that is rarely seen in Western cultures. Interpersonal relatedness includes such behaviours and attitudes as a respectful, obedient demeanour toward others, a belief in saving "face" (that is, allowing a "losing" party to suffer a loss and yet maintain esteem and reputation), and an emphasis on harmonious relationships. As we mentioned in Chapter 1, this dimension of personality reflects how people in Asian cultures tend to be more concerned about the impact of their behaviour on their family, friends, and social groups (known as *collectivism*), whereas people in Western cultures are more concerned with how their behaviour will affect their personal goals (known as *individualism*) (Cross & Markus, 1999; Hofstede, 2001). Thus, an Asian employee who is offered a promotion that would require relocating to another city may be concerned primarily with how the move would affect her family. On the other hand, the primary consideration of a Western employee might be how the move would increase her chances of someday becoming an executive in a major corporation.

Quick Quiz 13.2: The Nature and Nurture of Personality

1. Researchers using the quantitative trait loci approach collect information about _____ from their research participants.
   a. genes
   b. behaviours related to personality traits
   c. twins
   d. both a and b
2. Researchers obtain estimates of how heritable personality traits are by
   a. studying biochemical markers of personality.
   b. analyzing DNA in rats reared together.
   c. documenting family histories.
   d. studying twins.
3. People in Asian cultures exhibit qualities that suggest a personality dimension of _____ that is rarely seen in Western cultures.
   a. anxiety
   b. interpersonal relatedness
   c. separation distress
   d. agreeableness

Answers can be found at the end of the chapter.

HOW DO THEORISTS EXPLAIN PERSONALITY?

Maria is calm most of the time and gets along well with most people. Emily is excitable, and the slightest thing can make her "blow up." Annie loves parties and chats animatedly with anyone she happens to meet. Dmitry is reclusive and is rarely seen anywhere except the office. How do we explain such differences in personality style? Many theorists have devoted much attention to answering

Theories of personality, like all scientific theories, are based on theorists' observations and are used to generate research hypotheses.

What observations about personality does this photograph bring to mind?

this question. Let's take a look at the answers they have provided. The major explanations can be grouped into five distinct theoretical camps: psychoanalysis, humanism, social–cognitive learning, trait theory, and biological theory.

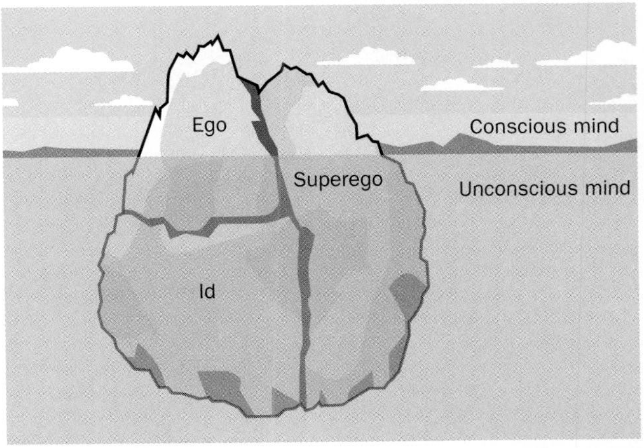

An iceberg can be used as a metaphor for Freud's conception of the mind. As an iceberg floats in the water, a huge part of it remains below the surface and only a small percentage is visible above the surface. Similarly, the conscious mind is what we notice above the surface while the unconscious mind, the largest and most powerful part, remains unseen below the surface.

Psychoanalytic Theories

Psychoanalytic theories are all based on or are variations of Freud's seminal ideas so we will cover these in some detail first before looking at more recent theories.

LO3 **Sigmund Freud** Undoubtedly the most famous of all psychologists is Sigmund Freud (1856–1939). Freud not only proposed an overarching theory of personality and psychotherapy but also founded the movement known as psychoanalysis and in the process of doing so essentially invented the field of psychotherapy.

As we mentioned in Chapter 1, the starting point for Freud's theory of psychoanalysis is the idea that the unconscious is the most powerful force in our personality. More generally, Freud described three layers of consciousness: unconscious, preconscious, and conscious. The *conscious* layer is simply what we are aware of at any given moment in time, whereas the *preconscious* is just below the surface of awareness. It is not currently conscious but can become so relatively easily. Because the conscious and preconscious layers are relatively unimportant in Freud's theory, we focus instead on the unconscious.

According to Freud, the *unconscious* contains all the drives, urges, or instincts that are outside awareness but nonetheless motivate most of our speech, thoughts, feelings, or actions. He believed that much of what we do and the reasons that we do it are hidden from our awareness and revealed to us only in distorted forms, such as slips of the tongue and dreams (Freud, 1900/1953, 1901/1960). He developed an elaborate system for interpreting the meaning of dreams, because he felt they were the best way to understand a person's unconscious.

Connection

Cognitive psychologists refer to mental processes that occur outside awareness as "implicit" or "automatic." Much of what we learn and remember is implicit.

See Chapter 6, LO1.

Freud also developed the notion that the human mind has three distinct "provinces," or regions, that involve control and regulation of impulses. The first province—developed in infancy—is the **id,** and it is the seat of impulse and desire. According to Freud, its sole function is to seek pleasure; it is therefore founded in the "pleasure principle" and operates on the "do it" principle. By the end of the first year of life, a sense of self, or **ego,** begins to emerge. Unlike the id, the ego is in direct contact with the outside world, and it operates on the "reality principle." If the id wants pleasure, the ego makes a realistic attempt to obtain it. The last part of the mind to develop, around age two or three, is the **superego,** the part of the self that monitors and controls behaviour. The superego "stands over us" and evaluates actions in terms of right and wrong; hence, it is our conscience. It operates on the "moralistic principle" and gives us a sense of what we should and should not do. Thus, the superego is the control centre of the personality and frequently applies the brakes to impulses of the id.

In a healthy person, the ego mediates this conflict between impulse and control. In fact, Freud believed that some people are mostly id-driven, whereas others are mostly superego-driven. People who are overly impulsive and pleasure seeking have a highly developed id. People who are overly controlling and repress their impulses have a highly developed superego. The healthiest person

id
Freud's term for the seat of impulse and desire; the pleasure-seeking part of our personality.

ego
Freud's term for the sense of self; the part of the mind that operates on the "reality principle."

superego
Freud's term for the part of the mind that monitors behaviour and evaluates it in terms of right and wrong; the conscience.

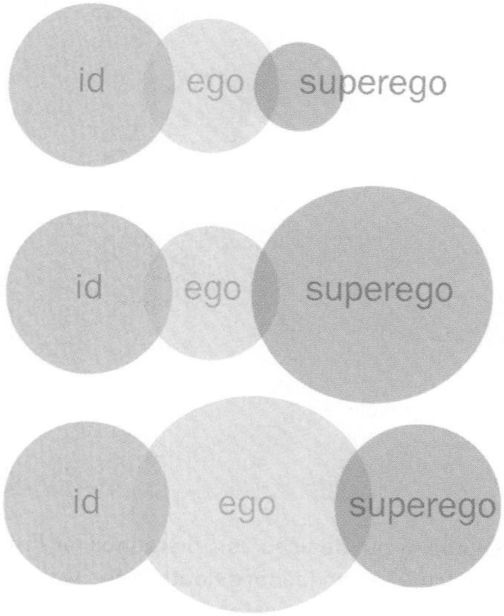

FIGURE **13.3**

THE RELATIVE INFLUENCES OF ID, EGO, AND SUPEREGO IN THREE TYPES OF PEOPLE. Freud argued that the relative sizes and strengths of the id, ego, and superego (as symbolized by the size of the circles) contributed to whether a person is overly impulsive, neurotically repressed and overcontrolled, or psychologically balanced and healthy. (*Source:* Feist & Feist, 2009.)

is one in whom the ego is most developed and can control in a realistic and healthy way the conflict between impulse and control (see Figure 13.3).

Another of Freud's major contributions to psychology is the concept of psychological **defence mechanisms** (Freud, 1926/1959). Although Freud first described these mechanisms, his daughter, Anna, developed them further (A. Freud, 1946). Just as the physical body has the immune system to protect it from foreign substances, they hypothesized that the mind also protects itself from harmful, threatening, and anxiety-provoking thoughts, feelings, or impulses. All defence mechanisms share two qualities: (1) They operate unconsciously; (2) they deny and distort reality in some way.

The most basic of all defence mechanisms is **repression** since it underlies all the other defence mechanisms. Repression is the unconscious act of keeping threatening or disturbing thoughts, feelings, or impulses out of consciousness. According to Freud, the impulses that are most likely to be repressed are sexual and aggressive impulses, because these are inherently the most threatening. Although repression may keep these impulses and thoughts out of awareness, they may be expressed in disguised or distorted form and reveal themselves through dreams, slips of the tongue, or neurotic behaviour.

Reaction formation occurs when an unpleasant idea, feeling, or impulse is turned into its opposite. This often results in exaggerated or compulsive feelings and behaviour (Freud, 1926/1959). For example, a woman may resent and even hate her mother, but because these feelings are not acceptable to her or to society, she turns them

defence mechanisms
unconscious strategies the mind uses to protect itself from anxiety by denying and distorting reality in some way.

repression
defence mechanism for keeping unpleasant thoughts, feelings, or impulses out of consciousness.

reaction formation
a defence mechanism that turns an unpleasant idea, feeling, or impulse into its opposite.

To honour Freud's contributions to psychology, his last home in London has been preserved as a museum. His patients would lie on this couch during treatment sessions.

into showy, exaggerated love. Homophobia is sometimes explained according to this defence mechanism: hatred and aggression toward homosexuals could be considered a reaction against fear of one's own latent homosexual impulses.

Another defence is **sublimation,** which involves expressing a socially unacceptable impulse in a socially acceptable and even desirable way. Freud believed that most creative achievements are motivated by sublimated impulses, usually sexual or aggressive. That is, unfulfilled sexual desire or aggressive impulses drive much creative output. Thus, for example, a man who is hopelessly in love with an unattainable woman may engage in sublimation, channelling his feelings into writing a novel whose main characters closely resemble him and the woman he desires.

sublimation
a defence mechanism in which a socially unacceptable impulse is expressed in a socially acceptable way.

One of Freud's most important and lasting ideas was that adult personality stems from early childhood experiences. This is, without a doubt, one of Freud's most controversial ideas. He called it a **psychosexual stage theory** because he believed that sexual feelings were key to each stage of personality development, even infancy. More specifically, Freud argued that as we move through each stage of life, a different region of our body is most erogenous—that is, a source of pleasure. He delineated four major stages of psychosexual development: oral, anal, phallic, and genital (see Figure 13.4).

psychosexual stage theory
Freud's stages of personality development; in different stages a different region of the body is most erogenous.

The *oral stage* is the first 12 to 18 months of life, when the mouth is the centre of pleasure. Infants suck, bite, and chew as a means of obtaining nourishment and a way of exploring their world. The *anal stage* takes place during the second and third year of life and involves the pleasure gained from holding and releasing one's bladder and bowels. Toilet training is the crucial event during the anal stage, and children learn to control their bladder and bowels. The third stage occurs from approximately ages three to six and is the *phallic stage* because the child discovers that the genitals are a source of pleasure (note that Freud used the male term *phallic,* which means "penis-like," to apply to both boys and girls). The phallic stage, however, was the most complex and controversial of all of Freud's stages. He argued that children not only discover pleasure from manipulating their genitals, but also harbour unconscious feelings of attraction for their opposite-sex parent and hostility for their same-sex parent. Desire for the opposite-sex parent and hostility toward the same-sex parent is known as the

Stage	Pleasure comes from . . .	Fixations may result in . . .
Oral (0–18 months)	The mouth and sucking, biting, chewing	Smoking and sarcasm
Anal (18–36 months)	The anus and bowel and bladder elimination	Obsessive and compulsive cleaning behaviours
Phallic (3–6 years)	The genitals (self-focused) and attraction for opposite-sex parent	Attraction to people like one's opposite-sex parent
Latency (6–puberty)	Not applicable; sexual feelings remain latent and dormant	Not applicable
Genital (puberty and up)	The genitals (self- *and* other-focused) and mature sexual behaviour (giving and receiving pleasure)	Immature sexuality that is either self- *or* other-focused

FIGURE **13.4**
FREUD'S THEORY OF PSYCHOSEXUAL DEVELOPMENT. Freud's theory focuses on distinct regions of the body being the main source of pleasure.

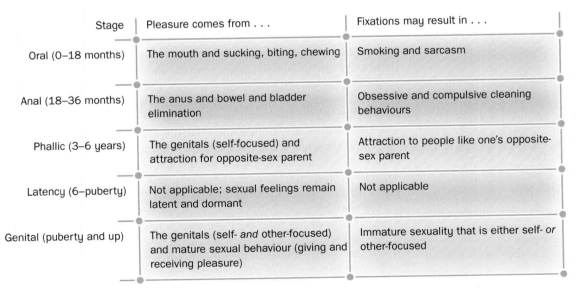

Oedipal complex. As children move through the phallic stage, they resolve the Oedipal complex by identifying with their same-sex parent and choosing to be more like him or her.

After the phallic stage, Freud argued that children go through a *latency stage,* which is not a psychosexual stage of development, but a period in which no region of the body is erogenous and the sense of sexuality goes beneath the surface (becomes latent). The last stage is the *genital stage,* which starts with puberty and lasts for the rest of one's life; sexual pleasure is interpersonal and exists between people outside the family. Freud argued that few people are healthy and balanced in their sexual relations as adults. Some remain selfish and focus on their own pleasure, whereas others give up their own pleasure and focus only on their partner's satisfaction.

fixation
a defence mechanism whereby a person continues to be concerned and even preoccupied with earlier stages of development.

A key offshoot of Freud's psychosexual stages was his idea of **fixation,** which is a defence mechanism whereby a person continues to be concerned and even preoccupied with an earlier stage of development. For example, someone with an oral fixation may continue in adulthood to get oral gratification from smoking or from being "biting and sarcastic." An anal fixation might be expressed in adulthood as obsessive or compulsive focus on cleanliness (which is why in the current slang, people who are compulsive are often called "anal"). A phallic or Oedipal fixation, for example, might be expressed as a person's continuously being attracted to people who resemble the opposite-sex parent in some way.

Connection

Some people compulsively clean or wash; others check to make sure doors are locked. Present-day clinical psychologists refer to such "anal fixations," when they disrupt someone's life, as obsessive–compulsive disorder.

See Chapter 15, LO9.

Freud is one of the most complex figures in the history of psychology. On the one hand, his name is one of the most widely recognized. His theories have had a significant and lasting influence on Western thought and culture. However, Freud is also one of the most controversial figures in the history of psychology. Some argue that his notoriety has fed popular misconceptions about the field of psychology (Stanovich, 2010). Over the last generation, many psychologists have dismissed Freud as a pseudoscientist, because he did not support his ideas with research that could be replicated (Dufresne, 2003). Others argue that just because his status as a scientist is questionable, it does not mean that his insights as a clinician have no scientific merit (Westen, 1998).

Freud believed that a fixation at the oral stage of development may lead to smoking in adulthood—in order to attain oral gratification.

Could the scientific method be used to test this hypothesis?

From a scientific perspective, Freud's theories are problematic in many respects. First, his theory is based entirely upon case studies. These cases rely on the recollections of his adult patients, not on the actual observation and study of children (Hergenhahn, 2009). His theory is focused almost entirely on male development with little mention of female psychosexual development. Even Freud's followers, as we see in the next section, did not agree with many of the details of his theory of psychosexual development. His theory is also criticized for the inclusion of ambiguous concepts that are difficult to operationally define and measure (Westen & Gabbard, 1999). Although the idea that adult personality has its origin in childhood is now widely accepted (Westen, Gabbard, & Ortigo, 2008), there is little to support the idea that personality is affected by fixations to earlier psychosexual development.

Freud became dogmatic about his ideas after he had published them. If any of his followers seriously challenged them, they were often kicked out of Freud's inner circle or official society. Some of these followers went on to develop their own theories of psychoanalysis. Among them were Alfred Adler, Carl Jung, and Karen Horney.

LO4 Psychoanalysis after Freud The first to break away from Freud was Alfred Adler (1870–1937), who saw himself as Freud's colleague rather than follower. But when he disagreed with Freud on the major motives underlying behaviour, he had to resign from the presidency of Freud's Vienna Psychoanalytic Society. Adler's first major assumption was that humans naturally strive to overcome their inherent inferiorities or deficiencies, both physical and psychological. According to him, **striving for superiority,** not sex or aggression, is the major drive behind all behaviour (Adler, 1956). Adler introduced the term *compensation* to explain how this process unfolds. All people, he pointed out, begin life as young, immature, and helpless. As they grow, they strive toward growth and completion. In the process, they attempt to *compensate* for their feelings of weakness or inferiority. Although all people do this to some extent, some develop an unhealthy need to dominate or upstage others as a way of compensating for feelings of inferiority—that is, they develop an **inferiority complex.**

striving for superiority
according to Adler, the major drive behind all behaviour, whereby humans naturally strive to overcome their physical and psychological deficiencies.

inferiority complex
an unhealthy need to dominate or upstage others as a way of compensating for feelings of deficiency.

Carl Jung (1875–1961) became more widely known than Adler. Jung's signature idea was that the unconscious has two distinct forms: personal and collective (Jung, 1918/1964). The **personal unconscious** consists of all our repressed and hidden thoughts, feelings, and motives, similar to Freud's notion of the unconscious. Jung also believed, however, that there is a second kind of unconscious, one that belongs not to the individual but to the species. He called it the **collective unconscious,** and it consists of the shared experiences of our ancestors—God, mother, life, death, water, earth, aggression, survival—that have been transmitted from generation to generation.

personal unconscious
according to Jung, all our repressed and hidden thoughts, feelings, and motives

collective unconscious
according to Jung, the shared experiences of our ancestors that have been passed down from generation to generation.

Jung hypothesized that the collective unconscious is made up of **archetypes:** ancient or archaic images that result from common ancestral experiences and show up most often in dreams, fantasies, hallucinations, myths, and religious themes. Jung postulated many archetypes, including the shadow, anima, and animus. The *shadow* is the dark and morally objectionable part of ourselves. We all have impulses that are dark and disturbing; in fact, most often we project evil and darkness onto our enemies and deny that we ourselves are evil or capable of it. The *anima* is the female part of the male personality, and the *animus* is the male part of the female personality. All people possess characteristics and traits—not to mention hormones—that are typical of both genders, but many men tend to deny and repress their feminine side, or anima. Many women likewise tend to deny or repress their masculine side, or animus. According to Jung, full personality development requires acknowledging and being receptive to these unconscious or less-well-developed sides of one's personality.

archetypes
ancient or archaic images that result from common ancestral experiences.

One of the first major female voices in the psychoanalytic movement was that of Karen Horney (pronounced "horn-eye"; 1885–1952). Compared to Freud, Horney focused more on the social and cultural forces behind neurosis and the neurotic personality, and indeed her approach is labelled "psychoanalytic social theory." The essence of Horney's theory is that neurosis stems from basic hostility and basic anxiety. *Basic hostility* is anger or rage that originates in childhood and stems from fear of being neglected or rejected by one's parents. Because hostility toward one's parents is so threatening, however, it is often turned inward and converted into *basic anxiety,* which Horney defined as "a feeling of being isolated and helpless in a world conceived as potentially hostile" (1950, p. 18).

Although basic anxiety in itself is not neurotic—it can give rise to normal behaviours—in some people it can result in neurotic behaviours. Horney argued that all people defend themselves against basic anxiety (isolation and helplessness) by developing particular needs or trends (see Figure 13.5). If these needs become compulsive and the person is unable to switch from one need to another as the situation demands, that person is neurotic (Horney, 1945). The three *neurotic trends* or needs are

1. *moving toward others* (the compliant personality: clinging to other people, belittling oneself)
2. *moving against others* (the aggressive personality: competing against others, prone to hostility and anger)
3. *moving away from others* (the detached personality: not responding emotionally, commitment shy)

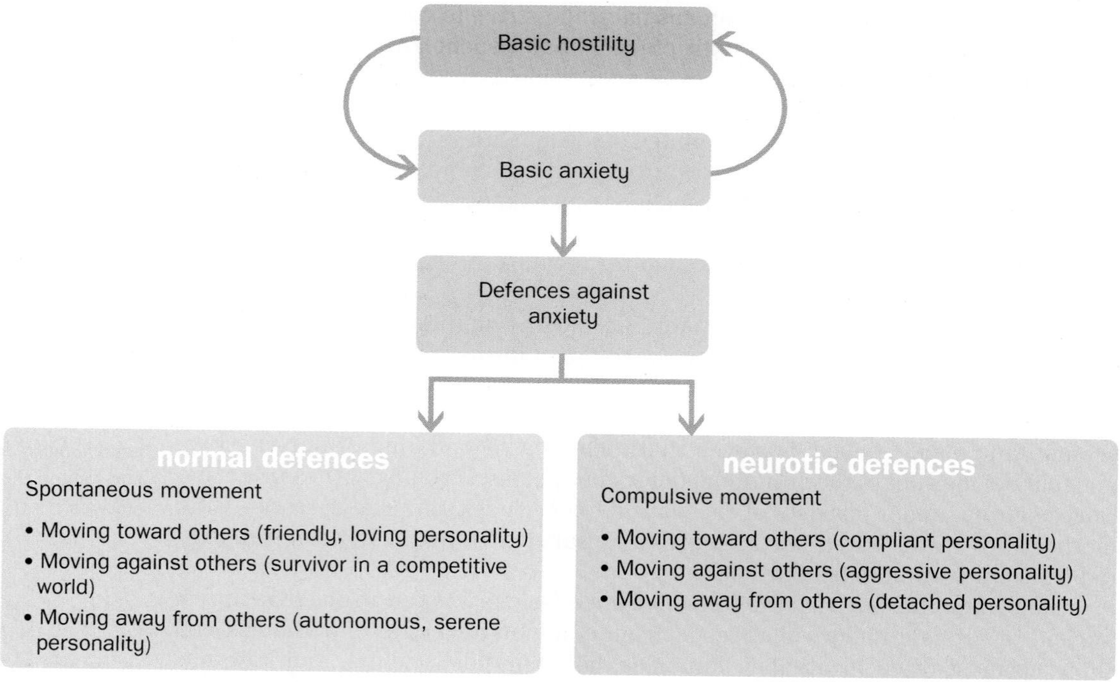

FIGURE **13.5**

INTERACTION AMONG HOSTILITY, ANXIETY, AND DEFENCES IN HORNEY'S THEORY. According this theory, hostility and anxiety mutually influence one another, and the person then defends him- or herself by developing either normal or neurotic defences. Horney maintained that we all may develop defences, but in neurotic individuals, these needs become compulsive and part of one's personality.

LO5 Humanistic-Positive Psychology Theories

A second major perspective explaining personality comes from a *humanistic approach*, which is optimistic about human nature, believing that humans are naturally interested in realizing their full potential. Humanists argue that psychology needs to study humans at their best as well as at their worst. As Abraham Maslow (1968, p. 5) wrote, "Freud supplied us with the sick half of psychology, and we must now fill it with the healthy half." The term *humanism* is not commonly used today, mostly because many adherents of this approach did not conduct empirical research. Yet the movement has been rekindled since the late 1990s under a new label: *positive psychology.* Positive psychology embraces and generates empirical research, but its fundamental ideas come from two major thinkers in the humanistic tradition: Abraham Maslow and Carl Rogers.

Abraham Maslow We discussed one of Abraham Maslow's (1908–1970) major ideas in Chapter 11: his hierarchy of needs (see Figure 11.4). An important concept that followed from his theory of needs was that of self-actualization, which stood at the top of the hierarchy. This term refers to people's inherent drive to realize their full potential (an idea that was influenced by Adler's notion of striving for superiority; Maslow, 1970). Only a very few people attain this highest level of the hierarchy of needs because only a very few are "fully human"—that is, living life at its fullest and achieving their full potential.

Based on an examination of historical figures whom he considered self-actualizing, Maslow identified a set of characteristics that he believed to be more common in self-actualizing individuals than in other people (Maslow, 1970). He listed 15 characteristics, five of which we summarize here:

Connection

A truly starving person is not concerned with art and beauty. Maslow's hierarchy of needs describes how the basic needs (such as hunger, thirst) must be satisfied before one can pursue the higher needs, such as self-actualization.

See Chapter 11, LO2.

1. *Spontaneity, simplicity, naturalness:* Self-actualizing people sometimes can appear quite childlike in their ability to be spontaneous and straightforward; they do not pretend to be what they are not.
2. *Problem-centred (have a "calling"):* Self-actualizing people often experience moments of profound personal importance or personal meaning (what Maslow called "peak experiences"), and these experiences shape the rest of their lives. A sense of what they were meant to do with their lives is suddenly revealed to them, and they devote the rest of their lives to it. These individuals are focused and secure in who they are and what matters most to them—and often their concerns have great philosophical, spiritual, political, artistic, or scientific meaning.
3. *Creativity (self-actualizing rather than specialized):* Problems confront us dozens, if not hundreds, of times each day. Self-actualizing people are able to readily solve problems with originality and novelty. By *creativity,* Maslow does not mean creativity as expressed in art or science (specialized creativity) but rather the kind of creativity that can be found in everyday life (self-actualizing creativity). For example, a woman who provides a loving home for her children, manages to schedule her children's various activities, works full-time as a well-loved college instructor, and organizes hot lunches at her children's school shows self-actualizing creativity.
4. *Deep interpersonal relations:* Self-actualizing individuals are likely to have few but profound relationships. They do not call 10 or 15 people their "best friends" or even "friends" but instead may have close relationships with only one or two people. These relationships, however, are intensely intimate—they share deep thoughts and feelings about themselves, each other, and the world.
5. *Resistance to enculturation:* Self-actualizing people are less likely than most people to be influenced by the ideas and attitudes of others. Their ideas are solidly their own; because they have a clear sense of direction in life, they don't look to others for guidance on what to think or how to behave.

In 1995, Craig Kielburger founded Free the Children (FTC), the world's largest network of children helping children through education when he was only 12 years old. He has received national and international recognition, recently becoming one of the youngest recipients of the Order of Canada.

Does Craig Kielburger fit Maslow's profile of a self-actualizing individual?

Carl Rogers Another key figure in the humanistic–positive psychology tradition was the psychotherapist Carl Rogers (1902–1987). Rogers developed a unique form of psychotherapy based on the assumption that people naturally strive toward growth and fulfillment and need unconditional positive regard for that to happen (Rogers, 1980). **Unconditional positive regard** is the ability to

unconditional positive regard acceptance of another person regardless of his or her behaviour.

Carl Rogers (second from right) leads a group therapy session. His client-centred therapy approach is discussed in Chapter 16.

respect and appreciate another person unconditionally—that is, regardless of their behaviour. This may sound easy, but in fact it is very difficult. It means that even if someone violates our basic assumptions of what it means to be a good, decent, and moral person, we still appreciate, respect, and even love him or her as a person. It requires that we separate person from behaviour—which can be difficult even for parents and their children. With children, unconditional positive regard means that they know their parents value and accept them even if they don't like eating spinach or hit their sibling when they get angry. To love people only when they do things that we want and like is to love them conditionally, or create **conditions of worth.** For example, suppose that Sarah gets angry at her little sister and pinches her. Her mom might reprimand her by saying that "nice girls don't pinch their little sisters." To gain her mom's approval, Sarah has to deny her true feelings of anger, and she may secretly believe that she is not a "nice girl" because she pinched her sister. As people become more and more responsive to *conditional positive regard,* they run the risk of becoming the type of person others want them to be, not the type of person they want to be. Rogers (1959) felt that conditions of worth can pose a serious barrier to self-actualization.

conditions of worth
the beliefs that a person's worth depends on displaying the "right" attitudes, behaviours, and values.

In contrast to Maslow, Rogers had a specific, measurable way of defining the self-actualizing tendency and psychological adjustment. To Rogers, all of us have two distinct ways of seeing and evaluating ourselves: as we really are and as we ideally would like to be. The first he called the *real self* and the second the *ideal self* (Rogers, 1959). Rogers then defined psychological adjustment as congruence between the real and ideal selves (see Figure 13.6).

Humanistic theories gained popularity in the 1960s and 1970s, largely as an appealing alternative to the negative determinism of psychoanalytic theories. Like psychoanalytic theories, critics argue these theories present concepts, such as self-actualization and unconditional positive regard, that are difficult to test scientifically. Addressing these criticisms, Martin Seligman and Mihály Csíkszentmihályi (2000) founded a new branch of psychology, *positive psychology,* which focuses on the empirical study of such things as positive emotions, strengths-based character, and healthy institutions (Seligman, 2004). Like humanist psychology, positive psychology seeks to enhance human fulfillment, but its methodology is scientific. Research has demonstrated that it is possible to be happier—to feel more satisfied, to be more engaged with life, to find more meaning, to have higher hopes, and probably even to laugh and smile more, regardless of one's circumstances (Seligman, 2004). As we saw in Chapters 11 and 12, positive psychology has produced important work on happiness, social support, health, and well-being.

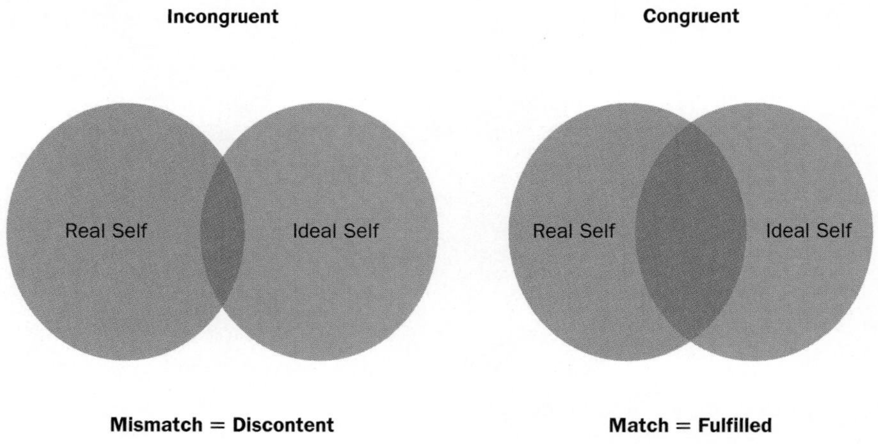

FIGURE **13.6**

CONGRUENCE OF REAL AND IDEAL SELVES. The more the ideal self overlaps, or is similar to the real self, the more fulfilled and happier the person is.

LO6 Social–Cognitive Learning Theories

A third major category of personality theory is based on the social–cognitive learning perspective. This perspective is founded on the ideas that people learn by interacting with their environments and that human thought processes are central to understanding personality. According to this perspective, each of us develops a unique personality because of our differing interactions with external stimuli, as well as the influence of our unique ways of thinking about the world and interpreting what happens to us. The research and writings of Albert Bandura and Walter Mischel exemplify this perspective.

Albert Bandura Bandura (1986) argues that three factors influence one another in shaping our personality. These factors include internal personal factors (such as our cognitive characteristics that have been rewarded in the past), the environment, and our behaviour. He terms this give-and-take relationship between factors **reciprocal determinism** (see Figure 13.7).

reciprocal determinism
the process by which personal factors, behaviour, and the environment all interact with one another to shape an individual's personality.

Consider the example of a child named Shane, who is acting out in school (behaviour). Shane doesn't like going to school (personal factor); therefore, he acts out in class (behaviour). This acting-out behaviour results in teachers and administrators of the school disliking having him around (environment). When confronted by the situation, Shane admits he hates school and other peers don't like him. These beliefs have been reinforced by the teachers' and peers' behaviours towards him. This results in Shane continuing to act inappropriately, forcing the administrators who dislike having him around to create a more restrictive environment for children who "act out." Each behavioural and environmental factor interacts with Shane, resulting in a continuous battle, and likely escalating his aggressive behaviour.

Another important principle in Bandura's theory concerns people's **self-efficacy,** or their beliefs about their ability to perform the behaviours needed to achieve desired outcomes (Bandura, 1997). According to Bandura, self-efficacy beliefs can impact an individual's level of accomplishment and well-being in numerous ways. For instance, self-efficacy helps determine the types of

self-efficacy
people's beliefs about their ability to perform the behaviours needed to achieve desired outcomes.

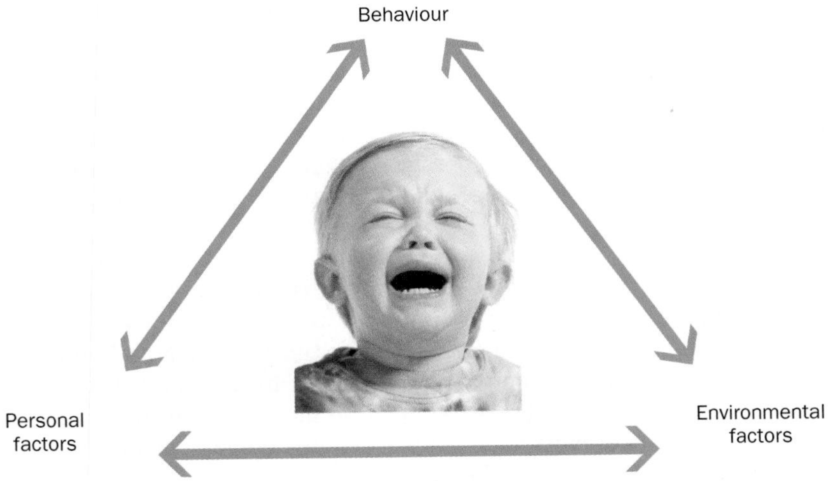

FIGURE **13.7**
RECIPROCAL DETERMINISM. Our personalities are shaped by the interaction of the environment, which consists of the physical surroundings and the potential for reinforcement; personal factors, such as thoughts or emotions that have been rewarded in the past; and behaviour, which may or may not be reinforced at a particular time and place.

Research has revealed that young women who have mastered martial arts skills in a self-defence training program show increases in their beliefs that they could escape from or disable a potential assailant (Weitlauf, Smith, & Cervone, 2000). But these self-efficacy beliefs were specific to this situation. Even though the women who mastered the self-defence skills enhanced their self-defence efficacy, they did not feel generally more capable in all areas of their lives.

tasks or activities people choose to engage in. Imagine that you have an opportunity to write an optional term paper in your introductory psychology class to improve your grade. Would you do so? Bandura would argue that you are more likely to write the paper if your self-efficacy is high—that is, you believe you can write an excellent paper because you have received high grades on the papers you have written in other courses in the past. You are less likely to write the optional paper if you have had bad outcomes in writing previous papers. In addition to determining types of tasks people engage in, self-efficacy beliefs also affect how much effort people will expend on an activity and how long they will persist with that activity, especially when it is particularly difficult. In general, people high in self-efficacy will exert greater effort and will be more persistent than people low in self-efficacy, who often expect to fail and tend to avoid challenges (Bandura, 1998). One issue many teachers face is in helping struggling learners. To get students to invest sufficient effort and persist on challenging tasks (like studying for a test), teachers must attempt to develop high self-efficacy within these students (Margolis & McCabe, 2004).

Connection

Bandura argued that people learn new behaviours by watching others and noting the consequences—a process he termed *observational learning.*

See Chapter 7, LO8.

Walter Mischel As we have seen earlier in the chapter, personality traits produce consistent behaviour over time and across situations. A hostile person, for example, may be less hostile in one situation (such as being run into by a child) than in another (such as being cut off in traffic). Yet, compared to a non-hostile person, he or she is likely to be more hostile in many—but not all—situations. Mischel says that people are not consistent across all situations (Mischel, 2009; Mischel & Shoda, 1995, 1999), as it would be pathological not to change one's behaviour when the situation changes. The qualities a person brings to each situation interact with the situation to make one person act somewhat differently when the situation changes. Figure 13.8 illustrates how people and situations interact according to Mischel's theory. The figure presents the probabilities of two individuals (A and B) acting in a hostile manner across nine different situations. As you can see, Person A is more likely to be

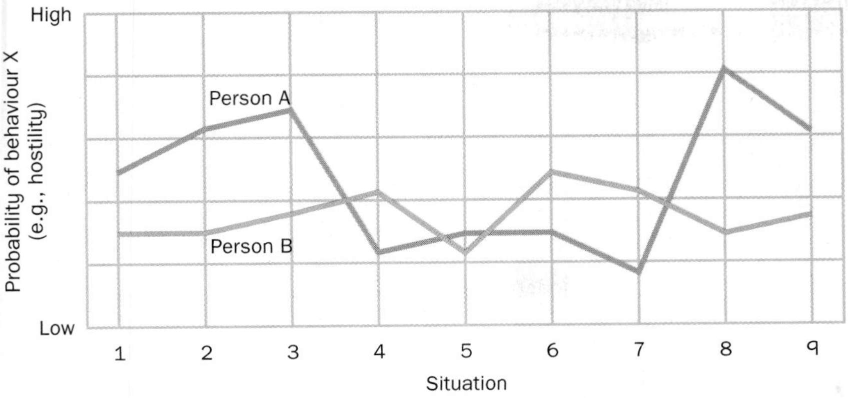

FIGURE **13.8**
HYPOTHETICAL PERSON-SITUATION-BEHAVIOUR INTERACTION. People respond to different situations differently, producing unique personality–situation profiles. Shown here are interactions between situations and hostility for Person A and Person B. (*Source:* Mischel & Shoda, 1995.)

Looking at the graph, who would you conclude is more hostile overall?

hostile in six of the nine situations, so we would label this person "hostile." But notice two things: (1) There are a few situations in which Person B is more hostile, and (2) Person B is more stable and consistent across all nine situations, whereas Person A is sometimes *very* hostile but at other times not hostile at all. This hypothetical situation demonstrates how the person, situation, and behaviour interact.

One major strength of the social–cognitive perspective, over psychoanalytic and humanistic theories of personality, is that many of its main principles have been tested under scientific conditions. The concepts in social–cognitive theory are easier to define and thus, better lend themselves to objective measurement. However, some argue that its focus is so much on the environment or situational factors that it fails to appreciate a person's inner traits, or the role of emotional or unconscious motives in our personality. It also fails to address how personality develops over time. Let us now turn to the empirically based approach to personality that has dominated the field for the last 20 years.

LO7 Trait Theories

A fourth general perspective that explains personality is the trait approach, which assumes that traits or dispositions are the major force behind personality. But which traits are most important? Between the 1930s and the 1980s, dozens of different measures of personality were developed, but almost none of them measured the same personality traits. Some psychologists argued for the central importance of hostility, authoritarianism, introversion, intelligence, repression, and impulsivity, while others cited psychopathic deviance, tolerance, or psychological insight. But until personality psychologists could reach a consensus on a set of traits that make up personality across cultures, no progress could be made in the study of personality, as it would mean different things to different people.

As far back as the 1930s, Gordon Allport (1897–1967) tried to figure out how many personality traits existed (Allport & Odbert, 1936). He began with the idea that language would be a good place to start looking. His argument was simply that if a word exists for a trait, it must be important. He approached the

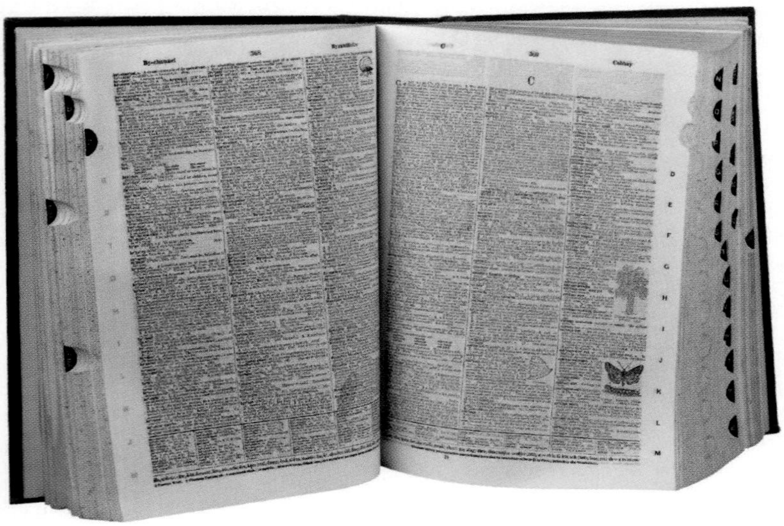

Gordon Allport's approach to studying personality was to analyze the language we use to describe people.

problem by taking an English dictionary and combing through it page by page and counting each time a term described a person. After going through and counting all the personally descriptive words, he came away with nearly 18 000 words in English. A few problems arose, however. First, some of these terms—such as *sad, angry, bored,* or *annoyed*—described temporary states. Others were personal evaluations (*wonderful, unhelpful*) or described physical traits (*tall, heavy*). And finally, others were essentially synonyms, such as *friendly* and *nice.* When he fixed these problems, he still ended up with more than 4000 English words that were personally descriptive. He went on to argue, however, that most individuals could typically be described with only about ten or so central traits, although he didn't really have any scientific evidence to back that claim.

Pioneering trait theorist Raymond B. Cattell (1965) sought empirical evidence for a compact way to describe personality. He had thousands of people rate themselves on numerous characteristics. He then used a statistical tool, called **factor analysis,** to look for groupings and commonalities in the data. Based on this research, he identified 16 factors or **source traits** that underlie human personality. He thought that these traits were the underlying source for the surface personality characteristics easily seen by others. These 16 source traits are dimensions with behavioural opposites located on each end of a continuum, such as *reserved* versus *outgoing,* and *relaxed* versus *tense.* These personality dimensions are shown in Figure 13.9. Cattell developed his own questionnaire, the 16 Personality Factor Questionnaire (16 PF; Cattell 1965) to measure individual differences on these traits and provide individual personality profiles.

factor analysis
a statistical tool used to identify clusters of traits that "go together" or are highly correlated with one another.

source traits
according to Cattell, the basic traits that underlie aspects of personality easily seen by others.

By the 1990s, personality researchers amassed evidence for the existence of five universal and widely agreed-upon dimensions of personality (Costa & McCrae, 1992; Digman, 1990; John & Srivastava, 1999). This perspective is known as the **Big Five** or **five-factor model;** the five dimensions are openness to experience, conscientiousness, extraversion, agreeableness, and neuroticism (see Figure 13.10). An easy way to remember these is to use the acronym O-C-E-A-N or C-A-N-O-E.

Big Five or five-factor model
a theory of personality that includes five dimensions: **o**penness to experience, **c**onscientiousness, **e**xtraversion, **a**greeableness, and **n**euroticism (OCEAN).

To what extent do our online personas reflect our "real" personalities? A commonly held assumption is that profiles on online social networking sites, such as Facebook, Twitter, and Instagram, display *idealized virtual identities* that do not reflect people's actual personalities. Back and colleagues (2010) had 236 users of social networking sites from Germany and the United States complete self-reports assessing the Big Five factors. Independent raters also rated the profiles of these individuals. Researchers found that individuals' self-reports correlated with the independent ratings of their personality as viewed from their profiles, suggesting that people use social media to communicate their real personalities.

In another study, researchers examined the relationship between the Big Five factors and the way people played the computer game *Sims 2* (Griebel, 2006). Thirty undergraduate university students volunteered to participate in the study, and they were administered a personality test assessing the Big Five before playing *Sims 2* for a total of ten hours over six weeks. Afterwards,

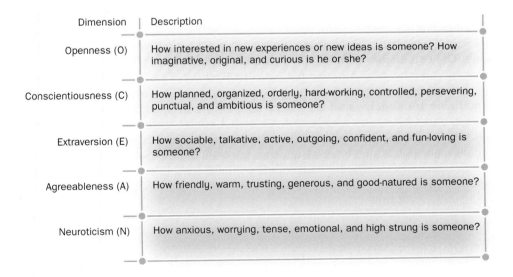

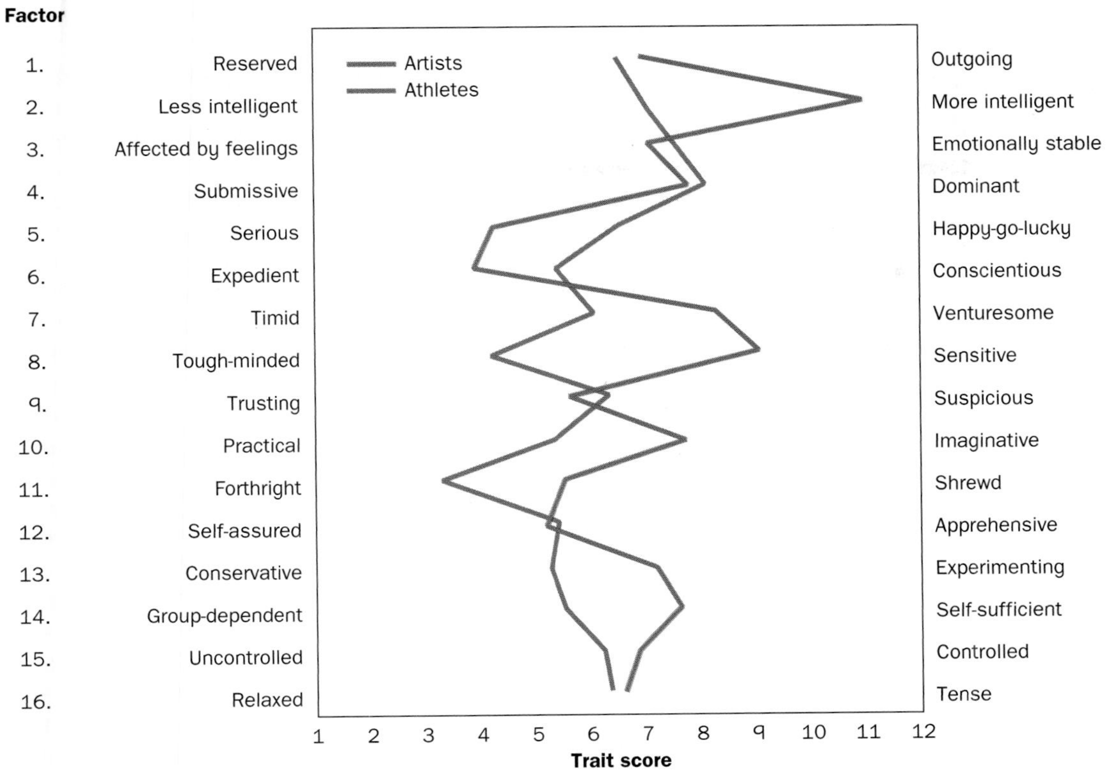

FIGURE **13.9**

CATTELL'S 16PF. Here we see personality profiles for two groups of people—athletes and artists—on Cattell's self-report measure of personality. Notice that artists, when compared to athletes, tend to be more intelligent, sensitive, and imaginative. Athletes appear to be more tough-minded and forthright. (*Source:* Based on data from Cattell, 1965.)

Dimension	Description
Openness (O)	How interested in new experiences or new ideas is someone? How imaginative, original, and curious is he or she?
Conscientiousness (C)	How planned, organized, orderly, hard-working, controlled, persevering, punctual, and ambitious is someone?
Extraversion (E)	How sociable, talkative, active, outgoing, confident, and fun-loving is someone?
Agreeableness (A)	How friendly, warm, trusting, generous, and good-natured is someone?
Neuroticism (N)	How anxious, worrying, tense, emotional, and high strung is someone?

FIGURE **13.10**

BIG FIVE DIMENSIONS OF PERSONALITY. The acronym OCEAN (or CANOE) will help you remember the five dimensions.

participants completed a questionnaire that asked detailed questions on how they played the game. Results indicated personality traits such as neuroticism, openness to experience, and conscientiousness correlated with specific game-playing behaviours. For example, participants who scored high on neuroticism were more likely to frequently change their Sims' careers and were more likely to enjoy making their Sims tease or insult other Sims. Participants who scored high

Is there any support for the idea of a national personality?

on openness were more likely to report that it was important for their Sims to live exciting lives, and worked hard at achieving their goals for their Sims. Participants who scored high on conscientiousness were more likely to report that it was important to keep their Sims' house clean and they were more likely to feel in complete control of their Sims' lives.

As we have already seen earlier in this chapter, the Big Five Factor theory has generated numerous studies on the universality of personality traits across cultures. An interesting question is: How do the personality traits of people from a particular culture match up with the cultural stereotype of what those people are like? One team of researchers examined perceptions of the personality characteristics of people from 49 cultures (Terracciano et al., 2005). They then compared those ratings to self-reports of people within those cultures. The researchers found that the self-reports did not match the cultural stereotypes. For example, Canadians were widely believed to be relatively high in agreeableness and low in neuroticism. However, Canadians' self-reports revealed that they were no more agreeable than—and just as neurotic as—people from other cultures.

Connection

Schemas or beliefs about how people are likely to behave based simply on the groups to which they belong are known as *stereotypes*.

See Chapter 14, LO2.

How many times have you thought that you (a Canadian) are different from the typical American? If you have had such thoughts, you are not alone. Many Canadians believe that they are different from Americans. Specifically, Canadians view themselves as being docile and compliant whereas they view Americans as rude, arrogant, and self-centred (McCrae & Terracciano, 2006). These shared perceptions of the personality characteristics of citizens of a particular country have been termed "national character" (McCrae & Terracciano, 2006). But are Canadians really different from Americans? Alas, no. Very few differences have been found between the personalities of Canadians and Americans, suggesting that perceptions of "national character" are unfounded stereotypes. McCrae and Terracciano (2006) argue that public awareness of such stereotypes might improve international relations.

The Big Five dimensions are more of a taxonomy, or categorization scheme, than a theory. The trait perspective has been criticized because it largely describes but does not explain personality. In the 1990s, Robert McCrae (1949–) and Paul Costa (1942–) proposed a theory around the Big Five personality dimensions. The two major components of their theory are basic tendencies and characteristic adaptations (McCrae & Costa, 1996, 1999). The Big Five personality dimensions, along with our talents, aptitudes, and cognitive abilities, are referred to as **basic tendencies** and they have their origin in biological forces. In fact, McCrae and Costa take a clear but somewhat controversial stance in arguing that these basic tendencies are due solely to internal or biological factors such as genes, hormones, and brain structures. Later on in this chapter, we will return to a discussion of the Big Five personality dimensions, examining how they are measured, how they relate to people's career and vocational choices, and how they change over time.

basic tendencies
the essence of personality: the Big Five personality dimensions plus talents, aptitudes, and cognitive abilities.

Biological Theories

The fifth way of explaining personality theoretically, biological theory, does provide explanations for McCrae and Costa's scheme. The biological theories of personality assume that differences in personality are partly based in differences in structures and systems in the central nervous system, such as genetics, hormones, and neurotransmitters. Among the most important of these theories for personality is the one proposed by Hans Eysenck (1916–1997), who argued for the fundamental importance of biology in shaping personality (Eysenck, 1947, 1982, 1990). Eysenck proposed three, rather than five, fundamental dimensions of personality. Two are included in the Big Five—neuroticism and extraversion. The third, psychoticism, is a combination of the three other traits from the Big Five of openness, conscientiousness, and agreeableness. Psychoticism consists of traits such as "aggressive," "cold," "antisocial," "impulsive," "egocentric," "non-conforming," and "creative." All three personality dimensions are hierarchical; that is, neuroticism, extraversion, and psychoticism each comprise more specific traits, which in turn comprise even more specific traits (see Figure 13.11).

Eysenck developed a model in which differences in personality are caused by the combined influences of genes, neurochemistry, and certain characteristics of the central nervous system (Eysenck, 1997). The main idea behind Eysenck's model is that differences in individuals' genome (DNA) create a different level of arousal and sensitivity to stimulation. These differences in genetics and levels of arousal and sensitivity lead to differences in the three major dimensions of personality: psychoticism, extraversion, and neuroticism (P-E-N). Personality differences in dimensions, in turn, lead to differences in learning, conditioning, perception, and memory. These cognitive-perceptual-learning differences lead to differences in social behaviours such as sociability, criminality, sexual behaviour, and creativity.

Evidence supports the connection between central nervous system arousal and personality traits, especially extraversion–introversion. Specifically, differences in cortical arousal and sensory thresholds lead to differences in extraversion–introversion. **Cortical arousal** refers to how active the brain is at a resting state as well as how sensitive it is to stimulation (Eysenck, 1997; Gale, 1983). Because they have higher baseline levels of cortical arousal, introverts require a lower stimulus level to arouse them and reach their "comfort zone" than do extraverts. Eysenck argued that lower thresholds to arousal imply greater sensitivity to stimuli. Stimulation, whether it is a new place or new people, can easily become overwhelming for an introvert. Therefore, introverts consistently shy away from or withdraw from stimulating environments. By the same token, extraverts, with low cortical arousal and high thresholds of arousal, seek out and enjoy highly stimulating experiences (Eysenck, 1990, 1997). Introversion or inhibition can thus be seen as a way of coping with an inherently aroused and sensitive central nervous system. Until recently, testing biological factors has been somewhat limited by the available technology. The advent of modern imaging

cortical arousal
level of activation in the brain.

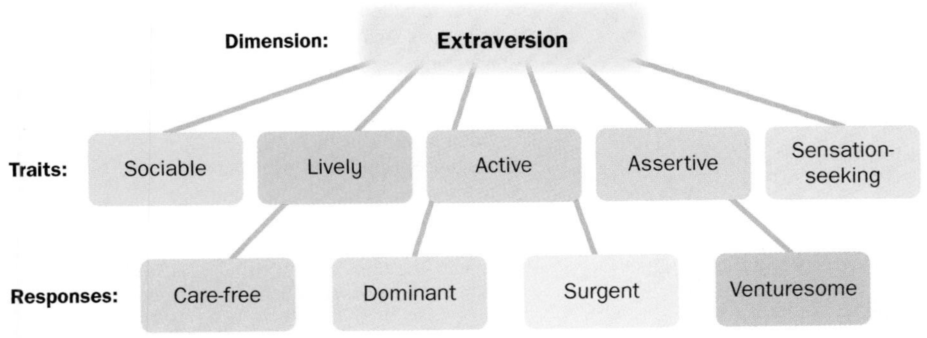

FIGURE **13.11**
EYSENCK'S HIERARCHY OF PERSONALITY TRAITS FOR EXTRAVERSION. For each of the three dimensions of personality, Eysenck developed a hierarchy of related traits and responses. (*Source:* Eysenck, 1990.)

techniques and neuropsychological testing techniques is allowing researchers to begin to explore the neurobiological basis of personality.

As you see, a number of different approaches have been proposed by different theorists. The primary assumptions, key ideas, and main criticism of each of the five approaches are presented in Figure 13.12.

	Assumptions	Theorist	Key ideas	Main Criticism
Psychoanalytic	Our personality resides in the unconscious and early childhood experiences lay the foundation for adult personality.	Freud Adler Jung Horney	Unconscious, Preconscious, Conscious Id, Ego, Superego Psychosexual development Striving for superiority Compensation Inferiority complex Personal unconscious Collective unconscious Archetypes: shadow, anima, animus Basic hostility, basic anxiety, defences against anxiety	Concepts are difficult to operationally define and test empirically
Humanistic	We have a natural interest in becoming the best person possible.	Maslow Rogers	Strive to become the best possible person Self-actualization Strive toward growth and fulfillment through unconditional positive regard Real self, Ideal self	Concepts are difficult to operationally define and test empirically
Social-Cognitive	A person's personality results from the interaction of environment, person factors, and behaviour. A person's behaviour changes in different situations.	Bandura Mischel	Reciprocal determinism Self-efficacy Behaviour results from the interaction of the cognitive and emotional qualities of the person and the particular situation he or she is in.	Overemphasizes the role of the environment
Traits	Traits are the major force behind personality.	Allport Catell 16 PF McCrae/ Costa	Ten traits Sixteen source traits **O**penness to experience **C**onscientiousness **E**xtraversion **A**greeableness **N**euroticism Five-factor model includes: Basic tendencies—biologically based Characteristic adaptations—culturally based	Describes personality more than it explains it
Biological	We have a biological foundation for our personality traits.	Eysenck	Personality is a product of both heredity and environment. **P**sychoticism **E**xtraversion **N**euroticism Differences in genetics, neurochemistry, and CNS cause personality differences.	Testing is limited by available technology

FIGURE **13.12**
SUMMARY OF FIVE APPROACHES TO PERSONALITY.

Quick Quiz 13.3: How Do Theorists Explain Personality?

1. Hatred and aggression toward homosexuals as a reaction to fear of one's own homosexual impulses would be an example of which Freudian defence mechanism?
   a. reaction formation
   b. psychosexual stages
   c. repression
   d. sublimation
2. According to Jung, the collective unconscious is made up of ancient or archaic images that result from common ancestral experiences called
   a. core-relational themes.
   b. the animus.
   c. the inferiority complex.
   d. archetypes.
3. The key assumption of humanistic theorists, such as Maslow or Rogers, is that people
   a. are driven by unconscious motives.
   b. strive toward growth and fulfillment.
   c. learn from observing others.
   d. none of the above.
4. The Big Five dimensions of personality are openness to experience, conscientiousness, extraversion, ______ and ______.
   a. depression; neuroticism
   b. agreeableness; neuroticism
   c. agreeableness; introversion
   d. anxiousness; introversion

Answers can be found at the end of the chapter.

Groundbreaking Research

Animal Personality

The question of whether animals have personality might seem to be stretching the definition of personality too far. If we claim that animals have personality, might we simply be projecting human qualities onto them, what scientists term *anthropomorphizing?* Most people who have owned more than one cat or dog can identify differences in the personalities of their pets. But even if we can see evidence of personality in animals such as dogs and cats, can we see it in other animals? Do mice have personality? Birds? Reptiles? Fish? Worms? What do you think? At what point does the term *personality* become meaningless?

ONLY HUMANS HAVE PERSONALITY

Until the 1990s, most psychologists would have argued that the term *personality* made sense only as a term applied to humans. But a graduate student at the University of California, Berkeley, changed this view. In the early 1990s Samuel Gosling was attending his required graduate seminar on personality psychology, which involved detailed discussion, readings, and debate about what personality means and how it should be defined. Here is what happened:

> My undergraduate degree had been in philosophy and psychology so in the service of understanding what personality means, I tried to adopt a reductio ad absurdum [reduction to absurdity] strategy, pushing the term personality until it no longer made sense. I thought I'd take a case where it clearly made no sense to use personality and then work backward to find out where the limits of personality lay. Animals seemed like a good example of something that clearly didn't have personality so I decided to start there. But the more I thought about it the less I could generate arguments for why personality could not be applied to animals. (Gosling, personal communication, November 9, 2005)

Most pet owners recognize distinct human-like traits in their beloved furry friends.

If Gosling had accepted his own assumption of the absurdity of animal personality, he would have never gone on to make important contributions to the field.

EVIDENCE FOR PERSONALITY IN OTHER ANIMALS

Gosling and his colleague Oliver John (1999) reported findings from 19 studies across 12 non-human species. Along with other researchers, they provided evidence for at least 14 major non-human species in which personality traits exist. They can be categorized along the same dimensions as human personality. The summary of these findings is presented in Figure 13.13. Keep in mind that the labels from the Big Five are general labels and the specific ones used in these studies vary somewhat. For instance, *neuroticism* is sometimes called *emotional stability, excitability, fearfulness, emotional reactivity, fear–avoidance*, or *emotionality*. *Agreeableness* is sometimes labelled *aggression, hostility, understanding, opportunistic, sociability, affection*, or *fighting–timidity*. In addition, *dominance–submission* is a trait that is often seen and measured in non-human animals, but it does not fit into any of the Big Five categories. These ratings of animal personality were made by one of two behavioural observation techniques: either by animal trainers who had extensive knowledge of the individual animals or by trained observers with no history with the animals but who were trained until they could reliably evaluate the dimensions in question.

It may not surprise you that primates and other mammals tend to share the largest number of personality traits with humans. However, chimpanzees, our closest relative, share with humans a distinct "conscientiousness" dimension. Such a finding suggests that conscientiousness—which involves impulse control and therefore requires highly developed brain regions capable of controlling impulses—is the most recently evolved personality trait. Thus, with the exception of chimps and horses, animals other than humans do not possess the required brain structures to control impulses and organize and plan their activities in advance. Even with chimps, the conscientiousness dimension was somewhat narrowly defined as lack of attention, goal directedness, and disorganized behaviour.

	Neuroticism	Extraversion	Agreeableness	Openness	Conscientiousness
chimpanzee	✓	✓	✓		✓
horse[a]	✓	✓	✓		✓
rhesus monkey	✓	✓	✓		
gorilla	✓	✓	✓		
dog	✓	✓	✓		✓[b]
cat	✓	✓	✓		✓[b]
hyena	✓		✓		
pig		✓	✓		
vervet monkey		✓	✓		
donkey		✓	✓		
rat[c]	✓		✓	✓	
guppy	✓	✓			
octopus	✓	✓			
chickadee[d]					

[a] Based on Morris, Gale, and Duffy (2002).
[b] Competence/learning is a mixture of openness and conscientiousness.
[c] Based on Blanchard et al. (2009).
[d] Based on Dingemanse et al. (2002).

FIGURE **13.13**

PERSONALITY DIMENSIONS ACROSS SPECIES. Ratings by trainers who know the animals or by trained observers produced these results, which suggest that animals do have personalities and that they share some of the same traits as humans. Note that domestic dogs and cats have a "competence" or "learning" dimension that is a mixture of openness and conscientiousness. Where no check mark appears, there is no evidence for that trait in that species. (*Source:* Gosling & John, 1999.)

Even animals like the octopus display behavioural tendencies similar to human personality traits.

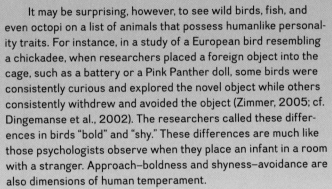

Working animals, like this guide dog, are chosen based upon personality traits, such as low neuroticism.

It may be surprising, however, to see wild birds, fish, and even octopi on a list of animals that possess humanlike personality traits. For instance, in a study of a European bird resembling a chickadee, when researchers placed a foreign object into the cage, such as a battery or a Pink Panther doll, some birds were consistently curious and explored the novel object while others consistently withdrew and avoided the object (Zimmer, 2005; cf. Dingemanse et al., 2002). The researchers called these differences in birds "bold" and "shy." These differences are much like those psychologists observe when they place an infant in a room with a stranger. Approach–boldness and shyness–avoidance are also dimensions of human temperament.

In another experiment, the researchers placed a bowl of worms in the room and then startled the birds by lifting a metal plate nearby. They then observed the amount of time it took for the birds to return to the worms. Once again, there were consistent individual differences: Some birds returned very quickly (bold) and others very slowly (shy). Even more interesting from the standpoint of personality is that these behavioural differences are consistent over long periods and appear to have a strong genetic component. It took, for instance, only four generations of breeding to produce noticeably bolder or shyer birds. Moreover, these behaviours are influenced by the same dopamine receptor gene that is involved in thrill seeking and openness to novel experiences in humans. If the same individual differences in traits (behavioural tendencies) exist in humans and other animals, they must share a common evolutionary history. In other words, these similarities between human and animal personality lend support to the argument that human personality is the product of evolutionary forces.

HOW THESE STUDIES CHANGED PEOPLE'S MINDS

Many researchers dismissed research about animal personality as anthropomorphic—merely projecting human ideas and values onto animals. When Gosling and others began this research in the early 1990s, there was considerable resistance to the idea that animals have personalities. Gosling himself began with the assumption that the idea of animal personality was absurd.

Yet top research journals are now publishing research on animal personality. More importantly, the potential benefits are being recognized. Research on genetics, health, and the biological and evolutionary basis of personality all benefit from an understanding of how animals differ in their personalities. Much of the early and current work on animal personality has a distinctly applied purpose—for example, selecting seeing-eye dogs or dogs that are suitable for bomb-detection tasks. As a result of ongoing research, it has become clear that individuals in most every species exhibit consistent differences in behaviour in a specific situation and that these differences remain constant over time. As such, the evidence very much fits the definition of personality: consistency of individual differences over time and across situations.

Challenge Your Assumptions

True or False? Many different kinds of animals have personality in the sense that humans do.

True: Primates, in particular, but most mammals and even non-mammals share personality traits with humans.

Quick Quiz 13.4: Groundbreaking Research: Animal Personality

1. Which of the human Big Five personality characteristics appears only in humans, chimpanzees, and horses?
   a. openness
   b. extraversion
   c. conscientiousness
   d. agreeableness

2. What is one real-world application of the work on animal personality?
   a. animal therapy
   b. dog show training
   c. selection of pets
   d. selection of seeing-eye dogs

Answers can be found at the end of the chapter.

LO8 HOW IS PERSONALITY MEASURED?

Defining and explaining personality are of prime importance, but you can only define and explain what you can measure. So how do psychologists measure and study personality? There are at least four distinct methods: behavioural observation, interviewing, projective tests, and questionnaires.

Behavioural Observation

The most direct and objective method for gathering personality data is to observe behaviour and simply count specific behaviours that are associated with particular traits, such as aggression, hostility, friendliness, anxiety, or conscientiousness. However, collecting valid data is more difficult than it might seem. For instance, choosing to rate the fairly straightforward example of "aggression" raises many questions. What specific behaviours will count as aggression? Hitting? Insulting? Sarcasm? How does a researcher quantify each behaviour—on a continuum from none to a great deal, or simply on the basis of whether it is present or not? Over what time period will the behaviour be observed? Will the people who are being observed see the raters? If so, will this affect their behaviour? Where will the behaviour take place: in a real-world setting or in a laboratory? Who will rate the behaviour? How do we know that different observers will view a given behaviour in the same way?

These questions address the issue of measurement in general and reliability in particular. If two or more raters are to accurately rate and agree upon their ratings, there must be **inter-rater reliability.** The researchers must first establish an exact definition of the trait they wish to measure, identify the behaviours that make up that trait, and practise rating it against experienced, expert, and reliable raters. The new raters are deemed "reliable" if their ratings compare well with established norms or expert ratings, usually with a correlation of .80 or higher.

inter-rater reliability
measure of how much agreement there is in ratings when using two or more raters or coders to rate personality or other behaviours.

When children or others, such as animals, who cannot evaluate or report on their own personalities are being assessed, behavioural observations are required. Advantages to behavioural observations do not depend on people's view of themselves, as self-report measurements do, and they are direct and relatively objective.

Despite these strengths, behavioural observations are costly and time-consuming. Moreover, not all personality traits can be observed by other people. Anxiety and depression, for instance, although they can be expressed through behaviour, are often experienced internally and subjectively—external observations can't tell the whole story. It is for these kinds of personality traits that a person's own reporting—that is, a self-report—is more reliable. Self-reports can be obtained in three ways: interviewing, projective tests, and questionnaires.

Interviewing

Sitting down with another person face-to-face is probably the most natural and comfortable of all personality assessment techniques. Interviewing is an ideal way to gather important information about a person's life. In fact, from the participant's perspective, interviewing is usually more engaging and pleasant than, for example, filling out a questionnaire. The clear advantage for participants is the open-ended nature of the interview, in which they can say anything they wish in response to a question. Of course, this is also a drawback of interviewing. What does a response mean? How are responses scored and by whom? What criteria are used? These issues are similar to those associated with behavioural ratings, but with interviews the "behaviour" is a verbal response to a question that must be coded reliably and accurately. Thus, the ease of interviews from the participant's perspective is offset by the difficulty of scoring responses reliably.

projective tests
personality assessment in which the participant is presented with a vague stimulus or situation and asked to interpret it or tell a story about what they see.

Rorschach Inkblot Test
a projective test in which the participant is asked to respond to a series of ambiguous inkblots.

Thematic Apperception Test (TAT)
a projective test in which the participant is presented with a series of picture cards and asked to tell a story about what is going on in the scene.

Projective Tests

Projective tests present an ambiguous stimulus or situation to participants and ask them to give their interpretation of or tell a story about what they see. These techniques are based on the assumption, stemming from psychoanalysis, that unconscious wishes, thoughts, and motives will be "projected" onto the task. By interpreting an entire series of such answers, a psychologist can identify consistent unconscious themes. The two most widely used projective tests are the Rorschach Inkblot Test and the Thematic Apperception Test (TAT).

In the **Rorschach Inkblot Test,** a series of ambiguous inkblots are presented one at a time, and the participant is asked to say what he or she sees in each one (see Figure 13.14). The responses are recorded and then coded by a trained coder (most often a psychologist or psychotherapist) as to how much human and non-human "movement," colour, form, and shading the participant sees in each card (Exner, 1974; Masling & Borenstein, 2005). Not only is the test used to measure unconscious motives, but its supporters also claim that responses can help them diagnose various psychological disorders, such as depression, suicidal thoughts, pedophilia, post-traumatic stress disorder, or anxiety disorders (Guarnaccia et al., 2001; Nash et al., 1993; Ryan, Baerwald, & McGlone, 2008; Sloan, Arsenault, & Hilsenroth, 2002).

Similarly, the **Thematic Apperception Test** consists of a series of hand-drawn cards depicting simple scenes that are ambiguous. The participant's task is to make up a story about what he or she thinks is going on in the scene. For instance, a TAT card might depict a male and female sitting next to each other on a sofa, with the woman talking on the phone. One person might tell a story of how this is a couple going through a stormy period in their relationship. The woman in fact is talking with one of her other male friends. Another person might tell a story of how the couple is trying to figure out what do that evening, and the woman is calling another couple about going to a movie tonight.

Like Rorschach responses, TAT answers are scored by trained raters. No interpretation of personality is ever based on just one inkblot or one TAT story. Rather, over a series of inkblots or TAT cards, a set of themes may emerge. One person might consistently see sexual

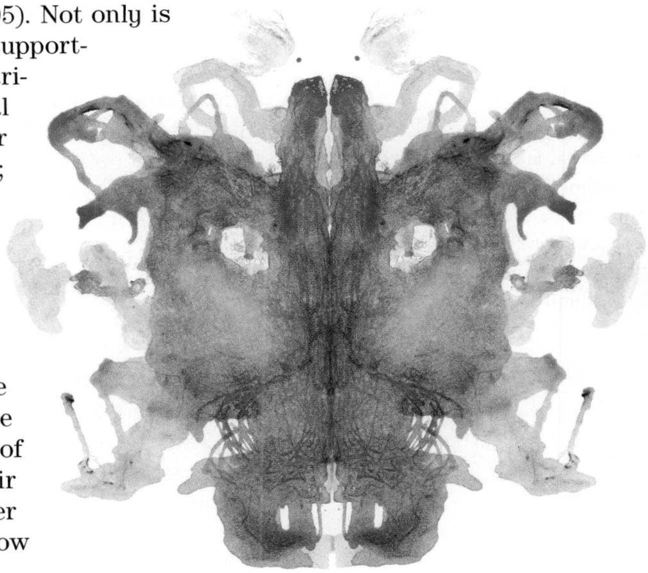

FIGURE **13.14**
AN INKBLOT SIMILAR TO THOSE FOUND ON A RORSCHACH INKBLOT CARD. In the Rorschach Inkblot test, a person is asked to interpret the inkblot however he or she wishes. After the participant has done this with a dozen or more cards, psychologists can form ideas about what kinds of thoughts, feelings, and motives are consistently being "projected."

objects in the inkblots; another might consistently make up stories that reveal conflict and aggression toward parents or authority in general. Although projective tests provide fascinating information, as with interviews their open-ended responses create difficulties in scoring. Inter-rater reliability is not as high as it should be, making conclusions drawn from projective techniques questionable (Huprich, 2008; Petot, 2000; Wood & Lilienfeld, 1999).

Personality Questionnaires

personality questionnaires
self-report instruments on which respondents indicate the extent to which they agree or disagree with a series of statements as they apply to their personality.

Because of the expense and time behavioural ratings and interviews require, along with the relative unreliability of projective tests, the most common way of measuring personality is asking participants to summarize their own behavioural tendencies by means of questionnaires. **Personality questionnaires** consist of individual statements, or *items;* respondents indicate the extent to which they agree or disagree with each statement as it applies to their personality. Responses are usually arranged on a *Likert scale,* which attaches numbers to descriptive responses, such as 1 "completely disagree," 3 "neither agree nor disagree," and 5 "completely agree."

The development of a personality questionnaire takes years of research and data collection before items are selected for the final version. The items first must meet the requirements of validity and reliability. That is, they must measure the trait or traits they claim to measure and must do so consistently over time and across questions dealing with the same traits.

rational (face valid) method
a method for developing questionnaire items that involves using reason or theory to come up with a question.

Questions are based on either the rational or the empirical method. The **rational** or **face valid method** involves using reason or theory to come up with a question. For instance, if we wanted to develop a new measure of anxiety, we might include an item like "I feel anxious much of the time." This is a "face valid" item because what it measures, anxiety, is clear and can be taken at face value. A frequently used personality questionnaire that uses the face valid method is the NEO-PI (Costa & McCrae, 1992). The problem with such questionnaires, however, is that because the questions are transparent, participants might give *socially desirable* or false answers rather than honest ones. For example, for the item "I am anxious much of the time," the person might not want to admit to frequently feeling anxious and hence might not answer honestly.

empirical method
a method for developing questionnaire items that focuses on including questions that characterize the group the questionnaire is intended to distinguish.

A second technique for selecting questions uses the **empirical method,** which disregards theory and face validity and focuses instead simply on whether a question distinguishes groups it is supposed to distinguish (Gough & Bradley, 1996). For instance, if the statement "I prefer baths to showers" distinguishes anxious from non-anxious people, it is used in a measure of anxiety. We would have to have an outside criterion of who is anxious or not, such as a therapist's evaluation of the anxiety levels. A standard way to empirically validate questions on an anxiety measure would be to develop a series of questions and then administer them to people known to suffer from anxiety disorders (as diagnosed by a therapist) and to people known to not suffer from anxiety disorders. If the questions are answered differently by the two groups, they are valid and should be included in the questionnaire. If they are not answered differently, they do not distinguish anxious from non-anxious people and should be discarded. For example, if we discover in initial testing that anxious people are more likely than non-anxious people to endorse the statement "I prefer baths to showers," we should include this item in our questionnaire on anxiety. We would include it even if we did not really understand why the two groups answer it differently. The evidence shows that it does distinguish the two groups, so it is used. This is the essence of the empirical method of making personality inventories.

Two of the most commonly used personality questionnaires in existence each were made using the empirical method: the Minnesota Multiphasic

Many personality questionnaires use Likert scales in order to easily quantify personality descriptions.

Personality Inventory (MMPI) and the California Personality Inventory (CPI). The MMPI is used by psychotherapists to assess the degree and kind of a person's psychiatric personality traits, such as depression, paranoia, or psychopathic deviance (antisocial personality; Tellegen et al., 2003). The CPI, however, is a measure of non-pathological or normal personality traits such as sociability, responsibility, dominance, or self-control (Gough & Bradley, 1996). Both the MMPI and CPI consist of questions that target groups answer differently than the general population. In "Psychology in the Real World" we describe how measures like the CPI have been used in career counselling and employee screening, including screening potentially dangerous police officers from police departments.

Psychology in the Real World

Personality and Career Interest and Job Performance

Would you want a surgeon operating on you who is known for being anxious and nervous? How about having a police officer in your hometown who is violent and aggressive? Would you want to buy something from a shy and socially awkward salesperson? Personality is important when it comes to jobs. Would you believe that personality tests do a better job of predicting your future success in your career than interviews, school credentials, or letters of recommendation? They do (Charmorro-Premuzic & Steinmetz, 2013). Conscientiousness in particular is generally the best personality predictor of how well you will perform in your job.

If you go to your university or college career guidance counsellor, he or she will very likely use personality tests in advising you in your career choices (Costa, 1996; Mount, Barrick, Scullen & Rounds, 2005). Government and business organizations also rely on them to select the right people for particular jobs (Carless, 1999; De Fruyt & Murvielde, 1999). Indeed, Hammer and Macdaid (1992) provide a list of occupations most and least similar to one's personality. Among other things, personality traits predict what kind of majors and careers we select, what kinds of employers select us, how people perform at jobs, and how likely they are to leave them once they get them.

Government and business organizations sometimes use measures of personality in screening job applicants.

What kind of person do you think would make an effective police officer?

PERSONALITY AND CAREER AND COLLEGE MAJOR INTEREST

The first stage of job selection—for college students at least—is picking a major. Larson and colleagues (2010) examined whether personality scores reliably differentiate majors in 368 undergraduate students using the Multidimensional Personality Questionnaire (MPQ; Tellegen, 2000). The MPQ is a self-report measure of personality that is scored on 11 primary personality traits, including social closeness, aggression (low agreeableness), harm-avoidance, and absorption. Social closeness involves enjoying being around people and having a wide circle of friends and is a part of extraversion on the Big Five. Aggression is the opposite of agreeableness on the Big Five, and absorption is similar to openness on the Big Five and describes a person who enjoys thinking and imagining, as well as trying new experiences. Harm-avoidance does not map onto the Big Five dimensions and is the preference to avoid situations that create fear in the person.

Results showed that education majors were higher than engineering majors on social closeness, whereas business majors were significantly lower on agreeableness than humanities and architecture/design majors. In addition, architecture/design majors were more absorbed than business majors. Elementary education majors scored highest on harm-avoidance and social closeness out of the nine majors. Similar research reported harm-avoidance is negatively related to realistic interests and specifically interests in mechanical activities (Staggs et al., 2007). In other words, mechanical and athletic majors are not as likely as other majors to be afraid or driven to avoid harmful situations.

PERSONALITY–ENVIRONMENT FIT AND JOB PERFORMANCE

Because there is so much research showing certain personalities match certain majors and jobs, researchers have proposed a theory of fit or congruence between personality and job. Holland calls this idea "congruence," in which he states that "people find environments reinforcing and satisfying when environmental patterns resemble their personality patterns" (Holland, 1985, p. 53). Industrial/organizational (I/O) psychologists also refer to this notion of congruence as "person–organization fit," or how well matched the person is to his or her work environment (Kristof-Brown, Zimmerman, & Johnson, 2005).

Numerous large-scale meta-analyses of over 1000 studies show that fit between personality and job does matter (Assouline & Meier, 1987; Kristof-Brown et al., 2005; Verquer, Beehr, & Wagner, 2003). The better the fit, the more satisfied people are with their jobs, the less likely they are to leave their jobs, and the more successful they will be.

Measures of fit and congruence allow employers not only to use personality measures to recruit and hire workers who best fit the job, but also to weed out people who might behave counterproductively. *Counterproductive work* behaviours can be defined as anything done by the employee that is intentionally negative for the organization (MacLane & Walmsley, 2010). Such behaviour might include such major infractions as betraying company secrets or employee theft, but may also involve minor transgressions such as working non-productively (such as spending too much time on Facebook or watching online porn).

What sort of personal characteristics have been linked with the counterproductive workplace behaviour? Of the traditional Big Five traits, people who are more conscientious, agreeable, and emotionally stable are less likely to engage in behaviours that harm their companies (Berry, Ones, & Sackett, 2007). In another example, a cluster of personality scales from the widely used California Psychological Inventory (CPI; Gough & Bradley, 1996) was able to reliably pick out police officers who consistently used excessive force and provided drugs to inmates (Hargrave & Hiatt, 1989). More specifically, the problematic officers scored unusually low on the CPI's self-control, socialization, and responsibility scales. These dimensions tap into what some psychologists refer to as conscientiousness—the tendency to plan and to be organized, controlled, and careful.

PERSONALITY AND SWITCHING JOBS

Personality traits also predict how long people stay in or switch their jobs. Two of the Big Five dimensions—openness to experience and agreeableness—appear to be most predictive of leaving jobs early in one's career. Recall that people high in openness to experience prefer new experiences over routine and that people high in agreeableness are warm, caring, and friendly. Researchers have reported that people high in openness and low in agreeableness are most likely to switch jobs and/or companies (Vinson, Connelly, & Ones, 2007; Wille, De Fruyt, & Feys, 2010).

In sum, people who are matched to their jobs make better, happier, more productive employees. Personality has wide-ranging influence over the kinds of careers we are interested in, how well various careers fit who we are, how long we stay, and how well we do in particular careers.

Challenge Your Assumptions

True or False? Your personality predicts future success in your career better than letters of recommendation, educational credentials, or interviews.

True: Although they are not as widely used, personality tests do a better job of predicting future success at jobs than traditional application materials such as educational credentials or interviews.

Social Network Measurement of Personality

As we have been discussing throughout the text, online social networking sites such as Facebook, Twitter, and Instagram have changed how we communicate and interact, but did you know that how you use them reflects on who you are and what kind of personality you have? Psychologists are getting close to using social network footprints and behaviour to measure personality (Ortigosa, Carro, & Quiroga, 2014). The content of an online profile, such as musical preferences or the number of online friends, can be used to predict personality traits (Kosinski, Stillwell, & Graepel, 2013; Kosinski et al., 2013; Marcus, Machilek, & Schütz, 2006; Özgüven & Mucan, 2013).

One fascinating finding is that what you "like" on Facebook strongly predicts your personality, as well as your intelligence, race, age, sexual orientation, and political affiliation (Kosinski et al., 2013). Analyzing the Facebook "likes" of 58 000 people, Kosinski, Stillwell, and Graepel (2013) found that liking the television comedy program *The Colbert Report* puts a person in the 87th percentile on openness but only the 23rd percentile on extraversion. In one of the largest studies to date, researchers surveyed more than 70 000 Facebook users with over 15 million status updates (Park et al., 2014). They found that people's self-reports on the Big Five traits correlated strongly with their friends' reports of their personality, as well as expected behaviours associated with those personality traits (e.g., extraversion and number of friends). Furthermore, analysis of the language used in status updates distinguished between individuals who were high and low on a trait, as shown in Figure 13.15 for extraversion.

Challenge Your Assumptions

True or False? Facebook "likes" reliably predict your personality traits

True: What we "like" on Facebook has been used to accurately predict our personality traits.

FIGURE 13.15

WORD CLOUDS GENERATED FROM FACEBOOK STATUS UPDATES FOR HIGH AND LOW EXTRAVERSION. The size of the word indicates the strength of the correlation with personality while the colour indicates how often the word was used. (*Source:* Adapted from Park et al., 2014.)

Quick Quiz 13.5: How Is Personality Measured?

1. The most objective method for gathering information about personality traits is to
   a. observe behaviour.
   b. conduct interviews.
   c. administer questionnaires.
   d. do genetic testing.
2. The Rorschach inkblot test is an example of which type of personality measurement?
   a. structure interview
   b. questionnaire
   c. projective test
   d. standardized test
3. Scales that use response categories ranging from 1 to 5 (with labels ranging from 1 for "completely agree" to 5 for "completely disagree") are called
   a. ratio scales.
   b. Likert scales.
   c. face valid.
   d. dichotomous.
4. Research has shown that personality assessment from social media sites like Facebook is
   a. unrelated to self-reports on personality questionnaires.
   b. inaccurate because people hide their flaws online.
   c. correlated with friends' reports of the Facebook user's personality.
   d. correlated with strangers' reports of the Facebook user's personality.

Answers can be found at the end of the chapter.

Evaluating Connections in Personality

Does Personality Change over Time?

Personality is at the centre of who we are. Recall our definition of personality at the beginning of the chapter: Personality is the unique and enduring manner in which a person thinks, feels, and behaves. Although it shows considerable stability over our lifetime, it also changes and develops between our infant and adult years. Hundreds of studies have looked at how personality traits change or don't change over the course of individuals' lives. Personality consistency and change illustrate many of the principles discussed in this chapter. Indeed, all definitions, theories, and measures of personality confront the question of consistency and change of personality.

Personality Consistency

When we talk about personality consistency, we mean relative consistency. In fact, that is one of the lessons learned from Walter Mischel's work on how qualities and traits interact with the specific situations to bring about different behaviour across different situations (Kammrath et al., 2005; Mischel & Shoda, 1999). No one is consistent all of the time or in all situations. Consistency is a matter of degree.

Longitudinal studies, those that examine the same people over a period of time, reveal high levels of stability of personality traits. Early in their collaboration, Costa and McCrae (1976) conducted a longitudinal study of personality, expecting to find that personality traits change over time. To their surprise, they found a high degree of stability over a ten-year period. Another set of longitudinal studies revealed very small changes in neuroticism, extraversion, and openness over a period of six to nine years (Costa et al., 2000; McCrae & Costa, 2003).

LO9

Most parents or observers of infants and toddlers are quick to project subtle signs of their children's interest or talent into the future. But do our personality and traits at age three portend future outcomes such as employment, mental illness, criminal behaviour, and quality of interpersonal relationships? Jack and Jeanne Block conducted some of the first long-term studies of human temperament and personality. They used most of the methods for assessing personality discussed in this chapter: interviews, behavioural observations, and personality questionnaires. They found, for instance, that children who were impulsive, aggressive, and tended to cry at age three were most likely to use drugs during adolescence (Block, Block, & Keyes, 1988).

Research from behaviour genetics has demonstrated that personality stability between adolescence and adulthood is largely due to genetic factors (Blonigen et al., 2006; Kruger & Johnson, 2008; Takahashi et al., 2007). More specifically, genetics contribute to the personality consistency we see from adolescence to adulthood, whereas environmental factors contribute to both stability and change in personality traits (Takahashi et al., 2007).

Personality Change

We all like to think we can change—that we have the power to change our destructive habits and become a better person. But can we? Research does support some degree of personality change as we move from adolescence through adulthood and as we adapt to changes in life circumstances. First, we consider changes across the life span.

Typical Personality Change across the Life Span

Recent research confirms that some degree of change in personality occurs normally from adolescence to adulthood and into old age (Allemand, Zimprich, & Hendricks, 2008; Roberts & Mroczek, 2008). The most impressive evidence comes from a meta-analysis of 92 studies that assessed personality change in over 50 000 individuals on the Big Five dimensions of personality (Roberts, Walton, & Viechtbauer, 2006). In general, people become steadily more agreeable and conscientious from adolescence to late adulthood (see Figure 13.16). In addition, people tend to become more assertive or dominant and emotionally stable from adolescence to middle adulthood and then level off on these personality dimensions. Finally, people generally become more sociable (social vitality) and open to new experiences from adolescence to early adulthood. These traits level off in adulthood and then decline in older adulthood. The same pattern of change is seen in cross-sectional research that examines personality differences in different age groups at the same time (Allemand et al., 2008). Together, these results make clear that personality is not set in plaster once we reach adulthood.

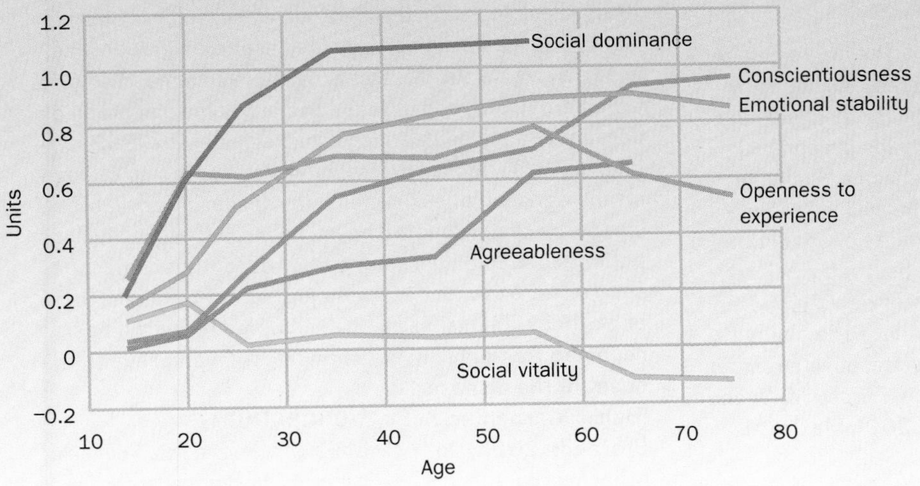

FIGURE **13.16**

PERSONALITY CHANGE FROM ADOLESCENCE TO LATE ADULTHOOD. This graph shows the results of a meta-analysis of personality change on the Big Five dimensions across 92 studies and involving more than 50 000 individuals. The scale of change is measured in standardized units. 0 units means no change. Emotional stability is the opposite end of neuroticism. (*Source:* Roberts, Walton, & Viechtbauer, 2006.)

Personality Change after Changes in Life Circumstances

Not only does personality show some degree of change during normal life-span development, but it also is open to change when we experience drastic changes in our lives, such as becoming a parent, suffering a brain injury, or developing Alzheimer's disease. Let's consider each of these circumstances.

Parenting and Personality Change. Few events change a person as much as becoming the primary caregiver for a totally helpless infant. How does such a major transition affect one's personality? The answer seems to be that it depends on many factors. Paris and Helson (2002) conducted a longitudinal study of female college seniors in their early 20s and followed them until they reached their 50s and 60s. They found that becoming a mother affected personality differently, depending on the woman's evaluation of motherhood. That is, if a woman liked being a full-time mother, then having children led to an increase in her flexibility, self-esteem, adjustment, resourcefulness, and control and a decrease in her dependence and fearfulness. If, however, she did not especially enjoy being a full-time mother, the opposite personality changes were observed.

Other researchers report that parenthood affects the personalities of mothers and fathers differently. For example, although self-concept in general seems to stay the same for both mothers and fathers, self-esteem goes down and irritability goes up in mothers but not in fathers (Onodera, 2003). Similarly, the gender of the parent interacts with the temperament of the child. Compared to having a child with an "easy temperament," having one with a "difficult temperament" is more likely to increase the father's but not the mother's anxiety (Sirignono & Lachman, 1985). The biggest personality change seems to come from increases in a personal sense of control and mastery if parents have an "easy" child and decreases on these dimensions if they have a

For some people, becoming a parent results in changes in personality.

"difficult" child (Sirignono & Lachman, 1985). Having a child who is difficult undermines the belief that parents can truly control the life and behaviour of their children.

Brain Injury and Personality Change. Do you remember Phineas Gage from Chapter 3? He was the railroad foreman who had a tamping iron shoot through his cheek and out the top of his skull, forever changing his personality (Macmillan, 2000). Current recent research on damage to the same part of the frontal lobes where Gage's injury occurred shows similar kinds of personality change. Based on ratings of personality (behavioural observations, Rorschach Inkblots, and semi-structured interviews), children and adults who suffer brain injury often lose the ability to control impulses, are socially inappropriate, have a temper, and are more prone to anger (Mathiesen, Förster, & Svendsen, 2004; Max, Robertson, & Lansing, 2001; Max et al., 2006; Parker, 1996; Rao et al., 2008).

Alzheimer's Disease and Personality Change. Alzheimer's disease is a major degenerative brain disease whose hallmarks are severe dementia and memory loss. It eventually affects personality and ultimately leads to death. Using the NEO-PI as a measure of the Big Five personality dimensions, various studies have shown that neuroticism increases and openness and conscientiousness decrease after the onset of Alzheimer's disease (Chatterjee et al., 1992; Clark et al., 2000; Strauss, Pasupathi, & Chatterjee, 1993). Two studies have also reported a decrease in extraversion (Strauss et al., 1993; Williams, Briggs, & Coleman, 1995), and at least one study has reported a decrease in agreeableness (Chatterjee et al., 1992; see Figure 13.17). Most studies, however, report no change on the agreeableness dimension. Research using other measures of personality have reported that Alzheimer's patients became less kind, generous, enthusiastic, and self-reliant and more irritable and out-of-touch (Petry et al., 1989; Talassi et al., 2007). Some research has reported that personality change can even precede the onset of the disease (Balsis, Carpenter, & Storandt, 2005). In other words, there is a biological basis for our personality. Changes in the brain are often accompanied by personality changes.

Connection

Children who are rated by their parents as being undercontrolled at age three are more likely than other children to have drinking problems, get in trouble with the law, and even attempt suicide at age 21.

See Chapter 10, LO7.

Research Process

Jack and Lucy before Alzheimer's diagnosis

1 Research Question

Does Alzheimer's disease change an individual's personality? Do different observers agree on the nature of personality change after a person develops Alzheimer's disease?

Lucy after diagnosis

2 Method

Eleven elderly men and 11 elderly women (mean age = 72) who met the criteria for Alzheimer's disease, based on cognitive testing and brain images, participated in this correlational study by Strauss and colleagues (1993). The primary caregiver (most often a spouse) and a secondary good friend or family member each rated the patient's personality using the NEO-PI. The NEO-PI measures the "Big Five" personality dimensions of neuroticism, extraversion, openness, agreeableness, and conscientiousness. Raters were asked to remember when the symptoms of Alzheimer's first started and then pick a period of a few years prior to that and rate the person's personality at that time. Approximately two to three months later, each rater was asked to evaluate the patient's personality again, but this time as he or she was then—after the onset of Alzheimer's.

Personality rating by Jack and his daughter

FIGURE **13.17**
PERSONALITY CHANGE AFTER ALZHEIMER'S DISEASE. (*Source:* M.E. Strauss, M. Pasupathi, & A. Chatterjee. (1993). Concordance between observers in descriptions of personality change in Alzheimer's disease. *Psychology and Aging*, 8, 475–480.)

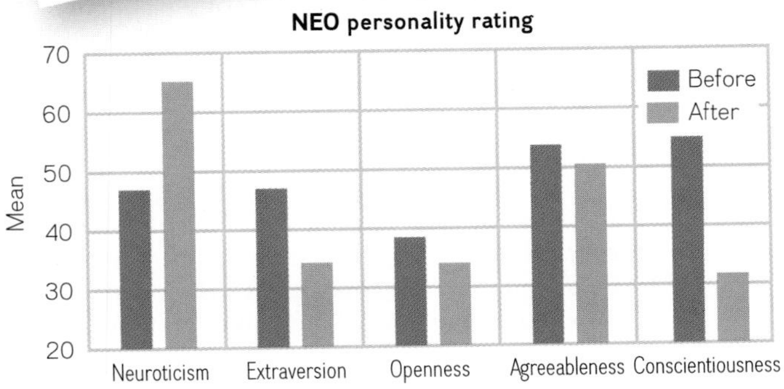

3 Results

Personality ratings of the person showed changes in three of the Big Five dimensions of personality after the onset of Alzheimer's disease. People were rated higher in neuroticism (anxiety) and lower in extraversion, openness, and conscientiousness. Agreeableness did not change. Independent ratings by secondary raters matched those of the primary raters and showed the same pattern.

4 Conclusion

Primary and secondary raters agreed that after the onset of the Alzheimer's disease people became more anxious, less extraverted, less open, and less conscientious. Other studies have replicated these general findings (Clark et al., 2000; Williams et al., 1995). Alzheimer's changes personality in predictable ways.

Quick Quiz 13.6: Evaluating Connections in Personality

1. Which personality trait tends to increase sharply from adolescence to adulthood but then taper off in late adulthood?
   a. conscientiousness
   b. neuroticism
   c. openness to experience
   d. repression

2. People who suffer brain injury, especially to the frontal lobes, often show which kind of personality change?
   a. They become more agreeable.
   b. They become less able to control their impulses.
   c. Their self-esteem decreases.
   d. They become more neurotic.

Answers can be found at the end of the chapter.

Chapter Review

DEFINING PERSONALITY

- Personality is the essence of who we are—both our uniqueness and our consistency. Personality traits function to change behavioural thresholds and make certain behaviours more likely and others less likely.

THE NATURE AND NURTURE OF PERSONALITY

- Personality is an expression of both nature and nurture. Personality traits have evolved through natural and sexual selection, in which genetic and environmental forces work in tandem in shaping an individual's personality.
- Studies of infant temperament offer another line of evidence for a biological basis for adult personality. Infants arrive into the world with different and unique ways of behaving.
- Although there are some cultural differences in personality, there appears to be a great deal of similarity across cultures.

HOW DO THEORISTS EXPLAIN PERSONALITY?

- Theories of personality organize and explain observations and also stimulate testable hypotheses. There are five perspectives that explain personality differences and development.
- The first theory, Freud's psychoanalytic theory, assumes distinct levels of consciousness. The most important of these is the unconscious, the level at which most thoughts, feelings, motives, and images reside. Freud developed the idea of psychological defence mechanisms, which defend us against psychological threats by unconsciously denying or distorting reality.
- Three followers of Freud broke their ties with him to establish their own views. Alfred Adler argued that striving for superiority is the primary motive underlying almost all behaviour. Carl Jung introduced the idea of the personal unconscious and the collective unconscious. Karen Horney developed a psychoanalytic social theory centred on three neurotic trends: moving toward others, moving against others, and moving away from others.
- Second, humanistic theory emphasizes psychological growth and health. Abraham Maslow developed a detailed concept of self-actualization—that is, the inherent tendency to strive to realize one's full potential. Carl Rogers developed the concept of unconditional positive regard to help people achieve self-fulfillment. The new field of positive psychology seeks to study factors, such as positive emotions, that enhance human fulfillment.
- Third, the social–cognitive learning theory of Albert Bandura suggests that personality is formed through

reciprocal determinism when the environment, person factors, and behaviours interact. Self-efficacy is also important to personality development. The theory of Walter Mischel is based on the belief that consistent personality characteristics interact with the environment to produce a person's unique behaviours.

- Fourth, trait theory argues for a universal and stable personality structure that consists of five dimensions of personality: openness, conscientiousness, extraversion, agreeableness, and neuroticism (O-C-E-A-N). These traits are normally distributed in the population, with most people falling somewhere between the two extremes on each trait.
- Fifth, biological theories such as those of Hans Eysenck are another perspective. Eysenck argued for three fundamental dimensions of personality: psychoticism, extraversion, and neuroticism (P-E-N). Eysenck's theory holds that differences in individuals' cortical arousal and sensitivity threshold lead to differences in introversion and extraversion.
- Confirming the importance of the biological basis of personality, personality psychologists and animal behaviourists have begun to explore the nature of animal personality. They have found not only that other primates and mammals exhibit many consistent and unique personality qualities but also that birds, fish, octopi, and even insects have personality traits that distinguish one individual from another.

HOW IS PERSONALITY MEASURED?

- Personality is measured in four major ways: observing and coding behaviour; interviewing; administering projective tests; and administering structured personality questionnaires. More recent research suggests that social networking sites might also accurately measure personality.

EVALUATING CONNECTIONS IN PERSONALITY

- Most of the major topics in this chapter can be connected by highlighting research demonstrating the stability and change in personality over time. Genetic forces contribute to personality stability, whereas environmental factors contribute to both stability and change.

Quick Quiz Answers

Quick Quiz 13.1: 1. b 2. c **Quick Quiz 13.2:** 1. d 2. d 3. b **Quick Quiz 13.3:** 1. a 2. d 3. b 4. b
Quick Quiz 13.4: 1. c 2. d **Quick Quiz 13.5:** 1. a 2. c 3. b 4. c **Quick Quiz 13.6:** 1. c 2. b

Social Behaviour

CHAPTER

14

CHAPTER OUTLINE

Challenge Your Assumptions

True or False?

- ☐ Being left out really hurts.
- ☐ I know whether I am prejudiced or not.
- ☐ People will sometimes risk their lives to help others.
- ☐ Attractive faces are anything but average.

LEARNING OBJECTIVES

- **LO1** Describe three types of biases in making attributions.
- **LO2** Define schemas and stereotypes and describe how they influence our perceptions about others.
- **LO3** Define attitudes and compare how cognitive dissonance and persuasion can lead to attitude change.
- **LO4** Compare the conditions that are likely to lead to (1) social facilitation and (2) social loafing.
- **LO5** Explain the difference between normative and informational influences on conformity, including findings from Asch's classic study.
- **LO6** Compare the findings from the classic studies by Stanley Milgram and Philip Zimbardo describing the ethical issues arising from their research.
- **LO7** Explain how in-group/out-group bias can lead us to view people differently.
- **LO8** Define prejudice and discrimination, and describe some of the factors contributing to their development.
- **LO9** List the biological factors that can influence aggression.
- **LO10** Explain how Bandura's social learning theory shows that aggression can be learned from others.
- **LO11** Define prosocial behaviour and describe the factors that contribute to the likelihood of helping in an emergency.
- **LO12** Compare the kin selection, reciprocal altruism, and social exchange theories of prosocial behaviour.
- **LO13** Define cooperation and describe how researchers study it in the laboratory.
- **LO14** List factors that enhance liking.
- **LO15** Describe some of the ways researchers define and measure love.

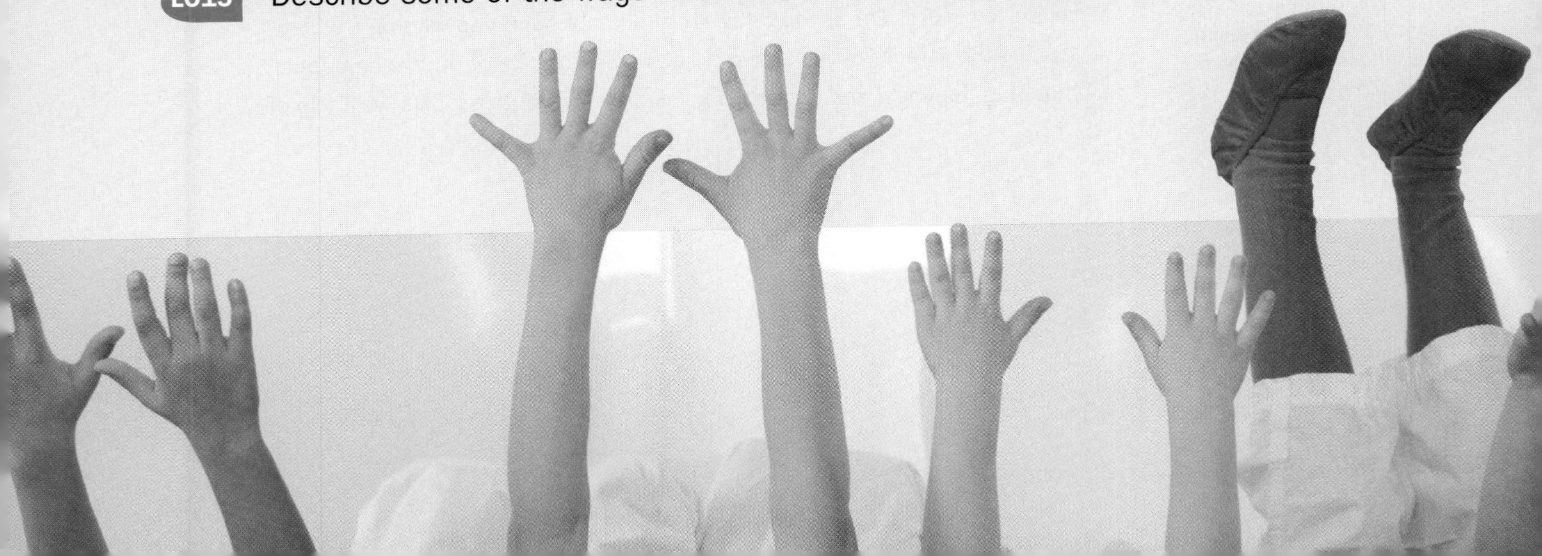

Thalia and her closest friend from high school, Deidre, chose to go to the same university. They roomed with other people, but they still saw each other frequently. Although their friendship felt a bit different, Thalia understood that they had different classes and some new friends. For years, Deidre had invited her to the family cabin to go skiing each winter, and Thalia took it for granted that she'd be going, even though she was always formally asked. When winter rolled around that first year, Thalia asked Deidre when they'd be heading to the snow. Deidre said softly, "I invited my new roommate this year." Thalia—stunned—felt as if she had been kicked in the stomach.

Being rejected hurts. In fact, social exclusion activates similar brain areas as physical pain. In one study on the neural basis for social pain, participants were brought into a lab with an fMRI scanner and were told they would be involved in an electronic ball tossing game called "Cyberball" (Eisenberger et al., 2003; Masten et al., 2009). Once inside the scanner, they could see, on a screen, a Cyberball game that was apparently in progress between two other research participants in scanners in different rooms. Actually, unknown to the participant, there were no other people playing the game. After watching the "others" play for a few throws, the participant joined in. For a while, the three players continued playing Cyberball together. After seven throws, however, the other players stopped throwing the ball to the participant and went on about their game. In effect, the participant was left out, as Thalia had been. Participants reported being upset about being excluded. What's more, the fMRI scans showed that the brain circuitry activated immediately after exclusion maps very well onto known brain circuitry for physical pain. This kind of *social pain* can be relieved by painkillers like Tylenol (DeWall et al., 2010) and may affect endocrine systems that support social connection (Maner, Miller, Schmidt, & Eckel, 2010). People who are more sensitive to physical pain are more sensitive to the pain of rejection, and these differences may have a genetic basis (Eisenberger, Jarcho, Lieberman, Naliboff, 2006; Way, Taylor, & Eisenberger, 2009). Further, people who trust their interaction partners and have higher self-esteem are less likely to experience social pain when excluded (Yanagisawa et al., 2011).

Challenge Your Assumptions

True or False? Being left out really hurts.

True: When we are excluded, it causes the experience of pain and activates similar brain circuitry as does physical pain.

social psychology
the study of how living among others influences thought, feelings, and behaviour.

Why does it hurt to be excluded? Like other social animals, humans form important bonds with other members of our species. We depend on other people to raise us and to cooperate with us in the presence of threats (Neuberg & Cottrell, 2006). As a result, the ways in which we relate to others play a huge role in our lives, and the need to belong is ingrained in our biology (Way et al., 2009). In this chapter, we will explore three key aspects of social behaviour: how we perceive and think about our social world, how the presence of others influences our behaviour, and how we relate to others. These topics are the focus of **social psychology,** which studies the effects of the real or imagined presence of others on people's thoughts, feelings, and actions. Exclusion is one of the topics we'll explore.

SOCIAL COGNITION

Our interest in other people is often about how they behave in a group and how their actions affect others. Therefore, many people ask: Why do we need a scientific study of social behaviour? Unlike other scientific disciplines, such as subatomic physics, social behaviour is an area of constant study through our day-to-day interactions with each other. However, our day-to-day interactions are rarely considered from an objective point of view. As you read through this chapter, you might be surprised about what science has revealed about our social worlds.

We are continually bombarded with information about the social situation that surrounds us. In order to make sense of it all, we must select, remember, and interpret information in order to make decisions. *Social cognition* refers to the way in which we think about our social world. As you will learn in this section, the way we see the social world strongly influences how we feel about it, and this, in turn, can guide our behaviour.

LO1 Attributions

In wondering why people do the things that they do, we often try to explain their actions (Kelley & Michela, 1980). **Attributions** are the inferences we make about the causes of behaviour, and they shape how we feel about others. Imagine that you are walking down a busy street and a young man asks you for spare change because he was robbed and needs bus fare to get home. Would you give it to him? How about if he told you that he couldn't be bothered to get a job? Would this change how you felt? The cause of his predicament would probably be a factor in your decision to help.

attributions
inferences made about the causes of other people's behaviour.

Pioneering social psychologist Fritz Heider (1958) made an important distinction between two types of attributions. Internal or *dispositional attributions* ascribe other people's behaviour to something within them, such as their personality, motives, or attitudes. For example, let's say that Chris flunked a test. A dispositional attribution would be "Chris flunked the test because he is too lazy to study." The person making this attribution assumed that Chris's flunking is a result of something about him, about his personal character or skills. But it is also possible that Chris's failing grade resulted from some external factor. Perhaps the test was too hard. People make external or *situational attributions* when they think that something outside the person, such as the nature of the situation, is the cause of his or her behaviour. If Jake says that Chris failed because the exam was too hard, Jake has made a situational attribution for Chris's grade.

We tend to evaluate our own behaviour in different ways depending on whether we have succeeded or failed. For instance, it is likely that Chris would attribute his failure on a test to something about the situation—say, the test was too hard or the professor unfair—rather than to his own abilities. If Chris had aced the test, however, it is likely he'd attribute his success to his own skills. This tendency to make situational attributions for our failures but dispositional attributions for our successes is known as a **self-serving bias.**

self-serving bias
the tendency to make situational attributions for our failures but dispositional attributions for our successes.

fundamental attribution error
the tendency to explain others' behaviour in dispositional rather than situational terms.

People tend to explain other people's behaviour in terms of dispositional attributions rather than situational ones, a bias in judgment known as the **fundamental attribution error** (Ross, 1977). This is not to say that dispositions don't matter, but rather that when making attributions of other people's behaviour, we tend to think that dispositional or personal characteristics matter the most. People living in Asian cultures, such as India and Japan, are much less likely to make the fundamental attribution error than are Europeans and North Americans (Choi, Nisbett, & Norenzayan, 1999). This seems to be due to a cultural tendency for Asians to explain behaviours—even things as extreme as murder—in situational or big-picture terms (Morris & Peng, 1994; Norenzayan & Nisbett, 2000).

Connection

Cultural differences in big-picture versus detailed processing are seen in performance on visual perception tasks too.

See Chapter 4, "Evaluating Connections in Sensation and Perception."

Meeting potential mates in a group of singles might make some people seem shy.

Would you make the fundamental attribution error in a situation like this and assume that shyness is a personality trait? Can you think of other situations where you would make this error?

It is perhaps not surprising that we have a bias for dispositional attributions since we notice individuals more so than their social surroundings. In other words, the "actors" are usually more obvious than the "stage." However, our tendency to rely upon dispositions to explain the causes of events has serious consequences, particularly in situations where someone has suffered a misfortune. **Blaming the victim** is an attributional bias that explains the cause of hardship by placing the blame on the victim rather than the situation. This type of attribution is sometimes used to blame the victims, rather than the perpetrators, of sexual assaults. In a survey of students at the University of Manitoba, it was revealed that participants who were more accepting of male sexual aggression against women were more likely to blame the victim (Morry & Winkler, 2001). Furthermore, a recent meta-analysis by researchers at the University of Toronto showed that, in cases of rape, blaming the victim was correlated with prejudicial attitudes such as sexism, racism, and classism (Suarez & Gadalla, 2010).

blaming the victim
an attribution that places blame on the victim of a crime, accident, or misfortune.

Many people believe that the world is a fair place with good people being rewarded and bad things only happening to bad people (Hafer & Bègue, 2005). Melvin Lerner, formerly of the University of Waterloo, has called this the **belief in a just world** (Lerner, 1980, Lerner & Simmons, 1966). Research suggests that people who hold strong just-world beliefs are also more likely to blame victims (Hafer, 2000). For example, people with strong beliefs in a just world believe that victims of serious illnesses, like AIDS and cancer, are responsible for their plights (Hafer & Bègue, 2005). When people's just-world beliefs are threatened by hearing about attacks on innocent people, they seek to maintain their just-world beliefs by derogating the victims of such attacks and distancing themselves (Hafer, 2000). People are in fact so motivated to maintain their beliefs in a just world that they will often engage in irrational thinking to preserve such beliefs. In one study, participants from the University of Calgary were more likely to attribute a man's misfortune (i.e., serious injuries sustained when hit by a car) to

belief in a just world
a belief that the world is fair with good people being rewarded and bad people punished.

Learning about attributional biases may make you less likely to make them. At the end of their first year, social science and commerce students at an Ontario university made dispositional attributions about the poor—blaming them for their poverty. However, by their third year, social science students were more likely to make situational attributions, whereas commerce students still made dispositional ones (Guimond & Palmer, 1996).

What are some of the consequences of our attributional biases?

his past behaviour when he was perceived to deserve the outcome (i.e., he was a bad person because he was having an affair) than when he was *not* perceived to deserve the outcome (i.e., he was not a bad person because he was not cheating on his wife), even though the two events (the affair and the accident) were completely unrelated (Callan, Ellard, & Nicol, 2006).

LO2

Schemas

Whether we are trying to determine if people are lying or simply trying to make sense of simple actions, our own notions of how the world works influence our perceptions of it. People develop models, or *schemas,* about the social world, which function like lenses through which we filter our perceptions. We first discussed schemas in Chapter 6 and defined them broadly as ways of knowing that we develop from our experiences with particular objects or events. In the area of social cognition, schemas are ways of knowing that affect how we view our social world.

We rely on schemas when forming impressions of other people, especially when we encounter ambiguous information. Imagine you are invited to dinner and notice that one of the guests has slurred speech and walks shakily across the room. You assume—reasonably—that she is drunk. Later you learn that she has Parkinson's disease, a neurological condition that affects motor coordination. Slurred speech and shaky walking are common symptoms of this disorder. You assumed that the woman was drunk because the schema of drunkenness was much more *accessible* to you than that of Parkinson's disease.

Stereotypes

Schemas of how people are likely to behave based simply on the groups to which they belong are known as **stereotypes.** When we resort to stereotypes, we form conclusions about people before we even interact with them just

stereotypes
schemas of how people are likely to behave based simply on groups to which they belong.

What stereotypes do these images bring to mind?

Connection

Another name for mental shortcuts we use in decision making is *heuristics*. Heuristics can be adaptive but they also can lead to flawed thinking.

See Chapter 8, LO11.

because they are of a certain ethnicity or live in a certain place. As a result, we end up judging people not by their actions, but by our notions of how they are likely to act.

People resort to stereotypes because they allow us to form quick—but often inaccurate—impressions, especially if we do not know someone very well. The human mind has a tendency to categorize and understand all members of a group in terms of characteristics that are typical of the group (Rosch, 1975). So if we meet someone new and learn that they belong to a particular (ethnic, social, political, or religious) group, we rely on what we think we know about the characteristics of that group so that we can anticipate how this new person might behave. When people avoid stereotyped thinking, fMRI scans show that the prefrontal cortex—an area involved in inhibiting inappropriate responses—is activated (De Neys, Vartanian, & Goel, 2008). This suggests that when you rely on stereotypes, you are not thinking carefully.

Is this the face of a leader? When Justin Trudeau was elected leader of the Liberal Party of Canada in April 2013, the Conservatives immediately ran a series of ads highlighting his youth and inexperience. Following in a similar vein, during the 2015 federal election campaign, they ran a series of ads denoting Trudeau as "Just not ready." Clearly, they were trying to connect him with people's negative stereotypes about young people as being irresponsible, flighty, with a sense of entitlement, and so forth. (Of course, the irony is that Trudeau was 43 when elected as prime minister—really not so young!)

Can you think of other examples of stereotypes used in the media?

Take a look at a few common stereotypes:

- Jocks are dumb.
- Women are bad drivers.
- Middle Eastern men with beards are probably terrorists.

With stereotypes, we have formed conclusions about people even before we interact with them. Stereotypes are often linked to something that is indeed factual but that does not characterize a whole group. For instance, the terrorists involved in the September 11 attacks in the United States, as well as the members of the Toronto 18 who plotted a terrorist attack on Parliament, were Middle Eastern men, many of whom had beards—but not all Middle Eastern men with beards are terrorists. Most serial killers are young, white men. Does that mean all young, white men are serial killers (Apsche, 1993)?

During his 2008 run for the U.S. presidency, Barack Obama faced numerous stereotypes associated with his name (which has Muslim roots), his mixed race, and his education. People who did not know much about him were more likely to believe rumours that he was a Muslim (although he is not). The implication that he was a Muslim activated the terrorist stereotype we just discussed. Some rivals stereotyped Obama as an elitist because he had gone to Harvard Law School. They tried to link him with stereotypical notions of well-educated people who are out of touch with average people, even though he had grown up in a low-income household and right out of college had worked with the poor and unemployed in Chicago.

Stereotypes paint dividing lines between people. As we will see in later sections of this chapter, they support notions of belonging and exclusion that can lead to unfair actions.

LO3 Attitudes and Attitude Change

People use the word *attitude* frequently, but what does it mean? Social psychologists define **attitudes** as a person's favourable or unfavourable feelings, beliefs, or actions toward an object, idea, or person (Olson & Zanna, 1993). Thus, attitudes have affective, cognitive, and behavioural components. The *affective* component includes the feelings or emotions associated with the belief; the *cognitive* component consists of the rational thoughts and beliefs that make up the attitude; and the *behavioural* component includes the motive to act in a particular way toward the person or object of the attitude. Consider Kellie, who is a huge Montreal Canadiens fan (see Figure 14.1). She loves the team (affective), knows all about each player (cognitive), and has bought season tickets to their home games (behavioural). Attitudes differ by how heavily each component is weighted. Some attitudes are more cognitive, such as your beliefs about the best way to slice a mango. Others may be more affective, such as your attitude about the death penalty.

Attitude: Canadiens fan

Affective component:	Enthusiasm about the Montreal Canadiens team
Cognitive component:	Knowledge about the players
Behavioural component:	Goes to all the team's home games

FIGURE **14.1**
ATTITUDE COMPONENTS. For a sports fan, a positive attitude is sometimes the only way to get through a losing season.

attitude
an individual's favourable or unfavourable beliefs, feelings, or actions toward an object, idea, or person.

Are people willing to switch attitudes based on evidence or a persuasive argument? What role do personality and persuasion play in our willingness to change attitudes? These are just some of the questions asked by social psychologists interested in attitude change. We examine two major reasons for changes in attitude: cognitive dissonance and persuasion.

Cognitive Dissonance One explanation for why and how we change our attitudes is cognitive dissonance, a theory proposed in the 1950s by psychologist Leon Festinger. **Cognitive dissonance** is the feeling of discomfort caused by information that is at odds with one's conception of oneself as a reasonable and sensible person (Festinger, 1957). Because we don't like feeling uncomfortable, we are motivated to try to reduce the discomfort. There are three options for decreasing the discomfort created by dissonance:

cognitive dissonance
the feeling of discomfort caused by information that is different from a person's conception of himself or herself as a reasonable and sensible person.

1. We can change our behaviour to make it consistent with dissonant cognition.
2. We can attempt to justify our behaviour by changing one of the cognitions to make it more consistent with our behaviour.
3. We can add new cognitions that are consistent with the behaviour and that therefore support it.

When people experience cognitive dissonance, they may go to extreme lengths to reduce it. In this way, they reduce their discomfort and maintain self-esteem. People often end up rationalizing or justifying their behaviour in order to reduce cognitive dissonance.

Festinger tested his theory with a simple, yet clever, experiment that has become a classic in the field of attitude change. He convinced undergraduate university students, who were participants in this experiment, to tell a lie to a fellow student. Participants arrived at the laboratory and were given two repetitive, incredibly monotonous tasks while an experimenter timed them and took notes. For 30 minutes, participants placed spools onto a tray and for an additional 30 minutes they moved wooden pegs a quarter of a turn clockwise, over

Strong attitudes about controversial issues, such as abortion, often reflect longstanding beliefs and consequently are difficult to change. **What strong attitudes do you hold? What are the cognitive, affective, and behavioural components of these attitudes? Can you imagine yourself changing such attitudes?**

and over again. Performance on these tasks was not actually part of the experiment; they merely provided an unpleasant experience, which was the basis of the lie participants were asked to tell. When the hour was up, the experimenter asked the participant to tell the next student, who was not an actual participant but a *confederate* (who worked for the experimenter), that the experiment was in fact a lot of fun. For telling this obvious lie, participants were given either $1 or $20. Participants in a control group were not asked to lie and were given no compensation. What Festinger wanted to determine was whether the compensation for lying altered participants' actual ratings of the experiment itself. Not surprisingly, the participants who were in the unpaid (control) group rated the task as being unenjoyable, since it was designed to be extremely boring. Those who were given $20 for telling the lie also rated the task very low. However, those that were given only $1 for telling the lie rated the task enjoyment much higher. The authors attributed this irrational behaviour (rating a boring task as fun) to cognitive dissonance since the $1 was not adequate compensation for the lie and therefore attitude was altered to fit with behaviour (see Figure 14.2; Festinger & Carlsmith, 1959).

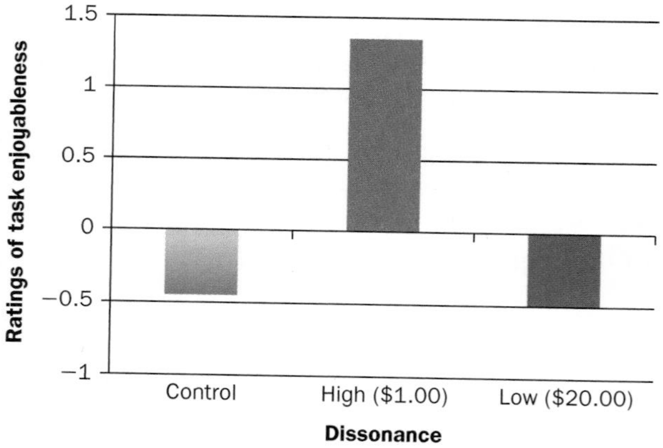

FIGURE **14.2**

CLASSIC STUDY OF COGNITIVE DISSONANCE. After completing a boring task, participants who were paid only $1 to tell a lie about how enjoyable the task was, changed their attitude towards the task and rated it as more enjoyable. Apparently, they reduced their cognitive dissonance about lying by convincing themselves that the task was enjoyable after all. In contrast, participants who were paid $20 to lie about the task's enjoyableness rated it no differently than a control group who was unpaid. (*Source:* Adapted from Festinger & Carlsmith, 1959.)

Smoking offers a classic example of an irrational behaviour in which many people engage. Smoking can cause lung cancer, emphysema, and heart disease. Still, many people continue to smoke. True, they are addicted. Cognitively, however, smokers must manage the conflict between their notion of themselves as rational beings and the fact that they engage in a very risky habit. To reduce the unpleasant feeling these dissonant thoughts and behaviours create, people who smoke may behave in one of the three ways that we just listed, as seen in Figure 14.3. People will work hard

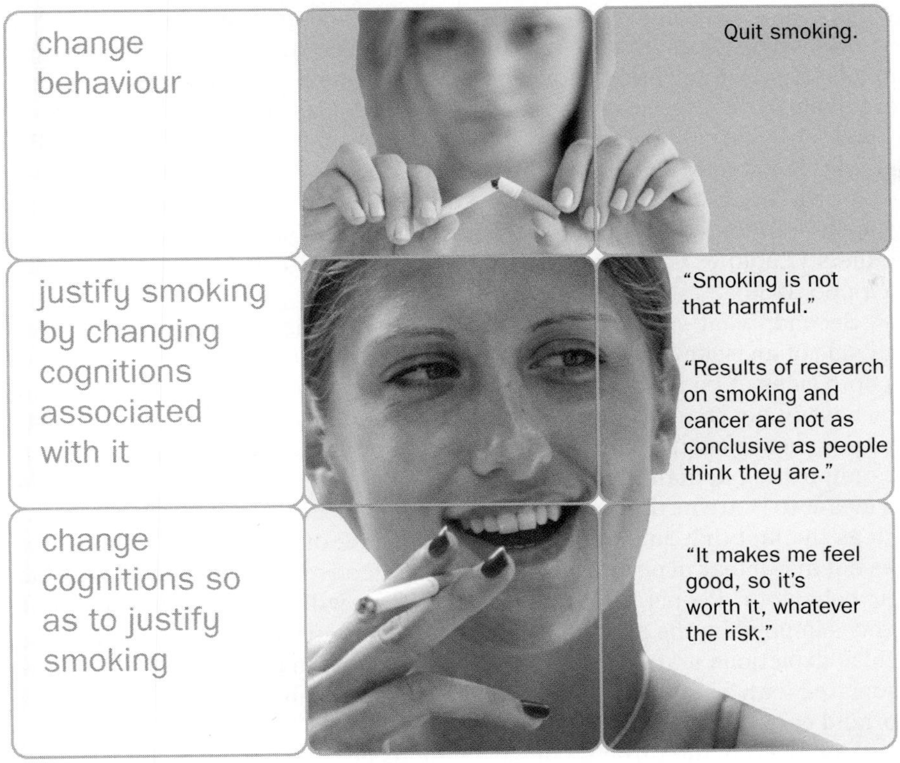

change behaviour
Quit smoking.
justify smoking by changing cognitions associated with it
"Smoking is not that harmful."
"Results of research on smoking and cancer are not as conclusive as people think they are."
change cognitions so as to justify smoking
"It makes me feel good, so it's worth it, whatever the risk."

FIGURE **14.3**
COGNITIVE DISSONANCE AND SMOKING. People smoke even though they know it's unhealthy. To reduce their cognitive dissonance, smokers might try one of these approaches, including quitting.

to rationally defend behaviours or strongly held positions in order to reduce the dissonance—the uncomfortable feeling—produced by opposing arguments.

Making use of the tendency toward dissonance around high-risk behaviours, such as smoking, is one approach to treating them. Simmons and colleagues (2013) created a Web-based program in which smokers watched a video of health information about the dangers of smoking (or a control video about nutrition). Then they were asked to make a video about themselves for the purpose of "promoting a healthy lifestyle," which would be shown to peers, in which they were asked to mention their smoking as well as other aspects of their lives. This potentially created dissonance, given the anti-smoking video they had just viewed. Consistent with the idea that people will change attitudes or behaviours to reduce dissonance, the smokers with the most dissonant situation (those who viewed the video about the health effects of smoking) had significantly higher scores on a "motivation to quit" questionnaire than those in the control conditions (Simmons, Heckman, Fink, Small, & Brandon, 2013).

Persuasion People can also use persuasion to change attitudes. **Persuasion** is an attempt by a person or group to change our opinions, beliefs, or choices by explaining or arguing their position. Persuasion is all around us all the time; friends, family, teachers, politicians, salespeople, and advertisers often want to change our minds about something. They attempt to talk us into something or convince us of their point of view. How successful they will be depends on many factors. The three criteria that we will focus on include who they are (source), the message being conveyed, and who we are (audience).

persuasion
the act of attempting to change the opinions, beliefs, or choices of others by explanation or argument.

First, how credible or believable is the persuader? Research suggests that we give more weight to people we perceive as experts (Heesacker, Petty, &

Cacioppo, 1983; Pornpitakpan, 2004). This is why people want to buy pain relievers promoted in commercials by famous TV doctors rather than unknown figures and advertisers tell us that "Four out of five dentists recommend . . ." And we're more likely to believe those who seem trustworthy, a trait that appears enhanced in those who argue a point of view contrary to their own self-interest (Petty, Fleming, Priester, & Feinstein, 2001). We are also more likely to be persuaded by people who are physically attractive and likeable to us, which is why advertisers spend millions of dollars to hire attractive, famous people to endorse their products (Eagly & Chaiken, 1975; Messner, Reinhard, & Sporer, 2008; Petty & Cacioppo, 1986).

Second, what should the message content focus on? Do you present only your side of an issue or both sides? The research suggests that messages containing both sides of an issue are usually more persuasive, especially when the audience has not yet committed to either side (Allen, 1991; Crowley & Hoyer, 1994). In addition, messages that attempt to persuade by arousing fear can be effective, but only if they actually create fear in the audience (Witte & Allen, 2000). Most ads meant to scare us don't actually do so. Simply citing statistics, for instance—such as the fact that smoking increases one's risk of lung cancer 20-fold—often does not instill fear in people and is not very effective at getting people to change their behaviour. People rarely believe that they will suffer the negative consequences implied by the ads. Ads on cigarette packages showing graphic images, such as depictions of damaged lungs, were adopted in Canada in 2000, and were associated with a significant reduction in cigarette sales and smoking behaviour (Borland et al., 2009).

Last, who is the targeted audience or receiver of the message? People are not equally malleable in their opinions or behaviour. The more people know about a topic and the firmer their prior opinions are, the less likely they are to change their attitudes (Eagly & Chaiken, 1998). Political campaigners know this well. Candidates often focus their efforts, especially near election day, on swing districts that either have not consistently voted one way in the past or have a mix of party preferences. In regions that have voted for the New Democrats for years, say, campaigning by Conservative candidates may be a waste of time.

Why does a message loaded with facts and logical arguments persuade some people and not others? In the elaboration likelihood model, Petty and Cacioppo (1986) propose that there are two routes to attitude change (see Figure 14.4). In the **central route to persuasion,** attitude change results from a person paying attention to the content of a message, carefully scrutinizing the merits of the message points or arguments. The person is engaging in effortful thinking (high elaboration) to make a decision. In contrast, in the **peripheral route to persuasion,** changes to attitudes result from people processing superficial message cues only (low elaboration), such as the expertise or attractiveness of the message source (i.e., cues that have nothing to do with the message itself). Attitudes changed through the central (high elaborative) route tend to be more persistent, predictive of behaviour, and resistant to attacks than those resulting from the peripheral (low elaborative) route (Petty, Haugtvedt, & Smith, 1995).

central route to persuasion attitude change that results from the effortful processing of the content of a message.

peripheral route to persuasion attitude change that results from low effort processing of superficial message cues, such as the characteristics of the message source.

Research suggests that people are more likely to follow the central processing route when the message is personally relevant for them (Petty & Cacioppo, 1986; Petty, Cacioppo, & Goldman, 1981). For example, undergraduates who think a new exam policy is likely to come into effect immediately would be more likely to pay attention to the strength of the arguments for such a policy in deciding whether they support it or not compared to those who think the new policy won't come into effect for another ten years. People also differ in their need for cognition. Some people take great pleasure in analyzing issues; others prefer not to use much mental effort (Cacioppo, Petty, Feinstein, & Jarvis, 1996). Because people sometimes pay attention to the content of the message and at other times, the superficial persuasion cues, many advertising campaigns use

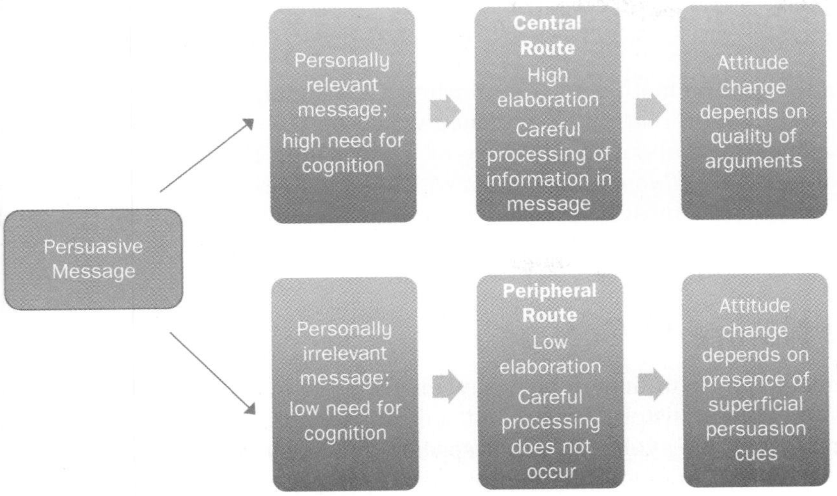

FIGURE **14.4**
THE ELABORATION LIKELIHOOD MODEL OF PERSUASION. According to this model, there are two routes to attitude change. On the one hand, if a message is particularly relevant for us and/or we take pleasure in thinking about arguments carefully, we are likely to be persuaded by carefully processing information in the content of the message. On the other hand, if the message is not relevant to us and/or we prefer not to think about things too much, persuasion is likely to come from the processing of superficial message cues. (*Source:* Based on suggestions from Petty & Cacioppo, 1986).

both types of information. For example, political campaigns often include ads of politicians smiling, shaking hands, and interacting with regular people. They also use ads presenting party platform ideas, such as plans for job growth and balancing the budget.

Quick Quiz 14.1: Social Cognition

1. Our tendency to conclude that Alex must have an aggressive personality because we see him hit Bobby once on the playground is an example of
   a. a stereotype.
   b. an attitude.
   c. blaming the victim.
   d. the fundamental attribution error.
2. "University professors are absent minded" is an example of
   a. an attitude.
   b. an attribution.
   c. a stereotype.
   d. a prejudice.
3. Janice is a university student who is active in politics. She considers voting to be very important for everyone, especially young people. So she volunteers five hours a week to staff a table at the student union encouraging students to register to vote, for any political party. Her stance toward voting would best be described as a(n)
   a. belief.
   b. attitude.
   c. attribution.
   d. bias.
4. LeBron considers himself to be a healthy person. He eats a healthy diet and exercises four days a week. Yet he is a smoker. His attitude toward smoking before he became a smoker was very negative. Now that he is a smoker, however, his attitude is not so negative. The change in his attitude is best explained by
   a. attribution.
   b. persuasion.
   c. bias.
   d. cognitive dissonance.
5. Social psychologists have demonstrated that three things matter most in whether an argument will persuade other people or not. The three things are
   a. source, message, and audience.
   b. source, believability, and audience.
   c. logic, believability, and audience.
   d. pressure to conform, source, and authority.

Answers can be found at the end of the chapter.

SOCIAL INFLUENCE

Imagine standing in an empty auditorium and singing your favourite song. Now imagine how different this experience would be if there were ten people in the auditorium. How about an audience of a thousand? This section of the chapter explores *social influence,* the way in which individuals affect each other's behaviour. Some of the most fascinating and controversial topics in social psychology, such as conformity and obedience, explore social influence.

LO4 The Nature of Groups

The social nature of human beings stems from the importance of group living in our evolutionary history. We are not solitary animals. Group living offered many advantages in the evolution of our species, such as increased safety in the presence of danger, cooperation with others to complete challenging tasks (such as hunting), and childrearing (Brewer & Caporael, 2006; Melis & Semmann, 2010). This heritage probably explains why people work to preserve group membership and why they modify their behaviour when in the presence of others.

What defines a group? The concept can be somewhat tricky to define. Are passengers on a city bus considered a group? How about fans at a hockey game? Hockey fans, whether they are rooting for the same or different teams, probably identify with each other more strongly than bus passengers do. Therefore, they might act quite differently towards each other (50 hockey fans are usually more excited than 50 bus passengers). Social psychologists recognize this distinction and define a group as a collection of two or more people who interact with each other, and are *interdependent.* In other words, their shared goals cause them to rely on each other (Aronson et al., 2004). In this section, we examine how the presence of other people influences behaviour and decision making, such as one's willingness to go along with the group. As we will see, social factors may push people to do things they might not otherwise do.

You may have noticed that sometimes you perform a task better with others around and sometimes you do worse. Such effects are seen in animals as diverse as humans, chimps, birds, and even cockroaches (Gates & Allee, 1933; Klopfer, 1958). The effect of having others present can depend on the situation or task at hand, how easy or difficult the task is, and how excited you are. **Social facilitation** occurs when the mere presence of others affects our performance. If a task is easy, the presence of others tends to improve performance whereas if a task is difficult, performance typically worsens. Over a century ago, Norman Triplett (1898) noticed that he rode his bike faster when he rode with others. In a laboratory test of the idea that the presence of others improves performance, Triplett asked children to wind a fishing reel as fast as they could. He tested them when alone and when in groups of other kids doing the same thing. Sure enough, they wound faster when other kids were present. Improvement in performance in the presence of others usually occurs for tasks that are easy, we know well, or we can perform well. On the other hand, if a task is particularly difficult, the presence of others impairs performance (Zajonc, 1969). Imagine having to solve arithmetic problems out loud in a room full of people. If you are like most people, you will likely make more mistakes while being watched because you would feel nervous. According to Robert Zajonc, knowing our behaviour is being evaluated by others creates arousal, and this is responsible for social facilitation (Zajonc, 1965).

social facilitation
when the presence of others improves performance on easy tasks, or impairs performance on difficult tasks.

Connection
Our level of arousal also affects our performance, according to the Yerkes–Dodson law.
See Chapter 11, LO2.

Performing a task *for* others is quite different from performing a task *with* others. When engaged in a cooperative activity, sometimes our individual performance cannot be separated from other group members. If you and five friends work together to push out a car stuck in a snow bank, your individual contribution cannot easily be distinguished from anybody else's. **Social loafing** occurs

social loafing
the phenomenon in which the presence of others causes one to slack off if individual effort cannot be evaluated.

when the presence of others causes individuals to relax their standards and slack off (Harkins, 1987). For example, if you are singing in a choir and there are dozens of other voices supporting yours, you are less likely to sing your heart out. You alone are not responsible for the sound, so the diffusion of responsibility alters your behaviour (you loaf). If you were singing a solo, you would belt it out—because all responsibility would rest on your shoulders.

LO5 Conformity

Social facilitation is a subtle way in which the presence of others changes our actions. More direct social factors also pressure us to act in certain ways. Society, for instance, imposes rules about acceptable behaviour, called **social norms.** Examples of social norms include "Boys don't cry," "Don't pick your nose in public," and "Don't be a sore loser." Norms vary by culture, too. Burping at the dinner table is considered rude in Canada but in some parts of East Asia, belching is seen as a compliment to the chef.

social norms
rules about acceptable behaviour imposed by the cultural context in which one lives.

Most of the time we abide by, or conform to, the social norms of our culture. **Conformity** occurs when people adjust their behaviour to what others are doing or adhere to the norms of their culture. The reasons for conformity vary, depending on the situation. **Informational social influence** occurs when people conform to the behaviour of others because they view them as a source of knowledge about what they are supposed to do. For instance, if the fire alarm went off during one of your lectures, and most other students were headed out the door at the back of the room, you might think that they knew the fastest way out and decide to follow. This is informational influence; you follow the group because they have information important to you. We do this all the time, especially as children. Other primates use informational social influence too—chimps look to other chimps to learn how to use unfamiliar tools (Whiten, Horner, & de Waal, 2005).

conformity
the tendency of people to adjust their behaviour to what others are doing or to adhere to the norms of their culture.

informational social influence
conformity to the behaviour of others because one views them as a source of knowledge about what one is supposed to do.

Sometimes we do things that go against our better judgment in an effort to preserve group membership. **Normative social influence** occurs when people go along with the behaviour of others in order to be accepted by them. A classic example is peer pressure, in which people engage in certain behaviours, such as drinking or trying drugs, in order to be accepted as a member of a particular

normative social influence
conformity to the behaviour of others in order to be accepted by them.

In nomadic cultures, such as in Mongolia, extended family groups have traditionally stayed together, sharing food, shelter, livestock, childrearing, and all other aspects of daily life.

How might communal living in isolated surroundings affect an individual's behaviour?

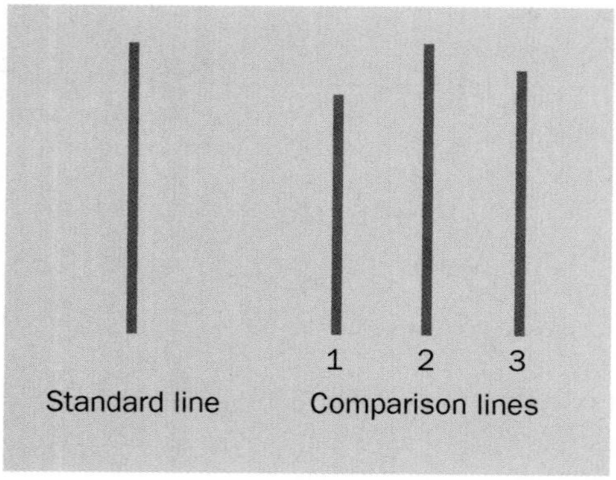

FIGURE **14.5**
STIMULUS LINES PRESENTED TO PARTICIPANTS IN THE ASCH CONFORMITY STUDIES. Each participant was asked to say which of the comparison lines (1, 2, or 3) matched the length of the standard line. The answers were always clear-cut; in this case, the answer is "2." The conformity manipulation involved the confederates in the group giving an obviously wrong answer (such as "1") and then seeing how the participant answered.

social group. This phenomenon is widespread. Look at yourself and your peers. Do you wear the same kinds of clothes? How many of you have similar hairstyles? Consider a more subtle example of normative social influence. You emerge from the theatre after going to a movie with friends, not sure whether you liked the movie or not, although everyone else in the group loved the film and is talking about it. By the end of the evening you may also be talking about what a great film it was and may have actually convinced yourself that it was great. We are not always aware of how other people shape our behaviour and beliefs.

One of the classic studies of social psychology, conducted by Solomon Asch in 1951, demonstrates the power of normative social influence. Asch devoted his career to the study of perception, specifically to investigating the fact that perception is not a direct function of the physical properties of stimuli. For example, he found that our perceptions of the angle of a line can be influenced by the frame around it (Witkin & Asch, 1948). Asch wondered whether the social world might also shape our perceptions. If pressured by the opinions of others, would people say they saw something that clearly wasn't there? Asch didn't think they would, but he was wrong.

Asch assembled several groups of six to seven people in the lab and told them he was researching visual acuity. He was really interested in conformity, but did not want to tell his participants the real object of the study in case that information changed their behaviour. Asch then showed the participants two cards—one with a standard line, the other displaying three lines of varying length. The participant's job was to pick the one line out of the three that matched the standard line. As you can see in Figure 14.5, the task was easy. This comparison process was repeated 18 times and, on each occasion, participants gave their answers out loud.

The one real participant didn't know that all of the other so-called participants were *confederates,* people who actually worked for the experimenter. The one real participant was always seated in the last chair and heard the judgments of all of the other group members before making a choice. On the first six trials everyone gave the obvious and correct answer. Starting on the seventh trial, however, the confederates started giving wrong answers. On the first of the rigged trials, the first confederate would glance at the cards and confidently say, "The answer is line 1," even when it clearly was not correct. The next confederate would nod in agreement and say, "Yes, it is line 1." After five or six people in a row gave the wrong answers—remember, this is a *very* easy task—it was the real participant's turn. Participants faced a choice: Agree with everyone else's clearly erroneous judgments or give the answer that they personally thought was correct.

While none of the participants agreed with the group all of the time, 76 percent of them went along with the group at least once when a group answer was clearly wrong. On average, participants answered incorrectly 37 percent of the time. Yet when left alone to do the task, participants made errors less than 1 percent of the time.

How does the design of this study make it a test of normative social influence rather than informational social influence? The answer is the lack of ambiguity in the task. Judging the lengths of the lines was really easy—there was no need for participants to look to others for information about the right answer. When participants worked alone, they rarely made errors. But in the situation just described, after all the confederates had given the same wrong answer, many participants conformed by also giving the clearly wrong answer.

groupthink
a situation in which the thinking of the group takes over, so much so that group members forgo logic or critical analysis in the service of reaching a decision.

Indeed, sometimes people go to great lengths to do what the group is doing, when it does not make sense, especially when the group is required to make a decision. This phenomenon, called **groupthink,** occurs when the thinking of the group takes over, so much so that group members forgo logic or critical analysis in the service of reaching a decision. Groupthink was first proposed by Irving Janis (Janis, 1983), who based his theory on careful analysis of historical examples of irrational decision making, such as the failure of the American military to anticipate the Japanese attack on Pearl Harbor during World War II. Janis proposed that groupthink is most likely to occur when certain conditions are met: The group is (1) close-knit and cohesive, (2) insulated from outside influences, (3) under the direction of a strong, directive leader, and (4) under pressure to reach a decision. Groupthink has been often indicated as a major factor in countless disasters, such as the sinking of the *Titanic* in 1912 and the contaminated water crisis in Walkerton, Ontario, in 2000 (Myers & Spencer, 2004). According to the U.S. Senate Intelligence Committee's report on intelligence failures leading up to the 2003 invasion of Iraq, the erroneous CIA assertion that Iraq possessed weapons of mass destruction—the primary justification for the invasion—was based on groupthink by an administration invested in finding a reason to attack Iraq (U.S. Senate, 2004).

Much of the support for Janis's groupthink theory comes from retrospective analysis of bad policy decisions by governments and corporations. However, this method of analysis is limited by the historical examples that researchers choose to analyze—after all, hindsight is 20/20. It is possible that groups make *good* decisions under conditions ripe for groupthink, but these good examples tend to be omitted from analysis. Furthermore, the difficulty in groupthink conditions means that performing experiments to test groupthink is challenging. Nonetheless, many researchers have attempted to experimentally manipulate groupthink factors, such as group cohesiveness, although with mixed results (McCauley, 1989). In one study of Australian undergraduate university students, cohesiveness actually *improved* decision making when group members were friends, while it hampered decision making if the group members were strangers (Hogg & Hains, 1998).

Culture affects conformity as well. In collectivist cultures, groups matter more than the individual, so any group-preserving behaviour (such as conformity) would be valued and encouraged. In Japan, for example, the company that one works for is elevated to the status of family. An employee is expected to make personal sacrifices for the company to preserve group unity (Miller & Kanazawa, 2000). Cross-cultural replications of the Asch experiments reveal that people in collectivist cultures like Japan are more likely to conform than are people in individualistic cultures (Bond & Smith, 1996).

Connection

In an individualistic culture, behaviour is determined more by personal goals than by group goals, whereas in a collectivist culture, behaviour is determined more by shared goals.

See Chapter 13, LO2.

Neuroscience research sheds light on the brain mechanisms involved in conformity. When people are made aware that their beliefs differ from those of most other people in a group, a brain region activated in reinforcement learning when we make an error becomes active (Klucharev, Hytonen, Rijpkema, Smidts, & Fernandez, 2009). In other words, the brain signals as though we've made a mistake when we deviate from the group opinion.

LO6 Obedience

Another kind of conformity, called **obedience,** occurs when people yield to the social pressure of an authority figure. Social psychological research on obedience emerged in response to real-life concerns in the aftermath of World War II. The horrific events of the Holocaust raised troubling questions: How could an entire nation endorse the extermination of millions of people? Were *all* Germans evil? Adolf Hitler did not act alone—a supporting cast of thousands was necessary to annihilate so many people. Former Nazi officers who testified in war trials after the war said they were "following orders." The same rationale was offered in 1993 by Canadian soldiers charged and convicted in the death of a civilian teenager in Somalia, and again in 2004 by U.S. soldiers who humiliated and tortured Iraqi prisoners at Abu Ghraib.

obedience
a type of conformity in which a person yields to the will of another person.

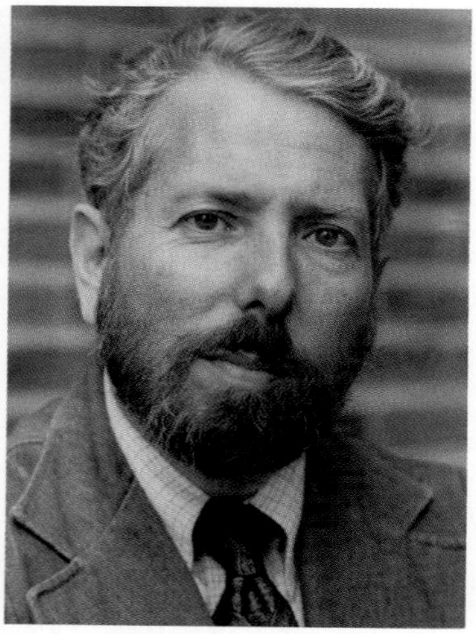

Stanley Milgram

Will people really do horrible things if an authority figure orders them to do so? One psychologist spurred into action by the Nazi atrocities was Stanley Milgram. A Jew whose family left Europe before Hitler's rise to power, Milgram spent much of his early academic life trying to make sense of the Holocaust (Blass, 2004). With the support of his graduate advisor, Solomon Asch, Milgram decided to investigate whether people would conform even when their actions could harm others.

Milgram recruited people from the community to participate in an experiment at Yale University. A participant arrived at the lab and sat down next to another supposed participant, who was a confederate. The experimenter, who looked very official in a white lab coat, then told both individuals that they would be participating in a study on the effects of mild punishment on memory. He then assigned them to be either a teacher or learner by asking them to pull a note that said either "teacher" or "learner" from a bowl. The drawing was rigged, however, so that the real participant always landed the "teacher" role and the confederate got the "learner" role. Then the experimenter showed both the teacher and learner to the room where the learner would sit. The learner's task involved learning and repeating lists of words. The learner was told that every time he made an error he would receive a mild electric shock, delivered by the teacher. With each mistake the shocks would increase in intensity. Both teacher and learner saw the chair where the learner would sit, which had restraints to make sure the electrodes had a good contact when he received the shock. The teacher then received a sample shock of very low voltage to get a sense of what the learner would experience. In actuality, this was the only real shock administered during the entire experiment.

Then they went to the teacher's room. The teacher sat at a table behind a panel of little switches. Under each switch was a label indicating voltage level, which ranged, in 15-volt increments, from 15 volts ("mild shock") all the way up to 450 (labelled as "XXX"), with 375 volts designated as "danger: severe shock" (see Figure 14.6a). The teacher was reminded that if the learner made mistakes he or she would have to deliver a shock, and with each mistake would have to increase the level.

The experiment began uneventfully. Then the learner made occasional mistakes. At lower levels of shock, the learner gave no real response to the shocks. As the teacher moved up the shock scale and the learner supposedly made more errors, the teacher and experimenter could hear a yelp of pain come from the learner with each shock. (In fact, the learner played a prerecorded tape of his responses to the shock.) At this point, many teachers would ask the experimenter if they should go on, and he would say, "The experiment requires that you go on."

Connection

Do you think participants were treated ethically in the Milgram study? What are the obligations of researchers to ensure the ethical treatment of participants in research?

See Chapter 2, LO9.

Before beginning the experiments, Milgram polled experts to see how many "teachers" they thought would go along with the experimenter's demands to administer high levels of shock. One group of experts, psychiatrists, predicted that only about 30 percent would administer shocks as high as 150 volts, less than 4 percent would go to the 300-volt level, and only one person in 1000 would go all the way to 450 volts. How far do *you* think most people would go in administering shocks?

The results differed drastically from these predictions. As shown in Figure 14.6b, at 150 volts, the point at which the learner yelled, "Get me out of here! My heart's starting to bother me! I refuse to go on! Let me out!" there was a drop in obedience—from 100 percent to about 83 percent. Some participants stopped, but many, although visibly uncomfortable, continued with the experiment. What is alarming is how many people went all the way up to the end of the shock scale, despite the yells and protests (and eventual silence) of the learner. Twenty-six of the 40 participants in the original experiment (65 percent) went all the way to 450 volts (Milgram, 1963, 1974). Men and women were equally likely to reach the 450-volt level.

Milgram's experiments show how powerful situations can make reasonable people do things that seem cruel and unusual. In fact, several "teachers"

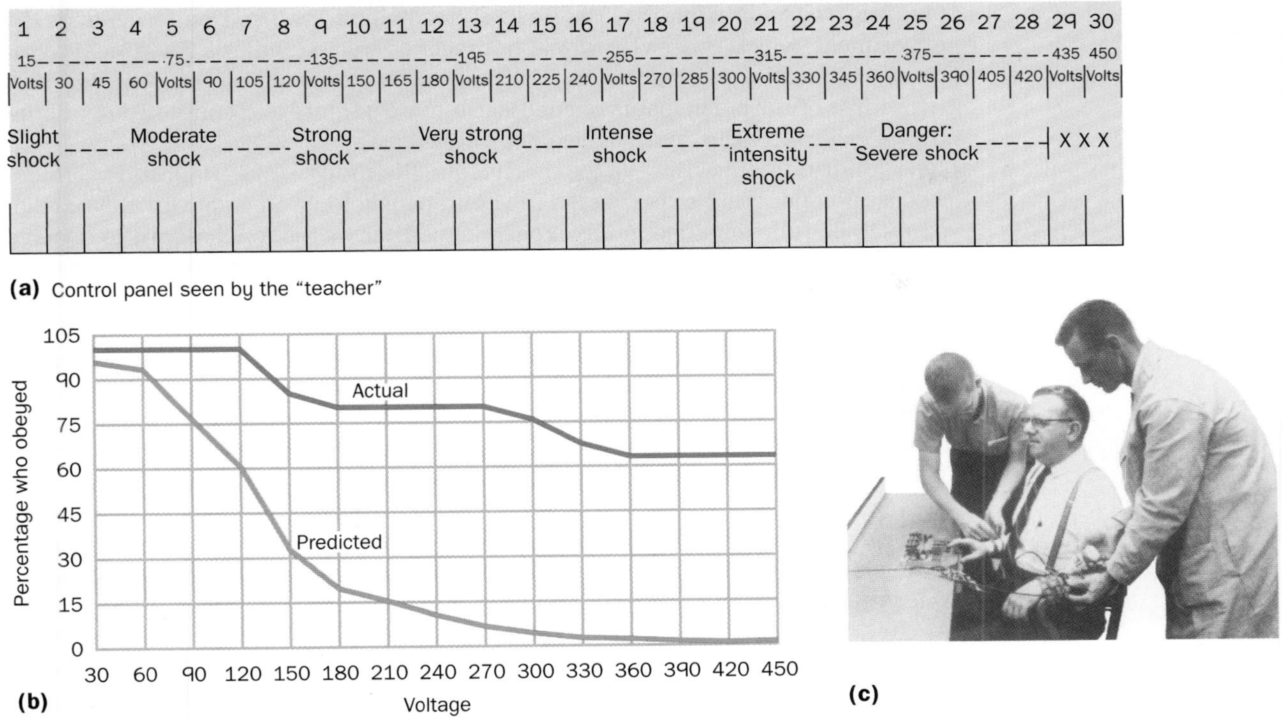

FIGURE **14.6**

MILGRAM'S STUDY OF OBEDIENCE. (a) This is the control panel seen by the "teacher." (b) Experts consulted by Milgram prior to the study predicted that at higher voltages, participants would refuse to administer further shocks to the "learner." As the graph shows, the experts were wrong. At the highest voltages, when the experimenter told them the experiment must continue in spite of the "learner's" protests, 60 percent of the "teachers" continued to administer "shocks." (c) The "learner" is strapped in for Milgram's study. (*Source:* Milgram, 1974.)

did protest and yet went on when the experimenter urged them to continue. When asked, "Who is going to take responsibility if that guy gets hurt?" the experimenter would say, "I have full responsibility, please continue." Somehow, the belief that someone else (the authority figure) was responsible for their actions alleviated feelings of guilt or concern in some of the participants. This is akin to former Nazi officers saying, "I was just following orders." But who really has the final responsibility?

Because participants clearly experienced mental anguish while taking part in the study, it sparked a fierce debate about ethics in research. Milgram contacted his participants later and asked whether they regretted having participated. Less than 2 percent did (see Figure 14.7).

You might think that you would never administer those shocks or that people today would know better. Not so. In 2006, social psychologist Jerry Burger conducted a modified version of Milgram's original study with college students. An important change from the original study was that when the participants began to protest, they were told to continue rather than told that they *had* to continue. Also, once participants passed the 150-volt range, the experiment stopped. By making these changes, the researchers were able to

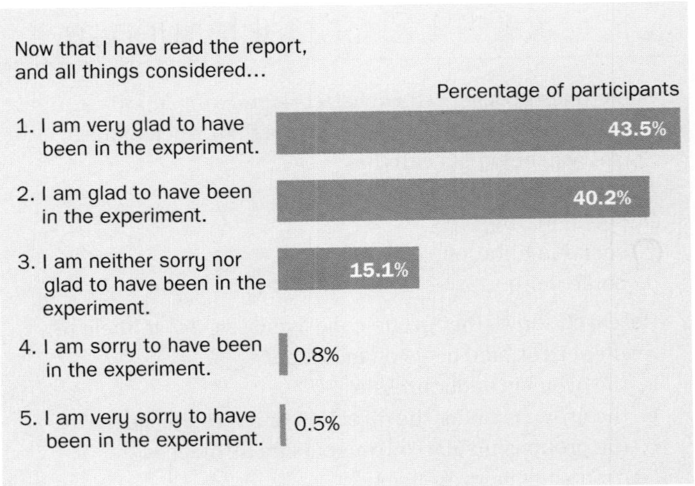

FIGURE **14.7**

QUESTIONNAIRE RESPONSES OF PARTICIPANTS IN MILGRAM'S OBEDIENCE STUDY. Despite the distress they experienced during the experiment, the majority of the respondents did not regret their involvement. (*Source:* Milgram, 1974.)

obtain permission from the American Psychological Association to conduct the experiment, which otherwise would not meet current standards for ethical treatment of human participants. As in Milgram's experiment, Burger reported that two-thirds of the participants obeyed the authority figure and continued to administer shocks after the "learner" began protesting.

Milgram's and Burger's experiments highlight some important ethical issues in conducting experiments in social psychology. In order for the participants to be fully engaged in the experiment, Milgram felt it necessary to deceive them about the purpose of the research. Any reasonable and moral human being, knowing the true intent of the experiment, would disobey the orders of the experimenter, right? Perhaps not. One of the most controversial experiments in social psychology revealed the dark side of human nature without any deception whatsoever. The Stanford Prison Study, conducted in the early 1970s in the laboratory of Philip Zimbardo, was a simple experiment whereby participants were recruited to spend two weeks in a simulated prison in the basement of Stanford University. The participants were all college students, and were pre-screened to ensure that they were as average, healthy, and otherwise as normal as possible. They were then randomly assigned to play the role of prisoners or guards, and the research team simply observed their behaviour. All of the participants knew the situation was entirely artificial and that they were being monitored by the experimenters. At first, the guards treated the prisoners well. However, after a few days there were escalating incidents of abuse of the prisoners by the guards. After only six days, the behaviour of the guards towards the prisoners deteriorated to the point that Zimbardo called off the experiment (Haney et al., 1973). Zimbardo was harshly criticized for letting the experiment go on as long as it did, but there were several important lessons learned from the Stanford Prison Study. First, it illustrated that role-playing, even if temporary and artificial, can profoundly guide behaviour. Furthermore, it showed that good people can commit evil acts when faced with powerful social situations, to the point that the situation can override individual personality and morality (Zimbardo et al., 2000). Both Milgram's and Zimbardo's controversial studies continue to inspire investigation and reinterpretation, including studies that suggest that people are more likely to follow authority not just for situational reasons but because they think the authority knew the right thing to do (Haslam & Reicher, 2012).

Quick Quiz 14.2: Social Influence

1. Sometimes people perform better—for example, ride a bike faster—when they are in groups than when alone. Social psychologists call this
   a. the Yerkes–Dodson principle.
   b. social loafing.
   c. social facilitation.
   d. conformity.
2. Research shows that group cohesiveness is *least* likely to result in irrational decision making if
   a. the group is under pressure.
   b. the group is under the direction of a strong leader.
   c. the group is insulated from outside influences.
   d. group members are friends.
3. When put in a situation where an individual has to say something about the length of a line that goes against what everyone else in the group has said, most people
   a. eventually conform at least once and go along with the group.
   b. always conform and go along with the group.
   c. never conform and go along with the group.
   d. pretend not to be paying attention.
4. In Milgram's study on obedience, under pressure from an authority figure, approximately what percentage of the participants gave the maximum punishment of 450 volts to the learner's incorrect answers?
   a. 25 percent
   b. 50 percent
   c. 65 percent
   d. 90 percent

Answers can be found at the end of the chapter.

SOCIAL RELATIONS

We constantly interact with other people. Sometimes these interactions lead to special connections with others that grow into friendship or even love. Other times we clash and find ourselves in conflict with others. In this section we discuss several different aspects of social interaction: exclusion and inclusion, prejudice and discrimination, aggression, helping, and attraction.

LO7 Exclusion and Inclusion

As a result of having evolved for group living, we humans tend to judge others and ourselves—judgments that stem from defending ourselves against other groups and competing with them for limited resources (Neuberg & Cottrell, 2006). That is, the machinery is in place for using cognitive and emotional processes to separate "us" from "them." Perceiving others as different from us has several consequences:

1. We sometimes evaluate and treat people differently because of the group they belong to.
2. Our actions are based on in-group/out-group distinctions ("us" versus "them").
3. It hurts to be excluded from our group.

When we show positive feelings toward people in our own group and negative feelings toward those in other groups, we are displaying **in-group/out-group bias.** Think back to the rivalry between your high school and its cross-town rival. Everyone who went to your school was part of your in-group, and you identified with them and felt pride belonging to that group. Everyone who went to the other school was part of the out-group, and you felt competitive whenever the two schools interacted. Moreover, you likely made many distinctions between students and groups at your school, but categorized everyone who went to the other school into one group: "them." This tendency to see all members of an out-group as the same is known as **out-group homogeneity.**

in-group/out-group bias the tendency to show positive feelings toward people who belong to the same group as we do, and negative feelings toward those in other groups.

out-group homogeneity the tendency to see all members of an out-group as the same.

Our tendency to view others from the perspective of in-groups and out-groups has a significant impact on how people feel towards immigration. In today's global climate, national borders are no longer the barriers they once were, and many countries' economies rely upon immigration to fill opportunities in the workplace. Canada, in 1972, was the first country in the world to adopt an official multiculturalism policy, which at its core aims to both preserve and share the cultural heritage of all ethnic groups. Many other countries have followed suit with their own multicultural policies, although these policies and their implementation have been fiercely debated. In 2010, German Chancellor Angela Merkel publicly declared multiculturalism in Germany "a failure" due to the lack of integration of immigrants into German society (Kinsman, 2010). Is it possible to celebrate cultural differences as well as share common societal values?

As you will learn later in this section of the chapter, we tend to be drawn to others who are similar to us, so some argue that the policies of multiculturalism, which focus on group differences, create a social dilemma. Researchers at McGill University interviewed Canadians from different ethnic backgrounds, including individuals of English, French, Jewish, Indian, Algerian, and Greek origins, in an attempt to examine the association between perceived similarity and willingness to associate with others based upon their ethnic heritage. Participants were asked to rate the similarity of their own ethnic in-group to other ethnic out-groups and were also asked how they would feel about becoming affiliated with an out-group member through family marriage, as a close friend, a neighbour, or a workplace colleague. Results indicated that ratings of perceived similarity were correlated with willingness to affiliate with ethnic out-groups (Osbeck et al., 1997). Findings like these have prompted some to suggest that more attention should be focused on similarities shared by ethnic groups, rather than highlighting the differences (Brodsky & Faryal, 2006).

One result of the human tendency to include and exclude others is that sometimes we get left out. As our chapter-opening scenario illustrated, rejection hurts. One possible reason it hurts to be left out is that our social connections are as important to us as our physical safety—so important that the brain's physical pain circuits also evolved to signal when we have been excluded from the group (see Figure 14.8; Eisenberger et al., 2003; MacDonald, Kingsbury, & Shaw, 2005; MacDonald & Leary, 2005; Masten et al., 2009). An interesting corollary of the pain finding is that, when people read friendly messages from those people with whom they feel socially connected, they feel physically warm and show brain activation patterns that correspond to the areas active during actual physical warmth (Inagaki & Eisenberger, 2013). Thus, there appears to be mapping of physical and social pain in our lived experience of others.

In modern life, we separate physical from social needs. But in early human evolution, these two needs were often intertwined. To be included in a social group meant you were fed, you were secure, and you could reproduce. Being excluded threatened not only survival but also the chance to reproduce (MacDonald et al., 2005). The need for connection runs so deep down the phylogenetic tree that you find it in social insects. When raised without social contact, cockroaches show behavioural deficiencies, including poor mating skills, reduced willingness to interact with others, and impaired foraging (Lihoreau, Brepson, & Rivault, 2009).

Humans also form social groups through social networks, which are webs of people who share common interests, professions, or familial relations (Christakis & Fowler, 2009). Both real-life and electronic social networks play an important role in social life. See "Psychology in the Real World."

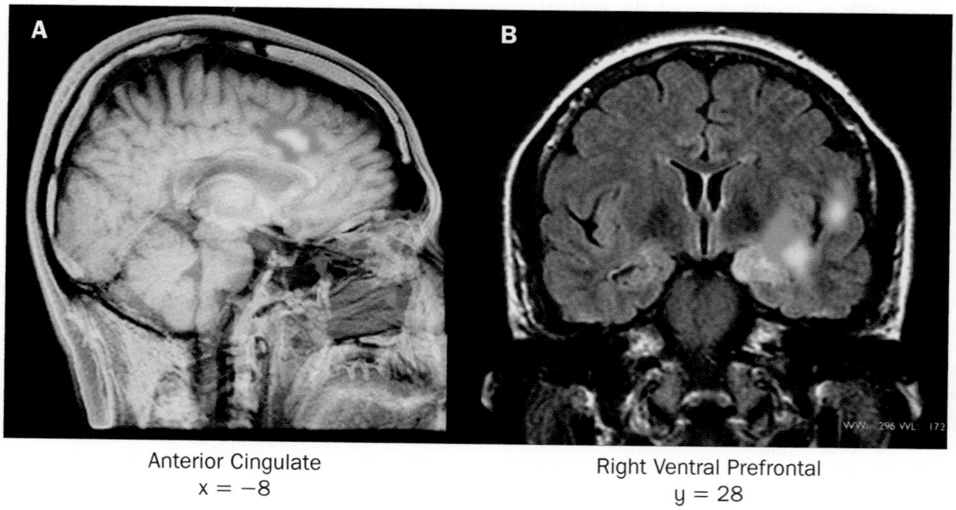

FIGURE **14.8**

BRAIN REGIONS ACTIVATED BY SOCIAL PAIN. Exclusion from an electronic ball-tossing game increased blood flow to the same areas of the brain activated by physical pain. The increase in activity in the anterior cingulate cortex (A) and in the right front section of the prefrontal cortex (B) shows up in these fMRI images as patches of orange and yellow. (*Source:* Eisenberger et al., 2003.)

The Social Psychology of Social Networks

Social networks form among people who share interests. You might be in one network as a function of your school, another by virtue of familial relationships, and yet another because of your musical taste. Networks are defined by associations among people that branch and spread beyond those people one knows directly (Christakis & Fowler, 2009).

Everything from physical health habits to moods can spread in a social network—often unbeknownst to all involved. By *spread* we mean that these behaviours are more common among members of a network than among people who are not in the same network. Eating behaviour, drinking habits, smoking, loneliness, happiness, and cooperative behaviour all spread in this way (Cacioppo, Fowler, & Christakis, 2009; Christakis & Fowler, 2007, 2008; Fowler & Christakis, 2008, 2010; Rosenquist, Murabito, Fowler, & Christakis, 2010).

How did social networks, such as Facebook and Twitter, play a key role in the revolutions in the Middle East and North Africa in the spring of 2011?

Nicholas Christakis and James Fowler (2009), pioneers in research on social networks, report that attitudes, behaviours, and habits move through social networks via the *three degrees rule.* For instance, your behaviour (say, your food preferences) can affect your friends (one degree) and their friends (two degrees) and their friends' friends (three degrees). So we are influenced by and influence our friends within three degrees of separation, but not much beyond that (Christakis & Fowler, 2009).

How does something like smoking behaviour spread in a network? Social psychological processes such as conformity and peer influence play a role; that is, you might be more likely to smoke if the people you know smoke and it is regarded as "OK" to smoke in your social circles. *Mimicry,* or the process by which we mirror the actions of others, may be one means by which our emotional behaviour can impact another person. In such cases, however, the behaviour gets distorted as it moves outward toward others, much as a message gets modified when it is passed among many people (Christakis & Fowler, 2009).

Real-life social networks have existed for ages, but social networking sites (SNSs)—electronic forums for interaction with friends and acquaintances—are relatively new. Although in their infancy, SNSs such as Facebook, Instagram, and Twitter are now a major means of social interaction among people ages 15–25. Between 2005 and 2010, there was a major shift from email as the major form of Internet use to SNSs such as Facebook (Judd & Kennedy, 2010). By January 2011, Facebook alone had more than half a billion users worldwide ("The Many Facets," 2011). Even though SNSs are electronic, they influence real-world social connections (Christakis & Fowler, 2009). For instance, SNS use contributes to perceptions of quality of social interaction and supports socialization (Yu, Tian, Vogel, & Kwok, 2010) and increases the likelihood of being exposed to differing political views, regardless of one's political affiliation (Kim, 2011).

Still, these two types of networks might work quite differently. Given how Facebook is arranged, ideas and preferences ("likes") instantly spread much more rapidly than they would in a real-world social network. It is possible that the three degrees rule may not apply to SNSs or that the limits of influence may be wider. Also, surveys of Facebook use show that people of all ages share much more private information publicly than they realize (Brandtzæg, Luders, & Skjetne, 2010). People readily disclose drug and alcohol use more freely on SNSs than they might in real-world public settings (Moran, Snelson, & Elison-Bowers, 2010). Indeed, certain people are more likely to make optimal use of privacy features than others—women more than men and younger people more often than older people (Litt, 2013).

People use SNSs to obtain what is known as *social capital* (Ji et al., 2010). Social capital is the value, or payoff (socially, professionally), one gains by connecting with others. Payoff for SNS use takes many forms. Many people use SNSs to get reinforcement for their views or images—in Facebook terms, one way to measure that is by means of receiving "likes" for one's postings. In fact, the number of "likes" received shapes future posting behaviour. A large-scale survey indicated that people who get reinforced by "likes" for disclosing personal information online (such as posting pictures, relationship status, whereabouts of social activities) are more likely to disclose even more in the future (Trepte & Reinecke, 2013). Also, we tend to "like" the posts of people who "like" our posts. Although many use SNSs primarily for enjoyment, some of the biggest factors that determine usage involve the behaviour of our "friends." Facebook use is affected by how many of one's peers are using it, as well as perceptions of reciprocity in liking behaviour (e.g., if you "like" their stuff, they will "like" yours; Lin & Lu, 2011). Here we see the power of social influence on SNS behaviour.

Both real and virtual social networks spread information to large numbers of people in a short period of time—often to powerful effect. In February 2011, the people of Egypt protested the authoritarian government of Hosni Mubarak. Within a matter of days, early reports and images of police violence against peaceful protestors had spread to millions of young Egyptians via Twitter and Facebook. This, along with other information, incited a revolution, which ultimately led to Mubarak's resignation.

LO8 Prejudice and Discrimination

We have discussed many processes that affect how we act in a group and how we view others. As we saw earlier in our discussion of social cognition, when trying to make sense of each other and deciding who is like us or who is different, we often rely on stereotypes to unfairly categorize people. Unfortunately, these stereotypes can fuel prejudice and discrimination.

prejudice
a biased, negative attitude based on an individual's group membership.

discrimination
negative behaviour towards another based upon group membership.

A **prejudice** is a biased attitude toward a group of people or an individual member of a group based on generalizations about what members of that group are like (Allport, 1954). Prejudicial thinking often stems from stereotypes rather than from careful observation of people's behaviour. Prejudices are generally negative and often based on insufficient information. **Discrimination** refers to negative actions directed towards another based upon that individual's group membership and is usually the result of prejudicial attitudes. However, discrimination can also result from institutionalized rules, such as a requirement that firefighters must be a certain height, which often discriminates against women and some ethnic groups.

Prejudices based on race-ethnicity are called *racism;* those based on sex are called *sexism*. If a male business executive does not seriously consider a highly qualified female applicant for a high-level management job because he is convinced that women are not capable of leading a company, his thinking is prejudicial. More precisely, it is sexist thinking. Not offering her an interview—even if she is the best-qualified applicant in the pool—is discrimination.

Probably the most powerful example of the arbitrary nature of prejudicial attitudes and discriminatory behaviour comes from the classic work in the 1960s by Jane Elliott, an American schoolteacher who decided to provide her Grade 3 students with a first-hand experience of prejudice and discrimination. Elliot's decision was spurred by the assassination of Martin Luther King Jr., whom the children had learned about weeks earlier as the "hero of the month." With no formal training in psychology, Elliott devised a simple experiment whereby she divided students into groups based upon eye colour. On the first day, she told them that blue-eyed people were superior to brown-eyed people, in that they were more intelligent, nicer, more trustworthy, and less wasteful. She allowed the blue-eyed children special privileges, such as extra time at recess. The brown-eyed children were made to wear collars and were not allowed to use the playground equipment and were only allowed one serving at lunch. In a matter of hours, her classroom was transformed; the superior blue-eyed children regarded the brown-eyed children with disdain and taunted them. The next day, Elliott reversed the roles and gave the brown-eyed children the special privileges while the blue-eyed

Does Canada have a racism problem? In January 2015, *Maclean's* magazine published an issue focusing on Canada's treatment of Aboriginal Canadians, suggesting that Winnipeg is fast becoming Canada's most racist city. They reported that Canada's First Nations are treated worse and live with more hardship than the African-American population in the United States, citing statistics such as unemployment (14 percent for First Nations versus 11 percent for African Americans), and high school dropout rates (23 percent versus 8 percent) (Gilmore, 2015). In response, Winnipeg mayor Brian Bowman (depicted above) held a press conference calling for all Winnipeggers to work together to combat racism.

What factors contribute to prejudice and discrimination towards our First Nations? How can we combat them?

children were now subject to restrictions, with the same results as the previous day. Not only did the children treat each other differently, but their academic performance on math and reading tasks was much poorer on the day when they were labelled as inferior (Elliott, 2006).

Jane Elliott went on to become a diversity trainer and has run this exercise as a workshop for numerous corporations and government agencies throughout North America. Her blue-eyed/brown-eyed exercise has become the subject of a number of television programs and films, including a 2005 documentary entitled *Indecently Exposed,* which explored Canadians' attitudes towards Native Canadians. Filmed in Regina, Saskatchewan, Elliott ran her workshop with a group of 22 Canadians, which included individuals from white and Aboriginal communities. No stranger to controversy, Elliott states, "Even nice Canadians are racist."

Prejudicial attitudes are learned early in life (when people are presented with racial-ethnic stereotypes, for example); and even if they are formally abandoned later in life, these reactions can become quite automatic (Banaji & Greenwald, 1995). Prejudices can operate outside conscious awareness, and they sometimes stand in stark contrast to one's conscious beliefs (Devine, 1989). Even a person who works hard at being fair may have a hard time overcoming biases that are automatic and deeply learned. There may also be an evolutionary basis for our automatic responses: The mechanism of recognizing group members may have evolved to preserve group harmony, cohesion, and close alliances, which could have been a means to enhance the survivability of individuals (Melis & Semmann, 2010; Neuberg & Cottrell, 2006).

Groundbreaking Research

The Study of Implicit Bias

Prejudice operates both inside and outside a person's awareness. Asking people directly about their racial-ethnic preferences provides information on their conscious beliefs at best; at worst, it provides answers that people think the researchers want to hear. Two social psychologists, Anthony Greenwald and Mahzarin Banaji, came up with a solution that has changed the way attitudes are measured.

TRADITIONAL APPROACHES TO THE STUDY OF PREJUDICE

For years studying prejudice meant surveying people about their conscious attitudes toward individuals from different racial-ethnic backgrounds. But over time, as it became less socially acceptable to display overt racism or show ethnic bias, people became less willing to openly acknowledge their prejudices. Prejudicial attitudes have actually declined steadily since the 1950s in North America. Still, when questionnaire respondents appear to be less prejudiced, it's impossible to know whether they are truly less prejudiced, are prejudiced but are hiding their biases due to social unacceptability, or have deeply rooted biases that are not accessible to conscious awareness.

Social psychologists now distinguish between *explicit* and *implicit* prejudice. Explicit ideas are plainly stated. Implicit views are indirect. An explicit reference to a desire to have sex with someone is "I want to go to bed with you." An implicit reference would be "Why don't you come by my place and watch a movie with me?" Measuring implicit knowledge and beliefs presents a challenge.

Mahzarin Banaji

Mahzarin Banaji had been interested in the relationship between explicit and implicit memory. She drew upon earlier research on *priming*, which showed that prior exposure to a word or image, even if it is not consciously recalled, leads to better recall of that word or image. Prior exposure leaves memory "traces" that can affect how we respond to information we encounter later (Jacoby & Dallas, 1981; Schacter, 1987). Banaji reasoned that this principle might apply to social cognition as well; that is, prior exposure—say from growing up in a racist society or from values at home—could ingrain certain biases. We may develop racist attitudes unknowingly (these are implicit) and later in life work to overcome them (these are explicit) (Baron & Banaji, 2006). The challenge for Banaji, then, was to disentangle the explicit and implicit sources of racism empirically.

Anthony Greenwald

INNOVATIONS IN MEASURING IMPLICIT BIAS

Banaji's graduate school advisor, Anthony Greenwald, developed a technique for measuring implicit biases and decided to apply it to racial words. He took European-American and African-American names and paired them with both pleasant and unpleasant words. He then took his own test to see how long it took to form associations between pairs of words. He was shocked at the difficulty he had pairing African-American names with pleasant words (Vedantum, 2005). When Banaji took the same test, she, too, was upset by the results, which looked about the same as Greenwald's. Banaji and Greenwald knew they were on to something. They dubbed the new test the *Implicit Associations Test (IAT).*

Greenwald and Banaji have applied the IAT to race concepts. Faster response times on the test indicate that people more readily associate two concepts; slower response times indicate a less automatic association. European Americans tend to respond more slowly to pairings of "Black" (words or faces) with positive words than they do to pairings of "Black" with negative words (Dasgupta et al., 2000; Greenwald, McGhee, & Schwartz, 1998). This is true even for people whose questionnaire responses seem to indicate that they do not hold racist attitudes. The reverse is true for African Americans. They respond more slowly to pairings of "White American" with positive words than they do to pairings of "White American" with negative words. Banaji and Greenwald (1995) have also reported evidence of implicit gender bias using the IAT; female and male college students more readily associated "fame" with male names than with female names.

REDUCING IMPLICIT BIAS

When social scientists heard about the IAT, their enthusiasm for the technique was immediate. The power of the findings was obvious: Even those of us who are convinced that we are not biased may harbour prejudices of which we are unaware. It became evident that researchers and the general population alike must deal with their own implicit prejudice and racism.

In the roughly 20 years since the IAT's publication, more than 600 published research papers, in areas ranging from marketing to neuroscience, have used the IAT technique. IAT scores predict suicidal tendencies, consumer preferences, political preferences, sexual orientation, symptoms of post-traumatic stress disorder, and drug and alcohol use (Anselmi et al., 2013; Greenwald, Poehlman, Uhlmann, & Banaji, 2009; Lindgren, Kaysen, Werntz, Gasser, & Teachman, 2013; Nock et al., 2010). Indeed, the IAT is an excellent teaching tool for anyone confronting his or her own implicit prejudice. Results from the test can be used to reduce prejudice and sensitize individuals and groups to the fact that these prejudices operate in subtle yet powerful ways. In 1998, Banaji, Greenwald, and Brian Nosek established a non-profit organization (Project Implicit) to help people apply the IAT technique.

Banaji lives by her own advice. She was so dismayed by her own performance on race- and gender-based IATs—in spite of being a minority woman herself—that she changed her behaviour. In addition to the non-profit work, she does little things to help undo her deeply held biases, such as displaying pictures of prominent black men and women from history in her office. You can try the IAT yourself at https://implicit.harvard.edu/implicit/demo/.

Connection

Priming is a kind of implicit memory that stems from prior exposure to the same or similar stimuli.

See Chapter 6, LO4.

Challenge Your Assumptions

True or False? I know whether I am prejudiced or not.

False: In spite of our best intentions or conscious beliefs, deeply held biases are often implicit, or outside our conscious awareness.

LO9 The Nature and Nurture of Aggression

Aggression is part of life. All animals compete with others, both within and outside their species, for survival. Almost every animal can be aggressive, and many animals kill others in order to survive. Humans are unique in that they often engage in aggression and violent behaviour when their survival is not at issue.

Aggression refers to violent behaviour that is intended to cause psychological or physical harm, or both, to another being. By definition, aggression is deliberate. A dentist who performs a root canal may hurt a patient, but we hardly would call that behaviour aggressive. Aggression is often provoked by anger, but not always.

aggression
violent behaviour that is intended to cause psychological or physical harm, or both, to another being.

There are several types of aggression. When aggression stems from feelings of anger, it is called *hostile aggression*. When aggression is a means to achieve some goal, it is called *instrumental aggression*. The hostile type of aggression is easy to understand. While you are driving, someone cuts you off on the road. You honk, and in response, the other driver makes an obscene hand gesture toward you (the hand gesture is an aggressive action).

Connection

How does hostility differ from anger? Hostility is a personality characteristic that sets the threshold for the emotion of anger.

See Chapter 12, LO5.

An example of instrumental aggression occurs in football when a defensive lineman smashes down a ball carrier to prevent the opponent from scoring. The goal is to prevent scoring by the other team, not to hurt the ball carrier. In this case, the aggressive action is considered to be justified by its instrumental goal.

Where does aggression come from, and why are people aggressive? Some people are more prone to violence than others. An individual's genetic disposition often plays a role, but genes by themselves are seldom enough to cause violent behaviour (Miczek et al., 2007). Caspi and colleagues (2002) found that when genetic factors combine with an abusive and neglectful environment, the likelihood of committing violence increases dramatically. Research on murderers has identified a cluster of traits shared by most of these individuals: being male, growing up in an abusive and neglectful household, having at least one psychological disorder, and having experienced some kind of injury to the head or brain (Pincus, 1999, 2001; Strueber, Lueck, & Roth, 2006–2007; Yang et al., 2010). In other words, the person's disposition interacts with certain environmental influences to make aggressive behaviour more likely.

Aggressive tendencies may be influenced by differences in brain functioning. Several brain areas are involved in aggression, including the hypothalamus, the amygdala, and the prefrontal cortex (Pincus, 1999). More specifically, the part of the prefrontal cortex responsible for impulse control often is functionally impaired in aggressive and violent people (Grafman et al., 1996). Amygdala damage is found frequently in murderers (DeLisi, Umphress, & Vaughn, 2009). Similarly, as a result of head injuries, psychopathology, or abuse, murderers may have problems with frontal lobe functioning, which involves impulse control, emotional intelligence, working memory, and attention (Strueber et al., 2006–2007) or reductions in the size of the hippocampus (Yang et al, 2010). Living in a constant state of fear can lead to neural systems being primed for unusually high levels of anxiety, impulsive behaviour, and vigilance, or a constant state of alertness (Bishop, 2007).

Two chemical messengers are consistently related to aggression: serotonin and testosterone. Serotonin has a broad range of effects on behaviour, one of which is keeping anger and anxiety in check. Low levels of serotonin make aggression more likely in both humans and animals (Moffitt et al., 1998; Raleigh et al., 1991). A number of lines of evidence point to testosterone's role. As the primary male sex hormone, it may account for the finding that boys are consistently more aggressive than girls at most ages (Maccoby & Jacklin, 1974). Relatively high levels of testosterone, whether in men or women, correlate positively with a propensity toward violence. Among both male and female prisoners, naturally occurring testosterone levels are higher in criminals convicted of violent crimes than in those convicted of non-violent crimes (Dabbs, Carr, & Frady, 1995; Dabbs & Hargrove, 1997).

Physical violence is more common in men than in women; the great majority of people arrested for criminal offences are men (Strueber et al., 2006–2007). Women are more likely to use non-physical forms of aggression, such as harsh words, "dirty" glances, and ignoring (Schober et al., 2009). However, women are certainly capable of high levels of physical aggression. A study at McGill University showed equal levels of aggression for men and women when they were provoked by a confederate (Hoaken & Pihl, 2000). Furthermore, within relationships, women actually show *higher* levels of physical aggression towards their partners (Thornton et al., 2010).

LO10

Social Influences on Aggression Situations that frustrate us and prevent us from reaching our goals are likely to make us aggressive. Moreover, the closer we are to our goal when we become frustrated, the more aggressive we are likely to be. A classic study by Harris (1974) demonstrated this effect. Confederates of the researchers cut in front of people in lines for movies or crowded restaurants. Sometimes they cut in front of the second person in line; other times they cut in front of someone farther back in line. The response of the person standing behind the intruder was much more aggressive when the confederate cut in front of the person second in line—closest to the goal.

Similarly, situations that lead to anger stimulate aggression, especially hostile aggression. Threats to our safety or the safety of our families fall into this category. Aggressive responses may be motivated by anger and/or fear. Road rage is a good example of such a situation, and aggressive driving is most likely to happen when people are angry (Nesbit, Conger, & Conger, 2007).

Observing aggressive people and the consequences of their actions can make us more aggressive. This is the fundamental idea behind Albert Bandura's *social learning theory*. Bandura's research demonstrated repeatedly that if children see adults punching an inflatable Bobo doll, they will do it too, especially if they see the adult being rewarded for the aggressive behaviour.

> **Connection**
> Social learning theory offers an explanation of modelling, the kind of learning in which we imitate the behaviour of others.
> See Chapter 7, LO8.

How does the Bobo doll research apply to real-life aggression? According to longitudinal studies of men and women, the more violence people watch on TV when they are children, the more violent behaviour they exhibit as adults (Huesmann, Moise-Titus, & Podolski, 2003). This correlational result does not tell us for sure that TV is the cause of the aggressive behaviour. However, more controlled experiments also suggest that watching TV violence leads to aggressive behaviour in some children. In a classic experiment, Wendy Josephson from the University of Winnipeg had Grade 2 and 3 boys watch either a violent police program or an exciting stunt bike race. Later the boys' aggressive tendencies were measured in a floor hockey game. Boys who watched the violent TV program showed more aggressive behaviours in their play than those who saw the non-violent show. This effect was most pronounced in children with aggressive personalities; those with less aggressive tendencies were less affected by viewing TV violence (Josephson, 1987).

Does violence in video games and other visual media increase the likelihood of aggressive behaviour?

Until recently, the evidence was overwhelming that exposure to violent programs or video games increased aggression in kids (Bushman & Anderson, 2001; Kirsh, 2006). Results from a recent meta-analysis suggest, however, that the effects of watching violence on aggressive behaviour have been exaggerated. It seems many of the studies fail to consider how other factors (such as sex, personality, and family violence) may also play a role in aggressive behaviour (Ferguson & Kilburn, 2009). For instance, having pre-existing violent tendencies or an aggressive personality are associated with aggressive behaviours after violent video game play (Markey & Markey, 2010). There is clearly a relationship between viewing violence and aggression, but the size of the effect is a matter of great debate (Anderson et al., 2010; Ferguson & Kilburn, 2010; Freedman, 2002).

So why is media violence linked to aggressive behaviour? One theory is that repeated exposure actually makes people less responsive to violence, rather than actually increasing aggression (or its emotional precursor—anger). The logic of such an approach is this: By repeatedly seeing and even participating in violent action (albeit in a virtual world), people may become desensitized to violence. In a study of desensitization to violence in people who play violent video games, the researchers randomly assigned more than 250 university students to play either a violent or a non-violent video game for 20 minutes (Carnagey, Anderson, & Bushman, 2007). Then they measured the participants' physiological responses to films of real-life violence, such as courtroom outbursts, police confrontations, shootings, and prison fights. The students who had played the violent video games showed less evidence of physiological arousal (as measured by heart rate and sweating) while watching films of real people being stabbed and shot than did the students who had played the non-violent games. A similar study showed that young men who had a history of playing video games showed reduced brain activation to real-life violence and that this reduced brain activation correlated with aggression in a behavioural task (Bartholow, Bushman, & Sestir, 2006). Such non-reaction to violence is disturbing.

LO11 Prosocial Behaviour

Just as people can harm others through aggression, sometimes people can be extraordinarily kind to others. **Prosocial behaviour** is behaviour that benefits others. In this section we will explore social processes that benefit others: altruism, empathy, and cooperation.

prosocial behaviour
action that is beneficial to others.

Sometimes humans do extraordinary things that benefit others at great cost to themselves. Consider the case of Éric Fortier of Gatineau, Quebec. In July of 2001, Fortier and his partner were camping with another couple in Katannilik Territorial Park Reserve in Nunavut when a polar bear attempted to claw its way through their tent. The animal was driven away by their screams but it later returned and attacked the other couple, savagely mauling them. Fortier, armed with nothing but a pocket knife, attacked the bear until it retreated into the woods. He and his partner then paddled eight kilometres across a river to find help for his friends, who later recovered. He was awarded the Medal of Bravery by the Governor General in 2002.

Would you confront an aggressive polar bear to help a friend? Would you place yourself in danger to help a complete stranger? How many people do you think would do so? What makes people help other people? Social psychologists have studied various factors that influence whether people will help others or not.

The Bystander Effect Late one night in 1964, Kitty Genovese was walking from her car to her apartment building in New York City after coming home from her job as a bar manager. As she approached the building, a man accosted her and stabbed her in the back. She screamed, "Oh my God, he stabbed me! Help me!" Fearing that her cries for help would be heeded, her attacker ran away. Lights went on in the apartment building, and a few people looked out, but no one called the police or came to help her. The man returned and renewed his attack. Genovese's screams were heard by numerous people, but still no one came to help. The 28-year-old Genovese died from her wounds before someone summoned the police. In another case in 2002, 19-year-old Breann Voth was attacked and killed in Port Coquitlam, British Columbia, while on her way to work. Her screams were heard by local residents for about ten minutes, yet no one called for help.

Even though these two cases happened in different cities, nearly four decades apart, the similarities are striking. How could so many people have ignored the screams of a young woman being so brutally attacked? What kind of attribution—either dispositional or situational—best explains this behaviour?

The Kitty Genovese case received a lot of publicity, and it spurred a great deal of research in social psychology. John Darley and Bibb Latané (1968) used the scientific method to try to understand why no one came to Genovese's rescue. First, they conducted an experiment in which research participants heard another participant having a seizure over an intercom (what they actually heard was an audiotape). The researchers led some of the participants to believe that they were the only ones hearing the person in distress, while others thought many participants heard it. Of those who thought they alone heard the distressed man, 85 percent tried to help. Of those who thought many other people also heard the distressed man, only 62 percent tried to help. The researchers concluded there is no safety in numbers. Specifically, the greater the number of bystanders who witness an emergency, the less likely any one of them will help. Latané and Darley called this phenomenon the **bystander effect.**

bystander effect
a phenomenon in which the greater the number of bystanders who witness an emergency, the less likely any one of them is to help.

In 1964, Kitty Genovese was attacked and killed while residents of her New York neighbourhood, shown in this photo taken after the murder, ignored her screams.
How does the research on the bystander effect explain why no one came to her aid?

One explanation of the bystander effect involves *diffusion of responsibility;* that is, when there are many people around, an individual's responsibility to act seems decreased. It makes sense when you think about it. When you alone witness an emergency, you know that you are the only source of aid. If several people are present, however, you might not regard it as your responsibility to help the person in need. Someone else might take care of it. Indeed, this is probably why no one helped poor Kitty Genovese. A lot of people were around, so everyone assumed "somebody else must have called the police!"

Several factors influence whether or not someone will intervene in an emergency. One is whether people actually notice the event. When people are in a hurry, they are less likely to notice an emergency (Darley & Batson, 1973). Moreover, when many people are present and doing nothing, a person is less likely to interpret an event as an emergency. This is an example of informational social influence, because in this ambiguous situation people look to others for clues as to what should be done. If everyone else is doing nothing, then maybe there's no emergency after all.

Even if we notice an event and interpret it as an emergency, we must decide that it is our responsibility to do something. In addition to a diffusion of responsibility, people often do a cost-benefit analysis to determine whether helping is worth the cost. Sometimes it is dangerous to be helpful. If you get to this step and decide it is worth helping, you still might not know how to help. For example, if you witness someone having a heart attack and want to help, you might not know CPR. Even if you've passed all the previous hurdles, you may not be able to help after all, though you could still call 911.

LO12 **Altruism** The term **altruism** refers to a selfless concern for and giving of aid to others. Because altruists often expose themselves to greater danger than those who selfishly protect themselves, helping poses risks to personal survival. For this reason, altruism makes no sense from an evolutionary perspective (Dawkins, 1989). So why do humans and other animals sometimes engage in altruistic behaviour?

altruism selfless attitudes and behaviour toward others.

Evolutionary theory offers two explanations for altruistic behaviour: kin selection and reciprocal altruism. **Kin selection** is the evolutionary mechanism that prompts individuals to help their close relatives or kin so that they will survive to reproduce and pass on related genes to their offspring (Hamilton, 1964). For instance, a dominant macaque monkey will share food with a subordinate monkey only if the two are close relatives (Belisle & Chapais, 2001; Furuichi, 1983). Individuals who help close relatives may be risking their lives, but they are also increasing the chances that if they do not survive, at least some of their genes will survive in their relatives.

kin selection individuals' tendency to help their own relatives as a way of ensuring that their genes get passed on.

Kin selection is more common in social animals, such as bees. Greenberg (1979) bred bees to have varied degrees of genetic relatedness and then released them near a nest watched by guard bees. Because the nest was crowded, not everyone could get in. Guard bees were much more likely to let in the bees that were closely related than those that were distantly related. There is evidence for kin selection in humans too. Burnstein and colleagues (1994) asked people to specify whom they would be most likely to help in life-and-death situations and

From an evolutionary point of view, true altruism has no clear survival advantage.

How can we explain altruistic behaviour?

non–life-and-death situations. People reported they would be more likely to help a relative in life-and-death situations, but not in non–life-and-death situations. In fact, when people are rescuing others from a burning building, they are much more likely to look for relatives first (Sime, 1983).

reciprocal altruism
the act of helping others in the hope that they will help us in the future.

Another evolutionary explanation for altruistic behaviour is **reciprocal altruism,** helping others in the hope that they will help you in the future (Trivers, 1971, 1985). It is easier for humans to survive when group members cooperate, and reciprocal altruism promotes such cooperation. That is, you might help another member of your group if you believe that you might benefit in some way as a result. From an evolutionary perspective, reciprocal altruism should be most common in species that are social, for only animals that live in groups have opportunities to benefit from reciprocal helping.

However, evolutionary mechanisms do not adequately explain all altruistic behaviour. Some social psychologists argue that in our relations with others we try to maximize our gains and minimize our losses (Thibaut & Kelly, 1959). This is the essence of **social exchange theory,** a non-evolutionary explanation of altruistic behaviour that says we help others because such behaviour can be rewarding, but we will help only if the rewards will outweigh the costs. How can helping be rewarding? For one thing, helping someone in need relieves our own distress at witnessing suffering. Also, helping someone is an investment in the future, because it is possible that they will help us when we need help. In this sense, social exchange is essentially the same as reciprocal altruism.

social exchange theory
the idea that we help others when we decide that the benefits to ourselves are likely to outweigh the costs.

Challenge Your Assumptions

True or False? People will sometimes risk their lives to help others.

True: People will sometimes put themselves at great risk to help others, without giving their own safety a second thought. These are rare acts of heroism, but they happen and are difficult to explain by current theories of altruistic behaviour.

According to social exchange theory, truly selfless altruism does not exist. What about Éric Fortier? Were his actions representative of selfless altruism? Or did he help because the guilt resulting from not helping would have been much worse for him to live with? Human and non-human primates may have both selfish and non-selfish motives for helping (de Waal & Suchak, 2010).

Whatever the cause of altruistic behaviour, psychological science is uncovering more and more evidence of the benefits of being kind and lending a hand. First, helping feels good, better than indulging ourselves, whether we are talking about sacrifices we make in our most intimate relationships (Kogan et al., 2010) or giving gifts or resources to strangers (Dunn, Aknin, & Norton, 2008). In fact, the joy of giving is seen even in toddlers (Aknin, Hamlin, & Dunn, 2012). A large-scale interview and questionnaire study showed that helping behaviour may be beneficial for health—it may help buffer against the effects of stress (Poulin, Brown, Dillard, & Smith, 2013). Specifically, the researchers found an overall connection between stress and mortality in the five-year period following the study: The more stress people experienced, the more likely they were to be dead five years after the study started—with a crucial exception. If people reported that they regularly lent a hand to others, this stress-mortality link was broken.

There are other benefits to being kind. When given the opportunity to think of others—to be generous, as it were—people are more likely to change behaviour if they see that the behaviour change is for the general good. In one clever but very simple study, Grant and Hoffman (2011) examined whether such an approach might help medical professionals increase hand washing (one of the major factors in preventing the spread of disease in health care settings). In one bathroom, they put a sign encouraging all employees to wash their hands, as it would help them (the employees themselves) not get sick. In another bathroom, they printed a similar sign, but this one said it would help them prevent others from getting sick. They only changed one word in the sign to change this meaning. They then kept track of how much soap was used in each bathroom, as a measure of hand washing. Surprisingly, more soap was used in the bathroom in which the sign emphasized the effects of hand washing behaviour on the health of others, which indicates that concern for others provided a greater motivation for behaviour change.

empathy
the ability to share the feelings of others and understand their situations.

Empathy C. Daniel Batson (1991) has proposed that true selfless helping occurs only when there is empathy. **Empathy** can be defined as sharing feeling and understanding about another person's situation. According to Batson's **empathy-altruism hypothesis,** people will offer selfless help only when they truly empathize with the victim. Consider the following example: A professor is talking with a student in his office. While pleading with the professor to postpone an upcoming test, the student begins to cry. Reacting to the student's distress, the professor becomes upset as well. The professor decides to help the student by postponing the test. Batson and his colleagues believe that two different motivations may underlie the professor's behaviour.

empathy-altruism hypothesis the idea that people help others selflessly only when they feel empathy for them.

The first motivation Batson calls the *egoistic motivation.* The professor may help the student in order to relieve the professor's own distress. This is not true altruism and would fit with social exchange theory, where the reward is reduction of distress. A second motivation, *empathic motivation,* may be that the professor's behaviour may spring from an altruistic desire to reduce the distress of the person in need. Unlike the person who is the egoistic helper, the empathic helper is serving another with the primary goal of helping the student through the crisis.

In order to understand the brain mechanisms of empathy, Singer and colleagues examined brain activation during a person's real pain experience and when witnessing the pain of a loved one (Singer et al., 2004). They created an experiment to study the response to a loved one's pain in the confines of an fMRI scanner. Singer obtained measures of functional brain activity in the female partner of a couple while the woman herself received a painful stimulus to her hand and then while she witnessed her male partner receiving the same painful stimulus (see Figure 14.9). The actual pain stimulus, which was a mild electric shock delivered by an electrode attached to the hand, activated a well-known pain circuit in the brain, involving the somatosensory cortex, insula, anterior cingulate cortex (ACC), thalamus, and cerebellum. When her partner was experiencing pain, only those structures in the pain circuit that are triggered by the emotional aspect of pain showed activation, most notably the front region of the insula and the ACC. So, when a partner experiences pain, people truly do feel it *with* their loved ones. Increasing evidence across various studies now supports the idea that the insula and anterior cingulate are key neural structures involved in empathy (Berhardt & Singer, 2012).

One week after the shooting on Parliament Hill in October 2014, a mosque in Cold Lake, Alberta, was vandalized, with windows broken and "Go Home" spray-painted on the walls. In response, dozens of people from the town showed up to help clean up and repair the damage. Some even posted signs of support for the Muslim community, such as "You are home" and "Love your neighbour."

How would you explain the actions of these community volunteers?

Research Process

1 Research Question

If empathy really is feeling what another person is feeling, are pain circuits in the brain activated similarly when someone feels pain and when empathizing with a loved one's pain?

2 Method

In a quasi-experimental study, Tania Singer and colleagues (2004) used fMRI to measure brain activation in women when they received a mild shock to the hand and also while they witnessed their partner receiving the same painful stimulus.

The partner sat next to the MRI scanner. The woman and her partner placed their right hands on a tilted board, which allowed the woman to see her and her partner's right hand with help of a mirror. On a large screen the woman saw visual cues that indicated whether she or her partner would get low pain or high pain. When administered, the shock lasted for 2 seconds.

3 Results

A mild shock was administered 3.5 seconds after the scan began, lasting for 2 seconds. The scans showed that self-pain activated all the structures in the pain circuit, while the partner's pain (the empathic pain condition) mainly activated the structures typically involved only in the emotional aspect of pain (anterior cingulate cortex, or ACC, and the insula).

The graphs show brain activation for the women as a change from a baseline (pain-free) state.

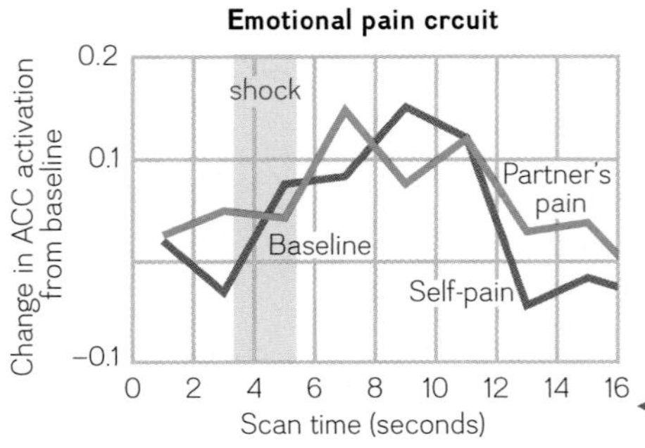

The similarity in patterns of activation in the ACC across these two conditions suggests that the women empathized with—that is, *felt*—their partner's pain.

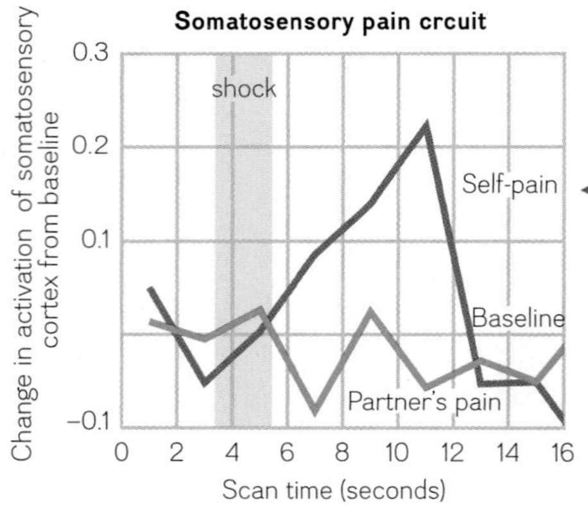

The difference in patterns of activation in the somatosensory cortex suggests that the women did not experience the same sensory aspects of pain when their partners received the shock as when they received the shock themselves.

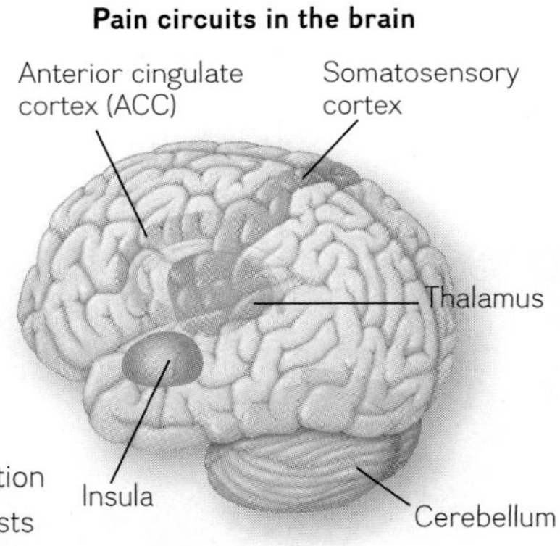

4 Conclusion

Experienced pain activates all pain networks in the brain (emotional and sensory), but empathic pain activates only the emotional pain network. When a loved one experiences pain, people truly do feel their loved one's pain, but that feeling may be more emotional than sensory.

FIGURE **14.9**

FEELING ANOTHER'S PAIN. Empathy for a loved one's pain involves brain circuitry that is activated by real pain. (*Source:* T. Singer, B. Seymour, J.O. O'Doherty, H. Kaube, R.J. Dolan, and C.D. Frith. 2004. Empathy for pain involves the affective but not sensory components of pain. *Science, 303,* 1157–1162.)

LO13 **Cooperation** Another type of prosocial action people engage in is cooperation. **Cooperation** occurs when two or more people or groups of people come together, working interdependently towards a common goal that will benefit everyone (Pennexr, Dovidio, Piliavin, & Schroeder, 2005). For example, you might form a study group with a few other psychology students to help one another pass a difficult final exam. Researchers often study cooperation by using **social dilemmas,** or situations in which the goals of the individual conflict with the goals of the group (Penner et al., 2005; Van Lange, Joireman, Parks, & Van Dij, 2013). Consider the following example. In the summer months, some communities face water shortages and impose watering restrictions, encouraging people to take shorter showers, not to water their lawns, and use washing machines and other appliances less frequently. Individual homeowners may not comply with these recommendations because they are inconvenient. But if everyone ignores the water restrictions, eventually the water could run out, leading to serious problems for everyone. This example highlights the two key aspects to all social dilemmas: (1) each individual benefits most from engaging in a non-cooperative behaviour (i.e., a behaviour that doesn't benefit the group) and (2) together, as a group, all individuals are better off if they engage in cooperative behaviour than if they don't (Dawes, 1980; Penner et al., 2005). Many of the most important environmental issues facing our global community today, such as overpopulation, global warming, and depletion of natural resources, are examples of social dilemmas (Van Lange et al., 2013).

cooperation
a type of prosocial behaviour in which two or more individuals, or groups, work together towards a common goal.

social dilemma
a situation in which the interests of the individual conflict with the interests of the group.

One way researchers study social dilemmas in the laboratory is by using a game called the *prisoner's dilemma*. Imagine that you and a friend have committed a serious crime. You are caught by the police and interrogated in separate rooms so that you cannot communicate with each other. The police are convinced you committed the crime but they need to build their case. You are told that if you confess and your partner does not, you will go free but your partner will get a ten-year sentence. If your partner confesses but you do not, you will get

A complicated social dilemma? On the one hand, mining oil from the Alberta tar sands benefits Canada's economy. On the other, it contributes to global warming by increasing greenhouse gas emissions, which affects all countries on the planet.

Can you identify some other social dilemmas?

a ten-year sentence and your partner will go free. If both of you confess, you will both receive a moderate sentence (five years). If neither of you confess, each of you will be convicted of a lesser crime and receive a light sentence (one year). In this game, you have to make a choice without consulting your partner—you can either confess or not. What would you do?

Clearly, the best outcome for you is to rat out your friend and confess (i.e., non-cooperative strategy). Of course, you run the risk that your friend will also confess and you'll receive a five-year sentence. But if you remain silent, you could end up receiving the long ten-year sentence if your friend confesses. The choice that will guarantee the best *mutual* outcome—short sentences for both—is the cooperative one where neither of you confess (see Figure 14.10).

The prisoner's dilemma has been used in hundreds of studies (Dawes, 1991). Some variations on the original game include repeating the game numerous times, playing with more than two people, playing between groups or networks of people, and using tokens, money, or course points instead of prisoner outcomes.

What happens when people play this game? Overall, there is a tendency to respond non-cooperatively (Lodewijkx, Rabbie, & Visser, 2006; Sally, 1995), but several contextual factors promote mutual cooperation. For instance, allowing people to communicate their intended choices to other game players increases cooperation (Dawes, McTavish, & Shaklee, 1977). Higher levels of cooperation occur when the game is played multiple times as opposed to one time, and when the game is played as a dyad rather than in larger groups (Sally, 1995; Tindale,

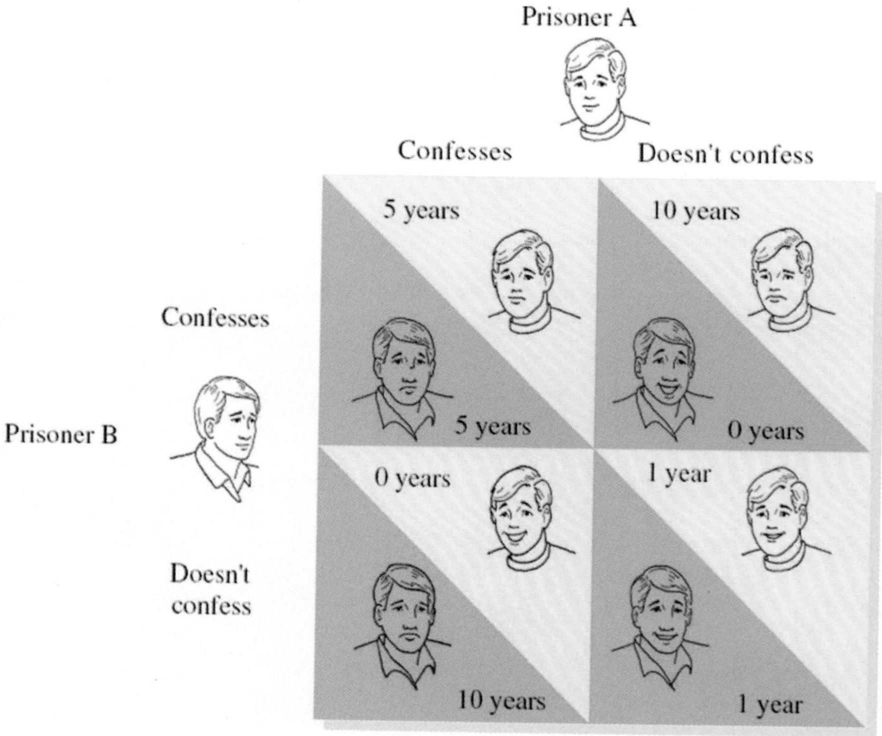

FIGURE **14.10**

THE PRISONER'S DILEMMA. In the original game, each of two criminals is offered immunity from prosecution in exchange for a confession. If neither confesses, both get off with a light sentence (lower right). If both confess, both receive a moderate sentence (upper left). However, if one criminal confesses and the other one doesn't, the confessing criminal goes free while the silent one spends years in jail. (*Source:* Myers & Smith (2015). *Exploring Social Psychology,* 4th Canadian ed. Figure 17-1, p. 259.)

How would you respond to this social dilemma?

Talbot, & Martinez, 2013). Also, influencing participants' perceptions of the game by simply changing its name can affect cooperation. In one study, participants who played the prisoner's dilemma, labelled as "the Community Game," cooperated twice as often as those who played the same game when it was labelled as "the Wall Street Game" (Liberman, Samuels, & Ross, 2004). Cooperation also increases when participants are able to reward one another for cooperative behaviour (Balliett, Mulder, & Van Lange, 2011). Personality factors play a role, too. People with a prosocial, cooperative orientation and those who more easily trust others tend to cooperate more in social dilemmas (Balliet & Van Lange, 2013; Bogaert, Boone, & Declerck, 2008). Moreover, people who initiate cooperation and always choose the cooperative strategy can influence the perceptions and actions of their group members, prompting some group members to cooperate more than they might otherwise (Weber & Murningham, 2008).

Liking, Attraction, and Love

What makes one person want to be with another? Is this process different for friends and lovers? What is love, anyway? In this section we will see how psychologists tackle questions of the human heart. Let's first examine how we come to like and be attracted to other people, and then we'll take a look at love.

LO14 **Familiarity, Similarity, and Attraction** Sometimes we like ideas or objects simply because they are familiar to us. *Mere exposure,* or direct experience with an object, idea, or person, increases our overall preference for it (Zajonc, 1968). The things that we come to like from exposure can be trivial, such as abstract symbols, or very meaningful, such as human faces. For example, Zajonc (1968) showed people nonsense words 1, 2, 5, 10, or 25 times; the more often they saw a word, the more they reported liking it. This effect was also true for repeated presentations of photographs of men's faces. In a later study, Zajonc showed that brief interactions with others increased liking between university students, even though the students did not speak to each other. The more frequent the interactions, the more the participants liked each other (Saegert et al., 1973). This effect is even more pronounced when participants have the opportunity to chat. In one experiment, strangers were instructed to speak about two or six topics, and the more they got to know each other, the more they liked each other at the end of the experiment (Reis et al., 2011).

People with similar ideas, values, and interests are more likely to like one another and share satisfying, long-lasting relationships (Keller, Thiessen, & Young, 1996). For example, researchers randomly assigned male university students to be roommates in a certain dorm at the beginning of the year. Those roommates who became real friends had common backgrounds, similar majors, and similar political viewpoints (Newcomb, 1961). People report that they like and want to help others who have similar personalities, attitudes, or beliefs (Wakimoto & Fujihara, 2004; Westmaas & Silver, 2006). There is a moderately strong correlation between the personality of a person's ideal partner and their own personality, and married couples also have strongly correlated age, levels of intelligence, and imaginativeness (Botwin, Buss, & Shackelford, 1997; Keller et al., 1996).

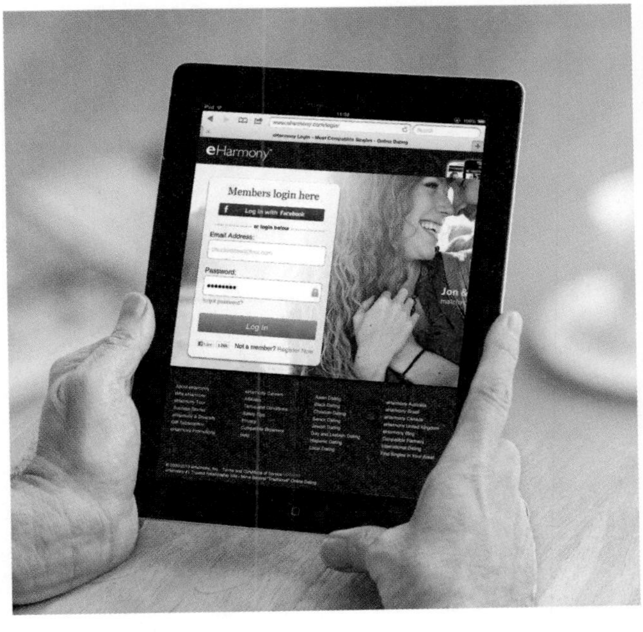

Can you meet your soul mate online? Although online dating has the advantage of providing access to large numbers of potential partners, there is *no* evidence to suggest that relationships developed online through dating sites are superior to those developed offline (Finkel, Eastwick, Karney, Reis, & Sprecher, 2012). Indeed, relationship research suggests that one of most important predictors of relationship success is how partners interact with each other—information online matching algorithms don't use!

One of the strongest factors influencing how much we like people is how much we think they like us, a phenomenon known as *reciprocal liking*. If we believe that another person does not like us, then we probably will not like them, despite how familiar and similar they might be. Reciprocal liking appears to influence our impressions very quickly—in one study of university students, reciprocal liking was evident with groups of students who interacted for only ten minutes (Chapdelaine et al., 1994). A more recent study had undergraduate students interact for only four minutes as part of a speed-dating session and then rate their feelings of romantic desire and chemistry. Results showed that if someone desired their date, these feelings were also reciprocated (Eastwick et al., 2007).

Physical Attractiveness Humans worldwide value physical attractiveness in partners (Buss, 1999; Etcoff, 1999; Miller, 2000). But what, exactly, is considered to be attractive? In research on attractiveness, people rate average and symmetrical faces as more attractive than less average and less symmetrical faces. *Average,* in this case, does not mean "common." Rather, *average* means that the size, location, and shape of each feature of the face—nose, eyes, mouth, cheekbones—are mathematically average in the population. They are neither too big nor too small, neither too far apart nor too close together. Look, for example, at the faces in Figure 14.11. These faces were produced by computer technology that morphed images of several real faces together. As more and more faces were averaged, people rated the faces as more and more attractive. People rated the eight-face composite as more attractive than the four-face composite; the 16-face composite as more attractive

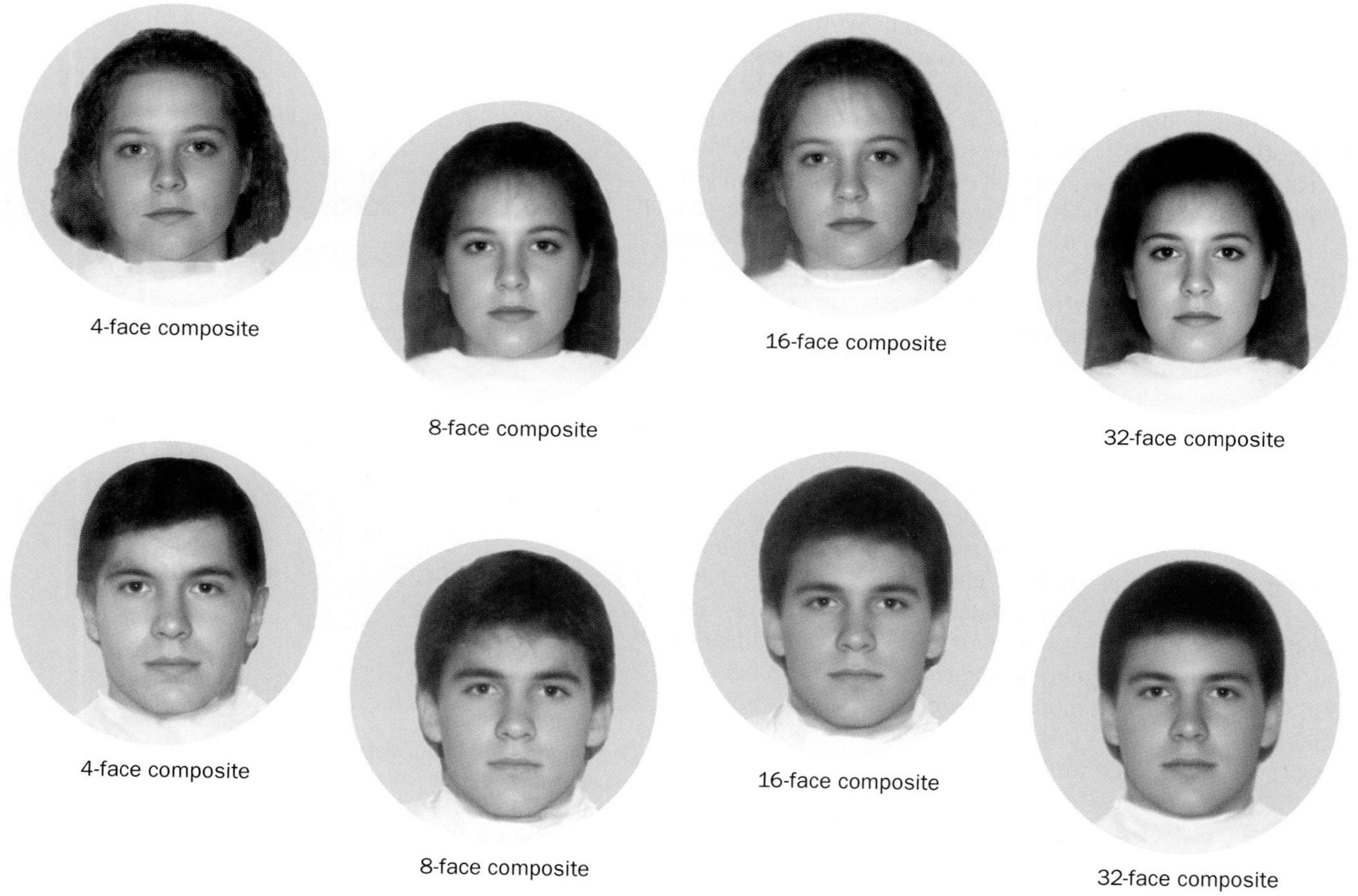

FIGURE **14.11**

RATING PHYSICAL ATTRACTIVENESS. The more faces that are morphed into one image, the more they move toward having average features. As they become more average in features, the faces are perceived as increasing in attractiveness.

than the eight; and the 32-face composite as more attractive than the 16 (Langlois & Roggman, 1990; Langlois, Roggman, & Musselman, 1994). Although exact standards for beauty vary by culture, there is much more agreement than disagreement between cultures in that average faces are preferred and rated as most attractive all over the world (Langlois & Roggman, 1990; Cunningham et al., 1995). Furthermore, infants as young as six or nine months of age also tend to prefer average faces over others, although they are too young for other people to have had much influence over their face preferences (Hoss & Langlois, 2003).

Averaged faces tend to be more symmetrical, and people seem to prefer symmetry when they rate faces for attractiveness (Etcoff, 1999). Moreover, symmetry is a rough indicator of genetic fitness; that is, symmetrical faces and bodies are signs of fewer genetic mutations (Miller, 2000).

Challenge Your Assumptions

True or False? Attractive faces are anything but average.

False: Probably for evolutionary reasons regarding fitness, people the world over tend to find faces that mathematically average the features of many faces the most attractive.

Sexual Attraction and Mate Selection What qualities do you look for in a prospective sexual partner? **Sexual strategies theory** suggests that men and women often approach relationships differently (Buss & Schmitt, 1993). In virtually all societies, men and women engage in both short-term matings (affairs, one-night stands) and long-term matings (marriages, extended companionships). Both are effective ways to increase one's reproductive fitness, but each strategy has strengths and weaknesses. Sex differences in attraction arise because *parental investment* is greater for women than for men (Trivers, 1972). Consequently, men devote a larger portion of their total mating effort to short-term mating than do women (Buss, 1999).

sexual strategies theory
the idea that men and women face different problems when they seek out mates, and so they often approach relationships in very different ways.

Buss (1999) found that men report wanting an average of 18 different partners throughout their lifetime, whereas women report only wanting four or five. Men value qualities that may signal fertility and accessibility (e.g., large breasts, wide hips compared to waist, youth), especially in short-term partners. This is less true in evaluating long-term partners. Women, in contrast, value men who can provide resources to support their offspring.

Connection

Men are more likely than women to be interested in casual sex.

See Chapter 11, LO4.

Mate selection factors might drive sexual partnerships, but these evolutionary pressures operate outside conscious awareness. Once people mate, it is the love that may develop between two people that keeps them together. But what is love?

LO15 **Love** As a concept, love is not easy to define. It takes many different forms and means different things to different people at different times in their lives.

Types of Love. Humans love in many different ways. We love our parents, lovers, friends, brothers and sisters, children, dogs, lattes, and music. How do we account for the variations? One well-known theory is Robert Sternberg's **triangular theory of love** (Sternberg, 1986). Sternberg proposed that three components—intimacy, passion, and commitment, in various combinations—can explain all the forms of human love (see Figure 14.12). *Intimacy* refers to close, connected, and bonded feelings in loving relationships. *Passion* refers to the drives that lead to romance, physical attraction, and sexual consummation and is accompanied by physiological changes and arousal. *Commitment* refers to both the decision to love someone—or not—and the decision to commit to love for the long term. Numerous studies support these three components (e.g., Hendrick & Hendrick, 1989; Sternberg, 1997). Research suggests that commitment is the most powerful predictor of long-term relationship satisfaction (Acker & David, 1992).

triangular theory of love
Sternberg's idea that three components (intimacy, passion, and commitment), in various combinations, can explain all the forms of human love.

Sternberg (1986) suggested that these three components are present in different amounts for different kinds of love. *Companionate love* exists when intimacy and commitment are high and passion is low. In *passionate love,* intimacy and passion are high and commitment is low. *Lust* is characterized by a lot of passion but no intimacy or commitment. For example, arranged marriages are all about commitment, at least in the beginning, with no intimacy or passion.

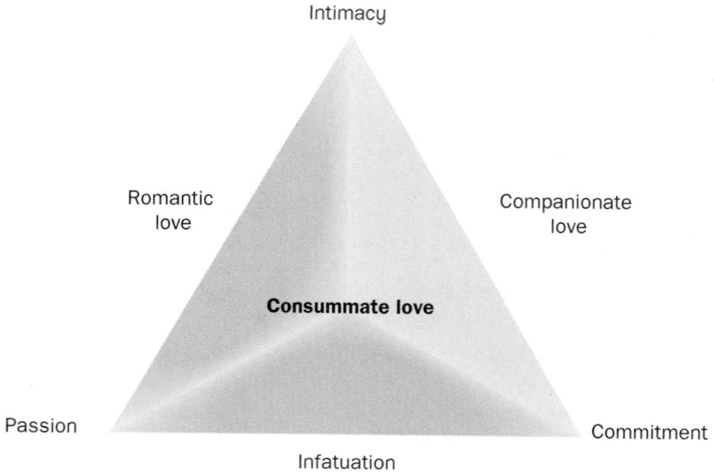

FIGURE **14.12**

STERNBERG'S TRIANGULAR THEORY OF LOVE. In Sternberg's model, all types of love are made up of three components: intimacy, passion, and commitment. Each type of love consists of a different balance of the three components. When all three exist in equal proportions, consummate love exists. (*Source:* Sternberg, 1986.)

Love as Attachment. Love is also closely connected to a well-known psychological phenomenon: attachment. Attachment, an important concept in human development, is an affection-based bond between infants and their primary caregivers that serves to protect infants from threats to their survival (Bowlby, 1969). Early research on attachment distinguished among three different attachment styles: secure, anxious-avoidant, and anxious-resistant (Ainsworth et al., 1978), as described in Chapter 10.

According to Cynthia Hazan and Phillip Shaver (1987), the attachment system established when we are infants appears to guide our adult relationships with others, including our intimate partners. Hazan and Shaver argued that the infant–caregiver attachment system underlies the important dynamics and individual differences in adult romantic relationships. By categorizing people's infant–caregiver attachment style based on an adult attachment interview, they found that securely attached adults report that they easily get close to others, readily trust others, and have more satisfying romantic relationships. Anxious-resistant adults tend to have less satisfying relationships, are more preoccupied with them, and fear that their partners do not want the intimacy they desire. Avoidant adults are uncomfortable being close to others and have less satisfying relationships (Hazan & Shaver, 1987).

Connection

Attachment is a bidirectional relationship requiring the active participation of infants and caregivers.

See Chapter 10, LO6.

Hazan and Shaver's model of attachment has been more recently refined by Kim Bartholomew at Simon Fraser University. She proposes that adult attachment styles can be categorized along two dimensions: self-image and image of others. In other words, individuals can be categorized based upon the extent that they feel worthy of love (positive versus negative self-image) and the degree to which they believe others will provide love and support (positive versus negative image of others). This categorization yields four distinct attachment styles, which are outlined in Figure 14.13. According to this model, individuals who have a positive image of the self and of others are classified as *secure* and tend to have satisfying romantic relationships. Those with a negative self-image but a positive view of others are classified as *preoccupied*, and tend to rely upon others' evaluations for their sense of self-worth, which is associated with high reliance on others in relationships. This attachment style is characterized by high levels of emotional expressiveness—for instance, individuals who score high on this style tend to cry more frequently. The *dismissing* style is defined as a positive self-image paired with a negative image of others, and it is correlated with low intimacy and self-disclosure in romantic relationships. In contrast to the preoccupied style, individuals high in the dismissing style tend to be confident and low on emotional expressiveness. A negative self-image combined with negative view of others is defined as a *fearful* attachment style. In many ways, romantic relationships with

Image of Others \ Self-Image	Positive	Negative
Positive	**Secure** Satisfying relationships, comfortable with intimacy (47%)	**Preoccupied** High reliance upon others, high emotional expressiveness, low self-confidence (14%)
Negative	**Dismissing** Dismissing of intimacy, high self-confidence, low self-disclosure (18%)	**Fearful** Fearful of intimacy, low self-confidence and disclosure (21%)

FIGURE **14.13**

THE FOUR-CATEGORY MODEL OF ADULT ATTACHMENT STYLES. Attachment styles are categorized based upon individuals' evaluation of the self and others, yielding four distinct attachment styles. According to this model, these dimensions characterize romantic relationships. The percentages in parentheses indicate the prevalence of each style in the population of undergraduate students used to validate the model. (*Source:* Bartholomew & Horowitz, 1991.)

this style are similar to those of the dismissing type, in that these individuals also avoid intimacy and do not disclose readily to others. However, like preoccupied individuals, fearful types tend to have low self-confidence and feel that they have little control in their relationships (Bartholomew & Horowitz, 1991). This four-category model appears to better characterize romantic relationships and is more widely used than Hazan and Shaver's original model.

Quick Quiz 14.3: Social Relations

1. Out-group homogeneity is the tendency to
   a. see people outside our group as looking or acting alike.
   b. see people inside our group as looking or acting alike.
   c. believe people outside our group think the same way we do.
   d. believe people inside our group think the same way we do.
2. Brandon believes women are not very good at math. However, as a computer scientist, he has always been able to treat women the same way he treats men at work. Which of the following best describes Brandon?
   a. Brandon is prejudiced against women.
   b. Brandon's behaviour is an example of discrimination.
   c. Brandon's beliefs are based on stereotypes.
   d. Both a and c are correct.
3. Measuring how long it takes a person to pair positive or negative terms with particular ethnic groups is used in social psychology as a measure of
   a. explicit racism.
   b. implicit racism.
   c. stereotypes.
   d. reaction time.
4. Sam was driving his car and recklessly caused an accident that seriously injured a driver in another car. Susan insulted an acquaintance because she believed the acquaintance had questioned her honesty. According to the definition of aggression in the book, who behaved aggressively?
   a. Sam
   b. Susan
   c. both Sam and Susan
   d. neither Sam nor Susan
5. The bystander effect says
   a. the more people who observe a person in need of help, the less likely any one person will help.
   b. the fewer people who observe a person in need of help, the less likely any one person will help.
   c. people stand by and wait for help when they need it.
   d. people are more likely to rescue people who are most closely related to themselves.
6. The world over, faces that have ________ are perceived as the most attractive.
   a. the smallest nose
   b. blue eyes
   c. features that are average in their dimensions
   d. eyes furthest apart

Answers can be found at the end of the chapter.

Evaluating Connections in Social Behaviour

Analysis of the Jonestown Cult

The tragic mass suicide of hundreds of members of the People's Temple in Jonestown, Guyana, illustrates many of the social-psychological concepts discussed in this chapter. In late November 1978, under the direction of the Rev. Jim Jones, members of this group fed a poison-laced drink to their children and then drank it themselves. More than 900 adults and children died; most were found lying together, arm in arm.

Most of the members of the People's Temple went willingly to their deaths. Why? After years of indoctrination and isolation from mainstream society, they had been led into complete commitment to Jones and the People's Temple. Jonestown had all the hallmarks of a cult. A **cult** is an extremist group led by a charismatic, totalitarian leader in which coercive methods are used to prevent members from leaving the group.

If we apply social-psychological theory to an analysis of these events, they become more comprehensible

cult
an extremist group led by a charismatic, totalitarian leader who uses coercive methods to prevent members from leaving the group.

because we can see that the members of the People's Temple were not very different from us. Four principles of social psychology—persuasion, conformity, obedience, and cognitive dissonance—can shed light on the tragedy of Jonestown (Osherow, 1999).

JIM JONES AND THE PEOPLE'S TEMPLE

Jim Jones founded the People's Temple in Indiana in 1958, preaching a message of brotherhood, racial integration, and freedom from poverty. His group helped feed and employ the poor. Jones presented a public image of a beloved leader who promoted a vision of racial harmony.

Throughout the 1960s, the group grew in size and popularity. Rumours surfaced that Jones used coercive methods to keep people from leaving the People's Temple. In the mid-1970s, after a great deal of bad publicity, Jones and his followers moved to a jungle outpost he called Jonestown in Guyana, South America. In 1978, U.S. Congressman Leo Ryan heard reports that the People's Temple was holding members against their will. He led a delegation of government officials, reporters, and concerned relatives to Jonestown to talk with residents about how they liked living there. Two families secretly informed Ryan that they wanted out. As Ryan's party and these two "defector" families tried to board their plane for the United States, Temple gunmen ambushed and killed five people, including Congressman Ryan. This ambush precipitated the mass suicide, an act that Jones and his followers had practised and rehearsed many times. It was their final act of rebellion against the system that they believed had forced them into exile.

THE ROLE OF PERSUASION

Jones was a charismatic figure. He sought out people who needed to hear his message: the urban poor, minorities, the elderly, ex-addicts, and convicts. Potential members of the People's Temple first encountered an almost idyllic scene in which blacks and whites lived, worked, and worshiped together in total harmony. Guests were greeted warmly and invited to share a meal. Jones also gave them miracles. He cured diseases; he made predictions that came true with uncanny frequency. Members were motivated to believe in Jones; they appreciated the racial harmony, sense of purpose, and relief from feelings of worthlessness that the People's Temple provided.

Jim Jones

Jones carefully managed his public image. He used letter writing and the political clout of hundreds of cult members to praise him and impress the politicians and reporters who supported the People's Temple as well as to criticize and intimidate its opponents. Most important, Jones limited the information available to members.

THE ROLE OF CONFORMITY AND OBEDIENCE

Conformity played a role in the People's Temple from the outset. Even getting into the group was not easy. People underwent a strict initiation process that actually drew members more firmly into the group. As they became increasingly involved in the People's Temple, they committed themselves more strongly to the group because they were required to donate their property and 25 percent of their income to the church. Before they entered the meeting room for each service, they wrote self-incriminating letters that were turned over to the church. If anyone objected, the refusal was interpreted as a "lack of faith" in Jones. All of these rules made the group more important than the individuals, making conformity to the group all the more likely.

As he gradually increased his demands, Jones also exposed cult members to the concept of a "final ritual," mass suicide. Rehearsals of this ritual served to test followers and their faith in Jones. In essence, Jones was making use of what social psychologists call the *foot-in-the-door* technique by getting people to agree to a moderate request (i.e., rehearsal). Once cult members had agreed to engage in frequent rehearsals of mass suicide, it became easier for them to go through with the real thing.

The suicides at Jonestown can be viewed as the product of obedience—people complying with the orders of a leader and reacting to the threat of force. In the People's Temple, whatever Jim Jones commanded, the members did. Jones was a forceful authority. By the early 1970s, the members of the People's Temple lived in constant fear of severe punishment—brutal beatings coupled with public humiliation—for committing trivial or even inadvertent offences. Milgram's experiments show us that the power of authority need not be so explicitly threatening to create compliance with demands. Nor does the consensus of the group need to be coercive, as Asch's experiments on conformity indicate. Yet Jones's power was both threatening and coercive.

Jones used threats to impose the discipline and devotion he demanded, and he took steps to eliminate any behaviour that might encourage resistance among his followers. As

These are some of the victims of a mass suicide at Jonestown, Guyana, in 1978. People's Temple leader Jim Jones used his status as an authority figure to persuade, intimidate, and indoctrinate his followers over several years, apparently convincing them that death was the only alternative to being captured and separated from the group.

Solomon Asch found in his experiments on conformity, if just one confederate expressed an opinion different from that of the majority, the rate of conformity drastically declined. This is minority social influence. In the People's Temple, Jones tolerated no dissent, made sure that members had no allegiance more powerful than their loyalty to him, and tried to make the alternative of leaving the church unthinkable. Anyone who dared to dissent was terrorized as a traitor, thereby squelching the possibility of minority social influence.

How did Jones do this? He used informers who reported indiscretions, split families to prevent allegiances, and forced parents to give over their children to the Temple. He thereby created conditions in which kin selection could not promote helping between members. Similarly, Jones worked to dissolve marital bonds by forcing couples into extramarital relations (sometimes with Jones himself). "Families are part of the enemy system," Jones said, because they weakened the individual's dedication to the cause. Not surprisingly, it was very hard to leave the cult. Not being able to defect or escape from the group, people had little choice but to conform.

THE ROLE OF COGNITIVE DISSONANCE

Cognitive dissonance helps explain why cult members believed Jones to the end and why so few defected. People did not become cult members all at once. Rather, the process of justifying their choice and becoming committed to Jones unfolded slowly over the course of weeks and months, sometimes years. Jones knew what he was doing. Starting the process with harsh acts of initiation is a perfect way to get people to rationalize their otherwise embarrassing behaviour. If people don't see the group they are about to join very positively, how could they possibly justify going through such humiliation in order to get in?

Even so, how could members not seek to escape and accept killing themselves and their children so easily? These acts were the product of a situation that made dissent impossible and faith in Jones and the Temple absolute. Once they were isolated from the rest of the world at Jonestown, escape was impossible. When escape is impossible, people rationalize their predicament. The members of the People's Temple reduced their cognitive dissonance by changing their attitude to conform with their behaviour. In this case, they told themselves that Jones was great and his message was wonderful. When the time to commit suicide finally arrived, most of the members clearly drank the juice quite willingly and by their own choice, so strong was their belief in Jones and his message.

Quick Quiz 14.4: Evaluating Connections in Social Psychology

1. The tragedy of Jonestown, where more than 900 committed mass suicide, can be explained by four principles of social psychology: persuasion, conformity, ________ and ________.
   a. attraction; aggression
   b. obedience; cognitive dissonance
   c. obedience; empathy
   d. discrimination; prejudice

2. After engaging in embarrassing behaviour, many cult members came to believe in the People's Temple even more. Such a process where attitudes are strengthened to align with behaviours can probably be best explained by
   a. obedience.
   b. cognitive dissonance.
   c. empathy.
   d. conformity.

Answers can be found at the end of the chapter.

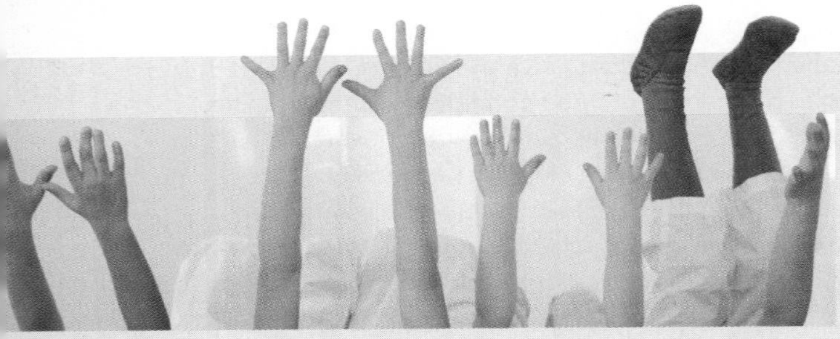

Chapter Review

SOCIAL COGNITION

- Social psychology is the study of the effects of the real or imagined presence of others on people's thoughts, feelings, and actions.
- We are constantly drawing conclusions about why people do what they do; that is, we make attributions. Sometimes we say internal qualities of the person were the cause of their behaviour. Other times we see outside forces in the environment as the cause of a person's behaviour.
- When forming opinions about others, we use schema about individuals based on what they are like or are likely to do based simply on the group they belong to. Opinions formed this way are stereotypes.
- Psychologists define attitudes as a person's favourable or unfavourable beliefs, feelings, or actions toward an object, idea, or person. People's attitudes and behaviours do not always match and are often resistant to change.
- One explanation for why and how people change their attitudes is cognitive dissonance, which is the feeling of discomfort caused by information that differs from one's conception of oneself as a reasonable and sensible person.
- Persuasion is another way in which attitudes can be changed. The elaboration likelihood model suggests attitudes change via two routes: central or peripheral.

SOCIAL INFLUENCE

- We act differently when other people are present than we do when we are alone. Sometimes our performance is improved when we are with other people; sometimes it is hindered. In addition, people adjust their behaviour in order to conform to what others are doing or to adhere to the rules of their culture.
- An individual can change the majority opinion of a group, but doing so takes perseverance and consistency.
- Obedience to authority can and has led to numerous instances of people doing things they otherwise would not, from soldiers in Nazi Germany and Abu Ghraib prison in Iraq to participants in Milgram's studies.

SOCIAL RELATIONS

- People hurt other people, help other people, and are attracted to and love other people.
- A prejudice is an attitude toward a group of people or an individual member of a group based on unfair generalizations about that group. Discrimination is negative behaviour directed towards certain people based on group membership. It is driven by prejudicial attitudes.
- Applying prejudice and discrimination to people based on their racial-ethnic group affiliations is racism. Racism operates both inside (explicitly) and outside (implicitly) our awareness.
- Aggression refers to violent behaviours that are intended to cause psychological and/or physical harm to another being. Aggression stems from a complex interplay of genetic and social forces.
- The more people who witness an accident or crime, the more likely it is that no one will call for help or intervene. This phenomenon is the bystander effect.
- People act in prosocial ways to help others in need. In life-and-death situations, kin selection explains why people are most willing to help those who are most closely related to them.
- Cooperation is another type of prosocial behaviour researchers study using the prisoner's dilemma.
- Relationships that are bound by similarities in personality, attitude, intelligence, and attractiveness tend to last the longest.
- People all over the world rate as most attractive those faces that possess average and symmetrical features. Sexual strategies theory suggests that men and women face different problems when they seek out mates, so they often approach relationships in very different ways.
- Sternberg's triangular theory of love states that all of the different forms of love each have three components: intimacy, passion, and commitment. Romantic love, for example, exists when intimacy and passion are present but commitment is absent.
- Attachment theory can be applied to adult romantic relationships. Adults with secure attachments to their partners report more satisfaction in their romantic relationships.

EVALUATING CONNECTIONS IN SOCIAL PSYCHOLOGY

- The People's Temple was considered to be a cult, which is an extremist group led by a charismatic, totalitarian leader who uses coercive methods to prevent members from leaving the group.

- Methods used by Jim Jones to ensure his followers' obedience and conformity included persuasion, rigid discipline and punishment of dissent, isolation, separation from family, and forced marital infidelity. Cult members resolved cognitive dissonance brought on by their situation through rationalization, telling themselves that Jones was a great leader with a wonderful message.

Quick Quiz Answers

Quick Quiz 14.1: 1. d 2. c 3. b 4. d 5. a **Quick Quiz 14.2:** 1. c 2. d 3. a 4. c
Quick Quiz 14.3: 1. a 2. d 3. b 4. b 5. a 6. c **Quick Quiz 14.4:** 1. b 2. b

Psychological Disorders

CHAPTER 15

CHAPTER OUTLINE

Challenge Your Assumptions

True or False?

- ☐ Mental disorders are relatively rare, and most families are free of mental disorders.
- ☐ Most people who suffer from mental illness are dangerous.
- ☐ Schizophrenia is a disorder of split personalities.
- ☐ Extreme stress can make you depressed.
- ☐ All the great artists in history can be viewed as psychologically disturbed.

LEARNING OBJECTIVES

LO1 List the criteria that distinguish "different" from "disordered" behaviour.

LO2 Describe the strengths and weaknesses of the *DSM-5*.

LO3 Describe the main characteristics of ADHD and autism spectrum disorder and list the factors that are thought to contribute to their development.

LO4 Explain the difference between positive, negative, and cognitive symptoms of schizophrenia.

LO5 List the factors that are thought to contribute to schizophrenia.

LO6 Describe the symptoms and potential causes of depression.

LO7 Describe the symptoms and potential causes of bipolar disorder.

LO8 Describe the different classes of anxiety disorders and list factors that are thought to contribute to their development.

LO9 Define obsessive-compulsive disorder and describe what causes it.

LO10 Define PTSD and describe who is most likely to be affected by it.

LO11 Distinguish between dissociative amnesia, dissociative fugue, and dissociative identity disorder (DID), and describe the controversy surrounding DID.

LO12 Describe the symptoms of the different types of personality disorders and list factors that are thought to contribute to their development.

It was a Sunday evening in the middle of winter—December 23, 1888. The artists Vincent van Gogh and Paul Gauguin, who were close friends, had had an intense argument. Over what, we do not know. What we do know is how it ended: Van Gogh, in a fit of rage, took a razor and cut off the lower portion of his left ear. He then wrapped the earlobe in a newspaper and gave it to a prostitute named Rachel, telling her to "keep this object carefully" (Runyan, 1981).

Why Van Gogh might have committed such a bizarre act has been the subject of much speculation. We do know, however, that he was not well either mentally or physically; diagnoses of his mental disorder have ranged from epilepsy to schizophrenia to alcohol poisoning. It is difficult to know for sure what he suffered from, but we know that his younger brother committed suicide and his sister spent 40 years in an insane asylum, diagnosed with "chronic psychosis." We also know that Van Gogh walked into a field near his home, shot himself in the chest, and died two days later at the age of 37. His last words were "the sadness will last forever."

What distinguished van Gogh from most others, of course, was his incredible gift for expressing his inner world and vision in artistic form. Van Gogh's searing, intense, and powerful paintings offer a glimpse into both his mental anguish and his genius. At the very least, his paintings and his life, fraught with psychological disorder, are fascinating to study.

Indeed, psychological disorders are compelling. They demand our attention, care, understanding, and treatment. But what are these disorders and how do they come about? In this chapter, we describe many psychological disorders and explain some of what is known about how they develop. As we discuss the causes of these disorders, we will focus on explanations that intertwine the biological with the environmental (Kendler, 2005; Moffitt, Caspi, & Rutter, 2005; Uher & McGuffin, 2010). We will begin by considering what it means for behaviour to be disordered and how disorders are diagnosed. At the end of the chapter we will explore the topic of creativity and psychological disorders and consider whether artists are more likely than the general population to suffer from a psychological disorder.

LO1 LO2 DEFINING PSYCHOLOGICAL DISORDERS

Creative artists such as Van Gogh and Gauguin are different from most people. So, too, are spelling bee champs, Olympic athletes, and class valedictorians. Yet *different* does not mean *disordered*. Does a young boy who has more than 5000 baseball cards and can tell you something about every one of them suffer from a psychological disorder? What about someone who washes his hands for 45 minutes ten times a day? How do psychologists distinguish behaviour that is simply different from behaviour that is disordered?

Human behaviour is complex and highly variable. Certain ways of behaving in the world are shown by more of the population on a regular basis and seem to be well adapted for functioning well in certain environments. These might be behaviours we call *normal*. Less common ways of behaving might be revealed through exceptional talent or might not be well suited for the environment. We might consider these less common behaviours disordered if they do not function well in the world. It is with this context in mind that we use the term *psychological disorders.*

Over time, understanding of and explanations for psychological disorders have gone through many significant changes. As discussed in Chapter 1, the medical model became the prevalent explanation for psychological disorders beginning in the 19th century and has lasted until now. The primary assumption of the medical model is that mental, like physical, illnesses are best diagnosed and treated as medical illnesses. Psychiatry is a branch of medicine, so it is not a coincidence that terms such as *illness, diagnosis,* and *therapy* or *treatment* are used in the context of psychological disorders. Borrowing from medicine, in their attempt to understand and treat psychological disorders, psychologists and psychiatrists aim to group them into a smaller set of categories. The first published classification system of mental disorders was by Emil Kraepelin, a German psychiatrist, who wanted to establish the biological nature of mental illness (Alic, 2001; Shepard, 1995). His first edition of *Compendium der Psychiatrie* was published in 1883. The first official classification system for diagnosing mental disorders in North America came in the United States in 1952 with the publication of the *Diagnostic and Statistical Manual (DSM).* However, it was not until its third edition, published in 1980, that diagnoses in the *DSM* became grounded in scientific evidence and clinical observations rather than theory. Currently in its fifth edition, the *DSM-5* has continued the tradition of defining disorders based on a combination of scientific evidence and clinical observations (American Psychiatric Association [APA], 2013). Although the *DSM* is used worldwide and most especially, in North America, a recent international survey of psychologists suggests that the *International Classification of Diseases (ICD),* published by the World Health Organization (WHO, 1992), is also extensively used, and is the preferred classification system in Europe and India (Evans et al., 2013). Like the *DSM,* the *ICD* is consistently revised; it is currently in its 10th edition (*ICD-10*).

How do psychologists define *mental disorder?* Following a long-standing tradition, the *DSM-5* defines a mental disorder as a **syndrome**—a set of related conditions—of clinically significant disturbances of thoughts, feelings, or behaviours. More specifically, they argue for the "4 Ds" of determining whether something is a mental disorder (APA, 2013). There has to be

- *disturbance* of thought, emotion, or behaviour,
- *dysfunction* of biological or developmental processes,
- *distress or disability* in everyday life (especially relationships or work), and
- *deviant* thought, emotion, or behaviour, but only if also dysfunctional; deviance alone is not enough.

Let's look at each of these a little more closely. Psychological disorders are distinguished by their clinically significant *disturbance* of psychological processes of thought, emotion, and behaviour. Mental disorders are distinguished from physical disorders that affect physiological and bodily structures and processes. For example, a person who has *hypothyroidism* (an underactive thyroid gland) may exhibit symptoms of depression. In this case, if the depressive symptoms appear to be due to hypothyroidism, which is a physical disorder, then a diagnosis of major depression is *not* appropriate. *Distressing* behaviour leads to discomfort, pain, or anguish, either in the person directly or in others, especially family members. The distressing element is one reason

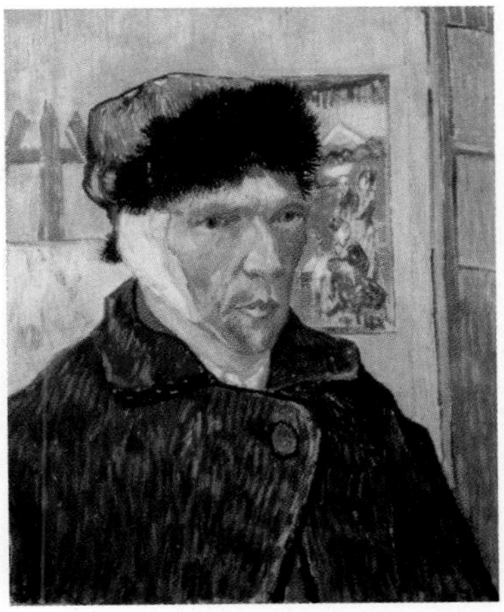

Van Gogh painted *Self-Portrait with Bandaged Ear* (1889) after cutting off part of his ear following a violent disagreement with his friend and fellow painter Paul Gauguin.

Is cutting one's ear off necessarily a sign of a psychological disorder?

Connection

Early conceptualizations of mental illness blamed demons and spirits. The modern medical model originated in the 1800s in Europe.

See Chapter 1, LO3.

syndromes
groups or clusters of related symptoms that are characteristic of a disorder.

Do you think this person has a psychological disorder? Recall the "4 Ds" used to classify psychologically disordered behaviour.

we say a person is "suffering" from a disorder. *Dysfunctional* behaviour interferes with everyday functioning, such as participating in everyday social relationships, holding a regular job, or being productive, and occasionally it can be a risk to oneself or others. *Deviant* literally means "different from the norm," or different from what most people do. It is important to point out, as the *DSM-5* does, that deviant behaviour can be classified as disordered only if it is also dysfunctional. Albert Einstein was deviant (or different from the norm) in his intelligence and creativity, but he was not suffering from a psychological disorder. Behaviours that possess only one or even two of these "4 Ds" are not typically classified as disordered. Finally, if a behaviour is culturally accepted it cannot be a disorder, such as hallucinations of shamans in some preliterate cultures.

The *DSM-5* describes 22 major categories of disorder, covering more than 350 distinct disorders (see Figure 15.1), some of which we will discuss in this chapter. For each distinct disorder, the *DSM-5* provides a list of criteria that psychologists and other mental health professionals use to diagnose a person with a particular condition and then develop an appropriate treatment plan. However, diagnosing a mental disorder can still often be difficult because symptoms rarely fall neatly into one category and sometimes symptoms are not severe enough to identify (Beidel, Bulik, & Stanley, 2014). The *DSM* criteria are also helpful to researchers who study disorders, allowing them to communicate with one another using the same terminology.

The *DSM-5* derives from a North American perspective of psychological illness. More than previous editions, the *DSM-5* tries to expand beyond the North American perspective by aiming to be consistent with international standards for disorder classification, such as the *ICD,* and discussing the prevalence rates of certain disorders in different countries. Some disorders, sometimes referred to as *culture-bound syndromes,* are found only in certain cultures. For instance, in some Southeast Asian cultures, certain men suffer from *koro,* the debilitating belief that one's genitals are retracting into one's body. In parts of the Middle East, some people suffer from *zar*—the belief that

Disorder	Description
1. Neurodevelopmental disorders	Conditions that begin early in development and cause significant impairments in functioning, such as intellectual disability, autism spectrum disorder, and attention deficit hyperactivity disorder.
2. Schizophrenia spectrum and other psychotic disorders	Characterized by distorted thoughts and perceptions, odd communication, inappropriate emotion, and other unusual behaviours.
3. Bipolar and related disorders	Disorders with major mood fluctuations, from mania to depression; also sometimes including psychotic experiences.
4. Depressive disorders	Characterized by extreme and persistent periods of depressed mood.
5. Anxiety disorders	Characterized by motor tension, hyperactivity, and apprehensive expectation/thoughts. Include generalized anxiety disorder, panic disorder, and specific phobia.
6. Obsessive-compulsive and related disorders	Characterized by obsessive thinking and compulsive behaviour.
7. Trauma- and stressor-related disorders	Disorders that develop after a traumatic event, such as post-traumatic stress disorder.
8. Dissociative disorders	Involve a change in consciousness, sudden loss of memory, or change of identity.
9. Somatic symptom and related disorders	Occur when psychological symptoms take a physical form even though no physical causes can be found.
10. Feeding and eating disorders	Include anorexia nervosa and bulimia nervosa (see Chapter 11).
11. Elimination disorders	Involve inappropriate elimination of urine or feces, such as bed-wetting.
12. Sleep-wake disorders	Consist of problems with the sleep-wake cycle, such as insomnia, narcolepsy, and sleep apnea (see Chapter 5).
13. Sexual dysfunctions	Problems related to unsatisfactory sexual activity, such as erectile disorder, premature ejaculation, and female orgasmic disorder.
14. Gender dysphoria	Occurs when there is a mismatch between a person's biological sex and gender identity.
15. Disruptive, impulse control, and conduct disorders	Characterized by problems controlling emotions and behaviours, such as conduct disorder and kleptomania.
16. Substance-related and addictive disorders	Involves persistent use of substances or some other behaviour (e.g., gambling) that leads to significant problems.
17. Neurocognitive disorders	Characterized by disordered thinking caused by conditions, such as Alzheimer's disease or traumatic brain injury.
18. Personality disorders	Develop when personality traits become inflexible and maladaptive.
19. Paraphilic disorders	Characterized by inappropriate sexual activity, such as pedophilic disorder.
20. Other mental disorders	Residual category for conditions not fitting into any of the above categories but are associated with significant stress or impairment, such as mental disorder due to another medical condition.
21. Medication-induced movement disorders and other adverse effects of medication	Problems with physical movement (e.g., tremors) caused by medication.
22. Other conditions that may be the focus of clinical attention	Include problems related to relationships, abuse, neglect, and others.

FIGURE **15.1**
MAJOR CATEGORIES OF MENTAL DISORDERS IN THE DSM-5. (*Source:* APA, 2013.)

they are possessed by spirits—and run around in fits of laughter, shouting, and singing (Watters, 2010).

Additionally, some disorders spread from culture to culture (Watters, 2010). For example, in China, anorexia nervosa has been extremely rare; when it was described, the fear of being fat was not a symptom. Sufferers most frequently complained of having bloated stomachs. However, a single widely publicized case of anorexia in 1994 that led to the death of a Hong Kong teenager suddenly made anorexia a much more commonly reported disorder—rates of the disorder had increased dramatically by the late 1990s. Moreover, because the journalists in Hong Kong who were covering the story tended to use the *DSM* to describe the disorder, with the increase in prevalence also came a change in symptoms. After the publicity surrounding this case, more and more Chinese people with anorexia began to complain mostly of their fear of being fat, not of bloated stomachs. In short, their disorder became more westernized.

Connection

Eating disorders, such as anorexia nervosa, meet the criteria for a psychological disorder.

See Chapter 11, LO3.

There has always been debate about the best way to approach categorizing psychological disorders. Critics have argued since the 1990s about the somewhat arbitrary designations of the *DSM*, and indeed the *DSM-5* has been met with controversy. Some critics claim the approach of classifying disorders on the basis of shared symptoms, which has long been the *DSM* approach, has resulted in too many categories and may be antiquated (Tavris, 2013). Some have also voiced concern about a tendency in the *DSM* to "medicalize" normal behaviour (Frances & Widiger, 2012). (See "Psychology in the Real World" for a discussion about the addition of Internet gaming disorder to the *DSM-5*.) Others have recently argued that the *DSM* ignores biology and that diseases should be classified by shared biological underpinnings (Jabr, 2013). Recently, research from more than 60 000 people worldwide suggests that five major psychiatric disorders (autism spectrum disorder, attention deficit hyperactivity disorder, bipolar disorder, depression, and schizophrenia) actually have a common genetic cause (Cross-Disorder Group of the Psychiatric Genomics Consortium, 2013). Moreover, recent evidence suggests—as with intelligence—that one general dimension or factor underlies all of the major psychological disorders (Caspi et al., 2014). Such findings imply that mental disorders are not as distinct and different as the *DSM-5* categories would imply.

Challenge Your Assumptions

True or False? Mental disorders are relatively rare, and most families are free of mental disorders.

False: Almost half of North American adults will suffer from a diagnosable mental illness of some kind during their lifetime.

How common are mental disorders? The answer is that they are surprisingly common. According to the results of the 2012 Canadian Community Health Survey (CCHS) on Mental Health, approximately 2.8 million Canadians (or one in ten) met the criteria for at least one of six mental or substance use disorders (see Figure 15.2; Pearson, Janz, Ali, 2012). Over the course of a lifetime, almost half (46 percent) of the adults in North America will suffer from at least one psychological disorder (Kessler et al., 2005). Similar percentages have been reported in New Zealand and Spain (Moffitt et al., 2010; Serrano-Blanco et al., 2010). In North America, more than half of those diagnosed will suffer from two or more disorders (Kessler et al., 2005). The existence of two or more disorders at the same time is termed **comorbidity.** Some recent research suggests that fear-based disorders (phobias and panic disorder) may often develop first and predict the onset of other disorders later in life (Kessler et al., 2012).

Connections

Dementia and Alzheimer's disease are cognitive disorders related to age. Other disorders, such as sleep disorders, can occur at any time in a person's life.

See Chapter 5, LO7; Chapter 6, LO9; and Chapter 10, LO13.

Unfortunately, it is estimated that as many as 40 percent of those experiencing a psychological disorder do not seek out any help, due in part to the *stigma* surrounding mental illness (Corrigan, Druss, & Perlick, 2014). In a survey released for the 50th anniversary of Mental Health Week in Canada in May 2001 (Canadian Mental Health Association, 2001), only half of those surveyed reported being willing to tell their friends or bosses if they were receiving treatment for depression. Moreover, over 50 percent of those who suffered from mood, anxiety, or substance use disorders reported feeling embarrassed

comorbidity
the occurrence of two or more disorders at the same time.

Psychology in the Real World

Is Overusing the Internet a Disorder?

In March 2010, police discovered that a couple in South Korea had starved their three-month-old daughter due to neglect caused by their constant preoccupation with the online multiplayer fantasy game *Prius Online.* The tragic irony is that in the parents' version of *Prius Online,* they were raising a virtual baby (Greenemeier, 2013)!

As this case demonstrates, some people just can't stay offline. For many people, this, in itself, may not be a serious problem. In some cases, however, people are online all day; they check their Facebook or Twitter feeds dozens or even hundreds of times a day, and they cannot continue their work or activities around the home without logging on. For them, Internet use has become so intrusive that it adversely affects their professional and personal lives in the real world.

As with all disorders, something becomes a problem once it causes clinically significant disruptions of everyday life. For the first time, the *DSM-5* includes a category called "Internet Gaming Disorder," but due to insufficient and inconclusive evidence, it is classified as a "Condition for Further Study." Any five of nine criteria must be present during a 12-month period for a diagnosis to be made:

1. Preoccupation with Internet games (not Internet gambling)
2. Withdrawal symptoms when games are taken away (e.g., irritability, sadness, anxiety)
3. Tolerance—that is, more and more time is needed to be satisfied
4. Unsuccessful attempts to stop or control one's habit
5. Loss of interest in previous hobbies and entertainment
6. Continued excessive use despite knowing of their psychological problems
7. Deceives family, friends, and therapists about how much one plays games
8. Use of Internet games to cope or escape from a negative mood
9. Jeopardized or loss of a significant relationship, job, or educational/career opportunity due to Internet gaming activity

Some of these criteria are, in fact, signs of addiction—namely, tolerance, mood regulation, and disruption of relationships, job, or school. Moreover, researchers have suggested that some people do experience behavioural withdrawal symptoms, such as emotions of irritation and anger, when the computer or smartphone is not available (Block, 2008). The Chinese government has labelled compulsive and disruptive Internet use "an addiction" (APA, 2013).

Connections

An addiction to drugs involves a loss of control over intake and continued use despite negative consequences.

See Chapter 5, LO10; and Chapter 7, "Evaluating Connections in Learning: Addiction as a Learning Disorder?"

Although there are more than 250 publications on gaming or Internet use disorder, and some evidence does suggest it may be addictive, mental health professionals do not completely agree on how excessive and dysfunctional Internet use should be classified (Petry & O'Brien, 2013). There is also some concern that inclusion of this disorder in the *DSM-5* will open the door for other "behavioural addictions."

In a review of the research from the United States, between 9.8 percent and 15.2 percent of high school and college students met the criteria for problematic Internet use (Moreno, Jelenchick, Cox, Young, & Christakis, 2011). Averages from studies across Europe and Asia report that 12 percent excessively play computer games, 10 percent abuse them, and 3 percent are dependent upon them. In China, prevalence rates for Internet use disorder range from 8 percent to 13.5 percent, with males outnumbering females about two to one (Wu et al., 2013). For Massively Multiplayer Online Role-Playing Games (MMORPGs), the rates of dysfunctional use were even higher, with 18 percent experiencing academic, health, or relationship problems (and 8 percent saying they spend more than 40 hours a week playing video games).

Worldwide, more people than ever before are relying on their mobile devices for texting, using social network sites, and perusing the Internet. Some psychologists describe *mobile addiction* as the excessive, impulsive checking and use of a mobile device (e.g., smartphone), especially in potentially dangerous or illegal contexts, such as while driving (Salehan & Negahban, 2013).

Whether these forms of technology dependency meet the criteria for mental disorders remains to be seen, but we know that overuse of such devices may have deleterious effects, such as impaired cognition and task performance while multitasking (Borst, Taatgen, & Van Rijn, 2010). As more and more of us engage our time in such multitasking, we are likely to feel the effects of such chronic distraction on a social level.

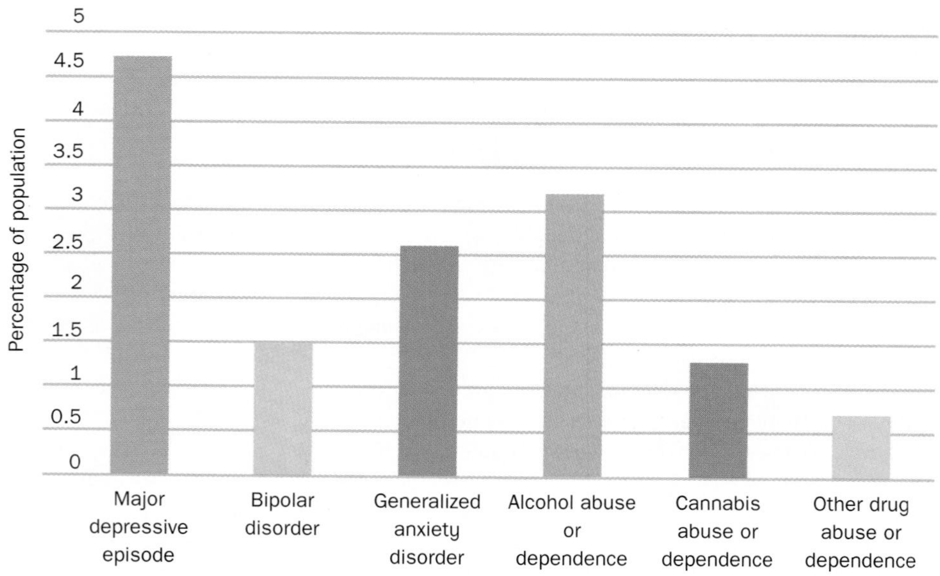

FIGURE **15.2**
PERCENTAGE OF CANADIANS 15 YEARS AND OLDER WHO EXPERIENCED A PSYCHOLOGICAL DISORDER OVER THE PREVIOUS 12 MONTHS. The Canadian Community Health Survey asked a sample of Canadians about the occurrence of several mental health problems over the preceding year. (*Source:* Statistics Canada, Canadian Community Health Survey (CCHS), Mental Health, 2012.)

Six-time Olympic medal winner Clara Hughes is an advocate for mental health. As the national spokesperson for Bell's Let's Talk Mental Health Initiative, she speaks openly about her own struggles with depression to help combat the stigma associated with mental illness.

about their problems and that they faced discrimination (Government of Canada, 2006). Surveys suggest that many Canadians hold negative attitudes towards those suffering from mental illness (Canadian Medical Association, 2008). One common misconception is that people with psychological disorders are unstable and dangerous. In fact, the majority of people with a psychological disorder never commit violent acts; they are more likely to be victims (Taylor, 2008). In 2009, the Mental Health Commission of Canada (MHCC) began an initiative, "Opening Minds," to change negative attitudes and discriminatory behaviours associated with mental health problems through education in partnership with many other Canadian organizations. Many high-profile Canadians, such as Olympic speed skating and cycling medalist Clara Hughes and former Vancouver Canucks' defenceman Kevin Bieksa, are also actively engaged in reducing stigma related to mental illness.

Let us now turn to look at some specific psychological disorders described in the *DSM-5*. We have selected a few to demonstrate the range of psychological problems people may encounter. As you will see, some of these are more common than others.

Challenge Your Assumptions

True or False? Most people who suffer from mental illness are dangerous.

False: Most people who suffer from mental illness are not dangerous to others or even themselves.

NEURODEVELOPMENTAL DISORDERS

Although most clinical diagnoses are reserved for adults (older than 18), a number of disorders are prominent in childhood. The *DSM-5* refers to these as *neurodevelopmental disorders,* which include intellectual disabilities (formerly called mental retardation) and learning disabilities. We discuss two of them: attention deficit hyperactivity disorder (ADHD) and autism spectrum disorder. See Figure 15.3 for an overview of these two disorders.

LO3 Subtypes of Neurodevelopmental Disorders

Jade can seldom work more than a few minutes on any given task, whether it is doing homework, reading, or even watching television. At school, she is constantly fidgeting in her chair and she blurts out whatever she is thinking. Jade's teacher regularly has to ask her to be quiet and stop disrupting others. Her homework is full of careless mistakes, even though she usually knows the answers. With these symptoms, psychologists would probably diagnose Jade as suffering from **attention deficit hyperactivity disorder (ADHD).** To receive the diagnosis of ADHD, the child must have displayed these symptoms before age 12. Between 5 percent and 10 percent of North American school-age children and 3 percent to 5 percent of children worldwide meet the diagnostic criteria of ADHD (Kessler et al., 2005; Polanczyk et al., 2007). Boys are more likely to be diagnosed with ADHD than girls by a ratio of about two to one (APA, 2013). ADHD begins in childhood but for about 30 percent, the symptoms continue into adulthood (Barbaresi et al., 2013).

attention deficit hyperactivity disorder (ADHD)
a neurodevelopmental disorder characterized by inability to focus attention for more than a few minutes, to remain still and quiet, and to do careful work.

Let's consider Antoine, who until age one behaved in ways that seemed "normal." At the end of that year, however, there were subtle signs that his development wasn't typical: He didn't babble or point to objects, he made very little eye contact, and he was hardly speaking at 18 months. When he did speak, he often simply repeated what someone else said and later he would say "you" when he meant "I." Moreover, he regularly flapped his hands. Finally, he became very interested in the details and sensory experience of objects. He often would smell and taste toys. Psychologists would diagnose Antoine with **autism spectrum disorder** (**ASD**, formerly known as autism, from *autos*, meaning "self"). Autism spectrum disorder is characterized by severe language and social impairment combined with repetitive habits and inward-focused behaviours.

autism spectrum disorder (ASD)
a neurodevelopmental disorder characterized by severe language and social impairment along with repetitive habits and inward-focused behaviours.

Disorder	Major symptoms	Behaviours
Attention deficit hyperactivity disorder (ADHD)	Inattention	Often fails to give close attention to details or makes careless mistakes, cannot sustain attention, does not listen when spoken to, does not follow through on instructions
	Hyperactivity	Fidgets with hands or feet, leaves seat in classroom when sitting is expected, inappropriate and excessive running or climbing, talks excessively
	Impulsivity	Blurts out answers before question is complete, cannot wait turn, often intrudes or interrupts others
Autism spectrum disorder	Impaired social interaction	Has impaired eye-to-eye gaze and facial expressions, fails to develop peer relationships, lacks sharing interests
	Impaired communication	Has impaired or severely delayed speech; language use is stereotypic or repetitive
	Repetitive and stereotypic behaviours	Shows preoccupation and repetitive interests or behaviours (such as finger or hand flapping), inflexible routines, or rituals

FIGURE **15.3**
SYMPTOMS AND BEHAVIOURS OF TWO NEURODEVELOPMENTAL DISORDERS. (*Source:* APA, 2013.)

People at the high-functioning end of autism spectrum disorder may have independent, productive lives in spite of their social impairments and narrow interests. One such individual is Temple Grandin, who earned a Ph.D. in animal science and became a professor at Colorado State University. A leading animal welfare advocate, Grandin has designed humane facilities for livestock and has written and spoken extensively about animal rights.

joint attention
the ability to make eye contact with others and to look in the same direction as someone else.

Evidence suggests that people with autism spectrum disorder are extremely sensitive to sensory stimulation and have trouble integrating multiple sources of sensory information, such as sight, sound, and touch (Iarocci & McDonald, 2006; Reynolds & Lane, 2008). Children with ASD also are more interested in inanimate objects than in people and social activities (Baron-Cohen et al., 2001) and have difficulty with joint attention. **Joint attention** is the ability to make eye contact with others and to look in the same direction as someone else. For example, if a mother points at something she is interested in, a child with ASD is less likely to look in the same direction. Researchers who were not aware of diagnoses and who closely examined eye contact made by children on their first-birthday home videos were able to correctly classify children as having autism spectrum disorder 77 percent of the time (Osterling & Dawson, 1994). Historically, approximately five to six children in 1000 met the criteria for ASD, but recent studies in North America, Europe, and Asia suggest a prevalence rate of 1 percent (Government of Canada, 2015). Some researchers believe the disorder may be over-diagnosed; however, the evidence suggests the rise is mostly due to increased awareness (Rutter, 2005; Wing & Potter, 2002).

Autism encompasses a range of disorders, from severe disability to high functioning. On the high-functioning end of the spectrum, children have impaired social interest and skills and restricted interests, but they may be quite advanced in their speech and have above-average intelligence (APA, 2013). For instance, children on the high-functioning end of the spectrum may engage adults in long-winded and "professorial" discussions on one rather narrow topic. Because Hans Asperger (1991/1944) first described this type of high-functioning autistic behaviour, it became known as Asperger syndrome. The *DSM-5* eliminated Asperger syndrome as a separate diagnostic category, although many people previously diagnosed as such still identify with the term and may call themselves "Aspies."

Causes of Neurodevelopmental Disorders

Neurodevelopmental disorders sometimes stem from genetic factors but often remain latent unless triggered by an environmental condition (Howe, 2010; Larsson, Larsson, & Lichtenstein, 2004). For ADHD, one of the environmental factors is whether the mother smokes while pregnant. However, smoking during pregnancy leads to conduct and impulse problems only if the child has one form of a gene for the dopamine reuptake transporter gene but not another (Kahn, et al., 2003). Neither prenatal smoke exposure alone nor the dopamine genotype alone is significantly associated with increased behaviour disorders. One environmental factor, long suspected by many parents to cause ADHD, is excessive sugar consumption. Controlled clinical studies, however, do not support a relationship between the amount of sugar consumed and hyperactivity, and this conclusion has held in many countries (Kim & Chang, 2011; Krummel, Seligson, & Guthrie, 1996; Whalen & Henker, 1998).

One consistent finding regarding brain activity of those with ADHD is low levels of activation. Brain activity in general is less pronounced in people with ADHD than in those without it (Zametkin et al., 1990; Zang et al., 2005). An under-stimulated brain explains the "paradoxical" effects of giving children with ADHD a stimulant to calm them down. The stimulant elevates their abnormally low nervous system activity and they require less stimulation and activity from the outside.

Head size is a marker of possible autism spectrum disorder. Often the brain is smaller than normal at birth but grows much faster during the first few years of life than the brains of non-autistic children (Courchesne, Campbell, & Solso, 2010). The brain of a five-year-old with ASD is the same size as that of a typical 13-year-old (Blakeslee, 2005). Although we do not yet know which genes are involved, this abnormal rate of brain growth is almost certainly due to genetic influences. In addition, the frontal lobes, where much processing of social information occurs, are less well connected in children with ASD than in non-autistic children (Belmonte et al., 2004). Finally, recent evidence shows that the amygdala in children with ASD is 13 percent larger than in children without the disorder (Bachevalier, 2011; Mosconi et al., 2009).

A promising theory about the origins of autism spectrum disorder is based on the mirror neurons (Ramachandran & Oberman, 2006). As we saw in earlier chapters, mirror neurons fire both when a person performs a particular behaviour (such as reaching for an object) and when he or she simply watches someone else performing the same behaviour. Mirror neurons are thought to be involved in many, if not most, social behaviours, such as observational learning, imitation, and even language learning. Because children with ASD are deficient in these skills, neuroscientists have predicted that mirror neurons malfunction in ASD children; research results show that this is indeed the case (Ramachandran & Oberman, 2006).

Quick Quiz 15.1: Neurodevelopmental Disorders

1. The occurrence of two or more disorders at the same time is known as
   a. bipolar disorder.
   b. comorbidity.
   c. dipolarity.
   d. syndrome.
2. Jolo is a five-year-old boy who does not speak, waves his arms around a lot, does not make eye contact, and does not seem to connect with other kids or adults. Jolo may have which disorder?
   a. autism spectrum disorder
   b. ADHD
   c. childhood depression
   d. theory of mind
3. Kelly fidgets a lot, blurts out what she is thinking, and makes many careless mistakes in her homework, even when she knows the answers. Kelly most likely would be diagnosed with which neurodevelopmental disorder?
   a. low IQ
   b. autism spectrum disorder
   c. anxiety disorder
   d. ADHD

Answers can be found at the end of the chapter.

SCHIZOPHRENIA

Some disorders result primarily from disturbances of thought and perception; as a group, they are known as **psychotic disorders.** They are characterized by an inability to distinguish real from imagined perceptions. One very serious psychotic disorder is **schizophrenia,** which involves profound disturbances in thought and emotion—in particular, impairments in perception, such as hallucinations. Emil Kraepelin, who coined the term *schizophrenia* (literally "split mind") in the 1890s, viewed the disorder as a split from reality, not a split attitude or split personality as is sometimes mistakenly assumed. Approximately 1 percent of the Canadian population is afflicted with this disorder at any given time, making schizophrenia much less common than depression (Goeree et al., 2005). Genetically, however, if a first-degree relative (a biological parent, sibling, or child) has the disorder, the odds of a person having the disorder rise to 10 percent (NIMH, 2007).

psychotic disorders
psychological disorders of thought and perception, characterized by an inability to distinguish between real and imagined perceptions.

schizophrenia
a psychotic disorder characterized by significant disturbances in thought and emotion, specifically problems with perception, including hallucinations.

Challenge Your Assumptions

True or False? Schizophrenia is a disorder of split personalities.

False: Schizophrenia and split personality (multiple personality, now known as dissociative identity disorder) are very different disorders.

LO4 Major Symptoms of Schizophrenia

For a diagnosis of schizophrenia, at least two of the following symptoms must persist for one month. Moreover, at least one of these symptoms must come from the first three (delusions, hallucinations, or disorganized speech; APA, 2013):

- Delusions
- Hallucinations

positive symptoms
the presence of abnormal thoughts and behaviours associated with schizophrenia, including hallucinations, delusional thinking, and disorganized thought and speech.

negative symptoms
the absence of normal thoughts and behaviours; symptoms include non-responsiveness, emotional flatness, immobility, catatonia, and the inability to complete tasks.

cognitive symptoms
problems with information processing, including working memory, attention, verbal and visual learning and memory, reasoning and problem solving.

hallucinations
convincing sensory experiences that occur in the absence of an external stimulus.

delusion
one of the symptoms of schizophrenia: false beliefs or exaggerations held despite evidence to the contrary, such as the idea that one is a famous person.

word salad
the speech of people with schizophrenia, which may follow grammatical rules but be nonsensical in terms of content.

- Disorganized speech
- Grossly disorganized behaviour or catatonic behaviour (immobile and unresponsive, though awake)
- Negative symptoms (such as not speaking or being unable to experience emotion)

The symptoms of schizophrenia fall into three major categories: positive, negative, and cognitive. **Positive symptoms** refer to the presence of abnormal thoughts and behaviours in schizophrenia that are not observed in people without the disorder, whereas **negative symptoms** refer to the absence of normal thoughts and behaviours. **Cognitive symptoms** involve deficits in information processing, particularly working memory and attention.

In general, poor integration of perceptual processes is a hallmark characteristic of schizophrenia. Look, for instance, at the pictures of watches in Figure 15.4. People with schizophrenia have more trouble putting the fragmented image together and perceiving it as a watch.

Positive symptoms include hallucinations, delusional thinking, and disorganized thought and speech. **Hallucinations** are convincing sensory experiences that occur in the absence of an external stimulus—in other words, the brain receives false sensory input. Auditory hallucinations are the most common form of hallucination in schizophrenia, typically taking the form of hearing voices in one's head. The following account from a person with schizophrenia describes an auditory hallucination:

> Recently my mind has played tricks on me, creating The People inside my head who sometimes come out to haunt me and torment me. They surround me in rooms, hide behind trees and under the snow outside. They taunt me and scream at me and devise plans to break my spirit. The voices come and go, but The People are always there, always real. ("I feel I am trapped," *New York Times*, March 18, 1986)

The important point about hallucinations is that patients experience them as real. It is not *as if* someone is talking to them; rather, they hear voices and are convinced that someone is living inside them. Indeed, this is a defining feature of psychosis (Nolen-Hoeksema, 2007). Similar to but distinct from hallucinations, **delusions** are false beliefs, often exaggerated claims, that a person holds in spite of evidence to the contrary, such as the idea that one is Jesus Christ.

Negative symptoms include non-responsiveness, emotional flatness, immobility or the striking of strange poses (catatonia), reduction of speaking, and inability to complete tasks. Traditionally, negative symptoms have been harder to diagnose and treat than positive symptoms.

Cognitive symptoms exhibited by people with schizophrenia include problems with working memory, attention, verbal and visual learning and memory, reasoning and problem solving, speed of processing, and disordered speech (Barch, 2005). For example, the speech of a person with schizophrenia often follows grammatical rules, but the content makes little sense. Such utterances are referred to as **word salad.** Similarly, patients sometimes make up new words, which are referred to as *neologisms.* In the following example, a woman who believed she was the only female professor at the "University of Smithsonian" (no such place) in England uses new words to produce a word salad:

> I am here from a foreign university . . . and you have to have a "plausity" of all acts of amendment to go through for the children's code . . . and it is no mental disturbance or "putenance." . . . it is an "amorition" law. . . . It is like their "privatilinia" and the children have to have this "accentuative" law so they don't go into the "mortite" law of the church. (Vetter, 1968, p. 306)

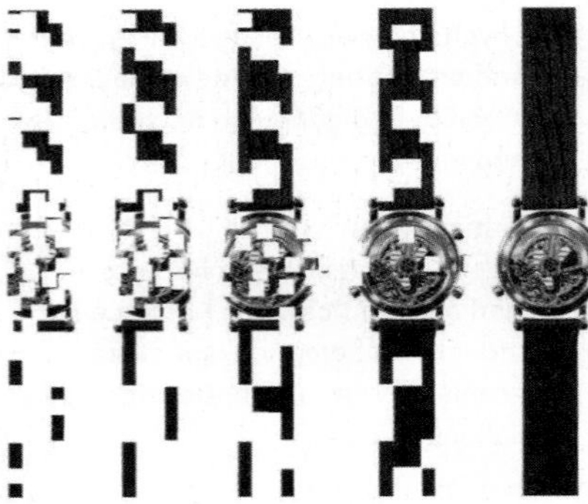

FIGURE **15.4**
INABILITY TO PERCEIVE FRAGMENTS IN SCHIZOPHRENIA. Perceiving fragments as parts of a whole can be difficult for people with schizophrenia. When normal subjects view fractured images like those above in sequence, they identify the object quickly, but individuals with schizophrenia often cannot make that leap swiftly. (*Source:* Javitt & Coyle, 2004.)

LO5 Nature and Nurture Explanations of Schizophrenia

Schizophrenia offers a perfect, though tragic, illustration of the dynamic interplay between biology and experience in the development of a psychological disorder. Historically, this explanation has been called the **diathesis–stress model.** *Diathesis* is the Greek word for "predisposition," so the diathesis–stress view is that biological predispositions plus stress or abusive environments together produce psychological disorders. Some researchers describe the diathesis–stress interaction between biological dispositions and environmental forces as a two-stage model (Kandel, 2000a; Lewis & Levitt, 2002). Stage one is the biological–genetic foundation, or disposition, and stage two is an environmental event that occurs at some point after conception, such as maternal infection, chronic stress, or using certain drugs (such as marijuana or amphetamines) at critical points in development (Fergusson, Horwood, & Ridder, 2005).

diathesis–stress model
biological predispositions *and* stress or abusive environments together produce psychological disorders.

Although genetic factors play an important role in the development of schizophrenia, they do not make it inevitable. The heritability rates are 70 percent to 85 percent, suggesting that the disorder is due largely to genetic influences (Cardno & Gottesman, 2000; Gebicke-Haerter, 2012; Harrison & Owen, 2003; Kandel, 2000a; Lewis & Levitt, 2002; Vyas, Patel, Nijran, Al-Nahhas, & Puri, 2010). Scientists have identified as many as 19 genes that contribute to schizophrenia, but the mechanisms they regulate have only recently been understood by neuroscientists (Harrison & Owen, 2003; Harrison & Weinberger, 2005; Mei & Xiong, 2008; Stefansson et al., 2009). The fact that one identical twin can develop schizophrenia, whereas the other genetically identical twin may not develop it, indicates that genes alone do not cause schizophrenia. Instead, genes are turned on or off by environmental experiences during brain development to produce the disorder (Gebicke-Haerter, 2012; Grossman et al., 2003; Moffitt et al., 2005; Petronis, 2004). Recent research has reported that there are up to 100 genes related to schizophrenia with epigenetic tags (methyl-groups; Gebicke-Haerter, 2012).

The more abuse and neglect (adverse experiences) children experience in their early home lives, the more likely they are to suffer from schizophrenia later (Edwards et al., 2003; Whitfield et al., 2005). Adverse experiences in the form of abuse and neglect often happen during the critical periods of brain growth and development (see Figure 15.5; Perry, 2002). In the child who suffered extreme neglect, notice the much smaller overall brain size as well as the enlarged ventricles (butterfly shapes) in the middle of the brain. These features are two of the major brain abnormalities characteristic of schizophrenia. One of the oldest findings on the brain and schizophrenia is the tendency of people with schizophrenia to have enlarged ventricles (the fluid-filled spaces in the brain; Lieberman et al., 2001).

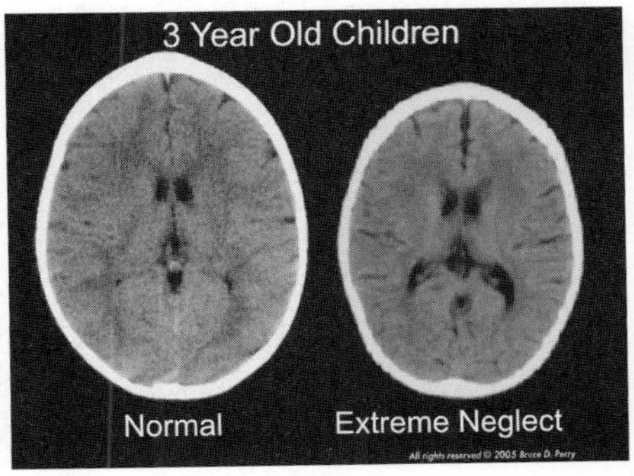

FIGURE **15.5**
EFFECT OF EXTREME NEGLECT ON BRAIN DEVELOPMENT. These MRI images show the brain of a typically developing three-year-old child who has had a normal amount of cognitive, social, and linguistic stimulation (left), and that of a three-year-old child who was deprived of regular social, linguistic, tactile, or cognitive stimulation (right). Growth is clearly stunted in the child who suffered from extreme neglect. Additionally, the dark butterfly-shaped structures (ventricles) are much larger in the child who suffered from extreme neglect. Enlarged ventricles are common in people with schizophrenia. (*Source:* Perry, 2002.)

Although we may not yet know their causes or how exactly they interact with environmental forces, certain biological and brain abnormalities are hallmarks of schizophrenia. In this section, we consider some of the better-known ones: maternal infection, dysfunctional prefrontal and hippocampus activity, enlarged ventricles, an excess of dopamine activity in the basal ganglia, and a deficiency in the neurotransmitter glutamate.

Maternal Infections and Schizophrenia During fetal development, neural growth can occur at a rate of 250 000 new neurons per minute and peak at approximately *3 million* per minute (Purves & Lichtman, 1985)! Consequently, what happens to both the mother and the fetus is crucial; any kind of disease or toxic substance experienced by the mother may dramatically affect neural growth in the fetus. If a woman contracts an infection during pregnancy, the risk of the child's developing schizophrenia later in life increases dramatically (Boska, 2008; Brown, 2006; Koenig, 2006; Moreno, Mitsumasa, et al., 2011). Prenatal exposure to infections and diseases such as influenza, rubella, toxoplasmosis, and herpes has been linked to increased risk of schizophrenia (Brown, 2006; Buka et al., 2001) and deficits in brain development (Moreno, Mitsumasa, et al., 2011; Short et al., 2010). The effect appears not to exist, however, during the first and second trimesters of pregnancy (months one to six; Selten, Frissen, Lensvelt-Mulder, & Morgan, 2010). So far it is unclear how these early life infections make the brain more vulnerable to schizophrenia, but a recent study found higher immune cell activity in the brains of adult schizophrenics as well as in individuals at risk for the disorder (Bloomfield et al., 2015). The link between the immune system, the brain, and schizophrenia has offered new insights into the causes of this disorder.

Schizophrenia and the Brain Abnormal brain development before birth may be responsible for many of the brain dysfunctions that are characteristic of schizophrenia (Lewis & Levitt, 2002). One mechanism by which maternal infections, for instance, may increase the risk of schizophrenia is by affecting the path neurons take when they migrate during fetal brain growth (Kandel, 2000a; Koenig, 2006). One of the most widely recognized brain abnormalities is a dysfunctional prefrontal cortex and its working memory; in people with schizophrenia, there is evidence of both reduced and excessive activity in that area (Andreasen et al., 1997; Barch, 2005; Goldman-Rakic, 1999; Weinberger et al., 2001; Vyas et al., 2010). Moreover, the genes in the prefrontal cortex that regulate how synapses function are dysfunctional in people with schizophrenia compared to those without the disease (Mirnics, Middleton, Marquez, Lewis, & Levitt, 2000). Often the hippocampus is smaller in people with schizophrenia, compared to those without the disorder (Barch, 2005; Harrison, 2004). See Figure 15.6 for an overview of these and other areas of the brain affected by schizophrenia.

Connection

During fetal development, the brain is extremely vulnerable to many different kinds of toxins.

See Chapter 10, LO2.

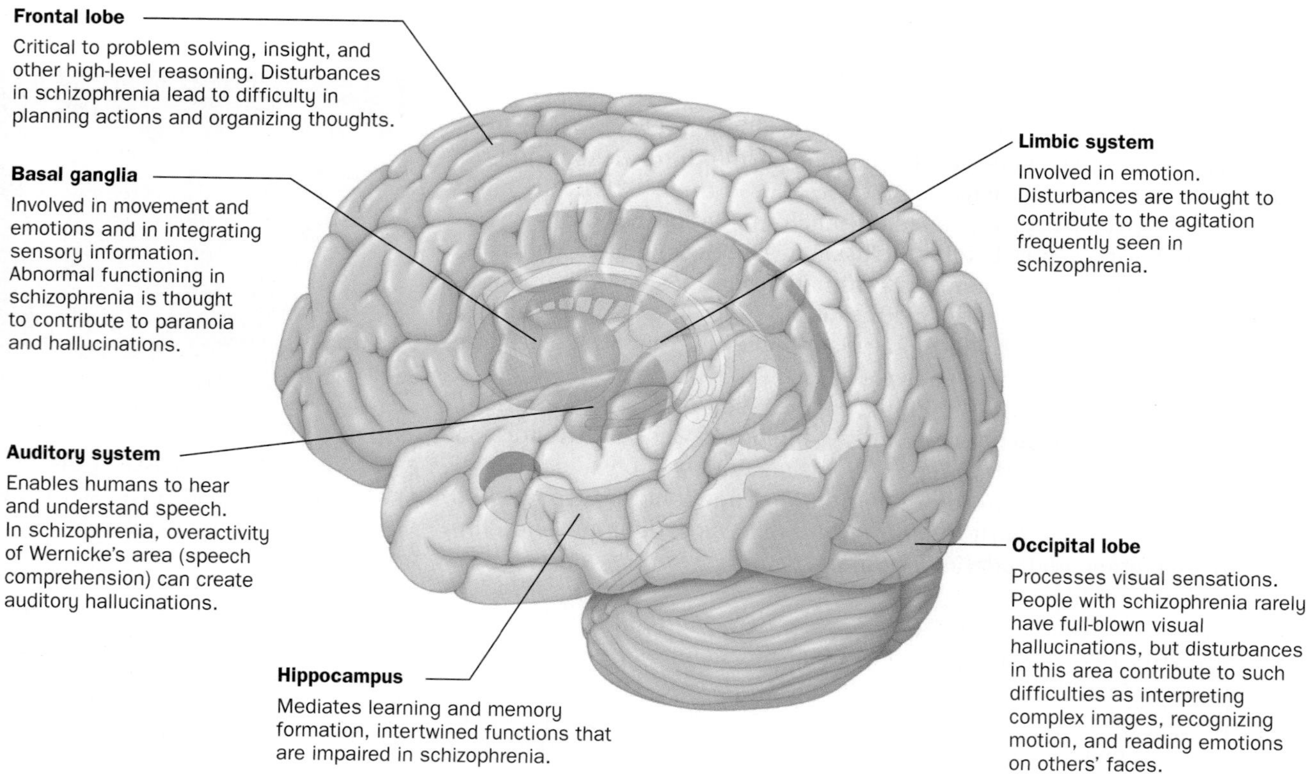

Frontal lobe
Critical to problem solving, insight, and other high-level reasoning. Disturbances in schizophrenia lead to difficulty in planning actions and organizing thoughts.
Basal ganglia
Involved in movement and emotions and in integrating sensory information. Abnormal functioning in schizophrenia is thought to contribute to paranoia and hallucinations.
Auditory system
Enables humans to hear and understand speech. In schizophrenia, overactivity of Wernicke's area (speech comprehension) can create auditory hallucinations.
Hippocampus
Mediates learning and memory formation, intertwined functions that are impaired in schizophrenia.
Limbic system
Involved in emotion. Disturbances are thought to contribute to the agitation frequently seen in schizophrenia.
Occipital lobe
Processes visual sensations. People with schizophrenia rarely have full-blown visual hallucinations, but disturbances in this area contribute to such difficulties as interpreting complex images, recognizing motion, and reading emotions on others' faces.

FIGURE **15.6**

AREAS OF THE BRAIN IMPAIRED BY SCHIZOPHRENIA. The structures highlighted here do not function normally in people with schizophrenia. Limbic system structures not shown here are the hypothalamus, amygdala, and cingulate gyrus. (*Source:* Javitt & Coyle, 2004.)

Brain problems in schizophrenia may not be simply a function of abnormalities in certain structures but may also stem from problems in the communications among groups of neurons. In people without schizophrenia, neural networks are efficiently clustered in close groups and move in and out of orderly and chaotic patterns of firing (Bassett, Verchinski, Mattay, Weinberger, & Meyer-Lindenberg, 2008). This process is essential for learning and memory. In people with schizophrenia, however, these networks are less clustered, less efficient, and more disorderly, especially in the frontal lobes (Bassett et al., 2008).

An obvious positive symptom of schizophrenia is hallucinations. What is going on in the brain during a hallucination? Brain imaging studies show that hallucinations activate the brain in ways similar, but not identical, to real external stimulation (Shergill et al., 2000; Shergill et al., 2003; Silbersweig et al., 1995). For example, activity in the auditory cortex of the temporal lobe and the visual cortex of the occipital lobe during visual and auditory hallucinations shows striking similarities to the kind of brain activity that occurs when visual and auditory stimuli are present. The part of the brain involved in interpreting and comprehending speech (Wernicke's area of the left hemisphere) is also activated during hallucinations (Stephane, Barton, & Boutros, 2001). Also noteworthy, however, is the lack of activity in the frontal lobes during the hallucination, which suggests that the person is unable to monitor and determine the source of the images or sounds (Shergill et al., 2003).

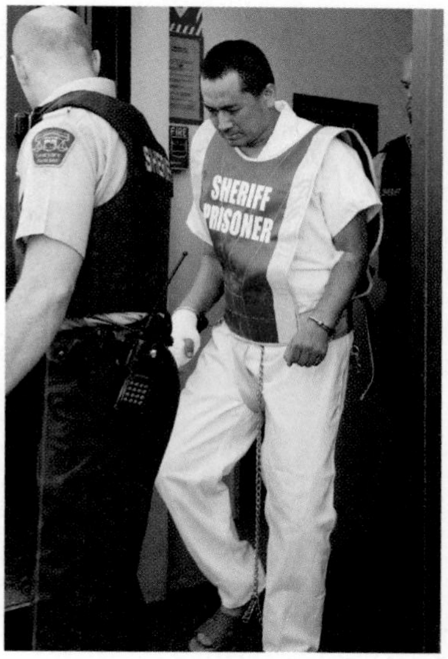

Vince Li beheaded a fellow passenger on a Greyhound bus and was later found to be suffering from schizophrenia and was not held responsible for his actions. Although tragic examples like this one suggest a link between psychological disorders and violence, we must remember that the media tends only to report on sensational cases, while research tells us that most people who have a psychological disorder are *not* violent.

Neurochemistry of Schizophrenia For decades, the prevailing view on the neurochemistry of schizophrenia was the *dopamine hypothesis,* which states that people with schizophrenia have an excess of dopamine in certain areas of the brain (Javitt & Coyle, 2004; Kegeles et al., 2010). The dopamine hypothesis was based on two findings. First, Nobel laureate Arvid Carlsson discovered that amphetamines stimulate dopamine release and therefore may mimic the hallucinations and delusions of schizophrenia (Javitt & Coyle, 2004). Second, early antipsychotic drugs that block dopamine receptors were somewhat effective at treating positive symptoms.

Groundbreaking Research

The Discovery of Dopamine

Before 1952, no one knew that dopamine is a neurotransmitter. The belief at the time was that dopamine was merely a precursor of epinephrine (Yeragani, Tancer, Chokka, & Baker, 2010). Moreover, most scientists were convinced that dopamine had no role to play in brain function (Carlsson, 1987). We now know, partly due to Arvid Carlsson's discoveries, that dopamine not only is involved in controlling our muscle movement and with the basic feelings of reward and pleasure but also is one of the main neurotransmitters involved in the development of schizophrenia.

Arvid Carlsson

THE EARLY YEARS

Even though he made important progress as a young researcher, Carlsson was denied tenure as a professor and for a while wondered whether to continue his research. He did continue, however, and his persistence paid off. A few years later, in the early 1950s he did the work on dopamine and its role in schizophrenia and Parkinson's disease that led to his Nobel Prize in 2000 (Benes, 2001).

Yet, nearly ten years after Carlsson's groundbreaking work on dopamine, many neuroscientists could not accept that it is a neurotransmitter, because they still believed neurotransmitters had to be electrical rather than chemical (Iversen & Iversen, 2007). Although the first drug treatments for schizophrenia were discovered by others, Carlsson's work helped support the view that schizophrenia is at least partly caused by excessive amounts of dopamine in the brain—a view now known as the dopamine hypothesis (Iversen & Iversen, 2007). Due to the central role that dopamine plays in schizophrenia, Parkinson's disease, and even ADHD, it is fair to say that the field of psychopharmacology would not be the same today without the early pioneering work of Arvid Carlsson.

NEW DIRECTIONS

There are, however, some problems with the dopamine hypothesis. As we discuss in more detail in Chapter 16, dopamine-specific medications (major tranquilizers) effectively treat only positive symptoms and even then are not entirely effective. In addition, only a minority of the people who receive the traditional drug treatment find it effective in managing their symptoms (Javitt & Coyle, 2004). When researchers became aware that another set of recreational drugs led to schizophrenia-like symptoms that did not directly involve dopamine, they turned their attention to these drugs. These drugs, PCP ("angel dust") and ketamine (an animal anesthetic, used recreationally as "Vit K" or "Special K"), do not affect dopamine production; instead, they impair the functioning of a different neurotransmitter, glutamate, and one of its receptors, NMDA. Glutamate is a major excitatory neurotransmitter that regulates the release of dopamine. PCP and ketamine block the action of glutamate, thus producing the same kinds of disturbances seen in schizophrenia (Harrison & Owen, 2003; Moghaddam, 2003). Glutamate deficiencies, then, may explain many of the symptoms of schizophrenia (Javitt & Coyle, 2004). A gene related to glutamate plays a role in prefrontal cortex functioning in schizophrenics, which further supports a role for glutamate in the disorder (Fallgatter et al., 2010).

These findings stimulated researchers to explore the role of glutamate in schizophrenia more fully. Not only is it crucial in learning, memory, neural processing, and brain development, but it also amplifies certain neural signals, making some stimuli more important than others (Goff & Coyle, 2001; Javitt & Coyle, 2004; Mayer, 2004). This process is crucial to selective attention—that is, focusing attention on some items of information while ignoring others. Thus, dysfunction in glutamate action would explain why people with schizophrenia have trouble with selective attention, cognitive control, and working memory.

Connection

People with Parkinson's disease gradually lose the ability to control their muscles and shake involuntarily. These symptoms result from the gradual death of dopamine-producing neurons.

See Chapter 3, LO8, LO9.

Quick Quiz 15.2: Schizophrenia

1. Which of the following is a negative symptom of schizophrenia?
   a. hallucinations
   b. delusions of grandeur
   c. catatonia
   d. disorganized speech
2. The heritability rate for schizophrenia is roughly
   a. 100 percent.
   b. 60 percent.
   c. 80 percent.
   d. 25 percent.
3. Low levels of which neurotransmitter might explain why people with schizophrenia have trouble with selective attention, cognitive control, and working memory?
   a. acetylcholine
   b. glutamate
   c. norepinephrine
   d. GABA

Answers can be found at the end of the chapter.

LO6 DEPRESSIVE DISORDERS

If schizophrenia and other psychotic disorders are expressions of thought and perceptual disturbances, then bipolar disorder and depression are expressions of disturbance in mood and emotion. The depressive disorders, bipolar disorders, and anxiety disorders are marked especially by disturbances in emotional behaviour that prevent people from functioning effectively in everyday life.

We all feel blue from time to time. Feeling sad after being rejected by a lover or failing an exam presents a normal response to life challenges, as does getting into a funk after a series of hard breaks. Yet being unable to leave your bed for days or failing to eat from a profound sense of despair or disinterest in doing anything—often without direct provocation—is something different altogether, and it may reflect an underlying disorder in psychological health.

According to the *DSM-5,* there are several forms of **depressive disorder.** What most people refer to as "depression" is formally called **major depressive disorder,** a chronic condition characterized by enduring changes in mood, motivation, and sense of self-worth. According to the *DSM-5,* to be diagnosed with major depressive disorder, one must have at least five of nine symptoms associated with major depression, which must continue for at least two consecutive weeks (APA, 2013):

depressive disorder
the highest-order category of the depressive disorders; it subsumes all forms of depression, including major depressive disorder and persistent depressive disorder.

major depressive disorder
a disorder characterized by pervasive low mood, lack of motivation, low energy, and feelings of worthlessness and guilt that last for at least two consecutive weeks.

1. Depressed (sad, listless) mood that stays low all day for several days
2. Reduced interest or pleasure in doing anything
3. Significant change in body weight (indicating dieting or overeating)
4. Sleep disturbances
5. Sluggishness or restlessness
6. Daily fatigue or loss of energy
7. Daily feelings of worthlessness, self-reproach, or excessive guilt
8. Lack of ability to concentrate or think clearly
9. Recurrent thoughts of death or suicidal ideation

Most importantly, symptoms must significantly impact daily functioning, in terms of both social and work-related contexts, and they must be a source of distress, in order to be the basis for a diagnosis of major depressive disorder. Approximately 12 percent of Canadians will have major depressive disorder at some point in their life (Patten et al., 2006), but the occurrence varies depending on age and sex. The disorder is three times more likely in 18- to 29-year-olds than in people over age 60 (Kessler et al., 2010). Females experience depression two to three times more often than males (teens and up; APA, 2013; Nolen-Hoeksema & Hilt, 2009). The World Health Organization lists depression as the leading cause of disability worldwide (WHO, 2012).

Other forms of depressive disorder have milder symptoms but last longer. One of these milder forms is **persistent depressive disorder** (**PDD,** previously called *dysthymia*). Most of the symptoms are the same as in a major depressive disorder, but they are less intense in PDD, though the depressive mood lasts most of the day and most of the time for at least two years.

persistent depressive disorder (PDD)
a form of depression that is milder in intensity but longer in duration than major depressive disorder.

Depression manifests itself differently in different people, but only rarely is it only about feeling blue. Although sadness is the emotion most associated with depression, many find the lack of interest in or ability to *feel* anything (positive or negative) to be the most disabling aspect of living with depression. The Pulitzer Prize–winning novelist William Styron, who went through a major depressive episode in his 60s, offered a poignant account of the experience in his book *Darkness Visible.* For Styron, as for many seriously depressed people, the feelings of despair reached a point at which ending his life seemed to be the only guaranteed source of relief:

> I had not as yet chosen the mode of my departure, but I knew that that step would come next, and soon, as inescapable as nightfall. . . . Late one bitterly cold night, when I knew that I could not possibly get myself through the

Arguably one of the most influential singer-songwriters of our time, Leonard Cohen has long battled depression. His music, poems, and novels are known for their artistic representation of melancholy.

What factors and symptoms are needed before everyday blues turn into a diagnosis of major depressive disorder?

> following day, I sat in the living room of the house bundled up against the chill. . . . I had forced myself to watch the tape of a movie. . . . At one point in the film . . . came a contralto voice, a sudden soaring passage from the Brahms *Alto Rhapsody*.
>
> This sound, which like all music—indeed, like all pleasure—I had been numbly unresponsive to for months, pierced my heart like a dagger, and in a flood of swift recollection I thought of all the joys the house had known; the children who had rushed through its rooms, the festivals, the love and work, the honestly earned slumber, the voices and the nimble commotion. . . . All this I realized was more than I could ever abandon, . . . I drew upon some last gleam of sanity to perceive the terrifying dimensions of the mortal predicament I had fallen into. I woke up my wife and soon telephone calls were made. The next day I was admitted to the hospital. (1990, pp. 63–67)

The kind of unbearable hopelessness we see in Styron's comments may be one reason that people with depression are at a higher risk of committing suicide than others. Indeed, suicide is a major risk for people with depression, and suicidal thinking is included as a symptom of depression (APA, 2013; Hawton, Comabella, Haw, & Saunders, 2013). However, a diagnosis of depression does not mean that a suicide attempt is inevitable. The presence of other psychological disorders, most notably substance abuse and schizophrenia, as well as psychosocial factors, such as family discord and abuse, are strongly associated with suicide risk (Rihmer, 2007).

Nature and Nurture Explanations of Depression

Depression is sometimes caused by a stressful or traumatic life event, such as physical or sexual abuse, but not always. For some people, depression just comes on, like using a switch to turn on a light. To the extent that this is true, the reason some people and not others develop depression stems from a combination of neurochemistry and life circumstance—the diathesis–stress model again (Bukh et al., 2009).

Abusive and extremely stressful environments increase one's risk for depression later in life. Researchers studying adverse experiences found that people who reported the most adverse childhood experiences were more likely to be depressed than people who reported no adverse childhood experiences (Anda et al., 2006; Pietrek, Elbert, Weierstall, Müller, & Rockstroh, 2013; Wang et al., 2010). Indeed, the role of stress in the development of depression is not trivial (Wang et al., 2010; Weinstein et al., 2010). In animals, experimental-induced stress kills neurons in the hippocampus, which can lead to symptoms of depression (Jacobs, 2004; Jacobs, van Praag, & Gage, 2000; Kendler, Karkowski, & Prescott, 1999). In humans, stressful events, especially social rejection, start a host of biological reactions, including activating the hypothalamic-pituitary-adrenal (HPA) system, which increases the likelihood of developing depression (Slavich, O'Donovan, Epel, & Kemeny, 2010). Indeed, recent evidence suggests that stress is associated with accelerated aging of cells, which in turn is associated with depression (Wolkowitz, Epel, Reus, & Mellon, 2010). Medications that make more serotonin available in the brain stimulate neural growth, which lessens the symptoms of depression (Malberg et al., 2000; Papakostos et al., 2008). This may be an important avenue for treatment, given that depression is associated with decreased brain density, which may reflect stress-related neuronal death (Lai, 2013).

Stressful life events, such as the death of a loved one, can trigger a major depressive episode in people who have a genetic predisposition for depression.

The physiological effects of depression may even be observable at the sub-cellular level. The mitochondria are structures inside cells (in this case, inside neurons) that play a key role in cell metabolism. Several studies point to mitochondrial dysfunction in specific brain tissues linked with the occurrence of depression, but it is not clear if this is a cause or an effect of the disease (Tobe, 2013).

Challenge Your Assumptions

True or False? Extreme stress can make you depressed.

True: Stress can cause depression and even premature aging of cells.

Stressful environments, however, appear to interact with particular biological dispositions and personality traits to produce depression, especially in people who have experienced stress, trauma, and abuse (Clark, 2005; Hankin, 2010; Krueger, 1999; Slavich et al., 2010; Uher & McGuffin, 2010). People who are deficient in the neurotransmitters serotonin and neuropeptide Y (NPY) are most susceptible to depression after experiencing extremely stressful situations (Lowry et al., 2008; Morales-Medina, Dumont, & Quirion, 2010; Risch et al., 2009). For example, a meta-analysis of 34 studies found support for an interaction between differences in serotonin genes, adverse experiences, and the development of depression (Uher & McGuffin, 2010). One of the 34 studies in this meta-analysis provides a nice example of the research into the nature–nurture origins of depression; see Figure 15.7 for more details.

Cognitive factors may also contribute to the development and maintenance of depression. People who suffer from depression engage in a negative thinking style (A.T. Beck et al., 1979). Specifically, people with depression tend to be more critical of themselves and others (e.g., "I'm no good") and to hold more pessimistic views of the future (e.g., "Nothing will ever turn out right for me"; R. Beck & Perkins, 2001). Such a negative style has been shown to predict onset and worsening of depressive symptoms (Alloy et al., 1999). In addition, a cognitive style involving *rumination*—brooding about everything that is wrong with your life—is associated with increased risk of developing depression, especially when combined with stressful experiences (Hyde, Mezulis, & Abramson,

Research Process

1 Research Question

How do genetic and environmental differences interact to affect the development of depression?

2 Method

Avshalom Caspi and colleagues followed a group of nearly 1000 people from age three until age 26 and measured life events experienced by the participants at different ages (Caspi et al., 2003). They also investigated genetic vulnerability by identifying forms (or alleles) of the gene for the serotonin transporter in the participants' genomes. (Recall from Chapter 3 that this transporter is responsible for synaptic recycling of serotonin, and therefore influences the amount of serotonin in the synapse.) This gene exists in two alleles, short (s) and long (l), and every individual inherits a copy from each parent.

3 Results

They found that people who had inherited two short forms (s/s) of the serotonin transporter gene were more likely to exhibit depressive symptoms following stressful life events than were those who had inherited the long form (l/l). For example, in the graph shown here, we see that if people experience a few major stressful events (no more than two), their risk of having a major depressive episode does not increase, regardless of which form of the serotonin transporter gene they carry. But if they experience three or four stressful events, the likelihood that they will have a major depressive episode nearly doubles or triples in those with the short form compared to those with the long form.

4 Conclusion

Depression is most likely in individuals who carry the short form of the gene *and* experience many severe life stressors. Neither condition by itself is likely to lead to depression.

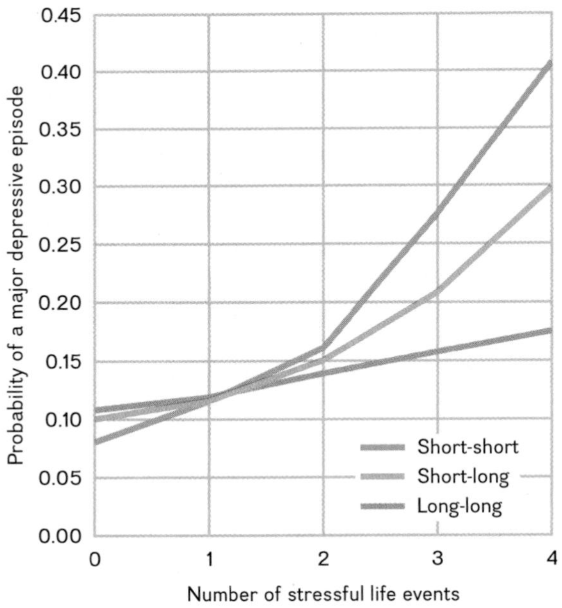

FIGURE **15.7**

GENE-ENVIRONMENT INTERACTION IN THE DEVELOPMENT OF DEPRESSION. Individuals with at least one short allele of the serotonin gene are more likely to experience depression than those with two long alleles. Those with two short forms of the gene are most vulnerable to depression if they experience at least three stressful life events. (*Source:* Caspi et al., 2003.)

2008). Some point to women's tendency to ruminate as an explanation for why women are more likely to develop depression than men (Nolen-Hoeksema, 2012; Nolen-Hoeksema, Wisco, & Lyubomirsky, 2008). A recent meta-analysis on gender differences in depressive rumination confirmed higher rates of rumination, brooding, and reflection in women than men, although this difference was small in adults (Johnson & Whisman, 2013). As we will see in Chapter 16, some successful forms of therapy focus on changing negative patterns of thinking to reduce depression.

Quick Quiz 15.3: Depressive Disorders

1. Latresha is not hungry, is extremely tired, and doesn't feel like doing much of anything. She might be coming down with a cold, or she might be suffering from which disorder?
   a. generalized anxiety disorder
   b. bipolar disorder
   c. major depressive disorder
   d. obsessive-compulsive disorder
2. Persistent depressive disorder is a form of depressive disorder that is
   a. milder in intensity but longer lasting than major depressive disorder.
   b. milder in intensity but shorter in duration than major depressive disorder.
   c. more severe in intensity but longer lasting than major depressive disorder.
   d. more severe in intensity but shorter in duration than major depressive disorder.
3. Which of the following statements is TRUE regarding depressive disorders?
   a. Men and women are equally likely to develop depressive disorders.
   b. Depressive disorders most likely result from a combination of stress and biological predisposition.
   c. Medications that make more dopamine available in the brain stimulate neural growth, and lessen depressive symptoms.
   d. Cognitive factors, like rumination, play little role in the onset and development of depression.

Answers can be found at the end of the chapter.

LO7 BIPOLAR DISORDER

People who suffer from **bipolar disorder** experience severe mood fluctuations, often cycling between very low (major depressive) and very high (manic or hypomanic) episodes. (At one time, this disorder was called "manic depression.") **Manic episodes** typically involve increased energy, sleeplessness, euphoria, irritability, delusions of grandeur, increased sex drive, and "racing" thoughts that last *at least once a week*. **Hypomanic episodes** are nearly the same symptoms but shorter in duration—they last *at least four days* (APA, 2013).

A useful mnemonic for remembering the symptoms of mania is D-I-G-F-A-S-T (Carlat, 1998):

D = Distractibility
I = Indiscretion
G = Grandiosity
F = Flight of ideas
A = Activity increased
S = Sleep (decreased need for)
T = Talkativeness

bipolar disorder
a disorder characterized by substantial mood fluctuations, cycling between very low (depressive) and very high (manic) moods.

manic episodes
one mood cycle in bipolar disorder, typically involving increased energy, sleeplessness, euphoria, irritability, delusions of grandeur, increased sex drive, and "racing" thoughts.

hypomanic episodes
consist of the same symptoms as manic episodes (e.g., increased energy, sleeplessness, euphoria, irritability, delusions of grandeur, increased sex drive, and "racing" thoughts) but are shorter in duration.

In 2006, Margaret Trudeau, former wife of Prime Minister Pierre Trudeau and mother of Prime Minister Justin Trudeau, went public with her lifelong battle with bipolar disorder. Since then, she has become an advocate for mental illness, with the goal of reducing stigma.

The *DSM-5* distinguishes between two kinds of bipolar disorder, depending on the severity of the mania (APA, 2013). *Bipolar I* is more severe because it involves meeting the criteria for mania (at least seven days), whereas *bipolar II* is less severe because it involves meeting the criteria for hypomania (at least four days). Recall that *hypo* means "below," so hypomania is not as severe as mania. Thus, the degree of depression is the same in bipolar I and II, but the mania is less severe in bipolar II than in I. Regardless of the differing degree of mania, both bipolar I and bipolar II are debilitating disorders, leading to significant impairment in work and social functioning (APA, 2013).

People with either form of bipolar disorder often find the initial onset of the manic phase pleasant, especially compared to the dullness and despair of the depressive phase. Unfortunately, the symptoms quickly become quite unpleasant and frightening. The manic upswing spirals out of control, often leading to frenetic activity, excessive energy, and grandiose thinking, in which sufferers think they have relationships with important people or have expertise in areas where they have none. Indiscretion occurs when a person says things that are somewhat inappropriate or gets involved in promiscuous sexual relationships.

Virginia Woolf, the groundbreaking early-20th-century novelist, suffered from bipolar disorder. She dealt with bouts of severe depression and frenetic mania, which ultimately led to her suicide in 1941. Virginia's husband, the writer Leonard Woolf, offered revealing descriptions of her condition while manic:

> She talked almost without stopping for two or three days, paying no attention to anyone in the room or anything said to her. For about a day when she was coherent, the sentences meant something, though it was nearly all wildly insane. Then gradually it became completely incoherent, a mere jumble of dissociated words. (quoted in Jamison, 1993, p. 29)

cyclothymia
a relatively mild form of bipolar disorder.

In an even milder but longer-lasting form of bipolar disorder called **cyclothymia,** both the manic and depressive episodes are less severe than they are in bipolar II disorder—that is, the hypomanic and depressive symptoms never reach the criteria for hypomania and major depression. Bipolar disorder affects men and women in roughly equal proportions.

Nature and Nurture Explanations of Bipolar Disorder

What causes bipolar disorder? As is true for other psychological disorders, multiple biological and environmental factors appear to interact in ways scientists are only now beginning to understand. The dynamic relationship between the environment and brain in bipolar disorder may be seen as early as prenatal development. Fetuses exposed to large amounts of alcohol may suffer permanent effects, including increased risks for bipolar disorder as well as depression, schizophrenia, alcoholism, intellectual disability, and drug abuse (Famy, Streissguth, & Unis, 1998; O'Conner & Paley, 2006).

The genetics of bipolar disorder are complex. Many variations of genes appear to play a role in the development of the disorder, the specifics of which are only beginning to be understood (Comer, 2007; Luykx et al., 2010; Shastry, 2005). Twin studies reveal that if one identical twin develops bipolar disorder, there is a 40–70 percent chance that the other twin will also develop the disorder (Müller-Oerlinghausen, Berghöfer, & Bauer, 2002; Shastry, 2005). Even if the chance is 70 percent that both twins will have the disorder, life events, such as stress and trauma, also play a role in the development of bipolar disorder (Müller-Oerlinghausen et al., 2002; Shastry, 2005).

Abnormalities in the brains of people who suffer from bipolar disorder may be a cause or a result of the biochemical, genetic, and environmental elements that contribute to the disorder. The prefrontal cortex, amygdala, hippocampus, and basal ganglia all may play a role (Müller-Oerlinghausen et al., 2002; Shastry, 2005). Overactivity in many of these regions is evident in the PET scan images displayed in Figure 15.8, showing up as red areas compared to the blue regions that indicate reduced activity during a depressive phase. There may also be problems in the connectivity among the key regions involved in emotional processing, such as the prefrontal cortex and amygdala (Chepenik et al., 2010).

Neurochemistry is also important to bipolar disorder. In both the manic and depressed phases, serotonin levels are low, but low serotonin may be coupled with high levels of norepinephrine in the manic phase and with low levels in the depressed phase (Comer, 2007; Müller-Oerlinghausen et al., 2002). In addition, thyroid hormones, which control metabolism, are sometimes present in either abnormally high or low levels in people with bipolar disorder (Bauer & Whybrow, 2001; Müller-Oerlinghausen et al., 2002).

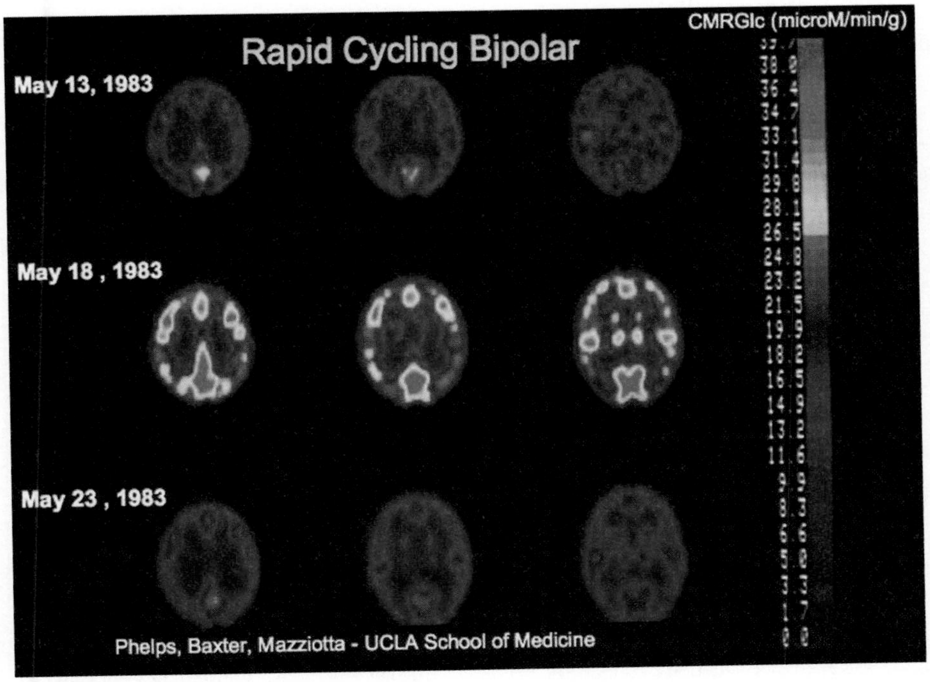

FIGURE **15.8**

THE BIPOLAR BRAIN. PET scan images show the brain of someone with bipolar disorder over the course of ten days. Blue and green indicate low levels of brain activity, and red and yellow indicate high levels of brain activity. The top and bottom images show the low activity of depression, whereas the middle images show an increased level of brain activity during mania.

Quick Quiz 15.4: Bipolar Disorder

1. David went home for Christmas break and he found that his mother, who was usually depressed, had just purchased dozens of bird houses from a local gift store. She'd had each custom wrapped and was planning to give them to all extended members of the family and all her neighbours, whom she claimed to love like family. She had spent thousands of dollars. What might be going on with David's mom?
   a. She won the lottery.
   b. She has bipolar disorder.
   c. She has an overactive hypothalamus.
   d. She is just depressed.
2. Which neurotransmitter is reduced in both the manic and depressed phases of bipolar disorder?
   a. acetylcholine
   b. dopamine
   c. norepinephrine
   d. serotonin
3. The difference between bipolar I and bipolar II disorder is that the
   a. manic episodes are less severe in bipolar I than bipolar II.
   b. manic episodes are more severe in bipolar I than bipolar II.
   c. depressive episodes are less severe in bipolar I than bipolar II.
   d. depressive episodes are more severe in bipolar I than bipolar II.

Answers can be found at the end of the chapter.

LO8 ANXIETY DISORDERS

Fear and anxiety are normal reactions to danger or future threat. These emotions create bodily changes—such as increases in heart rate—that support useful responses to danger. For some, however, fear and anxiety can get out of hand, occurring repeatedly in response to imagined threat and sometimes persisting for days. For about 26 percent of North Americans, though, anxious states can interfere with everyday functioning (Kessler et al., 2012; Anxiety Disorders Association of Canada, 2003). In this section we discuss five of the more common forms of anxiety disorders (see Figure 15.9).

Disorder	Major symptoms	Behaviours
Generalized anxiety disorder (GAD)	Pervasive/excessive anxiety lasting at least 6 months	Inability to relax
Panic disorder	Persistent worry about having a panic attack	*Panic attack:* Heart palpitations, trembling, dizziness, intense dread, and fear of dying *Panic disorder:* Prone to panic attacks, concerned about having a panic attack and about embarrassment of having a panic attack
Social anxiety disorder	Persistent fear of humiliation in the presence of others	Highly anxious, extremely self-conscious about appearance or behaviour or both, possibly housebound
Agoraphobia	Fear of not being able to escape or of help not being available if panic attack should occur in public place	Unwilling to leave home so as to avoid panic attacks
Specific phobias	Undue anxiety response to particular objects or situations	Intense fear or panic when confronted with particular situations or objects or even when thinking about them

FIGURE **15.9**

MAJOR SYMPTOMS AND CRITERIA OF SPECIFIC ANXIETY DISORDERS. (*Source:* APA, 2013.)

What overarching symptoms do all of these disorders share?

Generalized Anxiety Disorder

Generalized anxiety disorder (GAD) is a common anxiety disorder, characterized by a pervasive, excessive, and hard-to-control state of worry or anxiety that lasts at least six months (APA, 2013). People with GAD may also have trouble with sleep, body restlessness or agitation, difficulty concentrating, or muscle tension. Adults must exhibit at least three of the preceding symptoms to receive a diagnosis of GAD (APA, 2013). GAD affects between 3 percent and 9 percent of the North American population, although females are twice as likely as males to have GAD (Kessler et al., 2005; APA, 2013).

generalized anxiety disorder (GAD)
a state of pervasive and excessive anxiety lasting at least six months.

Unlike those suffering from other anxiety disorders, people with GAD often have been anxious throughout their lives and cannot recall when they began to feel that way (Barlow, 2004). In everyday language, we might call such a person a "worrywart"—someone who worries about anything and everything, often out of proportion to the actual threat. The writer, director, and actor Woody Allen has made a career out of his pervasive tendency to worry. Allen says he uses filmmaking and writing as a creative distraction from his anxiety (Briggs, 2005). The constant anxiety of GAD can be debilitating, however, preventing many people who suffer from it from being able to work at all.

Panic Disorder

The core of panic disorder is the panic attack. **Panic attacks** involve sudden changes in body and mind, characterized by an overwhelming sense of impending doom, heart palpitations, trembling, sweating, shortness of breath, dizziness, intense dread, nausea, and even a fear of dying (APA, 2013). Such attacks are associated with perceptions of threat and can occur for a number of reasons: fear of danger, inability to escape, fear of embarrassment, or fear of a specific category of objects. Panic attacks usually last about ten minutes but sometimes come and go over a period of an hour or more. Due to their physiological effects, people undergoing a panic attack may believe they are having a heart attack or are "going crazy."

panic attack
brief episodes of anxiety associated with a perception of threat and occurring because of fear of danger, an inability to escape, embarrassment, or specific objects.

Panic disorder is defined by frequent panic attacks and pervasive and persistent fear, worry, embarrassment, and concern about having more attacks (APA, 2013). The preoccupation with having another attack creates an anxious mood, which then increases the likelihood of more worrisome thoughts, and ironically, another attack. Thus, panic disorder creates a positive feedback cycle, wherein anxiety about future attacks hijacks the body's emergency response system and catapults it out of control. To receive a diagnosis of panic disorder, a panic attack must be followed by at least a month of persistent worry over future attacks, along with the development of potentially maladaptive behaviours to avoid attacks (e.g., avoidance of putting oneself in unfamiliar situations).

panic disorder
an anxiety disorder characterized by panic attacks and persistent anxiety about having more attacks.

People who have only occasional panic attacks without intense anxiety or fear about the possibility of future panic attacks do not qualify for the diagnosis of panic disorder. Approximately 7 percent of the Canadian population has experienced a panic attack in the past 12 months, whereas only about 1 percent to 4 percent of the population has panic disorder (Kinley et al., 2009). In North America, panic disorder is more common in women than men and less common in older adults. Overall, in Asian, African, and Latin American countries, the rates are very low—less than 1 percent—and the specific concerns or persistent worries appear to vary by culture (APA, 2013).

Social Anxiety Disorder (Social Phobia)

A **phobia** is a persistent and unreasonable fear of a particular object, situation, or activity (APA, 2013). Some people suffer extreme anxiety when they have to interact

phobia
an anxiety disorder marked by ongoing and irrational fear of a particular object, situation, or activity.

People with social anxiety disorder are extremely self-conscious and fearful of embarrassing themselves in front of others.

with other people, viewing each interaction as a possible opportunity to be scrutinized by others. **Social anxiety disorder,** or **social phobia,** is marked by a pronounced fear of humiliation or embarrassment in the presence of others, or severe self-consciousness about one's appearance, behaviour, or both. Consider the case of "Sarah," who hates going to the grocery store: She would not dare ask anyone working there how to find an item, out of fear that she might look as if she is stupid for not being able to find it herself. She doesn't want anyone to know she is anxious about being in the store. She is concerned that her voice might quiver when forced to say the obligatory "hello" to the cashier. This would make her seem really foolish and everybody would stare at her foolishness.

Fear like Sarah's can be paralyzing, making it very difficult to go out into public situations, even though in most cases the person recognizes that these fears are irrational. Unfortunately, the high degree of anxious arousal produced by social phobia may lead the person to act very nervously and thus, in a self-fulfilling way, exhibit behaviours that do indeed attract other people's attention.

social anxiety disorder (social phobia)
an anxiety disorder with fear of humiliation in the presence of others, characterized by intense self-consciousness about appearance or behaviour or both.

agoraphobia
an anxiety disorder involving fear of being in places from which escape might be difficult or in which help might not be available should a panic attack occur.

Agoraphobia

Agoraphobia is the most severe of all phobias (Bouton, Mineka, & Barlow, 2001). Contrary to popular belief, the primary "fear" in agoraphobia is not of being out in public. Formally, **agoraphobia,** is intense anxiety, fear, and panic about being in places from which escape might be difficult or in which help might not be available should a panic attack occur, such as in open spaces, in a public market, in line somewhere, outside of the home alone, or in enclosed spaces (e.g., movie theatres; APA, 2013). This fear of being unable to escape keeps people at home, where they feel safe. Panic attacks are associated with agoraphobia in about one-third of all cases.

Specific Phobias

Jennifer Aniston has spoken publicly about her fear of flying.

Only a few of us enjoy spiders, snakes, or heights, but most of us feel only mild levels of fear about such objects or experiences. Some of us, however, go beyond mild levels of fear. As many as one in eight people will develop a *specific phobia* for a particular object or situation, such as spiders (arachnophobia), heights, flying, enclosed spaces (claustrophobia), doctors and dentists, or snakes (Kessler et al., 2005). Specific phobias are marked by an intense and immediate fear, even panic, when confronted with very particular situations or objects; even thinking about those situations or objects may set off the fear reaction (APA, 2013). People with specific phobias will do almost anything to avoid coming into contact with the feared object or experiencing the feared event. Renowned Canadian pianist Glenn Gould, for example, limited most personal contact during the latter part of his life to phone conversations and letters because of his fear of being touched, a phobia known as haphephobia.

Nature and Nurture Explanations of Anxiety Disorders

How do anxiety disorders develop? Like all animals, humans have evolved fear mechanisms to determine whether a situation is safe or not and whether we need to try to fight or flee (LeDoux, 2000). Additionally, as is true for most complex traits, some people are more genetically disposed to anxiety than others. Anxiety disorders—and most other psychological disorders—result from the interplay between biological and environmental factors. Once again, we turn to examine integrated nature–nurture (diathesis–stress) explanations.

One biological factor that makes people vulnerable to anxiety disorders is their genetic heritage. Genetic heritability estimates for generalized anxiety, panic disorder, and agoraphobia range from 30 percent to 40 percent (Hettema, Neale, & Kendler, 2001; Maron, Hettema, & Shlik, 2010). Many different genes are likely involved in anxiety disorders (Leonardo & Hen, 2006), with some influencing the likelihood of developing one particular disorder, such as phobias, and others influencing the development of many different anxiety disorders, as well as other disorders (Kendler & Prescott, 2006). These latter types of genes with *broader effects* may be linked to the personality trait of neuroticism. People who are high in neuroticism—prone to worry, anxiety, and nervousness—are more likely to develop anxiety disorders than are people who are low in neuroticism (Eysenck, 1982; Hamer & Copeland, 1998). Degree of extraversion may play a role in some anxiety disorders as well. For instance, in panic disorder, people who are more introverted are more likely than those who are extraverted to avoid putting themselves in public situations (Rosellini, Lawrence, Meyer, & Brown, 2010).

Genes also likely affect the regulation of certain neurotransmitters implicated in anxiety (Dresler et al., 2013). Researchers have discovered that people who are prone to anxiety are deficient in receptors for GABA, a major inhibitory neurotransmitter (Charney, 2004; Nikolaus, Antke, Beu, & Muller, 2010). Deficiencies in GABA lead to excessive activation in certain brain regions, especially the limbic structures associated with fear. Moreover, the fact that some of the major medications for treating anxiety disorders work on GABA receptors is further evidence for GABA's role in anxiety. Some propose that these biological vulnerabilities produce intense physical sensations that may then be misinterpreted by anxiety-prone people (Antony, Ledley, Liss, & Swinson, 2006; Barlow, 2002; Gorman, Kent, Sullivan, & Coplan, 2000). For example, an anxiety-prone person with an overactive limbic system might be more likely to notice bodily changes, such as an accelerated heart rate and shortness of breath, interpret these symptoms as early signs of a heart attack, and react with intense worry. Studies suggest that people with panic disorder interpret bodily sensations more negatively than people with other anxiety disorders, as well as fearing these bodily responses more (Mathews & MacLeod, 2005; Olatunji & Wolitzky-Taylor, 2009; Taylor & Cox, 1998). Such *catastrophizing,* or imagining the worst possible outcomes, may exacerbate anxiety (A.T. Beck & Clark, 1988; Miranda & Mennin, 2007).

Anxiety disorders might also be the result of evolutionary adaptations gone awry. According to Seligman's (1971) *biological preparedness theory,* people are instinctively predisposed towards some fears. For example, people are more likely to form specific phobias for objects that were dangerous to our ancestors' survival, such as snakes, but not for contemporary threats, such as guns (Öhman, 2009). Consistent with this theory, research shows that people can be easily conditioned to fear common phobic objects, like snakes and spiders, but not neutral objects like flowers or mushrooms (Öhman, Dimberg, & Öst, 1985). People are also more easily conditioned to fear angry facial expressions (potential threats in our ancestral environment) than other types of facial expressions (Öhman, 2009; Woody & Nosen, 2008).

An ambitious study that is changing the way psychologists view the interaction between biology and environment in the development of psychological disorders, including anxiety disorders, is the Adverse Childhood Experiences (ACE) Study. For the ACE study, more than 17 000 participants have been interviewed about eight "adverse childhood experiences," including abuse, domestic violence, and serious household dysfunction (meaning that someone in the household abused drugs, had a psychological disorder, or committed criminal acts). Researchers correlated the adverse childhood experiences with health and mental health outcomes in adulthood.

The results were dramatic. The more adverse childhood experience participants reported, the worse the psychological outcomes. For example, someone who reported four or more adverse childhood experiences was two and a half times as likely to suffer from an anxiety disorder as someone who reported no adverse childhood experiences (Anda et al., 2006). Perry (2002) found that when children were removed from neglectful home environments at age one or two and placed in caring foster homes, the size of their brains increased dramatically. If they were removed from the neglectful environment after age four, however, there was little increase in brain size (circumference). If they were removed after age five, there was almost no increase (see Figure 15.10). Generally, for a child's brain size to be anywhere near normal, the child needs regular environmental stimulation by about age four.

In summary, people who have the bad luck of having a biological predisposition to anxiety *along with* the experience of chronic stress or abuse are

Connections

Brain development and language development, in particular, occur rapidly during critical periods, when we are biologically most receptive to a specific kind of input from the environment.

See Chapter 8, LO4; and Chapter 10, LO3.

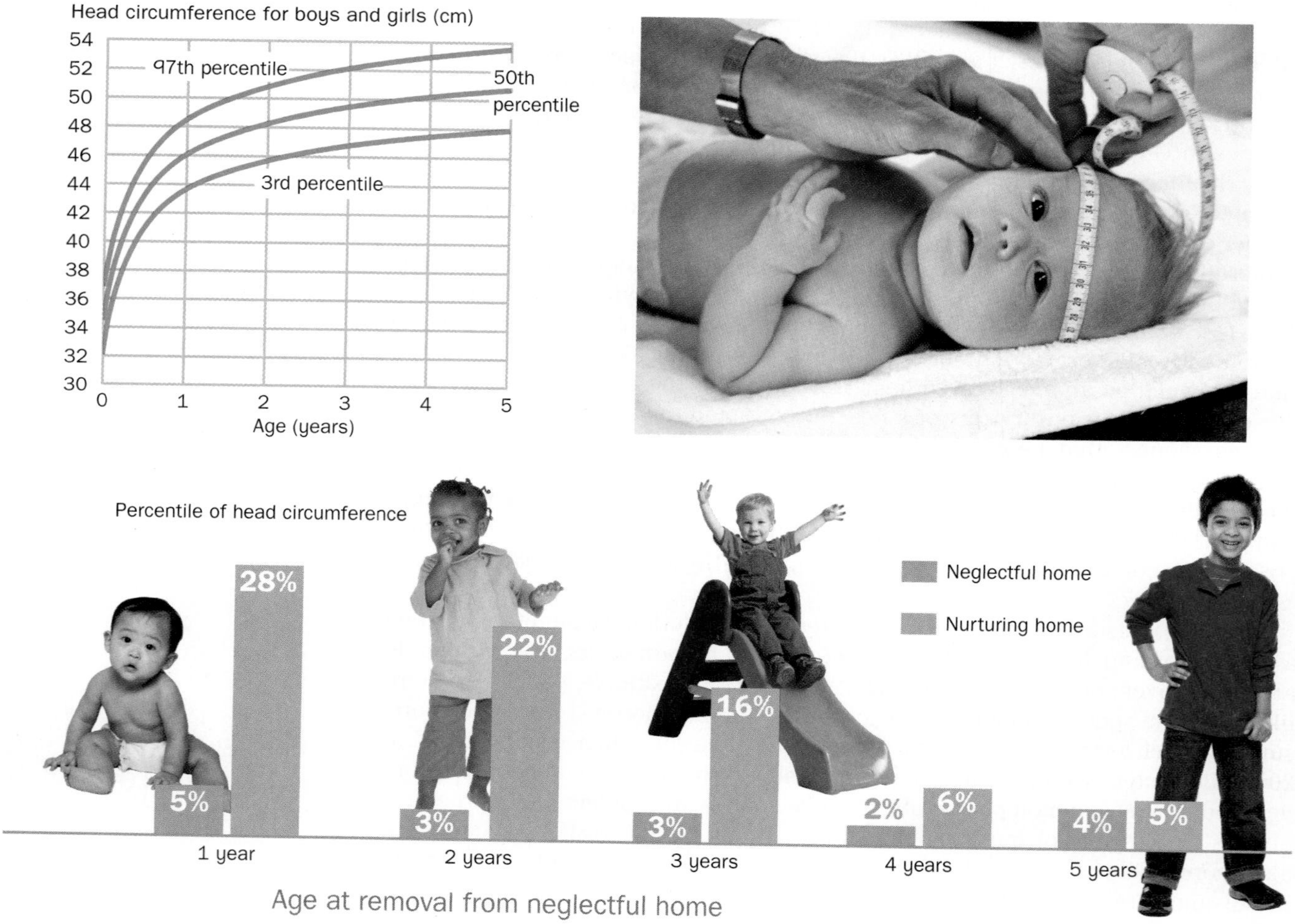

FIGURE **15.10**

EFFECTS OF NEGLECT AND REMOVAL FROM NEGLECTFUL ENVIRONMENTS ON CHILDREN'S BRAIN SIZE. Percentile of head circumference means the percentage of people in the population who have heads that are a particular size or smaller. Thus, the 30th percentile means that only 30 percent of people have that size or smaller. The younger the child is when he or she is removed from a neglectful home, the larger the brain/head size is after one year in a nurturing foster home. (*Source:* Perry, 2002.)

most likely to develop anxiety disorders. Those who have the biological predispositions *or* experience abuse are next most likely to develop these disorders, whereas those who have *neither* biological vulnerability nor chronically stressful experiences are least likely to develop these disorders.

Quick Quiz 15.5: Anxiety Disorders

1. Maya is preoccupied with fears of embarrassing herself in public, so much so that she avoids going shopping or out for walks in town. What disorder best describes this set of symptoms?
   a. generalized anxiety disorder
   b. specific phobia
   c. panic disorder
   d. social anxiety disorder
2. People who are prone to anxiety are deficient in receptors for _______, a major inhibitory neurotransmitter.
   a. GABA
   b. glutamate
   c. serotonin
   d. dopamine
3. Perry's ACE research has shown that if children who are raised in neglectful home environments are placed in caring and stimulating foster care at age five,
   a. their bodies recover but their brain size remains small the rest of their lives.
   b. their brains can bounce back and become average size.
   c. their brains show little increase in brain size.
   d. their brains show little increase at first but by age ten they are normal size.

Answers can be found at the end of the chapter.

LO9 OBSESSIVE-COMPULSIVE DISORDER

Obsessive-compulsive disorder (OCD) is a disorder that is manifested in both thought and behaviour. An **obsession** is an unwanted thought, word, phrase, or image that persistently and repeatedly comes into a person's mind and causes distress. People with OCD have thoughts that they cannot dismiss, especially negative thoughts that most people can disregard (APA, 2013). A **compulsion** is a repetitive behaviour performed in response to uncontrollable urges or according to a ritualistic set of rules. In short, obsessions are thought disturbances whereas compulsions are repetitive behaviours.

Obsessive-compulsive disorder most often involves cleaning, checking, or counting behaviours that interfere with everyday functioning. A man who is obsessed with security might check that the front door is locked 15 or 20 times before being able to drive away; a woman who is obsessed with germs might wash her hands dozens or even hundreds of times throughout the day. A famous example of OCD is the case of billionaire businessman and airplane innovator Howard Hughes, portrayed in the film *The Aviator*. Here, for example, are the explicit instructions Hughes gave his staff for removing his hearing aid cord from a cabinet:

> First use six or eight thicknesses of Kleenex pulled one at a time from the slot in touching the door knob to open the door to the bathroom. The door is to be left open so there will be no need to touch anything when leaving the bathroom. The same sheaf of Kleenex may be employed to turn on the spigots so as to obtain a good force of warm water. (quoted in Ludwig, 1995, p. 128)

Actor and comedian Howie Mandel wrote of his struggles with OCD in his autobiography *Here's the Deal: Don't Touch Me.*

obsessive-compulsive disorder (OCD)
a disorder in which obsessive thoughts lead to compulsive behaviours.

obsession
an unwanted thought, word, phrase, or image that persistently and repeatedly comes into a person's mind and causes distress.

compulsion
a repetitive behaviour performed in response to uncontrollable urges or according to a ritualistic set of rules.

People who suffer from OCD often know that their thoughts are irrational, or at least that their compulsive behaviours are excessive, but they cannot stop themselves. In some cases, compulsive behaviours stem from superstitions. For example, a man might feel the need to tap the wall 65 times before leaving a room for fear that not doing so will result in his parents dying. He knows rationally that there is no connection between wall tapping and the death of one's parents, but performs the ritual nevertheless. The 12-month prevalence rate of OCD in North America is 1.2 percent, and internationally it is between 1.1 percent and 1.8 percent (APA, 2013).

In OCD, too many thoughts are held in awareness, too much importance is ascribed to all thoughts (rational or irrational), and thinking about one's thoughts is excessive (Janeck at al., 2003). Research on cognitive performance in people with OCD reveals a preoccupation with conscious thinking; it is hard for people with this disorder to keep certain ideas or information out of awareness. Consequently, people with OCD have trouble with implicit learning but not with explicit learning (Goldman et al., 2008; Marker et al., 2006).

Connections

Implicit memory differs from explicit memory in terms of whether we are consciously aware of remembering. Similarly, some forms of learning occur automatically without conscious effort.

See Chapter 6, LO1; and Chapter 7, LO1, LO2.

Causes of Obsessive-Compulsive Disorder

Some scientists argue that the brain circuit that connects the caudate, the anterior cingulate cortex (ACC), and the limbic structures (such as the amygdala and hypothalamus) is working overtime in OCD (Aouizerate et al., 2004; Schwartz, 1999a, 1999b). The overactive ACC creates a perpetual feeling that something is wrong, which the limbic system structures translate into anxiety. In turn, anxiety stimulates more intrusive thoughts, which sometimes become compulsive actions. These actions occur as behavioural responses aimed at reducing the tensions or anxiety generated by the situation (from the caudate nucleus). Relief may be experienced, but only briefly, before the anxiety returns. The cycle goes on endlessly, due to the hyperactivity of the brain circuit—which is stuck in the "on" position. So this circuit involving the ACC, caudate nucleus, and limbic structures supports the obsessive thinking and compulsive responding (Fitzgerald et al., 2005; Guehl et al., 2008).

Quick Quiz 15.6: Obsessive-Compulsive Disorder

1. Rebecca has to count to seven chews every time she eats. If she is interrupted or loses count, she has to start all over again. This is an example of a(n)
   a. compulsion.
   b. obsession.
   c. anxiety.
   d. panic attack.

2. Joshua is constantly worried about getting sick from the germs everywhere he goes. He can't help but think about the germs, the germs, the germs. This is an example of a(n)
   a. compulsion.
   b. obsession.
   c. anxiety.
   d. panic attack.

Answers can be found at the end of the chapter.

LO10 POST-TRAUMATIC STRESS DISORDER

post-traumatic stress disorder (PTSD)
a type of trauma- and stressor-related disorder that involves intrusive and persistent cognitive, emotional, and physiological symptoms triggered by catastrophic or horrifying events.

Post-traumatic stress disorder (PTSD) is one of the trauma- and stressor-related disorders. PTSD involves a set of intrusive and persistent cognitive, emotional, and physiological symptoms triggered by exposure to a catastrophic or horrifying event—such as experiences of war, attempted murder, rape, natural disasters, the sudden death of a loved one, or physical or sexual abuse. In order to receive a diagnosis of PTSD, one must have directly experienced a traumatic event or witnessed such an event occurring to others, learned of a violent or accidental extreme trauma (e.g., death or sexual violence) occurring to a loved one, and/or repeatedly been exposed to or reminded of the details of such an event (APA, 2013). People suffering from PTSD experience a number of intrusive symptoms that last for at least one month. These may include recurring intrusive thoughts, feelings, or memories of the traumatic event, either while awake or dreaming, as well as *flashbacks,* vivid reactions in which the person feels as if he or she were experiencing the traumatic event all over again. There may be avoidance of situations or stimuli that might trigger the recollection of the event, as well as a number of persistent cognitive symptoms, such as a distorted view of oneself and self-blame associated with the trauma, as well as persistent emotional and physiological reactivity. For instance, people with PTSD are easily startled, may have hair-trigger tempers, and may be reckless or self-destructive.

War veterans are at increased risk not only for PTSD but also for depression, drug abuse, and suicide after returning home. The depth of despair in war-induced PTSD is seen in the following suicide note from an American Iraq war veteran who took his own life in June 2013: "All day, every day a screaming agony in every nerve ending in my body. It is nothing short of torture. My mind is a wasteland, filled with visions of incredible horror, unceasing depression, and crippling anxiety" (Cook, 2013). A 2013 survey of the Canadian military revealed that more than 5 percent of military personnel experienced an episode of PTSD within the past year (Statistics Canada, 2013). Rates of PTSD are even higher among those who have served in combat roles. Nine percent of Canadian Armed Forces personnel deployed to Afghanistan between 2001 and 2008 met the clinical diagnosis for PTSD within four years of their return (Boulos & Zamorski, 2014). Upwards of 24 percent of the U.S. veterans who served in Iraq have developed PTSD (Renshaw, 2011; Roehr, 2007; Tanielian & Jaycox, 2008). Research suggests the hypothalamic-pituitary axis, a major neuroendocrine system of the stress response (see Chapter 12), may be dysfunctional in war veterans with PTSD (Golier, Caramanica & Yehuda, 2012).

People of all ages can experience post-traumatic stress symptoms, including children who have experienced a serious trauma, such as extreme physical or sexual abuse (APA, 2013; Nixon, Ellis, Nehmy, & Ball, 2010). Compared to healthy controls, children with post-traumatic stress symptoms show reduced brain activity in the hippocampus while performing a verbal memory task (Carrion et al., 2010). The hippocampus plays a central role in learning and memory, so these results suggest that post-traumatic stress interferes with learning.

Following his return from the ill-fated United Nations' peacekeeping mission in Rwanda, Canadian General Roméo Dallaire blamed himself for being unable to stop the mass genocide. He developed post-traumatic stress disorder and attempted suicide before receiving proper medication and therapy. A recipient of the Order of Canada and retired senator, he now works tirelessly as an author, lecturer, and humanitarian to raise awareness about PTSD.

LO11 DISSOCIATIVE DISORDERS

dissociative disorders
psychological disorders characterized by extreme disruptions or gaps in memory, identity, or consciousness.

dissociative amnesia
a selective loss of memory, in the absence of brain damage, following a traumatic event.

dissociative fugue
a condition whereby a person forgets his or her identity and assumes a new one.

Daydreaming and being caught up in a great novel or movie are common everyday experiences in which we may lose our sense of time, space, and ourselves. **Dissociative disorders** magnify this effect: They produce extreme disruptions or gaps in memory, identity, or consciousness. These disorders lack a clear physical cause, such as brain injury, and often stem from extreme stress, trauma, or abusive experiences, especially during childhood. Although dissociative disorders are often associated with trauma, the *DSM-5* places them in their own category.

Dissociative amnesia is a condition characterized by a selective memory loss after a traumatic event. Often the memory loss is specific to the event itself, but some individuals suffer from more extensive loss of autobiographical memories. **Dissociative fugue,** a type of dissociative amnesia, is characterized by a loss of memory for one's own identity. The sufferer will often leave home and assume a new identity with no memory of his or her former life; after the fugue, there is no memory of the events that happened during the fugue state (Hennig-Fast et al., 2008). Dissociative fugue is extremely rare, occurring only in about two of every 1000 people (APA, 2013). The most dramatic dissociative disorder, however, is dissociative identity disorder and it will be the focus of this section.

Dissociative Identity Disorder

dissociative identity disorder (DID)
a dissociative disorder in which a person develops at least two distinct personalities, each with its own memories, thoughts, behaviours, and emotions. Some psychiatrists question the legitimacy of the disorder.

People with **dissociative identity disorder (DID)** develop at least two distinct personalities, each with a unique set of memories, behaviours, thoughts, and emotions. Consider the case of Eric, 29, who was found wandering around a shopping mall in Daytona Beach, Florida:

> Eric began talking to doctors in two voices: the infantile rhythms of "young Eric," a dim and frightened child, and the measured tones of "older Eric," who told a tale of terror and child abuse. According to "older Eric," after his immigrant German parents died, a harsh stepfather and his mistress took Eric from his native South Carolina to a drug dealers' hideout in a Florida swamp. Eric said he was raped by several gang members and watched his stepfather murder two men. (quoted in Comer, 2007, p. 208)

Eric had 27 distinct personalities, three of whom were female. Among these personalities were Dwight, a middle-aged and quiet man; Michael, an arrogant jock; Phillip, an argumentative lawyer; and Jeffrey, a blind, mute, and rather hysterical man.

Eric is a classic example of what used to be called "multiple personality disorder" but is now referred to as dissociative identity disorder (DID). The symptoms of DID include two or more distinct personality states, or "alters," amnesia, and self-destructive behaviours. People with DID may not remember anything about an experience or a particular period of their life. According to *trauma-dissociation theory,* individuals develop different identities to cope with the intense emotional pain resulting from a history of severe abuse (Putnam, 1989). In one study, more than 90 percent of people with DID reported having been either sexually or physically abused (Ellason, Ross, & Fuchs, 1996). Although it may not be diagnosed until adolescence, DID often develops in childhood (APA, 2013; Comer, 2007). Women are more likely to be diagnosed with DID than are men (APA, 2013).

However, the diagnosis of DID is somewhat controversial, with some psychiatrists claiming the diagnosis is not real but rather is produced unintentionally by therapists themselves (Putnam & McHugh, 2005). Many highlight the fact that the number of reported cases of DID has increased substantially from a few hundred before the 1970s to hundreds of thousands today, reflecting increased exposure to "multiple personalities" through popular North American culture, such as movies and books (Elzinga, van Dyck, & Spinhoven, 1998; Lilienfeld et al., 1999; Wilson, 2003). Further, there is a lack of solid research on the causes of the disorder. According to a recent review of a decade's worth of published cases of DID, the causes are still not well understood and actual occurrence rates are hard to identify (Boysen & VanBergen, 2013; Brand, Loewenstein & Speigel, 2013). In one survey, a majority of Canadian psychiatrists expressed reservations about including DID in the *DSM* and some have questioned the scientific evidence for the diagnosis, suggesting it is merely a "fad" (Lalonde et al., 2001; Pope, Barry, Bodkin, & Hudson, 2006).

In addition to increased prevalence, people diagnosed with DID today often report more "alters" than in the past (Elzinga et al., 1998). One view is that clients' and therapists' expectancies and beliefs are shaped by cultural factors, leading to over-diagnosis.

What role has popular culture played in the DID diagnosis?

Causes of Dissociative Disorders

People who suffer from dissociative disorders have one characteristic in common: they lived through a highly traumatic experience. They may have suffered sexual or physical abuse or survived a terrible accident or natural disaster in which a loved one was killed. Most explanations of dissociative disorder view it as a coping strategy that has gone awry (Putnam, 2006). The experience was so traumatic that the individual disconnects or dissociates the self from the event as a way of having it happen not to "him" or "her" but rather to "someone else." However, not everyone who experiences traumatic events develops a dissociative disorder. Also, some researchers and clinicians argue that DID results from a complex interaction of social-cognitive factors, including problems with attention and memory, disruptions in the sleep-wake cycle, and exposure to trauma or intense stress (Lynn, Lilienfeld, Merckelbach, Giesbrecht, & van der Kloet, 2012). Some theorists argue that particular personality traits, such as susceptibility to hypnotism, make some people more likely to develop dissociative disorders (Kihlstrom, 2005).

Quick Quiz 15.7: PTSD and Dissociative Disorders

1. Susan is the victim of a violent sexual assault. For the past month, she has been experiencing vivid flashbacks, feeling as if she is reliving the event all over again. It is likely that Susan is suffering from
   a. dissociative identity disorder.
   b. dissociative amnesia.
   c. post-traumatic stress disorder.
   d. bipolar disorder.
2. _______ produce(s) extreme splits or gaps in memory, identity, or consciousness.
   a. Dissociative disorders
   b. Bipolar disorders
   c. Mood disorders
   d. Post-traumatic stress disorder
3. Years ago, which disorder was known as multiple personality disorder?
   a. schizophrenia
   b. dissociative amnesia
   c. dissociative fugue
   d. dissociative identity disorder

Answers can be found at the end of the chapter.

LO12 PERSONALITY DISORDERS

personality disorders
maladaptive and inflexible patterns of cognition, emotion, and behaviour that develop in late childhood or adolescence.

As we saw in Chapter 13, personality consists of an individual's unique, long-term behaviour patterns. **Personality disorders** are maladaptive and inflexible patterns of cognition, emotion, and behaviour that generally develop in late childhood or adolescence and continue into adulthood. There are three distinct clusters of personality disorders: odd-eccentric, dramatic-emotional, and anxious-fearful (see Figure 15.11). Almost 15 percent of the general adult population (older than 18) and 20 percent of the young adult population (ages 18–25) suffer from some form of personality disorder (APA, 2013; Blanco et al., 2008; Lenzenweger, Lane, Loranger, & Kessler, 2007).

Odd-Eccentric Personality Disorders

schizoid personality disorder
an odd-eccentric personality disorder characterized by a desire to avoid close relationships as well as by emotional aloofness, reclusivity, and a lack of humour.

schizotypal personality disorder
an odd-eccentric personality disorder characterized by a desire to live an isolated and asocial life, but also by the presence of odd thoughts, perceptual distortions, and beliefs.

paranoid personality disorder
odd-eccentric personality disorder characterized by extreme suspicions and mistrust of others in unwarranted and maladaptive ways.

The three major odd-eccentric personality disorders are schizoid, schizotypal, and paranoid (APA, 2013). People with **schizoid personality disorder** do not want close relationships; are emotionally aloof, reclusive, and humourless; and want to live a solitary life. They always choose solitary activities; have little to no interest in sex; lack any close friends; and appear indifferent to praise or criticism from others. Similarly, a person with **schizotypal personality disorder** is also isolated and asocial, but in addition has very odd thoughts, perceptual distortions, and beliefs. For instance, people with schizotypal personality disorder may believe that stories on TV or in the newspaper were written directly about them. Moreover, the person dresses, acts, and appears in peculiar or eccentric ways.

People with **paranoid personality disorder** are extremely suspicious and mistrustful of other people, in ways that are both unwarranted and not adaptive. They may often test the loyalty of their friends and lovers because they regularly believe other people are trying to harm them. They may be regularly suspicious of their spouses' faithfulness even if there is no evidence they have been unfaithful. If someone does slight or insult them, they hold a grudge for an unusually long time. For example, if someone with paranoid personality disorder discovers that a colleague has just been promoted to a position she had wanted, she might

Cluster	Major symptoms	Personality disorders
Odd-eccentric	Lack of interest in social relationships, inappropriate or flat emotion, thought, and coldness	Schizoid
	Isolated, odd, and bizarre thoughts and beliefs	Schizotypal
	Extreme, unwarranted, and maladaptive suspicion	Paranoid
Dramatic-emotional	Wild, exaggerated behaviours, extreme need for attention, suicidal, seductive, unstable relationships, shifting moods	Histrionic
	Shifting moods, dramatic, impulsive, self-injury (e.g., cutting)	Borderline
	Grandiose thoughts and sense of one's importance, exploitative, arrogant, lack of concern for others	Narcissistic
	Impulsive, violent, deceptive, and criminal behaviour; no respect for social norms, ruthless	Antisocial
Anxious-fearful	Anxious and worrying, sense of inadequacy, fear of being criticized, nervousness, avoids social interaction	Avoidant
	Pervasive selflessness, need to be cared for, fear of rejection, total dependence on and submission to others	Dependent
	Extreme perfectionism and anxiety over minor disruption of routine, very rigid activities and relationships, pervades most aspects of everyday life	Obsessive-compulsive

FIGURE **15.11** **THREE CLUSTERS OF PERSONALITY DISORDERS AND THEIR MAJOR SYMPTOMS.** (*Source:* APA, 2013.)

conclude that the boss does not appreciate her and is actively trying to sabotage her career. When she sees co-workers talking later that day, she might assume that they are talking about her in a disparaging manner.

Dramatic-Emotional Personality Disorders

Another class of personality disorder involves dramatic and emotional disorders, of which there are four (APA, 2013). People with **histrionic personality disorder** want very much to be the centre of attention and often behave in very dramatic, seductive, flamboyant, and exaggerated ways. They can also be very emotional, intense, self-centred, and shallow in their emotions and relationships. Those with **borderline personality disorder** have out-of-control emotions, are very afraid of being abandoned by others, and vacillate between idealizing and despising those who are close to them. They are more likely than most to hurt themselves (cutting, burning, or attempting suicide) or suffer from eating disorders or substance abuse. Individuals with **narcissistic personality disorder** have an extremely positive and arrogant self-image, and most of their time and attention are self-focused. They have an exaggerated sense of self-importance and are grandiose. As a result, they often make unrealistic and unreasonable demands of others and ignore others' needs or wishes. They may be quite successful and climb the career ladder very quickly, but their narcissism often isolates them from others.

histrionic personality disorder
a dramatic-emotional personality disorder characterized by the desire to be the centre of attention and by dramatic, seductive, flamboyant, and exaggerated behaviours.

borderline personality disorder
a dramatic-emotional personality disorder characterized by out-of-control emotions, fear of being abandoned by others, and vacillation between idealizing and despising people who are close to the person with the disorder.

narcissistic personality disorder
a dramatic-emotional personality disorder characterized by having an extremely positive and arrogant self-image and being extraordinarily self-centred; other symptoms are an exaggerated sense of self-importance and grandiosity.

Perhaps the most captivating and intriguing of all personality disorders is **antisocial personality disorder,** which is marked by extremely impulsive, manipulative, ruthless, and callous behaviours. People with antisocial personality disorder often engage in criminal, deceptive, and violent behaviours. Indeed, although only about 3 percent of the population has this disorder, between 45 percent and 75 percent of male and 20 percent of female prison inmates are diagnosed with the disorder (Fazel & Danesh, 2002; Hare, 1993). Do not confuse *antisocial* with *asocial.* Antisocial personality is a potentially dangerous disorder, whereas being asocial simply means being shy and not enjoying social situations.

antisocial personality disorder
a dramatic-emotional personality disorder characterized by extremely impulsive, deceptive, violent, ruthless, and callous behaviours; a serious and potentially dangerous disorder.

Antisocial personality disorder was formerly known as *psychopathic personality disorder;* however, currently psychologists make a distinction between them. Most psychopaths meet the criteria for antisocial personality disorder, but the reverse is not necessarily true. Psychopaths show little empathy towards others and have difficulty forming close emotional bonds. They also show little fear of punishment, and within prison populations psychopaths are at high risk for reoffending (Hare & Neumann, 2009). Although psychopaths are overrepresented within the prison system, not all are involved in crime. Psychopaths act in their own self-interest without regard for others, which can be problematic in the workplace. The University of British Columbia's Robert Hare, a leading expert in psychopathy, co-authored a book in 2006 entitled *Snakes in Suits: When Psychopaths Go to Work,* describing the ways that psychopaths bully and manipulate others. Since psychopaths do not respond well to treatment, the authors strongly advise screening potential employees to avoid hiring people with these traits (Babiak & Hare, 2006).

Anxious-Fearful Personality Disorders

The third cluster of personality disorders consists of the avoidant, dependent, and obsessive-compulsive personality disorders. Each of these is characterized by persistent, high levels of anxiety, nervousness, and fear.

People with **avoidant personality disorder** are so afraid of being criticized that they avoid interacting with others and become socially isolated. They often feel inadequate and have low self-esteem and therefore tend to choose professions that allow them to be alone. People with **dependent personality disorder** fear being rejected and have such a strong need to be cared for. They feel safe only

avoidant personality disorder
an anxious-fearful personality disorder characterized by extreme fear of being criticized, low self-esteem, and avoidance of social interaction.

dependent personality disorder
an anxious-fearful personality disorder characterized by fear of being rejected and having a strong need to be cared for.

obsessive-compulsive personality disorder
an anxious-fearful personality disorder characterized by rigid habits and extreme perfectionism; more general than obsessive-compulsive disorder.

in relationships with others; ironically, however, they tend to drive others away because they are so clingy and demanding. People with **obsessive-compulsive personality disorder (OCPD)** are very rigid in their habits, extremely perfectionistic in how things have to be done, and frequently very rigid list makers and rule followers. This personality disorder is similar to the clinical disorder with the same name but is more general and does not have true obsessions and compulsions. Also, people with OCD know they have a problem, whereas people with OCPD are convinced their way is the right and only way things can be done. In short, obsessive-compulsive disorder (OCD) is usually focused only on cleanliness or checking, whereas OCPD is focused on all aspects of a person's life, as illustrated in the following case study of a 32-year-old accountant:

> For many years he has maintained an almost inviolate schedule. On weekdays he arises at 6:47, has two eggs soft-boiled for 2 minutes, 45 seconds, and is at his desk at 8:15. Lunch is at 12:00, dinner at 6:00, bed-time at 11:00. He has separate Saturday and Sunday schedules, the latter characterized by a methodical and thorough trip through the *New York Times*. Any change in schedule causes him to feel varying degrees of anxiety, annoyance, and a sense that he is doing something wrong and wasting his time. . . . [His] major problems are with women and follow the same repetitive pattern. At first, things go well. Soon, however, he begins to resent the intrusion upon his schedule a woman inevitably causes. This is most strongly illustrated in the bedtime arrangements. He must spray his sinuses, take two aspirin, straighten the apartment, do 35 sit-ups and read two pages of the dictionary. (Spitzer and colleagues, quoted in Nolen-Hoeksema, 2007, pp. 451–452)

Nature and Nurture Explanations of Personality Disorders

Research on murderers has identified a cluster of traits possessed by most of these violent criminals: being male, coming from abusive and neglectful households, having at least one psychological disorder (often antisocial personality disorder), and having suffered some kind of injury to the head or brain (Pincus, 1999, 2001; Strueber, Lueck, & Roth, 2006–2007). The frontal lobes and amygdala of many violent criminals are unusually disordered in size, activity, and function (Raine,

In the film *Monster*, Charlize Theron portrayed Aileen Wuornos, a prostitute who confessed to killing several men. Abandoned by her parents in childhood, Wuornos later ran away from her grandparents' home and turned to prostitution to support herself. At one of her trials, a psychiatrist testified that she was mentally ill with borderline personality disorder. Nevertheless, she was convicted of murder and later executed.

2013; Yang, Raine, Narr, Colletti, & Toga, 2009). Just being abused or having a psychological disorder or suffering a brain injury is not enough. To become antisocial and violent, a person usually has to experience all of these conditions.

Moreover, as a result of head injuries or living in a constant state of fear and abuse, or both, murderers almost always have moderate to severe problems of impulse control, social intelligence, working memory, and attention (Strueber et al., 2006–2007). Recall the principle of neuroplasticity from Chapter 3. Research on brain development suggests that living under a constant threat of abuse and stress changes the neural connectivity in the brain, making it less likely to develop many complex synaptic connections, especially in the frontal lobes. Being in a constant state of fear often leads to neural systems that are primed for unusually high levels of anxiety, impulsive behaviour, and a state of constant alertness. These are all conditions that might lead to violent or criminal behaviours. Finally, genetics interacts with abusive experience to create personality disorders. Different forms of one particular gene, for instance, when coupled with being abused as a child, make violent and antisocial behaviour in adulthood more likely (Caspi et al., 2002).

Connection

Neuroplasticity occurs when neurons and hence brain structure and function change as a result of input from the environment.

See Chapter 3, LO13.

Connection

How does our first environment—the womb—shape the expression of our genes?

See Chapter 3, LO2.

Quick Quiz 15.8: Personality Disorders

1. People with _______ personality disorder are so afraid of being criticized that they stay away from others and become socially isolated.
   a. borderline
   b. avoidant
   c. dependent
   d. psychopathic

2. Individuals with which kind of personality disorder are most likely to commit crimes and end up in jail?
   a. histrionic personality disorder
   b. narcissistic personality disorder
   c. antisocial personality disorder
   d. avoidant personality disorder

Answers can be found at the end of the chapter.

Evaluating Connections in Psychological Disorders

Creativity and Mental Health

Recall the mental anguish of Vincent van Gogh, whom we described at the beginning of the chapter. Ludwig von Beethoven, Wolfgang Amadeus Mozart, Robert Schumann, Virginia Woolf, Ernest Hemingway, William Styron, Jackson Pollock, Howard Hughes, Sylvia Plath, Salvador Dali, and the Nobel Prize–winning mathematician John F. Nash Jr. are other creative geniuses who have suffered from a psychological disorder. So many creative individuals have experienced psychological disorders that many people think creativity and disorders of the mind are connected. The term *mad genius* reflects this belief. To be clear, however, suffering from psychological disorders is not necessary to be creative. However—at least in art, literature, poetry, and music—there are higher rates of these disorders than in the general population (Ludwig, 1995; Post, 1994).

Exploring the connection between psychological disorders and creativity offers an opportunity to look again at the topics discussed in this chapter. We address two questions: (1) What is the evidence that creative people suffer from psychological disorders at a higher rate than the rest of the population? (2) Which disorders are more likely to be linked with creativity?

Evidence for a Relationship between Creativity and Psychological Disorders

To help us answer the first question, we can look at an impressive study of creativity and psychological disorder conducted by Arnold Ludwig. In a biographical study of 1005 eminent people in 18 professions, Ludwig (1995) examined the lifetime rates of psychological disorder across the professions and over lifetimes. Lifetime rate simply means the likelihood that a person will suffer a disorder at some point in her or his lifetime. Lifetime rates for any psychiatric illness are remarkably high for people in the arts: 87 percent of poets, 77 percent of fiction writers, 74 percent of actors, 73 percent of visual artists, 72 percent of non-fiction writers, 68 percent of musical performers, and 60 percent of musical composers (see Figure 15.12). Compare these figures with the 46 percent lifetime rate in the general population for any disorder (Kessler et al., 2005). The data from this large-scale study clearly indicate a higher prevalence of psychological disorders in creative artists than people in the general population.

Which Disorders Affect Creative Individuals?

Not all disorders are associated with creative ability. There is evidence, however, for a connection between creativity and many of the disorders we discussed in this chapter.

Autism Spectrum Disorder and Creativity

Some people with autism spectrum disorder are extremely gifted in one domain, such as music or math, a phenomenon known as savant syndrome (see Chapter 9). Most autistic savants do not produce great works of original genius because their amazing feats of calculation and recall are not original. However, some savants do produce truly creative works of art, usually math analyses, musical compositions, drawings, or paintings (Fitzgerald, 2004). One of the 20th century's greatest mathematicians, Srinivasa Ramanujan, showed clear signs of childhood autism (Fitzgerald, 2004). Composer Wolfgang Amadeus Mozart, also, may have been such a savant. A contemporary creative savant is Matt Savage (born in 1992), who was diagnosed with autism at the age of three. He is a professional jazz musician and composer who had recorded three albums by the time he was 14.

Asperger's syndrome, or what is now known as high-functioning autism, has been associated with creative ability in science, math, and engineering (Austin, 2005; Baron-Cohen et al., 2001). Baron-Cohen and his colleagues have shown that engineers, mathematicians, and physical scientists score much higher than non-scientists on measures of high-functioning autism or Asperger's syndrome and score higher than social scientists on a non-clinical measure of autism. Lastly, children with Asperger's syndrome are more than twice as likely as normal children to have a father or grandfather who was an engineer (Baron-Cohen et al., 1997; Baron-Cohen et al., 1998; Baron-Cohen et al., 2001).

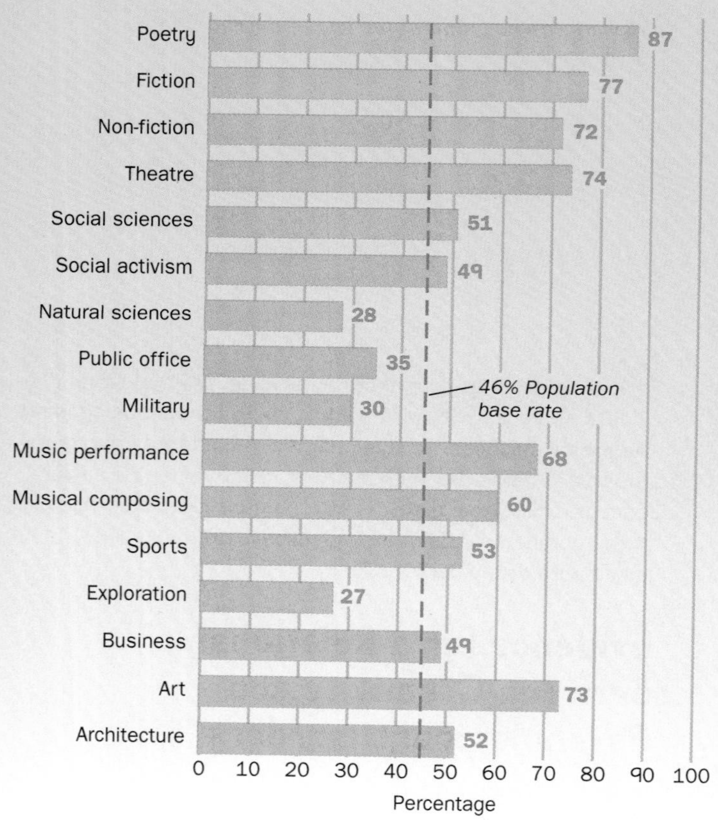

FIGURE **15.12**
LIFETIME RATES OF PSYCHOLOGICAL DISORDERS IN FAMOUS PEOPLE IN 16 DIFFERENT PROFESSIONS. (*Source:* Ludwig, 1995.)

Psychotic Symptoms and Creativity

Having unusual thoughts is common to both creative people and those with schizophrenia. For instance, much of the art of Salvador Dali, who claimed to be psychotic, consists of bizarre, dreamlike images—bordering on the kinds of delusions experienced by people with schizophrenia. John F. Nash Jr., the mathematician made famous by the book and movie *A Beautiful Mind,* was a creative person who also had schizophrenia (Nasar, 1998). He was creative despite, rather than because of, the psychotic episodes he experienced; all of his creative work preceded his schizophrenic symptoms and stopped after they began.

It is the milder psychotic symptoms, however, that are most strongly associated with creativity (Fink, Slamar-Halbedl, Unterrainer, & Weiss, 2012; Kinney et al., 2000–2001; Nettle & Clegg, 2006; Schuldberg, 2000–2001). Each of the following groups of people manifest unusual thought processes that are milder than those of schizophrenia: first-degree relatives of individuals with schizophrenia, people with schizotypal personality disorder, and those who score high on the normal personality dimension of psychoticism (see Chapter 13). These people are more likely to have unusual thought processes that develop into creative achievements that other people recognize to be significant (Burch et al., 2006; Fisher et al., 2004). Having a lot of ideas come to mind quickly can lead to many unusual associations that may be creative, but they may also be so unusual as to be similar to the bizarre associations seen in people with schizophrenia (Carson, Peterson, & Higgins, 2003; Eysenck, 1995; Fink et al., 2012). Recent evidence has uncovered variations in a gene (*neuregulin 1*) that appears to connect psychosis and creativity; it may partially explain why a maladaptive trait such as schizophrenia would continue in the gene pool (Keri, 2009; Venkatasubramanian & Kalmady, 2010).

Depression and Creativity

Emotional distress is a familiar companion to creative people. Many highly creative people have suffered from major depression (Ludwig, 1995). Across the 16 professions identified in Figure 15.12, the lifetime rate of depression was 30 percent, with poets (77 percent), fiction writers (59 percent), and visual artists (50 percent) having the highest rates. In addition, poets are 20 times more likely to commit suicide, a key indicator for depression, than most people (Ludwig, 1995). One recent study, in fact, found that social rejection combined with a biological disposition toward depression enhanced participants' artistic creativity (Akinola & Mendes, 2008). In less creative populations, there is often only a weak relationship between depression and creativity (Silvia & Kimbrel, 2010).

Although highly creative artists and writers may have a higher rate of depression than the general population, depressive episodes themselves do not generate much creative output. Recall that a complete lack of motivation is a common symptom of depression, so lower productivity would follow. Still, the experiences one has while depressed might inspire and motivate the creation of works of art as a way of understanding it.

Bipolar Disorder and Creativity

For more than three decades, studies of the relationship between psychological disorders and creativity have devoted more attention to bipolar illness than to any other condition (Andreasen & Glick, 1988; Bowden, 1994; Fodor & Laird, 2004; Jamison, 1993; Ludwig, 1995). Actors (17 percent), poets (13 percent), architects (13 percent), and non-fiction writers (11 percent) all exceed a 10 percent lifetime rate of bipolar disorder—10 times the rate in the general population (Ludwig, 1995).

There is a positive relationship between bipolar disorder and creative thought. For instance, some studies show that highly creative people are more likely than non-creative people to have bipolar disorder (Andreasen, 1987, 2006; Jamison, 1993; Jamison et al., 1980; Richards, 1994). Others report the other side of the coin: People with bipolar disorder are likely to be more creative than those without this condition (Fodor & Laird, 2004; Richards, 1994; Richards & Kinney, 1990). Indeed, many creative individuals throughout history have been bipolar (Jamison, 1993).

The manic phase is more likely than the depressive phase to generate creative behaviour (Andreasen & Glick 1988; Jamison et al., 1980). Few artists and writers are creative during their depressed phases; rather, they are creatively inspired during a milder form of mania, the hypomanic phase. A tragic example is the composer Robert Schumann whose output and episodes of mania and depression are graphed in Figure 15.13.

Challenge Your Assumptions

True or False? All the great artists in history can be viewed as psychologically disturbed.

False: Creative artists are at higher risk for mental illness over the course of their lifetimes, but there are many exceptions to the rule. There is no causal connection between the two.

Connection

Creative thinking requires novelty and problem-solving.

See Chapter 9, LO8.

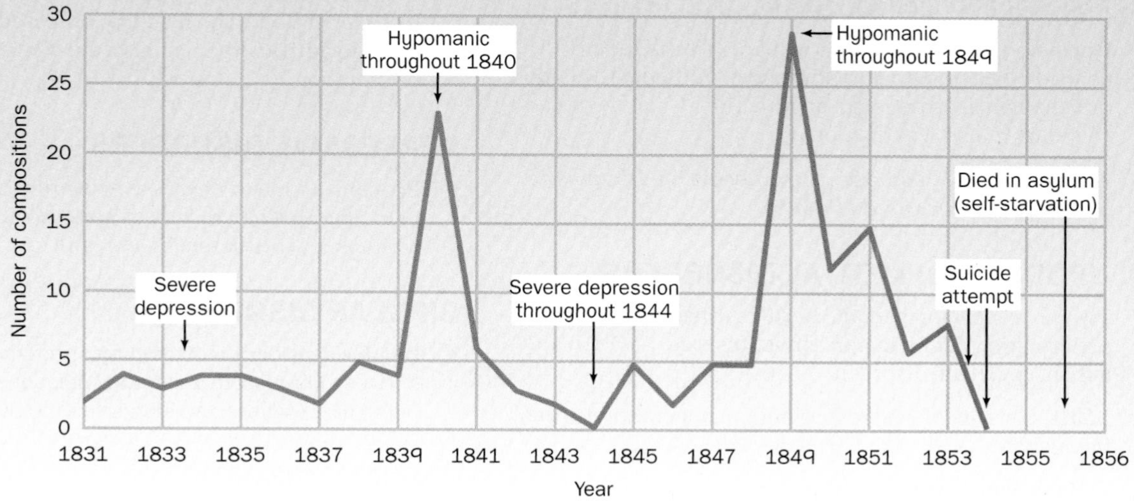

FIGURE **15.13**

BIPOLAR DISORDER AND CREATIVITY IN THE WORK OF ROBERT SCHUMANN. The composer's creative output coincided directly with the highs and lows of his disorder. His most productive years (1840 and 1849) were marked by his most hypomanic periods. (*Source:* Slater & Meyer, 1959.)

Quick Quiz 15.9: Evaluating Connections in Psychological Disorders

1. Research shows which psychotic disorder is most strongly associated with creativity?
   a. schizophrenia
   b. schizotypal personality disorder
   c. schizoid personality disorder
   d. split-personality

2. With respect to the relationship between bipolar disorder and creativity, the _______ phase is more likely to produce creative behaviour than the _______ phase. (Pick the best pair of words.)
   a. depressive; manic
   b. cognitive; depressive
   c. manic; depressive
   d. manic; affective

Answers can be found at the end of the chapter.

Chapter Review

DEFINING PSYCHOLOGICAL DISORDERS

- Psychologists agree on four general criteria for a psychological disorder: disturbance (of thought, emotion or behaviour), distressing, dysfunctional, and deviant (but only if also dysfunctional).
- A major tool for diagnosing disorders is the *Diagnostic and Statistical Manual (DSM-5).*

NEURODEVELOPMENTAL DISORDERS

- Two neurodevelopmental disorders affecting children are attention deficit hyperactivity disorder (ADHD) and autism spectrum disorder.
- ADHD consists of severe inattention, hyperactivity, and impulsivity.
- Children with autism spectrum disorder (ASD) show very inward-focused behaviours, with severe language and social impairment combined with repetitive habits and behaviours. They also have serious deficits in understanding other people's thoughts, feelings, and intentions.

SCHIZOPHRENIA

- Schizophrenia is a psychotic disorder of profound disturbances in thought, perception, and emotion.
- Positive symptoms of schizophrenia include hallucinations, delusional thinking, and disorganized thought and speech.
- Negative symptoms of schizophrenia include non-responsiveness, flattened affect, immobility or strange poses, reduction of speaking, and inability to complete tasks.
- Cognitive symptoms of schizophrenia include disordered thinking, including impaired attention and profound difficulty in monitoring conflicting sources of information.

DEPRESSIVE DISORDERS

- People with major depressive disorder experience a pervasive low mood, lack of motivation, low energy, and feelings of worthlessness and guilt.

BIPOLAR DISORDER

- Bipolar disorder involves substantial mood fluctuation between depressive and manic episodes, with bipolar I being more severe and longer-lasting than bipolar II.

ANXIETY DISORDERS

- Anxiety disorders occur when fears and worrying are out of proportion to the situation and interfere with everyday functioning.

- Generalized anxiety disorder, a pervasive state of anxiety lasting at least six months, consists of excessive worrying about relatively minor events of daily life.
- Panic disorder is extreme anxiety about having a panic attack.
- Social anxiety disorder (social phobia), a pronounced fear of humiliation in the presence of others, is marked by severe self-consciousness about appearance, behaviour, or both.
- Specific phobias involve an intense fear when confronted with particular situations or objects, such as spiders or heights.

OBSESSIVE-COMPULSIVE DISORDER

- Obsessive-compulsive disorder is a disorder of thought (obsession) and behaviour (compulsion).
- Obsessions are anxiety-producing thoughts that can preoccupy a person throughout the day and are beyond the person's control.
- Compulsions are repetitive behaviours, which are often rituals that people have developed to control the anxiety created by the obsessions.

POST-TRAUMATIC STRESS DISORDER

- PTSD involves a set of intrusive and persistent cognitive, emotional, and physiological symptoms triggered by exposure to a catastrophic or horrifying event—such as experiences of war, attempted murder, rape, natural disasters, sudden death of a loved one, or physical or sexual abuse.

DISSOCIATIVE DISORDERS

- Dissociative disorders entail the loss of a sense of time and space but also involve extreme gaps in memories, identity, or consciousness.
- People with dissociative identity disorder (DID) develop at least two distinct personalities, each of whom has a unique set of memories, behaviours, thoughts, and emotions. Some experts have reservations about classifying DID as a disorder.

PERSONALITY DISORDERS

- The schizoid personality is very emotionally cold, reclusive, humourless, or uninteresting; someone with schizotypal personality disorder expresses very odd thoughts and behaviour, is socially isolated, and has a restricted range of emotions.
- Paranoid personality disorder is marked by extreme suspiciousness and mistrust of other people, in ways that are both unwarranted and not adaptive.
- Those with borderline personality disorder suffer from out-of-control emotions, are very afraid of being abandoned by others, and vacillate between idealizing those close to them and despising them.
- People with dependent personality disorder fear rejection and have such a strong need to be cared for that they form very clingy relationships with others.
- Antisocial personality disorder is marked by extremely impulsive, deceptive, violent, and ruthless behaviours.

EVALUATING CONNECTIONS IN PSYCHOLOGICAL DISORDERS

- Creativity and psychological disorders are related, especially in the arts. Disorders such as depression, bipolar disorder, anxiety disorders, substance abuse, and suicide occur at higher rates in creative artists than in members of other professions and in the general population.

Quick Quiz Answers

Quick Quiz 15.1: 1. b 2. a 3. d **Quick Quiz 15.2:** 1. c 2. c 3. b **Quick Quiz 15.3:** 1. c 2. a 3. b
Quick Quiz 15.4: 1. b 2. d 3. b **Quick Quiz 15.5:** 1. d 2. a 3. c **Quick Quiz 15.6:** 1. a 2. b
Quick Quiz 15.7: 1. c 2. a 3. d **Quick Quiz 15.8:** 1. b 2. c **Quick Quiz 15.9:** 1. b 2. c

Treatment of Psychological Disorders

CHAPTER 16

CHAPTER OUTLINE

Challenge Your Assumptions

True or False?

- ☐ People can learn to not be afraid of flying.
- ☐ Shock therapy is never effective and is no longer used.
- ☐ Direct stimulation of neurons by electrical impulse is science fiction and is not used in treatment today.
- ☐ Talk therapy might make people feel better, but it does not change the brain.
- ☐ All effective psychotherapies involve people confronting the "root" childhood causes of their problems.

LEARNING OBJECTIVES

LO1 Identify and describe the techniques used by psychodynamic therapists to uncover unconscious motives.

LO2 Describe the goal of humanistic therapy.

LO3 Explain how token economies, systematic desensitization, and flooding are used to alter maladaptive behaviours.

LO4 Explain the approach of cognitive therapy in treating psychological disorders.

LO5 Describe how group settings are used in therapy.

LO6 Compare the differences and similarities between typical and atypical antipsychotic drugs.

LO7 Describe how the major classes of antidepressants and antianxiety drugs act at synapses.

LO8 Explain why bipolar disorder is often treated with several types of drugs.

LO9 Compare and contrast the procedures and effectiveness of prefrontal lobotomies, electric, and magnetic therapies in treating psychological disorders.

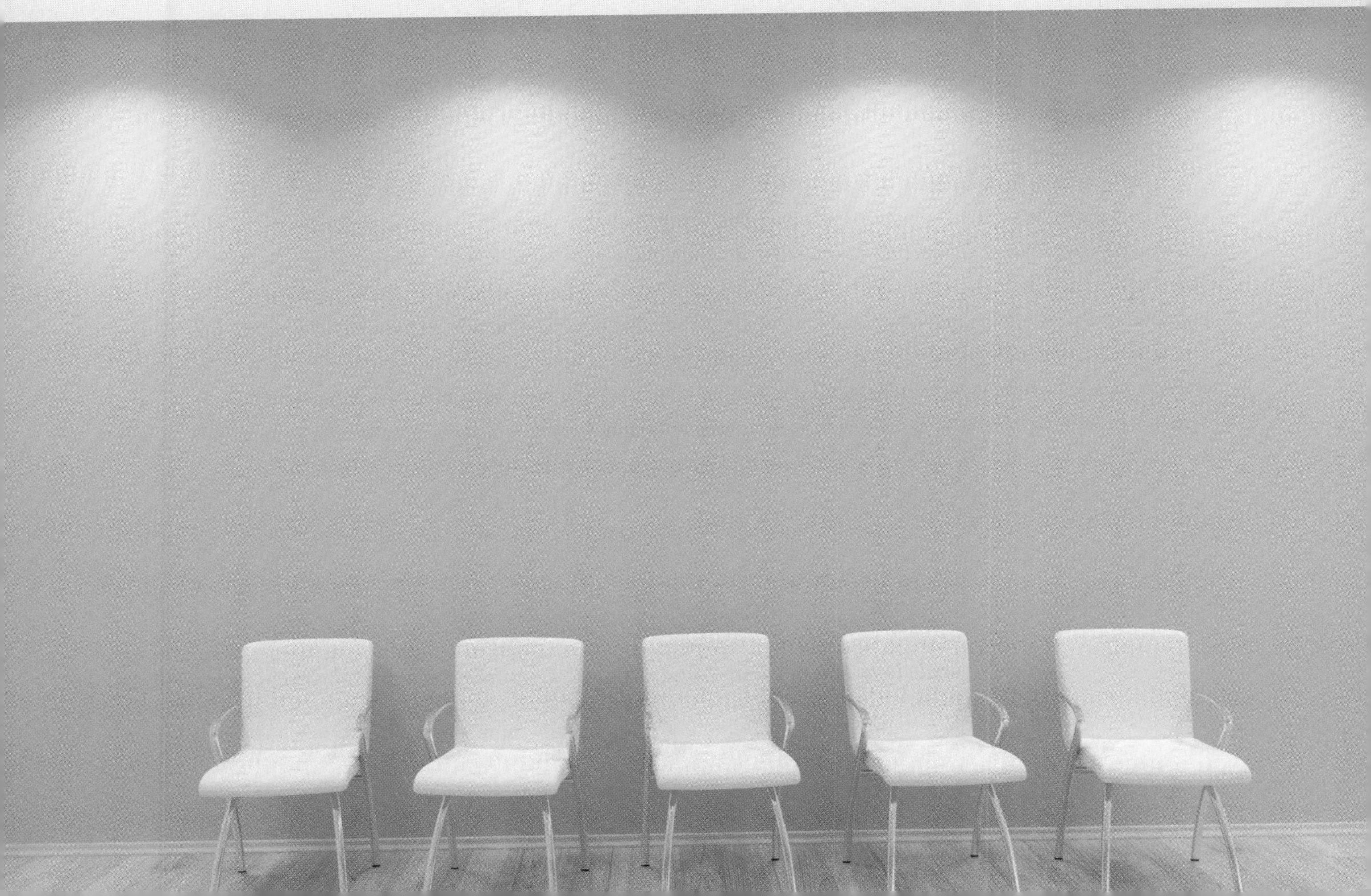

LO10 Summarize how therapies can be combined to treat psychological disorders.

LO11 Evaluate treatment effectiveness for psychological disorders.

LO12 List examples and evaluate the empirical evidence for emerging therapies.

LO13 Describe the goals and evaluate the effectiveness of prevention programs.

As you learned in Chapter 15, the causes of mental illness are often poorly understood. In many such cases, researchers have identified numerous potential causes, so treatment providers are often faced with conflicting points of view on how best to proceed. Changing pathological behaviour and thought is usually the goal of any approach, but what is the best way to do this?

One of the most shocking and controversial approaches was carried out in the 1950s under the direction of Dr. Ewen Cameron, a psychiatrist at the Allan Memorial Hospital in Montreal. Cameron practised an approach he called "psychic driving," which involved playing messages repeatedly to patients in order to replace their maladaptive thoughts and attitudes about themselves with those that were more beneficial (Cameron, 1956). In order to prepare patients for reception of these repetitive messages, Cameron thought it necessary to break down the individual's defences, or essentially wipe out their personalities and memories. In order to achieve this objective, Cameron used a variety of techniques, ranging from sensory deprivation, drug-induced comas, isolation, massive doses of insulin, and extreme doses of electroconvulsive shock therapy (Brown, 1997).

Many of Cameron's patients went on to suffer long-term damage resulting from the treatment they received while under his care. In particular, many experienced significant memory loss as a result of prolonged administration of electroconvulsive shocks. The plight of Cameron's patients came to light in the mid-1970s, when it was revealed that his work was secretly funded by the CIA in an alleged attempt to research Communist brainwashing techniques (Klein, 2007). The CIA and Canadian government awarded compensation to some of the most severely affected former patients, while others are still awaiting court decisions.

This disturbing example illustrates the vulnerable position in which sufferers of psychological disorders sometimes find themselves. It also underlines the importance of ethical standards in developing treatments. Cameron's psychic driving theories were not widely accepted by the scientific community, and his links to the CIA meant that his findings were long shrouded in secrecy. Today accepted treatments for disorders are tested using the scientific method and debated by the scientific and medical community. Psychiatrists, psychologists, and other mental health professionals draw on biologically based, psychological, and integrative treatments to help people with various kinds of disorders. Although we discuss the biological treatments and the psychological treatments separately for clarity, we must bear in mind that both categories of treatment can and do modify the brain.

TREATMENT APPROACHES

Making an informed decision about treatment for mental illness can be daunting, especially since we are often exposed to popular culture's portrayal of mental illness, rather than the views of the scientific community. For instance, mental illness is a theme in many popular films. Slasher films such as *Nightmare on Elm Street*,

Friday the 13th, and *The Silence of the Lambs* associate mental illness with homicidal violence. Some films and novels suggest that harmless personality quirks are inappropriately labelled as pathological and unnecessarily treated, such as the case in *One Flew Over the Cuckoo's Nest* (Wedding & Niemiec, 2003). Painting psychological disorders and their treatment in a negative light can be a significant barrier for some sufferers since they might be hesitant to admit to their illness and seek help, an issue we will revisit towards the end of the chapter. Even if an individual does decide to seek professional help for a disorder, the type of treatment is often influenced by the values and beliefs of the client. In a survey of patients who were newly prescribed antidepressant medication by their family doctors, those who were initially skeptical of the medication were less likely to adhere to drug treatment (van Geffen et al., 2010). Fortunately, there are a number of effective treatment strategies for psychological disorders, which will be the main topic of this chapter.

Different treatment strategies are offered by mental health professionals with specific training and certification. *Clinical psychologists* hold a doctoral degree, or Ph.D., with training in both research and clinical practice and work in clinics, hospitals, and private practice. Some clinical psychologists focus predominantly on research and work in universities. The treatment techniques most often used by clinical psychologists are often considered psychological, in that they rarely involve drug treatment or invasive techniques like surgery. *Counsellors* typically have doctoral degrees in counselling psychology and receive some of the same training as clinical psychologists, but with much less emphasis on research. *Social workers* typically hold master's degrees and use many of the same techniques as psychologists. Their focus is often on issues, such as parenting and substance use, which impact an individual's functioning in the community. *Psychiatrists* and *neurologists* also specialize in the treatment of mental illness, and have medical degrees as well as residency training. These professionals are licensed to prescribe pharmaceutical drugs, whereas most psychologists are not. *Family doctors* can also prescribe medication for mental illness, and in fact write more prescriptions for antidepressant and anti-anxiety drugs than psychiatrists do (Harman et al., 2000; Morrison et al., 2009).

Three major forms of treatment exist: psychological, biological, and integrative (see Figure 16.1). The psychological therapies include psychodynamic (psychoanalytic), humanistic, cognitive, and behavioural therapies. Drugs,

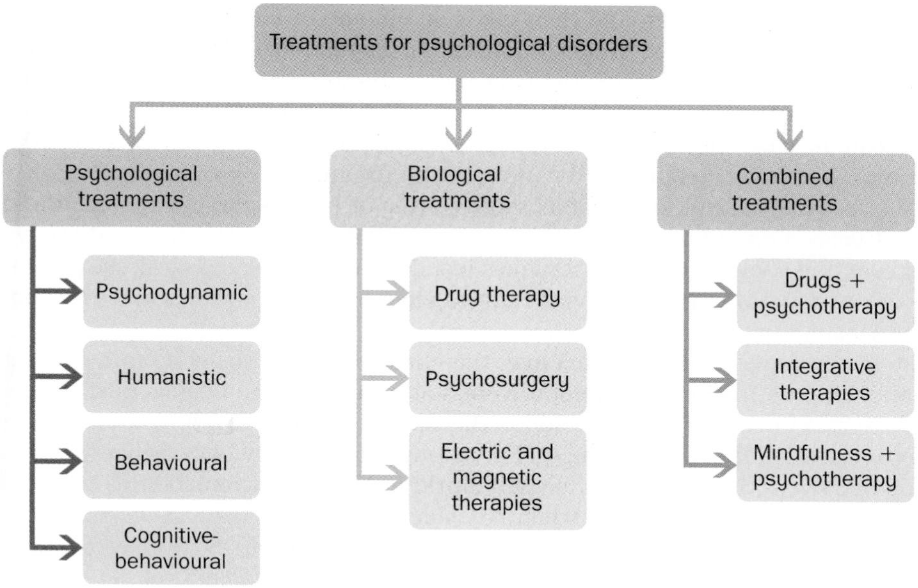

FIGURE **16.1**
THREE MAJOR APPROACHES TO THE TREATMENT OF PSYCHOLOGICAL DISORDERS.

surgical treatments, and electric and magnetic treatments comprise the biological approaches. The integrative therapies combine either drugs and psychotherapies or different variations of psychotherapy. Let's first consider the psychological treatments.

PSYCHOLOGICAL TREATMENTS

psychotherapy
the use of psychological techniques to modify maladaptive behaviours or thought patterns, or both, and to help patients develop insight into their own behaviour.

Psychotherapy is the use of psychological techniques to modify maladaptive behaviours or thought patterns, or both, and to help patients develop insight into their own behaviour. In psychotherapy a therapist and a client work together, or a therapist works with a group of people.

People may engage in psychotherapy for self-development as well as for the treatment of psychological disorders. In this chapter, we will focus on the use of psychotherapeutic techniques in treating disorders. There are several types of psychotherapeutic approaches, as outlined in Figure 16.1: psychodynamic, humanistic, behavioural, cognitive, and cognitive-behavioural. Each type of psychotherapy has its own explanation of what causes different disorders as well as how they should be treated.

LO1 Psychodynamic Therapy

psychodynamic psychotherapy
therapy aimed at uncovering unconscious motives that underlie psychological problems.

Inspired by Freudian psychoanalytic theory, **psychodynamic psychotherapy** aims to uncover unconscious motives that underlie psychological problems. The relationship between therapist and client in psychodynamic psychotherapy is that of a supportive partnership, in which the therapist listens to the client in a non-judgmental manner. The therapist's role is to help the client gain insight into the unconscious influences behind unwanted behaviours. To help the client access these unconscious influences, the therapist may use techniques such as free association or examine processes that might reveal unconscious motives, such as transference and repression. We will discuss how therapists may use these techniques and processes to help clients access the unconscious.

free association
a psychotherapeutic technique in which the client takes one image or idea from a dream and says whatever comes to mind, regardless of how threatening, disgusting, or troubling it may be.

One of Sigmund Freud's major contributions to psychology was his argument that "dreams are the royal road to the unconscious" (Freud, 1900/1953, p. 608). Freud's two major techniques for interpreting dreams in order to uncover their unconscious content were free association and symbols. In **free association,** the client recounts the dream and then takes one image or idea and says whatever comes to mind, regardless of how threatening, disgusting, or troubling it may be. After this has been done with the first image, the process is repeated until the client has made associations with all the recalled dream images. Ideally, somewhere in the chain of free associations is a connection that unlocks the key to the dream. The second technique for interpreting dreams is through *symbols;* that is, dream images are thought of as representing or being symbolic of something else. Classic examples of symbols are a snake symbolizing a penis and a cave representing a vagina. If the techniques just described are successful, the patient becomes aware of the disturbing thoughts in her or his unconscious and the problematic symptoms decrease.

transference
a process in psychotherapy in which the client reacts to a person in a present relationship as though that person were someone from the client's past.

In the process of **transference,** the client reacts to someone in a current relationship as though that person were someone from the client's past. While the client is in therapy, that person is the therapist, but it can be anyone in the person's present life circumstances. For example, a woman whose father was verbally abusive to her might find herself shirking her job responsibilities because she experiences extreme fear when her older male supervisor at work speaks with even a slightly raised voice. The supervisor thinks this is an overreaction, but he does not realize that the woman's response stems from her relating to him as if he were her father. If these reactions occur during a therapy session, as they often do, the therapist can use the transference to help the client understand how her behaviour and emotions in current relationships are influenced by her relationship with her father. By working through the unconsciously transferred feelings in the therapeutic setting, a client might be freed from their powerful grip in other settings.

Like transference, defence mechanisms are also central to psychodynamic theory and therapy. Freud described many different **defence mechanisms,** but all of them operate unconsciously and involve defending against anxiety and threats to the ego. The most basic one is **repression,** which involves forcing threatening feelings, ideas, or motives into the unconscious. In psychodynamic therapy, dream interpretation and transference are used to uncover repressed defences and unconscious wishes.

defence mechanisms
ways in which the mind protects itself from anxiety by unconsciously distorting reality.

repression
the unconscious act of keeping threatening thoughts, feelings, or impulses out of consciousness.

Some or all of these techniques may lead the client to catharsis. **Catharsis** is the process of releasing intense, often unconscious, emotions in a therapeutic setting.

catharsis
the process of releasing intense, often unconscious, emotions in a therapeutic setting.

Classical psychodynamic therapy, or psychoanalysis, as practised by Freud is not utilized much anymore (Kay & Kay, 2008), largely because it is too time-consuming and thus costly for most clients—classical psychoanalysis involves several weekly sessions over the course of several years! To help more people, modern forms of psychodynamic therapy frequently use shorter-term, more focused approaches (Levenson, 2010). For example, in *interpersonal therapy (IPT),* delivered over 12 to 16 sessions, the therapist might pay attention to the clients' most recent relationships and interpersonal behaviours that seem to be related to the onset and maintenance of depression (Weissman & Markowitz, 2002). Historically, criticisms of the psychodynamic approach have focused on the lack of rigorously controlled studies for its effectiveness. However, a recent meta-analysis suggests that scientific evidence for the efficacy of psychodynamic therapy is on the rise, and that it can alleviate symptoms in a wide range of mental disorders, such as depression, social anxiety disorder, and anorexia nervosa (Leichsenring, Leweke, Klein, & Steinert, 2015).

client-centred therapy
a form of humanistic therapy in which the therapist shows unconditional positive regard for the patient.

unconditional positive regard
the basic tenet of client-centred therapy; the therapist's genuine liking and empathy for the client, regardless of what he or she has said or done.

LO2

Humanistic Therapy

Humanistic therapies seek to help the client reach his or her greatest potential. The most prominent figure in humanistic therapy is Carl Rogers (1951), who developed **client-centred therapy.** Client-centred therapy holds that people have mental health problems because there is a gap between who they are and who they would ideally like to be. In client-centred therapy, the therapist must show **unconditional positive regard**—that is, genuine liking and empathy for the client, regardless of what he or she has said or done. The goal is to create an atmosphere in which clients can communicate their feelings with certainty that they are being understood rather than judged. Another fundamental element in client-centred therapy is listening with *empathy,* in that the therapist aims to reiterate what the client says so as to convey the situation from the client's point of view. These two elements of client-centred therapy enable the relationship with the therapist to be open and non-judgmental.

Carl Rogers (far right) leads a group therapy session.

If this unconditional positive regard is effective, the client will develop a strong sense of self-worth and the confidence to strive for self-fulfillment, which Rogers called *self-actualization*. In order for self-actualization to be achieved, an individual must feel valued by the self and others. Although aspects of humanistic therapy outcomes, such as self-actualization, are difficult to measure, limited research suggests that humanistic therapy is more effective than no treatment and, in fact, may be just as effective as cognitive-behavioural treatments, which we will discuss, shortly (Elliott, 2002). In particular, psychological disorders associated with low self-esteem and negative self-judgment, such as eating disorders, appear to benefit from humanistic therapy (Rieger et al., 2010). Additionally, research tends to support Rogers's view on the importance of the therapeutic relationship with studies showing strong positive associations between the quality of the client–therapist relationship and improvement outcomes, regardless of type of therapy used (Bohart, Elliott, Greenberg, & Watson, 2002; Cooper, 2004; Krupnick et al., 1996).

More recently, positive psychology has developed its own form of psychotherapy, generally referred to as *positive psychotherapy* (Rashid, 2008; Seligman, Rashid, & Parks, 2006). This therapy focuses explicitly on increasing a person's happiness, well-being, and positive emotions. Depression, for example, is treated not only by reducing helplessness, sense of worthlessness, and negative emotions but also by actively trying to create a greater sense of well-being and a sense of gratitude. Gratitude training, for instance, involves daily exercises in noticing and finding things in life for which one is grateful and thankful. People who regularly acknowledge what they have to be thankful for have a higher sense of well-being and happiness (Emmons & McCullough, 2003).

LO3 Behavioural Treatments

behaviour therapies
therapies that apply the principles of classical and operant conditioning in the treatment of psychological disorders.

token economies
a behavioural technique in which desirable behaviours are reinforced with a token, such as a small chip or fake coin, which can be exchanged for privileges.

In **behaviour therapies,** therapists apply the principles of classical and operant conditioning to treat psychological disorders. They focus on changing behaviour, rather than thoughts, feelings, or motives. The idea is to help clients eliminate undesirable behaviours and increase the frequency of desirable ones.

Token economies are based upon basic principles of operant conditioning and are used to treat maladaptive behaviours. This technique is based on a simple principle: Desirable behaviours are reinforced with a token, such as a small chip or fake coin, which the client can then exchange for privileges. Parents can use this approach with their children—if their room is messy and they clean it, they get a token. The kids can turn in five tokens for candy or a toy. The more this happens, the more likely they are to clean their rooms, or so the logic goes. In the realm of mental health, the technique was used with some success in the 1950s and 1960s to reduce undesirable psychotic behaviours in patients in mental institutions (Nolen-Hoeksema, 2007). Recent uses include treatment of substance abuse by people with schizophrenia. Each time the patients did not use drugs, they were rewarded with small amounts of money. Coupled with problem-solving and social-skills training, this token system helped control substance abuse in hospitalized patients with schizophrenia, who are generally very hard to treat (Bellack et al., 2006). Also, the use of token economies may encourage socially appropriate behaviours and enhance life skills in children with autism spectrum disorder (Matson & Boisjoli, 2009).

systematic desensitization
a behavioural therapy technique, often used for phobias, in which the therapist pairs relaxation with gradual exposure to a phobic object, generating a hierarchy of increasing contact with the feared object.

Systematic desensitization is a widely used application of behavioural treatment that is especially effective for treating simple phobias (Tyron, 2005). It is one of the earliest forms of *exposure therapy*—a class of techniques that involves confronting clients with what they fear in order to reduce their fear. Systematic desensitization pairs relaxation with gradual exposure to a phobic object. First, the therapist generates a hierarchy of increasing contact with the feared object, ranging from mild to extreme. Figure 16.2 shows a possible hierarchy for a person with

FIGURE **16.2**
HIERARCHY OF EXPOSURE TO SPIDERS (THE PHOBIC OBJECT) IN PATIENT WITH ARACHNOPHOBIA.

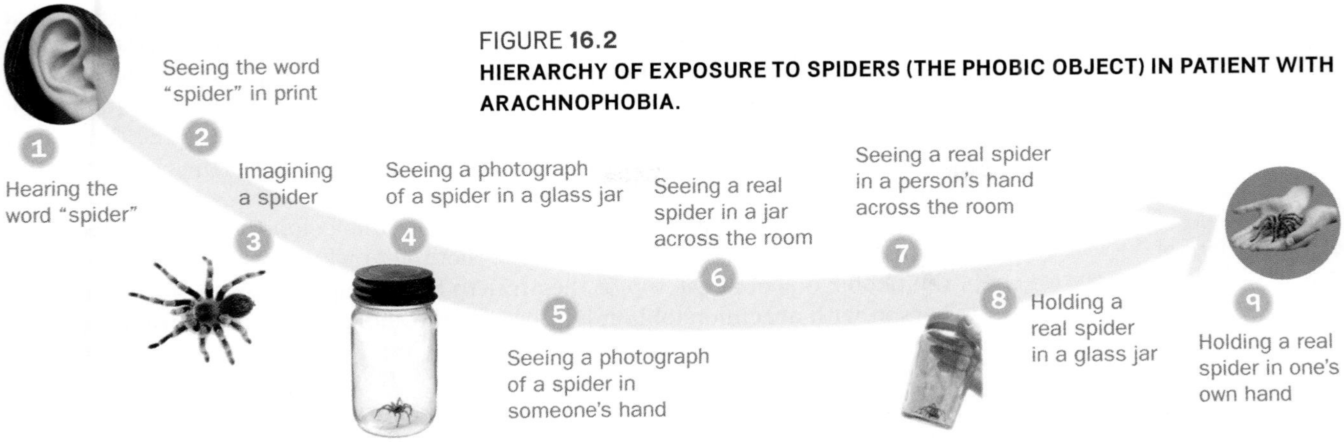
1
Hearing the word "spider"
2
Seeing the word "spider" in print
3
Imagining a spider
4
Seeing a photograph of a spider in a glass jar
5
Seeing a photograph of a spider in someone's hand
6
Seeing a real spider in a jar across the room
7
Seeing a real spider in a person's hand across the room
8
Holding a real spider in a glass jar
9
Holding a real spider in one's own hand

arachnophobia (a fear of spiders). In addition to increasing exposure, the therapist helps the client learn relaxation techniques that he or she can use when experiencing anxiety, especially anxiety related to the phobic object. The therapist works to help the client relax and then exposes the client to the phobic stimulus at gradually increasing levels of intensity. The idea is a clever one—to pair two incompatible body responses, relaxation and anxiety. It is sometimes called *counterconditioning*. The idea is that people cannot be both relaxed and anxious at the same time. By pairing an incompatible relaxation response with anxiety, a more adaptive response to feared stimuli is conditioned. And it works! Systematic desensitization often successfully treats phobias and some other anxiety disorders (Tyron, 2005).

Systematic desensitization can involve three types of exposure to a phobic object: imagined, real, or virtual. In imagined exposure, people simply imagine contact with the phobic object. In virtual reality exposure, the individual may be shown photographs or exposed to a virtual reality computer simulation. For instance, one type of virtual reality software allows clients to simulate flying during treatment for flying phobia, as depicted in Figure 16.3 (Wiederhold & Wieder hold, 2005). The most realistic level of exposure is in vivo exposure, in

Connection

Principles of classical and operant conditioning, including the powerful effect of reinforcement on learning, are the foundation of many behavioural therapies.

See Chapter 7, LO2, LO4.

Challenge Your Assumptions

True or False? People can learn to not be afraid of flying.

True: Behaviour therapy can teach people to not be afraid of flying.

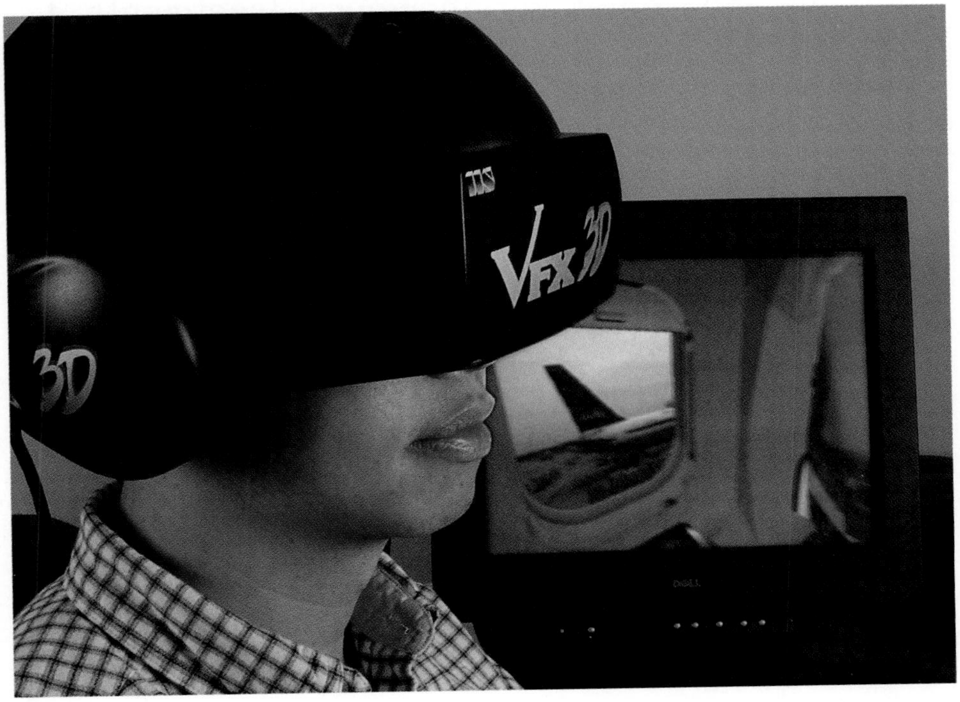
VFX 3D
3D

FIGURE **16.3**
SYSTEMATIC DESENSITIZATION IN TREATMENT OF FLYING PHOBIA. Because it is impractical and expensive to do therapy while on an actual airplane, simulating flying in a virtual reality format is an effective and cost-efficient way of systematically desensitizing people who are afraid of flying.

which the client makes real-life contact with the phobic object. Research suggests that in vivo exposure is generally more effective than imagined exposure when both are possible (Emmelkamp, 2004). Virtual reality therapy seems to be just as effective as in vivo exposure therapy (Opriş et al., 2012) and it has the advantage of being easier to arrange (i.e., the treatment session can held in the therapist's office) and control (i.e., the session can be easily terminated if the client feels too uncomfortable).

flooding
an extreme form of in vivo exposure in which the client experiences extreme exposure to the phobic object.

In contrast to systematic desensitization, implosion therapy, or **flooding,** is an extreme form of in vivo exposure therapy in which the client is exposed to the phobic object at the top of the anxiety hierarchy right away. For example, a person with arachnophobia might be asked to hold three hairy tarantulas until the client's anxiety and panic declines. Flooding therapies are based on the idea that some fears are maintained by avoidance. If you have a fear of heights, for instance, you typically never put yourself in high places where you would learn that the dire consequences you imagine do not happen. By repeatedly putting you in contact with the feared object or situation without any negative consequences, flooding allows extinction of the fear to happen. Although it can be distressing, the flooding technique is quick and effective (Craske & Mystkowski, 2006). However, one problem is that some clients may relapse after a short period of time (Craske, 1999; McNally, 2007; LaBorda, McConnell, & Miller, 2011).

There is ample research confirming the effectiveness of behavioural therapies, largely due to the relative ease with which behaviours can be measured in comparison to client insights obtained from other forms of therapy, such as the psychodynamic or humanistic approaches (Stanley & Beidel, 2009). In general, behavioural therapies are most effective for problems that are well-defined, such as specific fears, as opposed to vague feelings of fear or discontent, as experienced in generalized anxiety or depressive disorders (Wilson, 2011). In fact, behavioural therapies are sometimes criticized for not addressing the thoughts and perceptions that usually accompany behaviour. For this reason, many behaviour therapies are often combined with cognitive approaches, which we turn to examine next.

LO4 Cognitive and Cognitive-Behavioural Treatments

cognitive therapy
any type of psychotherapy that works to restructure maladaptive thought patterns.

Any type of psychotherapy that works to restructure irrational thought patterns is known as **cognitive therapy.** Typically, in cognitive therapy the therapist helps the client identify maladaptive thought patterns and then challenges these thoughts. Cognitive therapy (CT) is structured and problem-oriented, with the primary goal of fixing erroneous thought patterns. In using cognitive therapy, the therapist relies on what is known as the Socratic method: The therapist poses questions that help the client recognize erroneous logic that may support problematic thinking (Beck & Emery, 1985).

rational-emotive therapy
a cognitive therapy developed by Albert Ellis that aims to change emotions, such as guilt and sadness, by challenging the belief system that causes the emotions.

The two most influential figures in the development of cognitive therapies are psychologist Albert Ellis and psychiatrist Aaron Beck. The basis of Ellis's **rational-emotive therapy** is that emotions are the product of cognitions and that problematic emotions can be altered by challenging an individual's belief system. This therapy is approached using the *ABC model*—A is the activating event, B is the belief system, and C is the emotional consequence. For example, a man forgets his mother's birthday and feels profoundly guilty about it. In talking to his therapist, he reveals that the activating event (forgetting the birthday) led him to believe that he is a bad son, which resulted in the emotional consequence of feeling guilty. The therapist could then challenge the belief (he is a bad son) by pointing out that forgetting his mother's birthday is only one event that he could easily remedy with a belated gift. Furthermore, the therapist might point out that he has been kind to his mother in many other ways over his life.

By challenging the belief system, the aim is to change the negative emotional consequences.

Aaron Beck's approach to cognitive therapy is similar to Ellis's rational-emotive therapy in placing emphasis on changing thought processes. However, Beck's approach focuses more on changing flawed logic as an avenue to change. Let's consider the real-life case of Carlos, a 39-year-old man suffering from major depressive disorder. Carlos had tried several medications for his depression and had undergone one voluntary hospitalization, without satisfactory effects. His general practitioner (Dr. Hsu) recommended him for cognitive therapy. Many therapists believe that depressed people perceive events in such a way that they see only potentially adverse outcomes. Cognitive therapy for depression aims to point out the negative bias in such depressive thinking. Consider the following exchange between Carlos and his therapist, Dr. Walden (Gorenstein & Comer, 2002, pp. 54–55):

DR. WALDEN: You say you are a "basket case" and can barely function. What leads you to those conclusions?

CARLOS: Well, I've been hospitalized. That's how bad it's been. I just can't believe it.

DR. WALDEN: . . . Tell me again what led to the hospitalization.

CARLOS: I sort of panicked when the medicine didn't help, and I stopped going to work or anything else. Dr. Hsu figured that as long as I wasn't working, I might as well go into the hospital where I could try different drugs without having to manage all the side effects on my own. I also was pretty miserable at the time. I told Dr. Hsu my family might be better off without me.

DR. WALDEN: Do you think they would be better off?

CARLOS: I don't know. I'm not doing them much good.

DR. WALDEN: What would life be like for them without you?

CARLOS: It would be terrible for them. I suppose saying they'd be better off without me is going too far. As bad off as I am, I'm still able to do a few things.

DR. WALDEN: What are you able to do?

CARLOS: Well, I'm not in the hospital anymore. And I don't think I will be back either. . . . I mainly went in because I thought I could get better treatment or whatever. But it didn't pan out, so what would be the point of going back in?

DR. WALDEN: So the fact that you were in the hospital isn't really a sign that you are now or were ever a "basket case," which I take to mean someone who is completely helpless and cannot function.

CARLOS: . . . In looking back on it now, it was all basically voluntary. But that doesn't erase the fact that I am still a mess.

DR. WALDEN: How much of a mess are you?

CARLOS: I can't work, I can't help out at home. I can't even watch a television show. How much else do you want to know?

DR. WALDEN: A couple of minutes ago you said you were still able to do a few things. What are those?

CARLOS: I can drive to work and . . . I guess it's an exaggeration to say that I can't work at all. There are a few things I can do at the office.

DR. WALDEN: Like what?

Notice how Dr. Walden helps Carlos use his own logic to point out errors in the thinking that supports his notion of being worthless. For instance, Dr. Walden helps Carlos see that in spite of being hospitalized for depression, he was neither useless to his family nor totally unable to do things. Carlos came to realize that he really wasn't a "basket case" after all (Gorenstein & Comer, 2002, pp. 54–55).

cognitive-behavioural therapy an approach to treating psychological disorders that combines techniques for restructuring irrational thoughts with operant and classical conditioning techniques to shape desirable behaviours.

Often therapists integrate cognitive techniques for restructuring irrational thoughts with behavioural techniques to shape desirable behaviours in what is known as **cognitive-behavioural therapy** (CBT). As the name implies, the focus of CBT is to change both thoughts *and* behaviour. CBT entails restructuring thoughts, loosening the client's belief in irrational thoughts that may perpetuate the disorder, and offering incentives for acquiring more adaptive thought and behaviour patterns. One way to conceptualize CBT is to think of it as a tool for teaching skills that curtail *depressogenic thinking*, or thinking that tends to help generate or support depressed moods.

Cognitive-behavioural therapy focuses on changing a client's way of thinking in order to avoid irrational thoughts. Asking the client to break down problems into steps that can be tackled one at a time illustrates this approach.

CBT helps clients change the way they evaluate potential emotional threats. One way CBT does this is by encouraging reappraisal, which entails re-examining a situation that was previously seen as stressful. Through problem solving, clients can learn to adopt a new outlook on a situation. For example, a common depressogenic thought is that one is unable to do anything because all tasks seem insurmountable. A problem-solving approach to this kind of thinking would be to list the various steps in a given task and then work on each step until the task is completed. Not only will the client successfully accomplish the task, but that accomplishment may also have the further benefit of improving mood. Research on the cognitive processes involved in CBT in relation to treatment effectiveness show that people who engage in more problem solving during CBT reap more benefits (Chen, Jordan, & Thompson, 2006).

CBT has revolutionized the treatment of many psychological disorders; it has been successfully applied to disorders as varied as depression, phobias, post-traumatic stress disorder (PTSD), obsessive-compulsive disorder, eating disorders, and substance abuse. Because the goal of CBT is to change problematic thoughts and behaviours, one benefit to this approach is that clients learn coping techniques that they can use after treatment has ended. In fact, for depression and anxiety, the effectiveness of CBT is much longer lasting than drug therapies (Butler et al., 2006).

LO5

Group Therapies

group therapy therapeutic settings in which several people who share a common problem all meet regularly with a therapist to help themselves and one another.

Thus far, we have discussed therapy as an interactive session between a therapist and a client. However, sometimes therapies are delivered in group settings. In **group therapy**, several people who share a common problem all meet regularly with a therapist to help themselves and one another; the therapist acts as a facilitator. Group therapies often follow a structured process with clear treatment goals, such as learning to overcome social anxiety disorder or using CBT to treat eating disorders. The group serves as both a source of support and an aid to the therapeutic process, by allowing several people with a common problem to listen, discuss, and criticize one another. The interactions among participants become as much a part of the treatment as people's individual comments. These relationships become real-life contexts in which the various issues play out in front of the group. The presence of other people with the same problem also helps remove feelings of isolation.

support groups meetings of people who share a common situation, be it a disorder, a disease, or coping with an ill family member.

Groups can offer less structured therapeutic contexts as well. **Support groups** are meetings of people who share a common situation, be it a disorder, a disease, or coping with an ill family member. They meet regularly to share experiences, usually without programmatic treatment goals. They usually have a facilitator, a regular meeting time, and an open format. Support groups offer a sense of community, a forum for information exchange, and a place to share feelings for people who may have felt isolated by their situation. Support groups are widely available for people with all types of psychological disorders, as well as those living with chronic illnesses, such as diabetes and cancer.

Recently, group therapies have also taken the form of self-help groups over the Internet, especially for people who are experiencing problems that they are too embarrassed to discuss in face-to-face settings (Davison & Pennebaker, 2000).

Groups can be categorized in terms of their focus, such as eating disorders, substance abuse, treatment of OCD, or coping with bereavement and may be time limited or ongoing. Time-limited groups run for a set number of sessions, tend to follow a program of treatment, and usually do not add members after the first few meetings. Ongoing groups, in contrast, welcome new members as they appear. Alcoholics Anonymous (AA) and other substance abuse groups that follow AA's 12-step approach are examples of ongoing groups. Also in this category are "life support groups" in which people who are coping with, say, a spouse with a brain tumour or a son with major depressive disorder can meet and share their feelings about what they are going through.

How does group therapy compare to individual therapy? One advantage of group therapy is that it tends to be less costly. However, clients do receive less one-on-one time with a therapist. Despite this less individualized treatment, research suggests that group therapy is just as effective as individual therapy in relieving symptoms for a range of clinical problems, such as depression and anorexia nervosa (Nevonen & Broberg, 2006; O'Shea, Spence, & Donovan, 2015).

Psychological treatments have been used not only to alleviate psychological disorders but also to help prevent the development of such disorders. Given the difficulties in treating many psychological disorders and the costs to individuals and society of the large numbers of people suffering from such conditions, prevention programs are an increasing area of effort in psychology and medicine (see the "Preventing Disorders" section later in this chapter). Figure 16.4 summarizes the psychotherapies discussed in this section and lists what each therapy addresses as the causes of a disorder, as well as the therapy's treatment goals, and techniques.

Therapy	Cause of problem	Goal of therapy	Techniques
Psychodynamic	Disorders are symptoms of unconscious and repressed thoughts, feelings, and motives.	Work to uncover repressed and unconscious thoughts, feelings, and motives (defence mechanisms).	Dream interpretation, free association, transference Catharsis
Humanistic	Conditions are blocking personal growth.	Create conditions for optimal growth.	Unconditional positive regard, empathic listening
Behavioural	Maladaptive behaviour has been reinforced and rewarded.	Change reinforcers and rewards to change maladaptive behaviour.	Classical and operant conditioning; token economies; systematic desensitization
Cognitive	Irrational thoughts lead to disordered behaviours.	Change emotions/irrational thoughts.	Critical questioning (Socratic method)
Cognitive–behavioural	Maladaptive behaviours have been reinforced and irrational thoughts have developed.	Change thoughts and behaviour.	Restructure thoughts and offer incentives for acquiring more adaptive thoughts and behaviours; reappraisal

FIGURE **16.4**

CAUSES, GOALS, AND TECHNIQUES OF PSYCHOLOGICAL THERAPIES. Each major psychological perspective has its own theory of what causes psychological disorders, as well as distinct goals and techniques of treatment.

Quick Quiz 16.1: Psychological Treatments

1. José's therapist asks to hear about José's week. José tells him about some difficulty he is having with his wife and how he feels worthless in his marriage. The therapist expresses his empathy and understanding. He tells José he knows what it feels like to feel worthless and how uncomfortable that feeling is. What therapeutic approach is José's therapist taking?
   a. humanistic
   b. cognitive-behavioural
   c. cognitive
   d. psychodynamic
2. Which of the following methods is widely used for effective treatment of simple phobias?
   a. flooding (implosion therapy)
   b. token economies
   c. client-centred therapy
   d. systematic desensitization
3. Often therapists integrate cognitive techniques for restructuring irrational thoughts with behavioural techniques to shape desirable behaviours in what is known as
   a. cognitive-behavioural therapy.
   b. humanistic therapy.
   c. psychodynamic therapy.
   d. behaviour modification.

Answers can be found at the end of the chapter.

BIOLOGICAL TREATMENTS

Changes in brain functioning, particularly neurotransmitter signalling, have been implicated as potential causes in a number of psychological disorders. Therefore, one common approach to treatment is to remedy brain abnormalities by using biological treatments. The main focus of this section will be on the most common treatment approach, drug therapy, but we will also explore other biological treatments such as surgery and electric and magnetic therapies.

Drug Therapies

Connection

Do you need a caffeinated beverage to get you going in the morning? And more throughout the day to stay alert? People who require more and more caffeine or other drugs, including prescription drugs, have developed a drug tolerance.

See Chapter 5, LO10.

An overwhelming number of pharmaceutical drugs are available for the treatment of everything from mild anxiety to schizophrenia. Drugs used to treat psychological disorders are one of the most commonly prescribed drug classes in Canada, second only to cardiovascular drugs. Drugs are generally effective in managing symptoms, but do not usually cure disorders. Therefore, people who take drugs for mental illness are often prescribed them for long periods of time. Although the drugs used to treat various disorders vary dramatically in how they affect neuronal signalling, most exert their therapeutic effect by altering the signalling of one or more neurotransmitter systems (McKim, 2007). The challenge in developing pharmaceutical drugs is to produce therapeutic effects, but to minimize side effects.

LO6 **Drug Treatments for Schizophrenia** As you read in Chapter 15, the prevailing view for decades was that schizophrenia resulted from an excess of dopamine in the brain, which was based upon observations of individuals under the influence of amphetamine (or "speed"). Amphetamine stimulates dopamine release in the brain and, at high doses, produces hallucinations and delusions of grandeur similar to those seen in schizophrenia. More recently, the dopamine hypothesis has come into question, since other neurotransmitters appear to play a role in the disorder. Nonetheless, the major drugs used in treating schizophrenia are those that reduce the availability of dopamine in the brain (Javitt & Coyle, 2004). In the 1950s, researchers accidentally discovered that a class of drugs, the **phenothiazines,** helped diminish hallucinations, confusion, agitation, and paranoia in people with

phenothiazines
drugs used to treat schizophrenia; they help diminish hallucinations, confusion, agitation, and paranoia but also have adverse side effects.

schizophrenia. Later studies showed that phenothiazines block dopamine receptors in the brain.

The best-known phenothiazine is chlorpromazine (marketed as Thorazine). Another drug, haloperidol (Haldol), discovered at about the same time, showed similar effects on schizophrenic symptoms. The phenothiazines and haloperidol are known as **traditional antipsychotics,** because they were the first medications used to manage psychotic symptoms. Unfortunately, they have many unpleasant side effects. These include fatigue, visual impairments, and a condition called **tardive dyskinesia,** which consists of repetitive, involuntary movements of the jaw, tongue, face, and mouth (such as grimacing and lip smacking), and body tremors. Tardive dyskinesia is particularly problematic, as the effects are often irreversible, even after the drugs are discontinued (Trugman, 1998).

traditional antipsychotics
historically, the first medications used to manage psychotic symptoms.

tardive dyskinesia
repetitive, involuntary movements of the jaw, tongue, face, and mouth and body tremors resulting from the extended use of traditional antipsychotic drugs.

Some newer antipsychotic drugs, such as clozapine (Clozaril) and olanzapine (Zyprexa), do not have these side effects, and are called **atypical antipsychotics.** These drugs preferentially block a different type of dopamine receptor than the traditional antipsychotics do, which makes them less likely to create tardive dyskinesia (Potkin et al., 2003). Atypical antipsychotics also affect the activity of other neurotransmitters in the brain, such as serotonin (Dvir & Smallwood, 2008). Unfortunately, even these medications can produce some unpleasant or dangerous side effects, such as weight gain, increased risk of diabetes, a reduction in the number of certain white blood cells, and, rarely, a particular kind of cancer (Javitt & Coyle, 2004; Lieberman et al., 2005; Young, Niv, Cohen, Kessler, & McNagny, 2010).

atypical antipsychotics
newer antipsychotic drugs, which do not create tardive dyskinesia.

Connection

Schizophrenia and other disorders can be caused in part by genes that are expressed only under specific environmental circumstances.

See Chapter 15, LO5.

LO7 LO8

Drug Treatments for Depressive, Anxiety, and Bipolar Disorders Of all the medications for psychological disorders, drugs used to treat depression and anxiety are the most prevalent (Beck et al., 2005). There are five major categories of drugs used to treat depressive, anxiety, and bipolar disorders: monoamine oxidase (MAO) inhibitors, tricyclic antidepressants, selective serotonin reuptake inhibitors (SSRIs), benzodiazepines, and lithium.

All classes of antidepressant drugs work by increasing the levels of monoamine neurotransmitters in the synapse; however, they differ in their mechanisms and the neurotransmitter systems they target. The **monoamine oxidase (MAO) inhibitors** were among the first pharmaceuticals used to treat depression (Burgess, 2009). They work by reducing the action of the enzyme monoamine oxidase, which breaks down monoamine neurotransmitters (including norepinephrine, epinephrine, dopamine, and serotonin), thus prolonging their action in the synapse. This is thought to be the mechanism whereby they improve mood. Unfortunately, MAO inhibitors, such as phenelzine (Nardil) and tranylcypromine (Parnate) interact with many foods and over-the-counter drugs such as antihistamines and can produce dangerous increases in blood pressure. For this reason, their use for depression has declined (Fiedorowicz & Swartz, 2004; Yamada & Yasuhara, 2004). A transdermal patch, which allows administration of an MAO inhibitor without its having to enter the digestive tract, may provide some of the benefits of these drugs without the risks caused by their interactions with foods (Pae et al., 2007).

monoamine oxidase (MAO) inhibitors
a class of drugs used to treat depression; they slow the breakdown of monoamine neurotransmitters in the brain.

Tricyclic antidepressants such as imipramine (Elavil) and amitriptyline (Anafranil) were developed as an alternative to the MAO inhibitors, and are still popular for treating depression. These drugs work by blocking the presynaptic reuptake transporters for serotonin and norepinephrine, therefore increasing synaptic levels of these neurotransmitters. The tricyclics also have effects on other neurotransmitter systems, such as acetylcholine and histamine, which are responsible for the side effects associated with these drugs. Although the side effects of the tricyclics are less severe than MAO inhibitors, they can produce dry mouth, weight gain, irritability, confusion, and constipation (McKim, 2007; Zeino, Sisson, & Bjarnason, 2010).

tricyclic antidepressants
drugs used for treating depression, as well as in chronic pain management and in the treatment of ADHD.

Much evidence implicates the serotonin system in the symptoms of depression, so the development of new drugs that target only serotonin offered hope for

selective serotonin reuptake inhibitors (SSRIs)
drugs prescribed primarily for depression and some anxiety disorders that work by making more serotonin available in the synapse.

Connection

Transporter proteins on the presynaptic neuron, which are blocked by most antidepressants, remove neurotransmitter from the synapse into the terminal.

See Chapter 3, LO8, LO9.

benzodiazepines
a class of anxiety-reducing drugs that mimic the effect of the neurotransmitter GABA.

lithium
a salt that is prescribed for its ability to stabilize the mania associated with bipolar disorder.

treatments with fewer side effects. One class of drugs brought to the market in the 1990s, the **selective serotonin reuptake inhibitors (SSRIs),** make more serotonin available in the synapse. Like tricyclics, SSRIs inhibit the reuptake process, but are more selective for serotonin than noradrenaline, allowing more serotonin to bind with receptors on the postsynaptic neuron (see Figure 16.5). By allowing more serotonin to be used, the SSRIs alleviate some of the symptoms of depression. Fluoxetine (Prozac) and citalopram (Celexa) are two of the more widely used SSRIs and are among the most widely prescribed psychotherapeutic drugs in Canada.

Unlike the other classes of antidepressants, SSRIs do not have significant effects on multiple neurotransmitter systems, and therefore these medications create far fewer unpleasant side effects. Agitation, insomnia, nausea, and difficulty in achieving orgasm are the most common side effects produced by SSRIs (Waldinger et al., 2004). Another highly publicized but infrequent side effect of SSRI is an increased likelihood of attempting suicide, compared to other treatments for depression (Fergusson et al., 2005). The recently publicized cases of teens on SSRIs committing suicide often neglect to report that adolescents are usually in severely depressed states when they are prescribed SSRIs, suggesting that they might be likely to attempt suicide no matter which drug they were prescribed (Wessely & Kerwin, 2004). Widespread antidepressant use may be associated with a decrease in suicide rates worldwide, but the nature of that relationship is a matter of debate (Isacsson, Rich, Jureidini, & Raven, 2010).

The **benzodiazepines,** such as diazepam (Valium) and lorazepam (Ativan), are most commonly prescribed for anxiety. These drugs act by enhancing the effect of the inhibitory neurotransmitter GABA, producing both calming and sedation. Although they appear to work well for anxiety, they can have addictive properties, particularly in individuals with a history of substance abuse (Farré et al., 1998). Although SSRIs are prescribed primarily for depression, they are also prescribed for the treatment of certain anxiety disorders (Vaswani, Linda, & Ramesh, 2003).

The treatment of bipolar disorder presents many challenges, as the manic episodes have to be regulated, the depressive episodes prevented, and the shifts from one type of episode to the other controlled. Because no one drug can manage all these effects, treatment often consists of a combination of drug therapies. **Lithium**

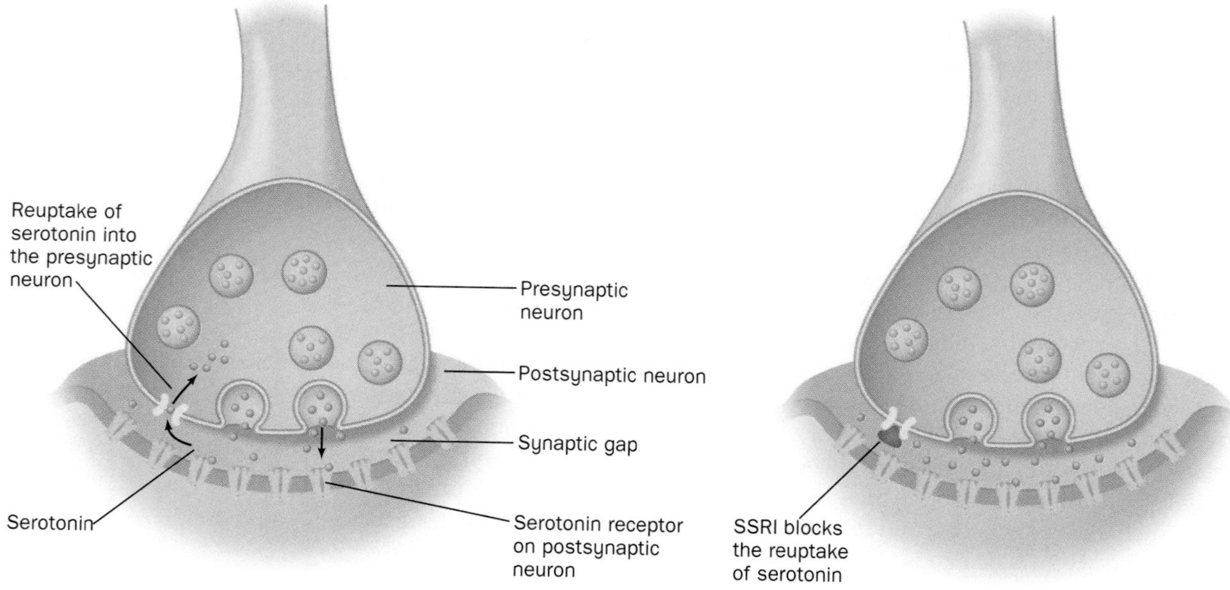

FIGURE **16.5**

THE EFFECT OF SSRIs ON REUPTAKE OF SEROTONIN. SSRIs increase serotonin levels by blocking the reuptake of serotonin into the presynaptic neuron. As a result, more serotonin stays in the synaptic cleft, where it can bind with receptors on the postsynaptic neuron.

has long been prescribed for its ability to stabilize the mania associated with bipolar disorder. We do not know how lithium works, although it appears to influence many neurotransmitter systems in the brain, including glutamate, the major excitatory neurotransmitter in the brain (Chuang, 2004; Jope, 1999). Taking lithium can be unpleasant and dangerous, as it can cause diarrhea, nausea, tremors, kidney failure, brain damage, and adverse cardiac effects (Aichorn et al., 2006). Some people develop tolerance to lithium after years of treatment, making the drug less effective (Post et al., 1998). Because of these problems, physicians often favour other drugs to treat the mania phase, including drugs prescribed to prevent convulsions, either alone or in combination with lithium. Antipsychotic drugs are sometimes used to manage the psychotic symptoms of bipolar disorder while antidepressants are used to manage the depressive phase (Bauer & Mitchner, 2004; Carney & Goodwin, 2005). The use of atypical antipsychotics in treating mood disorders in general (e.g., for anxiety, bipolar disorder, and depression) is increasing, partly because the dosage required to be effective is rather low and therefore has fewer side effects (Blier, 2005). Figure 16.6 summarizes the major drug therapies, the names of the medications that are used to treat specific disorders, and the various side effects of each medication.

Actor Robert Downey, Jr., has struggled with symptoms of bipolar disorder and drug abuse for a number of years.

Can you think of pros and cons for taking medications to treat bipolar disorder?

LO9 Psychosurgery

Recall from Chapter 1 the evidence from very early human history of attempts to cure insanity by trephining, which is drilling a hole in the skull to allow evil spirits to escape. Although psychological disorders are not now usually treated by surgical means, in the early 20th century physicians experimented with the use of surgery to disrupt the transmission of brain signals in people suffering from

Disorder	Class of drug treatment	Drug name	Side effects
Schizophrenia	Chlorpromazine	Thorazine	Fatigue, visual impairment, tardive dyskinesia
	Haloperidol	Halodol	Fatigue, visual impairment, tardive dyskinesia
	Clozapine	Clozaril	Weight gain, increased risk of diabetes, reduction of white blood cells
	Risperidone	Risperdal	Weight gain, increased risk of diabetes, reduction of white blood cells
Depression	MAO inhibitors	Nardil Parnate	Dangerous increases in blood pressure
	Tricyclic antidepressants	Elavil Anafranil	Dry mouth, weight gain, irritability, confusion, constipation
	SSRIs	Paxil, Prozac Zoloft, Celexa	Agitation, insomnia, nausea, difficulty achieving orgasm; rare cases of increased risk for suicide
Anxiety	SSRIs	Paxil, Prozac Zoloft, Celexa	Agitation, insomnia, nausea, difficulty achieving orgasm; rare cases of increased risk for suicide
	Benzodiazepines	Valium Librium	Can be addictive
Bipolar disorder	Lithium	Lithobid	Diarrhea, nausea, tremors, kidney failure, cognitive effects, adverse cardiac effects

FIGURE **16.6**

SUMMARY OF DRUGS USED TO TREAT PSYCHOLOGICAL DISORDERS. Most of the major psychological disorders can be treated with some form of medication, to varying degrees of effectiveness and with various side effects.

prefrontal lobotomy
a form of psychosurgery in which the connections between the prefrontal cortex and the lower portion of the brain are severed; it is no longer in use.

psychosis. In a procedure known as **prefrontal lobotomy,** they severed connections between the prefrontal cortex and the lower portion of the brain. Because the prefrontal cortex is involved in thinking (and, we now know, is crucial for working memory and planned action) and the lower areas are more concerned with emotion, they believed the surgery would modify behaviour and possibly disengage disruptive thought patterns involved in hallucinations and confused thinking. Typically, however, prefrontal lobotomies produced profound personality changes, often leaving the patient listless or subject to seizures; some patients were even reduced to a vegetative state (Mashour, Walker, & Martuza, 2005).

Rosemary Kennedy, the late U.S. President John F. Kennedy's younger sister, underwent a lobotomy when she was 23 years old to treat her erratic, often violent mood swings. Instead of producing the desired calming effect, the lobotomy left Rosemary mentally incapacitated. She would stare blankly at walls for hours on end and lost the ability to speak coherently (Lerner, 1996).

electroconvulsive therapy (ECT)
treatment of last resort for severe depression that involves passing an electrical current through a person's brain in order to induce a seizure.

After the introduction of the traditional antipsychotic medications, lobotomy fell out of favour. Moreover, the practice was widely regarded as cruel and inhumane. Today a very few, highly constrained forms of brain surgery are occasionally performed, but only as a last resort after other forms of treatment have been unsuccessful (Mashour et al., 2005).

Challenge Your Assumptions

True or False? Shock therapy is never effective and is no longer used.

False: Shock therapy can be effective, especially for the treatment of depression with psychotic symptoms, and is still used, even if as a last resort.

Electric and Magnetic Therapies

Although brain surgery for psychological disorders is rare, there are other ways to stimulate or decrease brain activation. Bizarre as it seems, electrical current can be used to help ease the suffering caused by certain psychological disorders. The application of electrical current as a medical practice goes back centuries: Apparently the ancient Romans used electric fish to treat headaches (Abrams, 1997). One of the more innovative applications of electrical stimulation may well hold the key to unlocking the mystery of depression and is discussed later in the chapter.

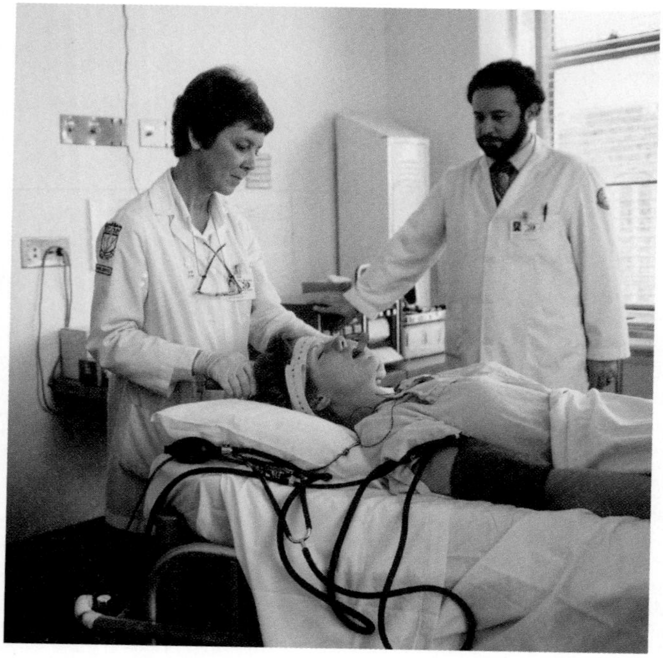

Challenging the assumptions of earlier generations of psychiatrists, more current therapists discovered ECT is an effective treatment for depression but not schizophrenia.

Electroconvulsive Therapy The notion of "shock therapy" conjures up images of barbaric torture of psychiatric patients, as in the case of Ewen Cameron's patients described at the beginning of the chapter. Yet electroconvulsive therapy is still used and can be effective for severe cases of depression in people who have not responded to other therapies (Fink, 2006). **Electroconvulsive therapy (ECT)** involves passing an electrical current through a person's brain in order to induce a seizure. The origins of ECT stem from the observation that people who have seizures become calm after they have them (Abrams, 1997). Physicians thought that ECT could be an effective treatment for schizophrenia because the induced seizures would calm the patient. Research eventually demonstrated, however, that ECT did not treat the symptoms of schizophrenia effectively at all, and it disappeared as a viable therapy for years. It resurfaced later as a treatment for people with severe cases of depression. In particular, ECT seems to be most beneficial for depression accompanied by psychotic symptoms, with some studies showing favourable response rates of 95 percent (Trevino et al., 2010).

Today, ECT is administered by connecting electrodes to the patient's head and passing an electric current (ranging from 60 to 140 volts) through the brain for one-third to one-half second. The voltage is not lethal because it is administered only to the head—indeed, the same voltage to the chest would be lethal. The treatment is called electro*convulsive* because the procedure produces a brief seizure, including bodily convulsions. To minimize the convulsions, patients today are given an anesthetic and muscle relaxant prior to ECT.

Standard ECT treatment involves up to 12 sessions over the course of several weeks. Some people report immediate relief of their depressive symptoms after treatment, although scientists do not fully understand how ECT works to relieve them (Nolen-Hoeksema, 2007). The downside to ECT is that it creates some permanent memory loss and other types of cognitive damage because it actually destroys some brain tissue. Using ECT on one side of the brain rather than both appears to reduce the risk of memory loss (Squire, 1977).

Repetitive Transcranial Magnetic Stimulation The idea of somehow stimulating or manipulating brain activity with an external application of energy has enduring appeal. Some practitioners have tried to find a way to do this without creating more harm. ECT was a good idea in some respects, but as just mentioned, it leaves people with memory damage and other negative effects. In **repetitive transcranial magnetic stimulation (rTMS),** physicians expose particular brain structures to bursts of high-intensity magnetic fields instead of electricity. Like ECT, repetitive transcranial magnetic stimulation is usually reserved for people with severe depression who have not responded well to other forms of therapy. Although some people experience relief from this therapy, it is not yet clear how much magnetic stimulation is optimal and for what length of time (Fitzgerald et al., 2006; Turner-Shea, Bruno, & Pridmore, 2006). TMS has also shown preliminary success in treating the negative symptoms of schizophrenia (Brunelin et al., 2010).

repetitive transcranial magnetic stimulation (rTMS)
treatment for severe depression involving exposure of specific brain structures to bursts of high-intensity magnetic fields instead of electricity.

Recently, innovative breakthroughs in neurology and psychiatry have led to the development of a very promising treatment for depression. This revolutionary approach has roots in both neurosurgery and the use of electricity to treat psychological disorders. We examine how it was discovered and how it works in "Groundbreaking Research."

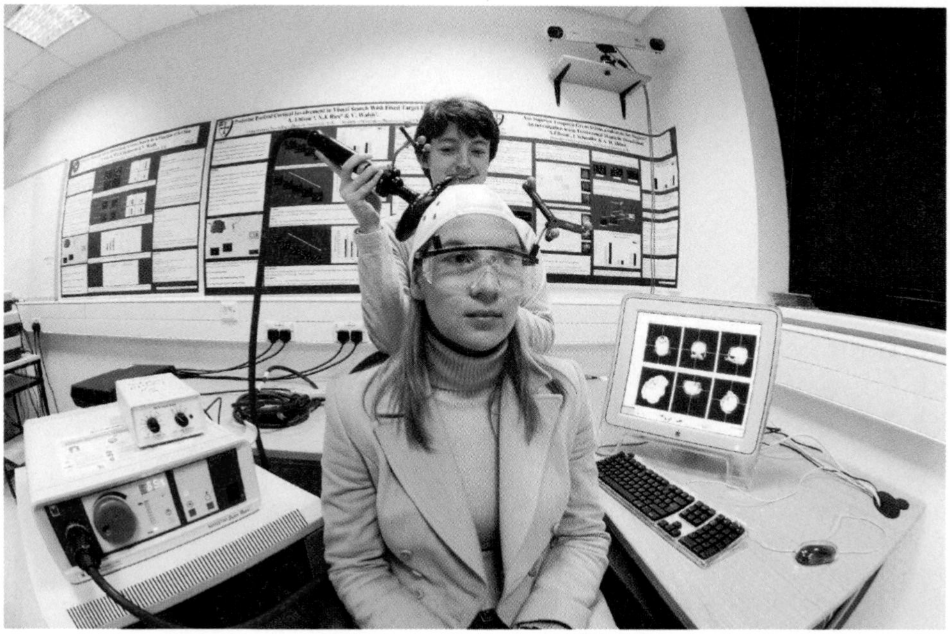

Repetitive transcranial magnetic stimulation exposes specific areas of the brain to bursts of high-intensity magnetic fields and may be used to treat people with severe depression when other options have failed.

Groundbreaking Research

Deep Brain Stimulation for the Treatment of Severe Depression

Helen Mayberg

The treatment of depression remains a major challenge. Few people are cured, although many obtain some relief from drugs, psychotherapy, repetitive transcranial magnetic stimulation, or ECT. Others, however, find no relief in any of these treatments. For them, depression is severe, unrelenting, and debilitating.

But there is hope. In her quest to understand the brain circuitry of depression, neurologist Helen Mayberg discovered what appears to be a neural switch that activates depression. In the process, she came upon a strikingly effective treatment for the disorder.

PREVAILING THINKING ABOUT BRAIN CIRCUITRY IN DEPRESSION

Most theorists on the brain mechanisms of depression hypothesized deficiencies in various neurotransmitters, based on how the effective drugs work. For example, the SSRIs increase serotonin availability; the MAO inhibitors affect dopamine, norepinephrine, and serotonin. In terms of brain regions, depressed people show reduced activity in certain brain areas, especially the cortex and areas involved in mood (Drevets et al., 1997; Mayberg, 2003; Shestyuk et al., 2005). Researchers and therapists therefore believed that deficiencies in these neurotransmitters were most important for understanding depression.

MAYBERG'S BREAKTHROUGH RESEARCH

Helen Mayberg took a different approach. As a young scientist, she trained with a neurologist who studied how various areas of the human brain work together. Her early training helped her see the brain in terms of the interactions among various areas rather than in terms of their individual functions alone. Early in her career, Mayberg studied depression in people with Parkinson's disease. Using PET imaging of brain activation, she and her colleagues found that these patients had reduced activity in both frontal cortex thinking areas and limbic emotional areas. But they also stumbled on a surprising phenomenon: Area 25 was hyperactive in these patients. Rather than discounting this unexpected finding, Mayberg tested it further. She found this same pattern of overactivation in Area 25 in depressed people with Alzheimer's, epilepsy, and Huntington's disease (Mayberg, 1997). Perhaps it played a role in depression more generally.

Finding overactivation in any brain area of depressed people was surprising, since many researchers have found that depression is related to underactivity rather than overactivity of certain cortical areas (Shestyuk et al., 2005). But Mayberg found *depressed activity* in frontal cortex areas, which fit with current models of depression, along with *overactivity* in Area 25.

Area 25 is located in the cingulate region of the prefrontal cortex, and it is surrounded by the limbic system. As such, it has connections with emotional and memory centres of the brain (see Figure 16.7). Mayberg reasoned that if Area 25 plays a key role in sustaining depressive thinking, one would see a reduction in activity in this area after successful treatment for the disorder. She and her colleagues performed PET scans of depressed people before and after a 15- to 20-week course of cognitive-behavioural therapy, an effective psychological treatment for depression. They did similar scans on people with depression taking an SSRI. Both groups of patients showed that reduced activity in Area 25 corresponded with clinical improvement of depressive symptoms

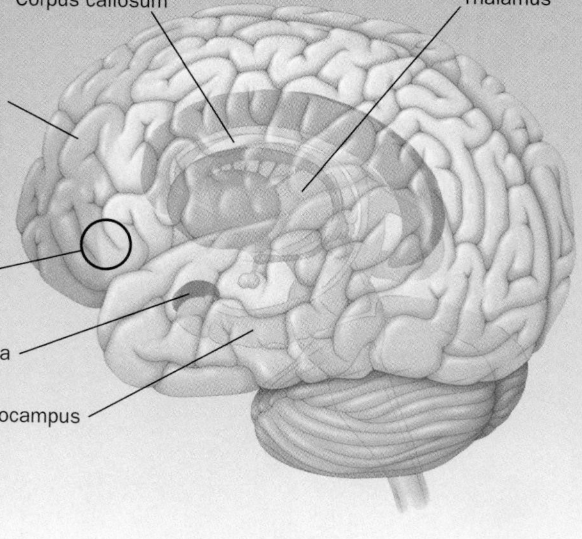

FIGURE 16.7

BRODMANN'S AREA 25, THE PREFRONTAL CORTEX, AND THE LIMBIC SYSTEM. Brodmann's Area 25 is located in the cingulate region of the prefrontal cortex, where it is surrounded by the corpus callosum and structures of the limbic system (amygdala, hippocampus, thalamus). The limbic system is important in regulating emotion and motivation.

(Goldapple et al., 2004; Kennedy et al., 2001). Mayberg also found activity in Area 25 when otherwise healthy people recalled sad memories (Mayberg et al., 1999).

Eventually, Mayberg and her colleagues amassed evidence that an overactive Area 25 is a general feature of depression. Moreover, successful treatment by an SSRI or cognitive-behavioural therapy reduced Area 25 activation. What seems most important about Area 25 is its connections with thinking areas of the prefrontal cortex and limbic structures involved in emotion (which are connected to each other). Area 25 thus may be a gateway between thinking and emotion. An overactive Area 25 may enable the type of negative thinking that feeds depressive states. Mayberg reasoned that if it were possible to close this gate, depression might cease. But how?

Mayberg knew scientists were implanting electrodes deep in the brains of people with Parkinson's disease to regulate activity in an area of the brain that produces the tremors (shaking) associated with that disease. Mayberg figured that she could apply the same technology, known as *deep brain stimulation,* to Area 25. She tried it with six patients whose severe depression had failed to respond to anything else. They implanted electrodes in Area 25 and used an external stimulator to deliver enough voltage to interrupt reducing neuronal activity in this area. For four of the patients, the depression ceased almost immediately (Mayberg et al., 2005). Shortly after activation of the electrodes, these patients said that they felt "sudden calmness or lightness," "disappearance of the void," or "connectedness." One of them described heightened awareness and greater perception of visual details and colours in the room.

Figure 16.8 illustrates the location of the implanted electrodes and the wearable pacemaker for stimulating them. Note that the treatment involves brain stimulation in the operating room as well as a method for stimulating the implants in daily life. Patients wear an external pacemaker that controls the delivery of electrical stimulation to Area 25.

In the following passage, Mayberg describes what happened when the stimulator was turned on to activate the electrode just implanted in Area 25 in the brain of a woman named Deanna. As the electrodes were being implanted in Area 25, Mayberg sat by Deanna's side and asked her to report, throughout the surgery, whatever she felt, however minor it might seem. What follows is Mayberg's account of what Deanna said when, unbeknownst to Deanna, the surgical team turned the stimulator on:

> "So we turn it on," Mayberg told me later, "and all of a sudden she says to me, 'It's very strange,' she says, 'I know you've been with me in the operating room this whole time. I know you care about me. But it's not that. I don't know what you just did. But I'm looking at you, and it's like I just feel suddenly more connected to you.' "
>
> Mayberg, stunned, signaled with her hand to the others, out of Deanna's view, to turn the stimulator off.

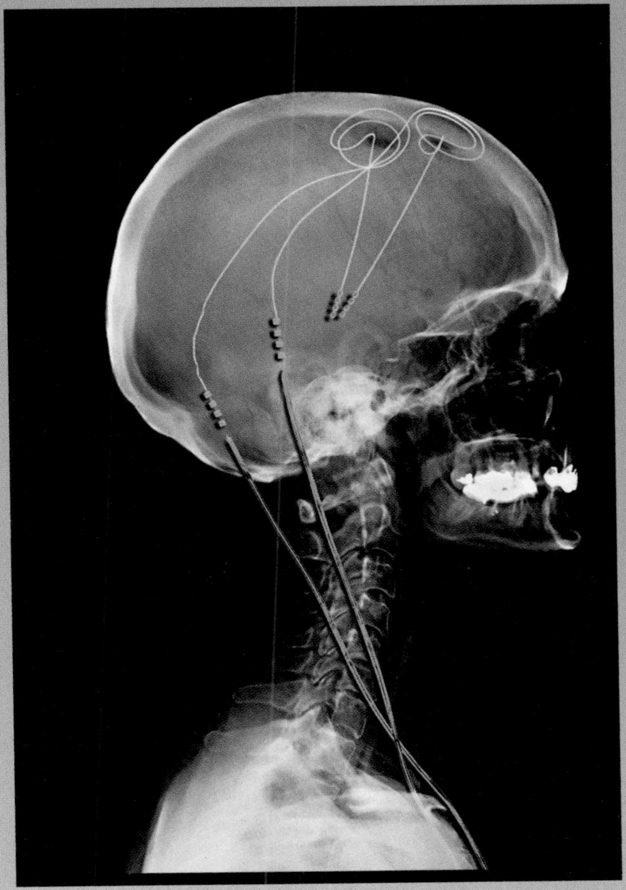

FIGURE **16.8**
DEEP BRAIN ELECTRODES AND STIMULATOR FOR STIMULATION OF AREA 25 IN DEPRESSED PATIENTS. A pacemaker implanted in the person's chest sends electrical impulses to electrodes projecting down into Area 25 of the frontal cortex.

> "And they turn it off," Mayberg said, "and she goes: 'God, it's just so odd. You just went away again. I guess it wasn't really anything.'
>
> "It was subtle like a brick," Mayberg told me. "There's no reason for her to say that. Zero. And all through those tapes I have of her, every time she's in the clinic beforehand, she always talks about this disconnect, this closeness and sense of affiliation she misses, that was so agonizingly painful for her to lose. And there it was. It was back in an instant." (Dobbs, 2006, April 2)

FOLLOW-UP RESEARCH

Although most people who have had the procedure experience dramatic improvements or complete elimination of their depression, a few do not. Large-scale clinical trials are underway in which Mayberg and others are studying the effects of stimulation of Area 25 on larger groups of people with treatment-resistant depression. Initial findings suggest that deep

Challenge Your Assumptions
True or False? Direct stimulation of neurons by electrical impulse is science fiction and is not used in treatment today.
False: Deep brain stimulation is a viable treatment for severe depression and other disorders.

brain stimulation offers relief for the symptoms of severe depression without impairing cognitive function, and the effects have lasted up to one year (Bewernick, Kayser, Sturm, & Schlaepfer, 2012; Lozano, Mayberg, & Kennedy, 2012; Mayberg, 2009; Rizvi et al., 2009; Schlaepfer, Bewernick, Kayser, Maedler, & Coenen, 2013). Moreover, follow-up research has expanded our understanding of the brain regions involved in treating depression with deep brain stimulation. For example, Schlaepfer (2013) has reported evidence that brain regions other than Area 25 involved in treating depression with deep brain stimulation include the medial forebrain bundle and the nucleus accumbens—regions intimately connected to reward and pleasure.

Quick Quiz 16.2: Biological Treatments

1. The antidepressant medications known as the SSRIs work by
   a. inhibiting monoamine oxidase.
   b. decreasing serotonin levels by inhibiting the reuptake of serotonin into the presynaptic neuron.
   c. increasing serotonin levels by inhibiting the reuptake of serotonin into the presynaptic neuron.
   d. reducing the activity of the neurotransmitter glutamate.
2. Your Aunt Julia has been in treatment for years for schizophrenia. She often has jerky spastic movements, which she tells you are from her medication, not the disorder itself. What side effect is she experiencing?
   a. intolerance
   b. reactive dysphoria
   c. tardive dyskinesia
   d. insomnia
3. Electroconvulsive therapy (ECT) is still in limited use for people with which disorder?
   a. schizophrenia
   b. obsessive-compulsive disorder
   c. generalized anxiety disorder
   d. major depressive disorder
4. Helen Mayberg was surprised to find that brain images of Area 25 showed ______ in people with severe depression and helped devise a way to treat them with deep brain stimulation.
   a. reduced activity
   b. overactivity
   c. tumours
   d. reduced blood flow

Answers can be found at the end of the chapter.

COMBINED APPROACHES

Some approaches combine different types of psychotherapy or combine non-traditional practices with traditional approaches. Sometimes the optimal treatment for a psychological disorder may be to combine drugs with psychotherapy. We will look at several combined approaches: drugs with psychotherapy, integrative therapy, and mindfulness training with psychotherapy.

LO10 Drugs and Psychotherapy

Given the dynamic interplay between biological and psychological influences in many psychological disorders, combined treatments might work better than either alone (Ganasen, Ipser, & Stein, 2010). The drugs can modify some of the debilitating effects of a disorder enough so that the patients can function sufficiently well to learn techniques that might help in changing their problematic thinking and behaviour. This approach works best for depressive and anxiety disorders, in which thinking is not severely impaired. For example, a combined therapy to manage depression might employ drugs to help manage the depressive state, along with CBT to help clients recognize and control the thought patterns that may push them into depressive states (Cuijpers, van Straten, Hollon, & Andersson, 2010; Teasdale et al., 2000).

Integrative Therapy

Some therapists take an *eclectic* approach to psychotherapy, which means that they draw on numerous techniques in their work with clients. These clinicians are typically trained in many methods and use those that seem most appropriate, given the situation, without loyalty to any particular orientation or treatment. This approach is known as **integrative therapy** (Norcross, Bike, & Evans, 2009; Prochaska & Norcross, 2007). For a client showing symptoms of simple phobia and suffering from depression, behavioural therapy may be best for treating the phobia while cognitive techniques may work better for the depression. Problems of self-esteem might best be treated with a humanistic approach.

The vast majority of practising clinical psychologists today say they take an integrative approach to treating disorders (Norcross et al., 2009; Norcross, Karpiak, & Lister, 2005). These practitioners share the experience that no one therapeutic approach is effective for all psychological disorders.

Prolonged exposure therapy is an integrative treatment program for people who have post-traumatic stress disorder (PTSD) (Foa et al., 2005; Powers, Halpern, Ferenschak, Gillihan, & Foa, 2010). It combines CBT with the imagined exposure form of systematic desensitization and relaxation. For clients with PTSD, this involves a course of individual therapy in which clients directly process traumatic events and thus reduce trauma-induced psychological disturbances. Thus, a person with combat-related PTSD might revisit traumatic war scenes in her mind (such as the death of a compatriot) and also engage in cognitive approaches with the therapist to reduce irrational thinking about her role in that event (e.g., she could not have saved him). This technique has been used effectively for the treatment of combat- and rape-related PTSD (Cahill et al., 2006; Foa et al., 1999, 2005; Nacash et al., 2007; Powers et al., 2010). Sometimes drugs prescribed for anxiety disorders are used in combination with prolonged exposure therapy to treat PTSD (Rothbaum et al., 2006).

integrative therapy
an eclectic approach in which the therapist draws on different treatment approaches and uses those that seem most appropriate for the situation.

Mindfulness Training and Psychotherapy

Some newer therapies integrate the non-traditional practice of mindfulness meditation with psychotherapeutic techniques to treat psychological disorders (Chiesa, Brambilla, & Serretti, 2010; Farb et al., 2010). In mindfulness meditation, the meditator is trained to calm the body and the mind and to notice the thoughts or feelings that might draw his or her attention, without getting pulled around by them and without clinging to them. These skills allow people to keep thoughts or emotions in perspective. We will explore three combined approaches in this vein: mindfulness-based cognitive therapy, dialectical behaviour therapy, and the four steps, a treatment for obsessive-compulsive disorder.

Connection

Mindfulness meditation practices help people become aware of everything that occurs in the mind and recognize it for what it is: a thought, an emotion, or a sensation that will arise and dissipate.

See Chapter 5, LO4.

John Teasdale and his colleagues pioneered the applications of mindfulness meditation to the treatment of major depressive disorder (Segal, Williams, & Teasdale, 2002; Teasdale et al., 2000). Their approach combines elements of CBT with mindfulness meditation to create a treatment known as **mindfulness-based cognitive therapy (MBCT).** Both mindfulness meditation and cognitive therapy involve restructuring one's thoughts. Standard cognitive therapy helps depressed people recognize their depressogenic thought patterns and has been very effective in reducing relapse when administered during depressive episodes. Mindfulness meditation develops skills for approaching thoughts non-judgmentally and enhances people's ability to realize that they are neither bound by their thoughts nor defined by them. To the extent that depression stems from recursive "negative" thought patterns in which the person becomes caught in a feedback loop that is reinforced by repeated episodes of depression, mindfulness meditation might help the patient break out of these loops (Farb et al., 2010; Teasdale et al., 1995).

mindfulness-based cognitive therapy (MBCT)
an approach that combines elements of CBT with mindfulness meditation to help people with depression learn to recognize and restructure negative thought patterns.

dialectical behaviour therapy (DBT)
treatment that integrates elements of CBT with exercises aimed at developing mindfulness without meditation and is used to treat borderline personality disorder.

Another combined treatment involving mindfulness is **dialectical behaviour therapy (DBT),** a program developed for the treatment of borderline personality disorder (Linehan, 1993). DBT integrates elements of CBT with exercises aimed at developing mindfulness without meditation. The training, which involves individual as well as group therapy, is designed to help clients develop a non-judgmental attitude toward their emotions and to accept their current behaviour. These skills and attitudes form the cornerstone of personality change, enabling the patient to learn how to regulate his or her own emotions (Linehan et al., 1991).

Jeffrey Schwartz (1997) has applied principles of mindfulness to the treatment of obsessive-compulsive disorder (OCD). Once again, the application is via a form of cognitive therapy that emphasizes the restructuring of maladaptive thought patterns. Schwartz's program, called the *Four Steps,* teaches people with OCD to use mindful thinking to break out of the rigid pattern of intrusive thoughts that plagues them. The Four Steps are self-instructional, although Schwartz uses them in conjunction with group therapy. The steps themselves involve a progression of cognitive and mindfulness exercises aimed at helping people with OCD to recognize intrusive thoughts as nothing but a symptom, and not a defining characteristic of the individual.

The Four Steps of Schwartz's approach are Relabel, Reattribute, Refocus, and Revalue (Schwartz, 1997). The goal of Step 1 is to learn to *relabel* intrusive thoughts and urges in one's own mind as obsessions and compulsions: "It's not me, it's the OCD" is how people describe it. Step 2, *reattribute,* involves ascribing the causes of those thoughts to the brain disorder involved in OCD, rather than one's own control. In Step 3, *refocus,* they learn to see that they can do something useful when an anxious thought occurs, rather than engage in a compulsive behaviour such as hand washing. They learn to understand anxious feelings in an entirely new way. The feelings of anxiety may not change, but their interpretation of what those feelings mean does change. Step 4, *revalue,* involves not taking the obsessive thought to mean all that much—it is just an obsessive thought, and it too will fade away. This is where mindfulness comes in.

Quick Quiz 16.3: Combined Approaches

1. Combining drugs with psychotherapy works well for which of the following disorders?
   a. depressive disorders
   b. anxiety disorders
   c. both a and b
   d. neither a nor b
2. Dialectical behaviour therapy (DBT) is a combined treatment program developed for the treatment of
   a. schizophrenia.
   b. borderline personality disorder.
   c. bipolar disorder.
   d. panic disorder.
3. "It's not me, it's the OCD" is how people describe a stage of which integrative treatment for obsessive-compulsive disorder?
   a. the 12 Steps
   b. cognitive behavioural therapy
   c. systematic desensitization
   d. the Four Steps

Answers can be found at the end of the chapter.

LO11 EFFECTIVENESS OF TREATMENTS

Consider some important questions about these treatments: How effective are these different therapies? Are some more effective for certain disorders than others? What outcomes and criteria do we use for assessing effectiveness? Just because something is called a therapy doesn't automatically mean that it is effective.

Evaluating the effectiveness of any treatment of psychological disorders is a challenging enterprise (Crits-Christoph & Gibbons, 2009). Part of the problem involves the difficulty in measuring clients' improvement. What measures should we use? Do we ask clients how they feel or do we measure changes in their behaviour? Do we ask their therapist? Or ask their friends and family? Although therapists sometimes agree on the criteria that indicate improvement, they often disagree on how these criteria should be assessed, or which measure should be used to assess them (Crits-Christoph, & Connolly, 1997; Lambert, Horowitz, & Strupp, 1997). Some argue that measurement is arbitrary and meaningless because it often doesn't tell us anything about how clients are functioning in everyday life (Blanton & Jaccard, 2006; Kazdin, 2006).

Measurement issues aside, even if we assess how clients are responding to treatment, and find that a client's symptoms have improved over the course of treatment, it cannot automatically be concluded that this improvement is due to the treatment. Sometimes people get better on their own, a phenomenon referred to as **spontaneous remission,** or natural improvement. And sometimes, just knowing that you are receiving a treatment and expecting that it will help you to get better can lead to improvement—a phenomenon known as the **placebo effect.** In clinical drug trials, the placebo effect is the reason why researchers include a *placebo condition,* or a group that receives a "sugar" pill, to compare outcomes with the treatment group that receives the actual medication. They want to be sure that it is the drug and not just the expectations of taking the drug that are leading to symptom reduction. Additionally, a statistical occurrence, known as **regression to the mean,** can make it look like treatment has been effective when it actually hasn't. Regression to the mean refers to when extreme scores become less extreme (or more average) on retesting. Most clients enter therapy when their symptoms are most extreme. As a result, if you measure their symptoms a few weeks later, chances are that most of them will score less extremely. In other words, it might look like the treatment has been effective when, in fact, the improvement could be explained by regression to the mean.

spontaneous remission
improvement in symptoms over time, naturally, without treatment.

placebo effect
improvement in symptoms as a function of expectations that the treatment is effective, rather than the treatment itself.

regression to the mean
a statistical phenomenon when extreme scores become less extreme on retesting.

Connection

Researchers conduct controlled experiments when they want to demonstrate that one variable is causing another.

See Chapter 2, LO5.

So how do researchers and clinicians combat these problems in evaluating treatment effectiveness? As you may have recognized, many of these problems can be addressed by designing studies that include control groups, random assignment of clients to condition, and placebo conditions (conditions where clients receive an equivalent intervention that is not expected to work but controls for client expectations). These types of studies are often referred to as *randomized controlled trials (RCTs).* It is on the basis of these types of scientifically rigorous studies that conclusions about the effectiveness of therapies can be made. With these ideas in mind, we turn now to examine the evidence for effectiveness of treatments: first for biological treatments, then for psychological therapies, and finally for integrative approaches.

According to proponents of dolphin therapy, swimming, touching, or feeding dolphins can calm children with ADHD and provide relief from depression. Yet, there is currently no empirical evidence to support these claims (Marino & Lilienfeld, 2007).

What evidence would the supporters of this therapy need to demonstrate its effectiveness?

Effectiveness of Biological Treatments

The SSRIs and tricyclics show comparable effectiveness in the treatment of depression (Kendrick et al., 2006). Both do a reasonable job of regulating depression and are preferable to the MAO inhibitors, given the undesirable, possibly dangerous, side effects of the latter. Of the various classes of antidepressants, the SSRIs have the fewest adverse side effects, and people seem to tolerate them better for long-term use (Nemeroff, 2007). Still, these drugs can take up to four weeks to take effect. Presumably, this is how long it takes synapses to produce enough new receptor sites to make use of the increased amounts of serotonin made available by SSRIs.

Recent studies, however, suggest that some of the more popular drugs for depression might not be as effective as was once thought. A study by Turner and colleagues (2008) suggests that the medical journals were biased in their publications of findings on the effectiveness of antidepressants. Nearly one-third of all U.S. Food and Drug Administration (FDA) studies—most of which reported negative results on antidepressants—were not published. As a result, for over a decade the impression of the effectiveness of these medications was overestimated (94 percent versus the more modest and more representative 51 percent). According to a large-scale meta-analysis, most widely used prescription antidepressants may be no better than placebos for people with mild to moderate depression. For those with severe depression, they are beneficial when compared to placebos (Fournier et al., 2010). The SSRI fluoxetine (Prozac) actually can harm certain kinds of neural growth and block synapse formation (Xu et al., 2010). A large, randomized trial in Romania compared the effectiveness and cost-effectiveness of drug treatment with Prozac and two kinds of psychotherapy (cognitive therapy and rational emotive therapy). They measured depression scores before, twice during, and six months after a 14-week treatment course. The psychological therapies were more effective than Prozac, as well as more cost-effective. It is not clear whether the same results would hold in North America (Sava, Yates, Lupu, Szentagotai, & David, 2009). Given that over 20 percent of North Americans take these drugs, some have challenged the assumption that the SSRIs are effective or that their effect comes through their increase in serotonin reception (Greenberg, 2013; Kirsch et al., 2002).

Lithium is still widely used for treatment of mania. Lithium does appear to have long-term effectiveness in treating bipolar disorder (Berghöfer et al., 2008). The evidence, however, for lithium's effectiveness in treating "acute" phases of mania is weak in spite of its regular use for this purpose (Reed, Novick, Gonzalez-Pinto, Bertsch, & Haro, 2009). Lithium does not appear to be superior to anticonvulsant or antipsychotic medications, or both, in regulating manic episodes. Moreover, these other medications have fewer toxic side effects than does lithium. Some research indicates that lithium may be most effective in preventing relapse and suicide in people with bipolar disorder, but many providers are not aware of this benefit (Carney & Goodwin, 2005).

The treatment of schizophrenia still presents a huge problem for mental health professionals. Both traditional and atypical antipsychotic drugs work best on the positive symptoms of schizophrenia, such as hallucinations and delusions, but are generally less effective on the negative symptoms, such as flattened affect, and the cognitive confusion that is characteristic of the disorder (Javitt & Coyle, 2004). One atypical antipsychotic, clozapine (Clorazil), does appear to be somewhat effective in treating the negative symptoms, but it also has a potentially serious side effect: diabetes (Javitt & Coyle, 2004). One of the major problems in treating schizophrenia, however, is persuading patients to continue taking the medication. Because of the unpleasant and often dangerous side effects of these drugs, patients often stop taking them. Up to 74 percent of people using traditional and atypical antipsychotics discontinue treatment (Lieberman et al., 2005; McEvoy, et al., 2006). Recent evidence that glutamate may drive the neurotransmitter system in schizophrenia offers hope for the development of more effective, less aversive drug therapies for the disorder (Patil et al., 2007).

ECT is regarded as a treatment of last resort for severely depressed people who have not responded to any other therapy. Although many patients report immediate relief with ECT treatment, its benefits usually last only as long as the treatments are maintained. Also, ECT can have severe side effects, including memory loss and confusion. ECT treatment to one hemisphere of the brain appears to work better than treatment to both hemispheres and creates fewer cognitive side effects (Sackheim et al., 1993). A controlled trial found that ECT and pharmacological therapy for depression were about equally effective in preventing relapse in people with major depressive disorder, but each form of treatment helped only about half the people studied (Kellner et al., 2006).

Effectiveness of Psychological Treatments

An increasingly prevalent view in psychiatry is that therapists need to make treatment choices based on the empirical evidence of their efficacy—that is, they need to be **evidence-based therapies** (APA Presidential Task Force, 2006). Yet very little research has addressed the issue of which psychotherapies work best for various disorders. Decades ago, a review of the literature on the effectiveness of various types of psychotherapies showed that people who received any kind of therapy were better off on a number of outcomes relevant to mental status than most people who did not receive therapy (Smith & Glass, 1977). The study revealed no significant differences between behavioural therapies and psychodynamic ones. Current meta-analyses of the effectiveness of psychotherapy continue to show that most forms of therapy are effective and few significant differences exist in effectiveness among general psychotherapy, cognitive-behavioural therapy, and psychodynamic therapy (Shedler, 2010). This conclusion is sometimes referred to as the **dodo bird verdict,** after the dodo bird in *Alice in Wonderland* (Luborsky, Singer, & Luborsky, 1975). The dodo bird proclaims, "Everybody has won, and must have prizes." The idea is that psychotherapy tends to work, but which kind of therapy one has appears not to matter too much. According to this view, *common factors* underlying the various approaches to psychotherapy, such as contact with a professional who shows empathy, contribute to client improvement and, thus, comparable treatment effectiveness (Laska, Gurman, & Wampold, 2014; Luborsky et al., 1975; Norcross & Wampold, 2011).

evidence-based therapies
treatment choices based on empirical evidence that they produce the desired outcome.

dodo bird verdict
the finding that most forms of therapy are effective and few significant differences exist in effectiveness among standard therapies.

However, this assessment does not mean there are no differences in effectiveness. As some argue, in many cases, the usefulness of psychotherapy also depends on *specific factors*, such as the nature of the disorder being treated and the state of the patient's mental health (Beutler, 2002). Some conditions are more responsive to psychological intervention than others although the mechanisms for change are often not well understood (Craighead, Sheets, Bjornsson, & Arnarson, 2005). Research suggests that personality disorders are best helped with psychodynamic psychotherapy (Shedler, 2010), phobias with behaviour therapy (Tyron, 2005), and schizophrenia with drug therapy (Javitt & Coyle, 2004). For instance, people with schizophrenia experience such disordered thinking that it may be very difficult to teach them to work with their feelings and thoughts in order to change their behaviour. That said, long-term group therapy appears to improve the basic life skills of people with schizophrenia (Sigman & Hassan, 2006).

People experiencing depressive and anxiety disorders are much more responsive to psychological approaches than are people suffering from schizophrenic disorders, but the approach needs to be matched up carefully with the disorder. Systematic desensitization, for example, is quite effective for treating a simple phobia but is inappropriate for treating depression. Length of treatment matters as well. As therapy continues, effectiveness declines (Howard et al., 1986; Kopta, 2003). Perhaps the potency of a psychological treatment begins to wear out after a certain point, or maybe only the harder-to-treat cases stay in therapy longer (Barkham et al., 2006).

Cognitive therapy (CT) and cognitive-behavioural therapy (CBT) have shown perhaps the greatest effectiveness of any form of psychotherapy for treating various psychological disorders, but they are especially effective for certain cases of depression and anxiety disorders (Kehle, 2008; Tolin, 2010; Venning, Kettler, Eliott, & Wilson, 2009). Recent data suggest that cognitive therapy is as effective as antidepressants in treating severe depression (Hollon et al., 2005). In one study (see Figure 16.9), experimental groups of individuals diagnosed with

Research Process

1 Research Question

Is cognitive therapy as effective as the more expensive anti-depressant medication in treating people with depression?

2 Method

Two hundred forty patients with moderate to serious depression participated in a 16-week experimental study. Half of them were randomly assigned to the anti-depressant medication condition, and the other half were randomly assigned to either the cognitive therapy or placebo pill condition. The medication group received Paxil (paroxetine) for 16 weeks and no psychotherapy. The cognitive therapy group received individualized cognitive psychotherapy on a regular basis for 16 weeks. Those in the placebo pill condition received the placebo for eight weeks and Paxil for the final eight weeks.

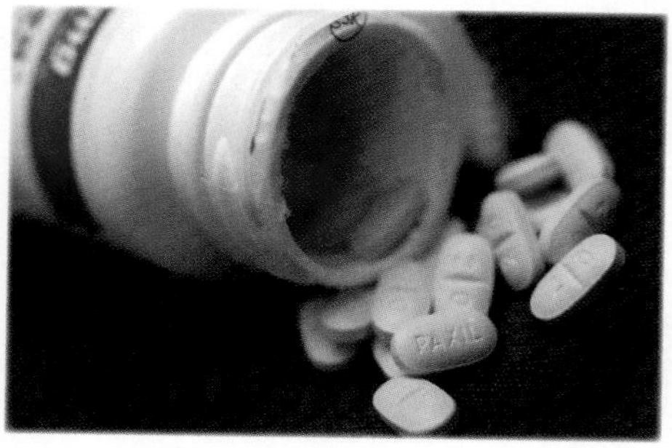

Depression scores were measured twice a week for all 16 weeks using a standard depression questionnaire, the Hamilton Depression Rating Scale. A score of 12 and above is representative of depression. Participants had to have initial scores of 20 or higher to be included in the study.

3 Results

The criterion for the absence of depression was a score lower than 12 on the Hamilton Depression Rating Scale. After eight weeks, 50 percent of the medication group, 43 percent of the cognitive therapy group, and 25 percent of the placebo group were no longer depressed, as the graph shows. After 16 weeks, 58 percent of both the medication and cognitive therapy groups were no longer depressed.

4 Conclusion

At eight weeks both cognitive and drug therapy were superior to a placebo condition in treating depression. After 16 weeks of treatment, cognitive therapy and drug therapy had been equally effective in treating depression.

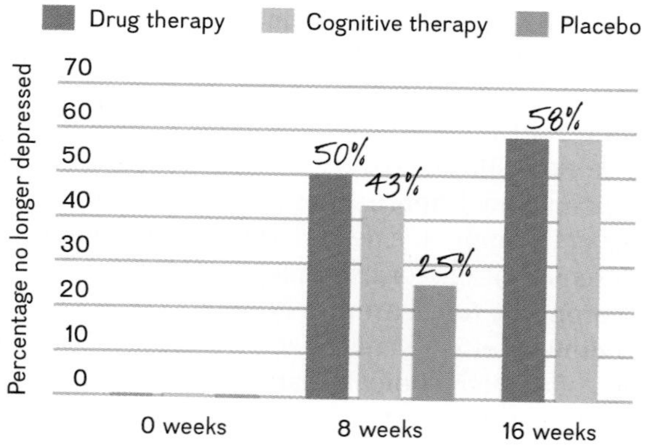

FIGURE **16.9**

COMPARING COGNITIVE THERAPY AND DRUG THERAPY IN THE TREATMENT OF DEPRESSION. Is cognitive therapy as effective as medications in the treatment of major depression? In practice, CT and drug therapy are often combined effectively to treat depression. (*Source:* R.J. DeRubeis et al. 2005. Cognitive therapy vs medications in the treatment of moderate to severe depression. *Archives of General Psychiatry, 62,* 409–416.)

depression received either cognitive therapy or drug therapy, while a control group was treated with a placebo. Cognitive therapy was as effective as drug therapy in treating depression, with fewer risks (DeRubeis et al., 2005). In the treatment of obsessive-compulsive disorder, CBT slows metabolism in the caudate nucleus, an area of the brain that is overactive in people suffering from this disorder (Linden, 2006). In short, psychotherapy can change the brain.

Behavioural treatments such as systematic desensitization are very effective in treating certain anxiety disorders, especially simple phobias, including performance anxiety and public speaking (Lazarus & Abramovitz, 2004; Tyron, 2005). In vivo exposure appears to offer the most effective treatment of simple phobias such as snake phobia, but people are more likely to drop out of such therapies than are people undergoing other forms of systematic desensitization (J. Buchanan & Houlihan, 2008; Choy, Fyer, & Lipsitz, 2007).

Challenge Your Assumptions

True or False? Talk therapy might make people feel better, but it does not change the brain.

False: Psychotherapy can and does change the brain.

Effectiveness of Combined Approaches

In spite of the logic for combining drugs with cognitive-behavioural therapy for both the treatment and the prevention of depression (Nolen-Hoeksema, 2007), few studies have systematically examined the relative benefits of drugs, psychotherapy, and the combination of the two. However, a 14-month study of mental health in more than 500 children examined the relative effectiveness of medication, behavioural therapy, and the combination of the two approaches in treating a variety of disorders (J.H. Edwards, 2002). For ADHD, the combination of drugs and behaviour therapy was superior to behavioural intervention and better than medication alone for most outcome measures (J.H. Edwards, 2002). Other research has reported that combining psychosocial intervention with atypical antipsychotic medication effectively reduces relapse rates and increases general functioning in those suffering from schizophrenia for up to 12 months after treatment (B. Kim et al., 2008).

Clinical research shows that prolonged exposure therapy (an integrative CBT approach) is effective, substantially reducing symptoms of PTSD over extended periods of up to 18 months after treatment is complete (Foa et al., 1999). Although it has still not been widely adopted by clinicians, prolonged exposure therapy shows substantial benefits compared to no therapy, supportive counselling, and other procedures designed to reduce stress (Cahill et al., 2006).

The advantage of mindfulness-based cognitive therapy (MBCT) compared with standard cognitive therapy is that it works when the person is in a non-depressive state, and so it might help prevent relapse. Breakthrough initial work on MBCT showed that it can prevent relapse in people who have had at least three previous depressive episodes. Participants who had recently completed successful drug therapy for their most recent bout of depression were randomly assigned to participate in MBCT or to continue with the treatment they otherwise would have received (treatment as usual), which included seeking help from other sources, such as family or a doctor (Segal, Williams, & Teasdale, 2002). Figure 16.10 shows that those who practised MBCT relapsed into depression only about half as often as those who received treatment as usual (Teasdale et al., 2000). More recently, MBCT was shown to be effective in preventing depressive relapse, regardless of the number of previous depressive episodes (Geschwind, Peeters, Huibers, van Os, & Wichers, 2012), and in reducing experiences of anxiety and stress in non-clinical samples (Kaviani, Javaheri, & Hatami, 2011). By restructuring thoughts, MBCT actually restructures synaptic connections involved in learning, memory, and emotion—another example of how experience can restructure the brain.

Borderline personality disorder has long been considered nearly untreatable, but dialectical behaviour therapy (DBT) became the first treatment effective in reducing the symptoms of this disorder (Soler et al., 2009). DBT reduces

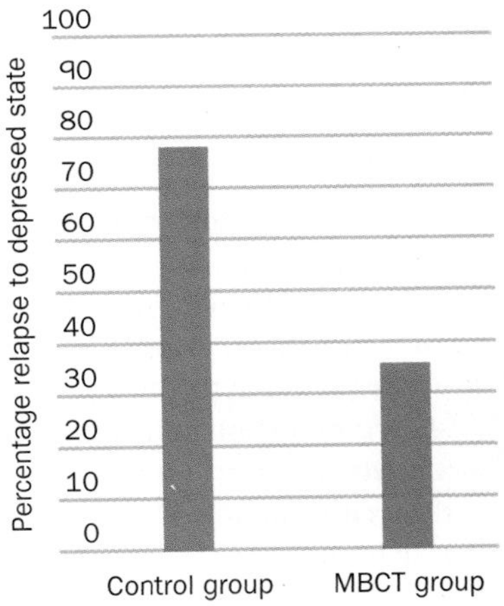

FIGURE **16.10**
EFFECTIVENESS OF MINDFULNESS-BASED COGNITIVE THERAPY (MBCT) FOR DEPRESSION. When people with depression were treated with mindfulness-based cognitive therapy, they were much less likely to experience a relapse compared to a comparison group of people with depression who received treatment as usual. (*Source:* Teasdale et al., 2000.)

self-inflicted harmful behaviours, lowers scores on depression questionnaires, decreases dysfunctional patterns associated with substance abuse, and increases the likelihood of staying in treatment (Koerner & Linehan, 2000; Kröger, et al, 2006; Linehan, Heard, & Armstrong, 1993). Most important, DBT reduces the risk of suicide attempts—the most disastrous risk associated with borderline personality disorder—much more than does non-behavioural psychotherapy (Linehan et al., 2006). Not only is DBT effective in treating borderline personality disorder, but it has also been adapted to treat eating disorders, conduct disorders, and domestic violence (Kristeller, Baer, & Quillian-Wolever, 2006; Nelson-Gray et al., 2006; Rathus, Cavuoto, & Passarelli, 2006). In a recent study of a group of people with a variety of diagnoses, participation in a weekly DBT course led to reductions in self-reported anxiety and depression and offered participants an increased sense of hope (Ritschel, Cheavens, & Nelson, 2012).

The last combined mindfulness technique is the Four Steps. It may take several months to progress through the Four Steps, but the treatment appears to work. In fact, Four Steps training not only helps break the thinking-behavioural cycles of OCD but also (or for this reason) changes the brain circuitry that appears to support repetitive thinking and behaviour (Schwartz, 2000). People with OCD have dramatically increased activity in the areas of the frontal cortex and caudate nucleus. These areas tend to be active in healthy people when events in one's environment deviate from what is expected (Schwartz, 2000). As people with OCD are constantly checking their environment for things that could be wrong, overactivation in the caudate nucleus area seems consistent with this disorder. PET studies reveal decreases in caudate nucleus metabolism in people who respond to the Four Steps treatment (Schwartz, 1999). This is consistent with other findings that CBT reduces overactivation in the caudate nucleus of people with OCD (Linden, 2006).

For all of the variety of treatments available, one of the most challenging aspects of psychological interventions is finding a therapist. The "Psychology in the Real World" feature offers practical information on how to choose a therapist.

Challenge Your Assumptions

True or False? All effective psychotherapies involve people confronting the "root" childhood causes of their problems.

False: Most effective psychotherapies, such as CBT, do not focus on childhood problems.

Quick Quiz 16.4: Effectiveness of Treatments

1. A therapist administers a new treatment for generalized anxiety disorder, a "scream" therapy where clients are encouraged to make as much noise as possible to release all their pent-up emotional fears. After six weeks of participating in this therapy, he finds that his clients show a reduction in their symptoms of generalized anxiety. He concludes that his treatment is effective in the treatment of GAD. Is the therapist justified in his conclusion?
   a. Yes—clients showed a clear reduction in symptoms of GAD.
   b. No—clients' improvement may be explained by regression to the mean.
   c. No—clients' improvement may be explained by the placebo effect.
   d. Both b and c explain his results.
2. Both traditional and atypical antipsychotic drugs work best on the ______ symptoms of schizophrenia, but are generally less effective on the ______ symptoms. (Pick the best pair of words to fill in the blanks.)
   a. negative; positive
   b. positive; negative
   c. cognitive; emotional
   d. emotional; cognitive
3. ______ exposure is a form of systematic desensitization that is very effective but has a high drop-out rate.
   a. Imagined
   b. Virtual reality
   c. Twelve-step
   d. In vivo
4. According to the research presented in Figure 16.9, which is more effective in decreasing depression—cognitive therapy (CT) or antidepressant medication (Paxil)?
   a. CT
   b. Paxil
   c. They are equally effective.
   d. Neither; the MAO inhibitors are best.

Answers can be found at the end of the chapter.

Psychology in the Real World

How to Choose a Therapist

As we read in Chapter 15, nearly 50 percent of the adult population at some point in their lives will suffer from a psychological disorder, whether it is phobia, depression, anxiety, schizophrenia, or something else (Kessler et al., 2005). However, only a subset of those who need therapy seek it out or receive it (Canadian Medical Association, 2008; Corrigan et al., 2014). Why? One reason has to do with the stigma of "seeing a shrink"—many people do not want their friends, family, or co-workers and bosses to know they are seeing a therapist. There is a stigma attached to the need for mental health treatment (Canadian Medical Association, 2008; Mental Health, 2001). Moreover, people often think they have friends and family who can help them so they don't need a therapist. In fact, therapists are trained professionals who have more knowledge, understanding, and training to deal with a whole range of mental health concerns than family and friends. These two forms of help, of course, are not mutually exclusive and should both be sought in unison.

Indeed, research on the effectiveness of treatment shows consistently that treatment is better than no treatment. In a large 1995 *Consumer Reports*' survey, 87 percent of people reported improvement in their mental health after receiving therapy (Seligman, 1995). Self-reported improvement was greatest for those who received longer-term therapy from a mental health practitioner other than their family physician (i.e., clinical psychologist, counsellor, social worker, or psychiatrist).

Suppose that you or a friend or family member is showing signs of difficulty coping or adjusting and would like to find a good therapist. How would you go about doing that?

A therapist's experience is important (Saisan, Smith, & Segal, 2010). You should look for someone who is trained and has experience in the area in which you are having difficulty. For instance, if you are experiencing obsessive-compulsive disorder, your therapist should have experience helping people with this disorder.

Note that these specialists are not qualified to practise therapy just because they have earned their primary degree (e.g., M.D., Ph.D., M.S.W.). They must also undergo several thousand hours of supervised training and pass a licensing exam before they can practise therapy. Therefore, at a minimum you want to make sure the therapist you are considering is licensed and in good standing. Each province has regulatory boards that can tell you whether complaints have been filed against particular therapists (e.g., B.C. College of Psychologists, B.C. College of Social Workers, etc.), although not all provinces have regulatory boards for all types of therapists, so examine qualifications carefully!

In finding a therapist, trusting your gut feeling is important. Relationships with therapists, after all, are relationships. Some work and some do not. Research tells us that the client–therapist relationship, sometimes referred to as the *therapeutic alliance,* can significantly affect the treatment outcome, affecting the client's beliefs about the treatment procedures, and their willingness to continue (Bohart & Wade, 2013). So it's important that you feel comfortable with and trust your therapist! You should feel comfortable setting up a trial period of perhaps five or six sessions and then determining whether you want to continue. All good therapists will respect your decision to go elsewhere if therapy is not working for you and won't try to make you feel guilty or convince you to stay. If they do, that is a red flag (Saisan et al., 2010).

The approach and orientation of the therapist may matter to you. Some approaches are very short-term and targeted, and others are very long-term and general. You have to decide which is right for you. Two of the more common approaches are cognitive-behavioural therapy (CBT) and psychoanalytic/psychodynamic therapy. Most therapists will take an eclectic or integrative approach, even if they were trained in a particular orientation. Even those trained in a particular orientation, such as psychodynamic or cognitive-behavioural therapy, may use techniques from different orientations if they feel that those will work best for a particular person.

Finally, once you make all of these decisions, you still need to find a therapist who fits your needs. The most common resources for assisting in finding a therapist are your family doctor, your family and friends, lists of providers recommended by your insurance plan, mental health associations, and counselling centres on campus. So ask a doctor or a friend when you are beginning to search for a therapist. Get advice from multiple sources and see whether there is any overlap. Once you have a recommendation, it is wise to speak with the therapist on the phone to get a sense of your comfort level with this person, or try an initial session. You should not feel obligated to continue with someone if you feel the connection is not right.

Canadian Mental Health Association
Mental health for all

Many mental health associations offer free referral services to help you locate qualified professionals in your community. One example of this type of referral service may be found at the British Columbia Psychological Association website: http://www.psychologists.bc.ca/content/find-registered-psychologist.

How would you go about locating a therapist for yourself or a family member? What resources are available in your community?

LO12 NEW DIRECTIONS IN TREATMENT

There are exciting new therapies on the horizon, but they are not yet fully developed and tested for widespread application. In this section, we briefly highlight a few of the more interesting new developments that appear to offer great promise for future treatment based on initial research.

Emerging Biological Therapies

optogenetics
a treatment that uses a combination of light stimulation and genetics to manipulate the activity of individual neurons.

One new possible treatment involves using light to stimulate neural activity in certain brain regions—a technique generally known as **optogenetics**, a combination of light (hence the "opto" prefix) stimulation and genetics to manipulate the activity of individual neurons (Deisseroth, 2010). Optogenetics was chosen as "Breakthrough of the Decade" by *Science* magazine in 2010. The technique has been used in various mental health–related applications, such as treating OCD and chemical dependency. In one recent study, researchers used light to stimulate neurons in the orbitofrontal region of the brain in mice and were able to decrease compulsive behaviours (Burguiére, Monteiro, Feng, & Graybiel, 2013). In another study using mice, researchers stimulated the neurons in the reward centre of the brain (the nucleus accumbens) that are activated by cocaine and, when silenced, greatly decreased the appetite for cocaine (Witten et al., 2010). Optogenetics may offer such precise access to specific areas of the brain that it may allow for carefully targeted stimulation-based treatments (some variation on deep brain stimulation), possibly replacing drug therapies that offer much less precise control of mood and behaviour (Touriño, Evan-Rothschild, & de Lecea, 2013).

Another potentially exciting future therapy is the regulation of specific genes involved in various mental disorders. A steady stream of recent research has confirmed the role of one particular gene (neuregulin 1) in the development of schizophrenia (Law et al., 2006; Mei & Xiong 2008; D.-M. Yin et al., 2013). Although still in early stages in animals, therapies based on this understanding may be quite beneficial in controlling some of the major symptoms of schizophrenia (Mei & Xiong, 2008; D.-M. Yin et al., 2013).

Some promising new areas of treatment make use of accidental findings of treatments used for other purposes. Consider the case of Botox, which is used for cosmetic purposes. Botox treatment for wrinkles involves injection of a very small amount of botulism toxin (a naturally occurring paralytic agent) into the facial muscles underlying common wrinkle areas (such as the area between the eyebrows), causing paralysis and relaxing nearby wrinkles. Botox works by blocking acetylcholine release from axons into the synapse, thereby inhibiting neuromuscular transmission. Once the Botox is injected, people frown less. As discussed in Chapter 11, there is fairly strong evidence for bodily feedback contributing to the experience of emotion, so if you reduce muscle feedback from the face, you reduce the emotional experience (Dimberg & Söderkvist, 2011). A handful of studies have shown that after Botox injections to the glabellar region (i.e., above the nose, between the eyebrows), people report feeling less strong emotions (Davis et al., 2010), because feedback to the brain from the facial muscles involved in certain emotions is reduced. There is evidence for significant improvements in mood for people who have major depressive disorder (Finzi & Rosenthal, 2014;

Optogenetics carefully controls electrical impulses to the brain that activate specific neurons. This technique offers promise for the treatment of psychological disorders in humans, such as compulsive disorders.

Wollmer et al., 2012). Botox may offer an easy new treatment for certain types of depression, but further research is needed to test the long-term effectiveness of this treatment. Botox treatment is not without drawbacks, however, as it can reduce one's ability to read other people's facial expressions, which is likely due to reduced facial mimicry during social interaction (Neal & Chartrand, 2011).

Connection

Acetylcholine (Ach) is a neurotransmitter involved in the control of muscles.

See Chapter 3, LO8, LO9.

Technology-Based Treatments

A number of new therapies make use of technology or the Internet to complement current therapies or make psychotherapeutic techniques available to people who might otherwise not have access to therapy or seek it out. These are the **technology-based therapies.**

technology-based therapies therapies that make use of technology or the Internet to complement current therapies or make psychotherapeutic techniques available to more people.

virtual reality therapies therapies that use virtual (digital simulation) environments to create therapeutic situations that would be hard to create otherwise.

In **virtual reality therapies,** virtual (digital simulation) environments create therapeutic situations that might be hard to create otherwise. For instance, virtual reality therapy has been used for the treatment of phobias, such as a fear of flying (as we saw in our discussion of behavioural therapy), or the treatment of PTSD by re-creating a traumatic situation, such as a battlefield (McLay, McBrien, Wiederhold, & Wiederhold, 2010; McLay et al., 2012; Ready, Gerardi, Backscheider, Mascaro, & Rothbaum, 2010; Riva, 2009). Both of these situations would be either costly or nearly impossible to replicate in real-life therapy (Cukor, Spitalnick, Difede, Rizzo, & Rothbaum 2009). Recent research shows virtual reality therapy to also be an effective treatment for social anxiety disorder (P.L. Anderson et al., 2013).

The Internet can be used as an online therapeutic environment as well. The virtual world, known as Second Life, provides a place for people to meet, interact, and develop a social milieu. This online program, which has been downloaded by 15 million users around the world, is a virtual environment where people interact with others in real time. It is mostly used recreationally but increasingly commercially and therapeutically as well (Lisetti et al., 2009). Therapeutically, the participants are clients and therapists, each of whom has an avatar (hence the name *avatar therapy*). Both people can talk through a headset to give their avatars a voice, or they can chat by text written on screen. Each participant can walk, fly, travel to different locations, and manipulate his or her own facial expressions and body language. As with other online games, participants encounter other avatars and interact with them.

One group of clinicians at Drexel University in Philadelphia is studying the effectiveness of Second Life treatment for social anxiety disorder, offering CBT in Second Life, in 12 weekly sessions (Yuen et al., 2013). Through avatars, a client meets with a therapist in a private, secure virtual room. Clients learn new techniques and get opportunities to practise. Second Life offers people with social anxiety—who avoid therapy that requires them to get out of the house and go to a new environment—a "safe" form of psychotherapy, because they are not directly observed or exposed to ridicule and embarrassing situations. Research on the effectiveness of Second Life is ongoing (Gorrindo & Groves, 2009; Ku et al., 2005; Yuen et al., 2013). Drawbacks to technology-based therapy, however, include its difficulty in ensuring confidentiality and in intervening if patients become an immediate danger to themselves or others.

Other digital therapeutic techniques make direct use of the Internet for both access to materials and the creation of online environments in which treatment can occur. Therapist-assisted *Internet-delivered cognitive behaviour therapy (ICBT)* is a promising new way to increase access to treatment for people with a variety of anxiety-related and depressive disorders, especially those who have difficulty accessing treatment because of mobility issues or living in remote areas. Heather Hadjistavropoulos and her colleagues at the University of Regina have designed such an online program where cognitive and behavioural strategies are delivered through 12 structured modules over the Internet and clients then complete homework assignments, communicating with a therapist once a week by telephone or email (Hadjistavropoulos, Alberts, Nugent, & Marchildon, 2014). Recent meta-analyses of randomized controlled trials indicate that electronic distribution may work just as effectively as face-to-face therapy for certain anxiety symptoms, including measures of panic disorder, social anxiety disorder, and generalized anxiety disorder, as well as depression (Andersson, Cuijpers, Carlbring, Riper, & Hedman, 2014; Andrews, Cuijpers, Craske, McEvoy, & Titov, 2010). Internet-based therapies provide a means to meet the growing demand for psychiatric care (Andrews et al., 2010), although they require the additional management of computer access for some clients and development of computer skills (Hadjistavropoulos et al., 2011).

Quick Quiz 16.5: New Directions in Treatment

1. Optogenetics has shown promise in the treatment of which of the following disorders?
   a. depression
   b. schizophrenia
   c. obsessive-compulsive disorder
   d. all of the above

2. Delivery of therapy using technology has many benefits, including
   a. increasing access to therapy.
   b. decreased cost to administer.
   c. teaching people how to use technology.
   d. a and b.

Answers can be found at the end of the chapter.

LO13 PREVENTING DISORDERS

The best and safest form of treatment for psychological disorders is prevention. *Prevention* focuses on identifying risk factors for disorders, targeting at-risk populations, and offering training programs that decrease the likelihood of disorders occurring. Many prevention efforts are underway in Canada, but the majority focus on the prevention of depression. In fact, in the wake of the economic recession of 2008–2009, the annual prevalence of major depression in Canada increased from about 5 percent to 7.5 percent (Wang et al., 2010).

Just as a healthy diet and exercise program can help prevent heart disease, prevention programs train people to behave in ways that help stave off depression and other psychological disorders. Preventing depression in at-risk groups, for instance, has decreased the onset of depression by as much as 25 percent (Beekman, Smit, Stek, Reynolds, & Cuijpers, 2010). This rate compares well to the success rate for those who receive therapy. Many prevention programs focus on children, because interventions earlier in life increase the likelihood of making a difference. A recent meta-analysis of more than 30 intervention programs for depression in teens found that shorter interventions and those that involve homework are the most effective (Stice, Shaw, Bohon, Marti, & Rhode, 2009).

Teen depression is a growing problem and the major cause of suicide in young people (Wessely & Kerwin, 2004). In a large-scale study of risk factors for adolescent depression, Van Voorhees and colleagues (2008) conducted face-to-face interviews of teens in Grades 7–12 in the home, obtained parent surveys, and measured depressive symptoms using a questionnaire. They found that several characteristics put teens at risk for a depressive episode: being female, being of a non-white race/ethnicity, having low-income status, being in poor health, and experiencing parental conflict. Teens who felt a connection among family members, warmth from their parents, and peer acceptance; who did better in school; and who participated in religious activities were less likely to have a depressive episode than others (Van Voorhees et al., 2008). Research on elementary school children reports similar findings (Dallaire et al., 2008).

In addition to poverty and unemployment, psychosocial factors—especially life stress and having a pessimistic outlook on life—increase the risk of depression (Southwick, Vythilingam, & Charney, 2005). For this reason, some intervention programs for teens focus on teaching them skills for dealing with stress, including developing a more optimistic outlook. One after-school program for teens at risk for developing depression is based on CBT. Participants have already experienced mild to moderate symptoms of the disorder; therefore, this program involves retraining in ways of thinking about adversity in life. Clarke and colleagues (1995) reported that compared to those who did not receive the training, those who participated were significantly less likely to become clinically depressed 18 months later (Clarke et al., 1995).

One of the most researched CBT programs, developed at the University of Pennsylvania—the Penn Resiliency Program (PRP)—is designed to prevent depression and other psychological disorders by also teaching resilience and skills for coping with stress, problem solving (flexibility in the face of adverse or challenging circumstances), and cognitive restructuring (learning to change one's perspective on events). In a meta-analysis of 17 interventions on nearly 2500 teenagers, Brunwasser and colleagues found that PRP participants had reported fewer depressive symptoms at post-intervention and both follow-up assessments compared with youths receiving no intervention (Brunwasser, Gillham, & Kim, 2009). More specifically, in a large-scale study of 697 early adolescents, the PRP was administered in weekly 90-minute sessions over a 12-week period (Gillham et al., 2007). PRP significantly reduced depressive symptoms at follow-up compared to a control group and to another intervention, which was not aimed at resiliency, in two of the three schools. Moreover, research on the PRP suggests that it successfully changes participants' negative cognitive styles, instilling optimistic outlooks (Seligman, Schulman, & Tryon, 2007). This is a crucial point—helping people look at things differently should prevent a relapse into depression (J.D. Teasdale et al., 2000). Thus, positive outlooks ingrained early in life ought to help prevent a lifetime of depression.

Another similar program based on CBT, *FRIENDS for Life*, is endorsed by the World Health Organization (2004), and targets the prevention of anxiety disorders in school-aged children (Barrett, 2004). Developed in Australia, it is a program designed to teach coping strategies to reduce anxiety and build resilience while also promoting self-esteem. Each session focuses on recognizing anxious feelings and physical reactions to anxiety, as well as challenging negative thoughts in anxiety-provoking situations and developing techniques for managing anxiety. Currently, used in British Columbia schools, it is delivered to students in Grades K–1, 4–5, and 6–7 by teachers in the B.C. school system (B.C. Ministry of Children and Family Development, n.d.). Although there are currently no studies confirming the program's effectiveness in Canada (Rose, Miller, & Martinez, 2009), some international research suggests that levels of anxiety remain lower on follow-up several months after receiving the program (Barrett & Turner, 2001; Barrett, Farrell, Ollendick, & Dadds, 2006; Liddle & MacMillan, 2010; Payton et al., 2008; Stallard et al., 2005).

Some people resist seeking mental health treatment.

Can you think of reasons it is important to promote public education about mental health?

Another population significantly affected by depression is the elderly. For some, aging is associated with dramatic life changes such as health problems and physical decline, which often prompt some individuals to seek assisted living for their elderly family members. Elderly people who relocate to nursing homes have to adjust to reductions in their independence and control over their lives (Raps et al., 1982). Newcomers to nursing homes are at the greatest risk for developing depression, likely due to the stress of change in control over their lives (Snowden & Donnelly, 1986). Given these known risks for depression in elderly nursing home residents, they are a population that can greatly benefit from depression prevention strategies.

Using a treatment program that had been successful in adolescents, Candace Konnert at the University of Calgary has investigated the impact of brief CBT on the prevention of depression in elderly nursing home residents. Compared to control participants, the CBT participants reported greater satisfaction with their treatment experience and had lower measures of depressive symptoms that persisted for six months (Konnert et al., 2009). Given that CBT appears to be effective in different age groups, it shows promise as a prevention strategy against depression.

Quick Quiz 16.6: Preventing Psychological Disorders

1. What is the safest and best form of treatment for depression?
   a. Paxil
   b. prevention
   c. group therapy
   d. cognitive therapy

2. Most successful prevention programs incorporate the principles of
   a. thought distraction.
   b. cognitive-behavioural therapy.
   c. poverty reduction.
   d. psychodynamic therapy.

Answers can be found at the end of the chapter.

Evaluating Connections in the Treatment of Psychological Disorders

Approaches to the Treatment of OCD and Anxiety Disorders

Obsessive-compulsive disorder (OCD) and anxiety disorders are a diverse group of conditions. Although they share the core symptoms of fear and anxiety, the *DSM-5* treats them as separate categories. Because they are so diverse, mental health practitioners use a wide variety of treatment strategies to help people with these disorders. Because of their varied symptoms and treatments, these disorders offer a useful context in which to illustrate the application of treatments discussed in this chapter.

Drug Therapies

Drug therapies play a major role in the management and treatment of OCD and anxiety disorders. The main categories of medications used for treatment include the antidepressants and the antianxiety drugs.

Antidepressants

Many doctors prescribe SSRIs for the treatment of anxiety disorders, such as social anxiety disorder and panic disorder, as well as for the treatment of OCD and post-traumatic stress disorder (PTSD). People who take SSRIs for these disorders report that these medications help them disengage from the repetitive cycle of anxiety-provoking thoughts that otherwise would snowball into anxiety. As a result, the SSRIs may help change patterns of thinking when combined with the thought restructuring of CBT and may allow people with OCD to apply cognitive techniques to learn how to think differently. Recent findings that people with OCD who take SSRIs often relapse suggest that combining these drugs with psychological treatments might be more effective than the drugs alone (Catapano et al., 2006). The SSRIs are also considered the first line of treatment for generalized anxiety disorder (Baldwin & Polkinghorn, 2005).

Other antidepressants are prescribed for OCD and anxiety disorders, but much less often. Most tricyclic antidepressants apparently do not work for people with OCD, for example, but do work for certain anxiety disorders. One tricyclic, clomipramine (CMI), however, is most effective on norepinephrine synapses and actually reduces the symptoms of OCD. Because tricyclics have numerous side effects, medical professionals tend to prescribe SSRIs instead (Bleier, Habib, & Flament, 2006).

Antianxiety Medications

Drugs that soothe the agitation of anxiety are used to treat anxiety disorders, especially for people who suffer from panic attacks. Occasionally physicians prescribe beta-blockers—drugs that block the action of neurotransmitters such as norepinephrine—to quickly calm the aroused sympathetic nervous system. One such drug is propanolol, which is often used to treat high blood pressure and other cardiovascular conditions. These medications calm the physiological symptoms of anxiety by bringing down heart rate, blood pressure, and rate of breathing.

The benzodiazepines (e.g., Valium) also calm the physiological arousal caused by anxiety and are widely prescribed for social anxiety disorder, panic disorder, and generalized anxiety disorder. They can also treat or prevent panic attacks in high-anxiety situations, but they are best used only occasionally. When regular users discontinue use of benzodiazepines, they experience withdrawal symptoms, such as insomnia, tremors, increased anxiety, tachycardia (rapid heartbeat), and sweating. Newer antianxiety medications, such as buspirone (used for generalized anxiety disorder) are less likely to create withdrawal symptoms, but they require longer continuous usage to be effective. The newer selective norepinephrine reuptake inhibitors, as well as SSRIs, are also used in the treatment of anxiety disorders (Dell'Osso et al., 2009).

Psychotherapeutic Treatments

As we have seen, cognitive-behavioural therapy helps people with anxiety disorders identify irrational thoughts and undo thinking patterns that support fear; it also helps them modify their responses to anxiety-provoking situations. CBT effectively treats specific phobias and social anxiety disorder in children as well as adults (Hirshfeld-Becker et al., 2010). According to a recent meta-analysis, CBT appears to be superior to other psychotherapeutic approaches in treating anxiety disorders overall (Tolin, 2010).

Group CBT therapy is very effective for the treatment of social anxiety disorder (Hofman et al., 2006; Tolin, 2010). Such contexts usually involve weekly meetings for about 12 weeks, as well as homework assignments each week. In addition to the normal benefits of CBT for reducing anxious thoughts and behaviours, the social factors involved in a group play a key role in the therapy's effectiveness. Because all the participants have gone through similar situations and can share their experiences, this support helps prevent feelings of isolation and helplessness. Also, group members provide examples of success. For instance, if someone in a social anxiety disorder group managed to go to a deli, order a sandwich, and pay the cashier and it went well, this provides an example that simple social transactions really can be done. Other group members might be inspired to try it themselves. Avatar therapy, with virtual reality group CBT, is now being used to treat social anxiety disorder as well (Riva, 2009).

Traditional psychodynamic therapies for anxiety disorders viewed anxiety as the main symptom of what was then commonly called neurosis. Neuroses, according to Freud, most often stemmed from repressed thoughts, feelings, and impulses that usually originated in childhood experiences. Therefore, the main approach of psychodynamic therapies is to uncover the unconscious thoughts, feelings, and impulses that lead to neurotic symptoms. Most commonly, this is achieved through dream interpretation, free associations, uncovering defence mechanisms, and catharsis. Symptom relief requires insight, and insight requires emotional release of repressed feelings. Although psychodynamic therapies have not been studied as extensively as CBT, recent randomized controlled trials suggest that in some cases, psychodynamic therapy may be just as effective as CBT in short-term symptom reduction, especially for social anxiety disorder and generalized anxiety disorder (Baardseth et al., 2013; Leichsenring & Klein, 2014). However, more empirical evidence is needed as long-term effectiveness (measured in terms of relapse) is less clear (Leichsenring & Salzer, 2014).

We have already discussed the use of systematic desensitization for the treatment of specific phobias. This process couples relaxation training with gradual exposure to the feared object and is very effective for the treatment of specific phobias such as fears of animals, flying, and heights (Aitken & Benson, 1984; Wiederhold & Wiederhold, 2005).

Combined and Integrative Therapies

As we have seen, sometimes medication can help people get "over the hump" of crippling symptoms so that a non-drug therapy has a chance to work. Such is the case with the combination of either antidepressants or antianxiety medications and CBT or systematic desensitization. Often the course of medication treatment is short term, until the psychotherapeutic training begins to take effect. Alternatively, the medication may be decreased slowly during the course of psychological treatment.

Combining drug therapy and psychotherapy offers hope for treating OCD. For example, in a review of the literature on children and teens who suffer from obsessive-compulsive disorder, Kaiser and Bouvard (2009) found that combining drug therapy with CBT was almost always as effective and sometimes more effective than either one alone. Although many people recommend combined therapies, a recent review of the treatment efficacy of combined therapies versus single therapy for anxiety disorders yielded little consistent evidence that combined therapy works better (Black, 2006). In fact, in some cases, drug mechanisms may inhibit the thought processes necessary to make a cognitive or behaviour therapy work, as may be the case with combined drug-exposure therapy for anxiety disorders (Otto, McHugh, & Kantak, 2010).

There is evidence that integrative psychotherapeutic approaches offer potential relief from a range of disorders. As already noted, OCD may be treated with mindfulness meditation practices and cognitive therapy. Mindfulness-based cognitive therapy shows promise in the treatment of generalized anxiety disorder (Evans et al., 2008). Also, dialectical behaviour therapy (DBT), which was developed to treat borderline personality disorder, has been used effectively to treat post-traumatic stress disorder (Wagner & Linehan, 2006).

Quick Quiz 16.7: Evaluating Connections in the Treatment of Psychological Disorders

1. Which drugs appear to help people with OCD disengage from the repetitive cycle of anxiety-provoking thoughts?
   a. SSRIs
   b. MAO inhibitors
   c. benzodiazepines
   d. lithium salts

2. Group CBT is very effective for the treatment of which anxiety disorder?
   a. generalized anxiety disorder
   b. social anxiety disorder
   c. panic disorder
   d. simple phobias

Answers can be found at the end of the chapter.

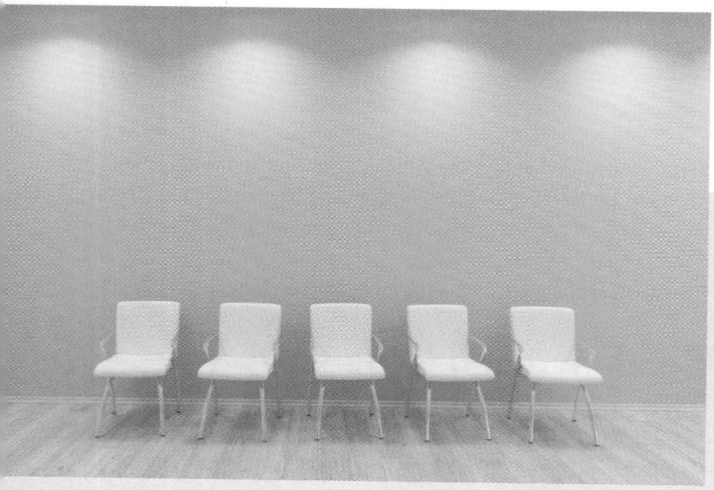

Chapter Review

TREATMENT APPROACHES

- Treatment strategies for psychological disorders can be classified into three main categories: psychological, biological, and combined approaches. Mental health professionals offering different treatments include clinical psychologists, counsellors, social workers, psychiatrists, and family doctors.

PSYCHOLOGICAL TREATMENTS

- Psychotherapy is the use of psychological techniques to modify maladaptive behaviours or thought patterns, or both, and develop insight into the client's behaviour.
- Psychodynamic therapies aim to uncover unconscious conflicts or motives underlying psychological problems or symptoms. Psychodynamic therapists use several techniques, such as free association, to access the unconscious.
- Humanistic therapy, such as client-centred therapy, helps clients realize their full potential. Therapists create an atmosphere in which clients can communicate

their feelings with the certainty that they are being understood rather than judged.

- Behaviour therapies apply the principles of conditioning to the treatment of disorders. Systematic desensitization, a widely used behavioural method, pairs relaxation with gradual exposure to a phobic object.
- Cognitive therapies work to restructure irrational thought patterns. Often therapists combine cognitive techniques for changing irrational thoughts with behavioural techniques to shape desirable behaviours in what is known as cognitive-behavioural therapy (CBT). CBT is a short-term psychological treatment that has been successfully applied to many disorders.
- Many treatments, including CBT, are administered as group therapy. Group contexts serve both as a source of support and as an aid to the therapeutic process, allowing several people with similar problems to listen, discuss, and criticize one another.

BIOLOGICAL TREATMENTS

- Drug therapies for schizophrenia include the traditional antipsychotics, which are rarely prescribed these days due to their adverse side effects, and the atypical antipsychotics. The atypical antipsychotics do not lead to tardive dyskinesia, but they are somewhat better at treating negative symptoms.
- Many different drugs are used to treat depression. The older antidepressants include the monoamine oxidase (MAO) inhibitors and the tricyclic antidepressants. The selective serotonin reuptake inhibitors (SSRIs) reduce reuptake of serotonin at the synapse and create far fewer unpleasant side effects than the older antidepressants.
- Lithium is prescribed to stabilize the mania associated with bipolar disorder. Due to the toxicity of lithium, medical professionals often prescribe other drugs to regulate manic episodes.
- Psychosurgery is brain surgery performed to treat psychological disorders. Prefrontal lobotomy was once used to reduce psychotic behaviour, but it is now considered an outdated and cruel procedure.
- Electroconvulsive therapy (ECT) involves passing electrical current through the brain to induce a seizure. Because ECT can lead to memory loss, the only currently acceptable clinical application of ECT is for cases of severe depression that fail to respond to any other treatment.
- Helen Mayberg discovered what may be a neural switch for depression, known as Area 25. Deep brain stimulation of Area 25 can provide sudden relief from depression in people who have failed to respond to all other treatments.

COMBINED APPROACHES

- Combined treatments are increasingly common in practice. These include methods that combine drugs with psychotherapy or combine various forms of psychotherapy with each other. Mindfulness practices have also been added to traditional treatments.

EFFECTIVENESS OF TREATMENTS

- Evaluating treatment effectiveness can be challenging. Randomized controlled trials allow researchers to rule out improvement due to the placebo effect and spontaneous remission.
- The SSRIs and tricyclics are equally effective in the treatment of depression. The SSRIs have the fewest adverse side effects, and seem to be tolerated better for long-term use.
- The evidence for lithium's effectiveness in treating bipolar disorder is weak in spite of its regular use for this purpose. It does not appear to be superior to less toxic anticonvulsants or antipsychotics in regulating manic episodes.
- Both traditional and atypical antipsychotic drugs work best on the positive symptoms of schizophrenia. Certain atypical antipsychotic drugs may relieve the negative symptoms.
- Although many patients report immediate relief with ECT, usually it is effective only as long as treatments are maintained. Also, the adverse effects of ECT on memory can be fairly severe.
- Psychotherapy is more effective for certain disorders than for others. CBT may be the most effective form of psychotherapy, especially for certain cases of depression and anxiety disorders.
- In some cases, the most effective treatments for many psychological disorders integrate one form of treatment with another.

NEW DIRECTIONS IN TREATMENT

- Some emerging therapies, such as optogenetics, gene manipulation, and even Botox, are "not yet ready for prime time" but show promise for the future.

- A number of newer therapies make use of technology or the Internet to complement current therapies or to make psychotherapeutic techniques available to people who might otherwise not have access to them or seek them out.

PREVENTING DISORDERS

- Prevention focuses on identifying the risk factors for disorders, targeting at-risk populations, and offering training programs that decrease the likelihood of disorders occurring. Most prevention efforts focus on depression.

EVALUATING CONNECTIONS IN THE TREATMENT OF PSYCHOLOGICAL DISORDERS

- The treatment of OCD and anxiety disorders illustrates how diverse approaches may be used to treat psychological disorders. Both psychological and biological therapies have been used, alone and together, to treat OCD and anxiety disorders.

Quick Quiz Answers

Quick Quiz 16.1: 1. a 2. d 3. a **Quick Quiz 16.2:** 1. c 2. c 3. d 4. b **Quick Quiz 16.3:** 1. c 2. b 3. d **Quick Quiz 16.4:** 1. d 2. b 3. d 4. c **Quick Quiz 16.5:** 1. c 2. d **Quick Quiz 16.6:** 1. b 2. b **Quick Quiz 16.7:** 1. a 2. b

Glossary

absent-mindedness a form of forgetfulness that results from inattention.

absolute threshold the lowest intensity level of a stimulus a person can detect half of the time.

accommodation the process by which people change existing schemas to incorporate new information (Chapter 10).

accommodation the process by which the muscles control the shape of the lens to adjust to viewing objects at different distances (Chapter 4).

acetylcholine (ACh) a neurotransmitter that controls muscle movement and plays a role in learning, memory, attention, sleeping, and dreaming.

achievement motivation a desire to do things well and overcome obstacles.

acquired immunity immunity provided by antibodies or cells produced in the body in response to specific antigens.

action potential electrical signal that travels along the length of the neuron; stimulates neurotransmitter release.

adaptations inherited solutions to ancestral problems that have been selected for because they contribute in some way to reproductive success.

adaptive behaviour adjustment to and coping with everyday life.

adolescence the transition period between childhood and adulthood.

adoption studies research into hereditary influence in which adopted people are compared to their biological and adoptive parents.

adrenal glands endocrine structures that release hormones important in regulating the stress response and emotions.

adrenal steroids fat-soluble hormones released from the adrenal gland; they have widespread and long-lasting effects.

adrenal-medullary system a major neuroendocrine pathway stimulated during stress in which the hypothalamus activates the sympathetic nervous system.

affective traits stable predispositions toward certain types of emotional responses such as anger.

afterimages visual images that remain after removal of or looking away from the stimulus.

aggression violent behaviour that is intended to cause psychological or physical harm, or both, to another being.

agonist drug that mimics the effect of a neurotransmitter at its receptors.

agoraphobia an anxiety disorder involving fear of being in places from which escape might be difficult or in which help might not be available should a panic attack occur.

alarm stage the phase of the general adaptation syndrome in which all of the body's resources respond to a perceived threat.

algorithm a step-by-step procedure or formula for solving a problem.

alleles different forms of a gene.

all-or-none principle the idea that once the threshold has been crossed, an action potential either fires or it does not.

allostasis process by which the body achieves stability through physiological change.

alpha waves pattern of brain activity when one is relaxed and drowsy; slower than beta waves.

altruism selfless attitudes and behaviour toward others.

Alzheimer's disease a degenerative disease marked by progressive cognitive decline and characterized by a collection of symptoms, including confusion, memory loss, mood swings, and eventual loss of physical function.

amacrine cells retinal cells responsible for modulating activity at the bipolar–ganglion cell synapse.

amnesia memory loss due to brain injury or disease.

amygdala a small structure located directly in front of the hippocampus; has widespread connections and is important for processing emotional information, especially that related to fear.

animistic thinking a belief that inanimate objects are alive.

anorexia nervosa an eating disorder in which people cannot maintain 85 percent of their ideal body weight for their height, have an intense fear of eating, and have a distorted body image.

antagonist drug that blocks the effect of a neurotransmitter at its receptors.

antecedent event a situation that may lead to an emotional response.

anterograde amnesia the inability to remember events and experiences that occur after an injury or the onset of a disease.

antigen any foreign substance that triggers an immune response.

antisense a synthetic DNA sequence used to block the expression of a gene.

antisocial personality disorder a dramatic-emotional personality disorder characterized by extremely impulsive, deceptive, violent, ruthless, and callous behaviours; a serious and potentially dangerous disorder.

anxious-avoidant attachment an attachment style characterized by infants who stay calm when their primary caregiver leaves and who ignore and avoid her when she returns.

anxious-resistant attachment an attachment style characterized by infants who are very distressed when separated from their caregiver and seek and reject contact with their caregiver on reunion.

aphasia deficit in the ability to speak or comprehend language.

appraisal the evaluation of a situation with respect to how relevant it is to one's own welfare; it drives the process by which emotions are elicited.

arborization the growth and formation of new dendrites.

archetypes ancient or archaic images that result from common ancestral experiences.

archival research research involving the use of already existing records of information.

assimilation the process by which people incorporate new information into already existing schemas.

association cortex cortical areas that do not produce movement or sensation when stimulated; involved in complex perception and thought.

association process by which two pieces of information from the environment are repeatedly linked so that we begin to connect them in our minds.

associative network a chain of associations between related concepts.

asylums facilities for treating the mentally ill in Europe during the Middle Ages and into the 19th century.

attachment the strong emotional connection that develops early in life between infants and their caregivers.

attention deficit hyperactivity disorder (ADHD) a neurodevelopmental disorder characterized by inability to focus attention for more than a few minutes, to remain still and quiet, and to do careful work.

attention the limited capacity to process information that is under conscious control.

attitude an individual's favourable or unfavourable beliefs, feelings, or actions toward an object, idea, or person.

attributions inferences made about the causes of other people's behaviour.

atypical antipsychotics newer antipsychotic drugs, which do not create tardive dyskinesia.

auditory nerve the nerve that transmits auditory information to the brain.

autism spectrum disorder (ASD) a neurodevelopmental disorder characterized by severe language and social impairment along with repetitive habits and inward-focused behaviours.

automatic processing encoding of information that occurs with little effort or conscious attention to the task.

autonomic nervous system (ANS) all the nerves of the peripheral nervous system that serve involuntary systems of the body, such as the internal organs and glands.

availability heuristic a device we use to make decisions based on the ease with which estimates come to mind or how available they are to our awareness.

avoidant personality disorder an anxious-fearful personality disorder characterized by extreme fear of being criticized, low self-esteem, and avoidance of social interaction.

awareness monitoring of information from the environment and from one's own thoughts.

axon a long projection that extends from a neuron's soma; it transmits electrical impulses toward target neurons.

babbling the sounds made as a result of the infant's experimentation with a complex range of phonemes, which include consonants as well as vowels; starts around five or six months of age.

basal ganglia a collection of structures surrounding the thalamus involved in voluntary motor control.

basic emotions set of emotions that are common to all humans; includes anger, disgust, fear, happiness, sadness, and surprise.

basic tendencies the essence of personality: the Big Five personality dimensions plus talents, aptitudes, and cognitive abilities.

basilar membrane a membrane that runs through the cochlea; contains the hair cells.

behaviour modification the application of operant conditioning principles to change behaviour.

behaviour therapies therapies that apply the principles of classical and operant conditioning in the treatment of psychological disorders.

behavioural genetics the scientific study of the role of heredity in behaviour.

behavioural measures measures based on systematic observation of people's actions or animals' activities either in their normal environment or in a laboratory setting.

behavioural neuroscience the study of the links among brain, mind, and behaviour.

behavioural thresholds the point at which a person moves from not having a particular response to having one.

behaviourism a school of psychology that proposed that psychology could be a true science only if it examines observable behaviour, not ideas, thoughts, feelings, or motives.

belief in a just world a belief that the world is fair with good people being rewarded and bad people punished.

benzodiazepines a class of anxiety-reducing drugs that mimic the effect of the neurotransmitter GABA.

beta waves pattern of brain activity when one is awake; a rapid, low-energy wave.

Big Five or five-factor model a theory of personality that includes five dimensions: **o**penness to experience, **c**onscientiousness, **e**xtraversion, **a**greeableness, and **n**euroticism (OCEAN).

binocular depth cues aids to depth perception that rely on input from both eyes.

biological constraint model view on learning proposing that some behaviours are inherently more likely to be learned than others.

biological psychology the study of the relationship between bodily systems and chemicals and how they influence behaviour and thought.

bipolar cells the retinal cell type that links the photoreceptors with the ganglion cells.

bipolar disorder a disorder characterized by substantial mood fluctuations, cycling between very low (depressive) and very high (manic) moods.

blaming the victim an attribution that places blame on the victim of a crime, accident, or misfortune.

blocking the inability to retrieve some information once it is stored.

bodily senses the senses based in the skin, body, or any membrane surfaces.

borderline personality disorder a dramatic-emotional personality disorder characterized by out-of-control emotions, fear of being abandoned by others, and vacillation between idealizing and despising people who are close to the person with the disorder.

bottom-up processing assembling a perceptual experience from its basic elements.

broad intelligence one of Carroll's three levels of intelligence that includes abilities such as crystallized and fluid intelligence, as well as memory, learning, and processing speed.

broaden-and-build model Fredrickson's model for positive emotions, which posits that they widen our cognitive perspective and help us acquire useful life skills.

Broca's area an area in the left frontal lobe responsible for the ability to produce speech.

bulimia nervosa an eating disorder characterized by binge eating and a perceived lack of control during the eating session.

bystander effect a phenomenon in which the greater the number of bystanders who witness an emergency, the less likely any one of them is to help.

Cannon-Bard theory of emotion theory that incoming emotional sensory stimuli travel to the thalamus, where the signal gets divided into a descending pathway to control body arousal and an ascending cortical pathway to control emotional experience.

cardiovascular system the heart, blood, and all the blood vessels.

case study a study design in which a psychologist observes one person over a long period of time.

catecholamines chemicals released from the adrenal glands that function as hormones and as neurotransmitters to control ANS activation.

category a concept that organizes other concepts around what they all share in common.

catharsis the process of releasing intense, often unconscious, emotions in a therapeutic setting.

causal inferences judgments about causation of one thing by another.

central nervous system (CNS) the part of the nervous system that comprises the brain and spinal cord.

central route to persuasion attitude change that results from the effortful processing of the content of a message.

cerebellum a hindbrain structure involved in body movement, balance, coordination, fine-tuning motor skills, and cognitive activities such as learning and language.

cerebral cortex the folded outer layer of brain matter in which much of human thought, planning, perception, and consciousness takes place.

child-directed speech changes in adult speech patterns—apparently universal—when speaking to young children or infants; characterized by higher pitch, changes in voice volume, use of simpler sentences, emphasis on the here and now, and use of emotion to communicate messages.

chromosome a coiled-up thread of DNA.

chunking the process of breaking down a list of items to be remembered into a smaller set of meaningful units.

cingulate gyrus a belt-like structure in the middle of the brain that plays an important role in attention and cognitive control.

circadian rhythms the variations in physiological processes that cycle within approximately a 24-hour period, including the sleep–wake cycle.

classical conditioning form of associative learning in which a neutral stimulus becomes associated with a stimulus to which one has an automatic, inborn response.

client-centred therapy a form of humanistic therapy in which the therapist shows unconditional positive regard for the patient.

clinical psychology the diagnosis and treatment of mental, emotional, and behavioural disorders and the promotion of psychological health.

closure the Gestalt tendency to see a whole object even when complete information isn't available.

cochlea a bony tube of the inner ear, which is curled like a snail's shell and filled with fluid.

cochlear nerve cell the neuron that synapses with hair cells; its axons make up the auditory nerve.

cognition the mental processes involved in acquiring, processing, and storing knowledge.

cognitive dissonance the feeling of discomfort caused by information that is different from a person's conception of himself or herself as a reasonable and sensible person.

cognitive psychology the study of how people perceive, remember, think, speak, and solve problems.

cognitive symptoms problems with information processing, including working memory, attention, verbal and visual learning and memory, reasoning and problem solving.

cognitive therapy any type of psychotherapy that works to restructure maladaptive thought patterns.

cognitive-behavioural therapy an approach to treating psychological disorders that combines techniques for restructuring irrational thoughts with operant and classical conditioning techniques to shape desirable behaviours.

collective unconscious according to Jung, the shared experiences of our ancestors that have been passed down from generation to generation.

collectivist culture a culture in which people tend to view themselves in connection to others; the needs of the group are more important than the needs of individuals.

coma a state of consciousness in which the eyes are closed and the person is unresponsive and unarousable.

comorbidity the occurrence of two or more disorders at the same time.

compulsion a repetitive behaviour performed in response to uncontrollable urges or according to a ritualistic set of rules.

concentration gradient the difference in the concentration of different ions across the neuronal cell membrane; creates a driving force for ion movement.

concept hierarchy an arrangement of related concepts in a particular way, with some being general and others specific.

concept a mental grouping of objects, events, or people.

concrete operational stage Piaget's third stage of cognitive development, which spans ages 6 to 11, during which the child can perform mental operations—such as reversing—on real objects or events.

conditioned response (CR) a behaviour that an individual learns to perform when presented with the CS.

conditioned stimulus (CS) a previously neutral stimulus that an individual learns to associate with the US.

conditioned taste aversion the learned avoidance of a particular taste or food.

conditioning a form of associative learning in which behaviours are triggered by associations with events in the environment.

conditions of worth the beliefs that a person's worth depends on displaying the "right" attitudes, behaviours, and values.

cones photoreceptors that are responsible for colour vision and are most functional in conditions of bright light.

confirmation bias the tendency to selectively attend to information that supports one's general beliefs while ignoring information or evidence that contradicts one's beliefs.

conformity the tendency of people to adjust their behaviour to what others are doing or to adhere to the norms of their culture.

confounding variable a variable whose influence on the dependent variable cannot be separated from the independent variable being examined.

conjunction fallacy an error in logic that occurs when people say that the combination of two events is more likely than either event alone.

consciousness an awareness of one's surroundings and of what's in one's mind at a given moment; includes aspects of being awake and aware.

conservation the recognition that when some properties (such as shape) of an object change, other properties (such as volume) remain constant.

consistency bias selective recall of past events to fit our current beliefs.

consolidation the process of establishing, stabilizing, or solidifying a memory; the second stage of long-term memory formation.

construct validity the degree to which a test measures the concept it claims to measure, such as intelligence.

contact comfort comfort derived from a baby's physical contact with his or her caregiver.

continuity the Gestalt tendency to see points or lines in such a way that they follow a continuous path.

continuous reinforcement reinforcement of a behaviour every time it occurs.

contralateral an anatomical term meaning opposite side.

contralateral neglect a condition in which individuals do not respond to one side of space, usually caused by damage to the right parietal lobe.

control group a group of research participants who are treated in exactly the same manner as the experimental group, except that they do not receive the independent variable or treatment.

conventional level the second level in Kohlberg's theory of moral reasoning, during which the person values caring, trust, and relationships as well as social order and lawfulness.

convergence a binocular depth cue; the way in which the eyes move inward as an object moves closer to you.

convergent thinking problems problems that have known solutions and require analytic thinking and crystallized intelligence to come up with the correct answer.

cooing the first sounds humans make other than crying, consisting almost exclusively of vowels; occurs during the first six months of life.

cooperation a type of prosocial behaviour in which two or more individuals, or groups, work together towards a common goal.

coping act of dealing with stress or emotions.

cornea the clear hard covering that protects the lens of the eye.

corpus callosum the nerve fibres that connect the two hemispheres of the brain.

correlation coefficient a statistic that ranges from −1.0 to +1.0 and assesses the strength and direction of association between two variables.

cortical arousal level of activation in the brain.

cortisol hormone produced by the body to mobilize the body's energy resources during stressful situations.

creativity thinking and/or behaviour that is both novel–original and useful–adaptive.

critical period a specific period in development when individuals are most receptive to a particular kind of input from the environment (such as visual stimulation and language).

critical thinking the process by which one analyzes, evaluates, and forms ideas.

cross-sectional design a research design in which different people of various ages are studied at one point in time to find age-related differences.

crystallized intelligence the kind of knowledge that one gains from experience and learning, education, and practice.

cultural relativism the idea that behaviour varies across cultures and can be understood only within the context of the culture in which they occur.

cultural test bias hypothesis the notion that group differences in IQ scores are caused by different cultural and educational backgrounds, not by real differences in intelligence.

cyclothymia a relatively mild form of bipolar disorder.

dark adaptation process of adjustment to seeing in dim light.

debriefing the explanation of the purposes of a study following data collection.

deductive reasoning reasoning from general statements of what is known to specific conclusions.

defence mechanisms unconscious strategies the mind uses to protect itself from anxiety by denying and distorting reality in some way.

delta waves type of brain activity that dominates Stages 3 and 4 sleep; slower than theta waves.

delusion one of the symptoms of schizophrenia: false beliefs or exaggerations held despite evidence to the contrary, such as the idea that one is a famous person.

dementia a loss of mental function, in which many cognitive processes are impaired, such as the ability to remember, reason, solve problems, make decisions, and use language.

dendrites finger-like projections from a neuron's soma that receive messages from other neurons.

dependent personality disorder an anxious-fearful personality disorder characterized by fear of being rejected and having a strong need to be cared for.

dependent variable in an experiment, the outcome or response to the experimental manipulation.

depolarization a change in the membrane potential of a neuron so that the inside of the cell becomes less negative.

depressants substances that decrease or slow down central nervous system activity.

depressive disorder the highest-order category of the depressive disorders; it subsumes all forms of depression, including major depressive disorder and persistent depressive disorder.

depth perception the ability to see things in three dimensions and to discriminate what is near from what is far.

descriptive designs study designs in which the researcher defines a problem and variable of interest but often makes no prediction and does not control or manipulate anything.

descriptive statistics measures used to describe and summarize research data.

developmental psychology the study of how thought and behaviour change and remain stable across the life span.

dialectical behaviour therapy (DBT) treatment that integrates elements of CBT with exercises aimed at developing mindfulness without meditation and is used to treat borderline personality disorder.

diathesis-stress model biological predispositions *and* stress or abusive environments together produce psychological disorders.

difference threshold the smallest amount of change between two stimuli that a person can detect half of the time.

discrimination negative behaviour towards another based upon group membership.

disorganized attachment an insecure attachment style characterized by infants who appear disoriented in the strange situation and show inconsistent reactions to the caregiver's departure and return.

display rules learned norms or rules, often taught very early, about when it is appropriate to express certain emotions and to whom one should show them.

dissociative amnesia a selective loss of memory, in the absence of brain damage, following a traumatic event.

dissociative disorders psychological disorders characterized by extreme disruptions or gaps in memory, identity, or consciousness.

dissociative fugue a condition whereby a person forgets his or her identity and assumes a new one.

dissociative identity disorder (DID) a dissociative disorder in which a person develops at least two distinct personalities, each with its own memories, thoughts, behaviours, and emotions. Some psychiatrists question the legitimacy of the disorder.

divergent thinking problems problems that have no known solutions and require novel solutions.

DNA (deoxyribonucleic acid) molecule that contains genes.

dodo bird verdict the finding that most forms of therapy are effective and few significant differences exist in effectiveness among standard therapies.

dominant genes genes that show their effect even if there is only one allele for that trait in the pair.

dopamine a neurotransmitter released in response to behaviours that feel good or are rewarding to the person or animal; also involved in voluntary motor control.

double-blind studies studies in which neither the participants nor the researchers administering the treatment know who has been assigned to the experimental or control group.

Down syndrome a chromosomal disorder characterized by mild to profound intellectual disability.

dreams images, thoughts, and feelings experienced during sleep.

drives the perceived states of tension that occur when our bodies are deficient in some need, creating an urge to relieve the tension.

drug replacement therapy a treatment for addiction that involves a less harmful form of the drug to avoid withdrawal.

dual coding theory theory proposing that visual and verbal information are processed by independent, non-competing systems.

Duchenne smile a smile that expresses true enjoyment, involving both the muscles that pull up the lip corners diagonally and those that contract the band of muscles encircling the eye.

educational psychology the study of how students learn, the effectiveness of particular teaching techniques, the social psychology of schools, and the psychology of teaching.

effect size a measure of the strength of the relationship between two variables or the magnitude of an experimental effect.

effortful processing encoding of information that occurs with careful attention and conscious effort.

ego Freud's term for the sense of self; the part of the mind that operates on the "reality principle."

egocentrism viewing the world from one's own perspective and not being capable of seeing things from another person's perspective.

electrical gradient the difference in charge across the neuronal cell membrane; it creates a driving force for ion movement.

electroconvulsive therapy (ECT) treatment of last resort for severe depression that involves passing an electrical current through a person's brain in order to induce a seizure.

electroencephalography (EEG) a method for measuring brain activity in which the electrical activity of the brain is recorded from electrodes placed on a person's scalp.

electrophysiology the study of electrical activity in the body.

embryonic stage the second prenatal stage, from two weeks to eight weeks after conception, when all of the major organs form.

emerging adulthood the transitional phase between adolescence and young adulthood; it includes ages 18–25 years.

emotion regulation the cognitive and behavioural efforts people make to modify their emotions.

emotional competence the ability to control emotions and know when it is appropriate to express certain emotions.

emotional response the physiological, behavioural/expressive, and subjective changes that occur when emotions are generated.

emotion-focused coping way of dealing with stress that aims to regulate the experience of distress.

emotions brief, acute changes in conscious experience and physiology that occur in response to a personally meaningful situation.

empathy the ability to share the feelings of others and understand their situations.

empathy-altruism hypothesis the idea that people help others selflessly only when they feel empathy for them.

empirical method a method for developing questionnaire items that focuses on including questions that characterize the group the questionnaire is intended to distinguish.

empiricism the view that all knowledge and thoughts come from experience.

enactive learning learning by doing.

encoding specificity principle the idea that memory is strongest when the conditions at recall match those present during encoding.

encoding the process by which we attend to, take in, and process new information.

endocannabinoids natural, marijuana-like substances produced by the body.

endocrine system system of glands that secrete and regulate hormones in the body.

enzymatic degradation a way of deactivating neurotransmitter from the synapse, whereby specific enzymes alter the neurotransmitter so that it can no longer bind to receptors.

epigenetics concerns changes in the way genes are turned on or off without a change in the sequence of DNA.

epinephrine also known as adrenaline, a neurotransmitter that arouses bodily systems (such as increasing heart rate).

episodic memory form of memory that recalls the experiences we have had.

ethics the rules governing the conduct of a person or group in general or in a specific situation—or more simply, standards of right and wrong.

ethology the scientific study of animal behaviour.

Eureka insight or insight solutions sudden solutions that come to mind in a flash.

event-related potential (ERP) a special technique that extracts electrical activity from raw EEG data to measure cognitive processes.

evidence-based therapies treatment choices based on empirical evidence that they produce the desired outcome.

evolution the change over time in the frequency with which specific genes occur within a breeding species.

evolutionary psychology the psychological approach that applies evolutionary principles to explain the development of mental characteristics and behaviours.

exhaustion stage the phase of the general adaptation syndrome when all resources for fighting the threat have been depleted and illness is more likely.

experiment a research design that includes independent and dependent variables and random assignment of participants to control and experimental groups or conditions.

experimental group a group consisting of those participants who will receive the treatment or whatever is predicted to change behaviour.

experimenter expectancy effects results that occur when the behaviour of the participants is influenced by the experimenter's knowledge of who is in the control group and who is in the experimental group.

explicit memory knowledge that consists of the conscious recall of facts and events; also known as declarative memory.

expressive-suppression a response-focused strategy for regulating emotion that involves the deliberate attempt to inhibit the outward manifestation of an emotion.

extinction the weakening and disappearance of a conditioned response, which occurs when the US is no longer paired with the CS.

Facial Action Coding System (FACS) a widely used method for measuring all observable muscular movements that are possible in the human face.

factor analysis a statistical tool used to identify clusters of traits that "go together" or are highly correlated with one another.

false memories memories for events that never happened, but were suggested by someone or something.

feature detectors neurons in the visual cortex that analyze the retinal image and respond to specific aspects of shapes, such as angles and movements.

fetal alcohol spectrum disorder a consequence of prenatal alcohol exposure that causes multiple problems, notably brain damage and intellectual disability.

fetal stage the third prenatal stage, which begins with the formation of bone cells eight weeks after conception and ends at birth.

fixation a defence mechanism whereby a person continues to be concerned and even preoccupied with earlier stages of development (Chapter 13).

fixation the inability to break out of a particular mindset in order to think about a problem from a fresh perspective (Chapter 9).

fixed interval (FI) schedule pattern of intermittent reinforcement in which responses are always reinforced after a set period of time has passed.

fixed ratio (FR) schedule pattern of intermittent reinforcement in which reinforcement follows a set number of responses.

flashbulb memory a vivid memory for an emotional event of great significance.

flexibility of thought the ability to come up with many different categories of ideas and think of other responses besides the obvious one.

flooding an extreme form of in vivo exposure in which the client experiences extreme exposure to the phobic object.

fluid intelligence the ability to think through a problem one has never confronted before and recognize patterns that may lead to a solution.

Flynn effect the trend of increasing IQ scores over the past century.

forensic psychology the field that blends psychology, law, and criminal justice.

forgetting the weakening or loss of memories over time.

formal operational stage Piaget's final stage of cognitive development, from age 11 or 12 through adulthood, when formal logic is possible.

fovea spot on the back of the retina that contains the highest concentration of cones in the retina; place of clearest vision.

fraternal twins twins that develop from two different eggs fertilized by two different sperm.

free association a psychotherapeutic technique in which the client takes one image or idea from a dream and says whatever comes to mind, regardless of how threatening, disgusting, or troubling it may be.

free-running rhythm the internally generated rhythm observed in individuals living in the absence of time cues.

frequency distribution a graph of the scores on a variable, arranged by the number of times each score was obtained.

functional fixedness mindset in which one is blind to unusual uses of common everyday things or procedures.

functional magnetic resonance imaging (fMRI) brain imaging technique that uses magnetic fields to produce detailed images of activity in areas of the brain and other soft tissues.

functionalism a 19th-century school of psychology that argued it was better to look at why the mind works the way it does than to describe its parts.

fundamental attribution error the tendency to explain others' behaviour in dispositional rather than situational terms.

GABA (gamma-aminobutyric acid) the major inhibitory neurotransmitter in the brain that inhibits postsynaptic neurons.

ganglion cells the retinal cell type that carries visual information from the eye to the brain; their axons make up the optic nerve.

gate control theory of pain idea that the spinal cord regulates the experience of pain by either activating or suppressing neural networks, called gates, that transmit pain sensations to the brain.

gender constancy the realization that gender is fixed and does not change over time.

gender identity the perception of oneself as male or female.

gender roles the behaviours, attitudes, and personality traits that are associated with being female or male.

gene-by-environment interaction research a method of studying heritability by comparing genetic markers, allowing researchers to assess how genetic differences interact with environment to produce certain behaviours in some people but not in others.

general adaptation syndrome (GAS) as defined by Hans Selye, a generalized, nonspecific set of changes in the body that occur during extreme stress.

general intelligence one of Carroll's three levels of intelligence; very similar to Spearman's concept of "g."

generativity a term Erik Erikson used to describe the process in adulthood of creating new ideas, products, or people.

genes small segments of DNA that contain information for producing proteins.

genius High intelligence combined with creative accomplishments that have a tremendous impact on a given field.

genome all the genetic information in DNA.

genotype the genetic make-up of an individual.

germinal stage the first prenatal stage of development, which begins at conception and lasts two weeks.

Gestalt psychology a theory of psychology that maintains that we perceive things as wholes rather than as a compilation of parts.

g-factor theory Spearman's theory that intelligence is a single general (g) factor made up of specific components.

glial cells central nervous system cells that provide structural support, promote efficient communication between neurons, and serve as scavengers, removing cellular debris.

glucocorticoids steroid hormones released by the adrenal glands; responsible for maintaining the activation of bodily systems during prolonged stress.

glucose a simple sugar that provides energy for cells throughout the body, including the brain.

glutamate the major excitatory neurotransmitter in the brain that excites postsynaptic neurons; important in learning, memory, neural processing, and brain development.

graded potential small electrical signals generated at the synapse by neurotransmitters; can trigger action potentials.

grammar the entire set of rules for combining symbols and sounds to speak and write a particular language.

group therapy therapeutic settings in which several people who share a common problem all meet regularly with a therapist to help themselves and one another.

groupthink a situation in which the thinking of the group takes over, so much so that group members forgo logic or critical analysis in the service of reaching a decision.

habituation-dishabituation paradigm a research method used to test babies' abilities to discriminate between a novel and familiar stimulus.

hair cells inner ear sensory receptors that transduce sound vibrations into neural impulses.

hallucinations convincing sensory experiences that occur in the absence of an external stimulus.

hallucinogens substances that create distorted perceptions of reality ranging from mild to extreme.

health behaviour approach explanation for illness or health that focuses on the role of behaviours such as diet, exercise, and substance abuse.

health psychology the study of the role that psychological factors play in regard to physical health and illness.

heritability the extent to which a differences in a characteristic are influenced by genetics.

heuristics mental shortcuts; methods for making complex and uncertain decisions and judgments.

hierarchies a way of organizing related pieces of information from the most specific feature they have in common to the most general.

higher-order conditioning a form of conditioning whereby a neutral stimulus is paired with a CS.

hindsight bias the tendency to overestimate our ability to predict an event, *after* the event outcome is known.

hippocampus a limbic structure that wraps itself around the thalamus; plays a vital role in learning and memory.

histrionic personality disorder a dramatic-emotional personality disorder characterized by the desire to be the centre of attention and by dramatic, seductive, flamboyant, and exaggerated behaviours.

homeostasis the process by which all organisms work to maintain physiological equilibrium or balance around an optimal set point.

horizontal cells retinal cells responsible for modulating activity at the photoreceptor–bipolar cell synapse.

hormones chemicals, secreted by glands, that travel in the bloodstream and carry messages to tissues and organs all over the body.

human language a communication system specific to *Homo sapiens;* it is open and symbolic, has rules of grammar, and allows its users to express abstract and distant ideas.

humanistic psychology a theory of psychology that focuses on personal growth and meaning as a way of reaching one's highest potential.

hyperpolarization a change in the membrane potential of a neuron so that the inside of the cell becomes more negative.

hypersomnia sleep difficulty characterized by sleeping more than ten hours a day for two weeks or more; includes urge to nap during inappropriate times.

hypnosis state characterized by focused attention, suggestibility, absorption, lack of voluntary control over behaviour, and suspension of critical faculties; occurs when instructed by someone trained in hypnosis.

hypomanic episodes consist of the same symptoms as manic episodes (e.g., increased energy, sleeplessness, euphoria, irritability, delusions of grandeur, increased sex drive, and "racing" thoughts) but are shorter in duration.

hypothalamic-pituitary-adrenal (HPA) axis a major neuroendocrine pathway relevant to the stress response involving the hypothalamus, pituitary gland, and the adrenal cortex.

hypothalamus a limbic structure; the master regulator of almost all major drives and motives we have, such as hunger, thirst, temperature, and sexual behaviour; also controls the pituitary gland.

hypothesis a specific, informed, and testable prediction of the outcome of a particular set of conditions in a research design.

id Freud's term for the seat of impulse and desire; the pleasure-seeking part of our personality.

ideational fluency the ability to produce many ideas.

identical twins twins that develop from a single fertilized egg that splits into two independent cells.

implicit memory kind of memory made up of knowledge based on previous experience, such as skills that we perform automatically once we have mastered them; resides outside conscious awareness.

imprinting the rapid and innate learning of the characteristics of a caregiver very soon after birth.

incentive any external object or event that motivates behaviour.

independent variable a factor that is manipulated by the experimenter under controlled conditions to determine whether it causes the predicted outcome of an experiment.

individualist culture a culture in which people tend to view themselves as autonomous individuals and to emphasize the needs of individuals.

inductive reasoning reasoning to general conclusions from specific evidence.

industrial/organizational (I/O) psychology the application of psychological concepts and questions to work settings.

inferential statistics statistical tests calculated on sample data to make conclusions about populations.

inferiority complex an unhealthy need to dominate or upstage others as a way of compensating for feelings of deficiency.

informational social influence conformity to the behaviour of others because one views them as a source of knowledge about what one is supposed to do.

in-group/out-group bias the tendency to show positive feelings toward people who belong to the same group as we do, and negative feelings toward those in other groups.

insomnia a sleep difficulty characterized by difficulty falling and staying asleep, as well as not feeling rested.

instinct an inherited behavioural tendency that has been preserved within a species because it helped ensure survival.

instinctive drift learned behaviour that shifts toward instinctive, unlearned behaviour tendencies.

insula a small structure inside the cortex that plays an important role in the perception of bodily sensations, emotional states, empathy, and addictive behaviour.

integrative therapy an eclectic approach in which the therapist draws on different treatment approaches and uses those that seem most appropriate for the situation.

intellectual disability significant limitations in intellectual functioning as well as in everyday adaptive behaviour, which start before age 18.

intelligence a set of cognitive skills that includes abstract thinking, reasoning, problem solving, and the ability to acquire knowledge.

interference disruption of memory because other information competes with the information we are trying to recall.

intermittent reinforcement reinforcement of a behaviour—but not after every response.

internal consistency the extent to which items within a test correlate with one another.

interneurons neurons that communicate only with other neurons.

inter-rater reliability measure of how much agreement there is in ratings when using two or more raters or coders to rate personality or other behaviours.

interval scale a scale of measurement in which the intervals between numbers on the scale are all the same size.

intimacy as defined by Erikson, the ability to fuse one's identity with another's without the fear of losing it.

introspection the main method of investigation for structuralists; it involves looking into one's own mind for information about the nature of conscious experience.

ions particles that carry electrical charge; found both inside and outside cells.

iris the muscle that forms the coloured part of the eye; it adjusts the pupil to regulate the amount of light that enters the eye.

James-Lange theory of emotion the perception of the physiological changes that accompany emotions that produces the subjective emotional experience.

joint attention the ability to make eye contact with others and to look in the same direction as someone else.

kin selection individuals' tendency to help their own relatives as a way of ensuring that their genes get passed on.

knockout an animal, usually a mouse, that has had a specific gene removed from its genome.

language acquisition device (LAD) an innate, biologically based capacity to acquire language, proposed by Noam Chomsky as part of his nativist view of language.

latent learning learning that occurs in the absence of reinforcement and is not demonstrated until later, when reinforcement occurs.

latent level Freud's deeper, unconscious level of dreams; their meaning is found at this level.

lateral hypothalamus region of the hypothalamus that promotes feeding.

law of effect the consequences of a behaviour increase (or decrease) the likelihood that the behaviour will be repeated.

learning enduring changes in behaviour that occur with experience.

lens the structure that sits behind the pupil; it bends the light rays that enter the eye to focus images on the retina.

lesioning intentionally damaging the brain with chemicals or electricity in order to determine the role in behaviour.

levels of processing the concept that the more deeply people encode information, the better they will recall it.

life satisfaction the overall evaluation we make of our lives and an aspect of subjective well-being.

light adaptation process of adjustment to seeing in bright light.

linguistic determinism hypothesis the proposition that our language determines our way of thinking and our perceptions of the world; the view taken by Sapir and Whorf.

lithium a salt that is prescribed for its ability to stabilize the mania associated with bipolar disorder.

longitudinal design a research design in which the same people are studied over time at various ages to find age-related changes.

longitudinal-sequential design a research design in which two or more age groups of people are studied repeatedly over time.

long-term memory the part of memory that has the capacity to store a vast amount of information for as little as 30 seconds and as long as a lifetime.

long-term potentiation strengthening of a synaptic connection when one neuron repeatedly fires and excites another neuron.

magnetic resonance imaging (MRI) brain imaging technique that uses magnetic fields to produce detailed images of the structure of the brain and other soft tissues.

major depressive disorder a disorder characterized by pervasive low mood, lack of motivation, low energy, and feelings of worthlessness and guilt that last for at least two consecutive weeks.

manic episodes one mood cycle in bipolar disorder, typically involving increased energy, sleeplessness, euphoria, irritability, delusions of grandeur, increased sex drive, and "racing" thoughts.

manifest level Freud's surface level of dreams, recalled upon waking.

mean the arithmetic average of a series of numbers.

measurement scale the categories or numbers assigned to each level of a variable.

measures the tools or techniques used to assess thought or behaviour.

mechanoreceptors receptor cells in the skin that are sensitive to different tactile qualities, such as shape, grooves, or vibrations.

median the score that separates the lower half of scores from the upper half.

meditation practices that people use to calm the mind, stabilize concentration, focus attention, and enhance mindfulness.

medulla a hindbrain structure that extends directly from the spinal cord; regulates breathing, heart rate, and blood pressure.

memory the ability to store and use information; also the store of what has been learned and remembered.

menarche the first menstrual period.

mental age the equivalent chronological age a child has reached based on his or her performance on an intelligence test.

mental representation a structure in our mind—such as an idea or image—that stands for something else, such as an external object or thing sensed in the past or future, not the present.

mental rotation the process of imagining an object turning in three-dimensional space.

mental set a tendency to continue to use problem-solving strategies that have worked in the past, even if better solutions are available.

meta-analysis a research and statistical technique for combining all research results on one question and drawing a conclusion.

metacognitive thinking the process that includes the ability first to think and then to reflect on one's own thinking.

microdialysis technique to measure released neurotransmitter by implanting a probe in the brain.

mindfulness a heightened awareness of the present moment, whether of events in one's environment or in one's own mind.

mindfulness-based cognitive therapy (MBCT) an approach that combines elements of CBT with mindfulness meditation to help people with depression learn to recognize and restructure negative thought patterns.

misattribution assigning memory to the wrong source.

misinformation effect alteration of memory by misleading information presented between encoding and recall.

mnemonic device a method devised to help remember information, such as a rhyme or acronym.

mode a statistic that represents the most commonly occurring score or value.

modelling the imitation of behaviours performed by others.

monoamine oxidase (MAO) inhibitors a class of drugs used to treat depression; they slow the breakdown of monoamine neurotransmitters in the brain.

monocular depth cues aids to depth perception that do not require two eyes.

monogenic transmission the hereditary passing on of traits determined by a single gene.

moods affective states that operate in the background of consciousness and tend to last longer than most emotions.

moral treatment the 19th-century approach to treating the mentally ill with dignity in a caring environment.

morphemes the smallest units of meaning in a language.

motivation the urge to move toward one's goals; to accomplish tasks.

motor neurons nerve cells that carry commands for movement from the brain to the muscles of the body.

multiple measurement the use of several measures to acquire data on one aspect of behaviour.

multiple-factor theory of intelligence idea that intelligence consists of distinct dimensions and is not just a single factor.

myelin sheath the fatty substance wrapped around some axons, which insulates the axon, making the nerve impulse travel more efficiently.

narcissistic personality disorder a dramatic-emotional personality disorder characterized by having an extremely positive and arrogant self-image and being extraordinarily self-centred; other symptoms are an exaggerated sense of self-importance and grandiosity.

narcolepsy sleep disorder characterized by excessive daytime sleepiness and weakness in facial and limb muscles.

narrow intelligence one of Carroll's three levels of intelligence that includes many distinct abilities.

nativist view of language the idea that we discover language rather than learn it, that language development is inborn.

natural immunity form of immunity that is the first response to antigens.

natural selection a feedback process whereby nature favours one design over another because it has an impact on reproduction.

naturalistic observation a study in which the researcher unobtrusively observes and records behaviour in the real world.

nature through nurture the position that the environment constantly interacts with biology to shape who we are and what we do.

needs inherently biological states of deficiency (cellular or bodily) that compel drives.

negative punishment the removal of a stimulus to decrease behaviour.

negative reinforcement removal of a stimulus after a behaviour to increase the frequency of that behaviour.

negative symptoms the absence of normal thoughts and behaviours; symptoms include non-responsiveness, emotional flatness, immobility, catatonia, and the inability to complete tasks.

neural migration the movement of neurons from one part of the fetal brain to their more permanent destination; this occurs during the third to the fifth month of pregnancy.

neurocultural theory of emotion Ekman's explanation that some aspects of emotion, such as facial expressions and physiological changes associated with emotion, are universal and others, such as emotional regulation, are culturally derived.

neuroendocrine system the hormonal systems whose activity is regulated by the nervous system.

neurogenesis the development of new neurons.

neurons the cells that process and transmit information in the nervous system.

neuroplasticity the brain's ability to adopt new functions, reorganize itself, or make new neural connections throughout life, as a function of experience.

neuroscience the interdisciplinary study of the structure and function of human and animal brains.

neurotransmitters chemicals that transmit information between neurons.

nodes of Ranvier uninsulated gaps between segments of myelin; the neuronal impulse travels by skipping from node to node, increasing the speed of conduction.

nominal scale a scale of measurement in which the levels of a variable are represented by categories.

non-REM form of sleep with few eye movements, which are slow rather than fast.

norepinephrine a neurotransmitter that plays an important role in the sympathetic nervous system, energizing bodily systems and increasing mental arousal and alertness.

normative social influence conformity to the behaviour of others in order to be accepted by them.

nucleus accumbens basal ganglia structure involved in reward.

obedience a type of conformity in which a person yields to the will of another person.

object permanence the ability to realize that objects still exist when they are not being sensed.

observational learning learning by watching the behaviour of others.

obsession an unwanted thought, word, phrase, or image that persistently and repeatedly comes into a person's mind and causes distress.

obsessive-compulsive disorder (OCD) a disorder in which obsessive thoughts lead to compulsive behaviours.

obsessive-compulsive personality disorder an anxious-fearful personality disorder characterized by rigid habits and extreme perfectionism; more general than obsessive-compulsive disorder.

olfactory bulb a forebrain structure that sends information either directly to the smell-processing areas in the cortex or indirectly to the cortex by way of the thalamus.

olfactory sensory neurons the sensory receptors for smell that reside high up inside the nose.

oligodendrocyte a type of glial cell that myelinates axons in the CNS.

one-word utterances single words, such as "mama," "dada," "more," or "no!"; occurs around 12 months of age.

operant conditioning learning based upon the consequences of behaviour.

operational definitions researchers' specific descriptions of the way that variables are measured or manipulated.

opioids neurotransmitters involved in reducing the response to pain.

opponent-process theory the theory that colour vision results from cones linked together in three opposing pairs of colours so that activation of one member of the pair inhibits activity in the other.

optic chiasm the point at which strands of the optic nerve from half of each eye cross over to the opposite side of the brain.

optic disc the point at which the optic nerve exits the eye; it contains no photoreceptors so forms a *blind spot*.

optic nerve structure composed of the axons of ganglion cells from the retina that carry visual information from the eye to the brain.

optogenetics a treatment that uses a combination of light stimulation and genetics to manipulate the activity of individual neurons.

ordinal scale a scale of measurement in which the numbers on the scale represent an ordered series (or rank order) along a continuum.

orexin a neurotransmitter important for arousal; it is absent in the narcoleptic brain.

originality the ability to come up with unusual and novel ideas.

out-group homogeneity the tendency to see all members of an out-group as the same.

pain a complex emotional and sensory experience associated with actual or potential tissue damage.

panic attack brief episodes of anxiety associated with a perception of threat and occurring because of fear of danger, an inability to escape, embarrassment, or specific objects.

panic disorder an anxiety disorder characterized by panic attacks and persistent anxiety about having more attacks.

papillae textured structures on the surface of the tongue that contain thousands of taste buds.

paranoid personality disorder odd-eccentric personality disorder characterized by extreme suspicions and mistrust of others in unwarranted and maladaptive ways.

parasympathetic nervous system the branch of the autonomic nervous system that usually relaxes or returns the body to a less active, restful state.

participant expectancy effects results that occur when the behaviour of the participants is influenced by their knowledge of the experimental condition.

peer-review the practice of judging the scientific merit of research through review by other scientists with expertise.

peers people who share equal standing or status and are at the same level, in terms of age, gender, skill, or power.

perception a psychological process: the act of organizing and interpreting sensory experience.

perceptual constancy the ability of the brain to preserve perception of objects in spite of changes in retinal image when an object changes in position or distance from the viewer.

perceptual set the effect of frame of mind on perception; a tendency to perceive stimuli in a certain manner.

peripheral nervous system (PNS) the part of the nervous system that comprises all the nerve cells in the body outside the central nervous system.

peripheral route to persuasion attitude change that results from low effort processing of superficial message cues, such as the characteristics of the message source.

persistence the repeated recall of pleasant or unpleasant experiences even when we actively try to forget them.

persistent depressive disorder (PDD) a form of depression that is milder in intensity but longer in duration than major depressive disorder.

personal unconscious according to Jung, all our repressed and hidden thoughts, feelings, and motives.

personality disorders maladaptive and inflexible patterns of cognition, emotion, and behaviour that develop in late childhood or adolescence.

personality psychology the study of what makes people unique and the consistencies in people's behaviour across time and situations.

personality questionnaires self-report instruments on which respondents indicate the extent to which they agree or disagree with a series of statements as they apply to their personality.

personality the unique and relatively enduring set of behaviours, feelings, thoughts, and motives that characterize an individual.

persuasion the act of attempting to change the opinions, beliefs, or choices of others by explanation or argument.

phenothiazines drugs used to treat schizophrenia; they help diminish hallucinations, confusion, agitation, and paranoia but also have adverse side effects.

phenotype an individual's observable characteristics.

phobia an anxiety disorder marked by ongoing and irrational fear of a particular object, situation, or activity.

phonemes the smallest units of sound in a language.

photopsins the light-sensitive proteins responsible for transduction in cones; different photopsins are sensitive to different wavelengths of light.

photoreceptors cells in the retina (called rods and cones) that convert light energy into nerve energy; they are transducers.

physical traces physical evidence of people's activities in a particular setting.

physiological measures measures of bodily responses, such as blood pressure or heart rate, used to determine changes in psychological state.

physiological reactivity model explanation for the causal role of stress-related bodily changes in illness.

pituitary gland the master endocrine gland that controls the release of hormones from glands throughout the body.

placebo a substance or treatment that appears identical to the actual treatment but lacks the active substance.

placebo effect improvement in symptoms as a function of expectations that the treatment is effective, rather than the treatment itself.

polygenic transmission the process by which many genes interact to create a single characteristic.

pons a hindbrain structure that serves as a bridge between lower brain regions and higher midbrain and forebrain activity.

population the entire group a researcher is interested in; for example, all humans, all rats, all Rhesus monkeys, all adolescents, all boys, all girls, all university students.

positive psychology a scientific approach to studying, understanding, and promoting healthy and positive psychological functioning.

positive punishment the addition of a stimulus that decreases behaviour.

positive reinforcement the presentation or addition of a stimulus after a behaviour occurs that increases how often that behaviour will occur.

positive symptoms the presence of abnormal thoughts and behaviours associated with schizophrenia, including hallucinations, delusional thinking, and disorganized thought and speech.

positron emission tomography (PET) brain imaging technique that measures blood flow to active areas in the brain.

postconventional level the third level in Kohlberg's theory of moral reasoning, in which the person recognizes universal moral rules that may trump unjust or immoral local rules.

postsynaptic neuron the neuron on the receiving side of the synapse, neurotransmitters bind to receptors on its membrane.

post-traumatic stress disorder (PTSD) a type of trauma- and stressor-related disorder that involves intrusive and persistent cognitive, emotional, and physiological symptoms triggered by catastrophic or horrifying events.

pragmatics the rules associated with the use of language across social situations.

preconventional level the first level in Kohlberg's theory of moral reasoning, focusing on avoiding punishment or maximizing rewards.

predictive validity the degree to which intelligence test scores are positively related to real-world outcomes, such as school achievement or job success, and thus have predictive value.

preferential looking a research technique used to test an infant's perceptual abilities by measuring which stimulus an infant gazes at longest.

prefrontal lobotomy a form of psychosurgery in which the connections between the prefrontal cortex and the lower portion of the brain are severed; it is no longer in use.

prejudice a biased, negative attitude based on an individual's group membership.

prenatal programming the process by which events in the womb alter the development of physical and psychological health.

preoperational stage the second major stage of cognitive development (ages two to five), which begins with the emergence of symbolic thought.

presynaptic neuron the neuron on the sending side of a synapse, it releases neurotransmitter.

presynaptic reuptake a way of removing excess neurotransmitter from the synapse, whereby neurotransmitter is returned to the presynaptic neuron for storage in vesicles for future use.

primary appraisal quick assessment of the meaning of a given environmental event for the individual.

primary reinforcers innate, unlearned reinforcers that satisfy biological needs (such as food, water, or sex).

priming a kind of implicit memory that arises when recall is improved by earlier exposure to the same or similar stimuli.

proactive interference disruption of memory because previously learned information interferes with the learning of new information.

problem-focused coping way of dealing with stress that aims to change the situation that is creating stress.

procedural memory kind of memory made up of implicit knowledge for almost any behaviour or physical skill we have learned.

prodigy a young person who is extremely gifted and precocious in one area and at least average in intelligence.

projective tests personality assessment in which the participant is presented with a vague stimulus or situation and asked to interpret it or tell a story about what they see.

prosocial behaviour action that is beneficial to others.

prosopagnosia a condition in which individuals do not recognize faces, often caused by damage to the right cortex.

protolanguage very rudimentary language, also known as prelanguage, used by earlier species of *Homo*.

prototypes the best-fitting examples of a category.

proximity the Gestalt tendency to group objects together that are near one another.

pseudoscience claims presented as scientific that are not supported by evidence obtained with the scientific method.

psychoactive drugs naturally occurring or synthesized substances that, when ingested or otherwise taken into the body, reliably produce qualitative changes in conscious experience.

psychoanalysis a clinically based approach to understanding and treating psychological disorders; it assumes that the unconscious mind is the most powerful force behind thought and behaviour.

psychodynamic psychotherapy therapy aimed at uncovering unconscious motives that underlie psychological problems.

psychology the scientific study of thought and behaviour.

psychoneuroimmunology (PNI) the science of how psychological factors relate to changes in the immune system.

psychophysics the study of how people psychologically perceive physical stimuli, such as light, sound waves, and touch.

psychosexual stage theory Freud's stages of personality development; in different stages a different region of the body is most erogenous.

psychosomatic theory the idea that emotional factors can lead to the occurrence or worsening of illness.

psychotherapy the use of psychological techniques to modify maladaptive behaviours or thought patterns, or both, and to help patients develop insight into their own behaviour.

psychotic disorders psychological disorders of thought and perception, characterized by an inability to distinguish between real and imagined perceptions.

puberty the period when sexual maturation begins; it marks the beginning of adolescence.

punishment stimulus, presented after a behaviour, that decreases the frequency of the behaviour.

pupil the opening in the iris through which light enters the eye.

quantitative trait loci (QTL) approach a technique in behavioural genetics that looks for the location on genes that might be associated with particular behaviours.

random assignment the method used to assign participants to different research conditions so that all participants have the same chance of being in any specific group.

random sample a type of sample in which every member of the population had an equal likelihood of being selected to participate in a survey.

range the difference between the highest and lowest score in a sample.

rapid eye movements (REM) quick movements of the eye that occur during sleep, thought to mark phases of dreaming.

ratio scale a scale of measurement in which there are equal intervals and an absolute zero point.

rational (face valid) method a method for developing questionnaire items that involves using reason or theory to come up with a question.

rational-emotive therapy a cognitive therapy developed by Albert Ellis that aims to change emotions, such as guilt and sadness, by challenging the belief system that causes the emotions.

reaction formation a defence mechanism that turns an unpleasant idea, feeling, or impulse into its opposite.

reaction range for a given trait, such as IQ, the genetically determined range of responses by an individual to his or her environment.

reappraisal an emotion-regulation strategy in which one re-evaluates an antecedent event so that a different emotion results.

reasoning the process of drawing inferences or conclusions from principles and evidence.

receptive field the area of visual space that stimulates activity of a particular neuron.

recessive genes genes that show their effects only when both alleles are the same.

reciprocal altruism the act of helping others in the hope that they will help us in the future.

reciprocal determinism the process by which personal factors, behaviour, and the environment all interact with one another to shape an individual's personality.

recovered memory a memory from a real event that was encoded and stored, but not retrieved for a long period of time until some later event brings it suddenly to consciousness.

reflexes inborn and involuntary behaviours—such as coughing, swallowing, sneezing, or vomiting—that are elicited by very specific stimuli.

refractory period the span of time, after an action potential has been generated, when the neuron is returning to its resting state and the neuron cannot generate an action potential.

regression to the mean a statistical phenomenon when extreme scores become less extreme on retesting.

rehearsal the process of repeatedly practising material so that it enters long-term memory.

reinforcer an internal or external event that increases the frequency of a behaviour.

reliability consistency of measurement over repeated occasions.

repetitive transcranial magnetic stimulation (rTMS) treatment for severe depression involving exposure of specific brain structures to bursts of high-intensity magnetic fields instead of electricity.

replication the repetition of a study to confirm the results; essential to the scientific process.

representative sample a research sample that accurately reflects the population of people one is studying.

representativeness heuristic a strategy we use to estimate the probability of one event based on how typical it is of another event.

repression defence mechanism for keeping unpleasant thoughts, feelings, or impulses out of consciousness.

research designs plans of action for how to conduct a scientific study.

research ethics boards (REBs) organizations that evaluate research proposals to make sure research involving humans does not cause undue harm or distress.

resistance stage in the general adaptation syndrome, extended effort by the body to deal with a threat.

resting potential the difference in electrical charge between the inside and outside of the axon when the neuron is at rest.

reticular formation a network of nerve fibres that runs up through both the hindbrain and the midbrain; it is crucial to waking up and falling asleep.

retina the thin layer of nerve tissue that lines the back of the eye.

retrieval the recovery of information stored in memory.

retroactive interference disruption of memory because new experiences or information cause people to forget previously learned experiences or information.

retrograde amnesia an inability to recall events or experiences that happened before the onset of a disease or injury.

rhodopsin the light-sensitive protein responsible for transduction in rods.

rods photoreceptors that function in low illumination and play a key role in night vision.

Rorschach Inkblot Test a projective test in which the participant is asked to respond to a series of ambiguous inkblots.

samples subsets of the population studied in a research project.

savant syndrome a very rare condition in which people with serious mental handicaps also show isolated areas of ability or brilliance.

scaffolding adjusting the level of support to fit a child's current level of performance on a task.

scatterplot a graph depicting a correlation between two variables.

schedules of reinforcement patterns of reinforcement distinguished by whether reinforcement occurs after a set number of responses or after a certain amount of time has passed since the last reinforcement.

schemas mental frameworks that develop from our experiences with particular people, objects, or events.

schizoid personality disorder an odd-eccentric personality disorder characterized by a desire to avoid close relationships as well as by emotional aloofness, reclusivity, and a lack of humour.

schizophrenia a psychotic disorder characterized by significant disturbances in thought and emotion, specifically problems with perception, including hallucinations.

schizotypal personality disorder an odd-eccentric personality disorder characterized by a desire to live an isolated and asocial life, but also by the presence of odd thoughts, perceptual distortions, and beliefs.

Schwann cell a type of glial cell that myelinates axons in the PNS.

scientific method the procedures by which scientists conduct research, consisting of five basic processes: observation, prediction, testing, interpretation, and communication.

scientific thinking the process of using the cognitive skills required to generate, test, and revise theories.

secondary (or conditioned) reinforcers reinforcers that are learned by association, usually via classical conditioning.

secondary appraisal self-assessment of the resources available to cope with stress.

secure attachment an attachment style characterized by infants who will gradually explore new situations when the caregiver leaves and initiate contact when the caregiver returns after separation.

selective attention the ability to focus awareness on specific features in the environment while ignoring others.

selective serotonin reuptake inhibitors (SSRIs) drugs prescribed primarily for depression and some anxiety disorders that work by making more serotonin available in the synapse.

self-actualization the inherent drive to realize one's full potential.

self-conscious emotions types of emotion that require a sense of self and the ability to reflect on actions; they occur as a function of meeting expectations (or not) and abiding (or not) by society's rules.

self-efficacy people's beliefs about their ability to perform the behaviours needed to achieve desired outcomes.

self-fulfilling prophecy a statement that affects events to cause the prediction to become true.

self-reports written or oral accounts of a person's thoughts, feelings, or actions.

self-serving bias the tendency to make situational attributions for our failures but dispositional attributions for our successes.

semantic memory form of memory that recalls facts and general knowledge, such as what we learn in school.

semantics the meaning derived from words and combinations of words in a language.

semicircular canals structure of the inner ear involved in maintaining balance.

sensation a physical process: the stimulation of our sense organs by features of the outer world.

sensorimotor stage Piaget's first stage of cognitive development (from birth to age two), when infants learn about the world by using their senses and moving their bodies.

sensory adaptation the process by which our sensitivity diminishes when our senses are constantly stimulated.

sensory memory the part of memory that holds information in its original sensory form for a very brief period of time, usually about a half a second or less.

sensory neurons nerve cells that receive incoming sensory information from the sense organs (eye, ear, skin, tongue, nose).

sentence phase the stage when children begin speaking in fully grammatical sentences; usually age two-and-a-half to three.

separation anxiety the distress reaction babies show when they are separated from their primary caregiver (typically shown at around nine months of age).

serial position effect the tendency to have better recall for items in a list according to their position in the list.

serotonin a neurotransmitter with wide-ranging effects: involved in dreaming and in controlling emotional states, especially anger, anxiety and depression.

set point the ideal fixed setting of a particular physiological system, such as internal body temperature.

sexual behaviour actions that produce arousal and increase the likelihood of orgasm.

sexual orientation the disposition to be attracted to either the opposite sex (heterosexual), the same sex (homosexual), or both sexes (bisexual).

sexual strategies theory the idea that men and women face different problems when they seek out mates, and so they often approach relationships in very different ways.

shamans medicine men or women who treat people with mental problems by driving out their demons with elaborate rituals, such as exorcisms, incantations, and prayers.

shaping the reinforcement of successive approximations of a desired behaviour.

short-term memory the part of memory that temporarily (for 2 to 30 seconds) stores a limited amount of information before it is either transferred to long-term storage or forgotten.

signal detection theory the viewpoint that both stimulus intensity and decision-making processes are involved in the detection of a stimulus.

significance level the standard used to decide statistical significance.

similarity the Gestalt tendency to group like objects together in visual perception.

single-blind studies studies in which participants do not know the experimental condition (group) to which they have been assigned.

Skinner box simple chamber used for operant conditioning of small animals.

sleep apnea sleep difficulty that results from temporary blockage of the air passage.

sleepwalking sleep difficulty characterized by activities occurring during non-REM sleep that usually occur when one is awake, such as walking and eating.

social anxiety disorder (social phobia) an anxiety disorder with fear of humiliation in the presence of others, characterized by intense self-consciousness about appearance or behaviour or both.

social desirability bias the tendency toward favourable self-presentation that could lead to inaccurate self-reports.

social dilemma a situation in which the interests of the individual conflict with the interests of the group.

social exchange theory the idea that we help others when we decide that the benefits to ourselves are likely to outweigh the costs.

social facilitation when the presence of others improves performance on easy tasks, or impairs performance on difficult tasks.

social learning theory a description of the kind of learning that occurs when we model or imitate the behaviour of others.

social loafing the phenomenon in which the presence of others causes one to slack off if individual effort cannot be evaluated.

social norms rules about acceptable behaviour imposed by the cultural context in which one lives.

social psychology the study of how living among others influences thought, feeling, and behaviour.

social referencing the ability to make use of social and emotional information from another person—especially a caregiver—in an uncertain situation.

socio-cultural perspective an approach to psychological research that emphasizes cross-cultural differences in thinking and behaviour.

softwiring the view that in contrast to hardwiring, biological systems—genes, brain structures, and brain cells—are inherited but open to modification from the environment.

soma the cell body of the neuron.

somatic nervous system peripheral motor nerves involved in control of voluntary movement as well as sensory nerves involved in the reception of stimuli from the external environment.

source traits according to Cattell, the basic traits that underlie aspects of personality easily seen by others.

spontaneous recovery the sudden reappearance of an extinguished response.

spontaneous remission improvement in symptoms over time, naturally, without treatment.

sports psychology the study of psychological factors in sports and exercise.

stagnation a situation in which an adult becomes more self-focused than oriented toward others and does not contribute in a productive way to society or family.

standard deviation a statistical measure of how much scores in a sample vary around the mean.

standardization the process of giving a test to a large group of people to establish norms or standards by which all other people who take the test are compared.

statistical significance a statistical statement about the likelihood that an obtained result occurred by chance.

statistics the collection, analysis, interpretation, and presentation of numerical data.

stereotype threat the process whereby anxiety about culturally held group stereotypes impacts negatively on individual test performance.

stereotypes schemas of how people are likely to behave based simply on groups to which they belong.

stimulants substances that activate the nervous system and produce arousal.

stimulus discrimination restriction of a CR (such as salivation) to the exact CS to which it was conditioned.

stimulus generalization extension of the association between US and CS to include a broad array of similar stimuli.

storage the retention of memory over time; the third stage of long-term memory formation.

stress a state when a situation overwhelms a person's perceived ability to meet the demands of that situation.

stressors events that trigger a stress response.

striving for superiority according to Adler, the major drive behind all behaviour, whereby humans naturally strive to overcome their physical and psychological deficiencies.

Stroop effect delay in reaction time when colour of words on a test and their meaning differ.

structuralism a 19th-century school of psychology that argued that breaking down experience into its elemental parts offered the best way to understand thought and behaviour.

subjective experience of emotion the changes in the quality of our conscious experience that occur during emotional responses.

subjective well-being state that consists of life satisfaction, domain satisfactions, and positive and negative affect.

sublimation a defence mechanism in which a socially unacceptable impulse is expressed in a socially acceptable way.

successful intelligence according to Sternberg, an integrated set of abilities needed to attain success in life.

suggestibility problem with memory that occurs when memories are implanted in our minds based on leading questions, comments, or suggestions by someone else or some other source.

superego Freud's term for the part of the mind that monitors behaviour and evaluates it in terms of right and wrong; the conscience.

support groups meetings of people who share a common situation, be it a disorder, a disease, or coping with an ill family member.

sustained attention the ability to maintain focused awareness on a target or idea.

sympathetic nervous system the branch of the autonomic nervous system that activates bodily systems in times of emergency.

synapse the junction between an axon and the adjacent neuron, where information is transmitted from one neuron to another.

synaptic pruning the degradation of synapses and dying off of neurons that are not strengthened by experience.

synaptic vesicles tiny sacs in the terminal that contain neurotransmitters.

synaptogenesis the formation of entirely new synapses or connections with other neurons.

syndromes groups or clusters of related symptoms that are characteristic of a disorder.

synesthesia an unusual sensory experience in which a person experiences sensations in one sense when a different sense is stimulated.

syntax the rules for arranging words and symbols to form sentences or parts of sentences in a particular language.

systematic desensitization a behavioural therapy technique, often used for phobias, in which the therapist pairs relaxation with gradual exposure to a phobic object, generating a hierarchy of increasing contact with the feared object.

tardive dyskinesia repetitive, involuntary movements of the jaw, tongue, face, and mouth and body tremors resulting from the extended use of traditional antipsychotic drugs.

taste buds structures inside the papillae of the tongue that contain the taste receptor cells.

taste receptor cells sensory receptors for taste that reside in the taste buds.

technology-based therapies therapies that make use of technology or the Internet to complement current therapies or make psychotherapeutic techniques available to more people.

temperament the biologically based tendency to behave in particular ways from very early in life.

teratogens substances that can disrupt normal prenatal development and cause life-long deficits.

terminals little knobs at the end of the axon that contain tiny sacs of neurotransmitters.

test bias characteristic of a test that produces different outcomes for different groups.

test fairness judgment about how test results are applied to different groups based on values and philosophical inclinations.

test-retest reliability the extent to which scores on a test are similar over time.

thalamus a forebrain structure that receives information from the senses and relays it to the cerebral cortex for processing.

Thematic Apperception Test (TAT) a projective test in which the participant is presented with a series of picture cards and asked to tell a story about what is going on in the scene.

theory a set of related assumptions from which scientists can make testable predictions.

theory of mind ideas and knowledge about how other people's minds work.

theta waves pattern of brain activity during Stage 1 sleep; slower than alpha waves.

thinking outside the box approach to problem solving that requires breaking free of self-imposed conceptual constraints and thinking about a problem differently in order to solve it.

three-stage model of memory classification of memories based on duration as sensory, short-term, and long-term.

threshold membrane potential of −55 mV, necessary for the generation of an action potential.

token economies a behavioural technique in which desirable behaviours are reinforced with a token, such as a small chip or fake coin, which can be exchanged for privileges.

top-down processing perception of the whole based on our experience and expectations, which guide our perception of smaller elemental features of a stimulus.

traditional antipsychotics historically, the first medications used to manage psychotic symptoms.

trait a disposition to behave consistently in a particular way.

transduction the conversion of physical into neural information.

transference a process in psychotherapy in which the client reacts to a person in a present relationship as though that person were someone from the client's past.

transgenic an animal, usually a mouse, that has a foreign gene inserted into its genome.

transience loss of information over time, the most common type of forgetfulness.

triangular theory of love Sternberg's idea that three components (intimacy, passion, and commitment), in various combinations, can explain all the forms of human love.

triarchic theory of intelligence Sternberg's three-part model of intelligence, including analytic, creative, and practical intelligence.

trichromatic colour theory the theory that all colour that we experience results from a mixing of three colours of light (red, green, and blue).

tricyclic antidepressants drugs used for treating depression, as well as in chronic pain management and in the treatment of ADHD.

t-test a particular type of inferential statistic designed to test differences between two means.

twin-adoption studies research into hereditary influence on twins, both identical and fraternal, who were raised apart (adopted) and who were raised together.

twin studies research into hereditary influence comparing pairs of fraternal and identical twins.

two-factor theory of emotion theory that the subjective experience of emotion is determined by awareness of physiological arousal as well as a cognitive process to assess the most plausible emotional state.

two-word utterances phrases children put together, starting around 18 months, such as "my ball," "mo wawa," or "go way."

tympanic membrane the eardrum.

Type A behaviour pattern a way of responding to challenge or stress, characterized by hostility, impatience, competitiveness, and time urgency.

ultradian rhythms the variations in physiological processes that repeat in a cycle of less than 24 hours; sleep stages follow this type of rhythm.

unconditional positive regard acceptance of another person regardless of his or her behaviour (Chapter 13).

unconditional positive regard the basic tenet of client-centred therapy; the therapist's genuine liking and empathy for the client, regardless of what he or she has said or done (Chapter 16).

unconditioned response (UR) the automatic, inborn reaction to a stimulus.

unconditioned stimulus (US) the stimulus that always produces the same unlearned response.

universal term referring to something that is common to all human beings and can be seen in cultures all over the world.

validity the degree to which a test accurately measures what it purports to measure, such as self-esteem, and not something else.

variable a characteristic that changes or "varies," such as age, gender, weight, intelligence, anxiety, and extraversion.

variable interval (VI) schedule pattern of intermittent reinforcement in which responses are reinforced after time periods of different duration have passed.

variable ratio (VR) schedule pattern of intermittent reinforcement in which the number of responses needed for reinforcement changes.

vegetative state a state of minimal consciousness in which the eyes might be open, but the person is otherwise unresponsive.

ventromedial hypothalamus region of the hypothalamus that promotes satiety.

viral-mediated gene transfer technique whereby a gene is packaged into a virus and injected into a brain region.

virtual reality therapies therapies that use virtual (digital simulation) environments to create therapeutic situations that would be hard to create otherwise.

visual acuity the ability to see clearly.

visual imagery visual representations created by the brain after the original stimulus is no longer present.

wakefulness degree of alertness reflecting whether a person is awake or asleep.

Weber's law the finding that the size of a just noticeable difference is a constant fraction of the intensity of the stimulus.

Wernicke's area an area deep in the left temporal lobe responsible for language comprehension.

word salad the speech of people with schizophrenia, which may follow grammatical rules but be nonsensical in terms of content.

working memory the part of memory required to attend to and solve a problem at hand; often used interchangeably with *short-term memory*.

Yerkes-Dodson law the principle that moderate levels of arousal lead to optimal performance.

young adulthood the development stage that usually happens by the mid-20s, when people complete the key developmental tasks of emerging adulthood.

zone of proximal development (ZPD) a range of tasks too difficult for a child to perform alone but possible with the help of others.

zygote the single cell that results when a sperm fertilizes an egg.

References

Aamodt, M.G. (2010). *Industrial/organizational psychology: An applied approach* (6th ed.). Belmont, CA: Wadsworth.

Aberg, M.A.I., Pedersen, N.L., Torén K., Svartengrenf, M., Backstrand, B., Johnsson, T., . . . Kuhn, H.G. (2009). Cardiovascular fitness is associated with cognition in young adulthood. *Proceedings of the National Academy of Sciences, 106,* 20906–20911. doi: 10.1073/pnas.0905307106.

Abrams, R. (1997). *Electroconvulsive therapy* (3rd ed.). New York: Oxford University Press.

Achter, J.A., Lubinski, D., Benbow, C.P., & Eftekhari-Sanjani, H. (1999). Assessing vocational preferences among intellectually gifted adolescents adds incremental validity to abilities: A discriminant analysis of educational outcomes over a 10-year interval. *Journal of Educational Psychology, 91,* 777–786.

Acker, M., & Davis. M.H. (1992). Intimacy, passion, and commitment in adult romantic relationships: A test of the Triangular Theory of Love. *Journal of Social and Personal Relationships, 9*(1), 21–50.

Ackerman, D. (1990). *A natural history of the senses.* New York: Vintage Books.

Adam, T.C., & Epel, E.S. (2007). Stress, eating and the reward system. *Physiology & Behavior, 91,* 449–458.

Adams, P. (1998). Hebb and Darwin. *Journal of Theoretical Biology, 195,* 419–438.

Adamson, L., & Bakeman, R. (1985). Affect and attention: Infants observed with mothers and peers. *Child Development, 56,* 582–593.

Adan, A., & Serra-Grabulosa, J.M. (2010). Effects of caffeine and glucose, alone and combined, on cognitive performance. *Human Psychopharmacology: Clinical and Experimental, 25,* 310–317.

Ader, R., & Cohen, N. (1975). Behaviorally conditioned immunosuppression. *Psychosomatic Medicine, 37,* 333–340.

Adler, A. (1931). *What life should mean to you.* New York: Capricorn Books.

Adler, A. (1956). *The individual psychology of Alfred Adler: A systematic presentation in selections from his writings* (H.L. Ansbacher & R.R. Ansbacher, Eds.). New York: Norton.

Adler, J. (Ed.). (2004). *Forensic psychology: Concepts, debates and practice.* Cullupton, England: Willan.

Adolphs, R., Cahill, L., Schul, R., & Babinsky, R. (1997) Impaired declarative memory for emotional material following bilateral amygdala damage in humans. *Learning and Memory, 4,* 291–300.

Adolphs, R., Gosselin, F., Buchanan, T.W., Tranel, D., Schyns, P., & Damasio, A.R. (2005). A mechanism for impaired fear recognition after amygdala damage. *Nature, 433,* 68–72.

Adolphs, R., Tranel, D., & Buchanan, T.W. (2005) Amygdala damage impairs emotional memory for gist but not details of complex stimuli. *Nature Neuroscience, 8,* 512–518.

Adolphs, R., Tranel, D., & Damasio, A.R. (1998). The human amygdala in social judgment. *Nature, 393,* 470–474.

Adolphs, R., Tranel, D., Damasio, H., & Damasio, A.R. (1994). Impaired recognition of emotion in facial expressions following bilateral damage to the human amygdala. *Nature, 372,* 669–672.

Ahima, R.S., Prabakaran, D., Mantzoros, C., Qu, D., Lowell, B., Maratos-Flier, E., & Flier, J.S. (1996). Role of leptin in the neuroendocrine response to fasting. *Nature, 382,* 250–252.

Aichorn, W., Huber, R., Stuppaeck, C., & Whitworth, A.B. (2006). Cardiomyopathy after long-term treatment with lithium—more than a coincidence? *Journal of Psychopharmacology, 20,* 589–591.

Ainsworth, M.D.S., Blehar, M.C., Waters, E., & Wall, S. (1978). *Patterns of attachment: A psychological study of the strange situation.* Hillsdale, NJ: Erlbaum.

Aitken, J.R., & Benson, J.W. (1984). The use of relaxation/de sensitization in treating anxiety associated with flying. *Aviation Space and Environmental Medicine, 55,* 196–199.

Akaike, A. (2006). Preclinical evidence of neuroprotection by cholinesterase inhibitors. *Alzheimer Disease and Associated Disorders, 20*(Suppl. 1), S8–S11.

Akinola, M., & Mendes, W.B. (2008). The dark side of creativity: Biological vulnerability and negative emotions lead to greater artistic creativity. *Personality and Social Psychological Bulletin, 34,* 1677–1686.

Aknin, L.B., Hamlin, J.K., & Dunn, E.W. (2012). Giving leads to happiness in young children. *PLoS ONE, 7,* e39211. doi:10.1371/journal.pone.0039211.

Albert, R.S., & Runco, M.A. (1989). Independence and the creative potential of exceptionally gifted boys. *Journal of Youth and Adolescence, 18,* 221–230.

Alexander, G.M., & Hines, M. (2002). Sex differences in response to children's toys in nonhuman primates (Cercopithecus aethiops sabaeus). *Evolution and Human Behavior, 23,* 467–479. doi:10.1016/S1090-5138(02)00107-1.

Alexander, G.M., Wilcox, R., & Woods, R. (2009). Sex differences in infants' visual interest in toys. *Archives of Sexual Behavior, 38,* 427–433.

Alic, M. (2001). "Kraepelin, Emil." Gale Encyclopedia of Psychology. Retrieved May 3, 2015, from Encyclopedia.com: http://www.encyclopedia.com/doc/1G2-3406000372.html.

Allemand, M., Zimprich, D., & Hendriks, A.A.J. (2008). Age differences in five personality domains across the life span. *Developmental Psychology, 44,* 758–770.

Allen, L., & Gorski, R. (2007). *Sex differences in the bed nucleus of the stria terminalis of the human brain* [e-book]. Cambridge, MA: MIT Press.

Allen, M. (1991). Meta-analysis comparing the persuasiveness of one- sided and two-sided messages. *Western Journal of Speech Communication, 55,* 390–404.

Allen, N.J., & Barres, B.A. (2005). Signaling between glia and neurons: Focus on synaptic plasticity. *Current Opinion in Neurobiology, 15,* 542–548.

Allison, D.B., Heshka, S., Neale, M.C., Lykken, D.T., & Heymsfield, S.B. (1994). A genetic analysis of relative weight among 4,020 twin pairs, with an emphasis on sex effects. *Health Psychology, 13,* 362–365.

Alloy, L.B., Abramson, L.Y., Whitehouse, W.G., Hogan, M.E., Tashman, N.A., Steinberg, D.L, . . . Donovan, P. (1999). Depressogenic cognitive styles: Predictive validity, information processing and personality characteristics, and developmental origins. *Behaviour Research and Therapy, 37,* 503–531.

Allport, G.W. (1937). *Personality: A psychological interpretation.* New York: Holt, Rinehart & Winston.

Allport, G.W. (1954). *The nature of prejudice.* Cambridge, MA: Addison-Wesley.

Allport, G.W., & Odbert, H.W. (1936). Trait-names: A psycho-lexical study. *Psychological Monographs, 47,* 1–171.

Alme, C.B., Miao, C, Jezek, K., Treves, A., Moser, E.I., & Moser, M-B. (2014). Place cells in the hippocampus: Eleven maps for eleven rooms. *Proceedings of the National Academy of Sciences, 111,* 18428–18435.

Al-Sahab et al. (2010). Age at menarche in Canada: results from the National Longitudinal Survey of Children & Youth. *BMC Public Health, 10,* 736.

Alt, K.W., Jeunesse, C., Buritrago-Tellez, C.H., Wächter, R., Boes, E., & Pichler, S.L. (1997). Evidence for stone-age cranial surgery. *Nature, 387,* 360.

Alterovitz, S., & Mendelsohn, G.A. (2009). Partner preferences across the life span: Online dating by older adults. *Psychology and Aging, 24*(2), 513–517.

Altman, J., & Das, G.D. (1966). Autoradiographic and histological studies of postnatal neurogenesis. I.A longitudinal investigation of the kinetics, migration and transformation of cells incorporating tritiated thymidine in neonate rats, with special reference to postnatal neurogenesis in some brain regions. *Journal of Comparative Neurology, 126,* 337–389.

Alzheimer Society of Canada. (2010). *Key facts about Alzheimer's Disease and related dementia.* Retrieved from http://www.alzheimer.ca/english/disease/stats-intro.htm.

Alzheimer's Association. (2008). *What is Alzheimer's?* Retrieved March 10, 2008, from http://www.alz.org/alzheimers_disease_what_is_alzheimers.asp#plaques.

Amabile, T. (1996). *Creativity in context.* Boulder, CO: Westview.

Amanzio, M., & Benedetti, F. (1999). Neuropharmacological dissection of placebo analgesia: expectation-activated opioid systems versus conditioning-activated specific subsystems. *Journal of Neuroscience, 19,* 484–494.

Amedi, A., Merabet, L.B., Bermpohl, F., & Pascual-Leone, A. (2005). The occipital cortex in the blind. *Current Directions in Psychological Science, 14,* 306–311.

American Association on Intellectual and Developmental Disabilities. (2010). *Intellectual disability: Definition, classification, and systems of supports* (11th ed.). Alexandria, VA: Author.

American Association on Mental Retardation (AAMR). (2002). *Mental retardation: Definition, classification, and systems of support* (10th ed.). Alexandria, VA: Author.

American Psychiatric Association (APA). (2013). *Diagnostic and statistical manual of mental disorders* (5th ed.). Washington, DC: Author.

American Psychological Association. (2009). *2009 Graduate Study in Psychology: Faculty and Student Data.* Retrieved on June 21, 2010, from http://www.apa.org/workforce/publications/09–grad-study/index.aspx.

American Psychological Association. (2010). *APA Affiliate and International Membership Totals 2001–Present.* Retrieved on June 21, 2010, from http://www.apa.org/about/archives/membership/affil-intl.aspx.

American Psychological Association. (2010). *Publication manual of the American Psychological Association* (6th ed.). Washington, DC: Author.

American Sleep Apnea Association (2006). *Sleep apnea information.* Washington, DC: Author.

Amichai-Hamburger, Y., & Vinitzky, G. (2010). Social network use and personality. *Computers in Human Behavior, 26,* 1289–1295.

Anda, R.F., Felitti, V.J., Bremner, J.D., Walker, J.D., Whitfield, C., Perry, B.D., et al. (2006). The enduring effects of abuse and related adverse experiences in childhood: A convergence of evidence from neurobiology and epidemiology. *European Archives of Psychiatry and Clinical Neuroscience, 256,* 174–186.

Anderson, C.A., Shibuya, A., Ihori, N., Swing, E.L., Bushman, B.J., Sakamoto, A., Rothstein, H.R., & Saleem, M. (2010). Violent video game effects on aggression, empathy, and prosocial behavior in Eastern and Western countries: A meta-analytic review. *Psychological Bulletin, 136,* 151–173.

Anderson, N.D., Lau, M.A., Segal, Z.V., & Bishop, S.R. (2007). Mindfulness-based stress reduction and attentional control. *Clinical Psychology and Psychotherapy, 14,* 449–463.

Anderson, P.L., Price, M., Edwards, S.M., Obassaju, M.A., Schmerts, S.K., Zimand, E., & Calamaras, M.R. (2013). Virtual reality exposure therapy for social anxiety disorder: A randomized controlled trial. *Journal of Consulting and Clinical Psychology, 81,* 751–760. doi: 10.1037/a0033559.

Andersson, G., Cuijpers, P., Carlbring, P., Riper, H., & Hedman, E. (2014). Guided Internet-based vs. face-to-face cognitive behavior therapy for psychiatric and somatic disorders: a systematic review and meta-analysis. *World Psychiatry: Official Journal of the World Psychiatric Association (WPA), 13*(3), 288–295. doi:10.1002/wps.20151.

Andreasen, N.C. (1987). Creativity and psychological disorder: Prevalence rates in writers and their first-degree relatives. *American Journal of Psychiatry, 144,* 1288–1292.

Andreasen, N.C. (2006). *The creative brain.* New York: Penguin Books.

Andreasen, N.C., & Glick, I.D. (1988). Bipolar affective disorder and creativity: Implications and clinical management. *Comprehensive Psychiatry, 29,* 207–216.

Andreasen, N.C., O'Leary, D.S., Flaum, M., Nopoulos, P., Watkins, G.L., Ponto, L.L.B., et al. (1997). Hypofrontality in schizophrenia: Distributed dysfunctional circuits in neuroleptic-naïve patients. *The Lancet, 349,* 1730–1734.

Andrews, G., Cuijpers, P., Craske, M.G., McEvoy, P., & Titov, N. (2010). Computer Therapy for the Anxiety and Depressive Disorders Is Effective, Acceptable and Practical Health Care: A Meta-Analysis. *PLoS ONE, 5*(10), 1–6. doi:10.1371/journal.pone.0013196

Anik, L., Aknin, L.B., Norton, M.I., Dunn, D.W., & Quoidbach, J. (2013). Prosocial bonuses increase employee satisfaction and team performance. *PLoS ONE, 8,* e75509.

Annese, J., Schenker-Ahmed, N.M., Bartsch, H., Maechler, P., Sheh, C., Thomas, N., Kayano, J., Ghatan, A., Bresler, N., Frosch, M.P., Klaming, R., & Corkin, S. (2014). Postmortem examination of patient H.M.'s brain based on histological sectioning and digital 3D reconstruction. *Nature Communications, 5,* 3122.

Anselmi, P., Vianello, M., Voci, A., & Robusto, E. (2013). Implicit sexual attitude of heterosexual, gay and bisexual individuals: Disentangling the contribution of specific associations to the overall measure. *PLoS ONE, 8,* e78990. doi:10.1371/journal.pone.0078990.

Anson, K., & Ponsford, J. (2006). Coping and emotional adjustment following traumatic brain injury. *Journal of Head Trauma Rehabilitation, 21,* 248–259.

Anthonisen, N.R., Skeans, M.A., Wise, R.A., Manfreda, J., Kanner, R.E., & Connett, J.E. (Lung Health Study Research Group). (2005). The effects of a smoking cessation intervention on 14.5-year mortality: A randomized clinical trial. *Annals of Internal Medicine, 142,* 233–239.

Antony, M.M., Ledley, D.R., Liss, A., & Swinson, R.P. (2006). Responses to symptom induction exercises in panic disorder. *Behaviour Research and Therapy, 44,* 85–98.

Anxiety Disorders Association of Canada. (2003). *Mental health and mental illness.* Retrieved from anxietycanada.ca/english/pdf/kirby.pdf.

Aouizerate, B., Cuny, E., Martin-Guehl, C., Guehl, D., Rougier, A., Bioulac, B., et al. (2005). Deep brain stimulation for OCD and major depression. *Neurology, 64,* A223–A224.

Aouizerate, B., Guehl, D., Cuny, E., Rougier, A., Bioulac, B., Tignol, J., et al. (2004). Pathophysiology of obsessive-compulsive disorder: A necessary link between phenomenology, neuropsychology, imagery and physiology. *Progress in Neurobiology, 72,* 195–221.

APA Presidential Task Force on Evidence-Based Practice, US. (2006). Evidence-based practice in psychology. *American Psychologist, 61,* 271–285.

Apsche, J. (1993). *Probing the mind of a serial killer.* International Information Associates.

Arbib, M., Liebal, K., & Pika, S. (2008). Primate vocalization, gesture, and the evolution of human language. *Current Anthropology, 49,* 1053–1063. doi: 10.1086/593015.

Arling, G.L., & Harlow, H.F. (1967). Effects of social deprivation on maternal behavior of rhesus monkeys. *Journal of Comparative and Physiological Psychology, 64,* 371–377.

Armenta, B.E., & Hunt, J.S. (2009). Responding to societal devaluation: Effects of perceived personal and group discrimination on the ethnic group identification and personal self-esteem of Latino/Latina adolescents. *Group Processes and Intergroup Relations, 12,* 23–39.

Armenta, B.E., Knight, G.P., Carlo, G., & Jacobson, R.P. (2011). The relation between ethnic group attachment and prosocial tendencies: The mediating role of cultural values. *European Journal of Social Psychology, 41*(1), 107–115.

Armitage, R., Smith, C., Thompson, S., & Hoffmann, R. (2001). Sex differences in slow-wave activity in response to sleep deprivation. *Sleep Research Online, 4,* 33–41.

Arnett, J.J. (2000). Emerging Adulthood. *American Psychologist, 55*(5), 469.

Arnett, J.J. (2004). *Emerging adulthood: The winding road from the late teens through the twenties.* New York: Oxford University Press.

Arnett, J.J. (2006). Emerging adulthood: Understanding the new way of coming of age. In J.J. Arnett and J.L. Tanner (Eds.). *Emerging adults in America: Coming of age in the 21st century* (pp. 3–19). Washington, DC: American Psychological Association.

Aronson, E., Wilson, T.D., Akert, R.M., & Fehr, B. (2004). *Social Psychology* (3rd Canadian ed.). Toronto: Pearson.

Arseneault, L., Cannon, M., Witton, J., & Murray, R.M. (2004). Causal association between cannabis and psychosis: Examination of the evidence. *British Journal of Psychiatry, 184,* 110–117.

Arseneault, L., Moffitt T.E., Caspi A., Taylor, A., Rijsdijik F., Jaffee, S.R., et al. (2003). Strong genetic effects on crosssituational antisocial behaviour among 5-year-old children according to mothers, teachers, examiner-observers, and twins' self-reports. *Journal of Child Psychology and Psychiatry, 44,* 832–848.

Artola, A. (2008). Diabetes-, stress- and ageing-related changes in synaptic plasticity in hippocampus and neocortex—The same metaplastic process? *European Journal of Pharmacology, 585,* 153–162.

Asch, S.E. (1951). Effects of group pressure on the modification and distortion of judgments. In H. Guetzkow (Ed.), *Groups, leadership and men.* Pittsburgh: Carnegie Press.

Asch, S.E. (1952). *Social psychology.* New York: Prentice-Hall.

Aserinsky, E., & Kleitman, N. (1955). Two types of ocular motility during sleep. *Journal of Applied Physiology, 8,* 1–10.

Asperger, H. (1991). "Autistic psychopathy" in childhood (U. Frith, Trans.). In U. Frith (Ed.), *Autism and Asperger syndrome* (pp. 37–62). New York: Cambridge University Press. (Original work published 1944.)

Associated Press. (2006, Oct. 24). Man with amnesia reunited with family. Retrieved from http://www.msnbc.msn.com/id/15373503/.

Association for Humanistic Psychology. (2001). *Humanistic psychology overview.* Retrieved from http://www.ahpweb.org/aboutahp/whatis.html.

Assouline, M., & Meir, E.I. (1987). Meta-analysis of the relationship between congruence and well-being measures. *Journal of Vocational Behavior, 31,* 319–332.

Atkins, D.C., Berns, S.B., George, W.H., Doss, B.D., Gattis, K., & Christensen, A. (2005). Prediction of response to treatment in a randomized clinical trial of marital therapy. *Journal of Consulting and Clinical Psychology, 73,* 893–903.

Atkins, D.C., Yi, J., Baucom, D.H., & Christensen, A. (2005). Infidelity in couples seeking marital therapy. *Journal of Family Psychology, 19,* 470–473.

Atkinson, G., Reilly, T., & Waterhouse, J. (2007). Chronobiological aspects of the sleep-wake cycle and thermoregulation. *Physiology & Behavior, 90*(2), 189.

Atkinson, J.W. (1964). *An introduction to motivation.* New York: Van Nostrand.

Atkinson, R.C., & Shiffrin, R.M. (1971). The control of short-term memory. *Scientific American, 225,* 82–90.

Austin, E.J. (2005). Personality correlates of the broader autism phenotype as assessed by the Autism Spectrum Quotient (AQ). *Personality and Individual Differences, 38,* 451–460.

Austin, M., Hadzi-Pavlovic, D., Leader, L., Saint, K., & Parker, G. (2004). Maternal trait anxiety, depression, and life-event stress in pregnancy: Relationships with infant temperament. *Early Human Development, 81,* 183–190.

Austin, S., Rutherford, A., & Pyke, S. (2006). In our own voice: The impact of feminism on Canadian psychology. *Feminism & Psychology, 16*(3), 243–257.

Averett, S.L., Argys, L.M., & Sorkin, J. (2013). In sickness and in health: An examination of relationship status and health using data from the Canadian National Public Health Survey. *Review of Economics of the Household, 11,* 599–633.

Baardseth, T., Godberg, S.B., Pace, B.T., Minami, T., Wislocki, A.P., Frost, N.D., . . . Wampold, B.E. (2013). Cognitive-behavioural therapy versus other therapies: Redux. *Clinical Psychology Review, 33,* 395–405.

Baars, B.J. (1997). In the theatre of consciousness: Global workspace theory, a rigorous scientific theory of consciousness. *Journal of Consciousness Studies, 4,* 292–309.

Baars, B.J., & Franklin, S. (2003). How conscious experience and working memory interact. *TRENDS in Cognitive Sciences, 7,* 166–172.

Babiak, P., & Hare, R.D. (2006). *Snakes in suits: When psychopaths go to work.* Regan Books: New York.

Bachevalier, J. (2011). The amygdala in autism spectrum disorders. In E. Hollander, A. Kolevzon, & J.T. Coyle (Eds.), *Textbook of autism spectrum disorders* (pp. 363–374). Arlington, VA: American Psychiatric Publishing.

Bachorowski, J. (1999). Vocal expression and perception of emotion. *Current Directions in Psychological Science, 8,* 53–57.

Back, M.D., Stopfer, J.M., Vazire, S., Gaddis, S., Schmukle, S.C., Egloff, B., & Gosling, S.D. (2010). Facebook profiles reflect actual personality, not self-idealization. *Psychological Science, 21*(3), 372–374.

Baddeley, A. (1986). *Working memory.* New York: Oxford University Press.

Baddeley, A. (2007). *Working memory, thought, and action.* New York: Oxford University Press.

Baddeley, A.D. (1998). The central executive: A concept and some misconceptions. *Journal of the International Neuropsychological Society, 4,* 523–526.

Baddeley, A.D. (2003). Working memory: Looking back and looking forward. *Nature Reviews Neuroscience, 4,* 829–839.

Baer, R.A., Smith, G.T., Hopkins, J., Krietemeyer, J., & Toney, L. (2006). Using self-report assessment methods to explore facets of mindfulness. *Assessment, 13,* 27–45.

Bagwell, C.L., Newcomb, A.F., & Bukowski, W.M. (1998). Preadolescent friendship and rejection as predictors of adult adjustment. *Child Development, 69,* 140–153.

Bailey, D.S. (2004). Why accreditation matters. *gradPSYCH, 2.* Retrieved from http://gradpsych.apags.org/apr04/accreditation.cfm.

Bailey, M.J., & Zucker, K.J. (1995). Childhood sex-typed behavior and sexual orientation: A conceptual analysis and quantitative review. *Developmental Psychology, 31,* 43–55.

Bailey, M.J., Dunne, M.P., & Martin, N.G. (2000). Genetic and environment effects on sexual orientation and its correlates in an Australian twin sample. *Journal of Personality and Social Psychology, 78,* 524–536.

Bailey, M.J., Kirk, K.M., Zhu, G., Dunne, M.P., & Martin, N.G. (2000). Do individual differences in sociosexuality represent genetic or environmentally contingent strategies? Evidence from the Australian twin registry. *Journal of Personality and Social Psychology, 78,* 537–545.

Baillargeon, R., & DeVos, J. (1991). Object permanence in young infants: Further evidence. *Child Development, 62,* 1227–1246.

Baird, A.D., Wilson, S.J., Bladin, P.F., Saling, M.M., & Reutens, D.C. (2007). Neurological control of human sexual behaviour: Insights from lesion studies. *Journal of Neurological Neurosurgery and Psychiatry, 78,* 1042–1049.

Baird, J.C., Wagner, M., & Fuld, K. (1990). A simple but powerful theory of the moon illusion. *Journal of Experimental Psychology: Human Perception and Performance, 16,* 675–677.

Baldwin, D.S., & Polkinghorn, C. (2005). Evidence-based pharmacotherapy of generalized anxiety disorder. *International Journal of Neuropsychopharmacology, 8,* 293–302.

Ball, K., Berch, D.B., Helmers, K.F., Jobe, J.B., Leveck, M.D., Marsiske, M., et al. (2002). Effects of cognitive training interventions with older adults: A randomized control trial. *Journal of the American Medical Association, 288,* 2271–2281.

Balliet, D., Mulder, L.B., & Van Lange, P.A.M. (2011). Reward, punishment, and cooperation: A meta-analysis. *Psychological Bulletin, 137,* 594–615.

Balsis, S., Carpenter, B., & Storandt, M. (2005). Personality change precedes clinical diagnosis of dementia of the Alzheimer type. *The Journals of Gerontology: Series B: Psychological Sciences and Social Sciences, 60B*(2), P98–P101.

Baltes, P.B., & Smith, J. (2008). The fascination of wisdom: Its nature, ontogeny, and function. *Perspectives on Psychological Science, 3,* 56–64.

Baltes, P.B., Reuter-Lorenz, P.A., & Rösler, F. (Eds.). (2006). *Lifespan development and the brain: The perspective of biocultural coconstructivism.* New York: Cambridge University Press.

Banaji, M.R. (2007). Unraveling beliefs. Retrieved June 18, 2007, from http://www.edge.org/q2007/q07_13.html.

Banaji, M.R., & Greenwald, A.G. (1995). Implicit gender stereotyping in judgments of fame. *Journal of Personality and Social Psychology, 68,* 181–198.

Bandura, A. (1969). *Principles of behavior modification.* New York: Holt, Rinehart & Winston.

Bandura, A. (1986). *Social foundations of thought and action: A social cognitive theory.* Englewood Cliffs, NJ: Prentice-Hall.

Bandura, A. (1997). *Self-efficacy: The exercise of control.* New York: Freeman.

Bandura, A., Ross, D., & Ross, S.A. (1961). Transmission of aggression through imitation of aggressive models. *Journal of Abnormal and Social Psychology, 63,* 575–582.

Bandura, A., Ross, D., & Ross, S.A. (1963). Vicarious reinforcement and imitative learning. *Journal of Abnormal & Social Psychology, 67,* 601–608.

Banks, M.S., & Salapatek, P. (1983). Infant visual perception. In P.H. Mussen (Ed.)., *Handbook of child psychology* (4th ed., Vol. 2). New York: Wiley.

Banuazizi, A., & Movahedi, S. (1975). Interpersonal dynamics in a simulated prison: A methodological analysis. *American Psychologist, 30*(2), 152–160.

Barac, R., & Bialystok, E. (2012). Bilingual effects on cognitive and linguistic development: Role of language, cultural background, and education. *Child Development, 83*(2), 413–422.

Barbaresi, W.J., Colligan, R.C., Weaver, A.L., Voigt, R.G., Killian, J.M., & Katusic, S.K. (2013, March 4). Mortality, ADHD, and psychosocial adversity in adults with childhood ADHD: A prospective study. *Pediatrics.* doi: 10.1542/peds.2012-2354.

Barbazanges, A., Piazza, P.V., Le Moal, M., & Maccari, S. (1996). Maternal glucocorticoid secretion mediates long-term effects of prenatal stress. *Journal of Neuroscience, 16,* 3943–3949.

Barbour, K.A., & Blumenthal, J.A. (in press). Exercise training and depression in older adults. *Neurobiology of Aging.*

Barch, D.M. (2005). The cognitive neuroscience of schizophrenia. *Annual Review of Clinical Psychology, 1,* 321–353.

Bargh, J.A., & Ferguson, M.J. (2000). Beyond behaviourism: On the automaticity of higher mental processes. *Psychological Bulletin, 126,* 925–945.

Bargh, J.A. (2014). Our unconscious mind. *Scientific American, 310*(1), 30–37.

Barkham, M., Connell, J., Stiles, W.B., Miles, J.N.V., Margison, F., Evans, C., et al. (2006). Dose-effect relations and responsive regulation of treatment duration: The good enough level. *Journal of Consulting and Clinical Psychology, 74,* 160–167.

Barlow, D.H. (2002). *Anxiety and its disorders: The nature and treatment of anxiety and panic* (2nd ed.). New York: Guilford.

Barlow, J.H., Powell, L.A., Gilchrist, M., & Fotiadou, M. (2008). The effectiveness of the Training and Support Program for parents of children with disabilities: A randomized controlled trial. *Journal of Psychosomatic Research, 64,* 55–62.

Baron, A., & Galizio, M. (2006). The distinction between positive and negative reinforcement: Use with care. *Behavior Analyst, 296,* 141–151.

Baron, A.S., & Banaji, M.R. (2006). The development of implicit attitudes: Evidence of race evaluations from ages 6 and 10 and adulthood. *Psychological Science, 17,* 53–58.

Baron-Cohen, S., Bolton, P., Wheelwright, S., Short, L., Mead, G., Smith, A., et al. (1998). Autism occurs more often in families of physicists, engineers, and mathematicians. *Autism, 2,* 296–301.

Baron-Cohen, S., Wheelwright, S., Skinner, R., Martin, J., & Clubley, E. (2001). The Autism-Spectrum Quotient (AQ): Evidence from Asperger syndrome/high-functioning autism, males and females, scientists and mathematicians. *Journal of Autism & Developmental Disorders, 31,* 5–17.

Baron-Cohen, S., Wheelwright, S., Stott, C., Bolton, P., & Goodyer, I. (1997). Is there a link between engineering and autism? *Autism, 1,* 101–109.

Barr, C.L., Kroft, J., Feng, Y., Wigg, K., Roberts, W. Malone, M., et al. (2002). The norepinephrine transporter gene and attention-deficit hyperactivity disorder. *American Journal of Medical Genetics, 114,* 255–259.

Barrett, L.F., Lane, R.D., Sechrest, L., & Schwartz, G.E. (2000). Sex differences in emotional awareness. *Personality and Social Psychology Bulletin, 26,* 1027–1035.

Barrett, L.F., Ochsner, K.N., & Gross, J.J. (2007). On the automaticity of emotion. In J. Bargh (Ed.), *Social psychology and the unconscious: The automaticity of higher mental processes* (pp. 173–217). New York: Psychology Press.

Barrett, L.F., Robin, L., Pietromonaco, P.R., & Eysell, K.M. (1998). Are women the "more emotional" sex? Evidence from emotional experiences in social context. *Cognition & Emotion, 12,* 555–578.

Barrett, P. (2004). *FRIENDS for Life: Group leaders' manual for children.* Bowen Hills, Queensland, Australia: Australian Academic Press.

Barrett, P.M., & Turner, C.M. (2001). Prevention of anxiety symptoms in primary school children: Preliminary results from a universal school-based trial. *British Journal of Clinical Psychology, 40,* 399–410.

Barrett, P.M., Farrell, L.J., Ollendick, T.H., & Dadds, M. (2006). Long-term outcomes of an Australian universal prevention trial of anxiety and depression symptoms in children and youth: An evaluation of the Friends program. *Journal of Clinical Child and Adolescent Psychology, 35,* 403–411.

Barth, J., Schumacher, M., & Herrmann-Lingen, C. (2004). Depression as a risk factor for mortality in patients with coronary heart disease: A meta-analysis. *Psychosomatic Medicine, 66,* 802–813.

Bartholomew, K., & Horowitz, L.M. (1991). Attachment styles among young adults: A test of a four-category model. *Journal of Personality and Social Psychology, 61*(2), 226–244.

Barton, J.J.S. (2008). Structure and function in acquired prosopagnosia: Lessons from a series of 10 patients with brain damage. *Journal of Neuropsychology, 2,* 197–225.

Bartoshuk, L.M. (2000). Comparing sensory experiences across individuals: Recent psychophysical advances illuminate genetic variation in taste perception. *Chemical Senses, 25,* 447–660.

Basak, C., Boot, W.R., Voss, M.W., & Kramer, A.F. (2008). Can training in a real-time strategy video game attenuate cognitive decline in older adults? *Psychology and Aging, 23,* 765–777.

Basbaum A.L., & Jessell, T.M. (2000). The perception of pain. In E.R. Kandel, J.H. Schwartz, & T.M. Jessell (Eds.), *Principles of neural science* (4th ed., pp. 472–491). New York: McGraw-Hill.

Bassett, E.B., Verchinski, B.A., Mattay, V.S., Weinberger, D.R., & Meyer-Lindenberg, A. (2008). Hierarchical organization of human cortical networks in health and schizophrenia. *Journal of Neuroscience, 28,* 9239–9248.

Basson, R. (2000). The female sexual response: A different model. *Journal of Sex & Marital Therapy, 26,* 51–65.

Batson, C.D. (1991). *The altruism question: Toward a social psychological answer.* Hillsdale, NJ: Erlbaum.

Batson, C.D., Fultz, J., & Schoenrade, P.A. (1987). Distress and empathy: Two qualitatively distinct vicarious emotions with different motivational consequences. *Journal of Personality, 55,* 19–39.

Bauby, J.-D. (1997). *The diving bell and the butterfly.* New York: A.A. Knopf.

Bauer, F., Korpert, K., Neuberger, M., Raber, A., & Schwetz, F. (1992). Risk-factors for hearing-loss at different frequencies in a population of 47 388 noise-exposed workers. *Journal of Acoustic Society of America, 6,* 3086–3098.

Bauer, M., & Whybrow, P.C. (2001). Thyroid hormone, neural tissue and mood modulation. *World Journal of Biological Psychiatry, 2,* 57–67.

Bauer, M.S., & Mitchner, L. (2004). What is a "mood stabilizer"? An evidence-based response. *American Journal of Psychiatry, 161,* 3–18.

Baumeister, R., & Leary, M. (1995). The need to belong: Desire for interpersonal attachments as a fundamental human motivation. *Psychological Bulletin, 117,* 497–529.

Baumrind, D. (1964). Some thoughts on ethics of research: After reading Milgram's "Behavioral study of obedience." *American Psychologist, 19,* 421–423.

Bavelier, D., Tomann, A., Hutton, C., Mitchell, T., Corina, D., Liu, G., et al. (2000). Visual attention to the periphery is enhanced in congenitally deaf individuals. *Journal of Neuroscience, 20,* 1–6.

B.C. Ministry of Children and Family Development. (n.d.). BC FRIENDS for Life. Retrieved from http://www.mcf.gov.bc.ca/mental_health/friends.htm.

Beadle-Brown, J., Murphy, G., & Wing, L. (2006). The Camberwell cohort 25 years on: Characteristics and changes in skills over time. *Journal of Applied Research in Intellectual Disabilities, 19*(4), 317–329.

Beauchamp, G.K., & Mennella, J.A. (2009). Early flavour learning and its impact on later feeding behaviour. *Journal of Pediatric Gastroenterology & Nutrition, 48,* S25–S30. doi: 10.1097/MPG.0b013e31819774a5.

Beck, A.T. (1976). *Cognitive therapy and emotional disorders.* New York: International Universities Press.

Beck, A.T., & Clark, D.A. (1988). Anxiety and depression: An information processing perspective. *Anxiety Research, 1,* 23–36.

Beck, A.T., & Emery, G. (1985). *Anxiety disorders and phobias.* New York: Basic Books.

Beck, A.T., Rush, A.J., Shaw, B.F., & Emery, G. (1979). *Cognitive therapy of depression.* New York: Guilford.

Beck, C.A., Williams, J.V., Wang, J.L., Kassam, A., El-Guebaly, N., Currie, S.R., Maxwell, C.J., Patten, S.B. (2005). Psychotropic medication use in Canada. *Canadian Journal of Psychiatry, 50,* 605–613.

Beck, R., & Perkins, T.S. (2001). Cognitive content-specificity for anxiety and depression: A meta-analysis. *Cognitive Therapy and Research, 25,* 651–663.

Beede, K.E., & Kass, S.J. (2006). Engrossed in conversation: The impact of cell phones on simulated driving performance. *Accident Analysis and Prevention, 38,* 415–421.

Beekman, A.T.F., Smit, F., Stek, M.L., Reynolds, C.F., & Cuijpers, P.C. (2010). Preventing depression in high-risk groups. *Current Opinion in Psychiatry, 23,* 8–11.

Beeman, M.J., & Bowden, E.M. (2000). The right hemisphere maintains solution-related activation for yet-to-be solved insight problems. *Memory & Cognition, 28,* 1231–1241.

Beidel, D.C., Bulik, C.M., & Stanley, M.A. (2014). *Abnormal psychology* (3rd ed.). Upper Saddle River, NJ: Pearson Education Inc.

Beirowski, B. (2013). Concepts for regulation of axon integrity by enwrapping glia. *Frontiers in Cellular Neuroscience, 7,* 1–22.

Belisle, P., & Chapais, B. (2001). Tolerated co-feeding in relation to degree of kinship in Japanese macaques. *Behaviour, 138,* 487–509.

Bell, A.P., Weinberg, M.S., & Hammersmith, S.K. (1981). *Sexual preference: Its development in men and women.* Bloomington: Indiana University Press.

Bellack, A.S., Bennett, M.E., Gearon, J.S., Brown, C.H., & Yang, Y. (2006). A randomized clinical trial of a new behavioral treatment for drug abuse in people with severe and persistent mental illness. *Archives of General Psychiatry, 63,* 426–432.

Belmonte, M.K., Allen, G., Beckel-Mitchener, A., Boulanger, L.M., Carper, R.A., & Webb, S.J. (2004). Autism and abnormal development of brain connectivity. *Journal of Neuroscience, 24,* 9228–9231.

Benes, F.M. (2001). Carlsson and the discovery of dopamine. *Trends in Pharmacological Sciences, 22,* 46–47.

Benet-Martinez, V., & Oishi, S. (2008). Culture and personality. In O.P. John, R.W. Robins, & L.A. Pervin (Eds.). *Handbook of personality: Theory and research* (pp. 542–567). New York: Guilford.

Benington, J.H. (2000). Sleep homeostasis and the function of sleep. *Sleep, 23,* 959–66.

Benjamin, J., Li, L., Patterson, C., Greenburg, B.D., Murphy, D.L., & Hamer, D.H. (1996). Population and familial association between the D4 dopamine receptor gene and measures of novelty seeking. *Nature Genetics, 12,* 81–84.

Benjamin, L.T. (2014). *A brief history of modern psychology* (2nd ed.). Hoboken, NJ: John Wiley & Sons, Inc.

Benjamin, L.T., Jr. (2007). *A brief history of modern psychology.* Malden, MA: Blackwell.

Bennett, C.M., & Baird, A.A. (2006). Anatomical changes in the emerging adult brain: A voxel-based morphometry study. *Human Brain Mapping, 27,* 766–777.

Bennett, E.L., Diamond, M.C., Krech, D., & Rosenzweig, M.R. (1964). Chemical and anatomical plasticity of brain. *Science, 146,* 610–619.

Bennett, P.J., Sekuler, R., & Sekuler, A.B. (2007). The effects of aging on motion detection and direction identification. *Vision Research, 47,* 799–809.

Beran, M.J., Smith, J.D., & Perdue, B.M. (2013). Language-trained chimpanzees (Pan troglodytes) name what they have seen but look first at what they have not seen. *Psychological Science Online First.* doi: 0.1177/0956797612458936.

Berenbaum, S.A., Korman, K., & Leveroni, C. (1995). Early hormones and sex differences in cognitive abilities. *Learning and Individual Differences, 7,* 303–321.

Berghöfer, A., Alda, M., Adli, M., Baethge, C., Bauer, M., Bschor, T., . . . Pfennig, A. (2008). Long-term effectiveness of lithium in bipolar disorder: A multicenter investigation of patients with typical and atypical features. *Journal of Clinical*

Psychiatry, 69, 1860–1868. doi: 10.4088/JCP.v69n1203.

Berhardt, B.C., & Singer, T. (2012). The neural basis of empathy. *Annual Review of Neuroscience, 35,* 1–23. doi: 10.1146/annurev-neuro-062111-150536.

Berkman, L.F., & Glass, T. (2000). Social integration, social networks, social support and health. In L.F. Berkman & I. Kawachi (Eds.), *Social epidemiology* (pp. 137–173). New York: Oxford University Press.

Berlyne, D. (1960). *Conflict, arousal, and curiosity.* New York: McGraw-Hill.

Bernat, J. (2006). Chronic disorders of consciousness. *Lancet, 367,* 1181–1192.

Berridge, K.C. (2004). Motivation concepts in behavioral neuroscience. *Physiology and Behavior, 81,* 179–209.

Berry, C.M, Ones, D.S., & Sackett, P.R. (2007). Interpersonal deviance, organizational deviance, and their common correlates: A review and meta-analysis. *Journal of Applied Psychology, 92,* 410–424.

Berry, J.W., Phinney, J.S., Sam, D.L., & Vedder, P. (2006). *Immigrant youth in cultural transition: Acculturation, identity, and adaptation across national contexts.* Mahwah, NJ: Erlbaum.

Berthoud, H.R. (2002). Multiple neural systems controlling food intake and body weight. *Neuroscience and Biobehavioral Reviews, 26,* 393–428.

Berzoff, J., Flanagan, L.M., & Hertz, P. (2011). Inside out, outside in: An introduction. In J. Berzoff, L.M. Flanagan, & P. Hertz, (Eds.), *Inside out, outside in* (3rd ed.). *Psychodynamic Clinical Therapy and Psychopathology in Contemporary Modern Contexts* (pp. 1–17). Lanham, MD: Roman & Littlefield Publishers, Inc.

Beutler, L.E. (2002). The dodo bird is extinct. *Clinical Psychology: Science and Practice, 9*(1), 30–34. doi:10.1093/clipsy/9.1.30.

Bewernick, B.H., Kayser, S., Sturm, V., & Schlaepfer, T.E. (2012). Long-term effects of nucleus accumbens deep brain stimulation in treatment-resistant depression: Evidence for sustained efficacy. *Neuropsychopharmacology, 37*(9), 1975–1985.

Bexton, W.H., Heron, W., & Scott, T.H. (1954). Effects of decreased variation in the sensory environment. *Canadian Journal of Psychology, 8,* 70–76.

Beyerstein, B.L. (1996). Distinguishing science from pseudoscience. The Centre for Professional and Curriculum Development, Victoria, B.C., Canada. Retrieved from http://www.sld.cu/galerias/pdf/sitios/revsalud/beyerstein_cience_vs_pseudoscience.pdf.

Bherer, L., Erickson, K.I., & Liu-Ambrose, T. (2013). A review of the effects of physical activity and exercise on cognitive and brain functions in older adults. *Journal of Aging Research.* doi: 10.1155/2013/657508.

Bialystok, E., Barac, R., Blaye, A., & Poulin-Dubois, D. (2010). Word mapping and executive functioning in young monolingual and bilingual children. *Journal of Cognition and Development, 11*(4), 485–508. doi: 10.1080/15248372.2010.516420.

Bialystok, E., & Craik, F.I.M. (2010). Cognitive and linguistic processing in the bilingual mind. *Current Directions in Psychological Science, 19,* 19–23.

Bialystok, E., Craik, F.I.M., & Freedman, M. (2007). Bilingualism as a protection against the onset of symptoms of dementia. *Neuropsychologia, 45,* 459–464.

Bialystok, E., Craik, F.I.M., & Ryan, J. (2006). Executive control in a modified antisaccade task: Effects of aging and bilingualism. *Journal of Experimental Psychology: Learning, Memory, & Cognition, 32,* 1341–1354.

Bickerton, D. (1990). *Language and species.* Chicago: University of Chicago Press.

Bickerton, D. (1995). *Language and human behavior.* Seattle, WA: University of Washington Press.

Bickerton, D. (2008). But how did protolanguage actually start? *Interaction Studies, 9,* 169–176.

Billig, M., & Tajfel, H. (1973). Social categorization and similarity and intergroup behaviour. *European Journal of Social Psychology, 3,* 27–52.

Binder, E., Droste, S.K., Ohl, F., & Reul, J.M. (2004). Regular voluntary exercise reduces anxiety-related behavior and impulsiveness in mice. *Behavioural Brain Research, 155,* 197–206. *Biography, Esref Armagan* (n.d.). Retrieved October 23, 2007, from http://www.esrefarmagan.com/bio.html.

Birch, L.L., & Fisher, J.A. (1996). The role of experience in the development of children's eating behavior. In E.D. Capaldi (Ed.), *Why we eat what we eat: The psychology of eating* (pp. 113–141). Washington, DC: American Psychological Association.

Birch, L.L., & Marlin, D.W. (1982). I don't like it; I never tried it: Effects of exposure on two-year-old children's food preferences. *Appetite, 3,* 353–360.

Birdsong, D. (2005). Interpreting age effects in second language acquisition. In J.F. Kroll & A.M.B. de Groot (Eds.), *Handbook of bilingualism: Psycholinguistic approaches* (pp. 109–127). New York, NY: Oxford University Press.

Birdsong, D. (2006). Age and second language acquisition and processing: A selective overview. *Language Learning, 56,* 9–49.

Bishop, S.J. (2007). Neurocognitive mechanisms of anxiety: An integrative account. *Trends in Cognitive Sciences, 11,* 307–316.

Biss, W.J., & Horne, S.G. (2005). Sexual satisfaction as more than a gendered concept: The roles of psychological well-being and sexual orientation. *Journal of Constructivist Psychology, 18,* 25–38.

Bjork, R.A. (2001, March). How to succeed in college: Learn how to learn. *American Psychological Society Observer, 14,* 3, 9.

Black, D.W. (2006). Efficacy of combined pharmacotherapy and psychotherapy versus monotherapy in the treatment of anxiety disorders. *CNS Spectrums, 11,* 29–33.

Blackmore, S. (1999). Meme, myself, and I. *New Scientist, 161,* 40.

Blakemore, S. (2008a). Development of the social brain during adolescence. *Quarterly Journal of Experimental Psychology, 61*(1), 40–49.

Blakemore, S. (2008b). The social brain in adolescence. *Nature Reviews Neuroscience, 9*(4), 267–277.

Blakeslee, S. (2005, February 8). Focus narrows in search for autism's cause. *New York Times.* Retrieved from http://www.nytimes.com.

Blakeslee, S., & Blakeslee, M. (2007). *The body has a mind of its own.* New York: Random House.

Blanchard, M.M, Mendelsohn, D., & Stamp, J.A. (2009). The HR/LR model: Further evidence as an animal model of sensation seeking. *Neuroscience & Biobehavioral Reviews, 33*(7), 1145–1154.

Blanco, C., Okuda, M., Wright, C., Hasin, D., Grant, B., Liu, S., & Olfson, M. (2008). Mental health of college students and their non-college-attending peers: Results from the National Epidemiologic Study on Alcohol and Related Conditions. *Archives of General Psychiatry, 65,* 1429–1437. doi: 10.1001/archpsyc.65.12.1429.

Blank, H., Musch, J., & Pohl, R.F. (2007). Hindsight bias: On being wise after the event. *Social Cognition, 25,* 1–9.

Blanton, H., & Jaccard, J. (2006). Arbitrary metrics in psychology. *American Psychologist, 61,* 27–41.

Blass, T. (2004). *The man who shocked the world: The life and legacy of Stanley Milgram.* New York: Basic Books.

Blaxton, T.A. (1989). Investigating dissociations among memory measures: Support for a transfer-appropriate processing framework. *Journal of Experimental Psychology, 15,* 657–668.

Bleier, P., Habib, R., & Flament, M.F. (2006). Pharmacotherapies in the management of obsessive-compulsive disorder. *Canadian Journal of Psychiatry, 51,* 417–430.

Blier, P. (2005). Atypical antipsychotics for mood and anxiety disorders: Safe and effective adjuncts? *Review of Psychiatry and Neuroscience, 30*, 232–233.

Bliss, T.V.P., & Lømo, T. (1973). Long-lasting potentiation of synaptic transmission in the dentate area of the anaesthetized rabbit following stimulation of the perforant path. *Journal of Physiology, 232*, 331–356.

Block, J., Block, J.H., & Keyes, S. (1988). Longitudinally foretelling drug usage in adolescence: Early childhood personality and environmental precursors. *Child Development, 59*, 336–355.

Block, J.J. (2008). Issues for DSM-5: Internet addiction. *American Journal of Psychiatry, 165*, 306–307.

Block, R.I., O'Leary, D.S., Hichwa, R.D., Augustinack, J.C., Boles Ponto, L.L., Ghoneim, M.M., Stephan Arndt, S., Hurtig, R.R., Watkins G.L., Hall, J.A., Nathan, P.E., & Andreasen, N.C. (2002). Effects of frequent marijuana use on memory-related regional cerebral blood flow. *Pharmacology, Biochemistry, & Behavior, 72*, 237–250.

Blonigen, D.M., Hicks, B.M., Krueger, R.F., Patrick, C.J., & Iacono, W.G. (2006). Continuity and change in psychopathic traits as measured via normal-range personality: A longitudinal–biometric study. *Journal of Abnormal Psychology, 115*, 85–95.

Bloomfield, P.S., Sudhakar, S., Veronese, M., Rizzo, G., Bertoldo, A., Owen, D.R., Bloomfield, M.A.P., Bonoldi, I., Kalk, N., Turkheimer, F., McGuire, P., de Paola, V., & Howes, O.D. (2015). Microglial activity in people at ultra high risk of psychosis and in schizophrenia: An [11C]PBR28 PET brain imaging study. *American Journal of Psychiatry*. DOI: 10.1176/appi.ajp.2015.14101358.

Blüher, M. (2010). The distinction of metabolically "healthy" from "unhealthy" obese individuals. *Current Opinion in Lipidology, 21*, 38–43.

Boeree, C.G. (2006). Personality theories. Erik Erikson, 1902–1994. Retrieved from http://webspace.ship.edu/cgboer/erikson.html.

Bogaert, S., Boone, C., & Declerck, C. (2008). Social value orientation and cooperation in social dilemmas: A review and conceptual model. *British Journal of Social Psychology, 47*, 453–480.

Bohart, A.C., Elliott, R., Greenberg, L.S., & Watson, J.C. (2002). Empathy. In J.C. Norcross (Ed.), *Psychotherapy relationships that work: Therapist contributions and responsiveness to patients* (pp. 89–108). Oxford: Oxford University Press.

Bohart, A.C., & Wade, A.G. (2013). The client in psychotherapy. In M.J. Lambert (Ed.), *Bergin and Garfeild's handbook of psychotherapy and behaviour change* (6th ed., pp. 161–188). New York, NY: Psychology Press.

Bollen, E., & Wojciechowski, F.L. (2004). Anorexia nervosa subtypes and the Big Five personality factors. *European Eating Disorders Review, 12*, 117–121.

Bolour, S., & Braunstein, G. (2005). Testosterone therapy in women: A review. *International Journal of Impotence Research, 17*, 399–408.

Bond, R., & Smith, P.B. (1996). Culture and conformity: A meta-analysis of studies using Asch's (1952b, 1956) line judgment task. *Psychological Bulletin, 119*, 111–137.

Bonnet, M., Decety, J., Jeannerod, M., & Requin, J. (1997). Mental simulation of an action modulates the excitability of spinal re-flex pathways in man. *Cognitive Brain Research, 5*, 221–228.

Book, A.S., Starzyk, K.B., & Quinsey, V.L. (2001). The relationship between testosterone and aggression: A meta-analysis. *Aggression and Violent Behavior, 6*, 579–599.

Boorboor, S. (2002). Integrating the incompatible: The rise of the incorporated immune system. (University of Rochester) *Journal of Undergraduate Research, 1*, 10–26.

Borland, R., Wilson, N., Fong, G.T., Hammond, D., Cummings, K.M., Yong, H.H., Hosking, W., Hastings, G., Thrasher, J., & McNeill, A. (2009). Impact of graphic and text warnings on cigarette packs: Findings from four countries over five years. *Tobacco Control, 18*, 358–364.

Born, J., Hansen, K., Marshall, L., Mölle, M., & Fehm, H.L. (1999). Timing the end of nocturnal sleep. *Nature, 397*, 29–30.

Bornstein, M.H., & Cote, L.R. (2005). Expressive vocabulary in language learners from two ecological settings in three language communities. *Infancy, 7*, 299–316.

Boroditsky, L. (2001). Does language shape thought? Mandarin and English speakers' conceptions of time. *Cognitive Psychology, 43*, 1–22. doi: 10.1006/cogp.2001.0748.

Borst, J.P., Taatgen, N.A., & van Rijn, H. (2010). The problem state: A cognitive bottleneck in multitasking. *Journal of Experimental Psychology. Learning, Memory, and Cognition, 36*(2), 363–382. doi: 10.1037/a0018106.

Boska, P. (2008). Maternal infection during pregnancy and schizophrenia. *Journal of Psychiatry and Neuroscience, 33*, 183–185.

Botvinick, M.M., Cohen, J.D., & Carter, C.S. (2004). Conflict monitoring and anterior cingulated cortex: An update. *Trends in Cognitive Sciences, 8*, 539–546.

Botwin, M., Buss, D.M., & Shackelford, T.K. (1997). Personality and mate preferences: Five factors in mate selection and marital satisfaction. *Journal of Personality and Social Psychology, 65*, 107–136.

Bouchard, C., Trudeau, N., Sutton, A, Boudreault, M.-C., & Deneault, J. (2009). Gender differences in language development in French Canadian children between 8 and 30 months of age. *Applied Psycholinguistics, 30*, 685–707.

Bouchard, T.J., Jr., & Loehlin, J.C. (2001). Genes, evolution, and personality. *Behavioral Genetics, 31*, 243–273.

Boulos, D., & Zamorski, M.A. (2014). Deployment-related mental disorders among Canadian Armed Forces personnel deployed in support of the mission in Afghanistan, 2001–2008: Surgeon General Report. Ottawa, ON: Department of National Defence.

Bourgeois, S., & Johnson, A. (2004). Preparing for dying: Meaningful practices in palliative care. *Omega: Journal of Death and Dying, 49*, 99–107.

Bouton, M.E., Mineka, S., & Barlow, D.H. (2001). A modern learning theory perspective on the etiology of panic disorder. *Psychological Review, 108*, 4–32.

Bowden, C.L. (1994). Bipolar disorder and creativity. In M.P. Shaw & M.A. Runco (Eds.), *Creativity and affect* (pp. 73–86). Norwood, NJ: Ablex.

Bowden, E.M., & Jung-Beeman, M. (2003). Aha! Insight experience correlates with solution activation in the right hemisphere. *Psychonomic Bulletin & Review, 10*, 730–737.

Bowden, E.M., Jung-Beeman, M., Fleck, J., & Kounios, J. (2005). New approaches to demystifying insight. *Trends in Cognitive Sciences, 9*, 322–328.

Bower, B. (2005, December 10). The Piraha challenge: An Amazonian tribe takes grammar to a strange place. *Science News, 168*(24). Retrieved from http://www.sciencenews.org.

Bowlby, J. (1969). *Attachment and Loss: Vol. 1. Attachment*. New York: Basic Books.

Bowlby, J. (1973). *Attachment and Loss: Vol. 2. Separation, anxiety, and anger*. New York: Basic Books.

Bowlby, J. (1980). *Attachment and Loss: Vol. 3. Loss, sadness, and depression*. New York: Basic Books.

Bowman, L.L., Levine, L.E., Waite, B.M., & Gendron, M. (2010). Can students really multitask? An experimental study of instant messaging while reading. *Computers and Education, 54*, 927–931.

Boyack, K.W., Klavans, R., & Börner, K. (2005). Mapping the backbone of science. *Scientometrics, 64*, 351–374.

Boyce, W., Doherty-Poirier, M., MacKinnon, D., Fortin, C., Saab, H., King, M., & Gallupe, O. (2006). Sexual Health of Canadian Youth: Findings from the Canadian Youth, Sexual Health and HIV/AIDS Study. *Canadian Journal of Human Sexuality, 15*(2), 59–68. Retrieved from http://www.sieccan.org/pdf/boyce_cjhs2006_sexualhealth.pdf.

Boyd, D. (2007). Why youth (heart) Social Network Sites: The role of networked publics in teenage social life. In D. Buckingham (Ed.), *MacArthur Foundation Series on Digital Learning—Youth, Identity, and Digital Media Volume* (pp. 1–26). Cambridge, MA: MIT Press.

Boylan, S., Cade, J.E., Dolby, V.A. et al. (2008). Maternal caffeine intake during pregnancy and risk of fetal growth restriction: A large prospective observational study. *British Medical Journal, 3*(337), a2332. Retrieved from EBSCOhost.

Boysen, G.A., & VanBergen, A. (2013). A review of published research on adult dissociative identity disorder: 2000–2010. *Journal of Nervous and Mental Diseases, 201*, 5–11.

Bradberry, C.W. (2007). Cocaine sensitization and dopamine mediation of cue effects in rodents, monkeys, and humans: Areas of agreement, disagreement, and implications for addiction. *Psychopharmacology, 191*, 705–717.

Bradley, R.M. (1972). Development of the taste bud and gustatory papillae in human fetuses. In J.F. Bosma (Ed.), *The third symposium on oral sensation and perception: The mouth of the infant.* Springfield, IL: Thomas.

Brain Observatory, UC San Diego. (2009). Retrieved March 15, 2010, http://www.thebrainobservatory.org.

Brain, Marshall (2003). How 3-D glasses work. Retrieved from http://science.howstuffworks.com/3-d-glasses2.htm.

Brand, B.L., Loewenstein, R.J., & Speigel, D. (2013). Patients with DID are found and researched more widely than Boysen and VanBergen recognized. *Journal of Nervous and Mental Disease, 201*, 440.

Brand, G., & Millot, J-L. (2001). Sex differences in human olfaction: Between evidence and enigma. *The Quarterly Journal of Experimental Psychology B: Comparative and Physiological Psychology, 54B*, 259–270.

Brandtzæg, P.B., Lüders, M., & Skjetne, J.H. (2010). Too many Facebook "friends"? Content sharing and sociability versus the need for privacy in social network sites. *International Journal of Human-Computer Interaction, 26*, 1006–1030.

Braver, T.S., & Barch, D.M. (2002). A theory of cognitive control, agingcognition, and neuromodulation. *Neuroscience and Biobehavioral Reviews, 26*, 809–817.

Breiter, H.C., Etcoff, N.L., Whalen, P.J., Kennedy, W.A., Rauch, S.L., Buckner, R.L., et al. (1996). Response and habituation of the human amygdala during visual processing of facial expressions. *Neuron, 17*, 875–887.

Breland, K., & Breland, M. (1961). The misbehavior of organisms. *American Psychologist, 16*, 681–684.

Breugelmans, S.M., Poortinga, Y.H., Ambadar, Z., Setiadi, B., Vaca, J.B., Widiyanto, B., et al. (2005). Body sensations associated with emotions in Rarámuri Indians, rural Javanese, and three student samples. *Emotion, 5*, 166–174.

Brewer, M.B., & Caporael, L.R. (2006). An evolutionary perspective on social identity: Revisiting groups. In M. Schaller, D.T. Kenrick, & J.A. Simpson (Eds.), *Evolution and social psychology* (pp. 143–161). New York: Psychology Press.

Brickman, P., Coates, D., & Janoff-Bulman, R. (1978). Lottery winners and accident victims: Is happiness relative? *Journal of Personality and Social Psychology, 36*, 917–927.

Bridges, K. (1932). Emotional development in infancy. *Child Development, 3*, 324–341.

Briggs, C. (2005). Allen uses films to avoid anxiety. *BBC News-Online.* Retrieved July 3, 2008, from http://news.bbc.co.uk/2/hi/entertainment/4539493.stm.

Brion, M., Pitel, A.L., Beaunieux, H., & Maurage, P. (2014). Revisiting the continuum hypothesis: Toward an in-depth exploration of executive functions in Korsakoff syndrome. *Frontiers in Human Neuroscience, 8*, 498.

Broadbent, D.E. (1954). The role of auditory localization in attention and memory span. *Journal of Experimental Psychology, 44*, 51–55.

Brodsky, A.E., & Faryal, T. (2006). No matter how hard you try, your feet still get wet: Insider and outsider perspectives on bridging diversity. *American Journal of Community Psychology, 37*, 311–320.

Brody, L.R., & Hall, J.A. (2000). Gender, emotion, and expression. In M. Lewis and J.M. Haviland-Jones (Eds.), *Handbook of emotions* (2nd ed., pp. 338–349). New York: Guilford Press.

Bronfenbrenner, U., McClelland, P., Wethington, E., Moen, P., & Ceci, S. (1996). *The state of Americans: This generation and the next.* New York: Free Press.

Bronner, M.B., Peek, N., Knoester, H., Bos, A.P., Last, B.F., & Grootenhuis, M.A. (2010). Course and predictors of posttraumatic stress disorder in parents after pediatric intensive care treatment of their child. *Journal of Pediatric Psychology, 35*, 966–974.

Broude G., & Greene, S. (1980). Cross-cultural codes on 20 sexual attitudes and practices. In H. Barry & A. Schlegel (Eds), *Cross-cultural samples and codes* (pp. 313–333). Pittsburgh: University of Pittsburgh Press.

Brown, A.S. (2006). Prenatal infection as a risk factor for schizophrenia. *Schizophrenia Bulletin, 32*, 200–202.

Brown, A.S., Begg, M.D., Gravenstein, S., Schaefer, C.A., Wyatt, R.J., Bresnahan, M., et al. (2004). Serologic evidence of prenatal influenza in the etiology of schizophrenia. *Archives of General Psychiatry, 61*, 774–780.

Brown, G.W., Harris, T.O., Kendrick, T., Chatwin, J., Craig, T.K., Kelly, V., Mander, H., Ring, A., Wallace, V., Uher, R., & Thread Study Group. (2010). Antidepressants, social adversity and outcome of depression in general practice. *Journal of Affective Disorders, 121*, 239–46.

Brown, K.W., & Ryan, R.M. (2003). The benefits of being present: Mindfulness and its role in psychological well-being. *Journal of Personality and Social Psychology, 84*, 822–848.

Brown, R.E. (1994). *An introduction to neuroendocrinology.* Cambridge: Cambridge University Press.

Brown, R.E. (2007). Alfred McCoy, Hebb, the CIA and torture. *Journal of the History of the Behavioral Sciences, 43*, 205–213.

Brown, R.T., Reynolds, C.R., & Whitaker, J.S. (1999). Bias in mental testing since Jensen's "Bias in Mental Testing." *School Psychology Quarterly, 14*, 208–238.

Brunelin, J., Poulet, E., Bor, J., Rivet, A., Eche, J., d'Amato, T., & Saoud, M. (2010). Transcranial magnetic stimulation (rTMS) and negative symptoms of schizophrenia. *Annales Médico-Psychologiques, 168*, 422–427.

Bruner, J.S., & Minturn, A.L. (1955). Perceptual identification and perceptual organization. *Journal of General Psychology, 53*, 21–28.

Brunet, A., Poundja, J., Tremblay, J., Bui, E., Thomas, E., Orr, S.P., Azzoug, A. Birmes, P., Pitman, R.K. (2011). Trauma reactivation under the influence of propranolol decreases posttraumatic stress symptoms and disorder 3 open-label trials. *Journal of Clinical Psychopharmacology, 31*, 547–550.

Brunwasser, S.M., Gillham, J.E., & Kim, E.S. (2009). A meta-analytic review of Penn Resiliency Program's effect on depressive symptoms. *Journal of Consulting and Clinical Psychology, 77*, 1042–1054.

Bryans, W.A. (1959). Mitotic activity in the brain of the adult white rat. *Anatomical Record, 133*, 65–71.

Buchanan, J., & Houlihan, D. (2008). The use of in vivo desensitization for the treatment of a specific phobia of earthworms. *Clinical Case Studies, 7*, 12–24. doi: 10.1177/1534650107300863.

Buchanan, T.W., & Tranel, D. (2008). Stress and emotional memory retrieval: Effects of sex and cortisol response. *Neurobiology of Learning and Memory, 89*, 134–141.

Buck, L.B. (2000). Smell and taste: The chemical senses. In E.R. Kandel, J.H. Schwartz, & T.M. Jessell (Eds.), *Principles of neural science* (4th ed., pp. 625–647). New York: McGraw-Hill.

Buckley, C. (2007, January 3). Man is rescued by stranger on subway tracks. *New York Times*. Retrieved from http://www.nytimes.com.

Buka, S.L., Tsuang, M.T., Torrey, E.F., Klebanoff, M.A., Bernstein, D., & Yolken, R.H. (2001). Maternal infections and subsequent psychosis among offspring. *Archives of General Psychiatry, 58,* 1032–1037.

Bukh, J., Bock, C., Vinberg, M., Werge, T., Gether, U., & Kessing, L. (2009). Interaction between genetic polymorphisms and stressful life events in first episode depression. *Journal of Affective Disorders, 119*(1–3), 107–115. doi:10.1016/j.jad.2009.02.023.

Bulik, C.M., Sullivan, P.F., Tozzi, F., Furberg, H., Lichtenstein, P., & Pedersen, N.L. (2006). Prevalence, heritability, and prospective risk factors for anorexia nervosa. *Archives of General Psychiatry, 63,* 305–312.

Bulkeley, K. (1997). *An introduction to the psychology of dreaming.* Westport, CT: Praeger.

Bullivant, S.B., Sellergren, S.A., Stern, K. Spencer, N.A., Jacob, S., Mennella, J.A., & McClintock, M.K. (2004). Women's sexual experience during the menstrual cycle: Identification of the sexual phase by noninvasive measurement of luteinizing hormone. *Journal of Sex Research, 41,* 82–93.

Bullough, V.L. (1998). Alfred Kinsey and the Kinsey Report: Historical overview and lasting contributions. *The Journal of Sex Research, 35*(2), 127–131. Retrieved from http://www.jstor.org/stable/3813664.

Burch, G., Pavelis, C., Hemsley, D.R., & Corr, P.J. (2006). Schizotypy and creativity in visual artists. *British Journal of Psychology, 97,* 177–190.

Burd, L., Roberts, D., Olson, M., & Odendaal, H. (2007). Ethanol and the placenta: A review. *Journal of Maternal-Fetal and Neonatal Medicine, 20,* 361–375.

Burgess, W. (2009). *The depression answer book.* Naperville, IL: Sourcebooks.

Burguière, E., Monteiro, P., Feng, G., & Graybiel, A.M. (2013). Optogenetic stimulation of lateral orbitofronto-striatal pathway suppresses compulsive behaviors. *Science, 340,* 1243–1246. doi: 10.1126/science.1232380.

Burnett, G.B., Moll, J., Frith, C., & Blakemore, S.-J. (2008). Development during adolescence of the neural processing of social emotion. *Journal of Cognitive Neuroscience 21,* 1736–1750.

Burnham, J. (Ed.) (2012). *After Freud left: A century of psychoanalysis in America.* Chicago, IL: University of Chicago Press.

Burnstein, E., Crandall, C., & Kitayama, S. (1994). Some neo-Darwinian decision rules for altruism: Weighing cues for inclusive fitness as a function of the biological importance of the decision. *Journal of Personality and Social Psychology, 67,* 773–789.

Burt, K.B., & Masten, A.S. (2010). Development in the transition to adulthood: Vulnerabilities and opportunities. In J.E. Grant & M.N. Potenza (Eds.), *Young adult mental health* (pp. 5–18). New York, NY: Oxford University Press.

Bushman, B.J., & Anderson, C.A. (2001). Media violence and the American public: Scientific facts versus media misinformation. *American Psychologist, 56,* 477–489.

Buss, A.H., & Plomin, R. (1984). Temperament: Early personality traits. Hillsdale, NJ: Erlbaum.

Buss, D.M. (1990). Toward a biologically informed psychology of personality. *Journal of Personality, 58,* 1–16.

Buss, D.M. (2003). *The evolution of desire: Strategies of human mating* (Rev. ed.). New York: Basic Books.

Buss, D.M. (2008). Human nature and individual differences: Evolution of human personality. In O.P. John, R.W. Robins, & L.A. Pervin (Eds.). *Handbook of personality: Theory and research* (pp. 29–60). New York: Guilford.

Buss, D.M., & Greiling, H. (1999). Adaptive individual differences. *Journal of Personality, 67,* 209–243.

Buss, D.M., & Schmitt, D.P. (1993). Sexual strategies theory: An evolutionary perspective on human mating. *Psychological Review, 100,* 204–232.

Butler, A.C., Chapman, J.E., Forman, E.M., & Beck, A.T. (2006). The empirical status of cognitive-behavioral therapy: A review of meta-analyses. *Clinical Psychology Review, 26,* 17–31.

Cacioppo, J.T., Fowler, J.H., & Christakis, N.A. (2009). Alone in the crowd: The structure and spread of loneliness in a large social network. *Journal of Personality and Social Psychology, 97,* 977–991.

Cacioppo, J.T., Petty, R.E., Feinstein, J., & Jarvis, W.B.G. (1996). Dispositional differences in cognitive motivation: The life and times of individuals varying in need for cognition. *Psychological Bulletin, 119,* 197–253.

Cahill, L., Haier, R.J., Fallon, J., Alkire, M.T., Tang, C., Keator, D., Wu, J., & McGaugh, J.L. (1996). Amygdala activity at encoding correlated with long-term, free recall of emotional information. *Proceedings of the National Academy of Sciences of the USA, 93,* 8016–21.

Cahill, S.P., Foa, E.B., Hembree E.A., Marshall, R.D., & Nacash, N. (2006). *Journal of Traumatic Stress, 19,* 597–610.

Caird, J.K., Willness, C.R., Steel, P., & Scialfa, C. (2008). A meta-analysis of the effects of cell phones on driver performance. *Accident Analysis and Prevention, 40,* 1282–1293.

Caldera, Y.M., Huston, A.C., & O'Brien, M. (1989). Social interactions and play patterns of parents and toddlers with feminine, masculine, and neutral toys. *Child Development, 60*(1), 70–76. doi:10.2307/1131072.

Calkins, M.W. (1898). Short studies in memory and in association from the Wellesley College Psychological Laboratory. I.: A study of immediate and delayed recall of the concrete and of the verbal. *Psychological Review, 5,* 451–456.

Callaghan, T., Rochat, P., Lillard, A., Claux, M., Odden, H., Itakura, S., & Singh, S. (2005). Synchrony in the Onset of Mental-State Reasoning. *Psychological Science (Wiley-Blackwell), 16*(5), 378–384.

Callan, M.J., Ellard, J.H., & Nicol, J.E. (2006). The belief in a just world and immanent justice reasoning in adults. *Personality and Social Psychology Bulletin, 32,* 1646–1658.

Calvert, S.L., Rideout, V.J., Woolard, J.L., Barr, R.F., & Strouse, G.A. (2005). Age, ethnicity, and socioeconomic patterns in early computer use. *American Behavioral Scientist, 48,* 590–607.

Cameron, D.E. (1956). Psychic driving. *American Journal of Psychiatry, 112,* 502–509.

Cameron, K., Salazar, L., Bernhardt, J., Burgess-Whitman, N., Wingood, G., & DiClemente, R. (2005). Adolescents' experience with sex on the web: Results from online focus groups. *Journal of Adolescence, 28*(4), 535–540.

Campbell, F.A., & Ramey, C.T. (1995). Cognitive and school outcomes for high-risk African-American students at middle adolescence: Positive effects of early intervention. *American Educational Research Journal, 32,* 743–772.

Campbell, F.A., Ramey, C.T., Pungello, E.P., Sparling, J., & Miller-Johnson, S. (2002). Early childhood education: Young adult outcomes from the Abecedarian Project. *Applied Developmental Science, 6,* 42–57.

Campbell-Sills, L., & Stein, M.B. (2007). Psychometric analysis and refinement of the Connor–Davidson Resilience Scale (CD-RISC): Validation of a 10-item measure of resilience. *Journal of Traumatic Stress, 20,* 1019–1028.

Campos, J., Hiatt, S., Ramsey, D., Henderson, C., & Svejda, M. (1978). The emergence of fear on the visual cliff. In M. Lewis & L. Rosenblum (Eds,), *The development of affect* (pp. 149–182). New York, NY: Plenum Press.

Campos, J.J., & Stenberg, C. (1981). Perception, appraisal, and emotion: The onset of social referencing. In M.E. Lamb & L.R. Sherrod (Eds.), *Infant social cognition: Empirical and theoretical considerations* (pp. 273–314). Hillsdale, NJ: Erlbaum.

Camras, L.A., Oster, H., Bakeman, R., Meng, Z., Ujiie, T., & Campos, J.J. (2007).

Do infants show distinct negative facial expressions for fear and anger? Emotional expression in 11-month-old European American, Chinese, and Japanese infants. *Infancy, 11,* 131–155.

Canadian Automobile Association. (2014). *Distracted driving.* Retrieved from http://distracteddriving.caa.ca/education/.

Canadian Centre on Substance Abuse. (2004). Canadian Addiction Survey (CAS). A national survey of Canadians' use of alcohol and other drugs: Prevalence of use and related harms. Retrieved on May 24, 2010, from http://www.ccsa.ca/eng/priorities/research/canadianaddiction/Pages/default.aspx.

Canadian Council on Animal Care. (1993). *Guide to the Care and Use of Experimental Animals, Vol. 1.* Retrieved from http://www.ccac.ca/en/CCAC_Programs/Guidelines_Policies/GUIDES/ENGLISH/toc_v1.htm.

Canadian Council on Animal Care. (2011). CCAC 2011 animal use statistics. Retrieved from http://www.ccac.ca/Documents/Publications/Statistics/CCAC_Animal_Use_Statistics_2011.pdf.

Canadian Council on Animal Care. (2013). CCAC Annual Report 2013–2014. Retrieved from http://www.ccac.ca/Documents/Publications/AnnualReports/2013-2014.pdf.

Canadian Institutes of Health Research, Natural Sciences and Engineering Research Council of Canada, and Social Sciences and Humanities Research Council of Canada. (2010). *Tri-Council Policy Statement: Ethical Conduct for Research Involving Humans.* Retrieved from http://www.pre.ethics.gc.ca/pdf/eng/tcps2/TCPS_2_FINAL_Web.pdf.

Canadian Medical Association. (2008). 8th annual national report card on health care. Retrieved from http://www.facturation.net/multimedia/CMA/Content_Images/Inside_cma/Annual_Meeting/2008/GC_Bulletin/National_Report_Card_EN.pdf.

Canadian Mental Health Association. (2001). An astounding 91% of Canadians say maintaining metal health is very important [Media release]. Retrieved from alberta.cmha.ca/files/2012/03/NewsRelease-010507.pdf.

Canadian Paediatric Society, Adolescent Health Committee. (2010). Sexting: Keeping teens safe and responsible in a technologically savvy world. *Paediatrics and Child Health, 15*(1), 41–42.

Canadian Paediatric Society, Psychosocial Paediatric Committee. (2003). *Impact of media use on children and youth* (Reference No. PP 2003–01). Retrieved from http://www.cps.ca/english/statements/CP/pp03–01.htm.

Canadian Psychological Association. (2000). *Canadian code of ethics for psychologists* (3rd ed.). Ottawa.

Canadian Psychological Association. (2010). *Annual report.* Retrieved on June 21, 2010, from http://www.cpa.ca/cpasite/userfiles/Documents/AR2010English.pdf.

Cannon, M., Caspi, A., Moffitt, T., Harrington, H., Taylor, A., Murray, R.M., et al. (2002). Evidence for early childhood pandevelopmental impairment specific to schizophreniform disorder: Results from a longitudinal birth cohort. *Archives of General Psychiatry, 59,* 449–456.

Cannon, W.B. (1929). *Bodily changes in pain, hunger, fear, and rage: An account of recent researches into the function of emotional excitement.* New York: Appleton.

Cannon, W.B. (1939). *The wisdom of the body.* New York: W.W. Norton.

Cannon, W.B., & Washburn, A.L. (1912). An explanation of hunger. *American Journal of Physiology, 29,* 441–454.

Canter, R.R., & Hirsch, J. (1955). An experimental comparison of several psychological scales of weight. *American Journal of Psychology, 68,* 645–649.

Cantor, J. (1998). Children's attraction to violent television programming. In J.H. Goldstein (Ed.), *Why we watch: The attractions of violent entertainment* (pp. 88–115). New York: Oxford University Press.

Caramagno, T.C. (1992). *The flight of the mind: Virginia Woolf's art and manic-depressive illness.* Berkeley: University of California Press.

Cardno, A.G., & Gottesman, I.I. (2000). Twin studies of schizophrenia: From bow-and-arrow concordances to Star Wars Mx and functional genomics [Review]. *American Journal of Medical Genetics, 97,* 12–17.

Carew, T.J., & Kandel, E.R. (1973). Acquisition and retention of long-term habituation in *Aplysia:* Correlation of behavioral and cellular processes. *Science, 182,* 1158–1160.

Carey, B. (2008). H.M., an unforgettable amnesiac, dies at 82. *The New York Times.* Retrieved from http://www.nytimes.com/2008/12/05/us/05hm.html?_r=0 on January 22, 2014.

Carlat, D.J. (1998). The psychiatric review of symptoms: A screening tool for family physicians. *American Family Physician, 58,* 1617–1624.

Carless, S.A. (1999). Career assessment: Holland's vocational interests, personality characteristics, and abilities. *Journal of Career Assessment, 7,* 125–144.

Carlo, G. (2006). Care-based and altruistically based morality. In M. Killen and J.G. Smetana (Eds.), *Handbook of moral development* (pp. 551–579). Mahwah, NJ: Erlbaum.

Carlsson, A. (1987). Perspectives on the discovery of central monoaminergic neurotransmission. *Annual Review of Neuroscience, 10,* 19–40.

Carlsson, I. (2002). Anxiety and flexibility of defense related to high or low creativity. *Creativity Research Journal, 14,* 341–349.

Carlsson, I., Wendt, P., & Risberg, J. (2000). On the neurobiology of creativity: Differences in frontal activity between high and low creative subjects. *Neuropsychologica, 38,* 873–885.

Carmody, T.P., Duncan, C., Simon, J.A., Solkowitz, S., Huggins, J., Lee, S., & Delucchi, K. (2008). Hypnosis for smoking cessation: A randomized trial. *Nicotine & Tobacco Research, 10,* 811–818.

Carney, S.M., & Goodwin, G.M. (2005). Lithium—a continuing story in the treatment of bipolar disorder. *Acta Psychiatrica Scandinavia, 111*(Suppl. 426), 7–12.

Carrion, V.G., Hass, B.W., Garrett, A., Song, S., & Rice, A.L. (2010). Reduced hippocampal activity in youth with post-traumatic stress symptoms: An fMRI study. *Journal of Pediatric Psychology, 35,* 559–569.

Carroll, J.B. (1993). *Human cognitive abilities.* New York: Cambridge University Press.

Carroll, J.L., & Rest, J. (1981, December). Development in moral judgment as indicated by rejection of lower-stage statements. *Journal of Research in Personality, 15*(4), 538–544.

Carson, S.H., Peterson, J.B., & Higgins, D.M. (2003). Decreased latent inhibition is associated with increased creative achievement in high-functioning individuals. *Journal of Personality and Social Psychology, 85,* 499–506.

Carstensen, L.L. (2006). The influence of a sense of time on human development. *Science, 312,* 1913–1915.

Carter, C.S., Mintun, M., Nichols, T.N., & Cohen, J.D. (1997). Anterior cingulate gyrus dysfunction and selective attention deficits in schizophrenia: [15O]H2O PET study during single-trial Stroop task performance. *American Journal of Psychiatry, 154,* 1670–1675.

Casey, B.J., Davidson, M., & Rosen, B. (2002). Functional magnetic imaging: Basic principles of and application to developmental science. *Developmental Science, 5,* 301–309.

Caspi, A. (2000). The child is father of the man: Personality continuities from childhood to adulthood. *Journal of Personality and Social Psychology, 78,* 158–172.

Caspi, A., Elder, G.H., & Bem, D.H. (1988). Moving away from the world: Life-course patterns of shy children. *Developmental Psychology, 24,* 824–831.

Caspi, A., Houts, R.M., Belsky, D.W., Goldman-Mellor, S.J., Harrington, H., Israel, S., . . . Moffitt, T.E. (2014). The p-factor: One general psychopathology factor in the structure of psychiatric disorders? *Clinical Psychological Science, 2,* 119–137. doi: 10.1177/2167702613497473.

Caspi, A., McClay, J., Moffitt, T.E., Mill, J., Martin, J., Craig, I.W., et al. (2002). Role of genotype in the cycle of violence in maltreated children. *Science, 297,* 851–853.

Caspi, A., Roberts, B.W., & Shiner, R.L. (2003). Personality development: Stability and change. *Annual Review of Psychology, 56,* 453–484.

Caspi, A., Sugden, K., Moffitt, T.E., Taylor, A., Craig, I.W., Harrington, H., et al. (2003). Influence of life stress on depression: Moderation by a polymorphism in the 5-HTT gene. *Science, 301,* 386–389.

Cassidy, T., McLaughlin, M., & Giles, M. (2015). Applying a resource model of stress to the cancer caregiver experience. *Clinical Nursing Studies, 3,* 59–66.

Castelli, D.M., Hillman, C.H., Buck, S.M., & Erwin, H. (2007). Physical fitness and academic achievement in third- and fifth-grade students. *Journal of Sport & Exercise Psychology, 29,* 239–252.

Castles, A., McLean, G.M.T., Bavin, E., Bretherton, L., Carlin, J., Prior, M., . . . Reilly, S. (2013). Computer use and letter knowledge in pre-school children: A population-based study. *Journal of Paediatrics and Child Health, 49,* 193–198. doi: 10.1111/jpc.12126.

Catapano, F., Perris, F., Masella, M., Rossano, F., Cigliano, M., Magliano, L., & et al. (2006). Obsessive–compulsive disorder: A 3-year prospective follow-up study of patients treated with serotonin reuptake inhibitors. *Journal of Psychiatric Research, 40,* 502–510.

Cattell, R.B. (1965). *The scientific analysis of personality.* New York: Penguin Group.

Cavallero, C., & Foulkes, D. (Eds.). (1993). *Dreaming as cognition.* New York: Harvester-Wheatsheaf.

CBS News. (2007, January 3). Bystander pulls off-daring subway rescue. Retrieved from http://www.cbsnews.com /stories/2007/01/03/national/main2324961 .shtml?source=search_story.

Ceci, S.J., & Williams, W.M. (1997). Schooling, intelligence, and income. *American Psychologist, 52*(10), 1051–1058.

Ceci, S.J., & Williams, W.M. (2007). *Why aren't more women in science? Top researchers debate the evidence.* Washington, DC: American Psychological Association.

Ceci, S.J., & Williams, W.M. (2010). *The mathematics of sex: How biology and society conspire to limit talented women and girls.* New York, NY: Oxford University Press.

Centers for Disease Control and Prevention (CDC). (2005). *Sexual behavior and selected health measures: Men and women 15–44 years of age, United States, 2002.* Retrieved March 12, 2008, from http://www .cdc.gov/nchs/data/ad/ad362.pdf.

Centers for Disease Control and Prevention (CDC). (2006). *Smoking and tobacco use fact sheet.* Retrieved May 16, 2008, from http://www.cdc.gov/tobacco/data_statistics/ Factsheets/cessation2.htm.

Centers for Disease Control and Prevention (CDC). (2007, August 8). *Smoking during pregnancy.* Retrieved February 23, 2008, from http://www.cdc.gov/tobacco/ health_effects/pregnancy.htm.

Centers for Disease Control and Prevention. (2007, May 31). *Fetal Alcohol Disorders* Retrieved April 25, 2008, from http://www .cdc.gov/ncbddd/fas/default.htm.

Chaffee, J. (1999). *The thinker's guide to college success* (2nd ed.). Boston: Houghton Mifflin.

Chahal, H., Fung, C., Kuhle, S., & Veugelers, P.J. (2013). Availability and night-time use of electronic entertainment and communication devices are associated with short sleep duration and obesity among Canadian children. *Pediatric Obesity, 8*(1), 42–51. doi:10.1111/j.2047-6310.2012.00085.x.

Chan, B.L., Witt, R., Charrow, A.P., Magee, A., Howard, R., and Pasquina, P.F. (2007). Mirror therapy for phantom limb pain. *New England Journal of Medicine, 357,* 2206–2207.

Chan, C., Brandone, A., & Tardif, T. (2009). Culture, context, or behavioural control?: English- and Mandarin-speaking mothers' use of nouns and verbs in joint book reading. *Journal of Cross-Cultural Psychology, 40,* 584–602. doi: 10.1177/0022022109335184.

Chan, G.C., Hinds, T.R., Impey, S., & Storm, D.R. (1998). Hippocampal neurotoxicity of Delta9–tetrahydrocannabinol. *Journal of Neuroscience, 18,* 5322–5332.

Chance, P. (1986). *Thinking in the classroom: A survey of programs.* New York: Teachers College, Columbia University.

Chang, E.C. (1998). Dispositional optimism and primary and secondary appraisal of a stressor: Controlling for confounding influences and relations to coping and psychological and physical adjustment. *Journal of Personality and Social Psychology, 74,* 1109–1120.

Chapdelaine, A., Kenny, D.A., & LaFontana, K.M. (1994). Matchmaker, matchmaker, can you make me a match? Predicting liking between two unacquainted persons. *Journal of Personality and Social Psychology, 67,* 83–91.

Chappell, M., & Humphreys, M.S. (1994). An auto-associative neural network for spares representations: Analysis and application to models of recognition and cued recall. *Psychological Review, 101,* 103–128.

Charmorro-Premuzic, T., & Steinmetz, C. (2013). The perfect hire. *Scientific American Mind, 24,* 42–47.

Charney, D.S. (2004). Psychological mechanisms of resilience and vulnerability: Implications for successful adaptation to extreme stress. *American Journal of Psychiatry, 161,* 195–216.

Chatterjee, A., Strauss, M.E., Smyth, K.A., & Whitehouse, P.J. (1992). Personality changes in Alzheimer's disease. *Archives of Neurology, 49,* 486–491.

Chaudhari, N., & Roper, S.D. (2010). The cell biology of taste. *Journal of Cell Biology, 190,* 285–296.

Cheah, C.S.L., & Nelson, L. (2004). The role of acculturation in the emerging adulthood of aboriginal college students. *International Journal of Behavioral Development, 28,* 494–507.

Chechik, G., Meilijson, I., & Ruppin, E. (1999). Neuronal regulation: A mechanism for synaptic pruning during brain maturation. *Neural Computation, 11,* 2151–2170.

Cheetham, C.E.J., Hammond, M.S.L., Edwards, C.J., & Finnerty, G.T. (2007). Sensory experience alters cortical connectivity and synaptic function site specifically. *The Journal of Neuroscience, 27,* 3456–3465.

Chemers, M.M., Hu, L., & Garcia, B.F. (2001). Academic self-efficacy and first-year college student performance and adjustment. *Science, 220,* 431–433.

Chen, J.V., Chen, C.C., & Yang, H-H. (2007). An empirical evaluation of key factors contributing to Internet abuse in the workplace. *Industrial Management & Data Systems, 108,* 87–106.

Chen, S.Y., Jordan, C., & Thompson, S. (2006). The effect of cognitive behavioral therapy (CBT) on depression: The role of problem-solving appraisal. *Research on Social Work Practice, 16,* 500–510.

Chepenik, L.G., Raffo, M., Hampson, M., Lacadie, C., Wang, F., Jones, M.M., . . . Blumberg, H.P. (2010). Functional connectivity between ventral prefrontal cortex and amygdala at low frequency in the resting state in bipolar disorder. *Psychiatry Research: Neuroimaging, 182,* 207–210.

Chia, E., Wang, J.J., Rochtchina, E., Cumming, R.R., Newall, P., & Mitchell, P. (2007). Hearing impairment and health-related quality of life: The Blue Mountains Hearing Study. *Ear & Hearing, 28,* 187–195.

Chiesa, A., Brambilla, P., & Serretti, A. (2010). Functional neural correlates of mindfulness meditations in comparison with psychotherapy, pharmacotherapy and placebo effect. Is there a link? *Acta Neuropsychiatrica, 22,* 104–117. doi: 10.1111/j.1601-5215.2010.00460.x.

Choi, I., Nisbett, R.E., & Norenzayan, A. (1999). Causal attribution across cultures: Variation and universality. *Psychological Bulletin, 125,* 47–65.

Chomsky, N. (1972). *Language and mind* (2nd ed.). New York: Harcourt Brace Jovanovich.

Chomsky, N. (1986). *Knowledge of language: Its nature, origins, and use.* New York: Praeger.

Chomsky, N. (2000). *New horizons in the study of language and the mind.* Cambridge: Cambridge University Press.

Chow, T.W., & Cummings, J.L. (1999). Frontal-subcortical circuits. In B.L. Miller & J.L. Cummings (Eds.), *The human frontal lobes: Functions and disorder* (pp. 3–26). New York, NY: Guilford Press.

Choy, Y., Fyer, A.J., & Lipsitz, J.D. (2007). Treatment of specific phobia in adults. *Clinical Psychology Review, 27*(3), 266–286.

Christakis, D., Zimmerman, F., DiGiuseppe, D., & McCarty, C. (2004). Early television exposure and subsequent attentional problems in children. *Pediatrics, 113,* 708–713.

Christakis, N.A., & Fowler, J.H. (2007). The spread of obesity in a large social network over 32 years. *New England Journal of Medicine, 357,* 370–379.

Christakis, N.A., & Fowler, J.H. (2008). The collective dynamics of smoking in a large social network. *New England Journal of Medicine, 358,* 2249–2258.

Christakis, N.A., & Fowler, J.H. (2009). Connected: The surprising power of our social networks and how they shape our lives. New York, NY: Little, Brown.

Chuang, D.M. (2004). Lithium protection from glutamate excitotoxicity: Therapeutic implications. *Clinical Neuroscience Research, 4,* 243–252.

Churchill, J.D., Galvez, R., Colcombe, S., Swain, R.A., Kramer, A.F., & Greenough, W.T. (2002). Exercise, experience and the aging brain. *Neurobiology of Aging, 23,* 941–955.

Chwalisz, K., Diener, E., & Gallagher, D. (1988). Autonomic arousal feedback and emotional experience: Evidence from the spinal cord injured. *Journal of Personality and Social Psychology, 54,* 820–828.

Cichetti, D. (2001). How a child builds a brain. In W.W. Hartup and R.A. Weinberg (Eds.), *Child psychology in retrospect and prospect.* Mahwah, NJ: Erlbaum.

Clancy, P.M. (1985). The acquisition of Japanese. In D. Slobin (Ed.), *The cross-linguistic study of language acquisition: Vol. 1. The data.* Hillsdale, NJ: Erlbaum.

Clark, A.E., Georgellis, Y., Lucas, R.E., & Diener, E. (2004). Unemployment alters the set point for life satisfaction. *Psychological Science, 15,* 8–15.

Clark, D.B, Thatcher, D.L., & Tapert, S.F. (2008). Alcohol, psychological dysregulation, and adolescent brain development. *Alcoholism: Clinical and Experimental Research, 32,* 375–385.

Clark, L., Bosworth, H., Welsh-Bohmer, K., Dawson, D., & Siegler, I. (2000). Relation between informant-rated personality and clinician-rated depression in patients with memory disorders. *Neuropsychiatry, Neuropsychology, & Behavioral Neurology, 13,* 39–47.

Clark, L.A. (2005). Temperament as a unifying basis for personality and psychopathology. Journal of *Abnormal Psychology, 114,* 505–521.

Clark, L.A., Watson, D., & Leeka, J. (1989). Diurnal variation in the positive affects. *Motivation and Emotion, 13,* 205–234.

Clark, R.D., III, & Hatfield, E. (1989). Gender differences in willingness to engage in casual sex. *Journal of Psychology and Human Sexuality, 2,* 39–55.

Clark, R.D., III, & Hatfield, E. (2003). Love in the afternoon. *Psychological Inquiry, 14,* 227–231.

Clark, W.R., & Grunstein, M. (2000). *Are we hardwired? The role of genes in human behavior.* New York: Oxford University Press.

Clarke, G.N., Hawkins, W., Murphy, M., Sheeber, L.B., Lewinsohn, P.M., & Seeley, J.R. (1995). Targeted prevention of unipolar depressive disorder in an at-risk sample of high school adolescents: A randomized trial of group cognitive intervention. *Journal of the American Academy of Child & Adolescent Psychiatry, 34,* 312–321.

Cobb, J.M., Fluster, Z., Leder, G., Seaver, A., Hendrick, J.L., & Hokanson, J.F. (2010). Information processing demands while texting on a simulated driving task. *Journal of Sport & Exercise Psychology, 32,* S72.

Coe, C.L., & Lubach, G.R. (2008). Fetal programming: Prenatal origins of health and illness. *Current Directions in Psychological Science, 17,* 36–41.

Cohen, J. (2010, April 2). Boxed about the ears, ape language research still standing. *Science, 328,* 38–39.

Cohen, J.D. (2005). The vulcanization of the human brain. *Journal of Economic Perspectives, 19,* 3–24.

Cohen, K.M. (2002). Relationships among childhood sex-atypical behavior, spatial ability, handedness, and sexual orientation in men. *Archives of Sexual Behavior, 31,* 129–143.

Cohen, S. (2004). Social relationships and health. *American Psychologist, 59,* 676–684.

Cohen, S., Alper, C.M., Doyle, W.J., Adler, N., Treanor, J.J., & Turner, R.B. (2008). Objective and subjective socioeconomic status and susceptibility to the common cold. *Health Psychology, 27,* 268–274.

Cohen, S., Doyle, W.J., Turner, R.B., Alper, C.M., & Skoner, D.P. (2003). Sociability and susceptibility to the common cold. *Psychological Science, 14,* 389–395.

Cohen, S., Tyrrell, D.A.J., & Smith, A.P. (1993). Negative life events, perceived stress, negative affect, and susceptibility to the common cold. *Journal of Personality and Social Psychology, 64,* 131–140.

Cohen, S., & Wills, T.A. (1985). Stress, social support, and the buffering hypothesis. *Psychological Bulletin, 98,* 310–357.

Colcombe, S.J., Erickson, K.I., Scalf, P.E., Kim, J.S., Praskash, R., McAuley, E., et al. (2006). Aerobic exercise training increases brain volume in aging humans. *Journal of Gerontology, 61,* 1166–1170.

Collins, A., & Loftus, E.F. (1975). A spreading activation theory of semantic processing. *Psychological Review, 82,* 407–428.

Comer, R.J. (2007). *Abnormal psychology* (6th ed.). New York: Worth.

Comery, T.A., Stamoudis, C.X., Irwin, S.A., & Greenough, W.T. (1996). Increased density of multiple-head dendritic spines on medium-sized spiny neurons of the striatum in rats reared in a complex environment. *Neurobiology of Learning and Memory, 66,* 93–96.

Conduct Problems Prevention Research Group. (1999a). Initial impact of the Fast Track prevention trial for conduct problems: I. The high-risk sample. *Journal of Consulting and Clinical Psychology, 67,* 631–647.

Conduct Problems Prevention Research Group. (1999b). Initial impact of the Fast Track prevention trial for conduct problems: II. Classroom effects. *Journal of Consulting and Clinical Psychology, 67,* 648–657.

Conger, R.D., & Donnellan, M.B. (2007). An interactionist perspective on the socioeconomic context of human development. *Annual Review of Psychology, 58,* 157–199.

Conrod, P.J., Castellanos, N., & Mackie, C. (2008). Personality-targeted interventions delay the growth of adolescent drinking and binge drinking. *Journal of Child Psychology and Psychiatry, 49,* 181–90.

Conrod, P.J., Pihl, R.O., Stewart, S.H., Dongier, M. (2000). Validation of a system of classifying female substance abusers on the basis of personality and motivational risk factors for substance abuse. *Psychology of Addictive Behavior,14,* 231–242.

Conroy, D.E., Ram, N., Pincus, A.L., Coffman, D.L., Lorek, A.E., Rebar, A.L., & Roche, M.J. (2014). Daily physical activity and alcohol use across the adult lifespan. *Health Psychology.* Advance online publication. http://dx.doi.org/10.1037/hea0000157.

Cook, C.C. (2013, July 6). Soldier's suicide note goes viral; family demands better for veterans. *CNN News,* retrieved from http://www

.cnn.com/2013/07/06/us/soldier-suicide-note/index .html?hpt=hp_t2.

Cooper, M. (2004). Towards a relationally-orientated approach to therapy: Empirical support and analysis. *British Journal of Guidance & Counselling, 32*(4), 451–460. doi:10.1080/03069880412331303268.

Cooper, S.J. (2005). Donald O. Hebb's synapse and learning rule: A history and commentary. *Neuroscience and Biobehavioral Reviews, 28,* 851–878.

Coplan, R.J., Karbeau, K.A., & Armer, M. (2008). Don't fret, be supportive! Maternal characteristics linking child shyness to psychosocial and school adjustment in kindergarten. *Journal of Abnormal Child Psychology, 36,* 359–371.

Corballis, M.C. (2010). Mirror neurons and the evolution of language. *Brain and Language, 112,* 25–35.

Correll, J., Park, B., Judd, C.M., & Wittenbrink, B. (2002). The police officer's dilemma: Using ethnicity to disambiguate potentially threatening individuals. *Journal of Personality and Social Psychology, 83,* 1314–1329.

Corrigan, P.W., Druss, B.G., & Perlick, D.A. (2014). The impact of mental illness stigma on seeking and participating in mental health care. *Psychological Science in the Public Interest, 15*(2), 37–70. doi: 10.1177/1529100614531398.

Cortoos, A., De Valck, E., Arns, M., Breteler, M.H.M., & Cluydts, R. (2010). An exploratory study on the effects of tele-neurofeedback and tele-biofeedback on objective and subjective sleep in patients with primary insomnia. *Applied Psychophysiological Biofeedback, 35,* 125–134.

Costa, P.T. (1996). Work and personality: Use of the NEO–PI–R in industrial/organizational psychology. *Applied Psychology: An International Review, 45,* 225–241.

Costa, P.T., & McCrae, R.R. (1976). Age differences in personality structure: A cluster analytic approach. *Journal of Gerontology, 31,* 564–570.

Costa, P.T., & McCrae, R.R. (1980). Influences of extraversion and neuroticism on subjective well-being. *Journal of Personality and Social Psychology, 38,* 668–678.

Costa, P.T., & McCrae, R.R. (1992). *NEO PI-R professional manual.* Odessa, FL: Psychological Assessment Resources.

Costa, P.T., Herbst, J.H., McCrae, R.R., & Siegler, I.C. (2000). Personality at midlife: Stability, intrinsic maturation, and response to life events. *Assessment, 7,* 365–378.

Costigan, C.L., & Dokis, D.P. (2006). The relations between parent–child acculturation differences and adjustment within immigrant Chinese families. *Child Development, 77,* 1252–1267.

Costigan, C.L., & Su, T.F. (2004). Orthogonal versus linear models of acculturation among immigrant Chinese Canadians: A comparison of mothers, fathers, and children. *International Journal of Behavioural Development, 28,* 518–527.

Côté, J.E., & Levine, C. (1987). A formulation of Erikson's theory of ego identity formation. *Developmental Review, 7*(4), 273–325. doi:10.1016/0273-2297(87)90015-3.

Cotman, C.W., Berchtold, N.C., & Christie, L.A. (2007). Exercise builds brain health: Key roles of growth factor cascades and inflammation. *Trends in Neurosciences, 30,* 464–472.

Coulson, E.J., May, L.M., Sykes, M.A., & Hamlin, A.S. (2009). The role of the p75 neurotrophin receptor in cholinergic dysfunction in Alzheimer's disease. *The Neuroscientist, 15,* 317–323.

Courchesne, E., Campbell, K., & Solso, S. (2010). Brain growth across the life span in autism: Age-specific changes in anatomical pathology. *Brain Research.* doi: 10.1016/j.brainres.2010.09.101.

Courtney, K.E., & Polich, J. (2009). Binge drinking in young adults: Data, definitions, and determinants. *Psychological Bulletin, 135,* 142–156.

Covington, M., & Omelich, C.L. (1987). "I knew I could before the exam": A test of the anxiety-blockage hypothesis. *Journal of Educational Psychology, 79,* 393–400.

Cowan, N. (2001). The magical number 4 in short-term memory: a reconsideration of mental storage capacity. *Behavioral and Brain Sciences, 24,* 87–185.

Cowan, N., Nugent, L.D., Elliott, E.M., & Saults, J.S. (2000). Persistence of memory for ignored lists of digits: Areas of developmental constancy and change. *Journal of Experimental Child Psychology, 76,* 151–172.

Coyne, J.C., Stefanek, M., & Palmer, S.C. (2007). Psychotherapy and survival in cancer: The conflict between hope and evidence. *Psychological Bulletin, 133,* 367–394.

Craig, W.M., &Pepler, D.J. (2007). Understanding bullying: From research to practice. *Canadian Psychology/Psychologie canadienne, 48*(2), 86–93.

Craighead, W.E., Sheets, E.S., Bjornsson, A.S., & Arnarson, E.O. (2005). Specificity and Nonspecificity in Psychotherapy. *Clinical Psychology: Science and Practice, 12*(2), 189–193. doi:10.1093/clipsy/bpi024.

Craik, F.I.M. (1979). The structure and organization of memory. *Annual Review of Psychology, 30,* 63–102.

Craik, F.I.M., & Lockhart, R.S. (1972). Levels of processing: A framework for memory research. *Journal of Verbal Learning and Verbal Behavior, 11,* 671–684.

Craik, F.I.M., & Tulving, E. (1975). Depth of processing and the retention of words in episodic memory. *Journal of Experimental Psychology: General, 104,* 268–294.

Craske, M. (1999). *Anxiety disorders: Psychological approaches to theory and treatment.* Boulder, CO: Westview Press.

Craske, M.G., & Mystkowski, J.L. (2006). Exposure therapy and extinction: Clinical studies. In M.G. Craske & D. Hermanns, & D. Vansteenwegen (Eds.), *Fear and learning: From basic processes to clinical implications* (pp. 217–233). Washington, DC: American Psychological Association.

Crawford, M., & Chaffin, R. (1997). The meanings of difference: Cognition in social and cultural context. In P.J. Caplan, and M. Crawford (Eds.), *Gender difference in human cognition. Counterpoints: Cognition, memory, and language.* New York: Oxford University Press.

Crews, F. (1996). The verdict on Freud. *Psychological Science, 7*(2), 63–68.

Crews, F.C. (1998). *Unauthorized Freud: Doubters confront a legend.* New York: Viking.

Crits-Christoph, P., & Connolly, M.B. (1997). Measuring change in patients following psychological and pharmacological interventions: Anxiety disorders. In H.H. Strupp, L.M. Horowitz, M.J. Lambert, (Eds.), *Measuring patient changes in mood, anxiety, and personality disorders: Toward a core battery* (pp. 155–188). Washington, DC: American Psychological Association. doi:10.1037/10232-006.

Crits-Christoph, P., & Gibbons, M.B.C. (2009). The evaluation of psychological treatment. In M.C. Gelder, N.C. Andreasen, J.J. López- Ibor, Jr., & J.R. Geddes (Eds.), *New Oxford textbook of psychiatry* (2nd ed., Vol. 1). New York, NY: Oxford University Press.

Cross, S.E., & Markus, H. (1999). The cultural constitution of personality. In L.A. Pervin & O.P. John (Eds.), *Handbook of personality theory and research* (pp. 378–396). New York: Guilford Press.

Cross-Disorder Group of the Psychiatric Genomics Consortium. (2013, April 20–26). Identification of risk loci with shared effects on five major psychiatric disorders: A genome-wide analysis. *The Lancet, 381,* 1371–1379, http://dx.doi.org/10.1016/S0140-6736(12)62129-1. Retrieved from http://www.sciencedirect.com/science/article/pii/S0140673612621291.

Crowley, A.W., & Hoyer, W.D. (1994). An integrative framework for understanding two-sided persuasion, *Journal of Consumer Research, 20,* 561–574.

Crump, T. (2001). *A brief history of science.* New York: Carroll & Graf.

Crystal, J.D., Maxwell, K.W., & Hohmann, A.G. (2003). Cannabinoid modulation of sensitivity to time. *Behavioural Brain Research, 144*, 57–66.

Csíkszentmihályi, M. (1990). *Flow: The psychology of optimal experience.* New York: HarperPerennial.

Csíkszentmihályi, M. (1996). *Creativity: Flow and the psychology of discovery and invention.* New York: HarperCollins.

Cuijpers, P., van Straten, A., Hollon, S., & Andersson, G. (2010). The contribution of active medication to combined treatments of psychotherapy and pharmacotherapy for adult depression: A meta-analysis. *Acta Psychiatrica Scandinavica, 121*, 415–423. doi:10.1111/j.1600-0447.2009.01513.x

Cukor, J., Spitalnick, J., Difede, J., Rizzo, A., & Rothbaum, B.O. (2009). Emerging treatments for PTSD. *Clinical Psychology Review, 29*, 715–726.

Cummings, J.H., Bingham, S.A., Heaton, K.W., & Eastwood, M.A. (1992). Fecal weight, colon cancer risk, and dietary intake of nonstarch polysaccharides (dietary fiber). *Gastroenterology, 103*, 1783–1789.

Cunningham, M.R., Roberts, A.R., Barbee, A.P., Druen, P.B., & Wu, C-H. (1995). "Their ideas of beauty are, on the whole, the same as ours": Consistency and variability in the cross-cultural perception of female physical attractiveness. *Journal of Personality and Social Psychology, 68*, 261–279.

Cunningham, W.A., & Zelazo, P.D. (2006). Attitudes and evaluations: A social cognitive neuroscience perspective. *Trends in Cognitive Sciences, 11*, 97–104.

Curcio, G., Ferrara, M., & De Gennaro, L. (2006). Sleep loss, learning capacity and academic performance. *Sleep Medicine Reviews, 10*, 323–337.

Curtiss, S. (1977). *Genie: A psycholinguistic study of a modern-day wild child.* New York: Academic Press.

Cusack, C.L., Swahari, V., Hampton, H.W., Ramsey, J., & Deshmukh, M. (2013). Distinct pathways mediate axon degeneration during apoptosis and axon-specific pruning. *Nature Communications, 4*, 2013/05/21/online VL-4 SP-1876PB at http://dx.doi.org/10.1038/ncomms2910 L3-0.1038/ncomms2910.

Cussler, E.C., Going, S.B., Houtkooper, L.B., Stanford, V.A., Blew, R.M., Flint-Wagner, H.G., et al. (2005). Exercise frequency and calcium intake predict 4-year bone changes in postmenopausal women. *Osteoporosis International, 16*, 2129–2141.

Cutting, A.L., & Dunn, J. (2002). The cost of understanding other people: Social cognition predicts young children's sensitivity to criticism. *Journal of Child Psychology and Psychiatry, 43*, 849–860.

Cytowic, R.E. (1989). *Synaesthesia: A union of the senses.* New York: Springer-Verlag.

Czech, C., & Adessi, C. (2004). Disease modifying therapeutic strategies in Alzheimer's disease targeting the amyloid cascade. *Current Neuropharmacology, 2*, 295–307.

Dabbs, J.M., Jr., Carr, T.S., & Frady, R.L. (1995). Testosterone, crime, and misbehavior among 692 male prison inmates. *Personality and Individual Differences, 18*, 627–633.

Dabbs, J.M., Jr., & Hargrove, M.F. (1997). Age, testosterone, and behavior among female prison inmates. *Psychosomatic Medicine, 59*, 477–480.

Dabbs, J.M., Jr., & Mohammed, S. (1992). Male and female salivary testosterone concentrations before and after sexual activity. *Physiology & Behavior, 52*, 195–197.

Dacey, D.M. (2000). Parallel pathways for spectral coding in primate retina. *Annual Review of Neuroscience, 23*, 743–775.

Dale, P.S., Dionne, G., Eley, T.C., & Plomin, R. (2000). Lexical and grammatical development: A behavioural genetic perspective. *Journal of Child Language, 27*, 619–642.

Dallaire, D.H., Cole, D.A., Smith, T.M., Ciesla, J.A., LaGrange, B., Jacquez, F.M., et al. (2008). Predicting children's depressive symptoms from community and individual risk factors. *Journal of Youth and Adolescence, 37*, 830–846.

Dallman, M.F., Pecoraro, N.C., & la Fleur, S.E. (2005). Chronic stress and comfort foods: Self-medication and abdominal obesity. *Brain, Behavior, and Immunity, 19*, 275–280.

Damasio, A.R., (2000). *The feeling of what happens: Body and emotion in the making of consciousness.* Chicago: Harcourt.

Damjanovic, A.K., Yang, Y., Glaser, R., Kiecolt-Glaser, J.K., Nguyen, H., Laskowski, B., Zou, Y., Beversdorf, D.Q, & Weng, N. (2007). Accelerated telomere erosion is associated with a declining immune function of caregivers of Alzheimer's disease patients. *The Journal of Immunology, 179*, 4249–4254.

D'Anglejan, A. (1979). Solving problems in deductive reasoning: Three experimental studies of adult second language earners. *Working Papers on Bilingualism, No. 17.*

Dardeno, T.A., Chou, S.H., Moon, H.S., Chamberland, J.P., Fiorenza, C.G., & Mantzoros, C.S. (2010). Leptin in human physiology and therapeutics. *Frontiers in Neuroendocrinology, 31*, 377–93.

Darke, P.R., & Ritchie, R.J.B. (2007). The defensive consumer: Advertising deception, defensive processing, and distrust. *Journal of Marketing Research, 44*, 114–127.

Darley, J.M., & Batson, C.D. (1973). "From Jerusalem to Jericho": A study of situational and dispositional variables in helping behavior. *Journal of Personality and Social Psychology, 27*, 100–108.

Darley, J.M., & Latané, B. (1968). Bystander intervention in emergencies: Diffusion of responsibility. *Journal of Personality and Social Psychology, 8*, 377–383.

Darwin, C. (1859). *The origin of species by means of natural selection.* London: John Murray.

Darwin, C. (1998). *The expression of the emotions in man and animals.* New York: Oxford University Press. (Original work published 1872)

Das, J.P., Kirby, J.J., & Jarman, R.F. (1975). Simultaneous and successive synthesis: An alternative model for cognitive abilities. *Psychological Bulletin, 82*(1), 87–103.

Dasgupta, N., McGhee, D.E., Greenwald, A.G., & Banaji, M.R. (2000). Automatic preference for White Americans: Eliminating the familiarity explanation. *Journal of Experimental Social Psychology, 36*, 316–328.

Davidson, R.J. (1994). On emotion, mood, and related affective constructs. In P. Ekman & R.J. Davidson (Eds.), *The nature of emotion: Fundamental questions* (pp. 51–55). New York: Oxford University Press.

Davidson, R.J. (2001). Toward a biology of personality and emotion. *Annals of the New York Academy of Sciences, 935*, 191–207.

Davidson, R.J. (2004). What does the prefrontal cortex "do" in affect: Perspectives on frontal EEG asymmetry research. *Biological Psychology, 67*, 219–233.

Davidson, R.J., Ekman, P., Saron, C., Senulis, J., & Friesen, W.V. (1990). Approach withdrawal and cerebral asymmetry: Emotional expression and brain physiology I. *Journal of Personality and Social Psychology, 58*, 330–341.

Davidson, R.J., Kabat-Zinn, J., Schumacher, J., Rosenkranz, M., Muller, D., Santorelli, S.F., et al. (2003). Alterations in brain and immune function produced by mindfulness meditation. *Psychosomatic Medicine, 65*, 564–570.

Davis, J.I., Senghas, A., Brandt, F., & Ochsner, K.N. (2010). The effects of BOTOX injections on emotional experience. *Emotion, 10*(3), 433–440. doi: 10.1037/a0018690.

Davison, K.P., & Pennebaker, J.W. (2000). Who talks? *American Psychologist, 55*(2), 205.

Dawes, R.M. (1980). Social dilemmas. *Annual Review of Psychology, 31*, 169–193.

Dawes, R.M. (1991). Social dilemmas, economic self-interest, and evolutionary theory. In D.R. Brown & J.E. Keith Smith (Eds.), *Frontiers of mathematical psychology: Essays in honor of Clyde Coombs.* New York: Springer-Verlag.

Dawes, R.M., McTavish, J., & Shaklee, H. (1977). Behavior, communication, and assumptions about other people's behavior in a commons dilemma situation. *Journal of Personality and Social Psychology, 35,* 1–11.

Dawkins, R. (1989). *The selfish gene* (New ed.). New York: Oxford University Press.

Day, H.I. (1982). Curiosity and the interested explorer. *Performance and Instruction, 21,* 19–22.

Deacon, H. (2006). Bilingual children. *Literacy Today, 49,* 17.

Deacon, T. (1997). *Symbolic species: Coevolution of language and the brain.* New York: Norton.

de Almeida, L.P., Ross, C.A., Zala, D., Aebischer, P., & Déglon, N. (2002). Lentiviral-mediated delivery of mutant huntingtin in the striatum of rats induces a selective neuropathology modulated by polyglutamine repeat size, huntingtin expression levels, and protein length. *Journal of Neuroscience, 22,* 3473–3483.

Deary, I.J., Graham, T., Wilson, V., Starr, J.M., & Whalley, L.J. (2003). Population sex differences in IQ at age 11: The Scottish mental survey 1932. *Intelligence, 31,* 533–542.

Deary, J.J., Strand, S., Smith, P., & Fernandes, C. (2007). Intelligence and educational achievement. *Intelligence, 35,* 13–21.

DeCasper, A.J., & Fifer, W. (1980). Of human bonding: Newborns prefer their mothers' voices. *Science, 208,* 1174–1176.

DeCasper, A.J., & Spence, M.J. (1986). Prenatal maternal speech influences newborns' perception of speech sounds. *Infant Behavior & Development, 9,* 133–150.

Deci, E.L., & Ryan, R.M. (1985). *Intrinsic motivation and self-determination in human behavior.* New York: Plenum.

De Fruyt, F., & Murvielde, I. (1999). RAISEC types and Big Five traits as predictors of employment status and nature of employment. *Personnel Psychology, 52,* 701–727.

de Graaf-Peters, V.B., & Hadders-Algra, M. (2006). Ontogeny of the human central nervous system: What is happening when? *Early Human Development, 82,* 257–266.

de Graaf-Peters, V.B., & Hadders-Algra, M. (2006). Ontogeny of the human central nervous system: What is happening when? *Early Human Development, 82,* 257–266.

Deisseroth, K. (2010). Optogenetics. *Nature Methods, 8,* 26–29. doi: 10.1038/nmeth.f.324.

DeKeyser, R., & Larson-Hall, J. (2005). What does the critical period really mean? In J.F. Kroll & A.M.B. DeGroot (Eds.), *Handbook of bilingualism: Psycholinguistic approaches* (pp. 88–108). New York, NY: Oxford University Press.

Delaere, F., Magnan, C., & Mithieux, G. (2010). Hypothalamic integration of portal glucose signals and control of food intake and insulin sensitivity. *Diabetes and Metabolism, 36,* 257–262.

Delahanty, D.L., & Nugent, N.R. (2006). Predicting PTSD prospectively based on prior trauma history and immediate biological responses. *Annals of the NY Academy of Sciences, 1071,* 27–40.

De Lisa, R., & Wolford, J.L. (2002). Improving children's mental rotation accuracy with computer game playing. *The Journal of Genetic Psychology,* 163, 272–282.

DeLisi, M., Umphress, Z.R., & Vaughn, M.G. (2009). The criminology of the amygdala. *Criminal Justice and Behavior, 36,* 1241–1252.

Dell'Osso, B., Buoli, M., Baldwin, D.S., & Altamura, A.C. (2009). Serotonin norepinephrine reuptake inhibitors (SNRIs) in anxiety disorders: A comprehensive review of their clinical efficacy. *Human Psychopharmacology: Clinical & Experimental, 25,* 17–29.

DeLongis, A., Folkman, S., & Lazarus, R.S. (1988). The impact of daily stress on health and mood: Psychological and social resources as mediators. *Journal of Personality and Social Psychology, 54,* 486–495.

Dembroski, T.M., MacDougall, J.M., Williams, R.B., Haney, T.L., & Blumenthal, J.A. (1985). Components of Type A, hostility, and anger-in: relationship to angiographic findings. *Psychosomatic Medicine, 47,* 219–233.

Dement, W. (1999). *The promise of sleep.* New York: Delacorte Press.

Dement, W., & Kleitman, N. (1957). The relation of eye movements during sleep to dream activity: An objective method for the study of dreaming. *Journal of Experimental Psychology, 53,* 339–346.

Demir, E., & Dickson, B.J. (2005). *Fruitless* splicing specifies male courtship behavior in *Drosophila. Cell, 121,* 785–794.

De Neys, W., Vartanian, O., & Goel, V. (2008). Smarter than we think: When our brains detect that we are biased. *Psychological Science, 19,* 483–489.

Derbyshire, S.W.G., Whalley, M.G., Stenger, A., & Oakley, D.A. (2004). Cerebral activation during hypnotically induced and imagined pain. *Neuroimage, 23,* 392–401.

Derry, G. (1999). *What is science and how it works.* Princeton: Princeton University Press.

Derryberry, D., & Tucker, D.M. (1994). Motivating the focus of attention. In P.M. Niedenthal & S. Kitayama (Eds.), *The heart's eye: Emotional influences in perception and attention* (pp. 167–196). San Diego, CA: Academic Press.

DeRubeis, R.J., Hollon, S., Amsterdam, J., Shelton, R., Young, P., Salomon, R., et al. (2005). Cognitive therapy vs medications in the treatment of moderate to severe depression. *Archives of General Psychiatry, 62*(4), 409–416.

Desmedt, A., Garcia, R., & Jaffard, R. (1999). Differential modulation of changes in hippocampal-septal synaptic excitability by the amygdala as a function of either elemental or contextual fear conditioning in mice. *Journal of Neuroscience, 18,* 480–487.

Devilbiss, D.M., & Berridge, C.W. (2008). Cognition-enhancing doses of methylphenidate preferentially increase prefrontal cortex neuronal responsiveness. *Biological Psychiatry, 64,* 626–635.

Devine, P. (1989). Stereotypes and prejudice: Their automatic and controlled components. *Journal of Personality and Social Psychology, 56,* 5–18.

de Vries, A.C., Kreukels, B.C., Steensma, T.D., & McGuire, J.K. (2014). Gender identity development: A biopsychosocial perspective. In B.C. Kreukels, T.D. Steensma, A.C.de Vries, B.C. Kreukels, T.D. Steensma, A.C. de Vries (Eds.) , *Gender dysphoria and disorders of sex development: Progress in care and knowledge* (pp. 53–80). New York, NY, US: Springer Science + Business Media. doi:10.1007/978-1-4614-7441-8_3.

de Waal, F.B.M., & Suchak, M. (2010). Prosocial primates: Selfish and unselfish motivations. *Philosophical Transactions of the Royal Society of London B, 365,* 2711–2722.

DeWall, C.N., MacDonald, G., Webster, G.D., Masten, C.L., Baumeister, R.F., Powell, C., . . . Eisenberger, N.I. (2010). Acetaminophen reduces social pain: Behavioral and neural evidence. *Psychological Science, 21,* 931–937.

de Win, M.M.L., Reneman, L., Reitsma, J.B., den Heeten, G.J., Booij, J., & van den Brink, W. (2004). Mood disorders and serotonin transporter density in ecstasy users—the influence of long-term abstention, dose, and gender. *Psychopharmacology, 173,* 376–382.

Dezutter, J., Wiesmann, U., Apers, S., & Luyckx, K. (2013). Sense of coherence, depressive feelings and life satisfaction in older persons: a closer look at the role of integrity and despair. *Aging & Mental Health, 17*(7), 839–843. doi:10.1080/13607863.2013.792780.

Dhabhar, F.S. (2014). Effects of stress on immune function: The good, the bad, and the beautiful. *Immunologic Research, 58;* 193–210.

Dhabhar, F.S., Saul, A.N., Daugherty, C., Holmes, T.H., Bouley, D.M., & Oberyszyn, T.M. (2010). Short-term stress enhances cellular immunity and increases early resistance to squamous cell carcinoma. *Brain, Behavior, & Immunity, 24;* 127–37.

Diamond, L.M. (2008). Female bisexuality from adolescence to adulthood: Results from a 10-year longitudinal study. *Developmental Psychology,* 44, 5–14.

Diener, E., & Seligman, M.E.P. (2004). Beyond money toward an economy of well-being. *Psychological Science, 5,* 1–31.

Diener, E., Suh, E.M., Lucas, R.E., & Smith, H.L. (1999). Subjective well-being: Three decades of progress. *Psychological Bulletin, 125,* 276–302.

Dietrich, K., Succop, P., Berger, O., & Hammond, P. (1991). Lead exposure and the cognitive development of urban preschool children: The Cincinnati Lead Study cohort at age 4 years. *Neurotoxicology and Teratology, 13*(2), 203–211.

Digman, J.M. (1990). Personality structure: Emergence of the Five-Factor Model. *Annual Review in Psychology, 41,* 417–440.

Dimberg, U., & Söderkvist, S. (2011). The voluntary facial action technique: A method to test the facial feedback hypothesis. *Journal of Nonverbal Behavior, 35,* 17–33.

Dingemanse, N.J., Both, C., Drent, P.J., Van Oers, K., & Van Noordwijk, A.J. (2002). Repeatability and heritability of exploratory behaviour in great tits from the wild. *Animal Behaviour, 64,* 929–938.

DiPietro, J.A., Hodgson, D.M., Costigan, K.A., & Johnson, T.R.B. (1996). Fetal antecedents of infant temperament. *Child Development, 67,* 2568–2583.

Dixon, R.A., Garrett, D.D., Lentz, T.L., MacDonald, S.S., Strauss, E., & Hultsch, D.F. (2007). Neurocognitive markers of cognitive impairment: Exploring the roles of speed and inconsistency. *Neuropsychology, 21*(3), 381–399.

Do, Y.K., Norton, E.C., Stearns, S., & Van Houtven, C.H. (2015). Informal care and caregiver's health. *Health Economics, 24,* 224–237.

Dobbs, D. (2006). Turning off depression. *Scientific American Mind,* 2006, *17,* 26–31.

Dobbs, D. (2006, April 2). A depression switch? *New York Times Magazine.* Retrieved from http://www.nytimes.com.

Dodou, D., & de Winter, J.C.F. (2014). Social desirability is the same in offline, online, and paper surveys: A meta-analysis. *Computers in Human Behavior, 36,* 487–495.

Doetsch, F., & Scharff, C. (2001). Challenges for brain repair: Insights from adult neurogenesis in birds and mammals. *Brain, Behavior & Evolution, 58,* 306–322.

Doidge, N. (2007). *The brain that changes itself: Stories of personal triumph from the frontiers of brain science.* New York: Penguin.

Dolcos, F., LaBar, K.S., & Cabeza, R. (2005). Remembering one year later: Role of the amygdala and the temporal lobe memory system in retrieving emotional memories. *Proceedings of the National Academy Sciences, 102,* 2626–2631.

Dolinoy, D., & Jirtle, R.L. (2008). Environmental epigenomics in human health and disease. *Environmental and Molecular Mutagenesis, 49,* 4–8.

Doll, R., Peto, R., Boreham, J., & Sutherland, I. (2004). Mortality in relation to smoking: 50 years' observations on male British doctors. *British Medical Journal, 328,* 1519–1528.

Domhoff, G.W. (2001). A new neuro-cognitive theory of dreams. *Dreaming, 11,* 13–33.

Dominguez, J.M., & Hull, E.M. (2005). Dopamine, the medial preoptic area, and male sexual behavior. *Physiology and Behavior, 86,* 356–368.

Donn, J.E., & Sherman, R.C. (2002). Attitudes and practices regarding the formation of romantic relationships on the Internet. *CyberPsychology & Behavior, 5,* 107–122.

Doty, R.L., Applebaum, S., Zusho, H., & Settle, R.G. (1985). Sex differences in odor identification ability: A cross-cultural analysis. *Neuropsychologia, 23,* 667–672.

Doupe, A.J., & Kuhl, P.K. (1999). Birdsong and human speech. *Annual Review of Neuroscience, 22,* 567–631.

Dresler, T., Guhn, A., Tupak, S.V., Ehlis, A., Herrmann, M.J., Fallgatter, A.J., . . . Domschke, K. (2013). Revise the revised? New dimensions of the neuroanatomical hypothesis of panic disorder. *Journal of Neural Transmission, 120*(1), 3-29. doi:10.1007/s00702-012-0811-1.

Drevets, W.C., Price, J.L., Simpson, J.R., Todd, R.D., Reich, T., Vannier, M., et al. (1997). Subgenual prefrontal cortex abnormalities in mood disorders. *Nature, 386,* 824–827.

D'Souza, J.F., Adams, C.K., & Fuss, B. (2015). A pilot study of self-actualization activity measurement. *Journal of the Indian Academy of Applied Psychology, 41,* 28–33.

Dubai, Y. (2004). The neurobiology of consolidations, or, How stable is the engram? *Annual Review of Psychology, 55,* 51–86.

Dufresne, T. (2003). *Killing Freud: 20th century culture and the death of psychoanalysis.* New York: Continuum.

Dunbar, R. (1996). *Grooming, gossip and the evolution of language.* London: Faber & Faber.

Dunbar, R.I.M. (2001). Brains on two legs: Group size and the evolution of intelligence. In F.B.M. deWaal (Ed.), *Tree of origin: What primate behavior can tell us about human social evolution* (pp. 173–191). Cambridge, MA: Harvard University Press.

Duncan, J., Seitz, R.J., Koldny, J., Bor, D., Herzog, H., Ahmed, A., et al. (2000). A neural basis for general intelligence. *Science, 289,* 457–460.

Duncan, S.C., Duncan, T.E., & Strycker, L.A. (2006). Alcohol use from ages 9 to 16: A cohort-sequential latent growth model. *Drug and Alcohol Dependence, 81,* 71–81.

Duncker, K. (1945). On problem-solving. *Psychological Monographs, 58,* ix. (Whole No. 270).

Duncko, R., Johnson, L., Merikangas, K., & Grillon, C. (2009). Working memory performance after acute exposure to the cold pressor stress in healthy volunteers. *Neurobiology of Learning and Memory, 91,* 377–381.

Dunham, Y., Baron, A.S., & Banaji, M.R. (2006). From American city to Japanese village: A cross-cultural investigation of implicit race attitudes. *Child Development, 77,* 1268–1281.

Dunn, E.W., Aknin, L.B., & Norton, M.I. (2008). Spending money on others promotes happiness. *Science, 319,* 1687–1688.

Dunn, E.W., Aknin, L.B., & Norton, M.I. (2008). Spending money on others promotes happiness. *Science, 319,* 1687–1688.

Dura, J.R., Haywood-Niler, E., & Kiecolt-Glaser, J.K. (1990). Spousal caregivers of persons with Alzheimer's and Parkinson's disease dementia: A preliminary comparison. *The Gerontologist, 30,* 332–336.

Durlak, J.A., Taylor, R.D., Kawashima, K., Pachan, M.K., DuPre, E.P., Celio, C.I., et al. (2007). Effects of positive youth development programs on school, family, and community systems. *American Journal of Community Psychology, 39,* 269–286.

Dvir, Y., & Smallwood, P. (2008). Serotonin syndrome: A complex but easily avoidable condition. *General Hospital Psychiatry, 30,* 284–287.

Dye, M.W.G., & Bavelier, D. (2004). Playing video games enhances visual attention in children. *Journal of Vision, 4,* 40A.

Eagly, A.H., & Chaiken, S. (1975). An attribution analysis of the effect of communicator characteristics on opinion change: The case of communicator attractiveness. *Journal of Personality and Social Psychology, 32,* 136–144.

Eagly, A.H., & Chaiken, S. (1998). Attitude structure and function. In D.T. Gilbert, S.T. Fiske, & G. Lindzey (Eds.), *The handbook of social psychology* (4th ed., Vol. 1, pp. 269–322). New York: McGraw-Hill.

Eastwick, P.W., Finkel, E.J., Mochon, D., & Ariely, D. (2007). Selective versus unselective romantic desire: Not all reciprocity is created equal. *Psychological Science, 18,* 317–319.

Ebstein, R.P. (2006). The molecular genetic architecture of human personality: Beyond self-report questionnaires. *Molecular Psychiatry, 11,* 427–445.

Edelman, S., Lemon, J., Bell, D.R., & Kidman, A.D. (1999). Effects of group CBT on the survival time of patients with metastatic breast cancer. *Psychooncology, 8,* 474–481.

Edmonds, C.V., Lockwood, G.A., & Cunningham, A.J. (1999). Psychological response to long-term therapy: A randomized trial with metastatic breast cancer patients. *Psychooncology, 8,* 74–91.

Edwards, J.H. (2002). Evidenced-based treatment for child ADHD: "Real-world" practice implications. *Journal of Mental Health Counseling, 24,* 126–139.

Edwards, V.J., Holden, G.W., Felitti, V.J., & Anda, R.F. (2003). Relationship between multiple forms of childhood maltreatment and adult mental health in community respondents: Results from the adverse childhood experiences study. *American Journal of Psychiatry, 160,* 1453–1460.

Eisenberger, N. (2013). Social ties and health: A social neuroscience perspective. *Current Opinion in Neurobiology, 23,* 407–413.

Eisenberger, N.I., Jarcho, J.M., Lieberman, M.D., & Naliboff, B.D. (2006). An experimental study of shared sensitivity to physical pain and social rejection. *Pain, 126,* 132–138.

Eisenberger, N.I., Lieberman, M.D., & Williams, K.D. (2003). Does rejection hurt? An fMRI study of social exclusion. *Science, 203,* 290–292.

Ekman, P. (1972). Universals and cultural differences in facial expressions of emotion. In J. Cole (Ed.), *Nebraska Symposium on Motivation 1971, Vol. 19* (pp. 207–283). Lincoln, NE: University of Nebraska Press.

Ekman, P. (1973). Cross-cultural studies of facial expression. In *Darwin and facial expression: A century of research in review* (pp. 169–222). New York: Academic Press.

Ekman, P. (1984). Expression and the nature of emotion. In K.R. Scherer & P. Ekman (Eds.), *Approaches to emotion* (pp. 319–343). Hillsdale, NJ: Lawrence Erlbaum.

Ekman, P., Davidson. R.J., & Friesen, W.V. (1990). The Duchenne smile: Emotional expression and brain physiology II. *Journal of Personality and Social Psychology, 58,* 342–353.

Ekman, P., & Friesen, W.V. (1969). The repertoire of nonverbal behavior—categories, origins, usage, and coding. *Semiotica, 1,* 49–98.

Ekman, P., & Friesen, W.V. (1971). Constants across cultures in the face and emotion. *Journal of Personality and Social Psychology, 17,* 124–129.

Ekman, P., & Friesen, W.V. (1978). *The facial action coding system.* Palo Alto, CA: Consulting Psychologist's Press.

Ekman, P., Friesen, W.V., & Hager, J. (2002). *The Facial Action Coding System* (2nd ed.). Salt Lake City, UT: Research Nexus.

Ekman, P., Friesen, W.V., O'Sullivan, M., Chan, A., Diacoyanni-Tarlatzis, I., Heider, K., et al. (1987). Universals and cultural differences in the judgments of facial expressions of emotion. *Journal of Personality and Social Psychology, 53,* 712–717.

Ekman, P., Levenson, R.W., & Friesen, W.V. (1983). Autonomic nervous system activity distinguishes among emotions. *Science, 221,* 1208–1210.

Ekman, P., & O'Sullivan, M. (1991). Who can catch a liar? *American Psychologist, 46,* 913–920.

Ekman, P., O'Sullivan, M., & Frank, M.G. (1999). A few can catch a liar. *Psychological Science, 10,* 263–266.

Ekman, P., & Rosenberg, E.L. (Eds.). (2005). *What the face reveals: Basic and applied studies of spontaneous facial expression using the Facial Action Coding System (FACS)* (2nd ed.). New York: Oxford University Press.

Ekman, P., Sorenson, E.R., & Friesen, W.V. (1969). Pan-cultural elements in facial displays of emotion. *Science, 164,* 86–88.

Elbert, T., Pantev, C., Wienbruch, C., Rockstroh, B., & Taub, E. (1995). Increased cortical representation of the fingers of the left hand in string players. *Science, 270,* 305–307.

Elder, G.A., Gama Sosa, M.A., De Gasperi, R. (2010). Transgenic mouse models of Alzheimer's disease. *Mount Sinai Journal of Medicine, 77,* 69–81.

Elder, S. (2014, July 27). A Korean couple let a baby die while they played a video game. *Newsweek.* Retrieved from http://www.newsweek.com/2014/08/15/korean-couple-let-baby-die-while-they-played-video-game-261483.html.

Ellason, J.W., Ross, C.A., & Fuchs, D.L. (1996). Lifetime Axis I and Axis II comorbidity and childhood trauma history in dissociative identity disorder. *Psychiatry, 59,* 255–266.

Elliot, J. (2006). Jane Elliot's blue eyes brown eyes exercise. Retrieved Nov. 1, 2010, from http://www.janeelliott.com/.

Elliott, R. (2002). The effectiveness of humanistic therapies: A meta-analysis. In D.J. Cain (Ed.), *Humanistic psychotherapies: Handbook of research and practice* (pp. 57–81). Washington, DC, US: American Psychological Association. doi:10.1037/10439-002.

Ellis, E., & Ames, M.A. (1987). Neurohormonal functioning and sexual orientation: A theory of heterosexuality–homosexuality. *Psychological Bulletin, 101,* 233–258.

Ellsworth, P.C., & Smith, C.A. (1988). Shades joy: Patterns of appraisal differentiating pleasant emotions. *Cognition & Emotion, 2,* 301–331.

Elman, J.L., Bates, E.A., Johnson, M.H., Karmiloff-Smith, A., Parisi, D., & Plunkett, K. (1996). *Rethinking innateness: A connectionist perspective on development.* Cambridge, MA: MIT Press.

Elms, A. (1993). *Uncovering lives: The uneasy alliance between biography and psychology.* New York: Oxford University Press.

Elzinga, B.M., Van Dyck, R., & Spinhoven, P. (1998). Three controversies about dissociative identity disorder. *Clinical Psychology & Psychotherapy, 5*(1), 13–23.

Emery, B., & Barres, B.A. (2008). Unlocking CNS cell type heterogeneity. *Cell, 135,* 596–98.

Emmelkamp, P.M.G. (2004). Behaviour therapy with adults. In M.J. Lambert (Ed.), *Bergin and Garfield's handbook of psychotherapy and behavior change* (5th ed., pp. 393–446). Hoboken, NJ: Wiley.

Emmons, R.A., & McCullough, M.E. (2003). Counting blessings versus burdens: An experimental investigation of gratitude and subjective well-being in daily life. *Journal of Personality and Social Psychology, 84,* 377–389. doi:10.1037/0022-3514.84.2.377.

Empana, J.P., Sykes, D.H., Luc, G., Juhan-Vague, I., Arveiler, D., Ferrieres, J., et al. (2005). Contributions of depressive mood and circulating inflammatory markers to coronary heart disease in healthy European men: The Prospective Epidemiological Study of Myocardial Infarction (PRIME). *Circulation, 111,* 2299–2305.

Employment and Social Development Canada. (2015). Learning—educational attainment. In *Indicators of well-being in Canada.* Retrieved from http://www4.hrsdc.gc.ca/.3ndic.1t.4r@-eng.jsp?iid=29.

Endo, T., Schwierin, B., Borbely, A.A., & Tobler, I. (1997). Selective and total sleep deprivation: Effect on the sleep EEG in the rat. *Psychology Research, 66,* 97–110.

Enzinger, C., Fazekas, F., Matthews, P.M., Ropele, S., Schmidt, H., Smith, S., et al. (2005). Risk factors for progression of brain atrophy in aging: Six-year follow-up of normal subjects. *Neurology, 64,* 1704–1711.

Epel, E.S., Blackburn, E.H., Lin, J., Dhabhar, F.S., Adler, N.E., & Morrow, J.D. (2004). Accelerated telomere shortening in response to life stress. *Proceedings of the National Academy of Sciences, 101,* 17312–17315.

Epel, E.S., Lin, J., Wilhelm, F.H., Wolkowitz, O.M., Cawthon, R., Adler, N.E., et al. (2006). Cell aging in relation to stress arousal and cardiovascular disease risk factors. *Psychoneuroendocrinology, 31,* 277–287.

Epel, E.S., McEwen, B., Seeman, T., Matthews, K., Castellazzo, G., Brownell, K.D., et al. (2000). Stress and body shape:

Stress-induced cortisol secretion is consistently greater among women with central fat. *Psychosomatic Medicine, 62,* 623–632.

Ericksen, J.A. (1998). With enough cases, why do you need statistics? Revisiting Kinsey's methodology. *The Journal of Sex Research, 35*(2), 132–140. Retrieved from http://www.jstor.org/stable/3813665.

Erikson, E. (1963). *Childhood and society.* New York: Norton.

Erikson, E. (1968). *Identity: Youth and crisis.* New York: Norton.

Erikson, E. (1982). *The life-cycle completed: A review.* New York: Norton.

Eriksson, P.S., Perfilieva, E., Bjork-Eriksson, T., Alborn, A.M., Nordborg, C., Peterson, D.A., et al. (1998). Neurogenesis in the adult human hippocampus. *Nature Medicine, 4,* 1313–1317.

Estes, R.E., Coston, M.L., & Fournet, G.P. (1990). *Rankings of the most notable psychologists by department chairpersons.* Unpublished manuscript.

Etcoff, N. (1999). *Survival of the prettiest.* New York: Anchor Books.

Evans, R.L. (1973). *Jean Piaget: The man and his ideas.* New York: E.P. Dutton & Co., Inc.

Evans, S., Ferrando, S., Findler, M., Stowell, C., Smart, C., & Haglin, D. (2008). Mindfulness-based cognitive therapy for generalized anxiety disorder. *Journal of Anxiety Disorders, 22,* 716–721.

Evans, S.C., Reed, G.M., Roberts, M.C., Esparza, P., Watts, A.D., Correia, J.M., & . . . Saxena, S. (2013). Psychologists' perspectives on the diagnostic classification of mental disorders: Results from the WHO-IUPsyS Global Survey. *International Journal of Psychology, 48*(3), 177–193.

Everett, D.L. (2005). Cultural constraints on grammar and cognition in Piraha: Another look at the design features of human language. *Current Anthropology, 46,* 621–646.

Everson, C.A., Bergmann, B.M., & Rechtschaffen, A. (1989). Sleep deprivation in the rat: III. Total sleep deprivation. *Sleep,12,* 13–21.

Exaptations. (2006). Retrieved November 28, 2007, from http://evolution.berkeley.edu/evosite/evo101/IIIE5cExaptations.shtml.

Exner, J.E., Jr. (1974). *The Rorschach: A comprehensive system.* New York: Wiley.

Eysenck, H.J. (1947). *Dimensions of personality.* London: Routledge & Kegan Paul.

Eysenck, H.J. (1982). *Personality, genetics, and behavior: Selected papers.* New York: Praeger.

Eysenck, H.J. (1990). Biological dimensions of personality. In L.A. Pervin (Ed.), *Handbook of personality: Theory and research* (pp. 244–276). New York: Guilford Press.

Eysenck, H.J. (1994b). *Test your IQ.* Toronto: Penguin Books.

Eysenck, H.J. (1995). *Genius: The natural history of creativity.* Cambridge: Cambridge University Press.

Eysenck, H.J. (1997). Personality and experimental psychology: The unification of psychology and the possibility of a paradigm. *Journal of Personality and Social Psychology, 73,* 1224–1237.

Eysenck, M.W. (1994a). Intelligence. In M.W. Eysenck, (Ed.), *The Blackwell dictionary of cognitive psychology* (pp. 192–193). Cambridge, MA: Blackwell Publishers.

Facione, P.A. (1990). *Critical thinking: A statement of expert consensus for purposes of educational assessment and instruction—The Delphi report.* Millbrae, CA: California Academic Press.

Fallgatter, A.J., Ehlis, A.-C., Herrmann, M.J., Hohoff, C., Reif, A., Freitag, C.M., & Deckert, J. (2010). DTNBP1 (dysbindin) gene variants modulate prefrontal brain function in schizophrenic patients—Support for the glutamate hypothesis of schizophrenias. *Genes, Brain and Behavior, 9,* 489–497.

Famy, C., Streissguth, A.P., & Unis, A.S. (1998). Psychological disorder in adults with fetal alcohol syndrome or fetal alcohol effects. *Journal of Pediatric Psychology, 155,* 552–554.

Fancher, R.E. (1985). *The intelligence men: Makers of the IQ controversy.* New York: Norton.

Fancher, R.E. (1996). *Pioneers of psychology* (3rd ed.). New York: Norton.

Fancher, R.E. (2009). The relationship between Charles Darwin and Francis Galton. *American Psychologist, 64,* 84–92.

Fantz, R.L. (1961). The origin of form perception. *Scientific American, 204*(5), 66–72. doi:10.1038/scientificamerican0561-66.

Fantz, R.L. (1963). Pattern vision in newborn infants. *Science, 140,* 296–297.

Farah, M.J., Shera, D.M., Savage, J.H., Betancourt, L., Giannetta, J.M., Brodsky, N.L., . . . Hurt, H. (2006). Childhood poverty: Specific associations with neurocognitive development. *Brain Research, 1110*(1), 166–174. doi:10.1016/j.brainres.2006.06.072.

Farb, N., Anderson, A., Mayberg, H., Bean, J., McKeon, D., & Segal, Z. (2010). Minding one's emotions: Mindfulness training alters the neural expression of sadness. *Emotion, 10,* 25–33. doi: 10.1037/a0017151.

Farber, N.B., & Olney, J.W. (2003). Drugs of abuse that cause developing neurons to commit suicide. *Developmental Brain Research, 147,* 37–45.

Farré, M., Terán, M.T., Roset, P.N., Mas, M., Torrens, M., Camí, J. (1998). Abuse liability of flunitrazepam among methadone-maintained patients. *Psychopharmacology, 140,* 486–495.

Fazel, S., & Danesh, J. (2002). Serious mental disorder in 23,000 prisoners: A systematic review of 62 surveys. *Lancet, 359,* 545–550.

Fehr, B., & Broughton, R. (2001). Gender and personality differences in conceptions of love: An interpersonal theory analysis. *Personal Relationships, 8;* 115–136.

Feinberg, I., Maloney, T., & March, J.D. (1992). Precise conservation of NREM period 1 (NREMP1) across naps and nocturnal sleep: Implications for REM latency and NREM/REM alternation. *Sleep, 15,* 400–403.

Feist, G.J. (1999). Personality in scientific and artistic creativity. In R.J. Sternberg (Ed.), *Handbook of human creativity* (pp. 273–296). Cambridge: Cambridge University Press.

Feist, G.J. (2004). Creativity and the frontal lobes. *Bulletin of Psychology and the Arts, 5,* 21–28.

Feist, G.J. (in press). Affective state and traits in creativity: Evidence for non-linear relationships. In M. Runco (Ed.). *Creativity research handbook* (Vol. 3). Cresskill, NJ: Hampton Press.

Feist, G.J., & Barron, F.X. (2003). Predicting creativity from early to late adulthood: Intellect, potential and personality. *Journal of Research in Personality, 37,* 62–88.

Feist, G.J., Bodner, T.E., Jacobs, J.F., Miles, M., & Tan, V. (1995). Integrating top-down and bottom-up structural models of subjective well-being: A longitudinal investigation. *Journal of Personality and Social Psychology, 68,* 138–150.

Feist, J., & Feist, G.J. (2009). *Theories of personality* (7th ed.). New York: McGraw-Hill.

Feldman, D.H. (2004). Child prodigies: A distinctive form of giftedness. In R.J. Sternberg (Ed.), *Definition and conceptions of giftedness* (pp. 133–144). Thousand Oaks, CA: Corwin Press.

Feldman, R.S., Quenzer, J.S., & Meyer, L.F. (1997). *Principles of neuropsychopharmacology.* Sunderland MA: Sinauer Associates.

Feldman-Barrett, L., Tugade, M.M., & Engle, R.W. (2004). Individual differences in working memory capacity and dualprocess theories of mind. *Psychological Bulletin, 130,* 553–573.

Feng, X., Shaw, D.S., Kovacs, M., Lane, T., O'Rourke, F.E., & Alarcon, J.H. (2008). Emotion regulation in preschoolers: The roles of behavioral inhibition, maternal affective behavior, and maternal depression. *Journal of Child Psychology and Psychiatry, 49,* 132–141.

Feng, Z., Hu, W., Hu, Y., & Teng, M. (2006). Acrolein is a major cigarette-related lung cancer agent: Preferential binding at *p53* mutational hotspots and inhibition of DNA repair. *Proceedings of the National Academy of Sciences, 103,* 15404–15409.

Fenson, L., Dale, P., Reznick, J.S., Bates, E., Thal, D.J., & Pethick, S. (1994). Variability in early communicative development. *Monographs of the Society for Research in Child Development, 59* (5, Serial No. 242).

Ferguson, C.J., & Kilburn, J. (2009). The public health risks of media violence: A meta-analytic review. *Journal of Pediatrics, 154,* 759–763.

Ferguson, C.J., & Kilburn, J. (2010). Much ado about nothing: The misestimation and overinterpretation of violent video game effects in Eastern and Western nations: Comment on Anderson et al. (2010). *Psychological Bulletin, 136,* 174–178.

Fergusson, D., Doucette, S., Glass, K.C., Shapiro, S., Healy, D., Hebert, P., et al. (2005). Association between suicide attempts and selective serotonin reuptake inhibitors: Systematic review of randomized controlled trials. *British Medical Journal, 330,* 396–402.

Fergusson, L., Horwood, J., & Ridder, E.M. (2005). Tests of causal linkages between cannabis use and psychotic symptoms. *Addiction, 100,* 354–366.

Fernald, A., & Morikawa, H. (1993). Common themes and cultural variations in Japanese and American mothers' speech to infants. *Child Development, 64,* 637–656.

Fernandez-Espejo, D., Junque, C., Bernabeu, M., Roig-Rovira, T., Vendrell, P., & Mercader, J.M. (2010). Reductions of thalamic volume and regional shape changes in the vegetative and the minimally conscious states. *Journal of Neurotrauma, 27*(7), 1187–1193.

Ferster, C.B., & Skinner, B.F. (1957). *Schedules of reinforcement.* Englewood Cliffs, NJ: Prentice-Hall.

Festinger, L. (1957). *A theory of cognitive dissonance.* Stanford, CA: Stanford University.

Festinger, L., & Carlsmith, J.M. (1959). Cognitive consequences of forced compliance. *Journal of Abnormal and Social Psychology, 58,* 203–210.

Fiedorowicz, J., & Swartz, K. (2004). The role of monoamine oxidase inhibitors in current psychiatric practice. *Journal of Psychiatric Practice, 10,* 239–248.

Field, T.M., Hernandez-Reif, M., Diego, M., Feijo, L., Vera, Y., & Gil, K. (2004). Massage therapy by parents improves early growth and development. *Infant Behavior and Development, 27,* 435–442.

Field, T.M., Schanberg, S.M., Scafidi, F., Bauer, C.R., Vega-Lahr, N., Garcia, R., et al. (1986). Tactile/kinesthetic stimulation effects on preterm neonates. *Pediatrics, 77,* 654–658.

Fields, H.L. (2005). *Pain: Mechanisms and management.* New York: McGraw-Hill.

Fields, R.D. (2005). Making memories stick. *Scientific American, 292,* 75–81.

Fields, R.D. (2008). White matter matters. *Scientific American, 298,* 54–61.

Filimon, F., Nelson, J.D., Hagler, D.J., & Sereno, M.I. (2007). Human cortical representations for reaching: Mirror neurons for execution, observation, and imagery. *NeuroImage, 37,* 1315–1328.

Finger, S. (1994). *Origins of neuroscience: A history of explorations into brain function.* New York: Oxford University Press.

Fink, A., Slamar-Halbedl, M., Unterrainer, H.F., & Weiss, E.M. (2012). Creativity: Genius, madness, or a combination of both? *Psychology of Aesthetics, Creativity, and the Arts, 6,* 11–18. doi: 10.1037/a0024874

Fink, M. (2006). ECT in therapy-resistant mania: Does it have a place? *Bipolar Disorders, 8,* 307–309.

Finke, R.A., Ward, T.B., & Smith, S.M. (1992). *Creative cognition: Theory, research and applications.* Cambridge, MA: MIT Press.

Finkel, E.J., Eastwick, P.W., Karney, B.R., Reis, H.T., & Sprecher, S. (2012). Online dating: A critical analysis from the perspective of psychological science. *Psychological Science in the Public Interest (Sage Publications Inc.), 13*(1), 3–66. doi:10.1177/1529100612436522.

Finnerty, G.T., Roberts, L.S.E., & Connors, B.W. (1999). Sensory experience modifies the short-term dynamics of neocortical synapses. *Nature, 400,* 367–371.

Finzi, E., & Rosenthal, N.E. (2014). Treatment of depression with onabotulinumtoxinA: A randomized, double-blind, placebo controlled trial. *Journal of Psychiatric Research, 52,* 1–6.

Fischer, A.H., & Manstead, A.S.R. (2000). Gender differences in emotion across cultures. In A.H. Fischer (Ed.), *Emotion and gender: Social psychological perspectives* (pp. 91–97). London: Cambridge University Press.

Fischer, G.G. (2004). Should I order an EEG? An overview of electro encephalography in the hospital setting at Gundersen Lutheran Medical Center. *Gundersen Lutheran Medical Journal, 3,* 26–29.

Fisher, J.E., Mohanty, A., Herrington, J.D., Koven, N.S., Miller, G.A., & Heller, W. (2004). Neuropsychological evidence for dimensional schizotypy: Implications for creativity and psychopathology. *Journal of Research in Personality, 38,* 24–31.

Fisher, S., & Greenberg, R.P. (1996). *Freud scientifically reappraised: Testing the theories and therapy.* Oxford, England: John Wiley & Sons.

Fitzgerald, K.D., Welsh, R.C., Gehrig, W.J., Abelson, J.L., Himle, J.A., Liberzon, I., et al. (2005). Error-related hyperactivity of the anterior cingulated cortex in obsessive-compulsive disorder. *Biological Psychiatry, 57,* 287–294.

Fitzgerald, M. (2004). *Autism and creativity.* Hove, England: Brunner-Routledge.

Fitzgerald, P.B., Benitez, J., de Castella, A.R., Daskalakis, Z.J., & Kulkarni, J. (2006). Naturalistic study of the use of transcranial magnetic stimulation in the treatment of depressive relapse. *Australian and New Zealand Journal of Psychiatry, 40,* 764–768.

Flaherty, M. (2005). Gender differences in mental rotation ability in three cultures: Ireland, Ecuador and Japan. *Psychologia: An International Journal of Psychology in the Orient, 48,* 31–38.

Flammer, E., & Bongartz, W. (2003). On the efficacy of hypnosis: A meta-analytic study. *Contemporary Hypnosis, 20,* 179–197.

Flavell, J.H. (1996). Piaget's legacy. *Psychological Science, 7,* 200–203.

Flege, J.E. (1999). Age of learning and second language speech. In D. Birdsong (Ed.), *Second language acquisition and the critical period hypothesis* (pp. 101–131). Mahwah, NJ: Erlbaum.

Flege, J.E., Munro, M.J., & MacKay, I.R.A. (1995a). Effects of age of second-language learning on the production of English consonants. *Speech Communication, 16,* 1–26.

Flege, J.E., Munro, M.J., & MacKay, I.R.A. (1995b). Factors affecting strength of perceived foreign accent in a second language. *Journal of the Acoustical Society of America, 97,* 2540–2551.

Flor, H., Elbert, T., Knecht, S., Weinbruch, C., Pantev, C., Birbaumer, N., Larbig, W., and Taub, E. (1995). Phantom-limb pain as a perceptual correlate of cortical reorganization following arm amputation. *Nature, 375*(6531), 482–484.

Florence, M.D., Asbridge, M., & Veugelers, P.J. (2008). Diet quality and academic performance. *Journal of School Health, 78,* 209–215.

Flynn, J.R. (1984). *The mean IQ of Americans: Massive gains.* New York: Harper and Row.

Flynn, J.R. (1987). Massive IQ gains in 14 nations: what IQ tests really measure. *Psychological Bulletin, 101,* 171–191.

Flynn, J.R. (1998). IQ gains over time: Toward finding the causes. In U. Neisser (Ed.), *The rising curve: Long-term gains in IQ and related measures* (pp. 25–66). Washington, DC: American Psychological Association.

Foa, E.B., Dancu, C.V., Hembree, E.A., Jaycox, L.H., Meadows, E.A., & Street, G.P. (1999). A comparison of exposure therapy, stress inoculation training, and their combination for reducing posttraumatic stress disorder in female assault victims. *Journal of Consulting and Clinical Psychology, 67,* 194–200.

Foa, E.B., Hembree, E.A., Cahill, S.P., Rauch, S.A., Riggs, D.S., Feeny, N.C., et al. (2005). Randomized trial of prolonged exposure for PTSD with and without cognitive restructuring: Outcome at academic and community clinics. *Journal of Consulting and Clinical Psychology, 73,* 953–964.

Fodor, E.M., & Laird, B.A. (2004). Therapeutic intervention, bipolar inclination, and literary creativity. *Creativity Research Journal, 16,* 149–161.

Foell, J. Bekrater-Bodmann, R., Diers, M., and Flor, Mirror therapy for phantom limb pain: Brain changes and the role of body representation. *European Journal of Pain, 18;* 729–39.

Foerde, K., Knowlton, B., & Poldrack, R. (2006). Modulation of competing memory systems by distraction. *Proceedings of the National Academy of Sciences, 103,* 11778–11783.

Fogassi, L., & Ferrari, P.F. (2006). Mirror neurons and the evolution of embodied language. *Current Directions in Psychological Science, 16,* 136–141.

Folkman, S. (1997). Positive psychological states and coping with severe stress. *Social Science and Medicine, 45,* 1207–1221.

Folley, B.S., & Park, S. (2005). Verbal creativity and schizotypal personality in relation to prefrontal hemispheric laterality: A behavioral and near-infrared optical imaging study. *Schizophrenia Research, 80,* 87–89.

Fombonne, E. (2003). The prevalence of autism. *Journal of the American Medical Association, 289,* 87–89.

Ford, C., & Beach, F. (1951). *Patterns of sexual behavior.* New York: Harper & Row.

Forgeard, M., Winner. E., Norton, A., & Schlaug, G. (2008). Practicing a musical instrument in childhood is associated with enhanced verbal ability and nonverbal reasoning. *PLoS ONE, 3,* e3566.

Forsten, B.L., Scotti, J.R., Chen, Y-C, Malone, J., Del Ben, K.S. (2007). Internet use, abuse, and dependence among students at a southeastern regional university. *Journal of American College Health, 56,* 137–144.

Foulkes, D. (1996). Dream research: 1953–1993. *Sleep: Journal of Sleep Research & Sleep Medicine, 19,* 609–624.

Fournier, J.C., DeRubeis, R.J., Hollon, S.D., Dimidjian, S., Amsterdam, J.D., Shelton, R.C., & Fawcett, I. (2010). Antidepressant drug effects and depression severity: Patient-level meta-analysis. *Journal of the American Medical Association, 303,* 47–53.

Fouts, R.S. (1997). *Next of kin: My conversations with chimpanzees.* New York: Avon.

Fouts, R.S., Fouts, D.H., & Schoenfeld, D. (1984). Sign language conversational interaction between chimpanzees. *Sign Language Studies, 42,* 1–12.

Fowler, J.H., & Christakis, N.A. (2008). The dynamic spread of happiness in a large social network. *British Medical Journal, 337,* a2338.

Fowler, J.H., & Christakis, N.A. (2010). Cooperative behavior cascades in human social networks. *Proceedings of the National Academy of Sciences, 107,* 5334–5338.

Frances, A.J., & Widiger, T. (2012). Psychiatric diagnosis: Lessons from the DSM-IV past and cautions for the DSM-5 future. *Annual Review of Clinical Psychology, 8,* 109–130. doi:10.1146/annurev-clinpsy-032511-143102.

Franco, O.H., de Laet, C., Peeters, A., Jonker, J., Mackenbach, J., & Nusselder, W. (2005). Effects of physical activity on life expectancy with cardiovascular disease. *Archives of Internal Medicine, 165,* 2355–2360.

Frangou, S., Chitins, X, & Williams, S.C.R. (2004). Mapping IQ and gray matter density in healthy young people. *Neuroimage, 23,* 800–805.

Frank, M.G., & Benington, J.H. (2006). The role of sleep in memory consolidation and brain plasticity: Dream or reality? *Neuroscientist, 12,* 477–488.

Frank, M.G., & Ekman, P. (1997). The ability to detect deceit generalizes across different types of high stakes lies. *Journal of Personality and Social Psychology, 72,* 1429–1439.

Franklin, V.L., Waller, A., Pagliari, C., & Greene, S.A. (2006). A randomized controlled trial of Sweet Talk, a text messaging system to support young people with diabetes. *Diabetic Medicine, 23,* 1332–1338.

Fratiglioni, L., Winblad, B., & von Strauss, E. (2007). Prevention of Alzheimer's disease and dementia. Major findings from the Kungsholmen Project. *Physiology & Behavior, 92,* 98–104.

Fredrickson, B.L. (1998). What good are positive emotions? *Review of General Psychology, 2,* 300–319.

Fredrickson, B.L. (2001). The role of positive emotions in positive psychology: The broaden-and-build theory of positive emotions. *American Psychologist, 56,* 218–226.

Fredrickson, B.L., & Branigan, C. (2005). Positive emotions broaden the scope of attention and thought-action repertoires. *Cognition & Emotion, 19,* 313–332.

Fredrickson, B.L., & Joiner, T. (2002). Positive emotions trigger upward spirals toward emotional well-being. *Psychological Science, 13,* 172–175.

Fredrickson, B.L., & Levenson, R.W. (1998). Positive emotions speed recovery from the cardiovascular sequelae of negative emotions. *Cognition & Emotion, 12,* 191–220.

Fredrickson, B.L., Tugade, M.M., Waugh, C.E., & Larkin, G.R. (2003). What good are positive emotions in crises? A prospective study of resilience and emotions following the terrorist attacks on the United States on September 11th, 2001. *Journal of Personality & Social Psychology, 84,* 365–376.

Freedman, J.L. (2002). *Media violence and its effect on aggression: Assessing the scientific evidence.* Toronto: University of Toronto Press.

French, S., Seidman, E., Allen, L., & Aber, J.L. (2006). The development of ethnic identity during adolescence. *Developmental Psychology, 42,* 1–10.

French-Belgian Collaborative Group. (1982). Ischemic heart disease and psychological patterns: Prevalence and incidence studies in Belgium and France. *Advances in Cardiology, 29,* 25–31.

Freud, A. (1946). *The ego and the mechanisms of defense.* New York: International Universities Press.

Freud, S. (1953). *The interpretation of dreams.* In J. Strachey (Ed. & Trans.), *The standard edition of the complete works of Sigmund Freud* (Vols. 4 & 5). London: Hogarth Press. (Original work published 1900)

Freud, S. (1959). *Inhibitions, symptoms, and anxiety.* In J. Strachey (Ed. & Trans.), *Standard edition of the complete works of Sigmund Freud* (Vol. 20). London: Hogarth Press. (Original work published 1926)

Freud, S. (1960). *Psychopathology of everyday life.* In J. Strachey (Ed. & Trans.), *Standard edition of the complete works of Sigmund Freud* (Vol. 6). London: Hogarth Press. (Original work published 1901)

Freund, A., & Ritter, J. (2009). Midlife crisis: A debate. *Gerontology, 55,* 582–591.

Friedlander, L.J., Reid, G.J., Shupak, N., Cribbie, R. (2007). Social support, self-esteem, and stress as predictors of adjustment to university among first-year undergraduates. *Journal of College Student Development, 48,* 259–274.

Friesen, W.V. (1972). *Cultural differences in facial expressions in a social situation: An experimental test of the concept of display rules.* Unpublished doctoral dissertation, University of California, San Francisco.

Frijda, N.H. (1986). *The emotions.* Cambridge, UK: Cambridge University Press.

Frith, U., & Frith, C. (2010). The social brain: Allowing humans to boldly go where no other species has been. *Philosohical Translations of the Royal Society B: Biological Sciences, 365,* 165–176.

Fruntes, V., & Limosin, F. (2008). Schizophrenia and viral infection during neurodevelopment: A pathogenesis model? *Medical Science Monitor, 14,* RA71–RA77.

Fuchs, A.H., & Evans, R.B. (2013). Psychology as a science. In D.K. Freedheim (Ed.), *Handbook of psychology. Volume 1: History of psychology* (2nd ed., pp. 1–31). Hoboken, NJ: John Wiley & Sons, Inc.

Furster, J.M. (1999). Cognitive functions of the frontal lobes. In B.L. Miller & J.L. Cummings (Eds.), *The human frontal lobes: Functions and disorders* (pp. 187–195). New York: Guilford Press.

Furuichi, T. (1983). Interindividual distance and influence of dominance on feeding in a natural Japanese macaque troop. *Primates, 24,* 445–455.

Furumoto, L. (1981). Mary Whiton Calkins (1863–1930). *Psychology of Women Quarterly, 5,* 55–68. doi: 10.1111/j.1471-6402.1981.tb01033.x.

Fuster, J.M. (2002). Frontal lobe and cognitive development. *Journal of Neurocytology, 31,* 373–385.

Fyhn, M., Hafting, T., Treves, A., Moser, M-B, and Moser, E.I. (2007). Hippocampal remapping and grid realignment in entorhinal cortex. *Nature, 446,* 190–194.

Gage, F.H. (2002). Neurogenesis in the adult brain. *The Journal of Neuroscience, 22,* 612–613.

Galanter, E. (1962). Contemporary psychophysics. In R. Brown (Ed.), *New directions in psychology* (pp. 87–157). New York: Holt, Rinehart & Winston.

Gale, A. (1983). Electroencephalographic studies of extraversion-introversion: A case study in the psychophysiology of individual differences. *Personality and Individual Differences, 4,* 371–380.

Gallagher, A.M., & Kaufman, J.C. (2005). *Gender differences in mathematics: An integrative psychological approach.* New York: Cambridge University Press.

Gallagher, M., & Lopez, S. (2007). Curiosity and well-being. *Journal of Positive Psychology, 2*(4), 236–248.

Gallagher, R.M., & Rosenthal, L.J. (2008). Chronic pain and opiates: Balancing pain control and risks in long-term opioid treatment. *Archives of Physical Medicine and Rehabilitation, 89*(Suppl. 1), S77–S82.

Galletti, C., & Fattori, P. (2003). Neuronal mechanisms for detection of motion in the field of view. *Neuropsychologia, 41,* 1717–1727.

Ganasen, K., Ipser, J., & Stein, D. (2010). Augmentation of cognitive behavioral therapy with pharmacotherapy. *Psychiatric Clinics of North America, 33,* 687–699. doi: 10.1016/j.psc.2010.04.008.

Gander, P.H., Barnes, R.M., Gregory, K.B., Graeber, R.C., Connell, L.J., & Rosekind, M.R. (1998). Flight crew fatigue III: North Sea helicopter air transport operations. *Aviation, Space, and Environmental Medicine, 69,* B16–B25.

Ganis, G., Thompson, W., & Kosslyn, S. (2009). Visual mental imagery: More than "seeing with the mind's eye." In J.R. Brockmole (Ed.), *The visual world in memory* (pp. 215–249). New York, NY: Psychology Press.

Garcia, J. (2003). Psychology is not an enclave. In R.J. Sternberg (Ed.), *Defying the crowd: Stories of those who battled the establishment and won* (pp. 67–77). Washington, DC: American Psychological Association.

Garcia, J., & Koelling, R.A. (1966). The relation of cue to consequence in avoidance learning. *Psychonomic Science, 4,* 123–124.

Garcia, J., Ervin, F.R., & Koelling, R. (1966). Learning with a prolonged delay of reinforcement. *Psychonomic Science, 5,* 121–122.

Garcia, J., Kimeldorf, D.J., & Koelling, R.A. (1955). A conditioned aversion towards saccharin resulting from exposure to gamma radiation. *Science, 122,* 157–159.

Garcia, J., McGowan, B.K., & Green, K.F. (1972). Biological constraints on conditioning. In A.H. Black and W.F. Prokasy (Eds.), *Classical conditioning II: Current research and theory* (pp. 3–27). New York: Appleton-Century-Crofts.

Gardner, H. (1980). *Artful scribbles: The significance of children's drawings.* New York: Basic Books.

Gardner, H. (1983). *Frames of mind: The theory of multiple intelligences.* New York: Basic Books.

Gardner, H. (1987). *The mind's new science: A history of the cognitive revolution.* New York: Basic Books.

Gardner, H. (1993). *Frames of mind: The theory of multiple intelligences* (2nd ed.). New York: Basic Books.

Gardner, H. (1999). *Intelligence reframed: Multiple intelligences for the 21st century.* New York: Basic Books.

Gardner, R.A., Gardner, B.T., & Van Cantfort, T.E. (Eds.). (1989). *Teaching sign language to chimpanzees.* Albany: SUNY Press.

Garrett, R.K., & Danziger, J.N. (2008). IM = Interruption management? Instant messaging and disruption in the workplace. *Journal of Computer-Mediated Communication, 13,* 23–42.

Garriguet, D. (2008). Beverage consumption of Canadian adults. *Health Report, 19,* 23–29.

Gates, M.F., & Allee, W.C. (1933). Conditioned behavior of isolated and grouped cockroaches on a simple maze. *Journal of Comparative Psychology, 15,* 331–358.

Gathercole, V.C.M., & Hoff, E. (2007). Input and the acquisition of language: Three questions. In E. Hoff & M. Shatz (Eds.), *The handbook of language development* (pp. 107–127). Oxford, England: Blackwell.

Gawryluk, J.R., D'Arcy, R.C.N., Connolly, J.F., & Weaver, D.F. (2010). Improving the clinical assessment of consciousness with advances in electrophysiological and neuroimaging techniques. *BMC Neurology, 10,* 11.

Gazdzinski, S., Durazzo, T.C., & Meyerhoff, D.J. (2005). Temporal dynamics and determinants of whole brain tissue volume changes during recovery from alcohol dependence. *Drug and Alcohol Dependence, 78,* 263–273.

Geary, D., & DeSoto, M.C. (2001). Sex differences in spatial abilities among adults in the United States and China. *Evolution and Cognition, 7,* 172–177.

Gebicke-Haerter, P.J. (2012). Epigenetics of schizophrenia. *Pharmacopsychiatry, 45*(Suppl. 1), S42–S48.

Geerlings, S.W., Beekman, A., Deeg, D., Twisk, J., & van Tilburg, W. (2002). Duration and severity of depression predict mortality in older adults in the community. *Psychological Medicine, 32,* 609–618.

Georges, E. (1995). A cultural and historical perspective on confession. In J.W. Pennebaker (Ed.), *Emotion, disclosure, and health* (pp. 11–22). Washington, DC: American Psychological Association.

Georgiadis, J.R., Kortekaas, R., Kuipers, R., Nieuwenburg, A., Pruim, J., Simone Reinders, A.A.T., et al. (2006). Regional cerebral blood flow changes associated with clitorally induced orgasm in healthy women. *European Journal of Neuroscience, 24,* 3305–3316.

Gerevich, J., Bácskai, E., Farkas, L., & Danics, Z. (2005). A case report: Pavlovian conditioning as a risk factor of heroin "overdose" death. *Harm Reduction Journal, 2,* 11.

Gershberg, F.B., & Shimamura, A.P. (1995). The role of the frontal lobes in the use of organizational strategies in free recall. *Neuropsychologia, 13,* 1305–1333.

Geschwind, N., Peeters, F., Huibers, M., van Os, J., & Wichers, M. (2012). Efficacy of mindfulness-based cognitive therapy in relation to prior history of depression: Randomised controlled trial. *British Journal of Psychiatry, 201,* 320–325. doi: 10.1192/bjp.bp.111.104851.

Gewirtz, J.C., & Davis, M. (2000). Using Pavlovian higher-order conditioning paradigms to investigate the neural substrates of emotional learning and memory. *Learning and Memory,* 7, 257–266.

Gibson, E., & Walk, R. (1960). The visual cliff. *Scientific American, 202,* 64–71.

Gibson, J.J. (1950). *The perception of the visual world.* Boston: Houghton Mifflin.

Gibson, J.J. (1966). *The senses considered as perceptual systems.* Boston: Houghton Mifflin.

Giedd, J.N., Blumenthal, J., Jeffries, N.O., Castellanos F.X., Liu, H., Zijdenbos, A., Paus, T., Evans, A.C., & Rapoport, J.L. (1999): Brain development during childhood and adolescence: A longitudinal MRI study. *Nature Neuroscience 2,* 861–863.

Gil, S. (2007). Body-image, well-being and sexual satisfaction: A comparison between heterosexual and gay men. *Sexual and Relationship Therapy, 22*(2), 237–244.

Gilbert, S.L., Dobyns, W.B., & Lah, B.T. (2005). Genetic links between brain development and brain evolution. *Nature Reviews Genetics, 6,* 581–590.

Giles, G.E., Mahoney, C.R., Brunye, T.T., Gardony, A.L., Taylor, H.A., Kanarek, R.B. (2012). Differential cognitive effects of energy drink ingredients: Caffeine, taurine, and glucose. *Pharmacology, Biochemistry, & Behavior, 102; 569–577.*

Gillham, J.E., Reivich, K.J., Freres, D.R., Chaplin, T.M., Shatté, A.J., Samuels, B., . . . Martin, E.P. (2007). School-based prevention of depressive symptoms: A randomized controlled study of the effectiveness and specificity of the Penn Resiliency Program. *Journal of Consulting and Clinical Psychology, 75,* 9–19.

Gilligan, C. (1982). *In a different voice.* Cambridge, MA: Harvard University Press.

Gilmore, Scott. (2015, January 22). Canada's race problem? It's even worse than America's. *Maclean's.* Retrieved from http://www.macleans.ca/news/canada/out-of-sight-out-of-mind-2/.

Givón, T. (2002). The visual information-processing system as an evolutionary precursor of human language. In T. Givón & B.F. Malle (Eds.), *The evolution of language out of pre-language* (pp. 3–50). Amsterdam: John Benjamins.

Givón, T., & Malle, B.F. (Eds.) (2002). *The evolution of language out of pre-language.* Amsterdam: John Benjamins.

Gjerde, P.F., & Cardilla, K. (2009). Developmental implications of openness to experience in preschool children: Gender differences in young adulthood. *Developmental Psychology, 45,* 1455–1464.

Gladwell, M. (2006, February 6). Troublemakers. *New Yorker.*

Glaser, R., & Kiecolt-Glaser, J.K. (2005). Stress-induced immune dysfunction: Implications for health. *Nature Reviews Immunology, 4,* 243–251.

Glassman, A., & Shapiro, P. (1998). Depression and the course of coronary artery disease. *American Journal of Psychiatry, 155,* 4–11.

Gleason, J.B. (2013). The development of language: An overview and a preview. In J.B. Gleason & N.B. Ratner, (Eds.), *The Development of Language* (8th ed., pp. 1–29). Upper Saddle River, NJ: Pearson Education Inc.

Gliksman, L., Newton-Taylor, B., Adlaf, E., & Giesbrecht, N. (1997). Alcohol and other drug use by Ontario university students: The roles of gender, age, year of study, academic grades, place of residence and programme of study. *Drugs: Education, Prevention and Policy, 4,* 117–129.

Godden, D.R., & Baddeley, A.D. (1975). Context dependent memory in two natural environments: On land and underwater. *British Journal of Psychology, 66,* 325–331.

Goel, V., & Vartanian, O. (2005). Dissociating the roles of right ventral lateral and dorsal lateral prefrontal cortex in generation and maintenance of hypotheses in set-shift problems. *Cerebral Cortex, 15,* 1170–1177.

Goeree, R., Farahati, F., Burke, N., Blackhouse, G., O'Reilly, D., Pyne, J., & Tarride, J.E. (2005). The economic burden of schizophrenia in Canada in 2004. *Current Medical Research and Opinion, 21,* 2017–2028.

Goff, D.C., & Coyle, J.T. (2001). The merging role of glutamate in the pathophysiology and treatment of schizophrenia. *American Journal of Psychiatry, 158,* 1367–1377.

Goldapple, K., Segal, Z., Garson, C., Lau, M., Bieling, P., Kennedy, S., et al. (2004). Modulation of cortical-limbic pathways in major depression. *Archives of General Psychiatry, 61,* 34–41.

Goldfield, B.A. (2000). Nouns before verbs in comprehension vs. production: The view from pragmatics. *Journal of Child Language, 27,* 501–520.

Goldin, P., McRae, K., Ramel, W., & Gross, J.J. (2008). The neural bases of emotion regulation: Reappraisal and suppression of negative emotion. *Biological Psychiatry, 63,* 577–586.

Goldman-Rakic, P.S. (1999). The physiological approach: Functional architecture of working memory and disordered cognition in schizophrenia. *Biological Psychiatry, 46,* 650–661.

Goldsmith, T.H. (2006). What birds see. *Scientific American, 295,* 69–75.

Goldstein, A.L., Faulkner, B., & Christine Wekerle, C. (2013). The relationship between internal resilience, smoking, alcohol use, and depression symptoms in emerging adults transitioning out of child welfare. *Child Abuse & Neglect, 37,* 22–32.

Goldstein, E.B. (2007). *Sensation and perception* (7th ed.). New York: Thomson-Wadsworth.

Goldstein, T., Bridge, J., & Brent, D. (2008). Sleep disturbance preceding completed suicide in adolescents. *Journal of Consulting and Clinical Psychology, 76*(1), 84–91.

Goleman, D.P. (1995). *Emotional Intelligence: Why it can matter more than IQ for character, health and lifelong achievement.* New York: Bantam Books.

Golier, J.A., Caramanica, K., & Yehuda, R. (2012). Neuroendocrine response to CRF stimulation in veterans with and without PTSD in consideration of war zone era. *Psychoneuroendocrinology, 37,* 350–357. doi: 10.1016/j.psyneuen.2011.07.004.

Gonzalez, J.J., Hynd, G.W., & Martin, R.P. (1994). Neuropsychology of temperament. In P.A. Vernon (Ed.), *The neuropsychology of individual differences* (pp. 235–256). San Diego: Academic Press.

Goodwin, C.J. (2012). *A history of modern psychology* (4th ed.). Hoboken, NJ: John Wiley & Sons, Inc.

Goodwin, D.W. (1995). Alcohol amnesia. *Addiction, 90,* 315–317.

Goodwin, P., McGill, B., & Chandra A. (2009). *Who marries and when? Age at first marriage in the United States, 2002.* NCHS data brief No. 19. Hyattsville, MD: National Center for Health Statistics.

Goodwin, P.J. (2004). Support groups in breast cancer: When a negative result is positive. *Journal of Clinical Oncology, 22,* 4244–4246.

Goodwin, P.J., Leszcz, M., Ennis, M., Koopmans, J., Vincent, L., Guther, H., et al. (2001). The effect of group psychosocial support on survival in metastatic breast cancer. *New England Journal of Medicine, 345,* 1719–1726.

Gopnik, A., Meltzoff, A.N., & Kuhl, P.K. (1999). *The scientist in the crib: Minds, brains, and how children learn.* New York: Morrow.

Gordon, P. (2004). Numerical cognition without words: Evidence from Amazonia. *Science, 306,* 496–499.

Gorman, J.M., Kent, J.M., Sullivan, G.M., & Coplan, J.D. (2000). Neuroanatomical hypothesis of panic disorder, revised. *The American Journal of Psychiatry, 157*(4), 493–505. doi:10.1176/appi.ajp.157.4.493.

Gorrindo, T., & Groves, J.E. (2009). Computer simulation and virtual reality in the diagnosis and treatment of psychiatric disorders. *Academic Psychiatry, 33,* 413–417.

Gosling, S.D. (1998). Personality differences in spotted hyenas (*Crocuta crocuta*). *Journal of Comparative Psychology, 112,* 107–118.

Gosling, S.D., & John, O.P. (1999). Personality dimensions in non-human animals: A cross-species review. *Current Directions in Psychological Science, 8,* 69–75.

Gosling, S.D., Ko, S.J., Mannarelli, T., & Morris, M.E. (2002). A room with a cue:

Personality judgments based on offices and bedrooms. *Journal of Personality and Social Psychology, 82,* 379–398.

Gosling, S.D., Sandy, C.J., John, O.P., & Potter, J. (2010). Wired but not WEIRD: the promise of the Internet in reaching more diverse samples. *Behavioral and Brain Sciences, 33,* 94–95.

Gosling, S.D., Vazire, S., Srivastava, S., & John, O.P. (2004). Should we trust Web-based studies? A comparative analysis of six preconceptions about Internet questionnaires. *American Psychologist, 59,* 93–104.

Goto, H. (1971). Auditory perception by normal Japanese adults of the sounds "l" and "r." *Neuropsychologia, 9,* 317–323.

Gottfredson, L. (1997). Mainstream science on intelligence: An editorial with 52 signatories, history, and bibliography. *Intelligence, 24,* 13–23.

Gottleib, N.H., & Green, L.W. (1984). Life events, social network, life-style, and health: An analysis of the 1979 National Survey of Personal Health Practices and Consequences. *Health Education Quarterly, 11,* 91–105.

Gottschalk, S. (2010). The presentation of avatars in Second Life: Self and interaction in social virtual spaces. *Symbolic Interaction, 33,* 501–525.

Gough, H.G., & Bradley, P. (1996). *California Psychological Inventory Manual* (3rd ed.). Palo Alto, CA: Consulting Psychologists Press.

Gough, H.G., & Bradley, P. (1996). *CPI manual* (3rd ed.) Palo Alto, CA: Consulting Psychologists Press.

Gould, E. (2008, May 25). Exposed. *The New York Times Magazine.*

Gould, E., Vail, N., Wagers, M., & Gross, C.G. (2004). Adult-generated hippocampal and neocortical neurons in macaques have a transient existence. *Proceedings of the National Academy of Sciences, 98,* 10910–10917.

Gould, S.J. (1997). Nonoverlapping magisteria. *Natural History, 106,* 16–22.

Government of Canada. (2006). *The Human Face of Mental Health and Mental Illness in Canada 2006.* Ottawa: Minister of Public Works and Government Services Canada.

Government of Canada. (2015). *Autism spectrum disorder (ASD).* Retrieved from http://healthycanadians.gc.ca/diseases-conditions-maladies-affections/disease-maladie/autism-eng.php.

Governor General Archives. Micaelle Jean biography. Retrieved January 22, 2010, from http://archive.gg.ca/media/fs-fd/G2_e.asp.

Gow, A., Whiteman, M., Pattie, A., Whalley, L., Starr, J., & Deary, I. (2005). Lifetime intellectual function and satisfaction with life in old age: Longitudinal cohort study. *BMJ: British Medical Journal, 331*(7509), 141–142.

Grafman, J., Schwab., K., Warden, D., Pridgeon, A., Brown, H.R., & Salazar, A.M. (1996). Frontal lobe injuries, violence, and aggression: A report of a Vietnam head injury study. *Neurology, 46,* 1231–1238.

Graham, S., & Lowery, B.S. (2004). Priming unconscious racial stereotypes about adolescent offenders. *Law and Human Behavior, 28,* 483–504.

Grant, A.M., & Hoffman, D.A. (2011). It's not all about me: Motivating hand hygiene among health care professionals by focusing on patients. *Psychological Science 22,* 1494–1499. doi: 10.1177/0956797611419172.

Grant, B.F., Hasin, D.S., Stinson, F.S., Dawson, D.A., Goldstein, R.B., Smith, S., et al. (2006). The epidemiology of *DSM-IV-TR* panic disorder and agoraphobia in the United States: Results from the National Epidemiologic Survey on Alcohol and Related Conditions. *Journal of Clinical Psychiatry, 67,* 363–374.

Graves, K.N. (2007). Not always sugar and spice: Expanding theoretical and functional explanations for why females aggress. *Aggression and Violent Behavior, 12,* 131–140.

Gray, J.L., & Thompson, P. (2004). Neurobiology of intelligence: Science and ethics. *Nature Reviews: Neuroscience, 5,* 471–482.

Green, D., & Swets, J. (1974). *Signal detection theory and psychophysics.* Oxford: Krieger.

Greenberg, G. (2013, September 3). The psychiatric drug crisis. *The New Yorker.* Retrieved from http://www.newyorker.com/tech/elements/the-psychiatric-drug-crisis?mobify=0.

Greenberg, L. (1979). Genetic component of bee odor in kin recognition. *Science, 206,* 1095–1097.

Greenberg, M.T., & Kusché, C.A. (1998). *Promoting alternative thinking strategies.* Boulder: Institute of Behavioral Sciences, University of Colorado.

Greenemeier, L. (2013, June). Real world. *Scientific American, 308,* 24.

Greenough, W.T., Volkmar, F.R., & Juraska, J.M. (1973). Effects of rearing complexity on dendritic branching in frontolateral and temporal cortex of the rat, *Experimental Neurology,* 41, 371–378.

Greenwald, A.G., & Banaji, M.R. (1995). Implicit social cognition: Attitudes, self-esteem, and stereotypes. *Psychological Review, 102,* 4–27.

Greenwald, A.G., McGhee, D.E., & Schwartz, J.L.K. (1998). Measuring individual differences in implicit cognition: The implicit association test. *Journal of Personality and Social Psychology, 74,* 1464–1480.

Greenwald, A.G., Poehlman, T., Uhlmann, E., & Banaji, M.R. (2009). Understanding and using the Implicit Association Test: III. Meta-analysis of predictive validity. *Journal of Personality and Social Psychology, 97,* 17–41. doi: 10.1037/a0015575.

Gregory, R.J. (2007). *Psychological testing* (5th ed.). New York: Allyn & Bacon.

Griebel, T. (2006). Self-portrayal in a simulated life: Projecting personality and values in the Sims 2. *Game Studies. The International Journal of Computer Game Research, 6*(1). Retrieved from http://gamestudies.org/0601/articles/griebel.

Grigorenko, E. (2000). Heritability and intelligence. In R.J. Sternberg (Ed.), *Handbook of intelligence* (pp. 53–91). New York: Cambridge University Press.

Grolnick, W.S., McMenamy, J.M., & Kurowski, C.O. (2006). Emotional self-regulation in infancy and toddlerhood. In L. Balter & C.S. Tamis-LeMonda (Eds.), *Child psychology: A handbook of contemporary issues* (2nd ed., pp. 3–25). New York: Psychology Press.

Groome, L., Mooney, D., Holland, S., Smith, Y., Atterbury, J., & Dykman, R. (2000). Temporal pattern and spectral complexity as stimulus parameters for eliciting a cardiac orienting reflex in human fetuses. *Perception and Psychophysics, 62*(2), 313–320.

Gross, C.G. (2000). Neurogenesis in the adult brain: Death of a dogma. *Nature Reviews Neuroscience, 1,* 67–73.

Gross, J.J. (1998). The emerging field of emotion regulation: An integrative review. *Review of General Psychology, 2,* 271–299.

Gross, J.J., & John, O. (1998). Mapping the domain of expressivity: Multimethod evidence for a hierarchical model. *Journal of Personality and Social Psychology, 74,* 170–191.

Gross, J.J., & Levenson, R.W. (1993). Emotional suppression—Physiology, self-report, and expressive behavior. *Journal of Personality and Social Psychology, 64,* 970–986.

Gross, J.J., & Levenson, R.W. (1997). Hiding feelings: The acute effects of inhibiting positive and negative emotions. *Journal of Abnormal Psychology, 106,* 95–103.

Gross, J.J., Richards, J.M., & John, O.P. (2006). Emotion regulation in everyday life. In D.K. Snyder, J.A. Simpson, & J.N. Hughes (Eds.), *Emotion regulation in families: Pathways to dysfunction and health* (pp. 13–35). Washington, DC: American Psychological Association.

Grossman, A.W., Churchill, J.D., McKinney, B.C., Kodish, I.M., Otte, S.L., & Greenough, W.T. (2003). Experience effects on brain development: Possible contributions to psychopathology. *Journal of Child Psychology and Psychiatry, 44,* 33–63.

Grossman, T., Striano, T., & Friederici, A.D. (2006). Crossmodal integration of emotional information from face and voice in the infant brain. *Developmental Science, 9,* 309–315.

Guarnaccia, V., Dill, C.A., Sabatino, S., & Southwick, S. (2001). Scoring accuracy using the comprehensive system for the Rorschach. *Journal of Personality Assessment, 77,* 464–474.

Guarraci, F.A., & Benson, A. (2005). "Coffee, Tea and Me": Moderate doses of caffeine affect sexual behavior in female rats. *Pharmacology, Biochemistry and Behavior, 82,* 522–530.

Guderian, B., Borreson, L., Sletten, L., Cable, K., Stecker, T., Probst, M., & Dalleck, L. (2010). The cardiovascular and metabolic responses to Wii Fit video game playing in middle-aged and older adults. *The Journal of Sports Medicine and Physical Fitness, 50*(4), 436–442.

Guehl, D., Benazzouz, A., Aouizerate, B., Cuny, E., Rotgé, J.-Y., Rougier, A., et al. (2008). Neuronal correlates of obsessions in the caudate nucleus. *Biological Psychiatry, 63,* 557–562.

Guilford, J.P. (1962). Potentiality for creativity. *Gifted Child Quarterly, 6,* 87–90.

Guilford, J.P. (1967). *The nature of human intelligence.* New York: McGraw-Hill.

Guilleminault, C., Kirisoglu, C., Bao, G., Arias, V., Chan, A., Li, K.K. (2005). Adult chronic sleepwalking and its treatment based on polysomnography. *Brain, 128,* 1062–1069.

Guimond, S., & Palmer, D.L. (1996). The political socialization of commerce and social science students: Epistemic authority and attitude change. *Journal of Applied Social Psychology, 26,* 1985–2013.

Guiraud, A., deLorgeril, M., Zeghichi, S., Laporte, F., Salen, P., Saks, V., et al. (2008). Interactions of ethanol drinking with n-3 fatty acids in rats: Potential consequences for the cardiovascular system. *British Journal of Nutrition,* April 29, 1–8. Advance online publication. Retrieved July 10, 2008.

Gunderson, E., Moline, J., & Catalano, P. (1997). Risks of developing noise-induced hearing loss in employees of urban music clubs. *American Journal of Industrial Medicine, 31,* 75–79.

Gunnar, M.R., Brodersen, L., Nachmias, M., Buss, K., & Rigatuso, J. (1996). Stress reactivity and attachment security. *Developmental Psychobiology, 28,* 191–204.

Gupta, A.S., van der Meer, M.A.A., Touretzky, D.S., and Redish. A.D. (2010). Hippocampal replay is not a simple function of experience. *Neuron, 65,* 695–705.

Gupta, S., Agarwal, A., Banerjee, J., & Alvarez, J.G. (2007). The role of oxidative stress in spontaneous abortion and recurrent pregnancy loss: A systematic review. *Obstetrical, Gynecological Survey, 62,* 335–347.

Gutteling, B.M., de Weerth, C., Willemsen-Swinkles, S.H.N., Huizink, A.C., Mulder, E.J.H., Visser, G.H.A., et al. (2005). The effects of prenatal stress on temperament and problem behavior of 27-month-old toddlers. *European Child and Adolescent Psychiatry, 14,* 41–51.

Guzman-Marin, R., Suntsova, N., Methippara, M., Greiffenstein, R., Szymusiak, R., & McGinty, D. (2003). Sleep deprivation suppresses neurogenesis in the adult hippocampus of rats. *European Journal of Neuroscience, 22,* 2111–2116.

Habib, M.K. (2007). Controlled biological and biomimetic systems for landmine detection. *Biosensors and Bioelectronics, 23,* 1–18.

Hackman, D.A., Farah, M.J., & Meaney, M.J. (2010). Socioeconomic status and the brain: Mechanistic insights from human and animal research. *Nature Reviews Neuroscience, 11*(9), 651–659. doi:10.1038/nrn2897.

Hadjistavropoulos, H.D., Alberts, N.M., Nugent, M., & Marchildon, G. (2014). Improving Access to Psychological Services Through Therapist-Assisted, Internet-Delivered Cognitive Behaviour Therapy. *Canadian Psychology, 55*(4), 303–311.

Hadjistavropoulos, H.D., Thompson, M., Ivanov, M., Drost, C., Butz, C.J., Klein, B., . . . Austin, D.W. (2011). Considerations in the development of a therapist-assisted Internet cognitive behavior therapy service. *Professional Psychology: Research and Practice, 42,* 463–471.doi:10.1037/a0026176.

Hafer, C.L. (2000). Do innocent victims threaten the belief in a just world? Evidence from a modified Stroop task. *Journal of Personality and Social Psychology, 79,* 165–173.

Hafer, C.L., & Bègue, L. (2005). Experimental research on just-world theory: Problems, developments, and future challenges. *Psychological Bulletin, 131,* 128–167.

Hafetz, J.S., Jacobsohn, L.S., García-España, J., Curry, A.E., & Winston, F.K. (2010). Adolescent drivers' perceptions of the advantages and disadvantages of abstention from in-vehicle cell phone use. *Accident Analysis and Prevention, 42*(6), 1570–1576. doi: 10.1016/j.aap.2010.03.015.

Haffenden, A.M., & Goodale, M.A. (1998). The effect of pictorial illusion on comprehension and perception. *Journal of Cognitive Neuroscience, 10,* 122–136.

Hafting, T., Fyhn, M., Molden, S., Moser, M-B., & Moser, E.I. (2005). Microstructure of a spatial map in the entorhinal cortex. *Nature, 436,* 801–806.

Haier, R.J., Jung, R.E., Yeo, R.A., Head, K., & Alkire, M.T. (2004). Structural brain variation and general intelligence. *NeuroImage, 23,* 425–433.

Hakuta, K., Bialystok, E., & Wiley, E. (2003). Critical evidence: A test of the critical-period hypothesis for second-language acquisition. *Psychological Science, 14,* 31–38.

Hale, B., Seiser, L., & McGuire, E.J. (2005). Mental imagery. In J. Taylor & J. Wilson (Eds.), *Applying sport psychology: Four perspectives* (pp. 117–135). Champaign, IL: Human Kinetics.

Halim, May Ling, Zosuls, K.M., Ruble, D.N., Tamis-LeMonda, C.S., Lurye, L.E., & Greulich, F.K. (2014). Pink Frilly Dresses and the Avoidance of All Things "Girly": Children's Appearance Rigidity and Cognitive Theories of Gender Development. *Developmental Psychology, 50*(4), 1091–1101.

Hall, C.C.I. (1997). Cultural malpractice: The growing obsolescence of psychology wit the changing US population. *American Psychologist, 52,* 642–651.

Hall, J.A., & Matsumoto, D. (2004). Gender difference in the judgment of multiple emotions from facial expression. *Emotion, 4,* 201–206.

Halpern, A. (1986). Memory for tune titles after organized or unorganized presentation. *American Journal of Psychology, 99,* 57–70.

Halpern, D. (2000). *Sex differences in cognitive abilities* (3rd ed.). NJ: Laurence Erlbaum Associates.

Halpern, D. (2004). A cognitive-process taxonomy for sex differences in cognitive abilities. *Current Directions in Psychological Science, 13,* 135–139.

Halpern, J.H., Pope, H.G., Sherwood, A.R., Barry, S., Hudson, J.I., & Yurgelun-Todd, D. (2004). Residual neuropsychological effects of illicit 3,4-methylenedioxymeth-amphetamine (MDMA) in individuals with minimal exposure to other drugs. *Drug and Alcohol Dependence, 75,* 135–147.

Hamann, S., Herman, R.A., Nolan, C.L., & Wallen, K. (2004). Men and women differ in amygdala response to visual sexual stimuli. *Nature Neuroscience, 7,* 411–416.

Hamilton, W.D. (1964). The genetical evolution of social behaviour I and II. *Journal of Theoretical Biology, 7,* 1–16, 17–52.

Hammer, A.L., & Macdaid, G.P. (1992). *MBTI career report manual.* Palo Alto: Consulting Psychologist Press, Inc.

Hammond, D., Fong, G.T., McDonald, P.W., Brown, K.S., & Cameron, R. (2004). Graphic Canadian cigarette warning labels and adverse outcomes: Evidence from Canadian smokers. *American Journal of Public Health, 9,* 1442–1445.

Han, J. (2004). Acupuncture and endorphins. *Neuroscience Letters, 361,* 258–261.

Han, Y., Yang, H., Lv, Y.T., Zhu, C.Z., He, Y., Tang, H.H., Gong, Q.Y., Luo, Y.J., Zang, Y.F., & Dong, Q. (2009). Gray matter density and white matter integrity in pianists' brain: A combined structural and diffusion tensor MRI study. *Neuroscience Letters, 459,* 3–6.

Haney, C., Banks, W.C., & Zimbardo, P.G. (1973). Interpersonal dynamics in a simulated prison. *International Journal of Criminology and Penology, 1,* 69–97.

Hankin, B.L. (2010). Personality and depressive symptoms: Stress generation and cognitive vulnerabilities to depression in a prospective daily diary study. *Journal of Clinical and Social Psychology, 29,* 369–401.

Hannigan, T.P. (1995). Body odor: The international student and cross-cultural communication. *Culture & Psychology, 1,* 497–503.

Hansen, R.A., Gartiehner, G., Lohr, K.N., & Daufer, D. (2007). Functional outcomes of drug treatment in Alzheimer's disease: A systematic review and meta-analysis. *Drugs & Aging, 24*(2), 155–167.

Hanson, J.L., Hair, N., Shen, D.G., Shi, F., Gilmore, J.H., Wolfe, B.L., & Pollak, S.D. (2013). Family poverty affects the rate of human infant brain growth. *PloS ONE, 8*(12), 1–9. doi:10.1371/journal.pone.0080954.

Hare, R.D., & Neumann, C.S. (2009). Psychopathy: Assessment and forensic implications. *Canadian Journal of Psychiatry, 54,* 791–802.

Hare, R.D. (1993). *Without conscience: The disturbing world of the psychopaths among us.* New York: Pocket Books.

Hargrave, G.E., & Hiatt, D. (1989). Use of the California Psychological Inventory in law enforcement officer selection. *Journal of Personality Assessment, 53,* 267–277.

Harkins, S.G. (1987). Social loafing and social facilitation. *Journal of Experimental Social Psychology, 23,* 1–18.

Harlow, H. (1958). The nature of love. *American Psychologist, 13,* 573–685.

Harman, J.S., Crystal, S., Walkup, J., & Olfson, M. (2003). Trends in elderly patients' office visits for the treatment of depression according to physician specialty: 1985–1999. *Journal of Behavioral Health Services & Research, 30,* 332–341.

Harmon, D. (2006). Free-radical theory of aging: An update. *Annals of the New York Academy of Sciences, 1067,* 10–21.

Harmon-Jones. E. (2003). Clarifying the emotive functions of asymmetrical frontal cortical activity. *Psychophysiology, 40,* 838–848.

Harris Interactive. (2008). *Cell phone usage continues to increase.* Retrieved from http://www.harrisinteractive.com/vault/Harris-Interactive-Poll-Research-Cell-Phone-Usage-Continues-to-Increase-2008-04.pdf.

Harris, A.J. (1999). Cortical origin of pathological pain. *Lancet, 354,* 1464–1466.

Harris, J.R. (1998). *The nurture assumption: Why children turn out the way they do.* New York: Free Press.

Harris, M.B. (1974). Mediators between frustration and aggression in a field experiment. *Journal of Experimental Social Psychology, 10,* 561–571.

Harris, T.O., Borsanyi, S., Messari, S., Stanford, K., Cleary, S.E., Shiers, H.M., Brown, G.W., & Herbert, J. (2000). Morning cortisol as a risk factor for subsequent major depressive disorder in adult women. *British Journal of Psychiatry, 177,* 505–510.

Harris, W.V. (2013). Thinking about mental disorders in classical antiquity. In W.V. Harris (Ed.), *Mental Disorders in the Classical World* (pp. 1–23). Leiden, The Netherlands: Brill.

Harrison, P.J. (2004). The hippocampus in schizophrenia: A review of the neuropathological evidence and its pathophysiological implications. *Psychopharmacology, 174,* 151–162.

Harrison, P.J., & Owen, M. (2003). Genes for schizophrenia? Recent findings and their pathophysiological implications. *The Lancet, 361,* 417–419.

Harrison, P.J., & Weinberger, D.R. (2005). Schizophrenia genes, gene expression, and neuropathology: On the matter of their convergence. *Molecular Psychiatry, 10,* 40–68.

Hart, B., & Risley, T.R. (1992). American parenting of language-learning children: Persisting differences in family-child interactions observed in natural home environments. *Developmental Psychology, 28*(6), 1096–1105. doi: 10.1037/0012-1649.28.6.1096.

Hart, B., & Risley, T.R. (1995). *Meaningful differences in the everyday experience of young American children.* Baltimore, MD: Paul H. Brooks.

Hasher, L., & Zacks, R.T. (1979). Automatic and effortful processes in memory. *Journal of Experimental Psychology: General, 108,* 356–388.

Haslam, S.A., & Reicher, S.D. (2012). Contesting the "nature" of conformity: What Milgram and Zimbardo's studies really show. *PLoS Biol 10:* e1001426. DOI:10.1371/journal.pbio.1001426.

Hassett, J.M., Siebert, E.R., & Wallen, K. (2008). Sex differences in rhesus monkey toy preferences parallel those of children. Hormones and Behavior, 54, 359–364. doi:10.1016/j.yhbeh.2008.03.008.

Hauser, M.D., Chomsky, N., & Fitch, W.T. (2002). The faculty of language: What is it, who has it, and how did it evolve? *Science, 298,* 1569–1579.

Hausmann, F., Arnold, K.E., Marshall, N.J., & Owens, I.P.F. (2003). Ultraviolet signals in birds are special. *Proceedings of the Royal Society, 270,* 61–67.

Hawkins, D.L., Pepler, D.J., & Craig, W.M. (2001). Naturalistic observations of peer interventions in bullying. *Social Development, 10*(4), 512–527.

Hawton, K., Comabella, C., Haw, C., & Saunders, K. (2013). Risk factors for suicide in individuals with depression: A systematic review. *Journal of Affective Disorders, 147,* 17–28.

Hayes, B.D., Klein-Schwartz, W., & Doyon, S. (2008). Toxicity of buprenorphine overdoses in children. *Pediatrics, 121,* 782–786.

Haynes, S.G., Levine, S., Scotch, N., Feinleib, M., & Kannel, W.B. (1978). The relationship of psychosocial factors to coronary heart disease in the Framingham study. I. Methods and risk factors. *American Journal of Epidemiology, 107,* 362–383.

Hazan, C., & Shaver, P. (1987). Romantic love conceptualized as an attachment process. *Journal of Personality and Social Psychology, 52,* 511–524.

Headey, B. (2008). Life goals matter to happiness: A revision of set-point theory. *Social Indicators Research, 86,* 213–231.

Headey, B.W., & Wearing, A.J. (1992). *Understanding happiness: A theory of subjective well-being.* Melbourne: Longman Cheshire.

Health and Human Services. (2004). *New surgeon general's report expands the list of diseases caused by smoking.* Retrieved August 19, 2008, from http://www.hhs.gov/news/press/2004pres/20040527a.html.

Health Canada. (2002). *National Population Health Survey: Canadians and healthy eating—how are we doing?* Retrieved November 21, 2010, from http://www.hc-sc.gc.ca/fn-an/surveill/nutrition/population/national_health_survey-enquete_nationale_sante-eng.php#12.

Health Canada. (2009). *Canadian Tobacco Use Monitoring Survey.* Retrieved June 29, 2010, from http://www.hc-sc.gc.ca/hc-ps/tobac-tabac/research-recherche/stat/_ctums-esutc_2009/w-p-1_sum-som-eng.php.

Hearnshaw, L.S. (1987). *The shaping of modern psychology: An historical introduction.* New York: Routledge and Kegan.

Heath, R.G. (1975). Brain function and behavior. *Journal of Nervous and Mental Disease, 160,* 159–175.

Hebb, D.O. (1949). *The organization of behavior: A neuropsychological theory.* New York: Wiley.

Hedden, T., & Gabrieli, J.D.E. (2004). Insights into the ageing mind: A view from cognitive neuroscience. *Nature Reviews Neuroscience, 5,* 87–96.

Hedges, L., & Nowell, A. (1995). Sex differences in mental test scores, variability, and numbers of high-scoring individuals. *Science, 269,* 41–45.

Hedges, S.M., Jandorf, L., & Stone, A.A. (1985). Meaning of daily mood assessments. *Journal of Personality and Social Psychology, 48,* 428–434.

Heesacker, M., Petty, R.E., & Cacioppo, J.T. (1983). Field dependence and attitude change: source credibility can alter persuasion by affecting message-relevant thinking. *Journal of Personality, 51*653–51666.

Hegelson, V.S., & Taylor, S.E. (1993). Social comparisons and adjustment among cardiac patients. *Journal of Applied Social Psychology, 23,* 1171–1195.

Heider, F. (1958). *The psychology of interpersonal relations.* New York: Wiley.

Hellige, J.B. (1996). Hemispheric asymmetry for visual information processing. *Acta Neurobiol Exp (Wars), 56,* 485–97.

Helliwell, J.F., Huang, H., & Wang, S. (2015). The geography of world happiness. In Helliwell, J.F., Layard, R. & Sachs, J. (Eds.), *World Happiness Report 2015.* New York: Sustainable Development Solutions Network.

Helliwell, J.F., Layard, R & Sachs, J. (2015). Setting the stage. In Helliwell, J.F., Layard, R. & Sachs, J. (Eds.), *World Happiness Report 2015.* New York: Sustainable Development Solutions Network.

Henderson, A. (2007). Sexual satisfaction among lesbian and heterosexual women: An ecological model. *Dissertation Abstracts International: Section B: The Sciences and Engineering, 67*(8-B), 4709.

Hendrick, C., & Hendrick, S. (1989). Research on love: Does it measure up? *Journal of Personality and Social Psychology, 56,* 784–794.

Hennig-Fast, K., Meister, F., Frodla, T., Beraldi, A., Padberga, F., Engel, R.R., Reiser, M., Möllera, H., & Meindl, T. (2008). A case of persistent retrograde amnesia following a dissociative fugue: Neuropsychological and neurofunctional underpinnings of loss of autobiographical memory and self-awareness. *Neuropsychologia, 46,* 2993–3005.

Herbert, A., & Rich, A. (1999). RNA processing in evolution: The logic of soft-wired genomes. *Annals of the New York Academy of Sciences, 870,* 119–132.

Herdener, M., Esposito, F., di Salle, F., Boller, C., Hilti, C.C., Habermeyer, B., . . . Cattapan-Ludewig, K. (2010). Musical training induces functional plasticity in human hippocampus. *Journal of Neuroscience, 30*(4), 1377–1384. doi: 10.1523/JNEUROSCI.4513-09.2010.

Hergenhahn, B.R. (2009). *History of psychology* (6th ed.). Belmont, CA: Wadsworth Publishing Company.

Hering, E. (1878). *Zur Lehre vom Lichtsinn.* Vienna, Austria: Gerold.

Herman, J.P., & Cullinan, W.E. (1997). Neurocircuitry of stress: Central control of the hypothalamo–pituitary–adrenocortical axis. *TINS, 20,* 78–84.

Hernandez-Reif, M., Field, T., Largie, S., Diego, M., Manigat, N., Seoanes, J., et al. (2005). Cerebral palsy symptoms in children decreased following massage therapy. *Early Child Development and Care, 175,* 445–456.

Herrnstein, R.J., & Murray, C. (1994). *The bell-curve: Intelligence and class structure in American life.* New York: Free Press.

Herz, R. (2004). A naturalistic analysis of autobiographical memories triggered by olfactory visual and auditory stimuli. *Chemical Senses, 29,* 217–224.

Hesse, E., & Main, M. (2006). Frightened, threatening, and dissociative parental behavior in low-risk samples: Description, discussion, and interpretations. *Development and Psychopathology, 18,* 309–343.

Hettema, J.M., Neale, M.C., & Kendler, K.S. (2001). A review and meta-analysis of the genetic epidemiology of anxiety disorders. *American Journal of Psychiatry, 158,* 1568–1578.

Hien, D.A., & Miele, G.M. (2003). Emotion-focused coping as a mediator of maternal cocaine abuse and antisocial behavior. *Psychology of Addictive Behaviors, 17,* 49–55.

Hilgard, E. (1965). *Hypnotic susceptibility.* New York: Harcourt, Brace, & World.

Hilgard, E. (1977). *Divided consciousness: Multiple controls in human thought and action.* New York: Wiley.

Hill, K.T., & Wigfield, A. (1984). Test anxiety: A major educational problem and what can be done about it. *Elementary School Journal, 85,* 105–126.

Hiller, H.H., & Chow, V. (2005). Ethnic identity and segmented assimilation among second-generation Chinese youth. *Sociological Studies of Children and Youth, 10,* 75–99.

Hillman, C.H., Buck, S.M., Themanson, J.R., Pontifex, M.B., & Castelli, D.M. (2009). Aerobic fitness and cognitive development: Event-related brain potential and task performance indices of executive control in preadolescent children. *Developmental Psychology, 45,* 114–129.

Hillman, C.H., Erickson, K.I., & Kramer, A.F. (2008). Be smart, exercise your heart: Exercise effects on brain and cognition. *Nature Reviews Neuroscience, 9,* 58–65.

Hindmarch I., Dawson, J., & Stanley, N. (2005). A double-blind study in healthy volunteers to assess the effects on sleep of pregabalin compared with alprazolam and placebo. *Sleep, 28,* 187–93.

Hinduja, S., & Patchin, J.W. (2008). Cyberbullying: An exploratory analysis of factors related to offending and victimization. *Deviant Behavior, 29,* 129–156.

Hines, L.M., & Rimm, E.B. (2001). Moderate alcohol consumption and coronary heart disease: A review. *Postgraduate Medical Journal, 77,* 747–752.

Hines, M., Fane, B., Pasterski, V., Matthews, G., Conway, G., & Brook, C. (2003). Spatial abilities following prenatal androgen abnormality: Targeting and mental rotations performance in individuals with congenital adrenal hyperplasia. *Psychoneuroendocrinology, 28,* 1010–1026. doi: 10.1016/S0306-4530(02)00121-X.

Hirshfeld-Becker, D.R., Masek, B., Henin, A., Blakely, L.R., Pollock-Wurman, R.A., McQuade, J., . . . Biederman, J. (2010). Cognitive behavioral therapy for 4- to 7-year-old children with anxiety disorders: A randomized clinical trial. *Journal of Consulting and Clinical Psychology, 78,* 498–510.

Hirst, W., Phelps, E.A., Buckner, R.L., Budson, A.E., Cuc, A., Gabrieli, J.D.E., Johnson, M.K., Lustig, C., Lyle, K.B., Mather, M., Meksin, R., Mitchell, K.J., Ochsner, K.N., Schacter, D.L., Simons, J.S., Vaidya, C.J. (2009). Long-term memory for the terrorist attack of September 11: Flashbulb memories, event memories, and the factors that influence their retention. *Journal of Experimental Psychology: General, 138,* 161–76.

Hirstein, William, & Ramachandran, V.S. (1997). Capgras Syndrome: A novel probe for understanding the neural representation of the identity and familiarity of persons. *Proceedings: Biological Sciences, 264*(1380), 437–444.

Ho, Y-C, Cheung, M-C, & Chan, A.S. (2003). Music training improves verbal but not visual memory: Cross-sectional and longitudinal explorations in children. *Neuropsychology, 17,* 439–450.

Hoaken, P.N.S., & Pilh, R.O. (2000). The effects of alcohol intoxication on aggressive responses in men and women. *Alcohol and Alcoholism, 35,* 471–477.

Hodgkin, A.L., & Huxley, A.F. (1939). Action potentials recorded from inside a nerve fibre. *Nature, 144,* 710–711.

Hoff, E. (2006). How social contexts support and shape language development. *Developmental Review, 26,* 55–88.

Hoff, E., Core, C., Place, S., Rumiche, R., Senor, M., & Parra, M. (2012). Dual language exposure and early bilingual development. *Journal of Child Language, 39,* 1–27. doi: 10.1017/S0305000910000759.

Hoff, T.L. (1992). Psychology in Canada one hundred years ago: James Mark Baldwin at the University of Toronto. *Canadian Psychology, 33,* 683–694.

Hofman, S.G., Schulz, S.M., Meuret, A.F., Moscovitch, D.A., & Suvak, M. (2006). Sudden gains during therapy of social phobia. *Journal of Consulting and Clinical Psychology, 74,* 687–697.

Hofstede, G. (1980). *Culture's consequences: International differences in work-related values.* Beverly Hills, CA: Sage.

Hofstede, G. (2001). *Culture's consequences: Comparing values, behaviors, institutions, and organizations across nations* (2nd ed.). Thousand Oaks, CA: Sage.

Hogan, T.P. (2007). *Psychological testing: A practical introduction* (2nd ed.). New York: John Wiley.

Hogeboom, D.L., McDermott, R.J., Perrin, K.M., Osman, H., & Bell-Ellison, B.A. (2010). Internet use and social networking among middle aged and older adults. *Educational Gerontology, 36*(2), 93–111. doi: 10.1080/03601270903058507.

Hogg, M.A., & Hains, S.C. (1998). Friendship and group identification: a new look at the role of cohesiveness in groupthink. *European Journal of Social Psychology, 28,* 323–341.

Hohmann, A.G., Suplita, R.L., Bolton, N.M., Neely, M.H., Fegley, D., Mangieri R., et al. (2005). An endocannabinoid mechanism for stress-induced analgesia. *Nature, 435,* 1108–1112.

Holland, J.L. (1985). *Making vocational choices: A theory of vocational personalities and work environments* (2nd ed.). Englewood Cliffs, NJ: Prentice-Hall.

Holland, P.C., & Petrovich, G.D. (2005). A neural systems analysis of the potentiation of feeding by conditioned stimuli. *Physiology and Behaviour, 86,* 747–761

Hollon, S.D., DeRubeis, R.J., Shelton, R.C., Amsterdam, J.D., Salomon, R.M., O'Reardon, J.P., et al. (2005). Prevention of relapse following cognitive therapy vs medications in moderate to several depression. *Archives of General Psychiatry, 62,* 417–422.

Holmes, J., Gathercole, S.E., & Dunning, D.L. (2009). Adaptive training leads to sustained enhancement of poor working memory in children. *Developmental Science, 12,* F9–F15.

Holmes, T.H., & Rahe, R.H. (1967). The social readjustment rating scale. *Journal of Psychosomatic Research, 11,* 211–218.

Holstege, G., Georgiadis, J., Paans, A., Meiners, L., van der Graaf, F., & Reinders, A. (2003). Brain activation during human male ejaculation. *Journal of Neuroscience, 23*(27), 9185–9193.

Hopfield, J.J. (1982). Neural networks and physical systems with emergent collective computational abilities. *Proceedings of the National Academy of Science, 79,* 2554–2558.

Hopson, J.L. (1998, September/October). Fetal psychology. *Psychology Today, 31,* 44. Retrieved from http://www.leaderu.com/orgs/tul/psychtoday9809.html.

Horn, J.L., & Cattell, R.B. (1966). Refinement and test of the theory of fluid and crystallized general intelligences. *Journal of Educational Psychology, 57,* 253–270.

Horney, K. (1945). *Our inner conflicts: A constructive theory of neurosis.* New York: Norton.

Horney, K. (1950). *Neurosis and human growth: The struggle toward self-realization.* New York: Norton.

Horrey, W.J., & Wickens, C.D. (2006). Examining the impact of cell phone conversations on driving using meta-analytic techniques. *Human Factors, 48,* 196–205.

Horwitz, A.V., White, H.R., & Howell-White, S. (1996). Becoming married and mental health: A longitudinal study of a cohort of young adults. *Journal of Marriage and the Family, 58,* 895–907.

Hosking, S., Young, K., & Regan, M. (2006). The effects of text messaging on young novice driver performance: Monash University Accident Research Centre, Report No. 246. Retrieved from http://www.monash.edu.au/muarc/reports/muarc246.pdf.

Hoss, R.A., & Langlois, J.H. (2003). Infants prefer attractive faces. In O. Pascalis & A. Slater (Eds.), *The development of face processing in infancy and early childhood: Current perspectives* (pp. 27–38). New York: Nova Science.

How a Swiss inventor hooked the world. (2007, January 4). Retrieved September 16, 2007, from http://www.swissinfo.org/eng/search/detail/How a_Swiss_invention_hooked_the_world.html?siteSect=881&sid=7402384&cKey=1167927120000.

Howard, K.I., Kopta, S.M., Krause, M.S., & Orlinsky, D.E. (1986). The dose-effect relationship in psychotherapy. *American Psychologist, 41,* 159–164.

Howard, M.A., & Marczinski, C.A. (2010). Acute effects of a glucose energy drink on behavioral control. *Experimental and Clinical Psychopharmacology, 18, 553–61.*

Howe, D. (2010). ADHD and its comorbidity: An example of gene-environment interaction and its implications for child and family social work. *Child & Family Social Work, 15,* 265–275. doi: 10.1111/j.1365-2206.2009.00666.x.

Howes, C., & Matheson, C.C. (1992). Sequences in the development of competent play with peers: Social and social pretend play. *Developmental Psychology, 28,* 961–974.

Huang, A., Chen, X., Hoon, M.A., Chandrashekar, J., Guo, W., Tränkner, D., Ryba, N.J.P., and Zuker, C.S. (2006). The cells and logic for mammalian sour taste detection. *Nature, 442,* 934–938.

Huang, H., Coleman, S., Bridge, J.A., Yonkers, K., & Katon, W. (2013). A meta-analysis of the relationship between antidepressant use in pregnancy and the risk of preterm birth and low birth weight. *General Hospital Psychiatry,* published online at prepublication at http://dx.doi.org/10.1016/j.genhosppsych.2013.08.002.

Hubbard, E.M., & Ramachandran, V.S. (2005). Neurocognitive mechanisms of synesthesia. *Neuron, 48,* 509–520.

Hubel, D., & Wiesel, T. (1962). Receptive fields, binocular inter action and functional architecture in the cat's visual cortex. *Journal of Physiology of London, 160,* 106–154.

Hubel, D., & Wiesel, T. (1979). Brain mechanisms of vision. *Scientific American, 241,* 130–144.

Hudson, W. (1960). Pictorial depth perception in subcultural groups in Africa. *Journal of Social Psychology, 52,* 183–208.

Huesmann, L.R., Moise-Titus, J., & Podolski, C. (2003). Longitudinal relations between children's exposure to TV violence and their aggressive and violent behavior in young adulthood: 1977–1992. *Developmental Psychology, 39,* 201–221.

Huet, N., & Mariné, C. (2005). Clustering and expertise in a recall task: The effect of item organization criteria. *Learning and Instruction, 15,* 297–311.

Huff, D. (1954). *How to lie with statistics.* New York: Norton.

Hull, C.L. (1943). *Principles of behavior: An introduction to behavior theory.* New York: Appleton-Century.

Hultsch, D.F., Hunter, M.A., MacDonald, S.W.S., & Strauss, E. (2005). Inconsistency in response time as an indicator of cognitive aging. In J. Duncan, L. Phillips, & P. McLeod (Eds.), *Measuring the mind* (pp. 35–58). New York: Oxford University Press.

Hultsch, D.F., MacDonald, S.W.S., Hunter, M.A., Levy-Bencheton, J., & Strauss, E. (2000). Intraindividual variability in cognitive performance in older adults: Comparison of adults with mild dementia, adults with arthritis, and healthy adults. *Neuropsychology, 14,* 588–598.

Hunt, M. (2007). *The story of psychology.* New York: Anchor.

Hunter, J.E., & Schmidt, F.L. (2000). Racial and gender bias in ability and achievement tests: Resolving the apparent paradox. *Psychology, Public Policy and Law, 6,* 151–158.

Hunter, J.P., Katz, J., & Davis, K.D. (2008). Stability of phantom limb phenomena after upper limb amputation: A longitudinal study. *Neuroscience, 156,* 139–149.

Huprich, S. (2008). TAT oral dependency scale. *A handbook of clinical scoring systems* *for thematic apperceptive techniques* (pp. 385–398). Mahwah, NJ: Erlbaum.

Huston, A., Wright, J., Marquis, J., & Green, S. (1999). How young children spend their time: television and other activities. *Developmental Psychology, 35*(4), 912–925.

Huttenlocher, J., Vasilyeva, M., Cymerman, E., & Levine, S. (2002). Language input at home and at school: Relation to child syntax. *Cognitive Psychology, 45,* 337–374.

Hyde, J.S. (1990). Meta-analysis and the psychology of gender differences. *Signs: Journal of Women in Culture & Society, 16,* 53–73.

Hyde, J.S. (2005). The genetics of sexual orientation. In J.S. Hyde (Ed.), *Biological substrates of human sexuality* (pp. 9–20). Washington, DC: American Psychological Association.

Hyde, J.S., Mezulis, A.H., & Abramson, L.Y. (2008). The ABCs of depression: Integrating affective, biological, and cognitive models to explain the emergence of the gender difference in depression. *Psychological Review, 115*(2), 291–313. doi:10.1037/0033-295X.115.2.291.

Hyde, K.L., Lerch, J., Norton, A., Forgeard, M., Winner, E., Evans, A.C., & Schlaug, G. (2009). Musical training shapes structural brain development. *The Journal of Neuroscience, 29,* 3019–3025.

Hyde, T.S., & Jenkins, J.J. (1973). Recall for words as a function of semantic, graphic, and syntactic orienting tasks. *Journal of Verbal Learning and Verbal Behavior, 12,* 471–480.

Hyman, S.E. (2005). Neurotransmitters. *Current Biology, 15,* R154–R158. *I feel I am trapped inside my head, banging against its walls, trying desperately to escape.* (1986, March 18). *New York Times.* Retrieved from http://www.nytimes.com.

Hyman, S.E. (2010). Emerging neurotechnologies for lie-detection: Where are we now? An appraisal of Wolpe, Foster and Langleben's "Emerging neurotechnologies for lie-detection: Promise and perils" five years later. *The American Journal of Bioethics, 10,* 49–50.

Iacoboni, M., & Mazziotta, J.C. (2007). Mirror neuron system: Basic findings and clinical applications. *Annals of Neurology, 62,* 213–218.

Iacoboni, M., Woods R.P., Brass, M., Bekkering, H., Mazziotta, J.C., & Rizzolatti, G. (1999). Cortical mechanisms of human imitation. *Science, 286,* 2526–2528.

Iarocci, G., & McDonald, J. (2006). Sensory integration and the perceptual experience of persons with autism. *Journal of Autism and Developmental Disorders, 36,* 77–90.

Ilieva, I., Boland, J., Farah, M.J. (2013). Objective and subjective cognitive enhancing effects of mixed amphetamine salts in healthy people. *Neuropharmacology, 64,* 496–505.

Inagaki, T.K., & Eisenberger, N.I. (2013). Shared neural mechanisms underlying social warmth and physical warmth. *Psychological Science, 24,* 2272–2280. doi: 10.1177/0956797613492773.

Inhelder, B., & Piaget, J. (1958). *The growth of logical thinking: From childhood to adolescence.* New York: Basic Books. *Institutional Review Board Guidebook.* (1993). U.S. Department of Health & Human Services. Retrieved January 10, 2008, from http://www.hhs.gov/ohrp/irb/irb_guidebook.htm.

Ipsos Reid Corporation. (2012). *The Ipsos Canadian inter@ctive Reid report: 2012 fact guide.* Retrieved from theexchangenetwork.ca/upload/docs/IpsosReid-Canadian%20Internet%20FactGuide.pdf.

Isacsson, G., Rich, C., Jureidini, J., & Raven, M. (2010). The increased use of antidepressants has contributed to the worldwide reduction in suicide rates. *British Journal of Psychiatry, 196,* 429–433.

Isen, A.M., Daubman, K.A., & Nowicki, G.P. (1987). Positive affect facilitates creative problem solving. *Journal of Personality and Social Psychology, 52,* 1122–1131.

Ishigami, Y., & Klein, R.M. (2009). Is a hands-free phone safer than a handheld phone? *Journal of Safety Research, 40,* 157–164.

Itri, J., Michel, S., Waschek, J., & Colwell, C. (2004). Circadian rhythm in inhibitory synaptic transmission in the mouse suprachiasmatic nucleus. *Journal of Neurophysiology, 92*(1), 311–319.

Iversen, S.D., & Iversen, L.L. (2007). Dopamine: 50 years in perspective. *Trends in Neurosciences, 30,* 188–193.

Iverson, L. (2003). Cannabis and the brain. *Brain, 126,* 1252–1270.

Izard, C.E. (1969). The emotions and emotion constructs in personality and culture research. In R.B. Cattell (Ed.), *Handbook of modern personality theory.* Chicago: Aldine Press.

Izard, C.E., Trentacosta, C.J., King, K.A., & Mostow, A.J. (2004). An emotion-based prevention program for Head Start children. *Early Education & Development, 15,* 407–422.

Jablensky, A., & Woodbury, M.A. (1995). Dementia praecox and manic-depressive insanity in 1908: A Grade of Membership analysis of the Kraepelinian dichotomy. *European Archives of Psychiatry and Clinical Neuroscience, 245,* 202–209.

Jabr, F. (2013, April 30). New DSM-5 ignores biology of mental illness. *Scientific American.* Retrieved from http://www.scientificamerican.com/article/new-dsm5-ignores-biology-mental-illness/.

Jackson, K.M. (2008). Heavy episodic drinking: Determining the predictive utility of five or more drinks. *Psychology of Addictive Behaviors, 22,* 68–77.

Jackson, L.A., von Eye, A., Biocca, F.A., Barbatsis, G., Zhao, Y., & Fitzgerald, H.E. (2006). Does home Internet use influence the academic performance of low-income children? *Developmental Psychology, 42,* 429–435.

Jacobs, B.L. (2004). Depression: The brain finally gets into the act. *Current Directions in Psychological Science, 13,* 103–106.

Jacobs, B.L., van Praag, H., & Gage, F.H. (2000). Adult brain neurogenesis and psychiatry: A novel theory of depression. *Molecular Psychiatry, 5,* 262–269.

Jacobs, J., Weidemann, C.T., Miller, J.F., Solway, A, Burke, J.F., Wei, X-X., Suthana, N., Sperling, M.R., Sharan, A.D., Fried, I., Kahana, M.J. (2013). Direct recordings of grid-like neuronal activity in human spatial navigation. *Nature Neuroscience, 16,* 1188–1191.

Jacobs, L.F. (2003). The evolution of the cognitive map. *Brain, Behavior, & Evolution, 62,* 128–139.

Jacobson, A.L. (1963). Learning in flatworms and annelids. *Psychological Bulletin, 60,* 74–94.

Jacobson, L.H., Kelly, P.H., Bettler, B., Kaupmann, K., & Cryan, J.F. (2006). GABAB(1) receptor isoforms differentially mediate the acquisition and extinction of aversive taste memories. *Journal of Neuroscience, 26,* 8800–8803.

Jacobson, S., & Jacobson, J. (2000). *Teratogenic insult and neurobehavioral function in infancy and childhood.* Mahwah, NJ: Erlbaum.

Jacoby, L.L., & Dallas, M. (1981). On the relationship between autobiographical memory and perceptual learning. *Journal of Experimental Psychology: General, 110,* 306–340.

Jacoby, L.L., Hessels, S., & Bopp, K. (2001). Proactive and retro active effects in memory performance: Dissociating recollection and accessibility bias. In H. Roediger, J.S. Nairne, I. Neath, & A.M. Suprenant (Eds.), *The nature of remembering: Essays in honor of Robert G. Crowder* (pp. 35–54). Washington, DC: American Psychological Association.

Jain, S., Dharap, S.B., & Gore, M.A. (2008). Early prediction of outcome in very severe closed head injury. *Injury: International Journal of the Care of the Injured, 39,* 598–603.

James, J., & Zarrett, N. (2006). Ego integrity in the lives of older women. *Journal of Adult Development, 13,* 61–75.

James, W. (1884). What is an emotion? *Mind, 9,* 188–205.

Jamison, K.R. (1993). *Touched with fire: Manic-depressive illness and the artistic temperament.* New York: Free Press.

Jamison, K.R., Gerner, R.H., Hammen, C., & Padesky, C. (1980). Clouds and silver linings: Positive experiences associated with primary affective disorders. *American Journal of Psychiatry, 137,* 198–202.

Janeck, A.S., Calamari, J.E., Riemann, B.C., & Heffelfinger, S.K. (2003). Too much thinking about thinking? Metacognitive differences in obsessive-compulsive disorder. *Journal of Anxiety Disorders, 17,* 181–195.

Janis, I.L. (1983). *Groupthink* (2nd ed., revised). Boston: Houghton-Mifflin.

Janssen, I., Shields, M., Craig, C.L., & Tremblay, M.S. (2010). Prevalence and secular changes in abdominal obesity in Canadian adolescents and adults, 1981 to 2007–2009. *Obesity Review, 12*(6), 397–405.

Jauk, E., Benedek, M., Dunst, B., & Neubauer, A.C. (2013). The relationship between intelligence and creativity: New support for the threshold hypothesis by means of empirical breakpoint detection. *Intelligence, 41,* 212–221.

Javitt, D.C., & Coyle, J.T. (2004). Decoding schizophrenia. *Scientific American, 290,* 48–55.

Jenkins, W.M., Merzenich, M.M., Ochs, M.T., Allard, T., & Guic-Roble, E. (1990). Functional reorganization of primary somatosensory cortex in adult owl monkeys after behaviorally controlled tactile stimulation. *Journal of Neurophysiology, 63,* 82–104.

Jensen, A.R. (1969). How much can we boost IQ and scholastic achievement? *Harvard Educational Review, 39,* 1–23.

Jha, A.P., Krompinger, J., & Baime, M.J. (2007). Mindfulness training modifies subsystems of attention. *Cognitive, Affective, & Behavioral Neuroscience, 7,* 109–119.

Ji, D., & Wilson, M.A. (2007). Coordinated memory replay in the visual cortex and hippo campus during sleep. *Nature Neuroscience, 10,* 100–107.

Ji, Y.G., Hwangbo, H., Yi, J.S., Rau, P.L.P., Fang, X., & Ling, C. (2010). The influence of cultural differences on the use of social network services and the formation of social capital. *International Journal of Human-Computer Interaction, 26,* 1100–1121.

Jiang, M., Green, R.J., Henley, T.B., & Masten, W.G. (2009). Acculturation in relation to the acquisition of a second language. *Journal of Multilingual and Multicultural Development, 30*(6), 481–492.

Jiang, X., Tien, G., Huang, D., Zheng, B., & Atkins, M.S. (2013). Capturing and evaluating blinks from video-based eyetrackers. *Behavior Research Methods, 45*(3), 656–663. doi:10.3758/s13428-012-0294-x.

Jimenez, R.T., Garcia, G.E., & Pearson, P.D. (1994). *The metacognitive strategies of Latina/o students who read Spanish and English.* Center for the Study of Reading, Technical Report No. 601. Urbana-Champagne, IL: College of Education.

Johansson, S. (2013). The talking Neanderthals: What do fossils, genetics, and archeology say? *Biolinguistics, 7,* 35–74.

John, O.P., & Gross, J.J. (2004). Healthy and unhealthy emotion regulation: Personality processes, individual differences, and life span development. *Journal of Personality, 72,* 1301–1333.

John, O.P., & Srivastava, S. (1999). The Big Five trait taxonomy: History, measurement, and theoretical perspectives. In L.A. Pervin & O.P. John (Eds.), *Handbook of personality theory and research* (pp. 102–138). New York: Guilford Press.

Johnson, D.F. (1997). Margaret Floy Washburn. *Psychology of Women Newsletter,* pp. 17, 22.

Johnson, D.P., & Whisman, M.A. (2013). Gender differences in rumination: A meta-analysis. *Personality And Individual Differences, 55*(4), 367–374. doi:10.1016/j.paid.2013.03.019

Johnson, R.E., Fudala, P.J., & Payne, R. (2005). Buprenorphine: Considerations for pain management. *Journal of Pain and Symptom Management, 29,* 297–326.

Johnson, W., Carothers, A., & Deary, I. (2009). A role for the X chromosome in sex differences in variability in general intelligence? *Perspectives on Psychological Science, 4,* 598–611.

Johnston, J.C., & McClelland, J.L. (1974). Perception of letters in words: Seek not and ye shall find. *Science, 184,* 1192–1994.

Jokela, M., Hintsa, T., Hintsanen, M., & Keltikangas-Jarvinen, L. (2010). Adult temperament and childbearing over the life course. *European Journal of Personality, 24,* 151–166.

Jope, R.S. (1999). Anti-bipolar therapy: Mechanism of action of lithium. *Molecular Psychiatry, 4,* 117–128.

Jordahl, T., & Lohman, B.J. (2009). A bioecological analysis of risk and protective factors associated with early sexual intercourse of young adolescents. *Children and Youth Services Review, 31,* 1272–1282.

Josephson, W. (1987). Television violence and children's aggression: Testing the priming, social script, and disinhibition predictions. *Journal of Personality and Social Psychology, 53,* 882–890.

Judd, T., & Kennedy, G. (2010). A five-year study of on-campus Internet use by undergraduate biomedical students. *Computers & Education, 55,* 1564–1571.

Juliano, L.M., & Griffiths, R.R. (2004). A critical review of caffeine withdrawal: Empirical validation of symptoms and signs, incidence, severity, and associated features. *Psychopharmacology, 176,* 1–29.

Jump, V.K., Fargo, J.D., & Akers, J.F. (2006). Impact of massage therapy on health outcomes among orphaned infants in Ecuador: Results of a randomized clinical trial. *Family & Community Health, 29,* 314–319.

Jung, C.G. (1918/1964). The role of the unconscious. In *Collected works* (Vol. 10; Trans. R.F.C. Hull). New York: Bollingen Foundation.

Jung, R.E., Gasparovic, C., Chavez, R.S., Flores, R.A., Smith, S.M., Caprihan, A., & Yeo, R.A. (2009). Biochemical support for the "threshold" theory of creativity: A magnetic resonance spectroscopy study. *The Journal of Neuroscience, 29,* 5319–5325.

Jusczyk, P.W. (1997). *The discovery of spoken language.* Cambridge, MA: MIT Press.

Jussim, L., & Harber, K.D. (2005). Teacher expectations and self-fulfilling prophecies: Knowns and unknowns, resolved and unresolved controversies. *Personality and Social Psychology Review, 9,* 131–155.

Kabat-Zinn, J. (1990). *Full catastrophe living.* New York: Delta.

Kabat-Zinn, J., Lipworth, L., & Burney, R. (1985). The clinical use of mindfulness meditation for the self-regulation of chronic pain. *Journal of Behavioral Medicine, 8,* 163–190.

Kabat-Zinn, J., Massion, A.O., Kristeller, J., Peterson, L.G., Fletcher, K.E., Pbert, L., et al. (1992). Effectiveness of a meditation-based stress reduction program in the treatment of anxiety disorders. *American Journal of Psychiatry, 149,* 936–943.

Kabat-Zinn, J., Wheeler, E., Light, T., Skillings, A., Scharf, M.J., Cropley, T.G., et al. (1998). Influence of a mindfulness meditation-based stress reduction intervention on rates of clearing in patients with moderate to severe psoriasis undergoing phototherapy (UVB) and photochemotherapy (PUVA). *Psychosomatic Medicine, 60,* 625–632.

Kagan, J. (2003). Biology, context, and developmental inquiry. *Annual Review of Psychology, 54,* 1–23.

Kahan, T.L. (2001). Consciousness in dreaming. A metacognitive approach. In T. Bulkeley (Ed.), *Dreams: A reader on religious, cultural, and psychological dimensions of dreaming* (pp. 333–360). New York: Palgrave Macmillan.

Kahn, R.S., Khoury, J., Nichols, W.C., & Lanphear, B.P. (2003). Role of dopamine transporter genotype and maternal prenatal smoking in childhood hyperactive-impulsive, inattentive, and oppositional behaviors. *The Journal of Pediatrics, 143,* 104–110.

Kahneman, D., & Tversky, A. (1973). On the psychology of prediction. *Psychological Review, 80,* 237–251.

Kahneman, D. (2002). Autobiography—Nobel Prize for 2002 in Economics. Retrieved December 15, 2006, from http://nobelprize.org/nobel_prizes/economics/laureates/2002/kahneman-autobio.html.

Kahneman, D., & Tversky, A. (1972). Subjective probability: A judgment of representativeness. *Cognitive Psychology, 3,* 430–454.

Kaiser Family Foundation. (2003). *Zero to six: Media use in the lives of infants, toddlers, and preschoolers.* Menlo Park, CA: Kaiser Family Foundation.

Kaiser, B., & Bouvard, M. (2009). Obsessive-compulsive disorder in children and adolescents: Efficacy of combined treatment. *Clinical Neuropsychiatry: Journal of Treatment Evaluation, 6,* 94–100.

Kalat, J.W. (2007). *Biological psychology* (9th ed.). Belmont, CA: Wadsworth.

Kaliman, P., Parrizas, M., Lalanza, J.F., Camins, A., Escoriheula, R.M., & Pallas, M. (2011). Neurophysiological and epigenetic effects of physical exercise on the aging process. *Ageing Research Reviews, 10,* 475–486. doi: 10.1016/j.arr.2011.05.002.

Kam, C.M., Greenberg, M.T., & Kusché, C.A. (2004). Sustained effects of the PATHS curriculum on the social and psychological adjustment of children in special education. *Journal of Emotional and Behavioral Disorders, 12,* 66–78.

Kam, C.M., Greenberg, M.T., & Walls, C.T. (2003). Examining the role of implementation quality in school-based prevention using the PATHS curriculum. *Prevention Science, 4,* 55–63.

Kaminski, J., Call, J., & Fischer, J. (2004). Word learning in a domestic dog: Evidence for "fast mapping" *Science, 304,* 1682–1683.

Kammrath, L.K., Mendoza-Denton, R., & Mischel, W. (2005). Incorporating *if . . . then . . .* personality signatures in person perception: Beyond the person–situation dichotomy. *Journal of Personality and Social Psychology, 88,* 605–618.

Kanarek, R.B. (1994). Does sucrose or aspartame cause hyperactivity in children? *Nutrition Reviews, 52*(5), 173–175.

Kanayama, G., Rogowska, J., Pope, H.G., Gruber, S.A., & Yurgelun-Todd, D.A. (2004). Spatial working memory in heavy cannabis users: A functional magnetic resonance imaging study. *Psychopharmacology, 176,* 239–247.

Kandel, E.R. (2000a). Disorders of thought and volition: Schizophrenia. In E.R. Kandel, J.H. Schwartz, & T.M. Jessell (Eds.), *Principles of neural science* (4th ed., pp. 1188–1208). New York: McGraw-Hill.

Kandel, E.R. (2000b). Nerve cells and behavior. In E.R. Kandel, J.M. Schwartz, & T.M. Jessell (Eds.). *Principles of neural science* (4th ed., pp. 19–35). New York: McGraw-Hill.

Kandel, E.R. (2001). The molecular biology of memory storage: A dialogue between genes and synapses. *Science, 294,* 1030–1038.

Kandel, E.R. (2004). The molecular biology of memory storage: A dialog between genes and synapses. *Bioscience Reports, 24,* 477–522.

Kandel, E.R. (2006). *In search of memory: The emergence of a new science of mind.* New York: Norton.

Kandel, E.R., Kupfermann, I., & Iversen, S. (2000). Learning and memory. In E.R. Kandel, J.H. Schwartz, & T.M. Jessell (Eds.), *Principles of neural science* (4th ed., pp. 1227–1246). New York: McGraw-Hill.

Kanner, A.D., Coyne, J.C., Schaefer, C., & Lazarus, R.S. (1981). Comparison of two modes of stress measurement: Daily hassles and uplifts versus major life events. *Journal of Behavioral Medicine, 4,* 1–39.

Kanner, L. (1943). Autistic disturbances of affective contact. *Nervous Child, 2,* 217–250.

Kanwisher, N. (2000). Domain specificity in face perception. *Nature Neuroscience, 3,* 759.

Karama, S., Lecours, A.R., Leroux, J-M., Bourgouin, P., Beaudoin, G., Joubert, S., et al. (2002). Areas of brain activation in males and females during viewing of erotic film excerpts. *Human Brain Mapping, 16,* 1–13.

Karlsen, P.J., Allen, R.J., Baddeley, A.D., & Hitch, G.J. (2010). Binding across space and time in visual working memory. *Memory and Cognition, 38,* 292–303.

Karni, A., Tanne, D., Rubenstein, B.S., Askenasy, J.J.M., & Sagi, D. (1994). Dependence on REM sleep of overnight improvement of a perceptual skill. *Science, 265,* 679–682.

Karraker, K.H., Vogel, D.A., & Lake, M.A. (1995). Parents' gender-stereotyped perceptions of newborns: the eye of the beholder revisited. *Sex Roles, 33,* 687–701.

Karwowski, M., & Gralewski, J. (2013). Threshold hypothesis: Fact or artifact? *Thinking Skills and Creativity, 8,* 25–33.

Kassin, S.M. (2008). Confession evidence: Commonsense myths and misconceptions. *Criminal Justice and Behaviour, 35,* 1309–1322.

Kassin, S.M., Meissner, C.A., & Norwick, R.J. (2005). "I'd know a false confession if I saw one": A comparative study of college students and police investigators. *Law and Human Behaviour, 29,* 211–227.

Kaufman, A.S. (1979). *Intelligent testing with the WISC-R.* New York: Wiley.

Kaufman, A.S., & Kaufman, N.L. (1983). *K-ABC interpretative manual.* Circle Pines, MN: American Guidance Service. (2nd ed., 2004, KABC-II).

Kaviani, H., Javaheri, F., & Hatami, N. (2011). Mindfulness-based cognitive therapy (MBCT) reduces depression and anxiety induced by real stressful setting in non-clinical population. *International Journal of Psychology and Psychology Therapy, 11,* 285–296.

Kawamura, Y., & Kare, M.R. (1987). *Umami: A basic taste.* New York: Dekker.

Kay, J., & Kay, R.L. (2008). Individual psychoanalytic psychotherapy. In A. Tasman, J. Kay, J.A. Lieberman, M.B. First, & M. Maj (Eds.), *Psychiatry* (3rd ed.). New York, NY: Wiley-Blackwell.

Kay, L.M., & Sherman, S.M. (2007). An argument for an olfactory thalamus. *Trends in Neurosciences, 30,* 47–53.

Kazdin, A.E. (2006). Arbitrary metrics: Implications for identifying evidence-based treatments. *American Psychologist, 61*(1), 42–49. doi:10.1037/0003-066X.61.1.42.

Keel, P.K., & Klump, K.L. (2003). Are eating disorders culture-bound syndromes? Implications for conceptualizing their etiology. *Psychological Bulletin, 129,* 747–767.

Keeler, R.F. (1983). Naturally occurring teratogens from plants. In R.F. Keeler & A.T. Tu (Eds.), *Handbook of natural toxins: Vol. 1. Plant and fungal toxins* (pp. 161–191). New York: Marcel Dekker.

Keenan, R.M., Jenkins, A.J., Cone, E.J., & Henningfield, J.E. (1994). Smoked and IV nicotine, cocaine and heroin have similar abuse liability. *Journal of Addictive Diseases, 13,* 259–269.

Kegeles, L.S., Abi-Dargham, A., Frankle, W.G., Gil, R., Cooper, T.B., Slifstein, M., . . . Laruelle, M. (2010). Increased synaptic dopamine function in associative regions of the striatum in schizophrenia. *Archives in General Psychiatry, 67,* 231–239.

Kehle, S. (2008). The effectiveness of cognitive behavioral therapy for generalized anxiety disorder in a frontline service setting. *Cognitive Behaviour Therapy, 37,* 1–7. doi: 10.1080/16506070802190262.

Keller, A., Litzelman, K., Wisk, L.E., Maddox, T., Cheng, E.R., Creswell, P.D., & Witt, W.P. (2012) Does the perception that stress affects health matter? The association with health and mortality. *Health Psychology, 31,* 677–684.

Keller, M.C., Thiessen, D., & Young, R.K. (1996). Mate assortment in dating and married couples. *Personality and Individual Differences, 21,* 217–221.

Kelley, H.H., & Michela, J.L. (1980). Attribution theory and research. *Annual Review of Psychology, 31,* 457–501.

Kelley, R., & Cornblatt, J. (2010, July 10). How creative are you? *Newsweek.* Retrieved from http://www.newsweek.com/photo/2010/07/10/creativity-test.html.

Kellman, P.J., & Arterberry, M.E. (2006). Infant visual perception. In D. Kuhn & R. Siegler (Eds.), *Handbook of child psychology: Vol. 2, Cognition, perception, and language* (6th ed., 109–160). Hoboken, NJ: Wiley.

Kellner, C.H., Knapp, R.G., Petrides, G., Rummans, T.A., Husain, M.M., Rasmussen, K., et al. (2006). Continuation electroconvulsive therapy vs pharmacotherapy for relapse prevention in major depression. *Archives of General Psychiatry, 63,* 1337–1344.

Kelly, M.M., Tyrka, A.R., Andeson, G.M., Price, L.H., & Carpenter, L.L. (2008). Sex differences in emotional and physiological responses to the Trier Social Stress Test. *Journal of Behavior Therapy and Experimental Psychiatry, 39,* 87–98.

Kelly, W.E., Kelly, K.E., & Clanton, R.C. (2001). The relationship between sleep and grade point average among college students. *College Student Journal, 35*(1), 84–86.

Keltner, D. (1995). Signs of appeasement: Evidence of distinct displays of embarrassment, amusement, and shame. *Journal of Personality and Social Psychology, 68,* 441–454.

Kempermann, G. (2006). Adult neurogenesis. In P.B. Baltes, P.A.Reuter-Lorenz, & F. Rösler (Eds.). *Lifespan development and the brain: The perspective of biocultural co-constructivism* (pp. 82–107). New York: Cambridge University Press.

Kempermann, G., & Gage, F.H. (1999). Experience-dependent regulation of adult hippocampal neurogenesis: Effects of long-term stimulation and stimulus withdrawal. *Hippocampus, 9,* 321–332.

Kendler, K.S., & Prescott, C.A. (2006). *Genes, environment, and psychopathology: Understanding the causes of psychiat-ric and substance use disorders.* New York: Guilford.

Kendler, K.S., Karkowski, L.M., & Prescott, C.A. (1999). Causal relationship between stressful life events and the onset of major depression. *American Journal of Psychiatry, 156,* 837–841.

Kendler, K.S., Kuhn, J.W., Vittum, J., Prescott, C.A., & Riley, B. (2005). The interaction of stressful life events and a serotonin transporter polymorphism in the prediction of episodes of major depression. *Archives of General Psychiatry, 62,* 529–535.

Kendrick, T., Peveler, R., Logworth, L., Baldwin, D., Moore, M., Chatwin, J., et al. (2006). Cost-effectiveness and cost-utility of tricyclic antidepressants, selective serotonin reuptake inhibitors and lofepramine: Randomized controlled trial. *British Journal Psychiatry, 188,* 337–345.

Kennedy, J.M., & Juricevic, I. (2006). Blind man draws using diminution in three dimensions. *Psychonomic Bulletin & Review, 13,* 506–509.

Kennedy, S.H., Evans, K.R., Krüger, S., Mayberg, H.S., Meyer, J.H., McCann, S., et al. (2001). Changes in regional brain glucose metabolism measured with positron emission tomography after paroxetine treatment of major depression. *American Journal of Psychiatry, 158,* 899–905.

Kenrick, D.T., Griskevicius, V., Neuberg, S.L., & Schaller, M. (2010). Renovating the pyramid of needs: Contemporary extensions built upon ancient foundations. *Perspectives on Psychological Science, 5,* 292–314.

Kensinger, E.A., Garoff-Eaton, R.J., & Schacter, D.L. (2007). How negative emotion enhances the visual specificity of a memory. *Journal of Cognitive Neuroscience, 19,* 1872–1887.

Kenyon, C. (2005). The plasticity of aging: Insights from long-lived mutants, *Cell, 120,* 449–460.

Keri, S. (2009). Genes for psychosis and creativity: A promoter polymorphism of the neuregulin 1 gene is related to creativity in people with high intellectual achievement. *Psychological Science, 20,* 1070–1073. doi:10.1111/j.1467-9280.2009.02398.x.

Kernberg, O.F. (2000). *Personality disorders in children and adolescents.* Poulsbo, WA: H-R Press.

Kessler, R.C., Avenevoli, S., McLaughlin, K.A., Greif Green, J., Lakoma, M.D., Pine, D.S., . . . Reis Merikangas, K. (2012). Lifetime comorbidity of DSMIV disorders in the US National Comorbidity Survey Replication Adolescent Supplement (NCSA). *Psychological Medicine, 42,* 1997–2010. doi: 10.1017/S0033291712000025

Kessler, R.C., Berglund, P., Demler, O., Jin, R., Merikangas, K.R., & Walters, E.E. (2005). Lifetime prevalence and age-of-onset distributions of *DSM-IV* disorders in the National Comorbidity Survey replication. *Archives of General Psychiatry, 62,* 593–602.

Kessler, R.C., Birnbaum, H., Bromet, E., Hwang, I., Sampson, N., & Shahly, V. (2010). Age differences in major depression: Results from the National Comorbidity Surveys Replication (NCS-R). *Psychological Medicine, 40,* 225–237. doi:10.1017/S0033291709990213.

Kessler, R.C., Chiu, W.T., Demler, O., & Walters, E.E. (2005). Prevalence, severity, and comorbidity of twelve-month *DSM-IV-TR* disorders in the National Comorbidity Survey Replication (NCS-R). *Archives of General Psychiatry, 62,* 617–627.

Key Learning Community. (n.d.). Retrieved July 13, 2007, from http://www.ncrel.org/sdrs/areas/issues/methods/assment/as7key.htm.

Khandaker, G.M., Dibben, G.R.M., & Jones, P.B. (2012). Prenatal maternal influenza and schizophrenia in offspring: What does this tell us about fetal programming of chronic disease? *Journal of Pediatric Infectious Diseases, 7,* 61–68. doi: 10.3233/JPI-120346.

Khatena, J. (1989). Intelligence and creativity to multitalent. *The Journal of Creative Behavior, 23,* 93–97.

Kiang, L., Yip, T., Gonzales-Backen, M., Witkow, M., & Fuligni, A.J. (2006). Ethnic identity and the daily psychological well-being of adolescents from Mexican and Chinese backgrounds. *Child Development, 77,* 1338–1350.

Kiba, T. (2002). The role of the autonomic nervous system in liver regeneration and apoptosis—Recent developments. *Digestion, 66,* 79–88.

Kiecolt-Glaser, J.K., Garner, W., Speicher, C., Penn, G., Holliday, J., Glaser, R. (1984). Psychosocial modifiers of immunocompetence in medical students. *Psychosomatic Medicine, 46,* 7–14.

Kiecolt-Glaser, J.K., Loving, T.J., Stowell, J.R., Malarkey, W.B., Lemeshow, S., Dickinson, S.L., & Glaser, R. (2005). Hostile marital interactions, proinflammatory cytokine production, and wound healing. *Arch. Gen. Psychiatry, 62,* 1377–1384.

Kiecolt-Glaser, J.K., Marucha, P.T., Malarkey, W.B., Mercado, A.M., & Glaser, R. (1995). Slowing of wound healing by psychological stress. *Lancet, 346,* 1194–1196.

Kiecolt-Glaser, J.K., McGuire, L., Robles, T.F., & Glaser, R. (2002). Psychoneuroimmunology and psychosomatic medicine: Back to the future. *Psychosomatic Medicine, 64,* 15–28.

Kihlstrom, J.F. (2005). Dissociative disorders. *Annual Review of Clinical Psychology, 1,* 227–253.

Kim, B., Lee, S., Choi, T., Suh, S., Kim, Y., Yook, K., & Lee, E.H. (2008). Effectiveness of a combined therapy of long-acting injectable risperidone and psychosocial intervention for relapse prevention in patients with schizophrenia. *Clinical Psychopharmacology and Neuroscience, 6,* 31–37.

Kim, H.K. (2005). Can only intelligent people be creative? A meta-analysis. *Journal of Secondary Gifted Education, 16,* 57–66.

Kim, J.J., & Yoon, K.S. (1998). Stress: Meta plastic effects in the hippocampus. *Trends in Neuroscience, 21,* 505–509.

Kim, K.H.S., Relkin, N.R., Lee, K.M., & Hirsch, J. (1997). Distinct cortical areas associated with native and second languages. *Nature, 388,* 171–174.

Kim, S., & Hasher, L. (2005). The attraction effect in decision making: Superior performance by older adults. *Quarterly Journal of Experimental Psychology, 58A,* 120–133.

Kimball, M.M. (1986). Developing a feminist psychology of women: Past and future accomplishments. *Canadian Psychology/ Psychologie Canadienne, 27*(3), 248–259.

Kimura, D. (2002, May). Sex differences in the brain: Men and women display patterns of behavioral and cognitive differences that reflect varying hormonal influences on brain development. *Scientific American, 12,* 32–37.

Kimura, D. (2007). "Underrepresentation" or misinterpretation? In S.J. Ceci & W.M. Williams (Eds.). *Why aren't more women in science?: Top researchers debate the evidence* (pp. 39–46). Washington, DC: APA.

King, D.E., Mainous, A.G. III, & Geesey, M.E. (2008). Adopting moderate alcohol consumption in middle age: Subsequent cardiovascular events. *The American Journal of Medicine 121,* 201–206.

King, L.A., Hicks, J.A., Krull, J.L., & Del Gaiso, A.K. (2006). Positive affect and the experience of meaning in life. *Journal of Personality and Social Psychology, 90,* 179–196.

Kinley, D.J., Cox, B.J., Clara, I., Goodwin, R.D., & Jitender, S. (2009). Panic attacks and their relation to psychological and physical functioning in Canadians: Results from a nationally representative sample. *Canadian Journal of Psychiatry, 54,* 113–122

Kinney, D.K., Richards, R., Lowing, P.A., LeBlanc, D., Zimbalist, M.E., & Harlan, P. (2000–2001). Creativity in offspring of schizophrenic and control parents: An adoption study. *Creativity Research Journal, 13,* 17–26.

Kinsey, A.C., Pomeroy, W.B., & Martin, C.E. (1948). *Sexual behavior in the human male.* Philadelphia: Saunders.

Kinsey, A.C., Pomeroy, W.B., Martin, C.E., & Gebhard, P.H. (1953). *Sexual behavior in the human female.* Philadelphia: Saunders.

Kinsman, J. (2010). Merkel's musings: Europe's multicultural problem is not ours. *CBC online.* Retrieved November 7, 2010, from http://www.cbc.ca/world /story/2010/10/19/f-vp-kinsman.html.

Kintaka, Y., Osaka, T., Suzuki, Y., Hashiguchi, T., Niijima, A., Kageyama, H., Fumiko, T., Shioda, S., & Inoue, S. (2009). Effects of gastric vagotomy on visceral cell proliferation induced by ventromedial hypothalamic lesions: role of vagal hyperactivity. *Journal of Molecular Neuroscience, 38,* 243–249.

Kirby, E.D., Muroy, S.E., Sun, W.G., Covarrubias, D., Leong, M.J., Barchas, L.A., & Kaufer, D. (2013). Acute stress enhances adult rat hippocampal neurogenesis and activation of newborn neurons via secreted astrocytic FGF2. *eLife, 2;* e00362.

Kirkham, T.C. (2005). Endocannabinoids in the regulation of appetite and body weight. *Behavioral Pharmacology, 16,* 297–313.

Kirkpatrick, L.A. (2005). *Attachment, evolution, and the psychology of religion.* New York: Guilford Press.

Kirsch, I. (2014). Antidepressants and the placebo effect. *Zeitschrift fur Psychologie, 222*(3), 128–134. doi:10.1027/2151-2604/ a000176.

Kirsch, I., Deacon, B.J., Huedo-Medina, T.B., Scoboria, A., Moore, T.J., & Johnson, B.T. (2008). Initial severity and antidepressant benefits: a meta-analysis of data submitted to the Food and Drug Administration. *PLoS Med, 5*(2), 45. doi: 10.1371/ journal.pmed.0050045

Kirsch, I., Moore, T.J., Scoboria, A., & Nicholls, S.S. (2002). The emperor's new drugs: An analysis of antidepressant medication data submitted to the U.S. Food and Drug Administration. *Prevention & Treatment, 5, ArtID23.* Retrieved from http:// www.journals.apa.org/prevention/volume5/ pre0050023a.html

Kirsh, S.J. (2006). Cartoon violence and aggression in youth. *Aggression and Violent Behavior, 11,* 547–557.

Kishiyama, M.M., Boyce, W.T., Jimenez, A.M., Perry, L.M., & Knight, R.T. (2009). Socioeconomic disparities affect prefrontal function in children. *Journal of Cognitive Neuroscience, 21*(6), 1106–1115.

Kisilevsky, B.S., Hains, S.M., Lee, K., Xie, X., Huang, H., Ye, H.H., . . . Wang, Z. (2003). Effects of experience on fetal voice recognition. *Psychological Science (Wiley-Blackwell), 14*(3), 220–224.

Kisilevsky, B.S., Muir, D.W., & Low, J.A. (1992). Maturation of human fetal responses to vibroacoustic stimulation. *Child Development, 63,* 1497–1508.

Klahr, D. (2000). *Exploring science: The cognition and development of discovery processes.* Cambridge, MA: MIT Press.

Klein, N. (2007). *The shock doctrine.* Toronto: Vintage Canada.

Klein, Perry, D. (1998). A response to Howard Gardner: Falsifiability, empirical evidence, and pedagogical usefulness in educational psychology. *Canadian Journal of Education, 23*(1), 103–112.

Klein, R.G. (1999). *The human career: Human biological and cultural origins* (2nd ed.). Chicago: University of Chicago Press.

Klopfer, P.H. (1958). Influence of social interaction on learning rates in birds. *Science, 128,* 903.

Klucharev, V., Hytonen, K., Rijpkema, M., Smidts, A., & Fernandez, G. (2009). Reinforcement learning signal predicts social conformity. *Neuron, 61,* 140–151.

Klüver, H., & Bucy, P. (1939). Preliminary analysis of functioning of the temporal lobes in monkeys. *Archives of Neurology and Psychiatry, 42,* 979–1000.

Knox, R. (2007, April 26). Kids' use of earbuds worries hearing experts. Retrieved from http://www. npr.org/templates/story/story .php?storyId=9797364.

Knutson, B., Adams, C.M., Fong, G.W., & Hommer, D. (2001). Anticipation of increasing monetary reward selectively recruits nucleus accumbens. *Journal of Neuroscience, 2,* RC159.

Kobayashi, M., Saito, S., Kobayakawa, T., Deguchi, Y., & Costanzo, R.M. (2006). Cross-cultural comparison of data using the odor stick identification test for Japanese (OSIT-J). *Chemical Senses, 31,* 335–342.

Koenig, J.I. (2006). Schizophrenia: A unique translational opportunity in behavioral neuroendocrinology. *Hormones and Behavior, 50,* 602–611.

Koerner, K., & Linehan, M.M. (2000). Research on dialectical behavior therapy for patients with borderline personality disorder. *Psychiatric Clinics of North America, 23,* 151–167.

Kogan, A., Impett, E.A., Oveis, C., Hui, B., Gordon, A.M., & Keltner, D. (2010). When giving feels good: The intrinsic benefits of sacrifice in romantic relationships for the communally motivated. *Psychological Science, 21,* 1918–1924. doi:10.1177/0956797610388815.

Koh, J.S., Kang, H., Choi, S.W., & Kim, H.O. (2002). Cigarette smoking associated with premature facial wrinkling: Image analysis of facial skin replicas. *International Journal of Dermatology, 41,* 21–27.

Kohlberg, L. (1981). *Essays on moral development, Vol. I: The philosophy of moral development.* New York: Harper & Row.

Kohn, P.M., Lafreniere, K., & Gurevich, M. (1991). Hassles, health, and personality. *Journal of Personality and Social Psychology, 61,* 478–482.

Kokko, K., Pulkkinen, L., & Mesiäinen, P. (2009). Timing of parenthood in relation to other life transitions and adult social functioning. *International Journal of Behavioral Development, 33*(4), 356–365.

Kolb, B., & Wishaw, I.Q. (2011). *An Introduction to Brain and Behaviour* (3rd ed.). New York: Worth.

Kole, M.H.P., & Stuart, G.J. (2008). Is action potential threshold lowest in the axon? *Nature Neuroscience, 11,* 1253–1255.

Konnert, C., Dobson, K., & Stelmach, L. (2009). The prevention of depression in nursing home residents: a randomized clinical trial of cognitive-behavioral therapy. *Aging and Mental Health, 13,* 288–299.

Kopell, B.H., Rezai, A.R., Chang, J.W., & Vitek, J.L. (2006). Anatomy and physiology of the basal ganglia: Implications for deep brain stimulation for Parkinson's disease. *Movement Disorders, 21,* S238–S246.

Kopta, S.M. (2003). The dose-effect relationship in psychotherapy: A defining achievement for Dr. Kenneth Howard. *Journal of Clinical Psychology, 59,* 727–733.

Koren, G. (2000). Caffeine during pregnancy?: In moderation. *Canadian Family Physician, 46,* 801–803. Retrieved from http://www.motherisk.org/prof/updatesDetail.jsp?content_id=327.

Kornell, N., & Bjork, R.A. (2007). The promise and perils of self–regulated study. *Psychonomic Bulletin & Review, 14,* 219–224.

Kornhaber, M.L., Fierros, E., & Veenema, S. (2004). *Multiple intelligences: Best ideas from research and practice.* Boston, MA: Pearson.

Kosinski, M., Matz, S. Gosling, S., Popov, V., Stillwell, D. (2013) Facebook as a social science research tool: Opportunities, challenges, ethical considerations and practical guidelines. *American Psychologist.*

Kosinski, M., Stillwell, D., & Graepel, T. (2013). Private traits and attributes are predictable from digital records of human behavior. *Proceedings of the National Academy of Sciences, 110,* 5802–5805.

Koslowski, B. (1996). *Theory and evidence: The development of scientific reasoning.* Cambridge, MA: MIT Press.

Kosslyn, S.M. (2002, July 15). What shape are a German shepherd's ears: A talk with Stephen Kosslyn. *Edge,* Retrieved from http://www.edge.org/3rd_culture/kosslyn/kosslyn_index.html.

Kosslyn, S.M. (2005). Mental images and the brain. *Cognitive Neuropsychology, 22,* 333–347.

Kosslyn, S.M., Van Kleeck, M.H., & Kirby, K.N. (1990). A neurologically plausible model of individual differences in visual mental imagery. In P.J. Hampson, D.F. Marks, & J.T.E. Richardson (Eds.), *Imagery: Current developments* (pp. 39–77). Florence, KY: Taylor & Frances/Routledge.

Kounios, J., Frymiare, J.L., Bowden, E.M., Fleck, J.I., Subramaniam, K., Parrish, T.B., et al. (2006). The prepared mind: Neural activity prior to problem presentation predicts subsequent solution by sudden insight. *Psychological Science, 17,* 882–890.

Kovács, A.M. (2009). Early bilingualism enhances mechanisms of false-belief reasoning. *Developmental Science, 12,* 48–54.

Kovács, A.M., & Mehler, J. (2009). Flexible learning of multiple speech structures in bilingual infants. *Science, 325,* 611–612. doi: 10.1126/science.1173947.

Krakauer, J., & Rackliff, R. (1997). *Into Thin Air: A Personal Account of the Mount Everest Disaster.* New York: Anchor Books.

Kramer, P.D. (1993). *Listening to Prozac.* New York: Penguin Books.

Krause, J., Lalueza-Fox, C., Orlando, L., Enard, W., Green, R.E., Burbano, H.A., Hublin, J.J., Hänni, C., Fortea, J., de la Rasilla, M., Bertranpetit, J., Rosas, A., & Pääbol, S. (2007). The derived FOXP2 variant of modern humans was shared with Neanderthals. *Current Biology, 17,* 1908–1912.

Kremer, S., Bult, J.H., Mojet, J., & Kroeze, J.H. (2007). Food perception with age and its relationship to pleasantness. *Chemical Senses, 32,* 591–602.

Kring, A.M., & Gordon, A.H. (1998). Sex differences in emotion: Expression, experience, and physiology. *Journal of Personality and Social Psychology, 74,* 686–703.

Kripke, D.F., Garfinkel, L., Wingard, D.L., Klauber, M.R., & Marler, M.R. (2002). Mortality associated with sleep duration and insomnia. *Archives of General Psychiatry, 59,* 31–36.

Kristeller, J.L., Baer, R.A., & Quillian-Wolever, R. (2006). Mindfulness-based approaches to eating disorders. In R.A. Baer (Ed.), *Mindfulness-based treatment approaches: Clinician's guide to evidence base and applications* (pp. 75–91). San Diego: Elsevier Academic Press.

Kristensen, P., & Bjerkedal, T. (2007). Explaining the relation between birth order and intelligence. *Science, 316,* 1717.

Kristof-Brown, A.L., Zimmerman, R.D., & Johnson, E.C. (2005). Consequences of individual's fit at work: A meta-analysis of person-job, person-organization, person-group, and person-supervisor fit. *Personnel Psychology, 58*(2), 281–342.

Kroeber, A.L. (1948). *Anthropology.* New York: Harcourt Brace Jovanovich.

Kröger, C., Schweiger, U., Sipos, V., Arnold, R., Kahl, K.G., Schunert, T., et al. (2006). Effectiveness of dialectical behavior therapy for borderline personality disorder in an inpatient setting. *Behaviour Research and Therapy, 44,* 1211–1217.

Krueger, R.F. (1999). Personality traits in late adolescence predict mental disorders in early adulthood: A prospective epidemiological study. *Journal of Personality, 67,* 39–65.

Krueger, R.F., & Johnson, W. (forthcoming). *Behavioral genetics and personality: A new look at the integration of nature and nurture.* In L.A. Pervin, O.P. John & R.W. Robins (Eds.), *Handbook of personality: Theory and research* (3rd ed.). New York: Guilford.

Krummel, D., Seligson F., & Guthrie, H. (1996). Hyperactivity: Is candy causal? *Critical Review of Food Science and Nutrition, 36,* 31–47.

Krummel, D.A., Seligson, F.H., & Guthrie, H.A. (1996). Hyperactivity: Is candy causal? *Critical Reviews in Food Science and Nutrition, 36*(1–2), 31–47.

Krupnick, J.L., Sotsky, S.M., Simmens, S., Moyer, J., Elkin, I., Watkins, J., & Pilkonis, P.A. (1996). The role of the therapeutic alliance in psychotherapy and pharmacotherapy outcome: findings in the national institute of mental health treatment of depression collaborative research program. *Journal of Consulting and Clinical Psychology, 64,* 532–539.

Kryger, M.H., Roth, T., & Dement, W.C. (2005). *Principles and practice of sleep medicine* (4th ed.). Philadelphia, PA: Elsevier/Saunders.

Krystal, A.D. (2005). The effect of insomnia definitions, terminology, and classifications on clinical practice. *Journal of American Geriatrics Society, 53,* S255–S263.

Ku, J., Kim, J., Jang, H., Park, S., Kim, S., Kim, C., . . . Kim, S.I. (2005). Relationship between social response to virtual avatar and symptom severity of patients with schizophrenia. *Annual Review of Cyber Therapy and Telemedicine, 3,* 3143–3149.

Kübler-Ross, E. (1969). *On death and dying.* New York: Macmillan.

Kubota, M., Nakazaki, S., Hirai, S., Saeki, N. Yamaura, A., & Kusaka, T. (2001). Alcohol consumption and frontal lobe shrinkage: Study of 1432 non-alcoholic subjects. *Journal of Neurology, Neurosurgery, and Psychiatry, 71,* 104–106.

Kubzansky, L.D., Sparrow, D., Vokonas, P., & Kawachi, I. (2001). Is the glass half empty or half full? A prospective study of optimism and coronary heart disease in the Normative Aging Study. *Psychosomatic Medicine, 63,* 910–916.

Kuczkowski, K. (2009). Caffeine in pregnancy. *Archives of Gynecology and Obstetrics, 280*(5), 695–698.

Kuhl, P.K., & Meltzoff, A.N. (1997). Evolution, nativism, and learning in the development of language and speech. In M. Gopnik (Ed.), *The inheritance and innateness of grammars* (pp. 7–44). New York: Oxford University Press.

Kuhl, P.K., Stevens, E., & Hayashi, A. (2006). Infants show a facilitation effect for native language phonetic perception between 6 and 12 months. *Developmental Science, 9,* F13–F21.

Kuhn, D. (1993). Connecting scientific and informal reasoning. *Merrill-Palmer Quarterly, 39,* 74–103.

Kuhn, D., Amsel, E., & O'Loughlin, M. (1988). *The development of scientific thinking skills.* Orlando FL: Academic Press.

Kuhn, D., & Pearsall, S. (2000). Developmental origins of scientific thinking. *Journal of cognition and development, 1,* 113–129.

Kuo, L.E., Kitlinska, J.B., Tilan, J.U., Li, L., Baker, S.B., Johnson, M.D., et al. (2007). Neuropeptide Y acts directly in the periphery on fat tissue and mediates stress-induced obesity and metabolic syndrome. *Nature Medicine, 13,* 803–811.

Kupfermann, I., Kandel, E.R., & Iversen, S. (2000). Motivational and addictive states. In E.R. Kandel, J.H. Schwartz, & T.M. Jessell (Eds.), *Principles of neural science* (4th ed., pp. 998–1013). New York: McGraw-Hill.

Kurdek, L. (2004). Are gay and lesbian cohabiting couples really different from heterosexual married couples? *Journal of Marriage and Family, 66*(4), 880–900.

Kurson, R. (2007). *Crashing through: The true story of risk, adventure and the man who dared to see.* New York: Random House.

Kusché, C.A., & Greenberg, M.T. (1994). *The PATHS Curriculum.* Seattle: Developmental Research and Programs.

Kwon, Y., & Lawson, A.E. (2000). Linking brain growth with the development of scientific reasoning ability and conceptual change during adolescence. *Journal of Research in Science Teaching, 37,* 44–62.

Kwon, Y., Lawson, A.E., Chung, W., & Kim, Y. (2000). Effect on development of proportional reasoning skill of physical experience and cognitive abilities associated with prefontal lobe activity. *Journal of Research in Science Teaching, 37*(10), 1171–1182.

Laborda, M.A., McConnell, B.L., & Miller, R.R. (2011). Behavioral techniques to reduce relapse after exposure therapy: Applications of studies of experimental extinction. In T.R. Schachtman & S. Reilly (Eds.), *Associative learning and conditioning theory: Human and non-human applications* (pp. 79–103). New York, NY: Oxford University Press.

Lachman, M.E. (2004). Development in midlife. *Annual Review of Psychology, 55,* 305–331.

LaFrance, M., Hecht, M.A., & Paluk, B.L. (2003). The contingent smile: A meta-analysis of sex differences in smiling. *Psychological Bulletin, 129,* 305–334.

Lagopoulos, J. (2007). Functional MRI: An overview. *Acta Neuropsychiatrica, 19,* 64–65.

Lai, C. (2013). Gray matter volume in major depressive disorder: A meta-analysis of voxel-based morphometry studies. *Psychiatry Research: Neuroimaging, 211,* 37–46. doi:10.1016/j.pscychresns.2012.06.006.

Lalonde, J., Hudson, J., Gigante, R., & Pope, H. (2001). Canadian and American psychiatrists' attitudes toward dissociative disorders diagnoses. *The Canadian Journal of Psychiatry / La Revue canadienne de psychiatrie, 46*(5), 407–412.

Lamb, R.J., Morral, A.R., Kirby, K.C., Iguchi, M.Y., & Galbicka, G. (2004). Shaping smoking cessation using percentile schedules. *Drug and Alcohol Dependence, 76,* 247–259.

Lambert, M.J., Horowitz, L.M., & Strupp, H.H. (1997). Recommendations and conclusions. In H.H. Strupp, L.M. Horowitz, M.J. Lambert (Eds.), *Measuring patient changes in mood, anxiety, and personality disorders: Toward a core battery* (pp. 491–502). Washington, DC: American Psychological Association.

Lambracht-Washington, D., & Rosenberg, R.N. (2013). Advances in the development of vaccines for Alzheimer's disease. *Discovery Medicine, 15,* 319–325.

Lamp, R., & Krohn, E. (2001). A longitudinal predictive validity investigation of the SB:FE and K-ABC with at-risk children. *Journal of Psychoeducational Assessment, 19,* 334–349.

Landry, R.G. (1973). The relationship of second language learning and verbal creativity. *Modern Language Journal, 57,* 110–113.

Lang, E., Berbaum, K., Faintuch, S., Hatsiopoulou, O., Halsey, N., Li, X., Berbaum, M., et al. (2006). Adjunctive self-hypnotic relaxation for outpatient medical procedures: A prospective randomized trial with women undergoing large core breast biopsy. *Pain, 126,* 155–164.

Lange, C. (1922). *The emotions* (I.A. Haupt, Trans.). Baltimore: Williams & Wilkins. (Original work published 1885)

Lange, P.G. (2008). Publicly private and privately public: Social networking on YouTube. *Journal of Computer-Mediated Communication, 13,* 361–380.

Langlois, J.H., & Roggman, L.A. (1990). Attractive faces are only average. *Psychological Science, 1,* 115–121.

Langlois, J.H., Roggman, L.A., & Musselman, L. (1994). What is average and what is not average about attractive faces? *Psychological Science, 5,* 214–220.

Lapsley, D.K. (2006). Moral stage theory. In M. Killen & J.G. Smetana (Eds.), *Handbook of moral development* (pp. 37–66). Mahwah, NJ: Erlbaum.

Larson, L.M., Wu, T., Bailey, D.C., Gasser, C.E., Bonitz, V.S., & Borgen, F.H. (2010). The role of personality in the selection of a major: With and without vocational self-efficacy and interests. *Journal of Vocational Behavior, 76*(2), 211–222.

Larsson, J., Larsson, H., & Lichtenstein, P. (2004). Genetic and environmental contributions to stability and change of ADHD symptoms between 8 and 13 years of age: A longitudinal twin study. *Journal of American Academy of Child and Adolescent Psychiatry, 43,* 1267–1275.

Lasagabaster, D. (2000). The effects of three bilingual education models on linguistic creativity. *International Review of Applied Linguistics in Language Teaching, 38,* 213–228.

Laschet, J., Kurcewicz, I., Minier, F., Trottier, S., Khallou-Laschet, J., Louvel, J., et al. (2007). Dysfunction of GABA-sub(A) receptor glycolysis-dependent modulation in human partial epilepsy. *Proceedings of the National Academy of Sciences, 104*(9), 3472–3477.

Laska, K.M., Gurman, A.S., & Wampold, B.E. (2014). Expanding the lens of evidence-based practice in psychotherapy: A common factors perspective. *Psychotherapy, 51,* 467–481. doi:10.1037/a0034332

Latané, B. (1981). The psychology of social impact. *American Psychologist, 36,* 343–356.

Latané, B., & Wolf, S. (1981). The social impact of majorities and minorities. *Psychological Review, 88,* 438–453.

Laureys, S. (2007). Eyes open, brain shut. *Scientific American, 296,* 84–89.

Lavelli, M., & Fogel, A. (2005). Developmental changes in the relationship between the infant's attention and emotion during early face-to-face communication: The 2-month transition. *Developmental Psychology, 41,* 265–280.

Lavie, N. (2007). The role of perceptual load in visual awareness. *Brain Research, 1080,* 91–100.

Lavie, N., Hirst, A., De Fockert, J.W., & Viding, E. (2004). Load theory of selective attention and cognitive control. *Journal of Experimental Psychology: General, 133,* 339–354.

Lavie, P. (2001). Sleep-wake as a biological rhythm. *Annual Review of Psychology, 52,* 277–303.

Law, A.J., Lipska, B.K., Weickert, C.S., Hyde, T.M., Straub, R.E., Hahimoto, R., . . . Weinberger, D.R. (2006). Neuregulin 1 transcripts are differentially expressed in schizophrenia and regulated by 5' SNPs associated with the disease. *Proceedings of the National Academy of Sciences USA, 103,* 6747–6752.

Lawless, H.T., Schlake, S., Smythe, J., Lim, J., Yang, H., Chapman, K., et al. (2004). Metallic taste and retronasal smell. *Chemical Senses, 29,* 25–33.

Lazar, S.W., Kerr, C., Wasserman, R.H., Gray, J.R., Greve, D., Treadway, M.T., et al. (2005). Meditation experience is associated with increased cortical thickness. *NeuroReport, 216,* 1893–1897.

Lazarus, A.A., & Abramovitz, A. (2004). A multimodal behavioral approach to performance anxiety. *Journal of Clinical Psychology, 60,* 831–840.

Lazarus, R.S. (1993). From psychological stress to the emotions: A history of changing outlooks. *Annual Review of Psychology, 44,* 1–21.

Lazarus, R.S., & Folkman, S. (1984). *Stress, appraisal, and coping.* New York: Springer.

Lazarus, R.S., Kanner, A.A., & Folkman, S. (1980). Emotions: A cognitive–phenomenological analysis. In R. Plutchik & H. Kellerman (Eds.), *Emotion: Theory, research, and experience: Vol. 1. Theories of emotion* (pp. 189–217). New York: Academic Press.

Leary, M.R., Kowalski, R.M., Smith, L., & Phillips, S. (2003). Teasing, rejection, and violence: Case studies of the school shootings. *Aggressive Behavior, 29,* 202–214.

Leary, M.R., Twenge, J.M., & Quinlivan, E. (2006). Interpersonal rejection as a determinant of anger and aggression. *Personality and Social Psychology Review, 10,* 111–132.

Le Bon, O., Hoffmann, R., Staner, L., & Armitage, R. (2009). Relationships between the number of ultradian cycles and key sleep variables in outpatients with major depressive disorder. *Psychiatry Research, 165,* 60–67.

LeDoux, J. (1996). *The emotional brain: The mysterious underpinnings of emotional life.* New York: Simon & Schuster.

LeDoux, J. (2003). *Synaptic self.* New York: Penguin.

LeDoux, J.E. (2000). Emotion circuits in the brain. *Annual Review of Neuroscience, 23,* 155–184.

Lee, K.A. (2006). Sleep dysfunction in women and its management. *Current Treatment Options in Neurology, 8,* 376–386.

Leichsenring, F., & Klein, S. (2014). Evidence for psychodynamic psychotherapy in specific mental disorders: a systematic review. *Psychoanalytic Psychotherapy, 28*(1), 4–32. doi:10.1080/02668734.2013.865428.

Leichsenring, F., & Salzer, S. (2014). A unified protocol for the transdiagnostic psychodynamic treatment of anxiety disorders: An evidence-based approach. *Psychotherapy, 51*(2), 224–245. doi:10.1037/a0033815

Leichsenring, F., Leweke, F., Klein, S., & Steinert, C. (2015). The Empirical Status of Psychodynamic Psychotherapy - An Update: Bambi's Alive and Kicking. *Psychotherapy & Psychosomatics, 84*(3), 129–148. doi:10.1159/000376584.

Leimgruber, K.L., Ward, A.F., Widness, J., Norton, M.I., Olson, K.R., Gray, K., & Santos, L.R. (2014). Give what you get: Capuchin monkeys (*Ceus apella*) and 4-year-old children pay forward positive and negative outcomes to conspecifics. *PLoS ONE, 9;* e87035.

Lemay, E.P., Jr., & Ashmore, R.D. (2004). Reactions to perceived categorization by other during the transition to college: Internalization and self-verification processes. *Group Processes & Intergroup Relations, 7,* 173–187.

Lenhart, A. (2009). *Teens and Mobile Phones Over the Past Five Years: Pew Internet Looks Back.* Retrieved from http://www.pewinternet.org/Reports/2009/14-Teens-and-Mobile-Phones-Data-Memo.aspx.

Lenneberg, E. (1967). *The biological foundations of language.* New York: Wiley.

Lennie, P. (2000). Color vision. In E.R. Kandel, J.H. Schwartz, & T.M. Jessell (Eds.), *Principles of neural science* (4th ed., pp. 572–589). New York: McGraw-Hill.

Lenzenweger, M.F., Lane, M.C., Loranger, A.W., & Kessler, R.C. (2007). DSM-IV personality disorders in the National Comorbidity Survey Replication. *Biological Psychiatry, 15,* 553–564.

Leonardo, E.D., & Hen, R. (2006). Genetics of affective and anxiety disorders. *Annual Review of Psychology, 57,* 117– 137.

Lepage, J-F., & Théoret, H. (2007). The mirror neuron system: Grasping others' actions from birth? *Developmental Science, 10,* 513–523.

Lerner, L. (1996). *The Kennedy women: The saga of an American family.* New York: Random House.

Lesch, K.P., Bengel, D., Heils, A., Sabol, S.Z., Greenburg, B.D., Petri, S., et al. (1996). Association of anxiety-related traits with a polymorphism in the serotonin transporter gene regulatory region. *Science, 274,* 1527–1531.

Leserman, J., Jackson, E.D., Petitto, J.M., Golden, R.N., Silva, S.G., Perkins, D.O., et al. (1999). Progression to AIDS: The effects of stress, depressive symptoms, and social support. *Psychosomatic Medicine, 61,* 397–406.

Lesku, J.A., Roth II, T.C., Rattenborg, N.C., Amlaner, C.J., & Lima, S.L. (2009). History and future of comparative analyses in sleep research. *Neuroscience and Behaviorial Reviews, 33,* 1024–1036.

Leuner, B., & Gould, E. (2010). Structural plasticity and hippocampal function. *Annual Review of Psychology, 61,* 111–140.

Leuner, B., Falduto, J., & Shors, T.J. (2003) Associative memory formation increases the observation of dendritic spines in the hippocampus. *Journal of Neuroscience, 23,* 659–665.

LeVay, S., & Hamer, D. (1994). Evidence for a biological influence in male homosexuality. *Scientific American, 270,* 44–49.

Levenson, H. (2010). *Brief dynamic therapy.* Washington, DC: American Psychological Association.

Levenson, R.W. (1988). Emotion and the autonomic nervous system: A prospectus for research on autonomic specificity. In H. Wagner (Ed.), *Social psychophysiology and emotion: Theory and clinical applications* (pp. 17–42). London: Wiley.

Levenson, R.W. (1994). Human emotion: A functional view. In P. Ekman & R.J. Davidson (Eds.), *The nature of emotion* (pp. 123–126). New York: Oxford.

Levenson, R.W. (2003). Blood, sweat, and fears: The autonomic architecture of emotion. *Annals of the New York Academy of Sciences, 1000,* 348–366.

Levenson, R.W., Carstensen, L.L., & Gottman, J.M. (1994). The influence of age and gender on affect, physiology, and their interactions: A study of long-term marriages. *Journal of Personality & Social Psychology, 67,* 56–68.

Levenson, R.W., Ekman, P., & Friesen, W.V. (1990). Voluntary facial action generates emotion-specific autonomic nervous system activity. *Psychophysiology, 27,* 363–384.

Levenson, R.W., Ekman, P., Heider, K., & Friesen, W.V. (1992). Emotion and autonomic nervous system activity in the Minangkabau of West Sumatra. *Journal of Personality & Social Psychology, 62,* 972–988.

Levine, D., McCright, J., Dobkin, L., Woodruff, A.J., & Klausner, J.D. (2008, March). SEXINFO: A sexual health text messaging service for San Francisco Youth. *American Journal of Public Health, 98,* 393–395.

Lewin, T. (2009, October 23). No Einstein in your crib? Get a refund. *New York Times.* Retrieved from http://www.nytimes.com/2009/10/24/education/24baby.html?_r=1&ref=education.

Lewis, D., & Levitt, P. (2002). Schizophrenia as a disorder of neurodevelopment. Annual Review of *Neuroscience, 25,* 409–432. doi: 10.1146/annurev.neuro.25.11270.142754.

Lewis, M.P., Simons, G.F., & Fennig, C.D. (Eds.). (2014). *Ethnologue: Languages of the World, Seventeenth edition.* Dallas, Texas: SIL International. Online version: http://www.ethnologue.com.

Lewontin, R. (1976). Race and intelligence. In N.J. Block & G. Dworkin (Eds.), *The IQ controversy: Critical readings.* New York: Pantheon.

Liberman, V., Samuels, S.M., & Ross, L. (2004). The name of the game: predictive power of reputations versus situational labels in determining prisoner's dilemma game moves. *Personality and Social Psychology Bulletin, 30,* 1175–1185.

Liddle, I., & MacMillan, S. (2010). Evaluating the FRIENDS programme in a Scottish setting. *Educational Psychology in Practice, 26*(1), 53–67.

Lidz, J., & Gleitman, L.R. (2004). Argument structure and the child's contribution to language learning. *Trends in Cognitive Sciences, 8,* 157–161.

Lieberman, J.A., Chakos, M., Wu, H., Alvir, J., Hoffman, E., Robinson, D., et al. (2001). Longitudinal study of brain morphology in first episodes of schizophrenia. *Biological Psychiatry, 49,* 487–499.

Lieberman, J.A., Stroup, T.S., McEvoy, J.P., Swartz, M.S., Rosenheck, R.A., Perkins, D.O., et al. (2005). Effectiveness of antipsychotic drugs in patients with chronic schizophrenia. *New England Journal of Medicine, 353,* 1209–1223.

Liebert, R.M., & Baron, R.A. (1972). Some immediate effects of televised violence on children's behavior. *Developmental Psychology, 6,* 469–475.

Lihoreau, M., Brepson, L., & Rivault, C. (2009). The weight of the clan: Even in insects, social isolation can induce a behavioural syndrome. *Behavioural Processes, 82,* 81–84.

Lilienfeld, S.O., Lynn, S.J., Kirsch, I., Chavez, J.F., Sarbin, T.R., & Ganaway, G.K. (1999). Dissociative identity disorder and the sociocognitive model: Recalling the lessons of the past. *Psychological Bulletin, 125,* 507–523.

Lin, K., & Lu, H. (2011). Why people use social networking sites: An empirical study integrating network externalities and motivation theory. *Computers in Human Behavior, 27,* 1152–1161.

Linden, D.E.J. (2006). How psychotherapy changes the brain—the contribution of functional neuroimaging. *Molecular Psychiatry, 11,* 528–538.

Lindgren, K.P., Kaysen, D., Werntz, A.J., Gasser, M.L., & Teachman, B.A. (2013). Wounds that can't be seen: Implicit trauma associations predict posttraumatic stress disorder symptoms. *Journal of Behavior Therapy and Experimental Psychiatry, 44,* 368–375. http://dx.doi.org/10.1016/j.jbtep.2013.03.003.

Lindsay, D.S., Hagen, L., Read, J.D., Wade, K.A., & Garry, M. (2004). True photographs and false memories. *Psychological Science, 15,* 149–154.

Linehan, M.M. (1993). *Skills training manual of treating borderline personality disorder.* New York: Guilford Press.

Linehan, M.M., Armstrong, H.E., Suarez, A., Allmon, D., & Heard, H.L. (1991). Cognitive–behavioral treatment of chronically parasuicidal borderline patients. *Archives of General Psychiatry, 48,* 1060–1064.

Linehan, M.M., Comtois, K.A., Murray, A.M., Brown, M.Z., Gallop, R.J., Heard, H.L., et al. (2006). Two-year randomized controlled trial and follow-up of dialectical behavior therapy vs therapy by experts for suicidal behaviors and borderline personality disorder. *Archives of General Psychiatry, 63,* 757–766.

Linehan, M.M., Heard, H.L., & Armstrong, H.E. (1993). Naturalistic followup of a behavioral treatment for chronically parasuicidal borderline patients. *Archives of General Psychiatry, 50,* 971–974.

Ling, R. (2010). Texting as a life phase medium. *Journal of Computer-Mediated Communication, 15,* 277–292.

Lippa, R. (1994). *Introduction to social psychology.* Pacific Grove, CA: Brooks/Cole.

Lisetti, C., Pozzo, E., Lucas, M., Hernandez, F., Selverman, W., Kurtines, B., & Pasztor, A. (2009). Second Life, bio-sensors, and exposure therapy for anxiety disorders. *Annual Review of CyberTherapy and Telemedicine, 7,* 19–21.

Lisetti, C., Pozzo, E., Lucas, M., Hernandez, F., Selverman, W., Kurtines, B., & Pasztor, A. (2009). Second Life, biosensors, and exposure therapy for anxiety disorders. *Annual Review of CyberTherapy and Telemedicine, 7,* 19–21.

Litt, E. (2013). Understanding social network site users' privacy tool use. *Computers in Human Behavior, 29,* 1649–1656. http://dx.doi.org/10.1016/j.chb.2013.01.049.

Locke, J. (1690/1959). *An essay concerning human understanding: Vol. 1.* New York: Dover.

Lockhart, R.S. (2002). Levels of processing, transfer-appropriate processing and the concept of robust encoding. *Memory, 10,* 397–403.

Lockhart, R.S., & Craik, F.I.M. (1990). Levels of processing: A retrospective commentary on a framework for memory research. *Canadian Journal of Psychology, 44,* 77–112.

Lockley, S.W., Dijk, D.J., Kosti, O., Skene, D.J., & Arendt, J. (2008). Alertness, mood and performance rhythm disturbances associated with circadian sleep disorders in the blind. *Journal of Sleep Research, 17,* 207–216.

Lodewijkx, H.F.M., Rabbie, J.M., & Visser, L. (2006). "Better to be safe than to be sorry": Extinguishing the individual-group discontinuity effect in competition by cautious reciprocation. *European Review of Social Psychology, 17,* 185–232. doi:10.1080/10463280601043430.

Loehlin, J.C., McCrae, R.R., Costa, P.T., & John, O.P. (1998). Heritabilities of common and measure specific components of the Big Five personality factors. *Journal of Research in Personality, 32,* 431–453.

Loeser, J.D., & Melzack, R. (1999). Pain: An overview. *Lancet, 353,* 1607–1609.

Loftus, E. (1996). *Eyewitness testimony.* Cambridge, MA: Harvard University Press.

Loftus, E. (2003). Make-believe memories. *American Psychologist, 58,* 864–873.

Logothetis, N.K., Pauls, J., Augath, M., Trinath, T., & Oeltermann, A. (2001). Neurophysiological investigation of the basis of the fMRI signal. *Nature, 412,* 150–157.

Long, M. (1990). Maturational constraints on language development. *Studies in Second Language Acquisition, 12,* 251–285.

Loomis, A.L., Harvey, E.N., & Hobart, G. (1936). Electrical potentials of the human brain. *Journal of Experimental Psychology, 19,* 249–279.

Lord, C., & McGee, J.P. (2001). *Educating children with autism.* Washington, DC: National Academy Press.

Lorenz, K. (1935). Der Kumpan in der Umwelt des Vogels. *Journal of Ornithology, 83,* 137–215.

Lorenz, K. (1937). The companion in the bird's world. *Auk, 54,* 245–273.

Lourenco, O., & Machado, A. (1996). In defense of Piaget's theory: A reply to 10 common criticisms. *Psychological Review, 103,* 143–164.

Lovaas, O.I. (1987). Behavioral treatment and normal educational and intellectual functioning in young autistic children. *Journal of Consulting and Clinical Psychology, 55,* 3–9.

Lovett, R. (2005, September 24). Coffee: The demon drink? *New Scientist.*

Lowry, C.A., Hale, M.W, Evans, A.K., Keerkens, J., Staub, D.R., Gasser, P.J., & Shekhar, A. (2008). Serotonergic systems, anxiety, and affective disorder focus on the dorsomedial part of the dorsal raphe nucleus. *Annals of the New York Academy of Sciences, 1148,* 86–94.

Lozano, A.M., Mayberg, H.S., & Kennedy, S.H. (2012). Response-deep brain stimulation and depression. *Journal of Neurosurgery, 116*(2), 313.

Lozoff, B., Beard, J., Connor, J., Felt, B., Georgieff, M., & Schallert, T. (2006). Longlasting neural and behavioral effects of iron deficiency in infancy. *Nutrition Reviews, 64*(Suppl.), S34–S43.

Lubben, J., & Gironda, M. (1996). Assessing social support networks among older people in the United States. In H. Litwin (Ed.), *The social networks of older people: A cross-national analysis.* London, England: Praeger.

Lubinski, D., & Benbow, C.P. (2006). Study of mathematically precocious youth after 35 years: Uncovering antecedents for the development of math-science expertise. *Perspectives on Psychological Science, 1,* 316–345.

Lubinski, D., Benbow, C.P. Webb, R.M., & Bleske-Rechek, A. (2006). Tracking exceptional human capital over two decades. *Psychological Science, 17,* 194–199.

Luborsky, L., Singer, B., & Luborsky, L. (1975). Comparative studies of psychotherapy. *Archives of General Psychiatry, 32,* 995–1008.

Luchins, A.S., & Luchins, E.H. (1969). Einstellung effect and group problem solving. *The Journal of Social Psychology, 77,* 79–89.

Luchins, A.S., & Luchins, E.H. (1970). *Wertheimer's seminars revisited: Problem solving and thinking.* Albany: SUNY Press.

Lucić, V., Yang, T., Schweikert, G., Förster, F., & Baumeister, W. (2005). Morphological characterization of molecular complexes present in the synaptic cleft. *Structure, 13,* 423–34.

Ludwig, D.S., & Kabat-Zinn, J. (2008). Mindfulness in medicine. *Journal of the American Medical Association, 300,* 1350–1352.

Lundqvist, T. (2005). Cognitive consequences of cannabis use: comparison with abuse of stimulants and heroin with regard to attention, memory and executive functions. *Pharmacology, Biochemistry and Behavior, 81,* 319–330.

Lutman, M.E., & Spencer, H.S. (1991). Occupational noise and demographic factors in hearing. *Acta Otolaryngologica, Suppl. 476,* 74–84.

Lutz, A., Greischar, L.L., Rawlings, N.B., Ricard, M., & Davidson, R.J. (2004). Long-term meditators self-induce high-amplitude gamma synchrony during mental practice. *Proceedings of the National Academy of Sciences, 101,* 16369–16373.

Lutz, B. (2007). The endocannabinoid system and extinction learning. *Molecular Neurobiology, 36,* 92–101.

Luykx, J.J., Boks, M.P.M., Terwindt, A.P.R., Bakker, S., Kahn, R.S., & Ophoff, R.A. (2010). The involvement of GSK3b in bipolar disorder: Integrating evidence from multiple types of genetic studies. *European Neuropsychopharmacology, 20,* 357–368.

Lykken, D. (1999). *Happiness: What studies on twins show us about nature, nurture and the happiness set point.* New York: Golden Books.

Lynn, R. (2006). *Race differences in intelligence: An evolutionary analysis.* Augusta, GA: National Summit.

Lynn, R. (2009). What has caused the Flynn effect? Secular increases in the Development Quotients of infants. *Intelligence, 37*(1), 16–24.

Lynn, S.J., Lilienfeld, S.O., Merckelbach, H., Giesbrecht, T., & van der Kloet, D. (2012). Dissociation and dissociative disorders: Challenging conventional wisdom. *Current Directions in Psychological Science, 21,* 48–53. doi: 10.1177/0963721411429457.

Maccoby, E.E. (2000). Perspectives on gender development. *International Journal of Behavioral Development, 24,* 398–406.

Maccoby, E.E., & Jacklin, C.N. (1974). *The psychology of sex differences.* Stanford, CA: Stanford University Press.

Maccoby, E.E., & Jacklin, C.N. (1987). Gender segregation in childhood. In H. Reese (Ed.), *Advances in child behavior and development.* New York: Academic Press.

MacDonald, G., & Leary, M.R. (2005). Why does social exclusion hurt? The relationship between social and physical pain. *Psychological Bulletin, 131,* 202–223.

MacDonald, G., Kingsbury, R., & Shaw, S. (2005). *Adding insult to injury: Social pain theory and response to social exclusion.* New York: Psychology Press.

MacKinnon, D.W. (1970). Creativity: A multi-faceted phenomenon. In J. Roslanksy (Ed.), *Creativity* (pp. 19–32). Amsterdam: North-Holland.

MacKinnon, D.W., & Hall, W. (1972). Intelligence and creativity. *Proceedings of the XVIIth International Congress of Applied Psychology,* Liege, Belgium (Vol. 2, 1883–1888). Brussels: EDITEST.

MacLane, C.N., & Walmsley, P.T. (2010). Reducing counterproductive work behavior through employee selection. *Human Resource Management Review, 20*(1), 62–72.

MacLean, K., Saron, C., Aichele, S., Bridwell, D., Jacobs, T., Zanesco, A., et al. (in press). Improvements in perceptual threshold with intensive attention training through concentration meditation. *Journal of Cognitive Neuroscience (Suppl).*

Maclean, K.A., Ferrer, E., Aichele, S.R., Bridwell, D.A., Zanesco, A.P., Jacobs, T.L., King, B.G., Rosenberg, E.L., Sahdra, B.K., Shaver, P.R., Wallace, B.A., Mangun, G.R., & Saron, C.D. (2010). Intensive meditation training improves perceptual discrimination and sustained attention. *Psychological Science, 21*(6), 829–839.

Macmillan, M. (2000). *An odd kind of fame: Stories of Phineas Gage.* Cambridge, MA: MIT Press.

MacWhinney, B. (1999). *The emergence of language.* Mahwah, NJ: Erlbaum.

Madden, M., & Lenhart, A. (2006). *Online dating.* Pew Internet & American Life Project. Retrieved from http://www.pewtrusts.org/uploadedFiles/wwwpewtrustsorg/Reports/Society_and_the_Internet/PIP_Online_Dating_0306.pdf.

Madigan, S., & O'Hara, R. (1992). Short-term memory at the turn of the century: Mary Whiton Calkins's memory research. *American Psychologist, 47,* 170–174.

Maes, H.M.M., Neale, M.C., & Eaves, L.J. (1997). Genetic and environmental factors in relative body weight and human adiposity. *Behavior Genetics, 27,* 325–351.

Maestripieri, D., Higley, J.D., Lindell, S.G., Newman, T.K., McCormack, K.M., & Sanchez, M.M. (2006). Early maternal rejection affects the development of monoaminergic systems and adult abusive parenting in rhesus macaques (*Macaca mulatto*). *Behavioral Neuroscience, 120,* 1017–1024.

Magnusson, D., & Stattin, H. (1998). Person-context interaction theories. In W. Damon (Ed.), *Handbook of child psychology (Vol. 1): Theoretical models of human development.* New York: Wiley.

Maguire, E.A., Woollett, K., & Spiers, H.J. (2006). London taxi drivers and bus drivers: A structural MRI and neuropsychological analysis. *Hippocampus, 16,* 1091–1101.

Mahdi, J.G., Mahdi, A.J., & Bowen, I.D. (2006). The historical analysis of aspirin discovery, its relation to the willow tree and antiproliferative and anticancer potential. *Cell Proliferation, 39*(2), 147–155.

Maier, N.R.F. (1931). Reasoning in humans: II. The solution of a problem and its appearance. *Journal of Comparative and Physiological Psychology, 12,* 181–194.

Maier, S.F., Watkins, L.R., & Fleshner, M. (1994). Psychoneuroimmunology: The interface between brain, behavior, and immunity. *American Psychologist, 49,* 1004–1017.

Main, M., & Hesse, E. (1990). Lack of resolution of mourning in adulthood and its relationship to infant disorganization: Some speculations regarding causal mechanisms. In M. Greenberg, D. Cicchetti, & E.M. Cummings (Eds.), *Attachment in the preschool years* (pp. 161–184). Chicago, IL: University of Chicago Press.

Main, M., & Solomon, J. (1990). Procedures for identifying infants as disorganized/disoriented during the Ainsworth Strange Situation. In M. Greenberg, D. Cicchetti, & E.M. Cummings (Eds.), *Attachment in the preschool years* (pp. 121–160). Chicago, IL: University of Chicago Press.

Makomaski Illing, E.M., & Kaiserman, M.J. (2004). Mortality attributable to tobacco use in Canada and its regions, 1998. *Canadian Journal of Public Health, 95,* 38–44.

Malberg, J.E., Eisch, A.J., Nestler, E.J., & Duman, R.S. (2000). Chronic antidepressant treatment increases neurogenesis in adult rat hippocampus. *Journal of Neuroscience, 20,* 9104–9110.

Malenfant, E.C., Lebel, A., & Martel, L. (2010). Projections of the diversity of the Canadian population: 2006 to 2031. Ottawa, ON: Minister of Industry.

Malenka, R.C., & Nicoll, R.A. (1999). Long term potentiation—A decade of progress? *Science, 285,* 1870–1874.

Maner, J.K., Miller, S.L., Schmidt, N.B., & Eckel, L.A. (2010). The endocrinology of exclusion: Rejection elicits motivationally tuned changes in progesterone. *Psychological Science, 21,* 581–588.

Mangels, J.A., Gershberg, F.B., Shimamura, A.P., & Knight, R.T. (1996). Impaired retrieval from remote memory in patients with frontal lobe damage. *Neuropsychology, 10,* 32–41.

Mann, T., Tomiyama, A.J., Westling, E., Lew, A-M., Samuels, B., & Chatman, J. (2007). Medicare's search for effective obesity treatments: Diets are not the answer. *American Psychologist, 62,* 220–233.

Marcia, J.E. (1966). Development and validation of ego identity status. *Journal of Personality and Social Psychology, 5,* 551–558.

Marcia, J.E. (2002). Adolescence, identity, and the Bernardone family. *Identity: An International Journal of Theory and Research, 2*(3), 199–209. doi: 10.1207/S1532706XID0203_01.

Marcia, J.E., Waterman, A.S., Matteson, D.R., Archer, S.L., & Orlofsky, J.L. (1993). *Ego identity: A handbook for psychosocial research.* New York: Springer-Verlag.

Marcus, B., Machilek, F., & Schütz, A. (2006). Personality in cyberspace: Personal web sites as media for personality expressions and impressions. *Journal of Personality and Social Psychology, 90,* 1014–1031

Marek, G.J., & Aghajanian, G.K. (1996). LSD and the phenethylamine hallucinogen DOI are potent partial agonists at 5-HT2A receptors on interneurons in the rat piriform cortex. *Journal of Pharmacology and Experimental Therapeutics, 278,* 1373–1382.

Marino, L., & Lilienfeld, S.O. (2007). Dolphin-assisted therapy: More flawed data and more falwed conclusions. *Anthrozoos, 20,* 239–249.

Markey, P.M., & Markey, C.N. (2010). Vulnerability to violent video games: A review and integration of personality research. *Review of General Psychology, 14,* 82–91.

Marks, R. (2006). The superlative, sensitive shark. Retrieved November 5, 2007, from http://www.pbs.org/kqed/oceanadventures/episodes/sharks/indepth-senses.html.

Markus, H., & Kitayama, S. (1991). Culture and the self: Implications for cognition, emotion, and motivation. *Psychological Review, 98,* 224–253.

Maron, E., Hettema, J.M., & Shlik, J. (2010). Advances in molecular genetics of panic disorder. *Molecular Psychiatry, 15,* 681–701.

Martin, C.L., & Ruble, D.N. (2004). Children's search for gender cues: Cognitive perspectives on gender development. *Current Directions in Psychological Science, 13,* 67–70.

Martindale, C. (1999). Biological bases of creativity. In R.J. Sternberg (Ed.), *Handbook of creativity* (pp. 137–152). Cambridge: Cambridge University Press.

Martini, L., & Whistler, J.L. (2007). The role of mu opioid receptor desensitization and endocytosis in morphine tolerance and dependence. *Current Opinion in Neurobiology, 17,* 556–564.

Maschi, S., Clavenna, A., Campi, R., Schiavetti, B., Bernat, M., & Bonati, M. (2008). Neonatal outcome following pregnancy exposure to antidepressants: A prospective controlled cohort study. *BJOG—An International Journal of Obstetrics and Gynaecology, 115,* 283–289.

Mashour, G.A., Walker, E.E., & Martuza, R.L. (2005). Psychosurgery; past, present, and future. *Brain Research Reviews, 48,* 409–419.

Masland, R.H. (2004). Neuronal cell types. *Current Biology, 14,* R496–500.

Masling, J.M., & Bornstein, R.F. (2005). *Scoring the Rorschach: Retrospect and prospect.* Mahwah, NJ: Erlbaum.

Maslow, A. (1968). *Toward a psychology of being* (2nd ed.). New York: Van Nostrand.

Maslow, A. (1970). *Motivation and personality* (2nd ed.). New York: Harper & Row.

Mason, J.W. (1971). A re-evaluation of the concept of "non-specificity" in stress theory. *Journal of Psychiatric Research, 8,* 323–333.

Mason. J.W. (1975). A historical view of the stress field. *Journal of Human Stress, 1,* 6–12.

Masten, C.L., Eisenberger, N.I., Borofsky, L.A., Pfeifer, J.H., McNealy, K., Mazziotta, J.C., & Dapretto, M. (2009). Neural correlates of social exclusion during adolescence: Understanding the distress of peer rejection. *Social Cognitive Affective Neuroscience, 4,* 143–157. doi: 10.1093/scan/nsp007.

Masters, J., & Barr, S. (2010). Young children online: E-learning in a social networking context. *Knowledge Management & E-Learning: An International Journal, 1,* 295–304.

Masters, W.H., & Johnson, V.E. (1966). *The human sexual response.* Boston: Little & Brown.

Masuda, T., & Nisbett, R.E. (2001). Attending holistically versus analytically: Comparing the context sensitivity of Japanese and Americans. *Journal of Personality and Social Psychology, 81,* 922–934.

Mateo, Y., Budygin, E.A., John, C.E., & Jones, S.R. (2004). Role of serotonin in cocaine effects in mice with reduced dopamine transporter function. *Proceedings of the National Academy of Sciences, 101,* 372–377.

Mathews, A., & MacLeod, C. (2005). Cognitive vulnerability to emotional disorders. *Annual Review of Clinical Psychology, 1*(1), 167–195. doi:10.1146/annurev.clinpsy.1.102803.143916.

Mathiak, K., & Weber, R. (2006). Toward brain correlates of natural behavior: fMRI during violent video games. *Human Brain Mapping, 27,* 948–956.

Mathias, J.L., & Wheaton, P. (2007). Changes in attention and information-processing speed following severe traumatic brain injury: A meta-analytic review. *Neuropsychology, 21,* 212–223.

Mathiesen, B.B., Förster, P.L.V., & Svendsen, H.A. (2004). Affect regulation and loss of initiative in a case of orbitofrontal injury. *Neuro-psychoanalysis, 6,* 47–62.

Maticka-Tyndale, E. (2008). Sexuality and sexual health of Canadian adolescents: Yesterday, today and tomorrow. *Canadian Journal of Human Sexuality, 17*(3), 85–95. Retrieved from EBSCO*host.*

Maticka-Tyndale, E., Harold, E.S., & Opperman, M. (2003). Casual sex among Australian schoolies. *The Journal of Sex Research, 40,* 158–169.

Matson, J.L., & Boisjoli, J.A. (2009). The token economy for children with intellectual disability and/ or autism: A review. *Research in Developmental Disabilities, 30,* 240–248.

Matsumoto, D., & Willingham, B. (2006). The thrill of victory and the agony of defeat: Spontaneous expressions of medal winners of the 2004 Athens Olympic Games. *Journal of Personality and Social Psychology, 91,* 568–581.

Matsumoto, D., Yoo, S.H., et al. (in press). Mapping expressive differences around the world: The relationship between emotional display rules and Individualism v. Collectivism. *Journal of Cross-Cultural Psychology.*

Matthews, K.A., Glass, D.C., Rosenman, R.H., & Bortner, R.W. (1977). Competitive drive, Pattern A, and coronary heart disease: A further analysis of some data from the Western Collaborative Group Study. *Journal of Chronic Diseases, 30,* 489–498.

Maurer, D., Mondloch, C.J., & Lewis, T.L. (2007). Effects of early visual deprivation on perceptual and cognitive development. *Progress in Brain Research, 164,* 87–104.

Mauss, I.B., Levenson, R.W., McCarter, L., Wilhelm, F.H., & Gross, J.J. (2005). The tie that binds? Coherence among emotion experience, behavior, and physiology. *Emotion, 5,* 175–190.

Max, J.E., Levin, H.S., Schachar, R.J., Landis, J., Saunders, A.E., Ewing-Cobbs, L., et al. (2006). Predictors of personality change due to traumatic brain injury in children and adolescents six to twenty-four months after injury. *Journal of Neuropsychiatry and Clinical Neurosciences, 18,* 21–32.

Max, J.E., Robertson, B.A.M., & Lansing, A.E. (2001). The phenomenology of personality change due to traumatic brain injury in children and adolescents. *Journal of Neuropsychiatry and Clinical Neurosciences, 13,* 161–170.

May, P.A., Gossage, J.P., Marais, A-S, Hendricks, L.S., Snell, C.L., Tabachnik, B.G., et al. (2008). Maternal risk factors for fetal alcohol syndrome and partial fetal alcohol syndrome in South Africa: A third study. *Alcoholism: Clinical and Experimental Research, 32,* 738–753.

Mayberg, H.S. (1997). Limbic-cortical dysregulation: A proposed model of depression. *Journal of Neuropsychiatry and Clinical Neuroscience, 9,* 471–481.

Mayberg, H.S. (2003). Modulating dysfunctional limbic-cortical circuits in depression: Towards development of brain-based algorithms for diagnosis and optimized treatment. *British Medical Bulletin, 65,* 193–207.

Mayberg, H.S. (2009). Targeted electrode-based modulation of neural circuits for depression. *Journal of Clinical Investigation, 119,* 717–725.

Mayberg, H.S., Liotti, M., Brannan, S.K., McGinnis, S., Mahurin, R.K., Jerabek, P.A., et al. (1999). Reciprocal limbic-cortical function and negative mood: Converging PET findings in depression and normal sadness. *American Journal of Psychiatry, 156,* 675–682.

Mayberg, H.S., Lozano, A.M., Voon, V., McNeely, H.E., Seminowicz, D., Hamani, C., et al. (2005). Deep brain stimulation for treatment-resistant depression. *Neuron, 45,* 651–660.

Mayer, M. (2004). Structure and function of glutamate receptors in the brain. *Annals of the New York Academy of Sciences, 1038,* 125–130.

McArdle, J.J., & Prindle, J.J. (2008). A latent change score analysis of a randomized clinical trial in reasoning training. *Psychology and Aging, 23,* 702–719.

McCabe, C., & Rolls, E.T. (2007). Umami: A delicious flavor formed by convergence of taste and olfactory pathways in the human brain. *European Journal of Neuroscience, 25,* 1855–1864.

McCauley, C. (1989). The nature of social infuence in groupthink: Compliance and internalization. *Journal of Personality and Social Psychology, 57,* 250–260.

McClain, C.S., Rosenfeld, B., & Breitbart, W. (2003). Effect of spiritual well-being on end-of-life despair in terminally-ill cancer patients. *Lancet, 361,* 1603–1607.

McClelland, D.C. (1985). How motives, skills, and values determine what people do. *American Psychologist, 40,* 812–825.

McClelland, J.L. (1988). Connectionist models and psychological evidence. *Journal of Memory and Language, 27,* 107–123.

McClelland, J.L., & Rogers, T. (2003). The parallel distributed processing approach to semantic knowledge. *Nature Reviews Neuroscience, 44,* 310–322.

McClelland, J.L., & Rumelhart, D. (1985). Distributed memory and the representation of general and specific information. *Journal of Experimental Psychology: General, 114,* 159–188.

McCrae, R.R. (2002). NEO-PI-R data from 36 cultures: Further intercultural comparisons. In R.R. McCrae & J. Allik (Eds.), *The Five-Factor Model of personality across cultures* (pp. 105–125). New York: Kluwer Academic/Plenum.

McCrae, R.R., & Allik, J. (Eds.). (2002). *The Five-Factor Model of personality across cultures.* New York: Kluwer Academic/Plenum.

McCrae, R.R., & Costa, P.T. (1996). Toward a new generation of personality theories: Theoretical contexts for the five-factor model. In J.S. Wiggins (Ed.), *The Five-Factor model of personality: Theoretical perspectives* (pp. 51–87). New York: Guilford Press.

McCrae, R.R., & Costa, P.T. (1997). Personality trait structure as a human universal. *American Psychologist, 52,* 509–516.

McCrae, R.R., & Costa, P.T. (1999). A Five-Factor theory of personality. In L.A. Pervin and O.P. John (Eds.), *Handbook of personality theory and research* (pp. 139–153). New York: Guilford Press.

McCrae, R.R., & Costa, P.T. (2003). *Personality in adulthood: A five-factor theory perspective* (2nd ed.). New York: Guilford.

McCrae, R.R., & John, O.P. (1992). An introduction to the Five-Factor Model and its applications. *Journal of Personality, 60,* 175–215.

McCrae, R.R., & Terracciano, A. (2006). National character and personality. *Current Directions in Psychological Science, 15*(4), 156–161.

McDaniel, M.A. (2005) Big-brained people are smarter: A meta-analysis of the relationship between in vivo brain volume and intelligence. *Intelligence, 33,* 337–346.

McEachin, J.J., Smith, T., & Lovaas, O.I. (1993). Long-term outcome for children with autism who received early intensive behavioral treatment. *American Journal on Mental Retardation, 97,* 359–372.

McEvoy, J.P., Lieberman, J.A., Stroup, T.S., Davis, S.M., Meltzer, H.Y., Rosenheck, R.A., et al. (2006). Effectiveness of clozapine versus olanzapine, quetiapine, and risperidone in patients with chronic schizophrenia who did not respond to prior atypical antipsychotic treatment. *American Journal of Psychiatry, 163,* 600–610.

McEwen, B.S. (1998). Protective and damaging effects of stress mediators. *The New England Journal of Medicine, 338,* 171–179.

McEwen, B.S., De Kloet, E.R., & Rostene, W. (1986). Adrenal steroid receptors and actions in the nervous system. *Physiological Review, 66,* 1121–1188.

McGaugh, J.L. (2000). Memory—a century of consolidation. *Science, 287,* 248–251.

McGrew, K.S. (2005). The Cattell-Horn-Carroll theory of cognitive abilities: Past, present and future. In D.P. Flanagan & P.L. Harrison (Eds.), *Contemporary intellectual assessment: Theories, tests, and issues* (pp. 136–181). New York: Guilford Press.

McKay, A., & Barrett, M. (2010). Trends in teen pregnancy rates from 1996–2006: A comparison of Canada, Sweden, U.S.A., and England/Wales. *Canadian Journal of Human Sexuality,* 19(1/2), 43–52. Retrieved from EBSCO*host.*

McKelvie, S.J. (1997). The availability heuristic: Effects of fame and gender on the estimated frequency of male and female names. *The Journal of Social Psychology, 137,* 63–78.

McKim, W.A. (2007). *Drugs and Behavior: An Introduction to Behavioral Pharmacology.* Upper Saddle River, New Jersey: Pearson Prentice Hall.

McKinley, M., Cairns, M., Denton, D., Egan, G., Mathai, M., Uschakov, A., et al. (2004). Physiological and pathophysiological influences on thirst. *Physiology & Behavior, 81*(5), 795–803.

McLaren, D. (2009). *Banded peak school: 2009–2010 annual report.* Retrieved from http://www.rockyview.ab.ca/publications/assets_publications/schooleducationplans/bandedpeak.pdf.

McLay, R.N, Graap, K., Spira, J., Perlman, K., Johnston, S., Rothbaum, B.O., . . . Rizzo, A. (2012). Development and testing of virtual reality exposure therapy for post-traumatic stress disorder in active duty service members who served in Iraq and Afghanistan. *Military Medicine, 177,* 635–642.

McLay, R.N., McBrien, C., Wiederhold, M.D., & Wiederhold, B.K. (2010). Exposure therapy with and without virtual reality to treat PTSD while in combat theater: A parallel case series. *Cyberpsychology, Behavior, and Social Networking, 13,* 37–42. doi: 10.1089/cyber.2009.0346.

McTiernan, A. (2005). Obesity and cancer: The risks, science, and potential management strategies. *Oncology (Williston Park), 19,* 871–881.

Mechelli, A., Crinion, J.T., Noppeney, U., O'Doherty, J, Ashburner, J., Frackowiak, R.S., et al. (2004). Neurolinguistics: Structural plasticity in the bilingual brain. *Nature, 431,* 757.

Mechtcheriakov, S., Brenneis, B., Koppelstaetter, F., Schocke, M., & Marksteiner, J. (2007). A widespread distinct pattern of cerebral atrophy in patients with alcohol addiction revealed by voxel-based morphometry. *Journal of Neurology, Neurosurgery, and Psychiatry, 78,* 610–614.

Medical Research Council of Canada, Natural Sciences and Engineering Research Council of Canada, Social Sciences and Humanities Research Council of Canada. (2005). *Tri-council policy statement on ethical conduct for research involving humans* (October 2005 ed.). Retrieved from http://pre.ethics.gc.ca/policy-politique/tcps-eptc/docs/TCPS%20October%202005_E.pdf.

Medina, A.E., & Krahe, T.E. (2008). Neocortical plasticity deficits in fetal alcohol spectrum disorders: Lessons from barrel and visual cortex. *Journal of Neuroscience Research, 86,* 256–263.

Mednick, S.A., & Mednick, M.T. (1967). *Remote Associates Test: Experimenter's manual.* Boston: Houghton Mifflin.

Medvec, V., Madey, S., & Gilovich, T. (1995, October). When less is more: Counterfactual thinking and satisfaction among Olympic medalists. *Journal of Personality and Social Psychology, 69*(4), 603–610.

Meerkerk, G., van den Eijnden, R.J.J.M., & Garretsen, H.F.L. (2006). Predicting compulsive Internet use: It's all about sex! *CyberPsychology and Behavior, 9,* 95–103.

Meeus, W., Iedema, J., Helson, M., & Vollebergh, W. (1999). Patterns of adolescent identity development: Review of literature and longitudinal analysis. *Developmental Review, 19,* 419–461.

Mehl, M.R., Vazire, S., Ramirez-Esparza, N., Statcher, R.B., & Pennebaker, J.W. (2007). Are Women Really More Talkative Than Men?. *Science, 317*(5834), 82.

Mehta, M.A., Sahakian, B.J., and Robbins, T.W. (2001). Comparative psychopharmacology of methylphenidate and related drugs in human volunteers, patients with ADHD, and experimental animals. In M.V. Solanto, A.F.T. Arnsten, & F.X. Castellanos (Eds.), *Stimulant drugs and ADHD: Basic and clinical neuroscience* (pp. 303–331). New York: Oxford University Press.

Mei, L., & Xiong, W.-C. (2008). Neuregulin 1 in neural development, synaptic plasticity and schizophrenia. *Nature Reviews Neuroscience, 9,* 437–452.

Melis, A.P., & Semmann, D. (2010). How is human cooperation different? *Philosophical Transactions of the Royal Society of London. Series B, Biological Sciences, 365*(1553), 2663–2674. doi:10.1098/rstb.2010.0157.

Melis, M.R., & Argiolis, A. (1995). Dopamine and sexual behavior. *Neuroscience and Biobehavioral Reviews, 19,* 19–38.

Mell, J.C., Howard, S.M, & Miller, B.L. (2003). Art and the brain: The influence of frontotemporal dementia on an accomplished artist. *Neurology, 60,* 1707–1710.

Meltzoff, A.N., & Moore, M.K. (1977). Imitation of facial and manual gestures by human neonates. *Science, 198,* 75–78.

Meltzoff, A.N., & Moore, M.K. (1983). Newborn infants imitate adult facial gestures. *Child Development, 54,* 702–709.

Melzack, R., Coderre, T.J., Katz, J., and Vaccarino, A.L. (2001). Central neuroplasticity and neuropathic pain. *Annals of the New York Academy of Sciences; 933,* 157–174.

Melzack, R., & Scott, T.H. (1957). The effects of early experience on the response to pain. *Journal of Comparative and Physiological Psychology, 50,* 155–161.

Melzack, R., & Wall, P.D. (1965). Pain mechanisms: A new theory. *Science, 150,* 971–979.

Melzack, R., & Wall, P.D. (1988). *The challenge of pain* (rev. ed.). New York: Penguin.

Menalled, L.B., & Chesselet, M.F. (2002). Mouse models of Huntington's disease. *TIPS, 23,* 32–39.

Mennella, J.A., & Beauchamp, G.K. (1996). The early development of human flavor preferences. In E.D. Capaldi (Ed.), *Why we eat what we eat: The psychology of eating* (pp. 83–112). Washington, DC: APA Books.

Mennella, J.A., Johnson, A., & Beauchamp, G.K. (1995). Garlic ingestion by pregnant women alters the odor of amniotic fluid. *Chemical Senses, 20,* 207–209.

Mental health: A report of the surgeon general. (2001). Retrieved from http://www.surgeongeneral.gov/library/mentalhealth/home.html.

Mental Health Commission of Canada. (2009). *Opening Minds.* Retrieved from http://www.mentalhealthcommission.ca/English/node/1587.

Merskey, H., & Bogduk, N. (1994). *Classification of chronic pain.* Seattle: International Association for the Study of Pain Press.

Merten, J. (2005). Culture, gender and the recognition of the basic emotions. *Psychologia, 48,* 306–316.

Messner, M., Reinhard, M., & Sporer, S.L. (2008). Compliance through direct persuasive appeals: The moderating role of communicator's attractiveness in interpersonal persuasion. *Social Influence, 3,* 67–83.

Meunier, M., & Bachevalier, J. (2002). Comparison of emotional responses in monkeys with rhinal cortex or amygdala lesions. *Emotion, 2,* 147–161.

Meynell, L. (2012). Evolutionary psychology, ethology, and essentialism (because what they don't know can hurt us). *Hypatia—A Journal of Feminist Philosophy, 27,* 3–27.

Michael, J. (1975). Positive and negative reinforcement, a distinction that is no longer necessary; or a better way to talk about bad things. *Behaviorism, 3,* 33–45.

Miczek, K.A., de Almeida, R.M.M., Kravitz, E.A., & Rissman, E.F. (2007). Neurobiology of escalated aggression and violence. *Journal of Neuroscience, 27,* 11803–11806.

Milgram, S. (1963). Behavioral study of obedience. *Journal of Abnormal and Social Psychology, 67,* 371–378.

Milgram, S. (1974). *Obedience to authority: An experimental view.* New York: Harper.

Millennials: Confident. Connected. Open to Change. (2010, February 24). Pew Research Center. Retrieved from http://pewresearch.org/pubs/1501/millennials-new-survey-generational-personality-upbeat-open-new-ideas-technology-bound.

Miller, A. (1996). *Insights of genius: Imagery and creativity in science and art.* New York: Springer Verlag.

Miller, A.H., Capuron, L., & Raison, C.L. (2005). Immunologic influences on emotion regulation. *Clinical Neuroscience Research, 4,* 325–333.

Miller, A.S., & Kanazawa, S. (2000). *Order by accident: The origins and consequences of conformity in contemporary Japan.* Boulder, CO: Westview Press.

Miller, B.L., & J.L. Cummings (Eds.). (1999). *The human frontal lobes: Functions and disorders.* New York: Guilford Press.

Miller, G. (2000). *The mating mind.* New York: Doubleday.

Miller, G.A. (1956). The magical number seven, plus or minus two: Some limits on our capacity for processing information. *Psychological Review, 63,* 81–97.

Miller, G.F. (2000). *The mating mind: How sexual choice shaped the evolution of human nature.* New York: Doubleday.

Miller, G.F., & Penke, L. (2007). The evolution of human intelligence and the coefficient of additive genetic variance in human brain size. *Intelligence, 35*(2), 97–114.

Miller, L.A., & Tippett, L.J. (1996). Effects of focal brain lesions on visual problemsolving. *Neuropsychologia, 34,* 387–398.

Miller, S. (2007). *Developmental research methods* (3rd ed.). Thousand Oaks, CA: Sage Publications Inc.

Milner, B. (1962). Les troubles de la mémoire accompagnant des lésions hippocampiques bilatérales. In *Physiologie de l'hippocampe* (pp. 257–272). Paris: Centre National de la Recherche Scientifique. English translation: P.M. Milner & S. Glickman (Eds.). (1965). *Cognitive processes and the brain: An enduring problem in psychology. Selected readings* (pp. 97–111). Princeton: Van Nostrand.

Milner, B., Squire, L.R., & Kandel, E.R. (1998). Cognitive neuroscience and the study of memory. *Neuron, 20,* 445–468.

Miranda, R., & Mennin, D.S. (2007). Depression, generalized anxiety disorder, and certainty in pessimistic predictions about the future. *Cognitive Therapy and Research, 31*(1), 71–82.

Mirescu, C., & Gould, E. (2006). Stress and adult neurogenesis. *Hippocampus, 16,* 233–238.

Mirescu, C., Peters, J.D., Noiman, L., & Gould, E. (2006). Sleep deprivation inhibits adult neurogenesis in the hippocampus by elevating glucocorticoids. *Proceedings of the National Academy of Sciences, 103,* 19170–19175.

Mirnics, K., Middleton, F.A., Marquez, A., Lewis, D.A., & Levitt, P. (2000). Molecular characterization of schizophrenia viewed by microarray analysis of gene expression in prefrontal cortex. *Neuron, 28,* 53–67.

Mischel, W. (2009). From personality and assessment (1968) to personality science, 2009. *Journal of Research in Personality, 43*(2), 282–290.

Mischel, W., & Shoda, Y. (1995). A cognitive-affective system theory of personality: Reconceptualizing situations, dispositions, dynamics, and invariance in personality structure. *Psychological Review, 102,* 246–268.

Mischel, W., & Shoda, Y. (1999). Integrating dispositions and processing dynamics within a unified theory of personality: The cognitive-affective personality system. In L.A. Pervin & O.P. John (Eds.), *Handbook of personality: Theory and research* (pp. 197–218). New York: Guilford Press.

Mishna, F., Cook, C., Gadalla, T., Daciuk, J., & Solomon, S. (2010). Cyber bullying behaviors among middle and high school students. *American Journal of Orthopsychiatry, 80*(3), 362–374.

Miyake, A., Friedman, N.P., Emerson, M.J., Witzki, A.H., & Howerter, A. (2000). The unity and diversity of executive functions and their contributions to complex "frontal lobe" tasks: A latent variable approach. *Cognitive Psychology, 41,* 49–100.

Miyake, K., Chen, S.J., & Campos, J.J. (1985). Infant temperament, mother's mode of interaction, and attachment in Japan: An interim report. *Monographs of the Society for Research in Child Development, 50,* 276–297.

Mizuno, S., Mihara, T., Miyaoka, T., Inagaki, T., & Horiguchi, J. (2005, March). CSF iron, ferritin and transferrin levels in restless legs syndrome. *Journal of Sleep Research, 14*(1), 43–47.

Moerman, D.E. (1998). *Native American Ethnobotany.* Portland, OR: Timber Press Inc.

Moffitt, T.E., Brammer, G.L., Caspi, A., Fawcett, J.P., Raleigh, M., Yuwiler, A., et al. (1998). Whole blood serotonin relates to violence in an epidemiological study. *Biological Psychiatry, 43,* 446–457.

Moffitt, T.E., Caspi, A., Taylor, A., Kokaua, T.J., Milne, B.J., Polanczyk, G., & Poulton, R. (2010). How common are common mental disorders? Evidence that lifetime prevalence rates are doubled by prospective versus retrospective ascertainment. *Psychological Medicine, 40,* 899–909. doi: 10.1017/S0033291709991036

Moffitt, T.E., Caspi. A., & Rutter, M. (2005). Strategy for investigating interactions between measured genes and measured environments. *Archives of General Psychiatry, 62,* 473–481.

Moghaddam, B. (2003). Bringing order to the glutamate chaos in schizophrenia. *Neuron, 40,* 881–884.

Moller, J., Hallqvist, J., Diderichsen, F., Theorell, T., Reuterwall, C., & Ahblom, A. (1999). Do episodes of anger trigger myocardial infarction? A case-crossover analysis in the Stockholm Heart Epidemiology Program (SHEEP). *Psychosomatic Medicine, 61,* 842–849.

Montague, D.P.F., & Walker-Andrews, A.S. (2001). Peekaboo: A new look at infants perception of emotion. *Developmental Psychology, 37,* 826–838.

Montgomery, G.H., DuHamel, K.N., & Redd, W.H. (2000). A meta-analysis of hypnotically induced analgesia: How effective is hypnosis? *International Journal of Clinical and Experimental Hypnosis, 48,* 138–153.

Moore, E.S., Ward, R.E., Wetherill, L.F., Rogers, J.L., Autti-Rämö, I., Fagerlund, A., et al. (2007). Unique facial features distinguish fetal alcohol syndrome patients and controls in diverse ethnic populations. *Alcoholism: Clinical and Experimental Research, 31,* 1707–1713.

Moore, R.Y., & Eichler, V.B. (1972). Loss of a circadian adrenal corticosterone rhythm following suprachiasmatic lesions in the rat. *Brain Research, 42,* 201–206.

Moradi, A.R., Herlihy, J., Yasseri, G., Shahraray, M., Turner, A., & Dalgleish, T. (2008). Specificity of episodic and semantic aspects of autobiographical memory in relation to symptoms of post-traumatic stress disorder (PTSD). *Acta Psychologica, 127,* 645–653.

Morales-Medina, J.C., Dumont, Y., & Quirion, R. (2010). A possible role of neuropeptide Y in depression and stress. *Brain Research, 1314,* 194–205.

Moran, E.M., Snelson, C., & Elison-Bowers, P. (2010). Image and video disclosure of substance use on social media websites. *Computers in Human Behavior, 26,* 1405–1411.

Moray, N. (1959). Attention in dichotic listening: Affective cues and the influence of instructions. *Quarterly Journal of Experimental Psychology, 11,* 56–60.

Moreno, J., Mitsumasa, K., Holloway, T., Lopez, J., Cadagan, R., Martinez-Sobrido, L., . . . Gonzalez-Maeso, J. (2011). Maternal influenza viral infection causes schizophrenia-like alterations of 5-HT2A and mGlu2 receptors in the adult offspring. *Journal of Neuroscience, 3,* 1863–1872. doi: 10.1523/JNEUROSCI.4230-10.2011.

Moreno, M.A., Jelenchick, L., Cox, E., Young, H., & Christakis, D.A. (2011). Problematic Internet use among US youth: A systematic review. *Archives of Pediatric and Adolescent Medicine, 165,* 797–805. doi: 10.1001/archpediatrics.2011.58.

Morey, R.A., Dolcos, F., Petty, C.M., Cooper, D.A., Hayes, J.P., LaBar, K.S., & McCarthy, G. (2009). The role of trauma-related distractors on neural systems for working memory and emotion processing in posttraumatic stress disorder. *Journal of Psychiatric Research, 43,* 809–817.

Morgenstern, N.A., Lombardi, G., & Schinder, A.F. (2008). Newborn granule cells in the ageing dentate gyrus. *Journal of Physiology, 586,* 3751–3757.

Morris, C.D., Bransford, J.D., & Franks, J.J. (1977). Levels of processing versus transfer-appropriate processing. *Journal of Verbal Learning and Verbal Behavior, 16,* 519–533.

Morris, J.S., Frilt, C.D., Perrett, D.I., Rowland, D., Yong, A.N., Calder, A.J., & Dolan, R.J. (1996). A different neural response in the human amygdala in fearful and happy facial expressions. *Nature, 383,* 812–815.

Morris, M.W., & Peng, K. (1994). Culture and cause: American and Chinese attributions for social and physical events. *Journal of Personality and Social Psychology, 67,* 949–971.

Morris, N.M., Udry, J.R., Khandawood, F., & Dawood, M.Y. (1987). Marital sex frequency and midcycle female testosterone. *Archives of Sexual Behavior, 16,* 27–37.

Morris, P.H., Gale, A., & Duffy, K. (2002). Can judges agree on the personality of horses? *Personality and Individual Differences, 33,* 67–81.

Morris, P.L., Robinson, R.G., Raphael, B., & Hopwood, M.J. (1996). Lesion location and post-stroke depression. *Journal of Neuropsychiatry and Clinical Neurosciences, 8,* 399–403.

Morrison, J., Anderson, M.J., Sutton, M., Munoz-Arroyo, R., McDonald, S., Maxwell, M., Power, A., Smith, M., & Wilson, P. (2009). Factors influencing variation in prescribing of antidepressants by general practices in Scotland. *British Journal of General Practice, 59,* e25–31.

Morrison, R.S., Maroney-Galin, C., Kralovec, P.D., & Meier, D.E. (2005). The growth of palliative care programs in United States hospitals. *Journal of Palliative Medicine, 8*(6), 1127–1134.

Morry, M.M., & Winkler, E. (2001). Student acceptance and expectation of sexual assault. *Canadian Journal of Behavioural Science, 33,* 188–192.

Mort, D.J., Malhotra, P., Mannan, S.K., Rorden, C., Pambakian, A., Kennard, C., & Husain, M. (2003). The anatomy of visual neglect. *Brain, 126,* 1986–1997.

Mortimer, J.A., Borenstein, A.R., Gosche, K.M., & Snowdon, D.A. (2005). Very early detection of Alzheimer neuropathology and the role of brain reserve in modifying its clinical expression. *Journal of Geriatric Psychiatry And Neurology, 18,* 218–223.

Moruzzi, G., & Magoun, H.W. (1949). Brain stem reticular formation and activation of the EEG. *Electroencephalography and Clinical Neurophysiology, 1,* 455–473.

Moscarelloa, J.M., Ben-Shahara, O., & Ettenberg, A. (2009). Effects of food deprivation on goal-directed behaviour, spontaneous locomotion, and c-Fos immunoreactivity in the amygdala. *Behavioural Brain Research, 197,* 9–15.

Mosconi, M., Cody-Hazlett, H., Poe, M., Gerig, G., Gimpel-Smith, R., & Piven, J. (2009). Longitudinal study of amygdala volume and joint attention in 2- to 4-year-old children with autism. *Archives of General Psychiatry, 66,* 509–516. doi: 10.1001/archgenpsychiatry.2009.19.

Moses-Kolko, E.L., Bogen, D., Perel, J., Bregard, A., Uhl, K., Levin, B., et al. (2005). Neonatal signs after late in utero exposure to serotonin reuptake inhibitors: Literature review and implications for clinical applications. *Journal of the American Medical Association, 293,* 2372–2383.

Moskowitz, J. (2003). Positive affect predicts lower risk of AIDS mortality. *Psychosomatic Medicine, 65,* 620–626.

Moss, M. (2013, February 20). The extraordinary science of addictive junk food. *New York Times.* Retrieved from http://www.nytimes.com/2013/02/24/magazine/the-extraordinary-science-of-junk-food.html?_r=0.

Motluk, A. (2005, January 29th). Senses special: The art of seeing without sight. *New Scientist, 2484,* p. 37. Retrieved from http://www.newscientist.com.

Moulden, H.M., Firestone, P., Kingston, D.A., & Wexler, A.F. (2010). A description of sexual offending committed by Canadian teachers. *Journal of Child Sexual Abuse, 19*(4), 403–418. doi:10.1080/10538712.2010.495046.

Mount, M.K., Barrick, M.R., Scullen, S.M., & Rounds, J. (2005). Higher-order dimensions of the Big Five personality traits and the Big Six vocational interest types. *Personnel Psychology, 58,* 447–478.

Müller-Oerlinghausen, B., Berghöfer, A., & Bauer, M. (2002). Bipolar disorder. *The Lancet, 359,* 241–247.

Mulvey, T.A., & Grus, C.L. (2010, August). *What can I do with a degree in psychology?* Paper presented at Annual Convention of American Psychological Association, San Diego, CA. Retrieved from http://www.apa.org/.

Munsinger, H. (1975). The adopted child's IQ: A critical review. *Psychological Bulletin, 82,* 623–659.

Murdoch, B.E. (2010). The cerebellum and language: Historical perspective and review. *Cortex, 46,* 858–868.

Murphy, K.A., Blustein, D.L., Bohlig, A.J., & Platt, M.G. (2010). The college-to-career transition: An exploration of emerging adulthood. *Journal of Counseling & Development, 88*(2), 174–181.

Murray, H.A. (1938/1962). *Explorations in personality.* New York: Science Editions.

Muscanell, N.L, & Guadagno, R.E. (2012). Make new friends or keep the old: Gender and personality differences in social networking use. *Computers in Human Behavior, 28,* 107–112.

Myers, D.G., & Spencer, S.J. (2004). *Social psychology* (2nd Canadian ed.). Toronto: McGraw-Hill Ryerson.

Myers, I.B. (1962). *Manual: The Myers-Briggs Type Indicator.* Palo Alto, CA: Consulting Psychologists Press.

Nacash, N., Foa, E.B., Fostick, L., Polliack, M., Dinstein, Y., Tzur, D., et al. (2007). Prolonged exposure therapy for chronic combat-related PTSD: A case report on five veterans. *CNS Spectrums, 12,* 690–695.

Nadarajah, B., & Parnavelas, J. (2002). Modes of neuronal migration in the developing cerebral cortex. *Nature Reviews Neuroscience, 3,* 423–432.

Nadkarni, A., & Hofmann, S. (2012). Why do people use Facebook? *Personality and Individual Differences, 52,* 243–249.

Naqvi, N.H., Rudrauf, D., Damasio, H., & Bechara, A. (2007). Damage to the insula disrupts addiction to cigarette smoking. *Science, 315,* 531–534.

Nasar, S. (1998). *A beautiful mind.* New York: Touchstone.

Nash, M.R., Hulsey, T.L., Sexton, M.C., Harralson, T.L., Lambert, W., & Lynch, G.V. (1993). *Adult psychopathology associated with a history of childhood sexual abuse: A psychoanalytic perspective.* Washington, DC: American Psychological Association.

National Eye Institute. (2002). *Vision problems in the U.S.: Prevalence of adult vision impairment and age-related eye disease in America, 2002.* Retrieved January 20, 2007, from http://www.nei.nih.gov/eyedata/pdf/VPUS.pdf.

National Institute of Mental Health (NIMH). (2007). *Schizophrenia.* Washington, DC: NIMH Publication # 06-3517.

National Institute on Alcohol Abuse and Alcoholism. (2005). *Heavy episodic consumption of alcohol.* Retrieved April 4, 2008, from http://www.collegedrinkingprevention.gov/NIAAACollegeMaterials/TaskForce/HeavyEpisodic_00.aspx.

National Safety Council. (2003). *What are the odds of dying?* Retrieved January 20, 2007, from http://www.nsc.org/lrs/statinfo/odds.htm.

National Science Foundation. (2002). Science and technology: Public attitudes and public understanding. In *Science and Engineering Indicators—2002* (Chapter 7). Arlington, VA: National Science Foundation.

National Sleep Foundation. (2008). *2008 Sleep in America poll.* Retrieved April 2, 2008, from http://www.sleepfoundation.org/site/c.huIXKjM0IxF/b.3933533/

Natural born copycats. (2002, December 20). *The Guardian.* Retrieved from http://www.mediaknowall.com/violence/nbk.html.

Nauta, W.J.H., & Feirtag, M. (1979). The organization of the brain. *Scientific American, 241,* 88–111.

Ndubakua, U., & de Bellard, M.E. (2008). Glial cells: Old cells with new twists. *Acta Histochemica, 110,* 182–195.

Neal, D.T., & Chartrand, T.L. (2011). Embodied emotion perception. *Social Cognition and Personality Science, 2,* 673–678.

Neisser, U. (1967). *Cognitive psychology.* Appleton-Century-Crofts: New York.

Neisser, U. (1998). Introduction: Rising test scores and what they mean. In U. Neisser (Ed.), *The rising curve: Long-term gains in IQ and related measures* (pp. 3–22). Washington, DC: American Psychological Association.

Neisser, U., Boodoo, G., Bouchard, T.J., Boykin, A.W., Brody, N., Ceci, S.J., et al. (1996). Intelligence: Knowns and unknowns. *American Psychologist, 51,* 77–101.

Neitz, J., Neitz, M., & Kainz, P.M. (1996). Visual pigment gene structure and the severity of color vision defects. *Science, 274,* 801–804.

Nelson-Gray, R.O., Keane, S.P., Hurst, R.M., Mitchell, J.T., Warburton, J.B., Chok, J.T., et al. (2006). A modified DBT skills training program for oppositional defiant adolescents: Promising preliminary findings. *Behaviour Research and Therapy, 44,* 1811–1820.

Nemeroff, C., & Rozin, P. (1994). The contagion concept in adult thinking in the United States: Transmission of germs and of interpersonal influence. *Ethos, 22,* 158–186.

Nemeroff, C.B. (2007). The burden of severe depression: A review of diagnostic challenges and treatment alternatives. *Journal of Psychiatric Research, 41,* 189–206.

Nesbit, S.M., Conger, J.C., & Conger, A.J. (2007). A quantitative review of the relationship between anger and aggressive driving. *Aggression and Violent Behavior, 12,* 156–176.

Nettle, D., & Clegg, H. (2005). Schizotypy, creativity, and mating success in humans. *Proceedings of the Royal Society (B).*

Neuberg, S.L., & Cottrell, C.A. (2006). Evolutionary bases of prejudices. In M. Schaller, J.A. Simpson, & D.T. Kenrick (Eds.). *Evolution and social psychology* (pp. 163–187). New York: Psychology Press.

Neugebauer, R., Hoek, H.W., & Susser, E. (1999). Prenatal exposure to wartime famine and development of antisocial personality disorder in early adulthood. *Journal of the American Medical Association, 282,* 455–462.

Nevonen, L., & Broberg, A.G. (2006). A comparison of sequenced individual and group psychotherapy for patients with bulimia nervosa. *International Journal of Eating Disorders, 39,* 117–127.

New York Academy of Sciences. (2003). *Adolescent brain development: Vulnerabilities and opportunities.* [E-briefing]. Retrieved March 13, 2008 from http://www.nyas.org/ebriefreps/main.asp?intSubSectionID=570#02.

New York Times—Health. (2009). Retrieved March 15, 2010, from http://www.nytimes.com/2009/12/22/health/22brain.html?pagewanted=1&_r=1&emc=eta1.

Newcomb, T.M. (1961). *The acquaintance process.* Oxford, England: Holt, Rinehart & Winston.

Newcombe, N.S., & Uttal, D.H. (2006). Whorf versus Socrates, round 10. *Trends in Cognitive Sciences, 10,* 394–396.

Newell, B.R., Cavenett, T., & Andrews, S. (2008). On the immunity of perceptual implicit memory to manipulations of attention. *Memory & Cognition, 36,* 725–734.

Newman, A.J., Bavelier, D., Corina, D., Jezzard, P., & Neville, H.J. (2001). A critical period for right hemisphere recruitment in American Sign Language processing. *Nature Neuroscience, 5,* 76–80.

Newport, E.L. (2003). Language development, critical periods in. In L. Nadel (Ed.), *Encyclopedia of cognitive science* (Vol. 2; pp. 733–740). London: Nature Group Press.

Neyens, D.M., & Boyle, L.N. (2007). The effect of distraction on the crash types of teenage drivers. *Accident Analysis and Prevention, 39,* 206–212.

Nichols, D.E. (2004). Hallucinogens. *Pharmacology & Therapeutics 101,* 131–181.

Nickerson, C., Schwarz, N., Diener, E., & Kahneman, D. (2003). Zeroing in on the dark side of the American dream: A closer look at the negative consequences of the goal for financial success. *Psychological Science, 14,* 531–536.

Nicoll, R.A., & Alger, B.E. (2004). The brain's own marijuana. *Scientific American, 291,* 69–75.

Nikolaus, S., Antke, C., Beu, M., & Muller, H.W. (2010). Cortical GABA, striatal dopamine and midbrain serotonin as the key players in compulsive and anxiety disorders—Results from in vivo imaging studies. *Reviews in the Neurosciences, 21,* 119–139.

Nilsson, L.G. (2003). Memory function in normal aging. *Acta Neurologica Scandinavica Supplementum, 179,* 7–13.

Nisbett, R.E., & Wilson, T.D. (1977). Telling more than we can know: Verbal reports on mental processes. *Psychological Review, 84,* 231–259.

Nisbett, R.E., Peng, K., Choi, I., & Norenzayan, A. (2001). Culture and systems of thought: Holistic versus analytic cognition. *Psychological Review, 108,* 291–301.

Nishida, A., Hisaoka, K., Zensho, H., Uchitomi, Y., Morinobu, S., & Yamawaki, S. (2002). Antidepressant drugs and cytokines in mood disorders. *International Immuniopharmacology, 2,* 1619–1626.

Nishimura, E.K., Granter, S.R., & Fisher, D.E. (2005). Mechanisms of hair graying: Incomplete melanocyte stem cell maintenance in the niche. *Science, 307,* 720–724.

Nishino, S. (2007). Clinical and neurobiological aspects of narcolepsy. *Sleep Medicine, 8,* 373–399.

Nishino, S., Okuro, M., Kotorii, N., Anegawa, E., Ishimaru, Y., Matsumura, M., & Kanbayashi, T. (2010). Hypocretin/orexin and narcolepsy: new basic and clinical insights. *Acta Physiology, 198*(3), 209–222.

Nithianantharajah, J., & Hannan, A. (2006). Enriched environments, experience dependent plasticity and disorders of the nervous system. *Nature Reviews Neuroscience, 7,* 697–709.

Nixon, R.D.V., Ellis, A.A., Nehmy, T.J., & Ball, S.-A. (2010). Screening and predicting posttraumatic stress and depression in children following single-incident trauma. *Journal of Clinical Child & Adolescent Psychology, 39,* 588–596.

Noble, K.G., Norman, M.F., & Farah, M.J. (2005). Neurocognitive correlates of socioeconomic status in kindergarten children. *Developmental Science, 8*(1), 74–87. doi:10.1111/j.1467-7687.2005.00394.x.

Noble, R.E. (2001). Waist-to-hip ratio versus BMI as predictors of cardiac risk in obese adult women. *Western Journal of Medicine, 174,* 240.

Nock, M.K., Park, J.M., Finn, C.T., Deliberto, T.L., Dour, H.J., & Banaji, M.R. (2010). Measuring the suicidal mind: Implicit cognition predicts suicidal behavior. *Psychological Science, 21,* 511–517.

Noda, H., Iso, H., Toyoshima, H., Date, C., Yamamoto, A., Kikuchi, S., et al. (2005). Walking and sports participation and mortality from coronary heart disease and stroke. *Journal of the American College of Cardiology, 46,* 1761–1767.

Nolen-Hoeksema, S. (2007). *Abnormal psychology* (4th ed). New York: McGraw-Hill.

Nolen-Hoeksema, S. (2012). Emotion regulation and psychopathology: The role of gender. *Annual Review of Clinical Psychology, 8*61–887. doi:10.1146/annurev-clinpsy-032511-143109.

Nolen-Hoeksema, S., & Hilt, L.M. (2009). Gender differences in depression. In I.H. Gotlib & Hammen, C.L. (Eds.), *Handbook of depression* (2nd ed., pp. 386–404). New York, NY: Guilford Press.

Nolen-Hoeksema, S., Wisco, B.E., & Lyubomirsky, S. (2008). Rethinking rumination. *Perspectives on Psychological Science, 3*(5), 400–424. doi: 10.1111/j.1745-6924.2008.00088.x.

Nolte, C., & Yollin, P. (2006, April 19). Officials salute city's majestic rise from rubble of '06—and the survivors. *San Francisco Chronicle,* pp. A1, A12.

Norcross, J.C., & Wampold, B.E. (2011). Evidence-based therapy relationships: Research conclusions and clinical practices. *Psychotherapy, 48,* 98–102. doi:10.1037/a0022161.

Norcross, J.C., Bike, D., & Evans, K. (2009). The therapist's therapist: A replication and extension 20 years later. *Psychotherapy: Theory, Research, Practice, Training, 46,* 32–41. doi: 10.1037/a0015140.

Norcross, J.C., Karpiak, C.P., & Lister, K.M. (2005). What's an integrationist? A study of self-identified integrative and (occasionally) eclectic psychologists. *Journal of Clinical Psychology, 61,* 1587–1594.

Norcross, J.C., Sayette, M.A., Mayne, T.J., Karg, R.S., & Turkson, M.A. (1998). Selecting a doctoral program in professional psychology: Some comparisons among PhD counseling, PhD clinical, and PsyD clinical psychology programs. *Professional Psychology: Research and Practice, 29,* 609–614.

Norenzayan, A., & Heine, S.J. (2005). Psychological universals: What are they and how can we know? *Psychological Bulletin, 131,*763–784.

Norenzayan, A., & Nisbett, R.E. (2000). Culture and causal cognition. *Current Directions in Psychological Science, 9,* 132–135.

Nottebohm, F. (1985). Neuronal replacement in adulthood. *Annals of the New York Academy of Sciences, 457,* 143–161.

Novak, M.A. (2003). Self-injurious behavior in Rhesus monkeys: New insights into its etiology, physiology, and treatment. *American Journal of Primatology, 59,* 3–19.

Nuechterlein, K., & Parasuraman, R. (1983). Visual sustained attention: Image degradation produces rapid sensitivity decrement over time. *Science, 220,* 327–329.

Oberauer, K., & Göthe, K. (2006). Dual-task effects in working memory: Interference between two processing tasks, between two memory demands, and between storage and processing. *European Journal of Cognitive Psychology, 18,* 493–519.

Oberman, L.M., & Ramachadran, V.S. (2007). The simulating social mind: The role of mirror neuron system and simulation in the social and communicative deficits of autism spectrum disorders. *Psychological Bulletin, 133,* 310–327.

Ochsner, K.N., Bunge, S.A., Gross, J.J., & Gabrieli, J.D.E. (2002). Rethinking feelings: A fMRI study of the cognitive regulation of emotion. *Journal of Cognitive Neuroscience, 14,* 1215–1229.

O'Cleirigh, C., Ironson, G., Fletcher, M.A., & Schneiderman, N. (2008). Written emotional disclosure and processing of trauma are associated with protected health status and immunity in people living with HIV/AIDS. *British Journal of Health Psychology, 13,* 81–84.

OCOL—Bilingualism in Canada. Retrieved January 22, 2010, from http://www.ocol-clo.gc.ca/html/biling_e.php.

O'Conner, M.J., & Paley, B. (2006). The relationship of prenatal alcohol exposure and the postnatal environment of child depressive symptoms. *Journal of Pediatric Psychology, 31,* 50–64.

O'Connor, S.S., Whitehill, J.M., King, K.M., Kernic, M.A., Boyle, L.N., Bresnahan, B.W., . . . Ebel, B.E. (2013). Compulsive cell phone use and history of motor vehicle crash. *Journal of Adolescent Health, 53,* 512–519.

Ogawa, H., Wakita, M., Hasegawa, K., Kobayakawa, T., Sakai, N., Hirai, T., et al. (2005). Functional MRI detection of activation in the primary gustatory cortices in humans. *Chemical Senses, 30,* 583–592.

Oh, J., Jeong, S., & Jeong, J. (2012). The timing and temporal patterns of eye blinking are dynamically modulated by attention. *Human Movement Science, 31*(6), 1353–1365. doi:10.1016/j.humov.2012.06.003.

Öhman, A. (2002). Automaticity and the amygdala: Nonconscious responses to emotional faces. *Current Directions in Psychological Science, 11,* 62–66.

Öhman, A. (2009). Of snakes and faces: An evolutionary perspective on the psychology of fear. *Scandinavian Journal of Psychology, 50*(6), 543–552. doi:10.1111/j.1467-9450.2009.00784.x.

Öhman, A., Dimberg, U., & Öst, L.-G. (1985). Animal and social phobias: Biological constraints on learned fear responses. In S. Reiss & R.R. Bootzin (Eds.), *Theoretical issues in behavior therapy.* New York: Academic Press.

Ohnishi, T., Matsuda, H., Asada, T., Aruga, M., Hirakata, M., Nishikawa, M., et al. (2001). Functional anatomy of musical perception in musicians. *Cerebral Cortex, 11,* 754–760.

Okagaki, L., & Sternberg, R.J. (1993). Parental beliefs and children's school performance. *Child Development, 64,* 36–56.

O'Keefe, J., & Burgess, N. (1996). Geometric determinants of the place fields of hippocampal neurons. *Nature, 381,* 425–428.

O'Keefe, J., & Dostrovsky, J. (1971). Hippocampus as a spatial map - Preliminary evidence from unit activity in freely-moving rat. *Brain Research, 34,* 171–175.

O'Keefe, J., & Nadel, L. (1978). *The hippocampus as a cognitive map.* Oxford: Oxford University Press.

Olatunji, B.O., & Wolitzky-Taylor, K.B. (2009). Anxiety Sensitivity and the Anxiety Disorders: A Meta-Analytic Review and Synthesis. *Psychological Bulletin, 135*(6), 974–999.

Olds, J., & Milner, P. (1954). Positive reinforcement produced by electrical stimulation of septal area and other regions of rat brain. *Journal of Comparative and Physiological Psychology, 47,* 419–427.

Oliver, M.B., & Hyde, J.S. (1993). Gender differences in sexuality: A meta-analysis. *Psychological Bulletin, 114,* 29–51.

Olson, J.M., & Zanna, M.P. (1993). Attitudes and attitude change. *Annual Review of Psychology, 44,* 117–154.

Omark, D., Omark, M., & Edelman, M. (1973). Formation of dominance hierarchies in young children. In T.R. Williams (Ed.), *Physical anthropology.* The Hague: Mouton.

Onodera, A. (2003). Changes in self-concept in the transition to parenthood. *Japanese Journal of Developmental Psychology, 14,* 180–190.

Opriş, D., Pintea, S., García-Palacios, A., Botella, C., Szamosközi, Ş., & David, D. (2012). Virtual reality exposure therapy in anxiety disorders: a quantitative meta-analysis. *Depression & Anxiety (1091-4269), 29*(2), 85–93. doi:10.1002/da.20910.

Orne, M.T. (1959). The nature of hypnosis: Artifact and essence. *Journal of Abnormal and Social Psychology, 58,* 277–299.

Ornstein, A. (2002). Religion and paranormal belief. *Journal for the Scientific Study of Religion, 41*(2), 301–311.

Orr, E.S., Sisic, M., Ross, C., Simmering, M.G., Arseneault, J.M., & Orr, R. (2009). The influence of shyness on the use of Facebook in an undergraduate sample. *Cyberpsychology & Behavior, 12*(3), 337–340. doi:10.1089/cpb.2008.0214.

Ortigosa, A., Martín, J.M., & Carro, R.M. (2014) Sentiment analysis in Facebook and its application to e-learning. *Computers in Human Behavior, 31,* 527–541

Osbeck, L.M., Moghaddam, F.M., & Perreault, S. (1997). Similarity and attraction among majority and minority groups in a multicultural context. *International Journal of Intercultural Relations, 21,* 113–123.

Oscar-Berman, M., & Marinkovic, K. (2003). Alcoholism and the brain: An overview. *Alcohol Research & Health, 27,* 125–133.

O'Shea, G., Spence, S.H., & Donovan, C.L. (2015). Group versus individual interpersonal psychotherapy for depressed adolescents. *Behavioural & Cognitive Psychotherapy, 43*(1), 1–19. doi:10.1017/S1352465814000216.

Osherow, N. (1999). Making sense of the nonsensical: An analysis of Jonestown. In E. Aronson (Ed.), *Readings about the social animal* (8th ed., pp. 71–88). New York: Worth/Freeman.

Ost, J. (2003). Seeking the middle ground in the "memory wars." *British Journal of Psychology, 94,* 125–139.

Oster, H. (2005). The repertoire of infant facial expressions: An ontogenetic perspective. In J. Nadel & D. Muir (Eds.), *Emotional development* (pp. 261–292). New York: Oxford University Press.

Osterling, J., & Dawson, G. (1994). Early recognition of children with autism: A study of first birthday home videotapes. *Journal of Autism and Developmental Disorders, 24,* 247–257.

Ottersen, O.P. (2010). How hardwired is the brain? Technological advances provide new insight into brain malleability and neurotransmission. *Nutrition Reviews, 68,* S60–S64. doi: 10.1111/j.1753-4887.2010.00350.x.

Otto, M.W., McHugh, R.K., & Kantak, K.M. (2010). Combined pharmacotherapy and cognitive-behavioral therapy for anxiety disorders: Medication effects, glucocorticoids, and attenuated treatment outcomes. *Clinical Psychology: Science and Practice, 17,* 91–103.

Ouellet, M-C., & Morin, C.M. (2006). Fatigue following traumatic brain injury: Frequency, characteristics, and associated factors. *Rehabilitation Psychology, 51,* 140–149.

Ouellet, M-C., Beaulieu-Bonneau, S., & Morin, C.M. (2006). Insomnia in patients with traumatic brain injury: Frequency, characteristics, and risk factors. *Journal of Head Trauma Rehabilitation, 21,* 199–212.

Owen, A.M., Coleman, M.R., Boly, M., Davis, M., Laureys, S., & Pickard, J.D. (2006). Detecting awareness in the vegetative state. *Science, 313,* 1402.

Oyama, S. (1976). A sensitive period for the acquisition of a nonnative phonological system. *Journal of Psycholinguistic Research, 5,* 261–283.

Ozer, E.J., Best, S.R., Lipset, T.T., & Weiss, D.S. (2003). Predictors of posttraumatic stress disorder and symptoms in adults: A meta-analysis. *Psychology Bulletin, 129,* 52–73.

Özgüven, N., & Mucan, B. (2013). The relationship between personality traits and social media use. *Social Behavior and Personality, 41,* 517–528.

Pace-Schott, E.F., Milad, M.R., Orr, S.P., Rauch, S.L., Stickgold, R., & Pitman, R.K. (2009). Sleep promotes generalization of extinction of conditioned fear. *Sleep, 32,* 19–26.

Pae, C.-U., Lim, H.-K., Han, C., Neena, A., Lee, C., & Patkar, A.A. (2007). Selegiline transdermal system: Current awareness and promise. *Progress in Neuro-Psycho-pharmacology & Biological Psychiatry, 31,* 1153–1163.

Pagani, L., Fitzpatrick, C., Barnett, T., & Dubow, E. (2010). Prospective associations between early childhood television exposure and academic, psychosocial, and physical well-being by middle childhood. *Archives of Pediatrics & Adolescent Medicine, 164*(5), 425–431.

Pahl, K., & Way, N. (2006). Longitudinal trajectories of ethnic identity among urban Black and Latino adolescents. *Child Development, 77,* 1403–1415.

Pahnke, W.N., Kurland, A.A., Unger, S., Savage, C., & Grof, S. (1970). The experimental use of psychedelic (LSD) psychotherapy. *Journal of the American Medical Association, 212,* 856–1863.

Paivio, A. (1986). *Mental representations: A dual coding approach.* Oxford. England: Oxford University Press.

Pallanti, S., Bernardi, S., & Quercoli, L. (2006). The shorter PROMIS questionnaire and the Internet addiction scale in the assessment of multiple addictions in a high school population: Prevalence and related disability. *CNS Spectrum, 11,* 966–974.

Pan, B.A., Rowe, M.L., Singer, J.D., & Snow, C.E. (2005). Maternal correlates of growth in toddler vocabulary production in low-income families. *Child Development, 76,* 763–946.

Panksepp, J. (2000). Emotions as natural kinds within the mammalian brain. In M. Lewis and J.M. Haviland-Jones (Eds.), *Handbook of emotions* (2nd ed., pp. 137–156). New York: Guilford.

Panksepp, J. (2005). Why does separation distress hurt? Comment on MacDonald and Leary (2005). *Psychological Bulletin, 131,* 224–230.

Pantev, C., Engelien, A., Candia, V., & Elbert, T. (2001). Representational cortex in musicians: Plastic alterations in response to musical practice. In R.J. Zatorre & I. Peretz (Eds.), *The biological foundations of music: Annals of the New York Academy of Sciences* (pp. 300–314). New York: New York Academy of Sciences.

Papakostos, G.I., Stahl, S.M., Krishen, A., Seifert, C., Tucker, V.L., Goodale, E.P., & Faca, M. (2008). Efficacy of bupropion and the selective serotonin reuptake inhibitors in the treatment of major depressive disorder with high levels of anxiety (anxious depression): A pooled analysis of 10 studies. *Journal of Clinical Psychiatry, 69,* 1287–1292.

Parasuraman, R. (1998). *The attentive brain.* Cambridge, MA: MIT Press.

Paris, R., & Helson, R. (2002). Early mothering experience and personality change. *Journal of Family Psychology, 16,* 172–185.

Park, G., Schwartz, H.A., Eichstaedt, J.C., Kern, M.L., Kosinski, M., Stillwell, D.J., Ungar, L.H., & Seligman, M.E.P. (2014, November 3). Automatic personality assessment through social media language. *Journal of Personality and Social Psychology.* Advance online publication. http://dx.doi.org/10.1037/pspp0000020.

Parker, R.S. (1996). The spectrum of emotional distress and personality changes after minor head injury incurred in a motor vehicle accident. *Brain Injury, 10,* 287–302.

Parker, S.T., & McKinney, M.L. (1999). *Origins of intelligence: The evolution of cognitive development in monkeys, apes, and humans.* Baltimore: Johns Hopkins University Press.

Partanen, E., Kujala, T., Näätänen, R., Liitola, A., Sambeth, A., & Huotilainen, M. (2013). Learning-induced neural plasticity of speech processing before birth. *PNAS Proceedings of The National Academy of Sciences of the United States of America, 110*(37), 15145–15150. doi: 10.1073/pnas.1302159110.

Partanen, E., Kujala, T., Tervaniemi, M., & Huotilainen, M. (2013). Prenatal music exposure induces long-term neural effects. *PLoS ONE, 8,* e78946.doi: 10.1371/journal.pone.0078946.

Pascual-Leone, A. (2001). The brain that plays music and is changed by it. *Annals of the New York Academy of Sciences, 930,* 315–329.

Patchin, J.W., & Hinduja, S. (2006). Bullies move beyond the schoolyard: a preliminary look at cyberbullying. *Youth Violence and Juvenile Justice, 4,* 148–169.

Patil, S.T., Zhang, L., Martenyi, F., Lowe, S.L., Jackson, K.A., Andreev, B.V., et al. (2007). Activation of mGlu2/3 receptors as a new approach to treat schizophrenia: A randomized Phase 2 clinical trial. *Nature Medicine, 13,* 1102–1107.

Paton, J.J., Belov, M.A., Morrison, S.E., & Salzman, C.D. (2006). The primate amygdala represents the positive and negative value of visual stimuli during learning. *Nature, 439,* 865–870.

Patten, S.B., Wang, J.L., Williams, J.V.A., Currie, S., Beck, C.A., Maxwell, C.J., & El-Guebaly, N. (2006). Descriptive epidemiology of major depression in Canada. *Canadian Journal of Psychiatry, 51,* 84–90.

Patterson, C.J. (2008). *Child development.* New York: McGraw-Hill.

Patterson, D.R. (2004). Treating pain with hypnosis. *Current Directions in Psychological Science, 13,* 252–255.

Paul, E.L., & White, K.M. (1990). The development of intimate relationships in late adolescence. *Adolescence, 25,* 375–400.

Paul, E.S., Harding, E.J., & Mendl, M. (2005). Measuring emotional processes in animals: The utility of a cognitive approach. *Neuroscience and Biobehavioral Reviews, 29,* 469–491.

Paulesu, E., Frith, C.D., & Frackowiak, R.S.J. (1993). The neural correlates of the verbal component of working memory. *Nature, 362,* 342–345.

Paulhus, D.L., & Landolt, M.A. (2000). Paragons of intelligence: Who gets nominated and why. *Canadian Journal of Behavioural Science, 32,* 168–177.

Paulozzi, L.J. (2006). Opioid analgesia involvement in drug abuse deaths in American metropolitan areas. *American Journal of Public Health, 96,* 1755–1757.

Paus, T., Keshavan, M., & Giedd, J.N. (2008). Why do many psychiatric disorders emerge during adolescence? *Nature Reviews: Neuroscience, 9,* 947–957.

Pavlov, I.P. (1906). The scientific investigation of the psychical faculties or processes in the higher animals. *Science, 24,* 613–619.

Pavlov, I.P. (1928). *Lectures on conditioned reflexes: Twenty-five years of objective study of the higher nervous activity (behaviour) of animals* (W.H. Gantt, Trans.). New York: Liveright.

Payne, J.D., & Nadel, L. (2004). Sleeps, dreams, and memory consolidation: The role of the stress hormone cortisol. *Learning & Memory, 11,* 671–678.

Payton, J., Weissberg, R.P., Durlak, J.A., Dymnicki, A.B., Taylor, R.D., Schellinger, K.G., et al. (2008). *The positive impact of social and emotional learning for kindergarten to eighth-grade students: Findings from three scientific reviews.* Retrieved from http://www.lpfch.org/sel/PackardES-REV.pdf.

Pearson, C., Janz, T., & Ali, J. (2013). Mental and substance use disorders in

Canada: Health at a Glance. *Statistics Canada*, Catalogue no. 82-624-X.

Pearson, J.D., Morrell, C.H., Gordon-Salant, S., Brant, L.J., Metter, E.J., Klein, L., et al. (1995). Gender differences in a longitudinal study of age-associated hearing loss. *Journal of the Acoustical Society of America, 97,* 1197–1205.

Pearson, N.J., Johnson, L.L., & Nahin, R.L. (2006). Insomnia, trouble sleeping, and complementary and alternative medicine: Analysis of the 2002 National Health Interview Survey data. *Archives of Internal Medicine, 166,* 1775–1782.

Peculiar institution. (2002). [Editorial]. *Scientific American, 286,* 8.

Pedersen, D.M., & Wheeler, J. (1983). The Müller–Lyer illusion among Navajos. *Journal of Social Psychology, 121,* 3–6.

Peigneux, P., Laureys, S., Fuchs, S., Collette, F., Perrin, F., Reggers, J., et al. (2004). Are spatial memories strengthened in the human hippocampus during slow wave sleep? *Neuron, 44,* 535–545.

Pelli, D.G., Farell, B., & Moore, D.C. (2003). The remarkable inefficiency of word recognition. *Nature, 423,* 752–756.

Penfield, W., & Boldrey, E. (1937). Somatic motor and sensory representation in the cerebral cortex of man as studied by electrical stimulation. *Brain, 60,* 389–443.

Pennebaker, J.W. (1995). *Emotion, disclosure, and health.* Washington, DC: American Psychological Association.

Pennebaker, J.W., Kiecolt-Glaser, J.K., & Glaser, R. (1988). Disclosure of traumas and immune function: Implications for psychotherapy. *Journal of Consulting and Clinical Psychology, 56,* 239–245.

Penner, L.A., Dovidio, J.F., Piliavin, J.A., & Schroeder, D.A. (2005). Prosocial behavior: Multilevel perspectives. *Annual Review of Psychology, 56,* 1–28. doi:10.1146/annurev.psych.56.091103.070141.

Peper, J.S., Brouwer, R.M., Schnack, H.G., van Baal, G.M., van Leeuwen, M., van den Berg, S.M., & Pol, H. (2008). Cerebral white matter in early puberty is associated with luteinizing hormone concentrations. *Psychoneuroendocrinology, 33*(7), 909–915.

Pepler, D.J., & Craig, W.M. (1995). A peek behind the fence: Naturalistic observations of aggressive children with remote audiovisual recording. *Developmental Psychology, 31*(4), 548–553.

Pereira, A.C., Huddleston, D.E., Brickman, A.M., Sosunov, A.A., Hen, R., McKhann, et al. (2007). An *in vivo* correlate of exerciseinduced neurogenesis in the adult dentate gyrus. *Proceedings of the National Academy of Sciences, 104,* 5638–5643.

Perlovsky, L.I., & Ilin, R. (2013). Mirror neurons, language, and embodied cognition. *Neural Networks, 41,* 15–22. doi: 10.1016/j.neunet.2013.01.003.

Perrin, J.S., Leonard, G., Perron, M., Pike, G.B., Pitiot, A., Richer, L., Veillette, S., Pausova, Z., & Paus, T. (2009). Sex differences in the growth of white matter during adolescence, *NeuroImage, 45,* 1055–1066.

Perry, B.D. (2002). Childhood experience and the expression of genetic potential: What childhood neglect tells us about nature and nurture. *Brain and Mind, 3,* 79–100.

Perry, R., & Zeki, S. (2000). The neurology of saccades and covert shifts in spatial attention: An event-related fMRI study. *Brain, 123,* 2273–2288.

Persky, H., Dreisbach, L., Miller, W.R., O'Brien, C.P., Khan, M.A., Lief, H.I., et al. (1982). The relation of plasma androgen levels to sexual behaviors and attitudes of women. *Psychosomatic Medicine, 44,* 305–319.

Persky, H., Lief, H.I., Strauss, D., Miller, W.R., & O'Brien, C.P. (1978). Plasma testosterone level and sexual behavior of couples. *Archives of Sexual Behavior, 7,* 157–173.

Pérusse-Lachance, É., Tremblay, A., Drapeau, V. (2010). Lifestyle factors and other health measures in a Canadian university community. *Applied Physiology, Nutrition, and Metabolism, 35,* 498–506.

Pesant, N., & Zadra, A. (2004). Working with dreams in therapy: What do we know and what should we do? *Clinical Psychology Review 24,* 489–512.

Pessoa, L. (2008). On the relationship between emotion and cognition. *Nature Reviews Neuroscience, 9,* 148–158.

Pessoa, L., Padmala, S., & Morland, T. (2005). Fate of unattended fearful faces in the amygdala is determined by both attentional resources and cognitive modulation. *NeuroImage, 28,* 249–255.

Peter, J., Valkenburg, P.M., & Schouten, A.P. (2005). Developing a model of adolescent friendship formation on the internet. *CyberPsychology & Behavior, 8,* 423–430.

Peterson, C. (2010). "And I was very very crying": Child self-descriptions of distress as predictors of recall. *Applied Cognitive Psychology, 24,* 909–924.

Peterson, L.R., & Peterson, M.J. (1959). Short-term retention of individual verbal items. *Journal of Experimental Psychology, 58,* 193–198.

Petot, J. (2000). Interest and limitations of projective techniques in the assessment of personality disorders. *European Psychiatry, 15,* 11–14.

Petronis, A. (2004). Schizophrenia, neurodevelopment, and epi genetics. In M.S. Keshavan, J.L. Kennedy, & R.M. Murray (Eds.). *Neurodevelopment and schizophrenia* (pp. 174–190). New York: Cambridge University Press.

Petry, N.M., & O'Brien, C.P. (2013). Internet gaming disorder and the DSM-5. *Addiction, 108,* 1186–1187. doi: 10.1111/add.12162.

Petry, S., Cummings, J.L., Hill, M.A., & Shapiro, J. (1989). Personality alterations in dementia of the Alzheimer type: A three-year follow-up study. *Journal of Geriatric Psychiatry and Neurology, 2,* 203–207.

Pettigrew, T.F. (1979). The ultimate attribution error: Extending Allport's cognitive analysis of prejudice. *Personality and Social Psychology Bulletin, 5,* 461–476.

Petty, R.E., & Cacioppo, J.T. (1986). The Elaboration Likelihood Model of persuasion. In L. Berkowitz (Ed.), *Advances in Experimental Social Psychology* (Vol. 19, pp. 123–205). New York: Academic Press.

Petty, R.E., Cacioppo, J.T., & Goldman, R. (1981). Personal involvement as a determinant of argument-based persuasion. *Journal of Personality and Social Psychology, 41*(5), 847–855.

Petty, R.E., Fleming, M.A., Priester, J.R., & Feinstein, A.H. (2001). Individual versus group interest violation: Surprise as a determinant of argument scrutiny and persuasion. *Social Cognition, 19,* 418–442.

Petty, R.E., Haugtvedt, C.P., & Smith, S.M. (1995). Elaboration as a determinant of attitude strength. In R.E. Petty & J.A. Krosnick (Eds.), *Attitude strength: Antecedents and consequences* (pp. 93–130). Mahwah, NJ: Erlbaum.

Petzinger, G.M., Fisher, B.E., McEwen, S., Beeler, J.A., Walsh, J.P., & Jakowec, M.W. (2013). Exercise-enhanced neuroplasticity targeting motor and cognitive circuitry in Parkinson's disease. *The Lancet Neurology, 12*(7), 716–726. doi: 10.1016/S1474-4422(13)70123-6.

Pfrieger, F.W. (2002). Role of glia in synapse development. *Current Opinion in Neurobiology, 12,* 496–490.

Phan, K.L., Wager, T., Taylor, S.F., & Liberzon, I. (2002). Functional neuroanatomy of emotion: A meta-analysis of emotion activation studies in PET and fMRI. *NeuroImage, 16,* 331–348.

Phelps, E.A. (2006). Emotion and cognition: Insights from the study of the human amygdala. *Annual Review of Psychology, 57,* 27–53.

Phelps, E.A., & LeDoux, J.E. (2005). Contributions of the amygdala to emotional processing: From animal models to human behavior. *Neuron, 48,* 175–187.

Phinney, J.S., & Ong, A.D. (2007). Conceptualization and Measurement of Ethnic Identity: Current Status and Future Directions.

Journal of Counselling Psychology, 54(3), 271–281. doi:10.1037/0022-067.54.3.271.

Piaget, J. (1954). *The construction of reality in the child.* New York: Basic.

Piaget, J. (1962). *Plays, dreams and imitation in childhood.* New York: Norton.

Piaget, J. (1972a). Intellectual evolution from adolescence to adulthood. *Human Development, 15,* 1–12.

Piaget, J. (1972b). *The child's conception of the world.* Totowa, NJ: Littlefield, Adams. Piaget, J., and Inhelder, B. (1967). *The child's conception of space.* New York: Norton.

Pierce, T. (2009). Social anxiety and technology: Face-to-face communication versus technological communication among teens. *Computers in Human Behavior, 25,* 1367–1372.

Pietrek, C., Elbert, T., Weierstall, R., Müller, O., & Rockstroh, B. (2013). Childhood adversities in relation to psychiatric disorders. *Psychiatry Research, 206,* 103–110. doi:10.1016/j.psychres.2012.11.003.

Pincus, J.H. (1999). Aggression, criminality, and the frontal lobes. In B.L. Miller and J.L. Cummings (Eds.). *The human frontal lobes: Functions and disorders* (pp. 547–556). New York: Guilford Press.

Pincus, J.H. (2001). *Base instincts: What makes killers kill?* New York: Norton.

Pinker, S. (2000). *Words and rules: The ingredients of language.* New York, NY: Basic Books.

Pinker, S. (2002). *The blank slate.* New York: Viking.

Pinker, S. (2004, Fall). Why nature and nurture won't go away. *Daedalus,* 1–13.

Pinker, S., & Bloom, P. (1992). Natural language and natural selection. In J.H. Barkow, L. Cosmides, & J. Tooby (Eds.), *The adapted mind: Evolutionary psychology and the generation of culture.* Oxford, England: Oxford University Press.

Pinker, S., & Jackendoff, R. (2005). The faculty of language: what's special about it? *Cognition, 95,* 201–236.

Pinsk, M.A., DeSimone, K., Moore, T., Gross, C.G., & Kastner, S. (2005). Representations of faces and body parts in macaque temporal cortex: A functional MRI study. *Neuroscience, 102,* 6996–7001.

Pinsker, H.M., Hening, W.A., Carew, T.J., & Kandel, E.R. (1973). Long-term sensitization of a defensive withdrawal reflex in *Aplysia. Science, 182,* 1039–1042.

Pliner, P. (1982). The effects of mere exposure on liking for edible substances. *Appetite, 3,* 283–290.

Plomin, R., & Caspi, A. (1999). Behavioral genetics and personality. In L.A. Pervin and O.P. John (Eds.), *Handbook of personality theory and research* (pp. 251–276). New York: Guilford Press.

Plomin, R., & Petril, S.A. (1997). Genetics and intelligence: What's new? *Intelligence, 24*(1), 53–77.

Plum, F., & Posner, J. (1980). *Diagnosis of stupor and coma* (3rd ed.). Philadelphia, PA: F.A. Davis.

Plunkett, K. (1997). Theories of early language acquisition. *Trends in Cognitive Sciences, 1,* 146–153.

Polanczyk, G., de Lima, M.S., Horta, B.L., Biederman J., & Rohde, L.A. (2007). The world wide prevalence of ADHD: A systematic review and metaregression analysis. *American Journal of Psychiatry, 164,* 942–948.

Polivy, J., & Herman, C.P. (1992). Undieting: A program to help people stop dieting. *International Journal of Eating Disorders, 11,* 261–268.

Pope, H.J., Barry, S., Bodkin, A., & Hudson, J.I. (2006). Tracking scientific interest in the dissociative disorders: A study of scientific publication output 1984–2003. *Psychotherapy and Psychosomatics, 75*(1), 19–24. doi:10.1159/000089223.

Popper, K. (1965). *Conjectures and refutations: The growth of scientific knowledge.* New York: Harper.

Porfeli, E.J., & Skorikov, V.B. (2010). Specific and diversive career exploration during late adolescence. *Journal of Career Assessment, 18,* 46–58.

Pornpitakpan, C. (2004). The Persuasiveness of Source Credibility: A Critical Review of Five Decades' Evidence. *Journal Of Applied Social Psychology, 34*(2), 243–281.

Porter, S., & ten Brinke L. (2010). The truth about lies: What works in detecting high-stakes deception? *Legal and Criminological Psychology, 15,* 57–75.

Porter, S. Bellhouse, S., McDougall, A., ten Brinke, L., & Wilson, K.A prospective investigation of the vulnerability of memory for positive and negative emotional scenes to the misinformation effect. *Canadian Journal of Behavioural Science, 42,* 55–61.

Porter, S., Woodworth, M., & Birt, A.R. (2000). Truth, lies, and videotape: An investigation of the ability of federal parole officers to detect deception. *Law and Human Behaviour, 24,* 643–658.

Porter, S., Yuille, J.C., & Lehman, D.R. (1999). The nature of real, implanted, and fabricated memories for emotional childhood events: Implications for the recovered memory debate. *Law & Human Behavior, 23,* 517–537.

Portman, T.A.A., & Garrett, M.T. (2006). Native American healing traditions. *International Journal of Disability, Development and Education, 53,* 453–469.

Posner, M.I., & Rothbart, M.K. (2004). Hebb's neural networks support the integration of psychological science. *Canadian Psychology, 45,* 265–278.

Posner, M.I., & Rothbart, M.K. (2007). Research on attention networks as a model for the integration of psychological science, *Annual Review of Psychology, 58,* 1–23.

Post, F. (1994). Creativity and psychopathology: A study of 291 world-famous men. *British Journal of Psychiatry, 165,* 22–34.

Post, R.M., Frye, M.A., Denicoff, K.D., Leverich, G.S., Kimbrell, T.A., & Dunn, R.T. (1998). Beyond lithium in the treatment of bipolar illness. *Neuropsychopharmacology, 19,* 206–219.

Potkin, S.G., Saha, A.R., Kujawa, M.J., Carson, W.H., Ali, M., Stock, E., et al. (2003). Ariprazole, an antipsychotic with a novel mechanism of action, and risperidone vs placebo in patients with schizophrenia and schizoaffective disorder. *Archives of General Psychiatry, 60,* 681–690.

Potter, J.W. (1987). Does television viewing hinder academic achievement among adolescents? *Human Communication Research, 14,* 27–46.

Poulin, M.J., Brown, S.L., Dillard, A.J., & Smith, D.M. (2013). Giving to others and the association between stress and mortality. *American Journal of Public Health, 103,* 1649–1655. doi: 10.2105 /AJPH.2012.300876.

Powell, J.L. (2012, November 15). Why climate deniers have no scientific credibility—in one pie chart [Blog post]. Retrieved from http://www.desmogblog.com/2012/11/15/why-climate-deniers-have-no-credibility-science-one-pie-chart.

Powers, M., Halpern, J., Ferenschak, M., Gillihan, S., & Foa, E. (2010). A meta-analytic review of prolonged exposure for posttraumatic stress disorder. *Clinical Psychology Review, 30,* 635–641. doi: 10.1016/j.cpr.2010.04.007

Pozzulo, J.D., & Lindsay, R.C.L. (1998). Identification accuracy of children versus adults: A meta-analysis. *Law and Human Behavior, 22,* 549–570.

Prabu, D. (1998). News concreteness and visual-verbal association do news pictures narrow the recall gap between concrete and abstract news? *Human Communication Research, 25,* 180–201.

Preckel, F., Holling, H., & Wiese, M. (2006). Relationship of intelligence and creativity in gifted and non-gifted students: An investigation of threshold theory. *Personality and Individual Differences, 40,* 159–170.

Premack, D. (1971). Language in chimpanzees? *Science, 172,* 808–822. *The prize in economics, 2002.* (2002). Retrieved November 15,

2006, from http://nobelprize.org/nobel_prizes/economics/laureates/2002/press.html.

Pressman, M.R., & Caudill, D.S. (2013). Alcohol-induced blackout as a criminal defense or mitigating factor: An evidence-based review and admissibility as scientific evidence. *Journal of Forensic Sciences, 58,* 932–940.

Price, S.P., Hilchey, C.A., Darredeau, C., Fulton, H.G., & Barrett, S.P. (2010). Energy drink co-administration is associated with increased reported alcohol ingestion. *Drug and Alcohol Review, 29,* 331–333.

Prochaska, J.O., & Norcross, J.C. (2007). *Systems of psychotherapy* (6th ed.). Belmont, CA: Wadsworth.

Prochazka, A. (2000). New developments in smoking cessation. *Chest, 117,* 169–175.

Profet, M. (1992). Pregnancy sickness as adaptation: A deterrent to maternal ingestion of teratogens. In J. Barkow, L. Cosmides, & J. Tooby (Eds), *The adapted mind* (pp. 327–365). New York: Oxford University Press.

Ptito, M., & Desgent, S. (2006). Sensory input-based adaptation and brain architecture. In P.B. Baltes, P.A. Reuter-Lorenz, & F. Rösler (Eds.), *Lifespan development and the brain: The perspective of biocultural coconstructivism* (pp. 111–133). New York: Cambridge University Press.

Public Health Agency of Canada. (2006). *Fetal alcohol spectrum disorder.* Retrieved from http://www.hc-sc.gc.ca/hl-vs/alt_formats/pacrb-dgapcr/pdf/iyh-vsv/diseases-maladies/fasd-etcaf-eng.pdf.

Pugh, M.V., & Hart, D. (1999). Identity development and peer group participation. *New Directions for Child & Adolescent Development, 84,* 55–70.

Pulver, C.A., & Kelly, K.R. (2008). Incremental validity of the Myers-Briggs Type Indicator in predicting academic major selection of undecided university students. *Journal of Career Assessment, 16*(4), 441–455.

Purves, D., & Lichtman, J.W. (1985). *Principles of neural development.* Sunderland, MA: Sinauer.

Putnam, F., & McHugh, P. (2005). Issue 3: Is multiple personality disorder a valid diagnosis? In R.P. Halgin (Ed.), *Taking sides: Clashing views on controversial issues in abnormal psychology* (3rd ed., pp. 42–53). New York: McGraw-Hill.

Putnam, F.W. (1989). *Diagnosis and treatment of multiple personality disorder.* New York, NY: Guilford Press.

Putnam, F.W. (2006). Dissociative disorders. In D. Cicchetti & D.J. Cohen (Eds.), *Developmental psychopathology: Vol. 3. Risk, disorder, and adaptation* (pp. 657–695). Hoboken, NJ: John Wiley.

Quaade, F., Vaernet, & F., Larsson, S. (1974). Stereotaxic stimulation and electrocoagulation of the lateral hypothalamus in obese humans. *Acta Neurochirurgica 30,* 111–117.

Quinn, P.C., Yahr, J., Kuhn, A., Slater, A.M., & Pascalils, O. (2002). Representation of the gender of human faces by infants: A preference for female. *Perception, 31,* 1109–1121. doi:10.1068/p3331.

Quiroga, R.Q., Reddy, L., Kreiman, G., Koch, C., & Fried, I. (2005). Invariant visual representation by single neurons in the human brain. *Nature, 435,* 1102–1107.

Radeau, M., & Colin, C. (2004). On ventriloquism, audiovisual neurons, neonates, and the senses. *Behavioral and Brain Sciences, 27,* 889–890.

Radford, A. (1997). *Syntactic theory and the structure of English: A minimalist approach.* New York: Cambridge University Press.

Raffaele, P. (2006, November). Speaking bonobo. *Smithsonian.* Retrieved from http://www.smithsonianmagazine.com.

Rahman, Q. (2005). The neurodevelopment of human sexual orientation. *Neuroscience and Biobehavioral Reviews, 29,* 1057–1066.

Raij, T.T., Numminen, J., Närvänen, S., Hiltunen, J., & Hari, R. (2005). Brain correlates of subjective reality of physically and psychologically induced pain. *Proceedings of the National Academy of Sciences, 102,* 2147–2151.

Raine, A. (2013). *The anatomy of violence: The biological roots of crime.* New York, NY: Pantheon.

Raleigh, M.J., McGuire, M.T., Brammer, G.L., Pollack, D.B., & Yuwiler, A. (1991). Serotonergic mechanisms promote dominance in adult male vervet monkeys. *Brain Research, 559,* 181–190.

Ramachandran, V.S., & Altschuler, E.L. (2009). The use of visual feedback, in particular mirror visual feedback, in restoring brain function. *Brain, 132,* 1693–1710.

Ramachandran, V.S., & Blakeslee, S. (1998). *Phantoms in the brain: Probing the mysteries of the human mind.* New York: Harper.

Ramachandran, V.S., & Hubbard, E.M. (2003, May). Hearing colors, tasting shapes. *Scientific American, 288,* 52–59.

Ramachandran, V.S., & Oberman, L.M. (2006). Broken mirrors: A theory of autism. *Scientific American, 295,* 63–69.

Ramanathan, L., Gulyani, S., Nienhuis, R., & Siegel, J.M. (2002). Sleep deprivation decreases superoxide dismutase activity in rat hippocampus and brainstem. *Neuroreport, 13,* 1387–1390.

Ramnani, N., & Passinghamand, R.E. (2001). Changes in the human brain during rhythm learning. *Journal of Cognitive Neuroscience, 13,* 952–966.

Ramus, F. (2013). What's the point of neuropsychoanalysis? *The British Journal of Psychiatry, 203*(3), 170–171.

Rand, K.L., & Ilardi, S.S. (2005). Toward a consilient science of psychology. *Journal of Clinical Psychology, 61,* 7–21.

Ranganathan, M., & D'Souza, D.C. (2006). The acute effects of cannabinoids on memory in humans: A review. *Psychopharmacology, 188,* 425–444.

Ransdell, S. (2010). Online activity, motivation, and reasoning among adult learners. *Computers in Human Behaviour, 26,* 70–73. doi: 10.1016/j.chb.2009.09.002.

Rao, V., Spiro, J.R., Handel, S., & Onyike, C.U. (2008). Clinical correlates of personality changes associated with traumatic brain injury. *Journal of Neuropsychiatry and Clinical Neurosciences, 20,* 118–119.

Rapoport, J., Chavez, A., Greenstein, D., Addington, A., & Gogtay, N. (2009). Autism spectrum disorders and childhood-onset schizophrenia: Clinical and biological contributions to a relation revisited. *Journal of the American Academy of Child & Adolescent Psychiatry, 48*(1), 10–18. doi: 10.1097 /CHI .0b013e31818b1c63.

Raps, C.S., Peterson, C., Jonas, M., & Seligman, M.E.P. (1982). Patient behavior in hospitals—helplessness, reactance, or both. *Journal of Personality and Social Psychology, 42,* 1036–1041.

Rashbaum, I.G., & Sarno, J.E. (2003). Psychosomatic concepts in chronic pain. *Archives of Physical Medicine and Rehabilitation, 84,* S76–S80.

Rashid, T. (2008). Positive psychotherapy. In S.J. Lopez (Ed.), *Positive psychology: Exploring the best in people, Vol. 4: Pursuing human flourishing* (pp. 188–217). Westport, CT: Prager/Greenwood.

Rathje, W., & Murphy, C. (2001). *Rubbish! The Archaeology of Garbage.* New York, NY: Harper Collins.

Rathus, J.H., Cavuoto, N., & Passarelli, V. (2006). Dialectical behavior therapy (DBT): A mindfulness-based treatment for intimate partner violence. In R.A. Baer (Ed.), *Mindfulness-based treatment approaches: Clinician's guide to evidence base and applications* (pp. 333–358). San Diego: Elsevier Academic Press.

Raz, A., & Shapiro, T. (2002). Hypnosis and neuroscience. *Archives of General Psychiatry, 59,* 85–90.

Raz, A., Fan, J., & Posner, M.I. (2005). Hypnotic suggestion reduces conflict in the human brain. *Proceedings of the National Academy of Sciences, 102,* 9978–9983.

Raz, N. (2000). Aging of the brain and its impact on cognitive performance: Integration of structural and functional findings. In F.I.M. Craik & T.A. Salthouse (Eds.), *The handbook* *of aging and cognition* (pp. 1–90). Mahwah, NJ: Erlbaum.

Read, J.P., Beattie, M. Chamberlain, R., & Merrill, J.E. (2008). Beyond the "binge" threshold: Heavy drinking patterns and their association with alcohol involvement indices in college students. *Addictive Behaviors, 33,* 225–234.

Ready, D.J., Gerardi, R.J., Backscheider, A.G., Mascaro, N., & Rothbaum, B.O. (2010). Comparing virtual reality exposure therapy to present-centered therapy with 11 U.S. Vietnam veterans with PTSD. *Cyberpsychology, Behavior, and Social Networking, 13,* 49–54. doi: 10.1089/cyber.2009.0239.

Rechtschaffen, A., Bergmann, B.M., Gilliland, M.A., & Bauer, K. (1999). Effects of method, duration, and sleep stage on rebounds from sleep deprivation in the rat. *Sleep, 22,* 11–31.

Reed, C., Novick, D., Gonzalez-Pinto, A., Bertsch, J., & Haro, J. (2009). Observational study designs for bipolar disorder—What can they tell us about treatment in acute mania? *Progress in Neuro-Psychopharmacology & Biological Psychiatry, 33,* 715–721. doi: 10.1016/j.pnpbp.2009.03.024.

Reed, G.M., Kemeny, M.E., Taylor, S.E., Wang, H.Y.J., & Visscher, B.R. (1994). Realistic acceptance as a predictor of decreased survival time in gay men with AIDS. *Health Psychology, 13,* 299–307.

Refinetti, R. (2006). *Circadian physiology* (2nd ed.). Boca Raton, FL: CRC Press.

Regier, T., & Kay, P. (2009). Language, thought, and color: Whorf was half right. *Trends in Cognitive Sciences, 13,* 439–446.

Regier, T., Kay, P., Gilbert, A., & Ivry, R. (2010). Language and thought: Which side are you on, anyway? In B.C. Malt & P. Wolff (Eds.), *Words and the mind: How words capture human experience* (pp. 165–182). New York, NY: Oxford University Press.

Reilly, D., & Neumann, D.L. (2013). Gender-role differences in spatial ability: A meta-analytic review. *Sex Roles, 68*(9–10), 521–535. doi: 10.1007/s11199-013-0269-0.

Reis, H.T., Maniaci, M.R., Caprariello, P.A., Eastwick, P.W., & Finkel, E.J. (2011, in press). Familiarity does indeed promote attraction in live interaction. *Journal of Personality and Social Psychology.*

Remafedi, G., Resnick, M., Blum, R., & Harris, L. (1992). Demography of sexual orientation in adolescents. *Pediatrics, 89,* 714–721.

Renaud, S., & de Lorgeril, M. (1992). Wine, alcohol, platelets, and the French paradox for coronary heart disease. *Lancet, 339,* 1523–1526.

Renshaw, K.D. (2011). Working with the new generation of service members/veterans from Operations Enduring and Iraqi Freedom. *Cognitive and Behavioral Practice, 18,* 82–84. doi: 10.1016/j.cbpra.2010.03.003.

Rexrode, K.M., Buring, J.E., & Manson, J.E. (2001). Abdominal and total adiposity and risk of coronary heart disease in men. *International Journal of Obesity, 25,* 1047–1056.

Rexrode, K.M., Carey, V.J., Hennekens, C.H., Walters, E.E., Colditz, G.A., Stampfer, M.J., et al. (1998). Abdominal adiposity and coronary heart disease in women. *Journal of the American Medical Association, 280,* 1843–1848.

Reynolds, C.F., & Redline, S. (2010). The DSM-V sleep-wake disorders nosology: An update and an invitation to the sleep community. *Journal of Clinical Sleep Medicine, 6,* 1–2.

Reynolds, C.R. (2000). Why is psychometric research on bias in mental testing so often ignored? *Psychology, Public Policy, and Law, 6,* 144–150.

Reynolds, S., & Lane, S.J. (2008). Diagnostic validity of sensory over-responsivity: A review of the literature and case reports. *Journal of Autism and Developmental Disorders, 38,* 516–529.

Rhoades, G.K., Stanley, S.M., & Markman, H.J. (2009). The pre-engagement cohabitation effect: A replication and extension of previous findings. *Journal of Family Psychology, 23,* 107–111.

Ricciardelli, L.A. (1992). Creativity and bilingualism. *Journal of Creative Behavior, 26,* 242–254.

Riccio, C.A., Waldrop, J.J.M., Reynolds, C.R., & Lowe, P. (2001). Effects of stimulants on the continuous performance test (CPT): Implications for CPT use and interpretation. *Journal of Neuropsychiatry and Clinical Neuroscience, 13,* 326–335.

Rice, M.L. (1989). Children's language acquisition. *American Psychologist, 44,* 149–156.

Richards, J.E., Reynolds, G.D., & Courage, M.L. (2010). The neural basis of infant attention. *Current Directions in Psychological Science, 19,* 41–46.

Richards, R.L. (1994). Creativity and bipolar mood swings: Why the association? In M.P. Shaw & M.A. Runco (Eds.), *Creativity and affect* (pp. 44–72). Norwood, NJ: Ablex.

Richards, R.L., & Kinney, D.K. (1990). Mood swings and creativity. *Creativity Research Journal, 3,* 202–217.

Richardson-Klavehn, A., & Bjork, R.A. (1988). Measures of memory. *Annual Review of Psychology, 39,* 475–543.

Rickwood, D., & Rylands, K.J. (2000). Predicting depression in a sample of older women living in a retirement village. *Australasian Journal on Ageing, 19*(1), 40–42.

Ridley, M. (2003). *Nature via nurture: Genes, experience, and what makes us human.* New York: HarperCollins.

Rieger, E., Van Buren, D.J., Bishop, M., Tanofsky-Kraff, M., Welch, R., & Wilfley, D.E. (2010). An eating disorder-specific model of interpersonal psychotherapy (IPT-ED): causal pathways and treatment implications. *Clinical Psychological Review, 30,* 400–410.

Ries, M., & Marks, W. (2005). Selective attention deficits following severe closed head injury: The role of inhibitory processes. *Neuropsychology, 19,* 476–481.

Rihmer, Z. (2007). Suicide risk in mood disorders. *Current Opinion in Psychiatry, 20,* 17–22.

Riis, J.L., Chong, H., Ryan, K.K., Wolk, D.A., Rentz, D.M., Holcomb, P.J., & Daffner, K.R. (2008). Compensatory neural activity distinguishes different patterns of normal cognitive aging. *Neuroimage, 39,* 441–454.

Riley, W.T., Rivera, D.E., Atienza, A.A., Nilsen, W., Allison, S.M., & Mermelstein, R. (2011). Health behavior models in the age of mobile interventions: are our theories up to the task? *Translational Behavioral Medicine, 1*(1), 53–71. doi:10.1007/s13142-011-0021-7.

Rinpoche, S. (1992). *The Tibetan book of living and dying.* New York: HarperCollins.

Risch, N., Herrell, R., Lehner, T., Liang, K.-Y., Eaves, L., Hoh, J., . . . Mirerikangas, K.R. (2009). Interaction between the serotonin transporter gene (5-HTTLPR), stressful life events, and risk of depression: A meta-analysis. *Journal of the American Medical Association, 301,* 2462–2471.

Ritschel, L.A., Cheavens, J.S., & Nelson, J. (2012). Dialectical behavior therapy in an intensive outpatient program with a mixed-diagnostic sample. *Journal of Clinical Psychology, 68,* 221–235.

Riva, G. (2009). Virtual reality: An experiential tool for clinical psychology. *British Journal of Guidance & Counselling, 37,* 337–345. doi: 10.1080/03069880902957056.

Rizvi, S., Kennedy, S.H., McNeely, H., Giacobbe, P., Mayberg, H.S., & Lozano, A.M. (2009). Functional outcome after 12 months of deep brain stimulation for treatment resistant major depressive disorder. *European Neuropsychopharmacology, 19,* S388–S389.

Rizzolatti, G., & Arbib, M.A. (1998). Language within our grasp. *Trends in Neuroscience, 21,* 188–194.

Rizzolatti, G., Fadiga, L., Fogassi, L., & Gallese, V. (1996). Pre motor cortex and the recognition of motor actions. *Brain Research: Cognitive Brain Research, 3,* 131–141.

Roberts, B.W., & Mroczek, D. (2008). Personality trait change in adulthood. *Current Directions in Psychological Science, 17,* 31–35.

Roberts, B.W., Walton, K.E., & Viechtbauer, W. (2006). Patterns of mean-level change in personality traits across the life course: A meta-analysis of longitudinal studies. *Psychological Bulletin, 132,* 1–25.

Robins, R. W., Gosling, S.D., & Craik, K.H. (1999). An empirical analysis of trends in psychology. *American Psychologist, 54*(2), 117–128.

Robinson, D.N. (1995). *An intellectual history of psychology* (3rd ed.). Madison: University of Wisconsin Press.

Robinson, G.E. (2004). Beyond nature and nurture. *Science, 304,* 397–399.

Robinson-Whelen, S., Tada, Y., MacCallum, R.C., McGuire, L., & Kiecolt-Glaser, J.K. (2001). Long-term caregiving: What happens when it ends? *Journal of Abnormal Psychology, 110,* 573.

Röder, B. (2006). Blindness: A source and case of neuronal plasticity. In P.B. Baltes, P.A. Reuter-Lorenz, & F. Rösler (Eds.), *Lifespan development and the brain* (pp. 134–157). New York: Cambridge University Press.

Roediger, H.L. (1990). Implicit memory: Retention without remembering. *American Psychologist, 45,* 1043–1056.

Roehr, B. (2007). High rate of PTSD in returning Iraq war veterans. *Medscape Medical News.* Retrieved July 5, 2008, from http://www.medscape.com/viewarticle/565407.

Roehr, B. (2007). High rate of PTSD in returning Iraq War veterans. Medscape Medical News. Retrieved July 5, 2008, from http://www.medscape.com/viewarticle/565407.

Roehrs, T., Zorick, F.J., & Roth, T. (2000). Transient and short-term insomnias. In M.H. Kryger, T. Roth, and W.C. Dement (Eds.), *Principles and practice of sleep medicine.* Philadelphia: Saunders.

Rogelberg, S.G., & Gill, P.M. (2006). The growth of industrial and organizational psychology: Quick facts. Retrieved December 6, 2007, from http://www.siop.org/tip/backissues/july04/05rogelberg.aspx.

Rogers, C.R. (1951). *Client-centered counseling.* Boston: Houghton Mifflin.

Rogers, C.R. (1959). A theory of therapy, personality, and inter personal relationships, as developed in the client-centered framework. In S. Koch (Ed.), *Psychology: A study of a science* (Vol. 3). New York: McGraw-Hill.

Rogers, C.R. (1980). *A way of being.* Boston: Houghton Mifflin.

Rogers, C.R., & Dymond, R.G. (Eds.). (1954). *Psychotherapy and personality change: Co-ordinated research studies in the client-centered approach.* Chicago: University of Chicago Press.

Roid, G.H., & Pomplun, M. (2005). Interpreting the Stanford-Binet Intelligence Scales, fifth edition. In D.P. Flanagan & P.L. Harrison (Eds.), *Contemporary intellectual assessment: Theories, tests, and issues* (pp. 325–343). New York: Guilford Press.

Rolland, J.P. (2002). Cross-cultural generalizability of the Five-Factor Model of personality. In R.R. McCrae & J. Allik (Eds.), *The Five-Factor Model of personality across cultures* (pp. 7–28). New York: Kluwer Academic/Plenum.

Rolls, E.T. (2000). The orbitofrontal cortex and reward. *Cerebral Cortex, 10,* 284–294.

Rolls, E.T. (2004). The functions of the orbitofrontal cortex. *Brain and Cognition, 55,* 11–29.

Rolls, E.T. (2006). Brain mechanisms under lying flavour and appetite. *Philosophical Transactions of the Royal Society of London, 361,* 1123–1136.

Rosch, E. (1973). Natural categories. *Cognitive Psychology, 4,* 328–350.

Rosch, E. (1975). Cognitive representations of semantic categories. *Journal of Experimental Psychology: General, 104,* 192–223.

Rose, H., Miller, L., & Martinez, Y. (2009). "FRIENDS for Life": The results of a resilience-building, anxiety-prevention program in a Canadian elementary school. *Professional School Counseling, 12*(6), 400–407.

Rosellini, A.J., Lawrence, A.E., Meyer, J.F., & Brown, T.A. (2010). The effects of extraverted temperament on agoraphobia in panic disorder. *Journal of Abnormal Psychology, 119,* 420–426.

Roseman, I.J. (1984). Cognitive determinants of emotion: A structural theory. *Review of Personality & Social Psychology, 5,* 11–36.

Rosen, L., Cheever, N., Felt, J., & Cummings, C. (2008). The impact of emotionality and self-disclosure on online dating versus traditional dating. *Computers in Human Behavior, 24*(5), 2124–2157.

Rosenberg, E.L. (1998). Levels of analysis and the organization of affect. *Review of General Psychology, 2,* 247–270.

Rosenberg, E.L. (2005). The study of spontaneous facial expressions in psychology. In P. Ekman & E.L. Rosenberg (Eds.), *What the face reveals: Basic and applied studies of spontaneous expression using the Facial Action Coding System (FACS)* (2nd ed., pp. 3–17). New York: Oxford University Press.

Rosenberg, E.L., & Ekman, P. (1994). Coherence between expressive and experiential systems in emotion. *Cognition & Emotion, 8,* 201–229.

Rosenberg, E.L., & Ekman, P. (2000). Emotion: Methods of study. In A. Kasdan (Ed.), *Encyclopedia of psychology* (pp. 171–175). Washington, DC: American Psychological Association and Oxford University Press.

Rosenberg, E.L., Ekman, P., Jiang, W., Coleman, R.E., Hanson, M., O'Connor, C., et al. (2001). Linkages between facial expressions of anger and transient myocardial ischemia in men with coronary artery disease. *Emotion, 1,* 107–115.

Rosenberger, P.H., Ickovics, J.R., Epel, E., Nadler, E., Jokl, P., Fulkerson, J.P., Tillie, J.M., & Dhabhar, F.S. (2009). Surgical stress-induced immune cell redistribution profiles predict short-term and long-term postsurgical recovery a prospective study. *Journal of Bone and Joint Surgery, American Volume, 91,* 2783–2794.

Rosenman, R.H., Friedman, M., Straus, R., Wurm, M., Kositchek, R., Hahn, W., & Werthessen, N.T. (1964). A predictive study of coronary artery disease. *Journal of the American Medical Association, 189,* 113–124.

Rosenquist, J.N., Murabito, J., Fowler, J.H., & Christakis, N.A. (2010). The spread of alcohol consumption behavior in a large social network. *Annals of Internal Medicine, 152,* 426–433.

Rosenthal, R. (1976). *Experimenter effects in behavioral research enlarged edition.* New York: Irvington.

Rosenthal, R., & Fode, K.L. (1963). The effect of experimenter bias on the performance of the albino rat. *Behavioral Science, 8,* 183–189.

Rosenthal, R., & Jacobson, L. (1968). *Pygmalion in the classroom.* New York: Holt, Rinehart & Winston.

Rosenthal, R., & Jacobson, L. (1992). *Pygmalion in the classroom* (Rev. ed.). New York: Irvington.

Rosenthal, R., & Rubin, D.B. (1978). Interpersonal expectancy effects: The first 345 studies. *The Behavioral and Brain Sciences, 3,* 377–386.

Rosenwasser, A.M. (2009). Functional neuroanatomy of sleep and circadian rhythms. *Brain Research Review, 61,* 281–306.

Rosenzweig, M.R., & Bennett, E.L. (1969). Effects of differential environments on brain weights and enzyme activities in gerbils, rats and mice. *Developmental Psychobiology, 2,* 87–95.

Rosenzweig, M.R., Krech, D., Bennett, E.L., & Diamond, M.C. (1962). Effects of environmental complexity and training on brain chemistry and anatomy: A replication and extension. *Journal of Comparative and Physiological Psychology, 55,* 429–437.

Rosenzweig, S. (1933). The experimental situation as a psychological problem. *Psychological Review, 40,* 337–354.

Ross, L. (1977). The intuitive psychologist and his shortcomings: Distortions in the attribution process. In L. Berkowitz (Ed.), *Advances in experimental social psychology* (Vol. 10), pp. 173–220. New York: Academic Press.

Ross, M., Heine, S.J., Wilson, A.E., & Sugimori, S. (2005). Cross-cultural discrepancies in self-appraisals. *Personality and Social Psychology Bulletin, 31,* 1175–1188.

Rotermann, M. (2005). Sex, condoms and STDs among young people. *Statistics Canada: Health Reports, 16*(3), *39–45.* Retrieved from http://www.statcan.gc.ca/pub/82-003-x/2008003/article/10664-eng.pdf.

Rotermann, M. (2008). Trends in teen sexual behaviour and condom use. *Health Reports, 19*(3), 1–5.

Rotermann, M. (2012). Sexual behaviour and condom use of 15- to 24-year-olds in 2003 and 2009/2010. *Health Reports, 23*(1), 1–5.

Roth, D.L., Fredman, L., & Haley, W.E. (2015). Informal caregiving and its impact on health: A reappraisal from population-based studies. *The Gerontologist, 55,* 309–319.

Rothbart, M.K., Ahadi, S.A., & Evans, D.E. (2000). Temperament and personality: Origins and outcomes. *Journal of Personality and Social Psychology, 78,* 122–135.

Rothbaum, B.O., Cahill, S.P., Foa, E.B., Davidson, J.R.T., Compton, J., Connor, K.M., et al. (2006). Augmentation of sertraline with prolonged exposure in the treatment of posttraumatic stress disorder. *Journal of Traumatic Stress, 19,* 625–638.

Rothenberg, D. (2005). *Why birds sing: A journey through the mystery of bird song.* New York: Basic Books.

Rowe, G., Hirsch, J.B., & Anderson, A.K. (2007). Positive affect increases the breadth of attentional selection. *Proceedings of the National Academy of Sciences, 104,* 383–388.

Rowland, N.E., Li, B-H., & Morien, A. (1996). Brain mechanisms and the physiology of feeding. In E.D. Capaldi (Ed.), *Why we eat what we eat: The psychology of eating* (pp. 173–204). Washington, DC: American Psychological Association.

Rozin, P. (1996). Sociocultural influences on human food selection. In E.D. Capaldi (Ed.), *Why we eat what we eat: The psychology of eating* (pp. 233–263). Washington, DC: American Psychological Association.

Rozin, P., & Fallon, A.E. (1987). Perspectives on disgust. *Psychological Review, 94,* 23–41.

Ruan, J. (2004). Bilingual Chinese/English first-graders developing metacognition about writing *Literacy, 38,* 106–112.

Ruble, D.N., Taylor, L.J., Cyphers, L., Greulich, F.K., Lurye, L.E., & Shrout, P.E. (2007). The Role of Gender Constancy in Early Gender Development. *Child Development, 78*(4), 1121–1136. doi:10.1111/j.1467-8624.2007.01056.x.

Ruf, C. (2013) Identified as arts prodigies, Ontario brothers now contributing to science. CBC News. Retrieved May 12, 2015 from http://www.cbc.ca/news/canada/hamilton/news/identified-as-arts-prodigies-ontario-brothers-now-contributing-to-science-1.1326362.

Ruff, H. (1999). Population-based data and the development of individual children: The case of low to moderate lead levels and intelligence. *Journal of Developmental & Behavioral Pediatrics, 20*(1), 42–49.

Rumbaugh, D.M., Beran, M.J., & Savage-Rumbaugh, S. (2003). Language. In D. Maestripieri (Ed.), *Primate psychology* (pp. 395–423). Cambridge, MA: Harvard University Press.

Runyan, W.M. (1981). Why did Van Gogh cut off-his ear? The problem of alternative explanations in psychobiography. *Journal of Personality and Social Psychology, 40,* 1070–1077.

Runyan, W.M. (1982). *Life histories and psychobiography.* New York: Oxford University Press.

Rushton, J.P. (1991). Mongoloid–Caucasoid differences in brain size from military samples. *Intelligence, 15,* 351–359.

Rushton, J.P. (1995). *Race, evolution and behavior: A life history perspective.* New Brunswick, NJ: Transaction Publishers.

Rushton, J.P., & Jensen, A.R. (2005). Thirty years of research on race differences in cognitive ability. *Psychology, Public Policy, and Law, 11,* 235–294.

Rushton, W.A.H. (1961). Rhodopsin measurement and dark adaptation in a subject deficient in cone vision. *Journal of Physiology, 156,* 193–205.

Russell, J.A. (1980). A circumplex model of affect. *Journal of Personality and Social Psychology, 39,* 1161–1178.

Ruthsatz, J., Ruthsatz, K., & Ruthsatz Stephens, K. (2014). Putting practice into perspective: Child prodigies as evidence of innate talent. *Intelligence, 45,* 60–65.

Rutter, M. (2002). Nature, nurture, and development: From evangelism through science toward policy and practice. *Child Development, 73,* 1–21.

Rutter, M. (2005). Incidence of autism disorders: Changes over time and their meaning. *Acta Paediatrica, 94,* 2–15.

Rutter, M. (2006). *Genes and behavior: Nature-nurture interplay explained.* Malden, MA: Blackwell.

Ruzgis, P.M., & Grigorenko, E.L. (1994). Cultural meaning systems, intelligence and personality. In R.J. Sternberg & P. Ruzgis (Eds.), *Personality and intelligence* (pp. 248–270). New York: Cambridge University Press.

Ryan, G., Baerwald, J., & McGlone, G. (2008). Cognitive mediational deficits and the role of coping styles in pedophile and ephebophile Roman Catholic clergy. *Journal of Clinical Psychology, 64,* 1–16.

Ryan-Harshman, M., & Aldoori, W. (2008). Folic acid and prevention of neural tube defects. *Canadian Family Physician, 54,* 36–38.

Rymer, R. (1993). *Genie: A scientific tragedy.* New York: HarperPerennial.

Saarni, C. (1984). An observational study of children's attempts to monitor their expressive behavior. *Child Development, 55,* 1504–1513.

Saarni, C. (1999). *The development of emotional competence.* New York: Guilford Press.

Sabbagh, L. (2006, August/September). The teen brain, hard at work: No, really. *Scientific American Mind, 17,* 21–25.

Sacco, R.L., Elkind, M., Boden-Albala, B., Lin, I-F., Kargman, D.E., Hause, W.A., et al. (1999). The protective effect of moderate alcohol consumption on ischemic stroke. *Journal of American Medical Association, 281,* 53–60.

Sackeim, H.A., Greenberg, M.S., Weiman, A.L., Gur, R.C., Hungerbuhler, J.P., & Geschwind, N. (1982). Hemispheric asymmetry in the expression of positive and negative emotions: Neurologic evidence. *Archives in Neurology, 39,* 210–218.

Sackeim, H.A., Prudic, J., Devanand, D.P., Kiersky, J.E., Fitz simons, L., Moody, B.J., et al. (1993). Effects of stimulus intensity and electrode placement on the efficacy and cognitive effects of electroconvulsive therapy. *New England Journal of Medicine, 328,* 839–846.

Sacks, O. (1985). *The man who mistook his wife for a hat.* New York: Summit Books.

Saegert, S., Swap, W., & Zajonc, R.B. (1973). Exposure, context, and interpersonal attraction. *Journal of Personal and Social Psychology, 25,* 234–242.

Sagan, C. (1987). The burden of skepticism. *Skeptical Inquirer, 12,* 38–46.

Saisan, J., Smith, M., & Segal, J. (2010, May). Psychotherapy and counseling: Finding a therapist and getting the most out of therapy. Retrieved from http://www.helpguide.org/mental/psychotherapy_therapist_counseling.htm.

Sakai, K. (2005). Language acquisition and brain development. *Science, 310,* 815–819.

Saklofske, D.H., Patterson, C.A., Gorsuch, R.L., & Tulsky, D.S. (2001). Discussion and guidelines for using the WAIS-III Canadian norms. In D. Wechsler, *WAIS-III Canadian technical manual* (pp. 35–41). Toronto: Psychological Corporation.

Salamone, J.D., Correa, M., Farrar, A., & Mingote, S.M. (2007). Effort-related functions of nucleus accumbens dopamine and associated forebrain circuits. *Psychopharmacology, 191,* 461–482.

Salehan, M., & Negahban, A. (2013). Social networking on smartphones: When mobile phones become addictive. *Computers in Human Behavior, 29*(6), 2632–2639.

Sally, D. (1995). Conversation and cooperation in social dilemmas. A meta-analysis of experiments from 1958 to 1992. *Rationality and Society, 7*, 58–92.

Salovey, P., & Mayer, J.D. (1990). Emotional intelligence. *Imagination, Cognition, and Personality, 9*, 185–211.

Sanderson, C.A., & Cantor, N. (1995). Social dating goals in late adolescence: Implications for safer sexual activity. *Journal of Personality and Social Psychology, 68*, 1121–1134.

Sapolsky, R. (1998). *Why zebras don't get ulcers: An updated guide to stress, stress-related disease and coping.* New York: Freeman.

Sarchione, C.D., Cuttler, M.J., Muchinsky, P.M., & Nelson-Gray, R.O. (1998). Prediction of dysfunctional job behaviors among law enforcement officers. *Journal of Applied Psychology, 83*, 904–912.

Sava, F.A., Yates, B.T., Lupu, V., Szentagotai, A., & David, D. (2009). Cost-effectiveness and cost-utility of cognitive therapy, rational emotive behavioral therapy, and fluoxetine (Prozac) in treating depression: A randomized clinical trial. *Journal of Clinical Psychology, 65*, 36–52.

Savin, H.B. (1973). Professors and psychological researchers: Conflicting values in conflicting roles. *Cognition, 2*(1), 147–149. Sawyer, R.K. (2006). *Explaining creativity: The science of human innovation.* New York: Oxford University Press.

Scarr, S. (1981). *Race, social class, and individual differences in I.Q.* Hillsdale, NJ: Erlbaum.

Scarr, S. (1985). An author's frame of mind [Review of *Frames of mind: The theory of multiple intelligences*]. *New Ideas in Psychology, 3*(1), 95–100.

Schaal, B., Marlier, L., & Soussignan, R. (2002). Human fetuses learn odors from their pregnant mother's diet. *Chemical Senses, 25*, 729–737.

Schacter, D.L. (1987). Implicit memory: History and current status. *Journal of Experimental Psychology: Learning, Memory, and Cognition, 12*, 432–444.

Schacter, D.L. (2001). *The seven sins of memory.* Boston: Houghton Mifflin.

Schacter, D.L., & McGlynn, S.M. (1989). Implicit memory: Effects of elaboration depend on unitization. *American Journal of Psychology, 102*, 151–181.

Schacter, S., & Singer, J.E. (1962). Cognitive, social, and physiological determinants of emotional state. *Psychological Review, 69*, 379–399.

Schaefer, E.J., Gleason, J.A., & Dansinger, M.L. (2005). The effects of low-fat, highcarbohydrate diets on plasma lipoproteins, weight loss, and heart disease risk reduction. *Current Atherosclerosis Reports, 7*, 421–427.

Schaie, K.W. (1996). *Intellectual development in adulthood: The Seattle Longitudinal Study.* New York: Cambridge University Press.

Scheier, M.F., Weintraub, J.K., & Carver, C.S. (1989). Coping with stress: Divergent strategies of optimists and pessimists. *Journal of Personality and Social Psychology, 51*, 1257–1264.

Schellenberg, E.G. (2004). Music lessons enhance IQ. *Psychological Science, 15*, 511–514.

Schellenberg, E.G. (2006). Long-term positive associations between music lessons and IQ. *Journal of Educational Psychology, 98*, 457–468.

Scherer, K.R., Banse, R., Wallbott. H.G., & Goldbeck. T. (1991). Vocal cues in emotion coding and decoding. *Motivation and Emotion, 15*, 123–148.

Scherer, K.R., Dan, E., & Flykt, A. (2006). What determines a feeling's position in affective space? A case for appraisal. *Cognition & Emotion, 20*, 92–113.

Schienle, A., Schäfer, A., & Vaitl, D. (2008). Individual differences in disgust imagery: A functional magnetic resonance imaging study. *NeuroReport, 19*, 527–530.

Schienle, A., Schäfer, A., Stark, R., Walter, B., & Vaitl, D. (2005). Gender differences in the processing of disgust- and fear-inducing pictures: An fMRI study. *NeuroReport, 16*, 277–280.

Schipani, D. (2014). *Real-life online dating success stories.* Retrieved from http://www.womansday.com/sex-relationships/dating-marriage/real-life-online-dating-success-stories-111464.

Schlaepfer, T.E. (2013). Neuromodulation of reward circuits with deep brain stimulation in treatment resistant depression. *Biological Psychiatry, 73*, 143s.

Schlaepfer, T.E., Bewernick, B., Kayser, S., Maedler, B., & Coenen, V.E. (2013). Rapid effects of deep brain stimulation for treatment-resistant major depression. *Biological Psychiatry, 73*, 1204–2014. doi: 10.1016/j.biopsych.2013.01.034.

Schmand, B., Eikelenboom, P., & van Gool, W.A. (2011). Value of neuropsychological tests, neuroimaging, and biomarkers for diagnosing Alzheimer's disease in younger and older age cohorts. *Journal of the American Geriatrics Society, 59*(9), 1705–1710. doi: 10.1111/j.1532-5415.2011.03539.x.

Schmidt, F.L., & Hunter, J. (2004). General mental ability in the world of work: Occupational attainment and job performance. *Journal of Personality & Social Psychology, 86*(1), 162–173.

Schmidt, F.L., & Hunter, J.E. (1998). The validity and utility of selection methods in personnel psychology: Practical and theoretical implications of 85 years of research findings. *Psychological Bulletin, 124*(2), 262–274.

Schmidt, M.E., & Vandewater, E.A. (2008). Media and attention, cognition, and school achievement. *The Future of Children, 18*, 63–85.

Schmithorst, V.J. (2009). Developmental sex differences in the relation of neuroanatomical connectivity to intelligence. *Intelligence, 37*(2), 164–173.

Schmithorst, V.J., Holland, S.K., & Dardzinski, B.J. (2008). Developmental differences in white matter architecture between boys and girls. *Human Brain Mapping, 29*, 696–710.

Schneider, J.A., Arvanitakis, Z., Bang, W., & Bennett, D.A. (2007). Mixed brain pathologies account for most dementia cases in community-dwelling older persons. *Neurology, 69*, 2197–2204.

Schober, G., Björkqvist, K., & Somppi, S. (2009). Identifying a new subcategory of aggression: Sex differences in direct non-verbal aggression. *Journal of Aggression, Conflict and Peace Research, 1*, 58–70.

Schooler, C. (1998). Environmental complexity and the Flynn Effect. In U. Neisser (Ed.), *The rising curve: Long-term gains in IQ and related measures* (pp. 67–79). Washington, DC: American Psychological Association.

Schredl, M., & Hofman, F. (2003). Continuity between waking activities and dream activities. *Consciousness and Cognition, 12*, 298–308.

Schuldberg, D. (1990). Schizotypal and hypomanic traits, creativity, and psychological health. *Creativity Research Journal, 3*, 218–230.

Schuldberg, D. (2000–2001). Six subclinical spectrum traits in normal creativity. *Creativity Research Journal, 13*, 5–16.

Schuler, J.L.H., & O'Brien, W.H. (1997). Cardiovascular recovery from stress and hypertension risk factors: A meta-analytic review. *Psychophysiology, 34*, 649–659.

Schulkin, J. (Ed.) (2005). *Allostasis, homeostasis, and the costs of physiological adaptation.* New York: Cambridge University Press.

Schultz, W.T. (2005). *Handbook of psychobiography.* New York: Oxford University Press.

Schulz, R., & Beach, S.R. (1999). Caregiving as a risk factor for mortality: The Caregiver Health Effects Study. *JAMA, 282*, 2215–2219.

Schwartz, G.M., Izard, C.E., & Ansul, S.E. (1985). The 5-month-old's ability to discriminate facial expressions of emotion. *Infant Behavior and Development, 8*, 65–77.

Schwartz, J.H. (2000). Neurotransmitters. In E.R. Kandel, J.M.Schwartz, & T.M. Jessell (Eds.), *Principles of neural science* (4th ed., pp. 280–297). New York: McGraw-Hill.

Schwartz, J.M. (1997). *Brain lock: Free yourself from obsessive-compulsive behavior.* New York: Harper.

Schwartz, J.M. (1999a). A role for volition and attention in the generation of new brain circuitry: Toward a neurobiology of mental force. *Journal of Consciousness Studies, 6,* 115–142.

Schwartz, J.M. (1999b). First steps toward a theory of mental force: PET imaging of systematic cerebral changes after psychological treatment of obsessive-compulsive disorder. In S.R. Hameroff, A.W. Kaszniak, & D.J. Chalmers (Eds.), *Toward a science of consciousness III: The third Tucson discussions and debates.* Boston: MIT Press.

Schwartz, J.M. (2000). The use of mindfulness in the treatment of obsessive compulsive disorder (OCD). Invited address presented at the Youth Mental Health Conference, New Zealand.

Schwartz, S.J. (2001). The evolution of Eriksonian and neo-Eriksonian identity theory and research: A review and integration. *Identity: An International Journal of Theory and Research, 1*(1), 7–58. doi:10.1207/S1532706XSCHWARTZ.

Schwartz, S.J., Zamboanga, B.L., & Jarvis, L.H. (2007). Ethnic identity and acculturation in Hispanic early adolescents: Mediated relationships to academic grades, prosocial behavior, and externalizing symptoms. *Cultural Diversity and Ethnic Minority Psychology, 13,* 364–373.

Schwarz, J.R., Reid, G., & Bostock, H. (1995). Action potentials and membrane currents in the human node of Ranvier. *Pflügers Archiv: European Journal of Physiology, 430,* 283–292.

Schwarz, S., & Hassebrauck, M. (2008). Self-perceived and observed variations in women's attractiveness throughout the menstrual cycle—a diary study. *Evolution and Human Behavior, 29,* 282–288.

Schwerdtfeger, A. (2007). Individual differences in auditory, pain, and motor stimulation. *Journal of Individual Differences, 28,* 165–177.

Scott, J. (2000). Rational choice theory. In G. Browning, A. Halcli, and F. Webster (Eds.), *Understanding contemporary society: Theories of the present* (pp. 126–138). New York: Sage.

Scott, T.H., Bexton, W.H., Heron, W., & Doane, B.K. (1959). Cognitive effects of perceptual isolation. *Canadian Journal of Psychology, 13,* 200–209.

Scoville, W.B., & Milner, B. (1957). Loss of recent memory after bilateral hippocampal lesions. *Journal of Neurololgy, Neurosurgury, and Psychiatry, 20,* 11–21.

Scruggs, J.L., Schmidt, D., & Deutch, A.Y. (2003). The hallucinogen 1-[2,5-dimet hoxy-4-iodophenyl]-2-aminopropane (DOI) infei31839_creases cortical extracellular glutamate levels in rats. *Neuroscience Letters, 346,* 137–140.

Scully, J.A., Tosi, H., & Banning, K. (2000). Life event checklists: Reevaluating the social readjustment rating scale after 30 years. *Educational and PsychologicalMeasurement, 60,* 864–876.

Sebastian, C., Viding, E., Williams, K.D., Blakemore, S. (2010). Social brain development and the affective consequences of ostracism in adolescence. *Brain and Cognition, 72,*134–145.

Segal, N.L. (2005). *Indivisible by two: Lives of extraordinary twins.* Cambridge, MA: Harvard University Press.

Segal, Z.V., Williams, J.M.G., & Teasdale, J.D. (2002). *Mindfulness-based cognitive therapy for depression.* New York: Guilford Press.

Segerstrom, S.C., & Miller, G.E. (2004). Psychological stress and the human immune system: A meta-analytic study of 30 years of inquiry. *Psychological Bulletin, 130,* 601–630.

Sehlmeyer, C., Schöning, S., Zwitserlood, P., Pfleiderer, B., Kircher, T., Arolt, V., & Konrad, C. (2009). Human fear conditioning and extinction in neuroimaging: A systematic review. *PLoS ONE, 4,* e5865.

Seifert, K.L., Hoffnung, R.J., & Hoffnung, M. (2000). *Lifespan development* (2nd ed.). Boston, MA: Houghton Mifflin.

Seligman, M.E.P. (1971). Phobias and preparedness. *Behavior Therapy, 2,* 307–320.

Seligman, M.E.P., & Csíkszentmihályi, M. (2000). Positive psychology: An introduction. *American Psychologist,* 55, 5–14.

Seligman, M.E.P., & Hager, J.L. (Eds.). (1972). *The biological boundaries of learning.* New York: Appleton.

Seligman, M.E.P., Rashid, R., & Parks, A.C. (2006). Positive psychotherapy. *American Psychologist, 61,* 774–788.

Seligman, M.E.P., Schulman, P., & Tryon, A.M. (2007). Group prevention of depression and anxiety symptoms. *Behaviour Research and Therapy, 45,* 1111–1126.

Seligman, M.P. (1995). The effectiveness of psychotherapy: The Consumer Reports study. *American Psychologist, 50*(12), 965–974. doi:10.1037/0003-066X.50.12.965.

Seligman, M.P. (2004). Can happiness be taught? *Daedalus, 133*(2), 80–87.

Selkoe, D. (2002). Alzheimer's disease is a synaptic failure. *Science, 298*(5594), 789–791.

Selten, J.P., Frissen, A., Lensvelt-Mulder, G., & Morgan, V.A. (2010). Schizophrenia and the 1957 pandemic of influenza: Meta-analysis. *Schizophrenia Bulletin, 36,* 219–228. doi:10.1093/schbul/sbp147.

Selye, H. (1937). The significance of the adrenals for adaptation. *Science, 85,* 247–248.

Selye, H. (1946). The general adaptation syndrome and diseases of adaptation. *The Journal of Clinical Endocrinology, 6,* 117–230.

Selye, H. (1976). *The stress of life.* New York: McGraw-Hill.

Selye, H. (1982). History and present status of the stress concept. In L. Goldberger and S. Breznitz (Eds.), *Handbook of Stress: Theoretical and Clinical Aspects* (pp. 7–20). New York: Free Press.

Sen, B., & Swaminathan, S. (2007). Maternal prenatal substance use and behavior problems among children in the U.S. *The Journal of Mental Health Policy and Economics, 10,* 189–206.

Seoane, A., Tinsley, C.J., & Brown, M.W. (2010, in press). Interfering with perirhinal brain-derived neurotrophic factor expression impairs recognition memory in rats. *Hippocampus, 21,* 121–126.

Serbin, L.A., Poulin-Dubois, D., Colburne, K.A., Sen, M.G., & Eichstedt, J.A. (2001). Gender stereotyping in infancy: Visual preferences for and knowledge of gender-stereotyped toys in the second year. *International Journal of Behavioral Development, 25*(1), 7–15. doi:10.1080/01650250042000078.

Serpell, R. (1982). Measures of perception, skills, and intelligence. In W.W. Hartup (Ed.), *Review of child development research* (Vol. 6, pp. 392–440). Chicago: University of Chicago Press.

Serrano-Blanco, A., Palao D.J., Luciano, J.V., Pinto-Meza, A., Lujan, L., Fernandez, A., . . . Haro, J.M. (2010). Prevalence of mental disorders in primary care: Results from the Diagnosis and Treatment of Mental Disorders in Primary Care Study (DASMAP). *Social Psychiatry and Psychiatric Epidemi-ology, 45,* 201–210. doi: 10.1007 / s00127-009-0056-y.

Shank, D.B., & Cotten, S.R. (2014). Does technology empower urban youth? The relationship of technology use to self-efficacy. *Computers & Education, 70,* 184–193.

Shanley, A. (2007). The future of Inuktitut in the face of majority languages: Bilingualism or language shift? *Applied Psycholinguistics, 28,* 515–536.

Shastry, B.S. (2005). Bipolar disorder: An update. *Neurochemistry International, 46,* 273–279.

Shaw, P., Greenstein, D., Lerch, J., Clasen, L., Lenroot, R., Gogtay, N., et al. (2006). Intellectual ability and cortical development in children and adolescents. *Nature, 440,* 676–679.

Shaywitz B.A., Shaywitz, S.E., Pugh, K.R., Constable, R.T., Skudlarski, P., Fulbright, R.K., Bronen, R.A., Fletcher, J.M., Shankweiler, D.P., Katz, L., et al. (1995). Sex differences in the functional organization of the brain for language. *Nature, 373,* 607–609.

Shea, D.L., Lubinski, D., & Benbow, C.P. (2001). Importance of assessing spatial ability in intellectually talented young adolescents: A 20-year longitudinal study. *Journal of Educational Psychology, 93,* 604–614.

Shedler, J. (2010). The efficacy of psychodynamic psychotherapy. *American Psychologist, 65,* 98–109.

Shekelle, R.B., Hulley, S.B., Neston, J.D., Billings, J.H., Borboni, N.O., Gerace, T.A., et al. (1985). The MRFIT behavior pattern study: Type A behavior and incidence of coronary heart disease. *American Journal of Epidemiology, 122,* 559–570.

Shen, H., Sabaliauskas, N., Sherpa, A., Fenton, A.A., Stelzer, A., Aoki, C., & Smith, S.S. (2010). A critical role for 4b $GABA_A$ receptors in shaping learning deficits at puberty in mice. *Science, 327,* 1515–1518.

Shepard, M. (1995). Kraepelin and modern psychiatry. *European Archives of Psychiatry and Clinical Neuroscience, 245,* 189–195.

Shergill, S.S., Brammer, M.J., Fukuda, R., Williams, S.C.R., Murray, R.M., & McGuire, P.K. (2003). Engagement of brain areas implicated in processing inner speech in people with auditory hallucinations. *British Journal of Psychiatry, 182,* 525–531.

Shergill, S.S., Brammer, M.J., Williams, S.C.R., Murray, R.M., & McGuire, P.K. (2000). Mapping auditory hallucinations in schizophrenia using functional magnetic resonance imaging. *Archives of General Psychiatry, 57,* 1033–1038.

Shermer, M. (1997). *Why people believe weird things: Pseudoscience, superstition, and other confusions of our time.* New York: W.H. Freeman.

Sheskin, D.J. (2007). *Handbook of parametric and nonparametric statistical procedures* (4th ed.). Boca Raton, FL: Chapman & Hall/CRC.

Shestyuk, A.Y., Deldin, P.J., Brand, J.E., & Deveney, C.M. (2005). Reduced sustained brain activity during processing of positive emotional stimuli in major depression. *Biological Psychiatry, 57,* 1089–1096.

Shields, M. (2006). *Overweight and obesity among children and youth.* (Health Reports, Vol. 17, No. 3). Retrieved from Statistics Canada website: http://www.statcan.gc.ca/studies-etudes/82–003/archive/2006/9277–eng.pdf.

Shiraev, E. (2015). *A history of psychology: A global perspective.* (2nd ed.) Washington, DC: Sage Publications, Inc.

Shomaker, L.B., & Furman, W. (2009). Interpersonal influences on late adolescent girls' and boys' disordered eating. *Eating Behaviors, 10,* 97–106.

Short, S.J., Lubach, G.R., Karasin, A.I., Olsen, C.W., Styner, M., Knickmeyer, R.C., . . . Coe, C.L. (2010). Maternal influenza infection during pregnancy impacts postnatal brain development in the rhesus monkey. *Biological Psychiatry, 67,* 965–973.

Siegel, S., & Ramos, B.M.C. (2002). Applying laboratory research: Drug anticipation and the treatment of drug addiction. *Experimental and Clinical Psychopharmacology, 10,* 162–183.

Siegel, S., Hinson, R.E., Krank, M.D., & McCully, J. (1982). Heroin "overdose" death: Contribution of drug-associated environmental cues. *Science, 216,* 436–437.

Siegler, R.S. (1994). Cognitive variability: A key to understanding cognitive development. *Current Directions in Psychological Science, 3,* 1–5.

Siegler, R.S. (2006). Microgenetic analyses of learning. In W. Damon & R.M. Lerner (Series Eds.) & D. Kuhn & R.S. Siegler (Vol. Eds.), *Handbook of child psychology: Volume 2: Cognition, perception, and language* (6th ed., pp. 464–510). Hoboken, NJ: Wiley.

Siegman, A.W., Anderson, R., Herbst, J., Boyle, S., & Wilkinson, J. (1992). Dimensions of anger-hostility and cardiovascular reactivity in provoked and angered men. *Journal of Behavioral Medicine, 15,* 257–272.

Sigman, M., & Hassan, S. (2006). Benefits of long-term group therapy to individuals suffering schizophrenia: A prospective 7-year study. *Bulletin of the Menninger Clinic, 70,* 273–282.

Silbersweig, D.A., Stern, E., Frith, C., Cahill, C., Holmes, A., Grootoonk, S., et al. (1995). A functional neuroanatomy of hallucinations in schizophrenia. *Nature, 378,* 176–179.

Silva, L.M., Cignolini, A., Warren, R., Budden, S., & Skowron-Gooch, A. (2007). Improvement in sensory impairment and social interaction in young children with autism following treatment with an original Qigong massage methodology. *American Journal of Chinese Medicine, 35,* 393–406.

Silventoinen, K., & Kapiro, K. (2009). Genetics of tracking of body mass index from birth to late middle age: Evidence from twin and family studies. *Obesity Facts, 2,* 196–202.

Silverman, I., Choi, J., & Peters, M. (2007). The Hunter-Gatherer Theory of sex differences in spatial abilities: Data from 40 countries. *Archives of Sexual Behaviour, 36,* 261–268. doi: 10.1007/s10508-006-9168-6.

Silvia, P.J. (2006). *Exploring the psychology of interest.* New York: Oxford University Press.

Silvia, P.J., & Kimbrel, N.A. (2010). A dimensional analysis of creativity and mental illness: Do anxiety and depression symptoms predict creative cognition, creative accomplishments, and creative self-concepts? *Psychology of Aesthetics, Creativity and the Arts, 4,* 2–10.

Sime, J.D. (1983). Affiliative behavior during escape to building exits. *Journal of Environmental Psychology, 3,* 21–41.

Simmons, V.N., Heckman, B.W., Fink, A.C., Small, B.J., & Brandon, T.H. (2013). Efficacy of an experiential, dissonance-based smoking intervention for college students delivered via the internet. *Journal of Consulting and Clinical Psychology, 81,* 810–820. doi: http://dx.doi.org/10.1037/a0032952.

Simon Fraser University—Natural Language Lab. Retrieved January 31, 2010, from http://natlang.cs.sfu.ca/.

Simon, H.A. (1978). Information-processing theory of human problem solving. In W.K. Estes (Ed.), *Handbook of learning and cognitive processe: Vol. 5. Human information processing* (pp. 271–295). Hillsdale, NJ: Erlbaum.

Simonds, J., Kieras, J.E., Rueda, M.R., & Rothbart, M.K. (2007). Effortful control, executive attention, and emotional regulation in 7–10-year-old children. *Cognitive Development, 22,* 474–488.

Simons, D.J., & Chabris, C.F. (1999). Gorillas in our midst: Sustained inattentional blindness for dynamic events. *Perception, 28,* 1059–1074.

Simonton, D.K. (1984). *Genius, creativity & leadership: Historiometric inquiries.* Cambridge, MA: Harvard University Press.

Simonton, D.K. (1997a). Creative productivity: A predictive and explanatory model of career trajectories and landmarks. *Psychological Review, 104,* 66–89.

Simonton, D.K. (1999). *Origins of genius.* New York: Oxford University Press.

Simpson, K. (2001). The role of testosterone in aggression. *McGill Journal of Medicine, 6,* 32–40.

Singer, T., Seymour, B., O'Doherty, J.O., Kaube, H., Dolan, R.J., & Frith, C.D. (2004). Empathy for pain involves the affective but not sensory components of pain. *Science, 303,* 1157–1162.

Sirignono, S.W., & Lachman, M.E. (1985). Personality change during the transition to parenthood: The role of perceived infant temperament. *Developmental Psychology, 21,* 558–567.

Sivonen, P., Maess, B., Lattner, S., & Friederici, A.D. (2006). Phonemic restoration in a sentence context: evidence from early and late ERP effects. *Brain Research, 1121,* 177–189.

Sjöström, P.J., Ranc, E.A., Roth, A., and Häusser, M. (2008). Dendritic excitability and synaptic plasticity. *Physiological Reviews, 88*(2), 769–840.

Skinner, B.F. (1938). *The behavior of organisms.* New York: Appleton.

Skinner, B.F. (1953). *Science and human behavior.* New York: Free Press.

Skinner, B.F. (1957). *Verbal behavior.* New York: Appleton-Century-Crofts.

Skinner, B.F. (1971). *Beyond freedom and dignity.* New York: Knopf.

Skinner, B.F. (1979). *The making of a behaviorist.* New York: Knopf.

Skinner, B.F. (1990). Can psychology be a science of mind? *American Psychologist, 45,* 1206–1210.

Skoe, E., & Kraus, N. (2012). A little goes a long way: How the adult brain is shaped by musical training in childhood. *Journal of Neuroscience, 32*(34), 11507–11510. doi: 10.1523/JNEUROSCI.1949-12.2012.

Slamecka, N.J., & McElree, B. (1983). Normal forgetting of verbal lists as a function of their degree of learning. *Journal of Experimental Psychology: Learning, Memory, & Cognition, 9,* 384–397.

Slater, E., & Meyer, A. (1959). Contributions to a pathography of the musicians: Robert Schumann. *Confinia Psychiatrica, 2,* 65–94.

Slavich, G.M., O'Donovan, A., Epel, E., & Kemeny, M. (2010). Black sheep get the blues: A psychobiological model of social rejection and depression. *Neurosciences and Biobehavioral Reviews, 35,* 39–45. doi: 10.1016/j.neubiorev.2010.01.003.

Sloan, P., Arsenault, L., & Hilsenroth, M. (2002). *Use of the Rorschach in the assessment of war-related stress in military personnel.* Ashland, OH: Hogrefe & Huber.

Smith, C.A., & Ellsworth, P.C. (1987). Patterns of appraisal and emotion related to taking an exam. *Journal of Personality and Social Psychology, 52,* 475–488.

Smith, D. (2006, April 25). Harvard novelist says copying was unintentional. *New York Times.* Retrieved from http://www.nytimes.

Smith, H. (2002). *The latest innovation in open fit hearing aids: Speaker-in-the-ear hearing aids.* Retrieved from Learning Disabilities Resource Community at http://www.ldrc.ca/contents/view_article/322/.

Smith, J. (2009, March 25). Number of U.S. Facebook users over 35 nearly doubles in last 60 days. Retrieved from http://www.insidefacebook.com/2009/03/25/number-of-us-facebook-users-over-35-nearly-doubles-in-last-60-days/.

Smith, M., & Glass, G. (1977). Meta-analysis of psychotherapy outcome studies. *American Psychologist, 32,* 752–760.

Smith, M., & Kollock, P. (Eds). (1999). *Communities in cyberspace.* London: Routledge.

Smith, N., Young, A., & Lee, C. (2004). Optimism, health-related hardiness and well-being among older Australian women. *Journal of Health Psychology, 9,* 741–752.

Smith, S.M., & Vel, E. (2001). Environmental context-dependent memory: A review and meta-analysis. *Psychonomic Bulletin & Review, 8,* 203–220.

Smyth, J.M. (1998). Written emotional expression, effect sizes, outcome types, and moderating variables. *Journal of Consulting & Clinical Psychology, 66,* 174–184.

Snarey, J.R. (1985). Cross-cultural universality of social-moral development: A critical review of Kohlbergian research. *Psychological Bulletin, 97,* 202–232.

Snow, D.R. (1996). *The Iroquois.* Cambridge, MA: Blackwell.

Snowden, J., & Donnelly, N. (1986). A study of depression in nursing homes. *Journal of Psychiatric Research, 20,* 327–333.

Snyderman, M., & Rothman, S. (1987). Survey of expert opinion on intelligence and aptitude testing. *American Psychologist, 42,* 137–144.

Society of Neuroscience. (2010). *Fact sheet.* Retrieved from http://www.neurosciencecanada.ca/files/Fiche_informations_EN.pdf.

Soler, J., Pascual, J.C., Tiana, T., Cebria, A., Barrachina, J., Campins, M.J., . . . Pérez, V. (2009). Dialectical behaviour therapy skills training compared to standard group therapy in borderline personality disorder: A 3-month randomized controlled clinical trial. *Behaviour Research and Therapy, 47,* 353–358.

Solms, M. (2000). Dreaming and REM sleep are controlled by different brain mechanisms. *Behavioral and Brain Sciences, 23,* 843–850.

Solms, M. (2002). Dreaming: Cholinergic and dopaminergic hypotheses. In E. Perry, H. Ashton, & A. Young (Eds.), *Neurochemistry of consciousness* (pp. 123–131). Philadelphia: Benjamins.

Solomon, S.G., & Lennie, P. (2007). The machinery of colour vision. *Nature Reviews Neuroscience, 8,* 276–86.

Song, S. (2006, March 27). Mind over medicine. *Time, 167,* 13.

Sorce, J.F., Emde, R.N., Campos, J., & Klinnert, M.D. (1985). Maternal emotional signaling: Its effect on the visual cliff behavior of 1-year-olds. *Developmental Psychology, 21,* 195–200.

Southwick, S.M., Vythilingam, M., & Charney, D.S. (2005). The psychobiology of depression and resilience to stress: Implications for prevention and treatment. *Annual Review of Clinical Psychology, 1,* 255–291.

Sowell, E.R., Thompson, P.M., Tessner, K.D., & Toga, A.W. (2001). Mapping continued brain growth and gray matter density reduction in dorsal frontal cortex: Inverse relationships during postadolescent brain maturation. *The Journal of Neuroscience, 21,* 8619–8829.

Spalding, K.L., Arner, E., Westermark, P.O., Bernard, S., Buchholz, B.A., Bergmann, O., et al. (2008, June 5). Dynamics of fat cell turnover in humans. *Nature, 453,* 783–787.

Spangler, G., & Grossman, K.E. (1993). Biobehavioral organization in securely and insecurely attached infants. *Child Development, 64,* 1439–1450.

Spanos, N.P., Williams, V., & Gwynn, M.I. (1990). Effects of hypnotic, placebo, and salicylic acid treatments on wart regression. *Psychosomatic Medicine 52,* 109–114.

Spearman, C. (1904). "General intelligence," objectively determined and measured. *The American Journal of Psychology, 15,* 201–292.

Spearman, C. (1923). *The nature of "intelligence" and the principles of cognition.* London: Macmillan.

Spelke, E.S. (1985). Preferential-looking methods as tools for the study of cognition in infancy. In G. Gottlieb, N.A. Krasnegor, G. Gottlieb, N.A. Krasnegor (Eds.), *Measurement of audition and vision in the first year of postnatal life: A methodological overview* (pp. 323–363). Westport, CT: Ablex Publishing.

Spencer, S.M., & Patrick, J.H. (2009). Social support and personal mastery as protective resources during emerging adulthood. *Journal of Adult Development, 16,* 191–198.

Sperling, G. (1960). The information available in brief visual presentation. *Psychological Monographs, 74,* 29.

Sperry, R.W., Gazzaniga, M.S., & Bogen, J.E. (1969). Inter hemispheric relationships: The neocortical commissures: syndromes of hemisphere disconnection. In P.J. Vinken & G.W. Bruyn (Eds.), *Handbook of clinical neurology* (pp. 273–290). Amsterdam: North-Holland.

Spiegel, D., Bloom, J.R., Kraemer, H.C., & Gottheil, E. (1989). Effect of psychosocial treatment on survival of patients with metastatic breast cancer. *Lancet, 8668,* 88–91.

Spinrad, T.L., Eisenberg, N., Cumberland, A., Fabes, R.A., Valiente, C., Shepard, S.A., et al. (2006). Relation of emotion-related regulation to children's social competence: A longitudinal study. *Emotion, 6,* 498–510.

Sprecher, S., Fehr, B., & Zimmerman, C. (2007). Expectation for mood enhancement as a result of helping: The effects of gender and compassionate love. *Sex Roles, 56,* 543–549.

Squire, L. (1987). *Memory and brain.* New York: Oxford University Press.

Squire, L.R. (1977). ECT and memory loss. *American Journal of Psychiatry, 134,* 997–1001.

Squire, L.R. (2009). The legacy of patient H.M. for neuroscience. *Neuron, 61,* 6–9.

Staggs, G.D., Larson, L.M., & Borgen, F.H. (2007). Convergence of personality and interests: Meta-analysis of the Multidimensional Personality Questionnaire and the Strong Interest Inventory. *Journal of Career Assessment, 15*(4), 423–445.

Stallard, P., Simpson, N., Anderson, S., Carter, T., Osborn, C., & Bush, S. (2005). An Evaluation of the FRIENDS programme: A cognitive behaviour therapy intervention to promote emotional resilience. *Archives of Disease in Childhood, 90,* 1016–1019.

Stanley, J. (1996). In the beginning: The Study of Mathematically Precocious Youth. In C.P. Benbow & D. Lubinski (Eds.), *Intellectual talent* (pp. 225–235). Baltimore: Johns Hopkins University Press.

Stanley, M.A., & Beidel, D.C. (2009). Behavior therapy. In B.J. Sadock, V.A. Sadock, & P. Ruiz (Eds.). *Kaplan & Sadock's comprehensive textbook of psychiatry* (pp. 2781–2803). Philadelphia, PA: Lipponcott, Williams & Wilkins.

Stanovich, K.E. (2010). *How to think straight about psychology* (9th ed.). New York: Allyn & Bacon.

Stanovich, K.E., & West, R.F. (1998). Individual differences in rational thought. *Journal of Experimental Psychology—General, 127,* 161–188.

Stanton, A.L., Danoff-Burg, S., Sworowski, L.A., Rodriguez-Hanley, A., Kirk, S.B., & Austenfeld, J.L. (2002). Randomized, controlled trial of written emotional expression and benefit finding in breast cancer patients. *Journal of Clinical Oncology, 20,* 4160–4168.

Starr, C., & Taggart, R. (2004). *Biology: The unity and diversity of life* (10th edition). Belmont, CA: Thomson–Brooks Cole.

Statistics Canada. (2001). Centre for Education Statistics, Statistics Canada. Retrieved May 1, 2011, from http://www.salic-slmc.ca/showpage.asp?file=langues_en_presence/langues_off/taux_biling&language=en&updatemenu=true.

Statistics Canada. (2004, June 15). Canadian Community Health Survey. *The Daily.* Retrieved from http://www.statcan.gc.ca/daily-quotidien/040615/dq040615b-eng.htm.

Statistics Canada. (2006). Census: The Evolving Linguistic Portrait, 2006 Census: Highlights. Retrieved January 22, 2010, from http://www12.statcan.ca/census-recensement/2006/as-sa/97–555/p1–eng.cfm.

Statistics Canada. (2006). Mortality, summary list of causes. Catalogue no. 84F0209X.Retrieved October 2, 2010, from http://www.statcan.gc.ca/cgi-bin/af-fdr.cgi?l=eng&loc=http://www.statcan.gc.ca/pub/84f0209x/84f0209x2006000–eng.pdf&t=Mortality,%20Summary%20List%20of%20Causes.

Statistics Canada. (2008). Adult obesity in Canada: Measured height and weight. Retrieved November 21, 2010, from http://www.statcan.gc.ca/pub/82–620–m/2005001/article/adults-adultes/8060–eng.htm.

Statistics Canada. (2009). Visible minority population, by age group (2006 Census). Retrieved from http://www.statcan.gc.ca/tables-tableaux/sum-som/l01/cst01/demo50a-eng.htm.

Statistics Canada. (2010). Internet use by individuals, by selected characteristics. CANSIM, tables 358–0123, 358–0124, 358–0125 and 358–0126. Retrieved May 31, 2011, from http://www40.statcan.gc.ca/l01/cst01/comm35a-eng.htm.

Statistics Canada. (2010). Youth Bilingualism in Canada. Retrieved January 22, 2010, from http://www.statcan.gc.ca/pub/81–004–x/2008004/article/10767–eng.htm.

Statistics Canada. (2011). *Canadian vital statistics, marriage database and demography division (population estimates).* Retrieved from http://www4.hrsdc.gc.ca/.3ndic.1t.4r@-eng.jsp?iid=78.

Statistics Canada. (2012). Canadian Community Health Survey (CCHS), Mental Health. Ottawa, ON: Author.

Statistics Canada. (2013). Canadian Forces Mental Health Survey. Ottawa, ON: Author.

Statistics Canada. (2013a). Table 358-0153—Canadian Internet use survey, Internet use, by age group, Internet activity, sex, level of education and household income, occasional (percent), CANSIM (database). Retrieved from http://www5.statcan.gc.ca/cansim/a47.

Statistics Canada. (2013b). Table 358-0152—Canadian Internet use survey, Internet use, by age group and household income for Canada, provinces and census metropolitan areas (CMAs), occasional (percent), CANSIM (database). Retrieved from http://www5.statcan.gc.ca/cansim/a26.

Steel, G.D., Callaway, M., Suedfeld, P., & Palinkas, L. (1995). Human sleep-wake cycles in the high Arctic: Effects of unusual photoperiodicity in a natural setting. *Biological Rhythm Research, 26,* 582–592.

Steele, C.M. (1997). A threat in the air: How stereotypes shape intellectual identity and performance. *American Psychologist, 52,* 613–629.

Steele, C.M., & Aronson, J. (1995). Stereotype threat and the intellectual test performance of African Americans. *Journal of Personality and Social Psychology, 69,* 797–811.

Steeves, V. (2014). *Young Canadians in a wired world, Phase III: Life online.* Ottawa, ON: MediaSmarts.

Steeves, V., & Wing, C. (2006). Canada's Internet generation: Connected, active and younger than ever. *School Libraries in Canada (17108535), 25*(4), 7–13.

Stefansson, H., Ophoff, R.A., Steinberg, S., Andreassen, O.A., Chicon, S., Rujescu, D., . . . Collier, D.A. (2009). Common variants conferring risks of schizophrenia. *Nature, 460,* 744–747.

Steffenach, H.A., Sloviter, R.S., Moser, E.I., & Moser, M.B. (2002). Impaired retention of spatial memory after transection of longitudinally oriented axons of hippocampal CA3 pyramidal cells. *Proceedings of the National Academy of Sciences, 99,* 3194–3198.

Stein, J.A., & Newcomb, M.D. (1999). Adult outcomes of adolescent conventional and agentic orientations: A 20-year longitudinal study. *The Journal of Early Adolescence, 19*(1), 39–65. doi:10.1177/0272431699019001003.

Steinberg, L. (2005). Cognitive and affective development in adolescence. *Trends in Cognitive Sciences, 9*(2), 69–74.

Steinberg, L. (2010). *Adolescence* (9th ed.). New York, NY: McGraw-Hill.

Steiner, B., Wolf, S., & Kempermann, G. (2006). Adult neurogenesis and neurodegenerative disease. *Regenerative Medicine, 1,* 15–28.

Steinhausen, H., & Spohr, H. (1998). Long-term outcome of children with fetal alcohol syndrome: Psychopathology, behavior, and intelligence. *Alcoholism: Clinical and Experimental Research, 22*(2), 334–338.

Stellar, E. (1954). The physiology of motivation. *Psychological Review, 61,* 5–22.

Stenberg, C.R., Campos, J.J., & Emde, R. (1983). The facial expression of anger in seven-month-old infants. *Child Development, 54,* 178–184.

Stephane, M., Barton, S., & Boutros, N.N. (2001). Auditory verbal hallucinations and dysfunction of the neural substrates of speech. *Schizophrenia Research, 50,* 61–78.

Sterling, P., & Eyer, J. (1981). Allostasis: A new paradigm to explain arousal pathology. In S. Fisher & H.S. Reason (Eds.), *Handbook of life stress, cognition and health* (pp. 629–649). New York: John Wiley.

Sternberg, R.J. (1985). *Beyond IQ: A triarchic theory of human intelligence.* New York: Cambridge University Press.

Sternberg, R.J. (1986). A triangular theory of love. *Psychological Review, 93,* 119–135.

Sternberg, R.J. (1991). Death, taxes, and bad intelligence tests. *Intelligence, 15*(3), 257–270.

Sternberg, R.J. (1995). For whom The Bell Curve tolls: A review of *The Bell Curve. Psychological Science, 6,* 257–261.

Sternberg, R.J. (1997). Construct validation of a triangular love scale. *European Journal of Social Psychology, 27,* 313–335.

Sternberg, R.J. (1998). Principles of teaching for successful intelligence. *Educational Psychologist, 55,* 65–72.

Sternberg, R.J. (2000). The concept of intelligence. In. R.J. Sternberg (Ed.), *The handbook of intelligence* (pp. 3–15). Cambridge: Cambridge University Press.

Sternberg, R.J. (2003). A broad view of intelligence: A theory of successful intelligence. *Consulting Psychology Journal: Practice and Research, 55,* 139–154.

Sternberg, R.J. (2005). The triarchic theory of successful intelligence. In D.P. Flanagan & P.L. Harrison (Eds.), *Contemporary intellectual assessment: Theories, tests, and issues* (pp. 103–119). New York: Guilford Press.

Sternberg, R.J. (2006a). *Cognitive psychology* (4th ed.). Belmont: CA: Thomson-Wadsworth.

Sternberg, R.J. (2006b). The Rainbow Project: Enhancing the SAT through assessments of analytical, practical, and creative skills. *Intelligence, 34,* 321–350.

Sternberg, R.J. (Ed.). (2004). *Definitions and conceptions of giftedness.* Thousand Oaks, CA: Corwin Press.

Sternberg, R.J., & Detterman, D.K. (Eds.). (1986). *What is intelligence? Contemporary viewpoints on its nature and definition.* Norwood, NJ: Ablex.

Sternberg, R.J., & O'Hara, L. (1999). Creativity and intelligence. In R.J. Sternberg (Ed.), *Handbook of creativity* (pp. 251–272). New York: Cambridge University Press.

Sternberg, R.J., Grigorenko, E.L., & Kidd, K.K. (2005). Intelligence, race, and genetics. *American Psychologist, 60,* 46–59.

Stevens, S.B., & Morris, T.L. (2007). College dating and social anxiety: Using the Internet as a means of connecting to others. *CyberPsychology & Behavior, 10,* 680–688.

Stewart, F. (2000). Internet acceptable use policies: Navigating the management, legal, and technical issues. *Information Systems Security, 9,* 46–53.

Stewart, J. (2008). Psychological and neural mechanisms of relapse. *Philosophical Transactions of the Royal Society, 363,* 3147–3158.

Stewart, J.H. (2005). Hypnosis in contemporary medicine. *Mayo Clinic Proceedings, 80,* 511–524.

Stewart, R.A., Rule, A.C., & Giordano, D.A. (2007). The effect of fine motor skill activities on kindergarten attention. *Early Childhood Education Journal, 35,* 103–109.

Stewart, V.M. (1973). Tests of the "carpentered world" hypothesis by race and environment in America and Zambia. *International Journal of Psychology, 8,* 83–94.

Stice, E., Shaw, H., Bohon, C., Marti, C.N., & Rhode, P. (2009). A meta-analytic review of depression prevention programs for children and adolescents: Factors that predict magnitude of intervention effects. *Journal of Consulting and Clinical Psychology, 77,* 486–503.

Stickgold, R. (2005). Sleep-dependent memory consolidation. *Nature, 437,* 1272–1278.

Stickgold, R., & Walker, M.P. (2007). Sleep-dependent memory consolidation and reconsolidation. *Sleep Medicine, 8,* 331–343.

Strack, F., Martin, L.L., & Stepper, S. (1988). Inhibiting and facilitating conditions of the human smile: A nonobtrusive test of the facial feedback hypothesis. *Journal of Personality and Social Psychology, 54,* 768–777.

Strassman, R.J. (1984). Adverse reactions to psychedelic drugs. A review of the literature. *Journal of Nervous and Mental Disease, 172,* 577–595.

Strauss, M.E., Pasupathi, M., & Chatterjee, A. (1993). Concordance between observers in descriptions of personality change in Alzheimer's disease. *Psychology and Aging, 8,* 475–480.

Strayer, D.L., & Drews, F.A. (2007). Cellphone-induced driver distraction. *Current Directions in Psychological Science, 16,* 128–131.

Strayer, D.L., Drews, F.A., & Couch, D.J. (2006). A comparison of the cell phone driver and the drunk driver. *Human Factors, 48,* 381–391.

Streissguth, A., Barr, H., Sampson, P., Darby, B., & Martin, D. (1989). IQ at age 4 in relation to maternal alcohol use and smoking during pregnancy. *Developmental Psychology, 25*(1), 3–11.

Strenze, T. (2007). Intelligence and socioeconomic success: A meta-analytic review of longitudinal research. *Intelligence, 35*(5), 401–426.

Stroop, J.R. (1935). Studies of interference in serial-verbal reaction. *Journal of Experimental Psychology, 18,* 643–662.

Strueber, D., Lueck, M., & Roth, G. (2006–2007). The violent brain. *Scientific American Mind, 17,* 20–27.

Stuart, E.W., Shimp, T.A., & Engle, R.W. (1987). Classical conditioning of consumer attitudes: Four experiments in an advertising context. *Journal of Consumer Research, 14,* 334–349.

Styles, E.A. (2006). *The psychology of attention* (2nd ed.). Hove, England: Psychology Press.

Styron, W. (1990). *Darkness visible: A memoir of madness.* New York: Vintage.

Suarez, E., & Gadalla, T.M. (2010). Stop blaming the victim: A meta-analysis on rape myths. *Journal of Interpersonal Violence, 25,* 2010–2035.

Suarez, E.C., Bates, M.P., & Harralson, T.L. (1998). The relation of hostility to lipids and lipoproteins in women: Evidence for the role of antagonistic hostility. *Annals of Behavioral Medicine, 20,* 59–63.

Suarez, E.C., Harlan, E., Peoples, M.C., & Williams, R.B., Jr. (1993). Cardiovascular reactivity and emotional responses in women: The role of hostility and harassment. *Health Psychology, 12,* 459–468.

Suarez, E.C., & Williams, R.B., Jr. (1989). Situational determinants of cardiovascular and emotional reactivity in high and low hostile men. *Psychosomatic Medicine, 51,* 404–418.

Subrahmanyam, K., Greenfield, P.M., & Tynes, B. (2004). Constructing sexuality and identity in an online teen chatroom. *Journal of Applied Developmental Psychology, 25,* 651–666.

Subrahmanyam, K., Šmahel, D., & Greenfield, P.M. (2006). Connecting developmental processes to the Internet: Identity presentation and sexual exploration in online teen chat rooms. *Developmental Psychology, 42,* 1–12.

Sullivan, K., Zaitchik, D., & Tager-Flusberg, H. (1994). Preschoolers can attribute second-order beliefs. *Developmental Psychology, 30,* 395–402.

Suomi, S. (2005). Genetic and environmental factors influencing the expression of impulsive aggression and serotonergic functioning in rhesus monkeys. In R.E. Tremblay, W.W. Hartup, & J. Archer (Eds.), *Developmental origins of aggression* (pp. 63–82). New York: Guilford Press.

Susskind, J.M., Lee, D.H., Cusi, A., Feiman, R., Grabski, W., & Anderson, A.K. (2008). Expressing fear enhances sensory acquisition. *Nature Neuroscience, 11,* 843–850.

Suvrathan, A., Bennur, S., Ghosh, S., Tomar, A., Anilkumar, S., Chattarji, S. (2014). Stress enhances fear by forming new synapses with greater capacity for long-term potentiation in the amygdala. *Philosophical Transactions of the Royal Society B-Biological Sciences, 369,* 20130151.

Swets, J.A. (1964). *Signal detection and recognition by human observers.* New York: Wiley.

Syed, M., & Azmitia, M. (2010). Narrative and ethnic identity exploration: A longitudinal account of emerging adults' ethnicity-related experiences. *Developmental Psychology, 46*, 208–219.

Synthesis on fetal alcohol spectrum disorder. (2007). In *Encyclopedia on Early Childhood Development.* Retrieved from http://www.child-encyclopedia.com/en-ca/fetal-alcohol-spectrum-disorder/how-important-is-it.html.

Szaflarski, J.P., Binder, J.R., Possing, E.T., McKiernan, K.A., Ward, B.D., & Hammeke, T.A. (2002). Language lateralization in left-handed and ambidextrous people: fMRI data. *Neurology, 59*, 238–244.

Tafti, M., Dauvilliers, Y., & Overeem, S. (2007). Narcolepsy and familial advanced sleep-phase syndrome: Molecular genetics of sleep disorders. *Current Opinion in Genetics & Development, 17*, 222–227.

Takahashi, Y., Yamagata, S., Kijima, N., Shigemasu, K., Ono, Y., & Ando, J. (2007). Continuity and change in behavioral inhibition and activation systems: A longitudinal behavioral genetic study. *Personality and Individual Differences, 43*(6), 1616–1625.

Takeuchi, H., Taki, Y., Sassa, Y., Hashizume, H., Sekiguchi, A., Fukushima, A., & Kawashima, R. (2010). White matter structures associated with creativity: Evidence from diffusion tensor imaging. *Neuroimage, 51*(1), 11–8.

Takeuchi, T., Ogilvie, R.D., Murphy, T.I., & Ferrelli, A.V. (2003). EEG activities during elicited sleep onset REM and NREM periods reflect different mechanisms of dream generation. *Clinical Neurophysiology, 114*, 210–220.

Talassi, E., Cipriani, G., Bianchetti, A., & Trabucchi, M. (2007). Personality changes in Alzheimer's disease. *Aging & Mental Health, 11*, 526–531.

Talati, A., Bao, Y., Kaufman, J., Shen, L., Schaefer, C.A., & Brown, A.S. (2013). Maternal smoking during pregnancy and bipolar disorder in offspring. *American Journal of Psychiatry, 170*, 1178–1185. doi: 10.1176/appi.ajp.2013.12121500.

Talmi, D., Grady, C.L., Goshen-Gottstein, Y., & Moscovitch, M. (2005). Neuroimaging the serial position curve: A test of singlestore versus dual-store models. *Psychological Science, 16*, 717–723.

Talwar, V., & Lee, K. (2008). Social and cognitive correlates of children's lying behavior. *Child Development, 79*(4), 866–881. doi:10.1111/j.1467-8624.2008.01164.x.

Tambs, K., Hoffman, H.J., Borchgrevink, H.M., Holmen, J., & Engdahl, B. (2006). Hearing loss induced by occupational and impulse noise: Results on threshold shifts by frequencies, age and gender from the Nord-Trøndelag Hearing Loss Study. *International Journal of Audiology, 45*, 309–317.

Tammet, D. (2006). *Born on a blue day: A memoir.* New York: Free Press.

Tang, Z., & Orwin, R.G. (2009). Marijuana initiation among American youth and its risks as dynamic processes: Prospective findings from a national longitudinal study. *Substance Use & Misuse, 44*, 195–211.

Tangney, J.P., Stuewig, J., & Mashek, D.J. (2007). Moral emotions and moral behavior. *Annual Review of Psychology, 58*, 345–372.

Tanielian, T., & Jaycox, L.H. (Eds.). (2008). *Invisible wounds of war: Psychological and cognitive injuries, their consequences, and services to assist recovery.* Santa Monica, CA: Rand Corp.

Tardif, T., Gelman, S., & Xu, F. (1999). Putting the "noun bias" in context: A comparison of English and Mandarin. *Developmental Psychology, 70*, 620–635.

Tare, M., & Gelman, S.A. (2010). Can you say it another way? Cognitive factors in bilingual children's pragmatic language skills. *Journal of Cognition and Development, 11*(2), 137–158. doi: 10.1080/15248371003699951.

Tarmann, A. (2002, May/June). Out of the closet and onto the Census long form. *Population Today, 30*, 1, 6.

Tashkin, D.R., Baldwin, G.C., Sarafian, T., Dubinett, S., & Roth, M.D. (2002). Respiratory and immunologic consequences of marijuana smoking. *Journal of Clinical Pharmacology, 42*, S71–S81.

Tavris, C. (2013, May 18). How psychiatry went crazy. *The Wall Street Journal*, C5.

Taylor, J.B. (2006). *My stroke of insight.* New York, Viking.

Taylor, P.J. (2008). Psychosis and violence: Stories, fears, and reality. *Canadian Journal of Psychiatry, 53*, 647–659.

Taylor, S.E. (1989). *Positive illusions: Creative self-deception and the healthy mind.* New York: Basic Books.

Taylor, S.E., Kemeny, M.E., Reed, G.M., Bower, J.E., & Gruene wald, T.L. (2000). Psychological resources, positive illusions, and health. *American Psychologist, 55*, 99–109.

Teasdale, G., & Jennett, B. (1976). Assessment and prognosis of coma after head injury. *Acta Neurochirurgica, 34*, 45–55.

Teasdale, J.D., Segal, Z., Williams, M.G., Ridgeway, V.A., Soulsby, J.M., & Lau, M.A. (2000). Prevention of relapse/recurrence in major depression by mindfulness-based cognitive therapy. *Journal of Consulting and Clinical Psychology, 68*, 615–623.

Teasdale, J.D., Segal, Z.V., & Williams, J.M.G. (1995). How does cognitive therapy prevent depressive relapse and why should attentional control (mindfulness) training help? *Behaviour Research and Therapy, 33*, 25–39.

Tellegen, A. (2000). *Manual for the Multidimensional Personality Questionnaire.* Minneapolis, MN: University of Minnesota Press.

Tellegen, A., Ben-Porath, Y.S., McNulty, J.L., Arbisi, P.A., Graham, J.R., & Kaemmer, B. (2003). *The MMPI-2 Restructured Clinical Scales: Development, validation, and interpretation.* Minneapolis: University of Minnesota Press.

Tellegen, A., Lykken, D.T., Bouchard, T.J., Wilcox, K.J., Segal, N.L., & Rich, S. (1988). Personality similarity in twins reared apart and together. *Journal of Personality and Social Psychology, 54*, 1031–1039.

Terracciano, A.A., Abdel-Khalek, A.M., Ádám, N.N., Adamovová, L.L., Ahn, C.K., Ahn, H.N., & McCrae, R.R. (2005). National character does not reflect mean personality trait levels in 49 cultures. *Science, 310*(5745), 96–100.

Terrace, H.S. (1987). *Nim: A chimpanzee who learned sign language.* New York: Columbia University Press. *Test Developer Profiles* (2001). Retrieved July 15, 2007, from http://www.mhhe.com/mayfieldpub/psychtesting/profiles/karfmann.htm.

Thagard, P. (2005). *Mind: An introduction to cognitive science* (2nd ed.). Cambridge, MA: MIT Press.

Thayer, S.E., & Ray, S. (2006). Online communication preferences across age, gender, and duration of Internet use. *CyberPsychology & Behavior, 9*, 432–440.

The many facets of Facebook. (2011, January 1). *San Francisco Chronicle*, D-1.

Thibaut, J.W., & Kelley, H.H. (1959). *The social psychology of groups.* New York: Wiley.

Thomas, A., & Chess, S. (1977). *Temperament and development.* New York: Brunner/Mazel.

Thomasius, R., Zapletalova, P., Petersen, K., Buchert, R., Andresen, B., Wartberg, L., et al. (2006). Mood, cognition and serotonin transporter availability in current and former ecstasy (MDMA) users: The longitudinal perspective. *Journal of Psychopharmacology, 20*, 211–225.

Thompson, P.M., Giedd, J.N., Woods, R.P., MacDonald, D., Evans, A.C., & Toga, A.W. (2000). Growth patterns in the developing brain using continuum mechanical tensor maps. *Nature, 404*, 190–193.

Thompson, R.F., & Madigan, S.A. (2005). *Memory: The key to consciousness.* Washington, DC: Joseph Henry Press.

Thompson, W.L., & Kosslyn, S.M. (2000). Neural systems activated during visual mental imagery. In A.W. Toga & J.C. Mazziotta (Eds.), *Brain mapping: The systems* (pp. 535–560). San Diego: Academic Press, 2000.

Thomsen, M., Hall, F.S., Uhl, G.R., & Caine, S.B. (2009). Dramatically decreased cocaine self-administration in dopamine but not serotonin transporter knock-out mice. *Journal of Neuroscience, 29,* 1087–1092.

Thorndike, E.L. (1905). *Elements of psychology.* New York: Seiler.

Thornton, A.J.V., Graham-Kevan, N., & Archer, J. (2010). Adaptive and maladaptive personality traits as predictors of violent and nonviolent offending behavior in men and women. *Aggressive Behavior, 36,* 177–186.

Thune, I., & Furberg, A.S. (2001). Physical activity and cancer risk: Dose-response and cancer, all sites and site specific. *Medicine and Science in Sports and Exercise, 33,* S530–S550.

Thurstone, E.L. (1938). *Primary mental abilities.* Chicago: University of Chicago Press.

Tikkanen, T. (2001). Psychology in Europe: A growing profession with high standards and a bright future. *European Psychologist, 6,* 144–146.

Till, B.D., Stanley, S.M., & Priluck, R. (2008). Classical conditioning and celebrity endorsers: An examination of belongingness and resistance to extinction. *Psychology & Marketing, 25,* 179–196.

Tindale, R.S., Talbot, M., Martinez, R. (2013). Decision making. In J.M. Levive (Ed.), *Group Processes* (pp. 165–192). New York, NY: Routledge.

Tobe, E.H. (2013). Mitochondrial dysfunction, oxidative stress, and major depressive disorder. *Neuropsychiatric Disease and Treatment, 9,* 567–573. doi: 10.2147/NDT.S44282.

Tobias, S., & Everson, H.T. (2002). *Knowing what you know and what you don't: Further research on metacognitive knowledge monitoring.* New York: College Entrance Examination Board.

Todd, P.M., & Gigerenzer, G. (2007). Environments that make us smart. *Current Directions in Psychological Science, 16,* 167–171.

Todman, D. (2008). *Wilder Penfield* (1891–1976). *Journal of Neurology, 255*(7), 1104–1105.

Toledo, S.E., & Toledo-Pereyra, L.H. (2003). Early American medicine. *Journal of Investigative Surgery, 16,* 311–314.

Tolin, D.F. (2010). Is cognitive-behavioral therapy more effective than other therapies? A meta-analytic review. *Clinical Psychology Review, 30,* 710–720.

Tolman, E.C., & Honzik, C.H. (1930). Introduction and removal of reward, and maze performance in rats. *University of California Publications in Psychology, 4,* 257–275.

Tomassy, G.S., & Fossati, V. (2014). How big is the myelinating orchestra? Cellular diversity within oligodendrocyte lineage: Facts and hypotheses. *Frontiers in Cellular Neuroscience, 8,* 1–11.

Tomkins, S.S. (1962). *Affect, imagery, consciousness: Vol. 1. The positive affects.* New York: Springer.

Tomkins, S.S. (1981). The quest for primary motives: Biography and autobiography of an idea. *Journal of Personality and Social Psychology, 41,* 306–329.

Tomkins, S.S., & McCarter, R. (1964). What and where are the primary affects? Some evidence for a theory. *Perceptual and Motor Skills, 18,* 119–158.

Tooby, J., & Cosmides, L. (1990). The past explains the present: Emotional adaptations and the structure of ancestral environments. *Ethology and Sociobiology, 11,* 375–424.

Tooby, J., & Cosmides, L. (1992). The psychological foundations of culture. In J.H. Barkow, L. Cosmides, & J. Tooby (Eds.), *The adapted mind: Evolutionary psychology and the generation of culture* (pp. 19–136). New York: Oxford University Press.

Tooby, J., & Cosmides, L. (2005). Conceptual foundations of evolutionary psychology. In D.M. Buss (Ed.), *The Handbook of Evolutionary Psychology* (pp. 5–67). Hoboken, NJ: Wiley.

Torrance, E.P. (1966). *The Torrance Tests of Creative Thinking-Norms-Technical Manual Research Edition-Verbal Tests, Forms A and B-Figural Tests, Forms A and B.* Princeton, NJ: Personnel Press.

Touriño, C., Evan-Rothschild, A., & de Lecea, L. (2013). Optogenetics in psychiatric diseases. *Current Opinion in Neurobiology, 23,* 430–435. doi: 10.1016/j.conb,2013.03.007.

Tracy, J.L., & Matsumoto, D.M. (2008). The spontaneous display of pride and shame: Evidence for biologically innate nonverbal displays. *Proceedings of the National Academy of Science, 105,* 11655–11660.

Tracy, J.L., & Robins, R.W. (2007). Emerging insights into the nature and function of pride. *Current Directions in Psychological Science, 16,* 147–150.

Tracy, J.L., & Robins, R.W. (2008). The nonverbal expression of pride: Evidence for crosscultural recognition. *Journal of Personality and Social Psychology, 94,* 516–530.

Tracy, J.L., Robins, R.W., & Tangney, J.P. (2007). *The self-conscious emotions: Theory and research.* New York: Guilford Press.

Transcripts of "Secrets of the Wild Child." (1997). Retrieved from http://www.pbs.org/wgbh/nova/transcripts/2112gchild.html.

Trautner, H.M., Ruble, D.N., Cyphers, L., Kirsten, B., Behrendt, R., & Hartmann, P. (2005). Rigidity and flexibility of gender stereotypes in childhood: Developmental or differential. *_Infant and Child Development, 14,* 365–380.

Treffert, D.A. (2006). *Extraordinary people: Understanding savant syndrome.* Updated version. Lincoln, NE: iUniverse Inc.

Treffert, D.A., & Christensen, D.D. (2005). Inside the mind of a savant. *Scientific American, 293,* 108–113.

Treisman, A. (1964). Verbal cues, language and meaning in selective attention. *American Journal of Psychology, 77,* 206–209.

Tremblay, K., & Ross, B. (2007). Effects of age and age-related hearing loss on the brain. *Journal of Communication Disorders, 40,* 305–312.

Trentacosta, C.J., & Izard, C.E. (2007). Kindergarten children's emotion competence as a predictor of their academic competence in first grade. *Emotion, 7,* 77–88.

Trepte, S., & Reinecke, L. (2013). The reciprocal effects of social network site use and the disposition for self-disclosure: A longitudinal study. *Computers in Human Behavior, 29,* 1102–1112. http://dx.doi.org/10.1016/j.chb.2012.10.002.

Trevino, K., McClintock, S.M., & Husain, M.M. (2010). A review of continuation electroconvulsive therapy: Application, safety, and efficacy. *Journal of ECT, 26,* 186–195.

Triandis, H.C. (1990). Cross-cultural studies of individualism and collectivism. In J.J. Herman (Ed.), *Nebraska Symposium on Motivation 1989, 37,* 41–133.

Triandis, H.C. (2003). Cultural syndromes and subjective well-being. In E. Diener, E.M. Suh (Eds.), *Culture and subjective well-being* (pp. 13–36). MA: MIT Press.

Triplett, N. (1898). The dynamogenic factors in pacemaking and competition. *American Journal of Psychology, 9,* 507–533.

Trivers, R.L. (1971). The evolution of reciprocal altruism. *Quarterly Review of Biology, 46,* 35–57.

Trivers, R.L. (1972). Parental investment and sexual selection. In B. Campbell (Ed.), *Sexual selection and the descent of man, 1871–1971* (pp. 136–179). Chicago: Aldine.

Trivers, R.L. (1985). *Social evolution.* Menlo Park, CA: Benjamin/Cummings.

Troisi, A. (2003). Psychopathology. In D. Maestripieri (Ed.), *Primate psychology* (pp. 451–470). Cambridge, MA: Harvard University Press.

True, M., Pisani, L., & Oumar, F. (2001). Infant–mother attachment among the Dogon of Mali. *Child Development, 72*(5), 1451–1466.

Trugman, J.M. (1998). Tardive dyskinesia: Diagnosis, patho genesis, pathogenesis, and management. *Neurologist, 4,* 180–187.

Tsai, J.L., & Chentsova-Dutton, Y. (2003). Variation among European Americans in emotional facial expression. *Journal of Cross-Cultural Psychology, 34,* 650–657.

Tsai, J.L., Chentsova-Dutton, Y., Friere-Bebeau, L., & Przymus, D.E. (2002). Emotional expression and physiology in European Americans and Hmong Americans. *Emotion, 2,* 380–397.

Tsai, J.L., Levenson, R.W., & Carstensen, L.L. (2000). Autonomic, expressive, and subjective responses to emotional films in older and younger Chinese American and European American adults. *Psychology and Aging, 15,* 684–693.

Tsakiris, M., Hesse, M.D., Boy, C., Haggard, P., & Fink, G.R. (2007). Neural signatures of body ownership: A sensory network for bodily self-consciousness. *Cerebral Cortex 17,* 2235–2244.

Tseng, W.S. (1973). The development of psychiatric concepts in traditional Chinese medicine. *Archives of General Psychiatry, 29,* 569–575.

Tugade, M.M., & Fredrickson, B.L. (2004). Resilient individuals use positive emotions to bounce back from negative emotional experiences. *Journal of Personality and Social Psychology, 86,* 320–333.

Tulku, T. (1984). *Knowledge of freedom.* Berkeley, CA: Dharma.

Tulving, E. (1972). Episodic and semantic memory. In E. Tulving & W. Donaldson (Eds.), *Organization of memory* (pp. 381–403). New York: Academic Press.

Tulving, E. (1985). How many memory systems are there? *American Psychologist, 40,* 385–398.

Tulving, E., & Thomson, D.M. (1973). Encoding specificity and retrieval processes in episodic memory. *Psychological Review, 80,* 352–373.

Turillazzi, E., Riezzo, I., Neri, M., Bello, S., & Fineschi, V. (2010). MDMA toxicity and pathological consequences: A review about experimental data and autopsy findings. *Current Pharmacological Biotechnology, 11,* 500–509.

Turner, E.H., Matthews, A.M., Linardatos, E., Tell, R.A., & Rosenthal, R. (2008). Selective publication of antidepressant trials and its influence on apparent efficacy. *New England Journal of Medicine, 358,* 252–260.

Turner-Shea, Y., Bruno, R., & Pridmore, S. (2006). Daily and spaced treatment with transcranial magnetic stimulation in major depression: A pilot study. *Australian and New Zealand Journal of Psychiatry, 40,* 759–763.

Tversky, A., & Kahneman, D. (1974). Judgment under uncertainty: Heuristics and biases. *Science, 185,* 1124–1131.

Tversky, A., & Kahneman, D. (1983). Extensional versus intuitive reasoning: The conjunction fallacy in probability judgment. *Psychological Review, 90,* 293–315.

Twyman, K., Saylor, C., Taylor, L.A., & Comeaux, C. (2009). Comparing children and adolescents engaged in cyberbullying to matched peers. *CyberPsychology & Behavior, 12,* 1.

Tyron, W.W. (2005). Possible mechanisms for why desensitization and exposure therapy work. *Clinical Psychology Review, 25,* 67–95.

Udry, J.R., Morris, N.M., & Waller, L. (1973). Effect of contraceptive pills on sexual activity in the luteal phase of the human menstrual cycle. *Archives of Sexual Behavior, 2,* 205–214.

Uher, R., & McGuffin, P. (2010). The moderation by the serotonin transporter gene of environmental adversity in the etiology of depression: 2009 update. *Molecular Psychiatry, 15,* 18–22.

Uhlhaas, P.J., & Singer, W. (2006). Neural synchrony in brain disorders: Relevance for cognitive dysfunctions and pathophysiology. *Neuron, 52*(1), 155–168.

Uhlhaas, P.J., Roux, F., Singer, W., Haenschel, C., Sireteanu, R., & Rodriguez, E. (2009). The development of neural synchrony reflects late maturation and restructuring of functional networks in humans. *Proceedings of the National Academy of Sciences of the United States of America,* 106(24), 9866–9874.

Uhlhaas, P.J., & Singer, W. (2010). Abnormal neural oscillations and synchrony in schizophrenia. *Nature Reviews Neuroscience, 11*(2), 100–113.

Umaña-Taylor, A.J. (2004). Ethnic identity and self-esteem: The role of social context. *Journal of Adolescence, 27,* 139–146.

United Nations Office on Drugs and Crime. (2009). World Drug Report 2009. Retrieved May 24, 2010, from http://www.unodc.org/unodc/en/data-and-analysis/WDR-2009.html.

U.S. Senate. (2004). Report of the Select Committee on Intelligence on the U.S. Intelligence Community's Prewar Intelligence Assessments on Iraq. Retrieved from http://www.gpoaccess.gov/serialset/creports/iraq.html.

Uylings, H.B.M. (2006). Development of the human cortex and the concept of "critical" or "sensitive" periods. *Language Learning, 56,* 59–90.

Vaidya, C.J, Zhao, M., Desmond, J.E., and Gabrieli. (2002). Evidence for cortical encoding specificity in episodic memory: Memory-induced re-activation of picture processing areas. *Neuropsychologica, 40,* 2136–2143.

Vaish, A., & Striano, T. (2004). Is visual reference necessary? Contributions of facial versus vocal cues in 12-month-olds' social referencing behavior. *Developmental Science, 7,* 261–269.

Valente, M., Placid, F., Oliveira, A.J., Bigagli, A., Morghen, I., Proietti, R., & Gigli, G.L. (2002). Sleep organization pattern as a prognostic marker at the subacute stage of post-traumatic coma. *Clinical Neurophysiology, 113,* 1798–1805.

Valkenburg, P., & Peter, J. (2007). Pre-adolescents' and adolescents' online communication and their closeness to friends. *Developmental Psychology, 43,* 267–277.

Valkenburg, P., & Peter, J. (2009). Social consequences of the internet for adolescents: A decade of research. *Current Directions in Psychological Science, 18,* 1–5.

Valkenburg, P.M., & Peter, J. (2007). Who visits online dating sites? Exploring some characteristics of online daters. *CyberPsychology & Behavior, 10,* 849–852.

Valkenburg, P.M., Peter, J., & Schouten, A.P. (2006). Friend networking sites and their relationship to adolescents' well-being and social self-esteem. *CyberPsychology & Behavior, 9,* 584–590.

Van Dongen, H.P., Maislin, G., Mullington, J.M., & Dinges, D.F. (2003). The cumulative cost of additional wakefulness: dose-response effects on neurobehavioural functions and sleep physiology from chronic sleep restriction and total sleep deprivation. *Sleep, 26,* 117–26.

van Geffen, E.C., Heerdink, E.R., Hugtenburg, J.G., Siero, F.W., Egberts, A.C., & van Hulten, R. (2010). Patients' perceptions and illness severity at start of antidepressant treatment in general practice. *International Journal of Pharmacy Practice, 18,* 217–225.

van IJzendoorn, M., & Juffer, F. (2005). Adoption is a successful natural intervention enhancing adopted children's IQ and school performance. *Current Directions in Psychological Science, 14,* 326–330.

van IJzendoorn, M.H., & Kroonenberg, P.M. (1988). Cross-cultural patterns of attachment: A meta-analysis of the strange situation. *Child Development, 59*(1), 147–156.

van Ijzendoorn, M.H., & Sagi-Schwartz, A. (2008). Cross-cultural patterns of attachment: Universal and contextual dimensions. In J. Cassidy, P.R. Shaver, J. Cassidy, P.R. Shaver (Eds.), *Handbook of attachment: Theory, research, and clinical applications* (2nd ed., pp. 880–905). New York: Guilford Press.

Van Lange, P.M., Joireman, J., Parks, C.D., & Van Dijk, E. (2013). The psychology of social dilemmas: A review. *Organizational Behavior and Human Decision Processes, 120*(2), 125–141. doi:10.1016/j.obhdp.2012.11.003.

Van Neste, D., & Tobin, D.J. (2004). Hair cycle and hair pigmentation: Dynamic interactions and changes associated with aging. *Micron, 35,* 193–200.

Van Voorhees, B.W., Paunesku, D., Kuwabara, S.A., Basu, A., Gollan, J., Hankin, B.L., et al. (2008). Protective and vulnerability factors predicting new-onset depressive episode in a representative of U.S. adolescents. *Journal of Adolescent Health, 42*, 605–616.

van Vugt, M., & van Lange, P.A.M. (2006). The altruism puzzle: Psychological adaptations for prosocial behavior. In M. Schaller, D.T. Kenrick, & J.A. Simpson (Eds.), *Evolution and social psychology* (pp. 237–261). New York: Psychology Press.

Van Wyk, P.H., & Geist, C.S. (1984). Psychosocial development of heterosexual, bisexual and homosexual behavior. *Archives of Sexual Behavior, 13*, 505–544.

Vandewater, E.A., Rideout, V.J., Wartella, E.A., Huang, X., Lee, J.H., & Shim, M. (2007). Digital childhood: Electronic media and technology use among infants, toddlers, and preschoolers. *Pediatrics, 119*, e1006–e1015.

Vandewater, E.A., Shim, M., & Caplovitz, A.G. (2004). Linking obesity and activity level with children's television and video game use. *Journal of Adolescence, 27*, 71–85.

Vaswani, M., Linda, F.K., & Ramesh, S. (2003). Role of selective serotonin reuptake inhibitors in psychiatric disorders: A comprehensive review. *Progress in Neuro-Psychopharmacology and Biological Psychiatry, 2*, 85–102.

Vaughan, R.M. (2008, February 8). The Q&A. *Globe Review.* Retrieved from http://www.theglobeandmail.com/.

Vedantum, S. (2005, January 23). See no bias. *The Washington Post.*

Veith, I. (1965). *Hysteria: The history of a disease.* Chicago: University of Chicago Press.

Venkatasubramanian, G., & Kalmady, S.V. (2010). Creativity, psychosis, and human evolution: The exemplar case of neuregulin 1 gene. *Indian Journal of Psychiatry, 52*, 282.

Venning, A., Kettler, L., Eliott, J., & Wilson, A. (2009). The effectiveness of cognitive-behavioural therapy with hopeful elements to prevent the development of depression in young people: A systematic review. *International Journal of Evidence-Based Healthcare, 7*, 15–33. doi: 10.1111/j.1744-1609.2009.00122.x.

Verquer, M.L., Beehr, T.A., & Wagner, S.H. (2003). A meta-analysis of relations between person-organization fit and work attitudes. *Journal of Vocational Behavior, 63*, 473–489.

Verschoor, E., Finlayson, G., Blundell, J., Markus, C.R., & King, N.A. (2010). Effects of an acute alpha-lactalbumin manipulation on mood and food hedonics in high- and low-trait anxiety individuals. *British Journal of Nutrition, 104*, 595–602.

Vertes, R.B., & Eastman, K.E. (2000). The case against memory consolidation in REM sleep. *Behavioral Brain Research, 23*, 867–876.

Vetter, H.J. (1968). New-word coinage in the psychopathological context. *Psychiatric Quarterly, 42*, 298–312.

Vinson, G.A., Connelly, B.S., & Ones, D.S. (2007). Relationships between personality and organization switching: Implications for utility estimates. *International Journal of Selection and Assessment, 15*(1), 118–133.

Vitello, P. (2006, June 12). A ringtone meant to fall on deaf ears. *New York Times.* Retrieved from http://www.nytimes.com.

Voderholzer, U., Riemann, D., Hornyak, M., Backhaus, J., Feige, B., Berger, M., & Hohagen, F. (2001). A double-blind, randomized and placebo-controlled study on the polysomnographic withdrawal effects of zopiclone, zolpidem and triazolam in healthy subjects. *European Archives of Psychiatry and Clinical Neurosceince, 251*, 117–123.

von der Goltz, C., & Kiefer, F. (2009). Learning and memory in the aetiopathogenesis of addiction: future implications for therapy? *European Archives of Psychiatry and Clinical Neurosceince, 259*(Suppl. 2), S183–S187.

Von Eye, A., & Mair, P. (2005). Developmental research design. In Celia B. Fisher & Richard M. Lerner (Eds.), *Encyclopedia of applied developmental science, Volume 2.* Thousand Oaks, CA: Sage Publications Inc.

Vyas, N.S., Patel, N.H., Nijran, K.S., Al-Nahhas, A., & Puri, B.K. (2010). Insights into schizophrenia using positron emission tomography: Building the evidence and refining the focus. *British Journal of Psychiatry, 197*, 3–4.

Wadlinger, H.A., & Isaacowitz, D.M. (2006). Positive mood broadens visual attention to positive stimuli. *Motivation & Emotion, 30*, 89–101.

Wagner, A.W., & Linehan, M.M. (2006). Applications of dialectical behavior therapy to posttraumatic stress disorder and related problems. In V.M. Folette & J.I. Ruzek (Eds.), *Cognitive–behavioral therapies for trauma* (2nd ed., pp. 117–145). New York: Guilford Press.

Wagner, T.D., & Ochsner, K.N. (2005). Sex differences in the emotional brain. *NeuroReport, 16*, 85–87.

Wahlbeck, K., Forsen, T., Osmond, C., Barker, D.J.P., & Erikkson, J.G. (2001). Association of schizophrenia with low maternal body mass index, small size at birth, and thinness during childhood. *Archives of General Psychiatry, 58*, 48–55.

Wahlsten, D. (1997). Leilani Muir versus the Philosopher Kings: Eugenics on trial in Alberta. *Genetica, 99*, 195–198.

Wakimoto, S., & Fujihara, T. (2004). The correlation between intimacy and objective similarity in interpersonal relationships. *Social Behavior and Personality, 32*, 95–102.

Waldinger, M.D., Zwinderman, A.H., Schweitzer, D.H., & Olivier, B. (2004). Relevance of methodological design for the interpretation of efficacy of drug treatment of premature ejaculation: A systematic review and meta-analysis. *International Journal of Impotence Research, 16*, 369–381.

Walker, M.P., & Stickgold, R. (2006). Sleep, memory and plasticity. *Annual Review of Psychology, 57*, 139–166.

Walker, R.W., Skowronski, J.J., & Thompson, C.P. (2003). Life is pleasant—and memory helps to keep it that way. *Review of General Psychology, 7*, 203–210.

Wallace, B.A. (2006). *The attention revolution: Unlocking the power of the focused mind.* Boston: Wisdom.

Wallentin, M. (2009). Putative sex differences in verbal abilities and language cortex: A critical review. *Brain and Language, 108*, 175–183.

Wallhagen, M.I., Strawbridge, W.J., Cohen, R.D., & Kaplan, G.A. (1997). An increasing prevalence of hearing impairment and associated risk factors over three decades of Alameda County Study. *American Journal of Public Health, 87*, 440–442.

Walsh, S.P., White, K.M., & Young, R.M. (2009). The phone connection: A qualitative exploration of how belongingness and social identification relate to mobile phone use amongst Australian youth. *Journal of Community and Applied Social Psychology, 19*, 225–240. doi: 10.1002./casp.983.

Walther, E., Bless, H., Strack, F., Rackstraw, P., Wagner, D., & Werth, L. (2002). Conformity effects in memory as a function of group size, dissenters, and uncertainty. *Applied Cognitive Psychology, 16*, 793–810.

Wang, J., Smailes, E., Sareen, J., Fick, G.H., Schmitz, N., & Patten, S.B. (2010). The prevalence of mental disorders in the working population over the period of global economic crisis. *Canadian Journal of Psychiatry, 55*, 598–605.

Wang, S., Zhang, Z., Guo, Y., Teng, G., & Chen, B. (2008). Hippocampal neurogenesis and behavioural studies on adult ischemic rat response to chronic mild stress. *Behavioural Brain Research, 189*, 9–16.

Wansink, B., Painter, J.E., & North, J. (2005). Why visual cues of portion size may influence intake. *Obesity Research, 13*, 93–100.

Wansink, B., Payne, C.R., & Shimizu, M. (2011). The 100-calorie semi-solution: Subpackaging most reduces intake among the heaviest. *Obesity, 19*, 1098–1100.

Warga, C. (1987). Pain's gatekeeper. *Psychology Today, 21,* 50–59.

Wason, P.C. (1960). On the failure to eliminate hypotheses in a conceptual task. *Quarterly Journal of Experimental Psychology, 12,* 129–140.

Wasserman, J.D., & Tulsky, D.S. (2005). A history of intelligence assessment. In D.P. Flanagan & P.L. Harrison (Eds.). *Contemporary intellectual assessment: Theories, tests, and issues* (pp. 3–38). New York: Guilford Press.

Waterland, R., & Jirtle, R.L. (2003). Transposable elements: Targets for early nutritional effects on epigenetic gene regulation. *Molecular and Cellular Biology, 23,* 5293–5300.

Watkins, K.E., Dronkers, N.F., & Vargha-Khadem, F. (2002). Behavioural analysis of an inherited speech and language disorder: Comparison with acquired aphasia. *Brain, 125,* 452–464.

Watkins, L.R., & Maier, S.F. (2003). When good pain turns bad. *Current Directions in Psychological Science, 12,* 232–236.

Watson, D., & Tellegen, A. (1985). Toward a consensual structure of mood. *Psychological Bulletin, 98,* 219–235.

Watson, J.B. (1925). *Behaviorism.* New York: Norton.

Watson, J.B., & Rayner, R. (1920). Conditioned emotional reactions. *Journal of Experimental Psychology, 3,* 1–14.

Watters, E. (2006, November 22). DNA is not destiny. *Discover.* Retrieved from http://discovermagazine.com.

Watters, E. (2010). *Crazy like us: The globalization of the American psyche.* New York, NY: Free Press.

Waxenberg, S.E., Drellich, M.G., & Sutherland, A.M. (1959). The role of hormones in human behavior: I. Changes in female sexual after adrenalectomy. *Journal of Clinical Endocrinology and Metabolism, 19,* 193–202.

Way, B.M., Taylor, S.E., & Eisenberger, N.I. (2009). Variation in the m-opioid receptor gene (OPRM1) is associated with dispositional and neural sensitivity to social rejection. *Proceedings of the National Academy of Sciences, 106,* 15079–15084.

Weathers, B. (2000). *Left for Dead: My Journey Home from Everest.* New York: Random House.

Weaver, D. (1998). The suprachiasmatic nucleus: A 25-year retrospective. *Journal of Biological Rhythms, 13,* 100–112.

Weaver, I.C.G., Cervoni, N., & Champagne, F.A. (2004). Epigenetic programming by maternal behavior. *Nature Neuroscience, 7,* 847–854.

Webb, W.B., & Agnew, H.W. Jr. (1970). Sleep stage characteristics of long and short sleepers. *Science, 168,* 146–147.

Weber, J., & Wahl, J. (2006). Neurological aspects of trepanations from Neolithic times. *International Journal of Osteoarchaeology, 16,* 536–545.

Weber, M.J., & Murnighan, J.K. (2008). Suckers or saviors? Consistent contributors in social dilemmas. *Journal of Personality and Social Psychology, 95,* 1340–1353.

Wechsler, D. (1944). *Measurement of adult intelligence* (3rd ed.). Baltimore: Williams & Wilkins.

Wechsler, D. (1958). *The measurement and appraisal of adult intelligence* (4th ed.). Baltimore: Williams & Wilkins.

Wechsler, H., Molnar, B.E., Davenport, A.E., & Baer, J.S. (1999). College alcohol use: A full or empty glass? *Journal of American College Health, 47,* 247–252.

Wechsler, H.L., Lee, J.E., & Kuo, M. (2002). Trends in college binge drinking during a period of increased prevention efforts. *Journal of American College Health, 50,* 203–217.

Wedding, D., & Niemiec, R.M. (2003). The clinical use of films in psychotherapy. *Journal of Clinical Psychology, 59,* 207–215.

Weedon, M.N., & Frayling, T.M. (2008). Reaching new heights: insights into the genetics of human stature. *Trends in Genetics, 24,* 595–603.

Weil, A., & Rosen, W. (1998). *From chocolate to morphine.* New York: Houghton Mifflin.

Weinberg, R.A. (1989). Intelligence and IQ: Issues and great debates. *American Psychologist, 44,* 98–104.

Weinberger, D.R., Egan, M.F., Bertolino, A., Callicott, J.H., Mattay, V.S., Lipska, B.K., Berman, K.F., & Goldberg, T.E. (2001). Prefrontal neurons and the genetics of schizophrenia. *Biological Psychiatry, 50,* 825–844.

Weinberger, M., Hiner, S.L., & Tierney, W.M. (1987). In support of hassles as a measure of stress in predicting health outcomes. *Journal of Behavioral Medicine, 10,* 19–31.

Weingarten, H.P. (1983). Conditioned cues elicit feeding in sated rats: A role for learning in meal initiation. *Science, 220,* 431–433.

Weinstein, A.A., Deuster, P.A., Francis, J.L., Bonsall, R.W., Tracy, R.P., & Kop, W.J. (2010). Neurohormonal and inflammatory hyper-responsiveness to acute mental stress in depression. *Biological Psychology, 84,* 228–234.

Weisinger, R., Denton, D., McKinley, M., & Miselis, R. (1993, November). Forebrain lesions that disrupt water homeostasis do not eliminate the sodium appetite of sodium deficiency in sheep. *Brain Research, 628*(1), 166–178.

Weissberg, R.P. (2005, August 20). *Social and emotional learning for school and life success.* Talk presented at the 113th Annual Convention of the American Psychological Association, Washington, DC.

Weissman, M.M., & Markowitz, J.C. (2002). Interpersonal psychotherapy for depression. In I.H. Gotlib & C.L. Hammen (Eds.), *Handbook of depression* (pp. 404–421). New York, NY: Guilford Press.

Weitlauf, J., Smith, R., & Cervone, D. (2000). Generalization effects of coping-skills training: Influence of self-defense training on women's efficacy beliefs, assertiveness, and aggression. *The Journal of Applied Psychology, 85*(4), 625–633.

Weldon, M.S., & Roediger, H.L. (1987). Altering retrieval demands reverses the picture superiority effect. *Memory & Cognition, 15,* 269–280.

Wenden, A.L. (1998). Metacognitive knowledge and language learning. *Applied Linguistics, 19,* 515–537.

Werker, J.F., & Byers-Heinlein, K. (2008). Bilingualism in infancy: first steps in perception and comprehension. *Trends in Cognitive Sciences, 12,* 144–151.

Werker, J.F., & Tees, R.C. (1984). Cross-language speech perception: Evidence for perceptual reorganization during the first year of life. *Infant Behavior and Development, 7,* 49–63.

Wermke, M., Sorg, C., Wohlschläger, A.M., & Drzezga, A. (2008, February 26). A new integrative model of cerebral activation, deactivation and default mode function in Alzheimer's disease. *European Journal of Nuclear Medicine and Molecular Imaging.*

Wertheimer, M. (1959). *Productive thinking.* New York: Harper.

Wessely, S., & Kerwin, R. (2004). Suicide risk and the SSRIs. *Journal of the American Medical Association, 292,* 379–381.

West, R. (2001). Theories of addiction. *Addiction, 96,* 3–15.

Westen, D., & Gabbard, G.O. (1999). Psychoanalytic approaches to personality. In L.A. Pervin & O.P. John (Eds.), *Handbook of personality: Theory and research* (2nd ed., pp. 57–101). New York: Guilford.

Westen, D., Blagov, P.S., Harenski, K., Kilts, C., & Hamann, S. (2006). Neural bases of motivated reasoning: An fMRI study of emotional constraints on partisan political judgment in the 2004 U.S. presidential election. *Journal of Cognitive Neuroscience, 18*(11), 1947–1958.

Westen, D., Gabbard, G., & Ortigo, K. (2008). Psychoanalytic approaches to personality. *Handbook of personality psychology: Theory and research* (3rd ed., pp. 61–113). New York: Guilford Press.

Westen, D., Gabbard, G.O., & Ortigo, K.M. (2008). Psychoanalytic approaches to personality. In O.P. John, R.W. Robins, & Pervin, L.A. (Eds.), *Handbook of personality: Theory and research* (3rd ed.). New York: Guilford.

Western's greatest controversy: Rushton. (2006, November 3). *The Gazette.* Retrieved from http://www.gazette.uwo.ca/articles.cfm?articleID=844&day=22&month=11&section=News&year=2006.

Westlye, L.T., Walhovd, K.B., Dale, A.M., Bjornerud, A., Due-Tonnessen, P., Engvig, A., . . . Fjell, A.M. (2010). Life-span changes of the human brain white matter: Diffusion tensor imaging (DTI) and volumetry. *Cerebral Cortex, 20,* 2055–2068.

Westmaas, J.L., & Silver, R.C. (2006). The role of perceived similarity in supportive responses to victims of negative life events. *Personality and Social Psychology Bulletin, 32,* 1537–1546.

Weston, D. (1998). The scientific legacy of Sigmund Freud: Toward a psychodynamically informed psychological science. *Psychological Bulletin, 124,* 333–371.

Whalen, C.K., & Henker, B. (1998). Attention-deficit/hyperactivity disorder. In T.H. Ollendick & M. Hersen (Eds.), *Handbook of child psychopathology* (pp. 181–212). New York: Plenum Press.

What causes Down syndrome. (2007). National Down Syndrome Society. Retrieved July 20, 2007, from http://www.ndss.org/index.php?option=com_content&task=category&sectionid=23&id=56&Itemid=234.

Wheeler, M.E., Petersen, S.E., & Buckner, R.L. (2000). Memory's echo: Vivid remembering reactivates sensory-specific cortex. *Proceedings of the National Academy of Sciences of the USA, 97,* 11125–11129.

White, A.M. (2003, Spring). What happened? Alcohol, memory blackouts, and the brain. *Alcohol Research & Health,* 186–196.

White, N.M., & McDonald, R.J. (2002). Multiple parallel memory systems in the brain of the rat. *Neurobiology of Learning and Memory, 77,* 125–184.

White, P. (2006). A background to acupuncture and its use in chronic painful musculoskeletal conditions. *Journal of the Royal Society of Health, 126,* 219–227.

White, R. (1964). *The abnormal personality.* New York: Ronald Press.

Whiten, A., Horner, V., & de Waal, F.B.M. (2005). Conformity to cultural norms of tool use in chimpanzees. *Nature, 437,* 737–740.

Whitfield, C.L., Dube, S.R., Felitti, V.J., & Anda, R.E. (2005). Adverse childhood experiences and hallucinations. *Child Abuse and Neglect, 29,* 797–810.

Whiting, B., & Edwards, C. (1988). *Children of different worlds: The formation of social behavior.* Cambridge, MA: Harvard University Press.

Whorf, B.L. (1956). *Language, thought, and reality: Selected writings of Benjamin Lee Whorf* (J.B. Carroll, Ed.). Cambridge, MA: MIT Press.

Wiederhold, B.K., & Wiederhold, M.D. (2005). Specific phobias and social phobia. In B.K. Wiederhold & M.D. Wiederhold (Eds.), *Virtual reality therapy for anxiety disorders: Advances in evaluation and treatment* (pp. 125–138). Washington, DC: American Psychological Association.

Wilensky, A., Schafe, G., Kristensen, M., & LeDoux, J. (2006). Rethinking the fear circuit: The central nucleus of the amygdala is required for the acquisition, consolidation, and expression of Pavlovian fear conditioning. *Journal of Neuroscience, 26*(48), 12387–12396.

Wilkening, F., & Sodian, B. (2005). Scientific reasoning in young children: An introduction. *Swiss Journal of Psychology, 64,* 137–139.

Wille, B., De Fruyt, F., & Feys, M. (2010). Vocational interests and big five traits as predictors of job instability. *Journal of Vocational Behavior, 76*(3), 547–558.

Williams, G., Cai, X.J., Elliot, J.C., & Harrold, J.A. (2004). Anabolic neuropeptides. *Physiology and Behavior, 81,* 211–222.

Williams, G.C. (1966). *Adaptation and natural selection.* Princeton, NJ: Princeton University Press.

Williams, J.H.G., Waiter, G.D., Gilchrist, A., Perrett, D.I., Murray, A.D., & Whiten, A. (2006). Neural mechanisms of imitation and "mirror neuron" functioning in autistic spectrum disorder. *Neuropsychologia, 44,* 610–621.

Williams, K.D., & Zudro, L., (2001). Ostracism: On being ignored, excluded, and rejected. In M.R. Leary (Ed.), *Interpersonal rejection* (pp. 21–53). New York: Oxford University Press.

Williams, P.A., Haertel, E.H., Hartel, G.D., & Walberg, H.J. (1982). The Impact of leisure time television on school learning: A research synthesis. *American Educational Research Journal, 19,* 19–50.

Williams, R., Briggs, R., & Coleman, P. (1995). Carer-rated personality changes associated with senile dementia. *International Journal of Geriatric Psychiatry, 10,* 231–236.

Williams, R.B., Jr., Haney, T.L., Lee, K.L., Kong, Y., Blumenthal, J.A., & Whalen, R. (1980). Type A behavior, hostility, coronary atherosclerosis. *Psychosomatic Medicine, 42,* 539–549.

Willis, S.L., Tennstedt, S.L., Marsiske, M., Ball, K., Elias, J., Mann Koepke, K., Morris, J.N., Rebok, G.W., Unverzagt, F.W., Stoddard, A.M., & Wright, E. (2006). Long-term effects of cognitive training on everyday functional outcomes in older adults. *Journal of the American Medical Association, 296,* 2805–2814.

Willis, S.L., Tennstedt, S.L., Marsiske, M., Ball, K., Elias, J., Koepke, K.M., et al. for the ACTIVE Study Group. (2006). Long-term effects of cognitive training on everyday functional outcomes in older adults. *Journal of the American Medical Association, 295,* 2805–2814.

Wilson, G.T. (2011). Behavior therapy. In R.J. Corsini & D. Wedding (Eds.), *Current psychotherapies* (9th ed., pp. 235–275). Belmont, CA: Thomson Brooks/Cole.

Wilson, N. (2003). Commercializing mental health issues: Entertainment, advertising, and psychological advice. In S.O. Lilienfeld, S.J. Lynn, & J.M. Lohr (Eds.), *Science, and pseudoscience in clinical psychology* (pp. 425–459). New York, NY: Guilford.

Wilson, T.D., & Dunn, E.W. (2004). Self-knowledge: Its limits, value and potential for improvement. *Annual Review of Psychology, 55,* 493–518.

Wimmer, H., & Perner, J. (1983). Beliefs about beliefs: Representation and constraining function of wrong beliefs in young children's understanding of deception. *Cognition, 13,* 103–128.

Winawer, J., Witthoft, N., Frank, M.C., Wu, L., Wade, A.R., & Boroditsky, L. (2007). Russian blues reveal effect of language on color discrimination. *Proceedings of the National Academy of Science, 104,* 7780–7785.

Wing, L., & Potter, D. (2002). The epidemiology of autistic spectrum disorders: Is the prevalence rising? *Mental Retardation and Mental Disabilities Research Review, 8,* 151–161.

Witkin, H.A., & Asch, S.E. (1948). Studies in space orientation. IV. Further experiments on perception of the upright with displaced visual fields. *Journal of Experimental Psychology, 38,* 762–782.

Witte, K., & Allen, M. (2000). A meta-analysis of fear appeals: Implications for effective public health campaigns. *Health Education & Behavior, 27,* 591–615.

Witten, I.B., Lin, S.-C., Brodsky, M., Prakash, R., Diester, I., Anikeeva, P., . . . Deisseroth, K. (2010). Cholinergic interneurons control local circuit activity and cocaine conditioning. *Science, 330,* 1677–1681.

Witthoft, N., Winawer, J., and Eagleman, D.M. (2015). Prevalence of learned grapheme-color pairings in a large online sample of synesthetes. *PLoS ONE, 10,* e0118996.

Woicik, P.A., Stewart, S.H., Pihl, R.O., & Conrod, P.J. (2009). The substance use risk profile scale: A scale measuring traits linked to reinforcement-specific substance use profiles. *Addictive Behaviours, 34,* 1042–1055.

Wolak, J., Mitchell, K., & Finkelhor, D. (2002). Close online relationships in a national sample of adolescents. *Adolescence, 37,* 441–455.

Wölfling, K., Flor, H., & Grüsser, S.M. (2008). Psychophysiological responses to drug-associated stimuli in chronic heavy cannabis use. *European Journal of Neuroscience, 27,* 976–983.

Wolkowitz, O.M., Epel, E.S., Reus, V.I., & Mellon, S.H. (2010). Depression gets old fast: Do stress and depression accelerate cell aging? *Depression and Anxiety, 27,* 327–338.

Wollmer, M.A., Boer, C., Kalak, N., Beck, J., . . . Kruger, T.H.C. (2012). Facing depression with Botulinum toxin: A randomized controlled trial. *Journal of Psychiatric Research, 46,* 574–581.

Wolpe, P.R., Foster, K.R., & Langleben, D.D. (2010). Emerging neurotechnologies for lie-detection: Promises and perils. *The American Journal of Bioethics, 10,* 40–48.

Wolraich, M.L., Wilson, D.B., & White, J.W. (1995). The effect of sugar on behavior or cognition in children. A meta-analysis. *Jama, 274*(20), 1617–1621.

Wood, J.M., & Lilienfeld, S.O. (1999). The Rorschach inkblot test: A case of overstatement? *Assessment, 6,* 341–351.

Woodcock, R.W., & Johnson, M.B. (1989). *Woodcock–Johnson Tests of Cognitive Ability–Revised.* Itasca, IL: Riverside.

Woodworth, R.S., & Schlosberg, H. (1954). *Experimental psychology* (Rev. ed.). New York: Henry Holt. *World's greatest living polyglot.* (n.d.). Retrieved May 31, 2007, from http://www.spidra.com/fazah.html.

Woody, S.R., & Nosen, E. (2008). Psychological models of phobic disorders and panic. In M.M. Anthony & M.B. Stein (Eds.), *Oxford handbook of anxiety and related disorders* (pp. 209–224). New York: Oxford University Press.

Work-related hearing loss. (2001). National Institute for Occupational Safety and Health, NIOSH, Publication No. 2001-103. Retrieved from http://www.cdc.gov/niosh/docs/2001-103/.

World Happiness Report, Commissioned for the United Nations Conference on Happiness on April 2nd, 2012 (mandated by the General Assembly of the United Nations) Edited by: John F. Helliwell, Richard Layard and Jeff Sachs New York: The Earth Institute, Columbia University.

World Health Organization. (1992). *International classification of diseases and related health problems* (10th rev.). Geneva, Switzerland: WHO.

World Health Organization. (2012). Depression [Fact sheet N°369]. Retrieved from http://www.who.int/mediacentre/factsheets/fs369/en/.

World Health Organization Report on Prevention of Mental Disorders. (2004). *Effective interventions and policy options summary report.* Department of Mental Health and Substance Abuse in collaboration with the Prevention Research Centre of the Universities of Nijmegen and Maastricht.

Wouters-Adriaens, M., & Westerterp, K. (2006). Basal metabolic rate as a proxy for overnight energy expenditure: The effect of age. *British Journal of Nutrition, 95,* 1166–1170.

Wright, S.C., Taylor, D.M., & Macarthur, J. (2000). Subtractive bilingualism and the survival of the Inuit language: Heritage-versus second-language education. *Journal of Educational Psychology, 92,* 63–84.

Wu, X., Chen, X., Han, J., Meng, H., Luo, J., Nydegger, L., & Wu, H. (2013). Prevalence and factors of addictive internet use among adolescents in Wuhan, China: interactions of parental relationship with age and hyperactivity-impulsivity. *PloS ONE, 8*(4), 1–8. doi:10.1371/journal.pone.0061782.

Wurtman, R.J., & Wurtman, J.J. (1995). Brain serotonin, carbohydrate-craving, obesity and depression. *Obesity Research* (3 Suppl.), 477S-480S.

Wurtz, R.H., & Kandel, E.R. (2000a). Central visual pathways. In E.R. Kandel, J.H. Schwartz, & T.M. Jessell. (2000). *Principles of Neural Science* (4th ed., pp. 523–545). New York: McGraw-Hill.

Wurtz, R.H., & Kandel, E.R. (2000b). Perception of motion, depth, and form. In E.R. Kandel, J.H. Schwartz, & T.M. Jessell (Eds.). *Principles of neural science* (4th ed., pp. 548–571). New York: McGraw-Hill.

Xu, F., & Garcia, V. (2008) Intuitive statistics by 8-month-old infants. *Proceedings of the National Academy of Sciences of the United States of America, 105,* 5012–5015.

Xu, F., Luk, C., Richard, M.P., Zaidi, W., Farkas, S., Getz, A., . . . Syed, N.I. (2010). Antidepressant fluoxetine suppresses neuronal growth from both vertebrate and invertebrate neurons and perturbs synapse formation between Lymnaea neurons. *European Journal of Neuroscience, 31,* 994–1005.

Yamada, M., & Yasuhara, H. (2004). Clinical pharmacology of MAO inhibitors: Safety and future. *NeuroToxicology, 25,* 215–221.

Yamamoto, B.K., Moszczynska, A., & Gudelsky, G.A. (2010). Amphetamine toxicities: classical and emerging mechanisms. *Annals of the New York Academy of Sciences, 1187,* 101–121.

Yanagisawa, K., Masui, K., Furutani, K., Nomura, M., Ura, M., & Yoshida, H. (2011). Does higher general trust serve as a psychosocial buffer against social pain? An NIRS study of social exclusion. *Social Neuroscience, 6,* 190–197.

Yang, Y., Raine, A., Han, C.-B., Schug, R.A., Toga, A.W., & Narr, K.L. (2010). Reduced hippocampal and parahippocampal volumes in murderers with schizophrenia. *Psychiatry Research: Neuroimaging, 182,* 9–13.

Yang, Y., Raine, A., Narr, K.L., Colletti, P., & Toga, A.W. (2009). Localization of deformations within the amygdala in individuals with psychopathy. *Archives of General Psychiatry, 66,* 966–994. doi: 10.1001.archgenpsychiatry.2009.110.

Ybarra, M.L., & Mitchell, K.J. (2004). Youth engaging in online harassment: Associations with caregiver-child relationships, Internet use, and personal characteristics. *Journal of Adolescence, 27,* 319–336.

Ybarra, M.L., & Mitchell, K.J. (2008). How risky are social networking sites? A comparison of places online where youth sexual solicitation and harassment occurs. *Pediatrics, 121,* e350–e357, doi: 10.1542/peds.2007.0693.

Yeragani, V.K., Tancer, M., Chokka, P., & Baker, G.B. (2010). Arvid Carlsson, and the story of dopamine. *Indian Journal of Psychiatry, 52,* 87–88. Retrieved from http://www.indianjpsychiatry.org/text.asp?2010/52/1/87/58907.

Yerkes, R.M., & Dodson, J.D. (1908). The relation of strength of stimulus to rapidity of habit-formation. *Journal of Comparative Neurology and Psychology, 18,* 459–482.

Yin, D.-M., Chen, Y.-J., Lu, Y.-S., Bean, J.C., Sathyamurthy, A., Shen, C., . . . Mei, L. (2013). Reversal of behavioral deficits and synaptic dysfunction in mice overexpressing neuregulin 1. *Neuron, 78,* 644–657. doi: 10.1016/j.neuron2013.03.028.

Young, A.S., Niv, N., Cohen, A.N., Kessler, C., & McNagny, K. (2010). The appropriateness of routine medication treatment for schizophrenia. *Schizophrenia Bulletin, 36,* 732–739.

Yu, A.Y., Tian, S.W., Vogel, D., & Kwok, R.C.-H. (2010). Can learning be virtually boosted? An investigation of online social networking impacts. *Computers & Education, 55,* 1494–1503.

Yuen, E.K., Herbert, J.D., Forman, E.M., Goetter, E.M., Comer, R., & Bradley, J. (2013). Treatment of Social Anxiety Disorder Using Online Virtual Environments in Second Life. *Behavior Therapy, 44*(1), 51–61.

Zajacova, A., Lynch, S.M., & Espenshade, T.J. (2005). Self-efficacy, stress, and academic success in college. *Research in Higher Education, 46,* 677–706.

Zajonc, R., Heingartner, A., & Herman, E.M. (1969). Social enhancement and impairment of performance in the cockroach. *Journal of Personality and Social Psychology, 13,* 83–92.

Zajonc, R.B. (1965). Social facilitation. *Science, 149,* 269–274.

Zajonc, R.B. (1968). Attitudinal effects of mere exposure. *Journal of Personality and Social Psychology, 9,* 1–27.

Zametkin, A.J., Nordahl, T.E., Gross, M., King, A.C., Semple, W.E., Rumsey, J., et al. (1990). Cerebral glucose metabolism in adults with hyperactivity of childhood onset. *New England Journal of Medicine, 15,* 1361–1366.

Zang, Y.F., Jin, Z., Weng, X.C., Zhang, L., Zeng, Y.W., Yang, L., et al. (2005). Functional MRI in attention-deficit hyperactivity disorder: Evidence for hypofrontality. *Brain Development, 27,* 544–550.

Zanna, M.P., Kiesler, C.A., & Pilkonis, P.A. (1970). Positive and negative attitudinal affect established by classical conditioning. *Journal of Personality and Social Psychology, 14,* 321–328.

Zatorre, R.J., Evans, A.C., & Meyer, E. (1994). Neural mechanisms underlying melodic perception and memory for pitch. *Journal of Neuroscience, 14,* 1908–1919.

Zeino, Z., Sisson, G., & Bjarnason, I. (2010). Adverse effects of drugs on small intestine and colon. *Best Practice & Research Clinical Gastroenterology, 24,* 133–141.

Zhang, L. (2010). Do thinking styles contribute to metacognition beyond self-rated abilities? *Educational Psychology, 30,* 481–494. doi: 10.1080/01443411003659986.

Zhang, Y., Jin, X., Shen, X., Zhang, J., & Hoff, E. (2008). Correlates of early language development in Chinese children. *International Journal of Behavioural Development, 32,* 145–151. doi: 10.1177/0165025407087213.

Zhao, Y., Montoro, R., Igartua, K., & Thombs, B. (2010). Suicidal ideation and attempt among adolescents reporting "unsure" sexual identity or heterosexual identity plus same-sex attraction or behavior: forgotten groups? *Journal of the American Academy of Child and Adolescent Psychiatry, 49*(2), 104–113.

Zhou, R., We, C., Patrick Rau, P.-L., & Zhang, W. (2009). Young driving learners' intention to use a handheld or hands-free mobile phone when driving. *Transportation Research Part F: Traffic and Behaviour, 12,* 208–217. doi: 10.1016/j.trf.2008.11.003.

Zhu, J., & Weiss, L. (2005). The Weschler Scales. In D.P. Flanagan & P.L. Harrison (Eds.), *Contemporary intellectual assessment* (2nd ed., pp. 297–324). New York: Guilford.

Zigler, E.F., Finn-Stevenson, M., & Hall, N.W. (2002). *The first three years and beyond.* New Haven: Yale University Press.

Zimbardo, P.G. (2007). *The Lucifer effect: Understanding how good people turn evil.* New York: Random House.

Zimbardo, P.G., Maslach, C., & Haney, C. (2000). Reflections on the Stanford Prison Experiment: Genesis, transformations, consequences. In Thomas Blass (Ed.), *Obedience to Authority: Current Perspectives on the Milgram Paradigm Obedience to Authority: Current Perspectives on the Milgram Paradigm.* Retrieved from http://www.prison-exp.org/pdf/blass.pdf.

Zimmer, C. (2005, March 1). Looking for personality in animals, of all people. *New York Times.* Retrieved from http://www.nytimes.com.

Zimmer-Gembeck, M., Hughes, N., Kelly, M., & Connolly, J. (2012). Intimacy, identity and status: Measuring dating goals in late adolescence and emerging adulthood. *Motivation & Emotion, 36*(3), 311–322. doi:10.1007/s11031-011-9253-6.

Zimmer-Gembeck, M.J., & Petherick, J. (2006). Intimacy dating goals and relationship satisfaction during adolescence and emerging adulthood: Identity formation, age and sex as moderators. *International Journal of Behavioural Development, 30,* 167–177.

Zimmerman, C. (2007). The development of scientific thinking skills in elementary and middle school. *Developmental Review, 27,* 172–223.

Zosuls, K.M., Ruble, D.N., Tamis-LeMonda, C.S., Shrout, P.E., Bornstein, M.H., & Greulich, F.K. (2009). The Acquisition of Gender Labels in Infancy: Implications for Gender-Typed Play. *Developmental Psychology, 45*(3), 688–701.

Zuber, B., Nikonenko, I., Klauser, P., Muller, D., & Dubochet, J. (2005). The mammalian central nervous synaptic cleft contains a high density of periodically organized complexes. *Proceedings of the National Academy of Sciences of the USA, 102,*19192–19197.

Credits

TEXT

Chapter 1

Figure 1.1: Adapted from Mulvey & Grus, 2010.

Chapter 3

Figure 3.4: Adapted from Laura King, *The Science of Psychology: An Appreciative View, 1st ed.*, Figs. 3.1, p. 68. Copyright © 2008 The McGraw-Hill Companies. Used with permission.
Figure 3.6: Richard H. Masland, "Neuronal cell types," *Current Biology*, 14(13), pp. 497–500. doi:10.1016/j.cub.2004.06.035. Copyright (2004) with permission from Elsevier.
Figure 3.7: Line art from Laura King, *The Science of Psychology: An Appreciative View*, 1st ed., Fig. 3.2, p.68. Copyright © 2008 The McGraw-Hill Companies. Used with permission.
Figure 3.14: From Michael Passer and Ronald Smith, *Psychology: The Science of Mind and Behavior*, 4th ed., Fig. 3.9, p. 80. Copyright © 2008 The McGraw-Hill Companies. Used with permission.
Figure 3.16: From Laura King, *The Science of Psychology: An Appreciative View*, 1st ed., Figs. 3.12, p. 82. Copyright © 2008 The McGraw-Hill Companies. Used with permission.
Figure 3.23: From Passer, M. W., & Smith, R. E., *Psychology: The Science of Mind and Behavior*, 4th ed. Fig 4.18, p. 117. Copyright © 2008 The McGraw-Hill Companies. Used with permission.

Chapter 4

Figure 4.5: From Michael Passer and Ronald Smith, *Psychology: The Science of Mind and Behavior*, 4th ed. Copyright © 2008 The McGraw-Hill Companies. Used with permission.
Figure 4.6: From R.H. Wurtz and E.R. Kandel (2000). Central Visual Pathways. In E.R. Kandel, J.H. Schwartz, and R.M. Jessell (2000), *Principles of Neural Science*, 4th ed. Copyright © 2000 The McGraw-Hill Companies. Used with permission.
Figure 4.8: Adapted from R.H. Wurtz and E.R. Kandel (2000). Central Visual Pathways. In E.R. Kandel, J.H. Schwartz, and R.M. Jessell (2000), *Principles of Neural Science*, 4th ed. P. 534. Copyright © 2000 The McGraw-Hill Companies. Used with permission.
Figure 4.9: © id work/iStock Exclusive/Getty Images RF.
Figure 4.18: Artist: Julian Jusim.
Figure 4.25: From Laura King, *The Science of Psychology: An Appreciative View*, 1st ed., Fig. 5.37, p. 188. Copyright © 2008 The McGraw-Hill Companies. Used with permission.
Figure 4.26: From Michael Passer and Ronald Smith, *Psychology: The Science of Mind and Behavior*, 4th ed. Copyright © 2008 The McGraw-Hill Companies. Used with permission.
Figure 4.31: From V.S. Ramachandran and E.M. Hubbard, 2003. "Hearing Colors, Tasting Shapes," *Scientific American*, 228, 52–59. Used with permission.
Figure 4.32: Based on W. Hudson, 1960. "Pictorial Depth Perception in Subcultural Groups in Africa," *Journal of Social Psychology*, 52, 183–208. Reprinted with permission of the Helen Dwight Reid Educational Foundation. Published by Heldref Publications, 1319 Eighteenth St., NW, Washington, DC 20036-1802. Copyright © 1960.
Solution to Figure 4.18: Artist: Julian Jusim.

Chapter 5

Figure 5.1: From S. Laureys 2007. "Eyes Open, Brain Shut," *Scientific American*, 296, 84–89. Art by Melissa Thomas. p. 87. Used with permission by Melissa Thomas.
Figure 5.2: From G. Teasdale and B. Jennett, 1976. "Assessment and Prognosis of Coma After Head Injury," *Acta Neurochirurgica*, 34, 45–55. Used with permission by Springer-Verlag.
Figure 5.3: Source: Owen, A. M., Coleman, M. R., Boly, M., Davis, M., Laureys, S., & Pickard, J. D. (2006). Detecting awareness in the vegetative state. *Science* 313 (5792). Sept 2006. p. 1402.
Figure 5.4: Source: Haffenden, A.M. and Goodale, M.A. (1998). The Effect of Pictorial Illusion on Prehension and Perception. *Journal of Cognitive Neuroscience*, 10 (1); Figure 1, p. 124. pp. 122–136. © 1998 by the Massachusetts Institute of Technology.
Figure 5.8: Reprinted from Timothy M. Monk et al., "Maintaining Safety and High Performance on Shiftwork," *Applied Ergonomics* 27(1), pp. 317–324. Copyright © 1996 with permission from Elsevier.
Figure 5.11: Adapted from H.P. Roffwarg, J.N. Muzio, and W.C. Dement, 1966. "Ontogenic Development of Human Dream-Sleep Cycle," Science, 152, p. 604, Figure 1. Reprinted with permission from AAAS.

Chapter 6

Figure 6.1: Carey, B. "H. M., an unforgettable amnesiac, dies at 82." December 4, 2008. The New York Times. Retrieved from www.nytimes.com.
Figure 6.2: Source: Kandel, Kupferman, & Iverson (2000). Learning and memory. In E. Kandel, J.H. Schwartz, & T.M. Jessell (Eds.). *Principles of neural science*, 4th ed., pp. 1227–1246, McGraw-Hill.
Figure 6.5: From A. Braddeley (2003). "Working Memory: Looking Back and Lookin Forward," *Nature Reviews Neuroscience*, 4, 835. Reprinted by permission from Macmillian Publishers, Ltd.
Figure 6.6: From R. Thompson and S. Madigan, 2007, *Memory: The Key to Consciousness*, p. 30. Princeton University Press. Reprinted by permission of Princeton University Press.
Figure 6.7: Adapted from L. Squire, 1987, Memory and Brain, Oxford University Press, Fig. 4.1, p. 155. With permission.
Figure 6.9: From Collins and Loftus, 1975, "A Spreading Activation Theory of Semantic Processing," *Psychological Review*, 82, 407–428. Used with permission by the American Psychological Association.
Figure 6.10: Craik & Lockhart. "Levels of Processing: A Framework for Memory Research." *Journal of Verbal Learning and Verbal Behavior*, 11, 1972, pp. 671–684.
Figure 6.11: Adapted from Craik and Tulving, 1975, "Depth of Processing and the Retention of Worlds in Episodic Memory," *Journal of Experimental Psychology: General*, 104, 268–294. Used with permission by the American Psychological Association.
Figure 6.12: From Slameck and McElree, 1983, "Normal Forgetting of Verbal Lists as a Function of Their Degree of Learning," *Journal of Experimental Psychology: Learning, Memory, and Cognition*, 9, 384–397. Used with permission by the American Psychology Association.
Figure 6.13: Adapted by Christopher Hoyt from line art from Laura King, *The Science of Psychology: An Appreciative View*, 1st ed., Fig. 3.2, p.68. Copyright © 2008 The McGraw-Hill Companies. Used with permission.
Figure 6.14: Excerpt in caption from Richard Douglas Fields. Brief excerpt from "How Memories Stick . . . to Long Term Memory," from the article "Making Memories Stick," *Scientific American*, 292, 75–81. Used with permission.
Figure 6.16: Figure 8-7: from *In Search of Memory: The Emergence of a New Science of Mind* by Eric Kandel. Copyright © 2006 by Eric. R. Mandel. Used by permission of W.W. Norton & Company, Inc.
Figure 6.17: Source: Moser, E.I., Kropff, E., and Moser, M. (2008). Place cells, grid cells, and the brain's spatial representation

system. *Annual Review of Neuroscience*, 31; 69–89. Reproduced with permission of Annual Review of Neuroscience.

Chapter 7

Figure 7.2: From R. Feldman, *Understanding Psychology*, 8th ed. Fig. 2, p. 189. Copyright © 2007 The McGraw- Hill Companies. Used with permission.
Figure 7.3: Source: Adapted from Pace-Schott, E.F., Milad, M.R., Orr, S.P., Rauch, S.L., Stickgold, R., Pitman, R.K. (2009). Sleep promotes generalization of extinction of conditioned fear. *Sleep*, 32(1); pp. 19–26. Figure 2, p. 22.
Figure 7.5: From King, *The Science of Psychology: An Appreciative View*, 1st ed., Fig. 7.4, p. 256. Copyright © 2008 The McGraw-Hill Companies. Used with permission.
Figure 7.8: From Weiten. School Sample Box for Weiten's *Psychology: Themes and Variations* (with Concept Charts), 7th, 7E. Copyright © 2007 Wadsworth, a part of Cengage Learning, Inc. Reproduced by permission. www.cengage.com/permissions
Figure 7.11: From King, *The Science of Psychology: An Appreciative View*, 1st ed., Fig. 7.8, p. 261. Copyright © 2008 The McGraw-Hill Companies. Used with permission.
Figure 7.14: From Garcia and Koelling, 1966. "The Relation of Cue to Consequences in Avoidance Learning," in *Psychonomic Science*, 4, 123–124. Used with permission.
Figure 7.15: From Bandura, Ross and Ross, 1963. "Various Reinforcements and Imitative Learning," from *Journal of Abnormal Social Psychology*, 67, 601–608. American Psychological Association.
Figure 7.16: From Bandura, Ross and Ross, 1963. "Various Reinforcements and Imitative Learning," from *Journal of Abnormal Social Psychology*, 67, 601–608. American Psychological Association.
Figure 7.18: Line art reprinted from G. Rizzolatti, L. Gadiga, V. Gallese, and L. Fogassi. "Premotor Cortex and the Recognition of Motor Actions," *Cognitive Brain Research*, 3, 131–141. Copyright © 1996 with permission from Elsevier.
Figure 7.19: Source: Siegel et al., 1982.

Chapter 8

Figure 8.2: From Laura King, *The Science of Psychology: An Appreciative View*, 1st ed., Fig. 3.18, p. 87. Copyright © 2008 The McGraw-Hill Companies. Used with permission.
Figure 8.3: From Sakai, 2005. "Language Acquisition and Brian Development," *Science*, 310, 810–819. Reprinted with permission from AAAS.
Figure 8.4: Hart & Risley. *Meaningful Differences in the Everyday Experience of Young American Children*. Fig. 2, Appendix B, p. 234. 1995, Paul H. Brookes Publishing Co.
Figure 8.5: From *The Symbolic Species: Co-Evolution of Language and the Brain* by Terrence W. Deacon. Copyright © 1997 by Terrence W. Deacon. Used by permission of W.W. Norton & Company, Inc.
Figure 8.6: From J. Winawer et al., 2007. "Russian Blues Reveal Effect of Language on color Discrimination," *Proceedings of the National Academy of Science*, 104, 7785–7789. Used with permission.
Figure 8.7: From R.N. Shepard and J. Metzler, 1971. "Mental Rotation of Three-Dimensional Objects," *Science*, 171, 701–703. Reprinted with permission from AAAS.
Figure 8.8: From James L. McClelland and Timothy T. Rogers (2003). "The Parallel Distributed Processing Approach to Semantic Cognition," *Nature Reviews Neuroscience*, 4(4), 2003. pp. 310–322. Reprinted by permission from Macmillan Publishers Ltd.
Figure 8.9: Source: Powell, James Lawrence. "Why Climate Deniers Have No Scientific Credibility—In One Pie Chart." DesmogBlog Project. http://www.desmogblog.com/2012/11/15/why-climate-deniers-have-no-credibility-science-one-pie-chart.

Chapter 9

Figure 9.3: Adapted from J.B. Carroll (1993). *Human Cognitive Abilities*, New York: Cambridge University Press. Used with the permission of Cambridge University Press.
Figure 9.8: Duncan, et al. "A neural basis for general intelligence." Science, 289, 2000. pp. 457–460.
Figure 9.9: Adapted from Grigorenko, 2000; Plomin & Petril, 1997.
Figure 9.10: Seifert, Hoffnung, & Hoffnung. *Lifespan Development*, 2e. 2000. Boston, MA: Houghton Mifflin.
Figure 9.13: King, L. *The Science of Psychology: An Appreciative View*, 1st ed., Figs. 9.3 and 9.4, p. 330. Copyright © 2008 The McGraw-Hill Companies. Used with permission of The McGraw-Hill Companies.
Figure 9.14: Luchins & Luchins. Weirtheimer's Seminars Revisited: Problem Solving and Thinking. 1970. Albany, NY: SUNY Press.
Figure 9.15: Source: Luchins, A.S., & Luchins, E.H. (1969). Einstellung effect and group problem solving. *The Journal of Social Psychology*, 77(1), Table 3. pp. 79–89.
Figure 9.16: Courtesy of Scholastic Testing Services, Inc. www.ststesting.com.
Figure 9.17: Carlsson, Wendt, & Risberg. "On the Neurobiology of Creativity: Differences in Frontal Activity Between High and Low Creative Subjects," *Neuropsychologia*, 38, 2000, pp. 873–885.
Figure 9.18: Finke, R. A., Ward, T. B., & Smith, S. M. Creative cognition: Theory, Research, and Applications. 1992. MIT Press.
Figure 9.19: Jauk, E., Benedek, M., Dunst, B., & Neubauer, A. C. "The relationship between intelligence and creativity: New support for the threshold hypothesis by means of empirical breakpoint detection." *Intelligence*, 41 (4), 2013, pp. 212–221. Elsevier Inc.
Solution for Figure 9.12b: Finke, Ronald A., Thomas B. Ward, and Steven M. Smith, *Creative Cognition: Theory, Research, and Applications*. Figure: "Creative Problem Solvin Using Mental Imagery," Copyright © 1992 Massachusetts Institute of Technology, by permission of The MIT Press.

Chapter 10

Figure 10.2: From C. Patterson et al., *Child Development*, 1st ed. P. 64. Copyright © 2008 The McGraw-Hill Companies. Used with permission.
Figure 10.3: From E. Mavis Hetherington, *Child Psychology: A Contemporary Viewpoint*, 6th ed. Figure 3.2, p. 89. Copyright © 2006 The McGraw-Hill Companies. Used with permission.
Figure 10.6: Santrock, J. *Children*, 10th ed., Fig. 5.16. Copyright © 2008 The McGraw-Hill Companies. Used with permission.
Figure 10.8 (c and d): OpenClipartVectors/pixabay.
Figure 10.15: Source: Baillargeon, R., & DeVos, (1991) Object permanence in young infants: Further evidence. *Child Development*, 62 (6), 1227–1246. Fig. 4, p. 1237. Reprinted by permission of Blackwell Publishing.
Figure 10.16: From C. Patterson et al., *Child Development*, 1st ed. Copyright © 2008 The McGraw-Hill Companies. Used with permission.
Figure 10.17: Source: Seifert, Hoffnung, & Hoffnung. *Lifespan Development*, 2e. 2000. Boston, MA: Houghton Mifflin.
Figure 10.22: Source: Harlow, H. "The Nature of Love," *American Psychologist*, 13, pp. 573–685, American Psychological Association, 1958.
Figure 10.23: Source: Field, et al. "Tactile/kinesthetic stimulation effects on preterm neonates," *Pediatrics*, 77, pp. 654–658. American Academy of Pediatrics, 1986.
Figure 10.25: From P. Shaw et al. (2006). "Intellectual Ability and Cortical Development in Children and Adolescents," *Nature*, 440, 676–679. Reprinted by permission from Macmillan Publishers, Ltd.
Figure 10.26: Data comes from the Canada, Youth and AIDS Study conducted in 1988 and the Canadian Youth, Sexual Health and HIV/AIDS Study conducted in 2002. (Source: Boyce et al., 2006.)
Figure 10.27: From *The Life Cycle Completed: A Review* by Erik H. Erikson. Copyright © 1982 by Rikan Enterprises, Ltd. Used by permission of W.W. Norton & Company, Inc.
Figure 10.28: Source: Adapted from Arnett, J. (2000). Emerging adulthood: A theory of development from the late teens through the twenties. *American Psychologist*, 55(5), Figure 2, p. 472. pp. 469–480. doi:10.1037/0003-066X.55.5.469.
Figure 10.29: Arnett. *Emerging Adulthood: The winding road from the late teens to the twenties*. New York, NY: Oxford University Press, 2004.

Figure 10.30: Source: Arnett, 2004.
Figure 10.33: Source: Schaie, 1996.
Figure 10.34: Reprinted with permission from Helpguide.org © 2001–2011. All rights reserved. For more information, visit www.Helpguide.org.
Figure 10.35: Steeves, Valerie. (2014.) Young Canadians in a Wired World, Phase III: Life Online. Ottawa: MediaSmarts. Figure 9, p. 20. © 2015 MediaSmarts, Ottawa, http://www.mediasmarts.ca, reprinted with permission.

Chapter 11

Figure 11.2: After Kent C. Berridge (2004). "Motivation Concepts in Behavioral Neuroscience," *Physiology and Behaviors,* 81, 179–209. Copyright © 2004 with permission from Elsevier.
Figure 11.3: From B. Smith, *Psychology: Science and Understanding,* 1st ed., Fig. 11.1 Copyright © 1998 The McGraw-Hill Companies. Used with permission.
Figure 11.6: From Michael Passer and Ronald Smith, Psychology: *The Science of Mind and Behavior,* 4th ed., Figs. 11.1 and 11.14, p. 377. Copyright © 2008 The McGraw-Hill Companies. Used with permission.
Figure 11.7: Source: R.D. Clark III & E. Hatfield. 1989. Gender differences in willingness to engage in casual sex. *Journal of Psychology and Human Sexuality,* 2, 39–55.
Figure 11.9: From J.A. Russell, 1980. "A Circumplex Model of Affect," *Journal of Personality & Social Psychology,* 39, 1161–1178. American Psychological Association.
Figure 11.10: From: Keltner, Dacher, "Signs of Appeasement: Evidence for the Distinct Displays of Embarrassment, Amusement, and Shame," *Journal of Personality and Social Psychology,* 1995, Vol. 68, No. 3, pp. 441–454, Fig. 1. American Psychological Association.
Figure 11.13: Breugelmans et al. "Body sensations associated with emotions in Raramuri Indians, rural Javanese, and three student samples." *Emotions,* 5, 2005, pp. 166–174. American Psychological Association.

Chapter 12

Figure 12.1: Holmes, T. H., & Rahe, R. H. (1967). "The Social Readjustment Rating Scale." *Journal of Psychosomatic Research,* Vol. 11, No. 2, 1967, pp. 213–218.
Figure 12.5: From H. Seyle, *The Stress of Life,* Fig. 12.4, p. 476. Copyright © 1976 The McGraw-Hill Companies. Used with permission.
Figure 12.7: Source: A.C. Pereira, D.E. Huddleston, A.M. Brickman, A.A. Sosunov, R. Hen, G.M. McKhann, R. Sloan, F.H. Gage, T.R. Brown, & S.A. Small (2007). An in vivo correlate of exercise-induced neurogenesis in the adult dentate gyrus. *Proceedings of the National Academy of Sciences,* 104, 5638–5643.)

Chapter 13

Figure 13.1: Source: https://bspace.berkeley.edu/access/content/group/0f4d90d8-c107-467d-000e-28cb28b3815b/Lecture%20Supplements/stats_meths/images/neuroticism.gif.
Figure 13.2: Plomin, R., & Caspi, A. (1999). "Behavioral genetics and personality." In Pervin & John (eds.), *Handbook of Personality: Theory and Research,* 2nd ed., 1999, pp. 251–276.
Figure 13.3: From Gregory Feist, *Theories of Personality,* 6th ed. Copyright © 2006 The McGraw-Hill Companies. Used with permission.
Figure 13.8: Adapted from W. Mischel and Y. Shoda (1995), p. 247. "A Cognitive-Affective System Theory of Personality," *Psychological Review,* 102(2), 246–268. American Psychological Association, doi:10.1037/0033-295X.102.2.246.
Figure 13.9: Source: Based on data from Cattell, 1965.
Figure 13.11: From Eysenck, 1990. In L.A. Pervin (ed.), *Handbook of Personality: Theory and Research,* 224–276. New York: The Guilford Publications, Inc.
Figure 13.13: Gosling, S.D., & John, O.P. "Personality dimensions in non-human animals: A cross-species review." *Current Directions in Psychological Science,* 8, 1999, pp. 69–75.
Figure 13.15: Adapted from Park, Gregory; et al. Automatic personality assessment through social media language. *Journal of Personality and Social Psychology,* Vol 108(6), Jun 2015, 934–952.
Figure 13.16: Roberts, B. W., Walton, K. E., & Viechtbauer, W. "Patterns of mean level change in personality traits across the life course." *Psychological Bulletin,* 132, 2006, pp. 1–25. American Psychological Association.
Figure 13.17: Adapted from Strauss, M. E., Pasupathi, M., & Chatterjee, A. (1993), p. 479. "Concordance between observers in descriptions of personality change in Alzheimer's disease." *Psychology and Aging,* 8(4), 475–480. doi:10.1037/0882-7974.8.4.475.

Chapter 14

Figure 14.2: Source: Adapted from Festinger & Carlsmith, 1959.
Figure 14.4: Source: Based on suggestions from Petty & Cacioppo, 1986.
Figure 14.5: From Michael Passer and Ronald Smith, *Psychology: The Science of Mind and Behavior,* 4th ed., Fig. 11a, p. 635. Copyright © 2008 The McGraw-Hill Companies. Used with permission.
Figure 14.6: From *Obedience to Authority: An Experimental View,* Figure 4, p. 28, by Stanley Milgram. Copyright © 1974 by Stanley Milgram. Reprinted by permission of HarperCollins Publishers and Pinter & Martin.
Figure 14.7: From *Obedience to Authority: An Experimental View,* Appendix 1, p. 195, by Stanley Milgram. Copyright © 1974 by Stanley Milgram. Reprinted by permission of HarperCollins Publishers and Pinter & Martin.
Figure 14.9: Source: T. Singer, B. Seymour, J.O. O'Doherty, H. Kaube, R.J. Dolan, and C.D. Frith. 2004. Empathy for pain involves the affective but not sensory components of pain. *Science,* 303, 1157–1162.)
Figure 14.10: Source: From David Myers and Steve Smith, *Exploring Social Psychology, 4ce.* Figure 17-1, p. 259. Copyright 2015 McGraw-Hill Ryerson.
Figure 14.12: From R.J. Sternberg (1986). "A Triangular Theory of Love," *Psychological Review,* 93, 119–135. Used with permission by Dr. Robert Sternberg.
Figure 14.13: Source: Bartholomew, K. & Horowitz, L.M. (1991). Attachment styles among young adults: A test of a four-category model. *Journal of Personality and Social Psychology,* 61; 226–244.

Chapter 15

Figure 15.1: Source: American Psychiatric Association. *Diagnostic and Statistical Manual of Mental Disorders,* 5th ed. 2013.
Psychology in the Real World: Source: American Psychiatric Association. *Diagnostic and Statistical Manual of Mental Disorders,* 5th ed. 2013.
Figure 15.2: Source: Statistics Canada, Canadian Community Health Survey (CCHS), Mental Health, 2012.
Figure 15.3: American Psychiatric Association. *Diagnostic and Statistical Manual of Mental Disorders,* 5th ed. 2013.
Figure 15.4: Javitt, D. C., & Coyle, J. T. "Decoding Schizophrenia." *Scientific American,* 290, 2004, pp. 48–55.
Figure 15.6: Javitt, D. C., & Coyle, J. T. "Decoding Schizophrenia." *Scientific American,* 290, 2004, pp. 48–55.
Figure 15.7: Caspi, A., et al. "Interaction between Serotonin Gene and Stress to Make Depression. Influence of life stress on depression: Moderation by a polymorphism in the 5-HTT gene." *Science,* 301, 2003, pp. 386–389.
Figure 15.9: American Psychiatric Association. *Diagnostic and Statistical Manual of Mental Disorders,* 5th ed. 2013.
Figure 15.10: From B.D. Perry, 2002, "Childhood Experience and the Expression of Genetic Potential: What Childhood Nelect Tells Us About Nature and Nurture," *Brain and Mind,* 3, p. 94 With kind permission of Springer Science and Business Media.
Figure 15.11: American Psychiatric *Association. Diagnostic and Statistical Manual of Mental Disorders,* 5th ed. 2013.
Figure 15.12: Ludwig, A. M. (1995). *The Price of Greatness. Resolving the Creativity and Madness Controversy.* 1995. The Guilford Press.
Figure 15.13: Slater, E., & Meyer, A. "Contributions to a pathography of the musicians: Robert Schumann." *Confinia Psychiatrica,* 2, 1959, pp. 65–94.

Chapter 16

Conversation between Dr. Walden and Carlos (p. 617): Source: Gorenstein & Comer, 2002, pp. 54–55.

Figure 16.9: DeRubeis, Hollon, Amsterdam, Shelton, Young, Salomon, Gallop "Cognitive Therapy vs. Medications in the Treatment of Moderate to Severe Depression." *Archives of General Psychiatry,* 62, 2005, pp. 409–416.

Figure 16.10: Teasdale, J. D., Segal, Z., Williams, M. G., Ridgeway, V.A., Soulsby, J.M., & Lau, M.A. "Prevention of relapse/recurrence in major depression by mindfulness-based cognitive therapy." *Journal of Consulting and Clinical Psychology,* 68, 2000, pp. 615–623.

PHOTOGRAPHS

Chapter 1

pp. 2–3: Masterfile RF; **p. 6:** © Punchstock/BananaStock; **p. 8:** David M. Goehring or CarbonNYC on Flickr/CC 3.0 Attribution; **p. 9:** Matthias Rietschel/AP Images; **p. 11:** Ben Curtis/AP Photo; **p. 12T:** Canadian Museum of Civilization, Artifact VII-C-1758, image S95-3306/Corbis; **p. 12B:** SSPL/The Image Works; **p. 13:** © Bettmann/Corbis; **p. 14:** Library of Congress, Prints & Photographs Division, Sigmund Freud Collection [LC-USZ62-72266]; **p. 15T:** Courtesy of The Unemployed Philosopher Guild, www.philosophersguild.com; **p. 15B:** David Buffington/Blend Images/Punchstock; **p. 16:** © Bettmann/Corbis; **p. 17 (William James):** © Bettmann/Corbis; **p. 17 (Mary Whiton Calkins):** Courtesy of the Wellesley College Archives; **(Margaret Floy Washburn):** Special Collections, Vassar College Libraries; **p. 19:** Petty Officer First Class Brien Aho/AP Images; **p. 21:** Chris F. Payne/McGill University Archives, PR000387 reproduced in McGill News, Vol.51, No.3, May 1970, p. 3; **p. 22:** © Glow Asia RF/Alamy; **p. 24 (Hippocrates):** © Stock Montage/Getty Images; **(William James):** © Bettmann/Corbis; **(Wilhelm Wundt):** © Bettmann/Corbis; **(James Mark Baldwin):** Courtesy of the University of Toronto Archives (B1965-0003); **(G. Stanley Hall):** © Bettmann/Corbis; **(Sigmund Freud):** Library of Congress, Prints & Photographs Division, Sigmund Freud Collection [LC-USZ62-72266]; **(Mary Whiton Calkins):** Courtesy of the Wellesley College Archives; **(B.F. Skinner):** © Bachrach/Getty Images; **(Donald O. Hebb):** Chris F. Payne/McGill University Archives, PR000387 reproduced in McGill News, Vol. 51, No. 3, May 1970, p. 3; **(Karen Horney):** © Bettmann/Corbis; **(Carl Rogers):** © Roger Ressmeyer/Corbis; **(Brenda Milner):** © Owen Egan; **(Martin Seligman):** Martin Seligman; **p. 26:** Image Source/Punchstock; **p. 27:** Library of Congress, Prints & Photographs Division [LC-DIG-ggbain- 03485]; **p. 28L:** © Natural History Museum, London/Science Source; **p. 28R:** © NHPA/Photoshot; **p. 29:** Frank Lukasseck/Corbis; **p. 31:** ML Harris/Getty Images; **p. 32:** Masterfile RF

Chapter 2

pp.34–35: Punchstock; **p.38 (book):** Areszpua/GetStock.com; **(The Thinker/Rodin):** © St. Nick/Shutterstock; **(Plato):** © INTERFOTO/Alamy; **(chimps):** © Ronald van der Beek/Shutterstock; **(head):** © Glow Images RF; **(baby):** © Image_Source_/iStock.com; **(marine life):** © Steven P. Lynch; **(graphene structures):** © Kim Steele/Getty Images RF; **(molecules):** Zeynep Mufti/iStock.com; **(butterfly):** Burke/Triolo Productions/Brand X Pictures/Getty Images; **p. 39:** Gary S. Chapman/Getty Images; **p. 40:** © chien321/Shutterstock; **p. 41 (clockwise from top):** Carl Lyttle/Getty Images; Zveiger Alexandre/iStock.com; Martin/Fotolia; © Tetra Images/Alamy RF; Editorial Image, LLC/Alamy; **p. 42:** © Shaun Curry/AFP/Getty Images; **p. 43T:** Photodisc/Getty Images; **p. 43B:** © STRINGER/SPAIN/Reuters/Corbis; **p. 45T:** Ufuk ZIVANA/Shutterstock; **p. 45B:** © Yuri Arcurs/GetStock; **p. 46:** © Somos RF/Getty Images; **p. 47:** Michael Nichols/National Geographic Image Collection; **p. 48:** © Bettmann/Corbis; **p. 49:** Jakob Helbig/Getty Images; **p. 50:** Peter Cade/Getty Images; **p. 51:** Image Source/Corbis; **p. 53 (left to right):** © PhotoAlto/PunchStock RF; © Bjorn Vinter/Getty Images RF; © Rob Melnychuk/Getty Images RF; © Goodshoot/Corbis RF; **p. 55 (face):** © Francisco Cruz/Purestock/SuperStock; **(Figure 2.11 photos):** © Ariel Skelley/Blend Images LLC; **p. 57:** Courtesy of the University of California, Riverside; **p. 58:** © Corbis RF; **p. 61 (self-reports):** Pressmaster/Shutterstock; **p. 61 (waitress):** © Stockbyte/Getty Images; **p. 61 (EEG headgear):** The McGraw-Hill Companies, Inc./Bob Coyle, photographer; **p. 62 (left to right):** broken3/Getty Images; Mark Andersen/Getty Images; JJ Studio/Shutterstock.com; **p. 63:** Courtesy of Dr. Matthias R. Mehl; **p. 66 (A):** PhotoAlto/Michele Constantini/Getty Images; **(B):** Frederick Bass/Getty Images; **p. 70:** Courtesy of Philip Zimbardo; **p. 71:** Marques/Shutterstock; **p. 72:** Wolfgang Flamisch/zefa/Corbis; **p. 73:** Wides & Holl/Getty Images; **p. 74:** Punchstock

Chapter 3

p. 77: Jack Hollingsworth/Getty Images; **p. 78:** © Images & Stories/Alamy; **p. 79 (torso):** © Suza Scalora/Getty Images; **(purple cells):** © phil morley/Getty Images RF; **p. 81:** © Randy Faris/Media Bakery RF; **p. 84:** © Andre Cezar/Getty Images; **p. 85:** James Woodson/Getty Images; **p. 86L:** Sernnovik/Dreamstime.com; **p. 86R:** James Woodson/Getty Images; **p. 88:** Hybrid Medical/Science Source; **p. 90:** © Corbis; **p. 92:** Jim Dowdalls/Science Source; **p. 93:** © Tina Carvalho/NIH-NIGMS; **p. 97:** Scott Houston/Sygma/Corbis; **p. 100:** © Federico Gambarini/epa/Corbis; **p. 101 (top):** © Peter Griffith/Getty Images; **(bottom, left to right):** Photodisc/Getty Images; Stockbyte/Getty Images; WEGNER, JORG & PETRA/Animals Animals; The McGraw-Hill Companies, Inc./Photo by JW Ramsey; **p. 102:** Kraig Scarbinsky/Getty Images; **p. 103:** © 2009 Kim in cherl/Getty Images RF; **p. 104:** © Karen Moskowitz/Getty Images; **p. 105:** ER Productions/Getty Images; **p. 111:** © Gary Malerba/CORBIS; **p. 113:** © Paul Avis/Alamy; **p. 114:** Digital Vision/PunchStock RF; **p. 115:** Courtesy of Jennifer Stamp; **p. 116 (MRI apparatus):** © Philippe Lissac/Godong/Corbis; **(MRI scan):** Photopix/Getty Images; **(PET scan):** © Department of Nuclear Medicine, Charing Cross Hospital/Science Source; **(fMRI scan):** ISM/Phototake; **p. 118:** ©Images & Stories/Alamy; **p. 120:** Jack Hollingsworth/Getty Images

Chapter 4

p. 122–123: Panoramic Images/Getty Images; **p. 125:** Bear Dancer Studios/Mark Dierker; **p. 126 (fly):** Cre8tive Studios/Alamy; **(candle):** The McGraw-Hill Companies Inc./Ken Cavanagh, photographer; **(watch):** © The McGraw-Hill Companies, Inc./Jill Braaten, photographer; **(perfume):** © Stockbyte/PunchStock; **(sugar):** FuzzBones/Shutterstock; **(face):** PhotoAlto/Alix Minde/Getty Images RF; **p. 127:** Thomas Hartwell/Corbis; **p. 131:** © Science Source; **p. 136:** © Michael Tran/FilmMagic/Getty Images; **p. 138 (railroad tracks):** Photodisc/Getty Images; **(flowers):** Creatas/PunchStock; **(balloons):** McGraw-Hill Education; **(lemons):** Humberto Olarte Cupas/Alamy; **p. 139:** © Mauro Fermariello/Science Source; **p. 141:** M. C. Escher's "Sky and Water I" © 2014 The M. C. Escher Company-The Netherlands. All rights reserved; **p. 142 (road):** © Royalty-Free/Corbis; **(moon):** NASA/JSC; **p. 145:** © Steve Allen/Brand X Pictures/Getty Images; **p. 146:** © Hector Mata/AFP/Getty Images; **p. 148:** PhotoAlto/Alix Minde/Getty Images RF; **p. 149:** © Corbis; **p. 152T:** © Jeff Greenberg/Alamy; **p. 152B:** The Tennessean, John Partipilo/AP Images; **p. 155:** ALEXANDER JOE/AFP/Getty Images; **p. 156:** © Ahn Young-joon/AP Photo; **p. 160:** BloomImage/Getty Images; **p. 161:** TENGKU BAHAR/AFP/Getty Images; **p. 162:** Panoramic Images/Getty Images

Chapter 5

pp. 164–165: Simon Jarratt/Corbis; **p. 167:** Chev Wilkinson/Cultura/Getty Images; **p. 169 (MRI apparatus):** © Martin Barraud/age fotostock; **(MRI of a brain):** Photopix/Getty Images; **(PET scan of a brain):** © Department of Nuclear Medicine, Charing Cross Hospital/Science Source; **(tennis racket and ball):** © Comstock Images/Alamy; **(floor plan of a house):** Ksenia Palimski/Shutterstock; **(comparative brain scans):** Owen, A. M., Coleman, M. R., Boly, M., Davis, M., Laureys, S.,

& Pickard, J. D. (2006). "Detecting awareness in the vegetative state." *Science*, 313(5792), p. 1402; **p. 173T:** Digital Vision/PUNCHSTOCK; **p. 173B:** Source: Simons, D. J., & Chabris, C. F. (1999). "Gorillas in our midst: Sustained inattentional blindness for dynamic events." *Perception*, 28(9), pp. 1059–1074. Figure provided by Daniel Simons. © 1999 Daniel J. Simons. All rights reserved. Image may not be distributed or posted online without written permission. www.theinvisiblegorilla.com; **p. 174:** Courtesy of David Strayer, Ph.D. Applied Cognition Lab, Department of Psychology, University of Utah; **p. 175:** © Oliver Multhaup/AP Photo; **p. 177:** © Cary Wolinsky/Aurora Photos/Getty Images; **p. 179 (eye):** © Dimitri Vervits/ImageState RF; **(woman):** © Tom Merton/OJO Images/Getty Images RF; **p. 184:** © Image Source/PunchStock RF; **p. 185:** © Anna Peisl/Corbis; **p. 187:** William Thomas Cain/Getty Images; **p. 190:** © Ingram Publishing/SuperStock; **p. 192:** Kirsty Pargeter/iStock.com; **p. 193:** Yurok/iStockphoto.com; **p. 194:** © Carlo Allegri/Getty Images; **p. 195 (tea pot):** Mehmet Salih Guler/iStock.com; **(cola):** Rafa Irusta/iStock.com; **(can):** P_Wei/iStock.com; **(tea):** Manuela Weschke/iStock.com; **(glass with ice):** Aleaimage/iStock.com; **(coffee):** Studioaraminta/iStock.com; **(mug):** Zveiger Alexandre/iStock.com; **p. 198:** Rod Rolle/Getty Images; **p. 200:** Simon Jarratt/Corbis

Chapter 6

p. 203: Vasiliki Varvaki/Getty Images; **p. 205:** © Owen Egan; **p. 208:** Jill Wellington, http://jillwellington.zenfolio.com; **p. 209 (baby foot):** © McGraw-Hill Education/Jill Braaten, photographer; **(smelling flowers):** © S. Olsson /PhotoAlto RF; **(eating peach):** ©Trinette Reed/Blend Images LLC RF; **(ear):** © McGraw-Hill Education/Eric Wise, photographer; **(eye):** © Barbara Penoyar/Getty Images RF; **(lightning):** © Jason Weingart Photography RF; **(reading paper):** © Hero/Corbis/Glow Images RF; **(military):** DoD/U.S. Air Force photo by Master Sgt. Mark C. Olsen; **p. 211:** © Joe Martin. www.mrboffo.com Used with permission; **p. 212:** Jason Todd/Getty Images; **p. 213:** Alex Wong/Getty Images; **p. 214:** Cohen/Ostrow/Digital Vision/Getty Images RF; **p. 217:** blue jean images/Getty Images; **p. 220:** © Peter Bregg Photography; **p. 222:** Stockbyte/PunchStock; **p. 224:** Steve Cole/Getty Images; **p. 228:** Tim Laman/Getty Images RF; **p. 233:** TT NEWS AGENCY/Reuters/Landov; **p. 235:** Stephanie Maze/Corbis; **p. 237:** Aaron Roeth Photography; **p. 238:** Vasiliki Varvaki/Getty Images

Chapter 7

p. 241: © Nicolas Ferrando/Corbis; **p. 243L:** Time & Life Pictures/Getty Images; **p. 243R:** © Pictorial Press Ltd/Alamy; **p. 245 (steak):** © Stewart Waller/fStop/Getty Images RF; **(bell):** © Photodisc/Getty Images RF; **(dog):** © McGraw-Hill Education; **p. 247:** Courtesy of Prof. Benjamin Harris, University of New Hampshire; **p. 248 (left to right):** © Don Farrall/Getty Images RF; © Martin Ruegner/Photodisc/Getty Images RF; © Design Pics/Leah Warkentin RF; © Design Pics/Don Hammond RF; **p. 249:** © Bachrach/Getty Images; **p. 250 (top to bottom):** © Hero/Corbis/Glow Images RF; Digital Vision/Getty Images; © Thinkstock/agefotostock RF; **p. 251:** Marc Debnam/Digital Vision/Getty Images; **p. 252 (running):** © Glow Images RF; **(man in car):** © Wealan Pollard/agefotostock RF; **(tickets):** © Kent Knudson/PhotoLink/Getty Images RF; **(surprise):** © McGraw-Hill Education; **p. 253:** Bettmann/Corbis; **p. 254 (bee):** © Don Farrall/Getty Images RF; **(screaming girl):** © Design Pics/Leah Warkentin RF; **(seat belt):** © Ned Frisk/Blend Images RF; **(sad child):** © Digital Vision/PunchStock RF; **p. 255:** Kim Gunkel/Getty Images; **p. 256 (top to bottom):** Sion Touhig/Corbis; **(slot machine):** WireImageStock/Masterfile; **(lecture):** Zucchi Uwe/dpa/Corbis; **(girl on phone):** leungchopan/Shutterstock; **p. 259:** Nina Leen/Time & Life Pictures/Getty Images; **p. 261 (Garcia):** © UCLA Psychology; **(dog food):** © Lew Robertson/Corbis RF; **(dog):** © McGraw-Hill Education; **(bell):** © Photodisc/Getty Images RF; **(dog):** iStockPhoto.com/Mark Coffey; **(boat):** © Ingram Publishing/SuperStock RF; **(nausea):** © Brand X Pictures RF; **(donut):** © Dynamic Graphics/PunchStock RF; **p. 264T:** © Jon Brenneis/Life Magazine/Time & Life Pictures/Getty Images; **p. 264B (two photos):** Courtesy of Albert Bandura; **p. 266:** © Virgo Productions/zefa/Corbis; **p. 269:** © Gary Salter/zefa/Corbis; **p. 270 (macaque):** © image100/PunchStock RF; **(nerve cells):** © Jim Dowdalls/Science Source; **p. 271:** © Inspirestock/PunchStock RF; **p. 272:** Elena Rostunova/Shutterstock

Chapter 8

p. 277: © PhotoDisc/Punchstock; **p. 279:** FINBARR O'REILLY/X90055/Reuters/Corbis; **p. 281T:** Onoky/SuperStock; **p. 281B:** Courtesy of Steven Pinker. Photo by Max Gerber; **p. 283:** Datacraft/Getty Images; **p. 287:** © China FotoPress/Getty Images; **p. 288T:** Russell Monk Photography/Getty Images; **p. 288B:** © Gwyn Photography/Getty Images; **p. 290:** Frans Lanting/Minden Pictures; **p. 291:** Courtesy of Daniel L. Everett; **p. 293 (top):** Digital Vision/Getty Images; **(centre left):** Matthieu Spohn/PhotoAlto; **(centre right):** © 2007 Getty Images, Inc.; **p. 293 (bottom):** Barbara Penoyar/Getty Images; **p. 294:** © Tara Moore/Stone/Getty Images; **p. 295:** © Dave and Les Jacobs/Blend Images LLC RF; **p. 301:** USGS photo by Don Becker; **p. 303:** McGraw-Hill Companies, Inc./Gary He, Photographer; **p. 304 (Tversky):** © Ed Souza/Stanford News Service; **(Kahneman):** © Sean Gallup/Getty Images for Burda Media; **(top right):** Eileen Bach/Getty Images; **p. 306:** © Andrew Rich/Getty Images RF; **p. 308:** © Du Cane Medical Imaging Ltd./Science Source; **p. 309:** © PhotoDisc/Punchstock

Chapter 9

p. 311: Robert Harding Picture Library/SuperStock; **p. 316T:** Francis Specker/AP Photo/The Canadian Press; **p. 316B:** © Kris Connor/Getty Images; **p. 318:** C.W. McKeen/Syracuse Newspapers/The Image Works; **p. 319:** Agencyby/GetStock.com; **p. 321 (both photos):** Courtesy of Nadeen & Alan Kaufman; **p. 323T:** Ciaproductions/GetStock.com; **p. 323B:** Commercial Eye/Getty Images; **p. 325:** Mika/zefa/Corbis; **p. 326:** Courtesy of Josh Tiessen Studio Gallery, www.joshtiessen.com; **p. 327T:** © Simone Brandt/Getty Images RF; **p. 327B:** © Science Photo Library/Alamy RF; **p. 330:** © Somos Images/Veer RF; **p. 336 (woman):** Purestock/SuperStock; **(table):** Image Source/Getty Images; **(jars):** TigerForce/Shutterstock; **p. 338 (Curie):** Time & Life Pictures/Getty Images; **(da Vinci):** Pixtal/age Fotostock; **(Woolf):** Popperfoto/Getty Images; **(van Gogh):** FPG Intl./Corbis; **(Einstein):** Library of Congress Prints and Photographs Division [LC-USZ62-60242]; **p. 346:** Robert Harding Picture Library/SuperStock

Chapter 10

p. 349: © Tom Merton/Getty Images RF; **p. 351:** arrowsmith2/Shutterstock; **p. 353:** David M. Phillips/Science Source; **p. 355 (embryo):** Anatomical Travelogue/Science Source; **(newborn):** © Francisco Cruz/Purestock/SuperStock RF; **(2 years):** © Purestock/SuperStock RF; **(4 years):** © RubberBall Productions/Getty Images RF; **p. 356:** Artiga Photo/Masterfile; **p. 358:** Photo by Sterling K. Clarren, M.D.; **p. 359** (left to right): © Image Source RF; © Image Source RF; © Image Source RF; © JGI/Jamie Grill/Blend Images LLC RF; © Pixtal/agefotostock RF; **p. 360:** Kevin Peterson/PhotoDisc/Getty Images; **p. 362:** Enrico Ferorelli; **p. 364:** © Corbis/SuperStock RF; **p. 365 (a and b):** Courtesy of Dr. Harry T. Chugani, Children's Hospital of Michigan; **(bottom):** Courtesy of Paul Thompson, Laboratory of Neuro Imaging, UCLA; **p. 366:** © Bettmann/Corbis; **p. 367:** Alison Barnes Martin/Masterfile; **p. 370:** © Tony Freeman/PhotoEdit; **p. 371:** Public Domain; **p. 374:** © Lee Lockwood/Time & Life Pictures/Getty Images; **p. 376:** H. Ray, Operation Migration Inc.; **p. 377:** Stockbyte/Getty Images; **p. 378:** Time & Life Pictures/Getty Images; **p. 380:** © Natalie Behring-Chisholm/Getty Images; **p. 381L:** © Steve Wisbauer/Getty Images RF; **p. 381R:** © IML Image Group Ltd/Alamy; **p. 383T:** Janis Christie/Getty Images; **p. 383B:** Design Pics/Leah Warkentin; **p. 386:** © Thinkstock/Getty Images RF; **p. 388:** Thinkstock/Getty Images; **p. 389:** Steven Vidler/Eurasia Press/Corbis; **p. 390 (left, top to bottom):** © Stockbyte/PunchStock RF; © Stockbyte/PunchStock RF; © Terry Vine/Blend Images LLC RF; © Bananastock/PictureQuest RF; **(right, top to bottom):** © David Buffington/Blend Images

LLC RF; © Blend Images LLC RF; © Laurence Moulton/PhotoAlto/PictureQuest RF; © Frare/Davis Photography/Brand X/Corbis RF; **p. 392:** © 2009 Jupiterimages Corporation RF; **p. 393:** Claus Andersen/COC/CP Photo; **p. 394:** © Ian Shaw/Alamy; **p. 395:** © Ted Streshinsky/Corbis; **p. 397:** Michael S. Yamashita/Corbis; **p. 398:** © Lars A. Niki; **p. 399:** Sarto/Lund/Getty Images; **p. 403:** © Tom Merton/Getty Images RF

Chapter 11

p. 407: Mike Powell/Getty Images; **p. 409 (left, top to bottom):** © didi/amanaimages/Corbis RF; © Royalty-Free/Corbis; © Digital Vision RF; **(right, top to bottom):** © Jose Luis Pelaez Inc/Blend Images LLC; Ryan McVay/Getty Images; Chris Ware/Getty Images; photogl/Getty Images; **p. 412:** Matthew J Parsons/Getty Images; **p. 414:** Richard Olsenius/National Geographic/Getty Images; **p. 415L:** © David Lodge/FilmMagic/Getty Images; **p. 415R:** © Fred Duval/FilmMagic/Getty Images; **p. 416:** Steve Gschmeissner/Science Source; **p. 418T:** © Dann Tardif/LWA/Corbis; **p. 418B:** Steve Cole/Getty Images; **p. 419:** The McGraw-Hill Companies, Inc./Jill Braaten, Photographer; **p. 420L:** © C Squared Studios/Getty Images RF; **p. 420R:** © Roberto Westbrook/Getty Images RF; **p. 421:** Dominic Chan/The Canadian Press; **p. 422:** The Canadian Press; **p. 425T:** Brand X Pictures/PunchStock; **p. 425 (Figure 11.8):** 2xSamara.com/Shutterstock; © Bananastock/PictureQuest; Elke Van de Velde/Getty Images; **p. 427 (7 photos):** Courtesy of Dr. Lenny Kristal and Robert Kong; **p. 429:** Martin Barraud/Getty Images; **p. 433T:** Courtesy of Erika Rosenberg; **p. 433B:** © Fine Art Images/Getty Images; **p. 437L:** Ken Graham/Getty Images; **p. 437R (top to bottom):** Darwin, C. (1872). The expression of the emotions in man and animals. London: John Murray. Figure 14; Darwin, C. (1872). The expression of the emotions in man and animals. London: John Murray. Figure 13; Darwin, C. (1872). The expression of the emotions in man and animals. London: John Murray. Plate 4; **p. 438:** Courtesy of Paul Ekman; **p. 439 (6 photos):** Courtesy of Erika Rosenberg; **p. 440:** KPPA/Reuters/Corbis; **p. 442:** © Andersen Ross/Blend Images/Corbis RF; **p. 446:** Mike Powell/Getty Images

Chapter 12

p. 449: Design Pics/Don Hammond; **p. 451:** Masterfile; **p. 453:** David Papazian Photography Inc./Brand X Pictures/Jupiterimages; **p. 454 (clockwise from top):** © Jose Luis Pelaez Inc./Blend Images LLC RF; © Image Source/Getty Images RF; © John A. Karachewski RF; © Royalty-Free/Corbis; **p. 455T:** PhotoAlto/Punchstock; **p. 455B:** Mike Powell/Getty Images; **p. 461:** Dirk Anschutz/Getty Images; **p. 462:** Steve Prezant/Corbis; **p. 463:** Andrew Olney/Digital Vision/Punchstock; **p. 465:** Diane Mcdonald/Getty Images; **p. 466:** © Randy Faris/Corbis; **p. 467:** © Keith Brofsky/Getty Images RF; **p. 470:** BananaStock/Alamy; **p. 471:** © Joaquin Palting/Getty Images RF; **p. 472:** © Zefa RF/Alamy; **p. 474 (top to bottom):** © Floresco Productions/agefotostock RF; © A. Minde/PhotoAlto RF; © Dave and Les Jacobs/Blend Images LLC RF; **p. 475:** Brian C. Weed/Shutterstock; **p. 476:** Brand X Pictures/PunchStock; **p. 477:** Brand X Pictures/PunchStock; **p. 478:** © Ingram Publishing/Alamy; **p. 479:** © Phanie/Alamy; **p. 480:** Design Pics/Don Hammond

Chapter 13

p. 483: TITUS/Getty Images; **p. 485:** Robert Glenn/Getty Images; **p. 487:** Design Pics/Don Hammond; **p. 489:** Noel Hendrickson/Getty Images; **p. 490:** Pixland/Corbis; **p. 492:** Peter Aprahamian/Corbis; **p. 494:** Ingram Publishing; **p. 497T:** Photo courtesy of Free The Children, www.freethechildren.com; **p. 497B:** Michael Rougier/Time & Life Pictures/Getty Images; **p. 499:** © Image_Source_/iStock.com; **p. 500:** © KOBI GIDEON/epa/Corbis; **p. 502:** Burke/Triolo/Brand X Pictures/Jupiterimages; **p. 504:** © Michael C. Gray/Shutterstock; **p. 507:** Courtesy of Jennifer Stamp; **p. 508:** © Brand X Pictures/PunchStock RF; **p. 509L:** Don Farrall/Getty Images; **p. 509R:** Don Farrall/Getty Images; **p. 511:** © Spencer Sutton/Science Source; **p. 513:** 7505811966/Shutterstock; **p. 514:** © Mario Tama/Getty Images; **p. 518:** Szefei/GetStock.com; **p. 519 (clockwise from top):** © iStockPhoto.com/Scott Griessel; © iStockPhoto.com/Scott Griessel; © iStockPhoto.com/Scott Griessel; Silverstock/Digital Vision/Getty Images; **p. 520:** TITUS/Getty Images

Chapter 14

p. 523: altrendo images/Getty Images; p. 526: sven hagolani/zefa/Corbis; **p. 527:** McGraw-Hill Companies, Inc./Gary He, photographer; **p. 528T (left to right):** Mareen Fischinger/Getty Images; Digital Vision/Getty Images; Peter Dazeley/Getty Images; **p. 528B:** Sean Kilpatrick/The Canadian Press; **p. 529:** Graham Hughes/The Canadian Press; **p. 530:** TIM SLOANAFP/Getty Images; **p. 531 (top to bottom):** © Tetra Images/Getty Images RF; © UK Stock Images Ltd/Alamy RF; **p. 535:** Anthony Plummer/Getty Images; **p. 538:** Courtesy of the Graduate Center, CUNY; **p. 539:** © 1968 by Stanley Milgram, copyright renewed © 1993 by Alexandra Milgram, and distributed by Penn State Media Sales; **p. 542:** Source: Eisenberger et al., 2003; © (left) Chris Gallagher/Science Source; (right) © BSIP/UIG via Getty Images; **p. 543:** © Ron Haviv/VII/Corbis; **p. 545:** Mike Deal/Winnipeg Free Press; **p. 546L:** © Harvard University News Office; **p. 546R:** Courtesy of Anthony Greenwald; **p. 549:** Shannon Fagan/Getty Images; **p. 550:** © NY Daily News/Getty Images; **p. 551:** Ashley Cooper/Corbis; **p. 553:** CTV NEWS Edmonton; **p. 555:** © Milesy/Alamy; **p. 557:** © IanDagnall Computing/Alamy; **p. 558 (8 photos):** Courtesy of Connor Principe and the Langlois Social Development Lab, University of Texas, Austin; **p. 562:** Bettmann/Corbis; **p. 563:** Bettmann/Corbis; **p. 564:** altrendo images/Getty Images

Chapter 15

p. 567: M. Spohn/PhotoAlto; **p. 569:** ©Art Media/Print Collector/Getty Images; **p. 570:** Ingram Publishing; **p. 574:** Adrian Wyld/The Canadian Press; **p. 576:** © Nancy Kaszerman/ZUMA/Corbis; **p. 578:** © Ingram Publishing/Alamy RF; **p. 579:** (left): © Muammer Mujdat Uzel/Getty Images RF; (right) © Living Art Enterprises/Science Source; **p. 581T:** John Woods/The Canadian Press; **p. 581B:** © Pressens Bild/Henrik Montgomery/AP Photo; **p. 584:** © Ann Johansson/Corbis; **p. 585:** © Philippe Desmazes/AFP/Getty Images; **p. 586:** © Ingram Publishing RF; **p. 588:** Fred Lum/Globe and Mail/The Canadian Press; **p. 589:** Courtesy of Drs. Phelps, Baxter, Mazziotta, UCLA School of Medicine; **p. 592T:** Masterfile; **p. 592B:** © Paul Buck/epa/Corbis; **p. 594T:** © Pixtal/agefotostock RF; **p. 594B (left to right):** © Kwame Zikomo/Purestock/SuperStock RF; © Digital Vision/Getty Images RF; © RubberBall Productions/Getty Images RF; © McGraw-Hill Education/Ken Cavanagh, photographer; **p. 595:** Charles Sykes/AP Photo; **p. 597:** © Europa Newswire/Alamy; **p. 599:** Lucian Milasan/Shutterstock; **p. 602:** © THE FILM COMPANY/AF archive/Alamy; **p. 606:** M. Spohn/PhotoAlto

Chapter 16

p. 609: Hofpils/Shutterstock; **p. 613:** Michael Rougier/Time & Life Pictures/Getty Images; **p. 615T (left to right):** © Geoff du Feu/Alamy RF; © Design Pics/Yuri Arcurs RF; © Burke/Triolo Productions/Brand X Pictures/Getty Images RF; ©Will Heap/Getty Images; © Dirk Freder/Getty Images RF; **p. 615B:** The Charlotte Observer, Christopher A. Record/AP Images; **p. 618:** © Royalty-Free/Corbis; **p. 623:** Jeffrey Mayer/Getty Images; **p. 624:** Will & Deni McIntyre/Science Source; **p. 625:** Simon Fraser/University of Durham/Science Source; **p. 626:** Courtesy of Helen Mayberg; **p. 627:** © Living Art Enterprises/Science Source; **p. 631:** Gleb Garanich/Reuters/Landov; **p. 634L:** © Joe Raedle/Getty Images; **p. 634R:** © Andrea Morini/Digital Vision/Getty Images; **p. 637:** Courtesy of the Canadian Mental Health Association, www.cmha.ca; **p. 638:** © John B. Carnett/Popular Science via Getty Images; **p. 641:** Maya Sherwood Photography/REX Features Ltd./The Canadian Press; **p. 644:** Hofpils/Shutterstock

Name Index

D

E

F

G

H

I

J

K

L

N

O

P

Q

R

T

X

Y

Z

Subject Index

D

E

F

G

H

I

N

O

Q

R

S

V

W

Y

Z